Improvement of the World

ALSO BY EDWARD CHALFANT

This book is the third volume in a trilogy of
the life of Henry Adams. The first two volumes
are available as well from Archon Books:

*Both Sides of the Ocean: A Biography of
Henry Adams, His First Life, 1838–1862*
published in 1982;

*Better in Darkness: A Biography of
Henry Adams, His Second Life, 1862–1891*
published in 1994.

Improvement of the World

A BIOGRAPHY OF
HENRY ADAMS
His Last Life
1891–1918

by
EDWARD CHALFANT

Archon Books
NORTH HAVEN   CONNECTICUT

This is volume three in a trilogy of the
life of Henry Adams. Volumes one and two
are listed opposite the title page of this
book.

Library of Congress Cataloging-in-Publication Data

Chalfant, Edward, 1921–
    Improvement of the world : a biography of Henry Adams, his last life,
1891–1918 / Edward Chalfant.
        p.   cm.
    Includes bibliographical references and index.
    ISBN 0-208-02232-5 (lib. bdg. : alk. paper)
    1. Adams, Henry, 1838–1918.   2. Historians—United States—Biography.
    I. Title.

E175.5.A2 C47   2000
973'.07'202—dc21
[B]   00-033147

The paper in this publication meets the minimum
requirements of American National Standard of
Information Sciences—Permanence of Paper
for Printed Library Materials, ANSI Z39.48-1984. ⊗

Printed in the United States of America

in memory
for James Thorpe III

CONTENTS

PREFACE ix

ACKNOWLEDGMENTS xi

PART ONE

1. BASEBALL AT ABOYNE 3
2. MOLECULES OR ATOMS, LIVING AND DEAD. . 24
3. ACTIVITIES OF DIFFERENT KINDS 47
4. THE LOOKOUT 68
5. VISION AND REVOLUTION 87
6. A PHENOMENON QUITE PECULIAR . . . 110
7. MY BUSINESS IS TO LOOK AHEAD . . . 134
8. UNDER COVER 158
9. VIOLENCE 183

PART TWO

10. BOTHERED BY THE SLAUGHTERHOUSE . . 209
11. UNDER THE SHADOW 231
12. AUTOMOBILING 245
13. VEHICLES OF ANARCHISM 260

vii

14. Every Object More Than Attained   .   . 281

15. None of My Business   293

16. The Second Traveling Copy   .   .   . 308

17. Unsatisfactory Works   331

18. To Worry Historians   350

PART THREE

19. Still in the Swim   373

20. "Chansons de Geste"   388

21. Room on the *Titanic*   409

22. Recoveries 427

23. Our Paris   449

24. War 463

25. Losses Misapprehended   478

26. Copies Given, Copies Found   .   .   . 498

27. Sins of the Heirs   522

abbreviations   545

notes   549

index   699

PREFACE

This book tells a complete story and is meant to be read by itself. It is also the concluding book of a trilogy.

From childhood, Henry Adams was exceptionally attentive to the future, to foresight, plans, and projects. The trait showed itself most importantly in a general plan he settled upon before he entered college. The plan could be described as a bundle of secret wants. He wanted to be four things: the leading American politician of his generation, a great writer, a Washingtonian, and a traveler.

Planning went hand in hand with exceptional speed in action. He moved so rapidly—albeit secretly and in highly unusual circumstances—that early in 1862, when not yet twenty-four, he found himself at the end of a first life, with chances to start a second. His speed did not desert him. In less than thirty years, between January 1862 and November 1891, he aimed at more difficult objectives, attained them, completed a second life, and prepared to start a third.

An underlying cause of these new beginnings was his genius for going to the heart of things. Another cause was even more controlling. He was interested in improvement, beginning with improvement of himself and improvements for his fellow Americans but extending to improvements for all human beings and especially learners, young or old, who might be disposed to improve their ideas and actions—and thus the world.

An adequate biography of such a person can only be a trilogy of biographies, each readable by itself, readable in any order, and so written as to tell in the form of three stories a long story that may qualify as a very great story—on the scale of legend, but anchored in the real. The component stories, it must be added, will be adequate only if the middle story is noticeably better than the first and the third and last is the best of all.

The first book of the present trilogy, *Both Sides of the Ocean*, appeared in 1982. The middle book, *Better in Darkness*, appeared in 1994 and flaunted the improvement principle in its title. This may have been rash. Storytellers can falter.

In its title *Improvement of the World*, this concluding book may be more rash. Yet it can be said in the title's defense that here Henry Adams is at his best. He—not the storyteller—makes the book superlative. The book begins, develops, and ends as the story of Adams's over-eventful last life. Yet it scarcely begins before it becomes in addition the story of a secret, permanent partnership between Adams and Elizabeth Sherman Cameron, the intelligent estranged wife of a United States senator—a partnership set in motion by the wife. Also it tells the story of the seven-year secret sharing by John Hay and Henry Adams of the office of secretary of state. It tells the story of a never-doubted great book, Adams's *Mont Saint Michel and Chartres*. It extends to the never-disclosed, complex story of a very great book, Adams's *Education*. It even tells the stories of the five copies of *The Education* that Adams is known to have annotated, copies that wandered as if they were refugees from a Russian novel, and wandered so much that the most important one can be deemed irretrievably lost.

When the last chapter has been written and read, questions may be asked. Does Adams occupy the central position in the final story? Or do both a man and a woman occupy the central position?

Mrs. Cameron and Henry Adams may have felt themselves caught in a drama in which they had to act the parts of heroine and hero. They possibly believed they had a story to live that could not be less than heroic. Perhaps they lived it to the full.

Adams has long since been recognized as a great writer. It may be time for him to be recognized as great for all his achievements, however many they were. But can justice be served if Elizabeth Cameron is not recognized as an accomplished writer and a great woman? It may help if this concluding book brings the merits of two persons more to the fore. Adams himself would require that the woman not be slighted.

ACKNOWLEDGMENTS

The opening chapters of this book were approved by James Thorpe III, president of Archon Books, prior to his wholly unexpected death in October 1994. Chapters 4–27 were all started with the help of his well-remembered, firm, very intelligent guidance and completed with the courageous support of Diantha Thorpe, his wife, the firm's successor chief. Much my greatest debts are to wife and husband.

The present trilogy—of which this book is the concluding volume—is the first biography of Henry Adams developed in its entirety since the opening of The Adams Papers at the Massachusetts Historical Society in 1955; the first developed since the preparation of Stephen T. Riley's *Microfilms of the Henry Adams Papers*, published by the Society in 1979; the first developed with the help of new evidence assembled by the editors of *The Letters of Henry Adams*, published by the Harvard University Press in six volumes in 1982 and 1988, plus its *Supplement*, published by the Massachusetts Historical Society in 1989; the only one that draws upon the huge array of information relating to Adams in the Worthington Chauncey Ford Papers at the New York Public Library, opened to researchers in 1986; the only one that is supported by the full array of evidence relating to Adams collected by his niece Louisa Hooper Thoron; and the only one that reflects all the evidence available to Aileen Tone, his companion in old age.

Thus the trilogy rests on incomparably improved evidence—evidence which requires a shift from received but mistaken visions of Adams to a different, credible vision which till now could not readily be made available in books but which was always more or less familiar to the persons who knew him best in life.

I have been especially assisted in getting evidence for the last book by directors, editors, librarians, and curators at the Massachusetts Historical Society, notably Stephen T. Riley, Malcolm Freiberg, Peter Drummey, and Brenda M. Lawson; by the editors of *The Letters of Henry Adams*, notably Charles Vandersee; by John D. Stinson and other specialists at the Manuscripts & Archives Division of the New York Public Library; and by the staffs of the Houghton Library at Harvard University, the John Hay Library at Brown University, the Boston Athenaeum, Columbia University Library, and the Library of Congress.

I owe many debts to Stephen Weissman, a leading New York dealer in rare books, and to Richard Stone, editor of the writings of John Jay Chapman and a close watcher of the rare book and manuscript markets.

In the absence of editing by James Thorpe, invaluable friends— Siegmund Levarie, Linton S. Thorn, Frederick M. Keener, and Ben Pleasants—gave my chapters strict, very helpful editing. Eleni (or Helen) Chalfant, my wife, read and suggested changes in every draft of each of the book's chapters. When all others had finished, Kathryn Collins subjected the text and notes to an editing more searching, strict, and helpful than previous ones. I have to commend her sharp awareness and rare editorial intelligence.

I owe an extraordinary debt to a series of persons, most notably Siegmund Levarie and Mary La Farge, for arranging an appeal on my part for a search in the area of Florence, Italy, for Henry Adams's Master Copy of *The Education of Henry Adams*. The search was conducted by Jean Grundy Fanelli, Ph.D., a highly qualified professional, with the assistance of her husband, Avvocato Luca Fanelli.

Evidently late in 1917, Adams gave his Master Copy to Aileen Tone. Ten years later, she left it in the library of her fiancé, Egisto Fabbri. She soon thereafter was barred from attempting its recovery.

In 1962, by mail, Miss Tone initiated a search of the library for the copy. The search was performed in good faith by Fabbri's niece, Principessa Tecla Caffarelli, who reported that the copy was not in the library. (For further details, see Chapter 27.)

Beginning in 1998, Jean and Luca Fanelli secured the full cooperation of Tecla Caffarelli's daughter, Signora Drusilla Gucci, who in time not only made a book-by-book search of the library but inquired among her relations to establish the library's history.

On the basis of Signora Gucci's findings, Jean Fanelli was able to send me "final information" on May 22, 1999, that the copy is not now in the library; that the library was moved "at least five times"; that the moves involved many sortings and possible scatterings of books; that World War II hurtfully impinged; that for a time the library was stored in cardboard boxes in a Florence cellar, with the result that mice and rats nibbled "quite a number" of books, which were then discarded; and that recently a caretaker sold from the remaining books all those that were thought to have any pecuniary value.

Independently the Fanellis made inquiries among the book dealers in the Florence area, with equally negative results.

I consider Dr. Fanelli's final report sufficient grounds for the conclusion that the Master Copy is irretrievably lost.

I believe, too, that all persons interested in Adams owe heartfelt thanks to Jean and Luca Fanelli for inquiries very well conducted and to Signora Drusilla Gucci for a search and inquiries as careful as the occasion required.

The following extracts appear by permission of the Massachusetts Historical Society: those from the collections of the papers of Henry Adams; those from the *Microfilms of the Henry Adams Papers*; those from *The Letters of Henry Adams* and the *Supplement* thereto; those from the Charles Francis Adams, Jr., the Elizabeth Cameron, the Cater, and the Lodge Family papers; those from materials in the Henry Adams Library; and those from other materials cited as owned by the Society.

The following extracts appear by permission of Faith Thoron Knapp and Gray Thoron: those from writings by Ward Thoron and late writings by Louisa Hooper Thoron; and all those from other materials cited as formerly or presently in the Faith Thoron Knapp Papers.

The following extracts appear by permission of the Houghton Library, Harvard University: those from the *Microfilms of the Henry Adams Papers*, Harvard reels; those from *The Letters of Henry Adams* and its *Supplement* that are dependent on Houghton Library holdings; and all other extracts based on Houghton Library holdings.

The following extracts appear by permission of the John Hay Library, Brown University: those from the *Microfilms of the Henry Adams Papers*, Brown reel; those from *The Letters of Henry Adams* and its *Supplement* that are dependent on John Hay Library holdings; and all those from other John Hay Library holdings.

The following extracts appear by permission of the Manuscripts & Archives Division, New York Public Library, Astor, Lenox and Tilden Foundations: those from the Worthington C. Ford Papers, the Macmillan Company Papers, and the Miscellaneous Personal Papers.

PART ONE

1

BASEBALL AT ABOYNE

Early on Friday, November 13, 1891, two middle-aged gentlemen, one American, one English, left a house in the Shropshire village of Much Wenlock, proceeded to Crewe, a railway junction south of Liverpool, and boarded the Scotch express with the object of staying that night at a hotel in Aberdeen. The American was Henry Adams. The Englishman was Adams's closest English friend, Charles Milnes Gaskell. A rich member of Parliament, Gaskell owned two remarkable houses.[1] The one they left that morning was originally the residence of the abbot at a Cluniac religious center, Wenlock Abbey.[2]

Their traveling together was the American's doing. Adams had arranged to pass a week with a Scottish couple, elderly Sir John and Lady Clark, at Tillypronie, their country house, situated on high ground west of Aberdeen. He had pressed Gaskell to join him. Gaskell obliged. Intimate with the Clarks, he would be a welcome added guest. Besides, he wanted to stay with Adams. He valued him immeasurably and thought him *the* American—the United States personified.[3]

The friends reached Aberdeen, slept, and arrived at Tillypronie. The Clarks were delighted to see them, but the weather was so inclement that hosts and guests were kept indoors.

Adams had first visited the Clarks in 1880, in company with his wife, Marian Hooper Adams, known familiarly as Clover. At the time, Mrs. Adams had described the Clarks as "profound liberals & radicals." She said their house—"looking far & wide over crimson moors & blue hills"—was "the perfection of good taste & luxury."[4]

In 1891, Adams would infinitely have preferred to arrive again with Clover. Tragically, she was present in spirit, absent in body. In the Virginia mountains in the summer of 1885, she had suddenly gone insane. Five months later, on December 6 in Washington, she killed herself with poison. The force of her act could be seen in a subsequent occurrence. On November 19, 1887, in Cambridge, Massachusetts, her only sister,

Ellen Hooper Gurney, killed herself by stepping in the path of an approaching train.

Clover's suicide had been reported in the press. Gaskell and the Clarks had quickly learned of it. Until the present, however, they had not had opportunities to scrutinize the widower. With the exception of a summer spent in Japan in 1886, Adams had stayed in America from the autumn of 1880 till August 1890. He then began a journey around the world. He went to Hawaii and stopped for long intervals at Samoa and Tahiti. By means of letters, he made a secret agreement to meet a friend in Europe. The friend was Elizabeth Sherman Cameron, the young wife of a senator from Pennsylvania, James Donald Cameron.

In time to meet Mrs. Cameron, Adams hastened by way of Fiji, Australia, and Ceylon to Suez, Marseilles, and Paris. A month later, he and she left Paris and crossed to London. Once free to do so, he went to Shropshire and sequestered himself at Wenlock Abbey with Gaskell, Lady Gaskell, and their daughter Mary. It is a fair guess that his hosts did not question him about his wife's tragedy, preferring nearer and safer topics. The same guess can be made about the Clarks.

At Tillypronie on November 18, 1891, the weather improved. Sir John went riding on a pony. Gaskell set off with a gun in search of rabbits. Averse to hunting but given to walks, Adams took a different path. He next day wrote to Mrs. Cameron, ". . . I got a two-hour stretch up over the moor and the heather, and I enjoyed the intense solitude of the brown hills where nothing spoke except the fresh wind and the occasional bark of a startled grouse. . . ."

The return to Tillypronie put Adams in mind of his wife's relations. The suicides of Marian Adams and Ellen Gurney interlocked with two other deaths: in 1881, the loss of Fanny Hooper, the wife of their brother Edward, to tuberculosis; and in 1886 the loss of Ephraim Whitman Gurney, Ellen's husband, to what was said to be pernicious anemia. In consequence, a survivor, Edward Hooper, was burdened in Cambridge, Massachusetts, with five motherless and auntless daughters: Ellen, Louisa, Mabel, Fanny, and Mary—all in their teens.

Adams viewed the welfare of his Hooper nieces as one of his prime responsibilities. At Tillypronie, he worried about Ellen, a sufferer from hay fever. With her in mind, he devised a simple plan. He told the Clarks he might arrange a vacation in healthful Scotland during the coming summer for himself, the nieces, and their father.

The Clarks meanwhile had studied Adams and found him too solitary. On Friday, November 20, when Adams was leaving, Sir John told him that he and Lady Clark would be pleased if he would return to their house as a remarried man. Adams felt the remark as kindly meant.

Wishing to answer with all possible brevity, he said he feared that any change in his situation might make a bad matter worse. On that note, he and Gaskell sped away.

The death of Marian Adams created a problem for her husband that he did not solve. A normal male, he differed sexually from other males only in having strong wishes and more than usual energy. The woman he married was the only woman he had wanted to marry. When she killed herself, Clover not only was irreplaceable; she was more than ever wanted. Her absence threw Henry into a condition of haunted restlessness which at best was painful and at times was dangerous.

Trying to make his condition bearable, he had turned to varied reliances. His main thought was to lead as nearly as possible the life he and Clover had wanted. By choice, they had not had children. Since 1877, they had lived in New England in summer, Washington in winter. Their summer home, Pitch Pine Hill, was a roomy cottage of their own design in Beverly Farms on the Massachusetts north shore. In 1885, their winter residence was a rented house in the capital at 1607 H Street, opposite the White House. They however had built a new house on an adjacent lot to the east, at 1603 H Street. On the fatal day, their new house was virtually ready for use.

In this ironic situation, Henry made drastic adjustments. He retained his ownership of Pitch Pine Hill, lent it to others in summer, but did not go there. He moved into 1603 H Street, used the study on the main floor as his main workroom, and reserved two top-floor rooms as his upstairs study and bedroom. He persuaded the State Department librarian, Theodore Dwight, to accept a bedroom and live with him. He otherwise converted the new house into a center for hospitality.

Friends were a saving reliance. Henry maintained his long-standing friendships with Clarence King, the country's leading geologist, and John Hay, the biographer—with John Nicolay—of Lincoln. Also he stayed in touch with three young women who had been Clover's most intimate friends: Rebecca Dodge (soon married to Charles Rae), Anne Palmer Fell, and Mrs. Cameron. He kept on terms of daily or near-daily contact with two families currently wintering in Washington, those of Congressman Henry Cabot Lodge and Civil Service Commissioner Theodore Roosevelt. When journeying to Japan in 1886 and again when journeying to the South Seas, the Indian Ocean, and at last to Paris, he took along the artist John La Farge and paid his expenses.

A last reliance was a costly work of art. Henry designed a bronze figure to be emplaced as a memorial for Clover and himself at their burial plot in Rock Creek Cemetery in Washington. He commissioned Augustus Saint Gaudens to model the figure and Stanford White to plan the stone work. The memorial was completed while its owner was in Samoa and Tahiti. He was sent photographs but had not yet seen it.

A complication was introduced by his wife's friends. Rebecca Dodge, Anne Fell, and Elizabeth Cameron regarded Marian Adams as their heroine. When she died, both Mrs. Fell and Mrs. Cameron were expecting babies. Both proved girls. Mrs. Fell named hers Marian. Mrs. Cameron wished to name hers Marian but was induced by her husband to substitute Martha—a Cameron name.

The bereaved widower learned the details about the names. To his way of thinking, both infants could be counted as Marians, which was a comfort; but under the stress of sexual deprivation, not to mention Mrs. Cameron's much-admired beauty and sometimes provoking manner, Henry increasingly felt sensations of being in love. He ceased feeling these sensations only after hurrying 12,000 miles from Tahiti to Paris to pass four weeks with his special friend. When he and Mrs. Cameron parted in London, she to return to Washington and her husband, he to join the Gaskells in Shropshire, his love for her had vanished or gone into abeyance. At fifty-three, he recovered his solitude.

Adams and Gaskell had met in 1863 in London. Two years later in Italy, Adams also met Gaskell's cousin and closest friend, Sir Robert Cunliffe, a young baronet. The meeting permitted the development of an unusual three-way friendship linking two Englishmen and an American. Cunliffe was well-off but not rich. Like Gaskell, he became a politician. In 1891, he too was a member of Parliament.

After leaving the Clarks, Adams and Gaskell retraced their route and parted at a station near Much Wenlock. Adams proceeded to Acton, Cunliffe's house in Wales, for a weekend reunion with the baronet.

Whenever he and she were in separate places, Adams had written letters to Mrs. Cameron, often in instalments; and she had replied. In secret, they still were corresponding. Their relation had lost an aspect of seeming love. What remained was mutual dependence. At Acton on November 21, he began an instalment by reporting: "We bade good-bye to our Scotch hosts [the Clarks] yesterday morning. They have been [as?] affectionate as possible, and in our parting talk Sir John amused me by another demonstration of the old-old wish, so familiar to me from my women friends, that I might find a *Frou-frou*, as he puts it,—a companion; he would like to see me remarry. . . ."

In reply, Mrs. Cameron would later say: ". . . [the Clarks] are quite right. You ought to marry. And it is I who say it to you!"⁵

Still later, Adams would protest. "I am past marriage. . . . I would not marry now—no! not even you. . . ."⁶

Their sharp exchange perhaps had uses, yet was beside the point.

Adams was not past marriage. He *was* married. When setting out for Scotland with Gaskell on November 13, he had taken a course adapted to his and Clover's wants. The course was oriented toward work.

A major branch of his work was labor as a historian. During the past three years, he had published a long narrative most easily referred to as his *History of the United States.* The narrative's central concern was the uniting of the American people in the period 1801 to 1815. Because he was also interested in the events of a preceding period, from the founding of the United States government in 1789 to the inauguration of President Jefferson in 1801, he wished to search for pertinent documents in archives in England, France, Holland, and Spain. For lack of time, he could not immediately go to Holland or Spain, but he intended to complete his investigations in the English and French archives without delay.

In Tahiti, he had begun a smaller but parallel project: a history of the Tahitians. He had collected information and drafted two chapters of a narrative titled *Memoirs of Marau Taaroa.* Later at Sydney, he had bought many books relating to the Tahitians and ordered them sent to Washington. Additional books about the Tahitians that he had bought in Paris were being packed for shipment. Wanting still other materials, he would enlist the London book dealers.[7]

Adams's most difficult problem as a writer was the development of his intended best book, to be titled *The Education of Henry Adams.* He had started it in 1890 in Washington.[8] Here an effort will be made to follow the process of its completion, but the effort will not be easy. There was nothing he was more secretive about than his work on *The Education.* None of his friends, not even Mrs. Cameron, had the least idea that he was writing it.

Adams's work as a politician had mainly related to great domestic and foreign crises, to choices of presidents, and to choices of secretaries of state. He had been so thoroughly involved in the business of the State Department that as a matter of course he knew the current minister to England, Robert Lincoln (son of the president); the first secretary of legation in London, Henry White; the current minister to France, Whitelaw Reid; the first secretary in Paris, Henry Vignaud; and the second secretary in Paris, Augustus Jay. This is not to say that Adams wanted the company of Ministers Lincoln and Reid.[9] Mere social encounters had no interest for him, and any favors he wished to ask could be performed for him inconspicuously by the secretaries.[10]

Washington excepted, London had more meaning for Adams than any other city. He had first seen the British capital in 1858 in the company of two Harvard classmates, Benjamin Crowninshield, a Bostonian, and Nicholas Anderson, an Ohioan. On the day he left Cunliffe at Acton and returned to town, November 23, 1891, the American whom Adams could most freely visit in London was Anderson's son Larz, currently serving as second secretary at the legation.

That day by letter, Adams disclosed to Mrs. Cameron that he would shortly be returning to Washington. He wanted his plan kept secret. ". . . do not betray my intention to anyone. . . ."

A friend whom Adams was hesitant to see in London was the expatriate writer Henry James. Adams's reason for hanging back was James's adaptation of his novel *The American* as a play for the London stage. Adams had attended the play with Mrs. Cameron a month earlier and had said adverse things about it. Yet hesitation ceased. Adams and James communicated. On cordial terms, they soon were sharing meals.

The historical documents Adams most needed to see in London were American and British diplomatic papers preserved at the Record Office. He engaged a copyist, Miss Byrne, who for usual fees could copy any papers he wanted copied. He soon made such inroads in the papers that Miss Byrne and several helpers were busied preparing heavy packages of copies for shipment to Washington.[11]

A physical problem required attention. Adams had been bothered for several months by a cyst on one of his shoulders. He consulted a London surgeon and was advised that an operation was necessary. Not wanting it known that he was in a surgeon's hands, he put it about that he would be gone for a time to Paris. The precaution taken, he secretly underwent the operation and spent a week recuperating at a private hospital at 17 Upper Wimpole Street. Larz Anderson knew his whereabouts and paid him visits.

On December 9, 1891, released from the hospital, Adams went to the office of the White Star Line and reserved passage to New York on the steamship *Teutonic*, to sail from Liverpool on February 3, 1892. He at once advised Mrs. Cameron that he would "probably take Stateroom W." She had crossed in November on the *Teutonic*. Possibly she had occupied Stateroom W. If she had, his impulse to reserve the space conformed to a pattern. During recent summers, she had borrowed Pitch Pine Hill and thus had lived in a house that he and Clover had built and long enjoyed. His taking a stateroom on the *Teutonic* that Mrs. Cameron had occupied would be same thing, turned around.

In no small part, Adams valued Mrs. Cameron for being a politician. A niece both of Senator John Sherman of Ohio and General William Tecumseh Sherman, a Union hero in the Civil War, she knew everyone who counted in America's national politics.

Her relation with Adams had a potential for a new beginning. She had been somewhat in love with him but not enough to lead to anything decisive. Much depended on her. Were her feelings to strengthen, he might adapt to her desires.

Henry and Marian Adams had been known to relatives and friends as ideally matched. Their marriage had been perfected by ownership of three Skye terriers, Boojum, Possum, and Marquis, and two fine horses, Prince and Daisy. The terriers formed different attachments. Boojum was Marian's, Possum Henry's, and Marquis theirs. As if in sympathy, Boojum died not long after his mistress. News that Marquis had died reached Henry while he was traveling in the Pacific. In London he heard from Theodore Dwight that Possum too had died. He answered on November 24: "So little Possum has followed Marquis to the next world. I am glad I had not to see him go, but as I expected it soon, I am not surprised. Indeed I wish only that Prince and Daisy might also have a peaceful end, as they are too old ever to be used again. Whenever I come back, I would rather begin perfectly fresh, with as little as possible of decrepitude. I like youth about me now that I have not to carry its anxieties."[12]

On December 13, 1891, having finished at the Record Office, Adams left for Paris but was stopped at the Channel by a storm. Boat service from Folkestone to Boulogne was suspended. He eventually crossed, arrived in Paris, and took rooms at the Hôtel Continental, over-looking the Tuileries gardens. By then it was etched on his mind that material progress in Europe remained extremely slow. Channel boats could not operate during storms. Although steam-driven, boats and trains could not keep their winter passengers from nearly freezing.[13]

Trains, boats, and ocean liners had important meanings for him. Not content with circling the earth, he was contemplating journeys to Central Asia, India, Persia, the south of France, the West Indies, and Central America. Yet his journeys were likely to be circumscribed. He believed it a mistake to travel alone and knew from experience that companions were very hard to recruit. He had found, moreover, that he was liable to desperate suffering from seasickness.

Apart from scattered moments with Henry James and Larz Anderson, Adams had recently been much alone. In Paris, he began the experiment of spending a month in utter solitude. He meant to survive it, even try hard to enjoy it.

When in Samoa, he had been troubled by toothaches. Still in need of help, he visited a Paris dentist, possibly an American.[14]

Day after day, he returned to the archives of the Ministère des Affaires Étrangèrs, read documents, and ordered copies.

During his earlier stay in Paris, he had bought French books and plays with the purpose of reading all the French literature and drama he had missed while writing his *History*. He had started reading his purchases while on the British side of the Channel. During his new interval in Paris, he commonly finished a volume a day. In the evenings, he dined alone in famous restaurants or scoured the boulevards to find others not advertised but equally good. Always alone, he attended plays, operas, and symphony concerts.

There was another woman in Adams's life, Lucy Baxter, a contemporary, formerly the companion of his mother. His attitude toward her resembled that of a forthright brother toward an intelligent sister. On December 22, 1891, he wrote to her: ". . . I am in absolute solitude. For the first time in my life I am here without a companion, and for a week I have not exchanged a word with anyone except the people at the Legation. This is dull. Yet I do not greatly object to solitude in Paris for a time. I have many years of arrears to pick up; a vast amount of reading to do; all the theatres to exhaust; and a good deal of reading of archives, to ascertain how many blunders I have foisted into history. Paris is an interesting place, and I am quite as much alive to its interest now as I was thirty years ago. Even the restaurants entertain me, and if I had anyone to show me what I want to see, I should wish no better than to be here."

Adams had been the first American historian to be granted access to the secret nineteenth-century records of the British, French, and Spanish governments as they related to the United States. Partly as a result of that triumph, he had formed friendly ties with two brothers from Brooklyn, Worthington Chauncey Ford and Paul Leicester Ford. The brothers belonged to a new breed of American historians bent on copying historical documents *en masse*. In Paris, Adams found Paul hard at work in one of the archives. Paul was confident of bagging documents in almost any amount. His prosperity reminded Adams that his own errand at the archives—finding supplementary papers for his *History of the United States*—was not greatly important. He finished his errand but at the same time shifted his attention to his history of Tahiti.

The reasons underlying his work as historian of Tahiti were mostly personal. Prior to the arrival of Europeans, the extended families who inhabited Tahiti were organized under hereditary great chiefs. At the time of Adams's arrival, Tahiti had become a French dependency. The island's most-respected native was not the abdicated puppet-king, Pomare V, and not his estranged wife, Queen Marau Taaroa, but instead was Marau's aged mother, Arii Taimai, a great chiefess of the Tevas, the island's most numerous and powerful family.[15]

Arii Taimai owed her status to being the granddaughter of Taura-atua i Patea, a Teva great chief who had lived to an advanced age and had treated her as his daughter. She married a visitor to the island, an English Jew named Salmon, no longer living. When Adams met her, she had devolved her responsibilities on the most capable of her sons, well-educated Tati Salmon, a four-hundred-pound giant. Adams became the guest of Tati and his mother and made such an impression on the chiefess that she took him into the family and gave him a Teva name, Taura-atua i Amo. The name's conferral made Adams a Teva great chief equal to any. He responded by suggesting the preparation of a book of Marau's memoirs, to be written by him and corrected by Marau and her mother. The suggestion illustrated Adams's practical genius and excellent manners. He naturally did not intend a mere volume of the daughter's memoirs. The pretence would be maintained, yet was always transparent. His true object was to elicit something unparalleled. He wanted to write the memoirs of Marau's mother, Arii Taimai.

In London, Adams had received word from Tati that he wished to come to Washington. Replying, Adams had named October 1892 as a good time to visit. He urged that Marau come too.[16] His invitation to Marau acted as a stimulus to himself as would-be historian of Tahiti.

The ancient Tahitians lacked written language. In its absence, they had strung their history on secretly-memorized genealogies going back through many generations. Simple in some respects, the genealogies were bewilderingly tangled in others. Adams had brought with him from Tahiti a mass of handwritten notes, many of which concerned the genealogies of the Tevas. Unavoidably his hardest work as historian of the Tahitians would be a study of tangles. One may suppose he resumed the labor in Paris.

With one important departure, Adams had carried out the plan he had designed in his teens. In the period 1870–1877, he was obliged to perform double duty in Massachusetts as editor of the *North American Review* and assistant professor of history at Harvard. In retrospect, the editorship did not matter, but the assistant professorship mattered greatly. He believed that human beings had two heavy responsibilities: bringing children into the world and educating them once born. It never left his mind that he had accepted the responsibility of being a teacher.

A second consideration was, if possible, more important. From an unknown early moment, Adams had been a fearer and hater of egoism.

For long-run purposes, the part of his fourfold plan that counted most for him was his aspiration to be a great writer. His impulse to write was powerful and destined him to produce three dissimilar books: an ambitious novel, an epic history, and a great book of a new kind.

His *Democracy/ An American Novel* appeared anonymously in 1880 and sold hugely in America and Europe. In 1891, its authorship remained an unsolved mystery. His *History of the United States* was published in four instalments in 1889–1891, signed as his. In date of conception, *The Education of Henry Adams* was almost as old as *Democracy* and the *History* but was redesigned and may best be thought of as twice-conceived. It would *not* be an autobiography.[17] Instead it would be the prototype of a new literary form that Adams discovered: the education. He completed his discovery of the form in 1869 when thirty-one. The form could be defined as a narrative of learning attempted by or imposed upon an actual or fictional person. The form was important for him for what such a book might *do*. He wished to write an education that would educate.

His discovery placed him in a clear-cut situation. Being a fearer and hater of egoism, he could not write an education about himself. Yet he had a ready alternative. He could write a prototypical education in which the actual Henry Adams was supplanted by a fictional Henry Adams. Before starting his journey around the world, he partly or entirely drafted the three opening chapters of *The Education*, eventually printed under the titles "Quincy," "Boston," and "Washington." These were chapters he could draft on a mere basis of memory, together with a clear idea of what he wished his book to achieve. When perfected, the chapters would provide a superbly engaging narrative of his earliest experiences. Broadly speaking, their protagonist would be his actual self when a boy. As the narrative proceeded, the actual Henry Adams would give way to the invented "Henry Adams." The transition would begin in earnest in the fourth chapter, "Harvard College."

From his perspective, the value of *The Education of Henry Adams*, when finished, would not inhere in its protagonist, an Adams who mostly never lived, or lived only on the printed page. Instead its value would inhere in benefits—or improvements—that might accrue to its readers. One of his traits was active sympathy with Americans younger than himself. The hero of the play by Henry James that he had seen in London, *The American*, was a mature citizen of the United States named Christopher Newman. What Adams disliked about the play is readily guessed. He saw little newness in Newman, and nothing of a Columbus. After seeing the play, he had written to Anna Lodge, the wife of Congressman Lodge, remarking rather pointedly that he had returned to Europe for one reason only: to find "a new young man."[18] His statement ironically mirrored an anticipation on his part that new young men could not be sought and found. They would have to be educated.

Another of Adams's traits was adapting books to serve different readerships. He had shaped *Democracy* to be read by multitudes. He originally meant his *History of the United States* to be widely read; but his wife died while the book was still in preparation; and after her death he contrived to change it in such a way that its meaning would probably be accessible only to a select company: readers of the future who were capable of breaking past its ingenious defenses.[19]

Rather narrowly, his *Education* was being written for males suited in age to attending universities but not necessarily enrolled therein.[20] This feature of the book did not indicate that Adams was indifferent to females or disbelieved in the education of women. It simply reflected a desire to address one audience at a time.

The decision of Henry and Marian Adams to build a house opposite the White House had had its beginnings in their negotiating to purchase a very large plot of ground at the corner of H Street and 16th Street. While advancing the negotiation, they had suggested to John Hay that the plot be divided to permit the building of a large corner house for Hay and his family, a mid-sized house for themselves on H Street, and a small house for Clarence King on 16th Street.

Hay vetoed the provision for King. Unassisted, the Adamses designed the interior of their house on H Street. With the Hays' consent, they called in a close friend, the architect H. H. Richardson. He made detailed plans for the house the Adamses had designed and freely designed for the Hays a large luxurious corner house.[21]

While at Tillypronie, Adams had mentioned in a letter to Hay that earlier he had gone to Birmingham, talked with the British politician Joseph Chamberlain, and seen his new house. "Chamberlain showed me his orchids and told me what he expected from Gladstone's new administration. . . . The Chamberlain house is very big, very costly, and rather American than English." He added suggestively: "England . . . suits me fairly well for the moment. . . . If you were only here, and we had a nice country-house for Mrs[.] Hay and the children and me, with poneys [*sic*] and an orchid and rose house, for all [of?] which we would get Chamberlain to pay, I should be quite happy. . . ."[22]

During the late 1880s, Adams, Mrs. Cameron, Hay, and Mrs. Lodge had formed a secret association they called the "family." In his letter to Mrs. Lodge, already noted, Adams used "family" in a new way to mean himself and all the Lodges, Camerons, and Hays—perhaps also the Roosevelts—in a body. Also he made a suggestion involving an English house. "What I seriously prefer is that all the family should come over next summer, and take a princely establishment somewhere within reach of London, for which Hay should pay; and which should provide amusement for all the husbands . . . while I should be properly and suitably petted and cared for by all the wives."[23]

Later, writing to Hay from Paris, Adams changed the subject and suggested their collaborating as writers of pseudonymous works. "I will come home, and immediately, if you will join me in writing, under any assumed name or character you please, a volume or two of Travels which will permit me to express my opinion of life in general, and especially of the French, their literature and their art." He explained: "My notion of Travels is a sort of ragbag of everything; scenery, psychology, history, literature, poetry, art; anything in short, that is worth throwing in; and I want to grill a few literary and political gentlemen to serve with champagne."[24]

Adams's suggestions consisted partly of froth, yet had meaning. He was trying to get his friends into motion. In ways his friends might like, he had begun to shape the future.

In Paris on December 26, 1891, while visiting the Augustus Jays, Adams was introduced to an American he may earlier have glimpsed but did not know. The other guests were Mrs. Griswold Gray and Mr. and Mrs. Theodore Wharton. During or after dinner, he and Edith Wharton had opportunities to talk. Writing to Mrs. Cameron two days later, he said: ". . . after a month of talking to oneself, one does not mind talking to some one else. Mrs[.] Wharton surprised me by her knowledge, especially of Paris on the literary and artistic side; she is very intelligent. . . ."

On the 29th, alone, Adams attended an opera, *Richard Coeur de Lion*, which to his ears was related to his *Education*. The link between the opera and his book was made possible by a series of occurrences dating from the creation of the United States government. The occurrences deserve step-by-step review. The series will lead to a revealing outcome.

In 1788, in keeping with a new Constitution, the American voters elected two of their leaders to serve four-year terms as first holders of new offices. The men elected were George Washington, to be president of the United States, and John Adams, to be vice president.

In 1792, both men were reelected. Washington took a severely disapproving view of nepotism and in no circumstances would have favored a young relative of his for public office. He however was in need of diplomats and chanced to notice the exceptionally developed abilities of Adams's eldest son, John Quincy Adams. On his own initiative in 1794, Washington chose young Adams, not yet twenty-seven, to be U. S. minister to Holland.[25]

While serving in that capacity, J. Q. Adams visited London. There he was persuaded by Mrs. John Singleton Copley, wife of the American painter, to sit for his portrait. The resulting likeness—a stunning picture—was shortly sent to America as a present from Mrs. Copley to a woman she much admired, Abigail Adams, the subject's mother.[26]

In 1797, John Adams succeeded George Washington as president. He retained his son in the foreign service but transferred him to Berlin as minister to Prussia. J. Q. Adams by then had married Louisa Catherine Johnson, an American born and raised abroad. Their first child was a boy, born in Berlin in 1801. At the urging of the father, the baby was named George Washington Adams, in memory of the recently-deceased first president. Soon father, mother, and baby traveled to America. When he reached his parents' house in Quincy, Massachusetts, ex-Minister Adams had been away for seven years.

After many vicissitudes, in 1824, J. Q. Adams was elected president. He served a term but was defeated by General Jackson in the election of 1828. He took his defeat very hard. (His father had similarly been defeated after one term in 1800, by Thomas Jefferson.) He left the White House but stayed for the moment in the capital. His sense of defeat was quickly transformed to profound disturbance. News came that, while traveling to Washington, his son George Washington Adams had thrown himself at night from a steamboat plying westward on Long Island Sound. The body was recovered.

Disturbance notwithstanding, J. Q. Adams returned to the government as a congressman and sustained a new career as a proponent of civil rights and foe of slavery. He had two other sons, John Adams II and Charles Francis Adams. John died in the 1830s, but C. F. Adams lived and had children. As a result, in the 1840s, aged J. Q. Adams became acquainted with his wife Louisa's favorite grandchild, the third-eldest, an active, good-natured boy named Henry.

From the time he could distinguish faces, grandson Henry knew his grandfather as two persons: a fighting old politician and a heroic youth in a portrait by Copley. There perhaps were times—even many times— when Henry believed that *he* was the Adams in the portrait.

J. Q. Adams died in 1848, and the portrait remained at Quincy, inherited by Henry's father. C. F. Adams was a capable writer. In 1880, he published a miniature bioqraphy of J. Q. Adams which Henry had occasion to read. The biography explained that in the 1790s J. Q. Adams wrote a series of articles. "One of these productions, when printed in the newspapers of America, met the eyes of President Washington, and touched him to such a degree that he marked the writer as a person fit for confidence in any emergency in the service abroad."[27] The appointment of J. Q. Adams as minister to Holland followed soon.

Over the years, Henry Adams tooks pains to learn the history of his Adams forebears in searching detail. He read the many volumes of his grandfather's diary as edited and published by his father. Also he read the miniature biography, already quoted. In Paris on December 29, 1891, impelled by memories of an Adams he had known well in person and through books, he attended a revival of an opera by the French composer André Grétry. He told the story in a letter to Mrs. Cameron: ". . . [I] hurried off to the Opéra Comique to perform an act of piety to the memory of my revered grandfather. Some people might think it a queer place for the purpose. . . . A century ago . . . Grétry produced his opera Richard Coeur de Lion. A century ago . . . President Washington sent my grandfather, before he was thirty years old, as Minister to the Hague, and my grandfather was fond of music to such an extent that . . . he tried to play the flute. Anyway he was so much attached to Grétry's music that when he was turned out of the Presidency he could think of nothing, for days together, but "Oh, Richard! oh, mon roy, l'univers t'abandonne" . . . . [In the opera, the minstrel Blondel remains true to Richard, whom all others have abandoned. Both he and Richard sing the song.] . . . as I had never heard the opera, I thought I would see it. . . . Nothing more delightfully rococo and simple could well be, than the music of Grétry. . . . I tried to imagine myself as I was then—and you know what an awfully handsome young fellow Copley made me. . . . Unluckily the Opera Comique[,] which used to be the cheerfullest theatre in Paris, is now to me the dreariest, and poor Richard howled mournfully as though time had troubled him."

While telling Mrs. Cameron some things, Henry omitted others. He avoided noting that when twenty-three he himself began a seven-year absence from America as a diplomat, albeit unofficial. He did not mention that he served in London, a capital far more important to the United States than the Hague or Berlin. He did not say that—like President Washington—he was interested in the possible existence of young men of sufficient ability to be "fit for confidence in any emergency." Nor did he disclose that he was writing a book that would need a Preface stating that the author's object was "to fit young men, in Universities or elsewhere, to be men of the world, equipped for any emergency."[28] Least of all did he explain that the words quoted were the key words in a Preface to The Education of Henry Adams—a Preface he had just written.[29]

No suggestion is meant that Henry Adams in 1891 was determined to educate into existence new versions of J. Q. Adams or Henry Adams. He had known from an early age that he would have to be an improvement—a new man—as compared with his grandfather. When fifty-three, he wanted the young readers of his incipient book to be improvements, as compared with himself. His book was attuned to the future. It looked forward to the advent of young men he could only dimly imagine.

* * *

Among the qualities that might be found in contemporary art and literature, none interested Adams more than signs of health. Earlier in Paris, he had gone with John La Farge to exhibitions of new French paintings. In the interval since, he had seen enough plays and read enough books to form a judgment of recent French literature. What he had encountered in French theatres, galleries, and books affected him as flaunting a self-conscious false pessimism that tended toward real pessimism without beginning to reach it. He drew the harsh conclusion that "the nerves of the French . . . are more diseased than anything on earth except the simple Norwegian blondes of Mr[.] Ibsen."[30]

As if to validate Adams's conclusion, on New Year's Day 1892, Guy de Maupassant went mad and attempted suicide. Adams noted the event in a letter to Mrs. Cameron. He said he was happy to have endured a month of almost unbroken solitude without himself going mad. He had reached the point of being startled by the sound of his own voice.[31]

Having finished at the French archives, he returned to London and took rooms where Larz Anderson lived, at 38 Clarges Street. As a courtesy, he inquired at the legation about Robert Lincoln. The minister was away, felled by influenza. The disease was epidemic.

He and Henry James resumed their meetings. James told him about a British writer from India, Rudyard Kipling, who on January 18 would be marrying an American, Caroline Balestier. Adams learned also that he and the Kiplings would soon be fellow passengers on the *Teutonic*. In part out of sympathy for James, Adams called on James's invalid sister Alice, who had come to London, evidently in final decline. She was not well enough to receive him, but he talked for two hours with her companion, Katherine Loring.

As always, Adams was writing letters. While writing continuously to Mrs. Cameron, he was maintaining correspondences with Hay, Edward Hooper, Theodore Dwight, Anna Lodge, Lucy Baxter, Rebecca Rae, Anne Fell, Mabel Hooper (the third-eldest Hooper niece), and a Washington lawyer-politician he trusted and greatly liked, William Phillips. The evident lack in the pattern was sustained correspondences with other Adamses.

Henry had three brothers, two older, one younger, and a younger sister. Of the brothers, the least troublesome to him was the eldest, John Quincy Adams II, a failed politician. The most troublesome was the second eldest, Charles Francis Adams, Jr., a failed railroad magnate. Brooks Adams was ten years Henry's junior. At first a kindly fellow, he suffered a breakdown in his thirties from which he emerged an apocalyptic philosopher. In different ways, Charles and Brooks were setting up shop as historians.

Some years earlier, Charles had suggested that Theodore Dwight be hired by the Adamses to catalogue and arrange the family's papers. Dwight was asked to work every summer. He accepted the assignment but did not perform it. In Paris on January 20, 1892, Henry received a letter from Charles about Dwight's negligence. The letter touched on Dwight's having lived with Henry in Washington at 1603 H Street.[32] Responding at once, Henry denied having had a voice in the question of Dwight's employment and said that the archivist, if not wanted, should be given notice. He said too, ". . . pray dismiss the idea that I want to have anyone live with me."

As before, Henry's intention to return to Washington was a secret known in America only to Mrs. Cameron.[33] Before sailing, he stayed for a week at Gaskell's main residence, Thornes House in Yorkshire.[34] As scheduled, on February 3, 1892, he boarded the *Teutonic* at Liverpool. As the ship crossed the Irish Channel, he wrote Gaskell a letter, to be posted at Queenstown, saying he expected "a week's misery."

In 1879 and 1880, he and Clover had crossed to Europe and back on the *Gallia*, a beautiful but unstable Cunard steamer. Still earlier, he had endured crossings on British vessels even more unstable. The lessons of past experience made his winter voyage on the *Teutonic* a revelation. The ship was very big and very steady. He later wrote to Gaskell: ". . . I felt a little wonder whether this world were the same that I lived in thirty years ago. In all my wanderings[,] this is the first time I have had the sensation. All the rest of the world seems more or less what it was, and Europe is less changed that any of the rest; but the big Atlantic steamer is a whacker."[35]

A mulatto major-domo, William Gray, and a black housekeeper, Maggie Wade—both permanently employed—had tended 1603 H Street while Adams was away. They were instructed by Mrs. Cameron to have all in readiness on February 11, 1892, when their employer would arrive from New York. Adams no sooner appeared than he called in workmen to repaint the interiors as needed. He meant the house to be used.

As if she were organizing a celebration, Mrs. Cameron assembled eight people, including her senator husband, their daughter Martha, Adams, and Hay, and hurried them to a week-long vacation at a plantation the senator had bought on St. Helena Island in South Carolina, at Coffin's Point.[36] Her undertaking lent cover to a deeply secret action. With Adams's consent, she initiated a "partnership" between him and her. She later used the word herself.[37]

The creation of the two-person partnership was simultaneous with the forming of a secret three-person political alliance between Adams and both Camerons, especially the senator.[38] A leading boss of Pennsylvania and a long-established cog in the Republican Party machine, Senator Cameron could seem almost the last person to be allied with Adams politically. Yet on some points they agreed; and somehow—although he was five years Adams's senior—Cameron was led to think, or led himself to think, that he should submit to Adams's direction.

The incumbent president of the United States was Benjamin Harrison, a Republican. The secretary of state was James G. Blaine. On reaching Washington in mid-November 1891, Mrs. Cameron had noticed that Secretary Blaine was concealing slight but unmistakable marks of having suffered a stroke. She knew her discovery would much interest Adams. In her first letter to him from the capital, she told him what she had seen.[39]

Mrs. Cameron was perfectly capable of acting without Adams's permission. When organizing her party of guests for the week at Coffin's Point, she included Blaine's daughter Harriet. The presence of Miss Blaine among the guests placed Adams in a challenging situation. In the past by anonymous and secret means, he had done heavy political damage to Harriet's father. He had importantly assisted in preventing Blaine's being nominated for president in 1876 and 1880, in bringing about his dismissal from the headship of the State Department in 1881, and in preventing his winning the presidential election of 1884. The motive of these actions had never varied. Adams had believed that pious and plausible James G. Blaine was corrupt from toe to crown.

In 1889, President Harrison had restored Blaine to his old place as head of the State Department. At St. Helena Island, remembering his own past victories and Mrs. Cameron's recent discovery, Adams found it easy to forget the satanic secretary of state and like the secretary's daughter.[40] For her part, Harriet entered the circle of Henry Adams's closer friends almost as if she had always been there.

Edward Hooper had already given his daughters the benefit of a first exposure to Europe. Adams did not know whether his brother-in-law was preparing a second expedition. Writing to his niece Mabel from South Carolina, he asked questions and urged a course of action. "Are you all going to Europe again next summer? Shall we take a joint palace near London, and improve our minds, or a moor in Scotland and improve our bodies? Your papa would look noble fishing for salmon, and I would chase the flying deer with enthusiasm. Suggest it to him, and I will write over to inquire for a quiet place. . . ."[41]

Adams's wife, her sister, and her brother had been very close to one of their cousins, William Sturgis Bigelow, known to them as Cousin Sturgis. In March 1892, Edward Hooper and Sturgis Bigelow traveled from Boston to New York and met Adams, who had come from Washington to join them. He escorted them to the capital; they stayed at his house; and with him they went to Rock Creek Cemetery. By then, Adams may have seen his and Clover's memorial several times, but the approvals given by Hooper and Bigelow counted as the memorial's acceptance.

In April, Hooper returned to Washington for a week with his three youngest daughters. During their visit, it was agreed that the five nieces and their father would go with Uncle Henry to Scotland, sailing on the *Teutonic* on July 6, 1892. Adams wrote to Sir John Clark, asking assistance in finding a rentable house near Tillypronie. Soon after, the uncle met the two oldest nieces in New York and led them to the capital for a week's visit without their papa.

Amidst these comings and goings, Clarence King arrived—in Adams's words—for "a week of discussion with me about tropical journeys to be made, and experimental worlds to be invented."[42] Details are lacking. The "tropical journeys" presumably pointed most toward Cuba. If the "experimental worlds" were utopias, the utopias must have diverged, some to accommodate King's aristocratic conservatism, others to suit Adams's democratic radicalism. That the two men were devoted friends was owing, not to matched outlooks or temperaments, but to shared love of experiments and love of science.

As he liked to do when in Washington, Adams was providing meals for friends and acquaintances. He was waiting news from Tati Salmon and Queen Marau. He was writing more letters. What did not appear in his letters was evidence of work. Yet there was work that he had to do. He had to draft chapters for his *Education*. He had to review his new documents relating to his *History of the United States*. And he had to make sense of his collection of materials relating to Tahiti. Because the French revolution had been inspired in part by explorers' glowing reports about Tahiti when first found, Adams decided to study the effects of the explorers' reports on Europe. As a means of camouflaging his more difficult labors, he said in some of the letters that he was reading books on the French revolution.[43]

Adams liked Washington in May and June and considered those months his summer. Writing to Sir John Clark on May 2, 1892, he explained: "Elsewhere I know no summer; only non-descript seasons. Nothing in the world is so lovely as this, and all the more because no painter ever discovered it, and no poet ever spoiled it."

Summer for Adams meant riding. Prince and Daisy had been retired, but he obtained a horse for the season and resumed his habit of riding out of town. The plans for the Rock Creek memorial called for plants, so he asked a gardener to set out "yews and things." On June 3, he rode to the cemetery to inspect his "small forest."[44] While coming back at a walk, the horse shied, lost its footing, fell, rolled onto him, and sprained his right ankle.[45] For the present, the sprain made normal walking and standing impossible.

Two of his Washington friends, William Phillips and John Slidell, were baseball enthusiasts. Not dissuaded by his bad ankle, they took him to a game, carrying him both ways as necessary. He wrote to Mrs. Cameron, ". . . I saw our club wallop the Cincinnatis." Later in June, he watched a game and reported to Hay, "I went to base-ball yesterday and saw the Senators rattle the Bowery Boys. . . ."[46]

A letter came from President Eliot of Harvard formally notifying Adams that he was to receive an honorary doctoral degree and would have to attend the Harvard commencement exercises on June 29.[47]

Adams responded by objecting, "You know that for ten years past I have not appeared in the world, even so much as in a drawing-room, and the idea of facing a crowd of friends and acquaintances in order to receive a distinction troubles me more than you, who are used to such things, will readily believe." He said also that a degree given to him would be regarded as "favoritism." As an alternative, he urged that degrees be awarded to John Nicolay and John Hay in recognition of their monumental biography of Lincoln.[48]

The issue of favoritism was real. Adams's father had been offered the presidency of Harvard and had served as an overseer. By virtue of his marriage to Clover Hooper, Adams himself became related to Edward Hooper and E. W. Gurney, respectively Harvard's treasurer and dean of the faculty. His brother John was currently a member of the Harvard Corporation. His brother Charles, currently an overseer, had suggested the honorary degree for Henry. One moreover can suppose that Henry had been given informal notice of the conferral long in advance, say in 1891 shortly after he arrived in London.[49]

To President Eliot, as to Charles, a doctorate seemed what Henry was due, in consideration of his *History of the United States*. Eliot countered Henry's objections by saying: "You are not conferring this degree on yourself. . . . To decline it would require a thousand explanations—to accept it is natural and modest."[50]

Henry put an end to discussion by advising Eliot that he had a sprained ankle, could not appear in person at the exercises as was required, and regretted his "enforced incompliance."[51]

The essential fact was that Henry did not want a degree in recognition of his work as author of his *History*. If he had thought that his *History* had been read at Harvard with a fiftieth of the care and intelligence with which it was written, he might have felt otherwise. As things stood, he knew the time was much too early for institutional recognition of his epic narrative to be anything better than a ceremonial emptiness. It did not improve matters that he disliked Harvard and disliked Eliot, and that he was forming an aversion to universities generally, whether in America or in Europe.[52]

In the 1860s purely by means of self-instruction, Adams had become a respected reader and critic of the writings of the world's leading geologists. He had formed very strong scientific interests: most notably interests in the evolution of human beings and in the changes of atmospheric temperature that resulted in ice ages.

When traveling, Adams liked to catch up on his reading. On July 6, 1892, with his servant William Gray and six Hoopers, he boarded the *Teutonic* and sailed eastward. During the voyage, he read a new book by Sir Robert Ball, *The Cause of an Ice Age*, published in New York. Ball reported that dates and durations of ice ages could not be firmly conjectured, still less established.[53] In the 1870s, as Adams very well knew, Clarence King had advanced a theory that the evolution of species— Charles Darwin notwithstanding—was caused by environmental changes, most obviously by changes of average temperatures in the atmosphere. For Adams accordingly, Ball's report was a disappointment.

When the *Teutonic* reached Liverpool, the British were totting up the results of an election. Adams's friends were losers. Gaskell had preferred not to seek reelection. Cunliffe had challenged a Gladstone supporter in Flintshire and was defeated.

The rentable house that Sir John Clark had found for Adams's party was Gordon Lodge, situated in the village of Aboyne, beside the Dee not far from Aberdeen. The Clarks insisted that Adams and the nieces spend portions of their time at Tillypronie. The invitation was the more urgent because Lady Clark, being ill and confined to her room, needed Ellen and Louisa to take her place when possible as hostesses.

The nieces were delighted with Scotland and were soon receiving visitors, paying calls, and generally doing things well-bred American girls were expected to do. Adams approved. He however had equipped the party with bats, balls, and gloves, with a view to the nieces' learning baseball. The long Scotch twilight of July and August proved a good time to play, and they played often for many hours.

The energetic uncle wanted to expand his nieces' freedom—break the barrier of custom that prevented them from exercising their bodies after outliving the games of early girlhood. One niece fully shared his revolutionary zeal. Louisa, known as Loulie, wrote to Cousin Sturgis and freely expressed her feelings.[54] She reported: "We're having a very jolly summer here, but we haven't done anything queer yet—I mean shot a deer on the wing or a keeper by mistake[,] nor fallen in love with a Highlander, nor have we been pulled into the river by salmon. In fact we don't have a chance to do anything of that sort, because women sportsmen—sportswomen rather, are somewhat looked down upon here. . . . Nobody has yet offered to teach us cri[c]ket. . . . I look at the boys playing and sigh as loudly as I dare but they don't pay the least attention. What we do play is baseball, and we make Uncle Henry keep his hand in[,] I can tell you. He's getting [to be] such an adept that you wouldn't know him. His forte is pitching, and his gestures and general appearance are getting quite professional. . . . He's in very good spirits, and he keeps us laughing all the time."

2

MOLECULES OR ATOMS,
LIVING AND DEAD

A dams needed to talk with Sir Alfred Lyall, an authority on India. Also he wanted to visit castles. Writing to Mrs. Cameron on August 25, 1892, he said he and the Hoopers had visited Cragievar, "a wildly fascinating genuine old Scotch castle, unaltered, and occupied by an insolvent Scotch Lord." He continued on September 2, ". . . this afternoon Sir John comes down to take us all to see Crathes and Drum, two old castles about halfway to Aberdeen. . . ." He revealed as well that he led an expedition himself. "The other day, being historically inclined, I took the whole outfit off to inspect Macbeth's Castle; for the hero was hunted up here, and killed on a hillside above Lumphanan. In his day, castles were earthworks,—a moat and a mound,—with wooden buildings; and Shakespeare's battlements were an anachronism. . . ." The expedition ended deliciously. ". . . Macbeth left in his moat and on his mounds a large harvest of wild raspberries."

Gaskell was at Inveroykel, his hunting lodge in Rossshire, not far from Inverness. He knew Sir Alfred Lyall and arranged a meeting at the lodge between Lyall and Adams. On his way to the meeting, Adams inspected Fyvie, another castle. He told Mrs. Cameron on September 15 that at Inveroykel he talked satisfactorily with Lyall, who proved "an interesting man, quite of the best Indian type." He did not say why he had sought a talk. The reasons deserve to be given.

Adams felt injuries suffered by the United States—also injuries suffered by the Adams family—as injuries to himself. Because he and his Adams forebears had been profoundly involved in diplomacy relating to wars and near-wars between the United States and Great Britain, he could appear to be narrowly concerned—or over-concerned—about rivalries between nations considered as states. He however was similarly concerned about rivalries between nations considered as economies, and it happened that the economy of the United States was susceptible to very severe damage originating in changes brought about or incurred by English financial institutions or their managers.

In London in the 1860s, Adams had formed cordial ties with English bankers, most notably Thomas Baring of Baring Brothers, the great London bank, and Thomson Hankey, governor of the Bank of England. The value of these ties for Adams partly lay in his experiencing bankers as human beings, rather than as figures mentioned in newspapers.

While he was journeying in the South Seas, Adams received news of a financial cataclysm. Baring Brothers failed, or rather failed and was revived by the Bank of England, the Rothschilds, and other intercessors. The news affected Adams personally. He was depending for cash on drafts against a Baring account.

Baring's near-destruction wrought havoc in the United States. A panic ensued in New York. Jay Gould took advantage of the panic to dislodge Henry's brother Charles from the presidency of the Union Pacific railroad. The annoyances Charles tended to inflict on Henry did not prevent Henry's feeling the blow to his brother as a blow to himself, and it mattered to him that the opportunity for Gould's maneuver had been afforded by a financial cataclysm in London.

In keeping with the Constitution, the money of the United States was gold and silver.[1] Paper money was in use but was redeemable in gold and silver at banks and was backed by gold and silver held by the Treasury Department. Unhappily, no device had been invented to protect the U. S. Treasury against outflows of its gold caused by changes of financial policy or practice abroad. A similar condition prevailed in India. The money of India was the silver rupee, and Indian silver was as much prey to English events as American silver and gold.

In 1892, Adams was watching for continued outflows of gold from the United States to London and indications of harm to the silver-based economies of the world, chiefly those of India and China. When he asked to meet Sir Alfred Lyall, his object was evident enough. He wished to engage Lyall in conversations centering around gold, silver, and ongoing English activities relating to all forms of money.[2]

When it first appeared, in February 1907, *The Education of Henry Adams* came as a complete surprise, a privately printed book loaned or given to a selection of officials, relatives, and friends. Opening the book, readers found a preface and thirty-five chapters. Further inquiry revealed that the book was written in two parts separated by a gap in time. Twenty chapters sustained a narrative of learning attempted and experienced by "Henry Adams" in the period 1838–1871.[3] Fifteen chapters sustained a narrative of learning by "Henry Adams" in the period 1892–

1905. The parts were noticeably dissimilar. The beginning narrative might sometimes test a reader's powers of comprehension. The closing narrative raised the stakes. It could be classed as reading of a high order of difficulty.

The two-part plan of *The Education* raises questions for biographers. When, where, and why did Adams decide to write the book as two narratives? Progress toward answers seems possible.

Writing from Scotland, Adams described his nieces to Mrs. Cameron as "school-girls." "You can imagine me passing day after day quietly, sometimes reading French Revolution, sometimes playing schoolmaster. . . ."[4] "The girls have lived just as though they were at home, doing lessons. . . ."[5] Typical lessons were studying the peerage, throwing baseballs left-handed, and shopping in Aberdeen. Instruction climaxed in a glimpse of American diplomacy. In late September, the party left Aboyne and went to London. Minister Lincoln treated the visitors to dinner, and First Secretary White led them to a stage show. ". . . the girls were amused, and in my office of educator I was glad to bring them to the Legation, a kind of . . . family hotel of mine, where I feel almost too much at home, whoever is the temporary occupant."[6]

While "reading French Revolution," Adams evidently had renewed his interest in the writings of Jean Jacques Rousseau.[7] When revealed in 1907, the Preface to *The Education* would begin with a passage Adams found in Rousseau's *Confessions*.[8] What needs particular notice is that Rousseau wrote his *Confessions* as two narratives separated by a break in time and that Benjamin Franklin did the same when writing his *Memoirs*. Adams evidently viewed the precedents as suggestive.[9]

Also suggestive were the fates of the classmates with whom Adams first went to Europe. Benjamin Crowninshield had died in January 1892. In London in September 1892, Adams learned that Nicholas Anderson too had died. As felt by Adams, it seems, the deaths threw youthful shared adventures into a newly-distant past and created a fracture—a break—in time.

Such things considered, Adams's decision to write *The Education* as two narratives can be conjecturally dated in late September 1892 in London. Once made, the decision was exceedingly important. It meant that henceforward he would be doing two things interconnectedly. He would be living. He at the same time would be going forward in experiences he knew would serve as bases for his second narrative.

The natural starting point for the first narrative was the one already adopted: the birth of Henry Adams in Boston on February 16, 1838. Possible starting points for the second narrative would be his week in a London hospital in December 1891 and his initial voyage on the *Teutonic*, sailing from Liverpool on February 3, 1892. Those were the moments that Adams in fact would use when writing Chapter XXI.[10] The big British steamer would itself provide the effective beginning, being the emblem of a new age.

A case can be made that *The Education* was in charge of Adams, and not the other way around. The second narrative begged to become the greatest story Adams could write. With a view to improving it, he was beginning to pitch his *actions* at a high order of difficulty.

Adams and the Hoopers returned to New York on another big White Star steamer, the *Majestic.* He accompanied them to Cambridge, turned around, and reached Washington in time to greet Tati Salmon. As he knew in advance, Queen Marau could not come. Adversities incident to her dead husband's will required her presence in Tahiti.[11]

The occasion that brought Tati to the United States was looming bankruptcy. To survive under French rule, the Tevas had gone into business as suppliers of oranges, sugar, and pearl shell. In 1892, business conditions were straitened worldwide, and the family was in need of cash. Tati hoped that arrangements helpful to the family could be made in America, most probably in New York.

Adams meant to give Tati every possible assistance, social and commercial. At 1603 H Street, the giant Tahitian dined with two of America's most irrepressible talkers, Theodore Roosevelt and Wayne MacVeagh. A Pennsylvania lawyer and former attorney general, Mac-Veagh was married to Senator Cameron's sister Virginia and had been Adams's most trusted political ally. Tati listened to the talkers. Partly because of his chiefly bearing and impressive size and perhaps more because he was content to listen, he won immediate social acceptance.

Thinking it best, Adams escorted Tati to New York and placed him in the hands of Clarence King, who knew some businessmen the Tahitian would want to meet. Adams returned to Washington and took delivery of a box Tati had shipped to 1603 H Street.

Left in New York without his adoptive brother, Tati felt adrift. He wrote to Taura-atua and said so. He mentioned having dined with King and John La Farge. ". . . Roosevelt came in afterward. . . ."[12]

The Tahitian's stay in New York overlapped Election Day. While Tati looked on, America's voters rejected the Republican, President Harrison, and elected his Democratic rival, ex-President Cleveland. The news depressed King and Roosevelt, both Republican loyalists. More depressing was the decline of business. King and Tati could not find importers willing to order anything the Tevas could supply.

Tati retreated to Washington. The box that had accompanied him from Tahiti had in it the two chapters of the *Memoirs of Marau Taaroa* that Adams had drafted while on the island. As returned to Adams, the chapters bore corrections by Marau.[13] Adams discussed the *Memoirs* with Tati, and the giant made a welcome discovery. He learned that Taura-atua i Amo—Henry Adams—already knew more about the history of the Tahitians than anyone else, Arii Taimai excepted.[14]

Adams had inherited a total of $400,000 from his Adams and Brooks antecedents.[15] Assisted by Edward Hooper, he was managing his own investments and garnering returns that much exceeded his expenses. He also was part-owner of an Adams Real Estate Trust managed by his elder brothers. With increasing anxiety, he was keeping track of a universal flow of gold to London. He viewed the flow as dangerous both to Americans and Tahitians. An index of his alarm was a gift in the guise of a loan. He lent Tati $13,000. The sum reflected the Tevas' most pressing embarrassments. Tati left on November 22, 1892, the carrier of a godsend. The Tevas had been rescued just in time.[16]

Adams was going forward with definite purposes. He intended to work. He meant to search in the South and in Cuba for a house adapted for use as a winter refuge. If winter absences slowed his work, he would compensate by working all the harder when back in Washington. At all times, he would harmonize his and the Camerons' activities.

During the past summer, Mrs. Cameron again had borrowed Pitch Pine Hill. After Tati left, on November 23, 1892, Adams started south with the Camerons for a second holiday at Coffin's Point. He and Senator Cameron were again together continuously. A possibility was growing that they might join in a political action.

In early December, Adams left South Carolina, reappeared at 1603 H Street, and began to work full-time. His labor on *The Education* remained completely secret.[17]

His writing the *Memoirs of Marau Taaroa* was not a secret. The project was known to the Camerons, Phillips, the Hoopers, and others. Without concealment, Adams studied his accumulated evidence, drafted chapters, and wrote to Tati and Marau concerning evidence he lacked.

Adams's letters to his Tahitian relations are missing.[18] All that survives is a transcript of the closing portion of a letter to Marau written late in 1892.[19] In the portion, Adams asks Marau to send him a Tahitian-English dictionary. He asks for the genealogy of her husband's family. And he asks questions about particular persons.

> My chief want now is the Pomare pedigree. Of course I have some of it, but every now and then I am puzzled. For instance, why did Tutaha of Haapape care to make young Otoo wear the Maroura and upset Teriirere? Tutaha's sister Tetuaraenui married Purea's brother Auri, which might give Tutaha an interest in Purea; but what interest had he in Otoo? He had . . . the same connection with Otoo as Teriirere, only one generation lower. . . .

The passage illustrated two truths. Tahitian words and names could seem dismayingly alien to persons not familiar with them, and Tahitian blood and marital relationships could seem discouragingly complicated. Yet Adams's questions would seem natural to Marau. They were pointed and might induce her to make an effort. They all but certainly would require her tapping her mother's memory.

When a young man, Clarence King had brought his scientific career to a high point by winning the appointment as founding director of a federal agency, the U. S. Geological Survey. He served long enough to get the Survey operating, then turned to private life, hoping to make a fortune in mining and to conduct independent research. He unluckily was burdened by illnesses; his efforts to win a fortune miscarried; and he complicated his life by secretly marrying a black woman by whom he had children and from whom he concealed his identity.

All the same, King achieved an important object. He contributed the lead article, "The Age of the Earth," to the January 1893 issue of the *American Journal of Science*. The article could be classed as geology. To reach his conclusions, however, King had had to join forces with the world's leading physicists. In his first sentence, he mentioned that in 1862 the British physicist William Thomson (later Lord Kelvin) had suggested that the age of the earth could be calculated from data about the planet's cooling—its "probable rate of refrigeration." King's article presented an estimate of the age of the earth based on Thomson's suggestion and data King himself had helped to develop about the cooling rate of diabase, a kind of rock.

There is no direct evidence that Adams read King's article. There does not need to be. It was a certainty that Adams would read everything King published. In the past, he had reviewed King's publications anonymously in the *North American Review* and the *Nation*.[20] In the present instance, he did something more difficult. Starting at the latest in January 1893, he began to study the principal writings of the leading physicists of Europe and America.[21]

When first introduced to geology by Professor Louis Agassiz in 1857–1858, Adams had learned about ancient glaciers that covered much of North America; hence his interest in investigations relating to changes of atmospheric temperature. In 1893, after reading King's article about the earth's cooling, he took particular interest in the study of heat and the study of electromagnetism. The authors he most read concerning electromagnetism were Michael Faraday, long dead, and James Clerk Maxwell, living and very active.[22] An all-round leader in physics, Maxwell was the foremost authority on heat. Adams read Maxwell's much-published *Theory of Heat* and closely studied his "kinetic theory" but did not immediately record how the theory affected him.

Monthly sailing ships provided direct transit from San Francisco to Tahiti. Tati had an easy voyage and arrived in time for the Tevas' Christmas party. Writing to Adams on January 11, 1893, he recalled that at the party Arii Taimai had led a toast by saying, "Taura-atua, my son, must remain before you all." Tati explained, "—(this is the way affection is shown. . . .)"

Marau was touched to learn of Taura-atua's rapid progress. On February 13, she wrote to tell him "how grateful I am for the trouble you take with our memoirs." She continued, ". . . the least I can do is to do my part of the work & to answer your questions as soon as possible." She knew he needed the words of certain old songs both in Tahitian and in literal English translations. She remarked, "You cannot really imagine how hard it is to translate tahitian into english [*sic*] or any other language & be able to keep a little of its charm." The difficulty was all the worse because the Tahitian language was rapidly dissolving. "There are so many words that we have lost all trace of, & a great many more that are not used today. . . ." Yet she promised, ". . . with mother's help . . . I will try my best."

By the March boat, Marau sent Adams three dictionaries. Also she said she had received something, evidently a list of questions.[23] She must have given the list to Tati. On May 7, he reported to Adams: "I have looked over your long questions about history and have answered them as far we could. . . . I have decided long ago that you know more of our history than any one, and that if you took the trouble to learn the language, and got to the root of the Tahitian names, you and our old mother, between you two alone, would finish the history of the island and [the] family in proper shape."

William Phillips was fifteen years younger than Adams. A Southerner given to amusing turns of speech, Willy enjoyed the trust of many federal officials. Early in 1893, he joined Adams as Washington assistant. His main function would be to gather important political intelligence. If outright spying had to be done, he would do it.

When possible during February and March 1893, in part to avoid the inauguration and the swarming of office seekers in the capital, Adams left Washington. He journeyed to Cuba with Phillips and asked about houses near Havana. He visited Anne Fell at her and her husband's orange grove in Florida. He returned three times to Coffin's Point, once as escort to Hooper and his daughters Ellen and Mabel. He was there in mid-March when Mrs. Cameron was away in Cleveland, consequent to the death of her elder brother Henry. In her absence, Senator Cameron, Adams, and growing Martha formed an impromptu household.

While moving about, Adams worked and worried. Phillips forwarded mail and additional books about Tahiti. Adams learned from newspapers that the flight of gold from the U. S. Treasury to London was continuing. And word came from New York that King was seriously ill.

On the chance that they might agree to join him, Adams wrote to the Hoopers proposing a visit to the World's Columbian Exposition in Chicago. The Hoopers proved unwilling. In late March, Adams returned to 1603 H Street and worked on the *Memoirs*. He invited Niece Louisa to visit him and sent the Hoopers a new proposal. He had concluded that Scottish hills were not high enough to relieve Ellen's hay fever. He accordingly proposed that they pass the coming August and September in the Alps. He wrote to Mabel: "If you would go to Switzerland, I could go over in May or June to find a house. . . ."

John and Clara Hay were financial supporters of Western Reserve University in Cleveland. The junior class wished to dedicate its 1893 yearbook to Mr. Hay. In support of the gesture, President Thwing wrote to Adams asking that he prepare a biographical sketch of Hay for the yearbook. Adams agreed "with pleasure" on April 1, 1893, only saying he needed a deadline and a suggestion as to length. He wrote the sketch before mid-May, and it was published soon after. Titled "Biography of John Hay," it filled five-and-a-half large pages. It bore no indication of authorship. One incidental passage excepted, it sustained a tone of factualness and measured praise.[24]

April Fool's Day was one of Adams's favorite occasions. He had promised Thwing the biography on that amusing anniversary.[25] Yet the work he submitted did not appear to be a joke or sportive exploit.

His sketch conforms—indeed over-conforms—to the requirements of a familiar genre: heroic biography as written by American patriots and respectful readers of the Bible. Its first paragraph concerns a Scottish John Hay who emigrated in the mid-1700s and founded a family in America. Two paragraphs later, amidst a parade of genealogical figures, a new John Hay is born. There follows a recitation of Hay's achievements as student, law apprentice, the younger of Lincoln's private secretaries at the White house, Union army officer, diplomat in Europe, editor of the *New York Tribune*; raconteur and poet; assistant secretary of state; and—with John Nicolay—author of a compendious book, *Abraham Lincoln/ A History*. The recitation includes a list of Hay's virtues: "his temper and tact, his wit, intelligence, discretion, and knowledge." It takes note of his marrying Clara Stone.

Reconsidered, Adams's sketch resembles a formal portrait framed in gold. It accentuates one idea—the idea with which it ends: that other Americans, for instance John Marshall, by writing a biography of Washington, had performed the "pious duty" of memorializing America's presidents; but Hay outdid them. His and Nicolay's *Lincoln* is painted as "probably the most considerable literary monument ever raised to a statesman or ruler in his own times by his own contemporaries."

Accentuation is heightened by avoidances. There is no mention of Hay's marrying money. His children do not appear. Nothing is said about his illnesses. No words appear about a tragic accident or other calamity. Yet Adams's sketch reads as if it were an encomium made necessary by a hero's recent death, of course after completion of the great work toward which the hero's heritage and his life had always marched. So there *is* a joke. Adams gave it a subtle form: a high piling up of the completest solemnity.[26]

He could joke about Hay because possessed of foreknowledge. He could foresee some of the principal contents of his *Education*. The book would include a straightforward evocation of the abilities and achievements of Clarence King. It also would set forth two myths. One would be a myth of a not-yet-decided sort about Hay as an American hero. The other would be a myth representing the elder Charles Francis Adams as a diplomatic slayer of British dragons.

Attention must be given to *The Education of Henry Adams* as it relates to heroism. The book was designed to concern a fictional Henry Adams different from the author, also named Henry Adams. The difference would be achieved by subtraction. As written, the book contains all sorts of biographical data about the actual Henry Adams. More often than not, the smaller facts offered about him are true. Yet the book's two narratives strip their fictional protagonist of *all* of the actual Adams's important achievements.

The presented "Henry Adams" is a fictional person who does not do much, a learner who is given ceaseless opportunities to acquire something called "education" and who comically does not get it. The method of the book has about it a madness much like the madness in the method of *Hamlet*. Whereas Shakespeare's play can be described as anti-chivalric, yet centers around a prince whose conduct at the end is ultra-chivalric, *The Education* is pro-heroic, yet centers around a learner whose only heroism is stumbling forward from one missed opportunity to another. By this highly original, inverted means, Adams's book can inculcate in its best readers a resource indispensable to all serious learners: a determination never to stop.

* * *

In November 1892, at the urging of President Harrison, representatives of twenty nations had attended a conference on silver held in Brussels. The U. S. delegates had been instructed to negotiate uniform use by all nations of gold and silver as money—or, failing that, an increase in the use of silver.

The main barrier in the way of agreement was England's insistence on preserving its gold-based monetary system, devised by Isaac Newton when director of the Royal Mint. Action being blocked, the conference adjourned in January 1893 with the intention of reconvening in May.

In March 1893, President Cleveland nominated John G. Carlisle, a senator from Kentucky, to be secretary of the treasury. Among the problems confronting the new administration, none was more pressing than the disappearance of gold from the government's vaults. In late March or April, the Treasury prepared new instructions for the chief delegate expected to attend the silver conference when reassembled. For unknown reasons and by unknown means, the instructions passed to Adams. If they were given to him with a view to his offering advice behind the scenes, a possible reason was a false supposition that he had become a Democrat. A second possible reason was positive knowledge in Washington that he was neither a Democrat nor a Republican. A more probable third reason was awareness that he was an expert on public finance and had written and edited leading works on the subject, including *The Life of Albert Gallatin* and a three-volume edition of Gallatin's *Writings*.

In Adams's opinion, the new instructions betrayed a lack of ideas about the proposal that the U. S. delegate should put before the conference. In response, he wrote an anonymous memorandum that exactly fit four sheets of legal-sized paper.[27] The memorandum began by saying, "The instructions assume that some proposition is to be made, either from the U. S. or from England or elsewhere, to serve as the starting point of negotiation." It explained what the American proposition would have to be, what latitude the American delegate would have to be accorded, and what backing he would need from the government and America's banks. The suggested proposition was the opening of all the world's mints to the free coinage of gold and silver.[28]

Adams's first purpose in writing the anonymous memorandum was to secure a worldwide settlement relating to gold and silver and thus promote financial stability and universal prosperity. His second purpose was to reduce or end the likelihood of a new great war in Europe comparable to the Franco-Prussian war of 1870. Such a war, he wrote, was "only prevented by the combination of moneyed interests."

As seen by Adams, the factors weighing most heavily against the achievement of a settlement were English intransigence and the weakness of the United States Government in managing its finances. He outlined reasons for believing that the English might give way, but he emphasized the importance of American weakness and made it the subject of his concluding paragraph.

> . . . if any good result is expected from negotiation, it is absolutely necessary that the [American] negotiator should be supported by vigorous defensive action of the government at home. As long as the United States Treasury stands wholly at the mercy of Europe, Europe will continue to disregard our demands. Every other government protects its Treasury. In no European country is the gold reserve at the mercy of a foreign demand. Until some means is devised and made effective for protecting the gold in the Treasury, the President cannot stand in a position to negotiate with effect, nor can his representatives abroad bring the bankers of Europe to reason.

The memorandum presumably was given to Secretary Carlisle. The resumption of the conference was postponed to November. The postponement was fatal to the conference, which never reconvened. It was fatal also to Adams's memorandum, the existence of which is known only because he kept his next-to-final copy.[29]

All the while, gold was flowing to London. On May 7, 1893, prices dropped sharply at the New York Stock Exchange. In America, signs were pointing toward a second panic more dangerous than the first.

As a rule when in Washington, Adams wrote his personal letters on paper engraved with his address and folded to permit the writer four small pages of space. On May 13, 1893, he wrote a tightly-composed, highly interesting letter that exactly fit eight pages. In this respect, the letter resembled his financial memorandum. On the basis of mere appearance, both the memorandum and the letter should be counted as additions to his important writings.

The circumstances in which the letter was written are uncertain but can be outlined with some likelihood of correctness. Adams knew a capable scientist in Washington, Samuel F. Langley, director of the Smithsonian Institution.[30] Perhaps at his dining table, Adams told Langley he had read Maxwell's *Theory of Heat*. Conversation turned to a passage in which Maxwell invented an imaginary being. Maxwell's passage becomes clear if read twice with care.[31]

> . . . it is impossible in a [gaseous] system enclosed in an envelope which permits neither change of volume nor passage of heat, and in which both the temperature and the pressure [of the gas] are everywhere the same, to produce any inequality of temperature or pressure without the expenditure of work. This is the second law of thermodynamics, and it is undoubtedly true as long we deal with bodies only in mass, and have no power of perceiv-

ing or handling the separate molecules of which they are made up. But if we conceive a being whose faculties are so sharpened that he can follow every molecule in its course, such a being . . . would be able to do what is at present impossible for us.

The meaning of the passage will be still clearer if it is borne in mind that in 1893 "molecule" and "atom" were interchangeable terms: both meant the smallest particle of matter. Maxwell chose to say "molecule."[32] Left to himself, Adams would have preferred "atom."[33]

After inventing his imaginary being, Maxwell went on to describe a vessel divided into chambers A and B by a partition in which there is a hole. He explained that if the very capable imagined being opens and closes the hole at such times that swiftly-moving molecules of gas pass from A to B and slowly-moving molecules pass from B to A, the redistributed molecules will "raise the temperature of B and lower that of A, in contradiction to the second law of thermodynamics."

Last details must be added. It appears that, when talking with Adams, Langley mentioned that Maxwell's imagined being had so teased the fancy of William Thomson that he nicknamed it "Maxwell's demon."[34] In 1879, Thomson had used the nickname when giving a lecture titled "The Sorting Demon of Maxwell" before the Royal Institution of Great Britain. Langley was aware that the lecture had been published, and he helpfully supplied Adams the book in which the nickname appeared.[35]

Adams read Thomson's lecture and wrote Langley to thank him for his help. The situation was complicated by several factors. Adams was fully as imaginative as Maxwell or Thomson. He was especially disposed to think of metaphors and parallels, and such was his turn of mind that he might think of parallels that mixed the serious with the comic. Adams, moreover, was an exceedingly attentive reader. When reading such a book as Maxwell's *Theory of Heat,* he read with an eye to what the author was saying and with an eye to the possibility that the author in particular passages might not express himself very well, might contradict himself, or even say things he did not mean. It is not suggested that Adams was a fault-finder. Just the opposite, he was a meaning-finder. He would try to learn the author's meaning even in the face of poor expression. He would search too for meanings the author failed to notice.

Maxwell and Thomson stood high among the world's physicists. They were rivals of Faraday. They could appear to tower over Adams. His proper attitude toward them could seem to be one of deference. But Adams, too, occupied a lofty station. He stood high among the historians of all time. He believed that history, while in some respects an art, was as much a science as geology or physics. On the premise that history was as high a pursuit as any other, or the highest, he would never look up to leaders in the other sciences. He instead would look across to them—either that or down.

At the same time, Adams understood that all minds were prone to error. Given a choice between an idea he suggested and one suggested by someone else, he might go to great lengths *not* to insist on the rightness of his own. His intellectual self-effacement would often be a consequence of excellent manners, but manners did not weigh as much with him as truth. One of his reasons for deprecating his own ideas was awareness that truth is hard to reach.

Beginning his letter to Langley, Adams wrote: "Many thanks for remembering the demon. He is not much of a demon, after all, and leaves me about as much in the dark as before he sorted."

With his usual excellent manners, Adams attributed his bafflement to himself. "The trouble is my brain, which does not sort. I cannot drive the kinetic theory into it."

He quoted two lines from Maxwell's *Theory of Heat*: "The molecules of all bodies are in a continual state of agitation. The hotter a body is, the more violently are its molecules agitated."[36] Also he took note of Maxwell's statement that the colder a body was, the less violently its molecules were agitated. He continued, ". . . in a body actually deprived of heat, the molecules cannot agitate at all, which contradicts the first of Maxwell's assertions."

Possibly not one reader in thousands would have noticed Maxwell's self-contradiction. Adams was entitled to congratulate himself. Instead he serio-comically remarked, "Evidently I am wrong. . . ."

He went on by treating Maxwell as having failed to find words that would say what he had in mind. "Clearly Maxwell must mean that *every molecule must have a definite minimum of heat inherent in it as matter*. That is, the molecule is the heat[,] plus other forms of energy, of matter [italics added]."[37]

Had he stopped there, Adams would already have completed a great letter. Writing on the assumption that matter is heat (or energy) and vice versa, he had proposed an amateurish, yet authentic, anticipation of Einstein's later statement, "The mass of a body is a measure of its energy. . . ."[38] Also, in making the proposal, Adams advanced a long step toward suggesting that the heat inherent in particles might be releasable as "atomic energy."

Adams had only started. He remarked afresh, ". . . I am obviously wrong. . . ." He said the proof of his being wrong was Maxwell's kinetic theory, which appeared to say that all heat whatever was in process of being lost. ". . . I understand that the kinetic theory contemplates the total dissipation of energy in any body as a necessary consequence of waste."

Writing these words, Adams repeated the second law of thermodynamics as Maxwell at points seemed to believe it could be stated. But to
Adams the second law seemed either ill-stated or part-mistaken. He
showed his opinion by producing, not a "sorting demon," but a molecule of his own selection. He said in his letter, "A molecule of hydrogen
gas is now bouncing about in the nebula of Orion." His posited molecule is alone in space and not part of a "body." ". . . the surrounding
temperature of space is presumed to have been −450° from eternity.
How then does the molecule bounce?" As nearly as Adams could learn,
Maxwell's answer would have to be that at −450° the molecule would
bounce very little. But Adams would not relent. He said again that, according to Maxwell, the molecule would lose *all* its heat. He concluded:
"Supposing it is lost, what is the status of the molecule[?] Obviously in
a series of years, say twenty million, at the observed rate of dissipation of
energy, many molecules must be dead."

Langley could hardly have expected a suggestion of the sort that
Adams had propounded. In his best vein of comedy, as if he thought his
idea not absurd, the historian entered a complaint. "Maxwell gives me
no definition of a dead molecule. I do not remember that Thomson
deals with the subject; yet a dead molecule must be something very different from a living molecule."[39]

The meaning of Adams's letter was unconcealed. He made clear his
belief that the principles of physics expressed by Maxwell were incomplete, not well-written, and not yet explanatory of the particles and bodies they concerned. He suggested that physics, when more developed,
would assert an equivalence between matter and energy. He upheld the
dignity of history, the science he himself had embraced, and did so by
thrusting forward two subjects that especially concerned historians: the
living and the dead.

Although assertive, his letter was friendly and highly acceptable. If
they could forgive his writing them comical letters, Adams could get
along happily with Langley and other scientists.[40] Meanwhile his letter
was one that properly could be written by a great historian. After all, he
was himself a student of "bodies." One such body was a united people,
the Americans. Prior to the arrival of European intruders, the Tahitians
were not united, hence not a body; but the Tahitians who lived in each
of the island's districts were united and were bodies. As for molecules
or atoms, Adams had studied individual Americans and currently was
studying individual Tahitians. In the past, moreover, he had published
conclusions not only about such dead atoms as Albert Gallatin, Thomas
Jefferson, and James Madison, but also about such still-living atoms as
Mrs. Ulysses S. Grant and Jay Gould.[41] He was speaking from experience.

* * *

Cleveland had chosen Walter Gresham of Illinois to be secretary of state and Thomas Bayard of Delaware to be ambassador—a new rank—to England. Gresham was a stranger to Adams. Bayard was a friend.

The Hoopers liked the idea of Adams's finding a house they could share with him in the Alps. Similarly the Camerons decided to pass the summer in Switzerland. Adams booked passage on the *Paris*, due to sail from New York on June 3, 1893. The Camerons would be passengers on the *Paris*, as would Ambassador Bayard and some harmless Blaines.

Senator Cameron was one of the dignitaries expected at the opening of the Columbian Exposition. He asked Adams to join him. On May 14, Uncle Henry wrote to Mabel Hooper: "I am trying to make up my mind to going to Chicago this week. It is a fearful effort, but Senator Cameron has, or means to have[,] a private car. . . . Yow yow!!"

The car materialized, and the senator's party made a quick visit to the Exposition. Adams advised Niece Louisa on May 28, "We were twelve consecutive hours at the show on Saturday [May 20] . . . ramping about in gondolas and chairs, and drinking beer by the barrel, and eating ice-cream and German cookery till life became a broken beer-jug, and we all came home to bed for a week."

In past years, Adams had traveled great distances to see extraordinary works created by human beings. In 1872 on the Upper Nile, he had seen the colossal figures at the temple of Abu Simbel. In 1886 in Japan, he had seen the imposing shrines built at Nikko for the first and third shoguns, Iyeyasu and Iye-mitsu. In 1893, he was aware that the buildings of the Chicago Fair had been designed by the country's leading architects. The knowledge did not prepare him for the Fair's amazing beauty at night, when its classically-shaped white pavilions were electrically illuminated. He realized that the pavilions were a mere stage set, to be taken down when the show was over. Yet he felt their beauty as one of humanity's great achievements.

He knew a leading Chicagoan, Franklin MacVeagh, brother of Wayne MacVeagh. On May 26, he wrote to Frank from Washington, "A man who has passed his life . . . always thinking and despairing of seeing his age rise to the creation of new art, or the appreciation of the old, cannot all of a sudden see his idea take shape in a form far more magnificent than he had ever dreamed it, without being for the moment stunned by the shock. . . . As I returned from the first visit to the Fair, every building in Chicago seemed to me to be twice the height it was before. I was crushed flat."

The voyage of the *Paris* to England began on rough seas. Adams felt queasy but appeared regularly for meals. Most of the other Americans became very seasick. Mrs. Cameron reacted so uneasily that on the ship's arrival she could scarcely go ashore.

Ambassador Bayard advanced to London amid a troop of compatriots. Adams was in the troop. He had earlier witnessed the arrival of two U. S. ministers in London: his father in 1861 and James Russell Lowell in 1880. Witnessing Bayard's arrival extended the pattern.

The Camerons stayed ten days in London before leaving for Switzerland. Adams stayed too. He met Gaskell and Cunliffe. Wanting his summer to end well, he booked return passage for the Hoopers and himself on a new ship, the *Lucania*, to sail in late September.

On June 27, 1893, prices crashed on the New York Stock Exchange. A devastating panic had begun. As if nothing had happened, Adams went to Scotland to see the Clarks. From Tillypronie on June 29, he wrote matter-of-factly to Mabel Hooper: "I leave here Saturday or Sunday; pass a day in London, and go direct to Geneva[,] where I rather expect to find the Camerons at a villa at Prangins. Then I shall try to investigate Switzerland for you. Henry James tells me much of it, on the strength of his brother William's experiences. They seem to prefer the Lake of Luzerne [*sic*] to the Lake of Geneva. . . ."

The Camerons' summer was already disrupted. A week before, on June 20, in view of the depletion of gold in the Treasury, President Cleveland had ordered Congress into special session. To be present, Senator Cameron would have to start toward Washington in late July.

Adams joined the Camerons at their rented villa in Switzerland. While Mrs. Cameron rested, he, the senator, and Martha went sightseeing in the Alps. Soon he and all three Camerons set off for Lake Lucerne. During the morning of July 22, they crossed the Furka Pass by carriage. Adams and the senator sat atop the carriage and talked about silver. President Cleveland wished Congress to repeal the provision of the Sherman Act of 1890 that required the Treasury to purchase silver in stated amounts at stated times. The president seemed to think that repeal of the provision would suffice to save the country from panic and general ruin of its banks and businesses.

In the afternoon, the party advanced to Lucerne.[42] There a letter reached Henry from his brother Charles.[43] It began:

> I am sorry to say that we [the Adamses] are in very serious financial trouble, and that the Trust is deeply involved. How deeply I cannot say, for,—to my great mortification I confess,—I have given no attention to the affairs of the Trust, leaving them wholly to John; and John,—owing to the stress to which he has been subjected,—is wholly broken down. . . . My own affairs at the same time call for my whole attention.
>
> Under these circumstances[,] Brooks and I think that you ought to return at once. . . . You cannot . . . delegate any outsider,—Hooper or an-

other[,—]to act for you. Any dirty linen must be washed in the bosom of the family.

There was no likelihood that Henry could himself be in financial trouble. As invested by him and Hooper, the capital he held in his own right was safe and paying good returns. Yet he could easily believe that financial trouble had overtaken his brothers. Equally he could believe that neither the president nor Congress had any idea how to rescue the country. In the circumstances, he had no choice. Both as a responsible Adams and a responsible though unofficial American politician, he had to go home and he had to act.

Cameron went to London. Henry escorted Mrs. Cameron and Martha to Homburg in Switzerland, left them there, reached London on July 27, and received a telegram from his brother Charles saying "Come soon."[44]

While in a cab on the Thames Embankment, he spied Cameron passing in another cab. He went to the steamship office, cancelled the reservations on the *Lucania*, and booked the earliest space to New York that he could get: a deck stateroom on an old vessel, the *Umbria*.

Cameron had engaged passage on another ship. Henry twice visited him. Knowing that the senator's Washington house was being renovated and would be uninhabitable, he lent him 1603 H Street for the rest of the summer. He and Cameron agreed to keep in touch by letter.

The Adamses were the leading family of Quincy, a country town in Massachusetts, seven miles south of Boston. The family's principal residence was a clapboard mansion, the Old House. In the absence of other takers, Brooks and his wife were occupying the mansion. John was living nearby in a house he had built for himself and his family. Charles had built a house even closer, at the top of President's Hill. He had recently bought an estate in rural South Lincoln, to which he expected soon to move. He meanwhile was living on his hilltop.

Henry appeared at the Old House early on August 7, 1893, a Monday. Brooks was away. His wife Evelyn—known as Daisy—welcomed Henry and gave him a room. Evelyn was Mrs. Lodge's sister. Anna Cabot Mills Lodge—known as Nanny—was Mrs. Cameron's closest friend.[45] These connections made a difference. Henry was back among his Adams relations, but in a way that reflected his having friendships.

John was angry with Henry for not accepting the honorary doctorate from Harvard and did not want to see him.[46] Henry visited Charles and learned the truth of the family's situation. All his brothers had borrowed heavily and invested in a market that was going to panic. As managers of the Real Estate Trust, John and Charles had bought properties that

could be sold only at prohibitive losses and would have to be held.
Charles was the brother most in debt. To tide himself over, he obtained
$900,000 from Frederick Ames, a multi-millionaire. Ames soon died, or
rather was killed by financial anxieties.[47]

Brooks returned. He told Henry his losses were so great that he
might have to depend on salaried work. A possibility he was considering
was service as a federal official. He meanwhile asked Henry to read a
"potential book" of his—an "incomplete manuscript"—"half legible
sheets." It lacked a title: Brooks could not think of one himself. It attempted a narrative of historical events, but he had not yet decided
which events to start or end with. All the same, Henry read the sheets
and responded encouragingly.[48]

In anticipation of a trip to Switzerland, the Hoopers had gone to
Beverly Farms and moved into Pitch Pine Hill. They wanted Henry to
visit them. He refused. Much though they might wish it, he would not
reenter his summer house.

The Senate was in session, Cameron was in Washington, and letters
were passing between him and Adams. They are missing. Presumably
each writer burned the other's letters as soon as received and read.

Adams had been studying press reports. On August 12, 1893, he
had written to Hay in Europe, "You are mighty lucky to be out of this
howling madhouse." He blamed the panic on England's money-lords.
By drawing gold to London, they had created gold famines in many
places. "England has tried her best to save herself by . . . forcing up the
price of gold on all her debtors. The squeeze has beggared us for the
moment. . . ." "True, I am pretty mad about it. In fact, I am furious, and
in no frame of mind to be judicial or historical."

Ten days later, Adams said in a letter to Gaskell that the panic in the
United States was a financial and political trick. "The scare is senseless;
a mere device of the capitalists to make us give up silver." He left it to
Gaskell to realize that the capitalists he was referring to were English.

On September 6, he told MacVeagh, ". . . I don't want my friends
to think me madder than I am, and I do want them, if possible, to understand why the madness of the times makes sanity impossible." ". . . I see
no alternative but a choice of sides. . . ."

Adams prefered a choice outside the pales of the Democratic and
Republican Parties. He confessed to Hay on September 8, "The amiable
but quite lunatic gold-bug has ended by making me a flat-footed Populist and an advocate of fiat-money."[49]

As Henry saw it, the truly shocking feature of the Adams family's
plight was the injury to John. The eldest son had proved a typical Adams

in pride of family, yet had been indolent, even lazy. In August and September, worry drained his resources. He made no effort to get better. Judging from his appearance, he did not have long to live.

Henry seemed not to do much. With Hooper, he went to Tuckanuck for a week's visit with Sturgis Bigelow. He visited Mrs. Lodge at the Lodges' house at Nahant, not far from Beverly Farms. After returning to the Old House, he partly idled. He and Evelyn found packs of cards and played double solitare.

Josiah Quincy, a neighbor of the Adamses, was leaving the office of assistant secretary of state. Brooks suggested himself for the place. He visited Washington and called on President Cleveland. He asked Henry to write to Wayne MacVeagh and urge him to send a letter of support to Secretary Gresham; Henry did as asked; and MacVeagh, in place of a letter, went to Washington and pled Brooks's case in person. The effort reflected MacVeagh's high opinion of Henry.[50] But Brooks's application was spurned by Cleveland and Gresham.

When writing to MacVeagh, Henry was candid about his wishes. He said, "I am far from eager to place any member of my family in office in Washington." ". . . my brother at Washington will be anything but a source of repose to me, and will probably drive me away. . . ." The government's decision not to use Brooks came as a relief. Yet Henry wanted to help Brooks. He told MacVeagh he had "other views" about his brother and hoped "to switch him on to another line."[51]

Panic had spread from the financial centers to every part of the country. Businesses and individuals were failing by thousands. Henry was not immediately told, but one person very hard hit was Clarence King. A bank he had started in Texas had closed its doors.[52]

In recent months, Henry Cabot Lodge had been promoted from the House to the Senate. Mrs. Lodge went to Washington to join him. At the same time, Mrs. Cameron rushed to America to attend her mother, who was gravely ill at Warm Sweet Springs in the Virginia mountains. To complicate matters, the Camerons' vacation house at Coffin's Point was damaged by a hurricane.

Beginning with his first trip to South Carolina, relations between Mrs. Cameron and Adams had become completely trusting on both sides. On September 15, 1893, he advised her that he would be in Washington on the 20th but would stay only briefly and would go to Chicago to pay the Exposition a leisurely second visit. Knowing his letter would be read only by her and knowing he could speak freely, he closed with a paragraph that could be read as partly comic and hyperbolic but none the less was a rhapsody of menace. He said he wanted the social order in the United States and Europe wrecked from top to bottom, and he wanted to help murder the chief lords of English capitalism. ". . . hating vindictively, as I do, our whole fabric and conception of society . . . I shall be glad to see the whole thing utterly destroyed and wiped away. With a communism I could exist tolerably well . . . but in a society of Jews and brokers, a world made up of maniacs wild for gold, I have no place. In the coming rows, you will know where to find me. Probably I shall be helping the London mob to pull up Harcourt and Rothschild on a lamp-post in Piccadilly."[53]

In the sense of hating and wanting to harm all Jews, Adams had not been and would never be an anti-Semite.[54] When not ignoring Jews, he simply disliked them.[55] He and Clover had preferred to avoid them.[56] The panic concentrated his attention on the most powerful bankers and money-managers in London. It happened that, after the failure of Baring Brothers in 1890, all the great English banks were controlled by "Jews and foreigners."[57] The man whose name was synonymous with English banking was the chief partner in N. M. Rothschild & Sons, Nathaniel Meyer de Rothschild. Adams and Lord Rothschild were almost of an age. By force of events, Henry was led to compare himself with his English opposite. On August 13, he had written to Willy Phillips, ". . . I ought to defy Rothschild for wealth, seeing that everyone owes me, and I nobody a thank-ye." Significantly, Adams thought of the banker, not as a Jew, but as a creditor and a person never in debt.[58]

As the panic grew worse, Adams came to see the bankers of London, New York, and Boston as mortal enemies. He changed his speech. When he wrote to Mrs. Cameron on September 15, he used an English locution and spoke about "a society of Jews and brokers" when what he meant was *bankers* and brokers.[59] The term he usually preferred was "gold-bugs." On September 25, he wrote to MacVeagh, "I am tired of Wall Street and State Street." "I go no further with the gold-bugs."

His concern was the control of money in vast amounts. He viewed America as under financial and economic siege. On that account, he became anti-capitalist, anti-banker, and anti-Rothschild. His motive was protective, and both national and personal.[60] He was watching stricken Americans as they weakened, tried to hang on, or died.

In the presidential election of 1892, more than a million votes had been cast for James B. Weaver, the candidate of a new force in American politics, the People's Party, usually referred to as the Populists. Although defeated, the Populists continued to urge, even demand, radical changes in the nation's life and government. One change they wanted was the free and unlimited coinage of silver, meaning that a citizen could take any amount of silver to the federal government's mints and get silver dollars in return, no questions asked.

President Cleveland's proposal that Congress repeal a section of the Sherman Act and end the government's purchases of silver was not a Democratic Party measure. It split the Democrats, split the Republicans, created new alignments of silver men and gold-bugs, and precipitated a furious debate in Congress.

Adams returned to Washington. He intended to act on his feelings. His means would be legitimate, to his mind, and confined to the field of public finance. On Monday morning, September 25, 1893, writing to MacVeagh, he said about Senator Cameron: "Don is in great force. . . . He swears . . . that he will make a speech, and do it today. I am curious to know what he will say if he gets up his courage to talk. If he really dares to talk to the Senate as he talks in private, he will take my breath away. . . ."

Cameron was not a senator who made speeches. He was not adapted to taking the floor and proposing legislation. Yet he did what he was not adapted to do. By reading a prepared text, he proposed an array of measures. His action took the press by surprise and brought on a storm of detraction. Next day, saying that Cameron had offered "A Remarkable Argument," the *New York Times* derogated his proposals as favors to senatorial allies.[61] The *New York Herald* reacted still more vigorously but in contradictory ways. The paper attacked him through four columns of print as a traitor to his constituents, yet also lampooned his action as a non-event. ". . . [he] entertained what few Senators could get near enough to hear him by reading a ten minutes' speech against repeal in his modest, scared schoolboy way. . . ."[62]

The speech became a national sensation. On Thursday, the *New York Sun* printed it complete.[63] Adams clipped a copy from the *Sun*, sent it to Hay, and half-suggested how the speech got written. "All the newspapers are full of violent diatribes against Don, who is as pleased as a hen with one chicken. . . . Quay [the other Pennsylvania senator] told him it was a good speech, and his wife must have written it. We who know him feel pretty sure that some one helped him, perhaps Wayne MacVeagh. . . ."[64]

Hay knew Cameron. He knew Adams even better. The materials Adams had sent him—the speech and Adams's comments—were a sufficient basis to warrant a conclusion. The speech was solely Adams's.

In part, his position could be defined in negative terms. He was against England's trying to impose her gold standard on all the world. He was against the controlling men in Lombard Street in London, Wall Street in New York, and State Street in Boston, meaning he was against the world's richest capitalists, bankers, brokers, and thieves. He was against President Cleveland's proposal to stop the U. S. government's purchases of silver. He believed that the proposal did not originate with Cleveland and had been taught to him by persons in the financial community. He believed also that, if passed, the proposal would be a surrender to English financial dictatorship, a source of worse trouble for the United States Government, a blow to American business in many parts of the country, and a heavy injury to Colorado and Nevada, the states in which silver was most widely mined.

Yet Adams's motives were mainly positive. He wished to help the victims of what he believed was a combination of English rascality and American incompetence. The need of the moment was leadership. Since the president had not recommended a program of measures adapted to the crisis in the United States, Adams wanted Congress to enact a program; and his purpose in writing a speech was to offer a program, either to be accepted as offered or replaced by a better.

Once presented by Cameron, the speech Adams wrote was issued in pamphlet form under the title *Remonetization of Silver.* Adams preserved a copy among his papers.[65] There can be no doubt that he had written every word that Cameron presented. Vocabulary, argument, and suggested measures were characteristic of Adams throughout.[66] The speech belonged to Cameron only in two respects, each admittedly considerable. The senator had been willing to offer it before the Senate as his own. He had agreed not only with its general tendencies but also with every line.[67]

As published in pamphlet form, the speech filled the better part of eight densely printed pages. It ended with a five-point program of measures for Congressional action. If carried out, the program would (a) give the Treasury the means to buy a new hoard of gold sufficient to meet its foreseeable needs; (b) expand the U. S. currency and rescue an industry, silver mining in the West, by initiating the free coinage of silver and by taxing the importation of foreign silver; (c) increase the flow of credit to farms and small businesses by eliminating taxes on state banks; (d) help the East and South by extending protections to the shipping industry; and (e) bring the Treasury much-needed new income by levying a duty on sugar. Moreover, by aligning the United States with the silver-based economies of India and China, the program would create a counterpoise to England in world finance.

Adams's program offered help to the country proportionate to its needs. Also his speech was valuable for treating the histories of the United States and Great Britain as open to analysis relating to money. Threaded through the speech was an outspoken sort of history. The most forcible passages were possibly the following.

> From the day when the Pilgrims founded Plymouth to the day when Penn founded Philadelphia; from the day when the tea was thrown into Boston harbor to the day when Washington was inaugurated President; from the day when Jefferson imposed his embargo to the day when the civil

war ended, and down to the day we passed the act now under discussion [the Sherman Act of 1890], the chief interest of our history in the eyes of America and Europe has been its successful protest against the ideas and interests of the moneyed power of England, whether that power was for the moment embodied in church or king, in a landed aristocracy or in a trading monopoly.

. . . ever since America was discovered, England has been controlled by its moneyed interests; and all Americans, at all periods of their history, have believed that the moneyed interests of England were selfish, cruel, and aggressive, as well as sordid, to a degree that made them dangerous to all the world and fatal to the weak.

. . . the moneyed interest of England never recoils before . . . difficulties. . . . If India suffers, India will have to submit. If the people [of India] are ruined, they will have to die. If the laboring class in England resists, it will be starved out, or will be shot down.

The British miners, half a million of them, are to be starved into accepting low wages in order that the British Government may enhance the value of the gold in which America pays the interest on her British debts. . . . The British Government may prefer to shoot its miners, as it has lately done. I do not think a Senator of the United States should legislate with a view to shooting his constituents.

I will not vote to ruin Colorado or Nevada. I will vote to help them, and in return I will ask their help to assist the other weak interests that are struggling throughout the Union for existence against heavy odds. I will vote in such a way as to lighten the many difficulties of the Southern States, and aid them to keep abreast of the national movement. I will give support to every portion of our Union, remote or near. . . .

3

ACTIVITIES OF DIFFERENT KINDS

Hoping fully to experience the Columbian Exposition, Adams asked his brother Charles to share the rent of a Chicago house for a month. Charles preferred a week. On October 1, 1893, the brothers started west. Henry was accompanied by Loulie, Phillips, and the housekeeper, Maggie Wade. Charles took his wife Mary, known as Minnie, and their youngest daughter Elizabeth, known as Elsie. Brooks went separately and roamed the Fair for a day but left, pleading rheumatism. Charles changed his mind and wanted a second week. Henry and his companions rejoiced. On October 8, Henry wrote to Mrs. Cameron that Maggie was "putting in eight hours a day, and vows she will see everything."

Seeing the Fair a second time, Henry beheld a "dream of beauty" conjoined with chaos. From Washington on October 18, he wrote to Lucy Baxter: "Chicago delighted me because it was just as chaotic as my own mind. . . . A pure white temple, on the pure blue sea, with an Italian sky, all vast and beautiful as the world never saw it before, and in it the most astounding, confused, bewildering mass of art and industry, without a sign that there was any connection, relation or harmony or understanding of the relations of anything anywhere. I wonder whether the twenty million visitors carried off the same sense that I did. Probably not. . . . They will think it education. Perhaps it is. Precisely what education is, I don't know. Perhaps to learn chaos when one sees it. . . ."

Writing on the 18th to Hay, Henry said of himself and the Exposition, "I revelled in all its fakes and frauds, all its wickedness that seemed not to be understood by our innocent natives, and all its genuineness which was understood still less." He dwelt on two exhibits. "I . . . looked like an owl at the dynamos and steam-engines." Dynamos and steam-engines exemplified electromagnetism and thermodynamics. Hovering near the machines helped Adams plan the second narrative of his *Education*. He nearly said so, telling Hay: "All the time I kept up a devil of a thinking. You know the tenor of my thought, so I will spare you; but if we ever write those Travels of ours, I've a volume or two to put in for the Fair."

Adams sometimes wrote in verse. Possibly while at the Fair but more probably afterwards in Washington, he remembered the headings of a satire he had published in 1875: *The Radical Club.*/ *A Poem, respectfully dedicated to "the Infinite."*/ *by an Atom.*[1] He also remembered Hamlet's saying, "O God, I could be bounded in a nutshell, and count my self a King of infinite space. . . . ." And he remembered Satan's self-congratulatory address to the sun in *Paradise Lost.* Jogged by his own words and words by Shakespeare and Milton, he hit upon an original line of thought and followed its path by developing some stanzas.[2] The result was a sort of poem: "Prayer to the Dynamo."[3]

The poem is far from easy to read. It has the look of a doodle or rumination that Adams wrote for himself. It carries forward ideas he had expressed on May 3, 1893, when writing to Langley, except that he uses "atom" to denote the smallest particle of matter.[4]

The work consists of a title and ten stanzas conforming to a five-line rhyme scheme. The title—"Prayer to the Dynamo"—has the merit of being easily remembered. It may indicate that while again at the Fair Adams at some point had found himself praying to a dynamo. Yet a reader permitted to see only the stanzas and not the title would be given no impression whatever that a dynamo might be involved.[5]

The stanzas are voiced by a human being—not Adams—acting as a representative of humanity.[6] Here the person will be referred to as the Speaker. The Speaker believes a contest is being waged between humanity and a "Power" or "Force" observable in the universe. As if uncertain how to address the Force, yet certain that the contest's result will be decided soon, the Speaker begins part-contradictorily:[7]

> Mysterious Power! Gentle Friend!
> Despotic Master! Tireless Force!
> You and We are near the End!
> Either You or We must bend
> To bear the martyr's cross.[8]

The Speaker assumes that prayer is appropriate. Yet the Speaker's tone is divided from the outset between the prayerful and the defiant, strongly tending toward the defiant. In later stanzas, the Speaker says that humanity's one "infinite" faculty is prayer but that prayer addressed to a Force is prayer wasted. The stanzas nowhere voice a completed prayer. They moreover suggest that humanity no longer worships a god of religion but clings to a belief in science, especially physics, as its remaining "God."[9]

A title adjusted to what the Speaker says would be "Contest with the Primal Force." The Force is introduced in the third stanza and is never supplanted. It is said to be "a shifting current," having properties of electromagnetism and light. Its relation to humanity is that of a mysterious adversary, perhaps a despot. Its range of action is "infinite," and its "play" is tireless, silent, deaf, and blind. The contest is a struggle for dominance. The contestants seem ill-matched. Humanity is enclosed within a boundary: "the finite sphere that bounds the impotence of thought." Moreover, humanity is unsure of its strength.

> What are we then? the lords of space?
> .   .   .   .
> Or are we atoms, whirled in space,
>   Shaped and controlled by you?[10]

Doubts and uncertainties notwithstanding, humanity is trying to win. The contest is close, and the upshot is a surprise. The Speaker directs attention away from the "Primal Force" and fixes it on "the Atom." Unlike the Force, the Atom can be held, tortured, and rent. Perhaps the Atom, by such means, can be made to impart a secret which, once known, will permit humanity to subdue the Force and gain perpetual dominance. The final stanza points the way.

> Seize then the Atom! rack his joints![11]
> Tear out of him his secret spring![12]
> Grind him to nothing!—though he points
> To us, and his life-blood annoints [sic]
>   Me—the dead Atom—King![13]

Readers are under no obligation to admire "Prayer to the Dynamo" as poetry.[14] The value of the rumination resides in its offering an instance of Adams's ability to think. Devising the stanzas helped him anticipate humanity's reaction to scientific findings about electromagnetism. When fifty-five, in October 1893, he sensed that the reaction would involve a powerful desire to demystify and smash the atom. He sensed too that the project would involve extremely dangerous and possibly suicidal risks.[15] His feat was secret. It seems worthy of notice and recognition.

Before and after his stay at the Fair, Adams projected a journey to India. He hoped to confer with knowledgeable Indians and see the world-wide commotion about gold and silver from the vantage point of Calcutta. He regretfully postponed the journey and never made it.

Earlier, on September 25, 1893, the day his speech was read by Cameron to the Senate, Adams had been hopeful that Congress would enact the program outlined in the speech or one much like it. He had written that day to Wayne MacVeagh about President Cleveland, ". . . his [i.e. the president's] gold fight is lost."[16]

Once back from Chicago, Adams plunged into "a bath of boiling politics." Excitement in Washington was greater than at any time since the formation of the Confederacy. On October 18, he exclaimed to Hay: "You never lost so much as in missing this silver fight. During the fortnight of my absence, matters have grown irretrievably worse. Cleveland has driven on the passions of the Senate until we are in a really dangerous temper. I fully expect that some one will be killed. . . . Oh, cock-a-doodle-doo! if I were not a pessimist and a fatalist, a populist, a communist, a socialist, and the friend of a humorist [meaning a friend of Hay's], where would I be at?"

During the next twelve days, chaos became disastrous. The country was experiencing the worst devastation of banks, businesses, farms, and households in its history. The federal government could fairly be expected to attempt saving action. President Cleveland had brought Congress into special session to pass a single measure but showed no impulse to propose a general program. Congress was constitutionally empowered to initiate a program but instead was debating the single measure the president had requested. The measure was adoption by the United States of a gold-based currency parallel to the English system and abandonment of silver as one of the metals used to back the country's paper dollars.

The conduct of the president and Congress affected Adams as a whip or goad. He was a private citizen. With the help of Senator and Mrs. Cameron and without his authorship being known, he had proposed within the U. S. government a program for immediate action. The program had merits too manifest to be denied. It awakened interest but not enough interest to win support in Congress. In Adams's view, the mood in Congress was one of opposition to serious thought and responsible action, and Cleveland and the legislators who favored the president's insufficient measure were acting as the dupes of England's moneyed interest—were compromising America's system of industry and finance—were sacrificing whatever the country had in the way of economic independence—in a word were betraying the United States.

Adams accordingly wrote a second speech for Cameron to read to the Senate. The new speech ended by challenging the Senate to vote on the program offered in the first. It used forcible language.

. . . the question . . . is whether Congress is or is not bound to think at all.

Already the action of Europe and European governments has spread ruin throughout the United States; has for six months paralyzed industry; has thrown our largest corporations into bankruptcy; has ruined several of our Western States, and through them has cost Eastern capitalists many millions of money invested in the West. . . . We [if willing to pass the president's bill] . . . are going to finish what Europe has successfully begun.

On Monday, October 30, 1893, the Senate completed its long debate. A senator who spoke against the president's measure was John Percival Jones of Nevada. A senator who read a prepared speech against it was James Donald Cameron. The vote was taken at 7:30 P.M. Cleveland's measure was adopted by a vote of forty-three to thirty-two. The winning bloc consisted of senators who represented states in which large banks and other capital-intensive businesses were situated. Among them were three Republicans: Lodge and Hoar of Massachusetts and Quay of Pennsylvania. Cameron, a Republican, was the only senator in the East who sided with the silver miners of Nevada and Colorado.

After the vote, Cameron led a party of five persons to Adams's house. One was an English currency expert, Moreton Frewen. Others were Jones, Lodge, and Senator Calvin Brice of Ohio, a Democrat—Adams's near neighbor at 1611 H Street. The four senators in the party had divided on the issue, Cameron and Jones against Cleveland's measure, Lodge and Brice for it. All were in high spirits. What they wanted was a chance to celebrate.

The mood of the hour needs explanation. The *New York Herald* had favored Cleveland's measure. On October 31, the day after the vote, the newspaper published a report from Washington:

REPEAL BILL
PASSED BY
THE SENATE.

Sound Money Victorious After
the Most Extraordinary
Struggle in the History of Congress.

Subordinate headlines read: "Bitterness in the Debate" and "Closing Hours Marked by Angry Personalities. . . ." Yet the body of the report tried to explain a surge of joy. "There is a feeling of grateful relief in the national capital to-night. It extends to all sides of repeal and all shades of politics. The tension was growing simply too great for human nature to bear. Even those who have been disappointed are glad it's over, while the friends of repeal are jubilant."

Cameron was one of the most jubilant senators. He was glowing in the light of sudden fame. That morning the *New York Sun* reported that

the Pennsylvanian had "read a statement" to the Senate. "Mr. Cameron
. . . spoke because his last speech in favor of free coinage was such a
marked success that he is beginning to regard himself as a public hero,
and was anxious to deserve his new reputation. It is said that since Mr.
Cameron came out of his shell he has received so many letters from his
own constituents and those of other Senators, commending, criticising,
and discussing his attitude, that he has found a new interest in life, and
is every day more and more convinced that he adopted the wisest
course. . . ."

The senator was well protected against suspicion that the speeches
he had read were the works of another person. That Adams had written
them was known only to Donald and Elizabeth Cameron and, probably,
to Virginia and Wayne MacVeagh.[17] Besides, Adams had talents of sympathy that permitted him to write as if he *were* a Pennsylvanian astray
from Republican orthodoxy. The chance of disclosure was zero.

Like the first, Adams's second speech was issued as a pamphlet.
Someone decided that the top of the pamphlet's first page should bear
a quotation from the speech that would make Cameron seem concerned
about free silver much more than—or even to the exclusion of—other
matters. The quotation read: "Free coinage of the American product of
silver is essential to our national prosperity."

The pamphlet had been printed before the vote was cast and was
given to reporters. The *New York Herald* echoed the quotation on October 31 by saying about the Pennsylvanian's share in the debate, "Don
Cameron then read a statement as to his position, in which he declared
that free coinage of American silver was necessary to national prosperity." The *Herald* went on to disagree. The paper took up the theme of
prosperity and announced that the country's new gold-backed currency
would work a miracle. "A great sigh of relief will go up from the business
men of the nation. . . . They can now go about their business with renewed hope for the future and restored confidence in the financial in-
tegrity of the government. . . . Those who have money may safely invest
it. . . . Those who have no money may borrow at a rate of interest
founded upon a sound and healthy currency. . . . Capitalists who have
money already invested in shops and factories and have been holding
off for the return of confidence may start up the now silent wheels, and
labor may return to its daily wage."[18]

Adams thought the occasion important but had to concern himself
about the role he had played in it. He took three steps. He preserved
among his papers pamphlet copies of the first and second speeches. He
preserved a hand-written partial draft of the October 30 speech. Later,
as part of the second narrative of *The Education*, he wrote an account of
the struggle in Washington and the celebration enjoyed at his house by

four senators and Moreton Frewen. A few words of the account should be quoted here. They typify *The Education* in speaking of "Henry Adams" in the third person. They illustrate the difficulty Adams created for himself by undertaking to write a book in which a fictional "Henry Adams" would figure continuously as a person of no importance. They make clear how far he, the author, would go toward annihilating the Adams of biographical and historical fact. Finally, they impart the misleading idea that the silver fight in Washington was rather mild.

> The struggle was rather less irritable than such struggles generally were. . . . On the evening of the final vote, Senator Cameron came back from the Capitol with Senator Brice, Senator Jones, Senator Lodge, and Moreton Frewen, all in the gayest of humors as though they were rid of a heavy responsibility. Adams, too, in a bystander's spirit, felt light in mind. . . ."[19]

The last statement was as false as possible. One can assume that Adams had arranged that Cameron bring selected visitors to the house. The purpose was unconcealed. To the extent that a private host could help warring senators shed their anger and remember the advantages of cordiality, Adams had wished to give assistance. Welcoming the arrivals, he necessarily acted the role of ill-informed amiable listener. Senatorial egos required the pretence. Yet the evidence is strong that, while the guests rejoiced, two Henry Adamses were present. One, a born conciliator, succeeded for the time in being pleasant. The other, a born patriot and politician, concealed the basic fact that he was heavy in mind, dissatisfied, and angry.

In his *History of the United States*, Adams had vividly shown that the American people could survive a crisis when nearly stripped of their government. Had President Cleveland and Congress done nothing to counteract the Panic of 1893, Adams might have felt forgiving. But the president and the majority blocs in the House and Senate had not done nothing. As Adams made clear in the October 30 speech, Cleveland and his coadjutors advanced a measure that would wreck the country's silver mining industry, crash the silver price, raise the gold price, prolong the drain of gold from the Treasury to London, shrink the country's already-diminished supplies of currency and credit, and generally work to bring on a lasting depression—all for the unconfessed purpose of surrendering America's economic independence to European dictation, coupled with dictation by America's currency dealers and America's most powerful and richest bankers.[20]

Adams's October 30 speech had been written by a man unwilling to be a loser. The system of American life and government that he believed in was being tossed away. Another system was being casually introduced. He foresaw that the result would be exacerbated distress. Feeling sure that his expectations were well-founded, he remained a stubborn promoter of his own ideas. His course pointed toward his writing a third speech.[21]

In 1884, a group of college and university history teachers had announced the founding of an American Historical Association. Adams had responded by paying for a life membership. In September 1885, accompanied by Clover, he went to Saratoga to attend the first annual meeting. He listened to the talks and discussions, the last excepted. What he heard inclined him against attending another meeting.

Adams's *History of the United States* had been the greatest feat achieved by an American historian till that time, both as research and as writing. Following its publication in 1889–1891, he had received a stunningly complimentary letter about it from his fellow historian Francis Parkman.[22] With that exception, his papers contain no letters of commendation or criticism from historians in the United States or elsewhere who read the *History* and wished to send him their opinions. Possibly he received such letters but destroyed them. A likelier possibility may be that no such letters were written.

A strong force behind the development of the American Historical Association was the zeal of Professor Herbert Baxter Adams of Johns Hopkins University—not related to Henry Adams. In 1891, with Professor Adams's approval, the Association chose Henry Adams as its vice president. The basis for the choice was his *History*. The choice was made while the author was traveling in the Pacific, was made without his knowledge, and could be criticized as designed less to promote the writing of history than to aggrandize the Association.

At its Annual Meeting in 1893, again without his knowledge, the Association chose Henry Adams to be its next president. A letter from Professor Adams informing Henry Adams of his election was delivered at 1603 H Street when he was writing his second speech for reading by Cameron to the Senate. The professor's letter reflected a complete mistake. Henry Adams had not wanted to be the Association's president. He should not have been elected.

The mistake was none of Henry Adams's doing. Yet he made an effort to erase it. He wrote to Professor Adams expressing thanks but saying he would be away and could not attend the 1894 Annual Meeting. Sent on October 28, 1893, his statement was tantamount to saying he would not perform the office. It was conditioned by Henry's belief that he would be going to India. His words were unequivocal. ". . . my present expectation is to be absent from the United States during the next twelvemonth."[23] On this basis, the Association was freed to name an acting president in Henry Adams's place.

Two events quickly persuaded Henry that he could not go to India.

The first was the silver vote in the Senate on October 30. The second was his receiving news that Clarence King had been arrested for disorderly conduct in New York on October 29, was found guilty and fined, and voluntarily entered the Bloomingale Asylum for the Insane.

Adams may have learned of King's arrest and confinement as early as November 1. He waited till the 5th and wrote to Hay: "Of course something remains untold, which I might learn in New York, but I don't care to ask. . . . Apparently he [King] is sane enough . . . and, if off his head, the trouble is physical rather than mental. . . ."

Adams's situation was very uncomfortable. King was immured in a Manhattan asylum. Hay was in Europe, reportedly unwell and wandering here and there in search of treatment. Adams was in excellent health but felt alone in Washington, which from his point of view had become the capital of a country betrayed by its official defenders, chiefly the president. Things being as they were, he could not leave. He told Hay: "I wish you were at home, or I were with you; but . . . I am more needed here than there, and I am waiting till December in the hope of seeing more clearly."

Knowing he must stay, he made a practical arrangement. Perhaps as early as November 3, 1893, he visited a Washington printing firm, Judd and Detweiler.[24] He asked the firm to print for him some copies of a book about Tahiti. Printing was to start at once and with good management could be done before the end of the year. By then, Congress would be back in session, the dimensions of the country's disorders would be more fully known, and a free-lance politician could better decide whether and how far he could stray from Washington.

Seven weeks later, on December 22, Adams had the printed book in his possession. It had the form of a 109-page narrative divided into thirteen untitled chapters. There was no preface and no table of contents. Seven genealogical tables supported the narrative. The pages were roughly the size of paper used in America for typing. Footnotes appeared on many pages. The number of copies printed is unknown and possibly was as few as eight.[25]

Casually looked into, the book could seem the memoirs of one of the world's living monarchs, prepared to please a select coterie of favored recipients. The title page read:

Memoirs
of
Marau Taaroa
Last Queen of Tahiti.

Privately Printed.
1893.

The text confirmed the impression. The word "I" appeared at points in the narrative as if Queen Marau were speaking.[26]

Memoirs of Marau Taaroa deserves better than casual examination. Strictly speaking, it is not a book. What Adams obtained from Judd and Detweiler was copies of proof-sheets of a work-in-progress. The sheets were readied when the work could appear to be complete but when, to Adams's mind, it was only complete enough to be reconsidered, preparatory to expansion and a final transformation.

Adams had all along been aware that he could recast the work, disengage it from Marau, transfer it to her mother, and print the result. The two versions would greatly differ. The sheets printed in 1893 could seem a book by a Europeanized Tahitian queen. The finished book would appear to speak for a person in no way European, the last of the ancient Tahitian leaders, a great chiefess of the Tevas.[27]

In view of Adams's intention, one might say his book would end in being simple. The case, however, was complicated. The best road toward that conclusion begins with a straightforward question: Who were the narrative's authors?

Marau and Tati were part-authors in the sense of being informants. Many points of Tahitian genealogy and history that are presented in the *Memoirs* were their contributions, conveyed directly to Adams. By the same logic, Arii Taimai was part-author. She was the person from whom the living Tevas had learned almost all they knew of Tahitian history. In large measure, the *Memoirs* were based on her testimony as spoken to Adams on the island through a translator or as passed by Marau or Tati to Adams through the mail. Yet the chiefess's most important connection with the work was as its *creator*, in the sense of having required— indeed forced—its being written.

In ancient days, the Tahitians had a system of life and government that was radically decentralized. The authority of the great chiefs who ruled the island's families and districts was formidable where it applied, but the chiefs could assert their authority only within definite, long-established bounds. When Arii Taimai was born, the system was under attack but still in force. In keeping with the system, she became great chiefess of the most powerful Tahitian family, rightful leader of much of the island's population, and governor in varying degrees of many of its districts. Thus, when he met her in 1891, Adams met a woman who in youth had wielded extraordinary, although limited, power. Their meeting permitted their quick discovery of an affinity that was rightly to be measured only as their actions measured it. She gave him a Teva name, Taura-atua i Amo, which—as he freely told people—had been the name of a very ancient Teva great chief.

Her giving him the name changed his sense of who he was. He was already Henry Adams, a very important American. Her making him Tauraatua i Amo made him also a most important Tahitian.

As Adams, he was—among other things—a historian. It was natural that, as a historian, he felt attracted to the moment in June 1767 when Captain Samuel Wallis of the British ship *Dolphin* sailed into a bay at an unknown island in the South Pacific, anchored, found himself surrounded by natives in canoes, and welcomed aboard a woman named Oberea, or Purea, who appeared to be a queen.[28] It was natural that Adams took a deep interest in the calamitous train of events that ensued—calamitous to the Tahitians, most of whom would die and the rest of whom would have to submit to colonial rule. It was natural, too, that Adams acquired in Australia, France, England, and the United States an astonishingly large collection of printed evidence about Tahiti. In other circumstances, he might have gone on to write a history of Tahiti comparable to *The Conquest of Mexico* or *The Conquest of Peru* by William Prescott; that is, an account of European intrusion written by a disinterested historian.

Adams was not disinterested. More than an onlooker might expect, he felt his Tahitian identity as real. In *Memoirs of Marau Taaroa*, his sense of being Tahitian is evident throughout. Pages here and there obliged the reader to believe that the writer is Marau; but the same pages are very evidently the work of a new-style Tahitian who has somehow obtained many important European records about the island and its people, has read them with close attention, and sifted from them large amounts of information never previously assembled. Though an exceptional Tahitian in learning, the author is typically Tahitian in sympathy. He writes in evident sympathy with his fellow Tevas and with all other Tahitians; and he writes, too, as if confident of their sympathy with him.

In history, sympathy is not necessarily at war with truth. The first version of Adams's Tahiti book is good evidence that a single narrative could satisfy both the requirements of Adams the historian and the Henry Adams made over by Arii Taimai into Taura-atua i Amo. The narrative also could suit the requirements of the American patriot who smuggled two anti-British speeches into the United States Senate. One can even believe that Henry Adams the patriot-politician was the person who decided to print at once a volume about the Tahitians and the destructive British.

The thirteen chapters Adams printed were apparently all the chapters he had written till that time. It was perhaps surprising to him that the thirteen formed a well-ended narrative. They told a story which, though interspersed with many other materials, was built around two stories of dominance, accidentally intertwined. At the time she went aboard the *Dolphin*, Purea, or Oberea—the Tahitian who was mistaken

by Wallis for the island's queen—was the former-great-chiefess of the
Tevas. Just then she was visiting a district not her own. She invited Wallis
to accompany her to Papara, the Teva's principal district. Had he complied, as she urgently made signs that he should do, Wallis would have
met her husband, Amo, and her son, Teriirere, born circa 1762. As it
happened, the captain and his associates did not see the husband and
learned nothing about the son.

Tahitian custom had displaced Purea as great chiefess in favor of
her son Teriirere from the moment he was born. Yet also custom had
encouraged Purea to require that things be done in her son's honor
while he remained an infant. She took the utmost possible advantage of
the rules in this regard and then went further. Displaying a kind of arro-
gance unexampled in previous Tahitian experience, she ordered the
building of a stone pyramid for her son on a promontory in Papara. The
pyramid covered an area of ground 267 feet by 87 feet, comparable to
the areas occupied by Europe's cathedrals. As a feat of labor, it possibly
exceeded the cathedrals, being built rapidly of coral rock shaped into
large blocks without the assistance of metal tools.

Again, had Wallis gone with Purea to Papara, he would have seen
the pyramid. While making the journey, he might have begun to sense
that Purea was not a queen but a district's former-great-chiefess; that
her authority was limited; and that she had unconscionably overstepped
the bounds set by Tahitian wisdom and precedent.[29]

Two years later, in 1769, Captain Cook arrived at Tahiti on the bark
Endeavor. He fully expected to be greeted by the supposed queen—
Purea, or Oberea. Adams explains in his second chapter: "Every Englishman in those days took comfort, when wandering over the world,
in the faith that kings and queens were a part of the divine system, and
that no intelligent race could hold up its head without them. A king or
a queen the English must have at Tahiti, and they had already settled
that Oberea was a queen."[30]

Cook was visited by Purea. He later met Amo and young Teriirere.
He assumed that the son was "heir apparent to the Sovereignty of the
Island."[31] But meanwhile he met a chief named Tutaha, or Tu (later
called Pomare), who seemed to have kingly powers. Moreover, while
making a tour of the island, Cook was twice astonished. He saw the pyramid erected to honor Teriirere, and nearby he saw human bones. The
bones were evidence of mass slaughter. Five months earlier, by surprise,
attackers from another district had killed many Tevas and driven Purea,
Amo, and Teriirere to the mountains. The surprise attack had given
Purea's story a continuation suited to Tahitian ideas of justice. She had
much exceeded her prerogatives as Teriirere's mother; other districts

had been outraged; and a successful onslaught had reduced her to her rightful size.

The story of British intrusion had only started. The chapters printed as *Memoirs of Marau Taaroa* tell in detail how the British inflicted kingship on Tahiti. Cook was the originator. The man he set up as king was Tu. In Adams's words: "Cook . . . deliberately intervened in support of the policy he had adopted of elevating Tu at the expense of the other chiefs. In his eyes Tu was King by divine right, and any attack on his authority was treason in the first place and an attack on British influence in the next."[32] The Tahitians recognized Cook's action for what it was. The later chapters of the *Memoirs* show "how desperately the unfortunate people struggled against the English policy of creating and supporting a tyranny."[33] Not surprisingly, the Tahitians who led in the struggle were Adams's fellow Tevas.

Few historical tragedies were worse than the one that Cook set in motion. According to Cook's estimate, there were 200,000 Tahitians in 1769. Their numbers fell to less than 20,000 by 1799 and to about 5,000 in 1803. The stupendous fatalities, as Adams explains, were mostly attributable to alien diseases (common colds, measles, dysentery, etc.) brought to the island by Europeans. Polynesians had no immunity to the diseases and were killed by them in thousands. But the fatalities were also attributable to the alien idea of kingship and to wars waged between Tahitian fleets and armies to assert or resist kingly authority bestowed by English captains with the backing of English guns and gunpowder, not to mention the backing of English missionaries and European drifters.

The Tevas resisted and survived but became favorite targets of English aggression. Purea, Amo, and Teriirere died early deaths, and the place of great chief passed to a son of Amo's by a second wife. The new leader was known to the English as Temarii and to the Tevas as Ariifaataia. He showed ability and considerably restored the Tevas in standing and power. Tragically he was killed in 1799 by burns he accidentally incurred by igniting gunpowder.

His death opened the way to a proposed overthrow of the Tevas. The missionaries provided arms to assist the attack. At the close of his narrative, Adams dwells on the missionaries' attitude. After the death of Ariifaataia, the Tevas had chosen a new great chief. The missionaries did not know who he was. They "did not care to know." They preferred to aid an attack "without knowing their own victim."[34]

A reader curious to learn the identity of the new Teva great chief can find help nowhere in Adams' text. Yet help is given in the last of his genealogical charts, Table VII. The chart says that Amo's brother Manea had two grandsons, Tati and Opuhara, and that Tati, born circa 1773, was Ariifaataia's successor.

Similarly, Table II makes clear that Tati was a nickname and that the actual name of Ariifaataia's successor was Taura-atua i Patea. The table shows, too, that Arii Taimai was his granddaughter.

Shown in neither the text nor the tables are the facts that most matter. Tahitian names of the sort considered were both names and titles. The most important of Arii Taimai's names was Taura-atua i Amo. In 1891, when she gave Adams that name, she did more than give him the name of a historic early Teva great chief. She gave him her own name—evidently the oldest and best she had! If ancient Tahitian ideas still had a bearing (and they apparently did), Adams—from the moment she gave him the name—replaced her as the great chief of the Tevas, superseding both her and giant Tati Salmon, her natural son.

The gift to Adams, as he learned, was munificent. Its true scope, it appears, was—for the present—kept secret. As felt by him, the gift was also interrogative. What could *he* give *her*? He knew that she, an authentic ancient, could not read or write. The inability supplied an answer. He could write a book that would serve as hers.

The chapters and tables printed in 1893 are all but silent about the last Teva great chiefs. They stop at a point in time when Taura-atua i Patea (with his brother Opuhara) and two persons named Taura-atua i Amo (one a woman, one a man) are, as history, still in the future. Yet the very last great chief is ever-present. He is the chief who wrote the chapters, developed the tables, and brought the British, historically, to account. In the secret circumstances, he could not have done less. And he greatly liked doing it.[35]

Adams paid heed to newspapers when they said things about him. On September 26, 1893, while reporting that Senator Cameron had read a speech and proved a traitor to his constituents, the *New York Herald* had published an editorial, "European Bomb Throwers." One can assume that Adams read the editorial. It began: "The attempt made on Saturday at Barcelona to slaughter Captain General Martinez de Campo and his entire staff adds one more to the list of terrible outrages committed by anarchists in all parts of Europe. Scarcely a week passes without the cable bringing stories of their dastardly work against some obnoxious potentate or other or against those whom they choose to designate as representing the capitalistic class."

Through the autumn, anarchists weighed on Adams's mind. On December 10, he affixed the label to himself.[36] Writing to Lucy Baxter, he explained: "I am, personally, an anarchist, but am tolerant in opinion within reasonable limits. My pet aversion is Grover Cleveland, but he lives so near me that I can't throw a bomb at him without breaking my own windows. Julius Caesar [in Shakespeare's play] was wholly wrong about fat men. They are not only loathsome but dangerous."[37]

The Camerons were going to Coffin's Point for Christmas. When Mrs. Cameron and Martha left on December 20, Adams did not go with them. He promised to follow in early January.

Brooks and Evelyn were visiting. Henry had said he would try to switch his brother to a "line" other than government work in Washington. As it happened, Brooks was changing lines unassisted. He was nursing his ambitions as apocalyptic philosopher. He wished to go to Europe and round out his "potential book." He meanwhile was promoting an international movement to restore the use of silver in the world's financial arrangements.[38]

That Brooks and Evelyn knew Henry was writing a history of Tahiti seems more than unlikely. After they had left, on December 22, Henry sent Marau two copies of the *Memoirs*, accompanied with a request that she and Tati correct and return them. Next day he advised Mrs. Cameron, ". . . I sent off my South Sea Idyll. . . ."

Freed to leave Washington, he prepared for two absences by replenishing his supply of paints, paper, and brushes for painting in water colors.[39] His first absence would be a new stay with the Camerons at Coffin's Point, the second a journey with Clarence King. Expecting that King would be leaving the asylum but would need protracted rest, he had suggested their going to the Bahamas or the West Indies. King had welcomed the offer. Apart from the shattering of his personal finances by the panic, his worst affliction was a spinal disorder, a painfully inflamed fifth vertebra.[40]

From Coffin's Point on January 16, 1894, Adams sent Hay a letter in which he called himself "a conservative anarchist." The two-word label had advantages. It set Adams apart from the anarchists, nihilists, syndicalists, socialists, and communists who were throwing bombs in Europe. It implied that an American radical could be labeled only with the help of paradox and the mixing of opposites.

In the same letter, Adams wrote a statement that Hay could believe and added some lines that he might not. "I have printed and sent to Marau a small volume of her Memoirs, hoping to encourage the family to supply more material, for I really enjoy writing that kind of history. It shows me, too, why I loathe American history. Tahiti is all literary. America has not a literary conception. One is all artistic. The other is all commercial." Writing similarly to Gaskell on January 23, he said he had been "printing (ultrissimo-privately) a small volume of South Sea Memoirs." ". . . it has amused me much more, and is much better reading, than my dreary American history, which is to me what Emma Bovary was to Gustave Flaubert."

Adams's lines need reply. If he loathed American history, one reason was overwork. Trying to make his *History of the United States* superbly interesting and responsive to available evidence, he had taken inordinate pains and had done so for many years. A second reason was America's fast-increasing attention to business. As led by Cleveland and Congress under the lash of England's money-lords, the country was being taught to be purely commercial.[41]

Compared to a history of the United States, a history of Tahiti was a tiny project, but not an easy one. Adams made statements about the finished chapters of his Tahitian history that pleased him but were untrue. His "South Sea Idyll" was not better reading than his *History*, nor was it easier reading. On the contrary, his Tahitian chapters could be read only by readers willing to concentrate. The narrative throughout was brilliant but difficult.

After a month with the Camerons at Coffin's Point, Adams joined King at Tampa. They crossed to Havana and learned to their chagrin that the only possible conveyance southward was a vessel departing for Santiago de Cuba. When they arrived, Santiago proved so unattractive that they thought of renting a house in the nearby hills. King knew Frederick Ramsden, the British Consul. Ramsden listened to their pleas and arranged the loan of a house, Dos Bocas, eight miles distant. On seeing the house, Adams thought it "our Paradise."[42] King had brought along his colored servant, Alexander. A Cuban cook, Pepe, was quickly recruited. Entry to heaven was effected with ease.

King spent much of their sojourn at Dos Bocas sampling rocks and inferring the outlines of Cuba's geology. Adams walked on the hills, painted, and made unavailing efforts to find a likable and buyable winter house. King later remembered him as being "simply delightful, genial and tropical in his warmth, physically active as a chamois."[43]

To complete their experience of paradise, the friends proposed to climb the nearest considerable mountain, Gran Piedra, "about four thousand feet high." Ramsden joined their enterprise and made needed arrangements. Adams, King, and Ramsden, with Blanco, a Spanish guide, and Sisto, a Cuban mulatto, spent the night on the mountain top. As described by Adams, the adventure involved no hardships whatever. "The sunset was indescribably fine. Such colors and shadows I never saw. . . . With one blanket I felt no cold. . . . When I woke at the first dawn, I was just as glad I had come as when I turned in at night. . . . The sun-rise was almost as fine as the sunset, and only at eight o'clock did we get started downward."

As usual when separated, Adams and Mrs. Cameron were exchanging letters.[44] The quoted lines about his night on Gran Piedra appeared in a letter he wrote to her on March 16, 1894. He carried the letter with him while returning to Havana, whence it passed through the mail to Coffin's Point.

When she replied on March 26, she felt cross with him for having gone off with King, apparently on the theory that King needed him more than she did, which, she said, was a "perfectly false assumption." Yet, mainly, she was not cross. On the contrary, she wanted to tell him what she truly thought of him.[45]

The words she allowed herself were unusual and had religious overtones. ". . . the everlasting truth prevails that you are of your sex a specimen apart, and that you are as true as the north star." "I have been doing such a lot of thinking lately about you and what you have been to me. I was in the darkness of death till you led me with your gentle guidance into broad fields and pastures green. Even sorrow and trouble lessen under your light—a light so calm and still. I wonder if any man was ever so *big* as you."[46]

The copies of *Memoirs of Marau Taaroa* reached Marau and Tati in early February 1894 and were read with amazement. Taura-atua's narrative told them important things they had not known. Following its discovery in 1767 by two European explorers—first the Englishman, Samuel Wallis, and next a Frenchman, Louis Bougainville—Tahiti had been moved to the center of Europe's attention. Descriptions of the Tahitians by Wallis and Commerson, a naturalist who accompanied Bougainville, were published in England and France. The descriptions appeared at the instant when the visionary ideas of Rousseau were in their highest ascendancy. The *Memoirs* outlined the consequence.

> The natural goodness of the human heart and the moral blessings of a state of nature were the themes of all Rousseau's followers, and at that time all Europe was following Rousseau. The discovery of Tahiti, as Wallis and Commerson painted it, was the strongest possible proof that Rousseau was right. The society of Tahiti showed that European society had no real support in reason or experience, but should be abolished, with its absurd conventions, contrary to the rights of man. The French philosophers seriously used Tahiti for this purpose, and with effect, as every one knows. Wallis's queen played a chief part in the European play, by exciting interest and sympathy. . . .

> . . . Tahiti really influenced Europe, and [Purea] . . . was without her own knowledge and consent directly concerned in causing the French Revolution and 'costing the head of her sister-queen, Marie Antoinette.[47]

The news that over-proud Purea had been held up for admiration in Europe as queen of an earthly heaven—"a model of humanity, sentiment, and conduct—the flower of a state of nature"—had different effects on Marau and Tati.[48] Being herself a queen by European rules, Marau was constrained to keep her dignity. Writing to Taura-atua on March 11, 1894, she reported that the copies of the *Memoirs* "arrived in a splendid condition" and that she had given one to Tati. "I am sure that he has perused it with as much pleasure as myself."

Tati did not labor under an imitatively European title. He told his adoptive brother, "The Memoirs have been studied over & . . . the amount of patience you must have taken to search for reports of the island, takes us all by surprise." "Why Tahiti was quite a place, in the old days." "Most of your reproduction[s] [i.e. quotations] are unknown to any one here." Tati said too that the chapters had been translated orally to Arii Taimai and that the few changes needed were "rectifications . . . in the spelling of the Native words."[49]

By mail in January, Henry had been advised that some properties were being sold by the Adams Real Estate Trust and that John had been persuaded to go to Europe for his health.[50] The news was good. Yet Henry continued to think that financial shock had turned his elder brothers to old men and that John's prospects were unimproved.

One of Henry's fixed convictions was belief in mountain air and exercise as helps to persons in need of renewal. Writing from Tampa on February 3, he had suggested firmly to Hay: "Try and get home by May. . . . My plans for the summer are now limited to the dream of an outing in the Yellowstone country." He did not yet say so, but his object was to repair Hay's health by having him join a trek on horseback from Yellowstone National Park through a seldom-visited wilderness to the Grand Tetons. It would be an ambitious journey.

King mended greatly in Cuba and wanted to swim in the Bahamas. He and Adams proceeded from Havana to Nassau, but Adams disliked the place and dragged King back to Havana. He had good reason for the move. Congress was debating reductions of the tariffs. If passed, lowered tariffs would make the United States a more profitable market for English businesses. As viewed by Adams, lowered American tariffs and America's abandonment of silver were complementary aspects of a program initiated in Europe, inimical to America's interests, and already half-adopted by America's witless rulers. In Havana, he could visit a U. S. consulate, scan recent issues of New York and Washington newspapers, and learn better what was happening.

He and King crossed from Cuba to Florida on April 10, 1894. King had business to do in Tampa that would detain him many days. Till

King's errand was completed, Adams stayed at an inn at Port Tampa. During the first days of his stay, he completed a third speech for delivery by Cameron to the Senate and mailed it to the senator.

The three speeches Adams wrote for Cameron to read to the Senate as his own have never been recognized for what they manifestly were: Adams's handiwork from start to finish and a unified series. His instinct when writing speeches for delivery by Cameron was to state ideas in simple sentences. In proportion as subjects were more serious, Adams's language would be simpler. The first paragraph of his third speech was as serious as possible.[51]

> . . . for a hundred years this matter of a protective tariff has been thrashed out between the two or three great [political] parties and the two or three great interests of the United States, and still it remains as serious as when it nearly broke the Union sixty years ago [in 1833, during the first administration of President Jackson]. In one sense it is now more serious than then. . . . The world . . . has become small. Interests which were then free for indefinite expansion are now cramped for space. The power of production, which was then slight, is now without limit. Races which then were beyond chance of contact are now in close competition. Capital, which then hardly existed as an organized force, is now massed in a common organization. . . . The capitalist has one set of principles; the laborer has another; the farmer has a third; and here in Congress, where all these interests and ideas meet and clash together, we are throwing ourselves from one to another without a notion where we are at last to rest.[52]

Senator Cameron had not been heard in the Senate since October 30, 1893. In reaction to the speech he had read on that great day, he had been stereotyped as an advocate of one thing only, the free coinage of silver. Because he had already given two speeches, his reading a third could not have the charm of novelty, and his past performances had proved that he had no abilities as a speaker.

The Pennsylvanian read Adams's third speech to the Senate on April 18, 1894. Word that he had the floor was taken as a signal for departure. Reporting next day from Washington, the *New York Herald* said of the senator: "He read from typewritten sheets, which he did not lift from his desk, and over which he leaned, little more than mumbling his words. He received the attention of a few Senators on the republican side, and almost emptied the chambers and the galleries."[53]

The *New York Sun* for April 19 published a summary of the speech clearly derived from the typewritten text. Possibly the reporter had been given a carbon copy. As a matter of course, the speech was published in the *Congressional Record*, but it evidently was never printed as a pamphlet. Among the reasons for the avoidance, the strongest and most plausible may have been that the speech was so wide-ranging and so strongly worded that there was positive risk of its attracting general notice, perhaps even intelligent notice.

Although the occasion for its being written was a proposed reduction of the country's tariffs, the speech mainly concerned the change in the world from nineteenth to twentieth century conditions and the course the United States might best take in a world astonishingly altered. It raised a question: ". . . whether we are to keep America in economical dependence on Europe, or whether we are to struggle for an independent position of our own." It favored a struggle for independence and insisted that the use of silver as money and the use of protective tariffs were necessary to that end. Especially it explained how necessary tariffs were for the American laborer.[54]

While reasserting Adams's position, the speech described the influences that were working to fix upon the United States a fate opposite to the fate that he was working for. It said that three "interests" were arrayed in favor of lowering the country's tariffs.

> First of all, and most powerful, is that remarkable cosmopolite moneyed interest, which belongs to no country, and more or less rules all, but which whether it is found in Europe or America, or in the remotest corners of the earth, has always its heart, its mass, its head, in the city of London. Next come the farmers of the [American] South and West, who have always, by the force of their own interests, been subject to the same magnet, because their market is London. . . . The third influence . . . is that of the class which, for want of any other name, I am obliged to call Mugwumps, who gravitate . . . towards what they believe to be English, and who take their impulse from the city of London, because the city of London, in finance, controls England.

> The only classes that stand beyond appeal or argument are the money lender and the Mugwump. The interests of the one, the sycophancy of the other, are bound to Europe. As long as Europe remains the center of capital[,] the money lender and the Mugwump must owe allegiance there.

By saying that the "cosmopolite moneyed interest" was present in the United States as well as Europe, the speech could be understood to point at a man it did not name. The man was America's most powerful banker, J. P. Morgan. Adams had known Morgan's parents and sister in London in the 1860s.[55] He knew that the younger Morgan's financial success on Wall Street had been based in considerable part on profitable ties with his father's London bank. In 1894, Adams could be sure that a broad swipe by Cameron at financial cosmopolites in America would raise a loud cry in the New York press. On April 19, the *New York Times* declared in a headline, "Mr. Cameron Exhibits Symptoms of Anglophobia." The New York editors were striking back.

Adams's third speech was unusual, and very assertive, with regard to an American epithet. "Mugwumps" had been adapted from a word in

Algonquian meaning "A great man: one who affects superiority, especially in political principles."[56]

As counter-applied by Adams with the help of Cameron, "Mugwumps" was given a wholly new meaning.[57] It became a label for sycophantic Grover Cleveland and members of Congress who had joined with him to inflict a mono-metallic currency on the already-injured United States. The changed meaning was noticed. On April 19, the *New York Sun* published what the senator had said concerning "Mugwumps."[58]

Adams was capable of holding grudges. He was capable also of finding means to express them. Socially he and the Camerons were as close as possible to the Lodges. He felt two deep grudges against Senator Lodge but would not let them show. Lodge had supported Blaine for president in 1884 and voted in favor of Cleveland's anti-silver bill in 1893. It was with Lodge much in mind that Adams in his third speech—obligingly delivered by Cameron—labeled a group or class of current American politicians as Mugwumps, meaning fawning courtiers of English capital.

4

THE LOOKOUT

Adams and King reached Washington on April 23, 1894. Three days at home sufficed for Adams to accomplish four things: gain an updated impression of the federal government, put a stop to his own political loquacity, invite his Hooper nieces to pay him a visit, and decide to leave the capital as soon as possible. On the 26th, he wrote to Hay: "To me, the whole thing here looks like a general Lunarium; a grand opera-bouffe of absolutely daft or imbecile human beings. I can't get over the impression at all. Gradually it is becoming an idée fixe with me, whenever I meet anyone, that I must say nothing to him because it is dangerous to irritate persons in their condition."

Loulie and Mabel arrived for a three-week lark. Though inclined to go about as a pair, the nieces were unalike. Just turning twenty, Loulie was spirited and very intelligent but often quiet. Newly nineteen, Mabel showed a gift for "attracting men of all ages."[1]

A package arrived: twelve copies of a pamphlet issued in Boston, *The Gold Standard: an Historical Study*, by Brooks Adams. A foretaste of Brooks's "proposed book," the pamphlet attempted to illuminate the world financial crisis by reviewing the history of money from ancient Roman times to the present.[2] In sentiment, it harmonized with the forcible speeches that Senator Cameron had read to the Senate.[3]

During the winter, Brooks had completed a draft of his book.[4] He was in doubt where to publish it. On May 9, he wrote to Henry from Boston, "The more I think of my book[,] the less I like bringing it out here. . . ." Many Bostonians knew that Brooks was advocating silver. They were reacting with aversion.[5] He accordingly asked Henry to help him find a publisher in London. Meanwhile, in hopes of studying banking where it started, he was leaving with Evelyn for Venice.[6]

That same day, May 9, Henry wrote to Bancel La Farge, son of John La Farge, "As soon as my girls go, I go. . . ."[7] He had revised his idea of visiting the Yellowstone country to include both Hay and King. The chance that either could join in the effort seemed slight. King liked the

68

idea but could not afford it.[8] Hay's plans would not bring him back to America till July.

On May 13, Adams asked Hay persistingly: "Why will you not go with me? If I start into the Yellowstone with a cook and a batterie de cuisine, guaranteed to travel not more than a mile a day, can we not become famous warriors and shall we not come back to burn our enemies at the stake—or steak, as you prefer? If we can go, I will see that you eat venison daily. . . . Perhaps we can take King with us."

The plan was no sooner re-proposed than it was jeopardized. On May 16, Loulie came down with mumps. Mabel wrote to their sister Ellen in Massachusetts: ". . . brilliant of her, wasn't it? She hasn't got it very badly, but she keeps to her room. . . ."[9]

The invasion of mumps required that Uncle Henry extend his interval in Washington, protect himself and others from contagion, and wait for Loulie to mend. For occupation, he turned to the documents he had collected in London and Paris relating to his *History of the United States*. The most interesting to him were some papers he had found in the archives of the French foreign office. They bore upon a statement he had made in his *History* about a Frenchman who appeared in Washington in 1812 under an alias, "Édouard de Crillon." In the *History*, he had called the man "an agent of Napoleon's secret police."[10] The new evidence proved that Édouard de Crillon was an unattached impostor. The discovery put Adams in a position to announce a factual error in his own work.

After staying six weeks instead of three, Loulie and Mabel went home. On June 12, 1894, writing to Lucy Baxter, Adams mentioned that his thermometer was touching 90°. He spoke of his younger brother. "As Brooks has now another hobby which ought to last him some years, I hope he is provided for. . . ." The hobby was Brooks's emerging book. Henry wished not to offer Brooks advice about what the book ought to say but wanted to look for evidence that might be useful. Apparently for that reason, he gave many of his volumes on the French Revolution to Western Reserve University, pulled together a new supply of books, and began a study of Roman authors in translation.[11]

The U. S. government was verging on bankruptcy. On June 21 in a letter to Cunliffe, Henry mixed personal news with comments on a crisis. "Mrs[.] Cameron and her sequela go next week [to Europe]. . . . The males must remain here a good while yet, for politics and finance wax daily more desperate, and the unfortunate government is at its wit's end. It came into office pledged to reduce taxation, and it has got to cram on the most unpopular taxes possible to fill a deficit that would be not less than £20,000,000, if its pledges were even partially kept. Hence much howling, shrieking of newspapers, scandal-mongering and chattering of the vast monkey tribe. Everyone scolds. Everyone also knows what ought to be done. Everyone reviles everyone who does not agree with him, and everyone differs, or agrees only in contempt for everyone else."

Several Republicans in Congress, Cameron included, sent messages to a national meeting of Republicans in Denver recommending that a free silver plank be added to the party's platform. Adams was not involved. Cameron wrote his letter of his own accord.

Adams accompanied Mrs. Cameron and her party to New York and when back in the capital mailed her some clippings from the *Washington Post* about her husband's letter. Not important in itself, the letter had the backing of the speeches Cameron had read to the Senate since September 1893. Cries accordingly were raised that James Donald Cameron should be the Republican candidate for president in 1896.[12]

On Monday, July 2, Adams went again to New York, this time with Theodore Roosevelt and Cecil Spring Rice. He passed Tuesday at Roosevelt's home, Sagamore Hill, on Long Island. On Wednesday, back in New York, he joined the newly-arrived Hays, with their daughters Helen and Alice, at the Brunswick House. He found them "very flourishing; the girls very bright and pretty, and all in good spirits."[13]

By chance, the Hays returned from Europe simultaneously with John Quincy Adams II. After a six-month absence, John wished to pass the summer in Massachusetts. He too put up at the Brunswick House. In gaslight near an elevator, Henry had an opportunity to look carefully at his eldest brother's face. What he saw convinced him that John had "an advanced case of Bright's Disease, and might die of apoplexy, or anything else, at any time." John apparently did not know he was seriously ill. No one else seemed able to see it. Rather than voice his conviction, Henry kept silent.

An accomplished outdoorsman, Willy Phillips had earlier explored the wilderness south of Yellowstone Park with Joseph Iddings, a geology professor at the University of Chicago. Adams secured the help of Phillips and Iddings as guides for his intended expedition.

King had signed a contract to inspect a silver mine in the northwest. He was scheduled to be free by August 1 and hoped to connect with Adams in the Yellowstone country thereafter.[15] King's hope made Hay reconsider. He agreed to join the undertaking, accompanied by his son Adelbert, a teenager ready for college.

In the United States, effective resistance to the proponents of the gold standard was contingent on assistance by organized labor. The most powerful labor organization in the country was the recently created

American Railway Union. On June 20, under the leadership of its president, Eugene Debs, the union had begun a boycott of all Pullman cars. The action shut down the midwestern railroads. President Cleveland responded by sending U. S. troops to Illinois. Debs was imprisoned. The strike was broken.

In a letter on July 6, Adams twitted Mrs. Cameron as if she meant to be a president's wife and intended to "shake hands with more people than Mrs[.] Cleveland." On July 13, after learning that the president had loosed the army against the railway workers, he wrote to her in earnest, "Cleveland has won another colossal victory for his friends the gold-bugs. . . ." "Your husband had better keep dead quiet now, till things take another turn. He is really helpless, and at most can only keep his head above water till time shall show whether we are to have a chance once more. Debs has smashed everything for the present. The working-man is so brilliant a political failure—so suicidal a political ally, that until he is dead and buried, the gold-bug must rule us. George M. Pullman and Andrew Carnegie and Grover Cleveland are our Crassus and Pompey and Caesar,—our proud American triumvirate, the types of our national mind and ideals."

In late July, railway traffic was sufficiently restored for Adams, Phillips, Iddings, and the Hays to meet at Chicago. They proceeded to Upper Geyser Basin at Yellowstone Park and went into camp on the 28th. By then, King's chance of joining them was spoiled. He had been badly delayed by the strike while trying to reach the silver mine.

In appearance, Adams had organized a summer expedition for no better purpose than outdoor enjoyment. After an interval of sight-seeing within Yellowstone Park, he and his friends started southward, aided by five assistants and twenty-five horses. They were gone four weeks, rode three or four hundred miles mostly through wilderness, pitched twenty-two camps, viewed the Grand Tetons, and safely returned. Along the way, Adams read Roman literature. He painted in watercolors and preserved two of the paintings.[16] He kept a close eye on Hay and his supposed poor health. Hay rebounded as if he had never been ill. His chance of returning to active life was manifest. Adams would not say so, but he—the organizer—had worked a remarkable cure.

When the party reached Mammoth Hot Springs, a letter from Edward Hooper was waiting for Adams, advising him that his brother John had died of "apoplexy, or something," on August 14, 1894, at Quincy.[17]

The Hays, Phillips, and Iddings had to go back at once to their usual haunts. Adams saw them off. Taking a northwestward direction alone, he went by rail to Seattle and by boat to Victoria in British Columbia. He had ideas of going to Alaska but learned that the ship would be late and decided to hurry east across the Rockies via the Canadian Pacific railroad. He stopped to inspect the Selkirk Glacier, traversed the plains, advanced by steamer through the lakes to Buffalo, and sped thence by rail to New York, arriving on September 20.

While traveling more than four thousand miles since leaving Yellowstone Park, he saw not a soul who knew who he was. In a letter to Mrs. Cameron from Banff Springs, he said the people he met were "commonplace." "Oh, I talk with them! You'll not believe it, but I do; and flirt with all the ladies who sell photographs and curios, and keep the hotels; and who are, by the bye, much the most amusing and instructive people I meet." His interlocutors judged him by his appearance and took him to be a traveling salesman. He later said in gratitude: "I pass invariably as a drummer. I am only happy to shelter myself under the disguise of so respectable a class."[18]

The journey raised the question of who—or what—Adams was. One way to approach the question was to notice a wish he had been careful not to have. In the early years of the Republic, two members of his family had been presidents. Throughout the years of his manhood, he had never wished that his father, he himself, or any of his brothers be president. In his view, two Adams presidents were enough and later Adamses had a duty to treat themselves, in silence, as disqualified.

His taking this view had not precluded his noticing the insufficiencies of the men who qualified. Since March 1869, six mediocrities—Grant, Hayes, Garfield, Arthur, Cleveland, Harrison, and Cleveland a second time—had occupied the White House. (Cleveland currently was different only in wreaking actual harm.) Henry had suffered from the six presidents' insufficiencies as keenly as anyone in the country. By various means, the latest being a series of "Cameron" speeches, he had tried at critical moments to offset the insufficiencies, as if he were himself a hidden alternative-president or president-in-reserve. Also important, or even more important, was his being pressed by events and by his sense of responsibility into a role which he might at times neglect but to which he tended to return with ever-increasing tenacity.

Ships at sea with deficient captains were ships in special need of a man at the bow or on a mast to serve as lookout. One of the roles of Henry Adams as politician had long since become that of lookout. As one of his duties, he had gone to places on America's perimeter: Europe, Canada, North Africa, Japan, Hawaii, Samoa, and Cuba. He had gone to places much beyond America's perimeter: notably Tahiti, Fiji, and Ceylon. Also he had traveled widely within the Union. On September 27, 1894, he told Gaskell that recently, by trekking a long distance in Wyoming, he had seen "a very wild, almost unknown, and most interesting series of mountain ranges." "The most beautiful is the Teton range. . . . Few travellers, and probably no tourists have ever been there, which was a sufficient reason for my wanting to go." The ranges were "quite unlike any mountain scenery I ever saw before." He assured Mabel Hooper that the mountains he visited were "American to the very snow." He had learned, too, that Canada was *not* American. "I was amused to find that when I went round through Canada to see the Selkirk glacier, it turned out to be distinctly European,—very fine indeed, but not in the least like the American."[19]

The role of lookout had applications to time. Adams had not become a great historian out of special interest in the past. Though interested in all time's aspects—present, past, and future—he was a man of the future. It was because he needed to learn where America was going that he had given most of the years of his second life to a systematic survey of a selected sample of the past. In his third life, his paramount duty as a politician would be to continue looking into America's future, and he would use every means he could summon. One means had been a journey from Yellowstone Park to Seattle and thence to New York, disguised without effort on his part as a drummer disposed to talk and especially to listen. It had been a beginning.

In New York, King's servant Alexander told Adams that King would shortly return to the city. In hopes of seeing him, Adams "waited three days, and sat in the Knickerbocker Club reading magazines to keep cool."[20] King failed to appear.

Adams went to Washington, spoke with friends, and read his mail.For political purposes, he had only two wholly dependable allies, Mrs. Cameron and Willy Phillips. Mrs. Cameron was still in Europe, buying furniture for her house. Situated diagonally across from Adams's at 21 Lafayette Square, the house was historic and very attractive.

In Adams's opinion, the effort to fight the gold-bugs had been lost during the previous spring and had to be dropped. Writing to Mrs. Cameron on September 25, 1894, he mentioned that Phillips had met her husband on a train from Harrisburg. "From what Phillips repeated of his [the senator's] conversation, I half-guessed that a presidential boom may be sometimes rather a troublesome tin-kettle tied to one's coat-tail. Let us hope that greatness enough has been achieved. . . . Silver is tearing the parties to pieces, but in the long run nothing can be more certain than that the money and organisation of the gold-bugs must win. The silver-populist has neither the brain, the courage nor the wickedness necessary for playing Julius Caesar. My idiot-brother Brooks is still wild to join the fight, but I hope to choke him off, as I hope you will choke off your husband."

Adams's mail included an announcement related directly to himself. Eleven months earlier, he had given the American Historical Association notice that he would be absent for a year and could not serve as president at the 1894 meeting. The Association did not name an acting president or other officer in his place. Just the opposite, the body continued to view Adams as its future chief. The announcement he received said that the Annual Meeting, originally scheduled for July 1894 in Saratoga, would be held after Christmas in Washington. He wrote to Hay on September 26: "My bête noire and namesake H. B. Adams of Johns Hopkins, has scored off me neatly. . . . I find a circular postponing the occasion till Dec. 27, *at Washington*. Really, he has put me in a tight place, but if King will go to Mexico I may escape."

Three ideas were uppermost in Adams's mind. He had been offered mid-winter use of a house owned by Consul Ramdsen near Santiago de Cuba and wished to accept the offer. He hoped to make a tour of the Windward Islands as far as Trinidad. And he wanted to go to Mexico. His ideas were well-adapted to King's inclinations. It happened too that a convenient ship, the *Mediana*, was plying regularly between New York and the Windward Islands.[21]

King appeared in New York. With regret, he advised Adams that he could not go to Trinidad; that he had to find immediate ways to earn money. Adams was dismayed but very anxious to travel. He wrote to Mrs. Cameron on October 2, "I shall sail alone on the Madiana [*sic*] four weeks hence. . . ."

He drew up a new, ambitious plan to circumnavigate the Caribbean. On October 6, he advised Mabel Hooper, ". . . I've a sort of an idea of visiting the islands, Martinique, &c, down to Barbadoes; then coasting the Spanish mainland to Colon at the isthmus of Panama; then coasting to Vera Cruz, and running up to the City of Mexico; then returning through Vera Cruz to Havana, and settling down for the winter at St[.] Iago. . . ."

Thinking he would soon be gone, he did not hire a cook. He wrote to Mrs. Cameron on the 10th: ". . . I am literally a hermit and hardly leave my empty house[,] which echoes like a church when I move. At the [Metropolitan] Club, where I take my meals, I see no one except my cousin Sydney Everett! Two of us are too many."

In the same letter, he spoke of Mrs. Cameron's husband. Passing the Camerons' house, he had spied the senator at his door. "We had half an hour's talk." "Your husband did not speak of his boom. . . . Upon my word, I hardly see how he can get rid of it. Things have so completely justified him, and the situation is becoming so much worse every week, that he will inevitably acquire the air of one of Michael Angelo's prophets. . . . I never saw such bold prophecies so quickly verified. . . . The stockmarkets [*sic*] tumble downstairs with bounds and bumps.

Wheat and cotton and corn and every other staple sells [*sic*] for less and less all the time."

Hay had gone to his summer house in New Hampshire and would soon be in Cleveland. On October 10, 1894, he complained to Adams half in earnest: "I am old and inert and worthless. I have no heart to work and worse still, I have attained to the miserable knowledge that the work is not worth doing even if I could do it."

Adams had an answer. He replied on the 12th: "Look about you, man! Look at—well! lots of things! Gresham, Bayard, Wayne McVeagh [*sic*], Tom Read, Cabot Lodge, Teddy Roosevelt, Debs and me! Be a hero in the strife!" As if Hay would want to be told, he added: "My old idea of writing travels has come back on me. Privately printed."

The cryptic disclosure was evidence that Adams was thinking of *two* of his books as "travels." One of course was his South Sea *Memoirs*. The other necessarily was his *Education*. In his mind the narratives in the latter had come to figure somewhat as journeys, fit for private printing. Possibly he was drafting more chapters.[22]

Mrs. Cameron had reserved space on a steamer to New York. Adams advised her on October 16, 1894: ". . . I shall expect you promptly on the 3d [of November], and shall try to catch your husband, to go with him to meet you. . . . Washington is pleasant now, and I am not sorry to linger a bit, to be with you. . . . I still adhere to my opinion that . . . opposition to the gold-bug must fail."

News had reached Adams of another death. During his sojourn at Tahiti, he had grown fond of Marau and Tati's sister Beretania, known as Prie, a sufferer from tuberculosis. A letter from Tati reported that Prie's struggle to live had ended. Adams felt her going as exceedingly sad. On the 28th, he confided to Gaskell: "I have lost a brother . . . but what has affected me also, though you will hardly believe it, is the death of my Tahiti sister, Beretania, a beautiful girl, or woman, who died of consumption a short time ago. . . . My Tahiti relationship is quite a real thing. . . ."

Confusion ensued. Adams learned that Mrs. Cameron would not reach New York till November 10. He and the senator went that day to the dock in New York, only to learn that she would arrive on the 17th!

Back at 1603 H Street, Adams waited and doubted. He wrote to Mrs. Fell, "I am now in a queer state of chaos and unrest, which seems to offer no end."[23] On the 16th, he wrote urgently to Mrs. Cameron: "I want to see you. I want to see Martha. I am tired of you both for not coming home." Next day they arrived, and he allotted two weeks to their company.

*   *   *

Brooks had sent Henry the first four chapters of a second draft of his book and had asked for criticisms and suggestions about a title. Henry read the chapters and returned them with comments—now missing—but left the problem of a title for Brooks and Evelyn to solve.[24]

Opportunely Henry acquired a companion on his prospective travels. Chandler Hale, at twenty-one, was a Washington drifter, son of Senator Hale of Maine, and, on his mother's side, grandson of Zachariah Chandler of Michigan—a leading Republican boss of the 1870s.[25] Chandler had often come to 1603 H Street in the evenings to play cribbage with Adams, who usually beat him.[26] Adams told him that he had taken space on the *Mediana* to Martinique. Chandler asked to go too, and Adams agreed. His only worry was that his young friend was liable to headaches and sunstroke.

King and Adams were exchanging letters. King believed that, if Adams and Hale would reverse their itinerary and go first to Mexico, he might connect with them when they reached the Windward Islands. On November 20, 1894, he sent Adams some suggestions concerning travel by Pullman car from Washington to Mexico City. Especially he suggested going by ship down Mexico's west coast from Acapulco to Panama, that being the most interesting route southward toward the islands.

As a result, Adams canceled his plan to go to Martinique and followed King's suggestions about Mexico, with the difference that he chose a route to Mexico via St. Louis. His duties as lookout remained in force, and St. Louis was an American city he had not seen. He *had* to see it.

Adams and Hale left for St. Louis on December 2. Possibly at the last minute and apparently for several reasons, Adams decided to serve *in absentia* as president of the American Historical Association. One reason was the body's legal status. The federal government had granted the Association a charter in 1889 that linked it to the Smithsonian Institution and required that it maintain its headquarters in Washington. To some extent, the charter made the Association an affiliate of the federal government. To the same extent, its president was a one-year holder of non-political national office.

A second reason had to do with science. In part because of their link to the Smithsonian, the members of the Association were inclined to think of themselves as practitioners of historical science. They still spoke of "history," but they emphasized that their sort of history was "scientific." As their president, Adams might quickly learn whether their protestations were a sham.[27]

A third reason related to much-noticed books. The previous April in a letter to Gaskell, Adams had mentioned a new book, *National Life and Character: a Forecast*, by Charles Henry Pearson. He had gone so far as to say, "I am satisfied that Pearson is right, and that the dark races are gaining on us, so that we may depend on their steadily shutting down on us, as they have already done in Haiti, and are doing throughout the West Indies and our southern States."[28]

By way of a reply, Gaskell had said he found only one idea in a book by Benjamin Kidd, *Social Evolution.*

Adams answered: "I will try to read Kidd, since everyone is talking about him, but on those matters I have my own prejudgments, and hate to see half-treatments, like Pearson's &c. We know too little yet to make a science of history. Another fifty years will do it, I've no doubt. I can wait. It will do no one any good. Did you ever read Karl Marx [i.e. Marx's *Capital*]? I think I never struck a book which taught me so much, and with which I disagreed so radically in conclusion."[29]

The passage was rich in implications. For Adams, Marx's *Capital* anticipated Pearson's *National Life and Character* in being a "half-treatment"—by which Adams partly meant a treatment adapted to the wants of a vested interest: the supposed proletariat in the case of Marx and white-skinned human beings in the case of Pearson.[30] In contrast, Adams wanted a treatment of history in which *all* interests were represented. Although he said that in fifty years there would be a science of history, that he could wait, and the science would do no one any good, he had said also that he had formed "prejudgments"—necessarily meaning he had *not* waited. For him, the science of history had existed for some time. Moreover, a full treatment of sorts was already present in his mind.

All these matters had been settled for Adams before he knew that the American Historical Association was to meet in December 1894 in Washington. They had sufficed to make him view his presidency of the Association as an opportunity. He at last had decided to seize it.

With Hale, Adams went to St. Louis, inspected the city, advanced to Chihuahua, stopped, and reached Guadalajara on December 11, 1894. He wrote to Mrs. Cameron next day that they arrived during "the fiesta of Santa Maria Purissima, the feast of the most mysterious mystery of the immaculate conception." ". . . . we strolled into the Cathedral at sunset, and the music soon let us know that some great function was at hand." His letter became emotional. "We sat two hours listening to the combination of orchestra, voices and two great organs of the latest and swellest Parisian work; and watching the swarm of Indians and half-breeds, swarthy and pathetic, the men in red or particolored serapes; the women with their shawls draped over their heads; and the babies playing on the floor, with an occasional howl at the most delicate notes of the organ. These sights always affect me. . . ."

That same day, Adams mailed in final form—with interlined corrections—a presidential address to the American Historical Association in the form of a letter to the body's secretary, Herbert Baxter Adams. The letter was intended to be read by the secretary at the meeting, and shortly was. A notable feature of the letter was good manners. President Henry Adams said in his opening paragraph, "Evidently I am fitted only to be an absent president, and you will pardon a defect which is clearly not official, but a condition of the man."[31] He said in closing that the remarks he had made in his letter were "only casual, and offered in the paradoxical spirit of private conversation." ". . . I have not expressed any opinion of my own; or, if I have expressed it, pray consider it as withdrawn."[32]

Attention should be directed to the situation within which Adams had written his letter. He had been publishing on historical subjects since 1867. Beginning in 1870 and continuing into 1891, at first in magazines, later in books, he had published important ideas relating to history as an art and a science. His efforts had climaxed in a *History of the United States* which offered not only a narrative of human events and conclusions about the direction being taken by human beings—more especially the Americans—but also a vocabulary used by the author for purposes of historical analysis. In December 1894, when his letter was read for him in Washington in his absence, there were American historians not connected with the universities and colleges, especially Worthington and Paul Ford, who had interested themselves in Adams's historical writings. There perhaps were university teachers of history here and there who had read the nine volumes of his *History of the United States* with a degree of appreciation. By and large, however, the history teachers of America had been too absorbed in teaching their students and working on their own projects to read his *History* or even ask what it said or suggested. In this respect, the members of the *American Historical Association*, resembled the governing authorities at Harvard. Much as Harvard had attempted to make Adams an honorary doctor before digesting his principal work, the Association had made him its president without doing him the honor of fully reading the "historical science" he had published.

This being the case, Adams had written a letter as president of the Association which was designed, not to claim for himself any of his already-published historical achievements, but instead to subject the Association's members to a test of their attention to business. His letter was short. It was more than generous. He treated the members of the association as representative of the world's historians at their best. And he raised five concerns:

—whether the historians would extend their inquiries to embrace all peoples in all places and times;
—whether the historians would develop a shared, agreed "theory," "hypothesis," "law," or array of "laws" asserting the truth about humanity's "historical evolution";
—whether their asserting such a finding would earn them the disfavor and opposition of any of the world's established and conflicting great interests (e.g. the Church, the State, Property, or Labor);
—whether, in the face of disfavor and opposition, the historians would divide into camps, or even abandon historical inquiry;
—and whether, more creditably, they would act together and uphold their discovery.

These five concerns might be quite enough for the members of the association to think about, but Adams brought up a sixth:

—whether the theory, hypothesis, law, or array of laws, once developed, would be optimistic (as Darwin's "conclusions" had seemed to be in the past) or pessimistic—in keeping with recent developments.

Adams viewed the sixth concern as exceedingly important. He said, ". . . I greatly fear [the theory] . . . would take its tone from the pessimism of Paris, Berlin, London and St. Petersburg. . . ."

There was always a problem, when reading or hearing Adams's words, about the way they might best be construed. In the give and take of conversation, and especially in situations involving ideas relating to history, he might make statements he only fractionally believed, or completely disbelieved, as a means of luring readers and hearers away from the seemingly safe but actually fatal shelters of intellectual passivity. In his presidential letter, as if he believed it, he suggested that history would become a science *only after it had offered a settled conclusion about its subject.* Going further, he threw in two hard-edged sentences:

Any science assumes a necessary sequence of cause and effect, a force resulting in motion which cannot be other than what it is. Any science of history must be absolute, like other sciences, and must fix with mathematical certainty the path which human society has got to follow.

Adams could anticipate that friends of his would be present at the December meeting. Two friends in fact attended: Ephraim Emerton and Justin Winsor. (Emerton had assisted Adams when he taught history at Harvard. Winsor was Harvard's librarian. He presided at the meeting in Adams's place.) It was not probable, however, that Emerton, Winsor, and other well-informed persons would try to persuade the members generally, after Adams's letter was read, that he was pulling their legs. The style of his hard-edged sentences was so severe that the sentences were sure to be received with entire solemnity. Thus a conclusion was sure to be drawn that Adams believed in the hideous idea that humans were automatons and that "human society" was riding on pre-established trolley tracks to ineluctable stops and at last to a car barn it could not choose. If only for that reason, a few members might feel outraged; and a few, in anger, might wish to differ.

Had the members of the Association read Adams's *History of the United States*, or, better, if they had read it with attention to its ideas, they would have known that his view of history was one which saw in human affairs an on-going contest between conservatism and innovation— between the inertia of established habit and the energy permitted by newfound visions. Similarly, if they listened carefully to his letter, the members would have realized that Adams was as much a believer in the reality of freedom as they were, very possibly more. The passage already quoted about a theory of history shared by all historians was so worded as to lead to an open-ended continuation. President Adams said he feared that, if developed, the theory "would take its tone from the pessimism of Paris, Berlin, London and St[.] Petersburg, *unless it brought into sight some new and hitherto unexpected path for civilization to pursue* [italics added]." The president himself was the first to say at the 1894 meeting that humanity might take a new and unexpected path.

The chief irony might turn out to be that the historians who had not read Adams's *History of the United States* would compound their omission by deciding to believe that Adams was horribly wrong about historical inevitability. By throwing in the hard-edged sentences, he had created abundant room for the members to invert his meaning.[33]

In Mexico, as previously in Cuba, Adams would sometimes say that he was seeking a purchasable winter retreat for himself, perhaps a former coffee plantation, a *cafetal*. His declarations were true as far as they went but did not account for the main features of his continual wanderings: their energy, breadth, and duration.

At Mexico City, he broached the subject of crossing the mountains by mule to Acapulco with the object of connecting with a steamer to Panama. On December 18, 1894, he wrote to Mrs. Cameron about his proposal, ". . . our Mexican acquaintances make very long faces, and threaten us with no end of discomforts." Yet he was bent on making the trip. "The country is beautiful. . . . I shall take a good outfit . . . and am assured that the country is now perfectly safe. . . . Don't scare Mrs[.] Hale by finding fault with all this."

After a week in Puebla, Orizaba, and Jalapa, Adams and Hale returned to Mexico City, intent on starting for Acapulco. They fell in with an American adventurer, Dewitt C. Foster, who claimed to have been twenty years in the Mexican army and claimed in addition to be a nephew of "old wicked Sam Ward," one of Adams's Washington contacts in 1869. Once offered suitable pay, Foster agreed to act as guide. Because of Hale's sensitivity to sun, Adams proposed "to ride only in the hours of morning and evening." For fear of missing the steamer, he "allowed ten days for a six-day journey." He wanted to travel in Mexican dress and, for the purpose, purchased "a full suit of leather riding-clothes after the style of the bull-ring."[34]

A day was lost to delays in getting mules. On December 29, the travelers set off on a mountain trail, achieved forty miles in eleven hours, stopped at Iguala, and tried to sleep. At 11:00 P.M., they were violently shaken. ". . . our Colonel-guide called 'Tremblor!' We had taken on a fairly first-class earthquake. . . ."[35]

Next day Adams was informed that they would have to ride fifty miles before 5:00 P.M. to catch a ferry across a river. They rode thirty before 1:00 P.M., but Hale "broke down with fatigue and sun." One problem was "fear of sunstroke."[36] A worse was disinformation. Adams realized that mule travel was slower than advertised. There were 250 miles of trail left to follow. Hale could not ride in bright sun. Days of rest were needed by men and mules. Arrival in Acapulco would require twelve days instead of six.

Patient as always, Adams advised Foster and the muleteers that the party would retrace its steps in darkness. He later wrote to Louisa Hooper: "Our journey back, stopping in the Indian huts, among the pigs and chickens; eating fresh tortillas and chile, which I preferred to our own canned stores; and sleeping chiefly on reeds, was very amusing to me. We did it nearly all by moonlight, resting and cleaning ourselves at Iguala; and on arriving here [at Cuautla], where a Frenchman has a good hotel, we stopped for a thorough rest; the first we have taken since we left Washington."[37]

The accident of attempting and abandoning a journey afforded Adams his best experience of the Mexicans. The people he met on the trail were doubtless told that he was a Yankee. Seeing his steel-and-silver spurs, tight leather trousers with white facings, leather jacket with white frogs, and sugar-loaf panama hat, they saw nothing unusual about the costume. They took him for another gentlemanly passer-by, to be welcomed and forgotten as an upperclass Everyman.

Adams observed his very likeable hosts with the eyes of an American lookout who was also an inveterate historian. From Cuautla on January 8, 1895, he reported to Cunliffe: "Mexico is exceptionally amusing, not in the romantic way I expected, but in a prosaic, grimy, Indian, scarlet-vermilion way of its own, impossible to describe, and disappointing to realize. It is another money-making machine, like the United States or

England or Italy, but uses peculiar and rather successful processes of its own, remnants of the Roman Empire, which still survives here in full flower. As far as I could judge, living as I have done, in their mud huts, and eating their tortillas and chile by their side, among the pigs and hens and dogs that fill the interstices of their cabins, I saw nothing whatever that I should not have seen in a like journey in the Spain of Hadrian. Every detail of the pottery, the mule-trains with their loads, the food, the clothes, and the roads where no wheel had ever passed, might have been Roman, and the people have the peculiar look, though all really Indians, that the Roman empire left forever on its slave-provinces."

Adams had intended to reach Acapulco by mule and Panama by ship preliminary to crossing the Isthmus and circling the Caribbean in a counter-clockwise direction ending in Cuba. Thwarted in the effort, he persevered by attempting the same journey, or something like it, in a mostly clockwise direction. After resting at Cuautla, he and Hale went to Vera Cruz and caught a steamer which took them southward to Tampico and then carried them northeastward a long leap to Havana.

As a matter of course while in Havana, Adams spoke with the American, British, and French consuls about the condition of Cuba. He was told that the worldwide depression had disastrously reduced the sale price of sugar. Also he learned from Count Maurice Sala, a retired French diplomat, formerly secretary to the French legation in Washington, that the Cuban archives had been moved ten years earlier to Seville. He rather wished to go to Spain and sift the documents in the Cuban archives. Instead, on a Spanish mail steamer, he and Hale proceeded eleven hundred miles to San Juan in Puerto Rico.

He was pleased to arrive. In a history that he had started in the form of letters to Mrs. Cameron, he mentioned that San Juan was unexpectedly attractive—"one of the most picturesque I ever saw, with its old walls and forts still perfect, and a fine harbor and sea-exposure, pretty suburbs, and a cleanliness very un-Spanish."[38]

Smallpox had broken out in Puerto Rico. To continue their journey, Adams and Hale would have to cross the island to its southern port, Ponce, take passage on an Italian steamer to Danish St. Thomas, and there—for fear of smallpox—be quarantined for fifteen days. The prospect of quarantine was unpleasant. Yet they elected to face it.

At St. Thomas, they submitted to seizure by a physician and were rowed to an airy prison. Adams cheerily explained: "All my historical ideas of quarantine were upset by the sight of this. Perched on the rocks above the harbor, the buildings look south over the sea to Santa Cruz on the horizon; west to Porto Rico [sic]; and north into the harbor and the town lying under the hills. . . . In the harbor are some vessels of war, Russian, Haitian, and French. Ocean steamers come in and go out. The sun is warm; the sky is clear; the waves are dancing fast and bright; blue isles and green mountains wear the purple noon's entrancing light; the place is clean, and the table is fair." ". . . of all the absurdities of travel[,] the absurdest is that I should find my Nirvana in a prison."[39]

For fifteen days, Adams loafed, bathed in the sea, painted, studied Spanish, smoked fine Havana cigars, and wrote excellent letters. He told Gaskell on February 16: "Here in the tropics they talk of nothing but sugar and coffee, low prices, ruin, and discontent. I ought to except Mexico where all is prosperity and satisfaction, but Mexico is a fragment of the later Roman Empire miraculously preserved as it must have existed two thousand years ago in Spain and Africa; and what ruins us, profits it. Here in the Antilles our civilisation struggles on, in a losing battle with barbarism, much as Froude described it, only worse. The negro, the half-breed, and the broken planter are the results of Columbus and the four hundred years of triumphant civilisation which we celebrated at Chicago. . . ."

Chance had decided that seven males be quarantined together at St. Thomas. In Adams's phrase, one was a "loathly German-American-Jew," traveling from Venezuela to Santo Domingo accompanied by a monkey.[40] Like many persons brought up as Christians, Adams was prey to a temptation to associate the Jews with Satan.[41] In this instance, he resisted the temptation. He said, "I find even the loathly Jew and his monkey rather picturesque."[42]

The comparative mildness of Adams's language could be attributed in part to paradisiacal surroundings. Part could be attributed to reflection. The previous September, when trying to advise Senator Cameron—via Mrs. Cameron—that the war with the gold-bugs was lost, he had studied himself and made a discovery. He had written to Lucy Baxter, "I have sought all over the world for some spot where life is easy, and money is superfluous, for I have long believed that the so-called civilisation—which is the Hebraisation, or commercial insanity—of our age must end in universal collapse and bankruptcy; but go where I will, I find that I carry myself with me, and that my Ego is the very product of the age I am trying to fly from."[43]

His discovery pointed toward a twofold conclusion: that he should be more accepting of himself and others. Yet he would never give up his efforts to initiate improvements, whether personal or large-scale.

Released, Adams and Hale took a British steamer that carried them into and out of several ports. In his history, Adams told Mrs. Cameron: "The islands are disappointing. All the English islands are mere sugar-farms without charm of color or life. Domenica [*sic*] alone has some air of the South Seas, and Martinique is really gay with the color and vivacity of the tropics, as Lefcadio [*sic*] Hearn describes it in his book, which you will find among my books of travel."[44]

On March 10, 1895, he wrote to Hay in stronger terms. ". . . the English are extraordinary people for taking the fun out of everything they touch. From the moment one loses sight of Porto [*sic*] Rico, nature, standing on her head, and kicking her heels in the air so that you mayn't lose one of her stunning beauties, seems just to flatten out when the English[man] takes hold of her with his trading paws. Heaven bless him! As I pass island after island which he has turned into a dreary Scotch sugar-manufactury, the very volcanoes seem to have turned into sugar-engines and have forgotten their capers. St[.] Kitts, Antigua, Monserrat [*sic*], Sta[.] Lucia, St[.] Vincent, are all as dreary as Aberdeen."

For the present, Adams seemed an idler lost to duty and responsibility. Yet his letters brimmed with a sense of achievement—the achievement of doing nothing and being away from Washington when doing nothing and being away were the right things for a man to do. He explained to Mrs. Cameron: "Much as I miss you and Martha, and sadly as I feel that my hair is fast whitening, and my fascinating period of life behind me forever, I cannot do the tragic. . . . Things are bound now to get better, however slowly,—or bust. Either way, I can breathe freer, and anyway I shall not have the sense of having said or done anything, good or bad. Selfishness is usually sense. Nobody has gained a hair this winter by anything he has said or done [in Washington]; and the man who has been out of it is the one most likely to be listened to hereafter.—Not that I want to be listened to! My poor brother Brooks is a warning against such ambition."[45]

Brooks was coming back from Europe to spend the summer at Quincy and work again on his book. Talking with Evelyn some months before, Henry had advised that course for Brooks. It had serious perils.

On March 14, 1895, writing to Mrs. Cameron, Henry had described his younger brother as "a little of a genius, with bad manners and sensitive nerves." "The silver business has brought Brooks's position in Boston to a crisis, and will drive him insane if he stays there." Being himself a fugitive from Boston and its environs, Henry could not offer to go there and give his brother company. "As I refuse even to enter the place, for fear of [a?] downright quarrel, or to talk with a Bostonian for fear of insulting him, or to talk of Boston, for fear of expressing my contempt and disgust for it, and its opinions and for everything it is, or ever was, or ever will be, Brooks is left without even my little aid or countenance, and writhes like a worm under the process of being stepped on."

There were dangers, too, in Brooks's paying visits to Washington. He would want to exhaust Henry's patience in endless conversations, or, rather, disputations. The amount of genius he possessed was only large enough to make him combatively unsure of his own ideas.

At Barbados, Henry and Chandler boarded a British steamer bound for Trinidad, the far point of their journey. A Scotchman, Colonel Mann, was among the passengers. Henry had met him and his handsome wife at St. Kitts. He had learned that the colonel was from the Deeside and had talked with him about the Clarks and other persons in Scotland. Also Henry liked Mrs. Mann. He told Mrs. Cameron what happened on the steamer. ". . . I took to her, and found myself actually making an effort to amuse her. It is so long since I have been able to make such an effort that I felt ashamed, as if I were a woman having a new baby at my time of life."[46]

Colonel Mann knew of a steamship line which offered passage from Trinidad, by way of Cartagena on the Spanish Main and Colon at the Isthmus of Panama, to New Orleans. The information permitted Henry to plan the last leg of his Caribbean circumnavigation. The plan afforded an interval in Trinidad, a place he found he liked.

In New Orleans on April 9, 1895, before starting toward Washington, Henry received a quantity of mail.[47] Included was a letter from a London genealogist, Chester Waters. The letter provided help concerning a problem that had dogged Henry since the 1860s. The problem centered in the fact that he was very deeply attached to his paternal grandmother, Louisa Catherine Johnson—the wife of John Quincy Adams.

In Washington the previous autumn, on November 11, 1894, Henry had received a letter from a Mrs. L. N. Walters of Georgetown, offering to sell him two miniature portraits painted in London by "Pell"— actually Charles Willson Peale. The persons depicted were Joshua and Catherine Nuth Johnson, the parents of Louisa Catherine Johnson. Mrs. Walters had inherited the portraits and was asking $600 for the pair.[48]

Henry arranged to see them. Writing to Charles on November 30, he mentioned the offer, said the portraits were "very nice work," but explained, ". . . I am not particularly in the market for that sort of art."[49] He rather cryptically added that he had written to a London genealogist, Chester Waters, and given him "a memorandum of certain names to be kept in mind."

Despite his reluctance, Henry bought the portraits.[50] It happened that Waters did not quickly attend to Henry's letter. When he at last replied, Waters recommended that Henry employ a young researcher in

London, Oswald Barron. Water's letter was the one that reached Henry in New Orleans. It is missing.

Next day, April 10, 1895, while traveling, Henry mailed a letter he would not mention to friends or relations. It was addressed to Barron. It too is missing, but its contents can be gleaned from other evidence. He made a request and promised the prompt arrival of a bank draft. He asked Barron to get him a record of the marriage of Joshua Johnson and Catherine Nuth and look for records concerning the bride and her antecedents. He advised Barron that Miss Nuth was English. He provided two scraps of data about her parentage.[51]

Henry had probably found the scraps in 1868 or 1869, when he had access to his grandmother's papers. The scraps had the form of a memorandum Louisa wrote, stating that her mother was an English-woman named Catherine Nuth and adding some slight hints about her mother's parentage. The information provided was extremely minimal.

While in appearance not important, the inquiry Henry had initiated affected his deeper feelings. He had long wanted to trace all his ancestors and had learned a great deal about many.[52] Yet he lacked information about Louisa's parentage, especially on her mother's side. He did not doubt that there had been an English mother named Catherine Nuth. He hoped Barron could get information about her. Until then, however, he would remain the victim of a paradox. He possessed masses of data about ancestors who did not much interest him. He had next-to-zero knowledge about some ancestors who interested him very much. Things were badly out of balance. He could almost have the feeling that he did not know who he was.

5

VISION AND REVOLUTION

When Henry arrived in Washington, on April 11, 1895, Brooks and Evelyn were already at 1603 H Street. They stayed "till about May 1," long enough for Brooks to say all he wished about his book.[1] He had completed a much-changed second draft but desperately lacked a title. Houghton Mifflin Company was reading the draft. In the event of rejection, he would send it to a firm in London he somehow had come to know about, Swan Sonnenschein and Company.

Henry invited his Hooper nieces to join him. Edward Hooper suggested to Abigail Adams, daughter of John Quincy Adams II, that she go too.[2] Abigail wrote to ask permission. Uncle Henry replied that he was "enormously pleased" that one of his own nieces "at last" wished to visit.[3] The strict truth was that Mary and Elsie, Charles's middle and younger daughters, had already been visitors. Abigail's arrival would enlarge Henry's collection of visitor-nieces to eight.

J. P. Morgan had saved the federal government from bankruptcy by arranging the sale of a bond issue to permit the Treasury's obtaining gold. Henry avoided naming Morgan in his letters but said he hoped London's "amiable gold-lenders" would "carry" the United States "another eighteen months before squeezing us again."[4] The hope was dismal. Clearly power continued to rest in the hands of money-lords in London. President Cleveland and Congress were impotent and adrift.

Henry considered Washington less dominated by money than London and New York. He told Gaskell: "Washington is an exceptionally social place. Of late years it has been a good deal injured by New York . . . but even New York loses half its grotesqueness here. . . . One might almost say that a person might have here some social consideration apart from—though hardly without—money . . . provided he or she were not clever or artistic."[5]

In 1887, a decision had been made that Charles—not Henry—should write a biography of their father. Charles put off his work on the project. In 1893, work was precluded by disaster: he lost $1,500,000. In 1895, he still viewed himself as "walking on the ragged edge." Yet he at last started work and wrote to Henry about his progress.[6]

Henry answered on April 16 by describing their father as an Adams too simple to be remembered, too capable to be forgotten. "He stands on the merits of his course and speech in one session of Congress, and his diplomatic papers and conduct. . . . His defects and limitations were as important, and as valuable, to him, as his qualities. . . . Had there been a little more of him, or a little less of him, he would have been less perfect. . . . From the moment he appeared anywhere—at Washington, London, Geneva—his place was never questioned, much less disputed. Russell, Palmerston, Disraeli, Bright, Cobden, Gladstone, Seward, and all the Americans, were bunglers in work compared with him, as his state-papers show. . . . His simplicity was like the purity of crystal, without flash or color."

Henry's answer reminded Charles that Henry was the son best prepared to memorialize their father. He asked Henry to write the needed biography, after all, so that *he* could write about their Adams grandfather.[7] (Charles had no idea that Henry was well along in writing a book, *The Education of Henry Adams*, which, as one of its lesser purposes, would establish a myth about their father, attributing to him a heightened degree of diplomatic prowess and importance.)

Henry proved uncooperative. Later Charles tried to elicit from him whatever records he had kept from the time when he and the minister were in England.[8] Henry lied and said he had no records.[9] His course was justified, perhaps, as self-protection.[10]

In time, Charles would warm to his task.[11] Indeed he would collect evidence in such quantities that he would end, not merely in writing and publishing a short biography of their father, but also in projecting a long biography of their father intended to serve as a history of the Civil War in its international bearings.[12]

Henry had welcomed so many people to midday "breakfasts" at his house that the gatherings had become a Washington institution. An especially agreeable guest had been a Chicago heiress, Mary Victoria Leiter. When Henry was returning from the Caribbean, Mary became engaged to George Curzon, an English diplomat. On his arrival in Washington, Henry asked Mary to introduce him to her fiancé.[13]

Marriages mattered. Earlier Henry had gained an advantage by giving breakfasts to Mary Endicott, who married the English leader Joseph Chamberlain. He would gain a second time by having given breakfasts to Mary Leiter, the future wife of George Curzon. The size of the gain could be foreseen. After marrying a Chicago fortune, Curzon might rise in English politics with wondrous speed.[14]

To help her sister, Lida Hoyt, whose nerves were ailing, Mrs. Cameron left the capital. Henry regretted her absence and worried about her health. He warned her: "The trouble with you is that your nerves too are beginning to go, and before they ought. Take care of them!"[15]

Henry was ten years older than Brooks. In the 1860s, he had led him to Antwerp to inspect the cathedral and, in Scotland, led him to medieval churches, forts, and abandoned Hermitage Castle. When Houghton Mifflin Company published Brooks's first book, *The Emancipation of Massachusetts*, in 1886, Henry read it and seemed to Brooks to be "almost the only man" who understood its underlying thesis.[16]

On May 14, 1895, Brooks notified Henry that Houghton Mifflin had rejected his draft.[17] He said he would send it to Sonnenschein in London and would soon write a preface. The sting of rejection showed in Brooks's letter. He called Boston "the modern Sodom."

Evelyn appended a note to her husband's letter. She told Henry: "You must help us to a name [i.e. a title for the book]. How do you like 'Ancient and Modern *Civilization*'—or the last word *alone?*" Since the title later adopted was *The Law of Civilization and Decay*, Evelyn should be credited with finding the path to its discovery.[18]

Eventually Brooks would tell Henry how the idea of the new book had first come to him. In 1888, while observing mass at Le Mans cathedral, he had suddenly felt that he "believed in the miracle" and that the emotions of the cathedral's builders survived in him. So inspired, he "resolved . . . to see . . . what it was that had made the crusades." He traveled to the Holy Land and experienced an even stronger feeling. The sight of the crusaders' huge abandoned castles and deserted Gothic churches overwhelmed him with a sense that the believers of the Middle Ages were soldiers excited and exalted by combat.[19] He tried to write a book but had no idea where the effort might lead.[20] In time, a contrast he perceived between the mentality of the crusaders and the mentality favored in commerce gave him a dark idea of social evolution. Freed to write, he in time developed a book that boldly illustrated the dark idea.

Being married to her sister Evelyn, Brooks saw much of Anna Lodge. In late May 1895, he learned that Mrs. Lodge, the senator, and their sons would be going to England in July and would travel on the Continent. Brooks persuaded Mrs. Lodge to plan visits to cathedrals in Normandy, to Mont Saint Michel in Brittany, and to the cathedral of Chartres near Paris. He also suggested that Henry go with them.[21]

When told about the tour and his projected role in it, Henry liked the plan but wished not to decide until he was better informed about Mrs. Cameron's intentions. She too had ideas of going to Europe. On May 25 by letter, he asked her whether he should accompany the Lodges. "As far as I can see, I can do nothing else, but I want first to learn how it stands with you, and what you will do."

On the 27th, Brooks advised Henry that his draft was in transit to London. A week later, he sent Henry a newly-written "Preface." He explained that the preface would serve as his "Book of Conclusions."[22]

When he opened Brooks's envelope, Henry found both the preface and a dedication of the book to himself. He replied on June 5, forbidding the dedication. He urged Brooks to review the preface and "strike out all the egoism you can reach." In addition, he sketched an uncertain prospect. ". . . *possibly* I shall go over with the Lodges, July 5, with the intent to return in October."

Henry was reviewing his intentions and thinking new thoughts. He remained convinced that the gold-bugs were victorious, yet was nursing hopes of resistance. Instead of leaving the country, he might stay home. "If the gold-bug government and society is to break down, I shall stay here to grin in its face. In case, by December next, the struggle should be still going on, with any chance of gold-bug defeat, I shall probably stay in Washington till the result is fixed."

He revealed too that he wanted a sharp clash with England. ". . . I see no dignified course for our government except that of a trial of strength. Towards that, all my little social buzz has been directed since September, 1893. I think it time that the political existence of England should cease in North America."[23]

Henry's problem was how to work a revolution in global politics. He wanted to organize a power sufficient to counterbalance the British Empire. He said that, if a free-silver administration was elected in the United States in 1896, it would be "thoroughly coached." *He* would set its policy. He continued: "I think I can effect that much. . . ." Yet the policy would need a capable, energetic champion in the White House. "All depends on the *man*,—the next President. The *policy* can only fail by wanting vigor."

Henry had designs. Even more, he had fears. His ideas were roaming to all the continents. Thoughts of past events were strongly affecting his attempts to foresee and shape the future. He confessed: "One's mind goes far, and dreams much over such a field of vision, but in the end it always loses itself in Asia. Russia is omnipotence. Without Russia, such a scheme might fail. I fear Russia much! Why can one never penetrate that polar mystery? What chance is there of repeating the diplomacy, the blunders and the disasters of 1812? What chance is there of achieving that success on which [President] Madison had a right to reckon, and which nothing but the unripeness of the age prevented his achieving? Our true point of interest is not India but Russia, yet Russia is impenetrable, and any intelligent man will deal with her the better, the less closely he knows her."

The central tenet of Brooks's dark idea of history was that nature vents its energy by creating new races, different and separate from one another, yet alike in being doomed to gravitate from barbarism to civilization before expiring.[24] The idea concorded with the sort of pessimism that Henry—in his letter to the American Historical Association—had said he deeply feared. If the author of the idea had not been his younger brother, he might have raised his voice against it. As things stood, he sought a way to praise.

He found the way by treating one of Brooks's subsidiary ideas as if it were his whole idea. To use a formula he would later print, Henry chose to assert that Brooks had "discovered or developed a law of history that civilisation followed the exchanges," meaning that civilization shifted—migrated—to the places to which gold and silver most tended to flow.[25] Not that Henry believed in the alleged law! He believed in it only enough to pose two questions. Could one find out how much gold had recently flowed from the United States to London? Could the outflows of coming years be predicted?

In early June 1895, Henry put the questions to himself, collected and analyzed the figures available to him, and grew dissatisfied with his answers. Worthington Ford was employed at the Treasury Department as chief of its Bureau of Statistics. Henry paid him a visit and obtained more figures. On June 15, he initiated a correspondence with Ford that brought them into partnership as researchers. The work they were starting involved laborious arithmetic. The figures available to them were in many instances wrong or confusing. Their findings would undoubtedly need amendment. Yet they intended to persevere.

The American Historical Association was launching a magazine, the *American Historical Review.* The first issue was planned to appear in October 1895. In early June, the editor, John Franklin Jameson, had written to ex-President Adams requesting an article for the issue.

The launching of the magazine could seem to reflect an assumption that the principal work of historians was a pouring forth of lectures, articles, monographs, and books. From the time in 1870 when he became a history teacher, Adams had made a very different assumption. He had supposed that the first task of historians was carefully to read the writings of current leaders in their field, test the validity of the leaders' writings by undertaking new research, and try to develop new conclusions, if needed, with the help of pertinent evidence, old or new. He had not changed his principles.[26] In June 1895, he was especially affected by the ways in which they applied to him. Was *he* the present leader among the American historians? Were other historians in the country reading his *History of the United States?* Did they understand the ideas at work in his narrative? Were they exerting themselves to find whether his assertions could be trusted?

Adams replied to Jameson on June 10, "To write an article is impossible." Yet he said he could supply "some unpublished material" and "a few lines of explanation." He intimated that the new material would correct a blunder he had made in his *History*, would relate to "scoundrels," and would amuse the magazine's readers.

On June 24, Adams sent Jameson a manuscript he described as an "article." It began with an extended statement about the prevalence of error in histories. It pointed to an error in Adams's own *History* concerning a Frenchman named Soubiran who passed himself off in Washington in 1812 as "Count Édward de Crillon." It corrected the error by quoting eight French documents in English translation. Four of the documents were by Soubiran. One, an autobiographical narrative, could have had few equals in world literature for seeming candor in combination with unchecked mendacity.

Jameson published Adams's "Count Edward de Crillon" in the inaugural issue. He possibly viewed the article as an amusing correction of a minor error. Obviously, however, the article conveyed a message. Implicit in Adams's pages was a request by him to other historians to read his *History*, find it mistaken if they could, and, if they could not, declare it to be true.[27]

Sonnenschein agreed to publish 1,500 copies of *The Law of Civilization and Decay* at the author's expense. Because the book would not be stereotyped, a second printing would not be possible.[28]

Mrs. Cameron waived all thoughts of Europe and planned to return with her husband and Martha to Henry's house at Beverly Farms. Henry felt he had better join the Lodges, as wished. They had reservations to Southampton on the steamer *New York*. He reserved a large stateroom on the ship and asked Rudyard Kipling to share it. With regrets on both sides, Kipling was obliged to forego a free luxurious voyage.[29]

Knowing that Henry was going to London, Brooks sent him letters of introduction to English financial experts. He said about one of them, Hermann Schmidt: ". . . [he] is, perhaps, the sharpest Jew in London. I consider him an economic genius. . . . He stands very close to the Rothschilds, and also to Henry Raphael, the ablest and most dangerous gold-bug in the world; at least I am told by all the men I know in London, that he [Raphael] is the most dreaded as an antagonist, and the most merciless of wreckers. He [Raphael] is deep in this gold business; probably at the bottom of it if the truth were known."[30]

On July 11, 1895, with the Lodges and Cecil Spring Rice, Henry landed at Southampton on the same dock at the same hour as his landing in 1893 with the Camerons and Ambassador Bayard. Because the Lodges would not leave England till late in August, Henry had weeks to spare. As a first venture after reaching London, he guided the Lodges' sons to Greenwich. He and the elder son, George Cabot Lodge, known as Bay, had formed a friendship. At the moment, Henry was calling himself "a conservative and religious anarchist."[31] Bay had adopted Henry's original term, "conservative anarchist." He liked to tell people that he and Henry Adams were the founders of that branch of anarchism.[32]

On July 19, Henry spoke with Sonnenschein at his office, came away with proofs of *The Law of Civilization and Decay* through page 160, and began to annotate them. He very possibly improved them.[33]

The English had held an election in which the Liberals lost to the Conservatives. Lord Salisbury headed the new government as both prime minister and foreign secretary. He asked George Curzon to serve in the Foreign Office as undersecretary. The Curzons accordingly were in London. They invited Adams to dinner. When he arrived, he was introduced to the home secretary, Herbert Asquith, who chanced to call. It was a fresh instance of his meeting important English politicians.

While still in London, he talked again with Sir Alfred Lyall about India and went to the City "to discuss the exchanges with bankers and brokers"—names not given. The bankers and brokers had conflicting opinions. He thought his own opinion best. He again believed that the gold-bugs would win and all others would lose.

Jointly the Gaskells and Cunliffes greeted Adams at Wenlock Abbey. Writing thence to Mrs. Cameron, Adams told her that her husband should retire from politics. ". . . you had better, with a good grace, submit to abandoning your senatorial dignities next year."[34]

As soon as possible, he journeyed to Scotland to see the Clarks. Tillypronie was rented, and the Clarks had moved to a cottage. Adams walked the eight-mile stretch from Dinnet Station to their temporary residence. On August 3, he wrote to his Hooper nieces about the effects of England's financial policies on the English. "Nearly every gentleman's estate in England is now for sale or to let, in fear of Sir William Harcourt's legacy duties. In Shropshire, the sweep is clean. . . . No one will buy, and the ruin of the old country squire is complete. . . . Altogether I never saw England so sad. The Jews alone are happy and rich. They swarm over London like centipedes."[35]

At Beverly Farms, Mrs. Cameron advised her husband to retire. His response included a decision that she and Adams had not anticipated. The senator decided to sell his Washington house and move his wife and daughter to Pennsylvania. She wrote to Adams on August 5: "... Donald ... considers himself out of the running—will not even be a candidate. ...." "He takes it calmly, and even with a sort of relief and talks of buying a 1000 acres in Chester Co. (Pa.) and building a house there and making his home there. Also he has secretly offered the Lafayette Sq. house for sale. The dark days are coming, I fear. I do not mind being out of politics—on the contrary—but to live in Penna!! Well, I wont [*sic*]. I'll travel."

A new letter from Adams to Mrs. Cameron was already in the mail. It contained his strongest assertion that she was "walking into nervous collapse." "You turn to me for help, and I am really more helpless than you are. ... As I have said again and again, you have merely to sit still and let things pass—they cannot hurt you. This is true, but I know also that reason has nothing to do with nerves. I should waste time and only bore you by arguing."[36]

In London on August 12, 1895, Adams talked with Hermann Schmidt—details not recorded. Also he revisited Sonnenschein, obtained the remaining proofs of *The Law of Civilization and Decay*, and read them. Next day, he wrote to Brooks. Not a person to hesitate, he told his unhappy brother:

> Whatever the public may think—or not think—or say—or not say,—you may take my word for it that the book is a great book.
> As this covers the whole case, I need say no more about it; and you may go to sleep at ease. Your work in life is done.

Without suggesting that Henry's lines to Brooks were insincere, one may place limits on what they meant. The work that Sonnenschein was readying for publication was a more powerful book than Brooks's relations and friends, even Henry, had imagined Brooks could write. It had the merit of being very different from any other book a reader would be likely to read. Yet Henry's praises were expressions more of love than of truth.

The Law of Civilization and Decay bears the marks of its author's long-past breakdown. As often as not, the book is a nightmare. It is most remarkable for its insistence that its readers be subjected to scenes of human beings murdered, hanged, burned alive, drowned, mutilated, starved, enslaved, displaced, plundered, and impoverished. It reflects a lapse of hope, a fall from happiness, the death of humor. What is left can be summed up in a phrase Brooks would shortly use in a letter to Henry: "the agony of consciousness."[37]

Henry was not the victim of a breakdown. He was capable of black forecasts when he thought them justified, but he was capable also of efforts to counteract the evils he foresaw. Admittedly, out of sympathy with Brooks, he would sometimes affect a pessimism much like his brother's. He wrote to Brooks on August 13, "As I am the blackest of pessimists, I was rather surprised to find Schmidt blacker still."[38] Yet, by nature and conviction, Henry was a sensible kind of optimist. He believed that human beings had the ability to form new visions with the help of which they might improve their destinies. In August 1895, the question most weighing upon his mind was what vision he and other Americans would best form, both to avoid being a nation of gold-bugs and to transform themselves to something better.

The four Lodges and Adams arrived at Amiens on August 18, 1895, in time "to visit the cathedral and hear the evening service."[39] Adams had a new experience. He wrote to Mrs. Cameron, "Though it is the third time I have seen Amiens, I never thoroughly felt it before."[40]

At Rouen, the party devoted two days to studying the city's three great churches. Again Adams studied buildings he had previously seen.

Thanks to ensuing stops at Caen, Bayeux, Coutances, Mont Saint Michel, Vitré, Le Mans, and Chartres, he saw buildings that were new to him. The experience affected him, in part, as a commentary on his past. At twenty, when first in Europe, he had been drawn strongly to cathedrals. Between 1858 and 1860, he had visited several. In August 1860, however, he had declined to take part in a visit to Brittany, preferring to stay in Paris and study French. The choice had cost him a probable opportunity to see Mont Saint Michel. In 1870, he was required to serve as Harvard's first full-time teacher of medieval politics and law. The subjects seemed so distant from cathedrals that his work as teacher acted as a positive bar against his going to see them. The pattern repeated. In 1879, when no longer a Harvard teacher, he and Clover journeyed to Canterbury, Amiens, and Rouen to see the churches. They would have gone to Mont Saint Michel, had it not been for bad weather and a chance of his gaining access in Paris to documents he needed for his *History of the United States*. That he went to Paris thereafter without traveling to nearby Chartres to see the cathedral could similarly be excused on grounds of duties.

Excuses seldom fully excused. In 1895, Adams could not have gone far on the route to Caen, Bayeux, and Coutances without feeling that in the past he had permitted himself *not* to go to places to which he ought to have gone. He saw Le Mans, where Brooks had the experience that led him to the Holy Land. By that measure, Henry was the actual younger brother, walking belatedly in Brooks's footsteps.

At the end of the route, Henry saw and entered a cathedral at Chartres which he said was "the finest thing in the world."[41] In between, he inspected Mont Saint Michel, to which he and Clover could have gone. His emotions while on the Mount—through Saturday, Sunday, and Monday, August 24–26, 1895—were so strong that he at once wished to learn more about the place by obtaining photographs and books.

The Lodges had a daughter Constance. Following the marriage of Brooks Adams to her Aunt Evelyn, Constance had insisted on addressing Henry Adams as "Uncle Henry."[42] Her brothers Bay and John took up the innovation. For this reason, Adams's corrective tour from Amiens to Paris by way of Mont Saint Michel and Chartres served as a reminder that he had a growing flock of nephews and was writing *The Education of Henry Adams*, a book for young men. By the same token, his traveling in Europe while Constance, Martha Cameron, and all his Hooper and Adams nieces stayed unadventurously in America reminded him that he was *not* writing an education for young women.

Biographers of Henry Adams have to ask when and why he decided to write his *Mont Saint Michel and Chartres*. The when was simple. He decided to write another book while he and Lodges were still at Mont Saint Michel.[43] The why was simple also. More than ever, Adams was functioning as America's lookout. His business was visions that might save. What mattered, he believed, was that someone see what needed to be seen. It might be better if younger persons—much younger than he—performed the feat. They might be women. Education for young women seemed to him fully as important as, but different from, education for young men. By that standard, *The Education of Henry Adams* was half a book. He would want to match it with a second half-book, identical in utility but fully adapted to female readers. *Mont Saint Michel and Chartres* was the needed second half-book.[44]

Adams could think of his days at Mont Saint Michel as a return to his wife. In the 1880s, Marian Adams became seriously interested in architectural designs by H. H. Richardson that were rooted in romanesque architecture of the middle ages.[45] At least as much as her husband, she would have gained by going to the Mount. It was unavoidable that Henry, when conceiving his *Mont Saint Michel and Chartres*, should think of the book, not as his, but as a book Clover could want to write; hence, like his novel *Esther*, a book he—unconfessedly—should write on her behalf.

His impulse to write the book was very strong. He started planning it at once. Some of his ideas spilled into his current letters. From Paris on August 29, 1895, he wrote to Mrs. Cameron, ". . . the trip was really an education." He knew his Hooper nieces had gone to the Continent with their father but did not know for certain what they had seen. On May 1, he wrote to Mabel: "I've a notion that you saw Chartres. . . . If not, I hope to take you there." He hurried to Beauvais, studied the cathedral, and told Mrs. Cameron it was "the most startling bid for architectural glory ever made." In the same letter, he looked forward to "Martha's education, when she and I go together to Chartres and Coutances." "Not that she will ever grow up to Coutances. The [cathedral's] austere outside, with the innate nobility and grace and infinite tenderness within, can only be felt by a finished life; but Martha must learn some history, and this is the way [for her] to understand her modern world."[46]

He planned his education for young women as a travel guide from Mont Saint Michel to Chartres, with whatever digressions and additions might be indispensable. The guide book could not be written in optimum form unless he could provide himself extended opportunities to travel and work in France. This necessity altered his view of Paris. On August 30, he had remarked to Mrs. Cameron: ". . . Paris never looked so sunny. In other respects I see little change from what it was in August, 1860, when I first lived here. More big streets and big houses; less in them." He changed his mind two days later only enough to write to Mabel: ". . . I love Paris so very little that I would not quite utterly destroy it, as I would destroy London; but would leave the Louvre, and Notre Dame, and the Café Riche or Véfour's. . . . Otherwise it is a tolerable place enough, except for the Jews and the Americans."[47] It took till September 12 for him to hint to Mrs. Cameron that the French capital would be his future place of summer residence. "Paris is the best summer-watering-place in Europe. It is the only city in the world which understands the world and itself. That I hate it is of course; it hates itself; but it at least amuses the pair of us."

Adams made his work on an education for women a secret kept even from Mrs. Cameron. Yet his urge to tell her about it was almost too strong for him to curb. He wrote to her from Tours on September 18: "The ultimate cathedral of the 13th century was deliberately intended to unite all the arts and sciences in the direct service of God. It was a Chicago Exposition for God's profit. It showed an Architectural exhibit, a Museum of Painting, Glass-staining, Wood and Stone Carving, Music, vocal and instrumental, Embroidery, Jewelry and Gem-setting, Tapestry-weaving, and I know not what other arts, all in one building. It was the greatest single creation of man. . . . Even its weaknesses are great, and its failures, like Beauvais and Le Mans, are [great?] because man rose beyond himself."

The person from whom the secret had most to be kept was Brooks, whose *Law of Civilization and Decay* was at the point of publication. Were he to learn of Henry's book, Brooks might think he had found an imitator and that the book would be an extension of his own. Alternatively, Brooks might think Henry wished to eclipse him, steal his ideas, or dress them for the public in more appealing garments.

Such fears—if Brooks had them—would be unfounded. Henry's incipient *Mont Saint Michel and Chartres* was an outgrowth of his and his wife's interests and ambitions. It would illustrate his own idea of history. But there was always the problem that Brooks was disturbed and in need of reassurance.

Once again, he gave Brooks the fullest possible support. From Paris on September 8, he sent his brother an account of his tour with the Lodges. He pled guilty to imitation *as a traveler.* "In modest imitation of you, we have taken vast draughts of Norman architecture. We have sat, or roamed, for hours and days through and about Mont St[.] Michel. Amiens, Rouen, Le Mans, and Chartres have been our happy homes. Caen and Bayeux are as the playgrounds of our childhood; and of all these familiar haunts the one that moved me most with a sense of personal identity with myself, was Coutances."[48]

In his letter, Henry echoed a feature of *The Law of Civilization and Decay* by treating New England as a continuation of impulses originated in Normandy and Brittany. Paying Brooks the compliment of writing a passage that Brooks could well have written, he said: "I have rarely felt New England at its highest ideal power as it appeared to me, beatified and glorified, in the cathedral of Coutances. Since then our ancestors have steadily declined and run out until we have reached pretty near the bottom. They have played their little part according to the schedule. They have lost their religion, their art and their military tastes. They cannot now comprehend the meaning of what they did at Mont St[.] Michel. They have kept only the qualities which were most useful. . . . So we get Boston."

Support from Henry was needed, for Brooks had fallen into one of his deeper glooms. In his newest letter to Henry, he repeated an estimate of Sonnenschein's that two hundred and fifty copies of *The Law of Civilization and Decay,* shipped to Macmillan and Company in New York, would "supply the American market to repletion." Brooks believed the publisher's estimate. He said he was telling Evelyn that his new book was the "crowning act to a life of folly." He was planning a trip to India, in order to be "far away for a few months until people have forgotten my indiscretion."[49]

Henry disagreed and predicted a great future for Brooks's *Law.* "I am inclined to think it will have plenty of readers. . . . That it must have a strong and permanent effect on the treatment of history, and probably on politics as a science, I cannot doubt; but it [the effect] may be slow and devious. All I can say is that, if I wanted to write any book, it would be the one you have written."[50]

The Camerons had varied their stay at Beverly Farms by going to Canada. The ravages of incompatibility were never more apparent. Writing from Quebec on September 1, 1895, Mrs. Cameron confessed to Henry that her summer with her husband had "not proved a successful experiment" and that she wished she had gone to Europe. She said of Donald: "His devotion to Martha is very nice, and she returns it by treatment which resembles his to me. She may revenge me yet, for she is openly indifferent to him and accuses him of being unkind to me. I attempt to talk to her about filial love and duty, and she agrees with all I say, then adds, 'Why does he treat *you* that way?' I am even a barrier between father and child."

When back at Beverly Farms, more unhappy than before, Mrs. Cameron received a letter from Henry written at Rouen and Caen and one from Mrs. Lodge written at Mont Saint Michel. She wrote to Henry on September 8, ". . . I gnash my teeth when I think that I might have been with you; might have seen all that with yr. eyes." She openly sought help. "I live on your letters. So give me life."

As steadily as hers to him, Henry's letters to her were crossing the Atlantic. He had told her he had been to Rheims and seen another cathedral. Obliged to go with the Lodges to see the chateaux in the Loire valley, he reported from Tours that he was "homesick for Mont Saint Michel and Coutances." "My single keen pleasure is the few glass windows still left in the Cathedral here [at Tours]. There are a dozen or two very exquisite and perfect ones, as good, I should think, as those at Chartres. . . ." He did not say so, but his study of cathedrals and stained-glass windows was becoming systematic.[51]

Her cry for "life" found him again in Paris. His best answer was news of starting homeward. ". . . I am to cross to London on Sunday, and resume my old quarters of 1891 at 38 Clarges Street."[52]

While still in Paris, he visited Auguste Rodin at his studio and spent an hour "looking at his marbles, and especially at a Venus and dead Adonis which he is sending to some exhibition in Philadelphia." On September 27, 1895, finishing a letter to Mrs. Cameron, he said he liked the sculptor's "decadent sensualities." ". . . but I must not have them. . . ." He explained that Rodin's figures "were hardly made for jeunes personnes like me and my breakfast-table company." If he appeared to say that, like Adonis, he was too young, he added that, like Adonis, he was dead. He classed himself with Queen Victoria. "I have not enough vitality left to be sensual. Victoria and I and our age are about equally genuine. We are beyond even vice."

Cuba and Puerto Rico were the remaining colonies of Spain in the Western Hemisphere. During his and Adams's stay near Santiago de Cuba in February and March 1894, King had been told by Cubans that a revolution was in the making. In February 1895, the revolution had begun. Long a supporter of Latin American colonials against European masters, King wrote an article, "Shall Cuba Be Free?" The article appeared in the September 1895 issue of *Forum*, a New York magazine. It urged official support of the insurgents by the United States. King sent a copy to Adams at his London address, the Morgan bank.

Adams reached London on September 29 and found King's article in his mail. On October 4, he wrote an important letter to Hay. What gave the letter importance was partly a likelihood that Hay would be appointed to high office by a Republican administration beginning in 1897 and partly Adams's willingness to speak to Hay about foreign policy. He began by approving King's article. He continued: ". . . the Jew question is really the most serious of our problems. It is Capitalistic Methods run to their logical result." Hay would realize that in Adams's mind the "Jew question" was the banking question and especially the English banking question, which was to say the dominance of English moneyed interests in the world's economy, with such results as the depression still prevailing in the United States and the impoverishment that helped explain the revolution in Cuba.[53]

The offices to which Hay would be best adapted were secretary of state and ambassador to England. If given either post, Hay would have to aim toward one of two objects: a rapprochement between England and the United States or an American severance from England. By temperament, Hay would prefer the rapprochement. Whatever he might prefer, there might remain the problem of domination of America by banks.

In his letter, Adams did not tell Hay what he thought should be done about the dominance, but he repeated a guess he had voiced to Hay in conversation. The guess was that ex-Minister Robert Lincoln was the American presidential hopeful most likely to please the banking syndicate which, for a commission, had saved the U. S. Treasury from complete depletion of its gold. The guess carried with it an implication that the Republicans, as tools of the New York banks, would win the election of 1896. ". . . I still think Bob Lincoln the likeliest man to suit the syndicate who owns us all."

*   *   *

Henry ascertained from Sonnenschein that printing of Brooks's *Law of Civilization and Decay* was nearly finished. He learned too that Brooks and Evelyn were shortly leaving for India. For Henry, it followed that, if promotion of the book was to be initiated by anyone, he himself would be the initiator.

From 38 Clarges Street in London on October 4, 1895, he began an aggressive campaign in favor of the book by writing to Mrs. Cameron: ". . . it is the first time that serious history has ever been written. He [Brooks] has done for it what only the greatest men do; he has created a startling generalisation which reduces all history to a scientific formula, and which is yet so simple and obvious that one cannot believe it to be new." That Henry wrote such things to Mrs. Cameron might seem evidence that he believed them. The statements were certainly evidence that the elder brother would go to great lengths to help the younger win the attention to which his book entitled him. Predictably, such attention would be very grudging. Henry believed that Brooks would be ignored and stigmatized by professors at universities and colleges. He summarized: ". . . [Brooks] is in History what Schopenhauer is in Metaphysics. I need not add that the world has got to ignore him, as it does Schopenhauer, and, if necessary, suppress him. No one who values his respectability and salary can venture to accept or . . . teach Brooks's law of history."

The most important of Henry's declarations about Brooks involved a declaration about himself. He told Mrs. Cameron in the same letter, "I have sought all my life those truths which this mighty infant, this seer unblest, has struck with the agony and bloody sweat of genius." The sentence asserted that Brooks had found the truths of history that Henry had always sought. It said, or at least implied, that Henry, in his capacity as a historian, had struck no truths at all, or none that mattered. Ostensibly straightforward, the sentence was false. It was true enough that Brooks in *The Law of Civilization and Decay* had propounded suggestions about human beings that many readers would find discomfortingly credible and hard to contradict. It doubtless was true as well that some of Brooks's suggestions had affected Henry as new. It was none the less a fact that Henry had made historical discoveries. He had a theory of history that he thought truer than his brother's. Moreover, he currently was acting on the theory, as in the case of deciding to write an education for women.

Henry's theory of history could be found anywhere and everywhere in his *History of the United States.* As his narrative made clear, he understood history as made, not by nature, but by human beings. He believed that the critically important reality was that human beings had ideas of the future: what he called "ideals"—visions of the possible. By acting energetically to attain what they saw as possible, human beings evolved. They formed new "nations" or "races." They freely remade themselves.[54] No theory could be simpler.[55]

Earlier, writing to Mrs. Cameron, Henry had spoken in passing about "the degradation of our politics and society[,] which is the certain course of our gold-bug development."[56] It might be gathered from his word "certain" that his attitude toward the degradation was passive, fatalistic, or necessitarian. But Henry's life story till then had been one of constant innovation, together with constant resistance to the unwanted. Besides, at Amiens and other places on the tour that ended at Chartres, what he did he think he witnessed?

As understood by him, Mont Saint Michel and the cathedrals were built by human beings who were imbued with a partly new ideal of getting to heaven. They built new churches—so they believed—in the presence of their Creator and in honor of the Virgin. The churches were part-way houses on the road to paradise. Each was a means. Yet, in the builders' eyes, the means above all other means was the Virgin. By her grace, if given, *anyone* could get to heaven.

Henry had arrived at Coutances and Chartres as the author of a great history of the American people. As understood by him, the Americans of 1800 had possessed a vision. Their vision was partly a thirst for wealth and power. Of the means developed at the time to make possible the achievement of wealth and power, none compared with an American invention, the steamboat, which as if by magic transformed the moving currents of North America's rivers into readily navigable waterways for passengers and cargoes, upstream as well as down.[57] But his *History of the United States* had a feature which its author could not forget. In the sixth chapter of his long narrative, he had said that "nothing was more elusive than the spirit of American democracy."[58] As storied by him, the Americans of 1800–1815 aspired not only to wealth and power but also to visionary ends which, while difficult for them to reach, and not easy to define, were very real and very high.

In 1895, Americans could be accused of striving *only* for wealth and power. They seemed inclined to become a nation without a complete ideal. Henry was resisting a threat that the nation might go blind. His books for young men and women would be offered as means toward the development of new capacities to see and reach high objects.

Mary Curzon invited Adams to pass a weekend at Reigate Priory and meet several other guests, notably Thomas Hardy. Adams had read none of Hardy's books. He paid the visit and met the novelist but took the role of listener.[59] In London on October 9, 1895, he listened again. ". . . Hermann Schmidt . . . dined with me, and talked gold and silver till midnight. Unless that most penetrating Jew deceives me, I know now all that anyone knows of foreign exchanges, South Africa and the future of mankind."[60] South Africa had figured in Schmidt's explanations because miners had found gold there. A chance existed that the gold famines created by England's money-lords would be lifted by sheer discovery and mining of the yellow metal.

Sonnenschein published Brooks's book next day. Henry bought a dozen copies at author's rates and started giving and sending copies to friends, English and American.

On October 12, he sailed for New York alone. He avoided everyone. In his first letter to Mrs. Cameron after debarking, he reported, "I . . . read Mme[.] de Sévigné all day and night in my cabin."[61]

A two-day reunion in New York with King, La Farge, and Hooper revealed that King was extremely short of money. In better times, King had bought from Adams a large painting of a whaling ship by Turner that Adams did not want. As a means of rescue, Adams offered to buy it back. He gave King $2,200, accepted the painting, and later made it a fixture at 1603 H Street on the east wall of the dining room.[62]

After a week at Beverly Farms with Martha but without her husband, Mrs. Cameron had been summoned by Donald to the Virginia springs. At an early date, all three Camerons returned to Washington.

Adams by then was in Washington, urging nieces and nephews to join him. He wrote to Gaskell on November 3: "The autumn is very beautiful here—quite marvelously beautiful—and, like the spring, more ideal and lyrical in expression than almost any other form of nature I have ever seen, in mere vegetation. I cling to the days as they pass, and all the more because there are no tourists to get between, or machinery to make money out of them."

A European diplomat whom Adams greatly liked was a friend of old standing, the Spanish minister, Enrique Dupuy de Lôme. On November 3, Dupuy and his wife called at 1603 H Street. What was said while they visited is unknown. To some extent, Adams may have been in the Spaniard's confidence.

The revolutionaries in Cuba had formed a nascent government and had sent delegates to the United States. Their errand was to induce the Cleveland administration to recognize their country as a belligerent—a *de facto* power. The delegates went to New York and conferred with Clarence King.

King wrote to Adams on November 13, "Would you like to know the Cubans who are coming to Washington to work [i.e. arrange?] belligerency, or would they be in your way?" Adams's reply is lost but was affirmative. Because Congress was not yet in session, the Cubans remained for the present in New York. Writing again to Adams, King named

names. "Gomez and Maceo are quite well. . . ." "Campos, if he continues to talk and give newspaper men his views, will lay a firm foundation
for belligerency for Congress to stand on."[63]

Mrs. Fell had written to Adams from Florida about freezing temperatures there. On November 17, Adams assured her, "Wait patiently another winter, and I think Cuba will be the fashion." "The affairs of the
world . . . have increased in interest with such startling rapidity that I
now live from month to month in full expectation of some great crash
which will make me smile."

Gold was flowing to London, and Adams and Ford were keeping
watch. Yet, for Adams, measurement of the flow had become a secondary consideration. He remarked to his co-researcher on the 19th, ". . . I
think we are about thirty or forty millions to the bad . . . but the political
situation is so much worse than the financial as to make the [financial]
calculation valueless for practical purposes."

The Hays returned to Washington on November 25. The Lodges
came four days later. The choice of a Republican presidential candidate
for the election of 1896 had become a burning issue. Lodge was backing
the speaker of the House, Thomas Reed. The Hays were rich supporters
of William McKinley, currently governor of Ohio.

A gap had opened between what Adams thought and what he was
willing to say. He wrote to Cunliffe on November 26: ". . . I hesitate to
start on my usual trip to the West Indies; and I hesitate the more because
the financial situation is . . . very unusual, not to say, unparalleled, and
I do not want to be caught again in a squeeze, and hurried home as in
'93. Finally, we have a Presidential election coming on . . . and although
I am out of all relation with parties, my friends are very deep in the
game."

What Cunliffe was not to know was that Adams intended to stay in
Washington—meant *not* to go to the West Indies. The phenomenon he
had in mind was the revolution in Cuba. As before, the high-ranking
official in Washington whom he could control was Cameron. On December 9, 1895, the senator notified his fellow Pennsylvanians that he would
not seek reelection. His lame-duck status reduced his usefulness to his
constituents, but it much increased his usefulness to Adams.

Cameron was a member of the Committee on Foreign Relations.
The chairman of the Committee was Senator Sherman of Ohio, the surviving uncle of Elizabeth Cameron and one of the persons instrumental
in bringing about her mistaken marriage in 1878 to a senator more than
twice her age. Adams had known John Sherman since 1867. There was
every prospect that Adams and Senator Cameron would enjoy the full
cooperation of Chairman Sherman if they wished to make arrangements
involving the Committee on Foreign Relations. The prospect was all the

better because Sherman, though capable and usually alert, was in his seventies and was losing his memory.

In knowledge of world affairs from ancient to present times, Adams had no rival in America. The foreign powers he was most considering were the British, Spanish, and Russian empires. He had also to think of England and Germany as manufacturing centers in need of markets. He had been exchanging ideas with William Rockhill, an American explorer, writer, and would-be diplomat. Writing to Rockhill on December 10, he prophesied concerning Europe's markets, "If I live and keep my mind ten years more, and the world moves at the same rate as since '93, I shall live to see Germany and England wrecked."[64] The prophecy was possible because events—so Adams believed—at last were turning decisively against Europe and favoring the United States.

During the previous June, Richard Olney, a Boston lawyer, had replaced Walter Gresham as secretary of state, the latter having died. Secretly, on July 20, 1895, a note written by Secretary Olney and approved by President Cleveland had been sent as instructions to Ambassador Bayard in London. The note invoked the Monroe Doctrine. It held that the United States was entitled to a deciding voice in the Western Hemisphere and by right could insist that an on-going dispute between Venezuela and Great Britain about the boundary between Venezuela and British Guiana be settled by arbitration. Bayard conveyed the substance of the note to Lord Salisbury at the Foreign Office.

Salisbury did not respond till November 26. For one reason and another, his response did not reach Secretary Olney till December 7. On seeing that the British government refused to arbitrate and questioned the legality of the Monroe Doctrine, Olney drafted a special message for President Cleveland to submit to Congress, together with Olney's original note and Salisbury's response. Cleveland submitted and published the message on December 17, 1895. It threatened war, if the British did not accede to arbitration.

Until that time, the citizens of both countries had not been told that the American challenge and the British counter-challenge went to extremes of vehemence. Like most other persons, Adams was amazed by Cleveland's special message and the attendant documents. His first impression was that the "great crash" had started. On that basis, he wrote to Secretary Olney that evening, December 17, to express "my strongest possible approval and support."[65] He wrote next day to Harriet Beale—(Harriet Blaine had married a drunkard, Truxtun Beale, and was already separated): ". . . the President's message lighted on me like a thirteen-inch shell. You may not imagine . . . how I read it with amazement; how I gasped and laughed and cried and could not sleep all night.

At last! Well, it was high time! So now, we'll talk with more than England. I shall stay here this winter. Do come back."

As Adams felt it, the crash involved a probability of war.[66] In part, the prospect affected him as an outbreak of *civil* conflict. He wrote to Gaskell: "So we are going to war! It sounds droll, to you and me. I remember how droll it sounded in '61, for my southern friends." Yet there was nothing droll in Adams's saying that Americans like himself were "hardened to civil war, and fall into its sharp drill almost easily." Unquestionably he would follow the lead of Cleveland and Olney. His one regret was that "Venezuela was only an accident, and the worst case for Cleveland to have chosen, because it is quite impossible to understand its merits. . . ."

Stocks plummeted in London, New York, and Boston. Adams enjoyed the drop as fit punishment for English and American plutocrats. It delighted him to learn that J. P. Morgan—a "dethroned monarch"—came to the capital and the president "did not send for him or see him." But messages from London indicated that England was heavily burdened by troubles in many parts of the world. It grew evident that Cleveland and Olney's action had been an ill-considered threat, nothing more. Ten days sufficed for Adams to describe what had happened as a "grand drunk."[67] The two countries would not fight.[68]

King's involvement with the Cuban delegates and his wanting Adams to befriend them were secrets Adams had wanted to reveal in some degree to Hay. On November 14, urging Hay to return to Washington, he had said: "Come and revolute Cuba. We are going to have a gay old circus. Unluckily my relations with Dupuy are so friendly that I cannot openly embrace his enemies."

In December 1895 or January 1896, the Cubans contacted Adams, and he arranged their coming to dine. Details are lacking. Presumably he received them alone, listened, and made no promises.[69]

As usual, he was doing several things. News had come from Tati that he was writing short biographies of Arii Taimai's grandfather and great uncle, Taura-atua i Patea and Opuhara. Tati would send the finished biographies to Adams as new evidence. Adams responded by seeking still other evidence. He sent Loulie Hooper a request for missionary records he knew she could supply from Cambridge.[70]

Phillips was helping Henry promote Brooks's *Law of Civilization and Decay*. During the Christmas season, Willy succeeded in giving copies to Secretary Olney and Justice Harlan of the Supreme Court. For Henry, the gifts were concurrent with a flurry of ideas. A hope possessed him that Cleveland might break free of the gold-bugs; that Olney might be the Democratic candidate for president in 1896; that the country was escaping dominance by bankers. The hope expired. Henry learned that Cleveland was "wabbling [*sic*] between the Jews and the Gentiles."[71] On December 30, he explained to Harriet: "If our presidential hippopotamus rolls over . . . he will leave nothing whole. Thus far, in three years, he has managed to destroy only his party and his friends. . . . If he flops once or twice more, he will end by upsetting the whole world, which will be fun to me, who am a sound conservative anarchist; but will incommode the good and wise."

Henry's letters gave an appearance of fully reporting what he was doing. Writing to Gaskell on January 23, 1896, he said he was bothered by a cold. "I am eager to go south, but never felt so uneasy, and unwilling either to go or stay. What with financial alarms, and Cuban excitements, which interest me exceedingly, and Venezuelan talk which bores me proportionally, and personal matters which luckily are the least of my concern, I drag on, from day to day, and blow my nose and mop my eyes. . . . At this season everyone is busy; no one comes near me; I am more solitary than a weasel in a hole, and the weather is not fit for a moulting crow."

Next day, Henry informed Brooks that *The Law of Civilization and Decay* was "passing through all the hands worth considering." "I am a little in fear lest the edition should be exhausted while you are in India. I would print another . . . if I had the power. . . ."

The Cuban delegates had conveyed to the administration and Congress a plea for recognition of Cuba as a belligerent. A simple dilemma was posed. The Cuban plea could be granted or refused.

Henry put it about that he was going to Florida. He told Brooks on the January 31, 1896: ". . . I hope to go south next week. . . . As far as I can see, the scrimmage is over. The nations . . . are settling down, afraid to fight. The gold-bugs have resumed their sway, with their nerves a good deal shaken, but their tempers or their sense unimproved." "Cleveland and Olney have relapsed into their normal hoglike attitudes of indifference, and Congress is disorganized, stupid and childlike as ever. Once more we are under the whip of the bankers. Even on Cuba, where popular feeling was far stronger than on Venezuela, we are beaten and hopeless."

In fact, Henry would not go south and was neither beaten nor hopeless. On February 1, he wrote to Macmillan in New York, attempting to arrange the company's issuing a new edition of Brooks's book.[72] Six days later, writing to Brooks, he mentioned bungling by Congress and indicated that he was doing something. "I am kept here by Cuba, which I appear to be running, for the faculty of bungling is the only faculty a legislative body possesses in foreign affairs. Of course, my share in it [the running of Cuba] is wholly behind the scenes. Even Cabot [Lodge] keeps aloof from me, or I from him; for I can't control him, and want no ally whom I can't control. So please do not allude to my doings either in letter or conversation."

Hay needed exercise, so he and Adams changed their habits. Adams told Harriet on February 8, ". . . [we] walk, every afternoon, as far as the boundary." The walks, two and a half miles long, afforded time to talk. Presumably Hay was the talker, Adams the listener.

All the while, a wholly secret American conspiracy had been in progress. It may best be called the Henry Adams Conspiracy. There were four or five conspirators: Henry himself, Elizabeth and Donald Cameron, Willy Phillips, and possibly Tom Lee. Conspiring had begun the previous autumn as soon as Henry and the Camerons were reunited. Since that time, Henry had placed their work on a firm basis by writing a secret paper which his confederates could read but were not to talk about except to each other.[73] The paper described itself as a "historical summary."[74] It recounted the revolutions in Europe, Asia, and America since 1815 and the interventions of the European powers in the same revolutions.[75] In addition, it recounted the history of the Monroe Doctrine and summarized the interventions of the United States in revolutions. It stated—much to the advantage of the Americans—the grounds on which the Europeans and the Americans had intervened. It ended by proposing a resolution to be introduced in Congress.

During the afternoon of Monday, February 10, 1896, the *Washington Evening Star* printed on its second page a report headed:

MORE ABOUT CUBA

Mr. Cameron's Resolution for Recognition of Independence

The report said that Senator Cameron of Pennsylvania had introduced a resolution for possible adoption by both houses of Congress and that his action came as a surprise. It quoted the text of the resolution. The essential words were: ". . . the good offices of the United States are earnestly recommended to the favorable consideration of the Spanish government for the recognition of the independence of Cuba."

Cameron's action reasserted and applied the Monroe Doctrine. It affirmed the right of the United States to support independence for colonial peoples throughout the Western Hemisphere. It supplanted a two-way dilemma with a three-way dilemma. Congress and the President could do nothing; they could choose a half-measure—mere recognition of Cuba's belligerency; or they could recognize Cuba's independence.

No Cubans had participated in the Henry Adams Conspiracy. When news of a proposed resolution favoring Cuban *independence* first appeared, the Cubans were as much surprised as everyone else.[76]

The practical bearings of the resolution were apparent. If Congress and President Cleveland united in urging the Spanish government to grant independence to Cuba, the Spanish government would have two alternatives. It could declare war against the United States, or it could grant independence to Cuba and thus end the civil war on the island between the revolutionary Cubans on the one side and a Spanish army— allied with Cuban "loyalists"—on the other. From the Spanish point of view, the first alternative involved huge risks. A war with the Yankees might go badly, and the Yankees might enjoy the support of many of the Central and South American republics.

While the Cleveland administration and Congress wondered what to do, conspirator Adams stayed contentedly in Washington. On February 17, he wrote to Cunliffe: ". . . I am more amused and in better temper than in these many years past. I have had real sport this winter, and feel young again. You had better sell all you have and buy with me in Cuba. I want to be a pretty creole."

On February 28, with deep misgivings, the Senate chose the mere half-measure. It passed a resolution favoring recognition of the revolutionary Cuba government as a belligerent and offering mediation to the Spanish government. That same day, Adams left with the Camerons and several guests for a month's vacation at Coffin's Point.

Willy Phillips stayed in Washington. He reported to Adams on March 18 that he had crossed paths with the Spanish minister and that Dupuy de Lôme would not look at him. He said too that the Senate was still very frightened, "lest we should stir Spain to war."[77] Adams replied on the 21st that their work had "gone all right so far." His one regret concerned the Spanish minister and his wife. "As for the poor Dupuys, my heart is sad. They have made a gallant fight, but I must . . . leave them to go under, without a word of sympathy."

When the month at Coffin's Point had ended and he had returned to the capital, Adams was told that Hay had agreed to take his daughter Helen and her friend Elizabeth Warder to Europe, leaving on May 20, 1896. Hay wanted Adams to go along.

Adams was very tempted. On Wednesday, April 1, he explained to Gaskell: ". . . I may take a passage with them. I need my annual month in Paris to keep me from mental extinction."

On Monday, April 6, the House of Representatives passed the timid half-measure favoring recognition of Cuba as a belligerent.

On Thursday by Pullman car, Adams, the Camerons, and Tom Lee left with three other persons for Mexico City. Their motive was easy to guess. Being conspirators, they wished to escape notice, and their preferred means of escape was short-term travel to another country.

6

A Phenomenon Quite Peculiar

In Mexico City, President Diaz assumed that Senator Cameron and his party were important persons and sent his carriage to help them pay a call. As one of the callers, Adams talked with Madame Diaz. Soon after, Cameron decided to travel briefly to Puebla and Jalapa. Thinking Martha too delicate to make the trip (she was a strapping girl of nearly ten), he arranged that she stay in the capital in care of Adams, Lee, and the maid. On April 27, 1896, Adams wrote to Phillips, "Martha could not be dragged through the dust and heat of the trip, and I was glad to escape it by playing nurse. . . ." An adventure followed. "This morning I took her out to Chapultepec and we passed the whole morning with Mme[.] Diaz and her sister Sophia Romero Rubens, who showed us all over the palace. . . ."[1]

Adams mentioned to Phillips that he wanted to make his two weeks in Mexico "an entire vacation from affairs." He said that efforts relating to Cuba were best suspended. "Our next innings on the Cuban matter can't come on at present. . . ." New efforts could begin with the reconvening of Congress. "I almost hope we can worry through to the recognition of independence next winter. . . ."[2]

The Cameron party reappeared in Washington on May 10. A letter from Bay Lodge had arrived for Adams. Young Lodge was studying in Paris and had learned from his mother that Uncle Henry might shortly be in Europe. In his letter, he explained, ". . . when Mama wrote me that you might come over in May[,] my self-control deserted me & I felt I must write & tell you how much I hoped you would come—& to Paris." He proposed that he and Adams travel to a cathedral they had not yet seen, perhaps the one at Bourges.[3]

Adams planned his next six months. He advised Gaskell on May 12 that he would board the *Teutonic* to begin "a pure lark to Europe." He and Hay had agreed to wander with Helen Hay and Elizabeth Warder as the ladies directed. Both were twenty-one. "They are nice girls, but restless as witches, and their broomsticks are long." Hay would take the witches home in July. Adams would stay abroad. ". . . I expect to . . . knock about till November . . . to escape our elections."[4]

Brooks and Evelyn were arriving from India. On May 14, Henry sent Brooks a letter timed to intercept him in New York. Henry previously had urged Brooks to get out a New York edition of *The Law of Civilization and Decay*. To the previous suggestion he added a new one much less simple. "If I were you, I would go back to Paris next autumn or earlier, and publish a French translation of your book, with some development of the first and last chapters, which seem to me now to be the least studied, though the most important."[5]

In time to join Henry for a few hours, Brooks and Evelyn came to Washington. On Monday, May 18, Henry left for New York with Hay and the girls. Mrs. Cameron saw Henry leave. Later that day, she drove with Brooks to the memorial Henry had placed at his and Clover's burial site in Rock Creek Cemetery. While she and Brooks were returning to Lafayette Square, a violent hot wind swept the capital, tearing and felling many trees. Afterwards she sent a note to Henry at his club in New York—the Knickerbocker—including mention of the storm. Next day she sent him a second note in care of the *Teutonic*. Meanwhile Willy Phillips found a letter from Tati Salmon in Adams's mail. He forwarded it to the ship, with a letter of his own.

In New York on Wednesday, King and Bigelow escorted Adams to the *Teutonic*. Adams went at once to his stateroom and wrote a letter to Mrs. Cameron for immediate mailing. He described a less than happy exchange. "For so many months that I have had you and Martha to take care of, I have now so many months without you, and I do not recognise myself in charge of Helen and the young Cleopatra."

Postal service was sometimes erratic. After the ship had sailed, Adams received what evidently was a *second* note from Mrs. Cameron. Two days later, the crew brought him a letter from Phillips and one from Tati. Phillips remarked: "Tremendous wind storm today. Many trees down. My! But it is hot!"[6] Tati sent bad news. Arii Taimai was ill. Marau was wholly idle. ". . . [she] has done nothing, to add to her 'memoirs'. . . ." Tati, however, had done what he had promised concerning Taura-atua i Patea and Opuhara. "I have written a short account . . . [telling] the little what [*sic*] is known of them. What the Europeans have said of them, you know better than I."[7]

The meaning of Tati's news was clear enough. In a short time, Arii Taimai would be dead. Marau was more than likely to drop the *Memoirs* altogether. Helped by Tati's "short account," Adams could extend his Tahitian history to the death of Opuhara in 1815, or even to the death of Taura-atua i Patea in 1849. He eventually would feel free to recast the narrative as if told by Arii Taimai.

While the *Teutonic* was still at sea, Adams began a letter to Mrs. Cameron saying in part that he had not received her first note from Washington. By a complex process, the first note later reached him. Both notes survive.[8] Writing them, Mrs. Cameron revealed the strength of her attachment. She said on May 18, "I watched you leave with the usual lump in my throat, which was too chokey to even tell you how lonely I already felt in anticipation." On the 19th, she confessed, ". . . I think of you every hour of every day, always with longing and gratitude beyond expression."

In appearance, the lark to Europe was necessitated by the whims of Helen Hay and Elizabeth Warder. After a stay in London and a day at Oxford, the girls led Hay and Adams to Paris. Bay Lodge awaited them. Helen and Bay were aspiring poets. On June 11, 1896, Adams wrote to Mrs. Cameron: ". . . having accomplished her first object of coming to Paris and reading each other's verses with Bay, [Helen] is quite indifferent about the next step. Elizabeth is as vague as Helen. . . ."

The actual necessity of the lark was political. The Republican National Convention would begin at St. Louis on June 16. Hay, a donor to McKinley's war chest, wished not to seem much concerned about the convention's results and not to be made a target of gossip and speculation. There was no doubting his state of mind. On June 12, Adams wrote to Mrs. Cameron, "Hay is deeply interested in his McKinley and watches for next week with zeal."

Though Hay and Adams were intimate friends and talk between them was unguarded and relaxed, they were politically unrelated. Hay was a staunch Republican. Originally a Republican and later an Independent, Adams had reinvented himself and become "a conservative and religious anarchist."[9] He would joke with Hay and others about his anarchism, but the only persons to whom he would fully explain his current political aims and projects were Mrs. Cameron and Willy Phillips.

Word reached Europe that the word "gold" had somehow been slipped into the language of the Republican Party platform. On Thursday, June 18, Adams wrote to Mrs. Cameron: "Our telegraphic news comes down only to Tuesday, announcing the total surrender of the great Ohio statesman to Wall Street. He [McKinley] could not help it . . . but it damns his administration before he is nominated."

Adams was writing from Antwerp. For lack of other guidance, the girls and Hay had thought best to let Uncle Henry plan their movements. His first suggestion was a rapid tour of Holland.[10]

News that McKinley had won the nomination was telegraphed from St. Louis on June 18. Phillips was keeping abreast of political gossip in

Washington.[11] He reported to Adams on the 20th that *Adams* figured in a rumor. He gave the revelation a comic turn.[12] "Your keeping company with a man who is *marked* as McKinley's Secretary of State, has been *re*marked [*sic*] on. It has been said that you have been promised the appointment of Ambassador to England if you will abjure your former creed and embrace the cause of gold." He turned to Cuba and used a code. "The papers are again stirring up excitement and insisting that Lee has made a report in favor of the Cubans. . . . Weightman told me last night that he had no doubt of the truth of the reported report. . . ." ("Lee" is surely Adams. "Weightman" may be impossible to identify. Is he a newpaperman? A politician? A diplomat?)

There were two developments. Hay and Adams had been teamed in a rumor about the topmost foreign policy appointments. The existence of a report by Henry Adams justifying intervention in support of Cuban independence had become *not* a secret to such an extent that word of it was appearing in the press.

Henry's high praise and assiduous promotion of Brooks's *Law of Civilization and Decay* had given Brooks a mistaken impression that he and Henry were turning into partners as historians and as politicians. In Washington after his brother left, Brooks obtained financial data from Ford.[13] He retired to Quincy and arranged to print a revised version of his pamphlet *The Gold Standard*—an action that he expected would enhance his credit among the silver Democrats. Similarly, he prepared a new version of *The Law of Civilization and Decay*, to be published by Macmillan in New York.[14] One of the main concerns of his book was the history of Byzantium. It was a subject on which he wanted Henry to be better informed. On June 13, speaking as one partner to another, he sent him a suggestion: "If you get a chance[,] go down to Italy and see the Byzantine things." The suggestion evidently reached Henry in Paris, following his return from Holland.

Wayne and Virginia MacVeagh happened to be in Paris. MacVeagh was serving as ambassador to Italy and had access to secrets relating to European politics. On July 1, Henry advised Mrs. Cameron that he and MacVeagh had had "a long talk." He gave no details.[15]

Henry took Hay and the girls to the Loire valley to inspect an assortment of chateaux, including Chenonceau and Chambord, which Henry had not previously seen. While there, he persuaded his companions to make a dash to Italy. In consequence, the party on July 6 sped to Basel and on the 7th to Milan.

On that day, July 7, 1896, Brooks was in Chicago, attending the Democratic Party Convention. Mrs. Cameron reported to Henry that his brother had "flown off to Chicago to shout for silver."[16] The actual purpose was not so tame. Brooks had arranged to seek the Democratic vice presidential nomination as running mate of John McClean, formerly a Republican silverite.[17] His high-flying ambition was short-lived. On July 8, Congressman William Jennings Bryan of Nebraska turned the convention into a religious revival meeting by delivering an oration climaxed with a cry that mankind should not be crucified "upon a cross of gold." Bryan's exploit won him the presidential nomination and made Brooks believe he had witnessed an "explosion" or "revolution."[18]

On the same day, July 8, Henry wrote to Mrs. Cameron from Milan, "I take for granted that the Democrats will get beaten, and that the gold men will control absolutely the next administration."

Secretive Henry had not told Hay, Helen, and Elizabeth that he was leading them to Italy so that he could visit early churches decorated with Byzantine mosaics. Without delay, he bustled his companions to Parma, to Bologna, and to an early church at Ravenna. On July 15 in Venice, he contrived to leave the others, hired a gondola, and glided across the lagoon to Torcello and Murano. That evening, he told Mrs. Cameron that he had gone in search of "Byzantine remains." ". . . Brooks and I . . . have been greatly exercised by the fact that the Roman Empire, one day, about the year 400, dropped to pieces without any apparent cause. It decaded [*sic*]. Everybody says so."

Without hesitation, Henry turned about and said the Roman Empire *did not fall!* ". . . it showed very curious energy for a corpse. It adopted a new and very strong, centralised religion just at that time." It did things "not usual for corpses to do." ". . . [the Empire] built Ravenna, which was the reason I wanted to see it." He had also seen the churches at Torcello and Murano. "It is a lovely excursion, as dreamy and weird as the Apocalypse, and the churches told me the same story as at Ravenna. There are two mosaic virgins over the apses of Torcello and Murano, as splendid as anything Gothic or Greek. Yet they are five hundred years later than Ravenna. For a dead empire, I hold this to be a phenomenon quite peculiar."[19]

The Byzantine mosaics in Italy were proofs to Henry that his own idea of history was the one he could believe. The idea was hopeful.[20] Not a Brooks, not a believer in declines from inspiration to usury, he saw a current or stream in human action such that new buildings supplanted old—new ideals were conceived—and death refused to die. He had studied the stream for many years and had recounted an instance of its movement in his *History of the United States*.[21] Sight of three churches in Italy—evidence he had not earlier considered—permitted him afresh to see its movement.

*   *   *

In recent days, Adams, Hay, Helen, and Elizabeth had been joined by a trio of young men, Adelbert Hay, Eugene Hale, and Reynolds Hitt. Someone proposed that the party return to Paris by sleeping car. Saying he disliked traveling by night, Henry sent the others ahead and returned by day, stopping to sleep at Milan and Basel. He rejoined his companions in Paris only to say goodbyes.

Using the Hôtel Westminster on the Rue de la Paix as his base, he began a forced interval of solitude. He wrote to Gaskell on July 24, 1896: "I read a volume or two every day, trying to find some sort of clue to where the devil I have got, in this astonishing chaos of a modern world. Newspapers I devour by the dozen, of all varieties; and I would even read philosophy and history if I could find anything which bore a resemblance to those antiquated studies."

Phillips had sent news from Washington about their Cuban efforts, which seemed to promise success.[22] Replying on July 26, 1896, Adams almost regretted helping the Cubans. Help was mandatory but meant tragic injury to Spain. "My heart bleeds for the Spaniards, whom I like more than any other people in Europe. . . ."

Cuba and Spain excepted, Adams's activities for the present were anything but tragic. He was lonely in Paris but comfortable and extremely busy. "My occupation is to read till noon; to get into the country and stroll till sunset; and to dine in the open air." ". . . solitude is now a habit."

Gradually Mrs. Cameron had awakened to the fact that her husband and his Cameron relations had the peculiarity of not communicating with one another. Similarly her husband would not communicate with her. She and Martha were staying with the senator at Donegal, a farm he had access to in Pennsylvania. Writing from the farm on July 19, she remarked to Adams: "At no time has he ever written [to] me—except incidentally—even when the absence has been of months duration, and he does not write [to] his children. They are strange people. . . ."

Adams had the opposite peculiarity of communicating with as many friends as possible. He had learned from Wayne and Virginia MacVeagh that they planned to spend some time at Bad-Homburg near Frankfurt. He had advised Mabel Hooper that he would shortly go there. "Paris," he confessed, "is too solitary even for me."

His experiences at Ravenna, Torcello, and Murano had reminded him of a difference he saw between oriental and occidental peoples.[23] On July 27, 1896, he wrote to Mrs. Cameron about the difference and used Elizabeth Warder as an example. ". . . my only objection to Elizabeth is that she *is* strong. . . . Is it Jew? I used to call her Cleopatra Jr. The face is more Greek than Jew, to my eye, but it is certainly oriental."[24]

He continued: "I have an instinctive fascination and terror for the [Greek] type, as I have for the Jew and the serpent, and I hardly know whether it attracts or repels me most. Our poor dear old blonde Aryan is such a fool! Only, here [in Paris] and in London, the Jew is such a howling horror and inevitable end of civilisation that my dread is far greater than the fascination."[25]

Casually in the same letter, Adams told Mrs. Cameron that the outdoor restaurants in Paris were good and "open-air music every afternoon is a great resource." He said next day in an added instalment that he was buying books on Byzantium and fourth-century Rome. "A few hundred dollars given to Byzantine art may redeem, in the last Judgment, the time I have wasted on political history."

Letters concerning the McKinley-Bryan race were reaching him from Mrs. Cameron, Phillips, Hay, and Brooks. He continued to believe that McKinley would win the election. He meanwhile became absorbed in the finances and politics of Europe. He wrote to Hay on July 28: "I am working like a little hornet to understand the subject here, and as a preliminary I read all the Paris newspapers, and every book I can find, previous to trying [Bad-]Homburg. The more I read, the worse I wonder. How the deuce do the Jews manage to make this chaos stand on end? It is a *tour de force*. . . ."[26] Managed chaos, he rather feared, might spell financial losses for him and his friends. He advised Gaskell, "In this situation an investment is sheer gambling."[27]

Directly from Brooks, Henry had learned that Brooks had gone to Chicago hoping the Democrats would want him as their vice-presidential candidate.[28] For Henry, the news was a new, unwelcome reminder of a disagreement that had existed since the early 1860s between him on the one side and his father and brothers on the other. The disagreement was deep. His father and brothers had continued to act as if Adams males had something to gain by seeking office. Oppositely he believed that a latter-day Adams could hope to exert strong political influence only if he combined useful political service, preferably anonymous, with avoidance of office. The disclosure that Brooks had acted on an office-seeking impulse irritated him extremely. In confidence, he burst out to Mrs. Cameron: "What a ticket: McLean and Adams! I prefer Bryan."[29]

A still deeper quarrel between Brooks and Henry was the one revealed to Henry by the test of Byzantium. During their brief meeting in Washington in May, Brooks had told him that he knew of "no Madonna like that of Torcello."[30] Since then, Henry had seen all the Byzantine remains in Italy that Brooks had seen. He had formed impressions and had begun to collect and study books on Byzantine art and history. A day was approaching when he would begin to explain to Brooks how differently they were reading the Byzantine survivals. The difference was so complete that, even if Henry expresssed it gently, Brooks would sense its completeness and would be hurt.

Early in August, Henry returned alone to Chartres and by way of contrast visited the great church of St. Denis north of Paris in which the original stained-glass windows did not survive. Also he visited the cathedrals at Senlis and Bourges. Midway in these proceedings, on August 4, he remarked to Mrs. Cameron that the United States was protected against limitless materialism only by its citizens' persistence in patriotism. It seemed to him that their patriotism did not redeem their materialism. In terms that might indicate disgust, anger, or both, he told her, "If there is such a thing in America as an earnest impulse, an energy or a thought outside of dollars and cents, I should like to see it before [my] imbecility sets in."

Senator Cameron's adult daughter Rachel had bought passage on the *St. Louis*, scheduled to leave Southampton for New York on October 10. News of her plan reached Adams. Wanting not to make another voyage alone, he too bought space on the *St. Louis*. By letter on August 9, 1896, he alerted Mrs. Cameron that he would return with "Rachel and her party."

Simultaneously, by letter, Mrs. Cameron sent Adams the unexpected news that she and Martha would be coming to Europe as soon as they could arrange it. One cause of the change was a nine-day heat wave during which temperatures in Pennsylvania steadily exceeded 100°.[31] Another was Martha's wilting in the heat. The senator resisted the idea that such realities justified flight by his wife and daughter to Europe. The wife explained to Adams, "I had to make a stand." Left unsaid was the principal cause of departure. To the utmost possible extent, Mrs. Cameron wished to be in Adams's company.

While her letter was in transit, Adams was arranging to spend a fortnight at Bad-Homburg with the MacVeaghs and a month thereafter with friends in England and Scotland. On August 11, writing again to Mrs. Cameron, he anticipated new efforts relating to Cuba. He implied that the island's freedom would be better secured during the tenure of a president other than Grover Cleveland. ". . . I shall take up the fight again as soon as Congress meets, but I am almost pleased to think that, as long as our monumental prize hog remains in the White House, all our efforts can effect nothing, and probably the present situation must last at least another year."

On August 13, 1896, Mrs. Cameron cabled to Adams, confirming that she and Martha were coming on the *St. Paul*, sailing on the 19th. He received the cable that day. Next day, as if nothing had happened, he left for Germany with MacVeagh. During the trip to Bad-Homburg, his trunk went astray. It contained his papers and much-needed books.

He knew very well that Mrs. Cameron would soon be in Europe, but he did not impart the news to her sister-in-law, Virginia MacVeagh. Keeping secrets in such cases had become a rule with him. In a letter meant for delivery to Mrs. Cameron on the *St. Paul* at Southampton, he explained, ". . . in my own family I never now mention one member to another." He at the same time made it clear that he would not go back with Rachel, and he admitted that he had joined the MacVeaghs because "tired of a solitary existence."

Rather than be noticed as rushing to Paris, Mrs. Cameron tarried in London and at Oxford. At Bad-Homburg, in a friendly spirit, Adams and MacVeagh disputed each other's opinions. Adams recognized that his anticipations of events might seem too grim and his anti-capitalist animosities too vehement. Yet he thought them justified. Writing to Lucy Baxter on August 26, he said he disliked the role of dismal prophet but was engaged in a deadly feud. "I hate to talk calamity, and nothing but the plainest evidence of its coming could make me do it. But as long as Wall Street and State Street, under the control of Lombard Street, govern me and the country, either Wall Street may kill me or I will kill Wall Street, for the enmity is mortal, and where Wall Street rules, there I die."

Given a choice between fear and hope, Adams would try to hope. An occurrence was troubling him painfully: a massacre of Armenians by the Turks. Yet he told Miss Baxter: ". . . Europe seems to me just now, like America, intensely alive. . . . The awful, unheard-of, absolutely unparalleled horrors of Armenia last year, are only now beginning to weigh on the European conscience, and the evident fact that western civilization stood by, and permitted the thing, solely in order to let the Czar of Russia show his power, and extend his sway, makes western Europe extremely ashamed. The popular irritation against the money-lending class . . . breaks out everywhere. . . . Society, to the very bottom, is quite seething with irritation, and the outbreak in America, where naturally outbreak comes easiest, is, I think, only the prelude to very lively times here [in Europe]."

Hopefulness showed too in his response to a French innovation. On August 26, telling Rebecca Rae he would soon come home, he said: "I shall not bring an *automobile* with me. These inventions infest France . . . make a horrid racket, and are particularly objectionable." He claimed to execrate them as "works of the devil." Yet he thought they might be improved—that some models "may succeed."

* * *

Adams's trunk was found. On August 29, 1896, he left Bad-Homburg and sped to Paris. Mrs. Cameron and Martha arrived. He wrote to Niece Mabel and Cecil Spring Rice but did not mention that he and Mrs. Cameron were seeing one another in a foreign capital in the absence of her husband. Except by being silent, he gave no indication that her late-summer flight to Europe had worked another metamorphosis in his and her relations. He said only that Martha was in Paris and that he and Martha would be going home together.[32]

He and Mrs. Cameron reserved passage on the *Paris*, to sail from Southampton on September 26. On September 13, leaving daughter and mother in Paris, he crossed to London bent for Scotland, to see the Clarks and the Gaskells at Tillypronie. From London, he sent a reminder: "Be sure to get here by the time I return."

About ten days later, three persons re-combined in London. As planned, on September 26, they began the novel experience of an ocean voyage by themselves. Senator Cameron met them on October 3 as they disembarked. The senator was all smiles. He explained that he had just "cleaned out the New York crowd at poker."[33]

Washington was thought by many to be a center of contagious illness. Adams wrote to Phillips, "I find all the women in a panic about fever in Washington. . . ."[34] After a day in New York, Mrs. Cameron went back with Martha and the senator to the Pennsylvania farm. Adams journeyed to the capital and his house.

A trolley line had been completed on H Street. Trolley cars were passing at all hours near Adams's windows. He told Hay, ". . . if it were not for the brimstone roar of the new electric tramway on which Apollyon cavorts at breakneck speed, beating gongs from afar, I should sleep in peace or at least in silence."[35] Yet he found that the gongs were "less disturbing than the old clatter of hoofs."[36]

A hurricane had swept through Washington. Adams was "in terror about the Cemetery." He feared that his and Clover's memorial had been damaged by falling trees. He visited the site and found nothing harmed. ". . . not a leaf of mine was disturbed."[37]

He had brought from New York copies of the American edition of Brooks's *Law of Civilization and Decay*, just issued by Macmillan.[38] On October 9, 1896, he sent a copy to Mrs. Cameron with an injunction: "Read the last chapter, which is mostly new." As before, he praised his brother's work unlimitedly. "The book is a very great book. . . . We can go to our graves in peace. . . ."

Graves were apropos. *The Century Illustrated Monthly Magazine* in New York wanted permission to describe the Adams memorial in an article. On October 14, 1896, Henry advised the editor, Richard Watson Gilder, that photographs of the bronze figure could be used, provided the article did not connect the figure with his wife or himself and did not try to make the figure "intelligible to the average mind." Without offering Gilder permission to repeat what he said, Adams said that his own name for the figure was " 'The Peace of God.' "[39]

Henry's statement was a mere device for preventing Gilder from publishing anything informative. Clover Adams had been a convinced agnostic. When he wrote the statement, Henry was perhaps a Christian but was so unbelieving that about eight months before he had written a parody of Genesis, ". . . let there be God!"[40]

Brooks had undergone a succession of new "break downs" and a "collapse."[41] His immediate problem was gout. He would shortly be going to England for treatment at Bath.[42] He and Evelyn planned to come to Washington before they sailed.

Election Day was near, and money in unprecedented amounts was being spent on McKinley's behalf. On October 14, Mrs. Cameron wrote to Henry from the farm, "I really fear that McKinley has it,—do you?"

In the past with respect to politics, Henry had treated Mrs. Cameron as the ally of her husband. Replying to her on October 16, he treated her as the ally of Henry Adams. He admitted, "I am intensely curious to get the election over, and see what we shall do with the situation. . . ." On some scores, he was non-committal. He said the United States might—or might not—"have a boom."[43] His feelings concerning Cuban independence had diminished in urgency. "Cuba seems to me now a perfectly sure thing. . . . Best keep hands off now." But on one score he was emphatic. "Diplomacy is to be the amusement of the future. I want much—muchissimo—to appoint our next ministers to England, France and Russia. Who would you select? Hay would answer for one. I think you or sister Anne [Mrs. Lodge] would do, but Cabot [Lodge] and your husband would kick."

Henry had broached the impossible idea of female diplomats. The idea could seem amusing. Yet it mirrored a fact. Elizabeth Cameron and Anna Lodge were far superior to their husbands in ability.

Two truths stood out. Henry had leagued himself with a woman who was to share equally with him in political efforts. Henry was paying continuous attention to public affairs on a global scale.

The leading Cuban revolutionist in Washington was Gonzalo de Quesada. On October 18, 1896, he paid Adams an evening call. Adams wrote next day to Mrs. Cameron: ". . . we had a full and deep Cuban discussion, and turned the subject over and over. Cuban matters are active just now. . . ." An agency especially active concerning Cuba was the Rothschild bank in Paris, which had an interest in the debts of the Spanish government. Adams told his partner: ". . . I draw the conclusion that [Alphonse] Rothschild is using the usual machinery either to save some of his money or to make some. Naturally I dread his success, as my chief desire in the Cuba matter is to strike at the Paris Jews and their whole political machine."

Adams knew many people but trusted them in very different gradations. He was trusting Mrs. Cameron absolutely. On October 23, he wrote to Hay and mainly said:

> There are distinct indications that the Parisian bond-holders of Spanish securities are now preparing to carry their campaign into our Treasury.

> The ways of governments are dark, and those of the Spanish government are more mysterious than those of Roentgen rays.

> . . . the Rothschilds can drive both Spain and us into any settlement they dictate.

> . . . [August] Belmont [in New York] is the only channel known to me through which to negotiate terms.

> . . . ultimately our American people must meet the bill, whoever is elected or defeated, and to me Bryan and McKinley are one. But what ought Congress to do?

> You can reflect on this chewing-gum till you return here; but then . . . bring an idea![44]

The passages were evidence of an important fact. Henry trusted Hay quite enough to raise sensitive questions but not enough to convey a full idea of what his own stake in each question really was.

In Paris and at Bad-Homburg, Adams and Wayne MacVeagh had agreed in predicting that McKinley would win the election. A letter to Adams was in transit from MacVeagh, asking a favor. The ambassador to Italy urged the private citizen in Washington, "After the election[,] drop me a line saying how it looks as to the new Sec'y of State—also as to Hay—Hitt—and any other of our friends in the new administration."[45]

Hay annually devoted autumn days to shooting ducks near Cleveland. On October 24, prior to receiving Adams's plea for an idea, he sent two ducks to 1603 H Street for his table. In a letter, he said about the election, "I would it were over and I were with you."

Mabel and Fanny Hooper were visiting Uncle Henry. Mabel was sick in bed. She had bronchitis and possible pneumonia.

Ailing Brooks left for Europe without journeying to Washington to consult with Henry. On the 27th in a letter to Lucy Baxter, Henry made remarks about himself and his surviving brothers. He said truthfully, ". . . Charles and I have never followed the same trail, and are long since out of sight of each other." He said untruthfully, "Brooks followed my path, and although he has gone faster and got ahead, I am only the more pleased, and glad to follow his lead. In his case, therefore, the risk of serious disagreement is nothing. . . ."

On October 28, Henry wrote again to Hay about Cuban matters. He said he had no ideas. ". . . I am still knocking my head on the Cuban question, and the more I knock, the more hollow it resounds." Yet his letter involved a statement and a question. "That we must recognise the independence of Cuba . . . is, I think, as nearly inevitable as any matter of future policy can be." "How would it do for Congress to recommend recognition and a treaty . . .?"

Hay may have replied to Adams's question in writing, but no reply has been found. Adams himself fell silent, or so it appears. During more than a fortnight, he wrote no letters that survive.

McKinley won the election of 1896 by a margin smaller than his adherents would have liked. Fanny Hooper left, and Edward Hooper came from Cambridge to assist Mabel's recovery. Adams broke his silence on November 15 by writing again to Lucy Baxter. His mood was philosophical and anti-European. "As Socrates or Pythagoras—or somebody else—used to say: One fool is much like another. So is one President, and even more so is one cabinet;—and yet, like as they are, I think them neither so like nor so fool as those in Europe, though undoubtedly less posted in general rascality—which is History."

His jibe at "History" reflected a letter—not extant—from the editor of the *American Historical Review*.[46] Jameson, it seems, wished to elicit from Adams a new written statement about history.[47]

Before replying to Jameson, Henry sent Gaskell a warning. "The election [in the United States] has resulted as I supposed it would, although the silver movement developed strength that rather astonished me. We have now a new administration to deal with, but an old situation. . . ." "We have, too, the Cuban matter on hand, which is beginning to look like a first-class cataclysm for Spain. I cannot see how she is to escape a catastrophe."[48]

Henry's trust in Gaskell was practically as complete as his trust in Mrs. Cameron. He told his English friend: "The autumn is pleasant and bright. I have been fussing over old literary odds and ends, and trying to keep myself occupied with trifles. . . . The best I can hope is to have one or two of my friends sent abroad so that I can have some one in Europe to amuse me. Probably John Hay will be offered something. Possibly he may accept it."

One literary odd-and-end that Henry had in mind was his Tahitian

Memoirs. He presumably was at work on closing chapters about Opuhara and Taura-atua i Patea.[49]

One of the trifles was Cuba's independence. Henry was revising his no-longer-secret "historical summary" for early printing.

Another trifle was his presidential letter of December 1893 to the American Historical Association. As has been mentioned, the Association published the letter in 1894 in its *Annual Report*. In 1896, the Association reprinted it as a pamphlet:

The Tendency of History.
by
Henry Adams,
President.

The persons who issued the pamphlet evidently included Jameson and especially Worthington Ford. A package of fifty copies was supplied to Adams. He felt the pamphlet as troubling.[50] In reaction on November 17, 1896, he wrote a letter to Jameson stating in courteous but unequivocal language that history had no tendency. He said that "the field of knowledge which is called History" was in a "chaotic and unintelligible condition" when he started to teach at Harvard in 1870, that it remained so in 1891 when publication of his *History of the United States* was completed, and that the same condition prevailed in 1896. "As History stands, it is a sort of Chinese Play, without end and without lesson." Speaking also about himself, he said things that Jameson might not want to believe. He explained that he wished to be viewed only "as a scholar, and not as a teacher."

The letter to Jameson could be read as Adams's second presidential letter to the American Historical Association. It could also be read as a letter of resignation.[51]

Congress was back in session. On December 8, 1896, as a member of the Committee on Foreign Relations, Senator Cameron introduced a joint resolution proposing (1) that Congress recognize "the independence of the Republic of Cuba" and (2) that the United States government "use its friendly offices with the Government of Spain to bring to a close the war between Spain and the Republic of Cuba." In support of his resolution, Cameron submitted to the Committee a report titled *Recognition of Cuban Independence.*[52]

From the moment Cameron submitted them, the resolution and report functioned as a public message to President Cleveland and Secretary Olney, challenging them to support independence for the Cubans.[53] The message was simultaneous with a financial turnaround. Newly-available data seemed to mean that the flow of gold from the United States to England would soon reverse. Adams wrote to Ford on December 16, "With a [trade] balance of $300,000,000 in our favor, the exchanges ought to be steadily favorable, and gold ought to flow constantly our way." Adams said too that he and Ford needed to meet. "I want to be posted as to the situation, so that I may have a notion of what is the best way to say nothing."

The Cameron resolution-and-report drew fire from leading figures in Massachusetts.[54] On December 22, 1896, the Committee published the report without mention of Adams's authorship. As printed, *Recognition of Cuban Independence* was a 25-page pamphlet. Confirmation that Henry Adams had written it appeared in the press. Charles Adams got wind of Henry's authorship. Charles was one of the leaders in Massachusetts who had been outraged by Senator Cameron's resolution. On December 24, he requested from Senator Lodge a copy of Henry's report and excused the request by saying that Henry would not comply if asked to send one. Charles said he wished to read the document. He further explained that he needed the copy for the Adams family archives.[55]

Of his circle of nieces, real and putative, Uncle Henry's favorites were Louisa and Mabel Hooper. In his opinion, Loulie had been avoiding him. He wrote to her, insisting that she to come to Washington. Writing to Mabel on December 30, he repeated that he wanted Loulie to visit. By way of news, he remarked, ". . . I read Byzantine history, and the early Christians."

Secretary Olney informed the press that any action taken by Congress in support of Cuban independence would be vetoed by President Cleveland.[56] In a letter to Gaskell on January 4, 1897, Henry kept silent about Olney's announcement but described his own situation as distressing and difficult. "I am a hermit without the repose of a hermitage. It is generally supposed that John Hay will be sent abroad in some diplomatic position, in which case I shall lose the only man whose society I depend upon." "I wish I were a Jew, which seems to me the only career suitable to the time."[57]

Loulie arrived, with the foreseeable result that Uncle Henry and Loulie devised a plan of future action by him and all the Hoopers. At roughly the same time, Uncle Henry began a series of letters to Uncle Brooks disagreeing with him about the conclusions to be educed from the relics of Byzantium. And on January 5, 1897, voluntarily, Henry sent Brooks his detailed report, *Recognition of Cuban Independence*.

Brooks had completed a cure at Bath and, with Evelyn, had gone to Paris. They would be renting a house there for the winter. Probably from Mrs. Lodge, they learned that Henry was the author of the much-publi-

cized report proposing Cuban independence. Brooks did not know that
Henry had mailed him a copy. Without saying who told him about the
authorship, Brooks asked Henry to send one. "I had some notion you
wrote the Cameron report and I want to see it very much. . . . I hear it
is supposed to be a great state paper."[58]

Loulie went back to Massachusetts. Uncle Henry wrote to Mabel on
January 12 about politics and said McKinley was weak. "Neither does the
noble Olney improve matters. . . ." Old Senator Sherman perhaps was
worse. ". . . the venerable Sherman is mixing things up with a pernicious activity almost as destructive as his total loss of memory. . . . No
one wants to face the responsibilities of office."

Henry himself felt strong. He was reminded of a previous time when
the Republicans ousted the Democrats and were put to the trouble of
creating a wholly new administration. Next day, he wrote to Lucy Baxter,
"I am constantly thinking of the winter of '60–61." He had a sense of
opportunity. "For the first time in my life, since 1861, I am fairly in the
middle of it, and see the machine grind." ". . . Cuba is all right. We are
not only going to free Cuba, but we are going to put her beyond the
reach of [the?] Havemeyers and the exploitation of New York capitalists."

Bay Lodge was in Berlin, writing poetry and reading philosophy. By
letter on January 17, 1897, Uncle Henry asked him to obtain certain
German financial pamphlets. Henry remarked, ". . . I am treading on
egg-shells. . . ." "I still hope that my neighbor [Hay] will pull off his
mission, for I want to stay with him in England. . . ."

The uncle's hopes remained high for another week. He wrote to
Mabel on the 28th: "My Cubans have won their fight. . . . My object is
to make another Santo Domingo or Colombia of [Cuba] . . . so as to
shut out Mr[.] Havemeyer and the New York and Boston civilisation.
Thus far we have wonderfully succeeded." Yet he voiced a complaint.
"Somebody—not you, but I suspect W. S. B. [i.e. Bigelow] or the Lodge
connections—talks of me too much. . . . Harriet Loring . . . met Hay the
other day, and . . . said that in Boston all the Cuban mischief was attributed to me." He said too that Hay was very much on his mind. "If Hay
goes to London . . . I shall probably go over with him to see him settled
in May Fair among the Jews."[59]

In Paris, Brooks was getting letters from Henry disputing or at least
questioning the historical conclusions he had published in the London
and New York editions of *The Law of Civilization and Decay*. Brooks did
not keep Henry's letters, but Henry kept Brooks's answers. That of January 19, 1897, indicated shock. Brooks said, "You have written to me a

number of times lately about your ideas on Byzantium. . . ." He protested. ". . . I have nothing to take back." ". . . I do not quite grasp what you mean by our civilization being a unity."

A later answer, sent on January 27, showed deeper perturbation. "I am . . . much interested in all your remarks about Byzantium. It may be I'm dull and slow, but I can't quite see it as you do." Perhaps as the only defense available, Brooks went on to reiterate the tenets of his idea of history.[60]

Niece Loulie had gone home to Boston with a plan that she, her sisters, and their father should start for Italy as soon as possible, that Uncle Henry should see them off at New York, and that later he should join them. The plan won acceptance.

To reinforce it, Henry wrote to Loulie on February 3 suggesting that the Hoopers travel fast to Sorrento. He said the place was "infinitely more beautiful" than Naples. He especially recommended its "dear old Byzantine cathedral and town lost on the top." Yet also he urged their making a further plan. "What shall we do with our summer? We ought to pass it near Paris . . . to learn a little French." He mentioned places where they could stay. One was St. Germain.

An economic boom was expected to follow the election of McKinley. It did not occur. Adams completed a review of the financial exchanges between the United States and England since 1870. By means of computations he designed himself, he discovered that England, while ostensibly profiting at the expense of other countries, had been suffering financially to such a degree that English foreign debts were being paid by disinvestment. Where before he had seen England as a profit-making financial predator, he found himself looking at England as an investment-dumping financial invalid. On February 4, he revealed his discovery to Ford. ". . . [England has] run steadily behindhand, and has been obliged, ever since 1890, to stop reinvesting and to sell out an increasing share of her holdings abroad." He asked the inevitable question: "How long can this last?"

Because the two sisters were ever-close, Uncle Henry's letters to Mabel Hooper counted as letters as well to Loulie, and vice versa. On February 11, 1897, he began a letter to Mabel by saying he was interested in the Hoopers' travel plans. ". . . I shall follow your steps to Italy. I am still waiting to know whether the Hays go to London, or anywhere; and whether Rockhill gets a post."

He went on to say that Mrs. Cameron would be going to Europe. He expected that the United States Government would let things slide. ". . . we shall drift along, and play pretend that we are doing

something. . . ." He spoke quietly of Cuba. "The pirate Phillips looks in
. . . with chunks of gossip. . . . Quesada comes now and then to tell me
what he learns, or hears, and to discuss the situation. . . ."

In the absence of Yankee intervention, Spanish soldiers were killing
many real or supposed revolutionaries in Cuba and were herding innocent Cubans into camps. Yet Uncle Henry wanted to keep the murders
and confinements of Cubans in perspective. He told Mabel: "It is as bad
as possible, and rather worse than anything in Armenia, but . . . peaceful
and well-governed India is worse off than the countries where people
are only massacred." As he described it, freedom was something human
beings truly wanted. He said the Cubans would fight even if their country was reduced to a wilderness. ". . . although Spain will no doubt exter-
minate half the people, with the help of Mr[.] Olney, I see no reason to
suppose that the rest will submit."

As head of the Bureau of Statistics, Ford could properly be seen as
the country's leading statistician. He studied Adams's newest figures and
agreed with them. On February 18, 1897, he confirmed that there had
been been "a long term of silent change in the direction of the current." ". . . I applaud your foresight and restudy your averages in the
light of conviction."[61]

For Adams, the meaning of the discovery about gold flow was that
the United States, though still caught in a depression, was stronger economically than Europe. Adams possibly was the first to know it. He told
Lucy Baxter on February 20, ". . . we are going to clean out Europe. . . ."
Yet he pictured the financial contest as a naval battle that was far from
over and might involve surprises. "She [Europe] has done her best to
sink us ever since the Baring failure in 1890 by withdrawing her investments. We have got to see what more she can do when the next spasms
come."

President-elect McKinley was business-minded. He could have asked
John Hay to head the new Cabinet as secretary of state. With a view to
pleasing businessmen, the incoming president offered the place to a
man without experience in foreign affairs, Senator Allison of Iowa. Allison elected to stay in the Senate, whereupon McKinley sought and
found a willing recipient in enfeebled Senator Sherman.[62]

Adams perfected his self-identification and called himself a Conservative Christian Anarchist. He first used the epithet during the morning
of February 24, 1897, in a letter to Anne Fell. He told her, ". . . the most
active field for a Conservative Christian anarchist will be Europe next
summer." ". . . if John Hay goes to England, his movements may affect
mine." "Somebody in Europe or America is going to get badly hurt,

economically and politically, and . . . I hope the victim will now be Europe—perhaps England."

Later that day, Adams sped to New York to usher the Hoopers aboard the *St. Paul*. He returned at once to Washington, possibly by sleeping car. On February 25, after more computation, he advised Ford that he could estimate the size of the holdings England had sold in the United States "since 1890." The sales had garnered "about £50,000,000."

By the time Adams returned, Mrs. Cameron was seriously ill. She had contracted a life-threatening form of "influenza." Adams later explained to Mabel, "Her heart went all to pieces."[63]

That day, perhaps in the evening, Adams sent Gaskell some news. ". . . my time of sailing will depend upon our new President, and his choice of Ambassador to England. After a long period of doubts and difficulties . . . the appointment of John Hay to England seems to be decided." Henry White would be first secretary. "Probably the whole crowd will have to go over as soon as possible after confirmation by the Senate, perhaps as early as April 1, in which case I shall take passage in the same steamer. . . ."

Much was decided; much remained in doubt. Adams described himself as "the scaredest man on the planet." ". . . I am not particularly disturbed by our Cuban and Spanish quarrels, though we are drifting directly into collision; but I do not at all like the economical outlook, and I am greatly worried by the severe and dangerous illness of my friend Mrs[.] Cameron, who has managed to break down under an attack of influenza which fell on the heart and scared us all into blue stone." If well enough, Mrs. Cameron might go abroad with the Hays and Adams as part of her convalescence. The role Adams sketched to Gaskell as his own was a subsidiary one. ". . . in our very small circle of families here, I generally find myself attached as guardian or errand-boy to the family which most wants companionship. Perhaps we shall all sail together, for we are all considerably dependent on each other. . . ."

On March 4, 1897, without incident, William McKinley was sworn in as president. Soon thereafter, old John Sherman was made secretary of state and John Hay ambassador to England. The vicissitudes of recent years had wholly united the Hays, the Camerons, the Lodges, and Adams as a "family." To the extent that the family had a central figure, it was Adams. Yet it also had a main reliance: helpful Phillips.

Mrs. Cameron and Mrs. Lodge were drawing constantly on Willy's ingenuities. When the Hays learned they would have to go to London, Willy arranged an easy move.[64] Yet Willy's relations with Adams were far closer than his relations with the others. He was Adams's intermediary with the Cubans and chief informant about developments within the federal government. He was a knowledgeable, ardent supporter of Adams's work relating to Tahiti. He was Adams's Washington lawyer and business manager. He was on good terms with Adams's constant visitors from out of town.

Adams moved ahead in his financial studies. He told Ford on March 10, ". . . the point on which I am most curious is that of so-called Cosmopolitan Capital, treated as a product, like wheat or iron." He said the gold-bugs in Europe and America had injured their own banks by pushing their countries' industries into competition. ". . . the capitalistic countries . . . in lowering the profits of industry, lower the profits of capital." "The collapse [of Baring Brothers in 1890] was wholly a result of competition of capital. . . ."

Because Secretary Sherman's failures of memory had become a matter of general comment, hopes were expressed that he might be given an unusually capable lieutenant. Adams understood that Rockhill would be made assistant secretary.[65] On March 15, with that prospect in mind, he assured Lucy Baxter that he was himself the outstanding winner. ". . . I come out very much on top. . . . With Hay in London and old John Sherman in the State Department with Rockhill for Assistant, I feel more in the stream than for thirty years past. . . ."

The praise Adams's *Recognition of Cuban Independence* had won as a great state paper was justified.[66] The report deserved to be read in tandem with his *History of the United States*. Both works were masterfully informative and superbly written. Both recounted the struggles of democrats in America and Europe against European oppressors. Yet the works were separated by a difference relating to the Adamses. In his *History*, Henry kept mention of his Adams forebears to a minimum. In his *Recognition of Cuban Independence*, he sank it to zero.

A main idea in his report was that the American Revolution and the Monroe Doctrine were two parts of one event; that neither could be sustained unless the other was sustained; and that, if sustained, the two would eventually result in the building of a democratic "system" throughout the New World in defiance of aristocracies and autocracies in the Old. Henry so shaped the text as not to mention that John Adams was a leader of the American Revolution and not to mention that John Quincy Adams was the writer of the Monroe Doctrine. This trick of historical effacement completed the removal—or seeming removal—of *three* Adamses from the report. Henry was the third, removed by the simple expedient of not signing what he had written.

The trick would work. It would prevent readers from wondering to what extent the course of world events had been controlled by Adamses.

It would prevent readers from realizing that the three Adamses were all still alive in the person of Henry. It would help readers concentrate on what mattered: Cuba's independence. It put a damper on talk about according the Cubans mere recognition as "belligerents."

In the privacy of his letter to Lucy Baxter, written on March 15, Henry celebrated his triumph. "My Cuban fight I regard as won, in less time, and more completely than I dared hope; and in all probability the insanity of Spain and the imbecility of France will end in a collapse that will emancipate Porto Rico too. In short, I rather hope to see my grandfather's work completed, and [all of] America really independent of Europe, even in Canada."

When well enough to begin to walk, Mrs. Cameron relapsed and was again confined to bed. At a time when her condition seemed at its worst, approximately on April 1, 1897, her husband rented their Washington house to the new vice president, Garret A. Hobart, for the four years of his term. Hobart's occupancy would begin on May 1.

Elizabeth Cameron and Rachel Cameron had known the house as their home. In a trice, they lost it. Rachel reacted secretly by consenting to marry Chandler Hale. Her doing so was understandable but would lead to an unhappy marriage and an eventual breakup.[67]

Mrs. Cameron reacted openly. Although too ill to sit up in bed, she declared she would go to Europe. Henry was visiting her every day at 4:00 P.M. She told him what she meant to do.

Brooks and Evelyn returned from Paris and came to 1603 H Street, arriving late on Friday, April 9. Writing next day to Lucy Baxter, Henry said he would be leaving Washington on Monday and that Brooks and Evelyn would "stay here after I go."

Henry's feelings, earlier sanguine, had become disturbed. He told Miss Baxter: "I have never felt more doubtful of my future, or of my return, but my circle here is broken to pieces. . . . At present, all that has interest for me is in Europe, or [is] going there. . . ."

On Monday, April 12, Henry left for New York, ready to sail on Wednesday with the Hays, White, Sturgis Bigelow, and Chandler Hale, who had been made secretary of embassy at Rome.

Anna Lodge was in New York. Henry arranged that she return to Washington and join with Evelyn to transfer Mrs. Cameron, Martha, a nurse, and a governess to 1603 H Street. Writing from New York, he told Mrs. Cameron how she and the others might best distribute themselves in his rooms.

Mrs. Cameron sent him a telegram: "Much better." He may not have believed it. On Wednesday, he sent her a last letter from the *St.*

Paul requesting that she direct a cable to him in London confirming that she was safely at his house.

Attempts by Anna Lodge and Evelyn Adams to move Elizabeth Cameron did not avail. She said she was leaving for Europe with Martha, the governess, and a nurse.[68] In care of the embassy in London, she sent Adams a cable stating that she would sail on the *St. Paul* on May 5. The underlying message was that she did not need Henry's house. She needed him.

The Hays, Adams, White, Bigelow, and Hale disembarked at Southampton on April 21. American well-wishers were at the dock. One was Henry James. Congratulatory speeches ensued. Hay later wrote, ". . . [Adams] so thoroughly disapproved of the whole proceeding that he fled to the innermost recesses of the ship. . . . Henry James stood by, and heard it all. . . ."[69]

Adams had cause to hide. He anticipated that his association with Hay would work to his political advantage. On that premise, he had to screen the association entirely from public notice.

Once in London, at Brown's Hotel, Adams checked his mail. Via the embassy, he had a cable from Mrs. Cameron. It said she would be coming on the *St. Paul*, arriving on May 11.

Telling no one about it, he pocketed the cable. He had promised to join the Hoopers in Florence. There was a question what to do. He visited the Hays at 5 Carlton House Terrace—the former residence of the Curzons, a veritable palace.[70] He found the ambassador and his dependents "sitting solemnly in the midst of their grandeur, having lost all the keys of their trunks."[71]

That evening, he took Chandler to dinner and was told an amazing secret. Young Hale divulged that he and Rachel were engaged.

Adams wrote to Mabel in Florence, explaining that Mrs. Cameron *might* soon arrive in England, in which case he would wait for her.

Bay Lodge was in London. During the next few days, Bay, Adams, and Bigelow kept one another company.

On April 23 and 28, Adams wrote new letters to Mrs. Cameron, addressed in care of Phillips. Their gist was that she should cancel her arrangement—not attempt a voyage till well enough to make it.

Letters were traveling in both directions. On April 19, Phillips had sent Adams some bits of news. "We here have been flambergasted [*sic*] over Rachel Cameron's engagement to Chandler." Henry's horses, Prince and Daisy, had died in Virginia; and Willy had paid their last bill. He had seen Horatio Rubens, of the Cuban delegates, and had talked with him about a certain Crowthers, to be identified in future letters only as C. He wished Adams to know that Mrs. Cameron was bearing up and could withstand the rigors of her voyage.

Near wars were in progress at the White House about the distribution of offices. In a new letter on April 30, Phillips noted that Theodore Roosevelt had won the appointment as assistant secretary of the navy. He touched on Crowthers. "I hope to get to C. early in June." He found room for a reference to someone best known as A. "I suppose that A. will now have a hand in our relations with England."

Rockhill was not made assistant secretary of state. He asked for the mission to China but was rejected. On May 3, Phillips sent Adams the news. Attentive to details, he mentioned receiving a "2nd letter" from Adams addressed to Mrs. Cameron. He said he had forwarded it to her at the Holland House, the hotel in New York to which she had been taken, before being carried to the *St. Paul.*

At the Holland House, Mrs. Cameron was examined and given a second opinion by a Dr. Janeway. He confirmed that she had a valvular heart disorder and recommended that she live quietly for six months. Once taken on board the ship, she began a letter to Adams that she would give to him at Southampton. It partly concerned Janeway's opinion and advice. In a second instalment, written when the voyage was ending, she resorted to a metaphor of an automobile that broke down.

> I am determined to make a good try at running our broken down machine—if it *won't* go, then I *can* re-adjust. . . . It is curious how one shuts up like a jack knife when anything becomes real, or sensitive. There is a long history of mental weakness & mental struggle. I have often wanted to tell you, but cannot. The moment it is of *you*, I cannot talk of you even to yourself. Above all, I cannot say any thing of all that I feel to you. Some day I shall go on my knees to you & humbly kiss your hand—Even then, you won't know the smallest portion of it, very dearest—Martha is prancing around in fine spirits & health, but broke out on Sunday with more bitterness than I cared to see about all her connections. She has seen more than I thought & remembers from further back—But for her very sake it must be *made* to work.

The automobile that broke down was her marriage. She thought the the only way to make it "go" was to leave her husband, taking their daughter with her. The occasion for her idea was not mere incompatibility. It was her husband's expelling her from a home on Lafayette Square that she had loved and had lovingly refurnished.

Her idea did not get at the controlling facts. Donald was rich and did not need the four years' rent. His evicting her had a meaning unrelated to real estate. His denying her the house was a sort of impromptu partial divorce without going to court. It was an indication that in his feelings she was not his wife.

*   *   *

Because Mrs. Cameron had not moved in, Brooks and Evelyn continued to use 1603 H Street. Brooks was especially pleased by the visits of Assistant Secretary Teddy Roosevelt, who often came for lunch.

On Monday, May 10, 1897, pleasure gave way to horror. Brooks sent a cable to Henry in London, in care of Baring Brothers, saying: "Willy Phillips drowned Sunday sailing."

The cable reached Western Union in London at 6:26 P.M., was delivered to the Baring bank, and redirected thence to Brown's Hotel early on Tuesday.[72] Henry also received a cable from Rockhill.

On Tuesday, Henry and Sturgis Bigelow went to Southampton. They were at the dock on Wednesday when passengers left the *St. Paul.* Mrs. Cameron was carried from the ship to an invalid compartment on the train to London. Later on Wednesday, Henry wrote to Mabel Hooper. He said that he, the Hays, and Bigelow were distressed by cables from Brooks and Rockhill saying that Phillips "drowned while sailing." The news had fallen heavily on its hearers. "It quite broke up poor Helen [Hay] . . . and I have not yet dared tell Mrs[.] Cameron. I imagine it gives the last blow to our Washington family, and will be a serious shock to Mrs[.] Lodge."

For Henry himself, the blow was worse than serious. He could not think, could not imagine what to do. He told Niece Mabel, ". . . I have instinctively pushed away the thought of how I am to provide for the difficulties this loss creates."

7

MY BUSINESS IS TO LOOK AHEAD

Hay had seen Henry Adams at the U. S. Legation in London in the 1860s when he unofficially was sharing the responsibilities of the English mission with his father, C. F. Adams, the official minister. When he himself was sent to the post, Hay regarded the Adams son as one of his predecessors in the office.[1]

In May 1897, the embassy's duties were light. The only matters at issue between England and the United States were bimetallism and a fur seals controversy. On the 17th on Hay's account, Adams attended a gathering of British bimetallists, took notes concerning the views expressed, and showed Hay the notes. Accommodation was disallowed in advance.[2] The speakers agreed that England's money-lords would not yield concerning silver except within "narrow limits of concession."[3]

Adams and Bigelow superintended the transfer of Mrs. Cameron to Paris, arriving on May 20. Adams put up at the Hôtel Vendôme. On the 20th, he wrote to Mabel that he would not be joining the Hoopers in Italy. He all along had hoped that he and they might share a summer residence near Paris. He assured her: ". . . if you have plans for resting anywhere, or coming to France for the summer, I will wait [for?] you here. . . . That chateau might turn up."

When it seemed best, Adams informed Mrs. Cameron that Phillips was dead. Details had come from Brooks by mail. Brooks said that Willy had not drowned; that accidentally a tightening main sheet had snared and broken his neck and pulled him off the boat, already killed.[4]

An unhappy message came from another quarter. Chandler Hale had gone to Rome and tried to function as a diplomat. The result was a breakdown. He had started a retreat to America.[5]

Hay was learning that State Department actions and instructions made little sense. He wrote to Adams on May 24: "I said when I started I could stand it a year— I begin to doubt it. It is utterly inconceivable the things they do and the things they say."

Replying next day, Adams advised that the State Department

needed "instruction—that's all,—and patience." He noted that Mrs. Cameron had taken Phillips's death "as well as possible." Firmly, he declared a severance. "Since leaving you, I've cut affairs, and dropped newspapers. Till November I want to hear no more so-called news."

In a new letter to Mabel, Adams offered to pay half the rent of a chateau, preferably near Paris. Mrs. Cameron might live close by. The Hoopers agreed to the arrangement, but finding an acceptable chateau took time. From Paris on June 3, Uncle Henry reported to Loulie that he had "ransacked St[.] Germain." "The French are still gloriously archaic. Their ways of life are those of the Renaissance. Ordinary picknicking is luxury compared with their country life, and, as for sanitary precautions, there are none outside of Paris, and none worth having, inside. All that one can hope for is a water-supply."

On the 3rd, he sent Mrs. Lodge a more general account of his conduct. ". . . in this career of the modern Rasselas, I have run away from Ambassadors and Bimetallists. . . . Even Cuba is lost to my sight. Phillips's death has shut the door to all view of what is happening, either in Cuba or in the State Department, and I guess I am the better for it. Yet I could dimly wish that other doors might open, as the old ones shut, but I find Paris alarmingly usual."

Searches at St. Germain yielded Henry a large villa for him and the Hoopers—the Pavillon d'Angoulême—and a place for Mrs. Cameron.

Brooks was planning a trip with Evelyn to Greece and Russia early in 1898. Writing from Quincy on June 1, 1897, he invited Henry to go too. Henry had reasons to accept. He was interested in Russia's nascent "State-Socialism" and wanted to meet Russia's finance minister, Sergei Witte. Yet he was certain to demur. If asked to choose between seeing a foreign country with Adams relatives, with friends, or with friends who were diplomats, he would much prefer the friends who were diplomats; and there remained a chance that Rockhill would win a place as a U. S. minister.[6] On June 11, Henry declined, telling Brooks: "Your plans are excellent, and I hope you may carry them out. . . . I make no plans, and do not care to fix movements ahead."

By then, Mrs. Cameron was ensconced at St. Germain and the Hoopers had arrived in Paris. Adams advised Mrs. Cameron on the 13th, a Sunday, that his nieces wanted him to act as their guide that afternoon "at Chartres" and that he would try to visit her next day.

On the 15th, he wrote to Mrs. Lodge, "Paris seems to have become my summer watering-place, and I seriously meditate an establishment here." His statements reflected an agreement that Mrs. Cameron and he had made the day before that when fully ready she would take a long-term lease on a Paris apartment, so that she and he could use it in alternation, as suited their convenience.

The foregoing considered, it could seem that Henry's treatment of Brooks and Evelyn had been negative. Yet in one respect the elder brother's treatment of the younger had been complimentary. His letter to Brooks of June 11 had included an analysis of world conditions possibly better than any he had achieved till that time. He had said: "The disruption of '93 has definitely rearranged society. . . . That another shock will come . . . everyone admits. . . . What form it will take is another matter. . . . In my own opinion, the centre of the readjustment, if readjustment is to be, lies in Germany, not in Russia or with us. For the last generation, since 1865, Germany has been the great disturbing element of the world, and until its expansive force is decidedly exhausted, I see neither political nor economical equilibrium possible. Russia can expand without bursting anything. Germany cannot. Russia is in many respects weak and rotten. Germany is immensely strong and concentrated. . . . Whether the first crisis of the struggle will come in economics or in politics, who knows? Whether it will come in my time, I doubt. Even when it does come, it will be only a phase in the larger movement which is either centralising or disorganising the world, or doing both at once."

Rockhill was assured by President McKinley that he would be given a mission, either to Greece or to China. The more probable, it seemed, was Greece. On June 27, 1897, on his and his wife's behalf, he sent an invitation to Adams. ". . . perhaps if we should go . . . [to Athens], we might hope to see you next winter."

On July 3 or thereabouts, Adams and the Hoopers started residence at the Pavillon d'Angoulême. The uncle later remarked to Cecil Spring Rice, "I have a house as large as an Ambassador. . . ."[7] He told Rebecca Rae that his hideout was "a queer old place, with huge cedars of Lebanon."[8] His motive in choosing the place could be described as anti-political and even reclusive. One of the advantages of the villa was proximity to a forest. He boasted to Cunliffe: ". . . newspapers rarely penetrate my fortress. A ride in the forest or a drive to Marly le Roi is my wildest effort. . . ."[9]

The nieces took lessons, this time to improve their French. Uncle Henry could speak French but said, "I wish I could jabber it. . . ."[10] By studying with the girls, he advanced in that direction.

He wrote to Brooks on July 29 that there was "little to be gained by thought and much by rest." ". . . it is much to have two months breathing space. . . ." Wanting a third month, he arranged an extension of the lease at St. Germain to the end of September.

Whenever he described himself as resting, Henry could be suspected of being busy.[11] He wanted added "rest" because engaged in a difficult labor. He was teaching himself Old French, a forgotten language that most people would be satisfied not to know.[12]

Living a half-mile from Adams helped Mrs. Cameron recover. Confident she would be well enough for the purpose, she planned a halfway return to her husband in the form of a winter's residence at the Holland House in New York. She and Martha would sail in November. If he felt moved to do so, Donald would join them.

Sharing the Pavillon d'Angoulême with Uncle Henry made Louisa and Mabel Hooper desirous of keeping his company as long as possible. It was decided that Edward Hooper should go home with three daughters and that Louisa and Mabel should go later with Mrs. Cameron. On September 12, 1897, Adams mentioned these details in a letter to Hay. He said too that he was "meditating a permanent establishment in Paris, or an escapade to hot climates."

Four Hoopers departed on September 16, leaving five persons in association at St. Germain. Without ado, Mrs. Cameron, Martha, Uncle Henry, Mabel, and Louisa became a momentary family. When their leases ran out, they returned to Paris. On October 2, they began a fortnight of pleasant wandering in Touraine "through all the castles and kings of Rabelais and Balzac." In his next letter to Hay, Adams reported that he and his babes were again in Paris, housed on the Rue de Rivoli at the Hôtel Brighton. Mrs. Cameron had taken an apartment at 61 Avenue Marceau. It seemed possible that Adams too would need an apartment, but his first concern was occupation for Louisa and Mabel. "If they want to go for a run in Langueduc and Provence, I shall take them off again for another fortnight before they sail. If they prefer Paris, we shall hang on, and in that case I may set up an appartement [sic] here and a cook, and make a season of it till March, when it will be time to go to Washington for a visit."[13]

Hay was well aware that Adams had fled his company and hidden himself in France. Comically the ambassador had written on September 5, "I wish we might meet some where, before I get too old to remember who you were." On September 28, he wrote more insistently: ". . . when am I to see you? This dwarfs all other questions." Finding that Adams held out no hope of an early return to London, Hay reacted on October 20 by asking a favor. "Mrs. Hay and two infantas want to go to Paris next week. . . . Do you think you could secure them lodgement in your tavern the Brighton . . . ?" He also spoke about a vacation. ". . . I shall take my leave later on, in a lump."

Louisa and Mabel elected to stay in Paris. To make room for them and later anticipated guests, Adams rented a big apartment at 16 Rue

Christophe Colomb. He and his nieces moved in on October 21. Mrs. Cameron's apartment was nearly opposite.

Mrs. Hay came to Paris mainly concerned about her husband's leave. When they were able to talk by themselves, Adams or Clara Hay—more probably Adams—voiced the thought of a journey up the Nile with agreeable companions. Henry James and Sir John Clark were named as desirable fellow vacationers. Adams was given a role in the plan only as a usable substitute for James or Clark, should either or both be unavailable. When disclosed to James and Clark, the plan would be attributed to Mrs. Hay, as if Adams had never heard of it.

A factor in the planning was news mailed from Scotland on October 7 that Lady Clark had died. Cunliffe had been at Tillypronie at the time and had written to Adams at once. Similarly, on October 24, Gaskell notified Adams that Francis Palgrave—Adams's former mentor in matters of art and poetry—was paralyzed and was expected to die very shortly. Inevitably the messages served Adams as reminders that Hay's health, although restored, needed considerate tending.[14]

Recently Adams had shown few signs of working on his books. Yet work on books had been his principal activity. In prospect, *Mont Saint Michel and Chartres* would need a chapter titled "La Chanson de Roland." He had reached the point of learning what the chapter would have to say. The evidence of his progress was a remark in a letter to Gaskell on October 31, 1897, that his reading of late had been "confined to old French, and Chansons de Geste."

The Education of Henry Adams presented a different problem. Such was the genius of the work that the success of its second narrative would require his waging a campaign of incessant learning by every means available. Books, magazines, and newspapers would figure among the means. Travel would rival or exceed them in importance. Yet the means to end all means would be friendships.

Recently Adams had received informative letters from his younger brother, from Ford, and from Hay. The letters were remarkable for the evident eagerness of their authors to lend Henry every assistance they could lend in the way of information and insight. In this respect, letters to him from an English official verged on the spectacular.

Adams liked Cecil Spring Rice without reservation, and the affection was reciprocated. Spring Rice's career in diplomacy had been shaped by postings in the United States, Japan, and Germany. At the embassy in Berlin, he was second secretary. He was officially constrained not to impart valuable information to *British* citizens, still less to Americans. In secret, however, his situation had become unusual. Five months earlier, on May 23, 1897, Adams had written him a letter beginning with a list of questions. An example was, "Will Europe make a supreme effort for empire, or will it deliberately accept the domination of Asia?" Obviously the questions had been meant as provocations. It did not diminish their provokingness that some were whimsically worded.

Spring Rice had replied on August 29 while on leave in the Lake Country. He began by speaking in personal terms but interrupted himself to say: "Politics will interest you immensely now. . . . When I left [Berlin,] the feeling was . . . something like this." There followed twelve paragraphs about Germany. They led to a conclusion: "Germany is become the most material of the mammon worshippers—but, in a way, for immaterial reasons: to maintain her military power, and to save herself from a socialist revolution."[15]

Once started on this path, Spring Rice prepared to write an even more serious communication. On November 7, 1897, from Berlin, he sent Adams an analysis of "the struggle going on here between the two great parties representing the interests of land and money." Showing every evidence of being well-informed and having arrived at reliable estimates, he turned attention to the German agrarians (i.e. the Junkers, who usually were soldiers), the manufacturers, the economists, the socialists, the Catholics, the government, and the Jews.[16]

The analysis was partly interesting as a comment on its addressee. One imagines that Spring Rice had written to Adams with the knowledge and consent of his superiors in Berlin and London. It apparently was thought that the person rightly to be trusted with British findings about Germany was Adams, an American private citizen currently staying in France. Yet the analysis could not have been intended only for him. In weight, breadth, and carefulness of wording, the British communication far exceeded what anyone would look for in a letter. A conclusion Adams would draw was that he should lend the communication to Hay as soon as possible and thus add it to the resources of the embassy in London and the State Department in Washington.[17] And a conclusion Hay would draw was that Adams was secretly the holder of a far-from-negligible position in international politics.[18]

With Martha, Mrs. Cameron crossed from Paris to London on November 18, 1897. She wrote that night to Adams: ". . . a whole channel of water lies between us. It gives one a different feeling—"[19]

Neither Sir John Clark nor Henry James could free himself to accompany the Hays to Egypt. On the 19th, Hay conveyed the result to Adams in Paris. "Do not think you have any *libre arbitre* about Egypt. Mrs. Hay says you *must* go. So says Helen. . . ."

Gaskell was staying with Adams, Louisa, and Mabel at 16 Rue Christophe Colomb. On the 21st, Adams and Gaskell escorted the nieces to

London; and on the 27th, by himself, Adams guided the nieces, Mrs. Cameron, and Martha to the *St. Paul* at Southampton.

Once back in London, he called on a lifelong friend from Boston, Alice Mason.[20] Next evening, he dined with a contemporary he had not previously met, Lady Randolph Churchill, originally Jennie Jerome, a New York socialite. He thought her "very good fun."[21] The meetings were instances of his readiness to be sociable. He liked seeing people and was reclusive only for a compelling reason. He knew that reclusiveness was the surest road to the completion of great books.

He returned to Paris on November 30 and began a fortnight of hard work. A letter from Ford awaited him. The Washington statistician had been dismayed to learn that Adams would not be home that winter. He had written, ". . . I shall miss your talks, and shall need them."[22]

In lieu of a talk, on December 1, 1897, Adams sent Ford a revised financial history of England. "She [England] began to withdraw her capital from America, Australia, &c, about 1887. . . . Why she did so I cannot conceive, and have asked in England in vain. It is admitted, but unexplained. Perhaps she had over-invested."[23]

The effect of England's withdrawals of capital was a story that must be repeated here. From 1887 forward, the withdrawals required proportionate shipments of gold to London. Gold famines resulted in many places. One of the famines precipitated the Panic of 1893 in the United States. The panic so injured Adams's brothers that John died and Charles and Brooks remained in straits. Moreover, the panic retained so strong a hold on Henry's mind that it was channeling his financial research and to some extent was governing his views.

In his December 1 letter to Ford, Adams disclosed an estimate and offered some comments. He calculated that in ten years since 1887 England had liquidated "about one fourth or one fifth of her probable holdings in America." He partly liked the change. ". . . it implies our rapid emancipation from the thrall of European capitalism. . . ." Yet even more he was alarmed by financial and political instabilities in every part of Europe, from England to Turkey. He therefore wanted "an American policy of withdrawal from what I dread as the coming convulsions of the world." "I want either to lock up the Treasury, crack on differential tonnage-duties; force down our foreign debts and obligations; and to develop American connections [i.e. with Latin America and Canada]; or, if we cannot do that, I want silver, pure and simple. Bimetallism would merely harness us to Europe. I am dead set against anything of the kind. . . ."[24]

Adams did not say so, but the revised idea he had developed of the financial history of England might require that he moderate his hatred of England's money-lords. Earlier he had understood the gold famines as results of rapacious designs on the part of such persons as Lord Rothschild and Chancellor of the Exchequer Harcourt. In December 1897, he had to consider the possibility that England's ten-year withdrawal of capital from other countries had been an unintended event—something that happened without anyone's having wanted it to happen, or even known what it was. In the light of this different vision, Nathaniel Rothschild might no longer seem a villain. He might be transformed to what he perhaps had tried to be: a circumspect banker who in the English way insisted on payment in gold.

Emotions were not easily given up. Adams would not quickly or fully recede from his anti-banker, anti-capitalist, anti-Rothschild, anti-English furies. Yet he deserved credit for original findings. If he could be criticized for having mislabeled Jews and non-Jews in the past as international robbers, he could also be praised for having performed original research that would permit him to counteract the mislabeling. His furies had had a basis in what he had believed was valid data. His recovery, if there were one, would have a basis in improved data he himself had taken pains to generate.[25]

Adams wanted to spend his fortnight in Paris "reading the Chanson de Rolland [*sic*] and eating cream-cheese."[26] He wrote to Mabel Hooper on December 3, 1897, "I study a great deal, and write, and think of people to see. . . . I am better off here than I should be in Washington, and Thérèse gives me uncommonly nice little meals."

An idea of his thoroughness as a learner can be gained by looking into his copy of a well-known anthology of Old French writings.[27] The copy belonged to the latest, most corrected edition:

Chrestomathie de l'Ancien Français
(VIIIᵉ-XVᵉ Siècles)
accompagnée d'une grammaire et d'une glossaire,
par Karl Bartsch.
Sixième édition
revue et corrigée par
A. Horning.

———

Leipzig,
F. C. W. Vogel.
1895

His annotations showed that, while reading the "Chanson de Roland" and other medieval works, he was expanding the Old French glossary at the back of the book with entries the editors had omitted.[28] It can seem unlikely that he already was translating passages into English for use in *Mont Saint Michel and Chartres*. Yet possibly he was.[29]

A young man he wished to meet in Paris was Bay Lodge's friend and Harvard classmate, Joseph Trumbull Stickney, known as Joe. Stickney was attempting an academic feat: to become the first American to earn a doctorate in literature at the Sorbonne. Roughly on December 10, he and two friends joined Adams for dinner at 16 Rue Christophe Colomb.

Brooks and Evelyn arrived from Boston on December 13. Being at loose ends, young Abigail Adams had come with them. Brooks was unwell but not too unwell to persist in his ambitions. His immediate problems were to persuade a Paris publisher to issue *The Law of Civilization and Decay* in French, somewhat expanded, and to hire a translator capable of readying a manuscript for the printer.

For ten days, Brooks, Evelyn, and Abigail stayed with Henry in his big apartment. Brooks still wanted Henry to go with him to Greece and Russia. Henry accepted the invitation but had not forgotten Rockhill. The latter had been appointed minister to several Balkan countries, chiefly Greece. In any plans Henry would make, the Rockhill family would continue to loom as a desired reliance.

Henry wished to help Brooks but, as a means of avoiding arguments, was frequently constrained to pretend agreement with his opinions. In the present instance, their discussions taxed Henry beyond endurance. He wrote to Mrs. Cameron on December 24: ". . . I have had my Brother Brooks with me for the last ten days, and of course have had to go over with him the whole field of the world's doings. . . ." Rather than strike at Brooks, Henry unleashed an angry commentary on Europe, Paris, London, Madrid, and Kaiser Wilhelm. ". . . I am . . . at a loss to understand how this rotten old barrack of Europe, and this utterly preposterous and empty phantasm of a city [Paris], continue to seem to hold themselves up before my eyes. . . . The besotted, self-satisfied stupidity of London; the cynical, Roman philosophy of Paris; the childish, monkeyish violence of Madrid;—it is all as unbalanced as Kaiser Willy's mind. As I see it, knowing what is going on in the extremities—in the Americas, in India, China, Australia and Africa,—it seems to me that the whole show must crumble to pieces. . . . Europe is bankrupt and imbecile. It's [*sic*] wealth is a delusion, and it's [*sic*] science a fraud, and its art a shadow."

In 1893, a rich promising young officer, Alfred Dreyfus, had been assigned to the French army's general staff. He was one of the first Jews to be admitted to that body. In October, 1894, he was secretly arrested. The fact of his arrest was leaked to an anti-Semitic Paris newspaper, *La*

Libre Parole. In December, a secret court-martial convicted him of passing army secrets to the Germans. Stripped of rank and sword, he was exiled for life to Devil's Island off the coast of French Guiana.[30]

Captain Dreyfus had not committed the treasonous crime for which he was convicted. The document construed as proof of his guilt was a handwritten list—a *bordereau*—that had come into the possession of the army during the previous summer. The prosecutors and judges believed the handwriting was his. Although similar, it was not.

Dreyfus's brother Mathieu knew that Alfred was innocent and tried to enlist support in his favor. In November 1896, Bernard Lazare, a Jewish critic, publicly alleged that the conviction had been a miscarriage of justice and that Captain Dreyfus was persecuted because he was a Jew. There followed a continual commotion in the press.[31]

Adams's earliest known mention of Dreyfus appeared in a letter written in November 1897, almost three years after the captain was convicted. It indicated a disposition to believe that Dreyfus was innocent.[32] Yet it and later remarks showed that Adams was part-inclined to take the case unseriously.[33] To some extent, he saw the hubbub in the press as an instance of French enthrallment in passing scandals and sensations.[34] At the same time, he recognized that he could not yet form a decided opinion. Some of the evidence had been published, but most of it had not. None of it had been satisfactorily reviewed by the press, and at the moment the air was filled with heated imprecations and blatant falsehoods.[35]

In January 1898, a court-martial tried a second officer suspected of passing army secrets to the Germans, Major Ferdinand Esterhazy. The accuser of Major Esterhazy was Colonel Georges Picquart, who had become head of French army intelligence subsequent to the trial of Captain Dreyfus and had later been removed. The court-martial was designed by the army to attract public attention and was staged in two parts, one public, one secret. It was only during the secret part that Picquart was permitted to testify. On January 11, amidst great public excitement, the judges found Major Esterhazy not guilty. It would later prove that it was Esterhazy, not Dreyfus, who had gone to the Germans bearing secrets.

One of Adams's friends in Europe was Aristarchi Bey, formerly the Turkish minister in Washington. On January 12, Bey dined with Adams. They "discussed the whole European situation" and the Dreyfus case. Next morning, Adams summarized Bey's view to Mrs. Cameron: ". . . [he] insists that, whether Dreifus [*sic*] is guilty or not, (and he has little doubt of the fact that he was, but this is no longer important except to him [Dreyfus]), the campaign which the Jews have made for him, the very large amounts of money they have spent on the press and the effort to pass by [i.e. by-pass] the government and control public opinion against it, has resulted in enormously stimulating the anti-semite feeling in France, which has now reached the point where violence has become only a matter of time. I believe Aristarchi to be right. The current of opinion is running tremendously strong, now that the whole extent of the Jew scandal is realised. For no one doubts that the whole campaign has been one of money and intrigue; and the French are very furious. Of course all the English and the Americans are with the Jews, which makes it worse."[36]

That Adams and Bey discussed the case as it related to the whole European situation accorded with Adams's exceptional needs. He was looking at Europe and at the Dreyfus case, not with the eyes of a disinterested onlooker, but with the eyes of a passionate American proponent of republicanism and democracy. For him, it was a fact of the first importance that France had come to the aid of the Americans in the 1780s when they were conducting their revolution—indeed that France was the only European power that had ever helped the United States. Seeing things in this perspective, Adams felt little interest in Dreyfus but was actively sympathetic to France.[37]

Violence flared on January 13. At day's end, Adams dined alone on or near the Boulevard Haussman. Early on the 14th, he wrote Mrs. Cameron an account of his doings which she would understand only with the help of newspapers. "When I strolled down the Boulevard after dark last evening, there was an ominous hum in the air that made me look about me; for, if anybody was going to visit Alphonse Rothschild, I've a sort of notion I'd like to go too. It appears that Zola kicked the boiler over. The situation is now worse than ever. For the first time in twenty years, the Army has put down its foot with a stamp that has scared Cabinet, Senate, Bourse and Boulevards. . . . Colonel Picquart found himself shut up in Mt[.] Valérien [a civil prison] before he could breakfast. But Zola howled; and the Bourse actually fought—Jews and Gentiles—till the police came in. A good day's work! and rioting too in Havana! and a new outbreak in India!"[38]

Emile Zola was France's leading novelist. On January 13, the day violence broke out, Georges Clemenceau, the editor of the newspaper *Aurore*, had prominently published a letter from Zola to Félix Faure, president of France, accusing the government and the army of conspiring against Dreyfus and shielding Esterhazy. For Adams as for all others, Clemenceau's publication of Zola's letter transformed a mere case into a world-famous "affair." It no longer was Dreyfus who was accused. It was the French government, the French army, and even a large portion of the French people.

Because the evidence was still mostly unpublished and almost entirely unexplained, Zola's accusation was a mere hypothesis. Adams accepted the hypothesis.[39] Accepting it was in one sense an advance, in another not. With Zola, Adams could believe that Dreyfus was innocent, but neither Zola nor Adams could know whether treason had been committed. On the basis of the evidence published till then, it was possible to believe that treason was not committed, only falsely asserted to help conspirators rid the army of a Jew. (The difference was important. Military secrets *were* sold to the Germans. French army intelligence had been right in attempting to find a traitor.)

In an important respect, Zola and Adams diverged. Zola clearly reveled in his hypothesis. Adams did not. As before, he tended to dislike all Jews. Yet he was *not* an anti-Semite in the sense of hating all Jews and wanting to injure them. Rather, as before, he was anti-capitalist, anti-banker, and anti-Rothschild. When he told Mrs. Cameron he might have liked to join any persons who wished to visit Alphonse Rothschild, he spoke as a Conservative Christian Anarchist and said—more or less— what many French anarchists were currently saying. When he said that Zola kicked the boiler over, he was referring to pent-up French anti-Semitism, which Zola's letter had released in the form of riots. When he said that in consequence the situation was worse than ever, he spoke as an American diplomat and friend of France who greatly feared the disappearance of France as a first-rate power. To him, it somewhat mattered that presumably innocent Dreyfus had been falsely convicted, expelled from the army, and imprisoned on Devil's Island; but it mattered incomparably more that the French army was showing signs of incapacity. Thus Adams's situation became one of hurt and distress. While other Americans hastened to experience a simple feeling that Dreyfus was innocent and deserved support, he understood that feeling, felt it very little, and strongly felt that the French army and government needed support because very probably at fault and drifting toward weakness, even collapse.[40]

Mrs. Cameron's attempt to meet her husband half way by living in New York created problems. She had written to Adams, "The eggs I am walking on have not smashed, but the tension keeps me so absorbed that I cannot concentrate on any thing else." Also she used a special word that Adams could decode. She said she was "homesick."[41]

On January 2, 1898, she had begun a week's return to Washington. One of her objects was to visit the State Department. She learned that Secretary Sherman, her debilitated uncle, viewed his secretaryship as "easy & delightful," and that Assistant Secretary William Day, who was doing Sherman's work, had become anxious to be relieved.

As Adams wished she would do, she visited his house and talked with

William Gray and Maggie Wade, his deserted servants. When writing to Adams about the visit, she said she felt "a sort of desperate desire to move my trunks in and stay there." Not doing so made her unhappy. "As I am now perfectly well, I don't fear any thing much—even a winter with Donald." "Alas! alas! that I am not with you."[42]

One of her terrors was that Adams's letters, which were reaching her every Saturday, would be delayed in transit when he was gone with the Hays to Egypt. She was writing weekly, as he was. On January 17, 1898, after returning to New York, she began a letter. She mentioned that Mrs. Wharton was "the most interesting woman I see." "Very intelligent, and so pretty to look at, too."

Next morning, when she was about to finish her letter, a newspaper was brought to her rooms. A few moments later, she told her distant partner: "The paper has just come up telling of anti-semitic riots in Paris. What fun! Hurray for Zola if he starts the ball. . . . What with riots in Paris, riots in Havana, anticipated riots in Madrid, the world is growing amusing again. Only I cannot *be* amused unless you are hear [*sic*] to be amused with me."[43]

Hay wanted to make his sixty-day leave an actual vacation.[44] He arrived in Paris on January 20 accompanied by wife, daughters Helen and Alice, and a young private secretary, Spencer Eddy. Adams awaited them at the Hôtel Brighton. That evening, Brooks and Evelyn took the Hays and Henry to see Coquelin in a new play by Rostand, *Cyrano de Bergerac*. As consolation for missing the performance, Henry sent Mrs. Cameron the play as printed.[45]

For Henry, return to Egypt was a risk. He and Clover had spent part of their wedding journey in 1872–1873 on the Nile. Sight of the river would inevitably remind him of that happy interval. Equally it might revive the shock and grief that had dogged him since her lapse into madness and suicide in 1885.

He had one upset. On February 2 at Cairo, the Hay party boarded a steam-driven riverboat and started for Memphis. Adams confided next day to Mrs. Cameron that the transition from shore to boat "came near knocking me quite off my perch." ". . . before I could catch myself, I was unconsciously wringing my hands and the tears rolled down in the old way, and I had to get off by myself for a few minutes to prevent Helen, who was with me, from thinking me more mad than usual. . . . A few hours wore off the nervous effect, and now I can stand anything, although . . . there is hardly a moment when some memory of twentyfive [*sic*] years ago is not brought to mind."[46]

From Adams's point of view, John and Clara Hay were uncomplicated people—as "simple as possible."[47] He was happy to assist them as companionable listener and experienced planner. Sometimes while the others in the party hurried to visit temples and tombs he earlier had seen, he stayed behind to write letters, paint, or read.[48]

Letters were reaching him from Mrs. Cameron. She had confessed on January 22 that her winter in New York was a "mistake." While touching on many subjects, she wondered what had happened to Clarence King. Her political news related mainly to Cuba. "Our brother McKinley keeps up the Peace cry—non-interference & all that[;] yet our fleet is gradually & very quietly concentrating around Key West."

She said in a postscript on the 25th: "I left this [letter] open for any news there might be. But I can see none. A [U. S.] warship has gone to Havana, but with Dupuy de Lôme's knowledge & consent."[49]

In Paris, Brooks was suffering torments. He had negotiated with Alcan, a well-known publisher, to issue a French edition of *The Law of Civilization and Decay*; but in his opinion the terms of the agreement were harsh.[50] He had engaged a translator, Auguste Dietrich, but the man had so limited a knowledge of English that Brooks gradually would find that he would have to translate the book himself.[51] Henry had slipped off to Egypt with the Hays; the French government had charged Zola with libel; a public trial was under way; and—as Brooks saw the matter—the French army had been betrayed by the French civil authorities. Indignantly, on February 14, he burst out to Henry, "Here are all the most distinguished officers in France, day after day brought up before a gang of dirty Jews, and badgered, and insulted, and held up to contempt with the connivance of the government. . . ."[52]

In Egypt, the travelers neared Assouan, the end-point of their journey. Henry passed his sixtieth birthday: February 16, 1898. On the 17th, a news bulletin arrived. It said that the American battle-ship *Maine* had exploded at Havana. On the 18th, Henry wrote to Mrs. Cameron: "What I heard yesterday about the destruction of the 'Maine' has made me turn yellow." The occurrence seemed mysterious and possibly unaccountable. ". . . as we have no particulars, I am the more depressed. How could the thing happen!"[53]

The *Maine* had exploded on February 15 while at anchor in Havana harbor. Whether the disaster was accidental or deliberate became a subject of intense speculation in many places. On the 20th, Brooks wrote to Henry from Paris: "I do not know when . . . I have regretted anything more than your absence during the last week. . . . In the first place, this business of the Maine, which I take to be part of a Carlist plot. . . . I wonder how Hay can be away from London. . . . Then comes this Zola business. . . . Anything like the bitterness of feeling, and the violence of the talk I have never heard. . . . The Nile is not the place for an hour like this."

The Hays' steamboat had turned downstream and would soon be at Cairo. Details about the explosion in Havana were still unavailable in Egypt, but news arrived from Paris that Zola had been convicted and sentenced to a year in prison. For Henry, the news was a last straw. He lost patience with almost everything in France, both bad and good. On the 26th, he part-comically remarked to Mrs. Cameron about Zola's prison sentence: "If he did not deserve it for the special offense, he did for his novels; and on the whole I think he had better have joined his friend Dreifus [*sic*] on the Devil's Island some time ago, with as much more French rot as the island would hold, including most of the press and the greater part of the theatre, with all the stock-brokers, and a Rothschild or two for example."[54]

Henry had told Mrs. Cameron that he had needed to get away from current affairs. ". . . Paris and Europe were becoming a bad nevrosis [*sic*]. . . ."[55] The worst strain on his nerves had been the frustration of his effort relating to Cuba. He had wanted the United States to recognize the independence of the Cubans voluntarily. The advantage of doing so had been manifest. Had Cleveland and Olney been willing to act or had McKinley and Sherman been willing to act, Spain could not have countered with a declaration of war—not without bringing the Latin America countries to the side of the United States in a pan-American alliance. There would have been small risk of war and an immense gain for American freedom.

At Shepheard's Hotel in Cairo during the evening of February 27, 1898, Adams and Hay listened to two well-informed Americans: James Angell, the U. S. minister to Turkey, and Hamilton Fish of New York, son of a former secretary of state. Adams listened with reluctance. He wrote to Mrs. Cameron, ". . . I heard what I have tried to put off so long, a little of the story of the 'Maine'. . . ."[56]

The story was hugely disturbing. It grew more so. In his usual quiet way, Adams asked Angell whether he knew at what hour the *Maine* had exploded. Angell gave the hour—9:40 P.M. Instantly Adams told the others: "Then the Spaniards did it."[57] As soon as possible, he retired to his room "and hid myself in bed." "Hardly had I turned off the stupid light, when a bang on my door started me up again." Hay's valet gave him a letter from Mrs. Cameron, sent from New York on February 11, four days prior to the explosion. She was transfixed by "this extraordinary Zola trial." "It convulses me—not with laughter—I have squasms, as Martha says, and after a column or more each day know less & less where any one is in it, or what it all means."

She sent news. Dupuy de Lôme had resigned and fled from Washington.[58] She was waiting for more news. "I watch the hours for the next newspaper, just as we did two years ago. . . . In the mean time, I find myself . . . in an exalted position. . . . I possess the only copy of Cyrano de Bergerac in New York."

Adams's portion was insomnia. He wrote to Mrs. Cameron next day, February 28: "Three long hours of midnight was the price I paid for my return to life from the tombs! As I am drawn back into the fascinating and horrible whirlpool of politics and finance, I thank the ill-luck that drove me away."

Someone suggested that Hay extend his leave and that the party go to Palestine, Lebanon, and Syria. Hay decided to forego the suggested trip, yet wished to return to London by way of Greece. Rockhill was in Athens. On March 4, 1898, wanting to visit him, Hay left with his dependents. Adams stayed in Cairo. The proposed journey was apparently his idea, and he was determined to make it.

He had reconsidered the news about the *Maine* and rather steadied himself. Next day, he told Mrs. Cameron: "My brother Brooks writes from Paris as though the world were coming to an end. His head is whisked round by the 'Maine' affair and the Spanish situation. You know how you and I have foreseen it all, these three years past, and we can afford to be cool."

Traveling where Adams wished to go could expose him to dangers. He hired a Muslim dragoman, Ibrahim, and with his help planned an itinerary that would take them to Alexandria, Jerusalem, Damascus, Smyrna, and Athens by April 1. By his own account, Adams was "a good traveller" if seasickness could be avoided. In the present case, he was venturing onto the Mediterranean in a small ship during a storm. He therefore took a precaution. "Having made friends with the chief-engineer[,] I bought out the second engineer's room . . . in among the engines [at the ship's center of balance]. . . . There I could lie all day and smoke and read and doze in peace and oil."

A different Jonah, he enjoyed being in the whale. "All night we rolled and tossed, and everything on the ship was on a rampage except me. In my den all was taut and steady, and not a pin broke loose."[59]

The port of access to Jerusalem was an unprotected roadstead. When the ship arrived, high winds and waves forebade the conveyance of passengers ashore. The ship proceeded to Beirut. There Adams landed and was told that the hotels were full and rail service to Damascus was interrupted by a blizzard.

He was happy, though cold. He wrote to Mrs. Cameron on March 12: ". . . my shivering Ibrahim has established me in a villa looking over gardens . . . onto a leaden sea, and mountains white with new-fallen snow. As I am thus imprisoned, and nothing will carry me anywhere, I sit down with my heaviest overcoat, feet positively icy, and fingers blue with cold, by an open window, to send you a despatch. Not that I can give you news of my future movements. Jerusalem will have to wait now till I die and go to the new one. . . ."[60]

Hay had written to Adams about a tour. ". . . [Rockhill] is looking forward with rapture to your coming next month. . . . He wants you to go with him to Constantinople, Sofia and the rest of his circuit, and I should think it would be a most amusing trip for you."[61]

The Rockhill-Hay proposal confirmed a pattern. Adams was functioning more and more as an unofficial diplomat closely linked with the official representatives of the United States in Europe.

As before, the diplomatic partnership Adams most wished to maintain was his secret and unlikely one with Mrs. Cameron. She reported to him from New York that her husband had left in a huff but had come back "apparently quite subjugated." In letters to Adams, she chronicled her states of mind and ended with a pleasing surprise.

> I cannot but feel that I really hold trumps now.
>
> My interest has been divided between our Maine & Mr Zola. . . . Can you solve that French problem? What does it all mean?
>
> . . . [Martha] is nervous, has no appetite, and yet is growing very fat. I think it is a question of hotel, pure & simple. I would take her away but I don't know where to go. The thought of your friendly house pursues me, but what would Mrs Grundy say?
>
> Donald actually talks of going abroad himself this summer. . . .
>
> I cannot see how war can be avoided. No one doubts that the Maine was blown up. . . .
>
> . . . I am sailing on the 30th of this month [March]. . . . It has come about perfectly smoothly, and I am coming as quick as the St. Paul can bring me. Donald will follow in May or June & spend the summer in England. . . . In the mean time, shall we come to Italy? or Paris? or London? or where??? Of course the absolutely necessary thing is that you shall be with us—or us with you. . . . I am cabling you . . . for the important [thing?] is that you shall be headed off from Russia.[62]

Like most Americans, Brooks felt that the destruction of the *Maine* portended war. Being in debt, he was anxious about renegotiating his loans in wartime. Even more, he was eager to be in Washington. He accordingly decided to postpone his travels with Henry and return to America. After reaching New York, he and Evelyn could go first to Henry's house. They might arrive when war-fever was running highest. He sent Henry word of the sudden change.[63]

As soon as trains resumed operation, Henry visited Damascus and the ruins of Baalbek. Later at Smyrna he received word that Brooks would not be coming to Athens.

The stop at Smyrna made possible a visit to Ephesus.[64] The few remains of the ancient city reminded Henry of the worst propensities of human beings. He wrote to Gaskell on March 30: "To see the clean sweep that mere changes in the channels of trade can make of the greatest cities of the world, is worth an effort. I do not know that I have ever felt a more acute sense of remoteness and desolation than today in the absolute wilderness that was formerly the center of art and life. . . . Nothing surprises me so much as the power of destruction in our race. They [human beings generally] seem to have made as much effort to destroy, as they ever made to create."

Because of errors by hotel-keepers, letters meant for Henry had been routed back to America, and he in reaction had ordered all his mail sent to Athens. He reached Athens on April 1 and next day wrote a letter to Hay urging him to rent a palace for the convenience of friends. "A Spanish war will hardly disturb me. Mrs[.] Cameron and Martha write me that they are coming over—in fact, they must be now at sea—and will arrive in London before this letter. Mr[.] Cameron is to follow, and Martha talks of ponies and our riding together in some English forest, instead of a French one. I ask no better. Find a ducal palace in the New Forest or the Dukeries, and ask us all to pass the summer."

That same day, April 2, 1898, Henry sent Brooks some words of reassurance. "As for my Washington house, the more you use it, the better. William and Maggy are longing for company. If you want the Beverly house, go to Edward Hooper about it."

In the same letter, Henry characterized himself as exceptional and foresighted. "I lose my head when other people are calm. The moment they get off their heads, I recover mine. For two years, the Cuban business drove me wild, because other people stupidly and brutally and wilfully refused to listen to its vital warnings. . . . As I told you in the Bryan campaign, my business is to look ahead. . . ."

He outlined his situation and disclosed his plans. "I never was afraid of a Spanish war. I'm not afraid of it now. . . . What I do fear is British finance." He also feared the Balkans. "My own wish is . . . to go up with Rockhill to the Balkan states, and try to get an idea of this great sorespot of Europe. That it is gangrened we know . . . . I want to find out whether the gangrene is spreading."[65]

When he traveled, Henry also read. In his current letters, he did not reveal what books he brought along or why he read them. One may guess that most of them related to the writing of *Mont Saint Michel and*

Chartres. One notices that, after the Hays left, he had visited Cairo's early mosques and saw their fine stained glass windows.[66]

Changes had occurred in relation to the *Memoirs of Arii Taimai.* By unknown means and at an unknown time, Henry had arranged that the chiefess, by dictating in Tahitian, would tell the story of her share in the island's history. Her story was to be translated and sent to him for use as the conclusion of the *Memoirs.* The arrangement was carried out in good time, before the onset of her last illness.[67]

Arii Taimai died on June 24, 1897.[68] Word of her death reached Henry in a letter from Tati Salmon—now missing—sent on July 12.[69] Presumably in Athens, he received a subsequent letter that Tati had started on February 12, 1898. In part, it concerned disputes among Arii Taimai's heirs about the division of property. Two of Tati's sisters had made extreme demands. "Marau has been the most troublesome, and I am afraid will be the *destruction of us all.* She will be a second Purea." "You are the only one I would write too [*sic*] of this, and you can imagine the state of mind I am in."

For Henry, the troublesomeness of Marau and the trust that Tati showed in him were guarantees that he could finish the *Memoirs* in the exact form he had wished the book to have. That he was silent about the guarantees in letters to Mrs. Cameron, Gaskell, and others did not indicate lack of interest. He was silent too about his progress in drafting *The Education of Henry Adams.* Perfect stillness was a sign that narratives would be completed.

Rockhill's wife Caroline and his elder daughter Dorothy welcomed Adams's arrival in Athena as an occasion for going to all the sites in Greece that he and they most wished to see. They made the arrangements, and Adams appreciated their kindness, but he had come with a particular motive. He hoped to feel what the ancient Greeks had felt in their more religious moments. For the purpose, his first ventures with Mrs. Rockhill and Dorothy were disappointments.

On April 5, 1898, after a climb on the Acropolis and a chance to look at the Parthenon, he wrote to Louisa Hooper: ". . . I cannot get to feel that Athens was ever a serious fact. Beautiful as a Greek temple was, I do not understand its fitness for worship; still less, for the residence of a God." ". . . [it] helps me to understand Greek history, but I did not come here to study history."

Hours at Eleusis and Sunium part-mended his unresponsiveness.[70] The great change came on April 19 on the slopes of Delphi. He wrote to Mrs. Cameron: "There is no excess at Delphi. The horror of the priestess' cavern is unseen and quite imaginary. The mountains are just imposing enough. The valleys are just far enough off, and the olive gives the tone of color. I was immensely pleased with the wonderful taste of it, as I always am with everything Greek. Only Delphi was the loftiest experiment they made, and the most daring." Still more strongly he wrote to Gaskell: ". . . [at Delphi] the Greeks . . . put all they had of faith and soul. . . . The place has [a?] quality of its own, unlike anything else in the world, and one hardly misses the buildings because clearly the religion of the place must have been anterior to them, and rather lessened than heightened by them."[71]

Mrs. Cameron was traveling toward Adams but had not learned his newest plans. She halted in Paris. Next she hurried to Venice on the chance that he could come there.[72] Writing thence on April 21, she told him she had rented a Paris apartment. (The address was 50 Avenue du Bois de Boulogne.) She meant to furnish it. ". . . then either of us can use it. . . ." She had already learned about his tour in the Balkans with Rockhill. She approved.

When she wrote, she did not know that one day earlier, on April 20, 1898, an ultimatum had been served on Spain by the United States government. The basis of the ultimatum was a joint resolution of Congress. The resolution recognized the independence of Cuba, demanded the withdrawal of Spanish forces from the island, empowered President McKinley to use the armed forces in support of the demand, and promised that Cuba would be self-governing when peace was arranged.

Spain responded on the 24th by declaring war on the United States. Mrs. Cameron learned the news. She wrote that day to Adams: "So war has come. How can you stay so far away from newspapers and from us? I want you to tell me what to think of it all."

They could meet soonest in Paris. She would be there sooner than he. Meanwhile, in sympathy with his Byzantine enthusiasms, she would hire a gondola and cross the lagoon to Torcello and Murano.

Mont Saint Michel and Chartres would rest on many bases but mostly on visits to churches, temples, and other sacred sites. When the Spanish-American War broke out, Adams was going to Constantinople in Rockhill's company with the intention of seeing the basilica of Santa Sophia.[73] Both city and church outran his anticipations. He wrote to Louisa Hooper on April 26. ". . . [Constantinople] is to me excessively interesting,—more so than any other city in the world. It is the epitome of universal history; the dust-heap where the human race has for ever [*sic*] dumped its vices and shame." "Naturally I rushed off at once to Santa Sophia. . . . I had not appreciated its possibilities. . . . I was lost in admiration of the astonishing cleverness of the men who, in the sixth century, when western civilisation had perished, and eastern was in full decadence, could build a structure that knocked cold all that Rome ever did, and all that the east ever has done. And yet it is the mere shell of what it was."

Rockhill sped them to Bulgaria. At Sofia on May 2, the minister and Adams were brought a garbled report saying that American warships had bombarded Cadiz in Spain. Adams wrote next day to Mrs. Cameron, "We promptly had a fit." "So far, good!" A later report from Spain said differently that an American fleet commanded by Admiral Dewey had clashed with a Spanish fleet off Cavite in the Phillipine Islands. The correction required a "change of hemisphere." From Serbia on May 5, Adams continued, ". . . Rockhill and I drink Dewey's health regularly every hour or two, and I guess that Cavite will serve. . . ."

He and Rockhill intended a stop at Bucharest in Rumania. A delay imposed by Serbian officials permitted Adams to reshape his plans. He deleted Rumania and advised Mrs. Cameron that he was going to Vienna and thence to Paris and London. "Diplomacy is likely to be amusing. . . . By all that is solemn, make London fit into your plans!" "Meanwhile, here I am at Belgrade, which is like being in the last century without picturesqueness. A deadly little place it is—a political, social and economical mistake from the start." ". . . at last things begin to move, and I want to join the dance."

Three weeks earlier from Athens, Adams had assured Mrs. Cameron that the changed posture of the United States with respect to Cuban independence was based on "our prodigious Cameron Reports." ". . . it was you and I who did all the real fighting against the odds when that hangman dog of an Olney went back on himself and us."[74]

Adams said too much. Secretary Olney had since vanished, together with President Cleveland. A Republican administration and a Republican Congress had come to power. They too had proved unwilling to take decisive action in Cuba's favor. If Adams's 1896 report was followed in April 1898, the willingness of Congress and McKinley to follow it was not traceable to what the report had said. Rather the willingness had been imparted physically—from Havana—by an explosion.

The situation was new. The outbreak of war and the naval battle that followed made Adams feel both elated and alarmed. From Belgrade on May 5, 1898, he sent Hay a letter expressing a wide range of ideas and feelings.

> I am dying of sheer curiosity to learn what Dewey has done at Cavite, for the Spanish account obviously omits all his serious work.
>
> . . . I expect . . . that diplomacy must now become pretty active, and as this is likely to be the last considerable settlement I shall witness, and as London

is likely to be the spot where one can see most, I intend to bestow on that commercial and rotten metropolis a portion of the coming summer. You may as well, therefore, resign yourself to that affliction.

. . . the worst and most nauseous dose Europe has yet had to suffer is the sight of our flag over Manila. . . . You have a new game to play, and I hardly see my clue. . . . I had not prepared myself for the new deal, and don't quite feel as though I knew the value of the cards or of the players.

For the most part, Adams's comments to Hay were candid.[75] Yet Adams faced the question, Who to trust? Adams viewed McKinley as the tool and creature of the America's capitalists. Hay admired McKinley unconditionally. On this score, the distance between Adams and Hay gaped extremely wide.

News had come that Mabel Hooper would soon be marrying Bancel La Farge, a son of John La Farge. For Uncle Henry, the news was a re-minder that older Loulie, soon to be twenty-four, had not found a hus-band. On the same day, May 5, 1898, he reacted by writing to Loulie with unprecedented frankness about her affairs—and his. He gave her an account of his ideas less modest than the one to Hay. "I wanted to see these so-called Balkan states in order to complete my knowledge of Europe, and to make up my mind whether America need bother about any immediate development of energy from hereabouts. Not much time was needed for settling that point. From here, America swells into gigan-tic proportions. She and Russia overshadow the earth. Western Europe quite disappears, and a new future world seems to take shape. . . ." "You remember my telling you a year ago that we had won the Cuban fight, but I could not yet say how much more. I am now going to see how much more." "Should I ever come back [to Washington], it will be to a new world. Our summer at St[.] Germain was a very fitting and tender farewell to the old one, and I meant it so."

En route to Vienna, Adams stopped at Budapest to take a look at Hungary's experiments in government. He wrote to Brooks on May 7, 1898: ". . . present Hungary is the child of State-Socialism in a most intelligent and practical form. . . . The forests, the mines, the banks, the very street-cars, and, for all I know, the babies and the pug-dogs, are, or might be, in principle, made, bred, and educated solely by and for the governing commissions or committees. . . . As one form of future society, it deserves a little attention, especially in connection with Russia; and, as it represents to me a possible future with which I sincerely wish I may have nothing to do, I recommend it to your notice."

The U. S. minister to Austria was Charlemagne Tower of Philadel-phia. Adams visited Tower on reaching Vienna and during an hour's conversation was pleased to learn that the minister was one of his former students. There was much to talk about, for the Austrian and Spanish royal families were related and might gain if the war between United States and Spain could be brought to an early close.

While in Vienna on May 9, Adams assured Mrs. Cameron that their country had changed in status. "We are already an Asiatic power! You and I hardly expected as much when we ran the December Report of '96. When the tide does run, it runs fast."

Brooks and Evelyn had arrived at 1603 H Street in late April 1898 just prior to the outbreak of war. They soon learned that Theodore Roosevelt had resigned as assistant secretary of the navy in order to command a unit of volunteer cavalry. Brooks wrote to Henry: "Poor Teddy has been completely carried off his legs. He has thrown up his place, and is going to take commission as lieutenant colonel of cowboys. We are all broken hearted about it. . . ."[76]

The idea that the United States should take advantage of the war with Spain to expand its territory and influence was an idea that many Americans were hastening to adopt. Henry reached Paris on May 16. He arrived an opponent of empire and a friend of peace. He wanted Hay to know his feelings. On the 17th, he warned the ambassador: ". . . this war is none of mine. My scheme was a very different one, and if war had followed, it would have been Spain's act, and all the Spanish American states would have been openly on our side. The Maine affair upset everything. The true culprits were Cleveland and Olney. . . ."

He had come to Paris mainly to join Mrs. Cameron.[77] While there, he wrote to Cunliffe reassuringly: "Paris still swarms with Americans in spite of the war, but most of my friends and relations have put on uniforms and expect to do some fighting. . . . My field of activity is much more on the side of making peace than war, and I hope that before the summer is over we may find a way out of the imbroglio."[78]

How much advice Adams could give Hay without giving him too much was a matter involving trial and error. From Paris on May 26, he sent Hay a set of terms he thought Spain might accept. "Spain recognises the independence of Cuba. She grants complete autonomy to Porto Rico. . . . The United States shall withdraw her forces from the Phillipines, on condition of retaining a harbor of convenient use for a coaling station. In consideration of these concessions, the United States will not exact a war indemnity."

Hay replied that he had thought of the same terms but would not venture an initiative. The reason was a change at home. John Sherman had been removed and William Day had been substituted as secretary of state. Day's appointment was a makeshift. All indications pointed toward an arrangement that would bring Hay to Washington to head the State Department and give it much-needed direction.

Adams planned to appear in London by June 1 and apparently did so. His immediate concern was to find a great house in the country, to be rented by himself and the Camerons with the object of affording the Hays a refuge away from London. On June 11, while seeking the house, he revealed to Brooks a panorama of worry. "I want peace. I want it quick. . . . I want it in order to recover our true American policy, which Congress has abandoned and which McKinley has betrayed. . . . I want it to save Cuba from the sugar-planters and the syndicates whose cards McKinley will play, and who are worse than Spain." "With these convictions, I am here to make peace if possible; but already the situation has run away with me. . . ." "As for the capitalists and their power, je m'en fiche pas mal [i.e. I do not care]. . . . It is the socialist—not the capitalist—who is going to swallow us next, and of the two I prefer the Jew."[79]

The great house Adams chose was Surrenden Dering, situated in Kent not far from London. While renting it with the Camerons, he retained rooms for himself in town on Clarges Street. His arrangements being made, he had only to put word about that an American summer country-headquarters was functioning in England and that guests, American and British, were wanted in any number. The Hays would stay there whenever it might suit them.

8

UNDER COVER

A Spanish fleet crossed from the Cape Verde Islands to the port of Santiago de Cuba and there found coal and apparent safety. On July 1, 1898, Yankee troops led partly by Colonel Theodore Roosevelt seized hills overlooking the port. Two days later while attempting an escape to sea, the fleet was destroyed by waiting U. S. warships. No longer having means to fight, Spain would have to sue for peace.

For Adams, good news from Cuba was followed by bad from Greece: Caroline Rockhill had died of typhoid. Fearing she had contracted the illness while helping him travel to places away from Athens, he wrote to Rockhill asking whether *he* had caused her death.[1] Rockhill replied that the illness started at a later time. Though relieved, Adams set his mind to moving Rockhill and his daughters to a place where they could better deal with their tragedy.

Hay was caught in the London season, but Clara assured Adams that the family would be coming to Surrenden Dering thereafter. On August 8, writing to Mabel Hooper, Adams mentioned that the Hays had arrived. Donald Cameron was at the house but did not cut a large figure. The work of providing for as many as twenty persons at once fell on his wife and Adams. Elizabeth Sherman Cameron had talents for directing guests and servants that befitted a niece of the general who had captured Atlanta, Savannnah, and Charleston.[2] Adams when young had performed domestic duties in comparable situations. In the present case, he did not grudge the effort. Yet he noticed its drawbacks. He remarked to Mabel on August 8: "It is no joke to run a hotel . . . and I am much struck by the demoralising effects of incessant attention to others. . . . One's energies are exhausted in housekeeping. One has no extra-energies to think of more distant things, to write letters, or to study or to think, at all."

On August 12, the war was officially declared to have ended. On the 15th by cable, President McKinley asked Hay to serve as secretary of state, replacing William Day, who would be sent to Paris to head a peace commission. Hay cabled acceptance and obtained the president's consent to complete his holiday at Surrenden Dering. His acceptance could be felt as a new justification for renting the house. It was as if the Camerons and Adams had had no motive except to provide a proper setting for an important public event. Yet the taking of the house had mainly reflected a reality very private and very secret.

If one may judge from her known actions and extant letters, the conduct of Elizabeth Cameron, beginning about the time of Martha's birth in 1886, had become that of a wife strongly resistant to sexual intimacy with her husband. Later Adams fell in love with her; and in the summer of 1890, prior to leaving for the South Seas, he told her what had happened. In early November 1891, after meetings with her in Paris and London, he wrote her a letter stating in pointed but acceptable language that, just as he could never have sexual relations with her, so also she could never have sexual relations with him.[3]

When Adams wrote the letter, Mrs. Cameron was crossing from Liverpool to New York on the *Teutonic*. Her principal reply took the form, not of words in letters, but of significant action. As has already been told, Adams returned to Washington in February 1892 and she immediately hurried him, with her husband, Martha, and others, to South Carolina. Till then she had not been in love with Adams in a way that would induce her to risk an affair. A gathering at her husband's vacation house would not seem an apt occasion for overtures of illicit love. Yet, beginning then, her and Adams's history became one of a man who had fully accepted the impossibility of their having sexual relations and a woman who—at a secret date entirely of her choosing—might prefer that such relations be one of the purposes of their arranging when possible to live near each other or live under the same roof; also their separating for long intervals to ward against possible gossip or accusation, not to mention public disgrace.

In the 1890s, as Mrs. Cameron well knew, adultery was criminal in America and Europe in the eyes of both religion and law.[4] Her disposition to commit adultery was a result of intensified love for Adams and mounting awareness of the emptiness of her marriage. By the time she and her husband appeared at Surrenden Dering in 1898, she had been unmarriedly married to Donald for twelve years. During a talk she and Adams had while running their hotel, she told him that her husband had had a "scrape" with a woman, was receiving letters from the woman that he wished not to receive, and was frightened by the possible results of his errancy.[5] The arrival of the woman's letters did not excuse whatever Mrs. Cameron and Adams may have done, or might begin to do, but her telling Adams about the letters made clear how inseparable she and Adams had come to be.

She and Adams did not know that nearly all their letters to each other would pass at future times under the eyes of biographers. When read in the 1990s, his letters to her from mid-November 1891 to the beginning of their stay at Surrenden Dering in 1898 would be useless for purposes of proving that he and she were lovers or when they became so. At most, they may show instead how well he could conduct an affair without letting the fact emerge in what he said in the mail. Oppositely, her letters to him, subsequent to their first visit to Coffin's Point, gradually became the writings of a woman frankly in love with the man to whom she was writing. The contrast did not mean she was less afraid of exposure than he. Perhaps they were equally fearful. But the basis of their intimacy was the strengthening of her desires. She wished him to know it. She was happy to say it.

Before obeying the president's summons to come home and be secretary of state, Hay had asked the opinions of the other adults then at Surrenden Dering. A discussion followed. McKinley seemed likely to be elected for a second term, ending in March 1905. It was foreseeable too that service as head of the State Department would expose Hay to positive danger. His health was good but precarious. Those asked none the less agreed that he should accept the appointment.[6]

During a talk by themselves or with Clara present, Hay told Adams that his willingness to serve depended on Adams's willingness to share the secretaryship and be "an associate in his responsibilities."[7] It was not suggested that Adams become an official: the sharing would be informal and secret. Adams assented.[8] He did not tell Mrs. Cameron about the new arrangement. Perhaps he was asked not to do so. He however disclosed it to Gaskell very sketchily and added a remark: "Evidently something is wrong with Hay—or with me."[9]

Rockhill had earlier served as third assistant secretary of state. He knew that Adams and Hay were close friends. On August 17, 1898, having learned that Hay would be secretary of state, he sent Adams a query: ". . . don't you think he could get me back in the department?"

The query reached Surrenden Dering when Adams was eating breakfast. In Adams's words, ". . . I threw it at once across the table to Hay. . . ." Hay read it, and a transfer for Rockhill became his and Adams's first order of business. Both men knew that, of the Americans versed in diplomacy, Rockhill was the one most familiar with China.[10]

While summoning many Americans to their great house, Mrs. Cameron and Adams also invited two Englishmen, Ralph Palmer and Cecil Spring Rice. Palmer was glad to flee his work as a London barrister. Again on leave, Spring Rice was being moved by the Foreign Office from Berlin to Constantinople. He had been privy to talks in London between

Hay and two high-ranking officials in the British government, Joseph Chamberlain and Arthur Balfour. One of his purposes in coming to Surrenden Dering was to deliver a message from Chamberlain to Hay.[11]

The eagerness of the British to accommodate Secretary Hay had a bearing on a difference between him and Adams. Over the years, Hay had become an Anglophile. He viewed the English-speaking peoples as uniquely beneficent and as superior to other peoples. His great wish was the achievement of union between the United States and the United Kingdom. He had made sympathy between the two powers the theme of his work as ambassador. He would do the same as secretary of state.[12]

Although he cared deeply about his English friends, Adams was very far from loving the English. He viewed the *Americans* as superior to other nations.[13] He wanted them to form friendly relations with other peoples, beginning with the Latin Americans, the French, the Spanish, and the British. Mainly he wanted the Americans to be independent.

Hay seemed not to notice the difference. Adams was glad to accept Hay as he was and try to help him. Yet Adams meant also to pursue his own objects. Unafraid of complexity, he would travel three secret roads. He would act alone. He would act in faithful partnership with Elizabeth Cameron. He would work with Hay.

After leaving politics, Cameron had taken a particular interest in the promotion of an American typewriter. One of his reasons for passing the summer in England was a schedule of business appointments on the Continent that he expected to arrange for the fall.

About September 1, 1898, the Hays returned to London. On the 8th, perhaps with Mrs. Cameron, Adams went to town, saw Hay, and wished him *bon voyage*. Adams would not sail till November and meant to give some of his time in the interval to other Adamses. Charles and his twin sons, John and Henry, came to Surrenden Dering, fresh from a bicycle tour on the Continent. About the time the visitors left, proofs of Brooks's *La Loi de Civilisation et de la Décadence* arrived from Paris. Helpful as always, Henry read them and mailed them with comments to Brooks at Quincy.[14]

On September 28 in London, *The Times* published a report that Henry Adams had been "suggested for Ambassador in London." Next day the Paris *Herald* reprinted the item.[15] A mere repetition of an old rumor, the report had no basis in any suggestion by Hay.[16] Yet it affected Henry as hurtful. It brought him into public notice at a time when, more than ever, he wished to be unseen and forgotten.

The lease at Surrenden Dering ran out on October 17. Henry and the Camerons moved to London and a week or so later journeyed together to the Hôtel Brighton in Paris. Henry said good-bye and took a train back to London.[17] Donald began his Continental tour as promoter of the typewriter. Mrs. Cameron hurried to her and Henry's fifth-floor apartment at 50 Avenue du Bois de Boulogne.

The apartment had at least four bedrooms. It would serve in part to house Henry's burgeoning Paris library, already delivered in boxes. That night, Wednesday, October 26, Mrs. Cameron wrote to Henry. She gave details. "Donald left an hour after your departure and I went at once to 50. Martha and Miss Lowe [the governess] joined me . . . and we worked all day there unpacking boxes and trunks. . . . You have no idea how nice it begins to look. . . . The table . . . is a brilliant success. . . . The hall rugs give an air of richness . . . and the dining room is charming with its new cabinet! *If* you were there!"[18]

She and Henry had parted with the expectation of being on opposite sides of the Atlantic till sometime in the spring, probably in May. Experience had taught her that the letters she wrote to him were always delivered and always safe in his hands. Yet she felt there were limits to what she could tell him in writing. She got around the limits by speaking in general. "I want to say a thousand things that I must not say. You will write soon, won't you?"

Adams slept on Wednesday in London. In the morning, he caught an early train to Crewe, was joined by Gaskell, and with him endured the long journey to Scotland. Sir John Clark awaited them in Aberdeen.

From the Palace Hotel on Friday, October 28, 1898, Adams reported to Mrs. Cameron: ". . . I am safely hidden. . . . But I rather dread emerging, and Washington looms rather absurdly big in the horizon."

From Tillypronie on Monday, he sent Rockhill a picture of what he would face at home. He gave no hint, indeed he denied, that he would have a political function. ". . . I expect to reach Washington in a fortnight. . . . I wish I could hear that you were going back there at the same time, for I am desperately alone—more solitary than I have been these thirty years. With Hay absorbed in work, Phillips dead, you away, the Camerons gone, and a new atmosphere in politics and society, I feel far more like seeking once for all my cheery final abode at Rock Creek Cemetery, than like chirping with nieces and quidnuncs at 1603 H Street."

Mrs. Cameron's letters were unceasing. She had told Henry on Saturday night, "It is a good thing Donald went away." She had added on Sunday night that she was too busy to see people, yet not "too busy to be homesick for you."

On November 4, Henry replied in dark tones. He said his heart was light "at hearing no more of my own name," yet sank into "horrible nightmares at the thought of the Square and its solitude."

That day, knowing he would board the *St. Louis* at Southampton on the morrow, she felt crushed. She asked him: ". . . how can I bear it? I thought it had reached its climax last year—that nothing could be harder. Well, I suppose that last year *was* worse[,] tho' today I do not feel that anything could be."

Writing to Rebecca Rae from Surrenden Dering, Adams had called the war with Spain "a queer war, with next to no one killed, and all the prisoners on one side."[19] Yet the war had immense results. Europe witnessed an assertion of American naval power. Spain lost her navy and her empire. Under cover of the conflict, the United States annexed Hawaii. U. S. troops seized Cuba, Puerto Rico, Guam, and part of the Philippines. In a glare of publicity, heroic Colonel Roosevelt consented to run for governor in his home state, New York.

Crossing on the *St. Louis* afforded Adams the novel experience of an electric lamp in his cabin. On November 11, 1898, at the dock in New York, passengers shouted to onlookers, asking whether Roosevelt had been elected. The exultant answer was yes.

Adams wanted to get home unnoticed. "Punctual as a true Dreyfussard, I arrived on Sunday afternoon at five o'clock, and came up by cable-car as it were incognito. . . . John Hay stumbled over me at my very doorstep, and came in to sit an hour. . . ." Later Spencer Eddy appeared and surprised Adams by saying there had been "some idea" in the State Department of making him—Adams—ambassador to England.[20]

Adams's actual status in the McKinley administration was evidenced by an observable routine. On November 21, he told Mrs. Cameron: "At four o'clock, Hay generally comes for a walk, and we tramp to the end of 16th Street discussing the day's work at home and abroad. Then at five we get back to Mrs[.] Hay's tea[,] where some one, agreeable or otherwise, generally drops in. About six I return to my den. . . ." Except when prevented by interferences such as bad weather, the secret co-secretaries continued their talks-while-walking.

They did not keep any records. Yet a comment is possible about the the scope of their talks. That Hay decided their scope was confirmed by a remark Adams made to Mrs. Cameron: that the subject of each talk was "the day's news and the morrow's prospects."[21] Hay was a creature of the present.[22] Where he was weak, Adams was strong. As much as other people, Adams liked to keep abreast of news and all sorts of gossip. Yet by nature and self-education, he belonged to the small minority of humans whose attention was ever-rooted in the future. That he was the country's best-informed historian was one of the proofs of the fact. He conducted historical inquiries, not as an antiquarian fixed on the past, but instead as a learner attuned to future times.[23] His inquiries helped him consider the question he felt was most important to him: What would the Americans—or, for that matter, what would all peoples—be best advised to do next?[24]

That winter, Adams devoted parts of his time to small tasks. He freed space on his shelves by giving books and bound volumes of historic American newspapers to Western Reserve University in Cleveland. He went through his wife's books, discarded some, and gave others to his Hooper nieces. He read his *History of the United States* and sent the publisher a battery of corrections. He catalogued his collection of Greek coins—a collection started by John Quincy Adams, expanded by Charles Francis Adams, and re-expanded by himself.

One task went unmentioned in his letters. While seeming not to do so, he transformed the *Memoirs of Marau Taaroa/ Last Queen of Tahiti* into a longer narrative: *Memoirs of Arii Taimai e/ Marama of Eimeo/ Teriirere of Tooarai/ Teriinui of Tahiti/ Tauraatua i Amo.*[25]

All the tasks were the pleasanter for Adams to perform because McKinley required the American commissioners in Paris to negotiate a peace treaty with Spain granting independence to Cuba. It was true that the commissioners required also that Spain cede Puerto Rico, the Philippines, and Guam to the United States. It was true as well that Adams had not favored these acquisitions. But he wanted the Cubans to be free, and McKinley's course seemed to assure that they would be.

An old treaty between the United States and England forbade each country to build, without the consent of the other, a canal linking the Caribbean Sea and the Pacific Ocean. Hay wished to modify the treaty to permit work on a U. S. canal in Nicaragua or Panama; he wished to settle differences with Canada about the boundary between Canada and Alaska; and he intended to bring Rockhill home as his official adviser with regard to China. He could achieve these and other objects only with the support of the Senate. His special need was the full support of Senator Lodge, chairman of the senate's committee on foreign relations. He did not have it.

Donald had led Mrs. Cameron to suppose that he meant to stay in Europe through the winter. She accordingly arranged Martha's admission to a Paris school. She then learned that Donald might return to America in December, leaving her and Martha in Paris. On November 25, 1898, she wrote to Adams, ". . . you will come over early!"

On the 29th, she announced that Donald was sailing in two weeks *from Genoa.* "Is not that astonishing!" ". . . it leaves us planted in Paris, in our own appartment [*sic*], with all the winter before us—and you on the other side! *Could* things be more exasperating! I feel so full of ideas and thoughts that I can scarcely write."

On December 4, prior to the arrival of her astonishing news, Adams began his first letter. He said Loulie was with him and he had done some silent listening. "Cabot [Lodge] came in at dusk, and Hay afterwards, and, for an hour they talked Senate and Treaty, and dreary Senatorial drivel. I sit silent. What do I care whether the Treaty is ratified, or whether we take the Philippines? I've won all my stakes. The Spaniards are almost out of Cuba, and are wholly out of Porto Rico. Our country has asserted its right and power even more emphatically than I tried to assert it."

Her news arrived next day and placed Adams under conflicting pressures. One was the necessity of maintaining the concealment of his and Mrs. Cameron's true relation. A second was the obligation to stay in Washington long enough to do for Hay all that could be done to help him through his first winter as secretary. A third was a large gap in Adams's preparations to write *Mont Saint Michel and Chartres*. He needed to see Monreale, the cathedral built in Sicily in the middle ages by the Normans. If he could get to Sicily, he would want also to see ancient Greek sites, especially at Syracuse and Taormina.

Hay and Adams were so conducting themselves as to make their adjoining houses a near equivalent of one household. A person to whom both men could turn as a confidante, though for different reasons, was Anna Lodge. In December, Adams suggested to Mrs. Lodge that all the Lodges should go to Italy in the early spring, accompanied by himself. He particularly suggested a foray into Sicily before the onset of hot weather. For her, the new plan resembled the old one that had taken the Lodges and Adams to Mont Saint Michel and Chartres.

For Adams, the new plan was indispensable, yet confining. He advanced it at the cost of making himself an appendage to the Lodges, committed to stay with them through the whole course of their journey. There was a question, too, whether Senator Lodge would be free to go.

In Paris, by arrangement with Mrs. Cameron, Palmer came from London to spend a few days with her and Martha at 50 Avenue du Bois de Boulogne. It was hardly usual for an unmarried male English visitor to stay in the Paris apartment of an American wife unattended by a husband. The comings and goings of the London barrister attracted notice, which perhaps was what Mrs. Cameron had wished to bring about.

After Palmer left, on January 4, 1899, she wrote to Adams emphatically: "What I want is you, you, you, and we can do plays and run around and shut our doors to this [American] colony here. They are worse than I thought them." She liked being an apartment dweller. "It is so comfortable and easy and independent. . . ." "All Paris has been excited about the man who was stopping with me!" "You have so many things here you will feel at home at once."

On January 8, Adams sprang news of his own. "Cabot [Lodge] . . . meditates an early start for Europe. In fact he has authorised and instructed me to engage March passage to Naples. . . . How will this suit you? Can you be in Italy in April? If so, we can meet in Rome or Naples;, but do not mention our plan till you hear it from sister Anne, or outside, for as yet it is much in the air."

Adams said nothing about going to Sicily to see Monreale. Neither did he disclose that he would soon be writing a book of a new kind, an education for young women titled *Mont Saint Michel and Chartres.* Yet he did say what she most wished to hear: that he could be expected to be in Europe by April, albeit in Italy, not in Paris.

Lodge vetoed passage to Naples because the ship was German. A revised plan was adopted. The Lodges and Adams would sail from New York for Southampton on March 25.

Adams and Mrs. Cameron gained greatly by the change. She could stay in Paris, and Adams could join her before going to Italy. On January 27, having learned of the revision, she told him: ". . . you and I can run about together and have *such* a good time. And I think you might remain in *our* appartement—at least for a while, don't you?"

Ford had left the government and taken a post at the Boston Public Library. On November 21, 1898, he had written thence to Adams: ". . . my great regret in leaving Washington is to be deprived of your chats. It is so rare to meet a man who inspires as well as explains, that I value the man in Washington who did both, and royally."

Adams said in reply that the world had "moved with bewildering rapidity." He believed the economic movement outran the political. ". . . the greatest revolution of all seems to me to be that astounding economical upheaval which has turned America into the great financial and industrial centre of the world, from being till now a mere colonial feeder of Europe. It was this that we saw impending three years ago, but without a suspicion of its imminence."[26]

From the start, Adams's winter in Washington was bleak. He had confessed to Rockhill on December 22: "I am pretty solitary . . . and have no companion but Hay. I miss Phillips terribly." There was no possibility of Rockhill's returning to the State Department. McKinley had filled all the places with presidential appointees. As the readiest alternative, Hay arranged that Rockhill be made chief officer at the Library of Congress. Unfortunately senators would go to disgraceful lengths to propitiate constituents. An unfit candidate in Massachusetts wanted the

opening at the Library. Senator Lodge supported the candidate. Rockhill's opportunity evaporated.

Frustration with regard to Rockhill was typical of Hay's trials. The
peace treaty with Spain was ratified by the Senate only after a struggle
and by a margin of one vote. The effort to settle differences with Canada
came to nothing. Hay negotiated a treaty with England to permit the
linking of the Caribbean and Pacific with a canal, but the Senate wanted
the treaty altered. Hay meanwhile had to humor McKinley's wife. Adams
told Mrs. Cameron on January 29: ". . . the irritation which counts double or treble all the rest, is the Court work at the White House; the
Cabinet dinners; and the duty of attendance on poor Mrs[.] McKinley.
This last must be terrible."

Servitude for Hay went hand in hand with relief for Adams. In the
same letter, he told Mrs. Cameron: ". . . I hug myself with delight that
no one knows my existence. Now I must send a long telegram to Rockhill
to explain the snags in the way of his appointment to the Library. Ain't
I just important? All the same, important or impertinent, I'm drearily
homesick for Martha and you."

Cubans were learning that the Yankee government assumed that
U.S. military occupation of Cuba and Cuban independence were equivalents. The Philippinos were learning a similar lesson. The official most
in the way of independence for both peoples was McKinley's incompetent secretary of war, Russell A. Alger. Hoping that he could help them
deal with Alger, the Cubans returned to Adams's house. Philippine
agents hovered near. On February 6, 1899, Adams reported to Mrs.
Cameron, "I have had constant communication with [such agents] . . .
through Rubens, my Cuban manager. . . ."

Henry almost believed that he and the Cubans could bring Alger to
reason. On the 27th, he recounted to Mrs. Cameron the brighter side
of a dark story. "Quesada and Rubens still come to consult me almost
daily, and, what is far more bewildering, they follow my advice. If it were
not for poor Alger, who is simply senile and irresponsible, and who always upsets tomorrow what he and we agreed upon yesterday, I should
feel that for once I had been allowed to have absolutely my own way in
the government on a policy so huge as that about Cuba since 1894,
which you and I fought out to a finish."

Martha Cameron had always known Adams by a funny name,
"Dordy Dobbitt," and had always heard her mother address him, and
speak of him, as "Dor." As nearly as Martha was allowed to know,
"Dordy Dobbitt" had two meanings. Part of the time, Adams was Dr.
Dobbitt, keeper of a school she went to; and the schoolhouse was his

study at 1603 H Street, which had a cupboard containing a dolls' house entirely hers. The rest of the time, she was a mother and Adams was her son, "Little Dordy," who was always growing younger, as well as smaller.[27]

In the winter of 1898–1899, Martha was nearing thirteen, and Adams wished not to continue as teacher. He had cautioned her in December about Dr. Dobbitt, "He's getting to be a horrid cross old nuisance, and ought to give up keeping school." Yet he had ended his letter: "Lots of kisses! Love to grandma. Affly your own Dordy."[28]

There was very little chance that Martha could think of the tie between "grandma" and Adams in any but an innocent light.[29] For other observers also, her mother and Dor lacked the appearance of adulterers.[30] Whether they were with Martha, or exchanging letters, or with friends, acquaintances, relations, or strangers, Mrs. Cameron and Dor were too much at ease, too harmonious, too amused and happy, and above all too clear in conscience either to be or seem to be wretched sinners, whatever they had done or might soon begin to do.[31]

Irritations mostly created by the Senate made Clara Hay declare that her husband would cease being secretary at the end of McKinley's present term. In sympathy, Adams studied the history of the Roman senate. Rockhill meanwhile wrote to Adams from Athens saying he wanted to go back to Tibet or, if Henry would go with him, to Caucasia.[32]

The imminence of Adams's departure for Europe made Hay anxious to speak. From the State Department on March 21, 1899, he sent his associate a short note. It mainly said, "If we should not meet again[,] I want to say how deeply I am in your debt. . . ."

Adams and the Lodges crossed to Southampton. Adams left his companions in London and went to Paris. On April 6, 1899, he informed Gaskell: "I am just now at the Hotel Brighton, 218 Rue de Rivoli, but my banker is Morgan, Harjes & Co[.,] Boulevard Haussmann, who will forward my letters." Writing to Hay on the 11th, he explained that he was staying "with Martha."

Dor would be in Paris for two weeks. Palmer had chosen the moment to return for a few days to 50 Avenue du Bois de Boulogne. Though he did not mention Mrs. Cameron in his letters, it is clear that Dor and she had opportunities to be by themselves.[33]

The Lodges came to Paris, ready to start for Italy. Mrs. Cameron hesitated but chose not to join the travelers. They left. On April 13, 1899, she advised Dor: "Tomorrow night I am going to dine & go to a play with W[illiam]. Vanderbilt—so have I fallen! Come back soon." Next day she ended a letter, "It seems a year since you left." "Good-bye, I *hate* to have you gone!"

In Rome, Lodge took Adams to call on an American couple, Winthrop and Margaret Chanler, with the result that Adams met the Chanler's eldest child, an enchanting girl named Laura. During later visits to the Chanlers, Adams by-passed the grownups, asked for Laura, spent time just with her, and made her a friend.[34] Shamelessly he told her things that were interchangeable with things he had earlier said to Martha, most notably that she, Laura, was his mother.

On April 17, he asked Mrs. Cameron to tell Martha about his behavior. "Tell her that the Chanler girl . . . and I are great friends, and are going doll-hunting. She is eleven, and thinks it is a great idea that I am only five-and-a-half, and growing downwards."

Laura changed the pattern. One day she asked Adams to stay for lunch. He and Laura's parents become well-acquainted. Mrs. Chanler later recalled the lunch as a complete success. "We discovered at once that we [the parents and Adams] immensely enjoyed one another's company and that we must be together as much as possible."[35]

That Adams became friends with Winthrop Chanler was a gain: the husband was a good fellow. The addition of Mrs. Chanler to Adams's life was an event. It was his first chance to learn what a Catholic American woman could be like. She was better educated than the other women he knew well. In time, she would elicit from him some of the best expressions of his ideas.

Adams's strong interests in the medieval Norman colony in Sicily and in the ancient Athenian colonies in Sicily and southern Italy proved infectious. He easily persuaded Senator Lodge, the senator's sons, and "Winty" Chanler to travel with him to a careful selection of Sicilian historic and archaeological sites. The party left Rome on April 22, 1899, intending to return by May 1.

On reaching Palermo, they went at once to the eleventh-century Norman cathedral. Adams began an account of their experience in letters to Mrs. Cameron. ". . . I saw Monreale and the mosaics, and . . . these were worth while. They make even Ravenna modest."

Downright astonishment began with the ancient Greeks. "Girgenti as a landscape is Athens with improvements." ". . . [it is] the most beautiful Greek ruin I know; far more charming than Athens or Corinth or even Delphi or Smyrna, and of course out of all comparison with places like Ephesus or Alexandria."[36]

By the time the party saw the remains of Syracuse, Adams's interest had become concentrated on the Greeks as "landscape-gardeners." "Girgenti and Syracuse were interesting studies in that profession, but yesterday came the climax at Taormina. Nothing in Japan compares with the vigor and genius which the Greeks put into this poor little colonial mountain-side. . . ." Adams seemed almost envious. ". . . the Greek is the only man who ever lived that could get the whole value out of his landscape, and add to it a big value of his own. His share counts for almost as much as the share of nature. The wretch was so complete an artist that big or little was equally easy for him to handle, and he took hold of [Mount] Etna as easily as he did of the smallest lump of gold or silver to make a perfect coin."[37]

The upshot was very high spirits. Adams crowned his pages to Mrs. Cameron with delighted lies. ". . . I am past literary ambition." "No one ever will be educated again. . . . We may as well be contented in our vulgarity, and be satisfied with dry champagne and the electric light, for at least the Greeks did not have these."[38]

Hay arranged that Rockhill head a Washington agency, the International Bureau of American Republics—later the Pan American Union. It was understood that the appointee's main duties would relate to Hay's work at the State Department. Rockhill started toward Washington. He contrived to meet Adams and the Lodges in Naples and travel with them as far as Rome. Writing thence on May 4, 1899, Adams suggested to Hay that Rockhill and his daughters live at 1603 H Street. ". . . it might be better and handier to you . . . that he should be close at hand like a private secretary."

Adams's experiences in Sicily gained in retrospect. On May 12 while still in Rome, he wrote to Mabel La Farge, ". . . Monreale and Taormina—are an education in themselves. . . ." He continued unrestrainedly: "Nobody but the Greeks ever knew anything about art. Nobody but the French ever knew anything about religion."

Mrs. Cameron wanted Dor back in Paris. Donald at any moment might require her and Martha's returning to America. In keeping with her wish, Adams propelled the Lodges northward ahead of schedule.[39] For reasons relating to his *Mont Saint Michel and Chartres*, which would partly concern Saint Francis, he shepherded them by way of Assisi and its thirteenth-century church. Irreligiously he reported to her: "The upper church is beautifully done . . . with every inch covered with fresco by Giotto or his fellows, in blues and gold and reds until, as one looks down from the high altar, the effect is that of a very charming ballroom. I felt as though I should ask Martha to give me a turn down the nave."[40]

By letter on May 16, Mrs. Cameron told Dor that she might have to sail for New York on July 1. "I am growing very impatient." "I love this Paris appartement, & the independence and the liberty,—and the balcony and the birds—how can I leave! You and I could do so much this summer! Well, all hope is not yet lost."

In Washington, Rockhill chose not to live at 1603 H Street. Hay was glad to have his help but did not treat him as a replacement for Adams. On May 18, Hay complained to his absent co-secretary: "The worst of my present job is that I can delegate so little of it. It is a grim, grey world you have left me to, with nobody to talk to, or to walk with, to keep me in the straight path by showing me the crooked."

On May 22 or thereabouts, presumably with the Lodges, Adams arrived in Paris.[41] The Lodges lingered, expecting to sail in mid-June. Adams stayed at hotels, first at the Westminster, then the Wagram. He and Mrs. Cameron were again together.

He was disclined to write letters.[42] He however received one from Mrs. Chanler that overflowed with kind feelings. "I wonder when we shall meet again—in what country or what continent. Soon I hope[,] before Laura outgrows your affection. . . . Laura sends a great deal of love to her little boy. . . . Your grandmother (I cannot see that I am anything else) wishes you a very pleasant summer. . . ."[43]

From the start, the Dreyfus case had been treated by the French anti-Semites as a god-sent opportunity to assail the French branch of the Rothschild family, their Paris bank at 19 Rue Laffitte, and its leading owner, Baron Alphonse de Rothschild.[44] This complication of the case was greatly re-complicated by the French anarchists, who hated Baron Rothschild while also hating the French anti-Semites.[45]

On June 3, 1899, a supreme French tribunal, the Court of Cassation, directed that Dreyfus be returned to France so that his case could be retried. The order meant that millions of persons in Europe and America would have to weather a new round of Dreyfus excitements.

The Dreyfus Affair was reshaping France and might reshape the entire world. Adams and Mrs. Cameron were in Paris and were constantly bombarded by the Affair's excitements. For them, it became much more than an interest. It approached being an occupation.

Henry received news from Brooks that he planned a trip with Evelyn to Russia, Siberia, and Peking in the autumn. He wanted Henry to join them. On June 12, Henry refused. He said: "I shall probably pass the summer quietly here alone. On the whole, if one must be alone, Paris is the best watering-place."

A letter from Loulie waited an answer. Writing from the Hôtel Wagram on the 25th, Uncle Henry offered a fictitious account of recent Parisian loneliness. ". . . I wander, week after week, in solitude, through the streets and the sales-rooms, hunting amusement." He mentioned other Americans. "Spencer Eddy is coming here to be Second Secretary. . . . Joe Stickney is here. Mrs[.] Cameron and Martha are just sailing for home."

The account was untrue. Mrs. Cameron and Martha were not to sail for another eleven or twelve days.[46] Thus for seven unbroken weeks, from May 22 through July 7 or 8, 1899, Dor was free to take meals and otherwise be at home at 50 Avenue du Bois de Boulogne.

On shipboard on July 11, three or four days after she and he said their goodbyes, Mrs. Cameron wrote to him: "I never cease thinking of 50, and I keep my watch at Paris time because I then can tell pretty well just what you are doing. You are *just* going to dinner now—exactly eight [o'clock] in Paris, but here we have just had tea."[47]

Donald made the mistake his wife had earlier made. He arranged that she and Martha stay at an American facility accessible to himself. The one he chose was the Oriental Hotel at the east end of Coney Island. Other than protection against the worst extremes of New York's summer heat, the hotel had little to recommend it.

The departure of mother and daughter from the Paris apartment had been Dor's signal to quit hotels and move in. He told Mrs. Cameron in his first letter, "It was not cheering to move down into your deserted rooms and to choke over a solitary breakfast." He accounted for his time. "I work on French all day." He mentioned going to Versailles to see a female couple he much liked, the actress Elsie de Wolfe and her stout companion, intelligent Elisabeth Marbury.[48] In new letters, he made similar assertions. "I labor over French six hours a day. . . ." "I study French or write letters." ". . . I study my French prepositions and walk in the Bois." ". . . I have done nothing all this month but study French prepositions and subjunctives. . . ."[49]

She knew, in part, what he really was doing. He had told her in conversation that he was going to write a travel book. Yet it was not till August 15 that he admitted to her in a letter: "I am seriously thinking of writing at last my *Travels in France with Nothing to Say*, and printing it privately. . . . I have it all in my mind. It would cost a year[']s work and about a thousand dollars."[50]

Even then, he did not tell her an important added truth. He was not the sort of writer who could study a subject, learn enough about it to write something worth saying, and then go on to something else. Rather he was the sort who would study a subject before, during, and after he wrote about it, would try to extend his knowledge as far as possible, and would always make sure his interest deepened.

The maid, Victorine, had relegated Mr. Adams to the blue bedroom. Mrs. Cameron thought her own room would be cooler. She advised Dor, "I am sure that my bedroom,—with the iron shutters closed all day—is the most comfortable to sleep in, & you had better try it." By way of news, she said that Governor Roosevelt had come to the Oriental Hotel and behaved like an obstreperous child. "Teddy spent Sunday here. . . . He is only two, and cannot grow up."[51]

The Brooks Adamses were in Germany. Word reached Henry that Evelyn had broken down and that she and Brooks had gone to Dresden, the nearest city, to await her recovery. Henry viewed Evelyn's illness as a reminder. He thought married women over forty needed continual protection against strains.[52] A case in point was Evelyn's sister, Mrs. Lodge. While abroad in the spring, "Sister Anne" had been quite ill.

Hay had gone to his summer home in Newbury, New Hampshire. He sent Adams a cry for help that had the form of a friendly letter, yet was historically important. He explained: ". . . the State Department, always impossible, has been a little Hell upon earth for the last few months. It was bad enough before you went away; but it has grown constantly worse, and there being no one to talk to, and call it names, makes the whole thing intolerable." The key problem was the Constitutional provision requiring that treaties be ratified by two-thirds of the Senate. "We have five or six matters now demanding settlement. I can settle them all, honorably and advantageously to our own side, and I am assured by leading men in the Senate that not one of these treaties, if negotiated, will pass. . . ."

Hay wanted Adams's ear. "I wish I might talk of it with you. I know of nobody to whom I might mention the matter who would not think it either pose or madness." There were passages in his letter that were not dark. He had lunched with Mrs. Cameron in New York and was told by her that she had met some New York politicians and tolerated their company—"like the cynical saint she is." He confessed to being fond of being secretary of state. "My nature, like the dyer's hand[,] has been so subdued to Washington that I pine for the purgatory I have left, even here, in the delicious air of these hills."[53] Yet he left no doubt that Adams's answer was sorely needed.

Adams was slow to reply. He perhaps needed time to think. He to some extent was distracted by the second Dreyfus court-martial, which had begun at Rennes in Normandy on August 4. There was also the melodrama of an urban siege. The French government had attempted a roundup of anti-Semites, had partly succeeded, but had met resistance from a die-hard leader, Jules Guérin, who barricaded himself and some followers in his house near the Gare de l'Est in the Rue du Chabrol. "Fort Chabrol" acquired a resemblance to a scene in the American Wild West. Unsure what to do, troops and police loafed nearby.

Events in France descended from very bad to even worse. At Rennes on August 14 while approaching the court, Fernand Labori, Dreyfus's chief lawyer, was shot in the back. His assailant—assumed to be an anarchist—eluded the police and remained at large. Dreyfus's other lawyer failed to win a suspension of the trial. The proceedings continued with small prospect of an acquittal.

Brooks had given up Siberia and Peking but wanted Henry to go to Russia with him and Evelyn. Also Brooks sent a manuscript. An article of his had been rejected by an American magazine, *Forum*, and he wanted an opinion.[54] Henry read the article. On Sunday, August 20, 1899, he wrote considered replies both to his brother and to Hay.

The lines he sent to Brooks were exceptionally Delphic. ". . . I am rather impressed by the fact that the cleverest men are saying least. . . . The immediate situation, whether in Europe or America, is rather a false one. . . . Dishonesty is the only possible policy, and if one must be dishonest, one had better hold one's tongue. If I were a socialist, I might be honest and loquacious at once, although the French socialists don't impress me that way—on the contrary. But we are not socialists, and at bottom we regard socialism as the hollowest humbug ever yet struck in history; if anything we are anarchists, and once more I repeat that our attitude towards the immediate present is one that admits of no transactions [i.e. no compromises]."

As for Russia, Henry would not go. "I loathe the country and the people. What I really want is to go there ten years hence. But every year is so much advantage, and some one year will produce a sudden enormous change. That is what I want to see."

His program for the moment was strict seclusion. ". . . I am growing old and you can't count any more on me for any purpose. I drift under cover, and have no idea but to get decently and quietly under ground. People naturally laugh at this—rather nervously,—but it's true. I want to get out of it. . . . I find Paris on the whole the easiest, most natural, and most ornamental sepulchre for the still living. Here I stay, and here you will probably find me. . . ."

Writing to Hay was difficult. Henry had two things on his mind: the secretary's woes and the breakdown of France. He turned first to the breakdown. ". . . the Dreifus business has proved to be even more grave than I feared, and has struck a blow at the republic . . . that seems to me fatal." ". . . [the] affair is a moral collapse that involves soldiers and civilians alike. . . ." "The army, the navy and the civil government have all admitted and proclaimed their incapacity to maintain France as one of the great powers. In that case, a new world must come."[55]

Hay's woes seemed open to treatment, provided the treatment was drastic. "Your business is to devise a set of arrangements by which you can run the machine along without settling anything. You want to invent a new modus vivendi for every dispute, which shall not need the approval of the Senate, and shall not leave any more record than is necessary. The process is more troublesome, but, with tact and good-nature, it does not seem necessarily less effective, than that of negotiating permanent treaties, usually unsatisfactory in the end."[56]

What Henry prescribed could be restated as three rules. Achieve a measure of international cooperation without negotiating treaties. Obviate record-keeping. Avoid the Senate. The rules ran contrary to American precedent. Yet Hay was likely to follow them when possible, almost as if he himself had been their author.

The French anarchists conscientiously objected to religion.[57] After dark on Sunday, August 20, 1898, to use Adams's term, a small "battle" was fought in Paris. ". . . my friends the anarchists . . . stormed a church and scared a sexton green."

Word spread that the anarchists were going to attack the anti-Semites at Fort Chabrol on Monday afternoon.

On Monday, Adams crossed Paris ready for combat. On Tuesday, he finished a report for Mrs. Cameron. "I went up . . . to see the fort in the Rue Chabrol and to lend a hand to the anarchists and the Dreifussards if they needed it." "I found the streets barred by a double line of troops and police, but the crowd[,] which more or less filled the Place in front of St[.] Vincent de Paul and the Rue Lafayette[,] was perfectly quiet, largely of women, and I heard not a cry or sound of excitement. I walked down [i.e. back] in disgust."

Mrs. Cameron was hoping she could spend some days in Washington at summer's end, with Martha and without Donald. She secured Dor's approval of her and Martha's staying at his house.[58]

More recently, at Donald's behest, she had left Coney Island, witnessed illegal gambling at the United States Hotel in Saratoga, and sought cooler air at Saranac Lake in the Adirondacks.

A bit at a time, Adams was letting others know that his work was taking new turns. On August 26, he confided to Gaskell, ". . . I stay quietly in doors when the mercury rises above 80°; and read mediaeval architecture." (He evidently was finishing chapters of *Mont Saint Michel and Chartres*.) He told Mrs. Cameron three days later,: "All last week I saw not a person. Plunged deep into an architectural study of Mont Saint Michel, I hardly went out of the house."

She had told Dor she was trying to wrest from Donald an agreement that she could return to Paris. Dor assumed she would prevail. At the same time, he grew vexed by the opacity of the Dreyfus Affair. He complained to her on September 5: ". . . the Dreifussards have put forward no theory to go upon. Sometimes they call [the original charge] . . . a mistake of judgment; sometimes a conspiracy of the staff. Both theories have been adopted or discarded in practice, and no one can tell us today whether the Dreifussards hold that there was no treason at all, or whether Esterhazy was a real traitor, or whether the bordereau was or was not a serious communication. . . . I grant the innocence of Dreifus, if that is wanted, without question. The party who is on trial now is not Dreifus but the army and people of France; and all I want to know is whether they are more rotten than other armies and other peoples."

In one part of his life, Dor felt dissatisfied. ". . . all has gone to disappoint us anarchists. We sacked a church, it's true, but Paris did not care. Paris seems indifferent to everything." In another part, he was content. ". . . I am living in the eleventh century. If you come over in October, I think I shall take occasion, in moving out, to run down to Normandy on an eleventh-century excursion, ending in Cherbourg to meet you and Martha."

William Gray and Maggie Wade had 1603 H Street in readiness for Mrs. Cameron, who expected to begin her stay on September 6, 1899. To her annoyance, she was prohibited. She wrote to Dor on the 3rd: ". . . I shall not stop with Maggie after all. Donald seems to think it might not be proper! So I'll go to the Arlington [a nearby hotel] and use your house as a sitting room."

On September 9, by a vote of five to two, the military judges at Rennes found Dreyfus guilty. News of the re-conviction and the split in the court was telegraphed throughout the world. Mrs. Cameron—delayed—was still in New York. She went to Washington on the 10th and rushed to Adams's house as soon as possible.[59] She reported: "Here I am in your own house, writing in your own room, at your own table. It seems too strange. After all, I thought I cannot harm any one but myself, and so I came. The Arlington seemed less inviting than 1603, where I could sit down and imagine that you might walk in at any moment. I arrived an hour ago." "I wish you knew *now* that I am here, and thought it all right."[60]

That she and he were a match was confirmed by their independent responses to the new Dreyfus conviction. She told Adams on the 10th: "It seems to me weak. Either he is or is not guilty, and in either case the [French] Government would be well out of it by a direct [i.e. unanimous?] verdict." Adams told her on the 12th: ". . . I had read the arguments rather carefully, to see what the theories on each side were, and had been meditating on the weakness of both. . . . Either there was treason; or there was not."

Impartial onlookers throughout the world were becoming satisfied that Dreyfus was twice convicted but innocent. Adams agreed, yet felt augmented sympathy with the disgraced French army. He also felt very angry. On September 18, 1899, writing to Mrs. Cameron, he remembered the Union's armed forces in the Civil War. "Since I grew up, say since the battle of Gettysburg and the capture of the Forts at New Orleans, I have had but one rule, which is to back the Army and Navy against everything everywhere on every occasion. That is why I am an anti-Dreifussard. When the army makes a mistake and shoots the wrong man, I am sorry, and would do all I could to redress the injustice; but the Army and Navy have saved and made me and mine so many times that I'm not going back on it, whatever it does. . . . This is Treason, I am happy to say. As far as I know, the fortunes of my race were made by Treason—or by suppressing it—by War. . . ."[61]

The Lodges were again in Paris. Mrs. Chanler had appeared. Adams was visiting every old church that could be reached by ordinary means of travel. He was furiously buying books. He excused his activities to Mrs. Cameron as an addiction. ". . . I dragged Cabot into the country two days running, to look at twelfth-century churches, for I am now all eleventh and twelfth century, and you will find a gay library of twelfth century architecture whenever you get back to your ancestral property. I caught the disease from dear old [H. H.] Richardson[,] who was the only really big man I ever knew; and as I grow older the taste becomes a habit, like *absinthe*. . . ."[62]

On September 19, President Loubet of France pardoned Dreyfus—an action to which Dreyfus consented, though it implied his having been guilty. Mrs. Cameron asked: "So Dreyfus is pardoned. What next?"[63]

Opportunely in Paris, "Mungo" Herbert, an English acquaintance, formerly secretary of legation in Washington, invited Adams to a dinner also attended by Charles Russell, England's chief justice. Russell talked about the second court-martial at Rennes. Adams wrote to Mrs. Cameron: "In five minutes he gave us a sharper picture of the whole circus than I have got from all the reports. I was relieved to find that he had taken count of all the questions that had puzzled me, and that they had puzzled him too. Dreifus himself the other day, after his release, in his first declaration, said that he had been condemned for a crime which another had committed. Then it was not a conspiracy [by the French army]. There was a traitor."[64]

The Affair was wholly clarified. A crime was committed: Dreyfus did not commit it. Yet, for Adams, the Affair was newly complicated. He realized that the participants had included the government of imperial Germany, and he asked Mrs. Cameron to notice what that government did not do. ". . . if it *was* Esterhazy [that sold secret military papers to the Germans], think of the German government deliberately prolong-

ing the martyrdom of Dreifus when it could have produced the papers—
which could have had no value."[65]

The point was ominous. When it came to Jews, governmental authorities in Germany might be as bad or worse than those in France.

Brooks informed Henry from Dresden that Charles had completed
a biography of their father, to be published by Houghton Mifflin Company. Brooks confessed, "I rather shrink from reading it."[66] Henry
shrank so extremely that he did not respond to Brooks's news.

A woman who would figure in Henry's *Mont Saint Michel and Chartres*
was Eleanor of Guienne—or Eleanor of Aquitaine. On October 3, Henry
mentioned her to Mrs. Cameron. "My only luxury has been to buy photographs of eleventh-century churches and church towers. I'm growing
frightfully learned on French art of the Crusades. I'm going to write a
drama on the Second Crusade with Queen Eleanor of Guienne for heroine, and myself to act Saint Bernard and reprove her morals."

To his surprise, Henry could not find French books about Eleanor.
He asked Brooks to search in Germany for works about her. Brooks soon
reported that there were none.[67] The moral was rather stunning. As writers about things medieval, Brooks and Henry were pioneers to a degree
that even they had not appreciated.

Separately Henry had made two remarks which bore on his interest
in education. On September 10, 1899, he remarked to Brooks that he
felt a "growing antipathy to Professors and Universities." On October
9, he told Mrs. Cameron about his studying church spires—or *flèches*, or
clochers—and in the next breath spoke, perhaps somewhat cryptically,
about a "guide-book." "I get into the country now and then. . . . I've got
several expeditions on hand: Etampes, Provins, St[.] Leu d'Esserents,
Evreux, Vendome, Auxerre, and no end of small villages, all to see
church-spires of the twelfth century. I've filled your drawers with photographs of *flèches*. I've a volume on Chartres that takes as much room as
a bed. What you're to do with all my stuff when you return, I don't know;
but I can't take it home. . . . Besides, I want the things here, especially
the photographs, for a guide-book."

His closing words could mean that his purchased books and photographs were serving him as a guide-book. Equally they could mean that
he had amassed a library as a necessary step toward *writing* a guide-book.
Assuming that he wanted Mrs. Cameron to read the sentence both ways,
several questions remained. Was the guide-book that Adams was writing
meant to provide helpful information concerning a scattering of buildings that readers might be inclined to visit? Might it lead readers in a
well-informed way along a path from a chosen point of departure to a

chosen point of arrival, say from Mont Saint Michel to Chartres? Or were questions of another sort in order? Was the guide-book—or was the path—a metaphor? Did Adams assume that all readers, just by living, were making journeys and could make better journeys if re-oriented toward new objects more worth reaching? Would particular new objects be suggested by Adams's guide-book?

On October 6, he made a proposal that could seem a joke. The recipient was Niece Loulie.[68] He told her: ". . . I've laid out occupation for all the summers to come. I mean to hire an automobile, and travel all over France, architecturating. Do you want to go? You had better not. The autos always jump over backwards and explode."

Augustus Saint Gaudens, America's leading sculptor, was in Paris. He and Adams had been friends since the 1870s, and they were paying each other friendly visits. On October 17, 1899, Saint Gaudens asked Adams and two Frenchmen, a lawyer and an architect, to join him for a quick visit to the cathedral of Amiens—the largest in France and the only large one built in a single effort in keeping with a single plan. They made the trip on October 20 and were met at Amiens by the local archivist, who served as guide.

The visit took rather unexpected turns. Adams told Mrs. Cameron: "If I did not know the Cathedral intimately, I had at least a bowing-acquaintance with it. . . . Nothing was ever younger or fresher, and I went all over it again, officially as it were, with more interest than ever. Curiously enough, it was new to St[.] Gaudens. As for the French lawyer, he had never even seen Saint Denis. I found it impossible to be *ingénu*;—not to patronize them. Is one odious! How can one help it? These *boutiquiers*—I except the architect and the *archiviste*—belong to a weird world of childish information. . . . As for Saint Gaudens, it was a new life. It overpowered him."[69]

While with the others at the cathedral, Adams evidently had been called upon for information. He could *not* have lectured, yet was as much as pressed to do so. The experience was definitive. It settled a question of manners. As author of two educations, one for young men, one for young women, he could not be odious. He could not step forward as the professor. He could never rise or stoop to teach. Impossible though it might seem, he would have to guide in such a way that all his readers would always be free.

Adams meanwhile was sparing no effort to learn. He had told Mrs. Cameron on October 16: "I am still wallowing in the twelfth century. Last week I ran down to Etampes to see the flèche. This week I must go to Chartres again." He in fact went on the 17th and "passed a long day studying [the cathedral] . . . so as to square it with the books. . . ." On the 20th, he went to Amiens with Saint Gaudens. On the 29th, he was again at Chartres, "to take a look at certain windows."

The look was a great success. "There was the usual service, and singing, all simple enough . . . but as I studied the windows and listened to the singing, I felt the charm as I never did before. Color counts for so much in idolatry. The glass window is as emotional as music. I am now deep in windows and have dropped *clochers.*"[70]

As a step toward writing a biography of their father more elaborte than the one just completed, Charles planned to rent a Washington house not far from Henry's and pass the winter reading documents at the State Department archives. Bay Lodge knew of the plan and informed Mrs. Cameron. Beginning a letter to Henry in New York on November 1, 1899, she relayed the news and asked, "Can you stand it?"

She intended to mail her letter on the 3rd, to go by the fastest ship. She ended it: "Wonderful! wonderful! I am to sail next Wednesday [the 8th], and shall cable you to that effect tomorrow morning. . . . It all came smoothly and easily, and I am now counting the days. Don't leave the appartement [*sic*]. Welcome us there like visitors. Two weeks from today we shall be together. I cannot write!"

Henry had been telling Brooks: "I don't want to go home. Washington is repulsive." Also he asked for help. ". . . try and find out for me what is the best statement of the Economical Theory of History in the works of Marx, Engels and the socialist authorities. Of course I've read Marx—at least, Capital—but I've not read Engels, and have never seen his works." Had he wished to be more frank, Henry would have specified that in 1894, or earlier, he had obtained an English translation of *Das Kapital* and looked into the first volume only long enough to be put off by Marx's hair-splitting distinctions.[71]

Brooks did more than identify the best statement of the theory. He sent Henry an authoritative book by the German socialist Eduard Bernstein and later another by Karl Kautsky. When Mrs. Cameron's cable reached him, Henry was reading the book by Bernstein. One may assume he cabled back, but the cable is lost. He however advised Brooks on November 5: "It is not likely that I shall sail for another month at least. Nothing will be doing in Washington before New Year, and here, on this side, things are rather interesting."

Reading Bernstein affected Henry, in part, as a means of reading himself. In the same letter to Brooks, he described an upsetting sort of learning. ". . . I have every day to re-educate myself, and try to forget all I was ever taught. . . . I have been pick-axeing into the socialist book you sent me. . . . Bernstein is, I suppose, a Jew like the rest, and a German Jew at that, with a preposterous German jargon of philosophy and a style worse than impossible; but he seems to prove that he is very much in my intellectual condition."[72]

The central idea Henry expressed in response to Bernstein carried irony very far. He had discovered that the socialists were preparing their own extinction. "I can now, with fair confidence formulate Marx's theory of histroy, as 'the survival of the cheapest, until it becomes too cheap to survive.' We are pretty cheap already, but the Trades Union is cheaper. Even an exceptionally intelligent socialist, like Bernstein, is only beginning to suspect how much cheaper socialism is than he and Marx. . . ."[73]

Mrs. Cameron expected to reach Paris on November 17, 1899. Between the time she and Martha sailed and the time they arrived, Henry evidently stopped writing letters. When and where he greeted mother and daughter is unknown. He possibly met them at Cherbourg.

On the 18th, breaking his silence, he gave the Élysée Palace Hôtel as his address and offered Brooks explanations of his staying in Paris that were new, even true. ". . . La Farge is coming out, and I've promised to wait for him. Also I hear that Charles is going to Washington. . . . Although . . . Charles seems to make less noise in the newspapers, he can hardly help treading on my toes . . . and as I do not want . . . to say anything unpleasant of him, I shall shorten my stay in Washington to the utmost." Mrs. Cameron appeared in the letter only as Henry's unnamed "propriétaire." Next day in a letter to Sir John Clark, she appeared only as Henry's unnamed "landlady."

Oddly, Henry alluded to Shakespeare. He told Gaskell on November 22 that he wished to write "a five-act drama, of the twelfth century, to beat Macbeth." "The more I study, the more I begin to understand that there was literary merit in Shakespeare. Macbeth and Othello are about all that is worth [anyone's?] having done since the Greeks."

When he again mentioned Mrs. Cameron, Henry was saying things that were better said than believed. He confessed to Lady Curzon on November 28 that he had "carried on a most compromising affair with the young and beautiful Mrs[.] Jack Gardner." He also told her that Mrs. Cameron—although "once as ambitious as Eve herself"—had drifted so far from politics that she retained "not a vestige of ambition" and did not regret "losing power."[74]

Adams had advised Gaskell that he would stay in Paris till Christmas.[75] In mid-December, a strongly worded letter came from Mrs. Hay. She said, "John misses you more than I can tell you. . . ." "Rockhill misses you awfully. . . ." "Please come home!!!"[76]

Yet Adams did not sail till twelve days after Christmas. A reason could be found in Shakespeare. *Macbeth* was perhaps not a work one would expect a man to turn to in the last days of the nineteenth century. Adams, however, had chosen that moment to reread the play.[77] He was interested in very powerful women, or rather in women who were discovering their power. He meant to keep his relations with Mrs. Cameron as far as possible from tragedy and for the present was succeeding, but he was living a Shakespearean drama, as well as wanting to write one. Somewhat in that spirit, he lingered till Twelfth Night in the company of a woman of forty-two who was admired by many as beautiful, who cared deeply about politics, and who as the days went by was freely learning what she wished to experience of love.[78]

9

VIOLENCE

A dams had left for Cherbourg on Saturday, January 6, 1900. Mrs. Cameron waited five days and began her first letter. "I feel as if you ought to be across several seas by this time—was ever week so long? And another ten days—or more—must pass before the first letter can come. It makes you and America seem very far away. Saturday I could not face people so I went over and wandered around the Luxembourg gardens all by my lone, looking at the ghost of the Pantheon appearing and disappearing through that thick fog, and wondering how far your train had carried you by that time. When you were being transferred to your ship I was sitting in Notre Dame listening to the music, very lonely, very miserable, very one sided and lame without the best half of me. I think that is all. I *had* to brace up."[1]

For Adams, the sight of fast-changing New York made Paris seem "a sort of Byzantine survival." He said so in his first letter, begun late on January 15 on a train to Washington. He said he was thinking of Paris "as I do of Chartres and Mont Saint Michel." All three were far away. "It is the calm of infinite astronomy."

He had received a telegram from Mrs. Hay saying King was waiting in Washington to see him. ". . . I bundled everything up, and caught the Limited. I am not used to being sought, and it disconcerts me. My nervous system is unequal to the strain of being telegraphed for."

On January 16 in the capital, he found time to write to Donald about Martha. He learned from Mrs. Lodge that Rockhill was "to marry again—in April—a Miss Perkins—or is it Parker—or somebody—of Connecticut." He dined in the evening with the Hays, King, Rockhill, and others, but he gave Mrs. Cameron no immediate account of King.[2]

With a view to being a permanent Paris summer resident, Adams had shifted a large balance to his Paris bank. He had made the acquaintance of an American lawyer in Paris, Edmond Kelly, who could serve as his agent. Especially he had started looking for furniture. In New York before catching the Limited, he joined Bigelow in looking at a Japanese collection awaiting auction. He liked a "dozen fine screens" and asked Bigelow to get them and have them sent to Washington.[3]

At the same time, Adams was brought abreast of Bigelow's openly-conducted mad pursuit of a great opera singer, Milka Ternina.[4] She was in New York. Bigelow had asked her to marry him; she had refused; yet they remained on such terms that he arranged that Adams meet her. The meeting fell through, but Adams promised to come back to hear her sing the heroine's part in Wagner's *Tristan and Isolde.*

Bigelow secured the screens. Adams was busy; Hay was sanguine. On January 22, 1900, Adams reported to Mrs. Cameron: "John Hay at once resumed his old habits, and went over all his year's diplomacy. I think I know what there is to know, and am surprised to find how little it is. . . . As I guessed, Hay has all his own way with foreign governments, and all his real energies are given to the Senate. Even the Senate is comparatively docile. . . . I can hardly believe that Hay will get his treaties through, but the senate thinks he will."

Adams's mild expressions masked increasing worry. Month by month, with Rockhill's help and in keeping with Adams's suggestion that he negotiate agreements informally, Hay was inducing England, Germany, and Russia to give part-acceptances to an "Open Door" policy with regard to China which Hay would eventually publicize as complete acceptances. Once in place, the new policy would give China a measure of protection against the foreign powers then vying to reduce the Celestial Kingdom to a patchwork of commercial bridgeheads and spheres of influence. Hay's initiation of the policy promised to make him a hero in the United States and a leader in world politics. Yet the protection given to China, while probably better than none, and perhaps the best that could be arranged, would be fragile and easily broken.[5]

More alarming to Adams than foreign inroads in China were British bunglings in a war against the Dutch settlers in South Africa. Fierce Boer resistance had revealed, at least to Adams, that British military management was grossly antiquated—had not improved since the American Revolution.[6] It seemed possible that other powers would intervene in the conflict. Adams told Mrs. Cameron on January 30: "Today's news reads grim. Indeed, if I were wise, I ought to run away from here, for my natural pessimism works now on Hay's natural pessimism, and his on mine, until we are both half out of our minds with anxiety. Of course it is an open secret that Russia, for months, has been representing to every [foreign] cabinet the inevitable necessity of joint intervention [in Africa]. . . . France must probably act with Russia and Germany. You see all the consequences without my lecturing. The happiest [consequence] would be the peaceful subsidence of England to the rank of France. The worst would be a violent convulsion which must end in her [the British empire's] total dismemberment."[7]

Donald replied to Adams's news of Martha by asking Adams to come to Coffin's Point.[8] Glad to be invited, Adams pondered the idea that he might go south, possibly taking Hay.

People had noticed that Hay and Adams's walks were too systematic and continuous to be unpolitical. The result for Adams was certainty that he should get away from Washington. On February 5, 1900, he explained to Mrs. Cameron: ". . . my relations with Hay make me suspected, and shut me out from the confidence of all the anti-administration elements; which is unfortunate but inevitable. As yet, no one has thought me worth attacking, but I can[']t stay here long."

After several false starts, Brooks and Evelyn had gone to Russia. They presumably were in St. Petersburg.

In Washington, Charles and his family were paying Henry visits. Charles talked incessantly about his biography of their father, to be published on February 17. Ten days prior to the event, Henry advised Brooks, ". . . he does not talk to me except of his patricide."

A subject Henry would not mention was his own exclusion from the book. Presumably at Henry's early insistence, Charles had so written the biography as not to say, or even hint, that Henry had accompanied their father through the seven years of his English mission. In that sense, the person killed was Henry, and *he* contrived the murder.

In 1900, as felt by Henry, the United States became a country unprecedented in the world. He remarked to Brooks: "A year of France and Italy had somehow dulled my sense. From the moment of landing in New York, I was conscious of a change of scale. Our people seemed to sling at least twice the weight, twice as rapidly, and with only half the display of effort. There is now almost no sense of effort, for instance, about our great railways; but the sense of energy is overpowering." There was a sense too of being "on top"—being the *highest* nation. How high was manifest in New York's newer buildings.[9]

None the less, Henry's attention was most fixed on the decline of England. Always likely to apprehend a great event sooner than others, he told Mrs. Cameron on February 13, "My real interest centres in the Transvaal. . . . My breath comes short as I listen for news. . . . I tell you, the church bells are tolling. The greatest empire the world ever saw is tottering to its grave." As if to prove him wrong, news came of British successes against the Boers. More pleased than displeased, he advised her on the 20th: ". . . the British seem to be getting ahead in the Transvaal. It was time! But what a comment on their previous transactions, and what a danger barely escaped!"

The Hays did not know that weekly letters were passing both ways between Adams and Mrs. Cameron. On February 19, 1900, Hay received a letter from her. He assumed its contents would be news to Adams and accordingly imparted to him what she had said.

Adams apprised her: "Hay got your letter yesterday, and told me your news. I rarely mention your letters to me, because it makes people jealous of me. Too many men still love you, and too many women are envious. Your fatal charms are still too vividly remembered. This is not pure compliment either. As historical fact, I close my eyes and shudder at the women who have succeeded to your empire."

Adams and Mrs. Cameron had successfully kept secret the strength of their attachment. Very differently, Adams's increasing contempt for Senator Lodge was revealed, yet not acknowledged. At the center of the situation was Adams's loyalty to Mrs. Lodge. He had reported to Mrs. Cameron on the 19th: ". . . every day I receive Hay's comments on Cabot, and once a week I receive Cabot's comments on Hay; and, what is much worse, I know that the brunt of it falls on Sister Anne, and that she is, as usual, at her wits' end to make her husband out not to be what he is."

The situation did not lend itself to improvement. Dor continued: ". . . it is quite useless for me to play pretend about Cabot. He knows by instinct my contempt; and sister Anne and Bay know it still better; in fact, our little family knew each other pretty well from the start. . . . Generally I take refuge in silence; but this time, silence is rather more expressive than words." "All this, of course, is profoundly secret."

A letter from Tati disclosed that Marau had wholly alienated her brothers and sisters.[10] In response, Adams decided later to ask a firm in Paris to print a small edition of his *Memoirs of Arii Taimai*.

He meanwhile took two precautions. He hired a contractor to grout the stonework at the Adams Memorial with lead; and, for reasons not much different, he secured Mrs. Cameron's letters in a metal box, with a note of instruction to his executors.

Niece Loulie returned to Washington on Uncle Henry's sixty-second birthday, February 16, 1900. As an amusement, he reactivated her Aunt Clover's photographic equipment and started taking portraits. Rather carelessly, while Loulie watched, he sat in a chair before a Japanese screen and photographed himself from a medium distance in profile by squeezing a shutter-tripping device with both his hands.[11] He went on to take more careful photographs of Loulie and several other people.[12] The one of Loulie, which he thought the best, was charmingly informal, though not perfectly in focus. The portrait of himself was very misleading. It showed him as old and possibly prophetic. It failed to reveal, indeed wholly concealed, his energy and animation.

Sometime in February, Uncle Henry looked into a volume of letters by Robert Louis Stevenson and was thrown into gloom by the Scottish writer's efforts to counteract his fatal illness with incessant false optimism. As if in protest, Henry wrote to Charles Warren Stoddard, "For the sake of the Blessed Virgin, can we not go down on our knees, as we did when I was young in the twelfth century, and confess our total ignorance, helplessness and misery?"[13]

Not important in itself, the outburst to Stoddard may have marked the date—February 21, 1900—when Adams began to write a poem, "Prayer to the Virgin of Chartres." Exactly how he wrote the poem is unknown. He possibly wrote it very slowly.

A copy of *Charles Francis Adams*, by his son Charles Francis Adams, was placed in Henry's hands, perhaps by Charles. Henry tried to read it and was reminded of occurrences of the distant past and roles he had played in them. On March 4, he wrote to Brooks about the narrow escape of the United States from a war with England in 1861–1862. No subject could be more fearful. "Looking back I grovel in the dust, and shake with terror at the immensity of the danger and the impotence of our efforts. I want to say nothing about it."[14]

Charles's book awakened Henry's dislike of biographical "analysis of character." "Our father would stand out better, larger and even truer, without definition. I do not like the microscope, or even the telescope[,] as a family ornament, and I loathe the photograph. . . ."

Continued attempts to read the book worsened Henry's ill-temper. Next day, he told Mrs. Cameron: "I've been trying to read my brother Charles's Life of our father, and it makes me sick. Now I understand why I refused so obstinately to do it myself. These biographies are murder, and in this case, to me, would be both patricide and suicide. They belittle the victim and the assassin equally."[15]

Henry had not returned to New York to hear Ternina sing. In March 1900, in the company of Ellen and Louisa Hooper, he made up for the omission. Writing on the 12th, he gave Mrs. Cameron a full acount. "The nieces took me to Philadelphia to hear Ternina as Ysolde, and Looly taught me what to say about it. . . . To me, the singular part of it was that the music of Ysolde should be interpreted to me by two young and perfectly pure girls. Another Americanism! I could not even hint to them what it meant, and they couldn't have hinted it to me if they had known. . . . Ternina put into it all she dared. I wished she had sung in Paris."

Mrs. Cameron had gone to Biarritz to lend support to her ailing sister Lida. At the same time, hoping to save Martha and herself from having to revisit America, she began the process of persuading Donald to make another trip abroad. She urged Dor on March 15: "*Do* try to find Donald somewhere. I want you to help about the summer."

She was preserving Dor's letters, even short notes. She learned from him in mid-March that he had kept her letters and put them in a box with a "direction" to his executors "to deliver them to you personally." She answered on March 19: "I am amused by the box of my letters. I had no idea that you kept them. Why not destroy them at once. Surely it is better. As for yours, I shall do the same & I promise you that no publisher or compiler shall ever get hold of them. They shall be destroyed."[16]

His message to her concerned the preservation of her letters so that they might be returned to her and the question of their survival placed in her hands. Her message to him was a mere first thought that came to mind. What counted was the truth. She had learned to her surprise that their correspondence was being kept and that control of it would one day pass to her—assuming he predeceased her. The outcome could be predicted. Destruction of their old and new letters was ruled out. Future letters would usually be saved.

On March 6, 1900, Henry assured Mrs. Cameron that Hay was "never in better health or spirits, and takes pounding with positive improvement of health—like massage." On the 13th, he took it back. ". . . [Mrs. Hay] says to me with conviction that she does not stay in office beyond this term under any circumstances." On the 20th, he disclosed a reason. "Hay seems to me very tired. Considering everything, I wonder only that he does not break down. . . . His treaties are all hung up. . . . He means to slip Joe Choate into his place, and quit."

Henry had informed Donald that he and others could not free themselves to go to Coffin's Point. Donald did not answer. Mrs. Cameron meanwhile said she could use some of the Japanese screens in Paris. Henry advised her on March 26 and 27: "In despair of direction or help from anybody[,] I engaged a room on the St[.] Paul for April 25, and apparently shall sail alone on that day." "I'm going to Paris to see you. I may as well bring the screens with me. . . . I wonder where I can put up? Perhaps Kelley [*sic*] may know of rooms, or an apartment to let, near you."

Concluding his letter, Henry promised to write again to her husband. He kept the promise and while so doing asked Donald to join him on the *St. Paul* and proceed with him to Paris. The gesture elicited a reply. Donald was grateful to be invited but wanted to spend the summer in America making money. He declared: "There is just before us an astounding era of prosperity. With my dull wits I may be able to catch on to some plunder—at least I mean to try!"[17]

The illness of Lida Hoyt was keeping Mrs. Cameron at Biarritz.[18] The illness worsened, and Mrs. Cameron persuaded her sister to travel to Paris with Martha and stay at 50 Avenue du Bois de Boulogne. By this means, she freed herself to plan a three-week run to Spain with an American couple, the Canfields, and yet reach Paris ahead of Dor. On March 26, 1900, before starting, she wrote to him: "I begin to feel that your vacation is over and it is time to ring the bell and call you in. I am more and more awake to the fact that without you I am no good. I have no energy, nor force, nor even amiability—which you used to think my strong point. I think that I am more apt to be distinctly depressing—yet whenever you are even within reach I seem to be able to spin around with quite a cheerful buzz. I lean on you very hard, and you supply all my momentum."[19]

In Madrid on April 4, she began a letter to him by saying that she and the Canfields would be returning in a moment to the Prado. She resumed the letter that evening in a state of extreme enthusiasm. "I have been at the gallery all day, & am much impressed by the Rubens[,] which I feel that I have never seen before. And by a Goya which no one ever speaks about but which is simply marvellous. Why didn't he stick to the nude only. . . . I am crazy about this gallery."

Brooks and Evelyn returned from Russia, came to Washington, stayed with the Lodges, and visited Henry. Brooks thought Henry irritable and feared that their long-standing friendship was at an end.[20] The fear was misplaced. Henry's irritation was caused by egoists. Mindful that Vice President Hobart had died, egoistical Governor Roosevelt was stating loudly that he would *not* permit himself to be placed on the Republican ticket in the election of 1900 as President McKinley's running mate; and in response to Senator Lodge's egoism, which was becoming gargantuan, an obedient Senate was wrecking Hay's treaties.

On April 22, 1900, Henry sent Rockhill some screens as a wedding present; and on the 25th he sailed. Once in Paris, he stayed at the Élysée Palace Hôtel near the Étoile. He soon moved to a ground floor apartment near the Trocadero at 20 Rue de Longchamps, within steps of the Paris Exposition. Also he looked for a firm that could print the Tahiti

Memoirs. He found one but at first said nothing in his letters about the edition.

As planned, Mrs. Cameron, Martha, and Mrs. Hoyt were at 50 Avenue du Bois de Boulogne. Mrs. Hoyt would shortly leave. Dor visited the pavilions of the Exposition, sometimes with Martha. Mrs. Cameron had warned him that the Paris fair would not compare in beauty with the one at Chicago. His first impressions were unfavorable. He thought the best things exhibited were the paintings.

Hay and Rockhill's effort to devise an international *modus vivendi* in China had run afoul of an unforeseen event, the Boxer Rebellion. Henry reacted on June 26 by urging Hay not to resign, should McKinley be reelected. In the same letter, he mentioned that he was reading St. Thomas Aquinas but did not explain his motive. Mrs. Cameron and Martha were the only persons who knew he was writing *Mont Saint Michel and Chartres.* He presumably had told them his plan of work. Having drafted the book's opening chapters, he was leaping forward to draft a last chapter about Aquinas. He would draft the many connecting chapters when he fully knew what they should say.

His secret efforts were conditioned by the untimely death of an Adams. He had originally had five nephews: John's three sons and Charles's twins. The twins were likable but gave no promise of high achievement. John's eldest son had died in boyhood. The youngest, a new Charles Francis Adams, was well-suited to business but not to politics nor to careers involving the arts or sciences. The middle son, George Caspar Adams, had been Henry's particular friend when a child and had been uncommonly amusing.

As an adult, George took to drink. Late in June 1900, a letter reached Henry from Brooks reporting that the nephew was *in extremis.* A letter from Charles said George was dying of "consumption"—a presentable explanation that Brooks would second when death occurred; but in Henry's view the actual illness was always whiskey.[21]

Posterity would not view George's death as significant. Its meaning for Henry was another matter. "Dear Dor," the salutation Mrs. Cameron invariably used in her letters, was a constant reminder to him—though he did not need reminding—that in addition to being Henry Adams he in secret had taken George as his alternate name. By the act, he had aligned himself not only with his father's eldest brother George, who died in 1829 by suicidal drowning, but also with his hard-drinking nephew George, who was drowning in alcohol in 1900. Each of the earlier Georges had shown signs of talent. One George would survive—by far the most talented of the three. If the Adamses were to be established as capable of achievements of the highest order, the last George could not rest. He had to make unheard-of efforts.

*   *   *

Charles and Henry were old enough to have memories of their paternal grandmother, Louisa Catherine Adams. Charles knew that her father was a Marylander, Joshua Johnson. He had learned that her mother was named Catherine Nuth. He had an impression that Catherine was a Marylander too, but he lacked evidence to support the impression. He accordingly wrote to Henry, asking what he knew of Catherine Nuth.[22]

Charles was seeking grist for the mill of his intended long biography of their father. He could not know that his request touched a sensitive nerve: Henry's secret feeling that he and Louisa Catherine Adams shared a single identity—were one person living in two successive forms. Neither could Charles know that the request trenched upon an inquiry that Henry had initiated in 1895—an effort to learn about their grandmother's mother and the latter's antecedents. Henry was far better informed than Charles. As has been noticed, he had found among their grandmother's papers a memorandum in her hand. The memorandum stated that her mother, Catherine Nuth, was an Englishwoman, daughter of a "Writer in the India Office" in London; that Catherine Nuth's mother was named Young; and that her Young grandfather had been a "partner in one of the great London breweries."

On this basis, Henry in April 1895 had sent twenty pounds to Oswald Barron in London and asked him to find a record of the marriage of Catherine Nuth to Joshua Johnson and to trace the Nuths and Youngs. Barron had set to work but had warned while starting that Nuth was a name "of great rarity" in England. He pursued his inquiries through records in many places for two years. At that point, he admitted that he had come to "a standstill." He had found none of the information his employer had requested. ". . . I have still money of yours in my hands and I feel that I owe you an ancestor."[23]

Replying to Charles on July 12, 1900, Henry imparted what he knew, only omitting Barron's name.[24] A troubling aspect of the case was that Barron had found no record of a marriage between Catherine Nuth and Joshua Johnson! "That young man reported to me investigations continued for two years through all the Parish records, and the India Office, and everywhere he could think; but not a trace has he ever found of Nuth or Young or Johnson, in marriage or out."

Henry suggested that Charles might start an investigation of his own. "Now *you* can try!" Yet if any Adams was likely to launch another effort, it would be Henry. For him, the parentage of Louisa Catherine Adams was *his* parentage. It mattered to him that she and he were descendants of a "Writer" in London who bore so rare a name as Nuth. He had to wonder whether Nuth was an immigrant to England. If so, where had he come from? Henry needed to know.

Although much cooler in summer than Washington, Paris occasionally became very hot. Mrs. Cameron and Martha suffered grievously in heat and wanted to escape to cool places. Besides, Martha had been unwell. On July 18, 1900, mother and daughter fled Paris and settled at a spa, Pougues Les Eaux, where Martha could begin a water cure.

Next day, Adams moved in at 50 Avenue du Bois de Boulogne. The apartment-for-alternate-use was ideal for him even in July and August. His overriding requirement was conditions favorable to work. He knew he could work in perfect comfort in temperatures as high as 81° or slightly higher; and he had found that, if fully aired at night, Paris apartments could be protected against heat all through the day simply by keeping the shutters closed and curtains drawn.

Rockhill, in addition to being a diplomat and explorer, was a researcher and translator. He sent Adams a copy of a translation he had just published, *The Journey of William of Rubruch to the Eastern Parts of the World, 1253–55, as Narrated by Himself*. A Franciscan friar, William of Rubruk had safely journeyed from the Holy Land to the Mongolian court and back, a feat which in Adams's judgment should have affected the traveler as a "daily miracle."

Adams welcomed the narrative as complementary to the thirteenth-century prose of the scholastic doctors and the historian Joinville. He wrote to Rockhill about William of Rubruch: ". . . I should call him a wonderfully good example of the men trained by all the great Orders to the practical work of the age. I can imagine him conscientiously and laboriously superintending the masons who were building the cathedral of Amiens. He makes me understand how those great churches got built; and how Albertus Magnus and Thomas Aquinas, and Duns Scotus[,] managed to pile up the enormous structure of their philosophy. The world never saw more patience or labor or sustained energy than these men showed. They did immense things, and I don't know but what Friar William's journey is as astonishing as anything that was done."[25]

A letter from Tati announced that his sister Moetia and her American husband, Dorence Atwater, were coming to Paris. The news made Adams wish he might get the *Memoirs of Arii Taimai* into print in time for Moetia's visit. His impulse ran counter to the work-habits of Paris printers, and he was sure to be disappointed.

Edward Hooper arrived for an extended visit. Since 1873, he had kept watch over Adams's investments. Both men knew that Adams had abundant surplus cash to spend on luxuries. Promptings by Hooper perhaps were one of the several reasons why Adams started to haunt the shops of Paris dealers, often to buy antique Chinese ceramics.

Mrs. Cameron and Dor, when possible, were writing to each other daily. On July 25, 1900, he mentioned to her that he had nearly finished his "metaphysical chapter" for *Mont Saint Michel and Chartres* and wanted Martha to read it. Writing also to Hay, he said he was studying St. Thomas Aquinas and scholastic dialectics in a fifth-floor apartment 127 steps above the street. His thoughts turned to steps because he habitually raced down the flights when going out.[26] The number he cited, 127, was an exaggeration indicative of high spirits.

The water cure for Martha did not work. Hooper was still at 50 Avenue du Bois de Boulogne. A visit by Palmer was impending. In the circumstances, Mrs. Cameron planned a stay for Martha and herself at a hotel at the Étoile favored by her and Dor, the Beau Site.

Langley appeared. He and Adams had met often in Washington since the days of the Chicago Fair. On July 29, he dined with Adams alone at the apartment.[27] At some point, without recording the fact, they went to the Champ de Mars to see an exhibition of dynamos much like the dynamos that had fascinated Adams at Chicago.[28]

Mrs. Cameron and Martha appeared on August 4 but soon went house-hunting in Normandy. They did not find a house. As the best alternative, they went to Switzerland and tried the experiment of living wherever impulse might direct.

Bay Lodge meanwhile had sent Adams news that he would be married to Elizabeth Davis in September. For unexplained reasons, the wedding was moved forward to August 18; upsetting stories reached Adams and Mrs. Cameron about Bay and Bessy's conduct; and there seemed a need for better information.

Simultaneously, Adams received news from Hay that he was in New Hampshire, very ill. Hay had dictated his letter to Clara. He said that there was no one else he could talk to; that Adams would have to come home; that Clara ordered it.[29]

A question had long hung over Adams: what he wanted to *be*; what station he aspired to; what role would meet his needs. The question was not his. It was asked or at least thought by friends, relatives, onlookers, and nearly everyone who knew anything about him. It made no difference that the question was needless; that he had long since reached high objects, that he had reached them repeatedly, and that currently he was reaching even higher. Nor did it help that he practically always succeeded. Almost all the persons who watched him were prepared to think of success as measurable only in terms of high political offices, other high institutional places, or great wealth.

In recent years, rather than ignore or evade the question, Adams had been meeting it with a formulaic comic answer. He liked to say that he had wanted to be a cardinal but no one had ever given him the necessary hat.[30] One beauty of the formula was complete self-erasure. It declared him to be a silly fellow who had abjectly failed.

An expression of his formula appeared in a letter to Loulie Hooper on September 2, 1900. He mentioned that Moetia had arrived and was charming, that Palmer had visited, and that Gaskell might come. He described himself as "hard worked" and implied that in the past he had not worked hard enough. With reference to her and her four sisters, he said: ". . . everytime I come down stairs, I have to climb all the way down from the eleventh century. I live in the twelfth. . . . This makes it awkward to run a great deal down to the street; and I haven't a lift to bring you all up. Poor things, you are such babies, and your dolls are so very stupid! but you don't know any better. If I had not failed in the ambition of my life to be a Cardinal, I would have done so much to make you intelligent!"

Dor's letters from Paris were more cheerful than Mrs. Cameron's from Switzerland. He reported to her on September 5, 1900, "Knowing that you may be back any day, I am working like a bob-tail rabbit." She said that day emphatically: "I'm growing old. Let's go south for the winter. No one writes. We haven't heard from Donald for three weeks. Even my sister has given out. You only never fail."[31]

Loulie wrote Uncle Henry an account of Bay and Bessy's marriage, and he relayed the story to Mrs. Cameron. She replied, "As usual, the only real information we get comes from blessed Loulie Hooper."[32] The information, whatever it was, led Adams to think of beautiful Bessy as even more a fool than impulsive Bay.

By returning to Paris on Sunday, September 16, Mrs. Cameron kept an agreement with the Swedish artist Anders Zorn to have her portrait painted. The finished painting would help to establish Zorn as a portraitist of fashionable women. She was shown full-face, seated on a sofa, wearing a most stylish, formal summer dress, and holding a fan. The background was suggestive of a Japanese screen. As a register of personality, the painting was a virtual blank.[33]

Work on the portrait was simultaneous with a change involving an apartment. Adams wanted to supplement the shared apartment at 50 Avenue du Bois de Boulogne with an apartment of his own nearby. One possibility was an airy high apartment overlooking the Étoile at 3 Rue de Traktir, a short walk east on the avenue. Mrs. Markwald, an American acquaintance, was renting it. She wanted to sublet it for a year. In late September, Adams met her terms and moved in.[34]

Rather than reoccupy 50 Avenue du Bois de Boulogne, Mrs. Cameron netted 3,000 francs by subletting it. She and Martha went to Pallanza in northern Italy.[35] Adams went on working, liked his " 'pied à terre' in the clouds," but had to absorb a shock. Sir Robert Cunliffe, an English gentleman, father of children, and a widower since 1898, had re-married to a woman of thirty-five. The news came from Gaskell. Adams replied on October 5: "You have clean knocked me out! How does one do that sort of thing? At thirty, it is an awful risk to face a young woman in—marriage. At sixty, it is worse. One kills oneself, and one cannot possibly explain beforehand." ". . . really one owes something to one's wife, not to mention one's children."

Adams was unconventional, yet moral. He still loved his wife, was averse to second marriages, was loyal to his wife's friends, and had joined with one of them in an arrangement so secret that it did not need explanation. From his perspective, Cunliffe's second marriage, if not immoral, bordered on the immoral. Inevitably it brought to mind the day in 1878 when Senator James Donald Cameron, a widower with grown children, married Elizabeth Sherman, not yet twenty-one. Compared to that performance, Adams's own dealings with Mrs. Cameron, and hers with him, could be regarded by both participants as intelligent, moral, and even redemptive.

Prior to his bout of illness in New Hampshire, Hay had remarked in a letter to Adams that the great foreign powers, chiefly England, Russia, Germany, France, and Japan, were using Washington as "a central Hello office"—a telephone exchange. The metaphor seemed hopeful. When he had recovered sufficiently to walk two miles a day, he wrote to Adams about the hectorings of America's newspapers. His tone was ironic. ". . . [the newspapers] expect us to make Russia honest and Germany unselfish; to insult England every hour and make certain of her cooperation whenever it is needed; to keep China whole and to smash her to pieces. That is our job and we shall do it. . . ."[36]

Hay meant to return to the State Department for a last winter but resign at the start of the next administration. Adams responded on October 5, 1900, with a metaphor of his own. He represented the great foreign powers as pigs and hogs, only different from each other in degrees of greediness, and he conferred on Hay the unlofty honor of being swineherd. ". . . in watching you herd your drove of pigs, I am at times astonished to see how, by hitting one on the snout and by coaxing another with a rotten turnip, you manage to get ahead, or at least not much backward. . . . True, your success has been surprising. You have been so right when everybody else was wrong, that I half believe you are too good to drive hogs; if anybody can be too good for a useful purpose."

Adams's metaphor of pigs and hogs was expressive of his ideas. He seriously believed that the imperial powers were guilty of juvenile, if not infantile, self-seeking. Yet he probably conceived the metaphor solely to assist his friend. Fully certain that Hay was going to quit, he wanted to help him feel that the office of secretary of state was servile and well worth leaving. Demotion to swineherd could affect Hay as comic. Laughter could ease a resignation.

Restored to health or something near it, Hay went back to Washington and renewed his victories as author of open doors to China. At the same time, John Sherman died. Mrs. Cameron construed the event as ending the period of her family's distinction. She wrote to Adams that when again in Paris she would want to dress in black.

Efficient as always, Adams had completed the Aquinas chapter for *Mont Saint Michel and Chartres* and was composing rhymed translations for use in other chapters. On October 27, 1900, he sent Martha a cryptic message: "St[.] Thomas and the Virgin have got married." The likeliest meaning of the line was that Adams had found a way of linking his last chapter with the earlier ones—either that or he had drafted many of the links and virtually completed the manuscript.

He earlier had informed Mrs. Cameron that he was planning a return to Washington. She mostly objected, slightly relented. In her newest letter, written on October 26, she stated a requirement. "Now don't talk about going home. I can't have it. I am certainly not negative about *that*. You must at least stay for Christmas. Indeed why should you go at all, *I* say. This broken summer and autumn makes me feel as if I had not seen you at all, tho' when I think of the usual separation of months and ocean[,] I realize that I cannot grumble."

In answer, Adams sent her a letter and an enclosure. The letter said in part: "Please read the enclosed translation of a Chanson by Thibaud de Champagne (about 1230) and tell me if it hitches anywhere. Martha too."[37] Titled "Chanson of Thibaud," the enclosure consisted of three rhymed nine-line stanzas ending with a courteous refrain. The stanzas were nothing if not presentable. Their burden was love so repelled and unrequited that its male victim had not begun to see a ray of hope.[38] Four lines were representative:

> Seldom the music of her voice I hear,
> Or wonder at the beauty of her eyes;
> It grieves me that I cannot follow there,
> Where at her feet my heart attentive lies.

In the past, Mrs. Cameron had received poems from Adams and
Hay, and recently she had been a reader of poems by Joe Stickney and
Bay Lodge. It seemed to her that Adams was the most a poet of the four.
On October 31, she told him her opinion. "You have the poetic quality
strong. I have always thought so and wondered why you did not do more.
When I think of Bay or Mr Stickney setting up as poets, while you—!
Dear me, what an unbalanced world it is."

That Adams was a poet was not in question. The confusing aspect
of the case was that his poetic capabilities showed least, or not at all,
when he wrote in verse. The moment he did so, he lapsed into the stan-
dardized rhymes, meters, and tricks of speech to which the better-adver-
tised English and American poets had descended by force of habit for a
half-century or longer. The moment he returned to prose, he regained
an extraordinary power to speak with intelligence, force, and feeling.
Thus Mrs. Cameron was right but wrong. Adams was more a poet than
any other man she knew. Yet, to read his poetry, she would have had to
turn away from the stanzas he sent her, ingenious though they were, and
read again the original prose of his principal books or his ever-arriving
letters.[39]

Ternina would soon be in Paris. Bigelow was waiting in Paris to greet
her. Bay and Bessy Lodge were expected also. Anticipating her own reappearance, Mrs. Cameron mused to Adams: "I hope that I shall see a
great deal of Dr Bigelow if his Ternina isn't there. And when she comes
might we not ask her to dinner? And when is Bay coming?" In a new
letter, she directed, ". . . you cannot sail till January, mind!" In a last
letter, she added, "We shall have to arrange a board system, you know,
for it is too absurd to think of my eating alone at one end of the avenue,
and you doing the same at the other."[40]

She and Martha arrived, and he regularly appeared for dinner at
6:00 P.M. at 50 Avenue du Bois de Boulogne.[41] Ternina was delayed. On
November 5, 1900, he advised Loulie: ". . . Ternina . . . is kept by doctors, or other reasons, in Munich or Vienna or wherever she is. As she is
to sail on the 17th[,] her visit here can now be only two or three days,
and I shall have hardly the chance to see her at all."

Knowing that Loulie would want to know his opinion of Cousin Sturgis's mad pursuit, he gave it. "There is a time for all things; even when
past fifty a man is at liberty to marry if he thinks best, but he is not at
liberty to give love as a reason."[42]

After attracting fewer visitors than anticipated, the Paris Exposition
was closing. Uncle Henry had not admired its architecture and may have
been prevented by work from seeing many exhibits. He used the last
days to return to one exhibit repeatedly. On November 7, he explained

his conduct to Hay. "It is a new century, and what we used to call electricity is its God. I can already see that the scientific theories and laws of our generation will, to the next, appear as antiquated as the Ptolemaic system, and the fellow who gets to 1950 will wish he hadn't. . . . The period from 1900 to 1930 is in full swing. . . . It will break its damned neck long before it gets through, if it tries to keep up the speed. You are free to deride my sentimentality if you like, but I assure you that I,—a monk of St[.] Dominic, absorbed in the beatitudes of the Virgin Mother—go down to the Champ de Mars and sit by the hour over the great dynamos, watching them run as noiselessly and smoothly as the planets, and asking them—with infinite courtesy—where in Hell they are going."

With sweeping self-dismissiveness, Adams summarized the Paris fair as "an education which I have failed to acquire for want of tutors." The truth was the opposite. He had had a tutor and had gained an education. At the perfect moment, he had gone to the Champ de Mars with Langley, who told him that the physical scientists were finding their subjects increasingly mysterious. The lesson was not wasted. Adams said to Hay, "The charm of the show, to me, is that no one pretends to understand even in a remote degree, what these weird things are that they call electricity, Roentgen rays, and what not. The exhibitors are dead dumped into infinity on a fork."[43]

Loulie was in Boston. Because Mabel had married and Loulie had not, Uncle Henry gave the unmarried older sister a heaping measure of support. The means he chose was expensive, aesthetic, and erotic. Among the many figures for sale at Auguste Rodin's studio, he found a small marble statue of Psyche holding a lamp and looking in the dark for missing Eros. Psyche wore no clothes. Her nakedness might offend the primmer residents of Boston, but Adams bought her and ordered her crated and shipped to Loulie as a present.

With excuses that reservations on steamers were hard to come by and that ships were delayed by storms, Dor was able to extend his and Mrs. Cameron's days together in Paris till January 21, 1901.[44]

He had arranged to lend his Rue de Traktir apartment to Bay and Bessy Lodge during his absence. He hoped to see them housed before he left for his ship, but their ship was late. When he was speeding to Cherbourg on one train, they sped toward Paris on another.[45]

On Friday, January 25, the newlyweds settled themselves at 3 Rue de Traktir. They noticed valuable books, Ming vases, and a Japanese screen with yellow dragons. Bessy wrote to Uncle Henry, "I can't possibly tell you how delighted we are with the apartment." Bay wrote too. "Here I am in your apartment and writing at your own table, surrounded by the Virgin Mary in many forms. . . ."[46]

That night, Bay, Bessy, and Stickney went to 50 Avenue du Bois de Boulogne to dine with Mrs. Cameron. She wrote to Dor on Monday that Bessy was "singularly beautiful, tall, languorous, mysterious with her Egyptian profile." "Bay is writing, but God knows what. . . ."

On Monday night, Mrs. Cameron took up Henry James's *Turn of the Screw.* She found it to be "something of a ghost story." "I read it through at a sitting and was glad to find that it kept me awake."[47]

On Tuesday, the concierge at 3 Rue de Traktir, an elderly woman, refused to permit the Lodges to get mail at that address. Mrs. Cameron learned about the refusal and at once wrote to Dor. She explained that the concierge had acted "on the ground that they had no right to be there." She thought the occurrence "French and funny." She hoped Bay would talk to the concierge and bring her around. If that failed, she herself would resort to other means.[48]

On Wednesday, the landlord, Monsieur Joly, a man of eighty-three, went to the building, met Dor's guests in the hall, and confirmed that they had "no right to be there." Bay and Bessy thought resistance out of the question. Without telling Mrs. Cameron, they went to the Left Bank and rented an attic apartment on the Rue de Bac. When she found out what they had done, Mrs. Cameron could have cabled to Dor. She waited till Monday, February 4, and sent him the details by letter. That she was becoming anxious showed in her misdating the letter as written on January 4.[49]

Queen Victoria had died while Dor was on the ocean. He and Mrs. Cameron exchanged reactions. She wrote with unvarnished skepticism, ". . . [the British] are terribly worked up and think that they are grief stricken."[50] Writing from New York on January 28, 1901, Dor slightly mourned. "Even I, who, for some years, belonged to Victoria's Court in what was supposed to be its best time, and who could never see anything but selfishness and bourgeoisie to admire in the old woman, and who never received from her or any of her family so much as a sign of recognition, am a very little touched to see her disappear so tragically, broken-hearted at the wretched end of a self-satisfied reign, and nobody care."

For him, New York principally meant Clarence King, who unluckily was absent. Ternina and Bigelow were present. He continued to Mrs. Cameron: "Sturgis Bigelow is giving his jools to Ternina who is always begging him to stop. She does not sing this week, so I've no excuse for staying on."

He found Washington unchanged. On February 5, he ironically advised her, "My secret conviction is that I'm buried out at Rock Creek; but my double certainly seems to be swearing as usual at 1603."

Loulie had joined him, to provide company through the winter. He saw enough of Hay to grow worried. On the 7th, he wrote to Brooks: "I think Hay very far from strong; and doubt his ability to remain in office, though I think he wants to stay, but I must talk with Mrs[.] Hay before knowing whether anything serious is the matter. Meanwhile, do not mention my opinion."

Starting in Paris, Dor had spoken strangely about praying to dynamos. In Washington, he kept it up. He told Mrs. Cameron, ". . . [I] pray to the dynamos persistently." He complained to Brooks on February 8, ". . . I have not even a dynamo to worship in this capital of the greatest nation that ever existed." That same day in a letter to Spring Rice, he spun a false history. "I passed nine months in Paris where I saw no one, and lived a religious and austere life. Every afternoon I went to the Exposition and prayed to the dynamos. There was nothing else to respect. They alone abode in an attitude and atmosphere of thought."[51]

He had had a disturbing experience. He told Spring Rice: ". . . on landing in New York I was led directly to look at a Velasquez which came straight from Castle Howard, and was one of the most superb pictures in England. Our aristocracy is revolting. Whether it is more revolting than yours I will not decide, for Dr[.] Johnson expressly said there was no precedence between lice and fleas; but when I was young, George Howard was a nice fellow with refined tastes. He ought to have sold his wife, not his Velasquez."

Re-exposure to the Hays and exacerbated worries about rising and falling empires gave Henry an impression of having nowhere to go. He continued to Spring Rice: "You ask about Hay! I can't tell you how he is. I should say that he had lost strength. . . . But the country, which was struggling with bankruptcy five years ago, is now reeking with new wealth and superfluous energy. Its contrast with Europe is as melodramatic as a Greek play; for Europe was gloomy and despondent. As for England, I dare not go there at all. I don't know what to say or where to look." And England was not the only tottering empire. "Russia is my worst problem. That colossal dwarf has got to show its real capacity soon, and if it breaks down, as I think it must . . . I cannot see anything but chaos ahead."

By February 11, Dor knew enough to be alarmed. He revealed to Mrs. Cameron, ". . . [Hay] can't now walk with me as far as the Scott statue without what he calls *angina pectoris*, and a high wind exhausts him between here and the Department." That night Helen Hay came for dinner. She brought news that her father was in bed again, this time with a cold.

Word of Bay and Bessy's difficulty with the concierge arrived on February 12. Dor wrote at once to Mrs. Cameron. His letter began fairly sensibly but became senseless as it continued. "Yes! The French are impossible. . . . If it were only concierges! but my printer does not print; my Rodin does not arrive, and my temper is permanently injured. . . . I foresaw what you tell me about the concierge; I told her that I had invited the Lodges as guests, and that she was to be as obliging as possible to them. I gave her a hundred francs for that purpose alone. If she persists, please call in Kelley [*sic*], and tell him to take it in hand. Of course I quit at once if I mayn't have guests as I please. Kelley must settle the matter with the proprietor, and if he [Joly] persists, Kelley must notify Mrs[.] Markwald that I return the apartment to her at once. Of course, my lease is for a year, and Mrs[.] Markwald must have her rent; but I have nothing more to do in Paris, and shall not be sorry for an excuse to leave it. If you are not there, I have no reason at all for staying, and should probably go in any case."

Dor was not merely writing a letter. He was committing "sudden violence," as he called it. He tried to attribute his act to boredom. ". . . life is an intolerable bore except when one is in love. I am sixtythree (*sic*) years old this week, and bored out of my wits."

On the 18th, he received Mrs. Cameron's history of Bay and Bessy's eviction. The details made matters worse. He replied: ". . . I am white with wrath. Your letter made me sick,—upset me so that I glared wildly at Cabot Lodge and Henry Watterson with hopes of a sudden impulse of homicidal mania, that at least I might kill some one. As between them and a Frenchman, the choice was small."

If earlier it had seemed that Dor might not be serious, it grew clear he was in earnest. He let Mrs. Cameron know that he was relieving her of further trouble in the matter. ". . . I write to Kelley [*sic*] today, and send him full powers, money and discretion to get me out, save what he can, and let me hear no more of Paris."

In a new letter to her on February 25, he provided information about a request. ". . . I have sent to Kelly a Power of Attorney to close up all my affairs at Paris, with a request that, if he succeeds in rescuing my things from the various robbers and ruffians who now control them, he should let Bessie and Bay have what books and embroideries they wish to take, and you whatever porcelains, bronzes or other things you will consent to receive in hospitality, which will save me storage." Kelly's duties extended to recovering the manuscript of the Tahiti *Memoirs* from the printer and inquiring after unclothed Psyche, who had vanished in the course of shipment.

Before seeing the news that brought on his violence, Adams had told Mrs. Cameron that he intended to write "a poem on the Virgin's miracles." On the day he first sent instructions to Kelly, he said things to her that could seem to mean the poem was finished. ". . . I have returned to verse and have written a long prayer to the Virgin of Chartres. . . . It is not poetry, and it is not very like verse, and it will not amuse you to read; but it occupies me to write; which is something—at sixtythree [sic]."

He enclosed a copy of his "Prayer," or rather the stanzas that then existed. He told her: "Here is my Prayer! No one but you has seen it. No one but you would care to see it."[52]

Lida Hoyt had learned from Donald that he would not reopen his house on Lafayette Square merely because the tenant, Vice President Hobart, had died and left it vacant. Lida forwarded the news to her sister in Paris. Its implication was that Mrs. Cameron should continue to think of Europe as her place of winter residence. On this assumption, prior to being told that Adams was ridding himself of his apartment at 3 Rue de Trakir, she had signed a three-year extension of the lease at 50 Avenue du Bois de Boulogne.

Dor's letters to Kelly and Mrs. Cameron cost them several days of fright but did not prevent their making effective use of their resources. Kelly sent Monsieur Joly an imperious letter stating that Mr. Adams, like his forebears, was the most distinguished of Americans; that his young "nephew," Mr. Lodge, was nearly as distinguished; and that an apology must be forthcoming.[53] The apology came; but even sooner, assisted by Adams's servant Jean Bailly, Mrs. Cameron hurried the Ming porcelains and silk embroideries from 3 Rue de Traktir to 50 Avenue du Bois de Boulogne. Kelly put the apology into her hands, and she sent it to Adams to show him how things had stabilized. But she made no effort to rescue his books.

The arrival of Dor's possessions much improved 50 Avenue du Bois de Boulogne. In a letter begun on March 13, 1901, Mrs. Cameron outlined the effect. ". . . your Ming makes me look like a museum. It is gorgeous. I feel rich and proud."

Her fighting spirit emerged in her contradicting Dor about where he would live. "Of course you will come back to Paris. I never heard such nonsense. Where else is there to go? I do not wonder at your annoyance, but do you escape it any where in one form or another? And why punish Martha and me for the vagaries of an old man of 83?"

The thing that most interested her was Dor's fury. She was not afraid to tell him how much he frightened her. "You yourself are as mysterious as the Sphinx. You have depths that frighten me when I get a glimpse into them."

The poem he had sent afforded her glimpses whenever she read it, but she felt unsure what the glimpses permitted her to see. "The Prayer you sent me stirred me profoundly, yet I only half know what it means. I know that the trouble it stirs up does not settle for hours and that I turn back and read again."

Adams may have been right to send Mrs. Cameron his "Prayer to the Virgin of Chartres," but no guarantee existed that she or anyone could read the poem and be certain what it meant. Of the thirty-six stanzas he supplied, the first fourteen and last twelve were spoken by a person—male, but either imaginary or miraculous—who had remained alive from the days when Chartres cathedral was new. The person confessed to being "weak, weary, sore in heart and hope," yet expected to live till 2600 A.D. or thereabouts, or at least felt able to foresee what would happen by that date. Ten middle stanzas were interjected as a separate "Prayer to the Dynamo."

If this biography is right, Adams had written the ten interjected stanzas in 1893 after scrutinizing dynamos at the Chicago Fair.[54] As has already been noticed, the stanzas were not a prayer and did not in a literal sense involve a dynamo. A further complication was that, as sent to Mrs. Cameron, the "Prayer to the Virgin of Chartres" was incomplete. Indispensable stanzas remained unwritten. Adams eventually would write them. Four in number, they would be the prayer to the Virgin to which all the thirty-six stanzas he supplied in 1901 could be read as an elaborate prolegomenon.

Mrs. Cameron knew Adams better than anyone then alive. She had read his *Democracy* and his *History of the United States*.[55] After her return from Italy, she and Martha had heard him read aloud from a draft of *Mont Saint Michel and Chartres*.[56] She was a reader capable enough to borrow a concluding volume of Gibbon's *Decline and Fall* from Kelly and find it so rewarding that she wished she had started at the first page of Volume I. Her estimate of Adams's "Prayer to the Virgin of Chartres" was unquestionably worth having, and its value might be the greater because the incomplete poem and his sudden violence were coevals, pertaining to a single moment.

After reading the poem several times, she concluded that, if meant as an expression of him—or his condition, thoughts, or feelings—the poem was a mistake. In her most forthright manner, she asked him: "*Are* you as weary as that? *Can* one be? Have you all the fatigue of the generations that preceded you to bear?" With equal directness, she treated the Virgin of his stanzas as a fiction well-adapted only to the wants of her worshipers in the middle ages. ". . . your Virgin is dethroned, *they* knew what she stood for, but it is too Pagan for today and no one understands."

*   *   *

Naked Psyche had turned up in Le Havre and was again in motion toward Boston. Hay could take walks only if he and Adams walked very slowly. King had contracted tuberculosis. On March 3, Adams wrote to Mrs. Cameron: ". . . I have been hit badly by Clarence King, who stopped here last week, sent south by his doctors, broken by pneumonia and gravely threatened by worse. I am very anxious about him. So, you see, my two friends, and I might say my only two friends, are agitating me by announcing that they don't know whether they are fatally ill or not, but will tell me in a month or two."

At the Capitol on March 4, 1901, Theodore Roosevelt and William McKinley were sworn in as vice president and president. Dor might gain by the return of Roosevelt, his wife, and children to Washington. He would *not* enjoy encroachment by his brother Charles as a neighbor. Charles had become a permanent winter Washingtonian.

Dor and Mrs. Cameron had planned that he rejoin her in Paris by May 1. Though no longer willing to live in Paris, he agreed to go to Italy. He advised her on March 15: "Sister Anne invited me to sail with her to Italy at the end of April. . . . Barring Cabot's interference, we shall therefore get to Italy early in May, with eyes on Bay and Bessy and Ravenna and the Dolomites. Can't you and Martha . . . be strolling somewhere about the Lido in May?"[57]

News had come from Boston that Edward Hooper was ill and confined to bed. Dor went on to say: "I imagine it is a case of slow decline of strength, and that care, rest, and iron will galvanise him again for a time; but he too will have to go abroad if he can."

As before, Dor refused to live in Paris. In a last instalment on the 19th, he informed Mrs. Cameron: "I write today to Kelly directing him to discharge Jean Bailly, and remove such of my property as you and Bay will consent to take. . . . Probably I shall have to pass through Paris first or last, but chiefly last. The printers annoy me more than the proprietors. A week at a hotel will be enough to dispose of them all, I trust, and there an end."

Aeschylus began his play *Prometheus Bound* by having Hephaestus, the god of fire and metallurgy, appear on the stage with two helpers, Force and Violence, to obey an order by Zeus that Prometheus be bound with nails and chains to a peak of the Caucasus. Here we may note the helpers. Force assists Hephaestus in the binding and speaks volubly as they proceed. Violence has no lines and presumably stands aside.

One of the ideas suggested is that violence is a last resort. A second is that violence is speechless. A third is that violence, while stronger than force, cannot be trusted and may sometimes light at random—hurt whatever may be near.[58]

For sixty-three years, Adams had been a paragon of self-control. Always energetic, he had often been forceful in his acts, but he had not been violent. When he erased 3 Rue de Traktir from his life, he perhaps tried to take careful aim and do what his feelings prompted him to do, yet his erasure of the apartment can seem to have been a random act. He said himself that the matter of the apartment was "superficial."[59] What then was substantial? What was deep?

The most private aspects of Adams's experiences were private to such a degree that observers might well despair of seeing into them. Yet a theory about what was troubling him could be suggested—a theory based on his age. It could seem that at sixty-three he felt too old for love; that he felt no longer suited to intimacy with Mrs. Cameron; and that the result was an interval of "white fury" directed at an aged Paris landlord who owned a particular apartment.[60] Mrs. Cameron might similarly be imagined to have felt that he was striking at their arrangement and bringing it to an end. But she did not have that idea. She could understand his not wanting to live again at 3 Rue de Traktir or even his wanting not to live in Paris, but she did not understand him to want a separation. He too did not want one.

A second theory could fix on Adams's temper. He was adapted to a particular sort of violence, the murder of a man. In 1901, a man he almost hated was Lodge. On February 8, he had described the senator as "a second-rate school-boy."[61] More expressively on February 25, he had told Mrs. Cameron that Lodge was "an indescribable product of New England and New Jersey immorality." A practical feature of Lodge's immorality had been daily annoyance for Hay as he attempted to manage the country's foreign affairs. Hay's trials considered, it can be tempting to think that Adams killed his tenure at a Paris apartment as a substitute for killing a senator from Massachusetts. It however was evident that his hatred of Lodge was small, as compared with his contempt. Really a murder-of-Lodge theory cannot be helpful.[62]

A third suggestion could have to do with impatience. It might be supposed that Adams came suddenly to resent his being called upon to redress the egregious error of James Donald Cameron's marriage by being the friend of the husband, the surrogate husband of the wife, and the alternative father of the daughter. He might be viewed also as suddenly restive in his capacity as the prop of John and Clara Hay. Yet the evident truth was that Adams was too loving to be impatient. He loved Hay and King unconditionally. Even stronger terms would suit his love for Mrs. Cameron. He began his letters to her without salutations. Within the letters, he never spoke to her by name. It thus might seem hard to guess how he addressed her when they were by themselves. Yet a conjecture is possible. One notices his letter to her of February 15,

1901. The letter began, "You poor martyred angel!" A single indication may suffice. Possibly in their close moments, he always spoke to her as "Angel." The word would carry with it assurance that neither she nor her marriage could impair his patience, and assurance in addition that her tie with him was blameless.[63]

What, then, accounted for the violence?

One may turn to some words he recently had emphasized. As sent to Mrs. Cameron, his "Prayer to the Virgin of Chartres" closed with the five words "Mother and Child in One!" Needless to say, the five words denoted Mary and Jesus. Yet they were also descriptive of Adams's own experience as understood by him. True, the mother with whom he felt as one was a grandmother. As he felt the tie, Louisa Catherine Adams had been his real mother, sole author, and earlier self.

A sixth word needs attention. For Adams, as for others, "dynamo" usually meant a device for generating electricity. Differently, in the title "Prayer to the Dynamo," he had used the word somewhat as a metaphor indicative of the physical universe. Yet sometimes he would use "dynamo" to mean the United States. From Washington on February 11, he had written to Mrs. Cameron, "As for me, I am running the shop." He then balanced the statement by telling her on February 18, "If you want to take charge of the dynamo[,] you can."

When the six words are brought together, Dor can be seen to be the mother's son who was born to run a dynamo, the United States. Yet a link is missing. A calculation is needed about the abilities of the son and whatever might make him waver.

Think of him as a self-guided dray horse pulling wagons. From an early age, whether as Henry, or George, or Dor, he voluntarily had drawn the heaviest wagons that his era, his country, his identity, and his talents could harness to mind and body. He drew them rapidly. In 1901, when he learned about Bay and Bessy's eviction, he went into a fury. At the same time, he watched himself get into the fury and saw himself act. It was important that he was able to watch, for what he watched had a helpful meaning. When taxed to the very utmost, *he had drawn too fast* and in consequence had committed an inanity: the murder of an apartment. The problem was not an apartment, not Paris. It was not place. It was pace.

In the future, the horse would go on, but with caution. By moving at a modified rate, he would not lapse again.

PART TWO

10

BOTHERED BY THE
SLAUGHTERHOUSE

Anna Lodge had become a Richard Wagner enthusiast. On March
20, 1901, Adams accompanied her to New York to hear Ternina
sing Brünnhilde in *Götterdämmerung*. What with the extreme idea of a
goddess's suicide, the chromatic music, Ternina's voice, and a conviction he formed that most members of the audience could not guess the
meaning of what they very attentively heard and saw, Adams responded
to the performance as "a world-shaking experience." He confessed to
Anne Fell: ". . . this American world, or rather this twentieth century,
strains my nerves to a point which needs rest." He seemed to feel he was
being given too many ideas. "My precious donkey-ears are glued to a
telephone which says all sorts of startling things."[1]

Telegrams arrived from Loulie in Boston. After midnight at his
house on Beacon Street, Edward Hooper had thrown himself from a
back upper-story window. His fall was broken by clothes lines, and he
was little injured.[2] Predictably, because his ailments were chiefly mental,
his doctors would commit him to an asylum. In reaction, Adams wrote a
"long calamity-wail" to Mrs. Cameron. His letter—no longer extant—
may have referred to the suicides of Marian Adams and Ellen Gurney as
ancillary causes of their brother's near-fatal act.[3]

President McKinley informed the Lodges that he would visit them
on July 1 at their summer home north of Boston. His announcement
quashed the Lodges' travel plan and Adams's hope that he could accompany them to Italy. He advised Gaskell on March 29 that the devil was
raging. A new plan had to be made. Hay was "very down." King was
critically ill. And Hooper was laid low—"probably for life."

Loulie and her sisters sent word that their father was improving.
Adams remembered similar news about their grandfather in 1885. He
told Mrs. Cameron on April 2, "Boston sends . . . such hopeful, not to
say confident reports, that I fully expect the worst."

Impending deaths did not prevent his reading newspapers. He noted that stress was increasing for millions of human beings: that American industrial and financial competition was hurting the Old World. He assured Mrs. Cameron: "Europe is wriggling like a mouse in a cat's mouth. She is a mouse or a rat or a parrot, as the case may be, but we are skinning her alive. . . . The situation is killing the Czar, and has driven the Kaiser mad, and has brutalised England, and Chinafied France; and it grows more intense every week." He gave instructions. ". . . be careful where you go. Don't get too far away! Don't let Martha get exploded by a bomb! Come home, and explode here!"

Mrs. Cameron had gone with Martha to Naples and thence to Sicily, principally to see Monreale. She had sent Dor a line of protest on March 26 from Syracuse. "It is almost time for you to start somewhere where we can meet you[,] if Paris is to be ostracized—but you really cannot mean it." Five days later from Palermo, she burst out: "I still protest about your French decision. It never occurred to me until you wrote to Kelly that you meant it. I protest from all sides. I have just re-rented for three years, but if you are not there I cannot stay. And where is there to go? *I* don't know of any place. You really must reconsider. I am delighted to have you give up the apartment. I never liked that anyway, but as to coming back there, you really must. Or you must find a place where I can go too."

She had seen the cathedral. "Monreale took my breath away—you never told me what it was, and I was stunned." And she was seeing a young English Rothschild. "The boy is Lionel, a son of Leopold's, and he is at Cambridge." ". . . I like the boy! A Jew, too!"[4]

With a mind to King, Adams had consulted their friend "Frank" Emmons and acquired a supply of books. He told Mrs. Cameron, ". . . I read tubs of geology. . . ."[5] On April 5, he held a dinner for available geologists, beginning with Emmons. Talk at dinner presumably concerned King, his achievements in science, and his fatal illness.

Adams wished to reexperience the disturbance of hearing Ternina in *Götterdämmerung*. He had written to Gaskell on March 29, ". . . I want once more to hear Ternina sing Brynhilde [*sic*], and I may come to London to risk it in May." He may have said the same to Mrs. Lodge. She had asked him to accompany her and the senator to Russia. She made a new suggestion that they first hear the operas of Wagner's *Ring*. Dor advised Mrs. Cameron on April 8: "Sister Anne thinks she will sail on July 3, and go to Baireuth, and thence to Russia; to this plan, I acquiesce." He inadvertently failed to say that he would not sail with the Lodges in July but would come to Europe much earlier.[6]

The financial markets were in chaos. In the same letter, Dor attributed the condition to the ever-increasing power of a banker in New York. He painted a vivid image. "London and Berlin are standing in perfectly abject terror, watching Pierpont Morgan's nose flaming over the ocean waves, and approaching hourly nearer their bank-vaults."

Mrs. Cameron returned to Naples and found an old letter from Adams asking her to meet him in Venice. Amazed, she replied on April 5: "Your letter confounds me. Are you actually going to Venice which you hate? And you are in earnest about Paris? What shall I do?"

Lack of hotel space drove her from Rome to Florence. She supposed Dor would sail by May 1. The prospect raised her spirits. She wrote on April 8: "How glad I shall be to see you! I wonder if I can linger in Italy so long— I may meet you in Paris but wherever it is still it will be meeting you, seeing you again." In the belief that he was coming on the very ship that would bring him the letter she had just completed, she ceased to write. Meanwhile, in Florence, she had met an interesting couple. The husband, Bernhard Berenson, was an authority on art.[7] He was Jewish. For her, much ice was being broken.

On April 15, 1901, King paused fleetingly at 1603 H Street.[8] He expected to go for treatment to the southwest, was cheerful, looked ten years older, and held out no hope whatever of survival.

By mail, Adams instructed Loulie in business management, to help her take charge of the Hoopers' money. Through his nephew Charles, he suggested a plan—later adopted—to move the Adams family's papers to the Massachusetts Historical Society for preservation, with a stipulation that they be withheld from inquirers for fifty years.[9]

Kelly had shifted the books from 3 Rue de Traktir to 50 Avenue du Bois de Boulogne. Writing to Bessy Lodge on April 16, Adams said the books would "have to be packed up and stored." Their rescue tended to suggest a better idea: that Adams should maintain two libraries, the large one in Washington, a much smaller one in Paris.

He had brought from Paris the all-but-completed first draft of *Mont Saint Michel and Chartres*. John La Farge was visiting. Dor advised Mrs. Cameron on April 22, ". . . I am reading him my Miracles of the Virgin!" (He meant Chapter XIII, "Les Miracles de Notre Dame.") The experiment might reveal how the writings of a non-Catholic about the Virgin would strike a Catholic born and bred. La Farge listened appreciatively, so much so that he became "quite upset." ". . . he almost had a husk in his voice. . . ."

Hay came daily for careful walks. Alexander Agassiz, the Boston entrepreneur whose copper mine in the midwest was Adams's main source of wealth, dropped by and joined with Adams in amazement at the rise of American industry and the fall of Europe's empires. Dor told Mrs. Cameron: ". . . I feel my poor old bald head creep with horror at the chances. Never since Adam left Paradise has there been such awful gambling and such chips on the table. No geological epoch was ever more suggestive of change. Positively I sit here, and look at Europe sink, first one deck disappearing, then another, and the whole ship slowly plunging bow-down into the abyss; until the nightmare gets to be howling. . . . My eyes can't quit it. Why don't the English run away—take to the boats—throw out rafts—send off rockets—fire off cannon? Why sink so, just stupid-drunk with beer! What horrible deity makes them blind and deaf!"

Donald informed Mrs. Cameron that he would stay in America through the summer. She decided she had to join him. On April 23, 1901, she cabled to Dor that she was going home in June. Her cable was ill-worded. It did not make clear that the decision was her own idea.

Uncertainty about Edward Hooper forced Adams to postpone his sailing. Late in April, Hooper was moved to McLean Hospital near Boston. Adams was freed, yet he worried. Letters had ceased to come from Mrs. Cameron. Beginning a letter to her on May 6, he said he was "seriously uneasy."[10] He added that he would sail on May 15, cable before he sailed, pause in London only to do errands, and come to Paris. Next day, he realized that he himself had stopped her letters by failing to tell her that his arrival was delayed. He confessed his mistake. He at the same time mistakenly assumed that Donald had ordered her home. On this erroneous basis, he retracted his refusal to live in Paris. "If you have to abandon Paris, I will take the apartment [at 50 Avenue du Bois de Boulogne]. . . . Paris is a pretty dreary place . . . but I am not better off elsewhere, and I can't stay always here."

Mrs. Cameron planned to sail with Lida on June 26 or July 6. She reached Paris on May 10 and found several of Dor's letters. They indicated that he and she were not going to meet at all! She wrote at once and was driven to tell him, ". . . as far as I can make out—[you] are not sailing till July 3rd, which means that I shall not see you."

There were many things to say. ". . . I saw much of the Berensons in Florence—think of me with Berenson!" Yet her great concern was their tie to one another. She feared a breakup. ". . . what am I to do? I am going to America, and perhaps for good. Since you won't return to Paris, why should I? And in that case, as I have rights of entry [at 3 Rue de Traktir], don't you want me to bring a lot of your things home to you?" "If this partnership is not to continue[,] you must certainly have yr. things." "Bay . . . took some of the porcelain." "But write, write, I feel all at sea."[11]

When Adams sailed from New York on the *St. Louis* on May 15, 1901, Mrs. Cameron knew from a cable, letters, and a talk with Kelly that she would have four weeks with Dor in Paris. In a letter begun in Paris on the 18th, she told him, "I never knew a more complete comedy of errors." "Dear, dear! it has not been funny." "Donald wrote that he would not come over[,] so I said that we would go there. Of course, I don't want to. Lida and I will go back together. . . . ."

By May 31, Adams was in Paris, settled at the Hôtel Beau Site and dining with Mrs. Cameron and Martha at 50 Avenue du Bois de Boulogne. He rented an automobile and hired a chauffeur. When convenient, he took mother and daughter on drives to places near Paris.

The manuscript of *Memoirs of Arii Taimai* was still at the printshop. Adams asked the printer to complete the edition.[12]

News came on June 24 that Adelbert Hay, during a reunion at Yale, fell late at night from a high window ledge and was found dead. His death seemed to portend untold evil for his parents.[13] Adams cabled, telling Hay he was "bitterly sorry" not to be with him.

Messages from the Hooper nieces shortly informed Adams that their father had died of pneumonia at the hospital.[14]

Mrs. Cameron and Martha left Paris for their steamer on June 29. Adams on the same day began an excursion with Bay and Bessy Lodge to Beauvais in the rented automobile. They saw the cathedral, but breakdowns slowed their arrival and forced their return by train. Adams concluded that the vehicle was underpowered. On July 3, he advised Mrs. Cameron that he had dismissed vehicle and driver. ". . . I shall never try anything short of 12 horses again."

He by then had reoccupied 50 Avenue du Bois de Boulogne. The printing of the *Memoirs* was advancing slowly. With a view to *Mont Saint Michel and Chartres*, he began to think of printers elsewhere.[15]

Senator Lodge obtained tickets for him, his wife, Bay, Bessy, and Adams to hear Wagner's *Ring* at Bayreuth. On July 21, 1901, Adams left Paris to join his hosts. In Bayreuth, he discovered that his landlady was Jewish, which he thought preferable to her being German. Ternina had come but would not be singing.

Lodge affected Dor as tolerable when away from Washington, but Dor was not looking forward to the operas, *Gotterdämmerung* excepted. He reported to Mrs. Cameron on the 26th: "Today comes a long session with the Valkyrie. I hope I shall get through without express profanity; but I am quite clear that for a delicate digestion like mine, with a tendency to insomnia, the Wagnerian beer-and-sausage should be taken in short gulps, and at concerts." He disagreed with Wagner's idea of opera as drama. "The literary-dramatic expression gives me the same spasms that a Church-of-England Bishop does, in the pulpit."

The last curtain fell on the *Ring*, and the Lodges' party set out for Salzburg and a week of Mozart. En route on August 3, from Nuremburg, Dor summarized for Mrs. Cameron the effect of Wagner's work. ". . . except to have seen it all, without cuts or abbreviations, I do not think I am better off." He said that "such a monstrosity of form" showed "loss of artistic sense." He equally recoiled from the changed face of Germany. One of his "first delights in art, way back in '59," had been a stop at Nuremburg. To his eyes, the Nuremburg of 1901 was artistically depraved. While still in the city, he told Mrs. Cameron: "It makes me happy to think that I shall never see it again. . . . In fact, I have had more than enough of Europe altogether, and I'm afraid my appetite for America is not voracious either. The world has lived too long. So have I. One of us two has got to go."

As befitted a member of the Senate Committee on Foreign Relations, Lodge planned a political trip to Russia. Differently, Mrs. Lodge and Adams wished to see the treasures in the Hermitage at St. Petersburg.

Bay and Bessy left Salzburg, bound for America. The elder Lodges and Adams set out for Moscow by way of Warsaw. The route permitted Adams many glimpses of Polish Jews. As nearly as he could judge from their clothes and bearing, they were outdated, obsolete human beings. It struck him that he too was outdated and obsolete. The thought made him very uncomfortable. On August 14, he sent Mrs. Cameron an evocation of Warsaw. "The Jews and I are the only curious antiquities in it. My only merit as a curio is antiquity, but the Jew is also a curiosity. He makes me creep."[16]

An American-made railroad car bore the party to Moscow. As seen from the car, Russia was a country of scattered log cabins variegated by cities five hundred miles apart. On the 17th, Adams continued his chronicle. ". . . I really want to see this big creature of a country, and big it certainly is. It dwarfs Europe instantly. . . . It is like America, and small things do not seem at home in it; but it is at least three generations behind us, economically and socially. . . . I'm satisfied already. Just looking out of the car window is enough."

In Moscow, the Lodges and Adams toured the Kremlin. Later, apparently alone, Adams witnessed mass at a new church. His account of the mass, written for Mrs. Cameron on August 21, drew on his historical resources. "As I watched it from the gallery, above the dense crowd, I thought that a crusader of the twelfth century . . . could have stood by my side and told me all about it without a sign of surprise. . . . The

Russian mass is a marvellous composite of the Jewish tabernacle and the first crusade. The robes are those of St[.] Louis, Godfrey of Bouillon, Solomon, Justinian,—I don't know who not—and the ceremonies those of Solomon's temple. I never saw anything more fascinating. Except the Athanasian Creed[,] I know nothing more Greek."

Even more than by the clergymen, Adams was fascinated by the congregants. "In some ways, I feel sure, the Russian of today is more primitive than the Frenchman or the German ever was. . . ." "I find my chief interest in watching the people in the churches and shrines. What I can't make out is whether the attitude is as completely passive as it seems, or whether there is an occasional gleam of fanatical fire. Thus far I've seen not a sign of individuality."

The party hurried to St. Petersburg. The first secretary at the U. S. legation, Herbert Peirce, was Mrs. Lodge's cousin.[17] With his help, the travelers visited the Hermitage for two hours and in the evening—five miles out of town—heard an opera "by a certain Boradin [*sic*], just like a Chinese play that has no beginning or end, but a ballet scattered about the middle."[18]

Senator Lodge was scheduled for interviews, notably with Sergei Witte. Mrs. Lodge and Adams returned to the Hermitage, where the paintings, to Adams's regret, were mostly Dutch. He shortly told Mrs. Cameron, ". . . I don't know that there is one touch of Michael Angelo [*sic*]." "You who know my sentiment for Dutch art and Dutch taste can conceive exactly what enthusiasm I feel here."[19]

The Lodges left on August 31 by a route via Berlin. Adams planned to return alone by way of Sweden. He meanwhile was brushed by deaths, past and anticipated. His surroundings reminded him that his grandmother's only daughter had died in infancy in St. Petersburg in 1812, and a letter from Hay brought him "very bad news of King."[20]

Mainly he was satisfied. In a letter begun on September 1, 1901, he assured Mrs. Cameron: ". . . I've got what I came for; I've done my Bayreuth, and retouched my Austria, and scraped the varnish off Russia. . . . The sum of my certainty is that America has a very clear century of start over Russia, and that western Europe must follow us for a hundred years, before Russia can swing her flail over the Atlantic. Whether she can do it then is no conundrum that I can settle. I imagine that my grandpapa, sitting here in his study ninety years ago, could see ahead to me now, better than I can see ahead to the year 2000, and yet it was not easy guessing even for him."

First Secretary Peirce wished to show Adams the best that Russia had to offer.[21] Next day, he led his visitor from St. Petersburg to the Summer Palace, which Catherine the Great inherited and improved. Later that day, Adams reported to Mrs. Cameron that it was the "prettiest royal residence I know." ". . . the park is as amusing as the palace. Poor Sister Anne [Mrs. Lodge] will be furious."

St. Petersburg was not done with him. The Swedish minister to Russia, Count Gyldenstolpe, had served as secretary of legation in Washington in 1885. Adams joined the Gyldenstolpes for a midday meal on September 3 and was told that certain ancient Greek terracotta figures found in the Crimea were unexampled in keeping their original appearance. The figures had been acquired by the Hermitage.

That evening, while dining with Peirce, Adams asked the secretary to inquire at the Hermitage about a Greek sphinx. The work was "said to be kept in the dark, under seal, to preserve its colors."

On the 4th, Adams and Secretary Peirce repaired to the Hermitage. For Adams, what followed was a return to ancient Greece. The director appeared with a case, broke its seals, and showed the Americans a miniature sphinx and a miniature Aphrodite—"just coming out of her opening shell, to make you scream with delight." In the afternoon, before boarding his ship for Stockholm, Adams tried to tell Mrs. Cameron what made the figures so arresting. "About the size of the usual figurine . . . these two little things seemed to be enameled with wax, and the color laid on, I imagine in the enamel; but of processes I know nothing. Only I know that the colors seem perfectly fresh, and yet refined, delicate and fluid to a degree that rivals true glazes." ". . . but it is the fascinating naïveté, of the work; the childlike charm of the touch; the divine youth of the art and the artist, that makes one curl up and wilt."

Adams passed September 6, 1901, in Stockholm. Next morning, he finished the chronicle he had been writing to Mrs. Cameron, mailed it, and went to a restaurant. While eating breakfast, he read in a newspaper that President McKinley had been shot but was still alive. The news paralleled what was reported after the shooting of President Garfield. One of Adams's first thoughts, perhaps the very first, was that McKinley would soon be dead and Theodore Roosevelt would succeed him. In the afternoon or evening, he ended a letter to Hay by saying: ". . . behind all, in my mind, in all our minds, silent and awful like the Chicago express, flies the thought of Teddy's luck!"

The details of the attack were not encouraging. On September 6, McKinley was greeting well-wishers at the Pan-American Exposition in Buffalo, New York. Within steps of his guards, he was shot twice at close range with a .32 calibre revolver by one of a file of persons who were walking toward him to receive a quick word and a handshake. As had happened in the case of Garfield, a bullet was still lodged in McKinley's body after the surgeons probed and closed his wounds.

There were the usual reports that the president would recover. Adams cannot be imagined to have believed them. He *can* be imagined to have believed that McKinley's death would injure a class of persons to whom he, Adams, was attached. The assassin, Leon Czolgosz, a son of Polish immigrants, was an anarchist in the European mold. He identified himself with a half-German alias, Fred Niemand, translatable as Fred Nobody. His crime perhaps made sense to him, but it harmed every anarchist in the United States, even if Christian and even if conservative. Adams was badly harmed. In the future, he would sometimes claim the role of anarchist; but Nobody's idiotic act gave the word an unwanted lack of helpful meaning; and there might be many times when Adams would feel himself an anarchist, yet keep silent.[22]

Mrs. Cameron's summer in America had begun at Coney Island. She hurried from there to Beverly Farms and looked at houses for rent. (Pitch Pine Hill had been occupied by Adams's nieces.) Martha had gone with Donald to his Pennsylvania farm. Mrs. Cameron joined them and was pleased to see that the place had been refurbished. Father, mother, and daughter tried to stay but were driven away by flies and heat. Donald chose flight to a rentable house at Beverly Farms.

On July 17, while still in Pennsylvania, Mrs. Cameron wrote to Dor, "It seems to be a recognized and established idea that I am to return [to Paris] in October." After the flight to Massachusetts, she contrived to pass some enjoyable days in Rhode Island. From Newport on August 27, she asked her faraway partner: "How is Europe, you pessimist? Is that still above water? No one will believe in disaster over here. . . . I wish I knew where you are."

She was again at Beverly Farms on September 7 when the president was shot. Next day she asked Dor: "Well, my dear, what do you think of all this? This is a how-de-do? Teddy and Cabinet are in Buffalo or on their way. . . ." "Think of Teddy in the White House—there is no limit to his luck. It has driven every thing else out of my head as well as out of the newspapers."

She hated McKinley for his share in the late-in-life misfortunes of her Uncle John. She went on to ask Dor, "How about meeting me in London?" "McKinley is better.— I am afraid he may live!"

On the North Sea en route to Stockholm, Adams had felt he crossed a north-south line to the east of which everything was under Russian influence and to the west of which everything was Yankee. The Swedish capital was evidence. It had "trees and a dry, blue sky, and hot sun, like Boston, and [was] just like it too in the looks of the people, for if ever there was a Yankeer [*sic*] than Yankee, he's a Swede."

A thought seized him that he should hurry by rail to Trondheim in Norway and thence by ship to Hammerfest, above the Arctic Circle and near North Cape. He easily proceeded to Hammerfest, ate reindeer, and saw some Lapps, whom he described as "lovely dirty little goblins in skins." He learned that in November the inhabitants simply turned on their electric lamps and went on "gaily catching fish."

Travel had often moved him to write beyond his usual powers. New scenes lent courage to his imagination and freed him to say things he could not have intended but said under impulsion from without. During the voyage from Trondheim to Hammerfest, he had looked from the ship at arctic mountains and had cried. In a new chronicle he had started for Mrs. Cameron on September 10, he explained: "This is the sadness of a life that never knew fun. These long mountains stretching their legs out into the sea never knew what it was to be a volcano. They lie, one after another, like corpses, with their toes up, and you pass by them, and look five or ten miles up the fiords between them, and see their noses, tipped by cloud or snow, high in behind, with one corpse occasionally lying on another, and a skull or a thigh-bone chucked about, and hundreds of glaciers and snow-patches hanging to them, as though it was a winter battle-field. . . ."

At Hammerfest, he read in a newspaper that McKinley's strength was gone and his condition hopeless. The return to Trondheim ended in the evening of September 16. He stepped ashore and saw bulletins saying McKinley had died and Roosevelt was sworn in. He ended his chronicle: "So Teddy is President! Is not that stupendous! Before such a career as that, I have no observations to make."

For the better part of eleven years, since August 1890, Adams had been a world-traveler. Since the Panic of 1893, he had been an active but very invisible politician. In both respects, his return to Paris in 1901 via Copenhagen and Bremen marked the beginning of curtailment. He would never make another far-reaching journey. When again at home, he would rejoin the Hays, but would want mainly to accord them his company and affection. So two Henry Adamses—the traveler and the politician—were much diminished. Yet two others—the Washingtonian and the writer—still lived. If possible, the writer had improved.

Journeys had ended; trips continued. Before going to England to meet Mrs. Cameron, Adams fitted in a long trip through southwestern France. He later reported to Loulie: ". . . [I] did my twelfth century like a crusader. I took the Brice girls to Tours, and chaperoned them to Langeais and Azay . . . went back to Angers . . . and down to Bordeaux and Toulouse and Albi; then back to Clermont Ferrand and to Bourges. I saw a deal of very fine glass, and some typical twelfth century churches.

They are things I ought to have seen forty years ago, but . . . I should not have understood them. . . ."[23]

During a stop in Washington in October 1901, Mrs. Cameron went to the White House and reported happily to Adams that Theodore and Edith Roosevelt were "as unaffectedly pleased to be there as anyone I have ever seen."[24] Mrs. Cameron was older than the president by less than a year. For her, continued relations with him were unproblematical. Hay and Adams were not so lucky. In the new Washington created by the murder of McKinley, each of them counted suddenly as much older.

As if to bridge the chasm, Roosevelt asked Hay to remain secretary of state as long as he himself might be president. Hay acceded to the request but took the liberty of repeating to Adams a telling example of the chief executive's offhand conversation. "Teddy said the other day 'I am not going to be the slave of the tradition that forbids Presidents from seeing their friends. I am going to dine with you & Henry Adams & Cabot whenever I like. But' (here the shadow of the crown sobered him a little) 'of course I must preserve the prerogative of the initiative. . . .' "[25]

Brooks meanwhile had reacted to Roosevelt's accession by planning to take Evelyn to Washington and move in at 1603 H Street. Writing to Henry on October 13, he admitted that his uninvited occupancy of the house might seem "rather cool." To justify it, he said, "I'm in for the new world." ". . . a nation is only great once."

In Paris, the printer had finished the edition of *Memoirs of Arii Taimai*. Henry sent a copy to Tati for approval or disapproval. He stacked the others in Martha's schoolroom at 50 Avenue du Bois de Boulogne. All were printed with wide margins on high-quality paper. Most were bound in blue cloth and bore on their backstrips a date in gold, "1901," and a reddish-brown leather label lettered in gold leaf to say "TAHITI." A few copies remained unbound.

Henry wanted to contact a London printer about an edition of *Mont Saint Michel and Chartres.*[26] He crossed the Channel on October 21, 1901, put up at Brown's Hotel, visited a printer, and connected with Mrs. Cameron and Martha.[27]

By November 2, Dor, mother, and Martha were in Paris, he at the Hôtel Beau Site. His accommodations must have seemed barren. Many of his Paris furnishings had been shipped by Kelly to Washington.[28]

Weeks passed. Writing to Niece Loulie on November 26, Adams said he had "a volume on Tahiti which I can do nothing with, until I hear from Tati." Rather than stay in Paris till January, he meant to leave before Christmas. Two chief concerns were King's condition and the effect of Adelbert's death on the Hays. On November 17, Hay had reported that King was dying penniless in Phoenix. He added, "If one of us could go out there and kill him, it would be a brotherly act."

Adams left for his steamer on December 21. King died in Pasadena on the 24th. A telegram from Emmons, delivered to Adams in New York, said the funeral would be held in New York on New Year's Day.

In a first letter to Mrs. Cameron from New York, Adams said he would attend the service before going to Washington. Also he noted that on shipboard he fell in with a couple, Mr. and Mrs. Fred Tams of Tuxedo Park, New York. "Mrs[.] Tams became my oldest friend. . . ."

As foretold, Brooks and Evelyn were in occupancy at Henry's house when he arrived. Brooks was a former Democrat anxious to be reborn as a pro-Roosevelt Republican. He had found a friend in Don Cameron and wanted the aging Pennsylvanian to attempt a return to politics either as senator or governor—a wholly impracticable idea.

In a new letter from Washington on January 5, 1902, Henry thought to tell Mrs. Cameron, "I was first mourner at King's funeral, among all our acquaintance. . . ." His place in King's affections was apparently well-known.

Henry that morning had performed the duty of an early visit to the executive mansion. Mrs. Cameron would need to know the details. "I went over to the White House, with Hay, and Edie [Edith Roosevelt] showed me over it, green-houses included, and the children thrown in. As you have done it all, I need not tell you about it. Theodore appeared only to say how-d'ye." The errand led to an agreement that five-year-old Quentin Roosevelt should go often to 1603 H Street to play with Martha's toys. In the afternoon, Hay and Adams took their "first regulation walk." Brooks and Evelyn dined elsewhere that evening, but Langley came and kept Henry company.

A risky development was an invitation to dine with the Roosevelts on January 10. Adams, the Hays, and the Lodges were invited. Adams did not know the name of the necessary fourth woman at the table.

On the fated evening, the Hays came in their carriage to Adams's door—"to pick me up and take me across to the slaughter-house." The Lodges were already at the executive mansion or shortly arrived. According to a letter Adams wrote to Mrs. Cameron on January 14, the fourth woman turned out to be "Mrs[.] Selmes of Minnesota, whom I must have known in the Hayes epoch, and who came on me like a ghost."

The guests waited twenty minutes for the Roosevelts "in the hideous red drawing-room." The meal in the private dining room was "indiffer-

ent" and "very badly served." ". . . Cabot was bright; Hay was just a little
older and a thought more formal than once we were; Edith was very
bright and gay; but as usual Theodore absorbed the conversation, and
if he tired me ten years ago, he crushes me now." Adams was treated as
old enough to deserve respect and uninformed enough to need instruction. "One condition is clear! Hay and I are shoved up to a distinct
seniority; we are sages." "Really Theodore is exasperating even to me,
and always was. His want of tact hurts Congressmen and Senators more
than it does me, but what annoys me is his childlike and infantile superficiality with his boyish dogmatism of assertion. He lectures me on history as though he were a high-school pedagogue. Of course I fall back
instantly on my protective pose of ignorance, which aggravates his assertions, and so we drift steadily apart."

Washington's new realities taught Adams that he could continue his
exertions as a writer and could speak with trusted men and women, or
children who came to enjoy the toys; but he would have to keep entirely
clear of conversations with politicians, Hay excepted.

A former student of his, Henry Osborn Taylor, had become an expert on things medieval. On January 15, 1902, he wrote to Taylor asking
whether some books he needed on medieval subjects could be obtained
for him in New York. Rather broadly, he explained, "My books are all
locked up in Paris in my bank-vault. . . ."

Taylor could not find the books.[29] Undismayed, Adams started a second draft of *Mont Saint Michel and Chartres*. His *History of the United States*
owed much of its superiority to his having written each of its volumes
three times and to his having subjected each draft to close scrutiny and
improvement. His procedure when completing *Mont Saint Michel and
Chartres* was still more strenuous. He meant to improve the book as
much and as long as his strength permitted.

Brooks and Evelyn went to visit Donald at Coffin's Point, intending
thereafter to spend an interval in Cuba. George Kennan, Gonzalo de
Quesado, and Montague White shared meals with Henry and satisfied,
or failed to satisfy, his strong appetite for information about China,
Cuba, and South Africa.[30] Henry watched Hay for signs of change. On
January 19, he wrote to Mrs. Cameron: "John seems to be quite well, for
him, and in good spirits; but he is singularly detached. His attitude
towards Theodore is that of a benevolent and amused uncle."

Henry was still more detached. He had become a political insider
who was also a political non-participant. A week later, on January 26, he
told Mrs. Cameron that he was "in the very heart of the world, with my
fingers close to the valves, and I pass my time entirely in the 12th century, as far away as mind can get!"

A treaty negotiated by Hay was sailing easily through the Senate. The treaty would complete the purchase of the Virgin Islands from Denmark—a process started by Secretary Seward in times forgotten. With an easy victory for Hay to talk about, Henry and his remaining friend could take their walks in a buoyant spirit. "Every day before five o'clock we prowl up Connecticut Avenue and discuss mankind. Really I think he sees no one else. As for Cabot I've not spoken to him, and Roosevelt I've not seen, though Mrs[.] Roosevelt has 'sent for me' to what she calls supper this evening . . . and I must go. . . ."[31]

Under pressures of many sorts, Henry had clarified his view of marriage. He wrote his fullest statement to Mrs. Cameron on January 27 after going to Mrs. Roosevelt's "supper." During the meal, the president was quieter; Edith made a favorable impression; and Henry came away prepared to pay her a most decided compliment. "Edith was very bright, and is really a charmingly simple and sympathetic White House head; the first, I think, in history." Yet also he framed an anarchic suggestion. ". . . I wish and wish that society would not insist that there is only one form of marriage. Why may not every man and woman make what contract they please, subject to proper provision for birth or death, and call it what they like!"

His letters to Mrs. Cameron told a story of alteration. He wrote on February 2, 1902, "The caitiff Rockhill is trying to get back to China! what a restless tom-cat he is." He added two days later, "Hay cares for nothing any longer, that I can see, and to me he shows no more appetite for conquest. The one and only great diplomatic battlefield for us is British Columbia and Manchuria. Hay is completely blocked on both. [Joseph] Chamberlain straddles British Columbia, and holds him off. Russia straddles Manchuria. Hay would have to break down both of them, and he is justly afraid even to whisper of it."[32] "Your Paris attic has certain merits; but even here I can drop back on the thirteenth century; and there I go!"

Marriage was again thrust on his mind by Helen Hay's engagement to Payne Whitney, a very rich New Yorker. They were married on February 6. Dor stayed away—as he told Mrs. Cameron—"on general principles." He had called on Helen ahead of time and had seen what he feared: a fiancée swamped in expensive wedding presents. "As she sat there, overwhelmed by tons of silver and gold, the evening before the wedding, blind with head-ache, I dropped the curtain and went back to my cave. My simple, foolish, helpless, unstylish, unfashionable little Helen has got to become either a New York swell, or a failure."

*   *   *

Henry was trying to refrain from saying anything whatever.[33] Hay had been given the duty of composing a eulogy on McKinley. Brooks had published a eulogy, and Hay paid it the compliment of adopting its ideas.[34] During walks, Henry learned about Hay's progress. At tea thereafter, he marveled at John and Clara's condition. He told Mrs. Cameron on February 18: "As to health and spirits, I have never seen either so well since years. How we fatten on graves!"

In the past, Henry had placed unlimited trust in Mrs. Cameron and incurred no penalties. The trust he and she had practiced led him to trust Mrs. Lodge. The president had a daughter Alice who shared her father's appetite for being noticed in the press. On February 28 or March 1, Mrs. Lodge came to 1603 H Street and asked a question. Had the questioner been anyone else, Adams might have saved himself from replying. He replied and on March 4 outlined the consequence to Mrs. Cameron. ". . . she came in, and sweetly asked me what I thought of Alice Roosevelt's going to England. Like a fool, I told her what I thought. On Sunday [March 2], Roosevelt announced to Mrs[.] Hay that Alice is not to go. He gave a harangue on the subject, concluding that 'H. A. is right! he says &c. &c,' straight from Sister Anne. Whom can I trust to hold a tongue? The puppets just rattle."

Not that Adams blamed "Sister Anne." Because Theodore Roosevelt was Theodore Roosevelt, it was perilous for anyone to go anywhere near him. Henry continued: "What can I do but hide? In my heart I knew that Sister Anne has the very same feeling as I, yet what could be more dangerous than to confide in each other? Such confidences are more fatal at sixty, than any live-intrigue at thirty."

As events proved, it was even perilous to be hospitable to little Quentin. The boy's visits to Henry's study gave Mrs. Roosevelt an idea. Adams disclosed it to Mrs. Cameron. ". . . Edith Roosevelt has sent for me to go to a child's party on Saturday. Why was I born? What for am I here? Wherefore is anything nothing?"

The weeks Brooks spent at 1603 H Street while Henry was still away had looked like office-seeking weeks, inspired by ideas that President Roosevelt might want the services of an Adams. No place was offered. Likewise Brooks's prodding of Donald was unproductive. Perhaps partly for these reasons, Brooks did not like Cuba when he got there. After shifting to Mexico, he liked Mexico so little that he and Evelyn planned an escape to Asheville, North Carolina.

From Mexico, Brooks wrote to Henry asking him to ask Rockhill to send a book to Asheville—a book containing material for a book Brooks hoped to start.[35] Rockhill sent the needed book.[36] On his way north,

Brooks stopped at San Antonio. Writing to Henry on February 23, he said: "I used to think I should like to hold a great office. . . . Last winter in Washington . . . I was very close to the machine, and I didn't care for it. It did not leave a pleasant taste in my mouth."

Brooks and Henry were differently situated with respect to Roosevelt. Brooks was disappointed and put off. Henry was only bothered. He had earlier explained to Mrs. Cameron. ". . . I am much too old to take Theodore seriously. . . . To me Theodore belongs to the class of my cousin William Everett, with far inferior intelligence, knowledge and memory, but far superior energies. His manner, temper, and even choice of words often mimic Will Everett's to a laughable degree. The parallel delights me all the more because it would infuriate to frenzy both Theodore and William[,] who certainly loathe each other."[37]

Roosevelt had launched an anti-trust suit against Northern Securities, a corporation of which J. P. Morgan was a principal organizer. The action came as a surprise. It reminded Henry of Cleveland and Olney's attack on the British in 1895. He told Mrs. Cameron: ". . . it is a Venezuela case over again, and I suspect that in this case as in the Venezuela message, the President had not a notion what he was doing. Cleveland was perhaps drunk, as the story goes; but Theodore is never sober, only he is drunk with himself and not with rum."[38]

Some particulars about the attack on Morgan so interested Henry that on February 24, 1902, he recounted them. ". . . Pierpont is furious because Theodore, suddenly, without warning, at a critical moment of the market when very large amounts of money were involved and borrowed on collateral, had hit him an awful blow square in the face. Theodore laughs at Pierpont. . . . Pierpont says that Roosevelt should have given him warning so that he could have had time to support the market. Theodore's reply is—and is the astonishing part of it—that he did give warning. True, he never spoke to [Elihu] Root[, the secretary of the treasury]; he did not consult his cabinet, or tell any member of it; but he sent for [Senator] Hanna [of Ohio] . . . to breakfast that morning, and told Hanna! He saw that Hanna didn't pay much attention to it! and now Hanna says he never heard it!"[39]

Dor had not said that Roosevelt lied. In a new letter, however, begun on March 2, he returned to "the Pierpont Morgan _débacle._" "You may have noticed my increasing and intense disgust of late. . . . Luckily I can write to you, as a safety valve; but I say no word to any man here, however intimate. . . . Theodore's vanity, ambition, dogmatic temper, and cephalopodic brain are all united on hitting everybody, friend or enemy, who happens to be near."

The new letter could seem to indicate that what disgusted Dor was mere added exposure to Roosevelt's self-centeredness. ". . . Theodore," he said, "is blind-drunk with self-esteem. He has not a suspicion that we are all watching him as we should watch a monkey up a tree with a chronometer." But a second annoyance for Dor was having to think the president dishonest. He invented an aphorism for the occasion. "God hates a liar is a lie. On the contrary[,] God loves liars and makes them prosper."[40]

Dor survived another White House dinner and a play at a theatre by saying not one word to the other males: Roosevelt, Lodge, and Root. He reported to Mrs. Cameron on March 9, 1902: "Theodore is living in a political fool's-paradise where not a breath of healthy air ever penetrates. Cabot and Root are obliged to stoke his furnace. . . . With all the vivacity of a happy nature[,] I talked with Sister Anne and little Edith. . . . At the theatre it was the same thing, only I hid myself in a corner and talked with Mrs[.] Root[,] who is a fool, but . . . is like many female fools, much more intelligent than the men."

Roosevelt's bellicosity increased. "If Root remonstrates, Theodore slaps his face too. Hay is already outside. Cabot himself is dragged by the heels. Congress is as sulky as Wall Street. Theodore is inflated with his own popularity; he wants to be candidate for the democrats too. . . . Luckily for a Christian Conservative Anarchist, he is not my President. Not that I have a candidate of my own, or care even to offer a wiser man in his place. . . ."

The world seemed to have developed a surplus of antipathies and did not need any more. "Sooner or later, England and Turkey and Austria and Poland and Finland and Russia and Japan, and the rest of the boiling, may boil." Thinking it time for a warning, Adams wrote to Gaskell about nations at cross-purposes. "In the crush of concentration which is squeezing the life out of everything weak, we may individually escape. At the same time, I tremble in my little shoes at the sight of these hostile peoples running at fearful speed on roads that run across each other. . . ."

Nations were frightening: heads of state were terrifying. "Here is America run by a school-boy barely out of college, and younger in nature than most school-boys who are not out of college. Germany is in the hands of a lunatic who ought to be shut up in an asylum. Russia and Italy are under young men [who are?] martyrs to melancolia [sic]. And now Spain is given to an idiot! or not given to him, as the case may be. Austria without an heir-apparent at all, and France alone with a serious executive government."[41]

*   *   *

Since leaving Beverly Farms in 1901, Mrs. Cameron had lapsed from good health to bad. She went south to Biarritz but did not much mend. Her friends the Canfields wished later to cruise in Greek waters on a rented yacht and asked her to go along. She agreed to go, at the cost of delaying the time when she and Dor could meet.

Writing from Biarritz on March 10, 1902, she complained about her husband: "Donald has written *once* since October,—and that scrap of a note was cross,—& so I don't know any thing about him. Martha and I write regularly, but without any notice whatever of our letters."

On the 15th, she said she hesitated to start a letter for fear of being dull. "*You* are not dull. Your letters are simply thrilling and make me regret more and more that I must miss the days of Teddy's administration. . . ." Her plan for the summer assumed that, if Donald would stay in America, she could take Martha to the Tyrol to make a start in German. She hoped Dor might join them. "I have no energy left. You must now brace up & provide 'go' for us both."

Niece Loulie was at 1603 H Street. Not a person to say meaningless things, Adams told Mrs. Cameron on March 11 that Loulie was his "type-writer and slave." What needed typing he did not say, but a possible guess relates to his *Tahiti.* Permission to distribute copies evidently had come from Tati, and Uncle Henry wanted copies sent to libraries, beginning about April 1.[42] Some would be sent in Tati's name, and typed letters might perhaps be sent in some cases.[43] If she was indeed pressed into service, Loulie was not ill-paid. She seized both a copy of *Memoirs of Arii Taimai* and a copy of its predecessor, *Memoirs of Marau Taaroa*—a valuable rare book.[44]

For three days running, Hay being absent, Mrs. Hay took Adams for carriage drives. On March 16, he advised Mrs. Cameron that he and Clara were having "a desperate affair." Evidently the two were weighing Hay's plight. Hay was expecting to be dismissed, yet equally could expect to be kept through another winter.[45] Meanwhile Adams was trying never to approach the president and never to come near Senator Lodge. "Sister Anne sees through me like a dirty window-pane, and Cabot knows why I avoid the White House and Massachusetts Avenue."[46]

Emmons sent Adams a biographical memoir he had written of King. Adams acknowledged it on March 17 and in his letter described King as "the most remarkable man of our time." The encomium was timely, for a memorial meeting was being planned at which persons who had known King well would speak about him.

Brooks had written from Asheville wanting permission to use some mathematical and scientific ideas of Henry's in the book he wished to write.[47] The result was a disclaimer. Henry replied on March 19, ". . . I have avoided meddling with science, being satisfied to know that the scientific men were bigger fools than I." Henry's words were untrue. He intended to go on meddling with science as capably as he knew how.[48]

Brooks and Evelyn returned to Washington. To Henry, the younger brother looked "old—old—old."[49] Before leaving the capital, Brooks made political inquiries but learned little that Henry did not know. Henry refused to talk. ". . . I kept my mouth shut to him."[50]

Looking back, Henry saw that he had carried silence very far. He wrote to Mrs. Cameron on April 6, "I've not exchanged ten words with Lodge or Roosevelt, and have not seen a statesman within my doors."[51] He thought he had had little choice. "It is not wholly my own fault. The intimacy of Hay's relations with me is very awkward indeed. As I am dead opposed to all his policy, except in Cuba . . . I am afraid of talking with anyone else. . . . From the first [i.e. from the time of McKinley's death], I have told him to get out; that he is in a false position, and that escape now would be a brilliant triumph. . . . At the same time, I know, though he conceals from me all that side of his relations, that he can't get out. He is one wheel in the old machine of Hanna and Pierpont Morgan, and Root is the other. Wall Street is in a desperate state of mind since Roosevelt so nastily struck it his foul blow on the Northern Securities; and Pierpont Morgan and Hanna insist that, at any cost, Hay and Root must stay."

At a fortunate moment, Brooks having left, Henry received an invitation from Mrs. Westinghouse to meet Lord Kelvin—earlier James Thomson—the British physicist who had nicknamed Maxwell's "demon." Henry valued the opportunity to inspect a man so important. He told Mrs. Cameron, "The honor is great, but unmerited."[52]

In Paris, Mrs. Cameron readied 50 Avenue du Bois de Boulogne for Dor's use. She assured him on April 9, "I miss you more and more—and I need you very much." She added on the 11th, "When I come back, I shall find you here!"[53] That said, she left for Greece.

Daily in Washington, Dor saw across the Square the house she had been deprived of. The sight reminded him that men were deformed by their occupations. On April 13, he wrote to her, "What makes a long residence in Washington so bad for one's temper is the horrible display of vanity, especially among the men." He specified: ". . . there are three professions—the preacher, the teacher and the speaker, which inevitably ruin the finest nature in a definite time. I was a pedagogue myself, and blush to this day at the marks I bear of it." He went on, ". . . it is now five years since you were thrown out!"

One of Dor's merits was continual striving for perfect accuracy of judgment, even about himself. In the same letter, he said he was a person only extraordinary in keeping a short distance ahead of other persons and being the index of what other persons were going to be. "I have never been at any time of life more than ten years ahead of the majority, and I have always been an atom in the mass. What I am, the mass is sure to become. . . ."

He wrote a last letter to Mrs. Cameron from America on April 27 and 29, 1902. It had the character of a report. One passage crowded three crucial matters into less than forty words. He said: ". . . I'm perfectly square with the Virgin, having finished and wholly rewritten the whole volume. I've sent Tahiti in Tati's name to half a dozen public libraries, and have started a historical romance of the year 1200." The last words of the passage might seem a cryptic reference to *The Education of Henry Adams*. They evidently referred instead to something new and much smaller, yet important.[54]

The great event of Adams's winter had been the one with which it started, the funeral of Clarence King. The death of Adams's friend affected Adams two ways at once. Perhaps as soon as he completed the new draft of *Mont Saint Michel and Chartres*, he began to write a talk titled "King" for possible reading at the projected memorial meeting in New York.[55] The central idea of the talk was that King had been "the ideal companion of our lives." He illustrated the idea in the talk by recounting some of his and King's adventures when they went to Cuba together early in 1894.

At the start of the talk, Adams said that he and others might want to dwell on the theme "How I first knew King." Nine sentences later, he said the theme was one he could not touch himself. ". . . I fear that the motive would cut too deep into King's life, not to mention my own. . . . We had ideals then, ambitions, and a few passions, which faded with time and are dead, even though they may not be buried; and his are not mine to handle."[56]

This rhetorical maneuver—suggesting a theme and then saying he would have to avoid it—bore upon a realization on Adams's part. Till then, his progress in writing *The Education of Henry Adams* had been slowed by uncertainty about the shape of its first narrative and especially the problem of its ending. King's death solved the problem by suggesting to Adams that he could end the narrative by telling how they met. A path was opened for him to him to complete the narrative. And a path was cleared for him to finish his talk, in case a memorial meeting occurred and a talk was needed.[57]

A time may come when crowds of educated Americans will know that Henry Adams wrote a great book—or at least the greatest book there is—about the Tahitians. In 1902, the persons who knew he had written, printed, and distributed the book were very few.[58] Probably no book by an American was ever launched into the world with so little attention permitted to the identity of its author.

If not told, American readers could not know that certain words printed in large type on its title page were relevant to Adams.

MEMOIRS

OF

ARII TAIMAI E

Marama of Eimeo

Terriirere of Tooarai

Teriinui of Tahiti

TAURAATUA I AMO

Paris

1901

As has been mentioned, the words "TAURAATUA I AMO" were one of the titles—and names—of Arii Taimai.[59] They were also the title-and-name she had given to Adams in 1891 when making him a great chief of the Tevas. Thus the title page of the book did two things. It stated the title of a book. For Tahitians, it acted as a reminder that two persons, Henry Adams being one, were bearers of a very great name.

From the time a copy reached Tati Salmon, the book was recognized in Tahiti as a work to be valued, read, and widely circulated. In 1920, a German translation was published through the agency of one of Tati's sisters.[60] At present the most available edition is the French translation, issued by the Musée de l'Homme in Paris in 1964.[61] There has never been an American edition designed for general sale.[62] The great barriers in the way of an American edition are the unfamiliarity and seeming difficulty of Tahitian names. To write the book, Adams had to learn and use hundreds of Tahitian names—names of districts, landmarks, families, persons, articles of use. Few Americans have undergone that initiation. Even if assured that a great Tahitian chiefess named Te vahine Airorotua i Ahurai i Farepua (and variantly nicknamed Purea, or Berea, or Oberea) was at one time a living human being, American readers might need the help of several readings of the narrative before believing that her formal name is perfectly natural and not impossible to recall.

Once sensed for what they are, the inducements to read Adams's book could hardly be greater. As printed in 1901, the book is a successful marriage of two narratives. One tells the history of Tahiti from the remotest past to the submission of the Tahitians to French rule in 1846 as remembered by the one surviving Tahitian to whom the history was still known. The other tells the history of Tahiti as learned by Adams with the help both of Tahitian memories and a quickly assembled library of European books and records, most of which were not known to the Tahitians. The two narratives are blended to make a single account, except that the conclusion is in Aɪii Taimai's words, translated from Tahitian. The overall effect is one of disaster and tragedy borne with fortitude and grace.

11

UNDER THE SHADOW

Adams boarded the *Philadelphia* at New York on May 6, 1902, thinking he faced a lonely voyage. He was discovered on the ship by Elsie de Wolfe with the actress Ethel Barrymore, and by Lida Hoyt with her younger daughter Elizabeth and a young cousin, Edith Hoyt. His discoverers perhaps assumed he was returning to Europe with no purpose except to return. He did not tell them that he was working; that he had with him the second draft of *Mont Saint Michel and Chartres* and some chapters—possibly nine—of *The Education of Henry Adams*.

He hurried to London and to Tours, where he joined Payne and Helen Whitney with a view to guiding them on drives in their powerful automobile, newly delivered from the Daimler factory. The machine was a wonder. It took them to Blois and back to Tours, 75 miles, without a breakdown. Adams became a convert. He later wrote to Mabel La Farge, "My idea of paradise is a perfect automobile going thirty miles an hour on a smooth road to a twelfth-century cathedral."[1]

Having just returned from Greece on the Canfields' rented yacht, Mrs. Cameron was in Venice. Adams wanted to see her but was worried about her health. From Tours on May 22, he urged, "Please come back well!" She expressed matching feelings and said she might stay for the moment in Italy. Health was indeed a problem, and critically so for her sister. Lida Hoyt was battling cancer. She wrote to Venice asking Mrs. Cameron to come to Paris and take charge of Elizabeth. As part of her response, Mrs. Cameron telegraphed to Dor that she would arrive in Paris on June 1.

Dor had gone alone to Le Mans by train to study the cathedral's glass, and he and the Whitneys were planning a trip by auto to Mont Saint Michel, Coutances, and other places. They cancelled the trip, and he directed a letter to Mrs. Cameron at Paris. "The only serious question is whether you go to America this summer. Answer me that, please! It is the only place where I cannot go with you."[2]

Stopping en route at Chartres, he headed for Paris, arrived, put up at the Hôtel Brighton, and began four weeks with Mrs. Cameron. The question of her summer could be settled only by eliciting a message from her husband. On June 21 or thereabouts, news came from Donald that he would soon be in England, that his wife and daughter were to meet him there, and that they would all go to Russia!

Sometime between June 21 and July 2, when she crossed with Martha to London, Dor let Mrs. Cameron into the secret of *The Education of Henry Adams.* He may have read her the first chapter. He may even have lent her the manuscript of the chapter. Whatever happened, she was interested to see that the book opened with the phrase "Under the shadow of Boston State House" and in the same sentence said a child was born and named Henry. To her mind, the idea of Henry's first appearing under a shadow was too perfect to be forgotten.

In London, she and Martha met Donald and learned that he was "not at all firm about going to Russia." He was in "great spirits" and wanted to rent a house or castle in Scotland—"not a little place"— something comparable to Surrenden Dering. He apparently assumed that his dealings with his wife and daughter would be more agreeable if Adams joined them at their imagined great residence. He wanted Adams to arrive there as soon as they did.[3]

Adams was pleased to be told that Russia was rejected and Scotland preferred. The knowledge that she could have Dor with her permitted Mrs. Cameron to search for a place "with some heart in the quest."[4] On July 6, she started a letter by telling him that Donald had made an offer for a suitable place on Scotland's west coast. She chose her words carefully. "Inverlocky (Castle, of course!) is *under the shadow* of Ben Nevis, and Fort William is its station [italics added]." She held back the letter till late on Monday, July 7, and closed it by exclaiming: "Got it!!! Will write E. C."

Dor replied that he would come "whenever you want me—really want me."[5] On Sunday, July 13, she urged, "Do come quickly." "Donald asks every day when I expect you." On Tuesday, she warned, "Don't think I'll let you escape when once I have you here." "Do come *soon!*"

Had she gained her wish, Dor would have taken the night express from London, arriving Wednesday morning, July 15. He was delayed and may not have arrived till two days later.

The summer of 1902, as described by Adams, was the "coldest, dampest, dreariest . . . since 1879."[6] In Scotland, the result was slippery paths and slick roads. On July 26 or 27, Adams sprained an ankle while on the moors. Soon after, Donald and Mrs. Cameron went driving in a four-wheeled carriage. Its wheels lost traction; it slid into a ditch; and

Mrs. Cameron was hurt in her spine and Donald in his legs. When restored to the castle, both were confined to their beds.

Adams had come to Scotland meaning to work. Prior to his mishap, he said, "I am doing nothing." "I read St[.] Thomas Aquinas. . . ." Afterwards, he said equivalent things: that he had his "Church philosophy" with him and was "deep in scholastic learning."[7]

On August 7, Donald and Mrs. Cameron were still laid up. A tutor had arrived to teach music to Martha and her mother's young cousin, Edith Hoyt. For Dor, it was a good chance to study. He used part of the day to inform Niece Loulie that he was planning a trip to Heaven with the help of Dante's *Paradiso*. "I've been reading Dante to learn the road. He tells all about it." What Uncle Henry did not say was that he was writing the third draft of *Mont Saint Michel and Chartres*.

At the start of September 1902, without notice and on crutches, Donald left Inverlocky, traveled to London, and sailed home. Langley had been asked to visit. Mrs. Cameron could not entertain male guests in her husband's absence. She and Dor alerted Langley that he could not come and new plans were necessary.

The easiest plan for Dor was a familiar one. He arranged to spend an interval with Sir John Clark at Tillypronie and three days at Wenlock with Gaskell as preludes to returning to Paris with his papers and books. Mrs. Cameron wove a complicated plan that had something simple as its principal object. It began with her declaring that she and Martha needed a cure at a spa on the Continent. Once ready to travel, she took Martha to London and hired a governess, Ms. Worthington, capable of managing a daughter in a mother's absence.

Without delay, mother and daughter, with Ms. Worthington, went to Vichy and began a cure. From Wenlock on September 20, Dor advised the mother: ". . . it is the pace, and not the liver, that kills." Mrs. Cameron had recovered enough from her injury to answer, "I am up to anything just now."[8] While at Vichy, she gave her plan new features. Her party would next perch in the Alps at the Caux Palace Hôtel sur Territet-Montreux. There Dor might join them. Later she and he would take Martha, with Ms. Worthington, to Karlsruhe to live with a German family and make progress in German.

In this defensible way, Mrs. Cameron could free herself to do what she wished: be in Paris near Dor and without Martha.[9] By the time she and he arrived, their apartment at 50 Avenue du Bois de Boulogne would be modernized. She had directed workmen to refinish walls and floors and install electric lights. The work was going forward.

*   *   *

Adams could not get rooms at the Beau Site and accepted a room at the Hôtel Columbia on the Rue Kléber. He tried to lure Joe Stickney away from the Sorbonne to make a tour of important medieval churches at Dijon, Vézelay, Auxerre, and Autun. Studious Joe would not go.

Mrs. Cameron, Martha, and Ms. Worthington arrived from Vichy on October 10 and left for Switzerland on the 16th. Adams and Mrs. Cameron were exchanging frequent letters.[10] He told her on October 17, ". . . I've been deep in my books and have hardly left my room. . . ." When convenient, he walked to 50 Avenue du Bois de Boulogne and used the schoolroom as his study. He was willing to mention his reading. Yet most of his effort, it appears, was given to writing.

Reynolds Hitt was serving at the Paris embassy and owned an automobile, a one-cylinder, nine-horsepower Renault. After riding in it with Hitt to Versailles and back, Adams thought it only adapted to local use. To be truly useful, automobiles needed much more power.

At Inverlocky, Henry had received a letter from Brooks saying that Worthington Ford had accepted a position at the Library of Congress.[11] Ford was synonymous with statistics. A kind of statistics Henry most wanted was statistics relating to the energy controlled by human beings in such forms as electricity generated in dynamos and motion imparted to automobiles by their engines. Replying to Brooks, Henry said, ". . . our country is established for at least a century as the centre of human energy." In his most provoking style, he predicted "an ultimate, colossal, cosmic collapse" by the year 2000—"but not on any of our old lines." "My belief is that science is to wreck us, and that we are like monkeys monkeying with a loaded shell; we don't in the least know or care where our practically infinite energies come from or will bring us to."[12]

Once hitched to the theme of energy, Henry would not let it go. Writing again to Brooks on October 7, 1902, he said he would return to Washington only in order "to get up a statistical bureau of Energy." As a first guess, he estimated that the energy at the disposal of human beings would increase between 1900 and 2000 in a ratio of 1,000 to 1,024,000. "You may consider this an impossibility. I see none. It is a trifle compared with the stupendous fact that in less than a century, starting with nothing, we are now working at least forty million horsepower a day."

John Hay and Elizabeth Cameron, being friends of the author, felt called upon to read most of the offerings of Henry James. The latest was a long novel, *The Wings of the Dove*. Hay was reading it with unalloyed pleasure and enthusiasm. Mrs. Cameron was reading it, thought it verbose, but kept on reading.

A letter from Clara Hay gave Adams notice that Reynolds Hitt was being shifted from Paris to Berlin, as second secretary. On October 20, 1902, Adams asked Mrs. Cameron, "Shall I take Hitt's apartment?" Situated at 23 Avenue du Bois de Boulogne, the apartment was on the top floor of a building owned by a Mrs. Whitcomb, an American. It offered every convenience that Adams could want.[13]

Writing to Mrs. Cameron again on October 22, Adams gave reasons for taking Hitt's apartment. He said he disliked "pigging in third-rate hotels like a card-sharper." "My situation is not dignified, or suitable or comfortable. . . ."

Mrs. Cameron had written on the 21st: "I am still struggling with Henry James['s] latest, which really I think he might [better?] not have published. It could be condensed into the pages of Daisy Miller & leave room for his adjectives." On the 22nd, she received Adams's question about the apartment. She favored taking it and suggested that she find a female servant for him—a *valet-cuisinier*—to insure his being properly fed. They already had agreed that he should join her and Martha at the Caux Palace Hôtel. She said that day in a new letter: "There is a sitting room & bedroom just next to my suite which I think I'll take for you when you come. Corner room & *such* views!"

Dor put the apartment question into Kelly's hands and journeyed to Switzerland. After he left Paris, a letter from Hay reached his bank. Hay needed rescue. "I shall never need you more than I do now." The problem was Roosevelt's torrential loquacity. Hay had spirited the president to his house for dinner without the knowledge of the press. "Theodore was in fine form. He began talking at the oysters and the chasse-café found him still at it. When he was one of us, we could sit on him— but who, except you, can sit on a Kaiser? Come home and do it, or we are undone. We shall lose discourse of reason through disuse."

Hay turned to James's *Wings of the Dove*. "It is sinfully good. . . . Of course, one must know one's alphabet and pay attention; but there are things in it of the first bricabrac. The little touches in the Venetian chapters are worth all the cost. It's the only thing I have read for a year: that's why I mention it."[14]

Adams and Mrs. Cameron conducted Martha and Ms. Worthington from Switzerland to Karlsruhe and without them went to Paris. A sixteen-day gap opened in Dor's letters. At the latest on Monday, November 10, 1902, he moved in at 23 Avenue du Bois de Boulogne. The apartment was livable. Hitt had not yet removed his furniture.

On that Monday, Henry broke his long silence. Writing to Hay, he promised to try to read *The Wings of the Dove* while crossing to New York. Writing also to Brooks, he dwelt insistently on energy. ". . . Philosophy,

Metaphysics, Mathematics, Dynamics, Chemistry,—all branches of human study since study began—have at last pretty well come on to this common ground." "Your economical law of History is, or ought to be, an Energetic Law of History. . . . If I were ten years old, I would educate myself to write that book, and teach that lesson, but I care too little now for God or man to teach anything."

Certain metaphors—atoms, dynamos, and automobiles—were taking very large places in Henry's imagination. In an earlier letter to Hay, he had said, "As an atom I consider myself a success."[15] In his new letter to Hay, he said differently, "I want to be a dynamo and run a planet, like Theodore and Kaiser William and Joe Chamberlain. . . ." He at the same time told Brooks that the United States, England, and France "now make an Atlantic system" and that the "system"—a virtual automobile—had a foreseeable history. "I cannot conceive how this machine can help running at accelerated speed." Moreover, many persons would own such machines. Writing twelve days later to Anne Fell, he said, "The only thing everyone must have in this world as a prime necessity of life is an automobile. . . ." The energetic law of history, it seemed, would conduce to economic democracy.

Mrs. Cameron returned briefly to Karslruhe. She wrote to Dor on December 1, 1902: "Here I am; you know the scenery. . . . Nothing is changed, except that it is darker and raining hard. . . ." "I feel as if you ought to knock on my door in another minute!"

Writing again next day, she asked, "What is the matter with the Stock Market over there?" Stocks had fallen sharply in New York.

At great expense, Dor bought a fine old portrait by Carle Van Loo of a beautiful Frenchwoman, Madame de Prie. He intended to make it a present to Mrs. Cameron and Martha. He wrote to the mother on December 3, "You are not to know anything about it till I sail. . . ." In the same breath, he declared *Mont Saint Michel and Chartres* completed. "I've finished Thomas Aquinas and the thirteenth century. I'm dying to know how it would look in type. . . ."

Mrs. Cameron considered his buying the portrait an approach to infidelity. She replied at once: "I am convulsed over Mme. de Prie! You wicked extravagant person, cannot you keep away from lovely frail French *ladies*[?] I am very keen to see her however, and quite excited." At the same time, she agreed about his completed book. "Do set up your St. Thomas,—why not?"

In Paris, with the help of photographs and financial assistance from Adams and Hay, the artist George Howland—Clarence King's half-brother—had painted a portrait of King for presentation as a gift to the Century Association in New York. Adams visited Howland and to the artist's surprise liked the portrait and agreed to take it with him on the *St. Paul* on December 27, to deliver it for acceptance.

Apropos of Madame de Prie, Dor had told Mrs. Cameron that he had never seen a living Frenchwoman who was beautiful. The remark gave its recipient a chance to teach him some French history. She replied on December 7: "I am afraid you will end by being in love with Madame de Prie! Of course those women were lovely. It was their *metier.* The revolution killed most of them, & mésalliances the rest. But I do think there is beauty left in France, only one must readjust one's standards somewhat and not look for our Anglo-Saxon type."

His intention to go home soon after Christmas aroused her to protest. "Why don't you wait? I'll lend you money!!!" She spoke too of Lida, whose cancer was being treated with rays. The results had been indecisive, and the doctors were about to use "a new & more powerful instrument just invented." Mrs. Cameron remarked, "Very mysterious, this X ray, and why *shouldn't* it succeed[?]"

She returned from Karlsruhe. Dor attended the Paris automobile show. On December 18, he advised Niece Loulie that his "little apartment" was "a pure joy." ". . . I am comfortable, though I've not set up a cook, and still eat at restaurants."[16]

His current reading included works of mathematics. He found them difficult and said he wondered whether medieval schoolmen or mathematicians were the "most unintelligible." Yet he believed that mathematical ideas helped him "get rid of primitive modes of thought." He was attracted to parabolic curves and was tempted to view the twentieth century as an ever-faster rush toward a disastrous accident.[17]

A great mathematician he had known in youth was Charles Peirce. He wrote to Mabel Hooper, ". . . Charley Peirce would just educate me. As it is, I am dying a block of ignorance." As if persistent ignorance were linked to hilarity, he explained: ". . . the world becomes more amusing every year. I am always in greater hopes of seeing it break its damn neck, which I calculate must happen by 1932. . . ."[18]

Before leaving for the steamer on December 27, he directed the concierge at his building to forward his mail to Mrs. Cameron at No. 50 on the other side of the avenue. He had long avoided expressing his feelings for her in written form. Yet, from Cherbourg, he assured her in a parting note: ". . . it is much in my heart that I may not see you again till May."

A storm tossed the *St. Paul,* and Adams became "ghastly seasick."[19] He may not have read much of James's *Wings of the Dove.* Yet he landed at New York as scheduled, on January 4, 1903.

He at once reversed his tactics of the previous winter by becoming exceedingly social. During a short stay in New York, he saw Lida and Elizabeth Hoyt, Mabel La Farge and her babies, Elisabeth Marbury and Elsie de Wolfe, Clara and Helen Hay, Lucy Frelinghuysen, Whitney Warren, Oliver Payne, Centre Hitchcock, Henry Higginson, and Robert Chanler. During the same time, he ran about with John La Farge.

On reaching Washington, he called on Anna Lodge. Hay took him for a walk. Edith Roosevelt required his dining at the White House with the Lodges and the Owen Wisters. "Theodore was less excited than a year ago, and occasionally let some one say a word or two."

Adams gave a dinner for the Wisters, with Bay and Bessy Lodge. A welcome visitor was Oliver Wendell Holmes, newly added to the Supreme Court. Writing to Mrs. Cameron, Adams said Holmes wore "that vague look of wondering bewilderment which you always see on the face of the Bostonian who for the first time has discovered America."[20]

Closing his letter, Adams continued to list his activities, which seemed never to stop. He called again on Anna Lodge and encountered Holmes a second time. The president dropped by, with Owen Wister and Leonard Wood. "Theodore rattled away as usual about all sorts of matters, big and little, but always announcing his own views, and never stopping to invite or consider those of other people." Langley shared dinner with Adams and reported being depressed "by heart-burnings and enmities which are rampant against him." Winty and Margaret Chanler would be arriving soon. "*Enfin!* you see my work is cut out. I've written to your husband. I've done all the duties I know of, except calling on the Michael Herberts and the Berty Peirces and Rebecca Dodge [Rae] and Chauncy [*sic*] Depew."

Mrs. Cameron's first letters from Paris were partly interesting for involving another married woman. She told Adams: "Mme. de Prie smiles down upon me softly. She is lovely." Her next letter was no different. "Mme[.] de Prie sends love. So do I."[21]

As tended to happen, Brooks and Evelyn had sailed eastward across the Atlantic while Henry was pitching westward. When Brooks called on her in Paris, Mrs. Cameron noticed the drift of his ideas and wrote to Henry, "You see [how] completely he is at variance with the doctrines you have been pounding into me." She asked Brooks and Evelyn to dinner. They came and Brooks said that Henry was avoiding him.[22]

Social whirls in Washington did not prevent Henry's doing what he wanted to do. He renewed his studies of Eloise and Abelard—"who was a much bigger fool than I." He talked continually with Hay about treaties and once about novel-writing, perhaps in connection with *The Wings of the Dove*.[23] With misgivings, he read part of *Mont Saint Michel and Chartres* to Bay Lodge. With greater misgivings, he listened to reports about his neighbor at the White House. On February 1, he summarized for Mrs. Cameron: "Our emperor is more irrepressible than ever; he tells his old stories at every cabinet dinner for two hours running and sits in the midst of a score of politicians and reporters describing his preparations for war with Germany. The joke is stale. We laugh but shudder."[24]

There was a printing firm in Baltimore, J. H. Furst and Company, that could print and bind small editions of books for authors willing to foot the bills. Adams contacted the firm—or possibly another much like it—and learned he could not afford to print *Mont Saint Michel and Chartres*. Part of his trouble was the printer's estimate. The cost of making 50 copies would be $1500. Another part was the fall of stocks in Wall Street. Adams's income was jeopardized.

He liked meeting people but knew Washington too well to be unaware of its dangers. There was a special danger that well-meaning friends would arrive at his house accompanied by seemingly innocent strangers. On February 10, 1903, he explained to Mrs. Cameron: ". . . the only profitable profession here is blackmail. . . . As you know, I have, since being alone, never allowed a woman to enter the house, unless I knew her. I have now extended the same law to men. Life is poisoned by terror of possible lies which cannot be disproved."[25]

As the days passed, he saw fewer people. "Of Roosevelt, I've seen nothing."[26] The Senate approved a treaty creating a commission to negotiate the Alaska-Canada boundary. Lodge was named to the commission and expected to go to Europe for its meetings. Dor would be on the same steamer. He told Mrs. Cameron on February 22: "I've nothing to tell you. I see no one; that is to say, no one I want to see."

One subject continued to trouble him: the lack of intelligence of Roosevelt as president. ". . . his mind is impulse, and acts by the instincts of a school-boy at a second-rate boardingschool. Mind, in [the] technical sense, he has not. I find it rather amusing to read Sister Ann's [*sic*] thoughts in her silence, and Mrs. Hay's in her face. One does not need to talk. The wireless system of messages and conversation is eloquent enough. But poor Edith Roosevelt, who thinks that everything her Theodore does is perfect, has to bear the load."

The only writing Adams confessed to doing was last touches on the manuscript of *Mont Saint Michel and Chartres*. "My great work on the Virgin is complete even to the paging, and I've no occupation."[27] He said nothing about the book's being printed. Yet he had numbered its pages. That was a sign he would print it, regardless of cost.

Hitt had returned to Paris and removed most of his furniture. On Dor's behalf, Mrs. Cameron brought in the most necessary replacements. Her health permitted her being active. She had written on February 9, ". . . I have not been so well for two or three years." The recovery at Inverlochy had left her somewhat stiff, but digitalis for her heart and the cure at Vichy had greatly helped her.

Assuming a joke would do no harm, Dor told Mrs. Lodge she should stay with him at his apartment when next they were both in Paris. She repeated the joke to Bay. He compounded it by informing his mother-in-law, Mrs. Johnny Davis, that women could not live with Adams in Paris for fear "they would lose their reputations." Mrs. Davis told Bay in reply that Adams had "cost too many women their reputations already." On March 15, Dor reported the details to Mrs. Cameron. He added: ". . . [Mrs. Davis] must have her eye on you. . . . She is awfully good fun, but in that respect she and I are too much alike;—we have both cost too many reputations, and I daren't go near her."

Irritations multiplied. The Century Association declined to accept the portrait of King as not up the standard of its collection. The portrait had to be taken to the U. S. Geological Survey as an alternative recipient. Information about King's interracial marriage was beginning to circulate, and the time was not far distant when even the Survey would think the portrait offensive and best removed.[28]

Hay's fortunes bore comparison with King's. Adams told Mrs. Cameron on April 5: "The change in Hay is to me the most trying. . . . He is now the statesman pure and complete. . . . All but the official is dead or paralysed. Socially or intellectually he is only a phantom, and shrinks from sight. Every day he comes still, and we pass a couple of hours together, but it is not a pleasure any longer to him, for the effort to keep in my world is more and more difficult for him; and the routine of office is his only real interest."

Falling stock prices in New York posed a problem which Adams solved with characteristic promptness. He informed Mrs. Cameron on April 12 that he meant to sell "his loose stock." The sales brought him cash. In the event of a panic, which seemed very likely, he could buy back the stocks at lower prices.[29]

As the time to sail approached, it struck him that what he had seen in America was "an innocent little childlike pantomime." To his way of thinking, the mark of his fellow Americans was an "astounding horizon of superficiality." On April 21, 1903, he complained to Mrs. Cameron: "Not one being here seems to exist but for the moment of personal occupation. . . . Neither life nor death affects them. They have reached the honey-bee stage, and exist only from habit." The habit that took precedence and absorbed almost all energies was that of "having more children."

In anticipation of his return to Paris, Mrs. Cameron had hired an

American servant for Dor named Sadie, presumably part-black or black. Sadie liked her new assignment and was impatient to meet her employer.

Mrs. Cameron was even more impatient. At a dealer's shop, she found something Dor might want, a "superb writing desk." She told him, "It is enormous, but *very* fine." In her next letter, she urged: "Do come soon! Devotedly E."[30]

Adams had written to Charles D. Walcott, director of the United States Geological Survey, asking for information about the date when the country's coal resources might be exhausted. Walcott had assured him that an estimate would be obtained from an expert. The expert, George Becker, eventually furnished a non-answer to the effect that coal would be mined in keeping with demand. Walcott sent Becker's letter to Adams on May 18. By then, Adams had sailed on the *New York*, arrived in Paris, appeared at his partly-furnished apartment, and made Sadie's acquaintance.

Walcott and Becker's letters interested him, and he preserved them for his files. For the present, he was not writing letters himself. He and Mrs. Cameron were together. They had much to do.

In retrospect, the winter Adams had passed in Washington could seem mysterious. A hidden feature could possibly be detected in his reaction to a manuscript. Bay Lodge had asked him to read a novel he was attempting, titled *The Genius of the Commonplace*. Adams had read the manuscript and advised Bay to put it aside.[31]

Written on April 22, 1903, Adams's reply contained two striking sentences about succeeding as an artful writer. "Anyone who wants to be an artist has got to study his defects, and the only way of studying one's own defects is to lay one's work aside until it is forgotten, and then to go over it again with no other thought than to see where it is wrong. . . . A man is generally artistic in proportion as he sees what is wrong, and most work is good in proportion not so much to what one leaves in it as to what one strikes out."

The sentences could be read as comments by Adams on his experience through the winter as author of chapters of his *Education* that he had earlier drafted, put aside, and avoided seeing till they were for the most part forgotten. If there had been nine chapters and if he read them with a view to their—and his—defects, his winter may have been one of exceptional but wholly secret productivity. A chance exists that in silence he completed second drafts of all nine.

These conjectures are the more necessary because Adams was writing a book which, while not having his life as its subject, had his life as its basis. It happened, too, that his life had not been one life and instead was three. Though linked, the three were radically different. His first life ended climactically, just after the *Trent* Affair of 1861–1862. As a basis for chapters of *The Education of Henry Adams*, it had the beauty of comparative simplicity and the further beauty of being easy for Adams to remember. Assuming he indeed had redrafted nine chapters, he had somewhat perfected the phase of his *Education* that was built on his first life; that is, the easiest of the three lives for him or others to consider. In that case, when he left for Europe, he faced the harder problem of writing chapters for the *Education* based on his second life. The problem would be harder because his second life was complex and possibly jumbled in memory.

The difficulty of his situation showed itself in his first extant letter written after his return to 23 Avenue du Bois de Boulogne. Addressed to Gaskell on June 5, 1903, it contained two inquiries. Adams asked whether he and Gaskell met in 1862 or 1863 and when William Evarts paid a visit to Cambridge University. The inquiries were fundamental. The answers would permit Adams to write Chapters X–XIII.[32] That done, he might hit on the ideas he would need for the chapters leading to the turning point, the moment in 1871 when he met Clarence King in such a way that they formed an ineradicable friendship.

Gaskell did not reply to the inquiries. On June 14, Adams repeated them. He said he needed the dates because he wished "to make some calculations." His letter contained references to Descartes and Newton, to Darwin and Lyell, to "Lord Kelvin with his radium and atheism," to the "laws of thermo-dynamics," to systems of stars "infinitely distant from the earth," and even to mathematical solutions reached "by non-Euclidean methods."

He had moved to a new vocabulary. He spoke of "space, energy, time, thought, or mere multiplicity and complexity." The calculations he wished to make concerned the Americans of the future. "Three hundred million people running an automobile of a hundred-million horse-power . . . is a new problem in planetary history." ". . . one arrives at the limits of the possible very soon; the difficulty begins with the impossible. We know so very little, and all wrong."[33]

Mrs. Cameron's residence abroad was continuing despite incessant fear that excuses for its continuance might run out. The best excuse was Martha's education. During a gloomy moment the previous fall, the mother had foreseen a new return to America as likely. She told Dor, ". . . America hangs over me & she [Martha] must make as big strides as possible before we go."[34]

Dor's enjoyment of his new Paris apartment, in contrast, promised to last. Writing to Niece Loulie on June 18, 1903, he said he lacked an automobile but was helped by a "lady's maid" and had "bought a Régence throne and a Régence or Louis XV writing-desk." He did not say what he meant to write while seated on his throne and at his desk, but he made clear that he was spending lots of money.

The approach of July brought heat and new fear for Mrs. Cameron's health. She could be active and felt strong, but the illness that had injured her heart in 1897 had left her with an abnormally low pulse. She would have to take precautions.

With Dor's approval, she sublet her apartment for a month to Mrs. Peter Cooper Hewitt and—accompanied by Martha and Ms. Worthington—went to Bad Nauheim for another cure. Leaving had its penalty. She wrote to him on July 6, ". . . I am desperately sorry we ever came!"

In reply, Dor turned her attention to the New York stock market. He noted that Calumet copper was down to 425 and noted two days later that "Steel Common" had dropped to 25. As if he were thinking aloud, he asked, "What does it mean?"[35]

She answered on July 18 that she feared another return to Donald. "America hangs over me!" Yet she found consolation in the fall of the market. "If Donald has lost money[,] perhaps he will think the trip too costly. Let us hope!!!"

Thanks to Sadie's ministrations, Dor ate at home during the day and ate only his evening meals "in town."[36] On Friday, July 24, 1903, stocks crashed in New York. He wrote to Mrs. Cameron next day, "The shock must be on the verge of '93."

She replied on Tuesday: "This *is* a smash-up, isn't it? I wonder where Donald stands in it?" She turned to health. "I am very well, but as I was well when I came here I cannot judge of the effects of the cure, except that my pulse was then 48, & is now 50, and I think that two beats were purchased too dearly by three weeks at Nauheim!"

Yielding to Martha's wish to go there, Mrs. Cameron extended their absence and went to St. Moritz. They found on arriving that the rooms she had reserved for them were given to the Vienna Rothschilds. She told Dor on August 10, ". . . I sat firmly on my luggage & made the proprietor move them to the 3rd floor where he proposed to relegate me. . . . If it had not been a Rothschild[,] I might have conceded the point, but I held my own."

Joe Stickney had won his doctorate at the Sorbonne and had gone for a time to Greece. On his way back, he paid Mrs. Cameron a visit at Bad Nauheim, during which he fell ill. He shortly reached Paris but was confused about Adams's address. Dor tracked him down in the Latin

Quarter. Joe had jaundice, but was well enough to go with Adams to dinners at Voisin's and Durand's.

Observers sometimes felt restive about Adams for being so well-to-do. It did not often occur to them that the principal cause of his financial security was his consistently making wise moves as an investor. He wrote to Gaskell on August 13, "Great fortunes have melted away since I left New York three months ago. . . ." He could speak in a quiet voice because his own fortune was intact.

Donald could be expected to be one of the market's heavy losers. Mrs. Cameron reported on the 15th, "I dare say Donald is feeling very poor,—& it looks worse ahead doesn't it?"

Dor said nothing in his letters about new chapters for his *Education*.[37] His silence was perhaps good evidence that he not only was drafting chapters but knew they were very good ones.[38]

Mrs. Cameron may have read that meaning between his lines. On the subject of his most original book, she stayed as silent as he.

At the altitude of St. Moritz—6,000 feet—she could walk but not climb. Ms. Worthington could do neither. She became unwell. The governess's plight forced departure. On August 24, 1903, Mrs. Cameron alerted Dor that she would arrive in Paris on the 27th about 5:00 P.M. and that he was to come to dinner. She said she and Martha were in "*brutal* health." "Above *all* I am glad to see *you* again!" She and he had been too long apart.

12

AUTOMOBILING

When a child, Henry had found a protector in his elder sister Louisa, and in early manhood he had helped his younger sister Mary as companion and tutor. He currently had reason for thinking of Louisa. She had died in 1870 of tetanus resulting from injury during a carriage accident. In the fall of 1903, he had the option of bringing a terrible death-by-accident into *The Education of Henry Adams* and may already have planned to give Louisa's death throes a central place in Chapter XIX, to be titled "Chaos."

Since 1868, Mary had lived quietly in Massachusetts. In the fall of 1903, she broke the pattern by bringing her daughter Dorothy to Paris. Henry welcomed their coming as occasion enough to get an automobile. He was hankering to try a model powered by electicity.[1] He rented one and hired a chauffeur.

During the following weeks, the automobile served triumphantly for Mary and Dorothy's purposes. Mrs. Cameron shared the use of the vehicle. It promised also to be a help to Mabel La Farge, who would soon be arriving with her husband and three small sons to begin a period of residence in France. On October 16, Adams reported happily to Anna Lodge, ". . . our machine is kept running up and down the Avenue like a tram." There were breakdowns but no accidents. The only drawback was the limited capacity of the auto's batteries. The vehicle could not go far, yet was ideal for use within the city.

Worry about Martha's future and her own prompted Mrs. Cameron to make a brief visit to America with the object of wresting financial concessions from Donald. She and Martha left for Cherbourg on October 21, 1903. She wrote to Adams en route: "I hate to go just now but I must—at least I ought to. As soon as I have a definite plan [to return,] I will let you know. . . . Goodbye. I just *hate* saying it!"

Soon after Mrs. Cameron left, Dor read in a newspaper— presumably the Paris edition of the *New York Herald*—that one of her nephews, Charles Sherman, a freshman at Yale, had suffered a fatal injury while rock-climbing near New Haven. In his first letter, sent on October 27, Dor reacted in terms that were at least heterodox and could seem convincedly irreligious. "I hear and see nothing but bad news. You will be met on landing by that of the death of your nephew at Yale, which seems pure malevolence of fate. If there were any possible excuse for such strokes!"

The loss of her nephew required that Mrs. Cameron go to Cleveland to attend Mrs. Henry Sherman, her bereaved sister-in-law. Together the two women joined Donald in Pennsylvania. He agreed to provide $12,000 a year for Mrs. Cameron and Martha's maintenance and opposed Martha's living in America.[2] On November 9, Mrs. Cameron advised Dor: "Things here are amiable but queer. I am to re-lease 50 [the Paris apartment]. . . . Martha is not to come out next year but [is] possibly to travel, and really I see no future but . . . indifference, and a great deal of Europe. There seems to be no lack of money. . . ."

Adams's letters said nothing about work. Mary and Dorothy departed. Bigelow was in Paris and used the automobile. Adams assured Mrs. Cameron: ". . . I am plutôt comfortable here, and the machine simplifies life enormously. Even the theatres are made easy." "Gradually Sturgis yields to Paris en électrique."[3]

In London, Macmillan and Company had published an authoritative three-volume biography of Gladstone by John Morley. Adams obtained a copy and read with burning interest "The American Civil War"—Chapter V of the second volume.[4] The chapter quoted documents he had never previously seen. He especially noticed Gladstone's statement, written in 1896, that Lord Palmerston, following the outbreak of rebellion in America in 1861, had "desired the severance [of the South from the North] as a diminution of a dangerous power [the United States], but prudently held his tongue."[5]

A quality that underlay Adams's phenomenal powers as a writer was excitability. In youth, he had met England's leaders: Prime Minister Palmerston, Foreign Secretary Russell, and Chancellor of the Exchequer Gladstone. During the period of crisis from May 1861 through October 1862, he had studied the three men as if his life depended on it, as in fact it had. He settled upon three judgments: that Palmerston was an active and dangerous enemy of the American Union; that Russell was Palmerston's dishonest catspaw; and that Gladstone differed in being not unfriendly to the Union.[6] In the 1890s, chiefly by reading biographies of Russell and other British politicians, Adams had formed an even lower opinion of Russell's conduct relating to the United States in 1861.[7] This experience of downward revision in no way prepared him for what he saw in 1903 in *The Life of William Ewart Gladstone*. At first he looked at the newly-published documents in stunned astonishment.[8] The documents were unanswerable evidence that his youthful appraisals of Palmerston and Gladstone had been grossly mistaken.

Fortuitously, the documents became available to him when he was planning or drafting the part of *The Education* in which they could best be used, Chapter X, "Political Morality." When written, the chapter would fully concede that Palmerston, the supposed worst enemy of the United States in the British Cabinet, had restrained his colleagues in their haste to recognize the independence of the newly-formed Confederate States. The chapter would also assert that Gladstone, the supposed near-friend of the Union, tried to force the hand of the British government in 1862 and precipitate recognition of the South in spite of Palmerston's resistance.[9]

Considered as material for a book aimed to assist young men of college age or thereabouts, the evidence in the Gladstone biography was beyond improvement. It raised questions about the difficulty faced by outsiders when trying to learn what politicians were doing. It raised questions about the psychology of such a man as Gladstone, a highly-educated, long-experienced politician whose secret actions of 1862, when opened for review in 1903, could well seem the behavior of a madman or a multiple personality. It even raised questions whether politics at critical moments might so bewilder politicians and observers of politicians that the proper attitude for observers, once such moments passed, might be one of extending forgiveness to politicians—or observers—who had erred.[10]

Almost simultaneously with the publication of the biography of Gladstone, new books by Henry James appeared. The one that interested Elizabeth Cameron was another long novel, *The Ambassadors*. She understood that in the strict sense of the word James no longer was writing his works; he was dictating them to secretaries. On November 15, she reported to Adams, ". . . [The] Ambassadors . . . worried me more than usual." "I wish he would stop dictating. I am sure it is that which is ruining his style." Yet she said the new novel's "touch of Paris" was "delicious."

The other book by James was a deviation from his usual work. Some years earlier, he had promised the children of the American sculptor William Wetmore Story that, if trusted with a large bundle of papers in their possession, he would write their father's biography. An English publisher, William Blackwood, paid him £250 in advance to write it. After years of delay, he hurried a two-volume work into existence by dictating in about two months a commentary sufficient to string the papers together, with such thoughts as they brought to mind. The book —*William Wetmore Story and His Friends/ from Letters, Diaries and Recollections*—could pass for biography.

Adams bought a copy. Among America's historians and biographers, none knew better than he the difficulties of finding evidence, discovering what it meant, and writing narratives fully consonant with its meaning. As he read James's volumes, he could see that James had made no effort to obtain evidence other than what Story's heirs had given him. He could see as well that James was little interested in Story and much interested in Boston and Cambridge, where Story passed his earliest years, and very interested in Italy, where Story set up as a sculptor, flourished, and died.

These limitations were disturbing to Adams somewhat in proportion to his hard work as a finder and reader of evidence. It happened, too, that he was five years older than James; that he had made Story's acquaintance early, in Rome in May 1860; and that he had taken so strong an interest in Story's statues that the sculptor had wished to know and weigh his opinions. The interest, moreover, had a sensitive consequence. A statue for which Story was credited, the "Medea" in marble, involved a positioning of a woman's arms which Adams remembered and to some extent re-used when he conceived the figure executed in bronze by Saint Gaudens for Marian and Henry Adams's grave site.

A consideration of another sort made Adams read James's volumes closely. Two of Story's lifelong friends were Charles Sumner and James Russell Lowell. James printed passages from thirty-four letters that passed between Story, Sumner, and Lowell. As it happened, Sumner and Lowell were also Adams's longtime friends.

A last consideration was a built-in comparison. James's book traversed a large number of matters which had appeared in already-drafted chapters of Adams's *Education*. It did not help that James's book was far inferior chapter by chapter to the book Adams was producing; and, if writing passable biography was the issue, it was Adams's opinion that James had flatly failed. Adams accordingly had the problem of choosing between silence about the failure and an expression of some sort to James.

On November 18, he wrote an unparalleled letter advising James that he had devoured the Story volumes and thought them a "*tour de force.*" Rather than criticize, he congratulated James for revealing a "painful truth" to the few who could see what was revealed: that the ambitious Bostonians of Story's time had resembled one another in being ignorant and shallow. Adams said: "One cannot exaggerate the profundity of ignorance of Story in becoming a sculptor, or Sumner in becoming a statesman, or Emerson in becoming a philosopher. Story and Sumner, Emerson and Alcott, Lowell and Longfellow, Hillard, Winthrop, Motley, Prescott, and all the rest, were [of?] the same mind,— and so, poor worm! was I."

Adams denied that James's book was biography and said it was something quite opposite, a form of collective autobiography. "So you have written not Story's life, but your own and mine,—pure autobiography,— the more keen for what is beneath, implied, intelligible only to me, and half a dozen other people still living. . . . Improvised Europeans, we were, and—Lord God!—how thin! No, but it is too cruel! Long ago,—at least thirty years ago,—I discovered it, and have painfully held my tongue about it."

Adams's letter could be described as impossible to answer because too dangerous to read.[11] Its underlying meanings were that James had committed a serious injustice by publishing a superficial book about a man not as superficial as the book, and had dishonored biography by pretending to practice it when unwilling to do so. The deadly phrase in Adams's letter—"improvised Europeans"—could hardly be applied to Adams, who had become a world citizen without any sacrifice of being an American. Yet it might apply to James as well as to Story.[12]

In every important respect except one, Adams's letter was a harsh rebuke. Its saving grace was that he put into it all he had in force of mind and power of expression and thus paid James the compliment of treating him as a writer deserving of the strongest censure a gentleman's manners might permit.

Mrs. Cameron and Martha reappeared in Paris on December 7, 1903. Less than three weeks later, on December 26, they and Dor left the city. Dor went to Cherbourg to board the *St. Louis.* Having sublet 50 Avenue du Bois de Boulogne to some Americans, the Livingstons, Mrs. Cameron started with Martha towards Rome, where they would pass the winter and Martha would make a start in Italian.

Dor's voyage was stormy, and he learned in New York that most of Chicago had been laid waste by an enormous fire.

Belatedly a committee of the Century Association was preparing a memorial volume in praise of Clarence King. The talk Dor had prepared about King was wanted for the volume. Once in Washington, he lent the manuscript to Hay, who pronounced it a "masterpiece" and said it would "give life to the whole book."[13] Valuable in itself, the talk was valuable also as an indication that Adams would sometimes be willing to appear again before the public as a writer of signed works.[14]

Hay had warned Adams that, for them as managers of America's foreign affairs, the winter would be "unusually nasty." He had offered a list of "horrors and poisons," including "Cuba, and Canada, and elastic currency, and the Isthmian Canal, and the Far East and Alaska."[15] One may assume that he and Adams reviewed the horrors and poisons, but Hay very soon came down with bronchitis. Intending a rapid recovery, he left for the South.[16]

Dor had promised Mrs. Cameron that he would improve his attitude toward President Roosevelt. He felt he had little choice. ". . . I must go home a warm Theodorist, or I must be ill-seen, and may even injure my intimates. . . ."[17] Though good, the purpose did not survive an early return to the White House.

Brooks and Evelyn were making 1603 H Street their headquarters. Evelyn prevailed on Henry to take her to a diplomatic reception. Roosevelt welcomed them "with warhoops" and required that Henry dine at his table with Secretary Root, Edward Everett Hale, and other listeners. Writing to Mrs. Cameron on January 10, 1904, Henry told what happened. "Desperate at the outlook, I flung myself . . . into the mad stream, trying to stem it, and Root tried to help me; but we were straws in Niagara. . . . We were overwhelmed in a torrent of oratory, and at last I heard only the repetitions of I—I—I—attached to indiscretions greater one than another. . . . How Root stands this sort of thing I do not know. . . . The worst of it is that it is mere cerebral excitement. . . . It has not the excuse of champagne. The wild talk about everything—Panama, Russia, Germany, England and whatever else suggested itself,— belonged not to the bar-room but to the asylum."

While concluding that Roosevelt had become excited to the point of insanity, Adams was himself made very fearful by an anticipated world event. Russia and Japan were vying to occupy Manchuria. In his view, Washington was the best place to foresee what Russia and Japan would do next. He continued his letter to Mrs. Cameron by divulging: "I have got to hide. Perhaps I may have to run. Yet the politics are so amusing that one wants to listen at the key-hole. I think this place is now the political center of the world. Everybody is interested,—excited,—and all are anti-Russian. . . . I am the only—relative—Russian afloat, and only because I am half crazy with fear that Russia is sailing straight into another French revolution which may upset all Europe and us too."

During the winter, Adams did important things. One was secretly drafting new chapters of his *Education*. Second was a mostly secret effort to bring about the printing of 100 copies of *Mont Saint Michel and Chartres* by J. H. Furst and Company in Baltimore. A soundless third was constant listening at the Washington keyhole for news about the expected Russo-Japanese war and the anticipated breakdown of Russia. Passages in his letters to Mrs. Cameron reflected ever-mounting fear. "The war is now accepted as inevitable. . . ." "Russia is in a terribly dangerous state. . . ." "The Tsar is almost Louis XVI over again. . . . Revolution is inevitable. . . . This conviction has turned me into a Russian. I don't want to see Russia go to pieces. Such a disaster would be worse than the collapse of France in 1870."[18]

Secretary Root resigned. Evelyn Adams had an operation and while convalescing lived with her sister, Anna Lodge. Henry hid, wrote letters, and worked. "Brooks runs about and instructs the great. I lock my doors and hold my tongue, for I am scared blue."[19]

Hay being away in the South, the Chinese and German ambassadors paid private visits to Henry Adams. ". . . I sat an hour with my friend Liang and talked war. Speck sat an hour with me and talked war. We are all about equally scared. . . . Speck is alarmed about Turkey and the Balkans and Austria. Liang is alarmed about China. I am in terror about Russia itself, and look to see the chaos of the Balkans extend to Vladivostock and Hong Kong." "If Russia breaks down, France must be isolated, and a victim. Either she must annex herself to Germany or to us. Either way she is sunk."[20]

On February 7, 1904, a fire in Maryland destroyed much of downtown Baltimore, and Japan began her war with a surprise naval attack on a Russian outpost at Port Arthur. The fire consumed the printer's copy of some chapters of *Mont Saint Michel and Chartres*. Henry was put to the trouble of providing new manuscripts for the printer.

Hay returned from the South. ". . . [he] came at four to walk, and talked an hour straight, about Russia and the situation. We fought over the whole field, as you may imagine. . . ." "You see how completely beside myself I am. To my wild imagination we are already deep in another and a bigger revolution like 1789."[21]

Brooks left for treatment at Hot Springs. The Berensons arrived with a note of introduction supplied by John La Farge. Henry did not want Berenson for a visitor but could not escape inviting him and his wife to the house. They came on February 15. Irritated by what he took to be the husband's "Jew deprecation," Henry treated Berenson as rudely as possible. He confessed to Mrs. Cameron, "In my own house I ought not to have done so." Yet the day was generally bad—"the worst day I've had for years." "People persisted in coming in."[22]

Gaskell had been ill. Henry wrote to him and very nearly mentioned *The Education of Henry Adams*. "Young men are needed. . . . The chance of a very great change in the world, is good, and everyone young should make ready for it. . . . I am doing my best, for one."[23]

Brooks and Evelyn went south. The Berensons went north. On February 24, Henry wrote to Mrs. Cameron that he was "profoundly glad of it." One meeting with the art historian had been one too many.

Although racked by a cough, Mrs. Cameron had left Rome to nurse a sick relative. Henry urged her on March 6, "Please go to bed and get well." On the 8th, he added that he and Hay were taking their daily walks. "Naturally there is much to discuss but I am always surprised at the little one knows."

Because Mary and Dorothy had come for a visit and were wanted at the White House, Henry was obliged to go with them and share a second meal with the president. The occasion revealed a change but not an improvement. "Theodore has stopped talking cowboy and San Juan. Every idea centres now on the election. . . ." The president would undoubtedly be the Republican candidate in the election of 1904, but most of his fellow Republicans in Congress were unhappy at the prospect. "That he has not a friend except Cabot, who is really loyal to him, has been too clear to me ever since I returned, but I am interested in watching his state of mind, because it makes clearer some very interesting characters of history. He is really *déséquilibré*, as the French say, and his daughter Alice is worse."[24]

Presumably with Hay's knowledge but on his own initiative, Adams was trying to help Russia by appealing through the German ambassador to Europe's rival monarchs as one another's blood relations. On March 14, 1904, he disclosed to Mrs. Cameron: "I entreat Speck to get the Kaiser to bestir himself, and to put the whole family-pressure on the poor little crétin Tsar. Nothing so agonizing was ever seen. Louis XVI was a mild tragedy beside it. . . . I believe that everyone in the circle of diplomacy thinks the same, but they [the rulers of Russia] are quite imbecile and helpless, just as they were in 1790. Mile by mile, day after day, they roll on, with the abyss straight ahead, and no one even squeaks."

A new world's fair, the Louisiana Purchase Exposition, would soon be opening at St. Louis. Clara Hay asked Adams to stay long enough to accompany the Hays to the fair. He assented, although it meant that Mrs. Cameron might return to Paris ahead of him. In a letter sent on April 11, he urged: "If you get to Paris by June 1, try and hire me an automobile, and a chauffeur. Twenty horse-power should be enough. I *must* have it, and you can use it. . . ."

By coincidence on April 11, Mrs. Cameron wrote to him on the same subject. Lionel de Rothschild had turned up in Rome equipped with a forty horsepower Mercedes. "Certainly no Christian has been so glad to see me for years. He took us around the country in the auto to see medieval castles & things, and now of course I want an automobile more than ever before. It seems a necessity of life."

Adams's impulse to rent a more adequate automobile mainly had to do with *Mont Saint Michel and Chartres*. Patient work had permitted him to re-copy the pages lost in the fire, and printing could resume. Yet he disliked the idea of treating the book as finished without his first seeing the great churches he had not visited and without his revisiting others, beginning with Chartres. To perform the errands without the help of an automobile would be slow and laborious. With such help, it might be swift and pleasurable.

His precautions relating to *Mont Saint Michel and Chartres* were of a piece with his sensitivity concerning the *Memoirs of Arii Taimai.* He and Tati had been corresponding steadily. Letters must have come from Tati thanking him for the book and extending the praise that it deserved. Yet, while keeping letters from Tati that concerned other topics, Adams kept none that praised the book or even spoke of it. His attitude apparently was that of an extreme perfectionist. He had been so anxious to raise the *Memoirs* to a state of perfection that he wished not to be informed, and not to admit, that he had done so.

A letter on a different subject was coming from Tati. Written on April 1, 1904, it said the Tevas would hold a feast to celebrate the completion of a church built in memory of Arii Taimai. Adams would figure in the proceedings. "Tauraatua[,] as head of the fighting chiefs, will have to be present or represented. . . ." On the assumption that Adams would not be free to attend, Tati asked, ". . . will you not write me a few words, which will be read out, to the people, by my son [Tauraatua], your namesake[?]"

Adams quickly complied. The necessity that he send an appropriate message arose from his rank. When she gave him the title-and-name Taura-atua i Amo, Arii Taimai had made him her "next of kin"—her nearest heir. Despite its importance, Tati perhaps could have set her action aside in silence. He did the opposite. He made arrangements that would cause the American Taura-atua i Amo to be the central personage at the feast: the one to whom all the speakers, as a matter of form, would be asked to address their words, and the one on whose behalf Tati himself would appear and preside.[25]

In October 1903 with the approval of Charles, Henry, and Mary, and under the title "Mrs. John Quincy Adams's Narrative of a Journey from St. Petersburg to Paris in February, 1815," Brooks had published in *Scribner's Magazine* the most remarkable paper left by Louisa Catherine Adams. Her narrative gave a clear, detailed account of a winter exploit by an American wife, a small son, and a nurse, when accompanied only by less-than-sufficient hired male protectors.[26]

Brooks had established himself as a writer. He needed subjects to write about. In a letter to Henry from Quincy on May 8, 1904, he mentioned that he was reading "our grandfather's papers." For Henry, the remark perhaps was warning enough that Brooks was starting an attempt to write a biography of John Quincy Adams. Brooks of course was free to write a biography of their grandfather, just as Charles was free to write biographies of their father, but it was a problem for Henry that his brothers should insist on producing less-than-excellent books on matters that directly affected him.

Mrs. Cameron was writing to Henry about her health, the value of water cures, and the value of automobiles. She had said on April 28, "If it were not for you, I should not go [to Paris] . . . but straight to Nauheim and finish up that business [an interrupted cure]. . . . Certainly *something* made me over last year, and I do not know whether it was Nauheim or St. Moritz or both." On May 1, she added, "But I need an automobile!!" On the 8th, she renewed the cry. ". . . my one desire in life is an automobile." ". . . I want my own!"

Henry intended to furnish her an automobile but first went to St. Louis with the Hays to see the fair. He enjoyed it and by May 26 was poised in New York, ready to reboard his favorite steamer, the *St. Louis,* and start again for Cherbourg. From the Knickerbocker Club, he sent a farewell message to Niece Loulie that touched on the relations best formed between men and women. "Slavery," he averred, "is the only institution that deserves respect. The woman wants a slave. She generally gets one. . . ."

Mrs. Cameron directed a letter to the *St. Louis,* timed to reach Dor the instant he arrived in Europe. She said she would be hurrying to Paris "to see as much of you as possible."[27] His schedule was such that he could stop at Coutances to visit old nearby parish churches. Once he and she were both in Paris, he inspected automobiles. Near the end of June, he bought an eighteen-horsepower Mercedes, hired a chauffeur—or *mécanicien*—named Morison, and rented a second auto capable of making trips with reasonable protection against mishaps.

Owning an automobile made him feel that the changes in the world since the 1830s were too great to have been experienced by a single human being. Writing to Anne Fell on June 27, 1904, he said he could not form a unified idea of his own history. "A world so different from that of my childhood or middle-life can't belong to the same scheme." "Out of a mediaeval, primitive, crawling infant of 1838, to find oneself a howling, steaming, exploding, Marconing, radiumating automobiling maniac of 1904 exceeds belief."

With Martha and a maid, Mrs. Cameron enjoyed a five-day drive from Paris to Nauheim in Dor's rented, second machine.

Left alone in Paris, Dor concentrated on his *Education.* Its two narratives would differ widely because tethered to different eras: a medieval past (1838–1871) and a modern present (beginning in 1892). He re-weighed the meaning of owning a Mercedes. It seemed to him that he was being driven at ever-increasing speeds toward the end of the world. On July 4, he explained to Cunliffe with cheerful nonchalance: "One might as well lead the way. . . . The end must be mighty near, to judge from the pace."

Under French law, unless given a number by the French authorities, an automobile could not leave France and return as French. The law further required the auto's being driven by two employees when leaving France. The strictures affected Adams. In hopes of lending the Mercedes to Mrs. Cameron outside of France, he applied for a number.

During a visit to Misses Marbury and de Wolfe at their villa in Versailles, Adams encountered some people he knew, including the Blacques, Eliot Gregory, and Berenson. Next day, he stated his reaction. "I fled in my own auto. Today it is in the shops, and likely to stay till the workmen choose to do what is wanted."[28]

On July 10, he took Mrs. Hewitt to Éperon in the Mercedes with complete success. "The machine went like a bird, but a kilometre a minute is too fast for comfort."[29] On the 13th, much encouraged, he set off on a four-day trip to Normandy to see more churches.

His language about his "mushine" sometimes indicated vexation.[30] More serious were the vexations of laboring alternately on his *Education* and *Mont Saint Michel and Chartres*. Chapters of the former being much in his mind, he said to Mrs. Cameron on July 21, ". . . [I] dread having to find something for that blamed machine to do." He offered to send the machine to her the following week. "You can return it when you're done with it." Also he inquired: "What are your plans? When do you go to St[.] Moritz?"

A possibility that appealed to Mrs. Cameron was a tour of northern Italy in September. On July 23, she suggested that Dor put off the loan of his auto till that time. He on the same day informed Gaskell that he owned a Mercedes. ". . . to my great relief and satisfaction, the inspector delays for weeks to give me a number, and the chauffeur always has a reason for sending the machine to the shops. Between them I am quite happy, and never have to go out-doors."

As he tended to do when writing to Gaskell, Adams fully expressed his fears. "You know how scared I have been about this [Russo-Japanese] war. The situation grows more intense every day, and its interest keeps me awake nights. . . . Russia is very rapidly foundering. . . . It is the greatest event that has taken place in our time, as a catastrophe. . . . Never has so great an empire sunk without dragging the world down with it. The confusion will be vast."

Knowledge that he would be keeping the automobile till late summer permitted him to take another trip. Its furthest object was the great abbey church on a hill at Vézelay at which Saint Bernard "preached the second crusade."[31] He left Paris on Thursday, July 28, and began a letter to Mrs. Cameron late on Monday. "All Thursday, Friday, and Saturday I was flying across the country like a mad flea. I had, for ten years, waited for a chance to get to Auxerre, Avallon, and Vezelay. Last Thursday I ran away as hard as I could; breakfasted at Provin's; got three clear hours at Troyes; and Friday morning got to Auxerre in time to see my *flèche*, and go on to breakfast at Avallon. The day was a squealer for heat, but I started off again at one o'clock, ran up to Vezelay like a cat, and at three o'clock had exhausted all my sights. I thought of going to Nevers, but decided on Bourges, a perfectly straight road of a hundred and twenty kilometres or so. I got there in time to give an hour to my windows."

He felt that Mrs. Cameron and he were attending to their respective duties. She was improving her and Martha's health. He told her on August 5: ". . . you must devote August to finishing your cure and giving Martha some mountain air." He was advancing in his *Education* and seeing more windows, portals, and spires. Being in a traveling frame of mind, he urged that Martha "read the adventures of Odysseus."

His attitude towards the Mercedes became divided between appreciation and chagrin. He explained to Gaskell: "To be private secretary or professor is nothing compared with being slave to an automobile. . . . I am off every day, and think it easy if I only run thirty or forty miles of an afternoon to visit a twelfth-century church or sixteenth-century glass."[32] On August 8, he wrote to Mrs. Cameron more gratefully, ". . . the machine has already enabled me to see a number of things I never should have seen without it, and which are uncommonly worth it." Trips to Chartres were very easy. He continued on the 10th: ". . . I've been down to Chartres. . . . It is eighty-eight kilometres, almost exactly the same as Fontainebleau via Versailles. Both trips take me two hours and three quarters, and in my opinion a real gentleman should not do them in less."

From St. Moritz on August 17, Mrs. Cameron sent him news that he had an admirer. "Mr. Berenson turned up yesterday & raved about you to my intense amusement[,] having heard *your* side of the question." In the same letter, she said she would need the Mercedes at Lake Como. "If you really want to send me the auto, could you let it meet me at Cadenabbia about the 10th Sept? But I insist on paying all expenses, and also that you won't send it if you have any use whatever for it, for you, or nieces."

Dor was using the Mercedes as much as possible. While her letter was in the mail, he was away on a six-day trip to Quimper and other places in Brittany, prefaced and concluded with visits to Chartres. The effort opened the way to an unqualified opinion. He assured her on August 20, "Chartres is far and away the greatest thing in the world, as I come back to it."

Three days later, he returned from another visit to Elsie de Wolfe and Elisabeth Marbury at Versailles with news for Mrs. Cameron that Berenson had been praising *her*. In Dor's view, such instances of praise were attempts at shrewdness. "Berenson," he reported, "has been slobbering you with praise to Miss de Wolfe. Apparently he is much of his race, and thinks flattery at second-hand infallible."

Being sixty-six, white-haired, and mostly bald, Adams tended to notice how age had changed him. He confessed to Gaskell on August 27 that, for him, reading had become a "labor." "Writing is better. It compels attention." His one diversion was "automobiling." "The auto is made for the aged. The sense of going—going—going—in the open air, dulls thought, and induces a sort of hypnotism . . . ."

As before, his acutest worries centered in Russia. He suggested: ". . . there is no Russian government. . . . This is what caused the war [with Japan]. The army repudiated the treaties made by the foreign department." He imagined that Russia could be transformed, but only over a long stretch of time. ". . . no way is now open except the total overthrow of the irresponsible Tsar, and the creation of a serious government. Fifty years is hardly enough for this. . . ." The worst hazard, be believed, was Russian militarism. ". . . I want a successful Russia, with a peaceful system, not a bomb."[33]

On August 29, Henry wrote to Hay about automobiling and Russia. ". . . I've ravaged France. I find that a gait of about 25 miles an hour on a straight country road hypnotises me as a chalk line does a hen." ". . . I have nothing to tell you. The war [between Japan and Russia] holds its path exactly as we foresaw, but more slowly. . . . Whatever is the result of the war, Russia has fifty years of reorganisation before her. . . . My blood curdles to think what will happen there if society breaks up; and there is nothing to hold it together except the ridiculous Tsar and the preposterous Church."

During their stay at Inverlochy Castle in 1902, Donald and Martha had been much noticed by Scottish Camerons. In 1904, Martha was invited to the Lochaber Ball, to occur in late September. She accepted the invitation. To arrive at the ball when wanted, she and the maid, Leonie, would have to be in London on September 28 in time to catch the express to Fort William.

Adams was expanding his survey of French church windows to take in as much glass as possible. He advised Mrs. Cameron: "Just back from Beauvais and Gisors[,] where I went to find more glass, having yesterday been to Andelys on the same errand. The quantity of 16th century glass is amazing, and much of it very fine indeed. . . . I should never have had the patience to hunt it by rail."[34]

The French authorities had at last supplied a number. Morison and a helper were ready to drive the Mercedes to Italy. There were problems about road maps and doubts whether a passable road led to Caden-abbia. Mrs. Cameron agreed to meet the drivers at nearby Carnobbio.

Morison and the helper found her, and mother and daughter began an Italian tour. The one thing Mrs. Cameron could not understand was Dor's unwillingness to join them. She wrote to him about it.[35] On September 9, 1904, he replied: "Remember that I loved Italy in 1859 and 1860, as passionately as you do, and that the Italy of 1900 is a torture to me. Hardly a feature is left. . . . I saw the middle-ages in their charm. You see a sort of tourist's middle-ages. . . . I should enjoy it like you if I were, like you, still sixteen."

Adams's intimates tended to honor him most, not for his powers of mind or his unexampled breadth of experience, but for extraordinary kindness. During the previous spring, Saint Gaudens had lived with Adams free of charge while at work in Washington on a bust of Hay. Out of gratitude, the sculptor created a bronze medallion on which Adams was caricatured as a porcupine armed with needles, yet also equipped with wings. He sent Adams the medallion. It bore a legend: "Porcupinus Angelicus Henricus Adamenso." Evidently the power attributed to the angelic porcupine was kindness without end.

Letters to Adams from Tahiti reflected the same reality. Tati had told very few of the Tevas that their lands had been saved from the auction block with money provided by Adams. The feast at Papara in memory of Arii Taimai occurred as scheduled. 2,800 people were fed for as many as three days. Foreigners looked on. In Tati's words:—"Several Americans and Englishmen were there, they asked, who was this Tauraa-tua, the speakers seem to be addressing. . . . Moetia told those who did not know you."

In this way, for Tahitians and foreigners, the feast became in part a public acknowledgment of Adams's rank.[36] Yet, for Tati, Adams was more than a great chief of the Tevas. He was the chief who saved the clan. ". . . had it not been [for] you, what life would we have had[?] I know what that means, but the young ones cannot."[37]

The Mercedes performed all but four days of Mrs. Cameron's planned tour and at that point lost its main brakes. By using the handbrake, Morison "crept" into Milan. There a mechanics' strike had closed the Mercedes shop. Mrs. Cameron met the emergency on her own initiative. She knew that Dor was done with the vehicle and meant to put it into storage. On September 20, she advised him, ". . . I shall ship the machine to Paris by train as soon as Morison can arrange it."

Although dogged by recurrent illness, including tooth troubles, Joe Stickney had returned to Harvard as a teacher of Greek.[38] In July, he had written Mrs. Cameron a letter so "curious" that she had not answered it.[39] At Milan, she received a letter—presumably from Lucy Stickney, Joe's mother—containing "more bad news!" She sent it to Dor with the injunction that he keep it for her.[40]

Mrs. Cameron and Martha returned to Paris; Martha and Leonie left for Scotland; and Mrs. Cameron and Dor were again by themselves. She needed a chance for long talks with him, for her and Martha's lives were about to change. In November, she, Martha, and Dor would return to America together. Because the Cameron house at 21 Lafayette Square was rented to a new tenant unwilling to leave it, there were problems about where to live. A house seemed an urgent necessity. Martha had reached an age that required her making her debut.

Mrs. Cameron crossed to London to meet Martha on her return and with her went to visit English friends. In Paris, Dor received news about Stickney. Of the young Americans who wished to be poets, Joe had been the most promising. A letter from his mother confirmed that he had a brain tumor, was incapacitated, could walk, and had improved. "Joe would send his love did he know I was writing."[41] Her letter was contradicted by a cable sent to Paris on October 12. It said, "Joe died last night." Its senders were Stickney's mother and Bay Lodge, his poetic rival and best friend.

Again Dor rented an electric auto. Mrs. Cameron had been visiting at Rufford Abbey, and he had avoided sending her letters at that address. On October 14, he directed a letter to her at Brown's Hotel in London, saying a cable had arrived about Stickney. He added that he would meet her train at the Paris station.

For three weeks, he wrote no letters that survive. On November 5 or thereabouts, presumably at Cherbourg, with Martha, he and Mrs. Cameron boarded a steamer, name uncertain. Their voyage would begin a transition to new arrangements they could not foresee.

13

Vehicles of Anarchism

Appearances would have been saved if Donald had met Mrs. Cameron, Martha, and Adams in New York when they left their ship. Instead he stayed at Coffin's Point in South Carolina; Adams repaired to the Knickerbocker Club at 319 Fifth Avenue; and Mrs. Cameron and Martha went to a hotel of their choosing—possibly the Holland House—and looked for a residence they could afford. They shortly moved to the Lorraine, a facility at Fifth Avenue and 45th Street best described as an upperclass boarding house.[1] Their rooms were comfortable and had telephones, but the food was very bad. For relief, mother and daughter would depend partly on invitations to meals with friends.[2]

For a year, first in New York and again in Paris, Adams had sought the acquaintance of a rich, well-placed New York matron, Mary Cadwalader Jones. (Her husband, Frederic R. Jones, was the brother of Edith Wharton.) Always eager to see her, Adams sped a note to her house at 21 East 11th Street. He sought meetings as well with John La Farge and Elisabeth Marbury. Perhaps from La Farge, he obtained the current address of Henry James, then visiting in America, and urged his coming to Washington, if convenient.

All usual enough, Adams's actions in New York were preparatory to a winter of more than usual hospitality in Washington. He apparently reached 1603 H Street on Saturday, November 19, 1904. Brooks was already there and Evelyn was expected. Henry called at the White House and spoke with Edith Roosevelt. He could not immediately summon the courage to call on Lucy Stickney and learn better what had happened to Joe, but he quickly visited Bay and Bessy Lodge and their children. The news of the moment was that Bay, in hopes of shocking any persons willing to read it, had written and published a drama in verse titled *Cain*. Adams obtained a copy and studied it on the assumption that its characters would be Bay as Cain, his brother John as Abel, and their parents as Adam and Eve. The assumption lent pungency to the drama. Adams thought it had interest.[3]

A letter came from Margaret Chanler, who was in Boston. On the 21st, Adams invited her to join him in Washington. "Elope and come!" he suggested. He added that for the sake of appearances she could arrange to be accompanied by his niece Abigail.

Appearances mattered. Mrs. Cameron was bent on precipitating a felicitous marriage for her daughter. Washington was the place where she intended to effect her purpose. In part for Martha's sake, she meant to live again as mistress of the house at 21 Lafayette Square from which they had been expelled in 1897. Meanwhile, as the readiest means of seeing Donald, she—with Martha—would return to Coffin's Point for Christmas. She also would make quick visits to Washington. While all this happened, she and Dor would need *not* to be talked about as persons who had been near-neighbors in Paris.

Clara Hay took Adams into her confidence about the question of her husband's future. Roosevelt had easily won the presidential election in November. He asked Hay to accept reappointment as secretary, and John wished to continue, but Clara forbade his continuing unless he was permitted a spring vacation abroad. She wanted Adams to share the journey. She had become convinced that John's ailments were extremely serious and had interceded because she was trying to save his life. In response, Adams agreed to help in any way she wished.[4]

Brooks left for a water cure at a Virginia spa, and Henry worked again on his edition of *Mont Saint Michel and Chartres*. Furst and Company was waiting for him to send a preface and prepare the index.[5] He completed the work in early December.[6] When readied, the copies would be dated on their title pages as issued in Washington in 1904.[7]

Mrs. Cameron was under pressures from her sister Cecil Miles and Lucy Stickney—Joe's mother—to visit them briefly in the capital; and she did so in mid-December. She however was most concerned that Dor accompany her and Martha to Coffin's Point.[8] He so arranged things that *Martha* invited him. On that basis, he bought a train ticket for December 23, joined daughter and mother for ten days of relaxation, and on January 3, 1905, was back at 1603 H Street.

The hundred copies of *Mont Saint Michel and Chartres* arrived from Baltimore—cost, $1,003.25.[9] Adams immediately gave copies to Hay, Anna Lodge, and Edith Roosevelt.[10] At the White House, Mrs. Roosevelt opened the book and noticed two words on the half-title page:

TRAVELS

—

FRANCE

She learned from the Preface that the book was "written for nieces, or for those who are willing, for the time, to be nieces in wish." That night she wrote to Adams that she was "glad to be a niece." She said too that he could not know how kind she thought him and how happily she had enjoyed traveling with him all evening.[11]

Adams had arranged with the printer to make *Mont Saint Michel and Chartres* closely resemble *Memoirs of Arii Taimai* in physical form.[12] The copies were bound in dark blue cloth and bore dark-red labels on their spines, lettered in gold. Each copy stood twelve inches high and ten wide.[13] The size resulted from margins ranging in width up to two-and-a-half inches. Adams needed the margins. He was not done with the book and wanted ample space in which to write corrections and improvements.

Nieces would prize copies because they were sumptuous in appearance and extremely easy—indeed friendly—to read. Ease of reading was achieved in part by omission. The title page omitted the name of the author. There was no table of contents. The chapters were headed only with Roman numbers. The chapter titles appeared only as running heads on the even-numbered pages. The text was supported with floor plans of churches and genealogical tables, kept as few and simple as possible. Passages quoted from Old French or Latin sources appeared with adjacent English translations by the author. The index listed both persons and subjects.

Good manners accounted for much of the book's readability. The author introduces himself in the Preface as an uncle inclined to take a summer-long journey in France with one of his nieces. He amusingly says he will do the talking and the niece must bring a camera and take the photographs. They are to start by going straight to Mont Saint Michel. The Preface ends, "The uncle talks."

Talk he does, through sixteen chapters and 338 pages, but the effect is that of a conversation. The niece's responses and suggestions are not given but are everywhere implicit in what gets said. She is as necessary to the book as the uncle. Were it not for her, the journey would not be taken and the book would remain unwritten.

Adams's distribution of copies reflected his situation and state of mind. On January 5, 1905, he advised Mrs. Cameron, "I have my Miracles de la Vierge ready for you, whenever you want it, but will keep it till you come." She would understand that his keeping the copy in Washington was part of a concerted effort by him and her to seem unrelated to one another.[14] Also she would assume that a copy had been reserved for Martha, who more than any other could be thought of as the "niece" for whom the book was written.[15]

In the same letter, Adams asked Mrs. Cameron for Mrs. Chanler's New York address. The point of the request was that he wished to give copies of his book to many women, young and old. Moreover, he would invite Mrs. Chanler and Laura to come to 1603 H Street as house guests and would invite Mrs. Jones and her daughter Beatrix to do the same.

On an early day, possibly January 5, he mailed copies to Louisa Hooper and Mabel La Farge. Writing on the 9th to Mabel, he hinted that there might be fewer copies than there were "nieces." Half in earnest, he said he was undecided whether President Roosevelt "counts in the class." The remark was a first sign that Adams in some cases would refuse to give copies, even if strongly urged.

Because Gaskell was his closest English friend, one might imagine Adams mailed him a copy at once. As a general thing, however, Adams wished not to hurry. He did not send Gaskell's copy till March.[16]

Henry Osborn Taylor was writing a compendious and authoritative work to be titled *The Mediæval Mind*. On January 6, though otherwise not in a rush, Adams had sent Taylor "my private folly," as he called it, and also offered a copy to John W. Burgess, a professor at Columbia University who had done him a favor. He explained to Burgess that his gesture was "purely personal and private" and that the book was "not to be published or put up for sale." Even more strongly, he insisted to Taylor that his folly could not be published. "I should bring on my head all the Churches and all the Universities and all the Laboratories at once."

Adams's brothers saved him from having to send them copies, Brooks by returning with Evelyn to Germany, Charles by taking his family to Egypt. Perhaps as early as January 6, Henry presented a copy to the French ambassador, Jean-Jules Jusserand. The gesture was personal; Henry liked him. Yet it would serve also as an international courtesy, an expression of America's regard for republican France.

Henry James began a week-long stay at Adams's "charming house" on Wednesday, January 10, 1905, and while there wrote to Mrs. Jones that his host was a "philosophic father."[17] Simultaneously John La Farge and Augustus Saint Gaudens came to Washington to attend a conference and took rooms in the house.

Mrs. Cameron and Martha appeared, in part because Martha would be attending a dance.[18] Except that she joined him for breakfast with Mrs. Lodge on Wednesday and possibly shared in a dinner Martha gave at the house on Friday, Mrs. Cameron saw nothing of Dor. When she left on Monday with Martha and La Farge, her copy of *Mont Saint Michel and Chartres* was still at his house.[19] Oppositely, James departed with a copy. He also carried off a set of front-door keys, which perhaps was a sign that his stay had been more-than-expectedly enjoyable.[20]

In one respect, Mrs. Cameron felt reassured. Writing to Dor from New York on January 16, she said she had seen no change whatever in the nation's capital. "It seemed to me just as small, just as provincial, and just as easy and pleasant as before. To my delight[,] Martha loved it, and was reluctant to come away." In other respects, the mother was less than satisfied. ". . . I scarcely had a word with you in Washington and I want one very much as a suspicion is forming in my mind that you are meditating something queer for the spring. Is it a journey? I want to talk to you about it, but when? Also I want my precious book. Will you send it off to me at once."[21]

Answering on the 18th, Adams imparted the deep secret that the Hays would start a vacation in March and he would be going with them. It was urgent that the secret be kept. To insure her keeping it, he said, "No woman has ever yet let out any confidence I trusted to her, but I would not trust a man." Urgency arose from the seriousness of Hay's condition. Adams believed the death of his friend had become a matter of a very few months, weeks, even days. He went so far as to say suggestively, "The vacation is innocent enough, but much may happen to prevent it."

Readers were sending Adams responses. Ambassador Jusserand described *Mont Saint Michel and Chartres* as "pages of poetry."[22] Henry Osborn Taylor said that Adams's faculty for presenting serious subjects in "an actually entertaining way" filled him with envy. One thing struck Taylor most. "The chapter on Abelard is immense."[23]

Taylor's impression reflected an aspect of the book that readers may have found surprising. Because the book's title named two great medieval buildings, readers began by assuming that architecture would be the book's concern throughout. Without question, readers appreciative of architecture would find the volume a feast. Yet the emphasis of *Mont Saint Michel and Chartres* was less on architecture than on persons. Thirteen of its sixteen chapters could be set apart as a giant commentary on the Virgin. The remaining chapters concentrated on Abelard, Saint Francis of Assisi, and Saint Thomas Aquinas. With justice, the book could be categorized as biography—or rather as four biographies: a long one of a woman, three short ones of men.[24]

Adams himself made important comments about the book. Writing to Gaskell four weeks earlier, he had said about *Mont Saint Michel and Chartres*: "It is my declaration of principles as head of the Conservative Christian Anarchists; a party numbering one member. The Virgin and St[.] Thomas are my vehicles of anarchism." On January 17, 1905, writing to Taylor, he said his interest in the middle ages was "scientific." Going into detail, he threw out some ideas that Taylor might have found hard to follow. "I am trying to work out the formula of anarchism; the law of expansion from unity, simplicity, morality, to multiplicity, contradiction, police. . . . I can see it in the development of steam-power. . . . Radium thus far is the term for these mechanical ratios. . . . The assumption of unity[,] which was the mark of human thought in the middle-ages[,] has yielded very slowly to the proofs of complexity. The stupor of science before radium is a proof of it."

Adams applied his phrase "vehicles of anarchism" to two persons: the Virgin and Thomas Aquinas. He could equally have applied it to two books: the one he had already printed, *Mont Saint Michel and Chartres*, and the one he was pressing to complete, *The Education of Henry Adams.* The book already printed contained a sizeable admixture of references to science. In *Mont Saint Michel and Chartres*, while saying much about architecture, art, literature, and feeling, Adams had found space to introduce Faraday, James Clerk Maxwell, and even Maxwell's demon.[25] He had thrown in such sentences as "Man is an imperceptible atom always trying to become one with God."[26]

If it was beginning to appear that Adams's newest writings would offer problems as well as pleasures to the reader, the problems could perhaps be solved most easily after the completion and printing of *The Education of Henry Adams*; and at that point the problems could perhaps be solved most easily by trying to learn what he meant by "anarchy." It might emerge that his "principles of anarchy" were the same as his principles of history, with one difference. Instead of stepping forward as a historian *writing* history, Adams—by writing and printing books of a new sort—would be an anarchist *making* history.

He had sent *Mont Saint Michel and Chartres* to Mrs. Chanler during the second week of January 1905. She responded by telling him that it was "the thing I most wanted and the book of all others I shall most enjoy."[27] Beginning on the 19th, with Laura, she paid him a visit during which he let her read a copy of *Memoirs of Arii Taimai.* On returning to New York, she wrote to say she regretted not having stolen it.[28] Her remark induced him to send her what she failed to steal.

After she had studied *Mont Saint Michel and Chartres* for three weeks, Mrs. Chanler reported to him, "I don't see how it can have been written. . . ." She had found in it "all the things I have felt & believed & thought." She called it an "externalising of my innermost consciousness"—which she had not known was "capable of expression." Not a person to hesitate, she had concluded that he was a convert to Roman Catholicism. ". . . I feel you that are a devout catholic & that you nestle in the folds of Our Lady's blue mantle."[29] Adams had not become a catholic, but he would not disabuse Mrs. Chanler of her error. On February 8, he simply assured her, "It is worth while to have only one reader, when she is a lioness."

Mrs. Chanler had a very good reason for supposing—mistakenly—that her friend shared her Catholicism. Adams was the sort of historian who could enter deeply into the feelings and beliefs of the persons he studied. He recognized that the Europeans of the middle ages fully believed in the Virgin as a living person, immortal, unlimitedly intelligent and considerate, and empowered to forgive. He fell in with their belief to the extent of saying in his book that the churches raised in Normandy and France in the middle ages were built at her command. For the purposes of the book, he treated her as real. He did not deny—indeed he affirmed—that her reality rested on faith alone; and in the closing paragraph he asserted, ". . . if Faith fails, Heaven is lost." But he kept the question of *his* faith or lack of it so completely out of sight that even a reader as acute as Mrs. Chanler might impulsively fill the void by inferring that he believed what all good Catholics had at one time believed, and what she more fully believed after gratefully reading his pages.

Had she been a non-Catholic or a Protestant, or a skeptic, agnostic, atheist, or adherent of a non-Christian religion, Mrs. Chanler might have seen that Adams's book from its first page to its last was readable as tragedy. Adams could fairly be charged with having told the inspiring and dismaying story of a great religion that failed. *Mont Saint Michel and Chartres* could be understood as perilously erected on a foundation of disbelief. To all who entered beneath its arches, it could say that the Christian faith has died and a new faith shall have to be born.

In 1898, some enterprising Americans had invented an engine of self-congratulation: a select body of not more than two hundred men to be called the National Institute of Arts and Letters. Its members were to create a still more select body, an American Academy of Arts and Letters, and were to do so by a four-stage process—"that seven members [of the Institute] be elected by ballot as the first members of the Academy, and that these seven be requested and empowered to choose eight other members, and that the fifteen thus chosen be requested and empowered to choose five other members, and that the twenty members thus chosen shall be requested and empowered to choose ten other members—the entire thirty to constitute the Academy. . . ."[30]

In 1905, as alphabetized, the list of the Institute's members in its Department of Literature began with two brothers, Charles Francis Adams and Henry Adams.[31] Formation of the Academy was advancing to its second stage. Seven members of the Institute had been elected to be members of the Academy: Samuel Langhorne Clemens, John Hay, William Dean Howells, John La Farge, Edward McDowell, Augustus Saint

Gaudens, and Edmund Clarence Stedman. On January 7, the seven
elected eight more. They included Henry Adams, Henry James, Charles
Eliot Norton, and Theodore Roosevelt.

Notice of Adams's election was sent to him on January 25.[32] He acceded to the honor.[33] Yet he could only have thought of the crowning
of his friends as more timely than his own. La Farge was unwell; Hay was
dangerously unwell; Saint Gaudens was threatened by cancer; and
Henry James, by producing a third long novel, *The Golden Bowl*, had
brought his career to an evident climax.[34] For Adams, oppositely, the
prospect was one of continued labor. The development of his *Education*
was testing his abilities to their utmost limit. Also it was stirring and
disturbing his emotions. To a degree that outsiders had little sense of,
his happiness was founded on a three-way friendship between King, himself, and Hay. He was ending the first narrative of *The Education* with the
meeting of himself and King. He meant to end its second narrative with
the death of Hay, and the portents were clear that Hay's death was in
the making.

On February 7, 1905, Mrs. Cameron wrote to say she was "sulky."
Dor had not been writing to her and had not answered her last letter.
Yet she was cheerful enough to assure him that *Mont Saint Michel and
Chartres* read "charmingly." ". . . I seem to hear you talk."[35]

Dor pled guilty to neglecting her and said the reason was incessant
visitors. One had been Cecil Spring Rice. In part because he liked to say
that he and his host were respectively nephew and uncle, Spring Rice
made off with a copy of the uncle's book.

Mrs. Chanler lent her copy to Edith Wharton. Also she disclosed
her possession of a copy to the president of Columbia, Nicholas Murray
Butler. A former medievalist and would-be biographer of Duns Scotus,
Butler urged her to ask Adams to send a copy for the Columbia library.
She wittily replied that Adams had a "rooted objection to the obviously
plausible." Not dissuaded, Butler asked her to prevail on Adams to send
him a personal copy that he might leave to Columbia when he died. She
forwarded Butler's modified plea, but Adams would not comply. He
wrote back on February 13 that the president was "not a niece."[36]

Mrs. Jones and Beatrix began their visit on February 16, Adams's
sixty-seventh birthday. Next day, Spring Rice wrote to him from the *Teutonic*, saying that *Mont Saint Michel and Chartres* was "wholly delightful."
"Martha told me you printed nothing which you hadn't first ascertained
she could understand. . . ." He called Adams a "poet."

Mrs. Cameron talked with Mrs. Jones after the latter's return to New
York and learned that while staying at Adams's house she "had the time
of her life."[37] Mrs. Jones too came away with a copy.

Still unwilling to be checked by Adams, President Butler borrowed Professor Burgess's copy and wrote to Mrs. Chanler: ". . . I am simply reveling in it." He insisted that she try again to extract a copy for "my library" from "the obdurate Mr. Henry Adams."[38] Mrs. Chanler sent the president's letter to Adams to plead its own case. She reported too that Mrs. Wharton had been "captivated."[39]

Niece Dorothy came to stay for the Inauguration. Mrs. Cameron and Martha were coming as well. It was expected that Dorothy and Martha would want to see the parade and take part in festivities, but Mrs. Cameron would not. The visit would be her first opportunity to live with Adams in his Washington house, and she intended to make the most of it. She had written to him well in advance: "I am not in the least keen about engagements. Let me stay at home as much as possible."[40]

Appearances would not be a problem. As occupants of guest rooms on Adams's second floor, Mrs. Cameron and Martha would have as predecessors Mrs. Chanler and Laura and Mrs. Jones and Beatrix. Moreover, Dorothy being present, Mrs. Cameron would be burdened with two girls to superintend. Thus onlookers could conclude that Mr. Adams had a very wide acquaintance and, in view of the inauguration, was of a mind to put up as many guests as his house could accommodate.

In her last letter from New York before her arrival, sent on March 2, 1905, Mrs. Cameron told Dor, "I am terribly keen about seeing you and talking over many things." She would be staying with him for eight or nine days, till March 11 or 12. A subject that she and he could not avoid would be his vacation with the Hays. Staterooms had been reserved on the Cunard steamer *Cretic*, scheduled to sail for Genoa on the 18th. Dor would be the Hays' only companion. Everything about the secretary's departure was being kept secret.

Mrs. Cameron and Martha paid their visit; Inauguration Day came and went; Roosevelt again was president; and time agreeably passed. As was necessary, Mrs. Cameron and Martha returned to South Carolina and began a second stay at Donald's house. The mother looked from the house at the Atlantic and thought about Dor's impending voyage. On March 13, she wrote to tell him: "So here *we* are, and you are off to the other side of this expanse of water. I don't like it, not one bit. But it cannot be helped, can it? The best part of the whole winter was our week with you in Washington."[41]

Next day, March 14, Dor told Mrs. Cameron, "I have been very solitary and low in mind since you departed. . . ." There was much bad news. Tati Salmon had come to San Francisco for an operation but had gone back to Tahiti without its being performed. In Paris, housekeeper Sadie had been discovered to be dying of cancer. At the Hays' house, there had been a sudden scare about "angina."[42] The European vacation was not called off, but Adams would have preferred not to take it. "I don't want to go. I like my spring here. . . ." Mrs. Cameron had little hope of returning to Europe. She knew a letter sent on the 15th would reach Adams before he sailed. In distress, she told him: "I think an American goodbye is worse than an annual foreign one, and I feel curiously like that spring eight years ago when I was ill and you sailed first. . . ." She spoke for both herself and Martha and seemed to say that two hearts were broken. "Goodbye, dear Dor, goodbye, goodbye. I feel that we shall not see you over there this year,— alas! Goodbye from both of us."

While still in Washington, Adams gave copies of *Mont Saint Michel and Chartres* to Langley, Edith Wharton, and Isabella Gardner. He sent one to Quincy for Brooks to read when again at the Old House.[43] Also he received a letter from Mrs. Jones asking why so good a book was not published. Replying on March 14, 1905, he said the book was "personal" and that he might be criticized for overreaching. ". . . I feel like a fool to risk such a piece of self-assertion. . . . At one breath, to set up for an architect, glass-worker, poet, theologian, metaphysician, mystic, and historian, is outrageous."

In New York on the 16th, he dined with Mrs. Jones. Next morning he learned from her that a copy was wanted by Richard Watson Gilder, the editor of *Century* magazine. Possibly Gilder's request involved an offer to publish the book in instalments. Whatever the details, the editor's action drew from Adams a statement about the value of printing privately. He asked Mrs. Jones to tell Gilder, ". . . if I had meant to publish I should have done so. . . ." He explained, ". . . the whole value, interest and decency of the indiscretion consists in being unpublished."[44]

At a dinner on March 17, Adams met one of his newer friends, Mrs. Tams, and was introduced to her daughter Violet, who he said "should be a niece."[45] The phrase was a sign that Mrs. Tams would be getting a copy. In Adams's lexicon, "nieces" could be mothers, grandmothers, even old men, but they apparently could not be university presidents or editors of nationally distributed magazines.[46]

Dor's last messages to Mrs. Cameron and Martha from New York were heavy with the misfortunes of others. He believed that Hay, Saint Gaudens, John La Farge, and Tati Salmon were all "condemned."[47] In a different sense, he himself was condemned. He was under irresistible compulsion to join the Hays on the *Cretic* and share their impending ordeal, whatever it might prove to be. He wrote to Martha, "The day is fine, and so am I, but I don't want to go aboard."[48]

* * *

When drafting and revising his *History of the United States*, Adams had used long manuscript paper that afforded him a lot of space per page. One may assume that the luggage he packed for his voyage on the *Cretic* contained a supply of such paper, plus necessary pencils, pens, and ink. The assumption is obligatory, because he had started the drive to finish *The Education of Henry Adams*. He had many chapters still to write, and the book was not of a kind that he or anyone could compose in two or even three drafts. Having reached sixty-seven, he felt he had not a moment's time to lose.

The voyage to Genoa was calm. Hay's scare in Washington, originally attributed to angina, had been discounted as a case of mere indigestion. Yet it appeared that Hay would best get a fresh diagnosis in Europe, preferably in Paris.

Apropos of Paris, on April 3, 1905, Dor wrote to Mrs. Cameron, "Of you I think most, as we approach our world. . . ."

The travelers paused in Nervi at the Eden Hotel. A local doctor was consulted, and he ordered Hay to go at once to Bad Nauheim for a cure. The diagnosis matched Mrs. Cameron's of 1897: a "heart-affection consequent on influenza and worry." Hay's case was not as bad as hers, but he was sixty-six, and she had been only forty.[49]

Adams accompanied the Hays to Bad Nauheim. What had started as a vacation had turned into treatment under a German doctor's direction. When a week had passed, Adams adopted the attitude that his presence was not needed; that he was free to start for Paris. He explained to Mrs. Cameron on April 23, "Anything to get out of Germany!"

Sadie had died in Paris on the day the Hays and Adams had sailed from New York.[50] Mabel La Farge and Mrs. Canfield had helped her as much as they could; and Mabel had recruited a replacement, Marie Herlem, whom Adams would later praise as excellent.

By some means never made clear in their letters, Mrs. Cameron had recently learned that Hay had arranged that he and Dor act as co-secretaries and share responsibility for the country's foreign affairs.[51] In Dor's view, Hay's illnesses had become fatal before they boarded the *Cretic*. It followed that neither was any longer a secretary. In this vein, Dor had already confided to Mrs. Cameron, ". . . I consider my job to be closed. . . ."[52] Writing to her again from Bad Nauheim, he told her he would soon be in Paris, "discharged from my last place, out of work, and alone."[53]

Adams arrived in Paris and passed some moments with Edith Wharton, who was not feeling well and would shortly leave. Chauffeur Morison reappeared. The Mercedes was brought from storage.

At Bad Nauheim, Hay received a communication from Spring Rice in St. Petersburg, in effect an intelligence report. Spring Rice said there would not be a revolution in Russia. ". . . we are told there is to be a general insurrection on May the 14[,] but as we have had several warnings of this kind lately & nothing has happened[,] we are skeptical." The Czarist government, he explained, was not bankrupt and the "reformers" lacked soldiers.[54]

As if they could proceed as usual, Hay sent Spring Rice's report to Adams. Simultaneously, Hay told Adams that his doctor forbade his seizing a chance to meet "His Awfulness," the Kaiser.[55] The reason for the interdict was only too evident. Hay was strong enough to go on living if he did nothing but rest. He was not nearly strong enough to see people or to conduct business.

Adams read Spring Rice's report. On May 3, he advised Hay: ". . . [Spring Rice] jumps to the conclusion that there can be no revolution. . . . How much revolution makes a revolution for Springy I don't know; but for my simple wants, as compared with eighteen months ago, eastern Europe has done about the most active bit of revolving as Europe has ever seen. One may be sure that it will go on. . . ."

To Adams's mind, impending revolution in Russia was not as frightening as possible war brought on by the unsolved problem of Germany's desire to expand. He told Hay: "One hardly sees a means of preparing any solution. . . . Yet war would be fatal to everyone, except perhaps to us; and victory would almost necessarily be fatal to Germany as well as to France and Europe. The difficulties of Germany are not such as war can relieve."

The recommended next step for patients who completed cures at Bad Nauheim was an after-cure, a period of unbroken rest. As it happened, Clara Hay had two things on her mind, a sick husband in Europe and the impending birth of a grandchild in America. Her concern about the grandchild assumed such proportions that she wanted John's after-cure to take the form of an interval at their summer place in New Hampshire. To make this possible, wife and husband reserved space on the steamer *Baltic.*

Adams offered the Hays his Mercedes, should they wish to come from Bad Nauheim to Paris by a novel means. John declined the offer, but Clara took an interest in radios. It occurred to her that if she could buy a "Marconi" to take with her on the *Baltic,* messages about the grandchild might be sent to her on shipboard.[56]

Brooks had returned to Quincy and opened *Mont Saint Michel and Chartres.* On May 12, 1905, he reported to Henry that he had read the last pages to Evelyn in his study "with an admiration, delight and emo-

tion which I can never hope to feel over any work of literature again."
Brooks said he had feared that their generation in the Adams family
would achieve "nothing of the first merit" but that Henry had proved
him wrong—that no work in English issued during the past century sur-
passed the unexpected book his brother had written. "I perhaps alone
of living men can appreciate fully all that you have done, for I have lived
with the crusaders and the schoolmen. . . ." Brooks went on to make
"one request." He asked Henry to publish his book in such a form that,
at a minimum, it could be distributed to libraries.

Letters passing between Henry in Paris and Mrs. Cameron in
America expressed well-matched, though opposite, ideas. Henry was saying he was "homesick" and wanted to be in Washington. She was saying
she and Martha were wanting "*so* much to go to Europe."[57]

In a new letter, she praised *Mont Saint Michel and Chartres*. "How
wonderful—quite wonderful—your book is! This may seem a tardy recognition, but you know that I am shy in praising you—always."[58]

Her compliment elicited a denial. Dor replied on May 13, "You are
very good and kind to say you like my talk;—for I deny that it is a book;
it is only a running chatter with my nieces and those of us who care for
old art."

His words were light and offhand. Yet the impulse behind them was
earnest and strong. He was reacting against publication, against universities, against the organized professions—and in favor of private talk, private printing, self-education, and independent discovery.

With Donald, Mrs. Cameron and Martha had left South Carolina
and gone to Pennsylvania to stay for a time at the farm. A great change
had occurred. Donald had agreed not to re-rent 21 Lafayette Square
when it was vacated by the tenant. Beginning on June 1, 1905, Mrs.
Cameron and Martha could use the house as they pleased.

In Paris, Adams was at work on *The Education of Henry Adams* but
silent about his progress. His lone close friend in or near the city was
Elisabeth Marbury. Through her, he heard of a potential added friend,
Anne Morgan—J. P. Morgan's daughter. What Adams hungered for,
however, was *many* new friends. On May 20, he told Mrs. Cameron, ". . . I
need terribly some social centre where I might get a sense of human
relation. . . ." The needed center could not be created in tumultuous
Europe. As he said, "The real volcano now is the Kaiser." The best possibility might be a new alliance between several houses in Washington,
beginning with his own.

Helped by Martha, Mrs. Cameron re-occupied 21 Lafayette Square
and made efforts to put its rooms more in order. She wrote to Adams
on June 4, "I feel that our being here is a great event—almost a resurrec-

tion." She said the return was "almost as delicious as going back into 50 would be."⁵⁹ But summer was coming, and the temperatures in the capital were on the rise. As a protection, mother and daughter made a temporary retreat to a tiny house that Mrs. Cameron contrived to rent in Rhode Island at ever-fashionable Newport.

Miss Marbury was a Paris theatrical agent. She needed someone to translate a French play into English for possible production. Adams agreed to be the translator and thus acquired a part-time occupation that would screen his work on *The Education*. A screen was needed, for he wished to give everyone—even Mrs. Cameron—a wrong impression that he was summering in Paris with nothing to do.⁶⁰

On June 5, writing at last to Brooks, Henry declined to publish *Mont Saint Michel and Chartres*. He gave four reasons: that Brooks was "audience enough"; that there were "already some fifty copies afloat"; that half of them had probably not been read; and that actual readers were next to unknown. "Thousands of people exist who think they want to read. Barring a few Jews, they are incapable of reading fifty consecutive pages, or of following the thought if they tried. I never yet heard of ten men who had ever read my history and never one who had read Hay's Lincoln." He admitted that such a reply could seem "contemptuous to my fellow men." ". . . perhaps it is so." Yet he ventured that "both they and my fellow-women . . . will like me better for not being on sale."

Dor's weekly letter to Mrs. Cameron that Monday, June 5, 1905, began with news of Paris traffic jams caused partly by autos and a visit by the king of Spain. Worse news concerned Hay. En route to Liverpool and the *Baltic*, the Hays came to Paris. On Friday in the Mercedes, Dor took them to the station to catch the train to London. Hay was unimproved. "Paris pulled him down at once. His nerves are gone. He is in no better physical condition than when he sailed."

Dor's letters looked much alike, but some were far more important than others. His present letter was one of his most important. It announced a new start in the world. "Even the Russian problem has taken a form altogether new."

Also the letter told what had happened to Dor and Hay's freedom to make foreign-policy decisions. Dor could have said that their freedom vanished the moment McKinley was shot. He instead spoke more openly. He said that Roosevelt, when president, wished to perform not only his own duties as chief executive but also those of all the Cabinet officers. "Theodore is his own Cabinet, and especially likes to play with foreign kings. Hay has had no choice but to hold the hats and look on. He had better go out, now that the excuse is good." From the first, Dor had favored ideas opposite to Hay's about what Hay should do in response to the president's takeover. He said in his letter, "Get out before you are kicked out! was my standing proverb."

Hay had answered that he "wanted to see himself kicked out." But Roosevelt's keeping Hay in service struck Adams as negative. He said of Hay, ". . . he merely stays kicked in." Not that Adams ever tried to force a resignation. "I have not meddled. On the contrary, I have assumed steadily that Hay would get back to his post."

The drawback of Dor's letter was that it openly said in writing things that were best said very privately in speech—or not at all. He accordingly advised Mrs. Cameron, "If you ever dare whisper one word of my letters, I'll kill you."

After landing at New York, Hay paid a brief business visit to Washington. When he at last reached his New Hampshire summer house, he had depleted his strength beyond recovery.

In Paris, Adams reviewed the maelstrom of world affairs. As was usual with him, retrospection gave way to anticipation. The problem was an approaching great war. On June 18, 1905, he told Mrs. Cameron: "You were the recipient of all my views long ago, and you can judge better than I whether I was right or not. I wanted to save Russia but hardly hoped it. The worst has happened now. Russia is ruined beyond salvation, and as a consequence Germany is playing the devil. I cannot see how such an unbalanced situation can last. France and England are in a chronic panic, and at any moment an explosion is possible. . . . War seems the only possible outcome. . . ."

In London on June 20, *The Times* reported that Sir Robert Cunliffe had died. A week later, the Paris edition of the *New York Herald* announced that Secretary Hay had been prostrated by an excess of urea in his blood. Adams read the announcement and reported to Mrs. Cameron, ". . . I fully expected it this week." He believed Hay's doctors were mystified by the case. "The doctors . . . had no idea what ailed him. I saw the same sort of physical collapse in my brother John and my brother-in-law Gurney. The doctors never explained it."

Hay died four days later, on July 1, 1905. On the 2nd, Dor confided to Mrs. Cameron: "I wrote Hay's epitaph last week. He was already dead for me. There is no more to say."[61]

For Mrs. Cameron, there was much to say. She wrote from Newport: "I cannot bear to think of the difference it will make in your life. . . . I cannot be what he was to you, but I can be less cranky than I often am." She said too that, while tending to her house in Washington, she had been pressed for time. ". . . I saw no one there, not even the Roosevelts, and heard no politics. And even if I had? It is all changed again even since then. You talk of automobile speed—I left there only ten days ago.

Already Russia is in full anarchy and revolution. . . . It is all as you said and 50 times worse, and your only mistake was in the time it would take—"[62]

The occasion moved her to exclaim that Newport was uninhabited. "As for people[,] there are none. Do you remember the Huron immortality where shadows of warriors with shades of bows and hatchets chased shades of game through shades of forests and rocks? It is a picture of American social intercourse." As a rule, she said, American men were "horrors" and American women were " 'animated.' " The mingling of such men and women was so lacking in purpose that the performance was a "ghosts' dance and a shadowy pleasure."[63]

Elisabeth Marbury and Anne Morgan had asked Adams to come from Paris in his auto to join them at Beauvais and revisit the cathedral. He went as asked and brought them to Paris. By then, the Mercedes had conveyed him and others in all directions for two months. After such hard use, it needed three or four weeks of repairs.

The hurts to Adams resulting from Hay's death were very deep. He described himself to Gaskell and to Mrs. Cameron as "stranded" and "alone." Even more strongly, he wrote to Clara Hay: "He and I began life together. We will stop together."[64]

As an essential part of his work, Adams had again been reading books by physicists. He had mentioned to Gaskell that his "recent study" turned on his trying to discover how soon the "world" would "break its neck." His first calculations had pointed to 1930–1940. They already were superseded. ". . . lately the figures show a rapid shortening up. In fact, it might happen tomorrow, according to the highest authorities in physics."[65]

Just how he or anyone could derive from the writings of physicists a timetable for the end of the world was a secret that Adams for the present was keeping to himself. Three things he did not keep secret were his belief that human events were moving at dangerous rates of speed; his wish to build a vast defensive "system" linking the United States, England, France, and the western half of Germany; and a conviction that Hay had been killed. He wrote to Mrs. Cameron on July 9 and 10. "If I read my radium right, the machine won't much outlast me." "My whole ambition was to detach France from Russia, and build her into our Anglo-American Atlantic system, whose mass would necessarily draw western Germany after it. . . ." "The Senate killed Hay. Our friend Cabot [Lodge] helped to murder him. . . ."

The charge of murder was timely. Friends were coming to Paris, among them the elder Lodges. When they appeared, what was Adams to say to a helpful murderer, the senior senator from Massachusetts?

The first friend to arrive was Mrs. Jones. She had brought new praises of *Mont Saint Michel and Chartres* and new demands that it be published. In reaction, Adams advised Mrs. Cameron that his "Talk" was being touted as "revelation." "The idea is absurd. I talked the talk to amuse Martha and my girls. I took the precaution to copyright it, that no publisher could copyright it against me. . . . The thing must remain Talk, not history."

Mrs. Cameron was not surprised by the excitement Adams's copies created. On July 9, 1905, she wrote to him: " 'I told you so' about your book. It is the best thing done in modern times and it will creep into the ken of the litterateurs and you will find yourself boomed in a new line. Don't you like it? Isn't it fun? I should think it would be."

The Lodges appeared, and Mrs. Lodge asked Adams to go with them to Chartres on July 14. Having been under the weather for several days, Adams was able to refuse by pleading ill health. On the 16th, he more honestly told Mrs. Cameron: ". . . I cannot venture myself any longer with Cabot. He has become physically repulsive to me. It is very hard. Of course one is perfectly transparent. She [Mrs. Lodge] sees every shade of my feelings. We keep up a sort of mask-play together, each knowing the other to the ground. She kept it up with Hay to the end. It has gone on for years, and may go on for more, but only on condition that I do not let my irritability show itself. At my age, one cannot be cautious enough."[66]

Mrs. Cameron would later tell Adams that his revulsion in the company of Lodge was "just as uncontrollable" as the shape of his nose. Speaking for herself, she said, "I have the faculty of liking people on the surface while despising them underneath. . . ." She even defended the senator. "Cabot *is* odious but he isn't *bête.*"[67]

While perhaps true, the defense could not comfort Adams. The murder of McKinley and the destruction of Hay had wholly stripped him of a huge political advantage he would have liked to have kept, and from his point of view their removals had differed only in that McKinley was killed fast by bullets and Hay was killed slowly by small hurts incurred while squabbling with the Senate and especially while being importuned for favors by never-satisfied Senator Lodge.[68]

Beginning on the day Adams joined her and Anne Morgan at Beauvais, Elisabeth Marbury had fallen into an alarming condition of partial paralysis from which she only slowly recovered. For Adams, Miss Marbury's sufferings were one blow too many. On July 24, 1905, he wrote to Mrs. Cameron, "I know not where to turn." He felt helpless, yet paradoxically never felt so interested. He said in the same letter: "The world is now more desperately interesting than it ever was. The disintegration, anxiety, explosions, terrors, are convulsing to anyone who watches our drift. We are sailing over an unknown ocean of possible torpedoes. . . ." Mrs. Cameron liked Newport because she could spend much of her time outdoors. Although she was looking forward to a winter at her house in Washington, she wished she could winter instead at her Paris apartment. "Truly," she told Dor, "it is Elysian Fields."[69]

In Paris, on August 11, Adams wrote a letter to Mrs. Chanler in which he spoke of the tendency of American men and women to run away from the work imposed upon them by the era into which they were born. He was thinking especially of the women. He explained: "Our fascinating old 12th century friends had a job that could be handled. There were never enough of them to fill a good-sized church, and the only force they controlled was a horse, without roads even for him. America has nearly a hundred million people running at least five-and-twenty million horsepower equivalent to the whole animal world since Eve. It worries me to see our women run away from the job."

Rather than merely generalize, Adams got down to cases. He turned to his own circle. "Sometimes, I admit, it is the man's fault. It was Don Cameron who ran away, not Mrs[.] Cameron. Still, Mrs[.] Cameron would like to run, like most other women."

He continued by saying that the reason he was throwing stones was because he would be going back to America. "I have always stuck to the job. . . . My knees knock together with dread and fear of next winter in Washington. I am isolated, superannuated, senile and silent. I have to bottle up my most effervescent antipathies, and am bored to suicide; but I am going to run the machine alone since my last ally [Hay] has had his life crushed out of him by it."

It of course was nonsense that Adams would act alone. On August 13, he outlined for Mrs. Cameron his view of the greatest danger at work in Europe. "The Anglo-German situation is acute. The Franco-German situation is worse because it requires military readiness as in actual war. . . . Germany may turn eastward. Let us hope she will; but her chance to wipe out France is now dazzling."

Two weeks later, he extended his analysis to include the United States. "We have got to support France against Germany, and fortify an Atlantic system beyond attack; for if Germany breaks down England or France, she becomes the centre of a military world, and we are lost. The course of concentration must be decided by force,—whether military or industrial. . . ." In the United States, the choice between forces was settled. ". . . we are industrial."[70]

Implicit in Adams's analysis was a proposal that he and Mrs. Cameron strengthen their association. His thoughts turned decidedly to marriage, or rather to his objections to marriage as an inheritance from the middle ages. He said to her on September 3, ". . . I wish society would do away with the mediaeval form of marriage . . . and substitute a simple contract of partnership. . . ." He had no wish that he and she be married in a way he would call "mediaeval." Yet he wished they could be sworn contractual partners in a way not yet encouraged by American law or public opinion.

Writing from Newport on August 20, 1905, Mrs. Cameron admitted to Dor, ". . . I am thinking too much of Europe all the time." During the next week, she realized she was suffering from cardiac asthma. She told him on the 27th that she was considering a rush to Bad Nauheim to fit in a cure. Thereafter they could return to America together.

By the time her letter reached him, he had booked passage on the *St. Louis*, to sail on October 28. If she were to come abroad, he would have to postpone his sailing. With the frankness that was usual between them, he advised her on September 5, ". . . I would rather be in Washington." Yet with the forbearance that also was usual between them, he said, ". . . I can wait your decision without trouble."

Mrs. Cameron made arrangements to sail on September 16. She was taking nitroglycerine and felt so improved that she had hopes of forgoing the cure in favor of autumn weeks at 50 Avenue du Bois de Boulogne. For his part, Adams waited at his apartment for an influx of women. Mrs. Cameron would arrive on September 24 and Mrs. Chanler on October 3. Mrs. Jones, momentarily away, would be back on October 10. Three mothers would bring three daughters: Martha, Laura, and Beatrix.

Everyone arrived as expected and placed strains on the Mercedes. In late October, Adams put the auto into storage and substituted a rented carriage. Although he was often in the company of Mrs. Chanler or Mrs. Jones, he is best imagined to have resumed the habit of passing a few hours every day with Mrs. Cameron and Martha, or with either of them alone.[71]

October 31 was a Tuesday. At a place he considered very unlucky, most likely on the sidewalk in front of 50 Avenue du Bois de Boulogne, Adams and Mrs. Cameron were spoken to by an American they slightly knew but would have preferred not to see.[72] Their interlocutor was Francis MacNutt, formerly an American resident in Rome and an official at the Vatican. He had been arrested in Rome for disorderly conduct and convicted. He had appealed and, in Mrs. Cameron's opinion, was "whitewashed" by the higher court.[73] While no longer in a position to live in Rome, he was free to return to the United States. He told Adams and Mrs. Cameron he would sail on the *Amerika* on November 18.

Without thinking, Mrs. Cameron said she would be sailing on the *New York* on the same day.[74] Her seeming friendliness may have been what emboldened MacNutt to do what he most wished to do. He asked

Adams to open paths for him and his wife in Washington, where he said they proposed to settle.

Adams was in peril of another experience of white fury. Just by accosting them, MacNutt had gained the considerable advantage of being able to speak in Washington of having talked in Paris with Henry Adams and Elizabeth Cameron—as if both were his close friends. He also had gained the different advantage of being able to tell listeners in the capital that he had seen Adams in Paris just as Adams could be expected to be seen, with the famous wife of former-Senator James Donald Cameron. Talk of the latter kind, while very damaging to Adams and Mrs. Cameron, would be even more damaging to Martha, whose greatest need, her marriageability considered, was unquestioned possession of a spotlessly respectable "background."

Somehow Adams and Mrs. Cameron got rid of MacNutt, and Adams went to his apartment. Late the next day, Mrs. Cameron sent a servant to him with a message, not extant and presumably oral, asking him to dinner. He replied at 6:45 P.M. with a note, doubtless sealed, saying he could not come—was "not fit."[75]

At 7:00 P.M. or thereabouts, she sent back a note asking whether the hindrance was a cold, indigestion, or MacNutt. She urged him to drive next morning in the carriage and said the carriage would be waiting for him. ". . . above all," she said, "let me know what the matter is. . . ."[76]

Answering at once with a second note, Adams said his unfitness was that he "didn't want to talk." He instead wanted to sleep and as preparation was going out for a meal. He added that he would not need the carriage.[77] At 7:30 P.M. when leaving for dinner, he sent a third note repeating that he would not need the carriage and suggesting they meet for breakfast at one or another of two favorite restaurants.[78]

She could not join him for breakfast. On Thursday she again sent him an invitation to dinner, presumably oral. He refused, writing to say he wished to "hide a little longer."[79]

Early on Friday, he sent a detailed explanation. He confirmed that he—"a white-haired and bald-headed old gentleman who must under no circumstances be agitated"—had been "agitated within an inch of his life." Since Wednesday, he had enjoyed two nights of sleep, each lasting as much as nine hours. Yet he was "still under such remnants of horror and disgust" that he dreaded "going back to the scene." On that account, he hoped that she and Martha could dine with him at some place well away from 50 Avenue du Bois de Boulogne.

Mrs. Cameron's reply was confident. ". . . the shock was great," she agreed. "But I suppose our worldly training is all thrown away, if we cannot learn to meet [i.e. defeat?] even a beast like that." Yet dinner on

Friday was impossible. She and Martha were promised for the opera with "two boys."[80]

On Friday, Adams went to Chartres and attended the vesper service. In a letter to Mabel La Farge, he mentioned his trip and said, "I've been hiding all the week, seeing nobody and going nowhere." If it was typical of him that he had treated his disturbance in solitude, it was also typical that his expedients were successful. He had to cure himself of violent feelings, mainly fury, horror, and disgust. His expedients were well-chosen.

The Japanese government had asked the government of the United States to act as mediator with a view to ending the war between Japan and Russia. The resulting conference at Portsmouth, New Hampshire, gave rise to the signing of a peace treaty on September 5, 1905. Secretary Hay had died too early to participate in the conference; and Elihu Root was appointed secretary in his place; but the official most active in bringing the conference to its very successful conclusion was President Roosevelt, who partly dictated the terms of the treaty.

Adams had never asked a favor of an American president. For that matter, he had never written a letter to an American president. On November 6, 1905, he did both. Marking the letter "*Private* and *Personal,*" he asked Teddy Roosevelt to decide what the owners of dwellings near the White House should say about Francis MacNutt.[81] He explained that he was trying to protect MacNutt's wife. He suggested that the president might be able to prevent MacNutt's coming to Washington by taking the matter up with the Catholic hierarchy.[82]

Adams told Roosevelt that MacNutt would sail "on the 18th in the 'Amerika.' " Adams and Mrs. Cameron still had reservations on the *New York*, to sail on the same day.[83] Adams waited till November 13 and then suggested to her that they postpone their sailing a week and go instead on the *St. Louis*, his favorite steamer.[84]

His suggestion was followed.[85] At Cherbourg on November 25, Dor, Mrs. Cameron, and Martha boarded the *St. Louis*. He had in his luggage a manuscript of *The Education of Henry Adams* brought nearly to completion. There is no evidence that his companions knew about the progress he had made in his book. He tended to be secretive in proportion to the importance of what he was secretive about. He had long behaved as if his *Education* would be his most important book and his chief vehicle of anarchism. On that assumption, he would keep the manuscript to himself, and he would try to finish and print it by the earliest possible date.[86]

This is the only photograph of Henry Adams taken during his third life that affords a good view of him full-face. His companion is Mabel Hooper, the third eldest niece of his deceased wife, Marian (Clover) Hooper Adams, and the niece who most resembled her aunt in face and figure. The photograph was taken for fun in a streetside "tin-type gallery." It may date from the spring of 1892, when Mabel and her two younger sisters visited their Uncle Henry in Washington. *Courtesy of Louisa Hooper Thoron*

Undated photographs of Elizabeth Sherman Cameron, wife of Senator James Donald Cameron of Pennsylvania and partner of Henry Adams throughout his third life, taken by Frances Benjamin Johnston, a professional photographer. Mrs. Cameron was born on November 10, 1857, and turned thirty-four in late

1891 when Adams began his third life. She seems about that age in the photograph to the left. The photograph above shows an older and perhaps more self-assured Mrs. Cameron. *Courtesy of the Library of Congress*

Snapshot taken at Surrenden Dering in the summer of 1898 at the time of John Hay's appointment as secretary of state and his secret arrangement with Henry Adams to share the office with him. Seated in front: Martha Cameron and Alice Hay. Seated higher, from left to right: John Hay, Clarence Hay, Edith Hoyt, and Helen Hay. Standing, from left to right, James Donald Cameron, Henry Adams, Spencer Eddy (Hay's private secretary), and Adelbert Hay. Possibly the snapshot was taken by Elizabeth Cameron, who does not appear. *Courtesy of Louisa Hooper Thoron*

Detail showing Henry Adams only, from a companion snapshot taken at the same time and place as the snapshot opposite. *Courtesy of Louisa Hooper Thoron*

Louisa Hooper, the second eldest niece of Adams's deceased wife, taken by Adams on the same day as the photograph opposite. Though rather out of focus, presumably by accident, the photograph admirably reflects Loulie's character. *Courtesy of the Massachusetts Historical Society*

Henry Adams in a picture taken and processed by Adams himself as a test run in February 1901 with equipment that belonged to his wife. He may seem serious, even solemn, but he is having a good time. His hands are squeezing a pneumatic bulb to activate the shutter of the camera. *Author's collection*

Henry Adams and Aileen Tone at Stepleton House in September 1914,
in a snapshot presumably taken by Elizabeth (Elsie) Ogden Adams, his
other companion at the time. In their company, he had recently fled the
close approach of the German army to Paris. He is looking at his watch
because delivery of the London newspapers is imminent.

The Scotch terrier belonged to Martha Cameron, then in Egypt. The
terrier liked to bite the gold-headed cane Aileen was using because of a
passing injury. She eventually gave the snapshot and the cane to the
author and his wife. *Author's collection*

14

EVERY OBJECT MORE
THAN ATTAINED

After the stormiest voyage he had known and after days of recovery
and shopping in New York, Adams, Mrs. Cameron, and Martha returned to Washington to begin an arduous winter. His particular concern was secret work on his *Education*. Pages not yet drafted would have
to be written. Others would have to be reconsidered, improved, rewritten, or rewritten several times. If guests were fewer, work could go faster.
He as usual would offer midday breakfast to many comers. Martha and
Mrs. Cameron might be the persons most likely to appear. Still, the re-
gime he set for himself was isolation and hard labor.

Mrs. Cameron intended to bring her daughter before the eyes of
every prepossessing unmarried young gentleman then present in Washington. As mother, she had the look of a new General Sherman. Adams
watched her campaign and saw that she and Martha "cut a wide swath."
He later said of the mother: ". . . I saw her grit her teeth and go in. She
meant to win, if it killed her,—as it will."[1]

For many winters, Langley had been Adams's best informant about
science and a favorite prospect for talk and dinner by themselves. Word
had come that Langley was seriously ill. A letter Adams wrote to him is
missing, but the reply survives. Langley confirmed that he had been ill
for weeks. He was silent about his copy of *Mont Saint Michel and Chartres*.
It perhaps was ominous that his main message was complimentary and
grateful. ". . . you can hardly enjoy my talks with you as much as I do
yours with me."[2]

The isolation Adams most wanted was isolation from Senator Lodge
and President Roosevelt. Writing to Gaskell on Christmas Day, 1905, he
remarked: "Roosevelt, I never see, and still less care to talk with. My
house is mostly frequented by women, children and anarchists who
make no noise and are not in politics."

Elisabeth Marbury and Elsie de Wolfe desired rooms in Adams's "hotel," as he was learning to call it, and he put them down for the week starting January 26, 1906. Until that time, it appears, he was able to work practically without interruption.[3]

Niece Dorothy had an advantage over Uncle Henry's other nieces in being a daughter of his surviving sister. Dorothy was to be married on February 7 in Boston. If she knew her uncle had a strict rule never to attend weddings, she autocratically ignored it and required his making the thousand-mile train journey to Boston and back.

Reexposure to Boston horrified him.[4] He described his birthplace as "green with mental mould." "It makes me sick to go around among people, as I would in a lunatic asylum, trying to say nothing for fear of explosion." Also New York wore on his nerves. He thought the city "rather terrific"—a "pandemonium" he could only "half like" and in which he was "never quite at ease." Even Washington was a hardship. In the capital, he said, ". . . one walks on pins."[5]

He thereafter was snared in White House initiatives. Because he attended a wedding in Boston, he could not refuse to attend Alice Roosevelt's wedding. The president himself had the idea that he and Edith should come to 1603 H Street. ". . . she & I are to dine with you . . . ," Roosevelt declared. ". . . you're in for it. . . ."[6]

Mrs. Jones and Beatrix arrived for a visit. On March 2, Adams served as a pallbearer at Langley's funeral. Roughly at the same moment, Mrs. Cameron left for Coffin's Point with Martha and several others, including Charles's youngest daughter Elsie.

For Mrs. Cameron, three months of exertion in the capital had led to a less-than-satisfactory result. Martha had taken a liking to a man her mother did not approve. An English aristocrat, Ronald Lindsay was one of the second secretaries at the British Embassy. He seemed to Mrs. Cameron too poor and perhaps not strong. On March 16, she suggested to Adams: ". . . do sample *him*. I fear that he is weak."

Without hurrying, Adams inveigled the prospect to dinner. When he reported his findings on March 28, he omitted everything else and confined himself to three words: "I like Lindsay." The judgment was so positive that one can suspect its being based both on Lindsay's evident personal qualities and what Adams guessed might be his potential as a diplomat.

When she came back from South Carolina, Mrs. Cameron was on such good terms with Donald that she could look forward to a new stay in Europe. In that respect, her winter was a cheering success. She and Dor made reservations to sail from New York on May 5.

In the form of a letter from her husband Bancel, bad news reached Uncle Henry that Niece Mabel had suffered a breakdown in France and was being moved to Switzerland for rest and treatment away from her children. According to Bancel, her illness took the form of intervals during which she became "excited & troubled." As a temporary arrangement, she would be accompanied by Adams's Paris servant, Marie.[7]

Niece Loulie had learned the news and was leaving at once by a German steamer. There was nothing Uncle Henry could do for Mabel that was not being done. In other circumstances, he would have preferred to postpone his sailing a week or two; but it was often his instinct to hurry toward difficulties, rather than flee them; and he wanted to be near Louisa, whom he viewed as the person best adapted to supervising Mabel's recovery. He accordingly moved his sailing forward to April 28. Mrs. Cameron did the same.

While still in Washington, Adams read an article in the *New York Times* in which he was mentioned as "the late Henry Adams," author of a *History of the United States* that was a "performance of the highest class."[8] The assurance that he had died delighted him. He informed Gaskell on April 23: "Everyone is dead. Yesterday I was struck by seeing my own name in the columns of the *New York Times* as *the late* H. A. *Tant mieux!* At least it is over. . . ."

Because Evelyn had made off with his copy of *Mont Saint Michel and Chartres*, Brooks had begged a fresh copy for himself. He later urged Henry to send copies for the Boston Athenaeum and for a Boston artist, John Briggs Potter.[9] Henry sent a copy for Potter and explained that he had already mailed copies to the Boston Public Library, to Harvard, and to the Athenaeum. He may also have sent copies to American libraries and universities in places other than Boston-Cambridge. His confidence in the book was rising.

His hopes for his *Education* had similarly improved. While writing to Gaskell about being dead, Adams said nothing about writing another book. Yet he outlined the occasion for the book's being written. He began by asking questions. "What is the end of doubling up our steam- and electric power every five years to infinity if we don't increase thought-power?" "Can our society double up its mind-power?" "As I see it, the society of today shows no more thought-power than in our youth, though it showed precious little then." What he wanted was positive effort to evolve human beings more broadly aware. ". . . [society] must do it or die, and I see no reason why it may not widen its consciousness of complex conditions far enough to escape wreck; but it must hurry. Our power is always running ahead of our mind, especially here [in America]."

The prescription was hopeful and reflected enterprise. Yet in two respects his letter to Gaskell spoke darkly. He noted that the United

States remained in the hands of Theodore Roosevelt, who was "amusing" but "exceedingly conservative." And he mentioned that San Francisco, which he said had "more style" than any other American city, had been destroyed by an earthquake and a fire.

Dor, Mrs. Cameron, and Martha once again crossed to Cherbourg, the Gare St. Lazare, and their Paris apartments. A strike of auto workers kept the Mercedes in storage, which perhaps was a help. Everything pointed toward Dor's having to stay at his desk for long hours. By a 98-page margin, *The Education of Henry Adams* was going to be longer than *Mont Saint Michel and Chartres.*[10] Many of the ideas he was presenting in the book would be unfamiliar to readers and might be difficult for them to grasp, and the style in which he was writing it was itself a new departure far from easy to sustain.

Mrs. Cameron extended her campaign by taking Martha to London for a stay at the Ritz. Soon she and Martha dined with King Edward and the U. S. Ambassador, Whitelaw Reid.[11]

In a Twainian mood, Dor twitted mother and daughter for consorting with "lovely Kings."[12] He retrieved the Mercedes and hired a chauffeur named Leon, but the machine broke down after one day's use and was sent back to the repair shop.

As a change of duties, he ordered Leon to the Channel to assist the absentees after leaving their Channel boat. Similarly he despatched Marie to the Paris station to meet their train and bring Mrs. Cameron a note asking that Dor be told "when your majesties receive your serfs."[13] Mrs. Cameron replied that he was wanted that same evening. Marie brought him the answer, and he hurried her to 50 Avenue du Bois de Boulogne with a second note: "Yes, I'll come to dinner."[14]

Mrs. Cameron's letters to Dor from England are missing.[15] Other letters indicate that their relations were unchanged. Writing to Mrs. Fell on June 23, 1906, he summarized an ideal existence. "I lead a hermit's life. . . . My machine rests happily at the shops, always being repaired. . . . My nieces do nothing but get married and break down. Mrs[.] Cameron is here with Martha much on her mind, Martha being twenty years old last Monday. We all dined in the Bois last night at a new restaurant. . . ."

Presumably Mrs. Cameron knew Dor was working and was not to be distracted. At the end of June for unstated reasons, she gave up her apartment.[16] An apartment could be had in Adams's building, but she chose not to take it and left with Martha for a cure at Bad Nauheim.[17] Many of her letters thence are missing.[18]

Adams's behavior was that of a man who, while secretly at work on a book relating to "thought-power," was much concerned about mathematics and physics. On July 8, he wrote to Gaskell in high spirits: ". . . what will the world be in 1950? Mathematically speaking, the world will be exploded. This is an algebraic certainty by rule of three or composition of sulphuretted hydrogen, or any other geometry; and I want to see it."

Isabella Gardner had learned that a Paris dealer had a medieval stained-glass window for sale. Tempted to buy it, she had asked Adams for assistance or guidance. He had looked into the matter and on June 13 had reminded her that, compared to the selling of medieval windows, the selling of used automobiles was "honest fraud." Yet in a second letter on the 24th, as if he felt no doubts, he stated, "The window is from Saint Denis, early 13th century."[19]

Because she had written a letter to Henry James but could not remember his English address, Mrs. Gardner sent the letter to Adams, asking that he add the address to the envelope and mail it. Adams did as asked and was rewarded by receiving from James a letter that transformed their relations.

Until that time, James had found Adams hospitable but had had no success in understanding him and had tended to paper over the gap by writing about him with grand, firm authority. An idea that had attractions for James was that Adams had written nothing of importance and was a pessimist because a failure. In November 1905, he had written to one of his nephews: "You tell me of being with H. Adams, and of his hospitality; of which it gives me great pleasure to hear—he being really very 'kind' in spite of his so irresponsible self-conscious xtravagant [sic] pessimism, the fruit, not wholly unnatural—of a disappointed and ineffectual personal career—I owe him a letter and mean to write him soon."[20]

That Adams was sometimes a self-styled pessimist was true, but not more true than that he remained a consistent optimist and that his being both the one and the other was a matter best looked into after it had shown itself more prominently in his books.

More important for the moment was the fact that James had a copy of *Mont Saint Michel and Chartres* and after many postponements had taken the trouble to read it. On July 30, 1906, he wrote Adams a letter that would have the effect of making them friends in the sense of full mutual respect and appreciation. James said: ". . . [I have] been reading you with the bated breath of wonder, sympathy & applause. May I say, all unworthy and incompetent, what honour I think the beautiful volume does you & of how exquisite & distinguished an interest I have found it, with its easy lucidity, its saturation with its subject, its charmingly taken and kept, *tone.* Even more than I congratulate you on the book[,] I envy you your relation to the subject."

One may suppose that Adams sent an immediate answer. It was his tendency to be prompt with replies. That no reply survives may be attributed to James, who felt such a dread of the preservation of personal letters that he burned large numbers of letters sent to him by other persons, including letters from writers who carefully preserved most or all of the letters he wrote to them.[21]

Adams had expected a summer of isolation.[22] Instead for a time he had the company of ailing John La Farge. Also Mrs. Gardner made an unlooked-for appearance. She had just survived an auto accident. Yet she wished to go with Adams in his Mercedes to as many old churches as they could reach. On Sunday, August 19, after La Farge had gone, she asked in a note, "How about Beauvais Thursday or Friday of this week?"

Mrs. Cameron finished her cure at Bad Nauheim and went to the Engadine in Switzerland. On Monday, she advised Dor that she and Martha had arrived at the Hotel Waldhaus in Vulpera but had moved to a nearby villa.[23] The reason was fear that Martha would be drawn into Jewish company. Mrs. Cameron went into detail. "The hotel was excellent but filled with German Jews of the most appalling description. I have never seen such a lot *any* where. I thought we could not bear it, but I *knew* we couldn't when Mr. Propper (he took the Curtis apartment in our house [at 50 Avenue du Bois de Boulogne]) wanted to introduce Martha to 'a charming American girl, Miss Rosenberg, of New York.' "[24]

That same day, Monday, August 20, 1906, Adams was scared "purple" by a punctured tire while returning from Verneuil—a trip of 150 kilometres that he made alone in search of windows. Telling Mrs. Cameron about the mishap two days later, he said, ". . . I am a wreck."

On Thursday, he conveyed Mrs. Gardner to Beauvais, and on Friday he took her and two of her protégés to Chartres. A burst tire delayed the completion of the second trip.

His sister Mary would be appearing soon with her younger daughter Elinor—the eleventh and last of his nieces by blood or marriage. On August 30, he informed Mrs. Gardner that he would be held in Paris by arrivals and would not be available for excursions. Next day, he and Leon were seated in their auto and "going slowly" along the Avenue du Bois de Boulogne nearly in front of No. 23 when an "auto cab came quickly round a blind corner without tooting or slackening speed" and struck the Mercedes "endwise."

Though not thrown out of his vehicle, Adams was hurled against the frame of the canvas top and cut by the metal. He made light of the matter but later told Niece Loulie that the effect was lasting. She reported, "For a month his nerves were shaken."[25]

Mrs. Gardner was sorry to hear of the injury to "that brilliant little Mercedes."[26] The part most damaged was the steering gear. An insurance company paid for its rebuilding. In good time, the machine was back in service.

Adams was saying nothing definite to anyone, not even to Mrs. Cameron, about his progress in *The Education*. Being far away and not in a position to look for signs of secret labor, she could tease him for being unoccupied. She had written to him, "If you are *very* idle[,] you can look for an apartment for me!"[27] She however was in no hurry to rent an apartment. Rather than come back to Paris, she arranged to go with Martha to Denmark and visit friends.

Dor did not search for an apartment. Writing on September 13, he reported: "Barely leaving my den except for meals, I have seen no one to speak of and done nothing. . . . So I've not found you an apartment nor anything else."

Denmark amused Martha. Mrs. Cameron hoped that her daughter was "forgetting poor Lindsay!" On September 18, she assured Adams: "I like Lindsay, but she is too young, & he is too poor [&] it won't do. I shall be terribly glad to get back and see you."

His telling Mrs. Cameron he had stayed in his den doing nothing was language indicative that he was as busy as possible. Yet what he said was also representative of a sort of behavior that for him was imperative. Going back as far as he could remember, it had been a necessary device of his to pretend that he was attempting or doing very little when he was doing incomparably more than his brothers, sisters, and other contemporaries, almost none excepted. He needed the device because his aspirations and activities placed him in a class of human beings not simply different but impeachingly different. What made things worse, and better, was that he always tended to achieve even more than he purposed to achieve.

One object he had formed in youth was to travel and see the world. His youthful ambition in this regard may have run to extremes. Yet he could hardly have guessed that he would succeed in going to places as far removed from each other as Nubia and Japan, Ceylon and Trinidad, Damascus and San Francisco, Australia and Cape North in Norway.

Another of his objects had been to establish himself away from Boston as a resident Washingtonian. This dream was very dear to him. Yet he could not have foreseen that he would end in being the owner-builder of a fine house on Lafayette Square and an across-the-square neighbor of America's ever-passing presidents.

A great political career was something that had been impossible for him to so much as plan. Two brothers were ahead of him in age, and both were politically-minded. Yet he had done just what he could not do. He had made it an object to become America's leading politician in his time. The means he chose was political service without the official holding of office, in combination with secrecy, anonymity, pretended uninvolvement, apparent unimportance, and even feigned non-existence. The result had been successes far beyond what could have seemed likely even to him, culminating in work as sharer with Hay in the management of the country's foreign affairs.

He had made it an object to become a great writer by writing three remarkable books: a satirical novel about American government and politics, an unexampled narrative history of the forming of the American people, and a book of a new kind, an *education*, seemingly about himself but actually about a fictitious Adams, an adventurous bumbler. As things happened, he wrote many remarkable books, including two he had never dreamed of writing. One was an unsurpassable history of Tahiti. The other was an *education* for young women in the form of a summer tour of the middle ages.[28] Moreover, he had come so far in *The Education of Henry Adams* that its completion in very good order seemed possible.

How soon he would tell Mrs. Cameron about his progress can only be guessed. She returned to Paris on or before September 23 and presumably stayed at a hotel. Cooperatively he and she found an apartment at 53 Avenue Montaigne for her use and for subletting at large profits to presentable Americans.[29] At the same time, they bought spaces on the steamer *New York*, scheduled to sail on November 3.

Gaskell and Adams had not seen each other for four years. Late in October 1906, rather than let the opportunity slip, Gaskell journeyed to Paris for a meeting.[30] He left, and on November 1, two days before leaving with Mrs. Cameron and Martha for Cherbourg and the *New York*, Adams wrote to him: "I shall be again on my way before you receive this letter, and look forward to another winter of vanishing interests. . . . I have won all the political stakes my youth played for, and have seen every object more than attained. The next game belongs to its own players. . . . Costless energy will be a condition new to nature. I worship it in the form of a bomb."

As with other letters by Adams, so with this: there were sentences that cried for commentary. A reader might suppose that the sentence about "costless energy" and the one about worshiping a "bomb" deserved attention. Yet the letter was most valuable for the words "and have seen every object more than attained." The truth was much too true! Adams's intentions were more than fulfilled. Yet he was still alive, still strong, and could anticipate more years of life. Soon the question would be, What to do after becoming more than successful in all his past ambitions?

When John died, Clara Hay decided to keep her Washington house as her winter residence. She donated many of her husband's books to libraries. Knowing she would want his company and advice, she wrote to Adams from Newbury urging him to join her in Washington and offering him space in her stable for an auto, should he rent or buy one.

On November 12, 1906, Adams reappeared at 1603 H Street If past years were a guide, Brooks and Evelyn were waiting for him when he arrived. He apparently told them that *Mont Saint Michel and Chartres* was his book about "unity" and that, to form a pair, he would soon be printing a book he was developing about "multiplicity."

Two weeks later, he wrote to Mrs. Chanler that his house was full of guests. Matters were complicated for him a day or two later when Maggie Wade had a breakdown—fortunately not lasting. Adams reacted by reducing visitors to a minimum.

When five weeks had passed, on December 19, he wrote a letter to Brooks containing more remarks about his new book. ". . . I hope soon to finish my study of Multiplicity to pair with Thomas Aquinas, and I rather imagine I had better die pretty quick before it gets read. I fear it is wicked." The remarks could be read as evidence that many chapters of *The Education* were already printed.

Mrs. Cameron and Martha left for the Christmas holidays. They did not get back on the Sunday when due but were said to be coming on a Monday—evidently January 7, 1907. The question of Martha's fondness for Ronald Lindsay had not lost its awkwardness.

At 9:00 A.M. that Monday, Adams sent Mrs. Cameron a reminder that she and Martha were expected at his house for dinner, that he was a man short, and that he "dared not ask Lindsay" without Mrs. Cameron's permission. "If you bar Lindsay, I must ask Barry or Berry."[31]

Clara Hay wanted to create a printed "Memorial" in her husband's honor.[32] She thought it should be a biography by Adams.[33] She evidently did not reveal her wish to him till early January 1907.[34]

Her wish could not be met with an outright refusal. Adams, Hay, and King had been "inseparable."[35] She was Hay's widow; and Adams's talk, "King," had been published in 1904 in New York in the *Clarence King Memoirs* published by a committee of the Century Association.

In some degree, moreover, her wish had to be granted. For Adams, the chance to work with Mrs. Hay was not a chance to be fumbled, much less lost. It had an aspect that Adams would especially appreciate. By helping her shape a memorial to her husband, he might get such a grip on things that he could hinder the public's learning that he and Hay had shared the secretaryship. He might forestall indefinitely the moment when that very unusual fact would be recognized and become an acknowledged part of America's history.

Yet her imposition of her wish was dangerous to him. It posed a threat to his independence as an author. It made inroads on his attention. And it was thrust upon him at the worst possible time.

If one may judge from the printed results, the first six chapters of his *Education* had earlier been put into type and corrected by Adams without haste. Their pages were nearly free of errors.[36] What Adams needed most was unhindered freedom to complete the book without change of schedule or method.

He declined to write Hay's biography. He told Mrs. Hay that biographies diminished their subjects and that her husband should not be diminished.[37] As a counter-idea, he suggested that extracts from a man's diaries and a selection of his personal letters (but not his business correspondence) could be tantamount to "a fairly continuous autobiography."[38] She possibly did not understand his advice. She seemed to agree with it. Together she and Adams turned their minds to the many letters Hay had written that might still be held by their recipients or otherwise be open to recovery; also to his diary.

At the same time under cover of total secrecy, Adams asked Furst and Company to advance the printing of *The Education* as rapidly as possible. Beginning with Chapter VII, proofreading and correction were so speeded that twenty-nine chapters were marred by a broad trail of uncorrected errors.[39] Worse, Adams sent some of the closing chapters to the printer when not entirely crystalized—when not quite in last draft.[40]

Adams later had occasion to write to President Thwing of Western Reserve University about Mrs. Hay's intended memorial. Thwing knew that she was looking for help in its connection. Adams told the president that she had turned to him "in despair." The expression was not too strong. Clara Hay was intelligent enough to sense that commemorating her husband would be a task both important and delicate. She assumed that Adams alone could perform it.[41]

Adams told Thwing important details. He had not guaranteed to Mrs. Hay that he could develop the compilation he had suggested. He only promised to "look over the material and try it out." Also he disclosed a difference of opinion. He said that he and Hay had disagreed about Hay's importance. ". . . I thought more of him that he did. . . ."

Where Hay might have wanted to suppress his papers or publish them only sparingly, Adams would wish to print as many as possible."[42]

President and Edith Roosevelt had not come to dinner at 1603 H Street. Adams decided to invite them but had to take precautions. Three presidents had been murdered; Roosevelt did not wish to be a fourth; and meals away from the White House involved augmented risks.

Monday nights were times when the president might seem likeliest to stay home. Adams won assurances from the president and Edith that they would come for dinner on Monday, January 21, 1907, at 8:00 P.M.

Knowing that Roosevelt's comings and goings were not to be advertised sooner than necessary, Adams waited till Sunday before inviting Ambassador and Madame Jusserand to come for dinner the following evening. He told Madame Jusserand that *Mrs.* Roosevelt would be a guest but did not tell her that the president would also be at the table.

Because she had already declined one invitation for that evening, Madame Jusserand replied that she and her husband could not come. She sent Adams her regrets early on Monday. He immediately appealed to the White House for assistance. The result was a message to Adams from Roosevelt's secretary saying that Ambassador and Madame Jusserand would indeed be coming at 8:00 P.M. White House pressure had cleared a way for the dinner to go forward.[43]

Other preparation being completed, Adams sent Mrs. Cameron a note stating that she would be "on duty" that night at his house.[44] One may assume that the dinner took place. The six participants could be described as three couples. Being conventional, the Roosevelts and the Jusserands needed no protection against Washington's ever-active perceivers and announcers of scandal. Mrs. Cameron was not asked as a necessary fifth guest. She was present as a chief sharer of the occasion and almost as if the table were hers.

She and Dor were an anarchic couple: she a woman whose husband was absent because indifferent; he a man whose wife was well-remembered but deceased. For her, the dinner with the president, his wife, and the Jusserands would serve as a very strong barrier against moralistic gossip in Washington society. That fact considered, the occasion was a kindness to her unparalleled in her experience. Dor had secretly engineered it. One may assume that both she and he understood its defensive value.[45]

At an unknown time, perhaps late in January, Adams added lines to the short Preface for *The Education*, ending it with a date: "February 16, 1907"—his sixty-ninth birthday.[46] He sent the Preface to Furst and

Company and by this means fixed a deadline before which all the copies of the book were to be delivered from Baltimore.

He set much too soon a deadline. As could be seen in *Memoirs of Arii Taimai* and *Mont Saint Michel and Chartres,* he could read proofs exceptionally well during normal hours. His hours had ceased to be normal. He was caught in work relating to Hay, and the sufferers were the proofs of *The Education,* some of which he read with less than minimum attention before returning them to the printer.

Rather than complain, he put a good face on a thoroughly bad situation. On January 28, he wrote to Gaskell: "I am doing my best . . . to close up my account with my world and generation. . . . I am, in a way, the literary executor of my circle, and, as the last survivor, I am harnessed to their funeral hearse."

He almost liked the role of executor. He saw it as a means of stepping quickly into the future. ". . . it consumes time. Also it hurries time, for already the century before 1900 is far off. . . ."

15

None of My Business

I n February 1907, Adams had to juggle antagonistically opposite projects. *The Education of Henry Adams* was the most ambitious flight of his
genius. *Letters of John Hay* was a memorial he conceived only when driven
to do so. He viewed it as entirely Mrs. Hay's. To get work started, he
prevailed on her to write to recipients of letters from her husband. Two
of them were the ambassadors to England and France, Whitelaw Reid
and Henry White. Another was Henry James.[1]

Mrs. Hay had a diary her husband had begun when starting work as
Lincoln's younger private secretary. She also had his personal letter
books, containing friends' letters he had saved. She entrusted the diary
and the letter books to Adams, turned the project over to him, and went
to California.[2]

An answer arrived from Ambassador Reid. Adams replied on February 12. He urged Reid to select from the letters in his possession those
which should appear in the memorial. He explained, ". . . I act . . . only
as a sort of reservoir for collection, and have merely to receive what you
choose to offer." He made clear that he had read Reid's own letters to
Hay, and he asked permission to copy parts of them. Going further, he
urged Reid to consider whether an old three-way correspondence between Hay, Reid, and William Evarts deserved to be put before the
public.

The indications were that work on Hay's letters would bring Adams
into closer association with Reid and White. Association with Reid might
not be easy. Recent letters by Hay had been critical of him.[3] In the past,
Adams and his wife had sometimes regarded him with suspicion, salted
with animosity. In 1882, Mrs. Adams had called him "a scheming tramp
from Ohio, sold to [James G.] Blaine, body and soul."[4]

On Monday or Tuesday, February 18 or 19, 1907, one hundred copies of *The Education* were delivered to 1603 H Street.[5] What Adams did
with the copies was in some ways private and cautious, in other ways

wholly secret. Because the secret aspect of his behavior became increasingly important with time, special pains will be taken here to reconstruct what happened.

For a beginning, he prevented other people from knowing how many copies had been printed.[6] He reserved copies for his own use but may not have reserved a set number.[7] He subjected one of his personal copies to a proofreading careful enough to fit the book for publication.[8] Because corrected with respect to spelling, punctuation, and other details, the copy might seem best designated the Corrected Copy. Here it will instead be called the Master Copy.[9] One may guess that Adams kept it in his main-floor study, but out of sight.[10]

On February 20, he mailed unmarked copies to his brothers and his sister.[11] With each copy he sent a letter.[12] Two of the letters are missing. The one to Charles survives. Henry asked Charles to read the book's "allusions" to himself with the assistance of the index. He urged him to cancel or revise the allusions if he found them objectionable. He said also, ". . . return me the volume." He did not say how many copies had been printed, but his directive that the copy be returned could be taken to indicate that they were few.

He had told Brooks that a book about "multiplicity" might soon arrive, but Brooks could not have anticipated the form the book was revealed to have when the package came. Charles and Mary were still more surprised. Reactions differed. Mary approved the book and returned it.[13] Brooks approved it but lost possession of the copy. The villainess who stole it was his wife. To settle the question of ownership, Evelyn wrote in the copy, "Evelyn Adams—Boston 1907."[14]

Being much older than Mary and Brooks, Charles could remember many events of Henry's boyhood. He read the first chapter, "Quincy," and was strongly affected. On February 25, he wrote excitedly to Henry, saying he could not help thinking that the chapter had been written "for me alone of the whole living world." "Lord!—how you do bring it all back!" ". . . oh dear!—oh dear! I'm a boy again."[15]

Brooks took the first chapter to be autobiography pure and simple. He described it to Henry as "your account of your childhood" and said he had read it "with great amusement and sympathy."[16] Charles formed the same impression, except that the chapter struck him as evocative but oddly reticent. He could remember a vivid episode in Henry's boyhood that Henry had failed to mention. Thus, in the elder brother's judgment, the chapter was indeed autobiography but deficient autobiography, partly notable for what Henry had not "let out."[17] At an unknown date, after paying it only limited attention, Charles approved the book. He did not return it.[18]

*   *   *

Henry next sought approval from others whom the book mentioned by name. He began with Donald Cameron, Anna Lodge, and President Roosevelt. Just then Mrs. Cameron and Martha were leaving for Coffin's Point on a friend's yacht. Henry gave the mother an unmarked copy to put before her husband. As could be expected, Donald looked at it, sent Adams *carte blanche* to publish whatever he pleased, and trusted Mrs. Cameron to take the copy back to Washington.[19] She was named in the book.[20] The copy was something she wished to have. One imagines she read it. There is evidence that she returned it.[21]

Mrs. Lodge was sick in bed. She apparently had heard from her sister Evelyn that Henry was letting people see copies of a new book he had written and privately printed—also that Evelyn had seized a copy. At breakfast time on March 5, a package was delivered to the Lodges' house at 1765 Massachusetts Avenue. The senator or his son John opened the package in the dining room. They found a book longer than *Mont Saint Michel and Chartres* but printed and bound to match it. Adams had inscribed the copy, "for/ Sister Anne/ with the love of/ Henry Adams/ March 1907."[22] A covering note—now missing—urged Mrs. Lodge and the senator to strike out or modify anything the book said about them. Young John looked into the book's index and saw entries for his parents and his brother Bay and Bay's wife but not for himself or his sister Constance. He lightly dismissed the book as "a total failure." The copy stayed long enough in the dining room for the senator to get absorbed in it and think it "fascinating." Word by then reached Mrs. Lodge upstairs that *The Education of Henry Adams* had arrived. She sent her husband an immediate order to relinquish it, and the copy was transferred to her possession.[23]

Next she sent Adams a plea that he give a copy to Constance. He quickly refused. He wrote in reply that the book had been printed "wholly for the purpose of getting it . . . to every friend who is drawn by name into the narrative, so that each one may correct or strike out any-thing unpleasant or objectionable."[24] In keeping with his rule, and per-haps at once, he dispatched a copy to Mr. and Mrs. George Cabot Lodge at 2346 Massachusetts Avenue. Bay's reaction was ecstatic. He scrawled a note of thanks in which he said that Adams at last had written a book about "the greatest subject in the world." Hasty and ambiguous, his broad phrase could be taken to identify the subject as education, the education of Henry Adams, or Henry Adams himself.[25]

The copy sent to the president was accompanied with Adams's usual instructions. On March 10, Roosevelt notified the author that nothing would be struck out or revised and that the copy would not come back. The reason was marital. ". . . I value my good understanding with my wife." Edith Roosevelt had snatched the copy "as her own."

* * *

Niece Loulie had come to 1603 H Street for her usual visit. Not being mentioned in the book, she was not entitled to being shown a copy—not if Uncle Henry adhered to his rule. On March 5, the day he sent copies to Anna Lodge and President Roosevelt, he gave Loulie a copy outright, apparently on condition that she keep quiet about his conduct.[26] The gift was a sign of status. If Bay Lodge had come to figure as the foremost of the uncle's various "nephews," Loulie had won first place among his ever-expanding troop of "nieces."

Adams was compunctious about seeking the approval of persons named in the book. He proceeded in some cases by asking friends to visit him and look into copies while relaxing in his library.[27] He appealed to other persons by mail—notably to President Eliot of Harvard. He sometimes got copies back.[28]

Approval was not the only problem. Adams anticipated that some persons who saw *The Education* would sense, even if vaguely, that the book was something extraordinary. He accordingly felt required to mis-represent or minimize it. When advising Henry Higginson that a book might arrive, he described its contents as "my last words of imbecility on man and matters." He described the contents to Gaskell as "reminiscences which are taking shape in my mind, and which are meant as my closing lectures to undergraduates in the instruction abandoned and broken off in 1877."[29]

Such deprecations were attuned to prevailing realities. In 1907 as in other years, aging writers were likely to burden the public with un-asked-for opinions. Despite the absence of students, former professors tended to continue giving lectures. It might take careful reading and thinking on Higginson and Gaskell's parts for them to realize that Adams's book was not an expression of opinions and was as far as possible removed from being a book of lectures. If they thought a second time, they might have realized that Adams was happy to lie about his book if lies would mitigate the offensiveness of throwing upon the world a new kind of narrative invented by himself, different from history, biography, and autobiography, and very carefully adapted to the needs of a particular class of readers: American males who felt themselves still young and were strongly disposed to learn.

In the long run, the responses to *The Education of Henry Adams* that were most deserving of respect might be those expressed by the readers for whom it was meant. Like *Mont Saint Michel and Chartres*, the new book was printed as simply as possible. Its title page bore the title and the place and date of issuance—Washington 1907—but did not name the author. A Preface followed. In its main passage, the Preface said that the author's object was "to fit young men, in Universities or elsewhere, to

be men of the world, equipped for any emergency."[30] The crucial words
were "young men"—as opposed to boys. The implication was that the
book was written to be read by males sufficiently gifted, developed, and
confident to undertake a course of education not possible within a university curriculum and more necessary than the education that universities were trying to foster.

Of the persons consulted about *The Education* in February and
March 1907, Bay Lodge came nearest to being a young man. Already in
his middle thirties, he was the father of three children. Really, for him,
the book had arrived much too late.

Meanwhile there were signs that things would happen to the book
that were not anticipated by its Preface. Women of different ages had
seized copies, and men no longer young were permitting themselves the
luxury of critical judgments. When replying to Adams about the copy
sent to the White House, President Roosevelt had remarked, "Of course
it is the most delightful book of the kind I know." The remark posited
the existence of many books of the kind. It suggested that Adams had
written an autobiography and had outdone other autobiographers in
coining things delightful. That the remark showed Roosevelt to be a
light-hearted, unthinking judge of a book he had hardly opened did not
lessen the remark's importance. The book was going to have a reputation, and the persons certain to claim an exclusive right to fix its reputation would be established *older* American men like Roosevelt and
Lodge—men not of the sort for whom the book was written.

Mary Jones did not appear in *The Education*. Adams again departed
from his rule. He sent her a copy inscribed "For Mrs. Mary Cadwalader
Jones with the affection of Henry Adams/ April 11, 1907."[31] In a letter
mailed that day, he explained—inaccurately—that the book till then
had been seen only by persons it named and that she would be the
secret exception. He pleaded, ". . . don't betray me!"

He mentioned to Mrs. Jones that the book was written in two parts,
intended to serve parallel purposes. "The motive of the first part is to
acquit my conscience about my father. That of the second part is to
acquit my conscience about Hay." True as far as they went, Adams's
comments reflected realities. Beginning in 1862, C. F. Adams had permitted his son to function as unofficial co-minister to England. In 1898,
Hay had arranged Henry's beginning seven years of work as secret co-
secretary of state. It had never been Henry's wish to recompense his
father by thanking him in print. Neither had he wanted to disclose what
Hay had done. Instead he had hoped to immortalize his father and Hay
as unaided heroes of diplomacy. As one of their lesser objects, the two

narratives of *The Education* performed these tasks. Each set forth a myth of unassisted greatness.[32]

Adams went on to tell Mrs. Jones that his own stake in *The Education* was confined to its last three chapters, which he said were tied to the last three chapters of *Mont Saint Michel and Chartres*—making six chapters, all told, which were "my little say in life." This added comment artfully mixed the false with the true. It lied, by masking the important fact that Adams had a stake in every chapter of both books. It told the truth, by hinting that both books were constructed of blocks of text each three chapters long. If she cared to, Mrs. Jones could confirm that this pattern of three-chapter blocks was present in both books, with interesting exceptions. In *The Education*, the second narrative—Chapters XXI to XXXV—hewed to the three-chapter pattern without stop; but the first narrative—Chapters I to XX—followed the pattern from Chapter I through Chapter 18 but broke it with a two-chapter block closing with the chapter "Failure." In *Mont Saint Michel and Chartres*, five three-chapter blocks were interrupted by an ambitious fourth-to-last chapter, "Les Miracles de Notre Dame," which stood alone.

Mrs. Jones prized her copy of *The Education* so highly she kept it in her bedroom. She read it intently but paused to write a letter assuring Adams that all he said about his father was "wonderful." "I didn't think any modern man could write so freely and yet so delicately. . . ." She made no claim to authority. Yet she said about the book, "I know [of] nothing at all like it any where."[33]

Steamship companies offered bargain winter rates through April 30. Adams saved $500 by reserving a suite on the *Philadelphia*, to sail on the 27th. Mrs. Cameron and Martha would cross on a later ship.

Adams had continued to seek approvals. Without result, he sent a copy to ailing John La Farge. The approval he needed most was that of Clara Hay. She appeared on four pages of *The Education*. Her husband appeared on fifty.

By April 11, 1907, Mrs. Hay had returned from California. At her and his earliest convenience, she and Adams discussed the memorial to her husband. Adams had read Hay's diary and had hand-copied the most usable portions.[34] Hundreds of letters were waiting for possible inclusion. Other letters were promised. Mrs. Hay knew nothing about *The Education of Henry Adams*. At some point in the discussion, Adams told her about the book, but only as a secondary issue.

On April 22, when about to leave for New York, he sent her a note and an unmarked copy. The note said he had printed "a few copies" for approval by the persons mentioned and that consent to publish had been given by his family, by President Roosevelt, and by President Eliot of Harvard. He assured her that the book would "lie unpublished till it seems worth while."[35]

Details required attention. Senator Lodge wanted a copy for himself. On April 22 or 23, Adams sent him one, inscribed to him simply "with regards." Lodge was very pleased to get it.[36]

Perhaps at the same time, Adams made a gift of a copy to Associate Justice Oliver Wendell Holmes of the Supreme Court, inscribed "with warm regards."[37] Holmes was named in *The Education* and was one of the few Americans who were actively interested in ideas.

When packing for his voyage, Adams put into his luggage copies of *Mont Saint Michel and Chartres* and *The Education* for an English writer he knew only slightly, Sir George Otto Trevelyan. Again the problem was approval. In the Preface to *Mont Saint and Chartres*, Adams had said that Lord Macaulay had a nephew—unnamed—who not only read his uncle's writings but in two praiseworthy volumes demonstrated that he had done so. The nephew was Trevelyan; the volumes were his biography of Macaulay; and Adams had brought uncle and nephew into his Preface to round out an opening paragraph about relationships between writers, readers, fathers, sons, uncles, nephews, and nieces. Since the paragraph was introductory both to *Mont Saint Michel and Chartres* and to *The Education of Henry Adams*, compunctious Adams felt he should visit Trevelyan and at least tell him about both books.[38]

A last necessity had to do with uncorrected errors still lurking in *The Education* and Adams's acute awareness that the book was not entirely finished and required improvement. In these connections, it helps to notice that the Preface to *The Education* begins by invoking Jean-Jacques Rousseau, together with his *Confessions*, and mentions Benjamin Franklin, known increasingly to Americans for his *Autobiography*. The references to Rousseau and Franklin had a basis in supposed literary rank. Adams thought them writers of the very highest order and saw their books not as great books but as very great books, meaning the exact sort of book he himself had in mind when designing his *Education*.[39] How close Adams had brought his book to being a very great book was something he possibly could not know. What he assuredly did know was that changes, even small changes, could transform a book remarkably in value.

He had been telling people that the copies of *The Education* were "proofs"—mere "sheets" of a "possible, projected book."[40] The expressions may have meant little to others. They meant a great deal to him. In his eyes, his *Education* was not yet a book. It remained a work in progress, crying for attention. Accordingly, when leaving for his voyage on the *Philadelphia*, he took with him one or more of his personal copies. Here one will be called the First Traveling Copy.[41] While away, he would read it and make new corrections where necessary; but his chief object would be to make tentative *improvements*, whether small or large. To his credit, he had hit upon a method of correction-and-improvement for his *Education* involving the use of successive copies. When he got back to Washington, he would compare the First Traveling Copy with his Master Copy, make new corrections in the latter as necessary, and make final improvements. If everything happened as expected, the only copy of real importance would still be the Master Copy.

Elisabeth Marbury was a fellow passenger with Adams on the *Phila-delphia*. A better friend could not be found. Miss Marbury, Miss de Wolfe, and Miss Morgan had formed a *ménage à trois*. Of the partners, Elisabeth seemed to him the ablest and most commanding.

In Paris, while picking up threads, Adams glimpsed Henry James and Edith Wharton, Laura Chanler, and Ambassador White. He talked with Wayne MacVeagh. He tried to sell his Mercedes and was told that open automobiles had become unwanted. Women favored closed ones.

As owner-editor of the *New York Tribune*, Ambassador Reid had acquired the habit of conducting his affairs efficiently. In response to the plea for Hay's letters, he had sent orders to assistants of his in New York to catalogue his letters from Hay and send several copies of the catalogue to him in London, together with the original letters. He reviewed the letters when they arrived and saw that a few were so sensitive that only Mrs. Hay could see them. He intended to speed the few to her, with a copy of the catalogue. Others he would mail to Adams in Paris with a copy of the catalogue marked in red to indicate which ones had gone to Mrs. Hay.

In letters explaining these intentions, Reid promised Adams that he would also send some guidelines about the dangers of publication. He meanwhile remarked that the celebrated letters of Horace Walpole seemed less interesting and less deft than Hay's.[42]

Reid's management took Adams by surprise. He had not expected that a mass of Hay's letters would be coming to him, by-passing Mrs. Hay. Neither had he foreseen an invitation. Reid wanted him to cross the Channel and share the comforts of his country house.

A letter came from Clara Hay. Adams and Mrs. Hay were unalike to the verge of incompatibility. His turn of mind was exploratory and experimental. Hers was timid. He was many-sided. She was simple. Although very quick to welcome such material innovations as autos and radios, she was conservative and conventional to the bone. Unconventional beliefs affected her as manifest errors. She particularly regretted the folly of persons who drifted into impiety. She might pray for such persons. She might try to set them right.

Her letter to Adams typified her simplicity. After touching on other matters, she said, "I have just finished reading The Education of Henry Adams and I was very much interested in it." She admitted there were things in the book that she did not understand. ". . . they were too deep for me." Yet she had formed an impression. The main basis of her impression was confidence that Mr. Adams was incapable of falsehood. It could not occur to her that the "Henry Adams" who appeared in *The Education* as the book's protagonist might in any degree be a fiction. She took for granted that Adams the author and "Henry Adams" the subject were identical and that for the most part he had wasted his life by vainly searching for a "Force" which, if found, would account for all events. She gathered too that he had read too many books. In her letter, rather than hesitate, she asked him, "Why,—instead of all those other books . . . did you not go back to your Bible?" She said, ". . . it is so simple—if you will only have faith as a little child! In the last months of his life[,] the Bible was John's constant companion. . . . Will you not try it before it is too late?"[43]

The most discriminating and industrious reader Adams knew was Gaskell. It apparently had been Adams's hope that he could take a copy of *The Education* to Europe and give it to Gaskell in England, but instead he mailed the copy from Washington. In Paris during the second week of May, he received a letter from Gaskell praising the book.

On May 15, 1907, Adams told Gaskell to keep the copy. He said the book would be held back "until we can get . . . Hay's 'Letters' published; and even then I prefer to publish the 'Mt[.] St[.] Michel and Chartres' before this last volume." A plan had been devised. To accommodate Mrs. Hay, *three* works would appear one after the other, ending with *The Education*. "Then I shall have survived, buried and praised my friends, and shall go to sleep myself. It is time."

That same day, May 15, Adams performed the difficult labor of replying to Mrs. Hay. Without being aware of it, she had done him a harsh injustice. He had read the Bible. Beginning in childhood, he had read it more than any other book. He had tried hard to follow its injunctions, most notably by honoring his father and mother.[44]

Yet her general view of him had been crudely right. It was true that he had become a universal historian intent on discovering the overall tendency of human feelings, thoughts, and actions. His desire to learn the story of humanity was a passion. The unusual thing about his passion was its not being self-serving. Dread of doing things for himself and hope of doing things for others had made him a researcher and thinker whose discoveries were as little *his* as possible. He had wholeheartedly wanted to reach conclusions that would lend themselves to being common property.

There might be risks in writing about such things to Mrs. Hay. He disregarded the risks and wrote to her in perfect honesty. "Long ago, I ceased seeking Truth or Force—which are the same thing—on my own account." He outlined the story of his passion. "All I have sought has been the direction, or tendency, or history, of the human mind, not as religion or science, but as fact,—as a whole, or stream,—and this with no view of its relation to me or my benefit." He admitted that he did not care what happened to him, if he could be of use to everyone else. "All my life I have tried to ignore self and selfishness either in this world or the next. . . ."

On May 19, 1907, Mrs. Cameron and Martha reached Paris and moved into their new apartment. Martha immediately collapsed. Her symptoms were lassitude and exhaustion. One could speculate that the underlying cause was separation from Ronald Lindsay. During recent months, she had left Washington twice to go to Coffin's Point and once to go to California. She had seen Lindsay after her last return to Washington but then had hurried with her mother to their steamer.[45]

Martha shared her mother's belief in water cures. Mrs. Cameron knew of an arsenical spring northwest of Venice in the Italian Alps at Levico. She proposed to take Martha there for a cure and rest. Dor thought their confidence in hydropathy misplaced but likable. On May 24, four days prior to their leaving, he said in a letter to Loulie that mother and daughter were "naturally mad."

Gaskell sent Adams a list of corrections needed in *The Education*. Adams advised his friend that he had entered them in a copy he had in Paris—the First Traveling Copy.[46] The copy survives and is accessible.[47] Some of Adams's annotations are exactly of the kind that he would be expected to make in a First Traveling Copy when he noticed simple errors he had not previously corrected in his Master Copy.[48] Other annotations correct errors pointed out to him by other persons, Gaskell being the conspicuous example.[49] But the bulk of the annotations were *improvements* made by an accomplished author in the course of an effort to transform an excellent book into a perfect book.[50]

By studying the First Traveling Copy closely, one can learn that Adams's opinion of his book is very high. His response is to do two things: improve the book by deletions, revisions, and additions, yet also try to keep it undisturbed and intact.[51] His improvements vary in size from as little as two letters to as much as forty words.[52] The result is a fuller, clearer, and more expressive book, made more likable and effective by a quieting of its tones.[53]

Because work on her husband's letters tired her, Mrs. Hay chose not to read a batch of letters supplied by Richard Gilder and mailed the originals, unread, to Adams in Paris. When he received an even larger package of letters from Reid in London, Adams saw that Reid too had trusted him with the originals.

The selection of letters for publication was increasingly becoming Adams's responsibility. He continued to say that Mrs. Hay would decide which letters would be included in the printed volumes. Yet he liked his freedom to choose and was shaping a compilation of writings that would have what he himself called "literary form."[54]

Mrs. Cameron regretted separation from Dor and was very distressed about Martha. She wrote from Levico that she had never seen Martha "so exhausted & miserable." The mother too was tired. She explained, "I can face illnesses—there is something to meet and lay hold of—but collapses whether of nerves or physique or both, knock me out." Fortunately, though still too weak for arsenical baths, Martha had an appetite and wished to read. ". . . [she] is deep in the Portrait of a Lady. It makes me old to see how she takes it."[55]

For Adams, Hay's letters to Reid opened the shutters of a window into their era that he had not expected to look through. The letters seemed to disclose more about Reid than about Hay. Studying them made Adams reconsider Reid's climb from newspaper work in Cincinnati to the ambassadorship in London. The chief puzzle was Reid's extraordinary self-esteem. On June 16, 1907, Adams told Mrs. Cameron, ". . . I sit in my den, and work over Whitelaw Reid's papers, and wonder whether Whitelaw is really and truly a great man, and whether President Harrison and Grover Cleveland and President Arthur were as great as he."

As revealed in Reid's papers, American politics became more obviously a "curious form of gambling" in which money invariably was lost. Vying to lift selected beneficiaries into the presidency, men like Reid and Hay had put large sums on the table. Writing again to Mrs. Cameron on June 20, Adams said: "I would give six-pence to know what Hay paid for McKinley. His politics must have cost!" The subject had literary possibilities. ". . . I could make a screaming novel out of it—to bust Democracy."[56]

Like her husband, Mrs. Hay had formed many acquaintanceships but had few friends. Her exchange with Adams about his *Education* did not diminish her impulse to write to him. In a new letter, she said she was at the mercy of political adversaries. "I find I have to be very careful in my way of living as I have enemies who are ready to say anything about me." Turning to other subjects, Mrs. Hay noted that Lindsay had been transferred and would soon be leaving Washington. She wondered whether Martha in consequence would be "inconsolable."[57]

At Levico, Martha was worse. Mrs. Cameron reported to Adams that her child was "weaker than I have ever seen her." Because Martha said she wished they could go to Scotland, Mrs. Cameron secretly read guide books and asked Dor for assistance. She wanted him to locate a "*possible* inn" in Scotland that she and Martha could use in August as a headquarters, when not paying visits.[58]

Word of Lindsay's transfer reached Levico and had astonishing effects. Mrs. Cameron advised Adams: "Perhaps Martha had better marry Lindsay after all. He by the way, hopes to leave America the 28th of June & be in Paris early in July. So you will see him before we do. Martha has taken a sudden turn & is *much* better."[59]

Adams reacted to the inquiry about a possible inn by suggesting that he join mother and daughter in Scotland as co-renters of a house. Mrs. Cameron replied: ". . . I don't want a house, it ties me down too much. You and I think Scotland a dreary place, but if Martha wants to go there I suppose she might as well."[60]

At every chance, Mrs. Cameron was seeking fresh allies for Dor and herself. Four Americans were coming to Levico: Ward and Ellen Thoron, and Frederic and Florence Keep. Mrs. Cameron judged Mrs. Keep to be an ally and sent Dor the good news. "Florence Keep turns out well. Under the stiff Boardman respectability[,] there is a vein of humor rather delicate & fine, an intelligent mind, and great evenness of temper."[61] There was no question of jealousy. If Mrs. Cameron had her way, Mrs. Keep and Henry Adams would soon be friends.

Ambassador White had withheld from Mrs. Hay a few of the many letters he had received from her husband. On July 3, he suggested to Adams an early meeting and said he would have with him some letters that were "too indiscreet for any idea of publication but which you may like to read." Presumably a meeting took place in Paris soon.

One result for Adams was new insights into the problem of writing Hay's biography. As much as ever, he wished not to be his friend's biographer. Yet he was being afforded opportunities to study evidence not usually disclosed. Seeing such evidence permitted him to ponder a new question: How much or little would he want to tell a biographer of Hay, should such a person come forward? While weighing the question, he felt an increasing desire to confer with Ambassador Reid.

The ambassador lived by turns in two houses, Dorchester House on

Park Lane in London and Wrest Park in the country, within easy reach by limousine. He preferred that he and Adams meet at Wrest Park. On July 17, Adams informed Gaskell that he would be coming to England in August, that he would have to talk with Reid, and that he wished to visit Sir George Trevelyan in Northumberland. Gaskell knew Trevelyan much better than Adams did. He might have an opinion about the possibility of a visit.

Mrs. Cameron and Martha had moved from Levico to an Alpine valley near Bolzano. They were in touch with Dor and well-posted about his plans. In her newest letter, the mother suggested, ". . . possibly we can all go to Wrest together." She said too that for beauty their Italian valley made the Engadine in Switzerland look like 30 cents. Part of the difference was the wild flowers. ". . . the flowers almost make me crazy." ". . . they are worth seeing if only to realize what they can be. The human form divine must make the creator wince."[62]

Adams paused in his work on the *Letters*. On July 22, he remarked to Gaskell that for the present his reading was all in "science and electrics." On the same day, he urged Reid to write an autobiography. The advice reflected an improved opinion of Reid's achievements.

Gaskell arranged an invitation for Adams to visit Trevelyan in Northumberland late in August. Trevelyan was advised that a copy of *Mont Saint Michel and Chartres* would soon be mailed to him. He wrote to Adams, "I look forward much to receiving your volume."[63]

Mrs. Cameron and Martha would be returning to Paris on the Orient Express, due early on Saturday, July 27, 1907. On Friday, Adams wrote to the mother at their apartment inviting them to lunch at Laurent's at 12:30 on Saturday. He implied that another male would be present. Three words were enough. ". . . I have Lindsay."[64]

Reid notified Adams that his wife was away and the best time for a meeting at Wrest Park would be the days following August 18. From Paris on August 1, Adams advised Gaskell that, during the latter part of the month, he would have to be at Wrest Park for several days to do "some literary work that is none of my business."

Together, Dor, Mrs. Cameron, and Martha crossed to London, put up for a night at the Ritz, and went to Wenlock Abbey. Gaskell and Lady Catherine welcomed them much as if they were a family. An invitation to visit friends of their own took mother and daughter back to London on August 14. From London, Mrs. Cameron sent Lady Catherine something new: a "thermos bottle for her morning coffee."[65]

After staying awhile with the Gaskells, Adams went to Wrest Park for three days with Reid. Writing to Mrs. Cameron on August 22, he said his host was as "genial as a dozen Dukes." On the 24th, he advised: "We are still alone here, and have done our work, besides talking vast volumes. Our confidential intimacy is amazing. . . ."

Reid's catalogue listed eighty-three personal letters from Hay to himself. The ambassador and Adams selected forty-eight for inclusion in the Hay memorial. Their effort was darkened by news from Washington that Elihu Root—the replacement secretary of state—had suffered a breakdown. According to the reports, he was a victim of overwork.

The weather in England had become truly abominable, the rainiest and coldest in memory. Rather than go to Scotland, Martha wanted to return to Paris, but the apartment at 53 Avenue Montaigne had been lent to Ellen Thoron. Somewhat against her will, Martha traveled with her mother to the Grant Arms Hotel in Grantown-on-Spey.

Adams journeyed to Northumberland, talked congenially with Sir George Trevelyan and his wife, journeyed to Tillypronie to visit Sir John Clark and connect with Gaskell, and at last journeyed with Gaskell back to Wenlock Abbey. Weather apart, Adams's stay in England and Scotland had been a success in all respects but one. Ambassador Reid and Sir John Clark had been barred by lack of hostesses from inviting Mrs. Cameron and Martha to stay at Wrest Park and Tillypronie simultaneously with Mr. Adams. Great Britain had not changed. Except at Wenlock Abbey, conventionality and formality reigned supreme.

Charles Adams for a dozen years had been president of the Massachusetts Historical Society in Boston. As president, he had written to Worthington Ford offering him a well-paid position as the Society's editor. Ford was interested but hesitant.[66]

While again at Wenlock Abbey, Henry Adams received a letter from Clara Hay that touched on deaths reported in the press. Saint Gaudens had died on August 7 at his studio in Vermont. In France on August 20, during an auto accident, a chauffeur had killed a pedestrian and sustained fatal injuries himself. The latter deaths disturbed Mrs. Hay because the chauffeur was employed by her daughter Helen.[67]

Henry returned alone to Paris and consulted with his travel agent about steamer space for Mrs. Cameron, Martha, and himself. A factor to consider was expense. Stocks had crashed horribly on Wall Street. The panic seemed as bad as that of 1893. Henry's income had shrunk a fifth and might shrink more.

Writing to Gaskell on September 14, 1907, a Saturday, Henry said that no one was in Paris. "Three wretched females ask me into the country for Sunday." The wretched females were Elisabeth Marbury, Elsie de Wolfe, and Anne Morgan. Henry would go to their villa as asked, but he meant to douse them cheerfully with pessimism, and he spoke of them as males. "I am going to comfort and encourage my fellow countrymen by assuring them that total ruin is at hand, and that next year we shall have no incomes and a socialist President."

Martha wished to remain in Scotland long enough to dance at the Inverness Assembly. Her mother assented but would rather have fled to Paris. On September 20, the eve of their departure from Inverness, Dor sent a letter to the mother in London. He said the travel agent had reserved two suites for them on the *St. Louis*.

Additional items of news gave Dor's letter exceptional interest. "Lindsay came up to see me Wednesday afternoon, and dined with me at La Rue's." "Copper has gone to the devil, and steel will follow, no doubt; but I've given away my auto, and am consequently well off."

Evidently Dor had been troubled by the deaths of Helen Whitney's chauffeur and the luckless pedestrian. Automobiles had undeniable advantages, yet sometimes killed.

16

THE SECOND TRAVELING COPY

Adams had indexed *The Education*. He knew that the president who preceded Theodore Roosevelt was William McKinley. In the index, he correctly listed the former president as "McKinley, William," and added the needed page numbers; but persons who turned to the first page listed would find the president represented as "James McKinley." The person at fault was surely Adams. He wrote "James" in his manuscript, and the compositor at the print shop put the error into type.

Many readers might think the mistaken "James" a slip too small for notice. Some might view it as a sign that Adams was beginning to suffer the illness that blighted his father's closing years: progressive loss of memory. Others might theorize that he was troubled by three murders; that when he was writing Chapter XV of *The Education* and came to McKinley, he remembered the presidents who were killed, Lincoln being the first, and unconsciously conflated the names of the second and third: James A. Garfield and William McKinley.

Adams corrected the error. On page 203 of his First Traveling Copy, he noticed "James McKinley," ran his pencil through "James," and wrote "William" in the margin.[1] He however saw the error, not as a reader, but as its maker. He may have seen that it reflected something more than a confusion of two presidents' names.

His *Education* had been written oppositely from most of his other works. To take a near-at-hand example, he had written *Mont Saint Michel and Chartres* mostly on the basis of specialized knowledge developed by visiting medieval buildings and consulting books and photographs. Admittedly there were parts of *The Education* that drew upon particular sources of data, but he had brought the book into being with the help of the entire range of his memories and imaginings. When writing it, he had tried to be aware, not of something, but of *everything*; and everything had included a plenitude of names.

Several names come to mind. In 1860, when Adams first arrived in Washington to pass a winter, the occupant of the White House was James

Buchanan. In 1868–1870, when Adams attempted permanent residence in Washington, he had occasion to study a daring maneuver, a "corner" in gold put into action on the New York Gold Exchange by an American, Jay Gould, but conceived by an Englishman, James McHenry. Late in 1870, Adams was banished to Cambridge, Massachusetts. There he met Henry and William James. After 1877, when he at last succeeded in returning to Washington, he gave most of his energy to a *History of the United States* which had much to say about James Madison as secretary of state and as president. This list of particulars could be extended but is already long enough to help explain why Adams made his McKinley error. When he was writing *The Education* and needed to speak of the slaughtered president, his mind was so crowded with overlapping names—James Madison, James Buchanan, James McHenry, Henry Adams, Henry James, William James, James A. Garfield, and William McKinley—that he produced an invention, "James McKinley," which on the one hand was a patent error and on the other was a faithful reflection of a mind beset, and occasionally overborne, by floods of experience.

Mrs. Cameron and Martha returned to Paris on September 25, 1907. On the same day, Berenson risked a letter to Adams asking for copies of *Mont Saint Michel and Chartres* and *The Education of Henry Adams*. He had been staying at Versailles with Elisabeth Marbury and Elsie de Wolfe. His hostesses had both books. Berenson started to read the earlier, learned also of the later, changed books, read—in his words—"the first hundred pages" of *The Education*, asked a question, and was told that the only way to get a copy of either book was to appeal to Adams. Had he wished to be cautious, Berenson might have asked for one. He was aware that Adams disliked him. He instead asked for both and said in his letter, "I am reduced to begging as you leave no other course open." "I wish I could see a great deal of you, but I dare say the attraction is not reciprocal."

Adams gave Berenson neither book. Replying on September 26, he elaborately lied. He averred that he had "no volumes to offer"; that he had printed a hundred copies of *The Education* but all were gone; that he had no power of "redistribution"; and indeed was "reduced to denying my own brothers and sisters." "Please accept this plea of bankruptcy. . . ."[2]

At a later time, Adams would say that Berenson had "the unpardonable fault of being intelligent and insupportable."[3] When lying to him in September 1907, Adams may have thought his lies flagrant enough to reveal themselves to Berenson as lies, in which case his refusal to give Berenson what he wanted would be an instance of one quick-witted person's sending another quick-witted person a refusal they both could accurately assess. Yet the important issue was neither lies nor the sending or non-sending of books. It was an important downward shift in Adams's estimate of the adequacy of his own knowledge.

What happened was in one way untroubling and simple. He read his First Traveling Copy of *The Education* with close attention to its last chapters. He found that three chapters—"The Grammar of Science," "A Dynamic Theory of History," and "A Law of Acceleration"—were susceptible of improvements. He made some eighty changes in the chapters, some tentative, many definite.

Perhaps at about the same time, he reviewed an earlier chapter, "Indian Summer." He came to a sentence that named a great American scientist. It read:

> The greatest of Americans, judged by his rank in science, Wolcott Gibbs, never came to Washington, and Adams never enjoyed the chance to meet him.

He saw nothing amiss in the sentence and continued reading. Towards the bottom of the page, "Wolcott Gibbs" reappeared as one of two Americans whose ideas had been met with "a conspiracy of silence." Seeing the name a second time, Adams reacted. In the margin, he pencilled what perhaps was a query, "Willard?" Uncertain what to do next, he erased what he had written but left traces of a capital W.

The pencilling-and-erasure had been caused by a realization. He had remembered that there were two American scientists whose last name was Gibbs. Their first names were Wolcott and Willard. He had seen that, when meaning to write the full name of one of them, he possibly had confused them and written the full name of the other.[4]

Much like the "James McKinley," the suspected error about a Gibbs had behind it an array of overlapping names. The difference was that this time the names of three Adamses were also involved and one of the three Adamses—Henry himself—had two names.

One must review the data. In 1838, when he was born, an Adams boy was named by his mother Henry Brooks Adams (which he changed in manhood to Henry Adams). In the 1840s, he learned that his father had had an eldest brother, George Washington Adams, who committed suicide by drowning in 1829. It appears too that when very young he read a history by George Gibbs, *Memoirs of the administrations of Washington and John Adams, edited from the papers of Oliver Wolcott, secretary of the Treasury*. Later, when a history teacher at Harvard, he attended faculty meetings and was afforded glimpses of one of Harvard's science teachers, Wolcott Gibbs. In 1888, he nicknamed himself George Washington but gave the nickname a comic coded form, Dordy Dobbitt. Ever since, he had answered to the name as used by Mrs. Cameron, notably in her letters, where she addressed him constantly as "Dear Dor"—the equivalent of Dear George. As if these complications were not enough, he became conversant in the 1890s with the activities of Senator Edward Wolcott of Colorado concerning the use of silver as money; sometime after 1900, seeking information about a prehistoric creature that interested him—"the ganoid fish, the *Pteraspis*"—he found the needed data in the writings of Charles D. Walcott, the American geologist; and in addition he was told by Langley about little-publicized but important discoveries of Willard Gibbs, a physics professor at Yale. Thus, when he wrote the chapter "Indian Summer," his mind was charged with eleven overlapping names some of which were deeply meaningful to him: George Washington, George Gibbs, George Washington Adams, a new George Washington (himself), John Adams, Henry Adams, Oliver Wolcott, Wolcott Gibbs, Edward Wolcott, Charles D. Walcott, and Willard Gibbs.[5]

The Gibbs he had intended to mention in *The Education* was Willard Gibbs. Seven times without variation, in "Indian Summer," in later chapters, and in the index, he had brought the full name into play as "Wolcott Gibbs." He had reviewed the occurrences when correcting his Master Copy in Washington and had seen "Wolcott" as correct. It was only in Europe when reading the First Traveling Copy that he sensed something wrong. Even then, he did not know for sure that he had confused two persons' names.

On October 10, 1907, a book by Charles Depéret on evolution, *Les Transformations du Monde Animal*, was published by Flammarion in Paris. Adams bought a copy, read it, and encountered passages that had affinities with passages in his *Education*. One such passage concerned the ganoid fish, the *Pteraspis*.[6] Struck to see that Depéret was interested in the species, Adams wrote in the margin of page 198 of his First Traveling Copy, "De Peret, *Transformations*, p. 95, 97, 107." In the margin on page 200, he similarly wrote, "De Peret. 97, 98."

Until that time, he had been content with his procedures as corrector and improver of *The Education*. The new marks he had made in the First Traveling Copy were neither corrections nor improvements. They instead were references. Each indicated that a passage in his own book could be compared to a purpose, at least by him, with one or more passages in someone else's book.[7]

From early youth, he had been accustomed to making copies of others' writings. It can be inferred that late in 1907 in Paris he copied onto appropriately-sized slips of paper the passages by Depéret that interested him. When he got back to Washington, he would insert the passages excerpted from Depéret's book into the Master Copy of *The Education*. Once followed in connection with other books he bought or already owned, this procedure would transform the Master Copy from a corrected and improved copy into a compendium of valued information. In one way, the transformation would be a step backward. The Master Copy would cease to be adapted to the needs of a publisher. An off-setting benefit was that Adams would have in one copy all the data relative to *The Education* that was pressingly interesting to him.[8]

On October 26, 1907, at Cherbourg, Adams, Mrs. Cameron, and Martha again sailed on the *St. Louis*. They reached New York when the Panic of 1907 was at its worst. American dollars were unobtainable by usual means. The Knickerbocker Club reluctantly lent Adams $25.00— enough to get the travelers to Washington. Donald was there to greet them. He shortly left for South Carolina with nothing but a train ticket and $2.00.[9]

Once at home, Adams gave Mrs. Hay the letters he had obtained for her husband's memorial while in Europe. For her part, Mrs. Hay had become apprehensive. Adams's practice of showing his *Education* to people mentioned in the book had affected her as a precedent to follow. She thought she might order a privately printed edition of her husband's *Letters*—as many as forty copies—for "communication to friends." Her purpose was explicit. She wanted "advice" from the "persons most interested in the publication."[10]

On December 6, when he had been a month in Washington, Adams wrote to Mrs. Jones that "three months very hard work" had brought him face to face with a mathematical equation: $a = x^2t$.[11] By then, it seems, he had obtained trustworthy assurances that the two Gibbses, Wolcott and Willard, were both great minds. So informed, he tried to solve the Wolcott/Willard problem in *The Education*. He opened his First Traveling Copy, turned to page 329, and let stand at the middle of the page the sentence already quoted about "Wolcott Gibbs" as the "greatest of Americans, judged by his rank in science." At the bottom of the page, he deleted a passing reference to "Wolcott Gibbs." On page 393, he looked at three sentences referring to "Wolcott Gibbs" and modified one of them by inserting eighteen confessional words. The result was the following (the insertion has been underscored):

> To Adams's vision, Wolcott Gibbs stood on the same plane with the three or four greatest minds of his century,—<u>the more so because in his ignorance he confounded him with another great mind,</u> Willard Gibbs.

This attempted solution of a problem, as Adams would eventually see, was simply not a solution. It brought into view a confusion in his own mind that readers of *The Education* would not need to know about. It over-critically asserted that he had confounded two Gibbs's names because of "ignorance." And it failed to do what was needed: wholly get rid of one Gibbs and bring another to the fore.

Adams moved to an altered strategy, part cautious, part assertive, regarding his books. He dropped the idea of early publication of *Mont Saint Michel and Chartres*. He faced the possibility that the book, though excellent, might be made more-than-excellent if he continued to widen his knowledge of France in the middle ages.

He dropped the idea of early publication of *The Education of Henry Adams* but began a small-scale experiment. On January 17, 1908, he advised his brother Charles, "Although I have no idea of publishing, I have all the stronger idea of consulting." "I feel free to ask wider advice. . . ."

He already had put copies into the hands of historians. One copy went to Seward's biographer, Frederic Bancroft, a resident of Washington, formerly the State Department's librarian.[12] Three others went to professors: John Burgess at Columbia, Edward Channing at Harvard, and John Stewart at Lehigh.[13] Adams's purpose was well-defined. He proposed to test whether there was a disposition among America's historians to develop historical ideas, as opposed to the perpetual finding and presentation of historical "facts."

Among Adams's friends, the one most interested in ideas was Mrs. Chanler. She was planning to come from New York to visit him on January 20 and 21. Her interests extended to science.

She came as planned. On the 21st, Uncle Henry mentioned in a letter to Niece Loulie that "Mrs[.] Winty" was at the house and Mrs. Tams was expected. He said he was idle. "Mrs[.] Lodge has withdrawn wholly from company outside her own house. Mrs[.] Cameron works hard for Martha, who is in bed every other day. I look out the window."

Evidently the theme of Adams and Mrs. Chanler's talks was mathematics as used in physics. After she left, he informed her, ". . . I discover that I am a pupil of Ernst Mach and an enemy of [Henri] Poincaré. . . . I think I will now burn the *Education*. . . ."[14]

In New York, Mrs. Chanler by then had spoken with a professor of mathematics, Michael Pupin, who had studied under Willard Gibbs at Yale. In a letter that crossed with Adams's, she reported that Pupin was "very learned" but "scorns our 4th dimension."[15]

Adams did not burn his *Education*. He however told Mrs. Chanler on January 30, apparently in earnest, "I am ashamed of it. . . ." This, in part, was his way of saying that he had learned enough about Wolcott and Willard Gibbs to know that Wolcott had to be fully excised.

In a new letter on February 3, he said he had had "no answer to my appeals to my own historian horde." ". . . the air is dead as dogs. Only the mathematicians show life. . . . I need mathematics horribly." He went on to divulge a stratagem which if carried out would require his privately printing both a letter and additional copies of *The Education*. He meant the stratagem as a goad. "In order to spur my Professors of history, I have drawn up a sort of circular to send them with the *Education*; for their minds cannot act unless directed, like static electricity." He enclosed his draft of the "circular" and urged her to ask Professor Pupin to read it.

She arranged that Pupin dine with her. On the 4th, she explained, ". . . after dinner I shall read him the [circular] letter & give him a pencil & pad for his notes. . . ."

On the 5th, Adams interjected a comment about *Mont Saint Michel and Chartres*. He knew that Mrs. Chanler still believed that the book was proof of Roman Catholicism in its author. "Say what you will," he protested, "the Chartres is heretical and worse."

Pupin, the expert auditor, disapproved Adams's circular letter. Mrs. Chanler reported on the 7th: "Prof. Pupin carried off the document & promised to write out on a separate sheet what you ought to have intended to say. It seems that your electrical mathematics are unorthodox & inadmissible in their present form."

Adams answered on the 8th that he was "not at all surprised." "Science is far worse than the Church. . . ."

She later informed him that he would be hearing directly from the professor, but Pupin's criticism has not been found. The circular letter also is missing. (It evidently concerned electricity and its chief early explorers, Benjamin Franklin and Michael Faraday.)

The clash of Adams's circular letter and Pupin's criticism could be mainly attributed to ill-matched motives. The professor had been consulted as a mathematician and scientist. He naturally wished to prevent anything being said by Adams that was unmathematical or unscientific. His motive was simple. But Adams was seldom simple. In this instance, he figured as a scientific historian, an ambitious educator, and a resourceful writer. His attempted letter to his fellow historians was serious, but there were no guarantees that it was not also humorous. Indeed the probabilities were all in one direction: that it was serious and exceedingly humorous. If serious humor of one sort proved dismissible on scientific grounds, he was certain to devise another sort. A hard man to discourage, he would make fresh efforts until he had written a message to the historians that he himself would approve and that promised to serve his object.

To everyone's surprise, Adams had been trying to arrange another journey for himself around the world. Mrs. Cameron had written to Gaskell, "He is talking of returning to Paris via Pekin & the Trans-Siberian[,] leaving here in March. . . ." As if the idea did not displease her, she added, ". . . isn't he wonderful?"[16]

Adams could afford the trip. His investments were continuing to provide him a more-than-sufficient income. Yet he could not go alone; and Ward Thoron, who wished to join him but had a wife and children, remained uncertain from week to week about his freedom to get away.

While waiting, Henry had been advised by Charles that the Massachusetts Historical Society had elected him to fill a newly-vacated place on its honor roll of the world's best living historians and that he had been nominated for the place by James Ford Rhodes, a retired businessman who was gaining wide approval as a historian of the United States. In gratitude, Henry sent Rhodes a copy of *Mont Saint Michel and Chartres* and explained in a self-deprecatory letter, "I doubt whether I could induce a score of people in America to read its last three Chapters, for which reason I do not publish what is to me the only thing worth reading I ever wrote."[17]

Rhodes liked the book so much he requested the loan of a copy of *The Education*.[18] Henry sent one. Rhodes read it and courteously returned it, together with penciled "suggestions." Though not a person to criticize, and even less a man of ideas, Rhodes felt prepared to notice Adams's remarkable ability to delineate historical personages. He observed approvingly, "A complete characterization of Sumner can be drawn from your pages." He said too that he could not "conceive of a better training than yours for a historian."[19]

Henry was pleased to get the copy back and still more pleased to receive suggestions. In a letter of thanks, he told Rhodes, "My own copy is now crammed with marginal notes, and will be further improved by yours, which will be its chief ornament."[20] The remark was an exception, for Henry as a rule was silent about his personal copies of *The Education*.[21] Also the remark was deceptive. It concealed the important fact that he was improving his *Education* with the help of two personal copies: a Master Copy and a First Traveling Copy.

The suggestions Rhodes sent are missing. One may may assume that Rhodes, to avoid disfiguring the borrowed copy with marks, listed his suggestions on a separate sheet or sheets of paper, and that Henry inserted the list in his Master Copy, preliminary to weighing the advisability of changes.[22] But no one can really know. All that seems sure about the Master Copy is that it was becoming crammed.[23]

Worthington Ford did not take the position as editor at the Massachusetts Historical Society. At least for the present, he wished to continue in a post he had won at the Library of Congress, a post that permitted his earning a salary by editing historical documents.

At about the same time, Ford lost touch with Henry Adams. Someone advised him that Henry was always in Paris. Yet he knew that Henry was writing books. He heard about *Mont Saint Michel and Chartres* and read the Library's copy. It filled him with "wonder and pleasure—wonder that a layman should enter so entirely into the spirit of the buildings." He heard too that Henry had privately printed another book titled an "Autobiography" or "My Influences," but the Library did not have it, and he could find no trace of copies.[24]

Early in 1908, talking with one of Henry's brothers, Ford was advised that Henry was in Washington and that the elusive book might be had by direct request. On February 17, 1908—one day after Henry's seventieth birthday—Ford wrote to him: "I have sought to obtain a reading of your volume on 'My Influences' . . . but can trace no copy within my reach. . . ." "May I come in some evening to chat[?]"

Henry replied that he had privately printed three books since 1900 and could not tell which one Ford wanted. He said too that he was reduced to his "last half-dozen copies" of the book Ford probably had in mind; also that he was "in despair" of recovering copies he had sent to people as loans. Yet he indicated that Ford could *borrow* what he needed, and he so framed his letter that the desired book's title—*The Education of Henry Adams*—did not appear.[25]

The occasion had been inspired by a rumor. Ford wrote again on the 19th and specified, "The particular book I had in mind I have heard of as an 'Autobiography' or as 'My Influences'—meaning the influences under which you fell at different periods of your life." Rather than wait for Ford to visit, Adams sent him *The Education* with a corrective letter. He said that he himself did *not* appear in the book. ". . . I was not thinking of myself at all in the *Education*. . . ." He denied that the book was autobiography or biography. ". . . [it] is meant for a novel—a story with a purpose, quite unlike biography." Reiterating a statement made in the book's Preface, he said that the story's protagonist, "Henry Adams," was not a human being but an artist's dummy on which to drape changes of clothing. "The *Ego* is a lay figure." Finally, he said the book was meant as "a private letter." "It has no other value."[26]

Much though he disliked explaining a book that was meant to be self-explanatory, Henry had thought of things he could say about *The*

Education that might be helpful. Presumably affected by one of the things he told Berenson—that he had printed one hundred copies—he had begun to tell people that in the book a centipede walks twenty steps downhill to a bottom called "Failure" and has to climb uphill fifteen higher steps to get a view of what it should have tried to see from the beginning. (The centipede's downward and upward movements correspond to the twenty chapters of the book's first narrative and the fifteen chapters of its second.) Henry included a version of the centipede metaphor in his new letter to Ford. He remembered to say, "Please return the volume when you have done with it."[27]

The plan to go to Paris via China and Siberia proved impracticable: Ward Thoron could not go. Niece Loulie arrived in Washington, and a new plan was developed. During the coming summer, she, Ward Thoron, and Uncle Henry were to attempt a tour of medieval churches in the south of France—a tour the uncle thought a precondition of his publishing *Mont Saint Michel and Chartres.*

Mrs. Cameron and Martha had paid their obligatory Christmas and New Year's visit to Coffin's Point. They went there again in March and raised the question of Donald's personal finances. On the 8th, the mother reported to Adams that her husband was carrying $400,000 of borrowed capital and that his securities had lost half their value. Pressed for cash, Donald meant to sell the house on Lafayette Square, which itself was encumbered by a $70,000 mortgage. She said her "one hope" was a complete absence of buyers.

To escape the rigors of winter, Mrs. Hay had gone to Thomasville, Georgia. She wished to order the private edition of her husband's *Letters.* Adams contacted Furst and Company on her behalf and secured an estimate of the cost. She found the estimate acceptable and wrote to Adams, ". . . when I get back I will make preparations to send the manuscript to him [Furst], as your work was satisfactory."[28]

The manuscript she spoke of had been long in preparation. Based mostly on copies Adams made with pen-and-ink, it was duplicated by typists employed by Mrs. Hay. Its form was such that Clara could easily read it and assess its risks. She was sure to notice that the typed pages were full of people's names.

Perhaps while she was at Thomasville, Adams furnished Mrs. Hay a concise statement to be printed at the start of the first volume. She called it a "Biographical Sketch."[29] Its thirty-nine paragraphs provided what Adams had earlier managed not to write: a fully serious and straightforward Hay biography. The paragraphs were very direct. They said of Hay when secretary of state: "His rule in diplomacy was to settle all questions, if possible, by word of mouth, and to write few papers. This practice reversed the old custom of American diplomacy, but reached results more rapidly. His name is attached to no state papers such as fill the records of Jefferson, J. Q. Adams, or Webster and Marcy; it is attached only to the results. . . ."[30]

Though willing to write it, Adams required that Mrs. Hay print the introductory biography without the slightest indication of its authorship and even without a heading. The provisos reflected Adams's tendency to self-effacement. Yet equally the biography reflected a tendency to self-assertion. Its paragraphs about Hay's work as secretary of state displayed knowledge of a kind that could have been acquired only by a sharer of the work.[31] Sooner or later, it would be noticed that a *co-secretary* must have written them.[32] When that happened, the hunt for Hay's anonymous biographer would have to proceed no farther than from Hay's door on 16th Street around the corner to Adams's on H Street. Really the biography was signed without a signature.[33]

During the autumn of 1907, William James learned that Adams had written a book called *The Education of Henry Adams.* James wrote to him requesting a copy. On December 9, while sending it, Adams asked its return and said, "I have so few copies that the people whose names are trifled with [James being one], have become more numerous than the copies." He remarked that his book was a portrait painted by John Singer Sargent. Trenchantly, he explained, "I am not there."

A correspondence followed. Writing on February 17, 1908, Adams inquired whether James had read "the Confessions of St[.] Augustine, or of Cardinal de Retz, or of Rousseau, or of Benvenuto Cellini, or even of my dear Gibbon." He offered the opinion that the earliest of the books was the best. ". . . I think St[.] Augustine alone has . . . a notion of writing a story with an end and object, not for the sake of the object, but for the form, like a romance." The implication was that Adams's book too was a romance; that his book told a story of heroic adventure that was given form by an "end" or "object."

James liked *The Education* enough to ask also for *Mont Saint Michel and Chartres.*[34] Adams claimed bankruptcy. "I have no more copies." He directed James to a copy he had sent to the Harvard library.[35]

Just then, Adams was reading a book by Owen Wister, *The Seven Ages of Washington: a Biography.* Like James, Wister lived in Cambridge. On March 20, Adams wrote Wister a letter thanking him for producing a fine biography of Washington and suggesting that it be doubled in size in a new version. He took occasion to add that, of the Americans of the eighteenth century, only two interested him greatly: Franklin and Washington. "They are a perpetual conundrum,—a wonder,—and their psychology passes my comprehension. Luckily Franklin has to a certain extent explained himself in that bit of autobiography which stands alone at the head of American literature. . . . Washington's breadth defies me, and his balance passes comparison."

When replying on March 27, Wister told Adams: "A day or two ago, William James showed me an autobiography you had sent him, of which I read chapters 12 and 13. I hope presently to be at the White House for a few days. May I then see this book, or—may I not?"

Adams immediately offered a copy, provided it be returned. Aware that Wister was much his junior, yet quick as always to place himself on a basis of equality with younger people, he confessed: "At seventy, I have become a student. . . . Unfortunately, I have not been able to find anyone in America, of late, who is willing to help me." He seemed almost to suggest that he and Wister collaborate.[36]

A few days later, a request for *The Education* arrived from James Laurence Laughlin, who had earned a doctorate in history at Harvard under Adams's supervision.[37] Adams offered a copy on condition it be returned. He at the same time disclosed the object—or one of the objects—that his book had been written to achieve. ". . . the pill is intended to show the necessity of purging education." ". . . our whole system of education is to be reconstructed . . . on some broad generalisation that will make it intelligible to the student; and I suggest that the department of history is the agent for doing it."[38]

Clara Hay notified Adams that she might come back from Thomasville during the week beginning March 16, 1908. He visited her after her return but during a long interval thereafter did not reappear at her door. She meanwhile was altering the manuscript of the memorial. On a Wednesday, possibly April 8 but more probably April 15, she sent him an altered manuscript together with a note telling what had happened: "You see I have suppressed all names. I thought it best, as it seems less personal."[39]

The memorial's full title was *Letters of John Hay and Extracts from Diary*. As printed, the materials would fill three volumes. The purpose of the volumes—stated by Adams metaphorically at the beginning of Volume I—was to erect a living statue of Hay by letting the reader view his available *personal* writings. These writings would suffice to "preserve the features and figure of the man as he moved or talked or showed himself to his friends and to society."[40]

Hay's diary entries were full of names. The following paragraph, written on April 19, 1861, a week after the outbreak of armed rebellion by the Confederacy, was typical.

> Wood came up to say that young Henry saw a steamer landing troops off Fort Washington. I told the President. Seward immediately drove to Scott's.

If permitted to see the paragraph as Hay wrote it, readers would have no trouble realizing that "the President" was Lincoln, "Seward" was the secretary of state, and "Scott's" was the headquarters of Winfield Scott, the highest ranking general in the Union army. But Mrs. Hay had altered the paragraph to read:

> W——— came up to say that young H——— saw a steamer landing troops off Fort Washington. I told the President. S—— immediately drove to S———'s.

As altered by Mrs. Hay for printing by Furst and Company, the paragraph could not be read at all. At a single stroke, or one may say by thousands of strokes, she had reduced her husband's personal writings to unparalleled gibberish.[41]

To confirm his being a permanent winter Washingtonian, Charles had built a house for himself at 1701 Massachusetts Avenue. He and his dependents arrived and occupied the house on March 7, 1908. Their living so near strengthened Henry's anxiety to be gone. He engaged space on the *St. Louis*, to sail for Cherbourg on April 25. Elisabeth Marbury would be a fellow passenger.

Henry wanted a contractor to install electric wiring and lights at 1603 H Street. Of his friends, one of those who had been hit hardest by the crash in the stock market was Elsie de Wolfe. She wished to stay in Washington for business reasons. Henry gave her free use of his house during his absence, and they agreed that she should redecorate all but one of the second-floor bedrooms in whatever manner seemed to her to be best. He would cheerfully pay the bills.

After reading it carefully once, Ford was reading *The Education* a second time. He wrote to Henry on April 9 and said it was "the most absorbingly interesting book I have met in two decades." ". . . such a character sketch as you give of Grant is worth all the biographies and autobiographies of the man. . . ." He detected a vein of "tragedy." Certain that Henry had written "a really great book," he wanted not to hurry through it, yet renewed his pledge to return the copy.

On April 10, because he would soon be leaving, Henry advised Ford and Wister to hold their copies of *The Education* till the coming winter. He happily accepted Ford's praise and named three writers—St. Augustine, Rousseau, and himself—as parts of a puzzle. He challenged Ford: ". . . do my favorite task! Read St[.] Augustine's Confessions; then read Rousseau's; then try to bring us [Augustine, Rousseau, and himself] together on one string. No Chinese puzzle is so amusing. No point in Darwinism is so vital."[42]

Frederic Bancroft wished to visit at 1603 H Street to get otherwise unobtainable information for a biography of Carl Schurz. Adams invited him to come any morning after 9:30. A fact of some importance to Adams was that, in January, Bancroft had been given a copy of *The Education.* The copy survives. It contains forty-four annotations by Bancroft. That Adams ever saw the annotations seems very doubtful. When they met in April, Bancroft may not yet have read the book.[43]

A week before Adams sailed, Mrs. Cameron left Washington to join Donald in Pennsylvania at the farm. The death of a relative obliged her to go briefly to New York. When she got back to the farm, she learned that Donald was going to Washington. She wanted to accompany him and get a last glimpse of Dor but decided to hold back. She sent him an explanation: ". . . I am trying so hard to please now that I dared not—or thought it unwise." As a safe alternative, she gave Dor some last instructions. "Tell Bessie [Marbury] that I put you into her hands—She won't like that!" "If the Brices are on your ship, make them take [i.e. rent] my apartment for three months. . . ."[44]

While Dor was crossing the ocean, Mrs. Cameron read in a newspaper that her sister Lida Hoyt had been struck by a hotel's revolving door in Richmond and had suffered a broken hip. She hurried to Richmond and immersed herself in Lida's problem, which was exceedingly serious. No other conveyance being workable, the invalid would have to be moved to her home on Long Island by yacht. Once there, she would be nursed as a victim of bone cancer. The disease had made her bones extremely easy to break.

In Paris on May 4, Adams dined alone at Paillard's at a table next to the table of an American capitalist, Peter Widener, and next day at the same restaurant he saw J. P. Morgan. He noticed that the banker, made acutely sensitive by his world-famous disfigured nose, avoided looking directly at other people.

By then, Adams had visited Edith Wharton, talked with Henry James, and agreed to lunch with William Dean Howells and James at Ambassador White's. He sent James a copy of *The Education*, requested that it be returned, and called the book a "shield of protection in the grave." "I advise you to take your life in the same way, in order to prevent biographers from taking it in theirs."[45]

Edith Wharton pressed Adams to join her and her dogs for dinner.[46] Mrs. Chanler and Laura arrived and wanted his company. Mrs. Jones and Beatrix were expected to arrive by the 26th. Adams meanwhile was seeing Lindsay. He wrote to Mrs. Cameron: "You and Martha may go hang, but Lindsay is the only satisfactory and sympathetic young man I know, and I only wish I were a girl and could marry him myself. I will try to marry him to Laura. . . ."[47]

The Calvin Brices wished to tour in their automobile with Adams as guide; and the Chanlers, Winty included, proposed to connect with the Brices and Adams by rail. The idea was to go north to churches in Normandy, west to Mont Saint Michel, and back to Chartres and Paris. The tour Adams designed included stops at a church at St. Pierre-sur-Dives and an abbey at Cerisy-la-Foret, which, he said, "complete my 12th century pilgrimages."

The Brices' party walked and boated around Mont Saint Michel, witnessed the famous tides, and spent a day inspecting the structures high above. At Chartres, Adams made a thorough re-study of the glass. Their adventure had a grim side. As always, baths were unobtainable in Normandy and Brittany. "But the weather was fine, and the automobiling perfect, and the apple-blossoms divine. . . ." He assured Mrs. Cameron from Paris, "Truly I am a new man!"[48]

He owed a letter to Niece Mabel. She was in Switzerland, slowly—very slowly—recovering from her breakdown. Of the Hooper nieces, she was the one who in face and figure strongly resembled Henry's wife. He did not baby her. She wanted a copy of *The Education*. He refused "because the Chartres is good enough for you." ". . . I don't carry a stack of volumes round on my back when I travel, and I have to refuse copies to everybody for that reason. . . . It is all nonsense. No one really reads either volume, as I can instantly see when they talk of it. They only play pretend like children, and ask for it because it is not for sale."[49]

Mrs. Cameron fired back at Dor for his remark about Martha's not marrying Lindsay. She replied on June 7 from Long Island: "Good Heavens, man, you do not suppose I am opposing Lindsay? On the contrary I wish Martha would marry him. So does she. But—Cameron like—she is resisting. . . . I can see her mind working. She is determined that she *wont* [sic],—and for the present she certainly wont [sic], but if she sees him again she will. There it all is in a nutshell."[50]

Loulie Hooper and Ward Thoron arrived in Paris on June 13. The trip they were to make with Adams would be long. While searching for an adequate automobile and a careful driver, he wrote to friends. On June 18, writing to Gaskell, he remarked about himself as an author, ". . . I think I have never written a chapter less than five times over, unless it were from sheer collapse." He spoke too about age and illness. "My little world at home is not in very good form. One's friends and connections are breaking down or dying in a rather promiscuous way, and I dread every fresh letter. There is more and more comfort in feeling oneself the oldest man alive. . . ."

Loulie, Thoron, and Uncle Henry left Paris roughly on June 26 and proceeded through Champagne and Bourgogne to Auvergne, hindered by only three flat tires. A circuit south and west took them to le Puy, Avignon, Montpellier, Narbonne, and Toulouse. At Bagnères-de-Bigorre in the Pyrenees, Loulie received an announcement that her sister Ellen had become engaged to John Briggs Potter. Among other things, the news meant that Ellen and Loulie would give up their house in Boston; that Loulie would lack a proper place to live; and that Uncle Henry could expect to see still more of her as a Washington visitor.

From Poitiers on July 17, Adams boasted to Mrs. Cameron that he and his companions had traveled 3,000 miles without discomfort. "I never have made so pleasant a trip, and have seen glass by acres." From Paris on the 20th, he added that Thoron had been "fussy but good-tempered" and Loulie "never irritated or irritating."

A letter to Adams was waiting in Paris from Edith Eustis, a neighbor on H Street. She put before him the possibility that both she and Mrs. Cameron would be absent from Lafayette Square during the coming winter. In reply, on July 23, he foresaw the possibility of his becoming a monument. "If you desert me on one side, and Mrs[.] Cameron on the other, I shall have nothing to contemplate but the vanishing Roosevelts opposite. If Mr[.] Bryan is elected President, I shall be left as a historical monument—such as the Washington Monument below—to overlook the past and present in equal isolation."[51]

In Boston, before leaving for Europe and the 3,000 mile journey, Loulie Hooper had lent Isabella Gardner her copy of *The Education*. Mrs. Gardner wrote to Adams about how she got the copy and about its dizzying effects. "I made her do it. . . . Every chapter [is] more interesting than the one before & at last all culminating in the 'Dynamic Theory of History' & the 'Law of Acceleration.'—It has set me whirling at such a rate that I am burning."[52]

Adams answered by assuring Mrs. Gardner that the book was "meant as experiment and not as conclusion." He said he was studying eight to ten hours a day. "I am more of a schoolboy at seventy than I was at seven. . . . The process is withering to self-esteem."[53]

When he told Niece Mabel that he did not carry copies of his books when traveling, Adams had told a fib. He had been equipped in Paris with his First Traveling Copy and at least three unmarked copies of *The Education*, one of which he had since lent to Henry James.[54] He had been studying science very intensively for the better part of a year. Signs of the labor could be found in the First Traveling Copy. In the margins, he had noted connections between passages in his book and pages in the following works by scientists other than Depéret. (He did not trouble to include needed accents in French words.)

> Oliver J. Lodge. *Modern View of Electricity.*
> Gustave Le Bon. *L'Evolution des Forces.*
> Henri Poincare. *La Science et l'Hypothese.*[55]

His marginal references would stand as evidence that he had kept the First Traveling Copy at hand in Paris and continued to write in it. They also were part of a pattern of evidence that one day he closed the copy, put it aside, and made a new beginning.[56] Taking up an unmarked copy he had with him, he treated it as another of his personal copies and started to enter annotations.

The copy he was starting to mark is best called his Second Traveling Copy. It survives. It contains ninety-two annotations—one in ink, the rest in pencil. All the annotations are in his handwriting, unhesitatingly written as if the results of mature reflection.[57]

His reasons for beginning afresh included a desire to put an end to the Wolcott/Willard confusion. On page 329 of the Second Traveling Copy, where "Wolcott Gibbs" first appeared, he drew a line through "Wolcott" and wrote "Willard" in the margin in large letters. For good measure, he deleted a "Wolcott" lower on page 329 and on page 394 a passage that said "Wolcott Gibbs" was "smothered by the usual conspiracy of silence."[58] The corrections would serve as reminders enough that when again in Washington he was to remove all the occurrences of "Wolcott" in the text of his Master Copy by deletion or by changes to "Willard."

Assuming that he later followed his instructions to himself and altered the Master Copy, one may say that *The Education* was so changed that the Gibbs confusion was entirely counteracted. If given in its changed form to a publisher, the book would be much improved. Readers would be spared not only an unneeded acquaintance with Wolcott Gibbs but also an unwarranted confession of ignorance by Adams which he might better never have thought, much less written on page 393 of his First Traveling Copy. For Adams had been the reverse of ignorant. He had burdened his heart and mind with feelings and information nearly to the limits of their capabilities.

At no small risk to himself, he every month was adding still more information. Evidences of his labor were annotations in the Second Traveling Copy. Opening the copy in a confident frame of mind, he skipped Chapters I–XIV as sufficiently improved. He read all the remaining chapters but concentrated on "Darwinism," "Twilight," "The Abyss of Ignorance," "Vis Inertiae," "The Grammar of Science," "The Dynamic Theory of History," and "A Law of Acceleration." As he read, he made fifty-one annotations that altered the text. More or less at the same time, he wrote forty-one marginal references linking *The Education* to the following works (again omitting needed accents):

Bouty. *La Verite Scientifique.* (8)
Bernard Brunhes. *La Degradation de l'Energie.* (2)
Deperet. *Transformations.* (1)
Duhem. *L'Evolution de la Mechanique.* (1)
[————]. *Life & Letters of Faraday.* (3)
Gaudry. *Essai de Palaeontologie Scientifique.* (2)
Rudolf Goldscheid. *Der Rich[t]erings und seine Bedeutung fur die Philosophie.* (1)
L. Houllevique. *Du Laboratoire a l'Usine.* (2)
Kelvin. *Jubilee Address.* (1)
Andre Lalande. *La Dissolution opposee a l'Evolution.* (2)
Gustave Le Bon. *L'Evolution des Forces.* (5)
Manville. *Les Decouvertes Moderne.* (1)
[Henri] Poincare. *La Science et l'Hypothese.* (1)
H. Poincare. *La Valeur de la Science.* (5)
Lucien Poincare. *L'Electricite.* (1)
Lucien Poincare. *La Physique Moderne.* (3)
J. Reinke. *Einleitung in die theoretische Biologie.* (1)
Roberti. *La Recherche de l'Unite.* (1)[59]

Reviewed in their totality, his marks in the Second Traveling Copy were signs that he was doing five things. He was making new improvements in *The Education*, including, as will be shown, one drastic improvement. He was studying a library of new, recent, and old books relating to science—the same library he had been studying when he closed his First Traveling Copy. He was discovering connections between passages in the books and passages he had printed in *The Education*. He was copying the discovered passages on slips of paper for later insertion in his Master Copy. And he was developing ideas for a possible short, new, and rather experimental work which he described to Mrs. Cameron as "a supplementary chapter of my Education," to be written for America's historians.[60]

At home, the eastern states were simmering through a torrid summer. Long Island was plagued with humidity and mosquitoes. Smoke from western forest fires was floating across the country. Natural adversities seemed never to relent.

Desperate for relief, Mrs. Cameron left her sister Lida to her nurses and sped Martha and herself to the Masconomo, a hotel at Manchester on the Massachusetts North Shore at which Dor had visited her in 1890 before he left for the South Seas. She wrote to tell him, "Here I am on the old camping ground after all these years."[61]

In Paris, Dor was seeing Lindsay and saw fit to advise him—and then inform her—that Mrs. Cameron was at the end of her resources and would have to come abroad for a month, perhaps to St. Moritz. Mrs. Cameron did not agree. On August 20, she told Adams from Manchester: "There is no question of coming abroad. I must be near enough to meet a hasty summons." She added that Martha was horrified by the prospect of childbearing and terrified by the "immutability" of marriage.

A shakeup in England's diplomatic corps enabled Lindsay to secure reassignment to the Foreign Office in London. As before, Adams was studying works of science. He claimed to be as solitary "as a stray comet." He said he was being "absorbed, like radium." Yet he did not view modern scientists as having plumbed the depths of their subjects. It delighted him to learn that Lord Kelvin, when dying, confessed to having "failed to understand anything at all."[62]

Mrs. Cameron's Paris apartment had been sublet through the summer. She arranged to re-rent it through December for $300 a month on the assumption that Lida would be slow to die. The assumption proved mistaken. A summons came. She hurried back to Long Island and sent Dor instructions to wait "until my next bad news."[63]

A letter from Dor was en route to her from Paris. It said that no close male American friend of his remained alive. On that account, he was preparing to call himself "the last surviving historical monument of Washington."[64]

Sir George Trevelyan had told Ambassador Reid that Adams had written an extraordinary book called *The Education of Henry Adams* and that copies were difficult to obtain. Recently, Reid had gone to America. During his return voyage to England, he was astonished to find that a fellow passenger, a neighbor of Adams's in Washington, Miss Brice, had a copy of *The Education* with her. She lent it to him, and he hastily read it. Later, from Wrest Park, he wrote to Adams saying he would "like very much" to have a copy. "How I envy you the leisure (& the industry) making such work possible!"[65]

Adams sent a copy at once, accompanied with a remark, "My views on education are radically revolutionary, but no one cares." Parenthetically, he told Reid that the Hay memorial had grown to three volumes. He avoided revealing that Mrs. Hay had made the *Letters* unreadable by reducing the personal names to initials followed by dashes.[66] On September 13 in a new letter to Reid, he said he needed to live two more years, if only to give himself time to decide whether his *Education* and *Mont Saint Michel and Chartres* should be consigned to the flames.

The remark partly had a basis in fear. On September 15, Adams told Mrs. Cameron that earlier, in July, he had experienced a first lapse of memory. It had occurred just after he entered the shop of a Paris antique-dealer. ". . . I happened to go into Audrain's place to ask a question, and, to my consternation, my French tumbled out all in a heap. The words came without connection." Embarrassed, he rushed away. By the time he got back to 23 Avenue du Bois de Boulogne, he had recovered his command of French. He none the less described his experience as a "first warning." He mentioned, too, that Faraday—England's "greatest genius"—began to lose his memory when he was only in his forties.

The arrival of a copy of *The Education* emboldened Ambassador Reid to speak more frankly. On September 17, he assured Adams that the book should be revised, not burned. "It is sure to be permanent and permanently useful. . . ." Yet, he said, it seemed "unduly pessimistic—especially in its closing chapters."

As Adams knew, the book's pessimism (or optimism) was a matter of delicate balances that could be adjusted by making changes in chapter titles. As they stood, the titles were simple but suggestive. Some formed obvious groups. Five titles—"Boston," "Washington," "Berlin," "Rome," and "Chicago"—were names of dissimilar cities. Two others—"Dilettantism" and "Darwinism"—made a discordant pair. "The Height of Knowledge" and "The Abyss of Ignorance" paired two extremes.

Partly in reaction to Reid's belief that the book was pessimistic, Adams opened his Second Traveling Copy, turned to Chapter XXIX, cancelled the chapter-title "The Abyss of Ignorance" and in large letters in the upper margin wrote a new title: "A Kinetic Theory of History." The change destroyed a pair of titles—"The Height of Knowledge" and "The Abyss of Ignorance"—by deleting its latter half. Simultaneously it created a new pair of titles—"A Kinetic Theory of History" and "A Dynamic Theory of History." The titles in the new pair were the most provoking and instructive in the book.[67]

When Adams changed its title, Chapter XXIX already included the essentials of a kinetic theory of history; but he thought it necessary that the chapter speak more plainly, both by means of a new title and by means of changes in its text. On the second page of the chapter, he looked at a passage involving Pascal, deleted four words, inserted seven, and gave the passage the following form (the inserted words are underlined; the quotations are from Pascal):

... one of the greatest minds, between Descartes and Newton,—Pascal,—
saw the master-motor of man in *ennui*: <u>a sort of kinetic theory of
progress</u>:—"I have often said that all the troubles of man come from his
not knowing how to sit still." Mere restlessness forces action. "So passes the
whole of life."[68]

That done, Adams advanced four more pages and looked at a paragraph
that described the universe as an "ocean of colliding atoms." Seeing an
opening, he inserted a new sentence in the middle of the paragraph:
"This offered a kinetic theory of history, without clue or direction,
which might have suited Pascal."[69]

The importance of these changes in a single chapter could not have
been greater. Writing *The Education*, Adams had produced a very great
book that was hard to read. It may be doubted whether anyone by then
had read it as it deserved to be read. Its best readers—Whitelaw Reid
and William James being examples—had tried to make reading easy for
themselves by seizing on one or another of the book's suggestions as if
the one suggestion were its only suggestion. Moreover, many readers,
being pessimists themselves (with or without knowing it), had fixed on
suggestions here and there in the book that they could hold up as evidence that *Adams* was pessimistic.

Until Adams drastically changed it, *The Education of Henry Adams*
could be alleged to be a book centering around one of its chapters, say
Chapter XXV, "The Dynamo and the Virgin." Similarly it could be alleged to espouse one theory: the one that readers could look to find in
Chapter XXXIII, "A Dynamic Theory of History." Somewhat plausibly,
the contents of the latter chapter could be alleged to be pessimistic.
Whitelaw Reid perhaps had leaned toward that opinion. But what would
future readers make of a book which in two slightly separated chapters
set forth both a "kinetic" theory of history and a "dynamic" theory of
history? The question was a mere beginning; for, if two theories were
emblazoned as findable in *The Education*, might not still other theories
be present in the book, lurking in its shadows, waiting to accost passing
readers when not expected?

Adams knew what was happening, and he had known what to do.
He had perfected his book. His changes in Chapter XXIX were so forceful that they promised to end all self-defeating easy readings and usher
in a time when readers of *The Education* would face the daunting fact
that the book sets forth a plethora of ideas and theories. At that point,
readers would either read the book thoroughly or avoid it.[70]

Lida Hoyt died on September 15, 1908. Mrs. Cameron attended the
funeral at Cleveland and went to the farm in Pennsylvania. Writing to
Dor on the 22nd, she justifiably reported, "It has been a disastrous summer in almost every way."

Writing on the same day, September 22, Adams informed her that on the 23rd, unless he learned from her by cable that she and Martha were coming to Paris, he would engage space on the *Kaiser Wilhelm II*, to sail from Cherbourg on October 28. He added that at Versailles he had encountered insupportable, intelligent Berenson. Also he said his momentary concern was having come upon a formula devised by Willard Gibbs. "I wish I knew what it means."

A fraction of Adams's time had recently been lost to dealings with idle members of America's richest, most privileged class, its "good society." Their center of activity was the Ritz on the Place Vendôme. On September 27, he assured Gaskell that he was ready to see his rich acquaintances impoverished and that always when going to the Ritz he wanted to carry a bomb. "Socialism may come when it pleases; it cannot be a greater bore than what it will sweep away. Nor can it be sillier, though it may be shabbier."

Had Donald not been trying to sell it, Mrs. Cameron would have returned to 21 Lafayette Square and waited there for Adams. That course being barred, she thought her best alternative was to take Martha to Europe for a two-month stay. She learned that Frederic and Florence Keep were coming home on the *Kaiser Wilhelm II*. She knew that the Keeps had a Paris apartment. Accordingly on September 27, she asked Dor to approach Mrs. Keep and ask whether she could occupy it.

Dor was studying French physics books that had much to say about Willard Gibbs.[71] On September 29, he told her his work had a result. "I have run my head hard up against a form of mathematics that grinds my brains out. . . . It is called the Law of Phases, and was invented at Yale. No one shall persuade me that I am not a Phase."

Mrs. Cameron reserved space on the *Adriatic*. She cabled to Dor on October 2, saying she and Martha would arrive on the 15th. By letter on the same day, she added, "We shall return here about Dec. 1st, and of *course* you must wait over for us, won't you?" Her assumption could not have been clearer. She supposed that she, Dor, and Martha would shortly be coming back to America together, possibly on the *St. Louis*.

A presidential election was in the making. The perpetual candidate of the Democrats, William Jennings Bryan, was about to lose to a Republican from Ohio, William Howard Taft. For Adams, the thought of a Taft administration was dismal. He had already lamented to Mrs. Chanler, ". . . the Titanic Theodore will go to somewhere, and that awful White House will look at me with its changed eyes."[72]

Florence Keep was delighted to provide Mrs. Cameron her apartment and only required that she accept it as a gift and retain the maid.[73] Mrs. Cameron and Martha appeared in Paris on October 15. The stage seemed set for an enactment of the mother's clearly-stated assumption.

Rather amazingly, her assumption proved mistaken. Dor had not been tentative about engaging space on the *Kaiser Wilhelm*. He had said he would engage it if not stopped in time by a cable, and no cable had come to him in the stated time.

Five days before his steamer was to leave, he informed Gaskell that he was going home to attend Roosevelt's "funeral services." "I have worked, too, like a dog; that is, with naps at frequent intervals. . . . It is no joke. The formulas of physics and chemistry today are in a different mental horizon from those of our day. Even mathematics talk a different language."

That Dor would start for home thirteen days after Mrs. Cameron and Martha arrived from home could seem an outrage. What had they come to Paris for, if not to see him and keep him company? And what were they to do in Paris after he left?

His answers to these questions did not appear in such letters as he currently was writing, but the questions had an answer. Lindsay had arrived from London. By leaving mother and daughter in Paris, Dor was settling the question of Martha's future. The time had come for her to accept or reject her English suitor.

Dor meanwhile would sail, bearing his First and Second Traveling Copies. His objects were evident. He intended to transpose the final improvements of *The Education* to his Master Copy. Simultaneously he would draft its "supplementary chapter." Thanks to a long interval of study, he would be able to begin the new work with correct statements about an American physicist, a Yale professor named Willard Gibbs.

17

UNSATISFACTORY WORKS

The *Kaiser Wilhelm II* carried Adams to New York by Election Day, November 3, 1908, in time to permit his witnessing Taft's victory. How the future president's administration would affect Adams depended mainly on the choice of a secretary of state. Ambassador White had returned from France, evidently to seek the appointment. He wrote to Adams on November 5, asking shelter at 1603 H Street.

When he arrived at his house on November 8, Adams found it illuminated with electric lights, as wished. Elsie de Wolfe had decorated three second-floor bedrooms in a luxurious modern style at odds with H. H. Richardson's interior architecture. Ambassador White would be the first visitor, or one of the first, to see the rooms.

The printing of Hay's *Letters* was nearly completed. Mrs. Hay gave Adams proofs of the biographical sketch, and he corrected and returned them. He wished to treat the project as solely hers. Yet he told her that its interest for him was great, even "excessive."[1]

In Paris, Lindsay had joined Martha and Mrs. Cameron every evening for dinner at the Keeps' apartment. He appeared as usual on October 31, and Martha snubbed him. Her suitor and her mother united in rebellion. In Mrs. Cameron's words: "The two worms turned and told her what they thought. She suddenly turned round and told him she would marry him." "I never saw such a sudden change."[2]

Adams sent Martha congratulations on her choice of a husband but soon wrote to Mrs. Cameron, ". . . I was thinking not so much of them as of you—or us."[3] It was understood that the mother again would permanently lose the house at 21 Lafayette Square when her daughter married. The prospect alarmed her. She wrote to Adams from Paris on November 15, "I dare not think of the future." She added from London on November 23: "You will have a hard load to carry this winter if you mean to carry me. I didn't think I would take it so hard."

Martha, Lindsay, and Mrs. Cameron made and cancelled a series of plans that presupposed a long engagement. Lindsay informed Adams on November 27, "The latest bright idea is that I come to America with them. . . ." The party would be arriving on the *Philadelphia*, due in New York on December 12. Lindsay hoped Adams would give him a room.

George Cabot Lodge had written and published *Herakles*, a 272-page neo-Sophoclean poetic drama with a large cast, including Prometheus. He put a copy into Adams's hands for approval. The work was a literary dead weight. Its many characters, beginning in Thebes and ending on a mountain in the Caucasus, failed to do or say anything which even very patient readers would be likely to think commendable for interest, sense, or feeling.

For Adams, disapproval was out of the question. He remained on terms of warm affection with Bay's mother; he had found a new close friend in Bay's wife; and as Uncle Henry he was locked into a relation with Bay himself that made Bay the not-to-be-criticized disciple and the uncle a revered master.

Adams read *Herakles* sufficiently to know what he should say. On December 2, 1908, he sent Bay a note stating that his drama was admirable for its "character-drawing," especially of Creon, and its "form," perhaps meaning its division into twelve scenes.[4] As further support, Adams bought copies and ordered that they be sent to a list of persons as gifts from himself.[5] By instructing Mrs. Jones to *read* her copy, he drew from her a compliment about the work which Bay was delighted to see.[6] And in a letter timed to greet Mrs. Cameron in New York, he said *Herakles* was "a very fine thing indeed, which no one in America will ever know enough to admire."[7]

Henry White had meanwhile come and gone without its being indicated that Taft might want him as secretary of state. Adams's current guests were Brooks and Evelyn, making their usual December visit. Brooks again needed assistance in producing a book. He was finishing a biography of John Quincy Adams, to match Charles's *Charles Francis Adams*. He had advised Henry in November, ". . . I will send you the chapters as they are copied and you can revise them for me." He explained that Charles and Mary had stakes in his venture. ". . . it is a job in which we all are interested[,] and you are the only one of us to whom I should care to submit a volume of this kind."[8]

Henry replied that he could not offer much help and did not have long to live. "I am making every effort to hang out two years more, for purposes of my own. . . ."[9] But Brooks was too self-centered to heed Henry's plea. During his and Evelyn's visit, he continued to assume that Henry would revise his chapters. Henry kept silent and did not name the purposes of his own that he had in mind.

Sometimes when alone in the evening, Henry entertained himself by playing unusual forms of solitaire. He especially enjoyed a monstrous variation called Napoleon at St. Helena. He described it to Niece Mabel by saying, ". . . two packs, ten cards on a row, four rows, and build on aces as you get them."[10]

Late in 1908, Americans took up jig-saw puzzles, an innovation promoted by Parker, a manufacturer of games. Not a person to miss out on a craze, Henry became a doer of jig-saw puzzles, with the secret addition that he was *writing* what he later called "a sort of jig-saw puzzle."[11] He had accumulated its pieces partly by copying and, where needed, translating extracts from published works. Most of the pieces related to science, some to history, a few to philosophy. He meant to arrange the pieces in each other's proximity with the help of explanatory passages, as if they might fit. The resulting puzzle might serve as the wanted "supplementary chapter" of his *Education.*[12]

Brooks and Evelyn left on December 13 in time for Lindsay to move in. For a week in two houses on the Square, Lindsay, Martha, Dor, and Mrs. Cameron experienced a sort of close association the eventual object of which would be a wedding, to occur in Europe in April. During the week, Dor was sometimes free to work. When it ended, Lindsay began a return voyage to London. It was agreed that Dor would accompany mother and daughter to Europe in March, to help chaperone Martha on the way to her wedding.

Adams and John Franklin Jameson were ex-presidents of the American Historical Association who lived in Washington. Being the editor of the *American Historical Review,* Jameson could appeal to experts everywhere in the country for assistance relating directly or indirectly to history. Similarly he could impose on Adams to offer meals to visiting historians. Thus it was not unusual that, on December 14, 1908, Adams asked Jameson to find "a young physico-chemist" to help him in relation to science and that, soon after, Jameson arranged that seven historians be regaled at Adams's dinner table on December 29.[13] As it happened, a physico-chemist could not be found, but Adams truly wanted one, and Jameson might have to try again.

Worthington Ford had returned his borrowed copy of *The Education.* After long delays, he agreed to leave the Library of Congress, move to Boston-Cambridge, and serve at the Massachusetts Historical Society as editor of publications. A project in need of his talents would be an edition of the writings of John Quincy Adams. Before departing, he arranged that Henry Adams join him for lunch.[14] A topic sure to come up when they met was Adams's edition of a parallel work, *The Writings of Albert Gallatin,* published thirty years earlier.

In a letter to Mrs. Jones on January 11, 1909, Adams said he was doing jig-saw puzzles. "I do puzzles daily. . . ." He apparently was both doing puzzles and writing his puzzler of a supplementary chapter.

Furst and Company had finished printing the *Letters of John Hay*, and Mrs. Hay had ordered the distribution of sets to a list of recipients. Events took a new turn. On January 16, 1909, writing from Cleveland, she advised Adams that Houghton Mifflin Company wished to publish a biography of her husband in the *American Statesmen Series* and needed help in finding an author. She thought Theodore Roosevelt might serve; she thought Senator Lodge might serve even better; and she reported that she was encountering "a good deal of criticism for leaving out names" in the *Letters* and not including an index. In self-defense, she protested pitiably, ". . . as there were some names I could not leave in [,] I think it best to leave them all out." ". . . of course when [the book] . . . is given to the public [,] I can put in the Historical names and then have an Index."[15]

Adams received Hay's *Letters*. He differed from other recipients in having access to the diary entries and many of the letters used in creating the book. So assisted, he began to write suppressed names into the margins of the volumes. This labor exacted perseverance in large amounts. By the time he reached the end of Volume III, he had inserted more than 2,100 names.[16] On January 21, he informed Mrs. Jones that he would let her read the *Letters* "with the names filled in." Yet thousands of blanks remained unexplained. There had been limits to what he could do.[17]

As he thought about it, the difference between what the memorial to Hay might have been and what it had become preyed on Adams's mind. He told Mrs. Jones on the 25th that he had intended the volumes to be a "thing unknown" in American literature: an "example of table-talk"—"grave and gay, frivolous and solemn, quick and unaffected, unconscious, witty, and altogether unlike the commonplace." "The result is what pleased God."

Henry was willing but not eager to read Brooks's attempted biography of John Quincy Adams. On January 29, 1909, he wrote to his hapless brother, "The sooner you send me your MS. the better." A typist had copied the drafts of such chapters as Brooks had written. The completed portion arrived at 1603 H Street on February 3. Without waiting to open the package, Henry sent Brooks a very large dollop of praise. "With your knowledge, your vigorous thought, and your energetic style, you cannot fail to make a great book."

Henry wanted Brooks's reaction to the new chapter he himself had drafted. He announced that a package would be coming to Boston. "In return, I send you my last plaything. . . ." He said his paper was "a study on the lines of my last two volumes."[18]

For Brooks, being trusted by Henry with a manuscript and asked for an opinion was an experience to be valued in proportion to its rarity. He opened Henry's package and found a 107-page manuscript written in a large form of Henry's beautifully legible handwriting, spaced to put roughly a hundred words on a page. The paper was dated at the end, "Washington./ January 1, 1909."[19] It bore a two-line title:

The Rule of Phase
applied to History

In American speech, "rule" and "law" were synonyms. Thus Henry's title comported with the title of the book believed to be Brooks's best, *The Law of Civilization and Decay*. It also chimed with titles Brooks had seen in *The Education of Henry Adams*: "A Dynamic Theory of History" and "A Law of Acceleration." So Brooks could assure himself that he and Henry were thinking identical thoughts.

On February 8, he informed Henry that his paper had come and he was "reading it slowly." He assumed Henry wished "to try an experiment to see if I understand." "My chief difficulty in forming an intelligent opinion is my ignorance of all your scientific postulates." He was a lawyer and writer to whom science was alien ground.

The younger brother did not know it, but a much greater difficulty hindered his efforts to read Henry's paper. Brooks was deficient in humor. Since his breakdown in the 1880s, he had kept going in life by being serious at all times. Henry, in contrast, was the most humorous Adams on record. His humor could show itself in protean forms and was not always easy to catch.

Brooks's letter of February 8 reminded Henry that humorless Brooks would not sense amusement unless told at least twice that it was under his nose. Patiently on February 10, Henry repeated: "The paper is a mere intellectual plaything, like a puzzle. It is not to be taken too seriously."

Meanwhile, without assistance, Brooks had seen that Henry's paper was inherently "incomprehensible." He reported this discovery on the 10th, telling Henry, ". . . I mean incomprehensible as treating thought as a substance." Setting aside this supposed limitation, and setting aside all that Henry said in his paper about science, Brooks moved forward to what he thought most important, saying, ". . . when you come to conclusions, I have little question that, in substance, you are right." Brooks took the paper to say that humanity resembled a fast-speeding comet after it entered the solar system. Doom was imminent. "We must burn as the comet burns when it nears the sun."

Brooks's sentence was a measure of his complete inability to read what Henry had sent him. Henry's paper said no such thing. True, the elder brother had brought a comet into "The Rule of Phase applied to History." Yet his paper said the comet turned 180° around the sun and sped away *unharmed* along a line in space parallel to the line on which it arrived. The two comets—the unharmed one Henry put into his puzzle and the burned one Brooks imaginatively read into the puzzle—were in keeping with the brothers' psychologies. Henry's was normal but unusually resilient. Brooks's had become abnormal and very dire.[20]

Some readers are drawn most unresistingly to writings they cannot understand. Brooks read Henry's paper again. On February 15, he wrote to tell him, ". . . I am so impressed by it that I have taken the liberty of having it copied for my own use. . . ." He said the typed copy would be finished in "a couple of days" and the manuscript would be returned to Washington promptly.

The copy was made. It was a 32-page double-spaced document titled "THE RULE OF PHASE APPLIED TO HISTORY."[21] What use Brooks might have for it was unclear. He had long been possessive of Henry's ideas, time, even properties.[22] He possibly began by feeling that he had to have a copy of Henry's paper merely in order to have it.

The man President-elect Taft chose to be secretary of state was Philander Knox, a former senator from Pennsylvania and U. S. attorney general who was an utter neophyte in foreign affairs. Adams wrote to Mrs. Jones: "Our dear Taft has begun by being ridiculous. The muddle in our State Department is a fatal beginning."[23]

A letter came from Reid about Hay's mutilated *Letters.* Reid complimented Adams for his "perfect" biographical sketch at the start of Volume I. He praised Adams for "the tact and skill and affectionate fidelity with which you have completed the whole big undertaking." He regretted the suppression of names and said, "I don't believe you like it any better than I do. . . ." Yet he doubted whether Adams could realize how "blind the omission of names makes the volumes."[24]

Following Lindsay's departure, Martha had lapsed into illness and irresolution. Word of the change reached her fiancé. Showing a decisiveness that Adams might admire, Lindsay informed his former host that he was coming back to Washington to "assume charge." When the news reached Adams, Lindsay's newest ship had already sailed.[25]

Adams looked afresh at Volumes II and III of the Hay *Letters* and saw that Mrs. Hay had excluded some letters that he and Reid at Wrest Park had decided were usable. It greatly embarrassed Adams that he had wasted Reid's time. On February 15, 1909, he wrote to the ambassador to report that Mrs. Hay had not told him "of her decision to omit certain letters, especially yours." He noted that he and Mrs. Hay had fallen silent about the memorial. ". . . with Mrs[.] Hay I have had no talk whatever, except to suggest that it would be easy to print a Key containing the suppressed names."

Adams meanwhile was being vexed by other Adamses. Charles was at his house a short walk away at 1701 Massachusetts Avenue. Brooks's biography of John Quincy Adams was ill-written, and within the biography the grandfather was doing things that such a grandson as Henry could review only at the cost of disturbance. In a long letter on February 17, he told Brooks he was suffering "nauseous indigestion of American history, which now makes me physically sick, so that only by self-compulsion can I read its dreary details." "Your picture of our wonderful grandpapa is a psychologic nightmare. . . ."

To Henry's way of thinking, J. Q. Adams had done himself immense harm by keeping a diary and by trying to improve other people by being didactic. For once, Henry compared their forebear and himself to his own advantage. "Thank God, I have done little preaching in my life. I have tried to tell stories, and sometimes to found them on a carefully concealed foundation of idea; but I trust I have never tried expressly to improve my fellow-insects. Senile as I am, I still hope I may cling to that salvation."

That Brooks had asked a typist to copy "The Rule of Phase applied to History" may have irritated Henry. Brooks's misreading the paper may have irritated him even more. In his long letter, Henry turned to the matter of his paper and made some statements obviously charged with feeling. He spoke about his new work in the past tense, as if it had died. ". . . you may do what you like with the paper I sent you, which was, in my point of view, only a sort of jig-saw puzzle, put together to see whether the pieces could be made to fit. Too well I knew the inadequacy of the public mind, to let me imagine that anyone could derive amusement from such trifles."[26]

Henry's assertion that he had never tried expressly to improve other people was at odds with his recent behavior. He had continued to feel that he should communicate with his fellow American historians. He was considering a plan to print copies of *The Education* as improved, send the copies with an introductory letter to selected professors of history, and shortly send the professors "The Rule of Phase applied to History," again with an introductory letter—all this with a view to challenging them to turn the country's universities into centers for the study of the history, or evolution, of ideas.

One way to find out that a plan was bad was to go a few distances toward trying it. To prepare for the printing of improved copies of *The Education*, Henry would have to transfer to a clean copy all the corrections and improvements accumulated in his Master Copy, which he described as "now wholly defaced by notes."[27] He had put off this labor while drafting "The Rule of Phase applied to History." He continued to put it off. He however drafted the letter needed to introduce the supplementary chapter to the professors.[28] Made up of eleven paragraphs, ten of which were long and detailed, the letter had a defect. Its contents and those of "The Rule of Phase applied to History" were over-duplicative.

An excellent judge of his own writings and a good judge of his own plans and actions, Henry could not have been long in seeing that his latest plan was ill-conceived. Three faults were obvious. Sending history teachers an improved form of *The Education* would be an abuse of the book, which was addressed to young men and well-adapted to their needs but ill-adapted to absorption by professors. Sending a book plus a supplementary chapter plus an introductory letter would place excessive demands on the professors' time. And sending "The Rule of Phase applied to History" had become impossible. The paper was a mere draft to which Henry had begun to see objections.

As promised, Brooks returned the manuscript of Henry's puzzle. Henry read it and began to write. By condensing and making improvements, including a changed ending, he created a second version of "The Rule of Phase applied to History" very different from and much better than the version he had earlier written.[29] Not that he had done all he needed to do: on the contrary, by patiently writing one thing after another, he was slowly groping and feeling his way. The direction in which he was moving was toward persuading the history teachers with a compact single instrument, a perfect work. That the second version of "The Rule of Phase applied to History" could not be the needed instrument was perhaps already evident, but it had beauties as compared with the first, and by writing it Henry had advanced long strides towards being able to design the instrument he sensed was possible: a small book that could be mailed to historians out of the blue and have very instructive effects.

During the first week of March 1908, Henry reached such a point in his work that he no longer needed certain papers. He could have put them in the trash. He instead made a package of the manuscript of the first version of "The Rule of Phase applied to History," the letter drafted to introduce the first version, and some pages of notes.[30] He took the package to Bay Lodge's house and told Bay he would value an opinion of the contents. Before leaving, he said Bay could keep or return the material, as he pleased.

Bay read the materials and saw that Uncle Henry had brought all terrestrial events from the earliest evidences of living beings to the present within a seven-phase formulation. He saw too that Uncle Henry wished to foment a re-orientation of America's universities by their history departments. In an undated letter apparently mailed on March 7, Bay responded with headlong enthusiasm. He said: "It's wonderful— and tremendous. The image is so big, so coherent, so comprehensive & clear & supremely convenient that I don't see how possibly the mind can do—to any purpose—without it, and what university education might do with it, is amazing just to dream of."[31]

Bay had read the material twice but was finding that the more he looked into it, the more it gave him ideas. The thought occurred to him that he should have a copy made and give Uncle Henry the copy. He asked in his letter, "Would you mind?"[32] Adams answered that no copy was necessary. He replied on March 8: "Do what you please with the MS. I don't believe I shall ever want it. . . ."

During four weeks starting on February 18, 1909, Henry sent Brooks six letters and eighty-two pages of comments about his biography of John Quincy Adams. Henry's comments praised the book's strengths, isolated its weaknesses, and identified the best and worst qualities of their forebear. The pages all survive. They amount to a book. They can be read in part as a great writer's manual explaining how to write—and not write—a biography.[33]

In the letters and comments, perhaps assuming Brooks would discard them, Henry wrote with an outspokenness he usually permitted himself only in talk. Two of the subjects that concerned him were the best way to shape a biography of John Quincy Adams and the touchy matter of territorial acquisitions by the United States government. The following paragraph is Henry Adams's reaction to Brooks Adams's account of the country's history during the presidency of Thomas Jefferson (1801–1809). The succeeding passages need no introductions.

> I have written and rewritten this story with disgusting frequency—in Gallatin, in Randolph, in my History, in an Aaron Burr which I burned,—until the mere repetition of it has become nauseous. I have turned myself inside-out like an india-rubber ball to make a case for everybody, and especially for J. Q. A.[,] whose case is the weakest of the lot, at least for me to defend, because I am most interested in the defense.[34]

> The history of the United States contains two episodes that I cannot and will not defend. One is that of Florida; the other, that of California, or the Mexican War. . . . In my history I had to tell a part of the Florida story and

it gave me the vomit. The last part is blacker than the first. At least our grandfather had the decency there to admit that he was a robber, which is a little better than Jefferson's attempt to be a thief; while the later robbery of California combined every possible mixture of both elements.[35]

J. Q. A. deliberately acted as the tool of the slave oligarchy (especially about Florida), and never rebelled until the slave oligarchy contemptuously cut his throat. To me it is a story that beats the tragedies of Hamlet, Othello and Macbeth all together; but I can't tell it—no, not I![36]

The fact seems [to be] . . . that J. Q. A. in 1830 [i.e. a year after being president] found his whole life a sentimental folly,—a bitter absurdity,—and that he went on deliberately to make another [life], which was founded on opposite ideas. . . . I want to get the good of this situation. . . . As the drama presents itself to my mind, the climax is the tragic failure of the early life. . . . I should try to paint that as dark as possible. The conclusion would show how the failure was turned into triumph by reversing every method and practice of the past. The construction of the play ought to be developed wholly by his own words and action. My own art would consist only in concealing my own art and myself.[37]

. . . in these eighteen years [1830–1848], and by efforts not essentially different from those of the wicked, he did organize a personal party—much as his only clever antagonist, John Randolph had done,—founded on sectional antipathies, in direct contradiction to all his protests of patriotism, and devotion to Union[,] previous to the Presidency.[38]

The peculiar characteristic of the cotton-planter was to be a damn fool. The old man was terribly fond of showing up this trait, with his sort of grim, satirical and bitter humor . . . .[39]

The most fatal mistake the cotton-planters made was the Mexican War, which Polk invented . . . in order to annex California, as he told George Bancroft. . . . He [Polk] had got Texas already, without war, and the cotton-planters could do nothing with California, but Polk butted into that rascality . . . which went far to save us all, and to smash the southern domination. In opposing the Mexican war[,] we [the Adamses] did right on moral grounds, but, had we succeeded, we should probably have saved the cotton-planters, for a good while, from ruin[,] which was the certain consequence of their own grasping and violent temper.[40]

More or less as an appendix to these and similar passages, Henry digressed to speak of Theodore Roosevelt's acquisition of a site for the Panama Canal.

. . . any nation has a right to be its own judge of the act of war. The only defence I could ever set up for Roosevelt's seizure of Panama was as an act of war . . . excused only on the ground that Colombia had rendered any other step impossible. And of this act of war he [Roosevelt] was the necessary judge.[41]

The overall message of Henry's pages was that Brooks should finish and publish the biography without fail. Yet the detailed points Henry made, perhaps sharpened here and there to provoke Brooks into fighting back, were so assertive and unsparing that Brooks could take them as indicating that the biography was a failure.

Brooks had enjoyed trying to draft the book. He was learning that biographies were hard to perfect.[42] He would soon tell Ford that his manuscript needed complete reconstruction.[43]

Henry said nothing to Brooks or to Bay about a new version of "The Rule of Phase applied to History." On March 17, 1909, he wrote to Jameson, asking him to find a qualified critic willing to read on a paid basis a paper involving physics with a view to "correcting its errors, or pointing out its defects." He made clear to Jameson that the paper would not be offered for publication in the *American Historical Review*. He said Jameson could reveal or conceal its authorship, as he preferred. The great necessity was to get detailed criticism by an expert. "I hunger for annihilation by a competent hand."

Ahead of time, on March 18, Lindsay and Martha were married and left for a brief honeymoon in Virginia. The wedding took place with so little noise that no trace of it appears in Henry's letters. The victory of the groom was achieved at a price. He conceded that Martha should go to Switzerland during the coming summer to take a cure.

On March 20, in a second letter to Jameson, Henry said he would be sailing from New York on the *Adriatic* on the 30th, would not be back before November, and would not need his paper criticized before that time. He explained that his object in writing the paper was "to suggest a reform of the whole university system, grouping all knowledge as a historical stream . . . and drawing a line between the University and technology." The paper accordingly was "didactic."

Jameson agreed to seek a critic but interpolated a request of his own. He wanted the loan of a copy of *The Education*. When Adams's paper and book arrived, he saw that the paper, handwritten on 118 long pages, very few words to a page, was as legible as if it were printed. Its title appeared as two lines: "The Rule of Phase/ applied to History." It was undated and bore no indication of authorship.[44]

Dor, Mrs. Cameron, Lindsay, and Martha were to sail together on the *Adriatic*. During her last days in Washington, Mrs. Cameron broke down. What mainly hurt her was what had hurt her in 1897 when Donald rented 21 Lafayette Square for four years to the new vice president. She was losing her home. In 1897, she had insisted on going abroad while very ill. This time she would do the same.

Dor advised Mrs. Jones that Mrs. Cameron was prostrated and her weakness "makes it necessary that I should act as garde-malade in case she can sail." "The doctor says she can't, so I know she will."[45]

*   *   *

Clara Hay tried to use her set of her husband's *Letters* and became dissatisfied. She learned that Adams had written a great many names into the margins of his set of the volumes. Knowing he was leaving for Europe and would not need them, she borrowed his volumes in order to copy in their proper places all the names he had restored.[46] It may not have occurred to her that her predicament was absurd. Perhaps she felt the memorial was becoming a nuisance. The odds were increasing that she would never arrange its publication.

Adams had given Jameson the second version of "The Rule of Phase applied to History," but he had not rid himself of the problem that the new version had helped him try to solve: that of writing the perfect message to be sent to America's historians. He accordingly disembarked from the *Adriatic* at Liverpool in a restless state of mind. He and Mrs. Cameron accompanied Lindsay and Martha to London, parted with them, and went on. Martha being married, Dor and her mother could live by changed rules. They immediately went to Paris.

Writing on April 11, 1909, from 23 Avenue du Bois de Boulogne, Dor told Mrs. Chanler that he had arrived two days earlier. Writing to Bay Lodge on the 12th, he said Mrs. Cameron was in Paris, resting at her apartment, which for once had no sub-tenant. Ten days later, he advised Bay reassuringly, "Mrs. Cameron is slowly emerging from the Niobe state." He added, ". . . I have at last solved my world and got it down to a sharp point,—a new chapter, quite ultimate."

His phrase "a new chapter" did not refer to the second version of "The Rule of Phase applied to History." Instead it referred to a book that Adams had conceived and meant to write. By traveling a road he did not identify to Bay, he had found the idea he needed. As he envisioned it, the book would join *Mont Saint Michel and Chartres* and *The Education of Henry Adams* as the last of a series. It would have the form of a much-extended personal letter. It would be privately printed and would be titled *A Letter to American Teachers of History*.

The time was a good one for hard work. Mrs. Cameron was getting better. Interruptions by friends in Paris were few. Lindsay and Martha could be expected to take care of themselves for a time in London. Even bad news from 1603 H Street was undisturbing. On April 29, 1909, Maggie Wade had died of apoplexy. She and Adams had been expecting it. Her slight stroke two years earlier had given them warning, and they had good-naturedly agreed that death was very near for one or the other of them, if not both.

The only questions that remained were what, precisely, to say in the new book and why, precisely, to say it. These were interesting questions. The present chapter will set forth, not the answers, but the situation Adams occupied, both as an American historian anxious to awaken the other American historians, and as an American historian in conflict with the scientists and philosophers of Europe.

He had said, "I have tried to tell stories, and sometimes to found them on a carefully concealed foundation of idea. . . ."[47] The story he had most in mind was his *History of the United States*. Its volumes had been read by many Americans for what they told, but for all practical purposes the volumes had never been read for the sake of their "foundation of idea." Yet such a foundation inhabited the volumes. It was concealed only in the sense that readers had failed to see it. The place to find it was not somewhere in the volumes but everywhere, for it had the form of a vocabulary of explanatory terms woven ceaselessly into the narrative. The terms were the parts of a theory of history. People interested in Adams's ideas were free to look again at his *History* and see what his theory was.

For him, "history" was a word denoting two things: past actions of human beings, and study of those actions with the help of evidence and with the intention of writing stories believed by the historian to be true. It has to be added that Adams believed history to be both the greatest of the sciences and the greatest of the arts.

Now to his vocabulary—his theory. He believed that:

—human beings are always in situations;
—they have means;
—they are conscious and think;
—they have ideals (this term embraces ideas, hopes, wishes, intentions, plans, purposes, and especially visions);
—they act (history is purposive);
—they confront or encounter obstacles;
—they sometimes fail, sometimes succeed;
—it is their ideals that give them "the energy of success";[48]
—they may *conserve* by doing only what has been done before, in which case humanity stands still while time flies;
—they may *innovate* by trying to realize new purposes or visions;
—by acting to realize such purposes or visions, they transform themselves and evolve into new orders of human beings;
—the business of historians is to study these transformations—"the workings of human development";[49]
—oppositely, study of the repetition of human habits and routines is the business of statisticians;
—for the most part, human beings exist and act as peoples, races, or nations (the terms for Adams are interchangeable);
—human beings in large numbers can act even when not organized or when only ill-organized;
—a great innovation may be either a new ideal or a new means;
—great innovations can be effected by individuals, an instance being John Fitch and Robert Fulton's invention, the steamboat;
—the Americans, while effecting a great innovation, large-scale democratic self-government, became a new nation possessed of new attributes;[50]

—the ideals of nations (or individuals) differ, with the result that human action is replete with cross-purpose; chaos supervenes; wars recur;

—the cause of change in history is attraction; it lies not behind in anterior actions but ahead in attractive possibilities seen by the active-minded;

—action to realize *new* ideals can effect progress and improvement;

—progress can be slowed, halted, and stopped by obstacles; stasis may ensue;

—progress can be unmade and reversed Satanically, as in the case of Napoleon's reinstitution of slavery in the French West Indies;

—human beings originally depended on heroes for government; and the histories of earlier nations were appropriately dramatic;

—histories of democracies are appropriately scientific;

—democracies can be assisted by leaders but can succeed without them, as in the case of the Americans' resistance to the British army which in 1814, to its great cost, captured the city of Washington and burned the White House;

—in democratic self-government, human beings have reached an ultimate beyond which it is impossible to go; yet the potential benefits of democratic self-government may be unlimited;

—there are "laws of human progress" and these laws are "matter not for dogmatic faith, but for study";[51]

—the situations of human beings include their bodies and all that surrounds or penetrates their bodies, with the result that human beings are always in a relation of sorts with Nature;

—the historian does not intend to discover or explain natural processes, yet cannot escape them;

—scientific historians (the historians of democracy) share with natural scientists the problem of the unity of science;

—only scientific historians can hope to understand history in its later moments, discover its "system," and "fix its relations to the system of Nature."[52]

All the above ideas were developed by Adams in time to appear in his *History* (1888–1890). His subsequent works are evidences that he continued to believe his theory of history, yet became more and more careful not to state it baldly, and never to preach.[53] It will help if his subsequent works are briefly re-examined, one by one.

His *Memoirs of Arii Taimai* (1901)—first recognized in the United States as a work of "prodigious value" in 1909—is a tragic history of cross-purposes: the purpose of the English, who required the Tahitians to have a monarch, and the counter-purpose of the Tahitians, who from times beyond recall had maintained themselves in comparative peace and prosperity by living dividedly in districts and systematically thwarting attempts by any great chief or chiefess to assert dominance over all the districts.[54] Part of the tragedy is that proponents of an intelligent ancient system of government are overthrown by proponents of a degraded European system handed down from medieval times. Another part of the tragedy is non-comparable weapons: the long spears of the Tahitians versus the invisible flying bullets of the English.[55]

In his *Mont Saint Michel and Chartres* (1904), Adams invites young American women to visit the Christians of France and of Europe generally in the eleventh, twelfth, and thirteenth centuries and sense the unparalleled energy and inventiveness imparted to Christian believers by an ideal of eventually going to Heaven, most possibly through the grace of the Virgin, and of meanwhile getting to Heaven on earth by building and entering beautiful churches and constructing logical systems of scholastic science. The point of the women's visit is to acquire knowledge of the immense value of ideals.

In *The Education of Henry Adams* (1907), Adams invites young American men to endure a 440-page narrative and the company of the amiable but always inadequate, forever re-educated dumbell-genius who is the humbled hero of the tale. The "Henry Adams" told about is mostly a fiction. The ordeal undergone by the fictional Adams and the young men invited to go with him is real in the sense of being representative of what it costs to learn. Implicitly a moral is drawn. The secret of learning is never to be stopped by failures and mis-tries.

The narratives in *The Education* concern learning imposed, learning by accident, learning by drift, and learning by deliberate attempt. The "Henry Adams" in the book tries to acquire a credible theory of history and hits upon a new idea: that history is accelerating.[56] By itself, this one idea is a sufficient ground for paying serious attention to Henry Adams's writings. It happens also to provide a bridge to what he wrote next.

The first version of "The Rule of Phase applied to History" (completed at the latest at the end of January 1909) has the aspect of a jig-saw puzzle, as Adams said. It is easily his most bewildering composition.[57] Yet if attention is fixed on its most evident message, the paper becomes simplicity itself.[58] The paper re-expresses with heavy emphasis the idea that history is accelerating.[59]

The second version of "The Rule of Phase applied to History" (finished at the latest on March 23 or 24, 1909) has never been printed and for accidental reasons has gone unnoticed. Perhaps better than anything else in Adams's writings, it illustrates the difficulty for him—indeed the hardship—of being America's leading historian. The main evidence of hardship is his drawing heavily on his comic powers. The paper is hard to read. It seems *not* to be a jig-saw puzzle. Its pieces are not numerous.

Because it brings serious issues forward for exhibition, it has to be serious. Yet it cannot be serious. Once understood, it turns out to be a parody of a learned lecture—a parody of just the sort that might be sprung by an ingenious, straight-faced American historian if inclined to mail a paper to a list of wholly earnest American historians without advising them that what they receive may be funny.[60]

The parody is fifty-two paragraphs long. In the first ten paragraphs, it may seem that Adams is speaking. Or would it be better to say that no one is speaking? "Facts" step forward and speak for themselves. The opening sentences set the tone:

> In the years 1876–1878, when the science of Chemistry was complete on its old atomic foundations, Willard Gibbs, Professor of Mathematical Physics at Yale, published in the Transactions of the Connecticut Academy his famous memoir on the "Equilibrium of Heterogeneous Substances," which, when brought to the notice of the Dutch chemists ten years afterwards, became in their hands a means of greatly extending the science of Static Chemistry. The name of Willard Gibbs has become in consequence more famous in science than that of any other American since Benjamin Franklin, but his Rule of Phases [*sic*] was expressed in mathematical formulas so difficult as to defy translation into literary equivalents, while the sense in which he used the word Phase was technical and so unusual as to mislead ordinary readers and double their difficulty of comprehension.

The parody explains that ice, water, and water vapor, according to Gibbs, are "phases" of a single "substance." But in paragraphs 4–8, ending with the word "result," the parodist changes terms, speaks of "solutions," and presents the idea that material substances can be *dissolved* into semi-material and non-material substances.

The speedy result is that a "hierarchy" of substances is put onto the blackboard. At the bottom are material substances: solid, liquid, and gaseous. Higher are semi-material substances: electricity, magnetism, and conceivably "animal consciousness." Higher still is the Ether, newly accepted by science, "a concrete substance, gifted, like ideal matter, with ideal rigidity, and, like mind, with ideal elasticity." Highest are "Space" and "Thought—or Hyper-space."

The reader is next informed (paragraphs 9–10) that there must be "Direction." An appeal is made to an image or figure suggested by Rudolf Goldschied: that law, rule, form, and order are all merely direction "regarded as stationary, like a frozen waterfall."

These preliminaries being completed, "facts" step aside and attention is invited to the devisings of a future physicist who will suggest a theory of history attuned to the hierarchy of substances. Without bothering to collect or study evidence, the future physicist makes short work of history. Assisted by received opinion, the physicist posits that a phase of history began when Galileo displeased the Church by saying the earth moved around the sun.

He names this phase the mechanical. He agrees that a religious phase preceded the mechanical. He dates the start of the religious phase from the first appearance of human beings. An anterior phase of instinct affords room for the pre-human evolution of animals.

He attaches spans of years to his phases. The mechanical phase is allotted 300 years: 1600–1900 A.D. The religious phase is allotted the square of 300 years: i.e. the 90,000 years preceding 1600. The instinctive phase is allotted the square of 90,000, which is so many preceding years that the number, being equivalent to eternity, is not stated. (It is mentioned parodically that the instinctive phase is analogous to things solid, the religious to things liquid, and the mechanical to things gaseous.)

The arithmetic is pursued forward as well as back. An electric phase is calculated to begin in 1900 and to last no longer than the square root of 300, or 17.33 years, till the spring of 1918. Last comes the ethereal phase, which will close in 1923.[61]

These conclusions are spun out in paragraphs full of scientific language and sporting a formula:

$$\frac{gt^2}{2}$$

The physicist is resisted only at one point in his performance. In paragraph 17, a historian (dismissively described as "eighteenth-century"—is it Adams?) exclaims that the physicist's phases were first discovered by two *historians*, Turgot and Comte, and that "by prior right" historians own that field of inquiry. It is quickly said in reply that the historians did not intelligently pursue the inquiry that Turgot and Comte initiated and that the historians' field of inquiry has been yielded to the physicists by default.

What America's professors of history would have made of Adams's second version, had he printed it and sent it to them in 1909, can perhaps be imagined. A small number might have laughed. The great majority would have been baffled. That a comet rushes into Adams's paper and out again might have seemed funny to the amused but would afford small help to the baffled. Yet the professors could share one firm judgment: that turning history into physics was very wrong.

Adams did not need to be told that history cannot be physics. He had long believed it. Impatience with physical scientists had shown itself in the first version of "The Rule of Phase applied to History." Adams had ended his jig-saw puzzle with a list of important things by which the physicists were perplexed. One was "Force." Eight others were "Heat,

Light, Magnetism, Electricity, Gravitation, Attraction, Repulsion, Pressure."[62]

In the improved second version, Adams deletes this heavy charge and restricts himself to presenting the physicists as over-confident and facile. The means he uses to register this complaint is the one already described. He turns an imagined physicist loose in a field of historical events he knows almost nothing about but nimbly explains. The device is Swiftian reduction to absurdity.

The attacks on physicists that Adams built into the versions of "The Rule of Phase applied to History" were sure signs that neither version was usable! The reason was evident. His interest did not center in physicists. It centered in historians. What he needed was a means with which to move his fellow historians towards taking their rightful place in the intellectual world. He could use as his means something drawn from physics; he could lampoon the physicists; but his imperative necessity was to awaken the historians' sleepy minds. For such minds, a hierarchy of substances, together with an accelerating sequence of historical phases, was much too intricate and complex. He needed something very simple, the simpler the better.

This was the point Adams reached before leaving for Europe with Mrs. Cameron, Lindsay, and Martha on the *Adriatic.* By the time he arrived in Paris or soon after, he found what he wanted. He was helped to make his discovery by two things especially: worry about the prevalence of pessimism and work on "The Rule of Phase applied to History."

Wanting not to be an optimist of the foolish sort, he—like Hay—had practiced a sort of hard-headedness he honestly could speak of as pessimism. For serio-comic purposes, or for sheer amusement, he had prophesied nearer and nearer dates for the world to end, halt, or go into reverse.[63] (While so prophesying, he was deluged by his brother Brooks with pessimistic utterances on the wrong assumption that they were of the same mind.) And he *was* pessimistic in one respect: he believed that European socialism was a form of pessimism-in-action and believed it would gain a foothold in the United States to the country's bitter sorrow. Yet consistently his conduct was that of an optimist who was also an active—even a fighting—anti-pessimist.

Work on "The Rule of Phase applied to History" taught him to look again at an invention that had been haunting his thoughts for sixteen years, since 1893. The invention was Maxwell's demon, the imaginary creature capable of distinguishing faster-moving and slower-moving molecules and sorting them into separate receptacles. In the first version of his paper, Henry had mentioned Maxwell four times and spoke once of the demon. In the second version, he referred to Maxwell as the "greatest recent authority" in physics (paragraph 23), mentioned him five times, and again spoke of the demon.

This increase of attention to Maxwell went hand in hand with the emergence of another name. In paragraph 41 of the second version, Adams interjected the remark: "The nineteenth century historian has neither the training nor the inclination to imitate Kelvin's methods or Clerk Maxwell's vectors. . . ."

From this remark, Adams needed to take only one short mental step and he would think seriously for the first time about Lord Kelvin's second law of thermodynamics. By inventing his demon, Maxwell had implied that, if events are to have direction, *energy must be lost*. But Kelvin outdid him. He said his second law was universal: it admitted of no exceptions: *all things whatever run down.*

Earlier this aspect of modern physics had not strongly impressed itself on Adams. It did so in 1909 in Paris. On May 2, he wrote to Gaskell: "I've been studying science for ten years past, with keen interest, noting down my phases of mind each year. . . . The last—thermodynamics— fetches me out on sea-level. . . . I'm sorry Lord Kelvin is dead. I would travel a few thousand-million miles to discuss with him the thermodynamics of socialist society. His law is awful in its intensity and rigidity of results."

Adams was seldom more excited. He had put aside his books about Gibbs. He was reading books about Kelvin. He was undertaking—so he thought—a "last" intellectual effort. The key words were "down" and "sea-level." The change was that he could read European *physics* as pessimistic. This revolution freed him to write.

18

TO WORRY HISTORIANS

M artha came to Paris in quest of a tiara to wear when presented to Edward VII at court. Lindsay came and escorted her back to London. On May 12, 1909, Adams advised Mrs. Lodge that Martha was "anything but stalwart." Her mother was considerably better. "Mrs[.] Cameron has picked herself up, and does the Roman matron business now, with fine effect. I think she will get natural again in a few months, but where or how she is to live, the Lord may know."

Writing three days later to Thoron, Adams spoke in terms partly pleased, partly grim. He was eager to work on his new book. "Mrs[.] Cameron is sitting in her apartment, staring vacantly into the future. Martha is trying to last through a London season, or a part of it. Brides cluck on every curb-stone. Widows ask me to dine. I swim in an ocean of pessimistic science, and squawk."

Reading about Kelvin was easy, but reading his works would be very difficult. On June 6, Adams told Gaskell that Kelvin had begun his career in 1849 "by proving that the universe . . . was flattening steadily, and would in the end, flatten out to a dead level where nothing could live." The proofs were technical and mathematical. ". . . I want Kelvin's writings, but I know I can't read a page of them."

The latest sensations in Paris were Isadora Duncan and Diaghilev's ballet company. Adams saw the Russian dancers—unclothed—with Edith Wharton and again with Mrs. Cameron. He later saw Ida Rubinstein impersonate Cleopatra more or less naked. He did not object to such performances and may have been happy to attend them.

Martha was presented at court in early June. She came to Paris and left with her mother for medical consultation at Lausanne. Adams meanwhile was at work on his book. He assured Thoron on the 10th, "I have now almost got my doctrine of the universe worked out to a point. . . ." He added on the 14th, "I've solved the universe for the four and twentieth time. . . ."

Berenson was in Paris. He and Adams had become quite friendly.

Together they looked at paintings, and Adams used some of the time to study his companion. He wrote to Bancel La Farge on June 28: ". . . [I] have fallen into the clutch of Berenson, who eviscerates the world with a satanic sneer. As I never could sneer, I am only competent to admire him."

Martha's ailment was diagnosed as nervous dyspepsia, and the proposed remedy was a water cure at Lausanne. Lindsay would join her there for his vacation. Adams planned to go as well but knew he could not make an appearance in Switzerland without spending several days with Bancel La Farge, Mabel, and the children.

To complicate matters, Ward Thoron was coming to Paris in hopes that he and Adams could resume their summer touring by auto in search of old glass. Where Thoron came, Loulie Hooper was likely to arrive. Though less than lovers, he and she had become more than friends. She too would be expected by Mabel and her husband in Switzerland.

Sturgis Bigelow was traveling in Europe with John Lodge, Bay's younger brother. Bigelow became ill and settled in Paris at the Hôtel Brighton, waiting to mend. John acted as one of his nurses but saw enough of Uncle Henry to learn that he was at work on a book. He relayed the news to his relatives in Massachusetts. Bay reacted excitedly. He wrote to the admired uncle on July 16, "References in a letter of John's to your last & greatest chapter has kindled the desire that always smoulders within me to see both you & it. . . ."

Though Adams's associates were many, the persons who most concerned him were Mrs. Cameron and himself. He told her on July 20, "You are my only real worry and anxiety, but I am also on my own mind a little." Her momentary problem was insomnia. His was back trouble—a touch of lumbago. Their deeper problem had long since been solved. By being together when possible and by writing constantly when apart, they had become intimates unanxious about their intimacy. Ailments worried them. Their love for each other did not.

In a letter to Adams sent from New York on July 22, 1909, John La Farge mentioned "Miss Loulie" and said he had been hearing about "a charming young woman of the name of Tone." Adams would soon learn that Aileen Tone—a New Yorker and a Catholic, educated in Paris—had become Loulie's closest friend.

Adams wrote to Bay Lodge on July 26: "I ought to be in Switzerland . . . but Paris grips me. . . . Ward Thoron arrived yesterday, zealous to go automobiling for glass windows. In my advanced decrepitude[,] I seem to be the only available young man. . . ."

Touring for windows was impracticable. Brooks and Evelyn were in

Paris and had claims on Henry's attention. They eventually left, and a plan was sketched that Uncle Henry, Thoron, and Loulie should go to Switzerland by automobile and see churches along the way.

Time permitting, Adams worked on his book. He liked to think his luxurious apartment was an artist's garret. He advised Mrs. Cameron on August 4, ". . . I begin to find vast content in the peace and protection of my modest attic."

Loulie arrived on August 9, and next day she lunched with Uncle Henry and Thoron at Laurent's, one of Adams's favorite restaurants. They would be leaving for Switzerland on the 15th. In the interval, Adams would serve as "dancing-bear to Mrs[.] Roosevelt," who lately had arrived in Paris.[1]

Equipped with a suitable automobile and driver, the travelers left Paris as planned, stopped at Rheims, inspected the cathedral, and proceeded towards Germany. At Heidelberg, they learned that Mabel wished them to postpone their visit. In accordance with Mabel's wishes, they headed for Lausanne to join Mrs. Cameron and Martha. Practically at the instant of their arrival, a telegram came from Edith Wharton in Paris. It said Bay Lodge had died and John was hurrying to Massachusetts.[2] Because Bigelow was ill and John was leaving, Adams started immediately for Paris, taking Thoron with him. He reached his apartment on August 29. A waiting message from Ambassador White said that Bigelow was worse. A letter from Mrs. Cameron, newly sent from Lausanne, reported that Martha was still unwell.[3]

At the Hôtel Brighton, a professional nurse informed Adams that Bigelow was sedated with morphine and could not receive him. Adams called on Edith Wharton, who had worries of her own. "Then I sat half an hour with Mrs[.] Roosevelt, who was just as full of bad news as all the rest, but whose spirits could not be subdued."[4]

During the rush from Lausanne to Paris, Adams had considered the letters he would have to write to Bay's mother and widow. He wrote both on the night of his arrival. The one to Anna Lodge said things a mother would need to hear. "Bay was my last tie to active sympathy with men. He was the best and finest product of my time and hopes. . . . You have lived, and will continue to live, in him."

The letter to Elizabeth Lodge was important. Adams was capable of language that not only expressed ideas and feelings but created new situations. Bessy's loss of her husband had reminded him of the loss of his wife. He reacted by making intimates of Bessy and himself. ". . . your miseries so acutely recall my own, of times that I shudder to remember. . . ." ". . . if you are like me . . . you will turn from one mood to another without rest, and will want affection at one moment as violently as you want solitude at the next." ". . . [Bay] had no greater admirer than I, but, for the moment, I am thinking most of you, and of your constant goodness to me, and whether I have any means of returning it." "If I owe to him one thing that has been worth to me more than another, it is you."

George Cabot Lodge was killed by a heart attack while vacationing with his father on Tuckanuck, an islet near Martha's Vineyard. There had been warning signs, but the son's health had seemed good enough to make his death on August 21 a complete surprise.[5]

As news of the calamity spread, friends took the view that Adams was one of the heavy losers. Writing to him from Virginia on August 24, Edith Eustis exclaimed, ". . . you have had so much trouble that I can't bear to think, that more has come to you. . . ."

Within the circle of the Lodges' friends, it had become an article of faith that Bay was a literary genius.[6] Mrs. Eustis wrote to Bigelow urging that something commemorative be written at once. ". . . *you* must work *now*, you & Mr. Adams & his friends, to make the world realize what his great gifts were."[7]

If the loss of Bay Lodge had been an isolated blow, Adams might have felt it less oppressively. At intervals from boyhood to the present, he had suffered unexpected deprivations of male friends and allies. On August 30, he summarized the effect to Mrs. Cameron: "I am utterly demoralised, and . . . wish I was dead. . . ."

They would not always say so, but Bay's admirers had valued him less for his poems than for his ebullient spirits and openness to new ideas. Henry James wrote to Adams, ". . . I immensely liked him . . . & as it was mainly in your house I did see him[,] I think of you as wretchedly wounded and deprived. . . ." Evidently intending an unqualified compliment, James added, "I recall him as so intelligent & open & delightful—a great and abundant social luxury. . . ."[8]

The closing words could appear to say that such persons as Bay Lodge were superfluous. Adams read the words as dismissive. It certainly helped that in his letter James told Adams what he had felt when reading *The Education*. He said that he had experienced Adams's book as a drenching in "suggestion & recall & terrible thick evocation"—that he had been caught in it "even as an indiscreet fly in amber."[9] But Adams would not let pass what James had said about vanished Bay. He replied on September 3, 1909, ". . . I believe we are all now social luxuries." What Adams had in mind was a collection of dead moths and butterflies. "Nothing matters much! Only our proper labels! Please stick mine on, in your wonderfully perfect way, and I will sit quiet on the shelf, contented, among the rest."

* * *

Adams had made his life in Paris the reverse of his life in Washington. By not hiring a cook and not having a spare room for guests, he had assured himself ample hours of solitude and perfect freedom to work. In the present instance, work was a speedy restorative. On September 9, he wrote good-humoredly to Margaret Chanler: ". . . I have been amusing myself with a fable for instructors of history. I've a notion of printing a Letter to Professors. Pure malice! but History will die if not irritated. The only service I can do to my profession is to serve as a flea."

Because Maggie Wade had died and William Gray needed an interval of rest, 1603 H Street was defended only by locks and an electric burglar alarm. Had he felt free to do as he pleased, Adams would have made arrangements to spend the winter in London. He instead felt he should return to Washington and help Bay's mother and widow. He saw and took to heart the letter from Edith Eustis to Bigelow saying Bay should be memorialized. The memorial that most suggested itself was a collected edition of his writings. Adams advised Mrs. Eustis in September 12, "I have little doubt that the Lodges will attend to the literary part." He avoided telling her that there also would have to be a biography. The reason? He believed *he* should write it.

Mrs. Hay had collected more letters by her husband and had reconsidered the edition of *Letters* that Furst and Company had printed at her request. The edition seemed to her much too personal. She wrote to Adams, ". . . when I am ready to give the letters to the public[,] I will have quite a number of interesting [new] ones, and I will leave out the more personal ones that are in the present volumes."[10]

A spirit of an opposite sort had seized Bessy Lodge. She had not immediately understood the letter Adams had written to her about her loss. The thought occurred to her that she should read the letter a second time. She did so and learned that its subject was not her lost husband but herself. She responded on September 13 by writing to Adams, "I have been reading your letter over again & must tell you how grateful & touched I am by what you say—the way you realize that I am the one who needs the love. . . ."

Dor had been assembling material for his "Letter to Professors." On September 17, he reported to Mrs. Cameron that Berenson had called and flattered him. He added next day, ". . . I've finished all my reading and all my writing. . . ." He had not written the book. He had merely finished writing English translations of passages in French and German that he meant to quote in the book.

Berenson had called with an object in mind: again he wanted copies of Adams's privately printed books. Adams not only gave him copies of the *Memoirs of Arii Taimai, Mont Saint Michel and Chartres,* and *The Education of Henry Adams*; he also lent him a manuscript and asked him to read and criticize it.[11] Flattery for flattery, none might be more acceptable than asking a person for advice. The manuscript lent to Berenson was the second version of "The Rule of Phase applied to History." It had floated from Washington to Europe. Why it floated was a tale worth hearing.

After Adams asked him to find a physicist willing to criticize a manuscript for pay, Jameson had contacted three experts in succession: Professor Wilder D. Bancroft at Cornell University, Professor A. G. Webster at Clark University, and Dr. Edgar Buckingham at the Bureau of Standards. The results were meager. Bancroft eventually furnished a one-page letter ending, ". . . the general argument seems legitimate." Webster refused to see the paper. Buckingham required a typed copy of the manuscript. Jameson had one made and sent it to him, whereupon Buckingham set a price of two hundred dollars for any work he might do. Rather than pay a fee he thought inordinate, Jameson recovered the typed copy.[12] Since he could use the copy as the basis for new appeals, he returned Adams's original. It found its way to Paris and to 23 Avenue du Bois de Boulogne in time for Adams to thrust it into Berenson's hands and ask for a criticism.

Berenson read and returned it, but what he said to Adams about it is unknown. Within the next few days, they met as guests at a party outside of Paris. Adams described his reader as "a quivering aspen, pale, shrunken, and coughing, but more cerebral than ever."[13]

Then or soon after, Adams told Berenson he was still interested in physics but had redirected his attention from Gibbs's rule of phase to Kelvin's second law of thermodynamics.[14] In late September, he asked Berenson to dine with him and some other guests at Voisin's.[15] In a follow-up letter, he inquired whether Berenson could provide him information about an Italian professor of physics named Ciamician. He said too that he needed the help of an Englishman, if there were one, capable of "explaining" Kelvin's works.[16]

These appeals to Berenson were written just prior to a moment when Adams fully clarified his sense of his own position. He till then had been making an assumption that he should not publish anything about physics without getting the advice of at least one physicist. More recently, he had suffered annoyances. One was a failed effort to persuade Paris book dealers to supply him the volume of Kelvin's writings in which the second law was stated in the Englishman's own words. A second was being forced to read about Kelvin in the writings of other physicists. Suddenly the assumption about getting the advice of a physicist ceased to apply. Adams realized that, to write the book he wanted to write, he would not need to learn more physics. The amount he already knew was enough to permit his doing what he meant to do: benefit the historians in America by quoting the scientists of Europe to show the degree to which European scientific thinking had become aggressively pessimistic. This was a program he could carry out on his own responsibility.

His one problem was that he still lacked the direct quotation from Kelvin that would serve as the cornerstone of his book. He wrote to Berenson, saying Paris book dealers could not supply Volume I of Kelvin's *Collected Mathematical and Physical Papers*.[17] In response, Berenson recommended Quaritch's in London.[18] Thereupon Adams did what he might better have done at the beginning: he wrote for help to Ralph Palmer. Without delay, Palmer alerted a London dealer. On November 3, 1909, Hugh Reese, Ltd., sent Adams the Kelvin volume.[19] By then, it appears, Adams—the quintessential American—was rapidly putting together a book largely made up of quotations from Europeans.

Donald had sold his Washington house; Lindsay had secured a London house at 6A Cadogan Square; and Martha returned from Lausanne in a state of nerves. With furnishings salvaged from 21 Lafayette Square and brought to England, Mrs. Cameron helped her daughter and son-in-law establish themselves in comfort. The mother's feeling appeared to be that if she could not keep her cherished house in Washington, she at least could insure that her daughter had a pleasant house abroad.

Thoron had been managing Adams's Washington affairs. On October 11, 1909, Adams informed him that he wanted William Gray to stay in service at 1603 H Street and hire added servants as needed. Writing next day to Mrs. Cameron, Dor said, "Taft and Knox between them have destroyed diplomacy. . . ." This was Dor's way of saying that Taft and Knox had closed all avenues to his taking part in the country's foreign affairs. In the same letter, he said he had discussed with Edith Wharton an article she was planning about Bay. Brief, her article was intended for a New York magazine.

Mrs. Cameron wished to come to Paris. Because her apartment had been sublet, she asked Dor to get space for her at a hotel. He found rooms at the Hôtel Crillon and on October 20, 1909, when writing to her about them, inquired, "When am I to sail?" She arrived on the 24th, stayed a fortnight, and went to Lausanne with Martha, who needed to consult her doctor.

During their absence, Dor wrote again to the mother about ships. He said in passing, "I eat too much, and get no exercise."[20] The signs were clear. He was finishing his book.

He had the help of a servant, Alexandre. When mother and daughter returned to the Gare de Lyon on November 23, Alexandre met them with a note from Dor, arranging a meeting next day for their midday meal.

Lunch had a practical result. Mrs. Cameron and Dor agreed to sail together on the *Adriatic* on December 29.

Before retiring as ambassador to France, Henry White invited Adams to dinner with Sir Alfred Lyall, Georges Clemenceau, and Louis Lépine, the prefect of the Paris police. Writing afterwards to Gaskell, Adams said he had enjoyed a long chat with Sir Alfred and that the Frenchmen were "very amusing." The dinner found Adams still interested in politics. "All my friends are now being kicked out of power as hard as possible, and I make the most of them while they last."[21]

Adams had not receded from anarchism. He viewed his newest work as at least a firecracker, though not a bomb. He told Gaskell he was writing "a little book . . . which I mean to explode under my colleagues in history."[22] In his next letter to Gaskell, sent on November 28, 1909, he said, ". . . I am going to print a little volume as soon as I get home, wholly for the amusement of worrying my dear Universities and irritating my rival professors. . . ." His word "Universities" was not misplaced. He had decided to send his book to the presidents, as well as the history teachers, at America's many universities.

On December 5, he wrote to Jameson asking for a list of the names and addresses—"at my expense"—of all the university presidents and history teachers in the country. He guessed the list might extend to three or four hundred names. Should there be a thousand, he said, "so much the better."

Two weeks later, he crossed to London and joined Mrs. Cameron and the Lindsays for Christmas. To excuse his conduct, he told Brooks, "I adore fogs."[23] Evidently the fogs were noxious and much writing had strained his eyes, for he suffered an attack of conjunctivitis.

He wrote from London to Sir John Clark at Tillypronie. The sight of Adams's "matchless clear and stately hand" moved Sir John to urge his coming for a visit, but Adams was gripped by the idea that he and Mrs. Cameron were needed in Washington.[24] He had told her, ". . . we must go home and stir it up."[25]

They crossed on the *Adriatic*. On January 7, 1910, Dor was back at the Knickerbocker Club, and Mrs. Cameron—one assumes—was back at the Holland House. She was firm in wanting to see Donald. When Dor left for Washington on January 10, she stayed in New York and sent Donald messages that would force a response.

After a day at his house, Dor apprised her that the Taft administration was "worse than I feared." "Never have I seen such a débâcle since

Cleveland's second term." "Nothing can be done. The whole concern is dropping to pieces."[26]

She replied, "I cannot say that it is a surprise." Irony obtained. "... to break up a solid party in the space of eight months is something of an achievement, and our dear Taft has a happy three years ahead of him."[27] She had heard from Donald and was going to Florida. He had promised to meet her at the Hotel Windsor in Jacksonville.

Bessy Lodge had returned with her children to Massachusetts Avenue. An urgent note from her was waiting for Adams. She said, "I can't begin to tell you what it means to me to have you here."[28] He visited her and on January 13, 1910, reported to Mrs. Cameron, "... she had best see no one but those who do not get on her nerves. ..."

He himself had a nerves problem. Brooks and Evelyn had come for a two-day visit, and Henry was having to listen while his brother voiced a stream of black commentaries. "... all his previous Jeremiads are as light compared to his present gloom."

Edith Wharton had sent Bessy the manuscript of her article on Bay. Bessy lent it to Uncle Henry. He returned it to her on the 14th with a letter saying it was "very sympathetic and appreciative." The article would appear in *Scribner's Magazine* in February.

The important fact was that Bessy trusted Adams as she trusted no one else. She and he agreed that there had to be a biography. She had letters of Bay's to her that she would not show to anyone. If Adams would write the book, she would supply him copied extracts.

Donald joined Mrs. Cameron in Jacksonville, "beaming and pleasant as if he had not let nine months go by without a sign of life." He said he could stay three days, after which she should go to the Royal Poinciana in Palm Beach, while he went to Charleston on business.[29] On January 21 and 22, 1910, she advised Dor from Palm Beach, "I am to stay here till called for." "I have some books & some sewing, so I can kill time in some way, I suppose. But I keep wondering why I am here—"

Dor had carried secrecy to such extremes that Mrs. Cameron did not know he had written another book. He broke the news on January 24 by telling her: "I'm amusing myself by printing a little volume to make fun of my fellow historians. The fun of it is that not one of them will understand the fun. ... I don't know that I should see the joke myself if I were not its author."

He also mentioned that Bay's poems would be published in collected form. He went on to say: "Bessy wants me to do a volume of Life. I assent readily, knowing that Cabot will do it, and will not let anyone else do it, however hard he may try to leave it alone."

When Dor said someone desired his doing something, one could guess that an act or word of his had awakened the desire. His pretence that Bessy had asked him to write the biography was too transparent to be believed. Not that Bessy was helpless. She and Adams had become complicitous. He was to shape the book as the two of them might wish.

At the Royal Poinciana, Mrs. Cameron caught sight of no one she wished to know. She reported to Adams on the 27th, "I, the chatterbox, never speak to a soul except the bell boy." For the present, the hotel was overrun by Irish Catholics. The husbands were good-looking. The women were "abominable," had "high strident voices," and played bridge or rocked in rocking chairs on the piazza.

Wayne and Virginia MacVeagh were at a nearby hotel. Because Virginia was Donald's sister, Mrs. Cameron was duty bound to visit them repeatedly. She found Wayne oppressive to listen to, perhaps in part because his brother Franklin was in Taft's Cabinet, mismanaging things as attorney general. Yet physically Palm Beach was such an attractive development that Mrs. Cameron wanted Dor to see it. In the same letter, on the 27th, she asked, "Why don't you come down?"

He thought the proper course was for her to be in Washington and stay at his house. He advised on January 30, "As you don't sleep, you will be better in the back room." The room he meant was the back bedroom on the second floor, down a flight from his own quarters and away from the never-ceasing annoyance of passing trolley cars. He placed no time limit on her desired Washington visit.

Perhaps misled or confused by the unexpected arrival in Paris of the manuscript of the second version of "The Rule of Phase applied to History," Adams had failed to inform Jameson that he had abandoned the parody and superseded it with an interesting, simple, short book.

Assuming nothing had changed, Jameson sent the typed copy of the second version to a fourth physicist, Professor Henry A. Bumstead at Yale, who had studied under Gibbs. Bumstead welcomed the paper as an instance of a historian's making an experimental effort to use in history the methods and ideas developed by his master in physics. While studying the paper, he discovered that Adams had included a wrongly chosen formula and some less than legitimate arithmetic; but he felt heartily supportive all the same and expressed his support by sending Jameson a 27-page typewritten criticism titled "Comments on Mr. Henry Adams's Paper, 'The Rule of Phase applied to History.' "[30]

The result was dramatic. On February 1, 1910, Jameson appeared at 1603 H Street bearing Wilder Bancroft's one-page comment, the 40-page typed copy that had been prepared for Dr. Buckingham, and the 27-page criticism by Professor Bumstead.[31]

For Adams, the documents were acutely distressing. As he viewed them, the two versions of "The Rule of Phase applied to History" did not rise to the level of inclusion among his works. They were mere transient papers he had written along a road that led to his fashioning a usable book which currently was in the press at Furst and Company. Yet Jameson had treated the second version of Adams's paper with the greatest respect; four physicists had been collared; and the last of the four had supplied a thorough criticism. Moreover, Jameson and his secretary had laboriously conjured up the list of presidents and history teachers that Adams needed, preparatory to mailing copies of his book: *A Letter to American Teachers of History*.

Adams presumably gave Jameson the many thanks that he was owed. After Jameson had gone, Adams hastened to thank Bumstead in a full, explanatory letter. He did not confess to utter ignorance of physics and mathematics. On the contrary, he said about the second version of his abandoned paper, ". . . I knew enough to know where certain blunders must be, though I never could know enough to correct them." He went on to disclose his motive. "What I have wanted, for the last twenty years, was to force some sign of activity into my own school of history, which seems to me as dead as the dodos. In my despair of galvanising it into life by any literary process, it occurred to me that some little knowledge of physico-chemical processes might show me a means of acting on it from outside." ". . . I have not abused your patience in order to amuse or annoy physicists, but only in order to worry historians."[32]

During Martha's pre-marital ditherings and first post-marital collapses, Mrs. Cameron had gained a great deal of weight. She had since lost some of it. At Palm Beach, she lost more. She reported to Dor on February 1, 1910, that she had shed seventeen pounds.

Furst and Company was printing. Dor replied on the 3rd: "My book is coming on rapidly and will announce the immediate dissolution of the world. I shall keep the back room ready for you."

Although she would have greatly liked another interval at 1603 H Street, Mrs. Cameron held fast to her resolve to stay where Donald had sent her. She refused to think that Dor was a sufferer in Washington. On February 7, she reminded him that his "establishment" and his "influence" were "the one permanent thing" in the capital.

She knew that her vegetating at Palm Beach seemed to Dor an error. She agreed on the 12th, ". . . I sit here no use to anyone[,] least of all to myself." Yet there was a compensation. "I have lost two more pounds. I shall have a lovely figure when next you see me."

Adams wanted to apprise Gaskell of the occasion for his printing another book. He explained on the 17th: "Throughout all the thought of Germany, France and England,—for there is no thought in America,—runs a growing stream of pessimism which comes in a continuous current from Malthus and Karl Marx and Schopenhauer in our youth, and which we were taught to reject then, but which is openly preached now on all sides. Next week I will send you a little volume I have written about it, not for the improvement of humanity, but only to prod up my own historical flock."

At Palm Beach, Mrs. Cameron continued to visit the MacVeaghs and listened while Wayne gave "long orations" against socialism "without commas or periods." It seemed to her that MacVeagh was a pessimist, but not so "paradoxical" as Dor, and "therefore less amusing." She sent Dor these details on the 24th and added that she was writing to Donald regularly "but of course never have an answer." Because the Florida sun was getting warm, she asked Dor to send her a straw hat.

Furst and Company produced many copies of Adams's book, possibly more than three hundred. In appearance, they matched the volumes of his *History of the United States.* Designed for easy reading, they were printed in large type, roughly 135 words to a page. The title page bore Adams's name.

A Letter
to
American Teachers
of
History

by
Henry
Adams

Washington
1910

The text filled 220 pages and was in four parts: a four-page prefatory letter, a chapter titled "The Problem" (encrusted with quotations from scientific writers), a shorter chapter titled "The Solutions" (likewise encrusted with quotations), and an index. The prefatory letter said the book invited an answer but did not require one. To leave no doubt that its message was personal and private, Adams signed a great many of the copies at the close of the prefatory letter.[33]

He began distribution on February 26, 1910. He sent Mrs. Cameron her copy, mailed the copies addressed to the presidents of universities, and dispatched copies to Brooks, both for him and for friends of his in Massachusetts.

On the 28th, Dor advised Mrs. Cameron that his little book was "a bitter bit of satire against his [MacVeagh's] dear socialism, but I do not admit that." The comment reflected a feeling Dor had that he could have expanded the book to include quotations linking pessimistic European science and socialism.[34] He had not done so. Yet he hoped readers would make the connection between the book and socialism without his having to make it for them.

Mrs. Cameron received her copy on March 1. She expected to have "great fun" reading it. Meanwhile she told Dor that she had firmly allied him and herself with two agreeable companions. Frederic and Florence Keep had turned up in Palm Beach. "I have promised . . . to sail with them on the Baltic on April 16th. Will that suit you? If so take a room."[35]

Dor's idea that he could write books for selected audiences—*Mont Saint Michel and Chartres* for young American women, *The Education of Henry Adams* for young American men in or or out of the universities, and his *Letter to American Teachers of History* chiefly to its stated addressees—ran counter to an idea firmly held not only by his friends but also by a large number of Americans who had read his *History*, met him, or otherwise learned about him. Their idea was that *any* book he wrote would interest a general readership. Somewhat in this spirit, MacVeagh caught Mrs. Cameron reading Adams's *Letter* and carried it off as adapted to reading by himself.

A day or two later, Adams visited his and his wife's grave site at Rock Creek Cemetery. When Mrs. Adams was buried there in 1885, the area surrounding the cemetery was rural. It had since become a suburb. On March 6, he mentioned to Mrs. Cameron that an "ocean of sordidness and suburbanity had risen over the very step of the grave." The change, or possibly something it suggested, reminded Adams that several of his experiences in the past had frightened him profoundly. He told her, "You have never felt fear, while . . . I am made sick by terror, and if I infect you with that disease, you might as well go to bed in a hospital and stay there."

Margaret Chanler was an early receiver of Adams's *Letter*. Among his friends, none was better equipped to apprehend ideas and follow arguments. She read the *Letter* and concluded that he not only agreed with the statements it contained by European scientists but endorsed them! It seemed to her that he had written something "wonderful & dreadful." "I should think your 'letter' would drive all sensible people into the bosom of the Mother Church." In closing, she saluted him as a "Prophet of Destruction."[36]

Adams answered on March 6 by assuring her that his *Letter* was a mere exhibit of quotations from the writings of other persons; that its meaning was as clear as possible; and that, far from being a pessimist, he was the only man in the United States who was not one.[37] His answer was serious, true, and helpful as far as it went, but did not affect the essential issue. That Mrs. Chanler had completely misread his book augured trouble for Adams. It indicated that Americans would have difficulty reading his *Letter* and would understand it in a sense directly opposite from the sense he intended.

Mrs. Cameron stayed at Palm Beach. She had said she was "full of worries" and wanted to tell Dor about them.[38] Yet her behavior was that of an estranged wife who had a definite idea of what she needed. On March 11, 1910, she informed him that she was going to Charleston "to try to arrange a modus vivendi with Donald." She remarked, "It is the old case of Mohamet and the mountain."

Having learned from Brooks that Henry had printed a new book, Ford wrote to 1603 H Street to beg a copy. Henry gladly sent one but told Ford that the book concerned university education and had to be sent first, not to friends, but to the persons at the universities responsible for teaching history. He said it contained the "strongest stimulant" he knew of, for affecting such education.[39]

A postcard from Mrs. Cameron led Dor to suppose she was en route to New York and news would follow. The news took the form of a letter from the Holland House. It partly concerned his book, which she said was "too deep" for her. ". . . but I know what fun you must have had in bringing the world to an end." She explained that she had stopped for a night in Charleston and come north with Donald. "My annals are the kind that cannot be told by letter." She asked Dor to say whether he would sail on an earlier ship if she wished to take one. And she promised, "We will have a long talk soon."[40]

When asked to go to Europe with Mrs. Cameron and the Keeps, Dor had reserved a room on the *Baltic*. He wished not to change ships. If a change was in order, he would want a later sailing, not an earlier. His reasons were evident. Responses to his *Letter* were arriving from university presidents; soon his mail might contain responses from history teachers that he would have to answer; and a publisher wished to talk with him about a book he allegedly had written titled *Memories*.

In a new letter, Mrs. Cameron declared: ". . . I will not desert Macawber if I can possibly help it." Her tone was urgent. "Donald wants me to go [abroad] as soon as possible. If he makes me pay my own hotel bill as he did at Palm Beach[,] I must get off at once."[41]

She arranged to sail on the *Oceanic* on March 26, 1910, more than two weeks earlier than Adams and the Keeps. Her letters to Adams seemed fragmentary. "The winter has been a failure and perhaps I would have done better not to have come over at all." "I *am* well—very— only a little fussed." "I feel awfully about leaving you behind, and personally I have no desire to start now myself."[42]

In "a suave temper," Donald saw her off in New York. She wrote to Dor from the *Oceanic* before it sailed, "He [Donald] seems old, and I hate to think of his loneliness, though he prefers it."[43]

Her behavior had an evident meaning related to money. From her arrival in New York to her departure for Europe, she had played the part of a wife determined to maintain appearances and do as nearly as possible what her husband preferred. One can suppose that her course ended in success: that she wrested from Donald an assured annual income for herself, apart from Martha, sufficient to keep her going. Her sailing early was Donald's idea. By taking Lida's two daughters with her, she lent herself the role of chaperone and gave her abrupt departure as perfect an appearance of respectability as the one she had maintained while killing time at Palm Beach.

Dor would learn the untold parts of her story soon enough. She would impart them when they were together and by themselves in Paris.

Adams preserved four letters from presidents of leading universities responding to *A Letter to American Teachers of History*. President Lowell of Harvard thanked Adams for the book and remembered the courses Adams taught while a member of the faculty. President Jordan of Stanford described the book as "very interesting," "subtle," and "very suggestive." He did not say he had read it. President Dodd of the University of Chicago read the book and said, "Your view that history teachers need to find themselves in the present anarchy of university teaching is certainly well founded." President Hadley of Yale read the book with positive interest. He said, "It is a long time since I have seen so much stimulating philosophic discussion condensed into so small a space." He asked, "Are we not taking the physicists too seriously?" And he favored history's being dealt with "directly from the historian's own standpoint."[44]

Adams perhaps received many letters from teachers but during the interval before he left for Europe preserved only one. Its writer was Edward Channing, his former student. Professor Channing said he was reading books, Adams's being the latest, which had thrown him into "a state of mental evolution" beyond his powers to describe. ". . . I feel that I know less than nothing and am doing something wrong."[45]

If the teachers who received Adams's *Letter* were silenced by it, the reason may have been intimidation. Adams had the reputation of standing easily first among America's living historians. By itself, this could be enough to cause hesitancy. But the teachers who opened the book were confronted by quotations from, and references to, a host of authorities recruited from the ranks of Europe's recent or still-living physicists, geologists, palaeontologists, biologists, psychologists, and philosophers. The following list of authorities and works that readers encountered in Adams's unlooked-for *Letter* is incomplete but representative.

> William Thomson (later Lord Kelvin), "On a universal Tendency in Nature to the Dissipation of Mechanical Energy."
> John Tyndall, "Heat as a Mode of Motion."
> Herv, Faye, *Origin of the World*.
> A. Dastre, *La Vie et la Mort*.
> Comte de Saporta, *Les Mondes des Plantes avant l'Apparition de l'Homme*.
> A. de Lapparent, *Traité de Géologie*.
> Albert Gaudry, *Essai de Paléontologie Philosophique*.
> Ludwig Hopf, *Human Species*.
> Paul Topinard, *L'Anthropologie*.
> J. de Morgan, *Les Premières Civilisations*.
> Eduard von Hartmann, *Philosophie des Unbewussten*.
> A. Lalande, *Dissolution*.
> Henry Bergson, *L'Évolution Créatrice*
> J. Joly, *Radioactivity and Geology*.
> Gustave Le Bon, *Physiologie des Foules*.
> Bernhard Brunhes, *Degradation*.
> Dr. J. Reinke, *Einleitung in die theoretische Biologie*.

Because Adams, without claiming credit for doing so, translated his quotations from the authorities into English where necessary, he made wholly readable a book that otherwise would have been intermittently unreadable for many of the persons for whom it was written. Yet the American history teachers who read it might experience a sensation, mistaken yet persistent, that it was sent to them from on high.

Adams had promised to serve history as a flea. The teachers who opened his *Letter* might instead feel assailed by Jupiter down-rushing in the guise of an army of European hornets.

As has been noticed, Adams had long been curious about changes in the temperature of the earth's atmosphere, with such results as the formation of polar glaciers. On returning from Paris to Washington, he had read an article, "The Climate of the Historic Past," sent to him by a geologist, geographer, and sociologist at Yale, Ellsworth Huntington. He had written to Huntington on January 11, 1910, to ask a question. He had seen it mentioned in an old French chanson that Charlemagne had married "under an olive-tree" in what later would be Paris. He wished to know whether temperatures in France were high enough in the middle ages to permit olive trees to grow in Paris.

Huntington received Adams's inquiry and soon after received a copy of his *Letter to American Teachers of History*. Being a geologist, he was less likely than Adams's chief addressees, the history teachers, to be intimidated by the opinion of Europe's scientists. Adams's book so interested him that he "read it straight through when I ought to have been sleeping." He wrote to Adams on March 20, took note of his question about French olive trees, did not answer it, but did him the service of offering a highly intelligent response to his book. While saying many things, he plainly stated a main idea that Adams had implied, yet not avowed, to be his own. The idea was assertive and optimistic. ". . . the historian or sociologist has as much right to impose a psychic theory of [human] elevation upon the world, as the physicist has to impose a law of degradation."

Adams thanked Huntington for his "long and valuable letter." He gave it as his opinion that the historians would have to "evolve some sort of science of sociology and social energy." He continued, "Such a science will have to accord with the science of physical energy, or it must be an independent science. This is the theme of my argument." He left it to Huntington to see that the new science—history reborn—might do well to be independent.[46]

In Huntington's response to Adams's book and in Adams's letter of thanks, there were no outbreaks of low spirits, pessimism, or despair. Within Adams's *Letter*, in contrast, there were litanies of appalling woe. It was despairing enough that Kelvin when young had announced his second law of thermodynamics by saying:

> "1. There is at present in the material world a universal tendency to the dissipation of mechanical energy.
>
> 2. Any restoration of mechanical energy, without more than an equivalent of dissipation, is impossible in inanimate material processes, and is probably never effected by means of organized matter, either endowed with vegetable life or subjected to the will of an animated creature.
>
> 3. Within a finite period of time, the earth must have been, and within a finite period of time to come, the earth must again be, unfit for the habitation of man. . . ."[47]

Subsequent European authorities were quoted by Adams to say that all life on earth will be extinguished; that the sun is shrinking and losing its powers of radiation; that energy imparted to the earth by the sun is stored by plants but wasted by animals and humans; that the tendency of evolution is *downward* to less-and-less capable organisms and is epitomized by humans, who are more intelligent than animals at the heavy cost of being unintuitive; and that progressive degeneracy is everywhere in evidence among living Europeans.

Ability to withstand this sort of testimony was possibly strong in some of America's universities, but it reportedly was weak in Adams's native city. As planned, Brooks had given copies of Henry's *Letter* to fellow Bostonians.[48] Brooks advised Henry in March that he had never known anything to "produce so deep and almost tragic an impression as this book." If the Bostonians were not pessimists before they read the *Letter*, they seemed eager to read it as their best chance to hurry the transition. Brooks said, "Poor Bigelow can hardly rally. . . ." And Brooks's osteopath, a highly-trained anatomist in charge of the osteopathic college, was "so shaken that I shouldn't wonder if he gave up instruction."[49]

An effect Brooks did not mention was that Bostonians, while being or becoming deep pessimists, were attributing their own views, not to themselves, but instead to Henry Adams, who did not share them. This misdeed was concurrent with another development: the birth of fame. Henry Adams was going to become famous sometime, beginning at some place. It appears that actual fame began to attach to him early in 1910 in Boston-Cambridge, but in a very mistaken form. There he was steeply lowered to evil eminence as America's killer of hope.[50]

A plea for help had come to Adams from an acquaintance, M. Alston Read of South Carolina. Like Adams, Read was descended from the Smith family of Charlestown, Massachusetts. His concern was a collection of old family letters reported to be in New York City. He asked Adams to obtain for him the address of the current owner of the collection and to write the owner a letter of assurance that the collection could be safely lent to him in South Carolina.[51]

Rather than do as asked, Adams sent Read's request to Ford at the Massachusetts Historical Society. He advised Ford that his great-grandmother Abigail Adams was a great-granddaughter of Thomas Smith of Charlestown; that confusions existed about the early Smiths; and that he wanted to leave Read's problem entirely in Ford's hands.[52]

By his own devices, Ford had obtained a stray copy of Adams's *Mont Saint Michel and Chartres*. During a visit to Nantucket, he had read the copy of *A Letter to American Teachers of History* that he had asked Adams to send him. He said in response to the *Letter*, ". . . you are upsetting apple-carts by the dozen. . . ."

The request from Read was something Ford felt well-adapted to deal with. "I will take up the Read matter with pleasure, and follow it to the end." Meanwhile he requested two additional books. "When you are ready to throw away a copy of your Pacific Islands (Tahiti) and the Education, place me at the head of the list."[53]

Adams mailed Ford copies of his *Tahiti* and *Education* and remarked that Catholic women had violently raided and exhausted his store of *Mont Saint Michel and Chartres.* He said about his *Letter.* "It struck me as funny. The few letters I have received do not seem to appreciate the humor."[54]

Publishers were vying to find someone able and willing to write a book-length biography of Hay. Ferris Greenslet, a stranger to Adams, was a chief editor at Houghton Mifflin Company in Boston. He would be arriving in Washington on March 25, intending to stay for three or four days. He wrote to Adams, asking the privilege of an interview about the unsolved problem of "arranging for a life of John Hay in the American Statesmen Series."[55]

Greenslet's request was followed next day by a letter from a Mr. Elbert Baldwin, representing a less-reputable firm in New York. He proposed that a biography of Hay be written by Adams in collaboration with "some one in Washington"—name not given.[56]

Like other people, Adams was susceptible to suggestion. He may have liked Baldwin's idea that two persons collaborate as writers of the biography. There is no evidence that he responded to Baldwin or met with him. He presumably met with Greenslet in his study and told him that, if Houghton Mifflin Company would find an author to write the Hay biography, he would provide assistance, provided his involvement was kept from public view.

The time was near when Adams would be sailing on the *Baltic* with the Keeps. The book most on his mind was his biography of Bay Lodge. Bessy was selecting and copying extracts from Bay's letters for his use. Presumably the publisher would be Houghton Mifflin. The Boston firm had issued Bay's poems and dramas.

Henry and Brooks were working jointly to arrange the transfer to Quincy of properties Henry owned that would embellish the Adams family mansion; also the consignment of the family's coin collection—accumulated by their grandfather and their father but augmented by Henry—to the Massachusetts Historical Society. While expediting these changes, Brooks learned that Henry was tempted to abandon Washington and wished in any case to reduce the number of possessions that seemed to him to be cluttering 1603 H Street. These were matters of serious concern to Brooks. Yet, from his point of view, they did not begin to compare in importance with Henry's paper "The Rule of Phase applied to History."

As seen by Brooks, Henry was the one Adams since John Quincy Adams who met the standard of performance set for posterity by the ablest Americans of the past. Brooks had not learned, or had wanted not to learn, that "The Rule of Phase applied to History" was written in two versions of which he had seen only the first. Still less could Brooks imagine that his typed copy of the first version was a relic of a mere unsettled moment in Henry's thinking—the interval prior to his discovering the plan of quotation-and-argument that underlay his *Letter to American Teachers of History*. Rather pathetically, because he had contrived to make himself the possessor of a typed copy of a manuscript by Henry that had not been printed, Brooks *had* to believe that "The Rule of Phase applied to History" was the best and deepest of his brother's writings, although it fitted neither description.

Apparently on April 1, 1910, Brooks felt an impulse to reread his great brother's imagined masterpiece. He reported to Henry that he had reread the paper on "Phase" and thought it "genius." Boldly he urged Henry to rewrite his volume of memoirs and bring it into conformity with the never-printed paper. ". . . make it ['Phase'] the base. That will satisfy me. Nothing else will."

Henry could not mend matters by telling Brooks that *The Education of Henry Adams* was not memoirs; that the versions of the "Phase" paper were both dead abandoned jokes; and that *A Letter to American Teachers of History* was a far better joke, well worth printing. The younger brother was so complete a pessimist that many sorts of things could not be explained to him. When sending Brooks copies of the *Letter*, Henry had taken pains to say that the "little book" was "a mere bit of amusement." The copies and the explanation had equally been wasted, and Henry had known why. ". . . [my book] can't help you in the least. Jokes never do."[57]

The slow *Baltic* carried its passengers safely to Liverpool. News awaited Adams in London that Sir John Clark had died at Tillypronie and that John La Farge was dying in New York.

A letter followed from Bessy in Washington, saying that she was sending the extracts she had copied from Bay's letters. "I tried to make them as varied and significant as possible. . . ." "I miss you more than you have any idea of & I love you very much. . . ."[58]

The Lindsays were at 60A Cadogan Square. Mrs. Cameron had much to do and might not wish to leave immediately for Paris. Dor similarly was tumbling in a "wild vortex" of activities. Writing to her early on Friday, April 29, 1910, he said he would try to come to the Lindsays' at 5:30 or 6:00 that afternoon and would try to see her in the morning before he caught his train. She was not to be disappointed if he appeared at neither place. She and he would be together very soon. ". . . come over to Paris when you are ready."

PART THREE

19

STILL IN THE SWIM

In a letter to Ford six weeks earlier, on March 22, 1910, Adams had mentioned Abigail Smith, his great-grandmother, "who married John Adams and wrote letters (which, by the bye, I always buy when I meet a copy, and shall be glad to buy if you meet one)."[1] Soon at a house in Boston on Newbury Street, Ford found the papers of Abigail's cousin Isaac Smith—a large collection. On April 16, he wrote to Adams, "In this collection[,] I find forty-six letters of Abigail Adams, eight of John Adams, and two of John Quincy Adams." Ford was having the letters copied and hoped to obtain the entire collection as an adjunct to the Adams family papers held by the Massachusetts Historical Society.[2]

The news about Abigail's letters moved her great-grandson Henry to impart information about a genealogical search that failed. He wrote to Ford from Paris on May 2: "The true object of my affections is not Abigail but Louisa Catherine (Mrs. J. Q.)[,] whom I have pursued for years with unholy devotion, backed by money and power, without success. Her mother's name was Catherine Nuth. Her father was a Writer in the India Office. Her grandmother was a Young, and Young was in a London Brewery. With all that, I have totally failed to find a trace of the Nuths or Youngs."[3]

Henry's lines were a confession and named the Adams he most loved. Yet nothing they said suggested that Ford should search for traces of London Nuths or London Youngs. Ford however was a responsive man. He would react by using his skills as a genealogical detective.

Adams arrived in Paris partly but not fully prepared to write *The Life of George Cabot Lodge*. The book would be very unusual for being written by an older writer in commemoratiom of a younger writer. It would be unusual too in that Adams would write the book in defense of Lodge's life and work although he completely disagreed with Lodge's guiding ideas.[4] He meant the book to be kind. It would end in being exceptionally forthright.[5]

He wrote a remarkable Chapter I, "Childhood," based on a stunning knowledge of Massachusetts families. His disposition was to finish with all possible speed. At the start of May, he received from Bessy Lodge the extracts she had copied from Bay's letters.

Adams advised her that the poems presented a problem. "Bay liked his Boston even less than I do. . . . All his poems express a more or less violent reaction against Boston, and ought to be read so. . . ." On that score, the incipient *Life* might say too much, but Adams was concerned that it "not say too little."[6]

While hurrying forward in the book, he resumed his Paris habits. The Whites invited him to dinner. In consequence, on May 6, 1910, he and J. P. Morgan ate a meal at the same table. On the 10th, he mentioned to Mrs. Cameron that Morgan's famous nose, increasingly deformed by infections, had become "most alarming."

Edward VII had died on May 6, and the British were staging a very elaborate funeral. Ex-President Roosevelt chanced to be in Europe, after an interval of hunting in Africa. The Europeans were extending him a welcome nothing short of imperial. President Taft appointed him to serve as chief official American mourner at the British ceremony. Writing to Mrs. Cameron on May 12, Adams referred to Roosevelt as "Kaiser Theodorus." On the 16th, he repeated the thought. "Tell Theodore he is to be our Emperor. By Jove, I believe he thinks so!"

Mrs. Cameron had to remain in London, for Martha was unwell. The mother not only remained; she had "the time of her life." Adams saw in her letters that she was "drinking life to the dregs of the London season" and associating "only with the very exalted."[7]

Adams came down with influenza. He must have had a mild case, for he was well enough to receive William James, who was traveling to Bad Nauheim for treatment of a heart condition. Adams and James had not met since the 1870s. It shocked Adams that James, overtaken by age and illness, looked like "a schoolmaster of retired senescence." On May 12, reporting to Mrs. Cameron, he said about his visitor: "When I last saw him[,] he was a delightful, sparkling, boy. Damn!"

Influenza did not keep Dor from work on the biography. He informed Mrs. Cameron on May 29: "I have arranged Bay's letters, &c, down as far as the Spanish war . . . with a thread of narrative and explanation. I can make nothing very good out of it. . . ."

He soon was writing Chapter IV, in which letters from Bay to Bessy first appeared. On June 16, he assured Bessy, "You have given me a wonderful selection of Bay's letters to you." He could not directly tell her that he had no belief in her husband's success as a poet. He could and did tell her that Bay's letters to her were "much better and more poetic than any poetry." "These letters are the only part of the volume that is, to me, worth writing, or doing, or feeling."

The *Life* was fairly easy to draft. Adams wrote to Anna Lodge on June 21, "The MS. is ready now, except for my own corrections. . . ." By "ready," he meant that Bay's story was told from birth to death, that it had taken form as nine chapters, and that the form would not change. Yet the book was very far from ready. Adams could not write a book without rewriting and improving it as often as necessary. He moreover had sought additional letters from two well-disposed persons: Langdon Mitchell, who, in the absence of Joe Stickney, had become the young poet on whose advice and good opinion Bay had most depended; and Marjorie Nott, a friend whom Bay had known since childhood. Mitchell had not replied. Marjorie had arrived in Paris and for Adams's use had brought some of her letters from Bay. All his letters were written in a rather unreadable handwriting. Marjorie believed they were more revelatory of their writer if read out of chronological order. She gave Adams her treasures in no order at all and left Paris before he could get her to establish their sequence and without giving him her next address.[8] Yet he managed to contact her; they corresponded; and he revised the *Life* to include parts of three letters from Bay to her that she had provided.[9]

Being in Europe, Adams needed the assistance of someone in America who could mail copies of his *Letter to American Teachers of History* to persons who requested copies. He imposed on Jameson to perform the task. He told the editor that copies could be found on a bookshelf in his study and on a shelf in the closet of his bedroom. William Gray was to let Jameson take as many as were needed.

Jameson took five and informed Adams that he would carry them with him to his summer house in Maine. He mentioned also that he was taking along "your delightful volume of Autobiography and shall read it again." He said he had read many autobiographies and felt sure that Adams's was "one of the great ones."[10]

Jameson's conduct was part of a pattern. In varied ways, people were hearing about Adams's *A Letter to American Teachers of History*. They were wanting it, trying to read it, trying to dismiss it, trying to oppose what they thought its thesis, and even finding ways to try to agree with it. Similarly people were hearing about his *Education*, wanting to obtain it, and assuming they could read it. Most of all, people were assuming that *The Education* was Adams's autobiobiography. The idea had become an *idée fixe*.[11]

Adams was aware that his *Letter to American Teachers of History* was a book that presupposed exceptional powers of comprehension in its readers. Of the fourteen men whose messages to him about his *Letter* are known to have reached him in Paris during the summer of 1910, the one whose response made the deepest impression on him was an *English* historian, Frederick J. Teggart, who was serving as curator of the Academy of Pacific Coast History at the University of California in Berkeley. He had borrowed a copy of Adams's *Letter* from a friend, read it with the attention he thought it deserved, and sent Adams a response fully equal to Adams's book as intelligent prose. Because he said he had become greatly indebted to Adams before seeing his *Letter*, one may assume that Teggart had read Adams's *History of the United States*. His object in writing to Adams was to suggest, as a counterpoise to Adams's *Letter*, some ideas of his own about history. He used one of his ideas to start his key paragraph:

> I believe that the true course for the student of history is to find the basis for all his interpretations in history itself. . . .

He used another to conclude his response.

> Men prefer light to darkness, and as a consequence biology and physics, by offering a promise of illumination to the human spirit, have won notable successes, while history, with all its intimate relations to life, has not even brought satisfaction to its immediate votaries.

Judging from what he said in his letter, Teggart had not realized that Adams had long since arrived at the same ideas and wrote his *Letter* to awaken readers to just such ideas by dialogic means.[12]

Whether Adams replied is unknown. All that can be affirmed is that he preserved Teggart's response and later said that *one* man had understood him, a historian in California who was English.[13]

Adams and Jameson had not forgotten that the physicist who provided a criticism of the second version of "The Rule of Phase applied to History" was to be paid for his trouble. For the purpose, Adams sent Jameson $150, a sum the editor thought too large. Jameson forwarded $100 to Bumstead, who considered the amount "very generous."

Bumstead seized the opportunity to write to Adams and praised his *Letter to American Teachers of History* as "a very remarkable book." ". . . it impresses me very much more than the essay on the Phase Rule applied to History. With the latter, I could not altogether avoid the feeling that there was something arbitrary and artificial in the analogies you drew. In the case of the 'Letter' however they are such as to cause the physicist to sit up and take notice. Whether or not they will have the same effect upon historians is a question . . . but I have for some time had the impression that historians were too much devoted to 'facts,' and nothing like so ready as we [the physicists] are to venture into the deep waters of speculation."[14]

* * *

At Bad Nauheim, William James finished reading a copy of Adams's *Letter*, given to him by Adams in Paris. Possibly giving him the copy was an error. Adams had failed to perceive that James, four years younger than himself, was mortally ill. He had no idea that James's responses from Germany—a letter and two postcards—would be the last substantive communications that James was strong enough to write.[15]

Henry Adams and William James liked each other but were philosophically ill-attuned. Adams knew he did not understand James's ideas.[16] James assumed he could understand Adams's *Letter*, but he really could not apprehend what it said. To him, Adams's book seemed an impiety. In his chief response, written on June 17, 1910, he addressed Adams with solemn frankness as an old man who had erred. ". . . I ask you whether an old man soon about to meet his Maker can hope to save himself from the consequences of his life by pointing to the wit and learning he has shown in treating a tragic subject."

The subject James had in mind was the life human beings might be able to devise for themselves while the universe in which they lived suffered a "constant radiation of unrecoverable warmth." He tried to do battle with Adams as if Adams *should* believe Kelvin's Second Law of Thermodynamics—indeed *had* to believe it. He explained, "It is customary for gentlemen to pretend to believe one another, and until some one hits upon a newer revolutionary concept [than the Second Law] . . . all physicists must play the game by holding religiously to the above doctrine." These things being said, James tried in several ways to show Adams that human beings would not have to experience evil consequences as the universe cooled, and might even be "happy and virtuous" when the life of the universe reached its "last expiring pulsation."[17]

For James, such a pronouncement as Kelvin's Second Law was not contestable. His view of the "tragic subject" could be characterized as one of intense, saving light against a background of general darkness. For Adams oppositely, Kelvin's Second Law lacked authority. Henry's guiding idea—soon disclosed in a letter to Brooks—was firm. ". . . as regards all recent literature, scientific, historic or whatnot, one must bear in mind that no *principle* whatever is accepted or admitted as proved. . . ." Henry fully liked the assumption that all principles or laws or axioms were tentative. "It suits me perfectly, if not you." ". . . we can . . . familiarise ourselves with the discussion. We cannot adhere to authority."[18]

At Quincy, Brooks was shifting from a belief long established in his mind to a new belief. His old belief was that the greatest Americans were

George Washington and J. Q. Adams.[19] His new one was that the greatest were Washington, J. Q. Adams, and Henry Adams.

Brooks thought Henry reluctant to impart his ideas and thought the ideas in dire need of fuller expression and wide publication.[20] He had sent a copy of Henry's *Letter to American Teachers of History* to his publisher, George Brett, the president of the Macmillan Company in New York. Soon Brooks advised Henry: "Brett wants to publish the volume. The difficulty is that you go too deep."[21]

Brett had studied the *Letter* and had asked Brooks to learn whether Henry would permit the book's publication under a changed title which would "show its importance and significance from the standpoint of the general public."[22] Brooks replied that he would be seeing Henry in Paris in July. He said too that Henry's *Letter* set forth "the most far reaching theory that has been advanced since Darwin."[23] But both the response by the publisher and the extreme claim made by Brooks rested on a false supposition that Henry's *Letter to American Teachers of History* contained a theory of history overtly stated by Henry as his. Brooks could not see that Henry in the *Letter* did not offer a theory—that instead Henry simply tried to bring America's historians abreast of a shockingly pessimistic discussion taking place between leading scientists, sociologists, and psychologists in Europe.[24] If America's historians reacted by developing a non-pessimistic theory of history, Henry would be able to feel that his *Letter* had taken effect, but his *Letter* did not directly tell them what their non-pessimistic theory would have to be.

True, those who could follow the *Letter* would find therein a grand theory-of-everything: Kelvin's Second Law of Thermodynamics, which Henry wanted America's history teachers to consider. But Brooks could not read the *Letter*, was not interested in Kelvin's Law, and was transfixed by what he imagined was Henry's grand theory-of-everything. The theory that transfixed the younger brother was the mad theory hurried into being by a physicist-turned-historian in the typed copy he owned of the inchoate first version of Henry's abandoned paper "The Rule of Phase applied to History"—a paper which Brett had never heard of, much less seen.

Brett appealed to Professor Channing and was urged by Channing to ask Henry's permission to publish the *Letter*. So encouraged, on July 16, 1910, the publisher wrote directly to Henry. Brett explained that he had "read and reread the work with great interest, much enlightenment and constant pleasure on account of its style." He plainly added that he wished to publish the book.

Brett was right to be pleased by Henry's style. All of Henry's works and letters since 1891 were expressed in variants of an attractively energetic style like no other in American letters and different from the styles of his earlier productions. Yet Brett's remark about the style of the *Letter* was unlucky. To value style apart from content was one of the surer ways to rouse Henry's combativeness.

Henry declined Brett's request for the book. He said its publication "would be purely mischievous, and could under no circumstances be beneficial." Also he revealed, perhaps to Brett's surprise, the completeness of his opposition to socialism. He said that his *Letter* was meant to exhibit the "scientific foundations . . . of socialism or collectivism, and to rouse the [American] Universities to the necessity of fighting for their lives." France and England, he continued, were already "socialised." Germany was restrained from socialism only by "military necessities." America was "not yet quite so deep, and I do not care to hurry our drowning."[25]

Apparently while in Washington, Adams had learned from Ward Thoron that his wife was leaving him. Because another man was involved, the case had exceptional interest for the capital's talebearers.[26] Adams wrote to Thoron about the breakup on June 10, 1910, and as consolation pointed to the troubles of others. ". . . I have hardly any other objects of interest than . . . friends struggling with broken lives, or with lives that are breaking up. . . . If I am not writing to Mrs[.] Cameron, I am working for Mrs[.] Lodge or Bessie, or Edith Wharton[,] whose husband has gone to pieces . . . ."[27]

Adams meanwhile acquired two supportive readers. Frederick B. Luquiens and Albert S. Cook were language teachers at Yale specializing respectively in Old French and Anglo-Saxon. Luquiens read *Mont Saint Michel and Chartres* and saw that it placed Old French writings in a new light as readable, interesting, and important. He noticed also that Adams's translations of parts of the *Song of Roland* into English were the best he had seen. He accordingly initiated a correspondence with Adams; Cook initiated another; and both men pressed Adams to arrange the publication of his book in a form small enough for tourists to use and cheap enough for students to buy.

False statements that no one would read his books had become a habit with Adams. So had statements that his books—*The Education* especially—were worthless.[28] Yet he admitted that *Mont Saint Michel and Chartres* was a good book, and even admitted being pleased that two teachers at Yale had discovered it.[29] Luquiens and Cook could not persuade him to publish the book, but their urgings much augmented his determination to improve it. Having a choice between readying a copy of *The Education* for publication and preparing to print a better version of *Mont Saint Michel and Chartres*, he chose the latter.[30]

* * *

In late July with two wards, Elizabeth Hoyt and Gladys Rice, known to Adams and others as the "twins," Mrs. Cameron crossed from London to Paris. She had shifted to an apartment at 80 Avenue du Bois de Boulogne. Adams made it his duty to supply transportation for her and the twins, whether by auto, carriage, or both.[31]

After much recasting, the manuscript of *The Life of George Cabot Lodge* seemed finished. For lack of her summer address, Adams had not mailed it to Bessy. On July 29, 1910, when an address was given him, he sent her the manuscript and the copies of letters she had supplied him. He assured her about the manuscript: "You will please treat it as your private property to handle as you please. You can burn it up if you like. . . . I have shown it to no person whatever. . . ." "You can strike out what you please, or put in what you please."

In Paris, Mrs. Cameron was crushed by news that Martha had been told by her doctor that she could not live in London, and Henry was crushed by having to talk with Brooks. He explained to Thoron on July 31 that he had no way to protect himself against his visiting brother except by "going him better." "Just now he is furious because Paris has run down until in a few years it will be uninhabitable. I have to prove to him that it is uninhabitable already. He screams that America has lost every vestige of mind or will; and I have to show him that she never had any. He wonders how I can stand living here. I prove to him that I can't. . . ."[32]

Henry further explained to Thoron that he was looking at America's politicians and university presidents—"our Tafts and Roosevelts, our Presidents Lowell and Hadley and Butler and Jordan and Woodrow Wilson; our Lodges and Pinchots and Beveridges and Bryans"—and had to infer that "the whole world has stopped advance, and is floating without movement in any direction." On the strength of this grim vision, he felt better. ". . . I am still in the swim."

Bessy had acquired her husband's bad habit of lofty utterance. She received *The Life of George Cabot Lodge* on August 19, 1910, read it that same day, and at once wrote to Uncle Henry to acknowledge the "grandeur, nobility, distinction, reserve, [and] immensity" with which he had treated the subject.

She took the manuscript to Bay's parents for them to read. Senator Lodge was if possible more pleased with the *Life* than Bessy. He reported to Adams on August 24,: "I cannot find words to tell you how much I like it—how delighted I am with it. No one else could have done it or given such an analysis of his character & his thought. It is the monument of all others which I should wish to see raised to his memory. . . ." Anna

Lodge read the book. On August 26, the anniversary of her son's death, she thanked Henry for writing "splendidly."

Adams was familiar with the tendency of relatives to want changes in books commemorative of deceased loved ones. Senator Lodge wanted one change. The father had written an account of Bay's death in a letter to Sturgis Bigelow. It occurred to him that Adams could obtain the letter. "If you will get it from him[,] you will have all the facts & can write the last page which nobody but you must write."[33]

Adams retrieved Lodge's letter from Bigelow, made a copy, and sent the copy to Lodge with the advice that the last paragraph of the letter would make "the best possible conclusion of the book." He noted that the letter was "somewhat intimate." Its tendency gave him occasion for an outburst about the *Life* as written. ". . . the book is all intimate, and biographies that should not be intimate would be no biographies at all. We cannot write about ourselves as though we were lumps of clay. . . ."[34] But Lodge decided that, after all, the intimate last paragraph should not be used to end the biography.

At about the same time, Adams received a request for a copy of *A Letter to American Teachers of History* from the librarian at Brown University, H. L. Koopman. Mr. Koopman had read a borrowed copy and asked whether he might "have a copy for my own." His letter did not stop there. He said, "I will take the liberty of adding that the library over which I have the honor to preside is about to occupy the new building which has been erected in honor of John Hay."[35] No surprise to Adams, the new building mentioned by Koopman was the John Hay Library. It had been constructed at Hay's Alma Mater after a bestowal of funds by Hay's widow. One may say that Clara Hay was superseding one memorial with another. Until depersonalized by Mrs. Hay, *Letters of John Hay* had been a memorial to Hay as intimate as its designer, Henry Adams, could make it. The volumes had reflected one thing more than any other: Hay's personal qualities. The new memorial, the John Hay Library, was expensive and imposing. It reflected the qualities of its donor, a woman to whom the personal had become repugnant. When the Library was dedicated late in 1910, her husband's *Letters* would be set aside and forgotten.

In 1861, in the days just preceding and following the outbreak of the Civil War, Henry Adams had written an article titled "The Great Secession Winter of 1860–61." He gave it to his brother Charles as a present, with assurances that Charles could do with it as he pleased. The recipient forgot the manuscript not long after being given it.

In 1910, Charles was delving for materials he could use for his intended, very-large-scale biography of his father. By accident, he recovered the manuscript of Henry's article.[36] He asked Ford to do with it whatever he thought best. As a first step, Ford published it in the *Proceedings of the Massachusetts Historical Society*, prefaced by remarks that Charles as president made at the June 1910 meeting of the Society.[37]

Charles assumed that Henry had forgotten the article. He sent him the printed result on September 9 with the comment that it "reads remarkably well, and has a distinct and considerable historic value." Henry very pleasingly replied that he had not "the faintest trace of a recollection" of the article, but whether Henry had forgotten the article can be doubted.[38] It was the most extended individual work he had written during his first life. When he received the article—27 long printed pages—he reacted as if he did not read it.[39] But Henry, it appears, had known and remembered what his article was worth from the time he wrote it. He later wrote to Ford asking that copies be sent in Charles's name to two men who would be greatly concerned about what it said.[40] One was Frederick Seward, the son of then-Senator William Henry Seward of New York, the central figure in the article. The other, John Bigelow of New York, was a key player in the *Trent* Affair of 1861–1862. Both were students of American history.

As a second step, Ford arranged the reprinting of Henry's article in a newspaper, the *Boston Transcript*. In consequence, many Bostonians—Evelyn Adams for one—were given a glimpse of a young man they had not imagined, the Adams of Henry Adams's first life; which was to say an American who was mostly anonymous when he lived, yet would grow famous with the passage of time; a politician-and-writer only twenty-three years of age who was ready to write the history of the American Union during the interval when it dissolved; and who later in the year would anonymously do things of even greater importance.[41]

Frederick Seward and John Bigelow received and read the copies of Henry's article. Seward described it as "singularly graphic, discriminating and just." He said it revealed things "as they actually were" during a time in the country's history which most historians neglected or blurred, "perhaps because of inability to describe it impartially." Bigelow valued the article for revealing things that had long remained unknown. He assured Ford that "it contains much that will be new to every man living that was born since 1850."[42]

Bay's *Life* being off his hands, Adams repeated his stratagem of doing something secret while doing something he was willing to show.

His open activity was reading about prehistoric settlements in Europe. He explained to Thoron: ". . . I read exclusively about the prehistoric man of Cro Magnon. Also about the Neanderthal skull. The ice-age is my special period. I was born in it."[43] His secret activity was work on the new version of *Mont Saint Michel and Chartres.* While doing it, he would seek assistance about particular difficulties from Luquiens, Cook, and Thoron, who was coming to Europe to immerse himself in medieval studies.

On September 27, 1910, the landlady notified Adams that he would have to vacate his apartment at 23 Avenue du Bois de Boulogne because the building was going to be demolished.[44] He found a substitute nearby at No. 88, one flight up from the street.[45] He described his new apartment as "much smaller and twice the cost."[46]

Bessy was staying with Anna Lodge in Massachusetts. She informed Uncle Henry that Bay would have preferred "not to have his bad health dwelt upon" in the *Life.* She and Bay's mother were agreed that part of a letter from Bay to Marjorie Nott "was written in a temporary depression & was not indicative of his general state of mind"—hence would have to be omitted. Perfection was the thing being looked for. "Mrs. Lodge and I feel that there should not be the slightest blemish & such we feel any over-emphasis of his failing health to be."[47]

Adams had agreed in advance to any changes in *The Life of George Cabot Lodge* that Bessy might make. It apparently did not occur to her or her mother-in-law that Adams had included information about Bay's physical ailments as a means of giving Bay good reason for depression. Once all details about physical ailments were elided, the depression ever-present in Bay's later writings (unavoidably quoted by Adams) would seem a purely emotional disability and one of a sort that was likely to irritate and put off a reader, even a sympathetic reader.

The issues were injury to the unhappy subject, George Cabot Lodge; injury to a careful author, Henry Adams; and injury to a well-balanced *Life.* As in the case of Hay's *Letters,* a dictate by a widow did the damage. Survivors could be good at doing harm.[48]

The twins had gone home, Martha had come to Paris as a preferable environment, and Mrs. Cameron was directing the transfer of Henry's belongings to 88 Avenue du Bois de Boulogne. Writing to Gaskell on November 13, 1910, he remarked that his brother Brooks was "desperate" and his brother Charles was "cynical." He pictured himself as idle. ". . . I have nothing to do, or to read, or to write."

Brooks liked to give Henry suggestions. During their meetings in July, he had failed to persuade Henry to write a large work setting forth his theory of history. He recently had proposed something more modest. ". . . print [i.e. publish] your Letter to Teachers—a little revised, so as to be clearly serious. . . ."[49]

Henry had printed hundreds of copies of his *Letter.* He would not print more. Yet he respected Brooks enough to say things to him that he might not say to others. In part, he replied by anatomizing the problem of honesty. He told his brother: "Truth is poison, to such an extent and so virulent, that not one of us dares touch it or even approach it. Yet silence is a sort of truth, and equally virulent,—sometimes, I think, more so."[50]

Charles had been a commander of cavalry when young and felt he was entitled to express opinions on military subjects. He had looked into the question of George Washington's military abilities and found that the Virginian was "a very poor soldier and no strategist at all." He had published a paper to that effect and sent Henry a copy for his information but did not know that Henry in 1874 had published a wholly opposite opinion.[51]

Rather than alert Charles to their disagreement, Henry recommended a little-known document. ". . . I hope you happened on Tim Pickering's criticisms of his [Washington's] military abilities, which I tumbled upon in the Pickering MSS in the Hist. Society's Collections. Tim was quite as sharp on George W. as he was on John Adams. The paper [about Washington] ought to be dated rather late, at all events, I should say, after 1800. I found it very amusing as coming from the military head of the New England Federalists."[52]

Taking the hint, Charles asked Ford's assistance, was furnished "about fifty typewritten pages" of criticisms of Washington by Pickering, read them, and reported to Henry, "I found them not only, as you state, 'amusing,' but most suggestive, not to say instructive." It rather astonished Charles that another man had set forth "the identical conclusions at which I had just arrived a century later." He appeared not to be sure which man was the more intelligent, Pickering or himself. "The similarity [of opinions] is almost startling."[53]

A cable from Mary Jones in New York to Adams in Paris announced the death of John La Farge. Earlier the artist's doctors had committed him to an asylum in Providence as insane. Adams had been sent a letter he wrote while mad. The letter's mere appearance had been horrendous. In such an instance, death was more than welcome.[54]

Niece Loulie was joined in Paris by Aileen Tone, her friend from New York, and Uncle Henry made the latter's acquaintance. Loulie had suffered a serious ear infection and had to go to Switzerland to rest. In her absence, the uncle continued to see Aileen.[55] He advised Loulie on November 27, "Miss Tone wanders about like a lost soul, now that she has not you to boss."

Thoron had come to Paris but was momentarily at Chartres, studying the cathedral's glass. Adams presumably had told him that he was revising his *Mont Saint Michel and Chartres.*

Ford meanwhile had been looking for London Nuths. He wrote to Adams: "The name you gave me—Nuth—has puzzled me much, as it is not an English form, but of German origin. Having found it in one or two places used for the more common form of Nutt, I traced a Joseph Nutt, brewer, of Wapping, who died May 18, 1739." Ford said he was sending the information because "sometimes a straw will serve as a pointer."[56]

The straw elicited a strong response. Adams wrote the history of his own defeat. "I applied to the India Office,—or what is left of it,—in London two years ago for a complete list of their Writers and officials during the 18th century, but they asked to know what I wanted it for, and . . . I withdrew the request when I found it a matter of favor. Thus I lost the chance of verifying the fact asserted by my grandmother that Nuth was a Writer in the India Office."

As he went on in his reply, Adams wondered good-humoredly whether he might be part-Jewish. Also, amusedly, he again identified himself with his Adams grandfather. "Should you pursue the search, you might have more success than I. Nutt or Nuth! Gentile or Jew! Who was he? and how came I to marry his daughter [i.e. his granddaughter]?"

Since straws were in order, Adams offered some straws of his own. ". . . for that matter, who the devil were the Johnsons? The first of the name ran away with a ward in chancery in his own vessel from the 'Pool,' which I take to be the Thames at London docks. She was[,] I think, named Baker."[57]

Miss Tone slipped away to join Loulie in Switzerland. On December 5, 1910, Adams began occupancy in the apartment at 88 Avenue du Bois de Boulogne. A chance loomed that Lindsay might be assigned to the embassy in Mexico City. Mrs. Cameron and Martha were in London, the mother unwell and in bed with bronchitis.

Having taken space on the *Adriatic,* due to sail for New York on January 4, 1911, Dor asked Mrs. Cameron to reserve rooms on the same ship. A plan was in the making for her and Martha to pass two months in the United States before proceeding to Mexico.

Lindsay's assigment to Mexico fell through. Because Martha could not remain in London, Dor suggested a stay by the Channel at Brighton or St. Leonard's—an expedient that helped his own mother and sister Mary in the 1860s when in flight from noxious London.

Mrs. Cameron returned to Paris, still unwell. The Lindsays would be visiting for Christmas, by which time she might be better.

*   *   *

A letter came from Charles containing news that gave Henry pause. A reception had been held in New York in honor of John Bigelow. As principal speaker, Charles had read a paper containing "disclosures." He explained to Henry: "I gave them, for the first time on any stage, the inside narrative of what took place in London, in September and October 1862, when Palmerston and Russell just failed to acknowledge the Confederacy. You, doubtless, retain a very distinct recollection of what then occurred. Only lately, in the *Life of Lord Granville*, has the curtain been lifted, and the inside wires which worked results at that time been put on view. Who would ever have supposed that it was Palmerston who then saved the situation? How astonished our good father would have been had he known the secret springs then at work in bringing about his own salvation!"[58]

Charles said his paper might appear in the *New York Independent*, in which case he would send Henry the printed text.[59] Henry meanwhile was free to consider his brother's boast that he, Charles, was the historian who first disclosed the unexpected truth that, in the fall of 1862, Lord Palmerston, above all people, had prevented the recognition of the Confederate States of America by Great Britain.

The boast was late. Henry had earlier studied amazing documents in Morley's *Life of Gladstone*. He had read the story of Palmerston's conduct as published in Fitzmaurice's biography of Lord Granville. He had made these matters the subject of most concern in Chapter X of *The Education of Henry Adams*. He had sent Charles a copy. Three and a half years had passed; but Charles had not read as far in the book as the end of Chapter X; or, if he had, he gave no sign of it in his letter. No record exists of Henry's replying to Charles about his mistaken boast. In difficult circumstances, the younger man preferred keeping silent.[60]

To Uncle Henry, the advantage of seeming to be idle had never been more apparent. He had recently written to Loulie, ". . . my name is Dormouse, and nothing annoys me so much as to wake up."[61]

Out of concern for Martha, Mrs. Cameron would not be returning to America. For Dor, the thought of going to Washington was dismaying on any terms. The capital had become "a dreary tomb"—"that town of oblivion where I have buried three generations."[62] Yet he could go back with a purpose. He was expecting "to print surreptitiously a few more copies of the Chartres."[63]

As planned, Dor, Mrs. Cameron, and the Lindsays spent Christmas together in Paris. Soon thereafter, Dor discharged Marie Herlem, his servant, and paid her racing debts, amounting to forty or fifty English pounds. How much she had stolen from him was not clear. She was revealed to have stolen and cheated in other directions. He made inquiries and paid reparations to all the discovered victims.

He went to the Channel and boarded the *Adriatic*. The Whites and other persons he knew would be fellow passengers. On January 5, 1911, he sent from the ship a parting letter to Mrs. Cameron, who had stayed in Paris and would be helping Martha.

He promised to be back "tomorrow" and said how it felt to go. "I feel a little twinge whenever I think of leaving you alone, but I have been left alone so often that it seems almost like going to sleep,—a kind of dormouse effect. I wish only that you would have let me keep on the carriage. Martha would have liked it. . . ."

20

"CHANSONS DE GESTE"

From Washington, Adams wrote to Furst and Company in Baltimore, asking how much the firm presently charged to print a 100-copy edition of *Mont Saint Michel and Chartres* and how long it took to produce the first edition. The company replied that the charge was $2.15 a page plus $60.00 for binding and that the first printing was completed in less than ten months. Being ready to start, the company added, "We hope to receive part of the copy on Monday."[1]

Ellen Thoron's attachment to a man who was not her husband had become the talk of Washington. Adams described "the Warder business" to Mrs. Cameron as "utterly astounding and inconceivable." "Society feels as though a bomb were sputtering under its table."[2] On January 19, 1911, he confided to Mary Jones: ". . . I feel a little like an owl in a mouse-nest, as though I were not much wanted. Most people here don't much want to be watched."

Thoron was at Chartres. Adams advised him that he hoped quickly to advance forty pages in his new *Mont Saint Michel and Chartres*. "I have preserved complete silence about my reprint, in order not to be bothered by requests to turn it into a text-book and guide-book. I'll burn Chartres itself before I degrade it to such a fate."[3]

Martha had returned to London. Writing to Dor from Paris, Mrs. Cameron anticipated being alive but not lively. "I lived through the loss of my all, so I suppose I can go on." She planned to go south with Annie Hickox, to rest and relax at Annie's apartment in Monte Carlo. ". . . I am going to be dull right along."[4]

Edward H. Davis, an associate professor of economics at Purdue University, was a boldly original thinker who could write with exemplary force and elegance. He borrowed a copy of Adams's *Letter to American Teachers of History* and found in it "a suggestion of great value." He wrote to Adams, saying that his *Letter* announced a need for "a basis which shall be common to all substantial thought and upon which may be developed a philosophy . . . broadly consistent and unexclusive." He said that publication of Adams's book was a necessity, and he asked to be informed when copies might be available.[5]

Frederick Teggart had responded to Adams's *Letter* by asserting that historians should develop their ideas on the basis of their own inquiries without regard to ideas developed in other fields. He reacted, one may say, exactly as Adams hoped all historians would react. Edward Davis responded in a way perhaps even better attuned to Adams's *Letter.* He raised broad questions. What were all inquirers in all fields to believe? And on what foundation were all inquirers to build a new philosophy?

Adams's response could seem inadequate. He sent Davis a copy of the *Letter,* said nothing about the basis for a new philosophy, but provided a summary of his own experience.[6] His account was stark—indeed was overdrawn. He said he had tried to ascertain "the state of mind" of his fellow Americans and to that end had published "eighteen or twenty volumes." Still trying to discover the nation's tendency of mind, he had made "one more effort," of which his *Letter* was a part. The result, he said, was "absolute silence." He had received scores of acknowledgments of his *Letter* "but not one whisper of interest—still less of discussion. . . ."[7]

What troubled Adams most was institutionalized American higher education. "We have run up huge skeletons of universities, with everything in them except ideas." He said the country's universities were avoiding "fundamental issues." ". . . they have come fairly up to the stone wall of Socialism . . . [and] what do they mean to do about it? Accept it?" He left no doubt that he considered Socialism "the abyss" into which the universities were falling without a struggle. Perhaps illogically, he concluded that publication of *A Letter to American Teachers of History* might hasten the fall.[8]

For all its inadequacies, Adams's response had the merit of eliciting from Davis something no one else had offered: a new suggestion. Davis argued in favor of what he called "an optimism." He sketched a widespread condition. ". . . people are *saying* one thing and *acting* another." ". . . it is possible—more, it is habitual—for ideas to be developed, in a sort of unrecognised form. . . ." "My belief is . . . that a fundamental principle is held (however un-awared-ly) by those who act, and that this principle will find utterance—replacing the outworn convention. . . ." He thus foresaw a new age. ". . . what is *truth* will become obvious." "As such, it must take its place as the basis of such teleological foresight as we are capable of employing in the determination of our actions."[9]

Adams welcomed Davis's optimism. He replied on February 3, "I am really grateful for it, because . . . it contradicts my contention that nobody really cares about the problems of our modern society." He said that in the 1870s, when teaching at Harvard, he had tried to exercise the students' minds by confronting them with assertions "which should compel the mind to fight." Perhaps he felt he again had moved someone to fight. He seemed to go along with Davis's idea that their fellow human beings were acting on new principles—new ideas they were not yet conscious of but eventually would recognize. Davis had found Adams out. He was a fellow optimist.[10]

No love was lost between Charles Adams, president of the Massachusetts Historical Society, and Dr. Samuel Abbott Green, the librarian and senior vice-president. In January 1911, Dr. Green asked Charles Adams to get a certain book for the Society's library.

Soon in Washington, Charles visited Henry and reported to Ford, "You can tell the Doctor . . . that I obtained from him [i.e. Henry] a copy of the 'Education of Henry Adams', which I will bring as an addition to the Library when I next come on."[11]

Ford felt obliged to undercut Vice-President Green and support President Adams. He assured the president with gentle malice: "The Doctor was very much pleased to hear about The Education of Henry Adams. He takes credit to himself for having obtained it."[12]

A conjecture may be justified that in Washington, after carrying the copy of *The Education* to his house, Charles read Chapter X and discovered that Henry had gotten ahead of him—had considered earlier the matters which he himself in his New York address, "The Most Critical Episode of the Civil War," had considered only later. Such a discovery would help explain why Charles, with respect to ever-capable Henry, was growing more and more disgruntled.

Oppositely, relations between Henry and Ford tended always to improve. Henry wrote to the editor: "The Nuth mystery thickens. To relieve responsibility on my shoulders, I enclose to you . . . such notes on the subject as I could pick out of my grandmother's papers." He pleaded genealogical defeat. "I did no better with Young than with Nuth, and neither Johnson nor Baker carried me far."[13]

Ford copied Henry's notes, returned the originals, and said in a covering letter that Louisa Adams's parentage was "hazy enough to gratify the most pronounced genealogist."[14]

Henry understood that Ford had agreed to investigate. He accordingly sent him two letters from Oswald Barron, the London genealogist, and a letter from a Mrs. Walters, who had sold the Adamses fine miniature portraits of Louisa's parents. In explanation, he said: "As you have taken up the Nuth problem, allow me to submit to you some of my old correspondence on the subject. I see that the Baltimore lady spells the name Neuth, but as she is fantastical on most points, she was probably so on that."[15]

Despite the advice of doctors, Mrs. Cameron prevailed on Martha to try again to live on Cadogan Square in London. While worrying about her daughter, Dor and Mrs. Cameron were worrying about three nieces and a young cousin.

Niece Loulie was again in Paris, in an apartment of her own. She had recovered from her ear infection but remained weak.

Niece Mabel had emerged from her breakdown enough to supervise her children's educations but was likely to need assistance, whether for herself, the children, or her husband.

Elizabeth Hoyt, Mrs. Cameron's niece, was suffering from neuritis and at times had only limited use of one arm. Dor had called on her in New York before coming to Washington. He thought her very agreeable and wanted her to visit at 1603 H Street as much as possible.

Edith Hoyt, known as Edie, was Mrs. Cameron's young cousin—so young she had been Martha's childhood playmate in Washington. She was educated abroad, was fatherless, lived in the capital, and wished to work for a living. Her doctors had advised her that her lungs were "threatened." As a means of recovery, she had been banished to the North Carolina mountains. A translator at home in French, German, and Italian, in addition to English, she affected many people as much too educated to be employable.[16]

With some misgivings, Mrs. Cameron was luxuriating on the Riviera. She appreciated the beauty of her surroundings but regarded the English and American residents as "derelicts." After visiting an English couple who had built a paradisiacal villa and lived in it for more than thirty years, she dismissively remarked to Dor, ". . . think of spending thirty years in Monaco."[17]

On February 9, 1911, Edie Hoyt wrote to Adams about her banishment and a translation she wished to send to Mrs. Jones in New York— "to see if Macmillan will publish it." Edie wanted to pay Adams a visit. "I hope I shall be allowed to go home by the middle of March and you will still be in Washington."[18]

On the same day, February 9, Mrs. Cameron informed Dor that, in London, Martha had suffered "another sharp attack of enteritis." She continued: "I am going to her, I think, when I leave here. *You* are in the midst of things, and I in a back-water."

When Edie Hoyt's letter reached Adams, Elizabeth Hoyt was ending a visit at 1603 H Street. Adams wrote to Mrs. Cameron: ". . . you had better send some money . . . according to Edie's wants. I suppose a few hundred dollars at a time is best, rather than any larger amount. As I am rotten with riches, and regularly swamped with bank[-]deposits, you can be generous, but don't mention me [to Edie]." He remarked that Elizabeth was "the gayest and laughingest of our whole crowd."[19]

Mrs. Cameron soon learned that Martha had "another sharp breakdown."[20] The mother declared an emergency. On February 20, ahe told Dor, ". . . I am . . . going straight through to London." She intended to move Martha to a place where there was better air and a sufferer could be outdoors. "I suppose it is my fault for urging her to try to remain in London against the doctors' advice."

Adams had encouraged Bessy Lodge to have *The Life of George Cabot Lodge* put into type.[21] In Washington, Senator Lodge joined Adams for dinner to discuss immediate publication. Adams advised Mrs. Cameron: ". . . I was beautiful and approved everything. . . . Sometimes I do it once too much, as in the case of John Hay's Letters. Bay's will be another case of the same sort but not so lurid." He at the same time confessed: "My real occupation is in reprinting secretly my Chartres, and trying to find out what new has been learned in seven years. This really amuses me. . . ."[22]

When writing at 88 Boulevard du Bois de Boulogne in Paris, Dor had been annoyed by glare, often a symptom of eye trouble caused by age.[23] At 1603 H Street, he overworked his eyes. While trying to speed the printing of the new *Mont Saint Michel and Chartres*, he began an effort to learn the history of a medieval chronicle attributed to Archbishop Turpin of Rheims. Thoron was collaborating with him. It interested them that the chronicle, an important one, was forged.[24]

In London, Mrs. Cameron saw that Martha's enteritis was the worst yet. "I sent at once for a specialist, and a nurse[,] and I hope that we shall soon get her in hand, as she is in no fit state to make the journey to Lausanne[,] where she really ought to go."[25] A specialist and a nurse were a mere beginning. Mrs. Cameron learned of a buyable property at Blandford in Dorsetshire three hours by train from London. Stepleton House was a stone structure that afforded sufficient space but lacked drains, electricity, and apparatus for winter heating.[26] A cable to Donald extorted a return cable to Martha agreeing to buy the property as a present to the Lindsays. Mrs. Cameron ordered the installation of drains and made ready to move daughter, attendants, and servants to Blandford and to safety.

Dor foresaw a new crisis on the New York Stock Exchange. Without disclosing his methods, he readied himself to survive it.

Langdon Mitchell belatedly sent Bessy Lodge in Washington "about forty letters" he had received from Bay.[27] Mitchell wrote also to Adams, saying he hoped the letters might be useful.[28]

Four of the new letters permitted Adams to revise Chapter IX of the *Life*—"The End." The revision was probably an improvement. Relations between the two poets had been friendly and brought out Bay's best qualities as a writer of letters. Yet the effect of the *Life* when finished was likely to be determined most by a striking letter in Chapter IX from Bay to his mother, written when Bay was too depressed to withstand with good temper the trials of a boat-and-rail trip from New York to Boston with his wife, their children, a governess, and a nurse. The trip involved the temporary loss of bags, one of which contained "Uncle Henry's manuscript" (the first version of "The Rule of Phase applied to History") and "all of mine" (the manuscript of Bay's *Herakles*).[29] That the elder Lodges and Bessy approved Adams's inclusion of this letter could seem astonishing; for the letter cast a long backward shadow in the narrative, as if there was something amiss all along, either in Bay or in the ideas he had lived by. The shadow made the *Life* a disturbing story.

Frederic and Florence Keep were pleasant, intelligent people who were living alternately in a Washington house and a Paris apartment. Fred had heart trouble, yet behaved as if he were perfectly well. He and Florence needed furnishings for their house and wished to import Dutch tulip bulbs for planting. With these wants in mind, they booked space on the *Lapland,* due to sail for Antwerp on April 22. Adams knew about their plan and wished not to make ocean crossings alone. He reserved space on the *Lapland* for the same date.

The new *Mont Saint Michel and Chartres* was being printed at a snail's pace, twelve pages a week. The slowness gave Adams time to reconsider the words of a song that Richard Coeur de Lion wrote when captured and held in Austria for ransom.[30] Adams had included some of its lines in Chapter XI, "The Three Queens." It occurred to him that he should print the entire song both in Old French and English.

On March 15, he informed Professor Luquiens, "In a frenzied moment I tried to translate Richard's Song into verse." He enclosed his rendering—seven stanzas—and asked for a criticism. Luquiens sent some small criticisms intended to perfect "your masterly translation."[31] So assisted, Adams expanded Chapter XI.

In London, Martha remained in bed. Mrs. Cameron reported, "She seems to me to be drifting into invalidism. . . ." The mother said too that putting Stepleton in order was a "biggish undertaking."[32]

After another week of anxiety, Mrs. Cameron declared that optimism was her only choice. "There is nothing between that & suicide.

Having escaped that two years ago, I have logically to try the other. Yet it is all as bad as can be." "Our one chance is this country house[,] which we are moving heaven & earth to prepare."[33]

Lindsay faced reassignment to a foreign post—the Hague, Brussels, Madrid, or Berne. Martha would be expected to accompany him, and a swift recovery was desired. On March 23, Mrs. Cameron felt able to say that her patient was "distinctly better." She told Dor, "I am planning to go to Paris next week to close the apartment there & to return here [to London] in short order to move Martha to Stepleton." "I am definitely going to spend the summer with Martha[,] so you must be prepared to come there too. It will be an empty barn, but there will be a bed for you at any time, so come."

Elizabeth Hoyt was ending a second visit at 1603 H Street. Dor advised Mrs. Cameron: ". . . [she] goes tomorrow. I am sorry to lose her, for she is an ideal companion. She is, like everyone, a wreck. She can't sleep more than two or three hours a night, and her nevritis [*sic*] goes and comes without stop." He had made financial precautions with Edie and Elizabeth much in mind. "I've hoarded two years income to provide . . . against others' fears."[34]

During her short stay in Paris, Mrs. Cameron arranged that Dor's apartment be put in order. She realized that much depended on Martha. ". . . I hope that when we move to the country she will . . . make the effort towards getting well which nobody but herself can do."

Mrs. Cameron acknowledged too that events were keeping her and Dor apart. "So things move on, but not just our way. I am old & tired—You[,] at any rate, have not an neurasthenic daughter!"[35]

Adams had lost his dislike of Berenson and felt a disposition to confide. He disclosed to his friend that he and his brother Brooks had "suffered agonies from contact with so-called optimists." Yet superficial American optimism seemed to Adams a mere annoyance if compared with its imaginable sequel. He said: ". . . I look forward with consternation to the possibility of a pessimistic America. Pessimism without ideas,—a sort of bankrupt trust,—will be the most harrowing form of ennui the world has ever known."[36]

Adams and the geologist Samuel Franklin Emmons had played together in Quincy when they were boys. When they were men, Emmons led Adams to his meeting with Clarence King. He died on March 29, 1911. Adams attended his funeral, once again as chief mourner.

He worried about Fred Keep and worried about the United States. On the 31st, he wrote to Thoron: ". . . Keep is tied down to a rigid regimen and has an attack of angina if he eats a custard pudding. The stock-exchange is worse than Fred, and has angina every other day. Business has quite ceased. As for our dear Taft, he is just what he was. The next presidential canvas is on the verge of beginning, and total chaos reigns."

Mrs. Cameron re-crossed the Channel from France to England during the worst storm she had ever known. As always, she and Dor were in touch by letter. She advised him on April 6 that Martha had "the troubled unhappy look of a nervous invalid."

The knowledge that she was writing to Dor for the last time before his return to Europe made him seem very near. She wanted them to be close. Yet she felt impelled to bring *three* persons together and keep them so. "I wish you could bring Elizabeth with you." "The truth is that she belongs to *our* atmosphere, not to her father's, and is not happy in Wall St. & Madison Avenue. I wish we could keep her."

In Washington, Adams had intruders to contend with. Ellen Warder Thoron sent friends to see him and beg him "to make Ward give her a divorce." He barred the friends, asked to speak with Ellen herself, and told her, "I never interfere in domestic affairs."[37]

Having little choice, he walked around the block to 1610 I Street and consulted his ophthalmologist, Dr. William Wilmer, about his eyes, which were "tired out, and have struck working." Adams was not in a good position to give his eyes a rest. Houghton Mifflin wanted him to do final work on *The Life of George Cabot Lodge*, and printing of the new *Mont Saint Michel and Chartres* was "three months behindhand."[38]

At the risk of irking the publisher, Adams asked that his name not appear on the binding of the *Life*, nor on its title page, but only on the false title page. There custom would call for smaller type. He got his way, with the result that when looked at by anyone in a hurry, the biography would be likely to seem anonymous.[39]

The Keeps and Adams sailed on the *Lapland*. When the ship paused at Dover, Fred went to London, and Dor received a letter from Mrs. Cameron. Replying to her from shipboard, he said her letter was "a tremendous relief and pleasure." "Allons! perhaps our next Chapter will be better than the last."[40]

Florence and Henry hunted for furniture and tulips in Amsterdam and proceeded to Paris. Fred awaited them. Louisa Hooper and Aileen Tone—"my two girls"—greeted Henry.[41] He thought Loulie resembled "an anaemic ghost."[42]

Because he wanted to eat at home and a cook, Mariette, had been found for him, he needed furniture for dining. Fred wanted furniture in quantity, and they sometimes shopped together.

Dr. Wilmer had insisted that his patient rest his eyes. Henry, however, was re-indexing the pages of *Mont Saint Michel and Chartres* that Furst and Company had printed.

Americans, including some Warders, were calling on Henry in Paris. He tended to lead such people to Hirsch, a dealer in antiques. He confided to Evelyn Adams: ". . . Europe is now swarming with people to be avoided. I live among them like a toad in a hole. I . . . can stand them . . . but only by taking them to be robbed by old Hirsch. In this way I have sold out everything in Hirsch's shop, till not a stick of forged furniture is left."[43]

On June 3, 1911, Fred Keep fell dead during an afternoon appointment for massage on the Avenue Kléber. He carried no identification. After desperate inquiries, Florence found his body at the morgue. She at first would not receive Henry. She wrote to explain that it was kinder to say " 'not at home' " than to "entertain you with tears."[44] To take her husband's remains to America, she arranged to sail for New York on June 24. She expected to be back in Paris by October.

Thoron was in England to do research. Henry sent him an ironic comment: "Fred could not think except as a gamble, and that I take to be the definition of the optimist. . . . The worst of it is that the optimist dies all right, and the others suffer." He told Mrs. Cameron more plainly, "I want no more *sudden widows*."[45]

A German expansion to the southeast seemed to impend. Adams mapped the danger for Gaskell. ". . . I see France cowering under the terror of the huge big storm-cloud gathering in central Europe, which must burst in a pretty determinable time. All the Jews and gamblers are watching Turkey, Austria, the Bagdad railway, and the Balkans." He hoped Germany would delay its attack for "ten years." "Thanks to the Virgin, I shall be in Heaven, and mighty glad not to be Germanised, but not sure even there."[46]

Eye trouble was limiting the things he could readily do. ". . . I am going blind, and can't read."[47] At 88 Avenue du Bois du Boulogne, new-made curtains permitted him to adjust the light. He often stayed indoors. ". . . I can only sit here, in half-light, neither reading, nor walking, nor writing, and only waiting for nothing."[48] It occurred to him that he might already have seen enough. He remarked to Gaskell, ". . . I have seen, or known, fourteen out of twenty[-]five American presidents . . . and I don't want to see any more."[49]

His Paris physician, Dr. Austin, and a Paris oculist, agreed that he had choroiditis. He informed Mrs. Cameron, "My eye-doctor says he doesn't know what causes choroiditis, but to save trouble they call it old age." He liked the eye-doctor. ". . . he's a good fellow, and doesn't bother me with remedies for the irremediable."[50] Yet treatment was attempted. On June 26, he informed Mrs. Lodge: "I've read nothing, heard nothing, seen nothing, and wear yellow glasses to keep off old age. That is doctors' sense!"

Weather permitting, he took meals at open-air restaurants in the Bois de Boulogne—most often the Pré Catalan—where he could talk with acquaintances. His sister Mary returned to Paris with Elinor and a friend of Elinor's, Ethel Clark. He led the two young women to the Bois and was "rather encouraged to find that I could still walk them off their feet."[51]

He all along had been reading. He suggested to Mrs. Cameron that she get Lindsay to bring her the English translation of Wagner's autobiography—"the most interesting book for a long time."[52] He read enough of a new German treatise on Thomism to believe he could put it aside. At an unknown date, perhaps soon in Paris, he found he could gain by using magnifying glasses.[53] His inclination was less to curb his reading than find the best ways to continue it.

The current U. S. ambassador, Robert Bacon, invited him to lunch with Henry White, Chauncey Depew, Walter Berry, and other Americans. There was much conversation but also much avoidance. Recounting his experiences to Mrs. Cameron on July 10, Dor voiced a premonition. "I notice that we talk no politics. A certain silence as of a coming deluge everywhere settles on us."

The silence was broken by noises. "The automobiles grunt by, like so many hogs, into the Bois and out of it, before my window. . . ."

Lindsay invited Adams to Stepleton, and Gaskell invited him to Wenlock Abbey. Adams put Gaskell off by claiming he was "too shakey to travel." A stronger preventive was work. Proofs were coming from Furst and Company, and he was returning them to Baltimore corrected. He moreover was reading a book by an English evolutionist, Alfred Russel Wallace, *The World of Life: A Manifestation of Creative Power, Directive Mind and Ultimate Purpose.* The book had affinities with Adams's *Letter to American Teachers of History.* Adams confessed to Gaskell: ". . . I have been reading with feverish interest a new volume by old Malay Wallace, Darwin's rival, who . . . is as much bothered as I am by his wicked past and Darwinian vagaries, and writes his 'World of Life' on the same lines that I took for my 'Letter to Teachers,' except that he frankly goes back to the God of Thomas Aquinas and Duns Scotus, who doesn't help me in the least."[54]

Lindsay would soon be ordered to his foreign post. Adams dreaded the change. ". . . then will come the lurid future."[55] Yet there were also dangers near at hand. On July 18, he advised Mrs. Cameron: "What I fear most is fatigue. Next comes heat."

He had rented an auto and had Loulie for a companion. He took her often to St. Cloud or nearby places "to see the sunset and the evening shadows." Mrs. Cameron would have been better company than any niece. He wrote to her very frankly, "I wish you were here, but even in the best of summers I have never had you here."[56]

Brooks and Evelyn made their customary July appearance, and Brooks concluded once and for all that Paris was uninhabitable. In a letter to Niece Mabel, Henry said he was eager to get Brooks "back to Boston, which is the only place that seems to suit him."[57]

Thoron returned to Paris and hunted in the libraries for medieval manuscripts. He brought copies of the more interesting ones to Adams. They were advancing their studies of the *Chronique de Turpin*, which Adams said they ought to publish.[58]

Adams worked well when dealing with many problems at once. He offered Gaskell examples. ". . . I devour books by the ton, but they are all of a kind that involve conundrums or puzzles. . . . E.G.: St[.] Augustine's views on Grace; St[.] Thomas Aquinas' view of Free Will; Darwin's ideas on Sexual Selection; Mâle's view of the Charlemagne window at Chartres and the Pseudo-Turpin of Rheims; the relative merit[s?] of a score of MSS. of the Pseudo-Turpin in the Bibliotheque National and the Arsenal; the extinction of the Tertiary Vertebrates and the action of the Glaciers; the meaning of the paintings in the Cro Magnon caverns. . . ."[59]

In part, his inquiries rested on his success as an investor. Confident that he could afford it, he provided money to speed a French exploration of a cave in the Dordogne once inhabited by Cro-Magnons.[60] On August 8, 1911, he assured Mrs. Cameron, ". . . [Henri Hubert] has charge of the digging, and I am to find a primitive man, thirty thousand years old, and a hairy elephant."[61]

Stocks had sagged on Wall Street. For leadership, Americans were looking to J. P. Morgan—also to ex-President Roosevelt, who was back in politics and loomed as a rival to President Taft in the election of 1912. Adams could not believe in T. R. as a "savior of society." In the same letter to Mrs. Cameron, he skeptically remarked: "Teddy and Pierpont Morgan are our only hope. United we fall."

After much labor, Brooks had drafted an account of the success of Minister Charles Francis Adams during the most hazardous period of his English mission, from May 1861 through October 1863. Two copies of the manuscript had been prepared. Brooks had left one with Ford in Boston. In Paris, he gave Henry the other and asked for an opinion.

The completion of Brooks's account meant that Charles, Henry, and Brooks had all written at length about their father. Charles was continuing to do so. He liked to state his ideas orally in public as soon as conceived. He liked also to restate them in book form. In August 1911, he sent Ford the final proofs of his latest book, *Studies Military and Diplomatic*, and suggested that Ford read page 411 and compare it with pages 134–53 of Henry's *Education* in order to see what Henry said about an English book, Lord Fitzmaurice's biography of Lord Granville. Charles went on to say that his brother was alerted to Fitzmaurice's disclosures "through me"; also that the disclosures were "very much an eye-opener" for Henry.[62]

Ford would understand what was at stake. He was to notice older Charles's superior prowess as a historian, and younger Henry's inferior prowess. If he neglected to look at the pages and trusted Charles to tell the truth, he might have granted that Charles opened Henry's eyes to things new to him; but if he read page 411 of *Studies Military and Diplomatic* and compared it with pages 134–53 of *The Education of Henry Adams*, he must have seen that Charles had conveyed a wrong idea of what the pages were about.

In 1864, Queen Victoria grew worried about imaginable actions by Lord Palmerston and Earl Russell in relation to Germany. That subject was at issue on page 411 of Charles's *Studies*. But Henry was not interested in Victoria's solicitude about Germany. He was interested in a series of actions the queen had seldom considered: Palmerston and Russell's—also Gladstone's—actions in relation to the United States. This was the subject Henry wrestled with on pages 134–53 of his *Education*. Thus the pages that Charles asked Ford to read did not connect. Perhaps because too weary in mind to keep things straight, the elder brother sent the editor on an errand to nowhere.[63]

Henry meanwhile was reading Brooks's manuscript, later published, somewhat revised, under the title "The Seizure of the Laird Rams."[64] In his account, Brooks did again what Henry had already done in some chapters of his *Education* and what Charles was doing in parts of his soon-to-be-issued *Studies Military and Diplomatic*. Brooks wrote the history of their father's work as minister. It spoke well for the youngest brother's narrative that Henry read it carefully and did not immediately say what he thought of it.

Mrs. Jones was in Paris. On August 2, 1911, Dor had written to Mrs. Cameron, "Everyone thinks that Paris is awful,—everyone except Mrs[.] Jones[,] who is delighted to get back. As for me, I've not enjoyed myself so much since I was a boy. I like heat at 80°. . . . Alexandre drives me about, from one end of the town to the other, to hold beautiful lady's hands like a sister only much more so. Ah! rendez-mois mes quatre-vingt ans!"

Mrs. Jones departed. Two couples—Adams and Aileen Tone, Thoron and Louisa Hooper—were left "quite alone."[65] Daytime Paris temperatures rose to scorching levels. Thoron said that even Washington heat was not "so severe." Yet he returned to the Bibliothèque Nationale and other libraries in search of manuscripts.[66] Adams assured Mrs. Jones that he and Ward had "ransacked every thirteenth-century MS. in the Bib. Nat. as well as in all the other libraries, and we know more about the Pseudo Turpin and his relics at St[.] Denis than the whole French Academy. . . ."[67]

Brooks and Evelyn had gone to Germany for a cure, were soon to be in London, and intended to return to Boston by way of Canada. Henry had nearly finished work on Brooks's manuscript. As was habitual with him, he also was thinking about the history of the earth's atmosphere and changes in its average annual temperatures. On August 8, affected by the heat in Paris, he told Mrs. Cameron, ". . . I would really like to know how warm it has been at the North Pole, and how many icebergs have been sent down to knock out our steamers to Quebec."[68]

Offhandedly, Henry added, "I hope to finish my last job of printing in another three months." The remark might seem only to mean that Furst and Company was sending proofs and that Henry was correcting them, indexing, and trying to finish while in Paris. Necessarily, however, the remark meant too that he had decided not to prepare and print a better version of *The Education of Henry Adams.*

That he had made this decision was tacitly confirmed by his report to Brooks on August 23 about "The Seizure of the Laird Rams." The manuscript represented Brooks at his best. Thoroughly documented and long enough to make two articles or a short book, his narrative firmly supported its main idea: that Minister Adams's work in England was a "masterpiece" both diplomatic and legal.[69] Being much more a lawyer than either Charles or Henry, Brooks had recounted the legal portions of the story with confidence. Henry reacted by suggesting that Brooks arrange the publication of his narrative in the *Proceedings of the Massachusetts Historical Society,* that he reorganize the narrative so that the diplomatic story was told first and legal story second as a separate chapter; also that he write a third chapter recounting their father's triumph in 1872 at Geneva, where ex-Minister Adams served on the board of arbitration that awarded the United States $15,000,000 in settlement of the Alabama Claims.[70]

Henry sent his reaction and the manuscript to Brooks's London address. He did not know that Ford had already promised to publish the paper in the *Proceedings.* Moreover, he misjudged his brother. He did not realize that Brooks had little left in the way of energy.

Brooks told Ford how Henry had responded to the paper. ". . . he returned it with a number of suggestions which I fancy would improve it to readers who are not lawyers, but of which I can't judge very well myself because . . . I have never been able to face the boredom of reading it. . . . I made a try the other night but I went to sleep at once." Yet Brooks advised the editor, ". . . it might be worth while to hold the paper back, if you have not put it into type, and let me see what I can do with it one of these days when I am in the mood."[71]

Later, perhaps with Ford's assistance, Brooks reconstructed his paper in two parts, as Henry had recommended; and Ford published it in the *Proceedings*. Also Brooks began work on the third part that Henry had wanted, relating to the Geneva tribunal.[72] But at that point the youngest brother faltered. The third part did not get written.

The Foreign Office assigned Lindsay to the Hague. Elizabeth Hoyt appeared at Stepleton. At the start of September, Mrs. Cameron and Elizabeth came to Paris for a week, saw Dor, and proceeded to Carlsbad for cures. Elizabeth was distressed about her arm. Dor was distressed about both women. He wrote to Mrs. Cameron on the 9th: "Your own cure is perhaps not as pressing as Elisabeth's [sic], but I hope you will do it seriously." He took occasion to mention how seldom he and Mrs. Cameron were together. "You are drifting pretty far away, but it is a sort of landmark to have you still drifting."

Adams liked to picture himself as a person who had lived longer than might be right but was buried in harmless studies. Reviewing his summer for Mrs. Lodge, he said, "Every night Thoron brought me a new batch of MS. from the Bibliotheque de l'Arsenal, and new books of Chansons, till I now know enough to write a heap of volumes like my Chartres." ". . . life has been solitary. As you know, my friends are dead, and my contemporaries ought to be."[73]

Martha mended enough to go to the Hague and seek a house. Adams wrote fewer letters than usual and, when not watching reports from Wall Street, where stocks again had fallen, seemed idly to be reading. On September 26, 1911, he told Gaskell, ". . . I took up my own volume of 'Education' and got interested in reading it. . . ."

He was reading his Second Traveling Copy, brought from Washington to be kept fixedly in his Paris library. His book affected him as redolent of a time long past. "It all reads alike. Ten years ago, or fifty years ago, reads like a hundred years ago. Everybody is dead or disappeared, and the world has spread without growing."

With Elizabeth, Mrs. Cameron returned to Stepleton. She wished to help the Lindsays get settled at the Hague and wished later to keep house with Elizabeth in Paris. Dor meanwhile sent little news. He was eating at his apartment. "Mariette seems to me to cook better than I deserve. . . ." His chauffeur lacked work. ". . . I've nothing for Alexandre to do. Looly alone uses him."

Mrs. Keep had come back to Paris.[74] Dor continued to pretend he was idle. On October 8, he told Mrs. Cameron why. "The days are too dark for reading and writing." Yet he admitted he was proofreading. "I am very slowly worrying through the last pages of the new imprint of Chartres. I am loaded with thirteenth-century MSS. and meditate vast erudition."

The world's largest steamship was the new *Olympic*, flagship of England's White Star Line. Dor reserved a stateroom on the vessel for its December 20 crossing. The prospect of being in America turned his mind to politics, of which he was heartily tired. In his next letter to Mrs. Cameron, he looked forward to the election of 1912. "My informants all say that Taft has absolutely no chance of reelection and the republican party is doomed. I don't see that it matters, since Theodore turned it into the Democratic party, and abjured its theories and principles, as well as its practices. I've set aside gold enough to last me my time."[75]

A pulse of energy was evident in Dor's letters. He assured Mrs. Cameron on October 22: "I wear dark glasses and look like the broken-down schoolmaster that I am. I burrow in the twelfth century still, and hope to dig back into the eleventh. I never learned so much about it as in the last six months."

The pulse grew very loud in a letter he wrote to Mrs. Jones. "I am living with Hugh Capet. I am a jongleur, screeching Chansons. I am trying to hope that I can get some more copies of my Chartres from the printer before I die at Roncevals or at Aliscans. . . ."[76]

He seemed to feel he was doing something heroic. And no wonder; for he was writing an amazing essay, "Chansons de Geste," which would run to 107 paragraphs, fill 173 pages of manuscript, and serve as an antechamber to *Mont Saint Michel and Chartres*.[77]

Adams's "Chansons de Geste" has gone unnoticed and has never been printed. It deserves close attention. It is the result of an exploit of literary and historical detection secretly conducted by Adams with Thoron's assistance. Adams set out to learn the authorship of the *Chanson de Roland* and the *Chanson de Willame*, a comparable medieval work discovered by George Dunn, an English collector, and published by him in 1903.[78] The difficulty of the inquiry was such that, in his essay, Adams quoted eighty Latin and Old French passages from nearly fifty texts, offered twelve translations of his own from Latin and Old French writings, and quoted writings by a half-dozen modern scholars. The result was an argument which might be clear to anyone who read it carefully but would be fully appreciated only by the few who could read the Latin and Old French passages that Adams wove into the argument but chose not to translate.[79]

The leading ideas set forth in the essay should be summarized, if only to make clear why Adams found the subject so interesting.

—Incursions by Vikings from the north and Saracens from the south wholly disrupted life in France during the century 850–950 A.D. After the disruption, the sole available means of reviving religious, political, and artistic activity in France was support of the Carolingian kings by the dukes of France.

—The dukes owned three abbeys, including the Abbey of Saint Denis just north of Paris—the burial place of Charlemagne's imperial predecessors. In 987, the incumbent duke, Hugh Capet, set the Carolingians aside and had himself crowned king of France. So doing, he unintentionally opened a path for a supremely talented French poet—name now unknown—to conceive a rhymed chant or *chanson* that he could sing at fairs for money.[80]

—At a date between 987 and 1050 but probably about 1020, the poet secured the help of a monk at the Abbey of Saint Denis—name now unknown—who could furnish him accounts of French history on the basis of which he could compose the intended *chanson*.[81]

—The poet wrote a *chanson* which celebrates the heroism of a French warrior, Vivien, while fighting infidels on a border of the Spanish March, a long-held French territory more or less equivalent to modern Catalonia. Dying Vivien sends a message to his uncle, Willame, the Count of the Spanish March, asking for rescue by both Willame and the king, residing near Paris at Saint Denis.

—The *Chanson de Willame* was a strong, even violent, incitement to French patriotism. It was such a success when heard that the poet asked the monk for material for a second *chanson*. The new information offered by the monk concerned an ambush sprung by Basque mountaineers against Charlemagne's army when returning from a visit to the Spanish March as far as Saragossa. One of Charlemagne's subordinates, a Breton named Hruolland, was killed in the ambush. The poet transformed Hruolland to a dying French hero named Roland, changed the Basque marauders into Saracen infidels, and invented supporting characters as needed. The resulting *Chanson de Roland* was an even greater success and was at least equally patriotic. It remains the starting point of French literature.[82]

—The poet's *Chanson de Willame* and *Chanson de Roland* were recited, freely recomposed, and altered by other *jongleurs* for as much as a century and a half before the texts were set down by copyists for preservation. As written, the texts are mere literary wrecks. Yet they are authentic wrecks of French masterpieces and are far superior to the compositions of other Old French poets.

Certain details need to be given, to explain why Adams and Thoron took particular interest in the Turpin chronicle.

—The *Chanson de Willame* and the *Chanson de Roland* ascribed to French possessions south of the Pyrenees both geography and history more fantastic than real.

—When the poet wrote the *chansons*, the facts of early French history had already been inextricably confused by persons anxious to cater to special interests. For example, Willame was remembered both factually as a lord of the Spanish March and fictionally as a lord of Orange in Provence, hundreds of leagues to the northeast.[83]

—The monks of Saint Denis felt strongly about their history. Archbishop Turpin had been recruited when young from their number and rose to be one of Charlemagne's aides. For this reason, in 1020 or thereabouts, the informative monk at Saint Denis insinuated Turpin into the poet's *Chanson de Roland* not only as an added character but as a martyr who dies in battle against the faithless Saracens.[84]

—In 1165, the Emperor Frederick I, Barbarossa, directed Anti-Pope Pascal III to canonize long-dead Charlemagne. Pascal felt he could not do so without obtaining evidence of Charlemagne's saintly character. He sent an agent to the Abbey of Saint Denis in quest of particulars. The monks furnished the agent an authentic letter by Archbishop Turpin and a chronicle allegedly by Turpin. According to Adams, the chronicle was "a flagrant and obvious forgery, fabricated at Saint Denis, but so great was the authority of the Abbey that all Europe accepted the so-called Turpin as genuine. . . ."[85]

A last detail has an importance of a different sort. Adams says in his essay that the *jongleurs* of medieval France boasted in their chants that the stories imparted were reliable because old and preserved at Saint Denis. "The regular literary formula required that the tale should have been preserved in a 'roll' . . . or in a chest or tomb . . . at Saint Denis for a hundred years. . . ."[86]

The detail matters because Adams soon would conceal a valued book in a trunk. He perhaps could be affected by his own writings.

Charles's book, *Studies Military and Diplomatic*, was published by the Macmillan Company in October 1911. Charles informed Henry that a copy was being mailed to him. He said the essays in the book had been assembled "at the suggestion and under the influence of our friend, Worthington C. Ford." He asked Henry to look at page 368 and remember a letter that Lord Fitzmaurice had included in his biography of Lord Granville. He added pointedly, "You are probably not aware of the fact that it was I who, through the medium and cooperation of Spencer Walpole, brought about the publication of that letter."[87]

A glance at *Studies Military and Diplomatic* sufficed for Henry to see that too many sons had written about their father. Charles's book contained two papers, "An Historical Residuum" and "Queen Victoria and the Civil War," designed to give the public new information about the English mission of the elder C. F. Adams. The papers did not have the force of Brooks's essay, "The Seizure of the Laird Rams." Yet they were written in an assured style that might suit the public and promote acceptance of Charles as the living Adams most worth reading.

For Henry, gloom was as good a defense when dealing with irritable Charles as when dealing with pessimistic Brooks. In his reply to his elder brother, Henry was silent about the letter Fitzmaurice published in his biography of Granville. He said nothing about Charles's book except that he had received it. He said gloomy things about the more recent inhabitants of the United States. He remarked: "Since the Civil War, I think we have produced not one figure that will be remembered a lifetime. The most prominent is our beloved Theodore." He seemed to view the alleged dearth as God-given. ". . . I think the figures have not existed. The men have not been born."[88]

Henry also said gloomy things about himself and Charles. ". . . I am dying alone, without a twig to fall from. . . . We leave no followers, no school, no tradition."[89] Perhaps his gloomiest thrust was to say that he and Charles were already forgotten. He said America was in a condition of "entire unconsciousness that I, or you, or George Washington ever existed." He recommended a particular course. ". . . we had better do our own epitaphs, and do them quick."

What Henry did not know, or knew but would not admit he knew, was that Charles had already written his autobiography.[90] In 1900, the elder brother had spun off a 300-page manuscript, rather critical and slashing. His epitaph was a long way toward being completed.[91]

Henry's answer reached Charles in mid-November. At the moment, Ford was preparing a paper about John Quincy Adams, to be read at a meeting of the Society. Ford was much assisted in writing his paper by a compilation of evidence that Henry had published in 1877 titled *Documents Relating to New-England Federalism. 1800–1815*.[92] Not realizing that praise of a work by Henry might damage his relations with the Society's president, Ford told Charles that he considered Henry's book a classic and a knock-out blow to critics of John Quincy Adams.

Charles did not like being told about Henry's excellent books. In reply, he let Ford know that he made "little account" of the purported "knock-out blow." He derogated Henry's compilation as "obsolete." "The volume . . . to which you refer is, I fancy, not often consulted. Certainly it is not a 'classic'."[93]

* * *

Houghton Mifflin Company published the *Life of George Cabot Lodge* in October 1911 and sent copies to Henry Adams and to Lodge's widow. Bessy read the book and was astonished afresh by "its great distinction & breadth." She wrote Adams a letter indicating that at a late stage of the book's development she had withdrawn permission to use a letter of Bay's to her that she had led Adams to think he might use. She apologized. ". . . I have no excuse—excepting that at times the complications of life . . . are too much for me—standing entirely alone as I do—& I do not hold myself together & I do back & fill."[94]

In reply, Adams described the ideal biographer. He told her that a biographer should be "invisible"—"a mere mirror" face to face with the subject—at most "a slight tone of color" in the story.[95]

One may assume that a copy of the *Life* reached Mrs. Cameron very quickly, that she read it at once, and wrote frankly to Dor about it. Unfortunately all the letters she sent him in the interval subsequent to April 8 and prior to December 21, 1911, are missing. He evidently received them. Perhaps he destroyed them as very medical.

He informed Mrs. Jones on October 27, "Mrs[.] Cameron and her hospital at Stepleton break up their household today. . . ." He was in a position to add: ". . . Martha migrates on Monday to the Hague. Her mother and Elisabeth [*sic*] get here a week later."

Edith Wharton was en route to Paris. News reached her about Mrs. Cameron. She wrote to Adams from Avignon, "I hear Lizzie is to be in Paris next week. We'll have wild times together. . . ."[96]

Once restored to her Paris apartment, Mrs. Wharton read a copy of *The Life of George Cabot Lodge*, presumably supplied by Adams. In a hurried note, she told him that she had spent her first night at home reading his book and "marvelling at the skill & wisdom with which you had dealt with a very difficult problem." She did not wish to say in writing what she thought the problem was. Instead she asked him to dinner. "I want to talk to you about it."[97]

Mrs. Wharton's approval of the *Life* gave Adams more-than-usual reason to write to her sister-in-law, Mrs. Jones. On November 3, he informed the latter that Houghton Mifflin had sent him copies. He did not like seeing them. "My eyes grow worse, but they reconcile me to anything if I am spared reading my own books." "Let us pray that no one may write our lives or publish our works."

Before his letter could reach her, Mrs. Jones obtained the *Life* and read it carefully. She had heard that Bessy forbade the use of some letters. Yet the biography Adams had written seemed complete. At 1:00 a.m., she told him: ". . . I know it is an ungodly hour for a letter, but I've just finished your Life of Bay[,] and . . . I may as well tell you how much I like it. The first thing I felt was the quality of distinction which is now almost never existent and then the restrained tenderness and the passionate sympathy with what he [Bay] had tried to do." She considered the book a kindness. "It is much to be able to do such a thing for a friend."[98]

Printing of the new *Mont Saint Michel and Chartres* was so nearly completed that Adams might have to do no more than read a few last proofs when again in Washington.

After a delay, Mrs. Cameron, Martha, and Elizabeth came to Paris together. Elizabeth seemed well. Martha did not. Dor thought her case emotional. He stated his view to Mrs. Jones. "I think the fears are the true disease. Every straw is a terror."[99]

In less that two weeks, Dor would go to Cherbourg and board the *Olympic*. Loulie would be going with him. By some means, he learned that another passenger on the ship would be his one-time student and friend Perry Belmont, who had been divorced from his first wife and was traveling with a second. Try as he might, Adams could not feel at ease with people who got divorced. He exclaimed to Mrs. Jones, "My only terror is the Perry Belmonts, for I don't in the least know what to do with them."[100]

When packing, he put into his luggage the text of the *Chanson de Willame* as published by its discoverer, George Dunn.[101] On shipboard or at home, he would start to translate the poem.

White Star ships bound for New York accepted passengers in England at Southampton, in France at Cherbourg, and in Ireland at Queenstown. Because too big to dock at Cherbourg, the *Olympic* would only anchor inside the breakwater. Vessels known as tenders would take passengers from a dock to the steamer. First-class passengers would be taken on a large tender, the *Nomadic*.[102]

Mrs. Cameron so busied herself with helping Martha, Elizabeth, and others that she reduced her hours with Dor to a frighteningly small allowance. He and Loulie left for Cherbourg on Wednesday, December 20, 1911. A violent storm was crossing Europe. Mrs. Cameron doubted that the *Olympic* could leave Southampton. On Thursday morning, she sent Elizabeth to the Morgan bank to make inquiries. Elizabeth came back with word that telegraph wires were down and the office of the White Star Line could not affirm that the ship had sailed.

Winds howled all day. Mrs. Cameron imagined that Dor was kept at Cherbourg but was not sure. At 8:00 P.M., December 21, she wrote him a note. "I try to tell myself that you are safer in Cherbourg than out at sea, but it does not comfort me much[,] for I know you are uncomfortable & will start fatigued & under the worst conditions."

She had no news to give him except that she and Elizabeth enjoyed making last use of Alexandre and the rented automobile. Her essential message was one of worry, almost of panic. She ended, ". . . I wish I knew where you are!"

21

ROOM ON THE *TITANIC*

Adams and Loulie waited all Wednesday night aboard the *Nomadic* at Cherbourg before the *Olympic* arrived from Southampton to take its passengers aboard. From Queenstown, Loulie sped a note to Mrs. Cameron to assure her that ship and passengers were safely on their way.[1]

Uncle Henry passed the voyage indoors. "I never left my palatial room except to take meals in the excellent restaurant. . . ." He said he took occasion to read "fourteen fierce novels."[2] Loulie punctuated his reading by paying visits. During a visit on Christmas Day, she had an experience she did not expect. "I was lying on his bed in his big stateroom looking at the ceiling. . . ." They were talking about best-selling novels. ". . . he was on the sofa between the portholes, the sun streaming into the cabin, books on books piled up near the sofa." She said that *he* wrote a " 'best seller' (his words)." He said it was titled *Democracy* and was published anonymously.[3]

To that point, Adams had done nothing new. He earlier had given Martha a copy of *Democracy* for her to read as written by himself.[4] But Loulie had long since begun to study him. She had learned how her uncles-by-marriage, E. W. Gurney and Henry Adams, had managed not to have children.[5] She had possessed herself of copies of both versions of Adams's Tahiti book. He had learned his lesson and gave her his *Mont Saint Michel and Chartres* and even a second copy of *The Education*. Before they set out for Cherbourg, he presented her a copy of the *Life of George Cabot Lodge*, inscribed, "Let us take ship & sail/ 16 Decr 1911."[6]

While lying in the stateroom, she realized he was doing something he till then had avoided: telling secrets and not stopping. "He was in his narrative vein, & I was electrified at being told. I could not look at him because of emotion."

He told her he had come to believe that books "depended for their success on advertizing." To prove it, he had written a second novel, *Esther*, "which he thought better than his first." ". . . he said he took the

409

theme from the building of [Boston's] Trinity Church and placed it [the novel] in New York." He said too that he created the heroine, Esther Dudley, by combining "two or three" women he knew. ". . . she was a composite . . . two or 3 in one, and he left me with the impression that it was 3 rather than 2." By his order, the novel was not advertised. Confirmingly, it did not sell.

Loulie was electrified because Uncle Henry had changed her role. By telling her secret after secret, he had made her his biographer, at least in the sense of giving her information that he was giving to no other young person; also in the sense of expecting her to develop an idea of his life and work that was well-informed and free of myth.[7]

In Washington on January 4, 1912, Adams started a letter to Mrs. Cameron by saying that returns to the capital were worse than departures. He had called on the Lodges, the Whites, Clara Hay, Edith Eustis, and his brother's family. Charles was out. Mrs. Lodge was unwell and in bed. Bessy Lodge and Mrs. Keep were away.

That afternoon, Mrs. Lodge got out of bed and came in her new auto to see him. "To my mind she looked about eighty, and feeble at that. She vows that nothing ails her except physical weakness, but if the weakness goes on, she will fade out, and just stop."

Mrs. Lodge left, and Adams began an errand. While crossing Lafayette Square, he was hailed by "a hippopotamus!" "It was the President himself[,] wandering about with Archie Butt, and I joined them as far as the White House Porch." Taft seemed "ripe for a stroke" and "showed mental enfeeblement all over." Adams wondered whether his own mind was enfeebled. He said the "nightmare" of thinking that everyone had deteriorated had gotten on his nerves. "Drat it!"

Last proofs of the new *Mont Saint Michel and Chartres* needed to be read. Adams mailed them to the printer on Monday, January 8, 1912. On Thursday, he exclaimed to Mrs. Cameron: "My final proof-sheets are sent; my final occupation is ended; since Monday I wake up every morning with the happy thought that I've nothing more to do in the world." His happy thought lasted till delivery of the next day's mail. It brought news from his Paris landlord that he would have to vacate his apartment at 88 Boulevard du Bois de Boulogne by July 1. He had been expecting the edict, felt inconvenienced, but was not alarmed.

In Paris, Mrs. Cameron heard the news. "They tell me you have had congé for your apartment! Oh! your prophetic pessimistic soul! You were right, as always. But it is a calamity. . . ." She listed the advantages of the "good spaces" he had lost: their looking out on an avenue—their facing gardens in front and back—sun streaming in—"new curtains!" She *was* alarmed. "I admit that I am upset."[8]

* * *

The 1912 version of *Mont Saint Michel and Chartres* arrived from Furst and Company on January 15. Adams mailed copies to seventeen libraries that Jameson had listed for him. He asked Jameson for an added list. The editor sent fifteen more addresses and requested a copy for himself.[9]

Adams meanwhile had received Mrs. Cameron's cries about his lost apartment. He assured her that her views about the loss were "very correct." Yet he was feeling cheered. ". . . I am looking forward to the amusement of fitting up a new one, which will give me occupation for the whole summer." He described the sort of place that a deteriorating man would want. "I might as well get one, this time, large enough to contain my social secretary and nurse."[10]

Recipients who opened the new version of Adams's book and compared it with the 1904 version could be excused if they got the impression that changes were minimal.[11] The most obvious was a date—"[December, 1904.]"—inserted above the opening line of the Preface. An inconspicuous addition was a table of contents. Evidently written at the last minute, it was inserted after the index at the end of the book.

Of the work's sixteen chapters, eleven reappeared without significant revisions.[12] There were scattered minor cuts and expansions.[13] In Chapter V, "Towers and Portals," Adams expanded a passage asserting that certain statues at Chartres cathedral are portaits of actual persons known to the parishioners who were living when the statues were put in place.[14] In Chapter IX, "The Legendary Windows," he greatly expanded his comments about particular windows at Chartres, most notably the window that repeats the fictional story of Charlemagne as a Christian warrior-saint.[15] In Chapter XI, "The Three Queens," as already noticed, he presented King Richard's prison song in full in Old French and English.[16] And in Chapter XVI, "Saint Thomas Aquinas," he added enough lines about Duns Scotus to pay appropriate respects to Aquinas's great successor.[17]

Careful review of all the changes could lead straightway to a not entirely surprising revelation. Throughout the year 1911, while giving time and effort to the printing of an updated and improved version of *Mont Saint Michel and Chartres*, Adams had concealed the fact that the book needed very little improvement and concealed the further fact that he was pouring large amounts of energy into a challenging secret enterprise, his essay "Chansons de Geste." He had concealed the essay not because he thought the ideas it advanced were weak or flawed. As its many pages showed, the essay was the work of a ground-breaking historian who feared his own ideas because convinced they were new and true.

The house Charles built for himself in Washington at 1701 Massachusetts Avenue was six blocks distant from 1603 H Street. When Henry had been home four days, Charles became embarrassed that they had not seen each other. He sent a hand-delivered letter saying he would come to dinner the following evening. He mentioned too that he was having eye troubles and that Dr. Wilmer had restricted his reading.[18]

One may assume that Charles came to dinner and that the brothers exchanged accounts of eye-strain, but evidence is lacking about another matter. At the November 1911 meeting of the Massachusetts Historical Society, Charles had read a paper, "The Trent Affair." When printed by the Society in 1912, the paper filled forty-two pages and was accompanied by an eighty-three page appendix of relevant letters drawn from the Adams family's collection, excerpts from newspapers printed in 1861, and letters by John Bright to Charles Sumner.

At an uncertain but early date, a member of the Society let it be known that he intended to write for publication in the *Proceedings* an answer to the president's paper. The objector was Richard Henry Dana—the third Dana of the name. He was riled by what he believed was bad history. In Dana's view, President Adams's paper was mistaken about what the English had done to the United States in the *Trent* Affair. Dana wished to make an issue of the error.[19] Charles, for once, was confronted with a serious historical mutiny.

Henry Adams kept more silent about some matters than others.[20] One of his completest silences concerned the initial and final versions of Charles's dubious paper and the abbreviated and unabbreviated versions of Dana's reply, "The Trent Affair: An Aftermath," read before the March 1912 meeting of the Society.[21] That Henry was wise to be silent can be inferred from the rival papers. If read in the light of Henry's writings about the treatment of the United States by the British government during the *Trent* Affair, Charles's paper failed to notice the only thing that for Henry—also for Dana—most mattered: an unprovoked English effort in 1861 to hurt the Union and help the Confederacy. With respect to this effort, Dana's paper was a documented reminder.[22] This is not to say that Henry assisted Dana's effort. Henry let Dana conduct his mutiny alone, which Dana was well-prepared to do.[23]

For many weeks early in 1912, the guest rooms on the second floor at 1603 H Street were taken by "nieces," "nephews," and other arrivals, and places at the dining table for noon-time "breakfast" were in steady demand.[24] When not attending to his guests, Henry worked at translations of the *Chanson de Willame*. His method was to assign himself a dozen verses a day. To spare his eyes, he wrote his English renderings in a very large form of his handwriting on large sheets of paper. He had no intention of translating the entire work. He wished to translate only parts that especially interested him or related to further inquiries he wanted to make in Europe.

Raymond Weeks, a professor of romance languages at Columbia, had established himself as an authority on the Chanson de Willame by publishing some learned articles. On January 25, Adams wrote a letter to Professor Luquiens at Yale. He revealed that he was translating parts of the *Chanson de Willame* but concealed his having developed a theory that the *Chanson de Willame* and *Chanson de Roland* were written by a single author and his having supported the theory in a detailed essay. He said he wanted to send Luquiens his partial translation when it was finished, so that Luquiens could "look it over"; he asked for information about an expert on the *Chanson de Willame*, Raymond Weeks; and he intimated that a new theory was possible about the two *chansons*. "The temptation is great to invent a theory that will apply. Such a literary problem has no parallel in history, and might even throw light on the problem of the Iliad itself. Yet the Chanson de Willame is so perplexing that as yet I wander in whole clouds of conjecture. . . . A totally new class of ideas rises up . . . which centres in the Abbey of St[.] Denis and the Capetian revolution of 987."

Being himself engaged in an effort to translate the *Chanson de Roland*, Luquiens was overjoyed to know that Adams was translating the other poem. He listed for Adams some Italian, French, German, and American books and articles that might assist him, and hastened to explain that Professor Weeks was a Harvard graduate.[25]

Not a person to act without obtaining the best available information, Adams wrote to Henry Osborn Taylor in New York, asking for an opinion of Weeks. Taylor replied that the professor was "a highly esteemed scholar, quiet, & serious[-]minded."[26]

So prepared, Adams on February 3 wrote to Weeks, saying that the professor's articles about the *Chanson de Willame* and related topics deserved to be reissued as "a standard book of reference." He gave Weeks no inkling that he was at work on a partial translation of the poem or that he had written an essay. He was at pains to give an opposite impression. "Naturally I have nothing to say; but merely as a matter of history, the relation between the twin poems of Roland and Willame is a point of capital importance."

Weeks sent Adams one of his articles—the only one he could easily supply. He said in a covering note, "I shall preserve your letter, not only for its contents, but also for the extreme beauty of your [hand]writing!"[27] The professor's reaction matched the reactions of many other persons who had received letters in Adams's handwriting. With remarkable frequency, his letters were being saved.

Edie Hoyt was back in Washington and visiting Adams, who found her "bright and well."[28] In Europe, Elizabeth Hoyt was less lucky. She remained a victim of painful, mysterious neuritis.

Mrs. Cameron had become as capable a money manager as Adams. She rented a Paris apartment at 6 Square du Bois be Boulogne, sublet it to a relative of the Vanderbilts for a comforting sum, and repaired with Elizabeth to the Hotel Montfleury at Cannes in hopes of a warm winter. The loss of Adams's ideal apartment continued to upset her. She explained, "I am afraid you will be driven to another *quartier*—and then!" She promised: "When I return to Paris[,] I shall hunt apartments [for you] hard. I ought to be there by the 20th of March."[29]

Life at Cannes was pleasingly monotonous. Mrs. Cameron was reading Herodotus. She reported having trouble with her eyes. ". . . I don't believe yours are much worse than mine. I am cut off from most things now, & spare them in every way."[30] But she did not spare them. She translated *Lady Windermere's Fan* into French. The labor was an exercise. It irked her that she could read and write French easily but was only slowly learning to speak it.[31]

She and Elizabeth planned an excursion to Corsica—a place Adams had not seen. On February 7, she asked him, "Have you made up your mind yet when to sail?"

From Washington on February 9, Adams sent Professor Weeks a copy of the new *Mont Saint Michel and Chartres*, together with what could appear to be an offhand summary of ideas about the *Chanson de Willame* and the *Chanson de Roland*. He said he had approached the subject "from the historical side" and had been "driven by historical necessities into my conclusions." "I have got to fit the Chansons into a certain society, and conversely to find the society which they fit." He said too that the question at issue was larger and more momentous than the invention of old songs. It was the making of a race, nation, or people. ". . . I can give [the songs] . . . no better company than the Capetian usurpation of 987 [by Hugh Capet] . . . and the astonishing literary activity and authority of the Abbey of Saint Denis. These two movements created France and its ideals. . . ."

Weeks's knowledge of the chansons was purely literary. He replied that he was "not qualified to judge as to the Capetian origin." Yet he agreed with Adams that the *Chanson de Willame* was "vastly more popular than the Roland, [and] more certainly primitive." He was reading *Mont*

Saint Michel and Chartres and reported that, as far as he had gone in the book, he had found not a single "false note."[32]

February 16, 1912, was Adams's seventy-fourth birthday. He celebrated partly by asking Weeks to name for him "any paper or essay" that touched on a seldom-considered question: whether the original setting of the *Chanson de Willame* was the Spanish March, as opposed to Orange, in Provence. He voiced this plea to Weeks in a letter that also involved ten excerpts from the Old French chant. Yet nowhere in the letter did he hint that he had written an essay on the subject and that what he wanted to learn was whether any other researcher had gotten ahead of him.

By then, Mrs. Cameron's question about Dor's sailing had arrived from Cannes. Because he had been comfortable on the *Olympic*, he was interested in a still larger steamer the White Star Line was soon to put in service. The new ship was being advertised as unsinkable because divided into sixteen water-tight compartments. As if he was deciding at the same moment he was writing, Dor replied: "I wonder whether the Titanic, on April 20, will suit. I think I shall take rooms on it, by way of venture."[33]

Adams's plan to cross to Cherbourg on the *Titanic's* first return voyage to Europe was contingent on Loulie's convenience. She soon agreed to join him on the voyage. Price was a consideration. Uncle Henry's space on the ship cost $600. A very different consideration was a British coal strike. Doubts were being voiced whether the White Star Line had coal enough to supply its ships, even its newest.

Mrs. Cameron and Elizabeth hurried from Nice to Corsica, scoured the island in search of glorious scenery, and found it. In Washington, Adams continued to translate verses of the *Chanson de Willame* and anticipated future work. On March 7, 1912, he wrote to Thoron, "I much want you to get down to Barcelona and do the geography of Willame."[34] The occasion for Adams's desire was a problem of names. During the past thousand years, place names in the Spanish March had entirely changed. Places referred to in the *chanson* might not be identifiable except by investigation on the spot.

By March 12, Adams had advanced far enough in his translation to justify a new letter to Luquiens. He told the Yale professor: "As I shall be pursuing the tracks of Willame next summer, I want to get him into my head, correctly, and with a certain confidence that I know all about him. Hence arises my attempt to translate." He asked Luquiens to review his English verses. As if the idea had newly occurred to him, he also said he was wondering whether the *Chanson de Willame* and *Chanson de Roland* were "composed by the same man, at the same time, for the same purpose."

The remarks to Luquiens implied a firm schedule of actions. Adams expected to reach Paris by April 27, to get access to a new apartment quickly, to arrange the moving of his possessions into it, and go to Barcelona to study geography—all before the onset of summer heat. When back in Paris, he could get settled in the new apartment.

Luquiens agreed to review the translation. He said he thought it "very likely that the same man composed the Willame and the Roland." As if afraid, he retreated at once to a safe, professorial position. "I don't see how anyone could prove it was *not* the same man."[35]

Adams sent Luquiens roughly 800 translated verses.[36] Luquiens combed them vigilantly for errors. He corrected some errors directly on Adams's manuscript in pencil.[37] He listed other errors and some points of difference in a four-page letter, typed and single-spaced. The spirit of his response was enthusiastically supportive.[38]

At Columbia, Professor Weeks had been prevented by conjunctivitis from trying to find for Adams a book or article connecting the *Chanson de Willame* and the Spanish March. Yet his eye trouble was not so bad that he could not continue reading Adams's "sparkling, charming volume"—the new *Mont Saint Michel and Chartres*.[39]

All along, Adams had known that Alexander Agassiz was mentioned in *The Education*. Yet Adams had failed to send him a copy and request his erasure, correction, or approval of what the book said about him. Agassiz had died in 1910, and his son George had became his literary representative and biographer. In January 1912, Adams sent George a copy of the book, which was gratefully received.[40]

The copies of *The Education* that Adams still held were matters of great importance to him. He had reduced his traveling copies to the status of utility copies, kept at hand for mere purposes of reference. The Second Traveling Copy remained in his Paris library. The Master Copy and the First Traveling Copy were at 1603 H Street. One may guess that the Master Copy was in his main-floor study, locked in one of the drawers of his very large, double-sided desk. One may guess that the First Traveling Copy was in the main-floor study within easy reach on a bookshelf. More than forty untouched or returned copies were also in the house, probably in his quarters on the top floor.[41]

Gaskell chanced to have two copies. It occurred to him that one of the two might better be given to the library of the British Museum in London. He wrote to Adams asking whether his "deeply interesting" book had been given to that library. If Adams had not sent a copy to the library, Gaskell said, he could readily do so himself.[42]

Gaskell's letter reached Adams on April 12, 1912, two days after the *Titanic* sailed. The White Star Line had managed to fuel its new ship for its maiden voyage, and word of the ship's departure had been cabled to New York. The news permitted Adams to tell his friend, "My ship, the Titanic, is on her way, and unless she drops me somewhere else, I should get to Cherbourg in a fortnight."

Adams did not consent to Gaskell's offer to give *The Education* to the British Museum. He instead suggested that both the copies in his friend's possession were better burned! He said, ". . . I hardly think my 'Education' is fit for any public. It is only proof-sheets, full of errors, and I've not given it to any library here." "Burn up the volumes when you are done with them!"

The injunction to Gaskell might seem a joke or self-effacement but was serious. Adams had made extraordinary decisions about his book.

The sub-tenant who had taken Mrs. Cameron's Paris apartment left a month ahead of time. Mrs. Cameron sped back to Paris to enjoy a month rent-free. She crowed to Adams, "There is nothing like capturing a Vanderbilt!" Unfortunately, while on the train, she hurt a foot. Unable to walk with ease, she postponed her hunt for Adams's new apartment. She assured him, "There is plenty of time ahead."[43]

Theodore Roosevelt was attempting to deprive President Taft of the Republican nomination for 1912 and bestow it on himself. Adams saw Roosevelt as trying to replay the role of Napoleon when leaving Elba and expected that few Republicans would assist him. Of the possible Republican candidates, Adams preferred Taft to Roosevelt. He believed neither could be elected.[44]

Mrs. Cameron went to Stepleton to see Martha and found her "pale" but better than "this time last year." In a letter that reached Adams on April 12 or the day after, the mother said, "I shall be in Paris when you arrive." "We will go apartment hunting together."[45]

Adams had come to think of Roosevelt as destructively unhinged. On Sunday, April 14, writing to Mrs. Jones, whom he was expecting to visit very soon in New York, he said, ". . . all my men-friends are wrecks. Except our dear Theodore, who is a wrecker."

To an exceptional degree, Adams had led a life mostly controlled by the person who was living it, rather than by external forces. The rule especially applied during the April days while the *Titanic* sped westward towards New York. He tried to put his affairs in order as they related to his *Education*.

With respect to two of his books, he occupied widely different situations. He had privately printed two versions of *Mont Saint Michel and*

Chartres. All the copies were models of educational, literary, and historical work. He could distribute them without the least hesitation.

In haste, he had finished the printing of 100 copies of one version of *The Education of Henry Adams.* At many points in the middle and later chapters, printing of the version was marred by uncorrected printer's errors and uncorrected errors attributable to himself, whether as author of the manuscript or as reader of the printer's proofs. The version, moreover, had turned out to be susceptible of improvement. Setting aside improvements made only in his Master Copy, Adams had entered 135 improvements—not mere corrections—in his First and Second Traveling Copies, including an improved chapter-title.

In the circumstances, all the printed copies of *The Education* that Adams had given to friends, all the copies he lent with requests that they be returned, and all returned and never-touched copies still on his hands at 1603 H Street had become an embarrassment to him. It hardly mattered that surplus copies in his possession had been expensive to print. Reputation was the decisive issue. With respect to reputation, surplus copies could seem much more costly than their printing had been.

He decided upon a course that had several aspects. One has been touched upon already: his telling Gaskell to burn the two copies in his possession. That small action had a large accompaniment. Presumably on Sunday, April 14, 1912, or a day or two earlier, he ordered the destruction of copies in his house, as many as thirty-five, or more.[46] An available procedure was to ask William Gray, his servant, to take the copies to the basement, preferably without being noticed, and burn them in the furnace whenever most convenient.

The destruction of many copies did not mean that Adams would never again have copies-for-distribution. He could expect that some of the copies he had lent would tardily float back to him, in which case he could lend them again, should he wish to do so.[47]

A completely separate matter was clean copies not burned and kept for his own use. He evidently saved five such copies.[48] One can assume that he shelved two with his First Traveling Copy in his main-floor study and two others on a shelf in his upstairs study. His purpose was to create easy-to-remember sets, one downstairs, the other upstairs. A lone clean copy was left.

Adams's bedroom was the center room at the front of the building on the top floor. Persons leaving his bedroom saw a door at the east end of the hall. The door permitted access to a cedar closet used for storage. A trunk in the closet contained clothes and other valuables that had belonged to Mrs. Adams. The trunk presumably was locked and may not have been opened for many years.[49]

At a very late moment, presumably on April 14, Adams performed an action wholly secret. He went to the storage closet, unlocked the trunk, put into it both the Master Copy and the fifth clean copy, and relocked the trunk.[50] By this means, he concealed the materials that an editor would need when readying a fully corrected-and-improved copy of *The Education* for use by a printer, preparatory to publication.[51]

The hiding of the copies had a constructive meaning. Adams meant his *Education* to be published in the form indicated by the corrections and improvements entered in the Master Copy, but only after his death. To make his intention clear, he had put the Master Copy and an Attendant Clean Copy in a trunk that could also be thought a tomb.[52]

Henry may have been strengthened in this intention by news that Charles had completed his *Autobiography* in final form. In preparation for the moment when the president of the Massachusetts Historical Society would die and the Society would have to publish a memoir in his honor, a 228-page typescript was being mailed to Ford in Boston.[53] Henry's *Education* was not an autobiography. It was the opposite. But Henry had ideas of fitness. A younger brother, he would not hurry his book into print before his elder brother's book. He would want his own book to wait.

There remained the important fact that *The Education* was Henry's best, most original, and most ambitious book. By hiding the Master Copy and the Attendant Clean Copy, he prepared for two eventualities. One was that he would go to Europe on the *Titanic*, return in the fall, take the Master Copy and Attendant Clean Copy from the trunk, and devote a few days to annotating the latter in such a way as to turn it into a Publisher's Copy that could go straight to a printer.

The second eventuality was a negative version of the first. He could imagine that he might never get back from Europe, or might not have time or opportunity to create a Publisher's Copy. He might get side-tracked into new interests, drift into illness, even die. In any of these cases, the best place of concealment for the Master Copy and the Attendant Clean Copy would be the trunk in the closet.

On Sunday, April 14, 1912, soon after 11:40 P.M., the *Titanic* sent signals of distress by "wireless." At high speed, the ship had grazed an iceberg and was damaged on its starboard side below the water line. Five compartments were flooding. In less than three hours, the ship would vanish in calm cold seas. There were not nearly enough life boats. Many hundreds of passengers and crewmen were sure to drown.

On April 15, like all the world, Adams learned that the ship and crowds aboard it had been lost. Always a politician, he noticed that the *Titanic* and President Taft were lost together: the president had sustained a heavy defeat in primary balloting in Pennsylvania.

Adams waited till Tuesday and wrote to Mrs. Cameron. "In half an hour, just in a summer sea, were wrecked the Titanic; President Taft; the Republican party . . . and I. We all foundered and disappeared." ". . . I turn green and sick when I think of it."[54]

He had discovered that he could not afford to listen while others discussed the ship and what had happened to the persons still aboard when it sank. He reported: "Last night the Lodges came to dinner; Jack White and a young Biddle came; Bessy brought Langdon Mitchell later. I listened to the talk. . . . Much was quoted from the talk elsewhere. . . . Through the chaos I seemed to be watching the Titanic foundering in a shoreless ocean."[55]

He had directed his travel agent to get comparable space for him on the *Olympic*, to sail on May 4. He informed Mrs. Cameron by cable and Loulie by telegram. He faced a two-week wait.

When Sunday came round again, he told Mrs. Cameron that the week had resembled the weeks of "the great defeats of the civil war." "The strain gets on my nervous system. . . . Only in history as a fairy tale, does one like to see civilisations founder, and to hear the cries of the drowning." He turned to the "supplementary foundering" of the dis-united Republicans and said of Roosevelt: "Our dear Theodore is not a bird of happy omen. He loves to destroy."

Adams's mind was fixed on the lost ship. "I find it impossible to shake off this nightmare, largely because everyone else talks about it."[56] He remembered a passage near the end of his *Education*: "Every day nature violently revolted, causing so-called accidents with enormous de-struction of property and life, while plainly laughing at man. . . ." He helplessly imagined an iceberg seeking a coming ship.[57]

Most dangerous to him was a letter he had written in the past. In 1901, he had advised Mrs. Cameron from Washington, ". . . I sit here, and look at Europe sink, first one deck disappearing, then another, and the whole ship slowly plunging bow-down into the abyss; until the night-mare gets to be howling."[58] The unsinkable *Titanic* did the same. It tilted bow-down and grandly slid from sight. The confirmation of the imag-ined by the real much augmented his fears of both.[59]

In appearance, he was unharmed. On April 22, he urged Loulie in normal tones, "Please find some books for the voyage!" Yet he acted as if aware that he had passed beyond the brink of danger. He was not reading newspapers. He was avoiding the Lodges, who liked to talk and by talking had made him irreparably nervous.

On Wednesday, April 24, Adams dined alone. William noticed that during dinner he did not use his right hand.[60] After dinner, William heard the noise of a fall. He hurried from the pantry to the dining room. Adams was on the floor, unable to rise, but able to speak. He was small and light enough to be lifted without difficulty. William and a female servant carried him up two flights to his bedroom and made him comfortable in his bed. There was no telephone, but William rushed to Mrs. Hay's phone next door and reached two doctors. Both came, completed their examinations, and said that Adams had suffered "a slight shock and must be kept very quiet." Mrs. Hay's physician, Dr. Hardin, arrived next. He agreed with his predecessors. Last to arrive was Dr. Yarrow, Adams's own physician. He brought in a nurse, forbade visitors, but "anticipated nothing serious."[61]

On Thursday, Dr. Yarrow found that Adams's right arm and leg were "perfectly well" but his right hand was "heavy." The symptoms seemed indicative of "a small clot or lesion" in the brain.[62]

From that point forward, Yarrow returned "three times a day."[63] It became apparent that Yarrow and Adams were good friends and that the doctor's efforts to help were not simply medical.[64]

Everyone wrote letters. Senator Lodge wrote to Sturgis Bigelow. Minnie—Charles's wife—wrote to Brooks and to Mary Adams Quincy. Anna Lodge wrote to her sister Evelyn—Brooks's wife. Charles's daughter Elsie wrote to Loulie. Clara Hay wrote to Mrs. Cameron.

Lodge's letters to Bigelow were frequent, detailed, and written to be read by Bigelow and relayed in the form of copies to Mabel La Farge in Switzerland and Mrs. Cameron in Paris.[65] By this means, a channel of almost daily communication was opened from the scene of the illness to a woman in Paris with whom the patient was known to have been in close relation. Though not a secret, the channel was invisible to the persons coming and going at 1603 H Street in Washington. Because it by-passed Henry's relatives, it spared the other Adamses the necessity of writing or cabling to Mrs. Cameron more than a minimum of times. It permitted Mrs. Cameron to get maximum information. Sadly for her, the information included advice that she must not write to Dor till told it would be appropriate for her to do so.[66]

Charles was away till Saturday, April 27, 1912. Presumably on Sunday, he came to 1603 H Street, entered Henry's room, and talked with him. On Monday, at Henry's direction, he sent 25,000 francs to Mrs. Cameron to pay bills and keep a balance on hand. Also Charles wrote her a letter. He said he would cable only if very necessary and would usually contact her by mail. He outlined salient points of the case. Dr. Yarrow was anticipating a complete recovery. A second nurse had been brought in, and a telephone had been ordered, to be installed in Henry's pantry or kitchen.[67]

Loulie arrived from Boston. Room had to be made for her, for she announced that she was staying.[68]

On May 2, Charles wrote again to Mrs. Cameron. He said that Henry was not anxious or worried, was rapidly recovering, was interested in political developments, and attributed his mishap to the " 'Titanic' disaster." Charles directed her to assume "entire charge" of Henry's affairs in Paris and to arrange the packing of his "papers, books, furniture, etc." and their removal to storage. He said he expected that Henry would stay in Quincy through June and go abroad on July 1 with a "companion and traveling secretary." "This is merely a program as it has arranged itself in my mind." Charles assumed that the companion-secretary would be a man. ". . . [Henry] must be perpetually attended. . . . Ward Thoron has been suggested as a person fairly worthy of consideration."

On May 4, Lodge informed Bigelow that Henry's blood pressure was 190 at the time of his "seizure" but had dropped to 150. "His physical condition is entirely satisfactory but mentally he is not quite right." ". . . he seems unable to coordinate his ideas. . . ."[69]

On May 7, Charles went to Boston. Writing to Mrs. Cameron next day from his Boston office, he said the patient was worse. Dr. Yarrow and Dr. Hardin were agreed that there had been "a further cerebral disturbance." Henry was "cheerful in a way, but restless." ". . . he continually evinces a desire to leave the bed."

In this new situation, Charles gave Mrs. Cameron new instructions. He said that during the one occasion when he was permitted to speak with him, Henry had been "explicit on one point." "He wished to have all his Paris belongings packed up and forwarded to this country, consigned directly to . . . Brooks Adams. I at the time suggested that they might be packed up and stored in Paris . . . for then I by no means despaired of his being able to return to Paris with an attendant companion. This expectation I have now abandoned. Accordingly . . . all his Paris belongings can be packed and forwarded at once. . . ."

When Charles's new instructions arrived, Mrs. Cameron was especially affected by the words "at once." The immediate dismantling and shipment of Henry's Paris establishment was a cataclysm for her fully as bad as her loss of her Washington house. Yet it seemed to be what Henry had ordered. If she could carry out the order, she would be satisfied. Her doing what he asked would be a loving service to him, even if ruinous to herself.

At the start of the year, Henry had said that his brothers had both become "older" than he was and that mentally Charles was "very shakey."[70] Recently too, Henry had pictured Senator Lodge as "broken down from mental feebleness."[71]

The description of Lodge was overdrawn. The senator's letters to Bigelow about Henry's condition were helpfully specific. Most of the information they contained came from Dr. Yarrow. Some of it could seem shocking. On May 7, Henry had said to the nurse then on duty "that he wanted her to write his mother, 'who', he said, 'you know, was lost on the Titanic.' "[72]

Yarrow had been friendly with Willy Phillips. On May 8, according to Yarrow as reported by Lodge, Henry acted as if Phillips were still alive. ". . . he said to the doctor: 'If you see Willie Phillips . . . will you give him a message?' The doctor said, 'I am not likely to see him but if I do I will give him the message.' "[73]

Yarrow returned during the evening of May 8 and found Henry in a "violent paroxysm." His physical condition had improved remarkably. "He struggled to get out of bed and wanted apparently to throw himself out of the window. . . . The doctor stayed until 10 o'clock himself and then had his assistant come and stay all night."[74]

Lodge interpreted the patient's behavior as alternations "between entire rationality and what amounts to delirium." ". . . his mind seems to be running back over the events of his life and confuses them with the present."[75]

Without disputing the opinion of the doctors that the blood supply in the patient's brain had been disturbed, a biographer may suggest that Adams was suffering severely from the strain of ideas. After the *Titanic* sank but before he himself sank helplessly to his dining room floor, he had remarked in a letter to Anne Fell that he had fifty times been on steamers that went to or near the place in the Atlantic into which the *Titanic* disappeared. He moreover told Anne that he had known every time that his ship was risking collision with Arctic ice. Fifty fears had been a great many. They had taught him too well that humans drowned.[76]

After he was carried upstairs to bed, Adams was occupied, not in confusing things, but in assembling things and bringing them together. He was most concerned about persons who drowned. He had not believed the story Brooks wrote to him in 1897 after Willy Phillips's death: that Willy was caught by a rope which broke his neck, killed him instantly, and snatched him overboard. The story Henry believed was the first one told: that Willy died by drowning.

When Henry wanted the nurse to write to his mother, he meant his grandmother, Louisa Adams, whom he counted as his real mother, and to whom he had wished to write in winter as a boy, when she was in

Washington and he in Boston. He thought of her, not because *she* drowned, but because her eldest son George vanished from the steamboat *Benjamin Franklin,* an indubitable suicide by drowning.

Henry had seen himself in part as a new George among the Adamses. Of course, it was not his grandmother but he himself—grandson Henry, the new George—that had claims to a stateroom on the *Titanic.*

Senator Lodge had been told that Henry had a paroxysm and tried to rise from bed, apparently wanting to throw himself from one of the bedroom's windows. Lodge must have wondered whether Henry was confusing himself with his brother-in-law, Edward Hooper, who had thrown himself from a window in Boston, attempting suicide. Henry, however, did not have suicidal impulses. Whether as Henry or as the new George among the Adamses, he was intent on staying alive. Rather obviously, his paroxysm was caused by his believing he was in bed on the *Titanic* when the ship and the iceberg were shortly to collide. He could tell night was coming. It was getting dark. He *had* to get out of bed, flee the stateroom, and stay on deck in hopes of reaching safety, possibly in a lifeboat. Yes, he violently tried to live.

As for his messages to his "mother" and Willy, they possibly said he had *not* drowned but that he could so well imagine what it was like that he might as well have. For him, the problem of icebergs and the chances of drowning had become all-too-familiar realities.

From the time they were boys, younger Henry had presented to older Charles the problem of being physically small, yet in other ways very big. Charles's way of solving the problem had been to assure himself that Henry was small and try to make him so. This was the way Charles was treating Richard Henry Dana in the matter of their rival papers titled "The Trent Affair." Dana was a new member of the Massachusetts Historical Society. He was big enough to engage the Society's president in battle and defeat him. Yet Charles had told Ford that Dana was "an amiable gentleman, but of very light weight." He went on to liken Dana to a pygmy battleship. "Carrying few guns, those he does carry are of small calibre."[77]

Brooks had never deceived himself about Henry's bigness. He had run up against problems of another sort: inability to understand him and inability to get him fully to disclose his ideas. Brooks had reacted by becoming desirous of acquiring tangibles—anything physical—that had belonged to his great brother. He had obtained from Henry some Adams heirlooms to embellish the Old House at Quincy. Next he would want Henry's Paris furniture, which belonged to a period of French furniture manufacture that could harmonize with the Adams mansion's interior.[78]

Of the persons concerned about Henry's fate, the men were the ones who entirely abandoned hope. Charles had effectively done so on May 7. On the 10th, Lodge informed Bigelow that he had been thinking that Henry was "not likely to live long" and that there seemed to be "no prospect of mental recovery." On the 11th, Brooks more definitely lamented to Ford, ". . . with Henry, I lose my strongest tie with the past, my most intimate friend, and the mind from whom I have drawn most since childhood."[79] For the youngest brother, Henry was already dead and had become a memory.

Charles wrote again to Mrs. Cameron on May 12, 1912. He reported that Minnie, Loulie, and Mrs. Lodge had visited Henry, "merely passing in and out of the room." The doctors were looking "grave." Minnie had taken charge of Henry's incoming mail.

Mrs. Hay wrote that day to Mrs. Jones. She mentioned that, when Charles visited him a second time, Henry treated the elder brother's presence in the room as "an intrusion." She said a third nurse had been summoned and Yarrow's assistant was staying at the house every night. All the bedrooms being full, Loulie was having to sleep at Charles's house but was in attendance near Uncle Henry every day.[80]

The wonders were Henry's muscularity and evident strength of will. Dr. Yarrow described his patient as "very strong" and said that when Henry was excited, the nurses could keep him in bed only "with great difficulty."[81]

The women at the scene had not lost heart. Clara Hay wrote again to Mrs. Jones on the 15th and said that Henry was "to be allowed to sit up in bed." He was well enough to ask Yarrow whether he could go to Quincy by July 1.

A cable from Bigelow to Mrs. Cameron on May 17, saying "mental condition growing worse," moved her to cable back to Bigelow and to Yarrow, asking whether she could come to Washington. The cable to Yarrow was garbled in transmission and was unreadable.[82] The one to Bigelow elicited a reply saying that Henry's ability to recognize her was "doubtful now" and would be "less likely later."[83]

A matching cable from Henry's sister Mary advised Mrs. Cameron not to think of a voyage. Mary Quincy said a visitor could "do nothing." She added that the Adamses were "moving him north."[84] There had been a flurry of family activity. Brooks had been in Washington on Saturday, May 18. He had seen Henry. It was agreed that Henry should be moved as soon as practicable.

Charles told Mrs. Cameron on May 21: ". . . I now regard the situation as quite hopeless. I do not think that he ever again will sustain a consecutive intelligence, or be able to speak of matters of business or arrangements to be made concerning himself." In the judgment of the eldest brother, the only place for Henry was a sanitarium.

Brooks was much concerned that Mrs. Cameron was burdened with the shipment of Henry's furniture. He felt that, being a lawyer, he was the person who should attend to "invoices, affidavits, etc." Charles accordingly cabled to Mrs. Cameron on the 24th, "Await letter before shipping Henry's household effects."[85]

Temperatures were rising in Washington, and Henry had been moved to a bedroom with a high ceiling. The idea of a sanitarium was dropped in favor of a family arrangement. There was an outer building on Charles's property in South Lincoln, Massachusetts, fifteen miles west of Boston, which could serve as "practically an independent hospital establishment." Henry could be taken from Washington to South Lincoln in a private railroad car. Charles communicated these details to Mrs. Cameron by letter on May 24. He in addition assured her that Brooks would be in Paris in six weeks.

Next day, May 25, Charles decided to wash his hands of the furniture matter. He advised both Brooks and Mrs. Cameron that Brooks was to assume complete responsibility.[86] Also on the 25th, Dr. Yarrow sent Mrs. Cameron a dark prognosis. He confessed, "I see very little hope for the future. . . ." He said that Henry's "mental faculties" would "never be the same."

Brooks took charge on the 25th by writing to Mrs. Cameron. He said he had not been told at an early stage about Charles's instructions. He was familiar with the difficulties of sending furniture to America and thought them burdensome. He encouraged Mrs. Cameron to leave Henry's furniture in storage till he could arrive.

Mainly Brooks was pessimistic. He thought Henry "helpless, hopeless." His brother had not "consciously" recognized him when they were together in Washington. Seeing him had been "most painful." "No one could wish him to live." "I wish I could give you any hope . . . but that I cannot do."[87]

22

RECOVERIES

Two days earlier, on Friday, May 24, 1912, Minnie had looked in on Henry and found "a marked improvement." She went next door and told her news to Mrs. Hay. On Sunday, Mrs. Hay wrote to Mrs. Cameron, saying that Mrs. Charles Adams had visited Henry on Friday and found that "for the first time she could understand what he said and his ideas and speech seemed to have a connection."

Henry's improvement thereafter was "distinct."[1] From Boston on June 7, Bigelow cabled to Mrs. Cameron, "EXTRAORDINARY IMPROVEMENT. . . . RECOVERY POSSIBLE."

Charles resisted the news. By letter from Boston on June 3, he assured Mrs. Cameron that the improvement was "very limited in its character." He said the disorder—"a clot" in the brain—was "most serious." He admitted that Henry wanted to have newspapers read to him but added, "He wanders off and has apparent hallucinations, in which travels in Africa and in Central Asia are a considerable feature." He said too that, once the transfer to Massachusetts was completed, the case would be placed under the management of Dr. Alfred Worcester of Waltham. The Hall cottage at the entrance of the avenue to Charles's house would serve as a "hospital annex." Visiting would be monitored. ". . . [Henry] will see the immediate members of his own family under Dr. Worcester's regulation. He will . . . receive such other visitors as Dr. Worcester may consider not prejudicial."

In a parallel letter from Boston on June 3, Brooks informed Mrs. Cameron that "no material improvement" was possible. On the 13th in Washington, Brooks saw Henry and spoke with him. Next day in a new letter, he advised Mrs. Cameron that his brother was "only the shadow of himself." "I apprehend that an excitement might be serious, and a shock be fatal. Poor man—I doubt not he would welcome that."

Senator Lodge borrowed a private railroad car from the president of the railroad connecting New York and Boston. On Sunday night, June 16, the car was coupled to the Federal Express in Washington. Henry stepped aboard, accompanied by Loulie, William Gray, amd nurses Hughes and Burnside. In South Lincoln next morning, "fully dressed," Henry "walked, with some assistance," to Charles's waiting automobile.[2]

Loulie had arranged to stay in Boston with Bigelow at his house on Beacon Street. She told Bigelow many details about Uncle Henry's recovery. On June 18, Bigelow cabled to Mrs. Cameron that she had "better begin writing."[3]

Dor and Mrs. Cameron were accustomed to timing their letters to cross the Atlantic on the fastest steamers. She had mailed her last letter to him on April 9 for conveyance from England on the *Titanic*. Shortly thereafter, she had gone to Paris, mainly to get everything ready for Dor at his apartment. His servants, Alexandre and Mariette, were—in her words—"sitting on the doorstep." When letters came saying that Dor was ill, her first impulse was to start at once for Washington.[4] The same letters required her to stay in Paris to ship his possessions to Brooks in Boston. She quickly got bids from shippers, signed a contract, and "arranged for all the formalities of invoices, consular certificates, valuation and insurance, also copies of his leases . . . dating back long before the time required by American law." When new orders came to stop the packing, she stopped it. When subsequent orders came to resume it, she had it resumed. Charles and Brooks had not understood that Henry's apartment had to be vacated by July 1. Mindful of the deadline, she took the responsibility of sending the shipment to Boston as originally contracted.[5]

When again at Stepleton and encouraged by Bigelow to write, Mrs. Cameron wrote at once. She told Dor about the shipment. "I finished everything up a week ago, packed my trunks, and rented my apartment, and now I am ready to come to America[,] where I hope to find you as good as new and ready to discuss all manner of interesting things with me—including Theodore!" The Republican Convention was taking place that very day. She thought it would make no difference whether Roosevelt or Taft became the Republican candidate. She said Theodore had already caused "the destruction of our party & political anarchy." "It is a wild and curious state of affairs."[6]

At South Lincoln, William rolled Henry by wheelchair to Charles's house and helped him walk. Charles was struck by Henry's saying that the noise of passing streetcars had become a torture to him in Washington and that "listening to the silence" in South Lincoln was a joy. On June 21, Charles repeated his brother's remarks to Mrs. Cameron. He mentioned that Henry could not write and could read only the headlines in newspapers. He again declared that Henry would need a "secretary-companion" and that the need would be permanent.

While Mrs. Cameron's first letter was en route to South Lincoln, Henry sent his first letter to her at Stepleton. Dictated on June 24 to Charles's secretary Miss Horne, the letter was addressed to "My Dear Mrs. Cameron" and was worded so cordially that it could seem impersonal. Henry said, "I see no probability that I shall be able to go back to Europe under any circumstances." ". . . the best I can hope for [is] to go back next winter for a time to Washington." He said also that, if his illness had not come upon him so rapidly, Mrs. Cameron would have become the owner of some or many of his Paris belongings. "I had intended that a quantity of things should remain with you. But I had to give the order in a half hour before I went out of my head. . . ."[7]

More than other Americans of seventy-four, Adams had earned a mental rest. Mostly by accident, he had been freed to take it. He remained in an other-than-normal state for twenty-six days, from April 28 till May 24, 1912. When he returned to normal, he was surprised to learn it was May. His thoughts had gravitated away from the horrific to the happy. He had ceased to worry about drownings. At the end, he reexperienced his travels to Japan and the South Seas with John La Farge, and he again imagined ambitious long journeys he had wished to take in Central Asia with Raphael Pumpelly.[8]

Mrs. Cameron had reconciled herself to the loss of Adams's Paris apartment and belongings. She took the view that she and he had an excellent apartment in reserve: her newest in Paris, at 6 Square du Bois de Boulogne. From Stepletion on June 27, she suggested to him: ". . . we will talk it all over when I see you, and we can also make our future plans. Mine is yours, as you know, and there is plenty of room for us both in #6."[9]

She reserved space on the *Adriatic*, scheduled to sail from Liverpool on July 11. Unhappily she received a cable on the 5th from Henry's nephew Charles directing her to postpone her sailing a week. She obtained a new reservation for the *Olympic* on the 17th.

She knew that Dor's Paris belongings were being held at Le Havre by a dock strike. As a precaution—possibly a very much-needed precaution—she cabled to the nephew, asking whether his uncle's things should be kept in France, after all. He cabled back that she should not change the shipper's orders. She of course complied.[10]

On July 8, she received Dor's first letter, much delayed in the mail. She began an immediate answer by saying that his letter made her "inexpressibly elated and happy." Apparently on July 9 or early on the 10th, she re-changed her steamer reservations, moving them back to the *Adriatic* on the 11th.

Brooks and Evelyn were to meet her in London on July 10. When they saw her, they listened to her inquiries about Henry but thought she had little to say.[11] In the circumstances, she felt a lie was best. The lie she chose was conveniently possible. She told them her husband had ordered her to come home at once by the *Adriatic*.[12]

Next day she began an uneventful voyage. She was met at New York by both her Hoyt nieces, Annie and Elizabeth. They brought news that their rich father, Colgate Hoyt, at sixty-four, was on the verge of marrying a woman from California who was thirty-three. For Mrs. Cameron, the news was a frightening surprise. Her nieces—children of her deceased sister Lida—were in danger of paternal neglect.

She met the emergency by saying she would attend the wedding and by going straight to Hoyt's house on Long Island to force her brother-in-law to settle incomes on his daughters, payable monthly. At the cost of a battle in his den, she got the settlements from him in writing. Satisfied, she went to Connecticut for the wedding and wrote to Dor to apprise him of what had happened. The arrival of her letters equipped Dor to tell a providentially-permitted lie that Mrs. Cameron had been brought home to witness Hoyt's marriage to a second wife.[13]

Minnie Adams wanted Mrs. Cameron to be a guest in her house at South Lincoln for a suitable period. She sent the guest full directions about conveyance by motorcar from Boston's South Station. The guest arrived on July 26 and stayed for a single night but insisted on staying thereafter at a Boston hotel, the Somerset. As before, Loulie was staying at Bigelow's house on Beacon Street. By parallel means, Loulie and Mrs. Cameron secured for themselves the right to visit the convalescent whenever they and he might prefer.

Although the fact was not to be admitted, Loulie and Mrs. Cameron were in America to give Henry company. He later said so to Berenson and said too that his companions were "Parisian."[14] Their company was sure to strengthen his inclination to return to Europe.

Raymond Weeks was a scholar without private means. He had found it impossible to live on the salary of an assistant professor at Columbia and was trying to close the gap by writing for pay. Yet, on June 9, 1912, he found time to write a four-page letter to Adams about the problem of the *Chanson de Willame*. He said Adams had stated the problem "in a startlingly clear manner, and one in which there is much new for me." Adams had been hoping to identify the castle that served Willame as his base. Weeks listed some thirty possible sources of new ideas or evidence and drew attention to "an ancient castle Balaguer, still visible from the sea, on the way from Terragona to Tortosa." The castle was mentioned "in an old chart for mariners."[15]

Delivered at 1603 H Street when Adams was disabled, Weeks's letter was later taken with other mail to South Lincoln. On July 15, Adams dictated a reply. He began by saying an illness had probably "put an end" to "serious study" by himself. He again avoided disclosing that he had written on essay on the origin of the *Chanson de Willame* and the *Chanson de Roland*. Yet he said he had "made a number of notes and abstracts, with the intention of working out for my own satisfaction a theory of mine as to the origin and the development of the chansons, and their relative age." He described his theory as "exceedingly simple"—which was true—and "not at all new"—which was false. On the latter ground, he suggested that abandonment of his theory would "not be a loss to the world."

Weeks had said in his letter that he had planned "a trip to Catalonia" but his salary had "never made it possible." Adams noted in reply that he had "planned a trip to Catalonia and the Spanish March for this year, but am now obliged to give it up." Yet Adams wanted the trip to be made. Since lack of money seemed to be the hindrance for Weeks, he offered to "join with any gentlemen" who might be willing to pay the expenses if Weeks would "go to Barcelona and follow up this study." Adams said the problem they shared was "next in interest" to that of the origin of "the Homeric poems." He did not have to add that identification of Willame's castle would bear comparison, albeit on a smaller scale, with Schliemann's discovery of Troy.

Weeks was exceptionally scrupulous. Replying on July 22, 1912, he apologized for having spoken about money. He rejected Adams's offer of assistance and said he could never seek or accept a research grant. His reason? Invariably grantors required that recipients bring back "Jason's fleece."

He was not hostile to Adams. He agreed that there might well be "something for us to discover" in the Spanish March and "that there must have been some Spanish proper name of a fortress" which could be connected with Willame. He estimated that "a year's work by either of us" would be needed to effect a discovery. But he threw back to Adams the work of going to Barcelona.[16]

Immediately after his and Mrs. Cameron's first talk at South Lincoln, Adams began to sketch European itineraries. On July 27, 1912, he dictated a letter to Spring Rice saying he wanted to visit the CroMagnon caves near the Pyrenees. In a letter to Berenson on August 1, he said his "ramblings" had ended. Yet he dictated the amazing phrase "when I get to Florence" and said he wished to visit Berenson at his house near Florence in Settignano. Next day, dictating a letter to Mrs. Keep, he outlined a plan that would take him to Washington in the autumn, to Rome in January, and to Paris in the spring.

By various means, especially massage, Dr. Worcester and the nurses were trying to hurry Henry's recovery. The patient's favorite means was walking. He often walked the quarter-mile to Charles's house and back. He timed his walks and tried to do them faster. On August 8, dictating a letter to Mabel La Farge, he said, ". . . I am now going about with some freedom, and even strolling in the woods under the eye of nurses or companions. . . . At a pinch, I could walk an hour, not fast, but so-so. At the same rate of recovery, I ought to appear next winter fairly myself."

Roughly on August 11, Mrs. Cameron went to Maine to join Elizabeth and visit friends. Adams succeeded in writing her a letter with pen and ink. He told her he was taken by automobile to the Lodges' house at Nahant, to sit on the verandah and see the ocean. His glimpse of the North Shore made him fearful. "I want to run away,—never to see that shore again." Yet his reaction was partly humorous. ". . . I sleep well," he noted, "and make a little gain in strength always, though strength seems to be my strong point anyway."[17]

The elder Lodges had been kept in Washington by the Senate's remaining in session. Adams was reconsidering his plans and was having difficulty guessing which plan was best. Going to Barcelona seemed impracticable, yet continued to attract him. He knew that, wherever he went, he would have to have someone with him and would always have to consider the other person's needs. In an uncertain state of mind, he advised Anna Lodge: "I am making plans for next winter,—Spain or Italy, which shall it be? I will be ready to start about Jan. 15. I hope to get Florence Keep to nurse me. You too?"[18]

Mrs. Cameron received Dor's handwritten letter on Saturday, August 17, 1912, at Northeast Harbor. She wrote at once to say she was "not only surprised but *thrilled* by having a letter in your own handwriting this morning." She added that she was returning to Boston and expected to see him at South Lincoln on Tuesday, the 20th.[19]

In Europe, Brooks had received "brilliant accounts" of Henry's recovery, including one from the ex-patient. The younger brother was thunderstruck. He wrote to Ford: ". . . [Henry] says he is about as well as before his stroke. His recovery is like a miracle."[20]

On August 24, after last talks with Henry, Mrs. Cameron went off to visit friends at Tuxedo Park and Lenox. Thereafter she would go to Cleveland, try to contact Donald, and start again towards Stepleton, where Martha would be wanting her assistance.

Henry turned his mind to his Paris possessions, which had arrived in Boston. They included eight large pieces of French furniture, valuable Chinese porcelains, two beds, fine linens, good table silver, his summer clothes, a fair number of books and a few papers, but no manuscripts. William wanted the linens and table silver for 1603 H Street. Henry needed the clothes and wanted some of the books. The remainder seemed best absorbed by covetous Brooks, who had gone to Germany for another cure but would be back on September 4.

While waiting for Brooks, Henry redoubled his efforts to get well. His illness had left him with a stubborn crick in his neck and had diminished his control of his right leg, arm, and thumb. He tried his usual reliances: walking and enjoying his surroundings. Writing to Moorfield Storey, he exclaimed: "Here the silence is thick. I love it. I walk for hours in the woods, devoured by gnats and mosqitoes, just gulping the silence."[21]

His doctors had said he had a stroke, but he was learning that the doctors no longer believed the diagnosis and were pulling away from it. Increasingly he was put to the trouble of being his own doctor and specifying the ailment. He wrote to Thoron, "That I had some five weeks fever and something strongly resembling paralysis of the right side, I know; but the doctors still profess inability to name [the disorder] . . . or to state the cause of it, or to define the state and nature of it."[22]

Brooks arrived in Boston, went to the shipper's warehouse, found the summer clothes for Henry and the linens and silver for William, and sent them to South Lincoln. He discovered that the furniture had been jostled in transit. Some pieces were damaged, and one or two small ones were damaged badly. Wanting to institute a claim against the shipper in Paris, he obtained Mrs. Cameron's itinerary from Henry and wrote to her about the claim. Being over-compunctious, Mrs. Cameron took his letters to mean that *she* was the person responsible for the damage.[23] Brooks meanwhile had an excuse for a new interest: the restoration of Henry's furniture to optimum condition.

Mrs. Cameron's efforts to contact Donald—"the man who owns me"— precipitated her husband's meeting her in New York at The Plaza just prior to her departure for England on the *Adriatic*.[24] His principal news when they met was his being attended by a Norwegian valet.

A special delivery letter to The Plaza and a telegram to the *Adriatic* were Dor's timely send-offs to her as she left New York. She replied by writing a short letter on shipboard and trusting it at Sandy Hook to the departing pilot, who assured her it would go back to New York and be delivered. It instead was conveyed to Ireland—a miscarriage that cost Dor a fortnight of anxiety.

Florence Keep still had the Paris apartment she and Fred had tried to furnish. Ordinarily she would not rent it. She was currently in America and had informed Adams that she would "probably not go abroad again for a year." On September 25, 1912, he stated the case in a new letter to Mrs. Cameron and went on to ask some questions. "Shall I take her apartment? I would rather take yours. Shall I urge Looly to go with me to Rome? Will you come down there?" The great problem was the one Charles had named, Henry's need of a person who could be with him continuously. Charles had thought of the person as a man. Henry thought of women but had no idea which woman might do—and be free to do. ". . . I wobble in vain for a guardian."

That same day on the *Adriatic*, September 25, Mrs. Cameron wrote to Dor and touched on the same subject. She said he already had a helper he could take to Washington: the more agreeable of his nurses. ". . . keep Miss Hughes with you—why not? A woman is a comfortable thing in a household and she is such a plump little cushion to rest upon."

Dor had been telling people that he could not read newspapers and magazines because the type was too small.[25] Mrs. Cameron knew however that he was reading books. She said in her letter that she had bought some books to read during her voyage—"among them Thayer's Life of Cavour, which is immensely interesting."

Presumably she did not know that William Roscoe Thayer had been named corresponding secretary at the Massachusetts Historical Society and was thus becoming closely associated with Ford.[26] She did know that Dor in youth had been in Rome, Naples, and Palermo when Cavour and Garibaldi were electrifying the world by attempting the unification of Italy. With that knowledge in mind, she urged him to read Thayer's book. "You might try it. You know it all, of course, but you can relive that period."

Brooks came to see Henry at South Lincoln on September 22, 1912, and found him looking "particularly well" and "very vigorous."[27] The sight made Brooks reconsider. He began inquiries the upshot of which was his writing to Henry emphatically: "I am certain that you have had no stroke. All the doctors are clear about that."[28]

Loulie looked extremely unwell. Uncle Henry knew she was worried. She presumably was in love with Thoron and waiting for a divorce to free him to remarry. Her beloved uncle was having to adjust himself to modern ideas about divorce. On October 1, he wrote to Thoron. He said, among other things, that Mrs. Keep had decided not to accompany him during the coming spring, "when I want to go to Rome." ". . . so now I propose to sail in the Adriatic, Feb. 18, with Looly and any volunteers that offer."

At South Lincoln, Mrs. Cameron had found a friend in Charles's daughter Elizabeth, or Elsie. At Stepleton, she received Henry's letter asking whether he should go to Rome with Loulie and whether she could meet him in Italy. She replied on October 5: ". . . take Elsie with you if you can—*and* Miss Hughes! She—Elsie—is a capable staff to lean on. I was so shocked by Loolie's appearance that I should be fearful of having her with you[,] lest you had to turn around and take care of her[,] instead of the reverse."[29]

Mrs. Cameron was familiar with the winter schedules of the White Star Line. She noted in her letter, ". . . the *Adriatic* sails for the Mediterranean [on] Jan. 7th [1913], and again in February." She went on to say: "If Donald does not send for me, I will meet you in Rome or Naples—or perhaps at Monaco, where I could board the steamer and go to Naples with you. I have rented my apartment to the Bliss's [*sic*] until April 1st. . . . It is yours from that time on—just as many of its contents are yours already."[30]

While these varied ideas of the future were floating in the air, Adams postponed his departure for Washington from October 15 to November 1. His motives were curative and aesthetic. He was enraptured by the colors of the leaves in the Massachusetts woods. Earlier, writing to Lindsay, he had said he was "galvanised into wandering all day in the woods, just to enjoy the light and color."[31] He assured Mrs. Jones on October 5, "This autumn weather would make the dead dance."[32] Next day he told Mrs. Cameron that the autumn was "glorious"—"raving with color." After ten more days, he recalled a ramble. "Yesterday afternoon I went geologising, two hours and a half, over the hills, through the woods, and round Walden Pond."

He wished to make his plans as far as possible in advance. Mrs. Cameron was keeping a large balance of his money in a Paris bank. On October 22, he suggested a use for the money. "I wish you would . . . go to Rome in February, take a large apartment, set up a carriage, and have all ready for me on March 5. I want to stay till May, then . . . go to San Moritz or some mountain for the hot weather, with a closure at Paris till I sail again." He further explained that she was to pay the expenses, hers as well as his, "out of my account."

The plan was open to objection. She replied from Stepleton on October 29: "You ask the impossible. Of all the places I have ever been in, Rome is the least abundant in available apartments & houses. I know of an apartment now, to be sure,—in the Barberini—but you would have to cable now, & take it for the whole winter." Another problem was that Dor proposed to travel with both Loulie and Elsie. ". . . I doubt that you could get *three* master rooms and I notice that both nieces are coming."

Before Adams could set out for Washington, the country's leading politicians combined to reduce his interest in American politics to zero.

President Taft secured for himself the place of Republican presidential candidate in an election he could not imaginably win. All eyes turned towards ex-President Roosevelt. Mrs. Cameron had seen him on Long Island while she was journeying, via detours, from Stepleton to South Lincoln. She had reported that he was as paunchy "as a Chinese grotesque figure."[33] In August, he accepted the nomination of a "Bull Moose" Progressive Party. He did not win a large following. On September 13, Dor called him a "droll Napoleon." "Without soldiers," he explained, "Napoleons are ridiculous."[34]

The Democratic standard-bearer was Woodrow Wilson, a former professor of history, political economy, and jurisprudence. Mrs. Cameron had seen from the start that he would be the next president. He had headed off a fourth presidential candidacy by William Jennings Bryan, the Democrats' three-time loser. She was anticipating a "reign of the college professor" but wondered in a letter to Dor what Wilson would do when obliged to have Bryan in his Cabinet—"to say nothing of Perry Belmont."[35]

Dor was a former assistant professor who had learned hard lessons while teaching history at Harvard. Six weeks before the election, he reminded Spring Rice, ". . . Mr. Wilson is a College Professor." He propounded a rule: ". . . a Professor is by essence incapable of acting with other men." The only recourse for Adams in such a case was complete avoidance. He told Spring Rice: "My instinct leads me to smile on Mr. Wilson, and go on smiling and have as little to do with him as possible. Yet I am all agog to know whom he can make his secretary of State. He can hardly be so grotesquely imbecile as Mr. Taft and Mr. Knox, but he may be as incapable in another way."[36]

During the next few days, Adams more and more believed that Mrs. Cameron was right: Bryan would turn up in Wilson's cabinet, necessarily as secretary of state. The prospect was sufficiently repellant to force a decision. Adams informed Jameson that he meant to leave the country before the new administration took office. ". . . I hope to pack up and git, the Lord knows where, but as far as possible, till the revolution is over. The new world will not concern me."[37]

Together on October 31, 1912, Uncle Henry and Loulie boarded a train in Boston and went to New York. He slept at the Knickerbocker Club, she at the Colony Club.[38] Next day they went on to Washington. The idea that governed their trip was one the uncle had accepted. He was always to be companioned.

Once in Washington, he could have rented a motorcar. Instead he bought a carriage upholstered in purple velvet that had belonged to Mrs. Sammy Howland and earlier to Perry Belmont.[39] He hired a coachman named Dawson. Each morning, Dawson drove Uncle Henry and Loulie to the wilds of Rock Creek Park to permit their taking walks.

Adams was serious about going to Italy. He asked Edie Hoyt to come every afternoon on a paid basis and read to him in Italian. The books she read were mostly new Italian novels. He learned more from them than he expected. He said in a letter to Berenson, "A pretty niece comes every afternoon to read Italian to me; and I am quite white with terror to find what mushy rot all Italian books are, that fall within my reach." The books contained a kind of "Italianismus," he said, that was "not worse, perhaps, than Germanism, but which very rapidly sickens." By way of contrast, he defined the sort of book he wished to hear. ". . . I would like to sauce my remaining days with a strong flavor,—not the harrowing sentimental, but the flavor of action. A story, true or otherwise, that would tell itself, and waste no words. . . ."[40]

While Henry was at South Lincoln, Charles had visited him every day for half an hour before dinner. Because they had seen little of each other for many years, the visits were a reversal of their habits and a chance for them to deal with each other in a new, friendly way. After Henry departed, Charles noticed that the Hall cottage had acquired "a very dreary aspect." On November 5, he wrote to Henry: "I do not like to go by it, especially in the evening, when no lights now gleam from the windows. I . . . miss you greatly."

Henry wrote in reply that he appreciated the care and shelter that Charles had given him. He urged his brother to come soon to Washington, "for my own sake as well as yours."[41]

Charles had revised his opinion of what had happened to Henry. He no longer believed that the cause of Henry's illness had been identified correctly by the doctors. Similarly, he changed his mind about Henry's need for a male assistant. In a new letter on November 8, he suggested to Henry that he might manage very well if helped by Elsie permanently. Charles thought Elsie too attached to her mother and too likely to stay home. "If . . . you have occasion for her [to help you] . . . she is entirely at your service."[42]

Another suggestion Charles wished to press concerned the following summer. He wanted Henry to plan a return to the Hall cottage and as an inducement reminded him that he had "two motors" and that one of his servants could act as "an assistant occasional chauffeur."[43]

Relations between the brothers had undoubtedly improved. Yet in one way their relations had worsened. For a dozen years, Charles had worked on his intended large-scale biography of their father by seeking new evidence and by writing and publishing preliminary papers. In June 1912, before Henry was brought to South Lincoln, Charles tried to start the biography. In mid-July, he advised Ford that he was "deeply involved in my *magnum opus.*" He however also said that he was studying the behavior of the British government towards the United States in 1861 and had formed opinions at variance with the ones his brother Brooks had published. He seemed disposed to abandon the biography and instead prepare a contentious paper. "I am getting deeper and deeper into the mire of controversy."[44]

In September, while Henry was at the Hall cottage, Charles was reminded by Frederic Bancroft that Henry in 1891 had published an essay —"The Declaration of Paris. 1861."—that concerned the matters in dispute between Charles and Brooks.[45] Charles read Henry's essay and discovered that his truly serious disagreement was with Henry. He accordingly began a paper titled "The Negotiation of 1861 Relating to the Declaration of Paris of 1856."

On October 10, Charles presided as usual at the monthly meeting of the Massachusetts Historical Society. During the meeting, he read his paper "by title," meaning he announced that it would be published in due course *as if* read by him to the October meeting. When published, his paper would run to nearly sixty pages. Its stated object would be to confute—or try to confute—an opinion published more than twenty years earlier by "Mr. Henry Adams."[46]

No evidence has been found that Charles, in conversation at South Lincoln or later by means of letters, told Henry he was preparing such a paper. Perhaps he kept silent. If he did, the precaution was for the best. Careful comparison of the younger brother's old paper with the older brother's new one would reveal something far more dangerous than a brotherly difference of opinion. The something was a difference in ability as historians. When it came to writing the history of what happened between England and the United States in 1861, Henry was an ever-improving master and Charles an incorrigible fumbler. If only for that reason, Henry would have to keep away from him.[47]

At Stepleton on November 4, Mrs. Cameron had started a letter to Dor by speaking about the likelihood of a general European war. She turned also to his wanting to rent a large apartment in Rome. She continued: "I have just under $4,000 of yours still to my credit in a special account waiting for me to go to Paris to have it transferred. I wrote you last week that I doubt if you could get an apartment in Rome sufficiently big for your requirements. Big salons—yes—but three or four or five bedrooms—no. There will be Loolie, Elsie, & I hope a trained nurse, besides yourself. It is almost impossible."

She was interrupted by a letter from Lucy Hewitt, inviting her to travel to Cairo in January 1913 "and go up the Nile for five weeks." She instantly told Dor: "Of course I shall go. I can be back at Naples about March 1st, and if you have arrived can go up to Rome to meet you. I am in a great twitter of excitement for I have wanted to go to Egypt all my life, and it was beyond me."

Her news about going to Egypt reached 1603 H Street about November 11, 1912. A confusion of messages followed. Word came that Sir James Bryce would be replaced as British ambassador to the United States by Sir Cecil Spring Rice. Evidently by a cable now missing, Adams was informed that Ronald Lindsay had hopes of being sent back to Washington. The hopes quickly died. To the mixed elation and dismay of the Lindsays and Mrs. Cameron, Ronald was promoted to a high but inappropriate post as undersecretary for finance in the government of Egypt, on leave from the British Foreign Service. He knew very little about finance. Throughout the foreseeable future, he and Martha would have to live every winter in Cairo, but the terms of his employment would permit their escaping Egypt's torrid summers each year for six full months. They planned to spend the months at Stepleton.

Dor presumably reacted by sending cables that were not saved. On November 28, when he at last wrote to Mrs. Cameron, he said the turning of events towards Egypt "brings a new theme into our poem." He added that she and the Lindsays had been directed "into strange paths where I cannot follow." Knowing Martha as he did, he had to believe that the Lindsays would absorb most or all of Mrs. Cameron's energy. "You will have full hands in helping them. . . ."

Loulie meant to go abroad with Uncle Henry in the spring but for the moment had reasons to be in Boston. She arranged to be replaced at 1603 H Street by Aileen Tone for a month, beginning in mid-November. The arrangement was a makeshift and could seem an imposition. Aileen was not a relative. She could not be thought of as a possible employee. She however was familiar with Adams's house. Loulie had brought her to 1603 H Street for a joint visit early in the year.

Miss Tone had become a pianist and singer while attending convent schools in Paris. In New York, she was singing in the chorus of the Schola Cantorum. The conductor, Kurt Schindler, had given her a music book, probably *6 Old French Christmas Carols*, prepared by himself and published in 1908. She put it among the things she would be taking to Washington. When it was almost time to catch her train, she went to Schirmer's music store and bought a music book that was new to her: a reprint of the first volume of a compendium originally published in 1853: *Échos du Temps Passé*, prepared by the librarian of the Paris Conservatoire, Jean-Baptiste-Théodore Weckerlin. On her arrival at 1603 H

Street, she left the Weckerlin book in the library so that Adams could inspect it, if so inclined, while she went upstairs.[48]

In Paris in 1901, Adams had taken Joe Stickney's sisters to a production at the Opéra Comique which featured alleged twelfth-century secular music. A Mme. Bréval sang the role of Griselidis. Adams reacted to the music as probably not authentic but thought Mme. Bréval "immense" and "great!" "Whether the music is worth hearing twice I doubt, but I must go again to hear her sing it."[49]

In November 1912, Adams knew there was such a thing as medieval music; but in his zeal to learn about poems, abbeys, cathedrals, visions in stained glass, and structures of scholastic theology, he had neglected to learn about their musical counterparts. He had written and printed a complete translation of the words of King Richard's prison song; yet it had never been impressed on his mind that the music of the song, and other songs, might be recoverable.

He opened the book Miss Tone left in the library. It began with a song by the Chatelain de Coucy dating from the 12th century. On three staves, Weckerlin provided the medieval air that a singer was to sing and a modern piano accompaniment in treble and bass. Also he prefaced the song with helpful data about the composer and the location of the manuscript in which the song could be found.

There was a piano in the library, an ordinary one, but a piano. When she returned to the room, Adams asked Aileen whether she could acquaint him with the song. She went to the piano and sang it. To his astonishment, it was "as good as the 12th century glass at Chartres,—but quite that!" To his greater astonishment, the next pages of the book presented a song by Count Thibaut of Champagne from the 13th century and said in a note that sixty-three songs by Thibaut were accessible in European archives. There followed two other 13th century songs, both by Adam de la Halle.[50] The pages caused a personal revolution. On November 16, Adams wrote to Thoron: "Miss Tone sings to me old French songs. . . . I want her to teach me the music of Aucassin and Marion, for the music is as fascinating as the words."

Brooks had hired an expert repairman to refurbish Henry's Paris desk and other large pieces. The desk appeared to date from 1720 or earlier. When repair work brought out the colors of the veneers, Brooks was startled by their beauty. He wrote to Henry, "These pieces were meant for some palace, and they give me a better notion of what that civilization was than I ever had before."[51]

The books shipped from Paris included remaining copies of Henry's *Memoirs of Arii Taimai*. Brooks advised Henry that he was keeping a copy for himself and a copy for the Adams family's library on the Quincy property. ". . . seventeen [copies] I send to you." "Most of the [other] volumes are on science, some on history."[52]

On December 1, without saying why he wanted it, Henry wrote to Brooks asking for "the little copy of the Poems of Thibaut . . . (2 vols), which is among the books sent from Paris." He said the volumes were "rare and rather costly." Lest they be damaged in the mail, he wanted them "carefully packed."

Brooks looked for the volumes and could not find them. He could only theorize that they had been stolen in Paris by the workmen who packed the books. He told Henry, "It is very vexatious." He later remarked, "Things do disappear in an astounding way." Perhaps in part as a consolation, he estimated that the six best pieces of Henry's Paris furniture could not be bought for "much less than "$25,000."[53]

In *Mont Saint Michel and Chartres*, Henry had said that Thibaut of Champagne "was a great prince and great poet who did in both characters whatever he pleased."[54] In his letters to Brooks, Henry did not explain that Thibaut was also the leading composer of the thirteenth century, nor did he say that he needed the *Poèmes* because he might soon be hearing a great deal of Thibaut's music. He seemed to suspect that, when dealing with Brooks, Charles, and other Adamses, he should not reveal how excited he could become about medieval songs.

As wished, Worthington Ford was bringing out an edition of *The Writings of John Quincy Adams*. He wanted also to edit for publication two series of old letters. On November 21, 1912, he wrote to Henry asking whether he could have permission to publish the letters of Elbridge Gerry to John Adams and the letters of William Vans Murray to John Quincy Adams. Henry instantly replied: "By all means! All the more because I recollect, as a boy, copying those letters for someone, and getting paid for it."[55]

In the thousands of pages of Henry's letters that recipients were preserving, references by Henry to his boyhood were rare to the verge of non-existence. His statement to Ford that he had been a paid copyist was not a mere exception; it amounted to a revelation.

In the world of American politics before the Civil War, there were no persons politicians needed more than copyists who patiently, with pen-and-ink, made correct copies of letters and other documents. That Henry when a boy became a paid copyist, perhaps a good one, helped explain why he enjoyed the indulgence of his grandfather, J. Q. Adams. It went a long way to explain why he, unlike his elder brothers, was given a writing table in his father's Boston library. It helped account for Henry's developing a handwriting characterized by Jameson as "copperplate."[56] It revealed a third-eldest son who had *worked*—who had found time to play with other boys, yet meant to earn his way in life, even though his parents were rich.

In New York, enthusiastic Episcopalians had undertaken to build a vast basilica, the cathedral of Saint John the Divine. The architect was Grant La Farge, a son of John La Farge. In June 1911, after the pillars of the apse had been put in place, the authorities controlling the building had recoiled against the basilica's Romanesque design as "*Moorish*," dismissed Grant La Farge, and asked a Boston architect, Ralph Adams Cram—no relation of Henry Adams—to design a Gothic cathedral around the stonework already completed.[57]

Cram and Adams had met. In 1910, Adams had trusted Cram with a copy of *Mont Saint Michel and Chartres* for presentation to a university.[58] Sometime in mid-1912, by asking Loulie Hooper to get one from Adams, Cram obtained a copy for himself.[59] These preliminaries opened a path for Cram to send Adams an extraordinary message. Saying he would soon be in Washington and wanted permission to call at 1603 H Street, he fully stated the purpose of the requested visit. "What I wish to propose is that Houghton, Mifflin Company should publish an edition [of *Mont Saint Michel and Chartres*] for sale at the official request of the American Institute of Architects. . . ."[60]

Cram was to be in Washington from the 8th to the 12th of December. 1912. Adams encouraged him to visit, but the date of the visit is unclear and perhaps was left to Cram's discretion.[61] The visit took place. Adams already knew what was proposed. He responded by telling Cram to take charge of the matter and not bother him again about it.[62]

In this summary way, Adams permitted the public issuance of one of his privately-printed books. Why he did so might seem a question, but answers were easily given. He liked to say that *Mont Saint Michel and Chartres* was the book he had written that he could most think well of. His having twice printed it was confirmation on his opinion. Besides, responsibility for its publication would be attributed to someone else —Ralph Adams Cram—and attributed still more to a reputable sponsor—the American architects as a body.

Loulie wished to stay in Boston through Christmas. The time had come for Miss Tone to leave. Uncle Henry had no one to replace her and wanted her not to go. In the pinch, he brought forward two ideas. He asked Miss Tone to stay with him indefinitely. He said that, with the help of others and beginning immediately, he wanted to obtain all the recoverable medieval French songs. The associates he had in mind were Aileen, Loulie, and Ward Thoron.

Adams's interest in medieval music was through-and-through historical. He wanted to hear the best-attainable approximation of medieval French airs as originally sung. If successful, his project would make Miss Tone the first American to sing the songs as sung originally and the first person to sing many of them in about six hundred years.

Miss Tone was in her mid-thirties. Her parents, Bernard and Katherine Tone, were well-to-do New Yorkers. If it came to that, she could happily continue to live with them. Living with Adams would be a great change for her, under partly stern conditions. The morning after the first occasion when he had given dinner to guests and she had been at his table somewhat as hostess, he had upraided her sharply for speaking during dinner about herself.[63]

After thinking about it, she had decided that she preferred his rule of self-effacement during meals with guests and was glad to try to do as he did. She had become fond of him and saw the chance of living with him as an opportunity. She saw too that, being fluent in French and acquainted with old church music in the Gregorian style, she would be a well-qualified aide in the effort to recover and hear old songs. So she promised to stay indefinitely and promised to work hard at their musical project.

Her consent was more or less simultaneous with a new experience of his severity. He told her that, while she stayed with him, she was never to read his books. The rule was to apply with special force to his *Education*. He mitigated its severity by making an exception: she could do as she wished about his *Mont Saint Michel and Chartres*.[64]

She evidently gave her consent on December 12, 1912. In direct response, he explained that, since she had endured him for a month, and since she promised to endure him indefinitely, he would treat her as an actual niece. The implication was that he would arrange an income for her, based on funds that were entirely hers. Meanwhile, perhaps on the 12th, he ordered a new Steinway grand piano.[65]

The first song in Weckerlin's volume began with the words "*Merci clamant de mon fol errement.*" In the days before Miss Tone agreed to stay, Adams had succumbed to a literary temptation and tried to translate the words.[66] He had written to Luquiens at Yale, asking help in completing a good translation. He had said too that he wanted to find the music of King Richard's prison song. He broadly declared that, if he could get to Europe, he would collect medieval French songs in great numbers. ". . . I will have all the music in the MSS. copied for the 12th and 13th centuries. . . ."[67]

The Library of Congress had long permitted Adams to borrow books. The books were brought to him, and retrieved, by the Library's horse-drawn wagon.[68] In the present instance, he wrote to the librarian,

Herbert Putnam, describing his needs. Putnam thought that Adams's needs would be best served if the library's person in charge of musical materials, Oscar Sonneck, called at 1603 H Street to be given full information "as to the scope of the inquiry."[69]

On December 13, Adams wrote to Thoron in Switzerland, saying that he had awakened to the availability of medieval music. "No one has touched it, or only to print it for cursed modern ears. I must search all over Europe for the music of Richard's Prison-song, which I want above all. . . . My only wish is to live long enough to discover it." No letter of Adams's had been more clamorous. "I want you to take up the job, and have every bit of 12th and 13th century music now to be found, photographed or copied for me. . . . I have not a minute to spare." Thoron was to start work at once with 5,000 francs. Adams and Miss Tone would be coming to Paris in March. "We will set up a College of the 12th Century. . . . Looly will be in it, and I hope Elsy Adams, and later Mrs[.] Keep."

Luquiens was away from Yale. After some delay, he answered from Ohio with information that for Adams was a new surprise. For one thing, the stanza Adams was translating was only the first stanza of a five-or-six-stanza song. For another, the song was not the oldest of the songs. There were older ones.[70] Since Adams had sent with his letter the text of the stanza, Luquiens furnished a translation. Also he urged Adams to consult some books about old music published within the past two years by a man named Aubry and a man named Beck.[71]

By the time Luquiens's letter came, Adams's attention had shifted entirely to music. On December 26, he confessed to Luquiens, "About music I am much more in the dark than about poetry, or glass windows, or architecture. . . ." He admitted wanting one thing more than anything else. "My objective-point is Richard's Prison-song, which, to a historian, is the oldest and greatest monument of English and French literature. . . . It has been almost ignored. I suppose I must go to England to get a photograph of any MS. of it."

These explanations drew from Luquiens the advice that Adams should avail himself of a French work, Gaston Raynaud's *Bibliographie des Chansonniers Français des XIIIe et XIVe Siècles*, published in Paris in 1884. There he might find the locations of manuscripts of songs that King Richard composed.[72]

Adams's theory of human action was in part a theory of motives and especially a theory of the power of ideas, ideals, or envisioned possibilities to bring strong new motives into play. In January 1913, he felt that the chance of recovering and hearing old music had given him a new motive, a new start, almost a second youth. He called Miss Tone "my best new niece" and told Mrs. Cameron, ". . . [she] has kept me alive."[73]

Before he heard from Luquiens, Adams learned about Raynaud's book from Oscar Sonneck, the specialist sent by the Library of Congress, He borrowed the Library's copy and notified Picard, his favorite book dealer in Paris, that he needed a copy.[74] He found listed in the book six manuscripts of musical works attributed to "*Roi (Le) Richart Ier d'Angleterre.*"[75] All pertained to the prison-song.

In a letter that soon arrived, Thoron reported having found in the library at Berne a manuscript of Richard's song "with staves." The manuscript did not provide the music but seemed proof that the music had once existed. Adams answered thankfully and said that he and Miss Tone were making progress. "In all we sing a dozen songs and shall invent Richard's, if we can't find it."[76]

By accident more than design, Houghton Mifflin Company had become Adams's current publisher. As one of the many volumes in its American Statesmen Series, the firm continued to sell Adams's *John Randolph*, first issued in 1882. *The Life of George Cabot Lodge* was one of the firm's recent books. *Mont Saint Michel and Chartres* would be brought out by the firm within the next twelve months.

Ferris Greenslet was Houghton Mifflin's chief executive for purposes of dealing with authors. On December 30, 1912, he had written to Adams about an agreement the firm had made with Mrs. Hay, securing her cooperation with Herbert Croly, a well-known journalist. Croly was to write "a Life of Mr. Hay, which we hope to publish both in the American Statesmen Series and also in independent form." Greenslet said Croly would be staying in Washington and would want to call on Adams to "discuss various matters pertaining to the biography." In advance, Greenslet thanked Adams for his help.

One may assume that Croly called at 1603 H Street, but one cannot assume that Croly persisted long in his intended work. The barrier in his way was one that Greenslet had mentioned in his letter to Adams. Mrs. Hay had stipulated that Croly could use her husband's privately-printed *Letters* "as a biographic base"—a phrase that might seem permissive—but was "not to print any portion of them *qua* letters"—a phrase that was seriously restrictive.

In his way, Charles was still attempting to get himself and Henry onto better terms. He recently had raised with Henry some questions about the inheritance of talent and ability in the Adams family.[77] In response, Henry had referred to the suicide of their father's eidest brother George by disappearing at night from a steamer on Long Island Sound.

". . . his drowning himself," Henry suggested, "showed a tragic quality far above the Adams average."[78]

Any idea that an Adams-by-blood had committed suicide was an idea Charles would try to prohibit. He waited a few days and took up the subject in a letter to Ford, asserting that George Washington Adams died accidentally. "It was gossiped that he had committed suicide, throwing himself from the steamer. There is, however, no evidence of this, and the more natural assumption is that, being restless in the night, he had left the cabin, going up on deck, and accidentally stepped overboard from an unguarded place in the gangway."[79]

The distance between Charles and Henry was partly a distance between two mentalities: the mentality of denizens of Boston-Cambridge and a mentality likely to be found in persons, Henry for one, who had left Boston and its environs to seek their fortunes in larger worlds. In mid-January 1913, Loulie arrived at 1603 H Street, recovered from a siege of grippe. Apparently with little warning, Uncle Henry's niece Abigail and her husband, Robert Homans, also arrived and stayed three days. Miss Tone took advantage of Loulie's presence to slip away to New York. During her absence, Henry received an overdose of Boston. After the Homanses departed, he permitted its effect to show. He told Mrs. Cameron: ". . . I got Miss Tone back . . . and shut down on visits, but my temper was ruined. All the piled-up hatred I have nursed for sixty years against Boston and Bostonians burst into frenzied rage."[80]

Charles knew nothing about Henry's rage. The affairs of the Massachusetts Historical Society had taken such a turn that a meeting would have to occur in Washington involving Senator Lodge, Justice Holmes, and other persons, in addition to Charles and Ford. Charles planned a dinner at his house for ten. He asked Henry, as one of the Society's nine current Honorary Members, to break his rule of avoiding dinners away from home and be good enough to appear.[81]

Henry thanked Charles for the invitation but refused to come on the ground that—new opinions by his doctor notwithstanding—he feared he might incur a second collapse at a dinner table. His note for the most part was courteous, but he used some hard-hitting words. He reminded Charles that J. Q. Adams fatally collapsed in 1848 on the floor of the House of Representatives. He went on to say, ". . . I particularly object to imitating our grandfather either in public or private. . . ." He seemed to spurn, not Boston, not Bostonians, but an Adams —indeed one of the Adamses who had been president.[82]

Lindsay and Mrs. Cameron were on such confidential terms that she was kept abreast of opinion in the Foreign Office and abreast of British fears of general war in Europe. In her letters to Dor, she said he and she should make plans only after giving thought to the coming war "and its contingencies." "The war," she insisted, "looms up nearer & nearer in spite of everyone protesting that they don't want it."[83]

To prepare for her trip to Egypt, she went to Paris, While there, she advised Dor, "The fear of war still paralyzes everything here." Yet war did not come, and she began the trip.[84]

The Hewitts had invited four other guests: Berenson, the Curtises, and a Columbia professor. All proved unavailable, and Mrs. Cameron became the lone companion of Lucy Hewitt, a "somnolent" wife, and Cooper Hewitt, an extremely rich but testy husband.[85] Rather than think ill of her predicament, she proposed to make the most of it by taking an active interest in Egypt and the sites she and the Hewitts might visit on the Nile.

When she sailed from Genoa for Alexandria, she knew that Dor had recovered his health but could not consider a voyage alone. Yet her feelings about him made her think of the impossible as if it might be possible. Soon she asked from Cairo: "What *are* your plans? Is any thing decided? Are you coming over? Why don't you jump on the Adriatic & come straight to Egypt. . . ." She said she could meet him in Cairo after the Hewitts and she completed their journey up the Nile. ". . . then we could return [to Paris] together via Rome? Martha would be *so* pleased, and it would be so easy & comfortable."[86]

She and Dor had known each other since early in 1881 and had been partners since February 1892. She knew he had been to Egypt with the Hays and ascended the Nile on a steamboat. She was uncertain whether they had gone up the river as far as Abu Simbel. (They hadn't.) By some chance or process of concealment, she had not been told that, in the course of their wedding journey in 1872–1873, Henry and Clover Adams had ascended the Nile on a sailing vessel as far as Abu Simbel, and that Henry had taken a stunning photograph of the temple. (In the photograph, the left-most of the huge stone human figures is shown in profile, looking into the distance as if space were time.)

She could not know it, but she felt an impulse to see Abu Simbel that matched the strong impulse Dor had felt forty years earlier. The ascent of the river by steam yacht was swift. The Hewitts' steamboat anchored at Abu Simbel. Some instinct told Mrs. Cameron to see the temple in the best way that might be open to her and to tell Dor what she had done while the adventure was new.

On February 1, 1913, she sent him an account of an experience at the temple which bore comparison with his experience in January 1873. Her account was short but ardent. "I do hope that you saw it, or you can never understand my raving enthusiasm. I never dreamed of any thing like it. After spending an afternoon there[,] I got up at five the next morning and went up there to see the sunrise."

Carved from a mountain on the river's west bank, the temple faced the rising sun. "A shaft of light struck the top of the temple first, then with the slow rapidity of a blush spread down to the heads of Ramses, then down, until in a short glorious moment the whole thing was warm rose-colored light. The level rays penetrated into the grim door—it faces due East—intentionally, of course—and the great figures . . . were illumined and clear."

She had not brought a camera. The experience she was recording was mostly interior. The figures most in her thoughts were Dor and herself. Her rising early to watch the sun illuminate the temple was a way of attempting to restore, affirm, or perfect their unity. Ways might be needed. This one was likely to succeed.

23

OUR PARIS

Thoron had gone to Paris and found two manuscripts providing the music of the prison-song. He did not cable word of his finds. Wanting them to be a surprise, he had an expert copy the scores. Picard mailed them to 1603 H Street.[1]

On February 2, 1913, Adams wrote to Martha in Cairo that he and others would be sailing on *La France* on March 27 and that he hoped to see her in Paris. Mrs. Cameron would learn the news when back at Cairo. Her plans called for departure from Egypt in late March.

Mrs. Keep had joined Adams's enterprise. On February 5, she, Miss Tone, and Adams were "greatly excited" by the delivery of Richard's music.[2] Adams sent Thoron a one-word cable: "BEAUTIFUL."[3]

He wrote at once to Mrs. Cameron, "Ward Thoron has found my music for the Prison Song, and I am in a hurry to get to Paris and go on with our studies." He said he and Miss Tone were "working furiously over our Richard and our Thibault" and had "a big repertoire." "Ward is discovering gold-mines for us, never exploited."

Richard Coeur de Lion was a great king who ruled when England's possessions included very large portions of what in 1913 was western and northern France. Adams was interested in *any* music Richard composed. After what must have been a moment of disappointment, he noted that the music of the king's song was "very simple." The description fit. To knowledgeable musicians, many medieval songs deserved attention. If considered solely for its music, Richard's song did not.[4]

The song being in hand, Adams formed new objectives. He wanted to hear a great many songs, do what he could to help select the most beautiful, and learn all he could about the composers. Especially he hoped to determine how the songs were meant to be sung—whether at an even beat or freely, perhaps in ways responsive to the words.

He and Miss Tone had developed for Thoron a list of books they would need in Paris.[5] They meanwhile accumulated books in Washington. Thanks to the Library of Congress and Thoron, they would soon receive facsimiles of parts of the archive of songs preserved in Paris at the Bibliothèque de l'Arsenal.[6]

Miss Tone had never worked before and thought their labors arduous. When it came to research, Adams was a hard-driving taskmaster for himself and others. His behavior bred results. To her eyes, the documentation they were able to assemble was astounding.[7]

The two authorities Luquiens had recommended, Pierre Aubry, a Parisian, and Jean-Baptiste Beck, an Alsatian German, had been rivals for the honor of being Europe's discoverers of medieval French music. In 1909, Aubry had produced the facsimile edition—*Le Chansonnier de l'Arsenal: Trouvères du XIIe-XIIIe Siècles*—parts of which were coming to 1603 H Street.[8] At about the same time, Beck published a theory of the correct transcription of the songs different from Aubry's. Each man disputed the other's claim to having been first on the ground. In 1910, they agreed to settle the question by fighting a duel. Aubry was killed accidentally while practising for the contest. For fear of opprobrium, Beck fled to the United States and became a professor of music at the University of Illinois.

Adams and his musical associates knew nothing about the intended duel and Aubry's accident.[9] Beck's professorship in Illinois seemed to them unaccountable.[10] To their delight, however, they learned that Beck was arriving in Washington, in part to lecture.

The usual shape of Adams's days had not changed. In the mornings, weather permitting, he and Aileen were driven to Rock Creek Park by Dawson, who waited while they completed long wintry walks in woods, over hills, and through ravines. Uncle Henry, she found, had "a sense of the north." He always knew where he was and at the pre-appointed time would emerge with her at a distant place where he had instructed Dawson to meet them.[11]

In the afternoons, Edie continued reading to Adams. He disliked being read to but believed that her reading was good for him. In the evenings, he and Aileen worked hard on songs, trying to understand how they were meant to be sung.

Thoron unexpectedly returned to America. He sent word he would stop briefly in Washington. The news was welcome. His arrival would permit the musical team to coordinate its intended future activities.

Beck's lecture was scheduled for an afternoon. Mrs. Jones was paying Adams a visit. Adams, Miss Tone, and Mrs. Keep attended the lecture. Writing to Mrs. Cameron on February 11, 1913, Adams described the *emigré* as "a wild French organist." According to Adams—whose word on such subjects was often suspect—Mrs. Keep was responsible for what happened. "Mrs[.] Keep instigated him [Beck] to get Miss Tone to sing for him; and he came back to dinner with us and Mrs[.] Jones. He went on all the evening playing and lecturing." "Thanks to Ward[,] who had worked like a woodchuck for us[,] we had even Richard's Prison Song. . . . It is fascinating,—that is, for us. . . ."

Aileen's closest friend in New York was Ruth Draper, an actress who was inventing and performing dramatic monologues, usually comic, sometimes satiric. Miss Draper had first appeared at 1603 H Street at a moment in 1911 when Adams chanced to have many guests. At the time, he had told Mrs. Cameron: "The most vital was Ruth Draper[,] who came last week to monologue at Emily Tuckerman's. I love Ruth Draper, and when she came in to breakfast, I went in to [i.e. attended] her monologue. She is a little genius. . . ."[12]

Miss Draper performed at Adams's house late on February 11. He exulted to Mrs. Cameron, "Tonight comes Ruth Draper, and we [shall] have an after-dinner séance for six. . . ." He was keeping up with the newest slang. "I'm no slouch. I do things *en artiste*."

The séance was repeated and improved upon. On the 23rd, a Sunday, Mrs. Chanler and the Henry Sedgwicks lunched with Adams, Aileen Tone, Ruth Draper, and Elizabeth Hoyt. Adams described the afternoon performance. ". . . we gave them a regular polite vaudeville. Three young women, all good-looking, capable and self-supporting, beat the record. Between monologues and 12th century songs and Elizabeth's humor, I never met the like. It was not mere amusement. . . . We were holding up against the world, and quite equal to it."[13]

The performances in Adams's house in February 1913 set a pattern. His ideal was private performance as opposed to public, and artistic performance as opposed to commercial. The things performed—Aileen's songs, Ruth's monologues, and Elizabeth's comic outbursts—were in different ways original. Adams provided the setting and helped make up an audience but mainly was an author or inventor. He was inventing something for his country, a new departure in music.

Henry needed a home for the valuable coins collected by his Adams grandfather, his father, and himself. Charles arranged that the coins be given to the Massachusetts Historical Society, where an appropriate curator, Dr. Malcolm Storer, could take them in hand.[14]

Like Henry, Charles was making an early voyage to Europe. He had been invited to lecture at Oxford on historical subjects. He wished to treat his stay in England as an opportunity to garner sensitive, privately-held documents relating to his father's dealings with the English in the period 1861–1872.[15] Handling and copying of the documents would be undertaken by Ford, who would accompany him. Ford was getting deaf.

If possible, his hearing problem increased his extraordinary love of work.

Henry wanted not to leave Washington without securing the services of a masseur willing to go with him to Paris. Mrs. Jones found one, a Belgian named Louis, and the way to departure was cleared.

On March 25, 1913, two days before he and his companions sailed, Henry inscribed a copy of the 1912 printing of *Mont Saint Michel and Chartres* as a gift from himself to "niece Aileen" and gave her the copy.[16] More or less simultaneously, but without telling her what he was doing, he sent his nephew Charles a letter directing that common stocks totalling $25,000 in value be set aside as belonging to Miss Tone and that she be credited with the income from the stocks, under young Charles's management.[17] Henry's act was a virtual adoption, meant to secure the "niece" through the rest of her life.[18]

Adams's voyage to Cherbourg on *La France* with four attendants—Aileen, Loulie, Elsie, and Louis—was comically luxurious. Henry James had produced a first volume of autobiography, *A Small Boy and Others.* Henry Adams did not read it. It instead was read to him in turns by three nieces.

Apartments were available in Paris for the party's use. One was Loulie's. The main one was Mrs. Cameron's, which out of consideration for Adams had been vacated early by Robert and Mildred Bliss. The third was Mrs. Keep's, at 53 Avenue Montaigne. Adams chose to stay a month at the third before moving to the main one, partly because Mrs. Keep had taken special pains to have her apartment ready for him but also because her apartment's location facilitated visits to shops.[19]

Mrs. Cameron had been detained at Cairo but would be coming to Paris with the Lindsays. At the most inconvenient possible moment, "exasperating Martha" came down with influenza.[20] When freed at last to travel, Mrs. Cameron accompanied her daughter and Ronald as far as Cannes and let them proceed without her to Paris and Stepleton. She wrote to Dor in explanation, "I would come up to Paris if you had not such a harem with you that one woman more w^d be superfluous."[21]

J. P. Morgan and Whitelaw Reid had died. Adams was their contemporary. With their deaths in mind, he replied to Mrs. Cameron on April 4, "I try to imagine myself as Parisian as you, and as young." He wanted her to change her mind and join him and two nieces at her own apartment. "There is still room for you at the Square. You can be my guest. . . ."

She preferred the opposite. She wished that, in her continued absence, he and Aileen and Elsie be *her* guests; also that they not pay rent, surely not the impressive rent she usually charged sub-tenants. She had no plans for herself but thought she might go to Italy. She seemed not jealous. On April 14, she congratulated Dor for having an ideal companion. "Miss Tone was a great invention, and she has the superlative merit of being handsome & being able to interest you."

Bessy Lodge had moved with her children to Paris. After a very short stay in America, Thoron had returned to Paris. In response to requests by Adams, he rented an auto and asked Bessy to find a piano.

On April 15, writing from Mrs. Keep's apartment, Adams told Mrs. Jones: ". . . I have organised my Scuola Cantorum for the 12th century, under the direction of Ward Thoron. . . . Elsie Adams is already at work in the Bibliotheque National copying Provencale scores of 1150. . . . Looly is converting the notation. Miss Tone is playing and singing the results."

Adams's report was misleading. When not directed by consensus, the school was directed by Adams. Thoron's actual chief function was that of obtainer of photographs of wanted scores. He rapidly obtained a great many and left for Lausanne.[22]

Four weeks later, on May 11, 1913, Adams wrote to Mrs. Cameron: "You know our Paris. Some one is always coming; some one is always gone. I sit here doing nothing."

As if ashamed of his fib, he became informative. "We have hunted through the Conservatoire till we have exhausted its resources. . . . We practice dozens of songs which no one else has touched for six hundred years. . . . We have two thousand songs, to be put in modern notation. . . . Many are very beautiful. . . . They are fascinating, and, like the stained-glass windows, their contemporaries, all our own, for no one else will ever want to hear them."

Mrs. Cameron's account of her experience at Abu Simbel had reached Adams before he left Washington. Without telling her, he brought with him to Paris prints of many photographs he had taken on the Nile in the winter of 1872–1873. Also he secretly arranged with Minnie Adams to send table silver and linens to Paris—presumably the same silver and linens that Mrs. Cameron had earlier been directed to remove from his Paris apartment and send to America.

Being at loose ends, Mrs. Cameron had gone to Florence, where she visited the Berensons, and thence to Marienbad in Bohemia, presumably to take a cure. A telegram caught up with her, requiring her return to Stepleton. Martha again had collapsed.

Adams sent more details about his school. He told Mrs. Cameron that he and his associates had passed a week in "wild pursuit of 12th century songs." "All the professors of the Conservatoire are now lecturing us." One of the lecturers was the librarian at the Conservatoire, Henri Expert—Weckerlin's successor. As a surprise, Adams diverged to say, "I have some old photographs of the Nile . . . which I shall send over [to Stepleton] to amuse you."[23]

There were threats to the success of Adams's musical enterprise. One was the general condition of Europe, another the failing condition of his eyes. He had confessed to Mrs. Cameron, ". . . we are very uneasy about war." He told Mrs. Lodge, "My eyesight does not extend beyond five minutes, and bad at that."[24]

War continued to recede. Adams's eyesight, though bad, was better than he said it was. All the while, he and his helpers had the advantage of American energy. When they talked to the professors at the Conservatoire, they discovered that the learned gentlemen were loath to make the small effort necessary to transpose a medieval song into usable notation. Adams wrote to Thoron on May 19, "All our great men end by saying 'Mais, c'est très difficile,' and tell us to do it ourselves. Such is France! the thing is easy as Yankee Doodle, but no one dare[s] touch it."

By then, the school—piano included—had moved from Mrs. Keep's apartment to Mrs. Cameron's, which had many rooms on two floors. The silver and linens had arrived. Adams meant them to be additions to Mrs. Cameron's properties. This was not a new idea. It was a fixed policy with him to give her furniture, paintings, Chinese ceramics, and other aids and comforts as a legacy, replacing in advance the legacy that he would not include in his will.

Mrs. Cameron received Dor's forty-year-old photographs, studied them carefully, and told him that she found them "most interesting." It was clear to her that she had seen one valley of the Nile and Henry and Clover Adams had seen another. Between 1873 and 1913, the river had been dammed and a famous temple at Philae—shown in at least one of the photographs—had been submerged in an artificial lake. Oppositely, at Abu Simbel, archeologists had revealed portions of the temple that in 1873 had been hidden. She told Dor, ". . . the sand-drift is removed, the stone birds uncovered, the terrace cleared, and a flight of steps leads to the fields below."

The drowning of the one site and the fuller exposure of the other seemed to affect her deeper feelings. She repeated herself, saying, ". . . the photos are *very* interesting."[25]

Many Americans had convinced themselves that Paris was not to be risked in July and August because likely to become very hot. Adams thought the reverse but, as a means of seeing Mrs. Cameron and Martha, proposed to rent a house near Stepleton and bring his nieces. Mrs. Cameron was well-posted about the limitations of Dorset. She informed him that no usable houses were available and that vicarages, though available, were unimproved and "still in the Middle Ages." As an afterthought, she remarked: "Of course you have read A Small Boy & Others, by Henry James. Now *there* is a book!"[26]

July came, and she insisted in a new letter, ". . . you must leave Paris."[27] Martha had similar ideas and asked to return to St. Moritz. While mother and daughter prepared a move to the Alps, Adams rented for six weeks from rich Americans—the Horace Havemeyers—a structure they retained as a shooting-lodge: the Château de Marivault, not far from the cathedral of Beauvais, at St. Crépin in Oise. At the same time, wanting to settle his plans, he bought space for himself and his nieces on the *Olympic*, to sail for New York on November 4.

Before moving to the chateau, Adams noted that Paris was so overrun by Americans that it was "much more American than Washington." Berenson appeared, listened to 12th century songs, and was "rather captivated." Dor assured Mrs. Cameron that Berenson's captivation seemed genuine. "He felt them, or said he did."[28]

On July 11, 1913, Dor and his party relocated at the chateau, perhaps bringing their rented piano. An expert in Paris, Amédée Gastoué, was transposing songs from Thoron's photographs. There seemed a possibility that Mrs. Cameron could stop at their "conventual establishment" while traveling to St. Moritz. Dor assured her: ". . . we are busy as mice. Of course I do nothing but smile; the others do the work."[29] But Martha kept her mother fully occupied. Mrs. Cameron was not free to come.

The mice used the auto to tour near the chateau and visit buildings. Adams wrote to Gaskell: "We are in a country where Richard Coeur de Lion and King John are much alive, but nobody has ever lived since. I can visit 12th century buildings every day, but no other buildings seem ever to have been built." Never-ceasing reminders of a past age made him possessive about the songs. "My chief joy is to guard them from anyone else. I wish Walter Scott were alive to share them with me, but he is my only companion in these fields, and I fear that even he never heard a note of music for Rebecca or Ivanhoe, or knew that it existed."[30]

Each song or group of songs was unknown territory till transposed and played. Adams liked to assume that the earliest—those from the time of the first crusade—were the best. Sadly all were lost. Some songs were poor. On August 12, Adams admitted to Thoron that there were "disappointments." "My Provençaux have proved, thus far, frauds. . . . In return, the Frenchmen have gained greatly. We have six or eight very first-rate Chatelains, Blondell &c., that rejoice my heart. Our Thibaut is a mine of wealth. We are beginning to find paths among them, and to learn how the society grouped them as artists. We know their styles."[31]

The music Adams's school wished to recover was secular with one exception, songs addressed to the Virgin, which became an exception on account of their beauty. In a last report to Thoron from the chateau, he wrote: "We are still working over what you left us. Only yesterday we adopted another Chanson à la Vierge out of your transcriptions." He mentioned a surprise. ". . . we find that our richest poet and musician next to the Chatelain [de Coucy] and—perhaps—Blondel, is a certain Vidame de Chartres, Guillaume de Ferrieres. . . . He must have been a precursor and teacher of Tibaut [sic] of Navarre[,] who stole bodily from him. This assumes that the [medieval] copyists knew what they were doing."[32]

Elizabeth Hoyt had come abroad to act as companion to Martha in Switzerland. She persuaded Martha to take an interest in mountain wild flowers. Freed to do a few things by herself, Mrs. Cameron left their high-perched residence and went down to the Palace Hotel at St. Moritz to dine with Madame Hubert, the wife of the archaeologist who was digging for Cro-Magnon remains with the help of Dor's money.

After dinner, Mrs. Cameron stayed awhile at the hotel and, without intending to, achieved a new understanding of who she was. A dance craze had swept the western world. Everywhere women and men were learning new dances, most famously the tango. At the hotel, she saw the dances. She wrote to Dor: "I had the curious sensation of feeling for the first time in my life that I was Early Victorian—a survival. Even I, hardened as I am, was shocked, and hurt."

Perhaps what hurt her was less what she saw done than its being done in public. "It was literally indecent—and horribly suggestive. In sex-less America it may go [i.e. be permitted?], but how about these Latin countries? Of course the dancers were principally American, but the spectators weren't. It seemed to me like an orgy. . . . I cannot put into words the sensation it gave me."[33]

Martha, Elizabeth, and Mrs. Cameron left Switzerland and proceeded towards Stepleton. Mrs. Cameron and Dor glimpsed each other in Paris. He was back at her apartment. Their chance was a dinner party there on September 2, 1913. Martha, Elizabeth, Aileen, Loulie, and Elsie were at the table. The preponderance of females was six to one.[34]

On any terms, hours with Dor had become difficult for Mrs. Cameron to arrange. In October, Martha would have to travel to Cairo to join Ronald for the winter. She was too unwell to travel alone and hoped a congenial female American contemporary could go with her. Elizabeth was not available; she was going home at once to New York. Martha and her mother thought Laura Chanler might be willing.

At Stepleton on September 17, Mrs. Cameron learned that *she* was to serve as Martha's traveling companion, with a stop at Paris. She told Dor: "Laura Chanler can't go to Cairo. It looks as if I would have to go—and quite aside from my own wishes, it isn't the best thing for Martha. She needs someone else. But I shall see you within a month, which is something."

The lectures that Charles Adams had given at Oxford in the spring were to be the occasion for his being awarded an honorary Oxford degree in the fall. His Oxford degree would place him first among the Adams brothers as a historian in the eyes of the public, or at least the English public. The degree could be thought hard-earned. Unlike any other Adams, he found ways to devise historical pronouncements supportive of high English self-esteem.[35]

Charles and Ford stayed in England through the summer. Charles's historical adventures had a dimension he appeared not to appreciate. In part because Ford was at his elbow, he was unearthing historical materials—English, Union, and Confederate—which would have the long-run effect of making it much more possible for biographers of his brother Henry to understand the complications that Henry had faced when he accompanied their father to England in 1861 and to outline what Henry achieved during his seven years in the English mission.[36]

In mid-August, Ford received from William Roscoe Thayer a confidential letter which would have been of the first importance to Henry Adams, had he been shown it. The occasion for the letter was a setback for Houghton Mifflin Company. Herbert Croly had decided not to attempt the biography of Hay. As a step towards persuading Thayer to undertake the biography, the firm had asked him to state his opinion of its viability. In turn, Thayer looked into the three privately-printed volumes titled *Letters of John Hay*.

If success in biography presupposed an easy affinity between the biographer and the person to be written about, Thayer's chances of success were very poor. He disliked Hay. He did not think well of the *Letters*. He told Ford: "The letters . . . could never serve as the backbone of a well-rounded consecutive biography. They simply report Hay in spots—no continuity, no evolution, no background, no perspective. There are dozens of his letters to Henry Adams which are tiresome & inane. In them, [Hay] . . . seems to regard a dinner with the Leiters or the Bradley Martins as his *summum bonum*."[37]

Houghton Mifflin Company made a provisional change of plans. If written by Thayer, the Hay biography would first appear, not as an addition to the *American Statesmen Series*, but by itself. Also Thayer would be assured a sizeable monetary reward.

Ford answered Thayer promptly. His answer is missing, but one of its main ideas can be adduced from Thayer's reply-to-the-reply, which survives. Ford had told Thayer that Hay probably had not functioned alone when secretary of state: that he had a secret male partner.[38]

Thayer was much affected by Ford's advice. In September 1913, when he was at the point of accepting Houghton Mifflin's offer, he explained to Ford: ". . . I quite agree with you as to Hay. He was a glorified amateur; but those seven years of his in the State Department happened to be epoch-making, and so he inherits the interest that attaches to them. My problem will be to discover how much he really controlled events, & how much he followed the suggestions of stronger men. Your hint of a probable Eger*ius* (or was it an Egeria?) does n't [*sic*] surprise me."[39]

Egerea was one of the *camenae*, the supernatural advisers in Roman mythology who bore comparison to the Greek muses. A "probable Egerius" would perforce be a highly persuasive *male* adviser. Thayer's question about an "Egeria" pointed to a *female* adviser. There can be no question as to the meaning of this dance of words. Ford had seriously suggested that Secretary Hay was guided, even governed, by Henry Adams. Thayer had flippantly asked in reply whether it would be truer to say that Hay was governed by Mrs. Lodge or Mrs. Cameron, the difference between the dictatresses being so slight that the two could be treated biographically as one.[40]

In his lost answer, Ford had doubted the wisdom of Thayer's writing about Hay after having written about Cavour. Thayer had prepared himself with reasons. "The subject interests me—not because Hay was great, or really a statesman, but because his career had those strongly contrasted vicissitudes which make a man interesting." "You say, 'But after Cavour?' Of course I have thought of that. But unless I am to remain idle the rest of my life, I shall have to tackle subjects far inferior to Cavour."

Thayer went on to liken biographers to portrait painters. ". . . if the biographer has the skill, & succeeds, he can produce a first rate biography of a second (or third) rate sitter." He did not mean that he would lower himself. "I would never waste time on a subject that did not appeal to me, and, in the case of a public man, did not possess historical significance."[41]

In a third letter to Ford, Thayer outlined his work. "The first need," he said, "is to orient myself . . . as to the persons now living who may be induced to furnish materials or reminiscences." He did not have to explain that Henry Adams would stand first on his list of proposed informants. Adams would *have* to be visited.[42]

*   *   *

Dor had come to the conclusion that Mrs. Cameron was out of sympathy with his passion for 12th century music and the 12th century in general. With the frankness they continuously practiced with each other, he told her on September 21, 1913, "We go on studying the Chatelain de Coucy and Blondel—but you don't care for the douzième. It's your seul défaut."

She replied next day from Stepleton. Her first concern was her travel arrangements. "I shall be in Paris about Oct. 12th to see you on our way to Cairo." She expected not to be back from Egypt before Dor and the nieces sailed on the *Olympic*, but she wanted to spend an interval in her apartment after they were gone, mainly to bring workmen in to refurbish it. When at last she turned to things medieval, her frankness was even franker than his. "I *do* like the douzième—I protest. I don't talk about it, because the rest of you talk [about] it so much, but I think I like it—and the 13th—as much as you do. But you leave me nothing to say."

Before she could start for Paris, Dor asked her a question about furnishings. "Shall I leave my linens and spoons and pots with you, or with a storage ruffian? I want to take nothing but clothes with me [to Washington]."[43]

The "pots" he referred to were very valuable Chinese porcelains. She did not make an issue of the linens and spoons, but later she wrote from Cairo: "I hope that you have packed up your Oriental porcelains— *all* of them. I only have four . . . so you can pack up all the rest. I really fear the responsibility."[44]

Before her letter from Cairo could reach him, Adams told Gaskell that his summer had been the "cheeriest and least depressing I have had for near thirty years." "I live in 13th century MSS. and 12th century poetry and music, and have it so entirely to myself that no one knows what it is, or cares to ask." French ignorance was instructive. "The intellectual Frenchmen, when you sing them the Chatelain de Coucy or Thibaut of Navarre, are warm in praise and naïf in astonishment, just as though I showed them a Cathedral . . . but they care as little for the one as for the other. . . ."[45]

On the same day, November 1, he made Mrs. Cameron a half-promise that he would return to Paris. "Perhaps I shall come back." His hesitancy had to do with a place to live. "If I do," he continued, "where the devil shall I go?" He seemed unable to conceive that he could re-occupy her apartment. Yet he knew very well that half the secret of his long season of cheerfulness had been the use of it. He exclaimed: "Once more, thanks for the apartment! it has been a haven of comfort and rest. I am deeply grateful."

Her plea about his porcelains reached him when he was poised to go to his ship. None of the porcelains had been packed. None would be. He replied: "I leave the potiches, &c, here. I've nowhere to put them. If you choose, smash them. . . . If I die, keep them. It is all I can leave you. If I come back, we will see."[46]

Had he not been been honor-bound to return Elsie to her parents in Washington and to give Miss Tone some home leave in New York, Adams would have had small reason to go back to 1603 H Street. Nearness to President Wilson and nearness to Secretary of State Bryan were for him strong reasons to stay away. Mentally he kept at a far distance from Wilson by pretending that the man's first name was Woodruff.[47]

He landed in America when Cram's edition of *Mont Saint Michel and Chartres* was being advertised in Boston but was not yet available in New York. Shortly in Washington, a copy reached him from Houghton Mifflin Company, or perhaps from Cram. He saw that Cram had introduced the book with a four-page Editor's Note. He described the Note as "flaming."[48]

As Adams perhaps knew, the judgment was unfair. There was nothing untoward in what Cram chose to say. Cram had called the book "one of the most distinguished contributions to literature." He had said it concerned "one of the greatest eras in all history" and was "heartening and exhilarating." He ascribed to it a practical importance: the power "to establish new ideals, new goals for attainment."[49]

On November 23, 1913, Adams thanked Cram for his effort and said that, from his own point of view, the book was "too intimate and personal" to be paraded before the public. At about the same time, he paid Cram the tribute of doing something one might think he could not do. With the impaired sight that was left to him, he combed the text of Cram's edition with microscopic attentiveness, made one improvement, and corrected thirty-one errors by the printer.[50]

What Adams did not do, though he had the chance, was to create a Publisher's Copy of *The Education of Henry Adams.* Neither did he take the trouble to see that the copies he had saved—a total of seven, two being the Master Copy and the First Traveling Copy—were safe in their places, downstairs, upstairs, and in the trunk in the storage closet. He seemed to be turning against the book.

Problematical Martha could not bear being alone at home in Cairo while Ronald was at work. When her mother was about to leave for Paris, she "quite on purpose" came down a second time with influenza. A cable to Edie Hoyt precipitated Edie's rushing to Cairo from Washington. By this means, Mrs. Cameron belatedly escaped to Paris. She arrived in time to join Edith Wharton and Berenson for an overseas Thanksgiving dinner.[51]

Adams had been Mrs. Cameron's sub-tenant at 6 Square du Bois de Boulogne for six months. He had succeeded in paying her an amount he thought appropriate. She had a use for the money. She informed him that very extensive improvements would be made at the apartment in December—"for which *you* pay." She said her account was "fat with money—but it will all go."[52]

In Washington, Adams had Loulie for company while Aileen returned to her parents and made the rounds in New York. His days were variegated by letters from Ford and a young Harvard historian, Samuel Morison. When replying to Morison, Adams remarked that Aaron Burr's conspiracy to form a separate American empire west of the Appalachians remained a mystery. "The New Orleans people held their tongues." Yet he felt sure the affair was "very nasty" and said that the "nastiest" participant was Andrew Jackson.[53] Replying with equal vigor to Ford, he said that Secretary Bryan was out of his head.[54]

Adams's usual words in the morning when coming down to start the day were either that he was "wuss" or "much wuss."[55] He liked to tell people that for him the end had long since arrived. He assured Wilbur Cross, the editor of the *Yale Review*, that his "active days" had passed. ". . . I can no longer write or read."

Knowing that Berenson had come to America and was in Boston, Adams urged him to accept a bed in Washington and promised more songs. "No one knows me," he admitted, "all my co[n]temporaries having died in the third crusade; but we still have some new songs of theirs. They [the songs], at least, are alive."[56]

Letters mailed in Boston and its environs on December 23, 1913, were not delivered in Washington till December 26. In that day's mail, Adams found a letter from Thayer about the problem of a Hay biography. The first lines of the letter concealed—indeed denied—that Thayer had begun work as his biographer in a merely professional or mercenary spirit and felt little respect for Hay. Also Thayer failed to say that the book would first be published apart from the series for which it had originally been solicited. He uncandidly explained: "Mrs. Hay writes me that she has been talking with you about the biography of Secretary Hay, which I have undertaken to write for the American Statesmen Series. I had been much interested by his versatile talents and varied career, and, after reading the three volumes of his privately printed Letters, I decided to see what I could make of his life."[57]

Thayer emphasized that Adams himself was the "one indispensable source" for disclosures about Hay's last years. He went on to say he had meant to delay visiting Washington till the spring but had been told by Mrs. Hay that Adams was "likely to go to Europe in March." He accordingly had changed his plans and would be in the capital for four or five days, beginning on January 14, 1914. He especially wished to learn all that Adams could tell him about "Mr. Hay's policy while he was Secretary of State."[58]

The last paragraphs of Thayer's letter concerned other subjects. Thayer said he had known Adams's *Education* only "in fragments," had long wanted a copy, and wished he could be given one. He said too that he was reading *Mont Saint Michel and Chartres*—presumably in Cram's edition. He offered a line of congratulation. "To say that our time has produced nothing else like it is slight praise."

As corresponding secretary of the Massachusetts Historical Society, Thayer had become the bosom friend of Ford, the Society's editor. At his leisure, he could borrow and take home the copy of *The Education* that Henry had given to Ford, or he could use the copy Charles had secured for the Society's Library. Obviously he was reaching for a copy of *The Education*, not because of need as Hay's biographer, but to become one of the book's proud few possessors.[59]

How easily Henry could see through Thayer's deceptiveness, which after all was deceptiveness of a very common sort, was perhaps a question not worth asking. Long accustomed to dealing with lies and dissemblings, Henry tended to notice them only to ignore them or react in ways he designed himself. In the present instance, he had known in advance that Thayer would write to him. Mrs. Hay had told him what to expect. Moreover, during the evening of December 23, Charles had come to visit; he and Henry discussed Thayer's future book; and he heard Henry say that Thayer would "not be permitted" to have the materials that would be needed for "a proper biography." As president of the Historical Society, Charles had formed bad impressions of the corresponding secretary. In a letter to Henry hand-delivered on the 24th, he said that Thayer was "wholly innocent of what he was about." He thought him "ignorant of American conditions."[60]

Henry was ready to answer Thayer's letter and did so at once. He said he would be "glad" to meet the biographer. In what could appear to be a forthcoming spirit, he stated that Hay had so closely allied himself with another man that the two had functioned as a unit. "The man who can steer you best is [Elihu] Root. . . . Root and Hay were politically one force. You can see there the whole drama."

What Thayer wanted was information. A warning seemed in order, so Henry noted that, when secretary of state, Hay "wrote little" and "intentionally conducted his affairs by word of mouth." "Come soon!" he suggested. "I am an old man."[61]

24

WAR

Nine months before, in February 1913, Thoron had informed Adams that he had consented to a divorce from his wife Ellen; and, in March, Ellen told Mrs. Keep that she had obtained the divorce. Mrs. Keep let Adams know right away.[1]

In December 1913, Mrs. Keep was informed that Mrs. Chandler Hale—Mrs. Cameron's step-daughter Rachel—had taken "legal steps to obtain a separation—but not [a] divorce." Mrs. Keep let Adams know, and he sped the news to Mrs. Cameron in Paris.[2] Its arrival helped, for Mrs. Cameron had been told by Mrs. John Monroe that Mrs. Luckemeyer had received a letter from New York which purported to disclose "an awful Washington scandal." As outlined by Mrs. Cameron, the alleged scandal was that Rachel had "caught Chandler and Mrs Reynolds Hitt in a false situation, & was divorcing him." Mrs. Cameron countered the allegation by informing Mrs. Monroe that Rachel was "not divorcing but merely separating from an irascible peevish husband." She advised Dor that her riposte, though true, would "do no good." ". . . that German Jewess [Mrs. Luckemeyer] will color the tale with erotic details, but you saved me from being taken unawares! Thank you!"[3]

All the while, Mrs. Cameron was readying to see Dor in Washington. Her apartment at 6 Square du Bois de Boulogne was fully refurbished. She rented it for three months to Gertrude Vanderbilt. That done, she reserved space on the *George Washington*, to sail for New York on January 18, 1914.

She received a cable from Donald: "Do not come." Her policy being one of compliance with her husband's wishes, she cancelled her reservation and, for lack of a better resource, moved into "gloomy rooms" at the Hôtel de Crillon.[4] She soon discovered that Dor had paid bills at her apartment that he ought not to have paid. On January 15, she expostulated with him: ". . . you are so generous that it amounts to dishonesty—it is hard to keep up with you." She said too that she was "furious" about losing access to her apartment *and* to America. She later assured him: "My main disappointment about not going to America is Washington—not Washington itself, but you. Of course, I scarcely have seen you since that visit to [South] Lincoln." She refused to count their subsequent meetings in Paris. "I can hardly call those glimpses of you here *seeing* you—they were only peeps."[5]

Thayer evidently met with Adams in Washington as scheduled, on January 14, 1914, in his main-floor study. The visitor hoped Adams might impart secrets about Hay's policies and efforts to implement them. He was thwarted. Adams told him very little.[6]

Adams owned things that could be very helpful to Thayer as Hay's biographer. One was his sheaf of letters from Hay. He did not produce it. He evidently wanted Thayer to seek letters first from Elihu Root, Henry White, Mrs. Whitelaw Reid, or others.

Thayer held to the opinion that Henry Adams was an "arch-egoist."[7] Not based on acquaintance or study of Adams's writings, the visitor's opinion rested solely on Boston-Cambridge omniscience. It flouted the well-known truth that Henry erred on the side of self-effacement and care for others.

Adams was aware of his traits and recently had pointed to one of them. He had told Louise Boit, ". . . I have a silly and feeble-minded antipathy to my own books, which leads me always to hide them when anyone is near."[8] The rule admitted exceptions. When Thayer entered the main-floor study, books written or edited by Adams were evidently in sight on its shelves. One was his copy of the *Letters of John Hay*, with many of its blanks filled in. It appears that Adams mentioned the copy to Thayer as something that someone at the Historical Society might want to reproduce—a hint which in time led to its getting into the hands of Ford, who obtained an unmarked set of the volumes and duplicated the entries Adams had made in the margins.[9]

Thayer had requested a copy of *The Education*. Adams could have refused. He could have told Thayer to borrow Ford's copy or use the copy in the Historical Society's library. Instead, saying it was a loan, he handed Thayer the First Traveling Copy.

Of the copies of *The Education* that remained at 1603 H Street, the First Traveling Copy had become the least valuable to Adams. All the corrections, usable improvements, and references it contained had been absorbed into the Master Copy. It had sunk to being a reference copy, useful but defaced. The same had happened to his Second Traveling Copy, which, with other books of his Paris library, was slumbering in Brooks's possession at the Old House in Quincy. All this considered, Henry's lending Thayer the First Traveling Copy was the reverse of a grand gesture. He lent the worst copy in his possession.

Thayer evidently was given no warning that there were markings in the copy, still less an explanation that they no longer were valued. Evidently, too, Thayer did not open the copy while he was still at 1603 H Street. It was only after he got away that he looked into it and began to wonder what he had been lent.

There is no evidence that Thayer ever notified Adams that, perhaps by accident, an *annotated* copy had left his house. What one finds on Thayer's part is silence, not about being the copy's holder, but about its containing annotations.

He had wanted only to get possession of a privately-printed book. As things developed, his behavior approximated that of an acquisitive person after committing an unintended, successful, grand-scale theft. He believed he had come away with the key to a literary kingdom.[10]

Adams was in Washington mainly with the purpose of waiting to go back to Paris. He never passed a duller season. Two events obtruded. Brooks sent him a large bill—$2,826.29—for the repair of his Paris furniture.[11] John Briggs Potter—the husband of Ellen Hooper—arrived from Boston to draw portraits of him and Aileen in crayon for which he paid more than Potter wanted.[12]

The most helpful experiences were walks and songs. On January 22, 1914, Adams wrote to Thoron ". . . Miss Tone walks me in the woods every morning, and sings me to sleep every evening, and I am quite happy. . . ." From Paris, Amédée Gastoué supplied more transcriptions of songs obtained by Thoron. Adams told Mrs. Cameron: ". . . Gastoué has sent us a big batch of new ones this week. . . . All are Chansons à la Vierge. . . . We use our evenings for the work. . . ."[13]

The Paris winter was the sunniest Mrs. Cameron had ever seen. She none the less wished to leave. The place she chose to visit was Ralph and Lisa Curtis's villa at Beaulieu on the Riviera. She knew that Ralph and Lisa's marriage had become very inharmonious and hoped that friction between husband and wife might work to her and Dor's advantage. She did not tell Dor what she hoped. Before leaving Paris, she merely advised him, "I shall probably return here for March."[14]

When he woke on February 16, 1914, Adams saw through his bedroom windows that snow was falling. A few hours later, he permitted himself a striking outburst in a letter to Mrs. Cameron. "I wonder what the weather was, seventy[-]six years ago today. This morning I felt quite baby-like, on waking up in a snow-storm. Perhaps I was born there. Anyway I am ready to die there. I hate snow."

The outburst sets a problem for Adams's biographers. Difficulty centers in a single fact. Adams's birth on February 16, 1838, was simultaneous with a snowstorm. For this reason, biographers need to know whether Adams gained access to the diaries his father kept in the 1830s and whether he read the entry his father had written on the day he, Henry, was born. The father's entry recorded the baby's birth and in addition recorded a preliminary experience, the father's walking through the snowstorm to fetch the doctor.[15]

Direct evidence that might solve the problem is lacking. In its absence, a circumspect biographer may guess three things: that Henry was told he was the son who would inherit his grandfather-and-father's coin collection; that he was told he would *not* inherit his father's diary; and that in consequence he left the diary strictly to others, principally to Charles.[16] These guesses may best be matched with another: that it became a by-word among the Adamses that Henry was born in a snowstorm—that he often was told so. In that case, the outburst he wrote in 1914 is simply evidence of his remembering what he was told. Also, of course, it is evidence that the snowfall in the morning of his seventy-sixth birthday was so suggestively timed by Nature that he had to exclaim about it.

Returning to Paris would require that Adams take with him at least two nieces, Aileen as "private secretary" and Elsie as manager of the household.[17] Both nieces had much liked Mrs. Cameron's Paris apartment. Considerately, Adams asked Mrs. Cameron questions so designed as to permit her an option. "Can you take me in again? Is there a country-house possible?"[18]

Mrs. Cameron could not take him in. Her apartment would be free in mid-April when Gertrude Vanderbilt moved out, but she wished to use it herself and secure an apartment just as good or better for Dor and the nieces. When she arrived at the Curtises' villa in Beaulieu, she saw signs of approaching separation. Ralph was in a "vicious temper," and Lisa was "out of spirits." Their large Paris apartment seemed more than likely to become available.[19]

Staying as Ralph and Lisa's guest proved upsetting. Mrs. Cameron ended her visit and moved to Monte Carlo, where she could relax in the company of Annie Hickox and Lady Randolph Churchill.

On March 6, 1914, a cable arrived from Dor. It is missing but evidently said he was leaving New York on April 18 on the *Olympic* and would need an apartment. Mrs. Cameron replied by letter. She advised him that Ralph was unwilling to rent the Curtises' Paris apartment but that she would be back in Paris in a week. "I shall find something and let you know." ". . . I have had enough of the Riviera."[20]

*   *   *

Brooks believed the Adamses owned papers injurious to them, and he wanted such papers destroyed before outsiders could see them. In support of the idea, he had recently said something that was untrue. He had told Ford, "My brother Henry has destroyed every scrap of writing he possesses, following the precedent of John Marshall. . . ."[21] The misstatement was not dishonest. Brooks was an honest man but on some subjects was both ill-informed and self-deceiving.

In fact, Henry had saved a great many papers. He kept letters in good order in desk drawers in his main-floor study.[22] The letters he most wished to protect were those he had received from Mrs. Cameron. During the time prior to Donald's telling her she could not come to America, he had placed thirty years of her letters in a metal box, to be given to her on her arrival in Washington. After she was barred from coming, Henry advised her that all her letters had been set apart and would either be given to her before his death or given to her by his executors.[23]

The plan comported with Henry's ideas about his health. He professed to be well. ". . . I cannot conceive what was the matter with me two years ago. . . . Apparently it was not old age or weakness."[24] Yet he saw his continued well-being as coexistent with a likelihood of death only months or weeks in the distance.

In a new letter to Ford, Brooks said something that very possibly was based on a letter from Henry now missing or a talk with him in Washington or Paris. Brooks remarked, "My brother Henry says that no biography of recent years has failed to injure its subject, and I rather agree."[25]

In Henry's current experience, autobiography—the supposed twin of biography—also was doing harm. He read *Notes of a Son and Brother*, the newly-issued second volume of Henry James's reminiscences. On March 7, he wrote James a letter of protest. He felt that James had written a book in which stuffy former realities were self-deceivingly re-remembered by the author as likable realities. Next day, writing to Mrs. Cameron, he reported having read James's "last bundle of memories" and being reduced to "dreary pulp." He wondered: "Why did we live? Was that all?" ". . . Henry James thinks it all real . . . actually still lives in that dreamy, stuffy Newport and Cambridge, with papa James and Charles Norton—and me! Yet why!"

James currently was living on Cheyne Walk in London. He received Adams's letter, replied to it, and destroyed it. Parts of James's reply could be quoted to Adams's disadvantage. James said Adams had sent him a message of "unmitigated blackness." He told Adams that he, James, was "that queer monster the artist, an obstinate finality, an inexhaustible sensibility"—as if Adams was *not* an artist, or not an artist in the same degree, and as if the only source of art, everywhere and always, was a "sensibility," and never anything in a sensibility's surroundings. It did not help that James said also that art was an "act of life" and that Adams, too, was performing such acts. Nor did it help much that James ended his letter, ". . . you understand—I admit indeed alone—your all-faithful/ *Henry James*."[26] The destruction of Adams's letter by James and the saving of James's reply by Adams would eventually unite to do Adams considerable harm.[27]

Berenson appeared in Washington, came daily for lunch, and listened for hours to twelfth-century songs. He and Adams had become good friends. Yet Adams could not be sure whether Berenson's "rapt attention" to the songs was a pose. On March 15, starting a letter to Mrs. Cameron, he asked: "Is it genuine; is it Jew? how can I tell! We hide our songs all we can. We never show them to the world."[28]

A cable arrived from Mrs. Cameron. Ralph had relented, and the Curtis apartment could be had for six months for $500 a month, beginning in April. Dor cabled his acceptance.

Martha threw everything into confusion by informing Mrs. Cameron that she had appendicitis. Next she said that she was better and that Ronnie would take early leave and escort her from Cairo to England.

The daughter's second announcement freed Mrs. Cameron to speed from the Riviera to Paris. There she made every preparation for Dor and the nieces except renting a piano. In her view, the right person to choose the instrument was Miss Tone.

In Washington, Adams heard that Donald had turned up, was staying with the MacVeaghs, and was looking "fit and young."[29] Adams did not see him. Similarly, he may not have seen his neighbor Mrs. Hay, who was mysteriously ill.

As usual in spring, the capital was a place much too beautiful to leave. On April 12, 1914, six days before sailing, Adams told Mrs. Cameron, "If I weren't afraid of the heat, I would never go." Next day to close his letter, he said he was sailing for one reason: "I am looking forward only to seeing you."

Accompanied by Aileen, Elsie, Loulie, and Mrs. Keep, he boarded the *Olympic* and began a "stunning voyage" to Cherbourg.[30] The news that greeted him in Europe was that Mrs. Hay had died. The death was reported as caused by pernicious anemia and heart trouble. Its actual cause was leukemia. She had not been told the diagnosis and did not realize that she was fatally ill. Her last conscious effort was to ask about Martha Lindsay's supposed appendicitis.

From Adams's perspective, the death of Clara Hay involved a possible benefit. Thayer might be freed to write a passable biography. Yet the death might also portend an unendurable calamity. The Hay property at the corner of H Street and Sixteenth Street might be sold to a developer as a site for a hotel or apartment house.

The danger somewhat receded. Alice Hay Wadsworth notified Adams that she and her brother Clarence would use the Hay house during the coming winter, and perhaps during later winters.

Located at 40 Avenue de Trocadero, the Curtis apartment afforded a view of the Tour Eiffel. Mrs. Cameron welcomed Dor but stayed only long enough to see that he and his helpers were comfortable. Then she sped to Marienbad for what she believed was an overdue cure.

Adams thought he was being treated in ways that, fully considered, were out of order and ridiculous. He wrote to Gaskell on May 2: "I was never so well cared for. Curious! everyone is absurdly civil and respectful,—absolutely deferential! Only I see the fun."

The treatment given him accorded with his changing place in the world. Although known in Massachusetts more to be misjudged and devalued than understood, he was growing famous. *Mont Saint Michel and Chartres* was receiving extremely positive reviews in America and England. Among the few readers who were seeing copies, *The Education of Henry Adams* was gaining a reputation as a book of still greater merit. Better still, the *Letter to American Teachers of History* had found its perfect reader. At Uncle Henry's direction, Miss Tone had sent a copy to Abraham Flexner. Without hesitation, Flexner performed the feat of realizing that the book was pervaded with "delicious humor." He wrote to Adams gratefully, "I had little idea when I picked up the volume that so rich a treat was in store for me."[31]

In a letter to Mrs. Cameron, Dor made ungenerous mistakes. With the Curtises in mind, he said, ". . . everyone hates people who rent their houses. . . . You too!" He went on to imply that she did not like his having surrounded himself with nieces and did not understand that he actually needed them.[32]

His mistakes did not make her angry. They made her talk. She spiritedly replied about the previous summer: "I *loved* feeling that you were in my shanty—but I hated taking that money from you! I hate any relation of that sort between you and me."

Although he may have been right to load her with beautiful, highly saleable possessions, she was being honest when she informed him that his Chinese porcelains, which she loved and enjoyed, made her uncomfortable. "I always have a cheap sensation when they are admired."

She had never doubted that he needed the nieces. "I have thanked heaven daily that you had them." Yet she admitted wanting to be with him by herself, apart from his attendants. "I sometimes long to have you alone, but I mean to arrange that."

She mentioned that Elsie was the only niece with whom she felt at ease. "Loolie & Miss Tone I admire but don't get at. Loolie is so polite, and Miss T. so gushing that I am held off at arm's lengths. But Elsie I can take to my practical New England stony heart. She isn't sentimental. Sentiment makes me shy."[33]

A European war seemed not only possible but almost imminent. On May 11, 1914, Adams remarked to Mabel La Farge that "all the governments" seemed to be "sliding into sheer idiocy." His attitude toward the sliding was a new one for him: indifference. He told Mrs. Cameron on the 16th, ". . . there is general preparation to dance for tomorrow we die, but as I mean to die tonight, or at any rate, before the general debacle, I don't much care."

The mood of the Europeans seemed to be one of weariness more than fear. Adams explained to Thoron on the 25th: "I expect every moment to see the skies fall. Nothing suggests tomorrow. The world is about to end. I assure you it feels quite like the fifth act, and everyone is sleepy." As if he were sleepy himself, he was keeping indoors. He said he was "happy to stay at home."

When in search of places to live, Dor and Mrs. Cameron depended on a Paris real estate agent, Frank Arthur. In late May, presumably on advice from Arthur, Dor motored to St. Rémy-Lès-Chevreuse in Oise and sought to rent the Château de Coubertin. The building amused him. He advised Mrs. Cameron, "If I am allowed to take it, you must go there. It is near Meridon."[34]

The chateau's owners accepted him as a tenant, to start occupancy in July. In Paris, meanwhile, he wrote few letters. In the only one that mattered, he summarized the attitude people were taking toward their life on earth and the attitude people were taking toward the life-beyond-death promised by Christianity. He told Gaskell: "No one anywhere, so-cialist, capitalist, or religionist, takes it seriously or expects a future." He saw a strong resemblance—also a dismaying difference—between contemporary life and life at a former time. "The life is that of the 4th century, without St[.] Augustin [sic]."[35]

Paris was the center of the earthly world. Its inhabitants seemed more unhappy than happy. Adams ventured to say: "All the women have nevrosis [sic]. Of the men I can't speak, since none ever come my way. I know that the streets are horribly jammed, if that is a pleasure, and that the Russian ballet is wonderful. . . ."[36]

Weeks passed with little change. Miss Tone disapproved his staying so much at home. On June 28, 1914, she induced him to drive to the Rue de Varenne to visit Edith Wharton and Walter Berry. Because she did not like Berry, she waited outside in the carriage.

Adams emerged from the building. News vendors nearby were crying a headline in French. He bought a newspaper and read that Archduke Ferdinand of Austria had been assassinated at Sarajevo. A moment later, in a voice that gave her a new idea of the meaning of the word, he told Aileen there would be "war."[37]

Uncle and nieces moved to the chateau. On July 5, en route from Marienbad to England, Mrs. Cameron joined them for a day. She later told Dor from Stepleton: "I left feeling that you could not have done better for yourself. . . . The place has atmosphere. . . ."[38]

Many Americans in Europe were alarmed. Mrs. Curtis asked Adams to let her regain her apartment by October 15. He consented and bought space on the *Olympic* for October 21, but he would have to find a place to live during the days between. Mrs. Cameron would have offered her apartment, beginning on the 15th; but Martha would be having her portrait painted during that week at Donald's expense, so no offer was possible. Meanwhile daughter and mother were planning another return to Switzerland. They would stop at 6 Square du Bois de Boulogne for a night and next day would take the best train to St. Moritz.

On July 28, 1914, Mrs. Cameron wrote to Dor from Paris and mainly said it was "very tantalizing" to be so near each other, yet not meet. "I wonder about the war," she remarked. "It looks serious."

Brooks and Evelyn Adams were in Europe, hastening to Bad Kissingen for their annual cure. Writing to Thoron on the 28th, Henry said that Brooks was going to Germany, Mrs. Cameron to Switzerland. He added: "They know best. I would rather go home." He said he expected a new kind of war. "I don't like risking two or three young women and a paralytic octagenarian to a siege of bombs and airships."[39]

Germany declared war on Russia on August 1 and on France two days later. On the 3rd, Germany invaded Belgium. England responded on the 4th by declaring war on Germany.

Brooks and Evelyn stayed just long enough in Paris to be prevented from going to Bad Kissingen. Martha and Mrs. Cameron reached Switzerland in time to be trapped. Mrs. Cameron asked for reservations back to Paris. The ticket agents told her no trains were running.

Gaskell offered Adams a house in England, should he want shelter from the "appalling catastrophe." Bessy wrote from Paris to Adams at the chateau, "I wonder how this terrible calamity has affected you. . . ." She said the Channel boats were being kept in port.[40]

Currency exchange ceased. Mrs. Cameron had trouble buying a Swiss postage stamp. She obtained one on the 4th and wrote to Adams: "As long as Italy remains neutral[,] we can get out that way eventually. If Italy is drawn in[,] we must remain here until the war is over." Her ideas were adapted to the lightning victory of the Germans in the war with France in 1870. She continued hopefully, ". . . though I hate Germans, I have confidence that they can wipe France out in no time at all, and that you will be quartering German officers in your château before a month is out."

The police at St. Rémy-Lès-Chevreuse suspected Miss Tone of being a spy. She, Adams, and Elsie were summoned for questioning. Uncle Henry explained that Miss Tone was "a friend of his niece." His testimony served but did not sit well with the interrogators.[41]

The police made a second demand: Adams had to fill out a request for permission to stay as a visitor. While complying, he grew agitated. He realized that he could not remember his mother's name. He had to ask Elsie and Miss Tone, "What *was* my mother's name?"[42]

Other French authorities very shortly commandeered the last horse at the chateau and Adams's rented automobile.[43]

On August 6, Adams complained that his "liver" was troubling him. He and the nieces hastened by train to the Curtis apartment, and he consulted his doctor. Also he sent Mrs. Cameron what she later said was a "long chatty telegram."[44]

The elder Lodges were in London. Bessy and her children had succeeded in joining them. Mrs. Jones was in Paris but soon would leave. Brooks and Evelyn were at the Hôtel Wagram on the Rue de Rivoli and wished not to return to England till they could travel comfortably. Unaware that Henry was in Paris, Brooks wrote to him at the chateau. The younger brother had become an enthusiastic Francophile. "I take back everything I have ever said about French degeneracy. . . . Here a great city has sent away every able bodied man. It has surrendered its transportation. It has submitted to martial law. I have not seen one disorderly person. I have not heard a murmur."[45]

Henry's first idea of wanting to go home had yielded to its opposite: he meant to stay. He advised Curtis on the 10th that he and the nieces had rented an auto and were expecting a piano. "We may have to bolt, but I think not. My young women adore the fun, and won't stir." He too was enjoying it.[46]

No letters were coming from Switzerland, but Dor assumed that the "refugees" would soon arrive, and he wished to wait for them.[47] He did not yet know that the border was closed and that Mrs. Cameron and Martha could not get back to Paris. Loulie had gone to Lausanne to visit Mabel, Bancel, and the children. She too was caught.

On August 12, Mrs. Cameron obtained another postage stamp. She asked Dor: "Are you going to try to get back to America, or brave the dangers of Paris again? I wish you wouldn't." No letters had come from him. She asked, "I wonder when I can hear from you?"

Brooks and Evelyn decided to leave. Henry advised Gaskell on the 13th that his brother and sister-in-law would start next day for London. His own plan was simple. "I shall not budge." "I hope soon to collect the refugees from Switerland." He reasoned that he and his nieces were the lucky ones. "All the world is worse off. We are at least awfully interested and absorbed. It is an appropriate ending to my life[,] which has of late seemed flat."

Gaskell believed that currency problems might affect Adams and offered him £100 to £200 in gold, should he get to England.

Letters that had been sent from the chateau on August 4 and 5 were delivered to Loulie in Switzerland on August 16. They permitted her to write to one of her brothers-in-law, Roger Warner: ". . . I expect to stick by Mabel until Dec. or Jan. with a minimum of Paris. . . . H.A.'s plans may modify mine but scarcely change them. I expect him to sail when he can, but I doubt that he can for some time."[48]

The Morgan bank in Paris succeeded in transferring money to Mrs. Cameron at St. Moritz. On August 20, she received an old letter from Aileen dated the 7th. It said Uncle Henry was in Paris and was thinking of going to England.

Martha offered a suggestion, with the immediate result that Mrs. Cameron wrote to Dor: "Martha would like to propose Stepleton to you. . . . There are plenty of rooms for you, and there is a *very* plain (and very elderly) cook, a house maid, & a parlor maid. . . ."

Martha could offer Stepleton to Dor because she would not be going there herself. She would be starting toward Cairo, accompanied by her mother. Mrs. Cameron explained: "This whole situation is very desperate. I don't want to go to Egypt but Martha insists." ". . . I now have money! I make no comments upon the war—what is the use? but I wish we had not left Stepleton."[49]

Telegrams were getting through. On August 21 or 22, Mrs. Cameron must have repeated by wire Martha's offer of her house and Dor must have answered by wire; for the mother said in a letter on the 22nd, "I cannot tell you how pleased Martha is that you will go to Stepleton." She spoke of a particular room. "The oak room is my den." She ended by saying, "I wish I were going your way."

Loulie learned by telegraph on the 25th that Uncle Henry, Aileen, and Elsie would leave Paris next day. He was at the Channel on the 26th and telegraphed to Mrs. Cameron from Dieppe. His message found her in Venice, seeking space for Martha and herself on a steamer bound for Alexandria. She answered by letter, "How I wish I were with you!" "I don't see *when*—if ever—I can come back."[50]

In London, Dor and the nieces found shelter at the Coburg Hotel. He advised Gaskell that "strain" had driven him from France. Yet he said he was "in no hurry" and wished to lead "a country life" for "a month or six weeks."[51]

A week later, on September 4, the fugitives shifted from London to Stepleton. The house was an astonishment. Dor told Mrs. Cameron: "If ever you were disposed to think yourself a success in life, it was, or should have been, yesterday afternoon at five o'clock, on seeing us arrive here. . . . To find ourselves suddenly at home, and such a home! it was a pleasure never to be felt but once." ". . . already Aileen Tone is singing . . . at your piano!"[52]

Mrs. Cameron and Martha moved from Venice to Genoa in search of an acceptable steamer. Dor was abreast of their movements. He wrote to Gaskell on the 9th: "Stepleton House is home. I am surrounded with my own things. The Lindsays are in Egypt, or, at least, Martha and her mother are at Genoa trying to get there."

As if in need of a restorative, Adams had reverted to Jane Austen. "I read Persuasion aloud of evenings." Probably Aileen was the actual reader. Uncle Henry merely listened and relaxed.

Mrs. Cameron wished not to become a compulsory third Lindsay. On September 13, 1914, she wrote to Dor from Genoa: "I am terribly reluctant to go to Cairo. . . . It is like turning my back on everything life has left—which isn't much." She closed on the 16th by saying, "I feel as if I were going off into space."

Many of the Americans who had been in Paris were already safe at home. Evelyn Adams wrote to Henry on the 17th, reporting that she and Brooks had arrived at Quincy.

At South Lincoln, Charles was finishing an eventless summer. It could seem ironic that he, a former cavalry colonel, brevet general, and survivor of battles, had been living peacefully in Massachusetts while mere Brooks, a lifelong civilian, had witnessed the mobilization of the French in Paris. It could seem still more ironic that Henry, physically the smallest brother, left for England only after German attackers had pressed close to Paris.

At Stepleton, Henry was content. He had seldom been happier. He wrote to Martha, ". . . we are as happy as fairy-stories here. . . ." "We have had all sorts of excitements. So have you—so has everybody."[53] Yet the sufferings of the Europeans seemed to him a gigantic and unrelievable disaster. On September 23, he wrote to Lindsay: "For the first time in my life, I am quite staggered. I have stiffly held my tongue and listened while everyone chatters, but as yet I see no light. I see none in the triumph of either party. If we wipe Germany off the map, it is no better."

For him, perhaps also for the nieces, black darkness of one kind in Europe coexisted with darkness of another kind in Washington. He admitted to Lindsay in the same letter, "We do not want to go home to the happy idiocy of Mr[.] W. J. Bryan."

Martha hoped that Dor would like her dog, a Scotch terrier she had left at Stepleton.[54] The hope was apropos. He had wanted a dog.

When the newspapers were due for delivery at Stepleton, he tended to be looking at his watch.[55] A continuous tension was at work in him between a strong desire to know everything about the war and a desire to ignore it. He explained to Mrs. Cameron on September 30: ". . . we know only what the newspapers tell us, and I try to think as little as I can, but you can conceive how ill I succeed."

When Dor's new letter reached her at Cairo, Mrs. Cameron was doing something that would remind her of him. She had somehow provided herself with the volumes of his *History*. She confessed to him in her reply: "I am re-reading with keen enjoyment a certain History of the United States. You may know it. It is wonderfully good reading, & I advise you when this war keys up your nerves beyond the bearing point to open the early pages and read that wonderful picture of the forests & streams, and of the material problems of our forebears."[56]

For war-related reasons, the *Olympic* would not make its scheduled October 21 departure for New York. The *Cedric* was substituted. In preparation for the voyage, uncle and nieces returned to London.

On the 20th, Henry James said in a letter to Edith Wharton that he had dined with Adams and "two young nieces, the natural and the artificial." James thought his friend "more changed and gone than had been reported, though still with certain flickers and *gestes* of participation, and a surviving capacity to be well taken care of; but his way of life, in such a condition, I mean his world-wandering, is all incomprehensible to me—it is so quite other than any I should select in his state."[57] James's report had value. It suggested that Adams had been very unwell. There had been an under-reported setback.

Mrs. Cameron had no letter from Dor in the weekly mail from England. She pressed ahead in his epic. She told him: ". . . I read a certain history. . . . It re-reads better than it read at first, and it gives a picture of Washington and America which no comic paper could outdo." She asked, "I wonder when I shall hear from you?"[58]

Dor perhaps cabled to her from New York after debarking from the

Cedric, but he did not quickly write. As quietly as possible, he reappeared at 1603 H Street.

An election took place. Jimmy Wadsworth—the husband of Alice Hay—was elected to the Senate from New York. He and Alice would be kept in Washington indefinitely. For Adams, the news was helpful.

Soon after, while at dinner with Aileen, he saw that William was behaving strangely. His servant had suddenly gone insane. When confronted with horrors in the past—even horrors as frightful as the breakup of the Union in 1861, or near-war with England later in that year, or the hideous death of his sister Louisa from tetanus in 1870, or the onset of Clover's insanity in 1885—Adams had always moved *toward* danger, the better to understand it and if possible be of use. In the present instance, he failed. He signaled to Aileen that he could not deal with William's problem—that *she* would have to do so. She somehow did, and the servant was committed to a mental hospital.

Whatever it may have been before, Dor's condition, physical and mental, had become precarious. On November 10, he sent Mrs. Cameron his news. He recounted William's breakdown. He affirmed that "Roosevelt and his following" had been "disposed of." He said affairs in America were "dull and flat and stupid, but so am I." And he stopped to remark, "The poor Kaiser strikes me as frantic."

That day or the next, Adams received a letter from his one-time correspondent, Edward Davis at Purdue University. Davis had the idea that the war had been caused by "pessimism as to the value of present civilization and its promise of permanency." He thought too that a "wholesale abandonment of one set of ideals" had begun, "in favor of another." He wanted Adams to reply to his opinions.[59]

Adams answered on November 11 that they could not correspond. He explained that the "present situation" was too "absorbing" to permit an old man to "draw conclusions." "It goes far beyond me. . . ."

During the previous June before moving to the chateau, Adams had obtained complete photographs of a manuscript of medieval songs. At every opportunity since then, he and Aileen had worked on the added songs. Writing to Mrs. Cameron on November 15, 1914, he said Aileen was taking him out for drives and bringing him back to "our MS. PC5." "It contains some five hundred songs which we study one by one. We are now near the end."[60]

His "five hundred" was an exaggeration and evidence of a return to good spirits. Feeling better made it easier for him to tell Mrs. Cameron about the strain imposed on him by the war. He confessed: "Last summer was no joke. I knew that unless I kept my mind off it, I should have [a?] nervous collapse. When I left Saint Remy[,] I had already broken down with nervous dyspepsia. . . . Stepleton lifted me over the gap, and I got home, but I had to keep off the thin ice. I read no papers and still avoid them."

His condition had two sides. There had been a heavy setback at the chateau. He accordingly likened himself to St. Augustine at Hippo when the saint despaired of earth and "wrote the City of God!" Yet all along there had been countervailing strength. He believed that he, Aileen, Elsie, Martha, and Mrs. Cameron were fortune's beneficiaries. "It has been a wonderful picnic. We have flitted from one strange scene to another. . . . We have really lived and seen life. I had no idea I had so much life left in me. . . ."

On Thanksgiving Day, November 26, he began a letter in instalments by speaking to Mrs. Cameron very directly about the war. ". . . when the world insists on killing itself, no one can stop it. As for me, I cannot even talk about it, for fear of doing harm."

Three days later, he added an analysis of the war's doomed inventors. "The Germans are half mad with solitude and isolation. I pity them, but it would be worse for them if they won. They are so deadly stupid. They make enemies out of sheer *dummheit.*"

25

LOSSES MISAPPREHENDED

While far apart at Cairo and Washington during the winter of 1914–1915, Mrs. Cameron and Adams tried to stay together. As before, they exchanged letters, his being parts of what can be called his perpetual confession. She pressed ahead in his *History of the United States* and felt anew the effects of his amazing honesty. She said the account he gave of American bungling and turpitude in the War of 1812 was "enough to send anyone to drink." "I retire into your history and blush that I am an American." At her "instigation," he meanwhile read Volume IV and said it showed "restraint" and an "absence of epithets."[1]

Both she and he wanted to avoid ensnarement in Europe's war. She wrote: "It is poisoning me through and through with hatred of the Germans. It is bad for one to hate so vindictively—it wears me out." A week later, she repeated herself. "This war is so on my nerves. . . . I find that I cannot read a newspaper at night, or my sleep goes. I hate to hear it discussed. . . ."[2]

He was similarly put off by newspapers. He believed that whatever news they contained had to be mostly bad. Looking into the faces of his guests and visitors, he saw distress. ". . . people now ask gloomily for my *Education*, to read the last chapter, God forgive me—and it! We all want gaiety. . . ."[3]

Spring Rice had come to Washington as ambassador, but Dor was not seeing him and was trying to keep completely silent. He assured Mrs. Cameron: "I write nothing except to you, and I fear I write nothing even then."[4]

A Catholic priest, Sigourney Fay, came to 1603 H Street, heard a number of songs, and took away a copy of the 1912 edition of *Mont Saint Michel and Chartres*. He sent Adams a thank-you note in which he explained at a stroke why Adams was exerting himself to hear forgotten songs and hear some of them a great many times. Fay wrote, ". . . the

478

wonderful music created for me an atmosphere far purer, and sweeter, than any in which this modern world revolves."[5]

For Dor, Mrs. Cameron's absence made Washington seem vacant. It almost made him feel she had died. He told her, "You can imagine me going on as when you had charge of the Square and our lives, only there is no longer a you."[6]

He was troubled also by other vacancies. He felt that the era to which he belonged had expired. Trusting that Gaskell might share the feeling, he said to his friend, "Our world is ended. . . ."[7]

He had similar feelings about his century. By writing his *History of the United States* in the period 1800–1817, he had engraved a special message on his mind: that in a single year, 1815, an old world had died and a new one had begun. He believed that a parallel death-and-birth occurred in 1715 and that another would occur in 1915. Indeed he refused to wait. Writing to Thoron in late December 1914 when the supposed metamorphosis was still ten days off, he declared, "The world has ended."[8]

Worst for him was the expiration of the Christian era. He felt he was living in a world that had lost its faith very early and had never quite renewed it. In his view, early Christianity died fast. He remarked to Henry Osborn Taylor, "The early Christian [faith] I take to have been abandoned long ago by the failure of Christ to reappear and judge the world." He viewed the replacement Christianity provided by Saint Augustine as impermanent and ill-built. He had taken to reading the Stoics and was disposed to say, ". . . the Augustinian adjustment seems to me only the Stoic, with a supernatural or hypothetical supplement nailed to it by violence."[9]

To his mind, Christianity was undergoing its second failure and was ending. The effect was an emptying of all history. He confessed to Taylor, "I need badly to find one man in history to admire."

An emptiness so vast could be crushing. Having no one to turn to, he feared he might lapse into senseless admiration of Jesus—senseless because belated. "I am in near peril of turning Christian and rolling in the mud in an agony of human mortification. All these other fellows did it,—why not I?"[10]

The Roosevelts had been known to Adams only as Republicans. A new Roosevelt, Franklin, a Democrat, was serving in Washington as undersecretary of the navy. During a visit to Mrs. Lodge, Adams met Franklin and his wife Eleanor. He mentioned them to Mrs. Cameron and said about Eleanor, ". . . [she] promises to be a favorite."[11]

For lack of evidence, the history of Adams's friendship with Eleanor Roosevelt can be reconstructed only scatteredly. One episode deserves special notice. Possibly when she and Adams were still new acquaintances, she heard a young man say to Adams that "he felt something was wrong with the Government, but nothing could be done because nobody seemed to care." The young man's words appeared to be directed against President Wilson. According to Eleanor's recollection, Adams replied: "Young man, don't get excited. I've watched people come into the White House and I've watched them go from the White House. Really what they do there doesn't matter a great deal."[12]

The reported episode was interesting for what it indicated about Adams's power to attract people. It was as if the young wife of an undersecretary, given the chance to find just one new friend during her first winter in Washington, could not prevent herself from listening to a spry old man she met who lived directly across from the White House and said things that lingered in memory.

If Adams's observations were correct, the war in Europe was making his fellow Americans "more dull and commonplace than ever." He told Mrs. Cameron that an "ant-nest" was more "a fecund centre of thought" than Washington. The capital ignored its most pressing needs. He exclaimed to Berenson, "Not one solitary vestige of a mental action ever comes in the sight." "The idea that the highest intelligences need immediate help most of all, is never suggested."[13]

One might think Adams could draw encouragement from the cries of individuals and institutions for copies of his *Education*. In New York, Florence La Farge borrowed Edward Martin's copy, read enough of it to find herself "flying through the spheres of thought," and wrote to Adams about her flights. By mail, he succeeded in getting the copy originally lent to John La Farge transferred to Florence.[14]

On January 16, 1915, Charles wrote from Boston, asking Henry to give him a copy for the Boston Public Library. The request had been set in motion by the librarian, Lindsay Swift, one of Henry's former students. Henry might be expected to grant it.

On the 19th in Washington, Charles brought Thayer to 1603 H Street for lunch. A third guest appeared: Underwood Johnson, director of the American Academy of Arts and Sciences. The guests wearied Henry to exhaustion by talking all at once. Thayer, seen for the second time, struck Henry as sensitive, although not highly intelligent. The biographer had been speeding through his work on *The Life and Letters of John Hay*. In order to review the passages Henry omitted when readying Hay's *Letters* for printing, he needed to see the originals of the letters Henry had received from Hay. Henry obliged and let him have the originals as a short-term loan.[15]

Next day in a note to Charles, Henry said he could not give his

Education to the Boston Public Library. He described the book as "an incomplete experiment which I shall never finish." He said— incorrectly—that the only copy accessible to the public was the one he had given Charles for the Historical Society. He said no copies remained for applicants. "None remain to distribute."

In a new letter to Mrs. Cameron, Dor pictured himself as the dormouse asleep at the tea-table in *Alice's Adventures in Wonderland*. His self-mockery could involve an implication that he knew a man in Washington, a mad hatter, who was insanely talkative.[16]

Mrs. Cameron made allowances for the time that would lapse between her mailing a letter in Cairo and Dor's receiving it. Eleven days in advance, she told him that she and the Lindsays would be thinking of him on February 16, 1915, his seventy-seventh birthday. She quietly added an observation. ". . . you, and Lincoln, and G. Washington make a February galaxy."[17]

In Mrs. Cameron's perfectly serious opinion, three Americans were stars of the first order of magnitude. All had been born in February. Washington and Lincoln were easy to characterize. Dor was very hard to characterize, or even loosely estimate. Unlike the others, he had lived to an advanced age. She thought he stood at the end of the series—that there would not be a fourth.

Senator Lodge had a way of coming to 1603 H Street for dinner. Dor celebrated his birthday by assuring Mrs. Cameron that the senator was no longer sane. Insistently Lodge talked about Woodrow Wilson. Dor listened and made a judgment. "As for our dear Cabot, I think he is off his balance, and his hatred of the President is demented."[18]

Adams was having esophageal troubles. In late February, Aileen had to go to New York. He wrote to her that he was dying as a result of eating lunch. Five days later, he told Mrs. Cameron he had undergone a "collapse" attributed to "dyspepsia."[19]

Different members of the Adams family responded differently when ill. Charles was not a man to coddle himself. For three days in Washington, he continued to ride his horse in bad weather despite being very sick. He paid for his obduracy with his life. On March 20, 1915, he died of what Henry said was "grippe" that "fell suddenly on his heart."[20] The actual illness was apparently pneumonia.[21]

The Massachusetts Historical Society owed unstinting honors to its departed president. Charles had reformed the institution, refinanced it, and rehoused it. Senator Lodge was named as his successor. Lodge proposed to honor Charles with a memorial address by himself, to be delivered at a meeting of the Society in Boston in a place that would accommodate many hearers. The meeting would occur in November.

There meanwhile was a funeral service for Charles in Washington, conducted privately at his house. Henry was expected to attend. He was grieved by his brother's death and even said that *he* should have died, not Charles.[22] Yet he refused to attend and sent Aileen in his place. During the evening of the same day, he and she devised an observance of their own. It consisted of her singing a *stabat mater* and part of a requiem mass.[23]

He and Aileen had worked on medieval songs till she had "sung them all, or all the best."[24] Since visitors seemed willing to hear such music, she and he arranged 102 songs as seventeen programs of six songs each. They ended each program with a song to the Virgin.[25]

The work of arranging programs felt natural to Adams and Aileen, and there might come a time in the future when Americans would flock to hear programs of medieval songs performed. In 1915, however, musical work of the sort that Henry had done could seem very unfitted for an Adams who had been born in Boston in 1838 with expectations of his becoming a New Englander and a Yankee.

The elder Lodges could be assumed to know what Adams was doing. After all, it was Mrs. Lodge who had led Henry to Mont Saint Michel and Chartres. But Mrs. Lodge and Senator Lodge were remarkably different human beings. The husband was nothing if not a Massachusetts man. He had seen a great deal of Henry Adams since the early 1870s and had become associated with Charles Adams only latterly. He had found in Charles much that he could admire. He was finding things in Henry that he disliked. Given a chance to ally himself with one of the brothers, he would opt for Charles and reject Henry, whose labors on out-of-date French songs could seem alien and outlandish.

Mrs. Cameron wished to get back to America and provide a home for Elizabeth Hoyt, who was reported to have had "a nervous breakdown."[26] Dor knew the particulars. With the needs of aunt and niece in mind, he rented for the coming summer a house in Dublin, New Hampshire, that had three double and four single bedrooms.[27]

The person likeliest to want a summer with Adams in New Hampshire was Mrs. Cameron. She merely felt she would have to get a separate house for herself and Elizabeth. She assured him: ". . . if a house could be found[,] it would be a wonderful opportunity of being near you. I hardly dare let myself think about it."[28]

Her and Dor's ideas about the summer were rooted in mistaken assumptions about the safety of ocean crossings at a time when German submarines were roving the seas in increasing numbers and with much success. When she made inquiries about ships, Mrs. Cameron was told not to try to go to America. She was advised to voyage, at most, from Egypt to the south of France. She could safely go thence to Paris and reoccupy her "green apartment in the Square."[29]

In the sense of reading each day's news, Dor had not been keeping abreast of the war. Yet he had formed new ideas about it—ideas which possibly could be arrived at only by a person who struck a balance between learning about events and considering events. He had written to Mrs. Cameron in February, ". . . I think the war is a consequence rather than a cause of our ubiquitous nervous collapse."[30] In April, he turned to two important matters at once: Germany's aggression and the aggressions of the international Socialists and Communists. He advised her: ". . . the man of the future is much less afraid of the kaiser than of the communard, and is shaking with terror either way. What a happy world we have invented!"[31]

On his way to New Hampshire, Adams visited Elizabeth Hoyt in New York and saw no trace of a nervous breakdown. With respect to company, living in the large rented house in Dublin promised to be nearly the same as living in Washington. The Henry Whites would be nearby, also Florence Keep, and such visitors as Margaret Chanler would sooner or later appear.

Three weeks of New Hampshire air gave Adams a feeling of being his proper self, only "shaky in the legs and bad in eyes." Unfortunately no letters came. While the dearth continued, he took occasion to give Mrs. Cameron a broad view of his situation and state of mind. ". . . I am alone on a mountain, waiting the end of the world, which . . . must come soon, and has in fact come for me long ago, for it is now just three years since I woke up out of my illness into a world which is quite another than the one I knew, and to which I can't accustom myself."[32]

The Germans had sunk a large British passenger steamer, the *Lusitania*. The loss of the vessel and many lives settled for Mrs. Cameron "the question of my attempting to get to America."[33] News reached her from Dor that Ward Thoron and Loulie Hooper were engaged and that, rather strangely, Loulie would stay at Biarritz till September before going home to be married. The delay seemed certain to increase the perils that Loulie would risk when crossing.

Unexpectedly in early June, Mrs. Cameron was informed that space was available for her on a ship departing for France. She accepted the offer, but Martha collapsed, and the departure was cancelled. A joint departure of daughter and mother was scheduled in its place, to occur on July 6, 1915. Under the new plan, Mrs. Cameron was to stay with Martha at Stepleton through all the latter part of the summer.

*　*　*

The newspapers reported that Henry James had become a natural-
ized British subject. His act was welcomed by the English as helpful to
the Allied cause in the war.[34] How Americans might feel about the
change was uncertain. At Dublin, Adams startled the other persons at a
gathering by saying excitedly about James: "He has thrown in his lot
with a dying country. England is done!"[35] Adams's statement could be
understood as a result of pertinacity as a historian. He had studied the
history of the English more fully than that of any other people but his
own. He saw England as sinking. He thought the elder country a ship
on which no intelligent American should be willing to go down.

James's action apart, the summer was uneventful for Adams. Mrs.
Cameron and Martha proceeded to Stepleton. Loulie returned to
America unscathed. Adams passed many weeks in healthful surround-
ings.

Margaret Chanler came to see him. She later confided in a letter to
her daughter Laura: "I had as you know paid Uncle Henry a little visit.
. . . He lives alon[e?] with his thoughts under the shade of [Mount]
Monadnock. I think the reason Aileen gets on so well is that she does
not intrude at all on his intellectual solitude. He is very much occupied
now with seeking a demonstration, a palpable proof of the existence of
God. . . . His attitude about the war is the one that most appeals to
me—one of silence and humility—bowing his head before the inscrutable destiny of nations. Praying!"[36]

For all her intelligence, Mrs. Chanler was ill-protected against self-
delusion and extreme misreading of first-hand experience. What she
had long wanted in Henry Adams was not the Adams before her eyes
but an Adams who unhesitatingly believed in God, craved God's help,
and was reaching to receive it. She needed to find in him her ideal
Catholic. While visiting at Dublin and thereafter, she succeeded in effecting the transformation delusively. Without intending it, Adams had
fed her madness. The assisting factor was mere avoidance. He now and
then had kept apart from a younger Catholic, Aileen, and from an older
one, Mrs. Chanler.

In July 1915, Senator Lodge started to read the "Autobiographical
Memoir" that Charles Adams had left to the Historical Society. The senator advised Ford that the memoir was "fascinating; delightfully written,
and with an honesty which is hardly to be equalled in the whole range
of biographies." He said the work should be published by the Society
"as a separate volume."[37]

Thayer had nearly completed *The Life and Letters of John Hay* and was
the more anxious to finish because he had lost the use of an eye. His

work as biographer had brought him into virtual partnership with Ferris Greenslet at Houghton Mifflin Company. On July 17, he wrote a letter to Henry Adams that touched a much-irritated nerve, the authorship of the anonymous novel *Democracy*. He said he had been told by Henry's brother Charles that Mr. and Mrs. Henry Adams, Clarence King, and Mr. and Mrs. John Hay had joined to form "an intimate coterie" called the Five of Hearts and that *Democracy* issued from the coterie—"Hay being the writer and you others the critics."

This preamble, which he may have known would be very disturbing to Henry, gave Thayer occasion to state that, after reading thousands of Hay's pages, he knew that Hay "could not have written 'Democracy.'" He continued: "Neither could King. You alone [Henry Adams] were up to the level of its substance, vocabulary and style."[38]

Thayer and Greenslet were perhaps insightful enough to anticipate that Henry would not admit that he wrote *Democracy*, and they probably did not much care whether he would help in that connection. They were after something bigger—big enough to induce Thayer to take the risk of telling Adams that his abilities placed him a full grade above the two men who had been his most valued male American friends.

Telling that to Adams was telling him what he did not wish to hear. The offense was all the worse because the assertion was true. Adams *was* more capable than King and Hay. Yet it was right of Thayer to be offensive, for he and Greenslet meant to prove to Adams that he was an author much too capable to be allowed to remain unpublished and especially that his *Education* had to be ceded without delay to a publisher, meaning Houghton Mifflin. Thayer's frontal attack had even the look of a frontal attack. He told Adams that he had "read, and reread your 'Education.'" He explained: "I cannot think of your determination not to publish it as being anything less than a great loss to American literature. And not to that only, but to autobiography, and to that small, rare group of books in which an epoch is personified in an individual. Let me urge you to reconsider, and to print the book during your lifetime."

The relative persuasiveness of Thayer's tactic depended most on the truth or falsity of its terms. If Adams's *Education* had been an autobiography and if the "Henry Adams" told about in *The Education* had been the actual Henry Adams, the Adams to whom Thayer had written might have agreed that his argument made sense. But fully as much as Mrs. Chanler, Thayer and Greenslet were given to self-delusion. They had imbued themselves with the mistaken idea that *The Education* was an autobiography and had allowed the idea to fill their minds till no other could enter.[39] It could not occur to them that Adams was both a writer and an originator; that his book was the prototype of a new literary form, the education; that in the long course of discovering the form, Adams had learned *not* to be an autobiographer; and that *The Education of Henry Adams* was relevant to autobiography only by being—as one of its lesser features—a potent anti-autobiography.[40]

Thayer and Greenslet could not see that the narratives in Adams's book, while sustaining an account of a third-person "Henry Adams," made use of small facts in the actual Adams's experience, yet were innovative literary devices which, while serving other ends, permitted Adams systematically to mute, neutralize, undercut, deny, or strip out *all* of his main achievements.[41] Why he had written a book so renunciative and abnegating was a great question. Thayer and Greenslet could not get to the question, much less suggest a possible answer; and via Thayer they had sent Adams an appeal that was sure to strengthen his resolve not to allow his book to be published.

He did not immediately answer Thayer's letter. When he did, on July 22, 1915, he seemed to say he had died. He said nothing about *Democracy*. "As for the Education, it has passed out of my control. Three years ago, I had to quit the world . . . and now I could no more resume it than I can recall my friends to life."

Adams may have meant his answer as final, but Thayer and Greenslet did not accept it. Instead the pursuers in Boston-Cambridge assured themselves that the thing to do with Adams was to go and talk with him. For them, the important question was what to say.

After more reading, Lodge notified Ford that he would soon return Charles's "Autobiography" to the Society. He said the manuscript required "a great deal of careful editing, which I know you will give to it." He said as well that the projected book was likely to "have a very considerable sale."[42]

Ford had suggested to Lodge that Charles's "memoir" and Lodge's Memorial Address should be published together. The senator liked the idea but was not ready to approve it. He replied, ". . . this can be decided when we meet." He had drafted the address and was having it typed. When he was satisfied with it, he said, he would send Ford a copy to permit its being printed, partly with a view to supplying the text to interested newspapers.[43]

On Saturday, September 18, Lodge advised Ford that "the autobiography and my address" were to appear together, as suggested, and that Houghton Mifflin would be the publisher. "I will write at once to Mr. Mifflin on behalf of the Society."[44]

On Tuesday, Lodge sent Mr. Mifflin's letter of consent to Ford. Lodge at the same time announced that he was coming to Boston on Friday and would give Ford the *Autobiography* and the "Memorial Address," which was "ready to go to the printer." The address was to appear at the front of the book as a very full introduction. Editorial details were left to the discretion of Ford and Greenslet.[45]

On Saturday, September 25, 1915, at her home on the Massachusetts North Shore, Anna Lodge died of a heart attack.

Her death had an importance for Henry Adams that few persons would openly acknowledge. She and Adams had formed a relationship so close that they addressed each other as brother and sister. Adams had long despised her husband. Increasingly her husband disliked Adams. While she lived, her husband and Adams play-acted that they were friends. She required it. Once she was dead, Lodge would reveal his dislike of Adams, albeit in forms many observers would fail to understand. Adams would go on concealing his low opinion of Lodge and might do so for many months. Yet eventually his true feeling would have effects.

Gaskell had been felled by illnesses. One of Adams's reliances when speaking or writing to friends not in good health was to say he was in a feebler state than he knew himself to be. In this vein, he had told his English friend on August 15, 1915, that he could "neither read nor write." He said as proof, "This is the first line I have put on paper for months."[46]

The words "months" was misleading. Since January 1, Dor had sent twenty-five handwritten letters to Mrs. Cameron. Beginning after July 2, a gap had opened in his letters to her. The gap extended to almost nineteen weeks. Her many letters to him indicate that letters sometimes came from him during the nineteen weeks but at other times did not.[47] One may infer that the few letters he sent to her during the gap were messages dictated to Aileen and that Mrs. Cameron did not keep them because they were not in his handwriting. One may also infer that Adams was suffering returns of old infirmities.

On September 25 just before her death, Mrs. Lodge completed and mailed a letter to Aileen, partly to pass along a gardener's report that the plantings at Adams's grave site in Rock Creek Cemetery were "in very good condition." The gardener had reported to Mrs. Lodge because she was supervising the upkeep of the site.[48] Her letter to Aileen arrived at Dublin together with the news that she had died.

Adams reacted by hand-writing a letter to Senator Lodge about lost wives. He stressed that he had not seen his wife for almost thirty years. "I have gone on talking, all that time, but it has been to myself—and to her. The world has no part in it. One learns to lead two lives, without education."[49]

The feelings brought out in Adams by the death of Mrs. Lodge were strong feelings of relatedness to her, the wife. Such feelings could not prevail against the senator's unconquerable self-centeredness. Lodge read Adams's letter as one of sympathy for him, the bereaved husband and new-made widower.

A note reached Adams from Lodge's daughter Constance, saying no letter of condolence had touched her father as much as his. Adams responded on October 5 with a note to the senator saying he had been prevented from replying to Constance by "my paralysed hand and arm."[50] Adams's condition could not be doubted. He was suffering intermittent arm-and-hand paralysis. It kept coming back.

On September 22, 1915, Mrs. Cameron and Martha had crossed from Stepleton to Paris. A week later, alone and in tears, Martha took the train for Marseilles, bound for Cairo and a reunion with her husband. It was a late beginning in self-reliance.

Renewed sight of Paris gave Mrs. Cameron an idea about the war's outbreak the summer before. On October 12, she wrote to Dor: "Do you remember those elaborate calculations of yours which worked out that the world would come to an end in 1917?" The only predictions Adams had made that were linked to elaborate calculations explicitly involving "1917" were in a sense not his. They were the parodic predictions worked up by an imaginary physicist-historian in the first version of "The Rule of Phase applied to History." Dor must have lent the version to Mrs. Cameron. (He had had an opportunity to do so in Washington early in 1909.) The idea that the world would end had stayed in her mind. In October 1915, wanting to twit Dor about it, she contradictingly said, "The acceleration was greater than you thought, & the blow struck three years earlier [i.e. in 1914, not 1917]."[51]

The importance of Dor's paper had not resided in its serio-comic details. It resided in the sheer suggestion that *a* world—theirs—was near its end. Mrs. Cameron was an excellent reader. She had grasped the suggestion and had not believed it. The result for her in 1915 was a fresh confirmation of his intelligence. Their world *had* ended! She happily confessed: "I would not believe you, but you are very aggravating, you are *always right*! Confound you!"[52]

For Adams, the great event of October 1915 was the publication of two volumes titled *The Life and Letters of John Hay*. He left Dublin and arrived in Washington in time to see the volumes when new, but he either postponed reading them or read them so slowly that his pace embarrassed him.[53]

On November 4, writing her weekly letter, Mrs. Cameron mentioned that physical difficulties were making it hard for her to use a pen.

She told Dor, ". . . between my troublesome eyes & my bad hand I can scarcely write at all." She made the remark in her usual handwriting, with all its very legible large shapes. Yet her hardships were real. To ease them, she when necessary hired a stenographer.[54]

On November 10, Dor's arm and hand were well enough to permit his writing her a full-length instalment. He began it: "Are you not surprised to see what looks like me! You may well be!" He turned to a question that keenly interested him: the uses of Thayer's book. He explained, "It does not matter whether you like it or not, so long as it helps to build up the legend of our Square. . . ." He outlined a large-scale proposal. He asked Mrs. Cameron to assemble volumes of letters drawn from those she and he had exchanged and those she had received from the Hays and Lodges. He treated the proposal as if it were practicable. ". . . if you have kept your letters, you must have tons which you can select to print. . . . You can easily choose volumes of them to be copied, and unite them by a mere thread of editing. You need not publish. . . . . Just lock them up, and name a literary executor."

Dor's proposal reflected a preference offset by a doubt. He told Mrs. Cameron that he was urging her to edit letters "as much because it would occupy and amuse you for years, as to immortalise you or us." He defined "us" by listing five persons beginning with her and Mrs. Lodge. "I do want you and Nanny to stand by the side of John Hay and Clover and me forever—at Rock Creek, if you like, but only to round out the picture." His doubt was whether she would be willing to associate herself with the Adams grave site. Rather than wait for her to reply, he reiterated his preference. ". . . I would like to feel you there, with Clover and me, and Nanny, and Hay, till the St[.] Gaudens figure is forgotten or runs away."

Really two suggestions were at issue: one that placed five persons around a bronze statue and another, less evident, which would eliminate the statue and so place the persons that Dor was at the center and the others were arranged about him. Dor favored the first. He was struggling not to admit his own centrality. Mrs. Cameron was certain to sense his resistance. She might wish to counteract it.

Before a large audience at the First Church in Boston on November 17, 1915, Senator Lodge delivered an extended Memorial Address lauding Charles Adams. A printed copy of the address was in the hands of Henry Adams in Washington soon enough to permit his writing to Lodge on the 18th: "A thousand thanks! You have done it with a good-feeling, a thoroughness, a conscientiousness, and an appreciation that puts us all at your feet."

Hearing the ring of such praise, one might wish to believe that Aileen read the senator's address to Henry and that she and he were extremely pleased. It seems more probable, however, that Henry sent his strongly-worded thanks after taking pains *not* to learn what Lodge had said. He knew Boston, and he knew Lodge.[55]

Two passages near the end of Lodge's address were hostile to Henry Adams in ways that Henry could anticipate. In each, Lodge contrasted Charles Adams with persons not named. The first passage said disdainfully: "We have had of late years, if not here [in America], at least in England, a group—it might almost be called a school—of paradox-makers who have achieved a now fading notoriety and who have certainly ardently admired each other. In the trick of paradox, no doubt, some cleverness has been shown and some passing amusement excited. But at bottom the whole busines is shallow, and, like all tricks constantly repeated, becomes tiresome."[56]

When Lodge spoke, hearers may have imagined that the senator had in mind only such well-known Europeans as Oscar Wilde and G. B. Shaw. Yet his words could also be taken to describe three men who earlier had lived simultaneously in Washington. Clarence King, John Hay, and Henry Adams had given an appearance of being each other's admirers. King had liked nothing better than paradox-making; Hay was a tireless inventor of lightly amusing turns of phrase; and Henry Adams often said things that respectable people might hear as ironic or uncalled-for. Moreover, Henry's wife had been much criticized in Boston—very unfairly—for an alleged tendency to avail herself of winters in Washington as opportunities to criticize Boston and Bostonians.[57]

Lodge's second passage appeared in the same paragraph of his address. It said about Charles Adams: "He saw with clear vision what was defective . . . in his own times and in his own country, but he did not on that account hold up with factitious admiration some long dead century, or some foreign country as an ideal where all was perfect, for he knew that such perfection existed nowhere and that the bygone century and the foreign country had their defects . . . which, if not worse than those of his own time and of his own land, were certainly quite as bad. He was not a pessimist, and professional pessimism had, for him, no attraction."[58]

Many hearers in Lodge's audience had read or heard about the 1913 edition of Henry Adams's *Mont Saint Michel and Chartres*. A scattering of hearers had read or heard about a book privately printed in 1907 titled *The Education of Henry Adams*. A few had read or heard about a small book by Henry Adams, *A Letter to American Teachers of History*, privately printed in 1910. The first of the three books could be dismissed—very unfairly—as a reactionary utopia, a dream of building in America a nostalgic simulation of eleventh, twelfth, and thirteenth century France.

The second could be dismissed—very unfairly—as a compendium of half-European pessimisms. The third *was* a compendium of European pessimisms. As its author, Henry Adams could be dismissed—very unfairly—as if he believed and endorsed the pessimisms.

That the senator had derogated Henry Adams was impossible to deny. Yet it was difficult to assert; for Lodge was the kind of person who in a speech at a public gathering could derogate Henry and his books, albeit disguisedly, and nine days later could say privately in a letter to Ford that Adams was his intimate friend—"no one more so."[59]

In November 1915, in part because the librarian, Herbert Putnam, had sought a copy and in part because he all along had meant to provide one, Adams took from its shelf one of the five clean copies of *The Education* that he had kept in 1912 and gave it to the Library of Congress. The gift was secret. Adams required that the "source" not be recorded.[60]

While sending it, Adams evidently informed Putnam that the book had the defect of "incompleteness." Putnam remarked in his letter of thanks that *The Education* had acquired a "unique repute." He went on to say, ". . . I fancy that its 'incompleteness' has struck no one as an imperfection. Nothing autobiographic can be complete."[61]

In mid-December 1915, Adams finished reading *The Life and Letters of John Hay* or reading enough to feel comfortable in writing Thayer a letter of praise. He told the biographer that his book, in addition to being "extremely readable" and "interesting," achieved a triumph for which he, Adams, was "wholly unprepared." Thayer had shown that three able women in Washington had tried to make the capital "a centre of art and taste"—"a new city." According to Adams, the women were "my wife, Mrs[.] Lodge and Mrs[.] Cameron, under the shadow of St[.] Gaudens' figure at Rock Creek."[62]

Adams's letter to Thayer functioned in Boston as a message to both Thayer and Greenslet. On December 22, each man wrote a reply. Thayer began his by assuring Adams, "You are the one person whose verdict really concerned me. . . ." As if the question was solely his own, he closed by asking, ". . . may I plead again for the publication of 'The Education.'?"

Greenslet excused his letter to Adams by echoing a rumor—or, more probably, by inventing one. "The rumor has reached the writer's ears that you are seriously considering the question of . . . publishing 'The Education of Henry Adams.' " The editor gave reasons for publishing the book without delay. *The Education* was mentioned in Thayer's *Life and Letters of John Hay*. It was an "autobiographic" supplement to Adams's own *Mont Saint Michel and Chartres*. And it was suitable as a follow-up to the publication of "the Autobiography of Charles Francis Adams with the introduction by Senator Lodge." Greenslet closed by offering to come to Washington during the "next few weeks to consider the details."[63]

If he felt any difficulty in replying to Thayer, Adams got around the difficulty by waiting a few days and writing to him about several matters, each substantial in a small way, but without saying a word about *The Education*.[64] Differently, Adams attempted a straightforward reply to Greenslet. He drafted it on left-over sheets of old Paris writing paper. No evidence has been found that he copied it onto up-to-date paper. He did not mail it.[65]

Adams made the draft a flat refusal. He said about himself and his book, ". . . I cannot recast it or remodel it, and certainly will not publish it as it stands."

Adams said in the draft that he wrote *The Education* "ten years ago"; that is, in 1905. His phrase could be criticized as misleading. It was true only with regard to some of the book's concluding chapters. Otherwise it was false.

Adams went further. He said his book was in an "incomplete, uncorrected, tentative form." This misstatement was at odds with the completeness and finish of a great many of the book's pages as printed and still more with Adams's many corrections and improvements—with all the work that had gone into the making of his hidden Master Copy, not to mention the strayed First and Second Traveling Copies.[66]

Seen as a whole, Adams's draft was a bundle of assertions he could write but could not send. As things stood, he had the alternative of waiting to hear that Houghton Mifflin's editor had arrived in the capital and wished to see him. He chose it.

Because Greenslet was put to the embarrassment of not receiving a reply, Thayer waited about six weeks and stepped in by writing Adams another letter. He pretended he had heard news. "Happening to be in the office of the Houghton Mifflin Company a day or two ago, I was greatly pleased to hear that they hoped to persuade you to consent to the publication of the 'Education' as a companion volume to 'Mont St. Michel and Chartres.' "[67]

Thayer had double reason for writing to Adams. He had received a commendatory letter from Mrs. Cameron, "who only regretted that my biography of Hay was not longer, giving still more of his correspondence." Mrs. Cameron's comment had reminded Thayer that Adams was very skilled at selecting letters, that letters had passed in great numbers between Adams and his intimates, and that many had been preserved. Thayer accordingly suggested to Adams that an "attractive" volume of letters could be published under the title *Henry Adams and his Friends*, if only Adams himself would select the letters.[68]

The idea of a book with that title had occurred independently to Americans in widely separate places.[69] The idea had a basis in one of Adams's achievements. Successive groups of persons had been brought together in Washington, and had stayed together, mainly because Adams possessed an ability to draw men and women into informal union and hold them there. Not John Hay but Henry Adams was the American other Americans had most occasion to learn about. Thayer knew it. Mrs. Cameron knew it even better.

Adams replied at once to Thayer, but again in an evasive way. He approved a book of his and his friends' letters. He only required that the selector be Mrs. Cameron and that *her* book—rather than *The Education of Henry Adams*—be the next work to appear. ". . . I want Mrs[.] Cameron's letters to precede all else."[70]

Mail delivery between Washington and Boston was dependably fast. Adams's letter to Thayer was dated Sunday, February 6, 1916. It very possibly was delivered to Thayer in Cambridge on Monday morning and was carried by him to Greenslet's office in Boston that afternoon. If so, Thayer's bringing Adams's letter to Greenslet comported with an action he had taken recently, perhaps within the past four or five days. He had secretly lent Greenslet a copy of Adams's *Education*.

In 1907, Greenslet may have leafed through a copy of *The Education* in New York; but he had never fully read the book; and he could not have anticipated being brought such a copy as the one that Thayer had placed before his eyes.[71] In Greenslet's later words, it contained "annotations, emendations, amendations, and other marginal writings by the author."[72]

Thayer's act placed Greenslet in the queer position of being an editor attempting to get a go-ahead from a writer to publish a book by that writer while having in his office without the writer's knowledge a copy of the selfsame book which contained 178 authorial markings.[73] But really the situation was even queerer; for, in the shared mistaken opinion of Greenslet and Thayer, the copy Thayer brought was Adams's *principal* copy: the one that set forth, apart from minor anomalies, *The Education* as Adams wanted a publisher to print it.

Greenslet was expected to attend the meetings of the Massachusetts Historical Society. Writing to Thayer on Monday, February 7, 1916, he said he would miss the February meeting because he was going to Washington. He had subjected Adams's *Education* to a "careful and complete reading." He admitted he had never read "a more fascinating book, or one that aroused in me more publishing covetousness." Moreover, he expressed his opinion of its author.[74]

Thayer and Greenslet differed about Adams. Thayer had visited him twice, had been helped by him, in a measure was liked by him, but had not receded from the idea that Adams was an "arch-egoist."[75]

Greenslet had met Adams once. He had formed his opinion of the man chiefly on the basis of *The Education* misread as autobiography. His opinion was condescendingly indulgent. In his letter, he told Thayer that he had found in Adams's book a "clear (but in many ways rather attractive) vein of ineffectualness" which he thought Adams was quite aware of. He guessed that Adams was reluctant to have *The Education* published because the book revealed his ineffectualness and especially revealed his not having been "entirely content with the role of inspirer of statesmen."[76]

A meeting between Adams and Greenslet occurred on Friday, February 11, 1916, at 1603 H Street.[77] The proposed linking of the books as if both were autobiographies was highly repugnant to Henry. One male Adams in Henry's generation had written at length about himself and preserved what he had written. Charles had done so by writing the long memoir—or *Autobiography*—that he had left to the Society and by writing and preserving volumes of private *Memorabilia*.

In contrast, Henry had written *against* himself. He had written and printed a long book in which he sacrificed himself and his three lives in the interest of assisting young male readers who might be willing to undergo the trials of self-education. The better to do something altruistic, he had done something self-destroying. He had not been a Charles. He had gone far in another direction. Yet there was one respect in which Henry could follow the example of his elder brother. Charles had wanted his memoir to be published posthumously. Henry could want the same for his *Education*.

Greenslet's proposal that Thayer introduce *The Education* was new. It held out an inducement to Henry greater than any other he could hope for. Predictably, Thayer would place the book somewhat in the context of the lives and works of the Washingtonians whom Henry had brought together. To that extent, Thayer could be relied upon.

Greenslet won his battle. Adams consented to the issuance of *The Education* after his death if introduced by Thayer. In addition, he agreed to leave his book to the Historical Society, agreed that the Society and Houghton Mifflin should cooperate in its publication, and agreed that all royalties should accrue to the Society.

Greenslet returned to Boston and wrote Adams a letter itemizing the terms of their agreement and requesting his acceptance. He said he had gone over the terms with Thayer and Ford. He specified that there would be "a Preface and Introduction by W. R. Thayer." Without showing the least awareness that the remark could irritate, he mentioned that he and his associates viewed Adams's book as "an outstanding one in the field of autobiographical literature."[78]

Rather than mail his letter to Adams, Greenslet sent it to Ford with a covering letter requesting that Ford either mail it or suggest changes. Ford received the materials on February 15, at 3:45 P.M.[79] He saw no need for changes and mailed the letter. One can assume it reached Adams on his seventy-eighth birthday, Tuesday, February 16, 1916, or the day following.

Most probably after receiving Greenslet's plea for signed acceptance of their agreement, Adams decided to inspect his "corrected" copy of *The Education*. He looked where he remembered having stored it— presumably in a locked drawer of his very large desk in his main-floor study.[80] It was not there.

Adams remembered a letter Gaskell had written to him, listing some errors in the book as printed. He looked for the letter in what he thought the desk's appropriate drawer. The letter was missing.

He knew he had sets of copies of *The Education*. He checked the sets, expecting to find two subsidiary annotated copies. Both were missing.[81]

He remembered having kept five clean copies in 1912 and having given one in November to the Library of Congress, but he found only three. One was missing.

When profoundly shocked, Adams tended not to cry out. The presumption is very strong that he said nothing to Aileen and nothing to Elsie. His shock is known only because he later mentioned it briefly to Gaskell. He told his English friend that he had looked for the copy of his *Education* he readied "near ten years ago" for use as the copy-text, were his book to be published. His exact words were "the copy I had corrected for that purpose." He confessed: "To my great annoyance, it had disappeared. Then I looked at my files for your letter of correction. That too was missing. Apparently some one—probably myself—has made free with my literary remains, for books are missing out of sets."[82]

The natural idea that he himself was the probable interferer had led him to wonder how much his sanity was impaired. He exclaimed to Gaskell, "Am I quite ga-ga, or only so-so!"[83]

Adams might better have spared himself his doubts about his sanity. He had not suffered a general impairment. All he had suffered was a limited array of interrelated losses.

Strictly speaking, they were not losses of books. Three clean copies were in plain sight at 1603 H Street. These were the copies he had found *not* missing. At a guess, two were stored in his upstairs study, and one was on a shelf in the main-floor study. Until he had felt compelled to look, he had not been noticing them. Ever since his recovery in 1912, he had wanted to keep his attention as much as possible away from *The Education*, away from its complicated history, and away from his small supply of copies.

The Master Copy and Attendant Clean Copy were not lost. They were safe in their hiding place: the trunk in the closet on the top-floor of the house—the trunk containing Clover's things.

True, the First Traveling Copy had not came back. Still held by Thayer, it was being guarded for him by Greenslet in the Houghton Mifflin office. Equally, the Second Traveling Copy had not come back. It remained asleep at Quincy among Henry's Paris books, neglected by Brooks and unlikely to be noticed. Yet both copies were extant. A letter would have sufficed for each to be recalled.

The real losses were of a completely different order. Henry had lost important memories relating to *The Education*. Some of them, one may say, went down with the *Titanic*. Others had vanished only recently. The main losses can be identified.

He had lost all recollection of having hidden his Master Copy and the Attendant Clean Copy in a place in his house where no one would be likely to find them while he continued to live.

He had lost all recollection of the features of the Master Copy that he had given it after correcting obvious errors. (One may infer that he had not filed Gaskell's letter-of-correction in his desk. He had inserted it in the Master Copy, presumably late in 1907. In 1916, he remembered the letter but could not remember where he had put it.)

He had lost all recollection of having made improvements in *The Education*, as opposed to mere corrections.

He had lost all recollection of copying passages from scientific books and inserting them in the Master Copy. Thus, at the critical instant in 1916, the Master Copy did not exist for him. What mentally existed in its place was the same copy in its early form, the form he had given it in the spring of 1907 when merely corrected—when minimally good enough to serve as a Publisher's Copy.

He remembered having annotated two other copies, but he did not remember their containing improvements, as well as corrections.

He had no memory of having lent the First Traveling Copy to Thayer in January 1914.

He had no memory of having taken the Second Traveling Copy back to Paris, probably in 1911, or of its being shipped with his other Paris books to Quincy in 1912. He had ceased to care about his Paris books.

No chance existed that he would ever take time at Quincy to rummage through them, come upon the Second Traveling Copy, and discover its astonishing markings.

The truly important question about Henry was an interior one: How great did he think his losses?

Grounds sufficient to suggest an answer can be found. They begin with his words to Gaskell. He told his friend that "books" had vanished from "sets" and that someone, probably himself, had "made free" with his "literary remains." In part, the statement was a way of saying he knew his memory had failed but failed narrowly, with particular regard to his *Education*.

His surviving memories about the book, such as they were, had led to what seemed a discovery of the loss of five valuable properties: a much-corrected copy, two other annotated copies, a clean copy, and a letter-of-correction.

The character of the properties conveyed an unavoidable meaning. His correction-and-improvement process had to have been ambitious.

The meaning, in turn, pushed him towards an ultimate question: Had he greatly improved his most original, most aspiring book?

For him, merely to sense the possibility of such a question was a very long step towards recapturing an overall memory that, yes, he had improved *The Education*, in fact improved it decisively.

In this way or a way much like it, he arrived at a mistaken but settled idea of his situation. His idea was made up of three misapprehensions: that, in their physical form, all the corrections he had entered in his printed copies were lost; that, in its physical form, the entire *improvement* was lost; and that the only resources he still had were three clean copies, troubled eyes, a weakened right arm and right hand, and a diminished fund of pertinent memories.

26

COPIES GIVEN, COPIES FOUND

A s his first action in an intended series, Adams took back his agreement with Greenslet about *The Education*. On February 18, 1916,
he warned the editor that he had new "wishes which may be obstacles."
The new wishes amounted to one wish: that nothing be done about the
book. His stating the wish had strong effects. Houghton Mifflin Company was pushed away. Greenslet and Thayer were barred from making
fresh entreaties. Thayer was dropped as intended writer of a preface-
and-introduction.

Adams was freed to begin anew, but his field of action was limited by
vision difficulties. Eye doctors in Washington and Paris had prescribed
corrective glasses. They did not help. As an alternative, he had equipped
himself with magnifying glasses of every sort and size.[1]

Choosing moments when Aileen and Elsie would not watch or interrupt, he began a complete secret reading of his *Education*. He shut himself in his top-floor study, placed pen and inkwell near at hand, opened
a clean copy, and tried to read rapidly.[2]

On page 8, he came to a man's name: "Vassal." He recalled that it
was misspelled, as printed, and had to be changed to "Vassall."[3] He
paused, reached for his pen, and again corrected it.[4]

On page 14, he deleted words indicating that "little Henry" inherited Louisa Catherine Adams's tea-pot, sugar-bowl, and cream-jug. The
change may or may not have been a new one.[5]

On page 31, he deleted all of a sentence remembering a drawback
of eastern Massachusetts in the 1840s: "There was not a trout-stream on
the coast, and no fly-fishing."[6] The deletion was new and prompted by
a rejoinder. In his address about Charles, Senator Lodge had said in
explicit reply to Henry's *Education*: ". . . there are trout streams in that
region even now, some carefully preserved; and in the 'forties' of the
nineteenth century they were more numerous and full of fish."[7] Perhaps
Henry had been told about the rejoinder. Perhaps he had read it. Thinking Lodge knew best, he cancelled his offending statement.

Yielding with respect to trout streams was apparently decisive. Henry stopped thinking about Thayer, Greenslet, and Houghton Mifflin Company. He turned his mind to the Massachusetts Historical Society and reconsidered its president, Senator Lodge.

In 1907–1909, Adams had corrected and improved *The Education* by reading a main copy (which became the Master Copy) and two assistant copies (the First and Second Traveling Copies). He had read the main copy only in Washington, the assistant copies only or mostly when away from Washington. In the assistant copies in some instances, he wrote annotations that were minimal or tentative. In the main copy, one can believe, his annotations were attemptedly full and final.

In late February 1916, Adams made use of the same procedure within the small world of 1603 H Street. After reading Chapters I–VIII in a main copy in his top-floor study, he read Chapters IX–XI in an assistant copy in his main-floor study.[8] He may have shifted to two copies in order to read even faster. He went on to read Chapters XII–XIV upstairs, XV downstairs, XVI–XVIII upstairs, and XIX–XX downstairs.[9]

He had reached the end of the first narrative. While reading in the assistant copy, he had annotated only sketchily and had made eleven changes. He possibly took the changes upstairs invisibly by writing the details on slips of paper and pocketing the slips. When reviewed upstairs, the eleven changes in the assistant copy grew to seventeen changes in the main copy.[10]

Eye trouble evidently impeded him. He re-visited William Wilmer, his ophthalmologist. Possibly Dr. Wilmer asked to see the typeface of the book his patient wished to finish reading. Adams spirited the assistant copy to Wilmer's house, presumably by having it carried by one of the servants.[11] To insure its safe return, he wrote his name and address on the copy's half title page.[12]

Wilmer held the assistant copy a while, and Adams raced to the end by reading upstairs in his main copy. He used his pen very sparingly. In the fifteen chapters of the second narrative—XXI to XXXV—he made only ten annotations.

All the changes he made were clearly recorded in the main copy. There were thirty-four. In a book of 460 pages, they formed a very thin, very broken trail.[13]

The copy survives. Studied hastily, the changes made in it can seem to represent a grotesquely inadequate effort by an aged author to ready a book for publication.[14]

Studied carefully, the same changes reveal themselves as signs of intelligent effort. They indicate that Adams wished to do one thing and not do others. He wished to *read* his book while he could—read it for the last time. Should impulse dictate, he might annotate here and there, but he did not intend to correct and improve the text. He intended mostly to leave it as he found it.[15]

He may have started reading without wanting to estimate how many corrections and improvements made earlier in the book had been washed away in his mind. Actual reading led him to confront the question. In the assistant copy, he came to a page where he earlier had made an improvement in the text involving Grant's secretary of state, Hamilton Fish. He remembered that an improvement had been possible at that point. Thinking to make one, he changed a sentence in the assistant copy by adding an awkward insertion.

Later in the main copy he so reworded the sentence that the awkwardness disappeared. The improvement so achieved was a good one, but not nearly as good as a clear, simple improvement he had devised in the First Traveling Copy in 1907 or 1908. Thus in this instance in 1916, with respect to surviving ability to remember, he was partly successful, mostly not. He may have sensed the fact.[16]

Not long after, in the main copy, he came to the first page that involved his confusion of Willard Gibbs with Wolcott Gibbs. This was the revision problem he had failed to solve in the First Traveling Copy and had fully solved in the Second. Seeing it afresh in 1916, he showed awareness of the problem. He changed a "Wolcott" to "Willard." On a subsequent page, he deleted a mention of "Wolcott."[17] He however had forgotten the solution he had achieved in the Second Traveling Copy. He seemed not to remember that the book concerned one Gibbs, Willard, and had to be shorn of Wolcott entirely. He left the relevant passages in a chaotic state of a sort a defeated annotator might prefer as an admission of helplessness.[18]

His plight was too evident to be blinked. He realized that he was in a state of memory loss that made re-correction and re-improvement of the book not merely difficult but impossible.[19] The practical upshot none the less was very positive. He decided that *The Education* deserved to be published even if only faintly amended—even with no better help than the marks in the main copy he had just closed.

In trying situations, Adams tended to act. At the moment, his impulse to act was strengthened by news from London that Henry James was failing in mind and body. Adams associated James with beloved Clover, who had known the novelist from an early time. The death of James would mean, in a measure, that Clover would again be dying. By the same token, it meant the time had come for important endings.

An ending Adams could bring about was his own extinction as a writer of books. He was helped by his concealed aversion to Lodge. He devised a stratagem that would make use of the senator, whether he liked it or not. Its purpose was to get *The Education* off the hands of its author very fast, with minimum effort.

The stratagem involved the following steps.

—Adams wrote two new things. One was an "Editor's Preface," the other a table of "Contents" listing the chapters of *The Education* and situating the additional preface at the start of the book.[20]

—In pencil, he signed the "Editor's Preface" with Lodge's initials, as if Lodge had written it. He added a question mark in pencil in the margin, opposite the initials.[21]

—He inserted the "Editor's Preface" and "Contents" in his new main copy, enclosed the copy in wrappings to make a packet, and sealed the packet, presumably with sealing wax.[22]

—He wrote Lodge a covering letter dated March 1, 1916. The letter concerned the packet and the eventual publication of the book.[23]

—He had Aileen take packet-and-letter to Lodge's house.[24]

— He asked Dr. Wilmer to keep the assistant copy as a gift.[25]

— On March 25, through an intermediary, G. L. Rives, and on condition that it not be catalogued or circulated before his death, he gave the New York Public Library the clean copy which to the best of his knowledge was the only copy then left in his house.[26]

The letter Adams sent Lodge with the sealed packet seemed candid and straightforward. Lodge would understand it to say that Adams was giving his *Education* to the Massachusetts Historical Society for posthumous publication; that he was asking Lodge to be the book's editor; and that he wanted the book published "as I leave it"; that is, in the exact form the furnished copy would prove to have when the packet was unsealed and opened.[27]

In fact, Adams's letter was deceptive. He had begun it by saying, "I send you herewith . . . a copy of my Education corrected and prepared for publication." The words could only be taken as assurance that the furnished copy was fully corrected. It wasn't. When the packet was opened, the copy would be revealed to be *unprepared* and almost wholly *uncorrected*. Until that moment, however, Adams's words would continue to deceive. The senator would remain assured that a fully adequate copy had been given to the Society.

Adams included in his letter a passage that requires close attention. He told Lodge, ". . . I have written a so-called Editor's Preface, which you have read, and which I have taken the liberty, subject to your consent, to stamp with your initials."

Future inquirers might view the passage as evidence that, during a visit to 1603 H Street, Lodge had been asked to read and approve the Editor's Preface so that Adams with a clear conscience could insert it in the copy of *The Education* that Aileen would carry to the senator's house, together with a letter. Alternatively inquirers might want to guess that Adams wrote the Editor's Preface in two versions, showed Lodge only the first, and destroyed it. But here a third conjecture is preferred: that Adams did not show Lodge the "Editor's Preface" in advance for his approval; yet he wanted the senator to perform the charade of being its author; so he worded the pages in a way that would tell Lodge that, as the price of the Historical Society's getting *The Education*, he had to accept the burden of being the pretended signer of an added preface he had not written and had never seen.[28]

The "Editor's Preface" was meant for eventual reading. It told the truth. It said that HA was obliged to permit the publication of his book despite its being "unprepared and unfinished"—"declaredly incomplete"—in short, that the copy in the sealed packet was *not* prepared for publication. So HA made very sure to put the "Editor's Preface" *inside* the packet, preparatory to sealing the packet and sending packet-and-letter to Lodge's house.

The "Editor's Preface" was the last of Adams's works. It would become important after his death for its immediate effects on the editors of *The Education* and for its future effects on the book's readers. It was important also at the time it was written.

Adams wrote it when he was seventy-eight and very sure of what he wanted. He meant it to introduce *The Education* in one way in order to prevent its being introduced in another. The way he wished to prevent was any way that would pair his book with his deceased elder brother's *Autobiography*, which, as he apparently knew, would shortly be arriving at the nation's bookstores.[29]

The "Editor's Preface" said nothing about Charles; nothing about the *Autobiography*. It introduced three books by Henry Adams—*Mont Saint Michel and Chartres*, *The Education of Henry Adams*, and *A Letter to American Teachers of History*—as closely interrelated. It especially linked two books of the three. It said that *Mont Saint Michel and Chartres* and *The Education* were studies and named their subjects. It said that their author viewed the one as deserving the subtitle "a study of thirteenth-century unity," the other as deserving the subtitle "a study of twentieth-century multiplicity."[30]

Henry Adams was nothing if not ingenious. By a few simple means—by writing an added preface, by keeping silent in it about Charles and his book, by listing in it only works of his own, and by flourishing the terms "unity" and "multiplicity"—he went very far towards taking charge of the discussion of his best last books through all futurity; and he attached a senator's initials to the exploit.[31]

Although possibly unavoidable, the "Editor's Preface" was regrettable. It said less than was needed. It advertised Henry Adams as an ordinary writer. While saying that two of his books were studies, it failed to say they were exemplars of a literary form he himself had discovered or invented: the education. So doing, it failed even to mention one of his strongest claims to literary glory.

The added preface had the appearance of providing a true, brief history of *The Education*. The history said that the author found the book difficult to write; that in 1912, when still dogged by the problems it had set him, he was incapacitated by an illness; and that the book was given to the Massachusetts Historical Society when "unprepared and unfinished"—"avowedly incomplete."[32] Thus, by omission, the history concealed an all-important matter: Adams's Master Copy. More generally, it concealed Adams's long-continued effort to reconsider an intended very great book and improve it in sufficient ways to *make* it a very great book.

The history also concealed a seeming disaster. It failed to disclose that, as nearly as he knew, Adams had mysteriously lost all the records of his book's improvement. This huge omission considered, the history was concealing enough to be downright false.

Yet the history was also true. It reflected Adams's honest knowledge that he could not re-correct and re-improve his work. It took its color from his certainty that he could give his best book to the public only in an unimproved and all-but-abandoned version. It had the hallmarks of a sincere apology.

For purposes of reference, the annotated copy of *The Education* that Adams sent to Lodge needs a name. If things had happened differently—if Adams had undergone fewer strains, if the *Titanic* had not been lost, if he had not been ill, if he had gone to Europe in 1912 and come back—he could have pulled the Master Copy and Attendant Clean Copy from their hiding place and transformed the latter into a Publisher's Copy with no more trouble than a few days' work.

He had wanted to create such a copy. It was because he wanted to create one that he hid the Master Copy with a copy free of marks.[33]

The right name for the copy Adams sent to Lodge accordingly is the Substitute Copy, meaning a substitute for the Publisher's Copy that Adams had failed to create. Admittedly the copy sent to the senator was a very poor substitute. That may help to justify a dismal name. Substitute Copy let it be.

A name is needed also for the copy that Adams let Dr. Wilmer keep.

Of the four copies so far found that Adams annotated, it alone bears his signature. It fairly begs to be called the Signed Copy.

Adams had not told Mrs. Cameron about his misadventure with his *Education*. He never would. He evidently believed that what happened to his book was not for her to know.[34] Yet there were feelings that he wished to express to her—perhaps to her alone. On March 1, 1916, the day he sent Lodge the Substitute Copy, he told her that news of James's death had come that morning. He felt moved to say in addition: ". . . [James] belonged to the circle of my wife's set long before I knew him or her, and you know how I have clung to all that belonged to my wife. I have been living all day in the seventies." ". . . indeed and indeed, we really were happy then."

His letter to Mrs. Cameron was nearly simultaneous with one to him from her. At Verdun in France, an immense battle was raging between German attackers and French defenders. She hated battles. She was engaged in full-time work helping refugees in Paris and expected to stay at such work indefinitely. Neither battles nor refugee work seemed to her fit material for her letters.

She had finished reading Thayer's *Life and Letters of John Hay* and had noticed a disparity between the Hay shown to readers in the biography and the Hay she knew in life. On March 2, 1916, she told Dor: "I think Mr. Thayer makes him a more decided, vigorous, character than he really was[;]—to me he seemed timid, un-self-asserting, and almost feminine in the delicacy of his intuitions & in his quickness."

Others were voicing reservations about the biography. From New York on March 6, Oswald Villard sent a confidential query to Ford in Boston. ". . . I write to ask if you share my great disappointment that Thayer should follow up his magnificent Cavour with so unsatisfactory a book?"[35] Ford wrote Villard an answer qualifiedly supportive of Thayer and unsupportive of Hay. ". . . [Thayer has] made all out of Hay that was possible, because to my mind Hay was a small man, and if he showed greatness in any direction, it was due rather to some influences from outside than to any quality of his own."[36]

Ford did not identify the alleged "influences from outside." His reticence was grounded in enthusiasm. He was interested in greatness. He had become acquainted with Henry Adams when himself a Washington resident. He had learned to think of John Hay as Adams's neighbor, close friend, and pliant satellite. He believed he had found greatness in Adams. He saw a complete absence of greatness in the satellite.

*   *   *

Again to accommodate Mrs. Cameron and her relations, should they need it, Adams rented for the coming summer a house in western Massachusetts that Mildred Bliss recommended as "the most beautiful house in America."[37] The house was huge. Called Ashintully, it was situated on high ground and afforded a view down the Tyringham Valley. Adams and his attendants would go there in May.

He meanwhile asked a favor of Mrs. Cameron and gave a reason. "Do please read my brother Charle[s]'s autobiography. . . . As a companion to my Education, and a sort of answer to it, my brother's views are so instructively humorous as to make me regret that I cannot destroy both."[38]

The reason could seem mistaken. Charles wrote his *Autobiography* before seeing Henry's *Education*. Thus the elder brother's book was not an answer to the younger's. Yet the facts had not been simple. Henry had conceived *The Education* when young. He had written part of his book before 1900 and thus could think of it as the earlier book of the two. Moreover, his book was incomparably the stronger and more ambitious. On these grounds, the *Autobiography* could be looked upon as a mere companion and answer.

Judging from his request to Mrs. Cameron, Henry had been reading the *Autobiography* himself, or was having it read to him. He at the same time was enduring visits by Lodge for meals. His letters were indicative of mounting exasperation. He told Mrs. Cameron, "I adore Cabot more than ever. . . . Cabot is now the darling of State Street. . . ." "Of course Aileen has been surrounded by troubles, and Elsie by anxieties, and Cabot by lunacies. . . ."[39]

In May as planned, Henry, Aileen, and Elsie journeyed to Massachusetts and took possession of their "stately pleasure-dome."[40] Mrs. Cameron's arrival was out of the question, but relatives and others arrived in abundance. A surprise addition was a Scotch terrier pup for Uncle Henry, surreptitiously obtained by Aileen and Elsie in connivance with one of the guests, Uncle Brooks.

At the same time, in Paris, Mrs. Cameron borrowed a copy of the *Autobiography*. Largely because Charles turned out to be almost the reverse of what she expected, she found the book "most interesting." She asked Henry for light. "His self depreciation . . . is pathetic. Didn't he really estimate himself better?"[41]

Like Mrs. Cameron, Dor hated wars, but he had studied many and had developed a keen sense of military realities. The wars he had studied most were the American Civil War and the War of 1812 between England and the United States. In 1914, he had amazed Aileen by telling her that the war in Europe would last four years.[42] The evident basis of his prophecy was his four-year study of Union setbacks and victories in 1861–1865 as reported in American newspapers sent to Europe.

Increasingly the war in France made him feel close to death. In March 1916, while still in Washington, he had explained to Gaskell: "Every letter I write, I consider,—for convenience—my last, and it is far more likely to be so than if I were in the trenches." After he moved to Ashintully, he claimed not to read newspapers. Battle news made him fear. He disliked having to fear, and the hugeness of the battles made them not only frightening but difficult to analyze.[43]

In August, Ford got possession of a newly-discovered daguerrotype of J. Q. Adams and had copies made of it. He sent a copy to Henry and sent with it a photograph he himself had taken of a commodious house on Portland Place in London that Minister C. F. Adams, his wife, and their three youngest children had occupied in the 1860s.

The pictures came to Henry as interesting surprises. He responded as follows.[44]

12 August, 1916

Dear Ford

The photographs certainly do carry me back a long way towards the beginning. That of my grandfather is admirable, and reminds me that once I was taken to Whipple's photographic rooms to see my baby brother daguerrotyped. He was in long clothes, asleep, on a sofa. The year was 1848, or 1849. That of my grandfather must have been before his stroke in 1846, but a glance at his diary ought to fix the day. Between the two, one covers a good lapse of time, and Brooks is still and always a blooming daisy.

The Portland Place house has not changed a brick in fifty years.

I can't say as much of the world about it, nor of those who lived in it. We have changed enough to satisfy a kaleidoscope, but you know all about it.

I hope your daughter's health goes on mending. I don't believe that, at my age, one ever mends, and the best one can do is keep out of sight and hearing, but one can do that,—if lucky.

Ever Yrs
Henry Adams

Adams's reply could be taken as evidence that he was well enough to enjoy being at his huge house and to want to go on living but not well enough to feel protected. His mood was hopeful, yet cautious.

The war continued. He studied it, and his spirits rose. The huge battle between the Germans and the French at Verdun had given way to a battle similarly huge between the Germans and the English along the Somme. On October 1, he wrote to Mrs. Cameron: ". . . I suspect your Germans are in convulsions. Verdun and the Somme correspond to Gettysburg and Vicksburg." Two days later, he prophesied to Gaskell: "As for the war-cloud[,] it is moving accurately on time. On my figures, based on 1863[,] it should take you till August, 1918, to reduce Germany to absolute extinction. . . . The last three months have seen immense progress. . . . The real work is done."

The stay in Massachusetts ended well. Adams admitted to Gaskell, ". . . this summer I have had the swellest house and the most guests I ever did have." He advised Mrs. Cameron, "We have seen millions of family. . . ." The irresistible attraction was Ashintully. ". . . all have wanted to see—our house."[45]

Once back in Washington, Adams did nothing notable. Because there was little to say and handling a pen was laborious, he was writing to Mrs. Cameron only monthly. In his December 1916 letter, he reported, ". . . Cabot Lodge, very grouchy, dines here. . . ." "As for me, I never talk at all, and seldom read papers. My nerves are a wreck and I sleep as I best can."

The New Year—1917—brought visits by Eleanor Roosevelt. Weather permitting, Adams kept to a healthy routine: ". . . a walk early in the morning before breakfast with a niece [Aileen], a drive till lunch with another [Elsie], a nap after lunch and another drive [again with Aileen], with a twelfth-century song before bed. . . ." He mentioned a construction site he passed on drives: the "new white marble mausoleum of Abraham Lincoln."[46]

A change occurred. Every Monday the British ambassador and his wife joined Adams and Aileen for lunch. Because the United States remained neutral in the war, Adams and Spring Rice could not talk diplomacy. The American willingly respected the ban and reported that the British visitor's behavior was "*quite* angelic."[47]

At an unknown moment, perhaps in February, Aileen became acutely aware that she was passing her fifth winter with Uncle Henry and was still obeying his requirement that no one speak in his presence about his wife. During a drive, she told him she wished their silence about his wife were broken. He replied that he would like nothing better! Soon he slipped into a habit of talking to her almost volubly about a woman she had never known: "your Aunt Clover."[48]

Lodge was coming for meals. His moods during his visits appeared to be frightened and black. Adams advised Mrs. Cameron in February that the senator was "more saturated with the terrors of the future than even my brother Brooks."[49]

The approach of spring raised the usual question of a plan for the summer. After hesitating, Adams decided to return to his own summer house. He told Mrs. Cameron that, for fear of German naval attacks on the Massachusetts North Shore, Pitch Pine Hill could not attract a high-paying tenant. ". . . [I] am making preparations to carry my infant household back to my house at Beverly Farms[,] where everyone will leave me alone . . . because they expect the Germans to bombard them at least three times a day, so rents are cheap."[50]

His desire to return to a summer house he had avoided for more than thirty years came as a surprise. It seemed an extension of the willingness he showed when asked by Aileen to permit their talking about his wife. Yet the extension involved a difference. He would be returning to Pitch Pine Hill on his own initiative.

The French philosopher Henri Bergson had come to Washington as a propagandist for the Allied cause. "Daisy" Harriman, a Democratic hostess in the capital, invited him to receive visitors at her home. Mrs. Chanler went to see him and required his calling on Henry Adams.

Dor outlined the result to Mrs. Cameron. "The great Bergson came in the other day and for an hour with infinite ingenuity I fought him off and made him talk philosophy. But at last he broke through all my entrenchments and gave me an hour's disquisition on the war, about which I honestly think I knew more than he did. . . ." Dor was not impressed. "Bergson is a funny little man, taking himself terribly seriously and taken so by all Society."[51]

Aileen wrote an account to Loulie and said that Bergson's visit lasted "an hour." She was present. ". . . [Mrs. Chanler] told Bergson he must see Uncle Henry & he invited him to *all* his meals but he was so dazzled by his success—poor modest philosopher—that he couldn't find time for a meal here but came for an hour one afternoon—and he and Henry talked charmingly—Uncle Henry forcing him to stand on his own ground of philosophy—and Bergson *struggling* to get off onto the war which is all he wants to talk about."[52]

Late in life, Aileen retold the story with emphasis on something neither Adams nor she had mentioned in their contemporary accounts. She said Adams was capable of excellent French and could have spoken in French to Bergson but spoke in English only and made the visitor do the same. She had seen him refuse to speak French before. She imagined he feared small mistakes might place him at a disadvantage.[53]

The meeting with Bergson was a special case, and Adams's conduct may have had a special motive. In 1917 as in other years, Europeans expected Americans to acquire philosophy from Europeans and not try to be philosophers themselves. Such expectations could be infuriating. If Bergson seemed to Adams to suppose that no American could be a thinker, Adams would counter with rudeness, and the kind of rudeness he preferred might well be constriction of their interchanges to a single language, his own.

* * *

Since the death of Hay in 1905, with one exception, Adams had done nothing important relating to the affairs of the United States government. The exception was his printing in his *Education* the passages that concerned the efforts made jointly by Hay and himself after Hay was named secretary of state. Because the co-secretaries made their efforts in ways that left as few records as possible, the passages in *The Education* about their work deserved scrutiny as evidence of extraordinary value with respect to a subject not easy to fathom.[54]

There was a limit to Adams's ability to keep silent in politics. At 8:00 P.M. on April 2, 1917, President Wilson went before a joint session of Congress to request a declaration of war against Germany. That night, Adams dictated to Aileen the conclusion of his April letter to Mrs. Cameron. He told of hearing sounds. "Before we sat down to dinner we heard the hoofs of the cavalry escort from Fort Myer, taking the president to the Capitol, and we had hardly finished our meal before the newsboys were crying the president's speech at every corner. Naturally Aileen Tone, being of an inquisitive temperament, insisted on reading it to me, amid my shouts of triumphant laughter over all my friends."

By quickly passing the resolution President Wilson had requested, the Senate and House placed the United States in partnership with England and France in the European war. As one of its myriad consequences, the Congressional resolution freed Adams to talk with Spring Rice unrestrictedly during the envoy's Monday visits to the house.

An important British commission headed by Arthur Balfour arrived in Washington. Adams arranged Balfour's coming with Spring Rice for a noontime meal. He crowed to Mrs. Cameron, ". . . through the alliance with Springy, we got Arthur Balfour. . . ." The commissioner's talk was confiding. ". . . [he] was very like himself . . . but he complains rather sadly of growing deafness. . . ."[55]

Adams remembered Beverly Farms as plagued in summer by clouds of mosquitoes. Well in advance, he directed that his house be generally refurbished and equipped with better screens.

He and the nieces arrived at Pitch Pine Hill in mid-May. He was speedily given opposite impressions. He told Mrs. Cameron: ". . . I found myself in my own parlor, which I had not seen for so many years that I can't remember how long, but which has not changed in the least since I left it." He also said, ". . . I wander every morning through the woods in search of something that I formerly knew, but it has been reformed out of existence in the attempt to destroy mosquitoes and gypsy moths which are the only real proprietors of the Shore."[56]

Presented a choice between the unchanged and the changed, he took the changed. He avoided the sleeping quarters he and Clover had used. He slept instead in an addition to the house built after her death to accommodate the Hooper nieces.

A letter came from Gaskell. For once, Adams replied politically. He told his English friend: ". . . we are, for the first time in our lives[,] fighting side by side and to my bewilderment I find the great object of my life thus accomplished in the building up of the great Community of Atlantic Powers which I hope will at least make a precedent that can never be forgotten. We have done it once and perhaps we can keep it up. Strange it is that we should have done it by means of inducing those blockheads of Germans to kick us into it. I think I can now contemplate the total ruin of our old world with more philosophy than I ever thought possible."[57]

Adams's joy accorded with his character. Although he was often said by himself, Mrs. Cameron, Hay, and others close to him to be a pessimist, and although he at times was rightly pessimistic about one thing or another, he had been from his beginnings a consistent, undaunted, practical optimist. In every situation, his concern had been to learn what good ideas could be had, and what helpful actions taken, by him and by other persons directly involved.

He knew what he was. During the previous summer at Ashintully, he had said in a letter to an acquaintance in Virginia that optimism and pessimism were the choices put before him and his brother Charles when young. He described an outcome that could seem complex on its surface but was simple underneath. "Charles being the elder had first choice. . . . He chose deliberately to back optimism. . . . I think I was really more of an optimist than he. . . ."[58]

Mrs. Cameron knew too. She had assured him, "Your dear old grumblings are more cheerful than anyone else's gayety."[59]

Especially but far from exclusively, Henry's optimism was linked to a great public object: peace in the world. He had been an explicit seeker of universal peace since December 1861. At the time, writing on the subject in a despatch to the *New York Times,* he had looked forward to "the unity and brotherhood of nations and races."[60]

For him, the real question in world affairs was not what to want but by what means to get it. In 1917, he at last was witnessing the unity and brotherhood of the English, the French, and the Americans. The gain was great. Compared to it, the loss of such old worlds as those of Queen Victoria, Napoleon III, and President Lincoln could be borne with smiles, when not with shouts of laughter.

There had been differences between his and John Hay's political ideas and wider differences between his and Theodore Roosevelt's. He had not wanted a merger of America with England, like Hay. He had not wanted an American empire, like Roosevelt. And he would happily have parted with his country's newly-acquired territorial excrescences.

What he had tried for by coaching Hay was a momentary universal peace informally brokered by Americans in Washington between representatives of all the great powers.[61] Yet he *wanted* something better. When a "Community of Atlantic Powers" came into existence in 1917, he thought its creation a sufficient improvement for the time being but saw more steps as needed. He assumed the stairway to permanent world peace would be long. He wanted it built and climbed.[62]

During his summer at Beverly Farms, Adams retained a chauffeur, rented an automobile, and took drives. He went to see Ward and Loulie Thoron at a historic house they owned nearby, The Lindens. He visited the Old House at Quincy and was shown his Paris furniture, restored to brilliance by Brooks's expert repairer. He could have called on Lodge at Nahant but did not do so. He noted to Mrs. Cameron in September, "Buried in the woods[,] I am invisible to any but the most insignificant sea birds, and have not even *heard* of Cabot, nor indeed of Bessy Lodge, who has not given a sign of life for months."[63]

Relations between Lodge and Adams had critically worsened. The senator hated President Wilson and liked to vilify him. Adams liked to be supportive of presidents when possible and was supporting Wilson gladly. Oppositeness had become complete.

At the moment, Adams was looking beyond the war to the next phase of things. He said in his September letter to Mrs. Cameron, "Behind all the killing comes the great question of what our civilization is to do next. . . ." If she fully considered his words, Mrs. Cameron might realize that the same question was behind all of Adams's best works: his *Education* and *Mont Saint Michel and Chartres*, his novel *Democracy*, his *History of the United States*, and his *Memoirs of Arii Taimai*. It was also behind his frequent cheerfulness and consistent intelligent optimism.

Cheer was the easier for him because Aileen and Elsie were doing all sorts of things he needed done. The lengths to which their assistance was being carried could be seen in some words he wrote to Mrs. Cameron: ". . . I have not touched money for years. . . ."[64]

The division of labor between the nieces had not changed. Elsie remained the businesswoman who ran the household. Aileen remained the hour-to-hour attendant who ministered to Adams's well-being and amusement. Her view of her responsibilities was enterprising. All along she had pressed him to do new things that he might like, or that she might like, with results good for both.

His passing remark that Aileen was inquisitive may help fill in the details of an occurrence that neither he nor she would speak about to other persons. The occurrence may best be dated conjecturally in November 1917 after their return from Beverly Farms to 1603 H Street. The supposable causes of the occurrence were her wanting to know more about Aunt Clover and her being the niece in charge of the top floor of the house. The place of the occurrence was the cedar closet on the the top floor that was used as a trunk room. The immediate object of the occurrence was to open the trunk containing Clover's things, most notably her Worth dress in green velvet.[65]

What evidently happened was simple. Inquisitive Aileen and uninquisitive Uncle Henry entered the closet and opened the trunk, only to find that Clover's things were pressed down by copies of *The Education of Henry Adams.* One copy was unmarked. The other copy was replete with corrections and improvements that Henry had written in the margins and the text. Also it was swelled by inserted pieces of paper bearing passages he had copied from new works relating to science. No available evidence indicates that Uncle Henry told Aileen what copies they were, or why there were two of them, or why they had been put into a trunk used for preserving Clover's things. Perhaps, until he knew what he intended to do with them, he shifted the copies to his upstairs study. Perhaps he did so instantly and in silence.[66]

In old age at her apartment in New York, Aileen Tone liked to tell about a terrible moment in Adams's house in Washington. Seven persons were at dinner: Ambassador and Lady Spring Rice, Senator Lodge and his daughter Constance, Adams's nephew-and-executor Charles (then a house guest), Uncle Henry, and herself. She remembered Lodge's vituperating so inordinately against President Wilson that Uncle Henry had to stop him by saying, "Cabot, I've never allowed treasonable conversation at this table and I don't propose to allow it now." The dinner was "finished in icy silence." There later was "some slight conversation." Two pairs of guests departed "soon after coffee."[67]

Adams liked to get off his letters to Mrs. Cameron at the start of each month. On Monday, December 3, 1917, Aileen was absent. She was paying a pre-Christmas visit to her parents in New York. Uncle Henry dictated to Elsie. He said nothing about Ambassador and Lady Spring Rice. He mentioned that Senator Lodge and Constance had come to the house the week before and that father and daughter had talked offensively. ". . . war is good for something, since it makes Cabot . . . prattle like a peacock. . . ." The account was hardly ill-tempered. ". . . on the whole Cabot's conversation has not essentially changed its character from what it was before—that is, of unbroken abuse of pretty much everybody in the world except himself, but especially of the president and his advisors."

A chasm of difference can seem to gape between Aileen's remembering a terrible moment and Adams's likening Lodge's talk to a peacock's prattle. To bridge the chasm, one might theorize that Adams was angry when he silenced Lodge at dinner but that several days went by before he dictated to Elsie, during which his anger cooled. But it can be suggested oppositely that his anger, great at first, remained great; moreover that, at the cost of giving Mrs. Cameron a tame account of an untame moment, and at the further cost of omitting the moment's main consequence, he withheld the fiery truth from Elsie, who had not been at the table during the terrible moment and was not a niece to whom he would disclose the deeper secrets of the house.

The cause of the terrible moment was the political identities of three men as understood by Adams. Each identity needs to be sketched.

Politically, who was Henry Adams in November 1917? An easy answer was at hand. As a result of Charles's death, Henry for more than two years had been the eldest member of America's most distinguished political family. But the easy answer was incomplete. His political identity was not limited to his being the eldest Adams. For reasons fully known to him but not fully known to the other persons present at the table, he could view himself as the best living representative of America's greatest politicians, reaching back to Benjamin Franklin and George Washington.

Everyone who knew Henry Adams knew in addition that John Adams, his great-grandfather, was the second president of the United States, and that his grandfather, John Quincy Adams, became president also. In similar fashion, many who knew Henry Adams knew that John Adams was the first U. S. minister to England; that J. Q. Adams too was minister to England; and that J. Q. Adams served for eight years as secretary of state under President Monroe. Many knew also that Henry's father, the elder C. F. Adams, was minister to England from 1861 to 1868, and that Henry served at the Legation, albeit unofficially, through all seven years. But, Henry excepted, no one still alive knew that in 1861 when England and the United States came within a hair's breadth of fighting a third war, Henry acted anonymously and very effectively through the press to help avert its outbreak. Gaskell perhaps excepted, no one still living knew that Henry had functioned in London from June 1862 forward as unofficial co-minister, sharing equally with his father in the more serious acts of the Legation. Other than himself, no one still living knew that in 1869 and 1870, while living in Washington, Henry again acted in secret to prevent war with England. Only he surely and fully knew that for seven years, from 1898 to 1905, he secretly had worked in partnership with Hay as unofficial co-secretary of state. He alone knew the extreme degree to which he had filled out his knowledge of the relations between the United States and other countries, especially England. And, Lodge excepted, none but he knew the degree to which he had informed himself about the *domestic* history of the United States, especially the history of efforts to dismember the Union and efforts to counter the intended dismemberments.

An instance of Henry's knowledge should be given. In his *History of the United States*, he had concisely but authoritatively disclosed the story of the Hartford Convention of 1814. While a war was being fought between the United States and England, delegates from several of the American states met at Hartford, Connecticut, to deliberate in secret about the possibility and advisability of breaking New England away from the Union. The meeting was chaired by George Cabot, a Massachusetts Federalist who inspired particular distrust in the mind of ex-President John Adams. A passage in Henry Adams's *History* disclosed the reaction of old John Adams in 1814 to reports of George Cabot's behavior at Hartford. In the passage, old Adams is described by a person who happened to visit him. The visitor heard him exclaim: "Thank God! thank God! George Cabot's close-buttoned ambition has broken out at last: he wants to be President of New England. . . ."[68]

In November 1917 in the eyes of Henry Adams, who was Henry Cabot Lodge, politically? A minimum answer had three parts. Currently he was a senatorial denunciator of President Wilson. Till July 1905, he had been the senator who most pestered Secretary Hay and hastened his death. And from youth he had been a loyal great-grandson of George Cabot, so loyal that he had produced a biography, *The Life and Letters of George Cabot*, published in 1877, which remained the standard work on the subject.

In Adams's eyes, Spring Rice's political identity was unique. Of the many Englishmen who had served as envoys to the United States, he was the first to serve after Great Britain and America became allied. In this sense, he had no predecessor.

The British envoy's presence at Adams's dinner table was emblematic of momentous change. It attested to the fact that two nations who twice had made war upon each other, and later had sometimes come very close to war, were transformed at last to friends. That Lodge saw fit to vent his anti-Wilson feelings in a friendly envoy's hearing had seemed to Adams a shameful parade of American dividedness and an imbecilic parade of insensitivity to international friendship. It had seemed an American enormity.

Adams had stopped it. The means he had employed was a reminder to Lodge that his forebears included a traitor. The means was savage but sufficed. Lodge desisted. People fled the scene.[69]

Lodge was not the sort of person who would accept Adams's act as the end of a very convenient association. If he felt mistreated, the senator would not show it. He soon was back at Adams's table as if nothing had happened. But something was sure to happen.

Of Adams's possessions, none mattered more to him than the lost-and-found Master Copy and Attendant Clean Copy. He can be thought to have waited for Lodge's return to Washington with the idea in mind that he should show him the recovered copies, disclose their history, and give them to him as designated future editor of *The Education of Henry Adams*. Evidently Lodge's arrival with Constance for dinner had been his first reappearance at 1603 H Street. One can believe that the senator's behavior at the table extinguished whatever willingness Adams had felt to give Lodge the copies or bestow them on the Society.

Very soon after the moment, Adams did something possibly wrong but well-adapted to his feelings. He reconsidered Aileen's upcoming visit to her parents. Without ado, he gave her the recovered copies to keep as her own, asked her to take them to her parents' house in New York, and told her not to read them while he continued to live. Thus he again arranged that no copies of *The Education* remain at 1603 Street. Much as he had done in March 1916, he got the book off his hands.

His action had a drawback. Without people knowing it, the Master Copy and Attendant Clean Copy were set astray in the world and made hostages to fortune. But Adams was not of a mind to hesitate.

Aileen saw the Attendant Clean Copy as something she might lend. Evidently in New York about December 1, 1917, she lent it to Susan Loring, the wife of William Loring, a Massachusetts judge and former student of Uncle Henry's. The Lorings' home was in Pride's Crossing, adjacent to Beverly Farms. The judge had come down with bronchitis. Soon, when they were again at home, Mrs. Loring began to read *The Education* aloud to her husband.

The judge liked the book and thought Adams had promised to give him a copy. He wrote Adams a light-hearted letter, saying, "I am not the only student who got more education fr. Henry Adams' courses in History than fr. the rest of his college course. . . ." He declared he would borrow a copy of Adams's "Letter to Students of History," as he called it, unless Adams first mailed him a copy—"when you send me the copy of The Education of Henry Adams you were good eno' to say you would let me have."[70]

Whether Adams had promised the judge he would be given a copy of *The Education* seems unlikely. Perhaps there was a misunderstanding. He answered on December 12, by which time Aileen was again at the house, poised to write what he dictated. He assured Loring, "If I promised to send you the *Education*[,] I was as great a fraud as the *Education* itself, for I have not a copy to send. . . ."

Adams's statement was true. Interestingly, too, it had a hidden meaning. When she heard him dictate it, Aileen was reminded of something known only to her. She—"niece Aileen"—was the last person to be given copies of Adams's best, most important book.

The recovery of two copies had been a surprise to her. His making them her property was another surprise. The principal basis of her receiving them—apart from her having precipitated their recovery—was the extraordinary fondness that he and she had come to feel for each other. Really the fondness decided the outcome. The copies could have gone to no one else.

She appreciated the twofold gift. She would show her appreciation partly by keeping quiet. She would keep so quiet that she would tell only a very few people that she owned *two* copies. Even to the few, she would never say—not in a manner that would create a record kept by her or by anyone else—how she had come to own them, why there were two, or what Uncle Henry told her about them.[71]

Adams evidently made silence easy for her by telling her nothing. She was left to value the copies according to their appearances. The unmarked copy seemed suited for heavy use. The other copy was suited for study. It was full of insertions in his handwriting. She thought it fascinating.[72]

Mrs. Cameron had left refugee work in Paris and was at Stepleton awaiting the arrival of Martha from Egypt. Martha had contracted a serious illness presumed to be dysentery. She needed a second diagnosis and treatment by better doctors. At the same time, Elizabeth Hoyt had crossed from Europe to Washington to do war work and had become a third niece-in-residence at 1603 H Street. Also a favorite nephew of Mrs. Cameron's, Henry Sherman, known as Hal, was sent to London in a military capacity. His being stationed within a train ride of Stepleton lent needed assurance to his aunt, whose worries on Martha's account and her own were multiplying. Mrs. Cameron felt well-adapted to refugee work in Paris. She felt little adapted to medical nursing at Stepleton. She thought it hard that she was having to forsake the one and embrace the other.

She and Dor had last been together three and a half years earlier, in April 1914. He had recently told her how separation was affecting him. ". . . I feel as though I were millions of ages away from you. . . ."[73] Her letters to him told the same story in different words. "I wish I were in a warm American house!" ". . . I wish I could spend Xmas with you."[74]

*   *   *

Christmas came and went. A month later, at midday on January 25, 1918, Uncle Henry and Aileen heard a ring of the front-door bell. Wanting to answer the ring himself, Adams hastened through the hall and down the steps to the door. Aileen heard him say "Rhinoceros!"[75]

Theodore Roosevelt had fared poorly in politics since leaving the White House in 1909. When he rang at Adams's house in 1918 accompanied by his wife Edith and daughter Alice, he was seizing a chance to glimpse a man he much liked and to enter rooms he could associate with his own best days. Edith and Alice were to stay for lunch. The ex-president had other engagements and would not be staying.

Adams later sent Mrs. Cameron an account of the Roosevelts' visit. ". . . all of them tumbled in here in their old way . . . as though nine years were a mere joke, and Theodore looking around the place snorted and puffed and said it was all 'just as it used to be,' while I welcomed him as a 'rhinoceros' and he roared 'Rhinoceros—ha, ha, he calls me Rhinoceros'!!!"[76]

Aileen had not forgotten that Loulie had a very close tie with Uncle Henry. She was trying to keep Loulie abreast of all that was happening at the house. She sent a letter on January 26, 1918, the day after the ex-President Roosevelt appeared. She happened to write just minutes after a different Roosevelt had departed. She said: "Mrs. Franklin Roosevelt has just been to lunch—straight from her canteen service—in uniform—and tells us she has five children . . . with every degree of grippe & cold, and *no* fuel after today except sticks of wood. The most *vivid* thing seems to be the great Theodore[,] who rushed in yesterday to see Uncle Henry— They behaved like children of five & six—called each other strange names and laughed wildly at queer jokes known only to each other—and then Theodore ran about the rooms saying *what* good times I've had in this house!!! After a sort of whirlwind visit of fifteen minutes . . . he rushed out again."[77]

To the dismay of many Americans, Mrs. Cameron for one, the Foreign Office recalled Ambassador Spring Rice from Washington to make room for a preferred successor. The ejected envoy seemed in good health. Rather than start towards London, he went to Canada. He wrote thence to Adams. On February 14, 1918, in Ottawa, he was felled by what his Washington doctor later told Adams was a "sudden death."[78]

Adams's physical condition was less easy to describe. To Aileen, he seemed energetic enough to be young. He also seemed more than old. He had the look of having undergone too many experiences, far beyond what could have been visited on a human being in one lifetime.

February 16, 1918, was his eightieth birthday. He received letters from Loulie and Gaskell. Aileen wrote to Loulie: "Your letter was just what Uncle Henry needed to finish off his birthday with a flourish. Instead of passing the 16th in a low state of mind as I rather expected—he took it triumphantly—with a kind of savage glee and was very amusing about it. Told everybody who came in. . . ."[79]

On the same day, a memorial service for ex-Ambassador Spring Rice was held in Washington. Aileen attended and saw President Wilson and Lord Reading, the new British envoy, plus the capital's other diplomats and what seemed "about half the British army." She all along was watching Adams to see how Spring Rice's recall and death affected him. She assured Loulie: ". . . [the] death was not exactly a shock—because nothing seems to come as a shock now to Uncle Henry—he seems to expect everything in a quite uncanny way. But . . . the loss of Springy is the worst thing that has happened."[80]

Adams and Spring Rice had enjoyed a closeness as politicians that had never before been possible between an American and an Englishman. Begun at Adams's house, the closeness continued in letters. Aileen thought the Englishman a marvel. She told Loulie: "His letters, since he had left, were perfectly *delightful*—and frequent—and of a frankness & originality & political interest that almost made the thing more intimate & charming than when he himself used to dash in & out— And Uncle Henry would answer the letters at once. . . ."[81]

Aileen saw Adams as hurt. "He feels more cut off and alone than I have ever seen him. . . . He said yesterday that he had counted on Springy's letters to amuse him & last easily *his* lifetime."[82]

Adams had the solace of a friendship with Gaskell which after almost fifty-five years was possibly the longest ever sustained between someone American and someone English. On February 19, dictating to Aileen, he sent Gaskell a letter which assumed that their correspondence would continue. He closed by saying, "Perhaps our next letters will grow more cheerful with the improvement of the world."

Yet if read with a close attention to its wording, the letter to Gaskell would reveal itself as felt by Adams to be his last to an English friend. The word "last" appeared in it three times; "passed" appeared twice; "past" and "passing" once apiece. The word choices could seem to be informed by a premonition. Perhaps, in his uncanny way, Adams was expecting another sudden death.

The letter to Gaskell was one of the best that Adams had sent him. Selected passages may indicate its interest. "I don't know whether you ever read . . . the last three chapters of my *Education*. . . . But . . . you might realize the enormity of time that has passed . . . since those chapters were written. Already I can see ahead quite far enough to satisfy my wildest desires, and even the temptation of seeing *more* does not tempt me to go on." ". . . I am, for the first time in fifty years, surrounded by talk of war and weapons which I cannot escape and which have less meaning to me now than they had then, although your British aeroplanes are sailing up and down under my windows. . . . It is only twenty years since my friend Professor Langley, at my table, talked about all these things as dreams of the future, and we're already wishing to heaven that they had remained dreams of the past. I am in a new society and a new world which is more wild and madder by far than the old one and yet I seem to myself to be a part of it—and even, almost to take share in it."

Word had come from Stepleton that Martha had undergone an operation meant as a last attempt to save her life. The outcome remained in doubt. In his March 1918 letter to Mrs. Cameron, Dor said he and the nieces were waiting for news "with *extreme anxiety*." He said too that he was sending Mrs. Cameron mere "chatter to fill up the time."

The things he chattered about were things that would interest her. He reverted to Springy's letters. "I wish very much that I was twenty years younger, and could collect and edit his letters to you, as well as the others that you have, for he was a charming letter writer, and almost the only man who would stand reading by the side of John Hay." He informed her that her house on Lafayette Square had become "a part of the Cosmos Club." He said Washington was much changed. ". . . you would hardly feel happy here and would find very few old friends."

He described another dinner. "Cabot Lodge came in to dine last night with Bessy, in very good form, as I thought, and not so atrabilious as he has been of late. He actually avoided abusing anybody. . . . Bessy was as handsome as usual, and Mabel La Farge, who is paying us a visit, listened to the conversation with respect. . . ."[83]

At last he mentioned the other Adamses. "Of my own family I have little or nothing to tell you except that they seem to me as blue as I could wish."

Thayer sent a belated letter, congratulating Adams for turning eighty. Patently wanting to lure Adams into a dialogue, he tried to flatter him by making a safe prediction. He foretold that two of Adams's works would always be read. ". . . the 'Mont St. Michel' and 'The Education' will remain outside of the whims of fashion in books."

Adams replied, chiefly to say that time was accelerating by huge amounts. "I am a much older man today than I was a week ago, and the gulf between me and my fellowmen seems wider and deeper." He did not seem to desire an answer.[84]

Thayer tried again. He borrowed and read Ford's copy of Adams's

Letter to American Teachers of History. On March 14, he wrote to Adams asking how he could buy a copy. "This seems like a very thinly disguised bid for an author's copy, but it isn't. I am so eager to have the book that I am willing to undergo this suspicion."

As before, Adams could not remember that Thayer was the possessor of the First Traveling Copy.[85] When it came to copies of *The Letter to American Teachers of History*, he wished to help. Copies had earlier been piled on a book-shelf in his main-floor study. Others had been stored "on the shelves in the closet of my bed-room."[86] If not moved, the latter copies were within Aileen's domain. Adams asked her to make a search. He assured Thayer, ". . . I have begged Miss Tone to seek in all her forgotten closets for some copies of the volume you mention[;] and now that she has found some, I do remember that many years ago I was driven by the hounds of Hell to utter a dying protest against everything as it is, and especially the historical school at Harvard College. . . ."[87]

Thayer may have reached the stage of no longer wanting replies and greatly wanting hard-to-get books. A copy of the *Letter* was mailed. This was what Thayer had said he was willing to be suspected of seeking: an author's copy of one of Adams's privately-printed works.

The spirit in which Adams sent the copy was positive. He assured Thayer, "You are . . . that wonderful object in creation, my last reader, and I give you herewith my final blessing. . . ."[88]

Mrs. Cameron's attachment to Adams remained as strong as ever. Since last seeing him in 1914, she had written him 182 letters and a telegram that survive. His letter of March 1, 1918, reached her at Stepleton on March 21. She instantly replied. Speaking for Martha, Lindsay, and herself, she explained: "We are in a perfectly indefinite stage of this horrible illness. . . ." She offered a reason for hope that Martha could live. "In a prolonged illness like this, death usually comes from exhaustion, and she is *not* exhausted. Her strength and tenacity of purpose remind me of her grandfather [Simon Cameron] and her father [Donald]. . . . Certainly nine women out of ten would have been dead by this time."

On March 27, she wrote again. As always, her lines were direct and unhesitating. Hope for Martha had waned. "Her life is hanging by a thread." "She is wasted to a skeleton."

Except for its salutation—"Dear Dor"—and its close—"Yrs ever/ E. C."—not a word in Mrs. Cameron's second letter related to Adams. Yet all the words related to Adams, for they conveyed a woman's feelings to the one man she deeply wished might read them. Her feelings were dark and were best expressed by her last lines. "Well, nothing matters but that thread of a life upstairs. If we can save that, nothing matters. If we cannot—well, it matters still less."

Stepleton and Lafayette Square were five time-zones apart. If Mrs. Cameron wrote her last lines approximately at noon, her doing so was simultaneous with Adams's usual time for waking from sleep. He did not wake up. Death caught him sleeping and may have approached so stealthily that he could not sense its happening.[89]

Mrs. Cameron's letters did not come in time for him to read them, but his powers of mind were such that he could know what the letters were going to say. In that sense, they came in time, and the closing words of the last were seen and understood.

27

SINS OF THE HEIRS

About six weeks before Adams died, Aileen briefly went to New York to sing at a mansion on the Upper East Side. What led her to do so is unknown, but Mabel La Farge appears to have had a part in it.

Mabel, recovered from her breakdown, had settled in Connecticut with her husband and sons. She was exchanging letters with a New Yorker she had earlier met in Europe. Egisto Fabbri was one of three fatherless nephews of an Italian who fled to America, became associated as a banker with Morgan, and amassed a fortune large enough to support many Fabbris. Because his American mother was not a Catholic, Egisto was raised as an Episcopalian, but by temperament he seemed better adapted to Catholicism. His aptitudes led him to architecture and love of medieval music. He designed a mansion at 7 East 95 Street for his sister-in-law, Mrs. Ernesto Fabbri. In 1917, the Fabbris celebrated the building's completion by staging musical entertainments in the library. A year later, on February 15, 1918, to benefit war orphans in Italy, they offered a program of "old Florentine music" that included "Three medieval Latin songs" sung by "Miss Aileen Tone."[1]

One may imagine that Mabel introduced Aileen to Egisto during Aileen's pre-Christmas visit to New York in December 1917. If so, Aileen's songs at the benefit in mid-February 1918 could be counted, not as the starting point, but as an early milestone in an expensive journey— expensive because the journey would end in her losing possession of the Master Copy and, ultimately, in its loss altogether.[2]

On Wednesday, March 27, 1918, Aileen was ready at 8:00 A.M. to accompany Uncle Henry on his pre-breakfast walk. Fifteen minutes went by, and he did not appear. She went upstairs to investigate, called at his bedroom door, heard no answer, went in, and found him in bed on his left side, his hands together before him. His expression seemed to indicate he was conscious. He was warm but could not be waked.

She left the room and instructed Mary Baily, the maid, to alert Elsie and Elizabeth Hoyt. Elsie telephoned Dr. Hardin. With Elizabeth, Aileen re-entered the bedroom. Elizabeth saw at once that Uncle Henry was dead. She noticed that Aileen was calm.

Dr. Hardin came quickly. His examination revealed a large stain on the left side of the head and face—evidence of a massive stroke. He said death occurred suddenly and painlessly at about 7:00 A.M.[3]

Being an Adams and manager of the household, Elsie wanted to make the funeral arrangements and otherwise take charge of practicalities. Aileen claimed a single prerogative: to decide what should be done to clothe the body. Knowing what she wanted, she went to the top-floor storage closet, opened the trunk containing Aunt Clover's things, and took out a long, finely-woven white shawl. At her direction, the body was later swathed in it. She saw the result and thought her hero had the dignity of a Roman emperor. Soon the casket was closed, and her act of love and veneration was concealed.[4]

Uncle Henry had not entered a church for purposes of worship since leaving college. He had told Aileen that he wished not to be carried when dead into St. John's Episcopal Church, two buildings to the east on H Street.[5] The remark may have been his way of asking that he not be made the subject of a funeral of any sort.

Elsie avoided arranging a public funeral but invited the clergyman in charge at St. John's Church, the Reverend Cotton Smith, to read a private service at 1603 H Street on Saturday morning, March 30. Dr. Smith had read the private service for Elsie's father in 1915 and on his own initiative had read psalms in a Puritan version. On Saturday, on the strength of things said to him by Elsie, he did for Henry what previously he had done for Charles.[6]

The burial at Rock Creek Cemetery in the afternoon differed from most American burials in committing a body to a grave site that would bear no names or dates. A paradox attached itself: fame could grow rapidly even if names and dates were omitted. The site was already well-known as the burial place of Mrs. Henry Adams. It would shortly become famous as that of both wife and husband.

Uncle Henry's executor, his nephew Charles, had come from Boston. He outlined what was going to happen. The deceased's holdings would be equally divided between the seven Adams nephews and nieces still living. On that account, 1603 H Street would soon be sold.

To Elizabeth Hoyt, the impending sale seemed an outrage. She said privately in a letter to Mrs. Cameron, "America is the most barbarous place on earth!"[7]

* * *

In his role as president of the Massachusetts Historical Society, Senator Lodge was mindful of money. Houghton Mifflin Company had paid large royalties to the Society as copyright-owner of Charles Adams's *Autobiography*. Lodge believed that even larger royalties might accrue when Henry died and the Society arranged with Houghton Mifflin or another company to publish his *Education*.

Lodge learned quickly of Henry's death.[8] He knew books sold best in autumn and during the Christmas buying rush. To his mind, the occasion called for speed, as well as perfect secrecy. That same day, Wednesday, March 27, 1918, he rushed the order to Ford at the Society. His letter was marked "Personal." Several passages were important.

> Mr. Henry Adams died suddenly this morning. The maid heard him get up and go into his bath room to take his bath. Then there was a long delay and they heard nothing more. Finally they went in and found he had gone back to bed and he was lying there apparently asleep with his eyes closed, and dead. He had died in a moment and painlessly. . . .[9]

> . . . he is a terrible loss to me for he has been one of the most intimate friends I had for 40 years. . . .[10]

> . . . he left to the Society his privately printed "Education of Henry Adams", which is his autobiography, to be published by the Society as that of his brother Charles was published.[11]

> . . . it is a very remarkable book, and I think a very great autobiography and will command a large sale.

> I leave it to you to decide when we should undertake the work, which you and I must do together. I should think that the sooner we get it ready for the press the better.

Ford received Lodge's letter the next afternoon. He found the packet that Adams had sent to Lodge and that Lodge had forwarded to the Society. An envelope was bound to the packet. He broke the envelope loose, opening it as he did, and read the letter it contained. Written by Adams and dated March 1, 1916, the letter affirmed that Adams was giving *The Education* to the Society and that the copy supplied in the packet was "corrected and prepared for publication." Without stopping to type a duplicate for his records, Ford sent the letter to Lodge. He sent with it a covering note in which he said about the letter: ". . . I have read it. . . . When you have read it, it might be filed here [at the Society] as part of the story."[12]

Lodge received and reviewed Adams's letter. On March 30 in a new letter to Ford, he declared, ". . . the autobiography . . . is all ready for the press, even to the [editor's] preface[,] which I am to sign." "Your work and mine . . . is merely to see it through the press with the utmost possible care."

Ford was a longtime friend of the Adams who had died.[13] If caught in a situation that required his deciding which interests to honor more and which less, he would place his and Henry Adams's interests first, those of the Historical Society and the Adams family next, and Senator Lodge's last; but he would do so in such a way as to appear to Lodge to be chiefly a great senator's respectful assistant.

Presumably on Friday, March 29, Ford broke the seals of Adams's packet, opened the copy of *The Education* that it contained, read Adams's hand-written "Editor's Preface" and "Contents," and leafed through the text to see how fully it was corrected and prepared for publication. He saw that Adams had *not* corrected or prepared the book in anything like a way that would fit it for publication. He reacted in two opposite ways at once. It rather irritated him that Adams's annotations were shockingly few. It thrilled him that the book had not been edited. The role of editor had fallen to *him*!

Apparently by telephone, he arranged to meet with Greenslet on Monday, April 1, 1918, at his office. April Fool's Day was decisive. In the morning, Ford drove a bargain with Greenslet which, though not accepted by Houghton Mifflin, nor by the Society, would be accepted soon by both with a minor change easy to foresee. Ford led Greenslet to believe that the book was all but ready for printing.[14]

In the afternoon, Greenslet wrote to Ford, asking for a reduction of the royalties but otherwise indicating that Houghton Mifflin was ready to proceed. He said, "If we may have the complete copy of the text and introduction in the course of two or three weeks, the book will be just in time for effective publication in the early autumn."[15]

Ford did his own typing. He had taken the trouble to type copies of Adams's "Editor's Preface" and "Contents" and had corrected the former slightly in pencil.[16] Late on Monday, he wrote to Lodge and sent the typed copies. While taking up matters not essential to this narrative, he took up or avoided others that were highly important. Each needs separate attention.

Ford avoided telling Lodge that Adams in the "Editor's Preface" had described *The Education* as "unprepared and unfinished"— "avowedly incomplete." (The words were too true. Lodge was not to heed them.)

Ford asked Lodge to read, sign, and return the typed copy of the "Editor's Preface." He urged: "Make such modification as seems to you fit. It [the original] was signed in pencil with 'H. C. L.' "[17]

Ford described Adams's marks in the sealed copy and suggested that he might do a little editing of his own. "The corrections in the volume . . . are few, and . . . I am not sure that it would not be well to make even more changes than he [Adams] has noted. For instance, on page 67 he uses the word 'sinfony.' There is no such word. . . . On the same page he uses the word in italics 'haus-fraus.' The italics show that he intended the foreign word, which would be 'haus-frauen.' If he wished to anglicize it, it would be as he has written it[,] but not in italics."[18]

Ford meant to use the Society's copy of *The Education* as the publisher's copy. In it he would duplicate Adams's changes in the sealed copy and add changes of his own making. Greenslet would not learn the origins of particular changes. Once printing was completed, the submitted copy would be returned to Ford, and he would destroy it.[19]

The procedure was something Lodge would have to know about. Ford disclosed it near the end of his letter in a way that mixed candor with deception. He said: "I shall take the liberty of transferring Mr. Adams'[s] corrections to the Society's copy and substitute his copy for it [on the Society's shelves,] as being the more interesting from these personal annotations. There are not many—hardly a dozen in all—and none of them of importance. It is quite a tribute to the finish of his work that the changes are so few." Deception entered with Ford's stating that Adams wrote "hardly a dozen" annotations in the sealed copy. Adams had written roughly three times that many.

Ford knew Lodge well enough to be confident that, if led to think he was being told everything an upper manager needed to be told, the senator would not try to peek into the editorial tent to see what a lower manager might be doing. Moreover, Ford had resources. He had the sealed copy. He had the Society's copy, free of marks. He had his own copy, free of marks. Best of all, he had nerve. As if to prove it, he had marked Adams's sealed copy in three places in pencil. One of his marks changed an index entry from "Ford, Worthington" to "Ford, Worthington C." The change was a signature. Ford had claimed *The Education* as principally his to edit.[20]

The near-agreement reached on Monday by Ford and Greenslet freed Thayer to show Ford his much-annotated copy of *The Education*. Thayer can be assumed to have moved the copy from the Houghton Mifflin office to Ford's office at the Society by Tuesday afternoon, April 2, 1918. He told Ford that he did not own the copy, that Adams had lent it to him in January 1914, and that for more than four years he simply had not returned it. Thayer expressed his and Greenslet's opinion that it was Adams's principal copy—the text as Adams wanted it published.[21]

Ford had been studying Adams's annotations in the sealed copy. He could not help but notice that Thayer's copy was marked in two handwritings.[22] Greenslet would later send Ford a partly inaccurate account of this intrusion.[23] Ford meanwhile noticed that scores of marks, some in ink, others in pencil, were in Adams's handwriting in the form it had before his illness. They tended to be improvements, not mere corrections, and many improved the book where improvement could not easily have been seen to be possible.[24]

Thayer and Greenslet notwithstanding, the copy could not be published as Adams left it. To anyone prepared to notice, there were anomalies enough in the copy to make it an enigma.[25] Adams had written encumbering references in the margins—references to writings by other authors.[26] He had left obvious misspellings uncorrected.[27]

Ford did not hesitate. By joining hands covertly with Thayer, he could work into *The Education* a host of corrections and improvements not to be found in Adams's sealed copy and in no way known to Senator Lodge, yet certainly made by Adams.

Covertness was required because Thayer's copy was long borrowed and could be viewed almost as stolen. Covertness would minister to speed, and Greenslet would be wanting the fully-edited book by April 30 at the latest. Covertness, too, would not require Ford to begin the deceiving of President Lodge. Editor Ford had already begun it on his own initiative. He would merely add new sin to old.

If possible, Corresponding Secretary Thayer was less hesitant than Ford. On Wednesday, he began a note to Ford on another subject with an amused, very friendly salutation, "Dear Accomplice."[28]

Lodge approved Ford's changes in the "Editor's Preface" and modified it himself. Notably, he crossed out the initials Adams had added to the text and wrote his signature: "Henry Cabot Lodge."

By these easy means, Lodge's important work as editor-in-chief was fully completed—with one exception. The senator had published a book in 1913, *Early Memories*, which he liked to think was the first volume of what eventually might become his two-volume autobiography. Being an autobiographer, he felt qualified to tell Ford that Adams's *Education* was "one of the most remarkable autobiographies which have been given to the world."[29] The notion that Adams was an autobiographer became a ruling idea for the senator, to the exclusion of other ideas. When possible, he avoided the title Adams had given his book. Indeed he resisted it. In letters to Ford, he referred to the work as "the autobiography," "the Autobiography," "this Autobiography," "his Autobiography," and "the Autobiography of Henry Adams."[30]

Ford noticed Lodge's insistence but did not quickly respond to it. On April 8, he advised Lodge that the publisher's copy would be ready in "three or four weeks." He said added changes would be made. "I am more than half way through in reading the 'Education'. . . . There is some misspelling of names which I shall correct . . . and there are some uses of words which strike me as peculiar. He always uses the word 'diplomate'. . . . The proper word is 'diplomat'. . . ."[31]

On April 12, Ford and Houghton Mifflin Company settled the terms of the future contract. Ford's work was not simple. He was evaluating annotations by Adams in two copies and developing changes himself. He was marking his own copy. He obtained details concerning errors that Frederic Bancroft had discovered. As a last step, he was marking the Society's copy, the one he had decided to sacrifice.[32]

Already significant damage had been done. Ford had corrupted the sealed copy with unidentified annotations of his own. Someone else had corrupted Thayer's copy with unidentified marks. And Lodge was being treated as if he were an editor seated too high above mere functionaries to be kept abreast of their activities, which, thanks to the seeming miracle of Thayer's copy, included a grand-scale deception.

On April 29, Ford was ready to sign the contract and deliver the Society's copy, completely marked, to Houghton Mifflin. He wrote to Lodge, assuring him that he would not have to see the submitted text. It would suffice if the senator were furnished "one set of the galley proofs." Should he wish to make changes, Lodge could make them on the proofs with minimum waste of time and energy.[33]

A troublesome reality still impended: Lodge's resistance to the title *The Education of Henry Adams*. One trouble was paired with another. As privately printed, the book had not named its author on the title page. On May 2, 1918, Ford ventured a suggestion. He voiced it in humble accents and in question form, but he knew in advance that Lodge would approve it, for he was only offering what the senator all along had been dictatorially requiring. Ford explained: ". . . to say merely 'The Education of Henry Adams' and stop there, gives no indication of the authorship, but if the two words 'an autobiography' be added, that will be serviceable to those who see the book and to catalogers. . . . Will there be any objection to that form?"

No objection was made. Immeasurable damage followed. A new kind of book, an *education*, went to the publisher as an established kind of book. Instead of bearing the arresting, teasing title that Adams had given it, the book was burdened with a combination of its title and a subtitle that negated the title's arrestingness and smoothed away its teasingness. The title page was made to say:

The Education of Henry Adams
An Autobiography

Adams's words would speak to the public. Lodge's words would interrupt before the public could properly listen.[34]

* * *

Lodge had told no one but Ford that *The Education* was being rushed to market. Ellery Sedgwick, the editor of the *Atlantic Monthly*, got wind of what was happening. He had seen a copy of the book. He asked Greenslet for permission to publish parts of it as articles. Greenslet alerted Ford. Ford and Lodge approved the arrangement, but Lodge wavered and asked Ford to consult nephew-executor Charles and Brooks Adams. The former consented. Brooks protested.

Far from thinking that Henry's book was an autobiography, Brooks saw it as "a fragment of several biographies" and as "disjointed comments on John Hay and King." He believed that Henry was important, indeed extremely important, but only in one way: as a man with a message. He felt he knew what the message was, and he hoped discerning readers might be able to find it in *The Education*. He wrote admonishingly to Ford: ". . . [Henry's] message was intellectual Chaos. That idea, even if it can be gathered from the book as a whole, can't be if the book is split into parts."[35]

A single blast of protest by Brooks sufficed to make Lodge quash the projected articles in the *Atlantic*. All the same, new damage was done. Brooks was led to ponder what he thought were Henry's failings and the failings of Henry's books.

For his part, Lodge feared that control of *The Education* might be seized by the governing body of the Massachusetts Historical Society, its Council. He instructed Ford to tell the Council that Henry gave the *Education* not to the Society but to him, President Lodge. Also he said he intended to consult another Adams. He explained. "The person who was most with Henry in these latter years was Miss Elsie Adams." ". . . her opinion would have a great deal of weight with me . . . as she talked with her Uncle about his books, including this one."[36]

Predictably in a new letter, Lodge told Ford he had learned from Elsie that her Uncle Henry would not have wanted "magazine publication."[37] While persuading himself that he and Elsie knew her deceased uncle's wishes about *The Education*, the senator permitted himself to think Miss Tone did not. Retroactively, he dismissed the latter as someone not-informed—indeed as never-existent.[38]

Although it was signed by Lodge, Greenslet disliked the "Editor's Preface." He wrote to Ford, ". . . its implication that 'The Education of Henry Adams' . . . will only be 'consulted by students' hardly does justice to one of the most readable and fascinating books in the world." He promised that employees in his office would develop jacket copy of a kind that would sell the book to the general reader.[39]

In anticipation of the start of printing, Lodge directed Ford to send him proofs marked to show "the slight changes" Adams had made in the sealed copy.[40] Ford complied and also sent Lodge a 28-item list of queries and new changes.[41] He did not reveal that the new changes were drawn from a copy of *The Education* brought in by Thayer.

Ford and Thayer lived in Cambridge. On May 3 on his way to work, Ford stopped at Thayer's house "to make a demand." Thayer was not at home, so Ford communicated his demand by letter. "My suggestion is that we [the Society] give to you our copy of the 'Education of Henry Adams,' which contains some manuscript notes, in exchange for the copy you 'hold.' " Ford said more. He conceded that the copy Thayer held was "undoubtedly the one which he [Adams] had in mind for a new edition." "It was his copy[,] and it came into your keeping legitimately. . . ." But he pointedly asked, ". . . did it come into your possession except by a fluke?"[42]

Thayer agreed to trade copies.[43] By this means, he became outright owner of a copy slightly annotated by Adams, and the Society took possession of the most-annotated copy known to Ford. Yet Ford won the Society a prize at very high costs. The false idea that the "Thayer copy" was Adams's principal copy had been wrongly conceded by Ford to be a true idea. By declaring the false to be true, Ford shut off any last possibility that he might look for other copies Adams might have annotated. The important reality that Adams had annotated *five* copies all extant, including two within easy reach—the actual Master Copy, owned secretly by Aileen Tone in New York, and the Second Traveling Copy, owned neglectfully by Brooks in Quincy—was rendered unthinkable. Any idea that Henry himself had fully corrected and thoroughly improved his greatest book was thrust into remote futurity as an idea that no one, Miss Tone excepted, could even begin to have.

Lodge read the galley proofs and made changes but became absorbed in what he thought were serious shortcomings in the book.[44] Adams had not provided detailed accounts of two diplomatic achievements: the negotiation of the Hay-Pauncefote Treaties with England preparatory to the cutting of the Panama Canal and the negotiation that settled the Alaska-Canada boundary. Relevant actions by Senator Lodge were left unmentioned. Wanting to right this imagined wrong, Lodge wrote Ford informative letters about himself for future study by historians.[45]

At the request of nephew-executor Charles, Ford planned a trip to 1603 H Street to survey the books in Henry Adams's library and identify those that might better be added to the Adams family's library at Quincy. In addition, voluntarily, Ford began a many-sided, vigorous effort to collect Henry's letters and other literary remains, with the intention of publishing such materials soon.

Brooks Adams learned of Ford's impending trip to Washington and asked Ford to obtain for him the remaining copies of Henry's *Letter to American Teachers of History*. Brooks was afire with an idea. To make possible recognition of Henry's "theory"—"the upshot of his life"—he wanted the Society to publish three of Henry's works in a uniform edition. Brooks told Ford that the *Letter* was Henry's "most remarkable book." He assigned it a central position. "The *Chartres* represents the inception of his theory; the *Letter to Teachers* its culmination; and the *Education* represents its downfall."[46]

Ford made his trip in late June. He flagged the books he thought should be moved to Quincy. He urged nephew-executor Charles to ship Uncle Henry's letters received—a very large collection—to the Adams Room at the Society. After returning to Boston, he made efforts to find out whether Brooks's proposal to issue three volumes of Henry's *Works* might be feasible. He learned that it was not.

Miss Tone had given Brooks the manuscript of an unpublished poem by Henry titled "Prayer to the Virgin of Chartres." On August 26, Brooks hoped to give Ford the manuscript for preservation by the Society, but he and Ford missed connections. Next day by letter, Brooks advised Ford about Henry's poem: ". . . I do not think it is one of his happier efforts. I should not suggest publishing it anywhere."[47] In Brooks's mind, Henry's unpublished writings fell into widely separate categories. Some were not to be published. Others *had* to be.

Being busier than ever as leader of the Republicans in Congress, Lodge could not chair the Society's meetings. They were chaired by Winslow Warren, the first vice-president. Warren had looked into Adams's *Education* and judged it "a monumental piece of conceit, entertaining, but of slight historical value" and unsuited to publication by the Society. The vice-president had the support of a member of the Society, Charles Pelham Greenough, who wanted the book "suppressed" because "worse than the C. F. A. volume."[48]

As things developed, Warren fell ill and could not chair the May meeting. Summer meetings were never held. When the next meeting convened, Henry Adams's volume would already be published. Speed could seem to have been the right option, and Lodge could seem vindicated.

To advertise its new books, Houghton Mifflin Company distributed a periodical: *The Piper/ A Monthly Chat with Booksellers & Book Buyers*. The issue for late-summer 1918 began with an "ANNOUNCEMENT *EXTRAORDINARY*" that described Henry Adams as "a profound and original thinker." His originality had been shown, perhaps to excess, in a title. "Fifteen years ago, he began the composition of the Autobiography which he has quaintly entitled 'The Education of Henry Adams.' " Booksellers and book buyers were urged to set the title aside and accord the book high rank among the world's best autobiographies.[49]

The Education went onto the market on September 19, 1918, or soon after. Ford had changed the text in two places on the basis of marks in the sealed copy (Adams's Substitute Copy) and in 179 places on the basis of marks in the copy brought by Thayer (Adams's First Traveling Copy).[50] To that point, Ford's editing worked to Adams's advantage. But Ford had made 113 additional changes on his and Lodge's initiatives.[51] Of these, as many as 39 were necessary.[52] The remaining 74 could be seen as damaging. A few concealed Adams's sometimes idiosyncratic spellings.[53] Others ran counter to his conversational style. Many resulted from misreadings of the passages they affected and caused the passages to make poorer sense.[54]

The book became the season's best-seller. It evidently gratified popular tastes. The *New York Evening Post* described it as "one of the most original, amusing and piquant books ever written."[55]

A person not gratified was Brooks. To his mind, Henry's *Education* was a literary mistake. He believed Henry joked in it about "subjects [which] can't be joked about or made funny." He believed that a reputation for having joked was "fatal to a public man" and to any thinker or man with a message, and he tended to state his opinion in strong terms. He would shortly explain to a confidant: "The 'Education' is seldom or never serious and . . . can't be taken seriousiy, for the author [Henry] don't [*sic*] want . . . to be taken seriously. He has assumed a pose. . . ." "Mark Twain could never be taken seriously, even if he died for it. . . ."[56]

Brooks found among his papers a 32-page typescript headed "THE RULE OF PHASE/ APPLIED TO HISTORY." He was very excited to have found it and apparently did not stop to read it.[57] He preferred to think the typescript was prepared by a Washington typist at Henry's request in 1912. (In fact, it was prepared by his own typist in Boston in February 1909.) He preferred to think it was a copy of Henry's last paper, completed in the winter of 1911–1912. (There was no such paper. What Brooks found was his own typed copy of the jig-saw puzzle Henry had dated January 1, 1909, had replaced with a better version, but wholly discarded when he hit upon the ideas he made use of when writing his *Letter to American Teachers of History*, printed in 1910.)

Brooks took the typescript to the Society and told Ford that he wanted the Society to publish a book in three parts. The first part would be an introduction to Henry by himself. The middle part would be Hen-

ry's *Letter to American Teachers of History.* The last would be the work
Brooks carried to the Society. Ford had not previously heard of it.
Brooks assured him that it was "the final word of Henry Adams' theory
of history."[58]

By letter, Ford outlined Brooks's project to Lodge. The senator replied that he had lunched at Thayer's house in Cambridge on November 11 and that talk during lunch had turned to Henry's *Letter to
American Teachers of History.* Theodore Richards of Harvard—a professor
of chemistry and a friend of Thayer's—had said the *Letter* should not be
published because in it Henry "had a great deal to say about thermodynamics and it was evident that he was inaccurate and did not understand
that subject." Lodge added a second opinion. "Mr. Thayer said that he
had looked into that question somewhat and that he was of that opinion
also[,] that what was said about thermodynamics could not be
trusted. . . ." Two opinions sufficed. Lodge ruled that it would "not be
judicious" for the Society to "reprint" Henry's *Letter.*[59]

Ford advised Brooks that a comment by Professor Richards about
Henry's knowledge of physics made publication by the Society impossible. Ford could have told Brooks to offer his project to Greenslet, who
had seen Henry's *Letter* and wanted to publish it; but Ford knew Brooks
well and possibly was aware of Brooks's strongest dislikes. Brooks had
had dealings with Greenslet and thought him a "little pig"—"the mean-
est and most narrow minded man . . . I have ever met."[60]

Ford wished to collect at the Society copies of all the important series of Henry Adams's letters. When ending a letter to Lodge, he asked:
"Would you have any objection to letting us [i.e. the Society] have copies of Mr. Adams'[s] letters to yourself? The copying could be done here
by photostat and would occupy only a few days, even if the number of
letters was large. Also would you have any objection to asking Mrs. Whitney if Henry Adams'[s] letters to John Hay could be sent on for
copying?"[61]

Lodge helped in some ways, but in another way his response became
a reminder that attempts to retrieve letters could lead with terrible effi-
ciency to the destruction of letters. Lodge reported finding "a large
packet of letters" that Adams had written to Mrs. Lodge. He said her
letters from Adams were "equal in number . . . to my own." A mostly
negative verdict followed. ". . . very few are suitable for publication. They
are very personal and very intimate and have a great deal to say about
other people—quite unlike most of his letters, which was all right when
he was writing to her but which would not do to publish at all because a
great deal of it was written in a jesting way, half in earnest and half in
jest, and they would be sadly misunderstood. Most . . . are very clever. If

there are any that would do [for publication], I will send them. . . . There is one that I shall most certainly send; a most interesting letter from Samoa in which he tells about seeing Stevenson."[62]

Brooks remembered that in 1910 he had sent to George Brett, head of the Macmillan Company in New York, a copy of Henry's *Letter to American Teachers of History*; that Brett had wanted to publish the book; that Brett asked Henry for permission; but Henry perversely balked. Within two weeks, Brooks found Brett's old offer to publish Henry's *Letter*.[63] On December 10, 1918, he wrote to Brett, harked back to the offer, and announced: ". . . I have control now and I want to know if you will take it [the *Letter*]. But I have something far more interesting to consult you about." "I have the last philosophic paper he [Henry] ever wrote. He sent it to me for my opinion only a few months before his stroke, which ended his active life. In my judgment[,] it is the ablest and most remarkable thing he ever wrote, and it is very short."

Brooks urged Brett to publish a book in three parts. First would be Henry's "biography"—"a notice . . . in which I should try to trace the growth of his mind." Second would be Henry's *Letter*. Last would be Henry's "final paper . . . called 'Phase.' " Brooks touted it as "the most brilliant of all."

Brooks viewed Brett as an old friend. He admitted to the editor that his own writings were viewed in Boston-Cambridge as "dangerous." He said that Henry's papers were viewed there as "worse." He frankly declared that he felt a grudge. ". . . I should like . . . to explain to Harvard College, among other folks, just what I think of them."[64] But he did not send Brett the "final paper . . . called 'Phase.' " For the moment, he let it stay in Ford's hands at the Society.

Brett accepted Brooks's proposal by return mail. Two days later, he sent Brooks a publishing contract. Brooks signed and returned the contract, and instructed Ford to speed the "final paper" to New York.

In a new letter to Brett, Brooks acknowledged that the submitted manuscript was not Henry's original but only a typed copy. ". . . be careful of it, for it is a copy sent me by my brother in 1912, for my criticism, and I have no other." Brooks mentioned too that Henry had "never printed" the paper and that many notables at Harvard "did not think it safe." "Richards, Walcott, Charles Eliot and the like, are, I understand, scandalized by it."[65]

When he said that Henry had sent him "The Rule of Phase applied to History" in 1912 and that Harvard magnates had been scandalized by the paper, Brooks believed both assertions. If someone had told him the truth, that Henry had sent the paper in 1909, that he quickly had written a second version, and that no one at Harvard had seen either version, Brooks would not have been affected. The basis of his newer actions was not mere honesty. He had passed beyond consideration of external facts and was responding exclusively to his own desires.

In New York, with astonishment that can only be imagined, Brett read the typescript and saw that Brooks had misrepresented what he had to offer. The work Brooks sent was not a paper but only the undeveloped sketch of a possible paper. Moreover, it was dated at the end, "Washington, January 1, 1909."[66]

If he wished, Brett could think himself confronted with a problem of publishing ethics. Also he could wonder how best to solve it.

Mabel La Farge knew Aileen had given Uncle Brooks the manuscript of Uncle Henry's "Prayer to the Virgin of Chartres." When an inquiry reached Mabel from Ford about any letters from Uncle Henry that might be in her possession, Mabel sent a guarded reply. "I shall be glad to show you all that might be of interest to publish. But I would like to bring them up to Boston . . . and to have the opportunity of going over a few questions with you in connection with them. . . ."[67]

Mabel shortly met with Ford. She told him she wished to publish a small book of Uncle Henry's letters and poems, with an introduction by herself. Ford agreed to act as her adviser. He gave her a copy of Henry's "Prayer to the Virgin of Chartres"; that is, a typed copy. He did not give her photographs or photostats of the manuscript.[68]

While beginning work on her book, Mabel received a report from Egisto Fabbri that he had "just finished the 'Education,' of which I should like . . . to say [to you] many things. Perhaps we may talk of some of these things by letter?"[69]

In reply, Mabel urged Egisto's coming to Connecticut. He remarked in a new letter that "what gives value and interest to the book [*The Education*] is that through the mist of questioning, uncertainties and searchings there shines the steady light of a high intelligence. Now I will be most eager to hear what you will say—"[70]

Mabel wrote her proposed introduction to Henry Adams under the title "A Niece's Memories." In advance of its appearing in her book, she published it in the *Yale Review*. Ford negotiated a contract for her with Houghton Mifflin Company; she signed it; also she sent Ford the manuscript of her book. It began with her "Memories," continued with Adams's "Prayer to the Virgin," and ended with some of Adams's letters to herself and his poem "Buddha and Brahma."

Ford disliked the book. He had already written to Lodge: "There seems to be almost a studied effort to make out that Henry Adams was about to become a Catholic. You may have seen the article by Mrs. La

Farge, who is herself a Catholic and writes only from that point of view."[71] The book seemed sure to do more harm than the article.

To Ford, the poem "Buddha and Brahma" represented Adams at his literary worst. He urged Mabel to omit the poem, and she did so.[72] He apparently urged in addition that Adams's "Prayer to the Virgin of Chartres" be moved to the end of her book. The change would reduce the book's tendency to make Adams seem an all-but-converted Catholic. Perhaps with some reluctance, Mabel made the change.[73]

The effort did not end well for Ford. He confided to Lodge: "I only learned by accident that she [Mrs. La Farge] had gone direct to the publisher with her 'second version' and do not know how much she has altered the first, which embodied about all that it should not embody—or imply." Ford went on to remark: "It is unfortunate to be maltreated by an enemy, more so by a friend, and most so by a member of the family."[74]

Coming from the pen of another person, the remark might seem unimportant. Because written by Ford, it carried a powerful message. As well as anyone then alive, he knew how much hurt one member of a family could wreak on another. He had been the eldest of three Ford sons until the middle son, Malcolm, murdered the remarkable youngest, Paul, at the cost of also immediately killing himself.[75]

Plain evidence that Brooks Adams had deceived him did not diminish the willingness of George Brett to fulfill his contract and publish a book of writings by Henry Adams. Anything by or about Henry Adams was sure to bring the Macmillan Company a profit. The gifted brother's *Education* was selling as fast as a sensational novel.

Brett returned the typescript, "THE RULE OF PHASE APPLIED TO HISTORY," to Brooks. He referred to the paper as "dry bones" of something Henry could have turned into "an intensely interesting little book." He remarked that "changes" were "necessary" and added caustically, ". . . I am somewhat doubtful as to the advisability of printing the date January 1/1909 in connection with this paper. . . ."[76]

The rebuke was wasted. Brooks no sooner received the typescript than he gave it to Ford and asked him to take charge of every aspect of the future book except the "life" of Henry—the "biography"—that he had himself contracted to prepare.

Ford learned from Brooks that Henry had improved his *Letter to American Teachers of History* and that his annotated copy was in his Washington library.[77] As it happened, nephew Charles and Brooks had given the library—all but a hundred volumes—to the Society. It had arrived but was still in cases, waiting to be unpacked. The annotated copy was quickly found. Brooks alerted Brett that it would be sent to New York by December 27 or 28, 1918, "ready for the printer."[78]

Someone, probably Ford, wanted to expand the emerging book to include the letter Henry wrote from Mexico in 1894, to serve as a presidential address to the American Historical Association. The letter had been published in the Association's *Annual Report* for 1894 under a title not of Henry's choosing. Brooks agreed to insert it in the book under its already-imposed title, "The Tendency of History."

When at last Ford wrote to Mrs. Cameron about the many letters she and Henry had exchanged, Henry had been dead for nearly ten months. Martha had died a month later, on April 28, 1918.[79]

The losses had hurt Mrs. Cameron so badly that she had pled with her nephew Henry Sherman to bring poison from London with which she could kill herself. He arrived without the poison.[80] Elizabeth Hoyt hurried from Washington to help. By degrees, Mrs. Cameron rallied.

Ford treated Mrs. Cameron as having special rights. He thought her correspondence with Henry deserved separate publication. He was bold enough to tell her: ". . . your long relations [with him] were closer than those enjoyed by any other person and called from him his best. I can easily believe that a correspondence arising from such relations would stand by itself and might lose its effectiveness by being diluted with other letters."[81]

She responded by giving the Society all her letters from Henry, plus other letters she thought relevant and helpful.[82] Ford steered her offerings into the Henry Adams Papers, as opposed to the Society's collections.[83] Later she gave to the Society, "in the charge of Mr. Worthington C. Ford," a great number of her letters to Henry that he had kept for her at 1603 H Street.[84] Partly to shield them against selective destruction, Ford made sure they were in chronological order and numbered their pages. There were 6,591 pages.

The truth emerged that Brooks could not write Henry's biography. Neither could anyone else. News was appearing on all sides that Henry had written things and done things till then unknown. Superficially credible outlines of his life, including the partial outline presented by Henry himself to readers of *The Education*, had already become incredible. New outlines that might accommodate the added data were not easy to construct. Information was destroying ideas.[85]

Brooks had the special handicap of not knowing Henry. The younger brother had so irritated the elder that Henry had made himself as inaccessible to Brooks as possible. Brooks in consequence had formed ideas that sounded true because he believed them but were misleading or flatly false. Examples abounded. "He [Henry] had no conception of how to publish books."[86] ". . . Henry was never, I fear, quite frank with himself or with others. . . ."[87]

To take the place of the "life" he could not write, Brooks tossed together a lengthy paper called "The Heritage of Henry Adams." To his credit, he believed that Henry was linked in important ways to John Quincy Adams and ultimately to George Washington. He tried to say so, but his paper tended to be wandering and scatter-brained.

Ford meanwhile had advanced to the typescript, "THE RULE OF PHASE APPLIED TO HISTORY." Henry's letters received and other files had arrived at the Society. Often a digger for evidence, Ford discovered in the files another typed copy of the paper, this one with comments by Henry A. Bumstead, a professor of physics at Yale. After delays, Ford contrived to send these materials to Bumstead, who sent them back with the advice that Henry's paper would have to be changed in one place, lest it be ridiculed on scientific grounds.

Ford compared the two typed copies as to wording and discovered that Henry had written his paper in two versions! He felt called upon to decide which version was the later. Had he been engaged in work entirely his own, he might have made thorough efforts to study the evidence; but speed was called for; his status was that of a subordinate; and Brooks was in charge. On this basis, Ford sent Brooks the second typed copy and declared that Brooks's typescript was Henry's later version. (It in fact was an approximation of the earlier version.) Ford noted too that it would be "safe" for Brooks to publish his typescript, "perhaps adding as a note Prof. Bumstead's comment."[88]

Brooks vetoed the addition of a note. Ford typed a fresh copy of "THE RULE OF PHASE APPLIED TO HISTORY."[89] While preparing it, he obtained from Bumstead assurance that a formula Henry had presented in his paper was "undoubtedly an error." Bumstead provided a different formula and new wording that could be substituted for Henry's formula and wording. Brooks himself made the substitution in the fresh manuscript Ford had typed. By this means, the way was cleared to publish as Henry's a silently doctored paper significantly different from the paper Henry had written.[90]

All along, Brett had urged Brooks to decide the title of his book. Brooks had suggested *Philosophy of Education* and *A Theory of Human Intellectual Energy*. Brett himself suggested *The Biology of History*. Something better seemed needed. Brooks went so far as to say, "The title is now the main question."[91]

Brett wanted the completed manuscript by April 15, 1919. Brooks asked that publication be delayed till the fall. The editor consented but set June 30 as the deadline for all contents. His deadline was met; and, on July 10, Brooks suggested as a title *The Philosophy of Democracy*. In a letter that is missing, he additionally suggested *The Degradation of the Democratic Dogma*. Brett delegated the book to an assistant named Henderson, who suggested *The Meaning of Democracy*. Brooks grew furious. Brett rushed to assure him that he could have any title he wanted.

The struggle elicited from Brooks a letter about what he called "this book of mine." It came into the open that the only theory that interested Brooks was his own, which was that the world had "reached the end"—that the "ultimate" had already come—that "the symptoms are of breaking"—that "we shall hit more or less of a tempest." Brooks wanted a title that would state *his* theory and he was sure he was coming close. He told Brett, "The only title I can think of that states the issue . . . is 'The Democratic Dogma and its Degradation', or some such title as that, which is clear and can't be put aside."[92]

Brett ordered his manufacturing department to issue the book with the following words on the title page:

THE
DEGRADATION OF THE
DEMOCRATIC DOGMA

by
Henry Adams

with an introduction by
Brooks Adams

It made no difference that Henry had not believed that democracy or its dogma had been degraded. It did not matter that his portion of the book was unrelated to democracy—that it concerned the problem set for historians by the newer theories of European and American scientists. All that mattered was that Brooks was victorious. He forced the adoption of a freakish title that said what he wished to say. For him, the title *was* the book. Its other contents, even the phrase "by Henry Adams," were accessory and incidental.

In April 1919, Elsie found a trove of letters that her father had assembled but thought lost. All were written between 1861 and 1865. They had passed between Charles and Minister Adams and between Charles and Henry. They began when the minister and Henry were en route to the U. S. legation in London and Charles was joining the Union army.

Elsie's discovery permitted Ford to prepare for Houghton Mifflin Company at high speed a two-volume collection of letters that became a new attention-catcher.[93] Titled *A Cycle of Adams Letters/ 1861–1865*, the volumes created impressions that, of the three Adamses whose letters appeared, Charles was the most admirable and Henry the least.[94]

Mabel La Farge's book was titled *Letters to a Niece and Prayer to the Virgin of Chartres*. Egisto Fabbri had known about the book from its inception. Mabel sent him a copy and assured him that the book was selling well. Egisto replied on January 14, 1921, ". . . when one looks back to the very beginning, how beautifully the idea has grown to its final and complete form!"[95]

In the same letter, Egisto made passing comments about Aileen. "I have not heard again from Miss Tone, but I feel convinced that if she sings Arab music it will be like one of the sources for the Gregorian. . . . We shall see."

The Fabbris owned a villa near Florence called Bagazzano. It was thought to have been a Medici hunting lodge. Not modernized, it could be occupied enjoyably only in the spring and fall. Egisto was using it as his home and a place to keep his library, but he tended to go to New York in winter and to Bar Harbor in Maine in summer.

Aileen lived in New York in winter, eleven blocks from the Fabbri mansion. She usually went in summer to Maine. As managed by executor Charles, the small fortune Uncle Henry had given her was yielding an income that promised to support her comfortably as long as she lived. She could afford to travel in Europe.

Egisto was at Bagazzano in October 1922, much busied as an architect. He had designed a house in nearby Serravalle for a friend, Ina de Vasconcellas, a Portuguese noblewoman. A much larger project followed. The church at Serravalle had been wrecked by an earthquake. The parishioners had asked him to design a new one, and he had already submitted drawings. The project especially thrilled him because many of the parishioners wanted "to take part in the building and contribute . . . the work of their hands."[96]

A visitor from America meanwhile had come and gone. Writing to Mabel, Egisto said, "Aileen spent a week here [at] the beginning of this month, and delighted in the beauty of everything, and sang to us. . . ."[97] During her visit, Aileen may have met Ina de Vasconcellas. She certainly learned about the projected church at Serravalle and the enthusiasm of the parishioners, which could seem a small-scale return to the church-building enthusiasm of the French in the middle ages.

Egisto stayed in Europe continuously while church-building went forward. During the summer of 1923, Aileen visited Egisto's sister Edith in Maine. Egisto soon reported to Mabel, "Aileen wrote me from Bar Harbor and I was very glad to hear that she had been able to go there and be with Edith even [for?] a short time. . . ."[98]

After last delays, *The Degradation of the Democratic Dogma* had been published in November 1919.[99] The Macmillan Company became aware that the elements of the book contributed by Brooks Adams were heartily disliked. A critic in the *New York Times*, for example, ridiculed the "preposterous introduction" and the "misfit title."[100] Thus an editors' question came to the fore. Could the book be reissued in such a way that Henry Adams was kept in and Brooks Adams shut out?

Brooks died in February 1927, and control devolved on the Macmillan Company. Free to act, its editors raked out Brooks's title, the many introductory pages by Brooks, the text of Henry's letter to the American Historical Association, and the title and date of his *Letter to American Teachers of History*. In 1928, the company published a 175-page book assembled from what was left. The book was titled

The Tendency
of
History

by
Henry Adams

It was easy to sell. Apart from Macmillan's edition, the Book League of America bought and distributed a special edition.

This double success could appear to benefit Henry Adams. Instead it intensified the effects of Brooks Adams's interference. Buyers of Macmillan's book found within its covers a single text three chapters long. There was no preface or introduction. The chapters were headed "The Problem," "The Solutions," and "The Rule of Phase Applied to History." The text was dated at the end, "Washington, January 1, 1909." No other date appeared.[101] So marketed, the book was a literary monstrosity not merely difficult to read but entirely opaque.[102]

Yet the public could very easily assign the monstrosity a meaning. The needed clue was the title imposed by the editors on their book: *The Tendency of History*. The title could be read two ways. It could be read as equivalent to *The Tendency of Events*. It could be read with attention to the presidential letter Adams wrote in 1894 to the American Historical Association, in which case it would be equivalent to *A Tendency to Be Feared in the Opinions Held in the Future by the World's Historians*. Needless to say, readers of the new book would understand its title the first way and never imagine the second. The same readers had already been told what tendency Henry saw in events. Because Macmillan had earlier issued *The Degradation of the Democratic Dogma*, Henry was America's leading "degradationist." He had become the famous man for whom the only tendency of events was down. Sale of Macmillan's *The Tendency of History* only strengthened and confirmed the misimpression. Brooks's original victory was made as destructive as possible. For a large segment of the public, Henry was fixedly recreated in a dismal image. He became a second Brooks.

Ford had wanted to publish a volume of Henry's letters as early as 1921. Brooks opposed such ideas. After Brooks died, control of the accumulated letters was delegated to a nephew, Henry Adams II—one of Charles's twins.

Ford left the Society. Nephew Henry found that Ford had put the letters between Henry Adams and Elizabeth Cameron in a location of their own in the Society's Adams Room. In 1929, he wrote to Ford: "In regard to the Henry Adams letters and Mrs. Cameron's letters which you placed in the room, I think these should be sorted out and a great many of them destroyed. Meanwhile . . . as my sister Elsie is taking a great deal of interest in the Manuscripts, I should think it would be a good thing if she ran over these."[103]

Ford diplomatically replied that Mrs. Cameron was alive and might want to see some of the letters. He kindly added, "I am very glad that your sister is taking an interest in the matter, for her judgment will be excellent—better, in fact, than the judgment of any man."[104]

Elsie desisted for a long interval but in 1937 resumed her labor. An important factor was attitude, and her attitude about the letters was as negative as possible. Her brother Henry disclosed to Ford: "I find that if Elsie does not like a few phrases in a letter, she then wants to discard the entire letter and also the entire series. She is very sweeping in her judgment."[105]

Elsie's desires proved sufficiently negative to be comprehensively self-defeating. Year after year, the Adams-Cameron letters escaped destruction. They continued to escape after 1941, when Ford died, and again after 1944, when Mrs. Cameron died. Their defender, in the end, was Henry Adams II. He became a firm admirer of his Uncle Henry and an active guardian of evidence, even in stressful situations.[106]

One important matter remained: Aileen's ownership of Adams's Master Copy. In 1925, she and Egisto secretly became engaged.[107] They hoped to marry at a not-distant time, but the prospect became disturbing to Egisto. In January 1926, he wrote to his sister Edith, ". . . I would give anything in the wide world if I could arrange my life without getting married. . . ." His letter continued, ". . . my imaginings of that tie fill me at times with a secret dismay. . . ."[108]

A year passed. The Serravalle church was nearly completed, and Egisto felt himself at the brink of conversion. He confided to Mabel, ". . . I am beginning to feel I cannot but be of the Church to whose affirmation I am giving all the energies of my life." At last, in May or June 1927, he was "received into the Holy Church."[109]

His and Aileen's engagement was still to be acted upon. She returned to Bagazzano, apparently in the fall. She brought with her the more remarkable of her privately-printed copies of *The Education*. She and Egisto agreed to own it jointly as a foretaste of their marriage. They agreed that it should stay for the present in his library.

Evidently in the spring of 1928, she returned to Europe to marry him. She hurried to Italy on a Paris-to-Rome express. The schedule kept the train at Florence for an hour. She was intercepted at the train by one of Egisto's sisters, possibly Ernestine. The sister was acting as family representative. She and Aileen talked in a compartment of the train. The sister told Aileen she was not rich enough to marry a Fabbri: she lacked the necessary *"dot."* It was implicit in the interception that the sister was acting and speaking with Egisto's full consent.

What was Aileen to do? She stayed on the train and went to Rome. She possibly did not request and at all events did not receive the book she had left with the other half-owner, her ex-fiancé.[110]

In New York more than twenty-three years later, an older Aileen Tone permitted two young married Americans to meet her at her apartment at 151 East 83 Street. From the moment they arrived, she warmly befriended them. By chance, they were offered and took an apartment across the street. She saw them frequently thereafter, treated them as intimates, helped them in innumerable ways, and often spoke to them as her "children." Yet ten years passed before she told them she had once owned an extraordinary copy of *The Education of Henry Adams.* She might not have spoken about the copy even then, were it not that she and the children were together in ideal surroundings, early in June.

Aileen was soon to begin her summer return to Maine. The children were at the point of starting another return to Europe. She had asked them to dine with her in the garden of the Cosmopolitan Club at 122 East 66 Street. The outdoor temperature during dinner was mild.

She got to talking about a man she had known named Egisto Fabbri. She said he lived much of the time in a villa not far from Florence named Bagazzano, originally a Medici hunting lodge; that she visited him there; that he and she became engaged; that she owned an extraordinary copy of *The Education*; that she took it to Bagazzano; and that they agreed to share its ownership as an anticipation of their marriage. They further agreed that the copy should stay for the time being in his library.

Aileen was saying things she had never said before. She seemed to be disclosing her deepest secret. While she continued to talk, she and the children moved to a corner of the club's brightly-lit sitting room. What most interested her was the contents of the copy. She said nothing about marks Adams had made in it, in pen or pencil, to correct or improve the book. She only described how she and Egisto had liked to sit side by side and read the many extracts from scientific books that Adams had written onto slips of paper and inserted at points in the text that concerned the same matters. By that means, he had turned his *Education* into a colloquy between other writers and himself. She and Egisto were fascinated by the juxtaposed opinions.

Unspoken realities permeated what Aileen was saying. It hung in the air that, of the copies of *The Education* that Adams might have reserved for his own use, the one she left at Bagazzano could have been the most important; and it had stayed in Fabbri's possession.

One of the children—the present writer—had been collecting and studying evidence relating to Henry Adams for nineteen years and was advancing step by step towards completing what he hoped might be an adequate biography. He wondered aloud whether the extraordinary copy that Aileen had left near Florence might be recovered. Aileen took up the idea at once. She was sure the copy was still at Bagazzano. She said she would write to a person who could find and send it. The person was Tecla, one of Egisto's nieces. She said she could get Tecla's address in Rome. She was eager to write the necessary letter, was confident and hopeful, yet also seemed somewhat doubting or afraid.[111]

Summer intervened. While in Maine, Aileen received a friendly letter from the niece. Tecla said that she would be going to Bagazzano in the fall and would "certainly" look for the copy.[112]

News came as expected—to New York in the fall. Aileen telephoned to repeat what it was. Tecla had gone through the library and had not found the copy.

Aileen had more to say. Without explaining why she thought so, she said the copy possibly was given to Ina de Vasconcellas, a Portuguese noblewoman. To preclude all chance of error, she spelled out the name, letter by letter.

Her voice was shaking. The subject was becoming unspeakable for her. She indicated that she would later talk about other subjects but that the things she had already said about the copy were her last. In haste, she and her hearer put down their telephones.[113]

Abbreviations

ABA   Abigail Brown Brooks (1808–1889)—HA's mother
AHA   American Historical Association
AHR   American Historical Review
AP   The Adams Papers, Massachusetts Historical Society
AT   Aileen Tone—HA's companion in old age
Autobiography   Charles Francis Adams/ 1835–1915/ An Autobiography, Bost & NY 1916
BA   Brooks Adams (1848–1927)—HA's younger brother
Beringause   Arthur F. Beringause, *Brooks Adams/ A Biography*, NY 1955
Bost   Boston, Massachusetts
Camb Cambridge, Massachusetts
Cater   *Henry Adams and His Friends/ A Collection of His Unpublished Letters*, compiled with a Biographical Introduction by Harold Dean Cater, Bost 1947
CaterP   Harold Dean Cater Papers, Massachusetts Historical Society
CFA   Charles Francis Adams (1807–1886)—HA's father
CFA2   Charles Francis Adams (1835–1915)—HA's elder brother
CFA2P   (plus box number)   Charles Francis Adams Papers (1890–1915), Massachusetts Historical Society
CFA3   Charles Francis Adams (1888–1964)—HA's nephew; son of JQA2
Clymer   Kenton J. Clymer, *John Hay/ The Gentleman as Diplomat*, Ann Arbor 1975
CMG   Charles Milnes Gaskell—HA's longtime close English friend
Degradation   Henry Adams, *The Degradation of the Democratic Dogma*, NY 1920—a posthumous compilation for which Brooks Adams bore sole responsibility
Democracy (1880)   [Henry Adams], *Democracy/ An American Novel*, NY 1880—published anonymously
Democracy (LoA)   *Democracy/ An American Novel*, as published in Henry Adams, *Novels/ Mont Saint Michel/ The Education*, NY: Library of America, 1983
Dennett   Tyler Dennett, *John Hay/ From Poetry to Politics*, NY 1934
EC   Elizabeth Sherman Cameron—HA's late-in-life partner; wife of James Donald Cameron
EHA (1907)   [Henry Adams], *The Education of Henry Adams*, privately printed, Wash 1907
EHA (1918)   [Henry Adams], *The Education of Henry Adams* Bost & NY: Houghton Mifflin Company 1918—first published edition, intrudingly and damagingly mis-subtitled *An Autobiography*

545

EHA (LoA)   *The Education of Henry Adams*, as published in Henry Adams, *Novels/ Mont Saint Michel/ The Education*, NY: Library of America 1983

F, II   *Letters of Henry Adams (1892–1918)*, edited by Worthington Chauncey Ford, Bost & NY 1938

FP (plus box number)   Worthington Chauncey Ford Papers, Manuscripts & Archives Division, NYPL

FTKP   Materials relating to HA owned by Faith Thoron Knapp

Garraty   John A. Garraty, *Henry Cabot Lodge/ A Biography*, NY 1953

GCL   George Cabot Lodge—friend of HA; elder son of HCL

Gwynn   *The Letters and Friendships of Sir Cecil Spring Rice*, Bost & NY 1929

HA   Henry Adams (1838–1918)—christened Henry Brooks Adams; dropped middle name in 1870 when thirty-two

HA2   Henry Adams (1875–1951)—HA's nephew; one of CFA2's twin sons

HA-1   Edward Chalfant, *Both Sides of the Ocean/ A Biography of Henry Adams/ His First Life: 1838–1862*, Hamden, 1982

HA-2   Edward Chalfant, *Better in Darkness/ A Biography of Henry Adams/ His Second Life: 1862–1891*, Hamden, 1994

HAL   Henry Adams Library, Massachusetts Historical Society

HA-micro (plus reel number)   *Microedition of the Henry Adams Papers*, 36 reels, Bost: Massachusetts Historical Society 1979, incorporating papers held by the Society, Brown University, and Harvard University (reel containing Brown materials is cited as HA-micro B; two reels containing Harvard materials are cited as HA-micro H)

HA/Thoron-micro   *Microedition of the Adams-Thoron Papers* (two reels), Bost: Massachusetts Historical Society, 1992

Hazen   *The Letters of William Roscoe Thayer*, ed. by Charles Downer Hazen, Bost & NY 1926

HCL   Henry Cabot Lodge—senator from Massachusetts; husband of HA's close friend Anna Cabot Mills Lodge;

HJ   Henry James

HJLetters   Henry James Letters, edited by Leon Edel (four volumes), Camb 1974–1984

HP   John Hay Papers, John Hay Library, Brown University

HUS (Scribner)   Henry Adams, *History of the United States . . .* (nine volumes variously titled), NY: Charles Scribner's Sons 1889–1891

HUS (LoA)   Henry Adams, *History of the United States . . .* (two volumes), NY: Library of America, 1986

JHLetters   Letters of John Hay and Extracts from Diary (three volumes), privately printed, Wash 1908; or facsimile edition, NY 1969

JQA   John Quincy Adams (1767–1848)—HA's grandfather

JQA2   John Quincy Adams (1833–1894)—HA's eldest brother

JTA   James Truslow Adams—first biographer of HA (not related to HA)

L, I, II, III   *The Letters of Henry Adams*, Volumes I-III [1858–1892], edited by J. C. Levenson, Ernest Samuels, Charles Vandersee, Viola Hopkins Winner, Cambridge & Lond: Harvard University Press 1982

L, IV, V, VI   *The Letters of Henry Adams*, Volumes IV-VI [1892–1918], edited by J. C. Levenson, Ernest Samuels, Charles Vandersee, Viola Hopkins Winner, Cambridge & Lond: Harvard University Press 1989

LCA   Louisa Catherine Johnson Adams (1775–1852)—HA's paternal grandmother; decisively influential in his life; wife of JQA

Levenson   J. C. Levenson, chief editor of L (see above)

LHT   Louisa Hooper Thoron (originally Louisa Chapin Hooper)—HA's favorite niece-by-marriage; expert on HA; wife of Ward Thoron
LoA   Library of America
Lond   London
LP (plus box number)   Henry Cabot Lodge Papers, Massachusetts Historical Society
LTimes   *The Times* of London
MC   Martha Cameron—daughter of Elizabeth Cameron and James Donald Cameron
MHA   Marian (or Clover) Hooper Adams (1843–1885)—HA's wife
MHALetters   The Letters of Mrs. Henry Adams/ 1865–1883, ed. by Ward Thoron, Bost 1936
MHS   Massachusetts Historical Society
MP   Macmillan Company Records, Manuscripts & Archives Division, NYPL
MSM&CH (1904)   Henry Adams, *Mont Saint Michel and Chartres*, privately printed, Wash 1904
MSM&CH (1912)   Henry Adams, *Mont Saint Michel and Chartres*, privately printed, revised & expanded, Wash 1912
MSM&CH (1913)   Henry Adams, *Mont-Saint-Michel and Chartres*, Bost: Houghton Mifflin Company 1913—first published edition
MSM&CH (LoA)   Henry Adams, *Mont Saint Michel and Chartres*, as published in Henry Adams, *Novels/ Mont Saint Michel/ The Education*, NY: Library of America, 1983
NAR   The North American Review
NY   New York City
NYPL   New York Public Library
NYTimes   *New York Times*
O.[year].[page]   *Supplement to THE LETTERS OF HENRY ADAMS/ Letters Omitted from the Harvard University Press Edition*, Bost: MHS, 1989—bound in two parts
SKETCHES   *Sketches for the North American Review, by Henry Adams*, edited by Edward Chalfant, Hamden 1986
Thayer   William Roscoe Thayer, *The Life and Letters of John Hay*, Bost & NY 1915
Wash   Washington, D. C.
WJ   William James

NOTES

E ach chapter rests on a body of principal sources and a scattering of additional sources. I have headed each chapter's notes with a list of its principal sources. As necessary, I have gone on to cite additional sources. In all cases of quotation, the source is given.

I also have written "comments," some long. The pertinence of each will be apparent if it is read in conjunction with the narrative.

The most important sources relating to Henry Adams are writings he published, privately printed, or otherwise preserved; his letters; and letters written to him. Many of the letters, both by him and to him, appear in the *Microfilms of the Henry Adams Papers* compiled by Stephen T. Riley, published in 1979, and in the *Microfilms of the Adams/Thoron Papers*, published in 1992. Because the letters as filmed are virtual equivalents of the manuscripts, I have coordinated my notes with the films. Unfortunately the films are accessible in few places.

The vast majority of the letters by Adams quoted in the narrative appear in printed form in *The Letters of Henry Adams* edited by J. C. Levenson and others, published in six volumes in 1982 and 1988, or in the two-part *Supplement*, published in 1989. The *Letters* are widely available. Unfortunately the *Supplement* is much less so.

1. BASEBALL AT ABOYNE

Letters by and to HA are in HA-micro 9, 10, B, or H, unless otherwise indicated.

PRINCIPAL SOURCES

   (1) eighteen letters, EC to HA, 12 Nov 1891–7 Aug 1892.
   (2) twenty-four letters, HA to EC, 12 Nov 1891–4 Aug 1892.
   (3) nine letters, HA to Hay, 14 Nov 1891–6 Jul 1892.
   (4) five letters, HA to Lucy Baxter, 16 Nov 1891–7 Aug 1892, L, III, 570–72, 591–93; L, IV, 8–9; O.1892.1–3.
   (5) thirteen letters, HA to CMG, 26 Nov 1891–24 Jul 1892.
   (6) four letters, HA to Clark, 23 Apr 1892–29 May 1892, L, IV, 6–7, 9–10, 13–14; O.1892.9–10.
   (7) three letters, HA to Eliot, 12, 16, & 16 Jun 1892, L, IV, 21–22, 26–28; F, II, 10–11.

LESSER SOURCES; CITATIONS; COMMENTS

   1. "Gaskell" is used for convenience. His full surname was Milnes Gaskell, as if the names were hyphenated.

2. Present-day historians call the site Wenlock Priory. In 1891, its owner and HA knew it as Wenlock Abbey.

3. Mary Ward, CMG's daughter, told me in 1962 that her father would not have liked to visit the United States but that he liked "to have *America* come to him." Her emphasized word left no doubt that for her father HA *was* America.

4. MHA to her father, 8 Aug 1880, AP.

5. EC to HA, 6–7 Dec 1891.

6. HA to EC, 13–25 Dec 1891.

7. A list of Tahiti-related books in the Henry Adams Library at the Massachusetts Historical Society appears as Appendix IV in Max I. Baym, *The French Education of Henry Adams*, NY 1951. A fuller list of HA's Tahiti-related acquisitions is possible and would be useful.

8. HA's starting his *Education* is evidenced by his echoing its opening words in a letter to EC, saying, "I too was in Arcadia born—or in Hancock Place, beneath the shadow of the State House Dome. . . ." The letter is dated only "Wednesday." Levenson and his associates date it [6 Aug 1890]. See O.1890.8. A more probable date is [late June-early July 1890]. See HA-2, Chap. 25, note 51.

9. Later Reid and his wife invited HA to lunch. For details, see HA to EC, 28 Dec 1891–8 Jan 1892.

10. As his letters to her show, HA imposed on the London legation for help in getting jewelry sent to EC through State Department channels. He possibly asked the Paris legation for help in similar connections.

11. Byrne to HA, 15 Apr 1892.

12. Readers may think it unlikely that HA could seriously believe that Possum would go to "the next world," but he was so capable of holding unusual beliefs that in this instance what he believed might best be considered an open question.

13. Summarizing what he saw in France and Great Britain in 1891–1892, compared with what he had seen at much earlier times, HA wrote to Hay, 9 Jan 1892, ". . . in Europe I see no progress—none! They have the electric light, voilá tout!"

14. An American, Thomas Wiltberger Evans (1828–1897), had practiced dentistry in Paris from the time of the Second Empire. See "US Winners of French Award," NYTimes, 3 Sep 1993. It is easy to believe that the Adamses availed themselves of Evans's services as early as 1862, and that HA sought them in 1891.

15. For HA's first use of "chiefess," see L, IV, 307. Evidently the word is English usage. Compare American dictionaries and the *Oxford English Dictionary*.

16. HA's first letter to his Tahitian relatives, Tati Salmon's reply, and HA's letter to Salmon of 6 Dec 1891 suggesting that Marau too come to Washington are missing; but the sequence of letters is made clear in Salmon's second letter to HA, 10 Feb 1892, saying: "I could see the difference she [Arii Taimai] has made between your first message, & the present one, she merely treated the first as a simple act of politeness on your part, where as [*sic*] the last, it affected her." In the same letter, Salmon says HA was "the first" of the family's foreign visitors "that has really shown acts of remembering us." He appears to have been assured by HA that a meeting in Washington in October would be possible. He adds: "Please informed [*sic*] me of your movements, for Oct or Nov—or even Dec., I will do my best to come along, & bring along Marau. . . ."

17. HA's view of autobiography had two sides. He stood ready to say that

"the interest of autobiography" is "the only interest that lasts forever, and holds its own in history." See HA to Charles W. Eliot, 13 Nov 1886, L, III, 45. Yet it was a cardinal principle with him that ego-centrism, whether in action, speech, or writing, had to be avoided when possible.

18. HA to Anna Lodge, 25 Nov 1891.

19. HA-2, 555–56, 862–63, 865, 870–71, 873.

20. *EHA* (1907), vi; (LoA), 722.

21. It bears emphasis that the house plans Richardson drew reflected dissimilar impulses. The Adamses had hoped to bring *three* households into cooperation and provide more or less modest accommodations for each. The Hays tended in the direction of grandeur.

22. HA to Hay, 14 Nov 1891. As HA and Hay knew, Chamberlain could meet high costs. He had married a rich American, Mary Endicott. When single, Mary had sometimes shared HA's midday "breakfasts" at 1603 H Street.

23. HA to Anna Lodge, 25 Nov 1891.

24. HA to Hay, 9–13 Jan 1892. HA's prescription for "Travels" comes close to being a factual description of a small book of travel letters he wrote from Europe to CFA2 in 1860. Thus the prescription can be taken as evidence that, in the first days of 1892, HA was thinking of his experiences in 1860 and contemplating Chaps. V and VI of *The Education*.

25. HA's contemporary letters make clear that he wished to visit Holland but are silent about a motive. The motive may be a given. He can be viewed as wanting to find papers relating to JQA's service as minister to Holland in the 1790s.

26. Intended by Mrs. Copley as a surprise, the portrait was successful in that respect and in all others. See Andrew Oliver, *Portraits of John Quincy Adams and His Wife*, Camb 1970, xx, 37–41.

27. *Memorial Biographies of the New England Historic Genealogical Society*, Bost 1880, I, 114.

28. *EHA* (1907), vi; (LoA), 722.

29. Of the six paragraphs of the Preface, the first four could have been written in Paris in December 1891. I believe they are best dated in that month. The last two have the appearance of an addition. Also see Chap. 14.

30. HA to EC, 28 Dec 1891–8 Jan 1892.

31. HA wrote a still grimmer account of his Paris stay. See HA to Lucy Baxter, 4 Oct 1892:—"That I did not go insane was a pleasing and constant surprise to me. When I escaped to England in January[,] I was at the end of my strength."

32. CFA2's letter is missing. Its principal contents can be inferred from HA's reply.

33. When asking her not to betray his plan of return (letter of 14–28 Nov 1891), HA explained, ". . . I want to reserve my plans to myself for reasons that belong to my family affairs." Evidently the family member he had in mind was CFA2, and the affair was CFA2's wanting him to receive a Harvard degree. See note 49.

34. Gaskell and Cunliffe's affection for HA showed in their conduct. The former joined him in London prior to his coming to Thornes. The latter went to Liverpool to see him before he boarded the *Teutonic.*

35. HA to CMG, 26 Feb 1892. With still greater emphasis, HA told his brother Charles that the *Teutonic* "knocked me silly." See HA to CFA2, 12 Mar [1892].

36. In *The Education*, HA says he first visited Coffin's Point at the senator's behest, in February 1893. See *EHA* (1907), 290; (LoA), 1024. The account is fiction. HA made his first visit in February 1892. As the general tenor of his letters to EC about his visits makes clear, he made the visit strictly because EC wished him to do so.

37. EC to HA, 10 May 1901:—"this partnership."

38. I believe it is a fair assumption that HA formed his political alliance with the Camerons at the earliest chance, in South Carolina in February 1892, but positive evidence of the alliance's existence first appears in HA's papers dating from the late summer of 1893.

39. EC to HA, 12–17 Nov 1892:—"He has had a stroke. I feel sure of it. Otherwise he looks well."

40. On the eve of the 1892 Republican nominating convention, Blaine suddenly resigned from his secretaryship, tried to prevent the party's nomination from going again to Harrison, sought it for himself, and failed. HA reacted in carefully chosen, deceptive ways. As a means of maintaining good relations with the Hays, Camerons, Lodges, and Roosevelts, all of whom were Blaine's intimates, HA told EC (letters of 5 & 11 Jun 1892) that he wanted Blaine to be elected president, but only for the pleasure that the change might afford young Harriet. And for purposes of British public consumption, HA assured CMG (letter of 13 Jun 1892) that Blaine was ordered by the Republican managers to oppose Harrison and loyally obeyed.

Behind these transparent pretenses, one can see HA's true opinion: that Blaine was a spent force and that his unsuccessful maneuver was a last outbreak of unbridled egoism and betrayal.

41. HA to Mabel Hooper, 21 Feb 1892.

42. HA to Clark, 23 Apr 1892.

43. His claim was weightier than might appear. In 1894, when he no longer needed them, he would give Western Reserve University "approximately 120 books on the French Revolution and the Napoleonic period." See L, III, 187n1.

44. HA to EC, 9 Jun 1892.

45. Recounting his mishap, HA wrote to EC, 5 Jun 1892, ". . . my horse shied at a nigger, caught his hind-foot in a deep, muddy rut, and in half a second rolled over, catching my right leg under him." The passage includes one of the few instances till then of HA's using the epithet "nigger."

46. Letters, HA to EC, 9 Jun 1892 & 23 Jun 1892.

47. Eliot to HA, 9 Jun 1892.

48. HA to Eliot, 12 Jun 1892.

49. CFA2 conveyed his suggestion to the university through Hooper. See L, IV, 27n3. It seems possible that Hooper sent HA news of the intended conferral in a Thanksgiving-time 1891 letter that is known to be missing. It seems equally possible that a late 1891 letter from CFA2, now missing, informed HA that the conferral of a degree would be suggested in recognition of his *History*. Whatever happened, HA was careful to arrive in Washington without his return being known to anyone in Quincy or Cambridge.

He kept away from both Quincy and Cambridge till late on June 29, 1892, after Harvard's commencement had ended. On the 29th, starting from New York, he traveled to Cambridge to stay with the Hoopers till he and they would have to go to New York to board the *Teutonic*. While in Cambridge, he noted that his right foot was "not yet strong enough for use." "I can walk very short distances all right, but a few rods are a serious job. . . ." See HA to EC, Friday, [1 Jul 1892].

50. Eliot to HA, 14 Jun 1892. The letter ties the intended degree specifically, but not only, to HA's *History*.

51. HA to Eliot, 16 Jun 1892.

52. Relations between HA and his former students were a very different matter from his relations with Harvard College and especially from his relations with President Eliot, who when hiring him in 1870 had shown the attitudes of an overbearing employer.

On June 22, 1892, Western Reserve University gave HA an honorary degree as doctor of laws. His acceptance was required; his appearing was not. The institution's president, Charles F. Thwing, was one of HA's former students. Writing to HA about the degree, Thwing adverted to his teaching medieval institutions at Harvard in the 1870s but said nothing about his *History*. See Western Reserve University to HA, 22 Jun 1892; Thwing to HA, 27 Jun 1892.

Thus HA could construe the Western Reserve award as a token of esteem from his former students and an acknowledgement of his work at Harvard as a teacher of the history of law and author of "The Anglo-Saxon Courts of Law." HA accepted the award after Harvard's commencement took place and after Thwing's letter, sent to Washington too late to reach him, had been forwarded to Hooper's house in Cambridge. See HA to Thwing, 1 Jul 1892, L, IV, 37.

53. HA's copy is in HAL. It is inscribed by him: "Henry Adams Teutonic Room 94." A passage relevant to his interest in ice ages says (38), ". . . of any periodic ice age, either tertiary, mezazoic, or azoic, the evidence is most doubtful, and of periodic changes, no evidence exists."

54. Louisa Hooper to Bigelow, 7 Aug 1892. She retrieved her letter at a later time. I copied it in 1965 at her suggestion.

2. MOLECULES OR ATOMS, LIVING AND DEAD

Letters by and to HA are in HA-micro 10, 11, B, or H, unless otherwise indicated.

PRINCIPAL SOURCES

(1) twenty-four letters, EC to HA, 7 Aug 1892–10 Sep 1893.

(2) fifteen letters, HA to Hay, 10 Aug 1892–28 Sep 1893.

(3) forty letters & notes, HA to EC, 11 Aug 1892–[15 Sep] 1893.

(4) thirteen letters, HA to CMG, 12 Aug 1892–22 Aug 1893.

(5) six letters, HA to Phillips, 20 Sep 1892–13 Sep 1893.

(6) eight letters, HA to Louisa Hooper, 26 Oct 1892–14 Jun 1893.

(7) five letters, HA to Mabel Hooper, 6 Nov 1892–29 Jun 1893.

(8) transcribed portion of letter, HA to Marau Taaroa, [Dec? 1892], L, IV, 82–83.

(9) [HA], "Biography of John Hay," *The Reserve* [yearbook published by the junior class of Adelbert College, Cleveland, Ohio], XIII (1893), 9–14.

(10) [HA], 4-page memorandum beginning "The instructions . . . ," HA-micro Miscellaneous.

(11) letter, HA to Langley, 3 May 1893, L, IV, 99–101.

(12) [HA], *Remonetization of Silver. Speech of Hon. J. D. Cameron, of Pennsylvania, in the Senate of the United States, Monday, September 25, 1893.*, Wash 1893— HA's copy, MHS. (For attribution to HA, see note 65, below.)

LESSER SOURCES: CITATIONS: COMMENTS

1. The Constitution of the United States says in Art. I, Sec. 8, that Congress shall have the power to "borrow Money on the credit of the United States" and

to "coin Money, regulate the Value thereof, and of foreign Coin." It further says in Art. I, Sec. 10, that no state shall "make any Thing but gold and silver Coin a Tender in Payment of Debts." It nowhere specifies that the *federal* government shall not make anything but gold or silver coin a tender in payment of debts. It is silent about two key questions: the creation of paper money by the federal government, and approval by the federal government of the use of paper money as a tender in payment of debts.

2. Principal source 12 is evidence of HA's having followed the movement of gold continually since 1890.

3. As privately printed by HA, the chapters of *The Education* begin with dates. Their titles appear only as running heads. Chapter XX is dated "1871." It can be objected that the chapter's contents reach onward to events occurring as late as 1877. In reply, it can be urged that the *principal* contents of the chapter, those in its concluding paragraphs, are properly dated 1871.

The date "1871" for Chapter XX lends a measure of justification, or at least excuse, for HA's dating Chapter XXI "1892" and titling it "Twenty Years After." The title repeats the title of the famous novel *Vingt Ans Après* by the elder Alexandre Dumas as usually translated into English. Many readers would know that *Vingt Ans Après* carries forward a story of three friends that Dumas began in his earlier novel *Les Trois Mousquetaires*. The same readers would apprehend that HA's book tells a story of three friends: Clarence King, John Hay, and the protagonist.

4. Letters, HA to EC, 28 Jul 1892 & 11 Aug 1892.

5. HA to Lucy Baxter, 21 Sep 1892, O.1892.21–22.

6. HA to EC, 1 Oct 1892.

7. HA wrote the opening chapter of *Memoirs of Marau Taaroa* after his return from the South Seas. The chapter draws on materials published by Europeans immediately following the discovery of Tahiti. In the chapter, HA makes the point that what was found in Tahiti appeared to Europeans to bear out with astonishing fidelity the ideas they currently were learning from Rousseau. One might conclude accordingly that there are two works by HA that should be read with Rousseau in mind: his Tahiti book (both versions) and *The Education*. But HA had brought Rousseau's ideas to the fore in the opening pages of his *Life of Albert Gallatin*. Also he can be said to have answered Rousseau's ideas implicitly in his *History of the United States*. For all these reasons, he can be viewed as an American writer who paid Rousseau the compliment of very serious attention and long-sustained reply.

8. As a rule, when he wanted to include in his writings materials translated into English from other languages, HA wrote the translations himself. He had a copy of Rousseau's *Confessions*, Paris, 1886, HAL. Presumably he translated from it the passage with which he begins the Preface to *The Education*.

9. In the Preface to *The Education*, HA names two writers: Rousseau and Franklin. He does not refer explicitly to Franklin's *Memoirs*, but he points in that book's direction by speaking of Franklin as "a model" of "self-teaching." See *EHA* (1907), v; (LoA), 721.

10. In *The Education*, HA dates the hospital stay as having occurred in January 1892. See *EHA* (1907), 276; (LoA), 1009. This minor fiction permits him to begin Chapter XXI with the date "1892." Also see note 3, above.

11. Marau Taaroa to HA, 10 Aug 1892, saying that "for this year" her leaving Tahiti "is not to be thought of."

12. Salmon to HA, 9 Nov 1892.

13. Marau Taaroa to HA, 10 Aug 1892:—". . . I have already worked at them [the chapters of the *Memoirs*] although very little, & the only reason for my not sending them before is that I have had very little confidence in the post & have had no one to send them by. I promise to send it by Tati. . . ."

14. Salmon to HA, 7 May 1893.

15. HA to BA, 2 May 1903.

16. Salmon to HA, 2 Jul 1893.

17. In his letters in the period January-June 1893, HA makes no overt reference to *The Education*. In his letter to Louisa Hooper, 6 May 1893, he however remarks: ". . . I silently took John Hay by the hand, and led him up to the baseball ground, where we saw our team whack the New Yorkers." The remark seems to echo the most famous passage of *The Education*, in which HA's paternal grandfather silently takes grandson Henry by the hand and leads him to school. The remark possibly is evidence that HA had so nearly perfected Chapter I of *The Education* by early May 1893 that it was influencing his other writings.

18. One may conjecture that HA's letters to his Tahitian relatives were in large part questionnaires. The conjecture may help explain both the disappearance of the letters and the survival of a partial copy of one of them.

19. Principal source 8.

20. For HA's reviews of King's publications, see HA-2, 909–10, index entries under HA, *Writings*, sub-section headed "writings & publications about science."

21. For an account of the relation between King's geology and its underpinnings in contemporary physics, see Thurman Wilkins, *Clarence King/ A Biography*, NY 1958, 326–32.

22. Chap. XXI of *The Education* (the opening chapter of the second narrative) begins with a paragraph that includes the following statement: ". . . education should try to lessen the obstacles, diminish the friction, invigorate the energy, and should train minds to react, not at haphazard but by choice, on the *lines of force* that attract their world [italics added]." At first sight, the statement may seem to draw imaginatively on Newton and things mechanical; but a long paper, "On Faraday's Lines of Force," occupies a large portion of the text in James Clerk Maxwell's *Scientific Papers*, Camb England 1890. In view of the phrase "lines of force" so strongly emphasized in Maxwell's book, HA's statement must be read as attentive to Faraday, Maxwell, and things electromagnetic. By the same token, the second narrative in *The Education* must be read from beginning to end as based in part on knowledge of *modern* physics.

23. Marau Taaroa to HA, 11 Mar 1893.

24. Principal source 9. The incidental passage (10) makes fun of the village of Warsaw, Illinois, calling it "one of the many western towns which then aspired to the rank of a future metropolis, and which the course of time has not carried perceptibly towards its object." The passage may reflect HA's originally negative opinion of Chicago. He foresook that opinion and expressed an approving one on 20 May 1893 after first visiting the Columbian Exposition. One perhaps can thus infer that he wrote the biography of Hay before that date.

25. In 1861, HA celebrated his secret arrangement to act as London correspondent of the *New York Times* by sending the editor a preliminary despatch dated April 1. In 1879, he arranged that his anonymous novel *Democracy* be published on April 1, 1880. That he made an April Fool's Day promise in 1892 to write a sketch of Hay is clearly a deliberate extension of the pattern.

26. HA had written a serious short biography, his miniature life of Gallatin. See HA-2, 368, 374–75, 785, 794–95. That he would write a second is very doubtful, for he much disliked repeating himself in his writings. He however could

want to write a parody of serious short biography. Hence the interesting work on Hay.

27. Principal source 10.

28. Ibid. HA's second paragraph reads: "On the part of the U. S. it is plain that only one proposition could be wholly acceptable: i.e. the opening of all mints to the free coinage of both metals at the present ratio." HA adds that, if offered, the proposition would be rejected by the English, whereupon the English would be obliged to offer a proposition and discussion could follow.

In other words, HA favors the presentation of what he believes is the proposition that is right for all the world; he expects the English to resist it; and he believes that progress towards acceptance of the American proposition can be made.

29. Principal source 10. Written in ink, the next-to-final copy is unsigned, untitled, and undated. It is slightly disfigured by two small insertions and a correction. One may assume that the final copy differed only in accommodating the changes. The final copy may now be somewhere in the National Archives, unidentified.

30. The title of the chief officer of the Smithsonian Institution was secretary. Langley had held the post since 18 Nov 1887. How long he and HA had known each other is not known.

31. The passage is taken from the New York Public Library's copy of James Clerk Maxwell, *Theory of Heat*, new ed., NY 1875, 328. The copy was given to the library by HA's friends Worthington and Paul Ford. Their gift is a reminder that in the 19th century books by leading scientists were read as a matter of course by intelligent Americans not formally trained in the sciences.

32. Abraham Pais, *Inward Bound/ Of Matter and Forces in the Physical World*, Oxford & NY, 1986, 72n:—"By 'molecules', Maxwell meant our 'atoms'—terminology was not uniform in those years."

33. In 1875, when publishing his satire *The Radical Club./ A Poem, respectfully dedicated to "The Infinite./ By an Atom.*," HA had used "an Atom" as his pseudonym. One may assume that his adoption of the pseudonym reflected his being an Adams, his being the smallest son in his generation in the Adams family, his being one of the descendants of Adam, and his being a creature who feels at a very far remove in size from the Creator described in the dedication as "The Infinite."

34. Thomson used "demon" in the unpejorative Greek sense of supernatural creature.

35. I am indebted to J. C. Levenson and his associates for tracing HA's mention of a "demon" in his letter to Langley to Thomson's lecture as published in 1889. See L, IV, 101n2.

Langley conceivably knew that Thomson invented the nickname, not in response to Maxwell's *Theory of Heat*, but in 1867 after seeing a letter from Maxwell to Peter Guthrie Tait involving mention of "a finite being" able to inspect the paths and velocities of molecules. See Abraham Pais, *'Subtle is the Lord'/ The Science and the Life of Albert Einstein*, Oxford 1982, 61n.

36. Maxwell, *Theory of Heat*, op. cit., 306.

37. While treating Maxwell's book as sometimes deficient in expression, HA clearly viewed it as mainly deficient in explanation. He responded to the contradiction he found in Maxwell's statements as indicative that something was omitted in Maxwell's thinking, and he posited the omitted something to be inherent minimum atomic heat.

38. Einstein's statement is drawn from Pais, *Inward Bound*, op. cit., 104, where Pais presents it as translated from "the second of his [Einstein's] 1905 papers on relativity." HA's "definite minimum of heat" anticipates the "rest energy" of the atom implicit in Einstein's theory of special relativity.

39. Read as friendly talk, HA's introduction of living and dead molecules (or atoms) qualifies as successful farce. Farce is achieved partly by saying the exactly wrong thing. As HA may have known, Maxwell had taken the very firm position that "molecules are neither born nor die." See Pais, *Inward Bound*, op. cit., 178, quoting Maxwell's article, "Atom," *Enc. Brittanica*, 9th ed., 1875.

Read as a serious suggestion, HA's introduction of living and dead molecules qualifies as successful prophecy. His suggestion exactly anticipates terms that would appear in later years in scientific discussion of a certain category of atoms. For example, see Pais, 122, quoting from Frederick Soddy, *The Interpretation of Radium*, NY 1920, 114: "If the destroying angel selected out of all those [human beings] alive in the world a fixed proportion to die every minute, independently of their age . . . and chosen purely at random . . . then our expectation of life would be that of the radioactive atoms."

40. As his contemporary letters show, HA was on excellent terms not only with King but also with Alexander Agassiz, George Agassiz, Arnold Hague, and Raphael Pumpelly—all distinguished geologists.

41. That HA was capable of thinking of humans as living or dead molecules or atoms is a matter of record. In his "Prayer to the Dynamo," interjected in his poem "Prayer to the Virgin of Chartres," he writes the words ". . . Me—the dead Atom. . . ." See L, V, 209. (The words hark back to his having used "An Atom" as a pseudonym for himself. See note 33, above.)

42. Details of the day's journey are drawn from the account in *EHA* (1907), 294; (LoA), 1028. The account mentions "letters" to HA "from his brothers," but there apparently was only one letter, written by CFA2 on behalf of all three brothers. See note 44.

43. CFA2 to HA, 7 Jul 1893. For an error concerning this letter, see note 44.

44. In 1919, BA said he telegraphed and wrote from Quincy to HA in Switzerland in 1893. See *Degradation*, 90.

His statements clouded the mind of his biographer, who quotes some words about the condition of JQA2—"complete collapse and a sort of nervous prostration"—as if they appear in a letter by BA to HA, 7 Jul 1893. See Beringause, 102n5. But there is no such letter by BA to HA. The words appear in a letter of that date by CFA2 to HA.

Levenson and his associates appear similarly to have been too much affected by BA's statements. Although BA claimed he telegraphed to HA *in Switzerland*, they attribute to BA a telegram HA received *in London*. See L, IV, 114–15n1.

The only relevant contemporary evidence is HA's quoting in his letter to EC, Thursday, 27 [Jul 1893], two words of the telegram he received in London. The telegram itself is missing. There seems every likelihood that its sender was CFA2.

45. Many women who figure in this narrative had nicknames, including shared nicknames. With some exceptions, I have avoided using the nicknames. Notable exceptions are CFA2's wife, Mary Ogden Adams, known as Minnie; HA's favorite niece-by-marriage, Louisa Hooper, known as Loulie (variously spelled); CFA2's youngest daughter, Elizabeth Ogden Adams, known as Elsie; George

Cabot Lodge's wife, Elizabeth Davis Lodge, known as Bessy (often spelled Bessie); HA's housekeeper in Washington, Maggie Wade (often spelled Maggy); and one of HA's servants in Paris, Sadie.

46. Abigail Adams Homans, *Education by Uncles*, Bost 1966, 20–21. Mrs. Homans says in error that HA was in Cambridge at Edward Hooper's house during Harvard's commencement on June 29, 1892. This was just what HA took pains to avoid. He timed his arrival at Hooper's house to occur at 6:00 P.M., well after the exercises were completed. See HA to EC, Tuesday, 29 [actually 28 Jun 1892], L, IV, 34.

47. Edward Chase Kirkland, *Charles Francis Adams, Jr.,/ 1835–1915, The Patrician at Bay*, Camb 1965, 177.

48. *Degradation*, 90–91. The dealings HA and BA had with one another at Quincy in August-September 1893 must be adduced from sources written at later times. The sources deserve close attention, item by item.

(a) In April 1894, BA published a pamphlet: *The Gold Standard/ An Historical Study*. After learning that HA approved it, BA wrote to him, ". . . I suppose you recognized the last half of the last chapter of my book." See BA to HA, 6 May 1894. The remark may seem to indicate that the pamphlet was extracted from a complete manuscript that HA had read in the summer of 1893. It will appear, however, that what HA read was something very incomplete.

(b) In his 6 May 1894 letter, BA also said: "What with one thing and another[,] I have worked like a horse—and I have done my book—at least as far as the sketch is concerned." The remark affirms that a manuscript had been incomplete. By dint of a winter's effort, BA had transformed it to a "sketch"; i.e. a first draft.

(c) Soon after, BA reported, "I am now quite ready to print my book, indeed it cannot wait longer than to be re-written. . . ." See BA to HA, 30 Jun 1894. In this case, BA affirms that the draft is not ready to go to a printer. A *readable* draft must be prepared.

(d) In his 30 June 1894 letter, BA said too that he meant "to recast my book completely." He had decided where in history his narrative would begin but remained uncertain where it would end. ". . . I mean to plunge in with Augustus [in ancient Rome] and come right down to date, ending with Italy probably . . . but of this I am not sure."

(e) BA went to Europe in the summer of 1894. After his return, he wrote to HA: "Reading over ones [*sic*] own work is a shock to ones [*sic*] vanity. I have been looking through my manuscript the last six weeks . . . . It is very far from what I supposed it to be. . . . I am rewriting it from beginning to end, and I suppose it will take me most of the winter. See BA to HA, 14 Nov 1894. The passage affirms that the completed "sketch" was in no sense a finished book.

(f) Soon after, BA reported to HA: "I find the copy you read very crude and badly put together, and I am taking it all apart and recasting it entire." See BA to HA, 19 Nov 1894. Because the word "copy" has several meanings, BA may appear to say that HA had read a complete copy, but other evidence will affirm its being incomplete.

(g) BA quickly warned his brother: ". . . I think I will send you my first four chapters to look through. I particularly want your advice as to a preface, or [a] concluding chapter, and also as to a name [i.e. a title]." See BA to HA, 22 Nov 1894. The passage supports the inference that BA in 1893 had shown HA only some *opening* chapters.

(h) HA read the rewritten opening chapters and returned them with criticisms. BA responded with thanks but needed more assistance. "I should like to show you my last chapters as well as my first. I want you to suggest a name [i.e. title], and I also want to have your opinion on a sort of final word . . . such as I put in at the beginning of the first copy you read." See BA to HA, 5 Dec 1894. The passage is important. It affirms that HA had not seen *last* chapters in 1893. It affirms too that the material HA read in 1893 began with a statement of the intended purport or thesis of the manuscript.

(i) BA completed the much-recast second draft in May 1895 and sent it to London for publication. He remarked to HA that work on the book had occupied him "for eight years"; i.e. since 1887. See BA to HA, 27 May 1895. Assuming BA's statement to be true, the partial manuscript shown to HA at Quincy in 1893 represented a six-year effort. (Much of the effort had taken the form of travel.)

(j) HA annotated a copy of the London edition (the copy is at MHS). He wrote at the close, "This chapter has lost greatly in the omissions made in the original draft." The comment applies to a draft of *recent* date. See item (h), above.

(k) At an unknown time, HA wrote Chap. XXII of *The Education*. He said therein that by August 1893—"with the advantages of ten years' study"—BA had "swept away much rubbish in the effort to build up a new line of thought for himself"; that BA "had discovered or developed a law of history that civilisation followed the [money] exchanges, and having worked it out for the Mediterranean was working it out for the Atlantic." See *EHA* (1907), 296; (LoA), 1033. HA's phrase "ten years' study" (i.e. since 1883) is evidently a deliberate exaggeration meant to work in BA's favor.

HA's account does not describe a manuscript. It says only that by August 1893 BA had "discovered or developed a law of history"; that he had "worked it out" in connection with "the Mediterranean" (i.e. in relation to the Greeks, Romans, Venetians, etc.); and that he also was "working it out" in connection with "the Atlantic" (i.e. in relation to the British, Germans, French, Americans, etc.). The words used do not suggest a book. They suggest continuing inquiry and a preliminary sort of writing.

The account in *The Education* may in one respect be misleading. There is no contemporary evidence that BA in 1893 was using the phrase "law of history" in the statement at the start of the incomplete work that he showed to HA. It thus seems possible, even probable, that HA in his account is fictionally throwing back to 1893 an all-important term that BA did not use till 1895, the year when "law" belatedly appeared in the title of BA's book—the title he could not invent himself and wanted others, HA especially, to invent on his behalf.

(l) In 1919, BA published an account of his dealings with HA at Quincy in 1893. See *Degradation*, 88–94. Beginning his account, BA says he showed HA only an "incomplete manuscript" (90), some "half legible sheets" (91), "my potential book" (91). He says too that HA read the sheets "carefully" (91). In my view, BA with these words settles what happened in Quincy in 1893 in all its important features.

There remains the important fact that two of HA's brothers, CFA2 and BA, indulged in the vice of pretending to remember long-past conversations verbatim. BA's 1919 account of his dealings with HA at Quincy in 1893 is not limited to the testimony quoted immediately above. It includes an 800-word conversation he alleges he had with HA in 1893. In the conversation, "incomplete manuscript" is replaced by plain "manuscript," "potential book" is four times replaced by "book," and the "book" is mentioned as if ready for printing.

On its face, the alleged conversation BA published in 1919 is arrant fiction devised in part—whether consciously or unconsciously—to shift events of later years back to August-September 1893.

The fictional conversation brings to mind a passage in Abigail Homans's *Education by Uncles*, op. cit., 49, in which she says about HA: ". . . his rule about any form of repetition [of conversations] was drastic and unequivocal: 'You ought to be shot for quoting what anyone says—you never get it straight and it may do endless harm.' And then he would add, 'Have your own ideas but keep off other people's.' " (It may not have occurred to Mrs. Homans that, while giving an account of HA's advice, she herself twice did what he suggested she never do.)

That the conversation presented by BA in 1919 was fiction did not prevent its later being read as fact by authoritative commentators. See Beringause, 101–03; also Charles A. Beard's Introduction to BA, *The Law of Civilization and Decay*, NY 1943, 5–7.

The result was mistaken received opinion that what BA asked HA to read in 1893 was a titled complete draft. See, for example, Levenson and his associates, L, IV, xviii:—". . . Brooks asked Henry to read in draft his *Law of Civilization and Decay*. . . ."

49. Levenson and his associates assert that in August-September 1893, as a consequence of reading a draft of BA's *Law of Civilization and Decay* and engaging in "long talks" with him, HA "became converted to silver coinage and to an apocalyptic view of the modern world." See L, IV, xviii–xix. The assertion is open to innumerable objections. The chief objections should be stated.

Concerning the alleged draft of BA's book, see note 48, above.

HA could not be "converted to silver coinage." The U. S. government had been minting silver coins since 1792. That HA had ever been been opposed to such minting is inconceivable.

Neither could HA be "converted" by BA to the free and unlimited coinage of silver. Writing his memorandum suggesting the appropriate U. S. position with respect to this issue (principal source 10), HA had said the previous spring that the only position the U. S. could rightly take was insistence on the free and unlimited coinage of gold and silver at the current ratio at all mints throughout the world.

Whether HA's anti-capitalism was "apocalyptic" may be debated, but he gave his anti-capitalism expression in speeches that antedated BA's more or less parallel writings. See note 65.

50. BA to HA, 8 Oct 1893. See also MacVeagh to HA, 21 Apr 1900, HA-micro 16:—"Each year now finds me feverishly anxious to see all I can of the few men for whom I really care[,] and you have long known your high place in that very limited company."

51. Three letters, HA to MacVeagh, 31 Aug, 6 Sep, 25 Sep 1893, L, IV, 123–24, 130.

52. Wilkins, *Clarence King*, op. cit., 338–39.

53. In HA's available letters—whether published or unpublished—written during the interval embraced by this book, there are by my count 402 occurrences of the word "Jew" or variants such as "Jewess," "Jewish," "Judaic," "Hebrew," etc. The dates of the occurrences make clear that the subject had little or no interest for HA until great public events seemed to him to require that he react. The first such event was the Panic of 1893, the second the Dreyfus Affair. Each seemed to him to affect the vital interests of the United States.

His phrase "a society of Jews and brokers" is the lone instance of his using "Jew" or a variant in 1893. (For 1892, see note 55, below.)

His notion that he wanted to help a London mob kill an English money-manager—Rothschild, Harcourt, or both—was new. It appeared in three letters in quick succession: HA to Hay, 8 Sep 1893; HA to EC, Friday [15 Sep 1893], and HA to Hay, 21 Sep 1893. It was a fantasy conceived in reaction to English *financial* tyrants.

The fantasy was not aimed at English money-managers because some or all of them were Jews. HA would have felt equal fury and hatred if none of them had been Jews.

His fantasy was a helpful index of the vehemence of his feelings. Yet it was interestingly at variance with his conduct. In the single instance in all his life when he would try to join a mob, he would do so sportively prepared to assist French anarchists in an anticipated attack on French *anti-Semites*! See Chap. 9.

54. Present-day opinions that HA was an anti-Semite are in my view mistaken and highly over-reactive misreadings of the evidence. Opinions, of course, partly rest on definitions. I accordingly have tried to define very carefully what I think HA was and was not in his thoughts and actions relating to the Jews and the anti-Semites of his time. It helps to notice that he viewed the anti-Semites objectively and from a distance, as unrelated to himself.

55. In his letters between mid-November 1891 and the end of 1892, HA had used the word "Jew" or variants only twice.

When aboard the *Teutonic* on 3 Feb 1892, he wrote to Gaskell (HA-micro 9), "My two hundred fellow-travelers are Jews." The statement is hyperbolic. To me, it seems more an expression of long-established and habitual dislike than of active, new hostility.

On 22 Oct 1892, he wrote to EC from Washington, ". . . all us Puritan New Englanders are children of the wandering Jew." In subsequent letters, HA says: to EC (11 Feb 1898), "We are all wandering Jews . . ."; to EC (1 Jan 1899), "I am the wandering Jew!"; to CMG (6 Apr 1999), "I loathe [tourist travel] . . . but wandering Jews—or Gentiles—have no choice . . ."; to EC (15 Jul 1903) "It's rather a happy life, something like the Wandering Jew. . . . I picked out a Jew and Jewess for foreign [at a restaurant], but they took the next table and howled Yankee . . ."; and to EC (3 Sep 1905), "My first experiment in Washington was in May, 1850. Since then I've made new ones . . . till it seems to me that the Wandering Jew was a humorous trifler." The expressions seem to posit, at the least, a sense HA had of fellowship between some Americans, beginning with himself, and the wandering Jews of legend and history.

That patterns both of dislike and sympathy could appear in his letters should come as no surprise. He was not a simple man.

56. There was a notable exception: HA and MHA's friendship with Lady Goldsmid. See HA-2, 381, 798–99.

Accidents of life had brought HA into association with persons who were entirely or partly Jewish by descent, and his dealings with some of them had been affectionate, on his part and theirs. The most important instances are HA's dealings with Francis Palgrave and with the children of Arii Taimai and her deceased husband, Alexander Salmon. (Palgrave was raised a Christian. HA's adoptive brothers and sisters in Polynesia were raised as Christians.) For further details, see HA-2, index entries for Palgrave, Marau Taaroa, Tati Salmon, Perry Belmont, and Charles and Hartman Kuhn.

57. Bradford Perkins, *The Great Rapprochement/ England and the United States*,

1895–1914, NY 1968, 76: —". . . [the] collapse of Baring left control of all the great banking houses in the hands of Jews and foreigners. . . ."

58. The English banker and HA were alike in avoiding notice. See Youssef Cassis, *City Bankers/1890-1914*, Cambridge Univ. Press, 1994, 91:—". . . [Lord Rothschild] . . . reigned from the shadows while his brother Alfred occupied the more conspicuous positions." Presumably HA was aware of the parallel.

59. The best evidence that the English had a history of using "Jew" in place of "banker" or "moneylender" is Portia's line in *The Merchant of Venice* when she is first in the presence of two strangers: Antonio, a merchant and ship-owner, and Shylock, a banker or moneylender. She asks (1623 folio), "Which is the Merchant heere? and which the Jew?"

HA can appear to have acquired this trick of speech, or an adaptation thereof, while living in England in 1861–1868.

Of the 402 occurrences of the word "Jew" and variants in his letters in the period embraced by this book, a clear majority—219—are rightly read in my view as terms referring, not to Jews as Jews or to Jews generally, but to the richest and most powerful bankers, brokers, capitalists, or their relations, whether Jewish or not Jewish. It must be added that HA uses the terms in this way only in his most private letters, where they function often as a form of shorthand. He avoids the terms, so used, in works written for publication, such as his "Cameron" speeches and his *Recognition of Cuban Independence*.

60. For his motive as personal, see HA to Hay, 5 Nov 1893:—". . . I can't forgive them [the gold-bugs] their massacre of my friends[,] who are being cleaned out and broken down by dozens."

61. See "Cameron's Obliging Speech," *New York Times*, 26 Sep 1893, 5. The newspaper reported that Cameron had scarcely spoken in the Senate since last elected. "The Pennsylvania Senator is not in the habit of making speeches. He is supposed to think a good deal, but the public is seldom given an opportunity to hear his thoughts uttered. . . . His speech to-day [*sic*] is taken as an evidence simply of his desire to serve his friends in the Senate . . . to whom he is under obligations for good 'turns' done in the past."

After listing Cameron's friends (Senators Butler, Wolcott, Vest, and Brice), the *Times* continued: "To those who know something of the inclinations which rule Mr. Cameron's actions, it seems not unlikely that he decided that the generous thing for him would be to make a speech advocating all the things his friends would like to see accomplished. . . ." "It did not take Mr. Cameron long to read this wonderful presentment. All his friends were in the chamber, and it was remarked that they seemed to be amused at his effort."

62. *New York Herald*, 26 Sep 1893, 9. The paper's alarm was clearly shown in the headlines: "CAMERON DEFIES HIS CONSTITUENTS./ Pennsylvania's Senator Treats with Contempt His Party's Demand for Repeal./ Proclaims Adherence to Silver./ His State Wants Sound Money, but His Senatorial Chums Have Greater Influence./ Business Men Must Speak./ Senators Should Be Made to Realize How Earnest Is Their Demand for Speedy Action."

63. *New York Sun*, 28 Sep 1893, p. 3, under the headings "THE REPEAL DEBATE. Senator Cameron's Speech. . . . / *From the Congressional Record, Sept. 26.*"

64. HA to Hay, 28 Sep 1893. HA was willing to suggest to Hay that Cameron's speech was written partly or wholly by someone else, but there is no evidence that he was willing to suggest the same to members of his family.

BA was supplied the speech, presumably by HA's sending him a pamphlet copy. BA took it to be Cameron's own work. He wrote to HA, "I have read Mr[.] Cameron's speech and was so delighted that I ventured to write him a little note." See BA to HA, 26 Sep 1893.

65. Principal source 12. "Remonetization of Silver" was the first of three speeches read by Cameron to the Senate on 25 Sep 1893, 30 Oct 1893, & 18 April 1894 respectively. Consistent in style and content, the speeches were manifestly the work of a single writer.

Levenson and his associates say about the first speech (L, IV, 131n2): "A partial draft of Cameron's speech, in HA's hand, is at the Massachusetts Historical Society." The statement is mistaken. The draft in HA's hand is an attempt—perhaps an initial attempt—to draft the *second* speech, the one delivered before the Senate by Cameron on 30 Oct 1893. See HA, *Note Book/Manners & Customs*, HAL. Because it is sufficient evidence that HA wrote the second speech, the draft in HA's hand is also sufficient evidence that he wrote all three.

The first and second speeches were off-printed as pamphlets. In 1955, while reading the Henry Adams Papers at the Massachusetts Historical Society, I found a copy of each pamphlet among the papers then boxed as "Miscellaneous." When the Henry Adams Papers were filmed in the 1970s, the two pamphlets were not included in the roll labeled "Miscellaneous." I regard the omission as an editorial mistake. It seems to me that HA kept the pamphlets among his papers to indicate his being their author.

66. HA's *Remonetization of Silver* makes no reference to Jews. It is explicitly directed against "moneyed power" and "moneyed interests." The terms apparently reflect a conscious determination by HA to make wealth the issue and to avoid making issues of religion or race.

67. HA built into the speech two of his long-standing ideas: that Pennsylvania was the one state whose interests as a rule were identical with those of the Union generally, and that Pennsylvania had played the role of mediator between the other states—or between the country's sections—when they were at odds. I believe that these ideas especially met with Cameron's approval.

3. ACTIVITIES OF DIFFERENT KINDS

Letters by and to HA are in HA-micro 11, B, or H, unless otherwise indicated.

PRINCIPAL SOURCES

(1) thirteen letters, HA to EC, 8 Oct 1893–16 Apr 1894.

(2) nine letters, HA to Hay, 18 Oct 1893–11 Apr 1894.

(3) three letters, HA to CMG, 16 Nov 1893–23 Jan 1894.

(4) seven letters, EC to HA, 26 Dec 1893–10 Apr 1894.

(5) HA, "Prayer to the Dynamo" as included in "Prayer to the Virgin of Chartres," appended to HA to EC, 25 Feb 1901, HA-micro 17; also L, V, 206–12.

(6) same, as included in HA's MS. of "Prayer to the Virgin of Chartres" in notebook titled "The Yellow Ribbon," HA-micro Miscellaneous.

(7) [HA], *Speech of Hon. James Donald Cameron of Pennsylvania in the Senate of the United States, Monday, October 30, 1893*—HA's copy, MHS; together with HA's partial MS. of same in *Note Book/Manners and Customs*, HAL. (See Chap. 2, note 65, above; also note 44, below.)

(8) [HA], *Memoirs of Marau Taaroa/Last Queen of Tahiti,* Wash (privately printed) 1893.

(9) [HA], speech beginning "Mr. CAMERON. Mr. President, for a hundred years . . . ," *Congressional Record,* 18 Apr 1894, 3819–20. (New attribution. See Chap. 2, note 65, above.)

LESSER SOURCES; CITATIONS; COMMENTS

1. For the date of composition, see note 3, below.

2. The links between the headings of HA's satire, Hamlet's lines (II, ii—1623 Folio), Satan's address (IV, 32–113), and HA's stanzas should be evident to readers. See principal sources 5 & 6.

3. "Prayer to the Dynamo" appears among HA's writings only within his "Prayer to the Virgin of Chartres." Principal sources 5 & 6 are the surviving MSS.

As published by Mabel Hooper La Farge in *Letters to a Niece,* Bost & NY, 1920, 128–30, "Prayer to the Virgin of Chartres"—including "Prayer to the Dynamo"—inaccurately follows principal source 6. HA's spelling, capitalization, and punctuation are changed. Most disturbing is the change from a dash to a hyphen between the last words of the last line of "Prayer to the Dynamo." The version published by Ernest & Jayne Samuels as editors of HA, *Novels/Mont Saint Michel/ The Education,* NY: Library of America, 1983, 1204–05, reproduces Mrs. La Farge's defective version.

In both principal source 5 and principal source 6, "Prayer to the Dynamo" is set off as a distinct entity. Yet the poem has usually not been read as a separate work, and its date of composition has not been a matter of concern. I suggest it was written in October 1893, that HA later matched it with his "Prayer to the Virgin of Chartres," and that he so shaped the latter that it could include the former.

In support of the date, one can say (1) that HA had just had his first known experience of seeing dynamos; (2) that one of his traits was celerity: he tended to act or write soon rather than late; (3) that "Prayer to the Dynamo" involves mention of interests of his that were strong in 1893, including electricity, light, and the atom; (4) that the "dead Atom" mentioned in the last stanza parallels the "dead molecule" prominent in his letter to Langley of 3 May 1893; and (5) that the letter to Langley, with its mention of Maxwell's "demon," and HA's letter to Hay of 18 Oct 1893, with its phrase "a devil of a thinking," are consonant with "Prayer to the Dynamo," in which humanity figures as thinker, perhaps even *demoniac* thinker. See L, IV, 99–101, 134.

One notices also the passage in HA's *Education* about the Chicago Fair, especially the sentences beginning, "One lingered long among the dynamos, for they were new, and they gave to history a new phase." See *EHA* (1907) 298–99; (LoA), 1033. The sentences leave no doubt that for HA dynamos meant Chicago and October 1893.

4. HA's choice of "atom" is partly humorous. He was not above puns. "Adams," "Adam," and "Atom" had put temptations in his way too great to be resisted. See HA-2, 892, all pages indexed under "Adam"; and 909, all pages indexed under *Radical Club. A Poem. . . .*

5. The title "Prayer to the Dynamo" can be defended as suitable to the poem if the words "the Dynamo" are read as a metaphor suggesting the universe, with its internal rotations, its electromagnetic currents, its permeation by light, its mystery, and its unaccountability.

6. It needs emphasis that the person so acting is not HA. The poem is one of many instances of his attempting to reach conclusions without regard to himself and his own interests.

7. The extracts quoted here are taken from principal source 5.

8. The stanza ends with an image of crucifixion. The image may involve both a king that is and a king that may come to be. See note 15, below.

9. "God" appears only in stanza 8 in the phrase "by the God we now hold tight." In context, "God" cannot mean God as usually meant. It *can* mean "thought" believed in as "God." "Thought" appears in the poem (stanza 6). "Science" does not. It can be urged, however, that for HA in 1893 "thought" and "science" were often synonymous.

10. To avoid the repetition of "space," HA later changed "in space" to "apace." See principal source 6. The change appears in the MS. as an ink correction. Whether it is an improvement may be debated.

11. By raising the question whether molecules could die, HA in his letter to Langley had verged on asking whether molecules (or atoms) could also be analyzed into parts, dismembered, or killed.

12. The two lines owe some of their force and much of their meaning to HA's ending them with "spring." The metaphor can suggest that the atom is metallic and that at its center it is bent or coiled like a spring under tension. The metaphor can suggest too that the atom at its center is a source of energy much as springs are sources of water. Thus the metaphor can also suggest a *flow* of energy.

Because the metaphor embraces the metallic and the liquid, the meaning of the lines is helpfully imprecise. The lines do not assume that the nature of the atom is known. They instead suggest that a secret is going to be learned.

13. It is impossible to believe that HA wrote the expression "Me—the dead Atom" without remembering his authorship in 1875 of *The Radical Club/A Poem . . . by an Atom*. It is equally impossible to believe that he wrote the word-sequence "Atom—King" without being reminded of his friendship with Clarence King. Although evident, the references are inoperative in the poem. Readers trying to grasp the meaning of the poem may best treat both references as irrelevant.

14. HA did not value the poem as poetry. He treated it as not good enough to be shown by itself to anyone, and only good enough to be quoted within a longer poem and to be described therein as "curious." See the first line following "Prayer to the Dynamo" in principal source 5 or 6.

15. The concluding stanza begins with an image which readers would associate with the Tower of London: torture on a rack by order of a monarch. There follows an image familiar to readers of Prescott's *Conquest of Mexico*: Aztec extrications of the hearts of still-living human sacrifices. A Biblical image comes next: a victim ground by millstones. Considering that the first stanza invokes a crucifixion, the poem as a whole must be viewed as dealing with the violent.

The expression "the Atom" in the last stanza appears in part to be a title interchangeable with "King."

The capitalization of "Atom" may suggest that the Atom is the first creation of the Force and a kind of Son—a touch both Biblical and Miltonic.

The stanza makes clear that, when seized and bereft of its heart, "the Atom" may bleed and its blood may "annoint" (*sic*) the Speaker of the poem. Moreover, the anointing blood may have power to make the unroyal royal, and a coronation may be effected by which the Speaker may suddenly become a replacement Atom! The stanza also suggests that the Speaker's coronation may

be instantaneously fatal, in which case both Atoms die and the human Atom—
the new King—plays the ironic simultaneous roles of dead winner and second
loser.

All things considered, the poem anticipates that the seizure and dissection
of the atom will occur and be momentous but will have as its first properties its
being violent and its being exceedingly unsafe for humans beings when they try
it.

16. L, IV, 130.

17. Although there is no evidence that they knew the secret, there are
strong reasons for believing the MacVeaghs were told. HA had trusted Wayne
MacVeagh with secrets in the past. Mrs. MacVeagh was Cameron's sister. For
Cameron, EC, and HA, telling the MacVeaghs the new secret was the obvious
best protection against their guessing HA's authorship and imparting their
guess to other persons.

18. Issue of 31 Oct 1893. The quoted words are preceded by headlines
saying, "Money May Now Be Safely Invested, Mills and Factories May Resume
and Labor May Return to Its Wage."

19. *EHA* (1907), 300–01; (LoA), 1034–35.

20. Principal source 7, p. 8:—"The influence, whatever it is, which is responsible for the present bill, certainly does not command the confidence of a
majority of the Senate."

In effect, HA restated this sentence and made it fully explicit in the following lines of *The Education*:—". . . [Adams] fell headlong into the extra-session of
Congress called to repeal the Silver Act. The silver minority made an obstinate
attempt to prevent it, and most of the majority had little heart in the creation of
a single gold standard. The Banks alone, and the dealers in exchange, insisted
upon it. . . ." See *EHA* (1907), 300; (LoA), 1034.

21. For lack of other choices, parts of HA's neglected program would later
be adopted. An instance is the duty on sugar introduced in the tariff bill passed
by Congress in 1894.

22. Parkman to HA, 28 Jan 1891, HA-micro 8.

23. L, IV, 137.

24. The printer is named in a letter, Phillips to John La Farge, 13 Jul 1896.
See Ira N. Hayward, "From Tahiti to Chartres: The Henry Adams-John La Farge
Friendship," *Huntington Library Quarterly*, August 1958, 349.

25. Levenson and his associates say there were "ten copies" (L, IV, 149n1).
They do not cite a source, and I know of none. Yet ten may be correct. HA
evidently sent two copies to Tahiti for correction and return. One came back
and is in HAL. It bears corrections and additions by Tati Salmon and HA. It
presumably was used as a copy text when the final version, *Memoirs of Arii Taimai*,
was privately printed in Paris in 1900–1901. The other apparently was not returned and may be the copy described as "dans la bibliothèque océanienne du
Père O'Reilly." See HA, *Mémoires d'Arii Taimai*, Paris 1964, xx. There originally
was an unmarked duplicate in HAL. It was sold to Parkman Howe and is now
owned by the University of Florida. A copy given to La Farge is owned by the
Huntington Library. A copy given to Hay is owned by Brown. Harvard owns a
copy given by HA to Phillips, a copy obtained from HA by LHT, and a copy
donated by a book collector. A copy given to EC, whereabouts uncertain, may
be the one given to Harvard by the collector. These copies number only eight.

26. E.g., see page 63:—"I have before me, among the late King's papers, a
quantity of genealogical matter, but all so contradictory and so little capable of
proof that it will not hold together."

27. Except possibly Tati Salmon at a late date, HA told no one that he meant to transfer the book from Queen Marau to Arii Taimai. Phillips was the American friend most interested in HA's Tahiti work. He was misinformed. Writing to La Farge in 1896, he said, ". . . when the work is complete, he [HA] intends to print it in a manner suitable to the dignity of the memoirs of a Queen." See Hayward, "From Tahiti to Chartres," op. cit., 349.

28. Purea was a nickname. Her complete Tahitian name was Te vahine Airorotua i Ahurai i Farepua. Her shorter Tahitian name was Airorotua. See principal source 8, p. 48.

29. Purea's behavior moved HA to say in the *Memoirs of Marau Taaroa*, 48:—"If a family must be ruined by a woman, perhaps it may as well be ruined thoroughly and brilliantly by a woman who makes it famous." The line is the most memorable in the book. When he transformed the *Memoirs of Marau Taaroa* into the *Memoirs of Arii Taimai*, HA kept the line but so reorganized the text that the line lost its centrality.

30. Principal source 8, p. 10.

31. Ibid., 66.

32. Ibid., 72.

33. Ibid., 103.

34. Ibid., 109.

35. HA gave Phillips a copy of the book. The result was a letter from Phillips, now missing. HA replied (O.1894.1):—"I'm really glad you like Marau. It's the kind of history I like to write. . . ."

36. HA's calling himself an anarchist preceded by five months the earliest record of BA's making a parallel claim. See BA to HA, 6 May 1894: "Think of me—the *anarchist.*"

37. The reference is to lines in Shakespeare's *Julius Caesar* (I, ii—1623 folio):

> Let me have men about me, that are fat,
> Sleeke-headed men, and such as sleep a-nights:
> Yond *Cassius* has a leane and hungry looke;
> He thinkes too much: such men are dangerous.

In HA's opinion, it seems, fat Grover Cleveland thought too little and was dangerous for that reason.

38. Three letters, BA to HA, 8 Oct 1893, 15 Oct 1893, & 25 Nov 1893. See also Chap. 2, note 48, above.

39. HA preserved watercolors he painted during his stays at Coffin's Point and in Cuba. See reproductions in L, IV, following 150.

40. One may assume that HA proposed to pay their expenses and later did so, but evidence is lacking.

41. The vehemence of HA's anti-banker animus in evident in two letters. See HA to Hay, 4 Jan 1894:—"When the Rothschilds have failed, and the Bank of England has suspended, I shall begin to look for light. . . ." See HA to CMG, 23 Jan 1894, saying he detests the age in which he is living, "with all its infernal Jewry." "I want to put every money-lender to death, and to sink Lombard Street and Wall Street under the ocean."

(The word "Jewry" is the only occurrence of "Jew" and its variants in his writings during the period embraced by this chapter.)

42. HA to EC, 16 Feb 1894.

43. King to Hay, 16 May [1894], HP.

44. EC had written to HA on his fifty-sixth birthday, 16 Feb 1894: "I hope you see the papers, for they are full of the fall in silver, the petitions of India for the re-openings of the mints and many silver items which all point the same way. Last of all, the discovery of a gang in Cincinnati who have been carrying on *your* scheme of coining a better silver dollar than Uncle Sam does, and making money galore at it." Her reference was to HA's second speech, read to the Senate by her husband on 30 Oct 1893. There HA had explained: "The new policy [suggested by President Cleveland] looks to a further fall in the value [i.e. price] of silver bullion. Any fall, which causes much further decline, must render silver coin a very dangerous medium for the Government to use as money. With modern appliances, and with little capital, a skillful mechanic could coin a silver dollar identical with the Government dollar—perhaps not to be distinguished from it—in any quantity, and with little risk of detection."

The importance of EC's reference to the speech lies in her attributing the explanation about counterfeiting exclusively to HA.

Clearly she fully knew the story of his sole authorship of the speeches her husband read to the Senate. And clearly she regarded HA's speech-writing with approval.

45. Her impulse to tell him was perhaps the stronger because her husband had left Coffin's Point and was again in Washington.

46. HA could not escape seeing that EC was calling him her savior, and he could not read her phrase "pastures green" without remembering both the phrase "green pastures" in the twenty-third Psalm and the phrase "pastures new" at the end of Milton's "Lycidas"—a poem that acts as a redemption.

47. Principal source 8, p. 7.

48. Being genealogically-minded Polynesians, Marau and Tati could feel their relationship with Purea as close. She was their great-great-great-great-aunt-by-marriage.

49. Salmon to HA, 9 Mar 1894.

50. BA to HA, 1 Jan 1894; CFA2 to HA, 19 Jan 1894.

51. The simplicity of style sustained throughout the three speeches should not be taken as evidence that they were written by Cameron. The simplicity was of a kind that required a powerful intellect and exceptional mastery of language.

52. HA was a scientific historian but not an anthropologist and not a biologist. He freely used "race," "people," and "nation" as synonyms. All three terms were important to him, if only because history in his opinion was made for the most part by nations or peoples or races, as distinguished from individuals.

53. *New York Herald*, 19 Apr 1894, 7. The report is especially valuable for saying Cameron "read from typewritten sheets." One may assume that all three of HA's speeches were typed at Cameron's direction and that HA's manuscripts were destroyed.

54. In London in the 1860s, HA had been converted to British ideas of free trade. A measure of the degree to which he rethought his ideas as the start of his third life is his return to American protectionism. The near-failure of Baring Brothers was the first stimulus to reconsideration. The ensuing crash in New York was another. The principal determinant was the Panic of 1893. It changed his mind.

55. Entries in HA's engagement books, HAL, dated 15 Jan, 14, 27 May 1862; 27 Jun 1866; & 29 Jan, 4 Jul, & 29 Dec 1967.

56. See "mugwump" in the *Century Dictionary*, then newly issued.

57. Having redefined the word in a speech, HA used it in his letters. See

HA to EC, 6 Jul 1894:—". . . your husband . . . the only safe and reactionary mugwump in the country . . . alone represents the interests of capital." Also HA to Louisa Hooper, 29 Sep 1894—"My winter plans are vague as a mugwump's politics." And HA to EC, 2 Oct 1894—"The next Congress will not be aristocratic, still less mugwump."

58. *New York Sun*, 19 Apr 1894, 5.

4. THE LOOKOUT

Letters by and to HA are in HA-micro 11, 12, B, or H, unless otherwise indicated.

PRINCIPAL SOURCES

(1) fourteen letters, HA to Hay, 26 Apr 1894–10 Mar 1895.

(2) five letters, HA to CMG, 28 Apr 1894–16 Feb 1895.

(3) twenty-four letters, HA to EC, Thursday [17 May 1894]-10–14 Mar 1895. (The letter headed "Thursday" is filmed at the end of 1893 in HA-micro 11 but omitted from L and O. With regard to its date, see note 9, below. The letter beginning "Yarrow" is filmed in HA-micro 12 at the start of November 1895. It should be dated [? May 1894]. It is omitted from L and O.)

(4) twenty-two letters, EC to HA, Tues [Jul 1894]-30 Mar 1895.

(5) letter, HA (as president of AHA) to Herbert Baxter Adams (as secretary of AHA), 12 Dec 1894, L, IV, 228–34.

(6) same as printed in *Annual Report of the American Historical Association for the Year 1894*, Wash 1895, 17–23, under a title, "The Tendency of History," not written by HA but based on terms used in the second paragraph of his letter.

LESSER SOURCES; CITATIONS; COMMENTS

1. LHT to the author, 21 Nov 1963.

2. The phrase "proposed book" is BA's. See *Degradation*, 96.

3. It needs emphasis that BA believed that Cameron wrote the speeches he had read to the Senate. See Chap. 2, note 64, above.

4. See Chap. 2, note 48, above.

5. Prior to publishing his pamphlet, BA had revealed his leanings in an article, "Gold Supply and Demand," *Boston Herald*, 21 Mar 1894. He soon after said that some Bostonians who had espoused bimetallism had begun to "squirm under the literature they have helped to bring into being." See BA to HA, 9 May 1894. BA named no names, but a person he must have had in mind was Lodge. The latter's action had been two-sided. He had both voted for Cleveland's gold standard and joined in the cry for universal bimetallism.

6. BA's research effort in Venice came to nothing. See his *Law of Civilization and Decay*, NY 1896, 167–68.

7. O.1894.16.

8. King to HA, 11 May [1894]:—". . . what I would not give (if I had not pawned everything), to go off to the Yellowstone with you. . . ."

9. Transcript of letter, Mabel Hooper to Ellen Hooper, [17] May 1894, author's collection. Ellen Hooper lent the original to LHT with permission that I copy it. Comparison of Mabel's letter with HA's letter to EC dated "Thursday" and beginning "Looly says she has mumps . . ." (see principal source 3) permits firm dating of both letters.

10. *HUS* (Scribner), VI, 186. For HA's correction, see *HUS* (LoA), II, 422–23.

11. HA to Thwing, 2 May 1894, L, IV, 187 & 187n1.

12. For details about Cameron's letter, see L, IV, 197n1.

13. HA to EC, 6 Jul 1894.

14. See HA to CFA2, 24 Sep 1894, written almost twelve weeks later. In *The New Century Dictionary* (1927), Bright's disease is defined as "kidney disease, attended with albuminuria."

15. King wanted HA to go with him to the mine, but HA demurred. See King to HA, 4 Jun [1894], filmed out of sequence in HA-micro 11 as if dated in January.

16. See "Grand Teton. From Pacific Creek Camp. 8 August 1894" and "Showery Evening at Cache Creek. 29 August 1894," L, IV, following 150.

17. Hooper to HA, 25 Aug 1894. According to Hooper, JQA2 had been thought to be the victim of "malarial fever." He eventually had a slight stroke. A severe stroke followed. On August 14, he "had another stroke of apoplexy, or something, and died within an hour."

18. Letters, HA to EC, 13 Sep 1894 & 25 Sep 1894.

19. HA to Mabel Hooper, 6 Oct 1894.

20. HA to EC, 25 Sep 1894.

21. Ever since Clover Adams's death in 1885, King had been trying to arrange HA's going with him to Mexico. Recently he had urged their going to Martinique and Trinidad. See letters, King to HA, 11 May [1894] & 22 Jul [1894].

22. The final version of HA's Tahiti book bears on its half title page the words "Travels/ Tahiti." Both versions of his *Mont Saint Michel and Chartres* say on their half title pages, "Travels/ France." Because the books were printed and bound to seem uniform with each other and are uniform in appearance with *The Education of Henry Adams* as privately printed, it can come as almost a surprise or puzzle that the half title page of *The Education* does not also say "Travels."

23. HA to Anne Fell, Friday, [16 Nov 1894]. The conjectural date given by Levenson and his associates—[9 Nov 1894]—seems to me to be one week too early. See O.1894.23.

24. Letters, BA to HA, 22 Nov 1894 & 5 Dec 1894.

25. Hale had served when only nineteen as assistant secretary of the U. S. delegation to the International Bimetallic Conference in Brussels. See *Who's Who in America*, VIII [1914–1915]. It seems more than likely that he became well-acquainted with HA shortly after returning from the conference.

26. HA to EC, Saturday, 23 [Dec 1893].

27. In his "Report of Proceedings of the Tenth Annual Meeting of the American Historical Association," Herbert Baxter Adams characterized the meeting as a "scientific convention" held by one of the country's "scientific bodies." See AHA, *Annual Report* for 1894, 1.

28. HA to CMG, 28 Apr 1894. In this instance, echoing Pearson, HA uses the word "races" in a way keyed to pigmentation of the skin.

29. HA to CMG, 15 Jun 1894. HA's annotations in the first volume of Karl Marx, *Capital*, trans. by Moore and Aveling, Lond 1887, HAL, show mounting impatience with Marx's hair-splitting definitions. E.g., 34: "This beats me. Nothing more German was ever written than this complication of Value, Values, and forms of value."

30. What HA learned from Marx's *Capital* is clear only up to a point. By

linking Marx's book with Pearson's, he indicated that he was finding that books were becoming partial in two senses: the sense of being incomplete and the sense of being partisan. He possibly also learned to discount Marx's socialist theorizing as sophistical and fallacious.

31. Quotations from the letter appear as printed in principal source 6. HA's capitalization and punctuation are normalized in this version without affecting the sense.

32. Under a title "The Tendency of History" not of HA's choosing, the letter would shortly be published at the front of the *Annual Report of the American Historical Association for the year 1894* and in 1896 for unknown reasons would be off-printed as a pamphlet. (For details, see Chap. 6.) In 1919, the letter would be included in a fast-selling volume, *The Degradation of the Democratic Dogma*, for which Brooks Adams bore responsibility. (For details, see Chap. 27.)

Unfortunately, from 1894 to 1919, the letter was mistaken for a sort of Rosetta stone which interested persons could use to decipher a supposedly otherwise not decipherable philosophy of history thought to be locked in HA's inscrutable mind. (E.g. see Charles A. Beard's Introduction to BA's *Law of Civilization and Decay*, NY 1943, 13–14.) But as the words quoted here plainly state, HA's letter did *not* set forth his philosophy of history. Instead it concerned a professional situation faced by America's historians. Specifically it expressed HA's fear of, and opposition to, what he took to be the pessimism of Europe.

33. The sentences suggested in effect that history would not be a science until historians had become as capable of foretelling human events as astronomers were of calculating where the planets would be at future times. The suggestion was absurd for obvious reasons. Human beings were not planets; and sciences were sciences before, as well as after, their practioners arrived at conclusions.

That HA saw the suggestion as absurd can be assumed. He wrote it. His very evident motive was to give members of the association an opportunity to sense the absurdity as well as he could. He did indeed write his letter "in the paradoxical spirit of private conversation." This was a spirit that reached for contradiction.

34. HA to EC, 25 & 27 December 1894.

35. HA to Louisa Hooper, 6 Jan 1895.

36. HA to CMG, 16 Feb 1895.

37. HA to Louisa Hooper, 6 Jan 1895.

38. EC to HA, 8–10 Feb 1895.

39. HA to EC, 12–18 Feb 1895.

40. HA to EC, 12 Feb 1895.

41. A year earlier, HA had used the phrase "infernal Jewry." See Chap. 3, note 41, above.

42. There are four occurrences of the word "Jew" and its variants in HA's writings during the period embraced by this chapter. The two quoted here occur in HA to EC, 12–18 Feb 1895.

43. HA to Lucy Baxter, 26 Sep 1894. "Hebraisation" in one of the four occurrences mentioned in note 42.

44. HA to EC, 8 Mar [1895].

45. HA to EC, 10–14 Mar [1895].

46. Ibid.

47. For HA's presence in the city, see telegram, HA & Hale to Mary Leiter, [9 Apr 1895], together with HA's letter to same, 11 Apr 1895, L, IV, 267–68.

48. Mrs. Walters to HA, 11 Nov 1894, attached by HA to his letter to Ford, 11 Feb 1911, FP 15.

49. HA held a generally low opinion of portraits.

50. HA to Phillips, 19 Dec 1894. HA anticipated that "Pell" would prove to be Charles Willson Peale. See L, IV, 227–28, notes 2 & 3; also L, VI, 193n2.

51. Barron to HA, 1 May 1895, attached by HA to his letter to Ford, 11 Feb 1911, FP 15. Also see HA to CFA2, 12 Jul 1900, HA-micro 16.

52. For an example of HA's knowledge of his Adams forebears, see HA to CFA2, Saturday, 16 May [1896].

5. VISION AND REVOLUTION

Letters by and to HA are in HA-micro 12, 13, B, or H, unless other wise indicated.

PRINCIPAL SOURCES

(1) fifteen letters, HA to CMG, 25 Apr 1895–1 Apr 1896.

(2) seven letters, HA to Hay, 26 Apr–14 Nov 1895.

(3) eighteen letters, HA to EC, 11 May–19 Oct 1895.

(4) eight letters, EC to HA, 26 May–[18 Sep?] 1895.

(5) fourteen letters, HA to BA, 5 Jun 1895–18 Feb 1896.

(6) HA, "Count Edward de Crillon," *American Historical Review*, Vol. I, No. 1 (Oct 1895), 51–69.

(7) [HA], *Recognition of Cuban Independence*, Senate Report No. 1160, 54th Congress, 2d Session, ordered to be printed 21 Dec 1896, 1–25. (HA's authorship is universally conceded. The report was first attributed to him in JTA, *Bibliography of the Writings of Henry Adams*, NY 1930.)

LESSER SOURCES; CITATIONS; COMMENTS

1. HA to Lucy Baxter, 15 Jun 1895, L, IV, 286–87.

2. LHT to the author, 19 Jan 1965; Abigail Adams Homans, *Education by Uncles*, Bost 1966, 41.

3. HA to Abigail Adams, 22 Apr [1895].

4. HA to CMG, 25 Apr 1895.

5. Ibid.

6. CFA2 to HA, 22 April 1895.

7. Letters, CFA2 to HA, 12 May 1895 & 26 May 1895. HA had already said he would "never touch" their father's biography. See HA to CFA2, 26 Apr 1895.

8. Five letters, CFA2 to HA, 11, 15, 29 Nov 1895; 31 Jan, 16 Feb 1896.

9. For the lie, see HA to CFA2, 2 Feb 1896. The question of records was not simple. HA had long since destroyed his diaries of the 1860s, or those that most mattered, but also he had kept materials of great importance. See note 12.

10. CFA2 had preserved the bulk of HA's early letters. HA knew it and asked (letter of 2 Feb 1896) that his letters be returned to him when not needed. The request was part-and-parcel with an important consideration: HA wished *not* to be mentioned in the biography of CFA. Also see Chap. 9.

11. CFA2 to HA, 16 Feb 1896.

12. CFA2 was aware that HA had a complete run of the *Index*, the weekly newspaper published by the Confederacy in London. When CFA2 explicitly asked for it, HA instantly sent it. See CFA2 to HA, 18 Feb 1896; HA to CFA2, 21 Feb 1896.

13. The wedding took place on 22 Apr 1895 in Washington. Presumably HA did not attend. As a rule, after his wife died, he refused to go to weddings.

14. Two months after the wedding, Hay wrote to HA: "It is curious what a step Curzon made in marrying. Last year he was never thought of for Cabinet rank—now it is a matter of course." See Hay to HA, 27 Jun [1895].

15. HA to EC, Thursday, 16 [May 1895].

16. BA to HA, 7 Mar 1887.

17. When writing his introduction to a reprint of the New York version of BA's *Law of Civilization and Decay*, NY 1943, Charles A. Beard misread BA's 14 May 1895 letter as dated 14 May 1894. See p. 8. The one-year error permitted Beard to form a very wrong impression of the pace at which BA's book was developed.

18. As the text of the published book makes clear, "law," "civilization," and "decay" were words BA used increasingly when writing his later chapters and the preface. One accordingly may guess that Evelyn and her husband found all the materials for the needed title simply by paying closer attention to what BA had written.

19. Three letters, BA to HA, 21 Sep, 13 Oct, 23 Dec 1895.

20. BA to HA, 24 Jun 1895.

21. In a letter to Wayne MacVeagh, 10 Oct 1895, O.1895.40–41, HA later sketched what happened.

22. BA to HA, 2 Jun 1895.

23. HA's saying he wanted a "trial of strength" might be taken to mean that he wanted an American declaration of war with England. But HA was a diplomat. He understood shades of difference in *diplomatic* trials of strength. His phrase may best be taken to indicate his favoring a diplomatic challenge to England so peremptory that England could escape from war only by making a concession sufficient to make war unnecessary from the American point of view.

The matter is complicated by HA's saying he thinks it time that "the *political* existence of England should cease in North America [italics added]." Clearly he favored a total severance of the ties between England and Canada.

The problem he had most in mind was the shattering effects of England's financial management on the economic well-being of the United States. One accordingly may infer that he wanted an American challenge requiring that England (a) make a financial concession and (b) sever its remaining ties with Canada. By demanding two things, the United States might get one. The one that mattered more had little to do with Canada and much to do with England's squeezing gold from her debtors in the Western Hemisphere and throughout the world.

24. The version of BA's *Law of Civilization and Decay* published in London in 1895 became a rare book. The definitive version is the French translation, published in Paris in 1899. It too is a rare book. I accordingly have keyed this chapter to the second version in English, published in New York in 1896 and many times reprinted.

BA's ideas relating to "nature" and its venting "energy" by creating races can be found at innumerable points in the preface and ensuing chapters. An unhelpful phrase, "oscillations between barbarism and civilization," appears in the preface. The phrase is unhelpful because it suggests movement in two directions. Elsewhere BA makes it clear that he sees races as gravitating or evolving in one direction only. His book illustrates the "law" with examples, most notably the evolution of a society of farmer-soldiers centered in Rome into a commercial

"Roman" empire centered in Constantinople, and the evolution of a society of Norman farmer-soldiers into a commercial "British" empire centered in London and controlled by usurers.

25. *EHA* (1907), 296; (LoA), 1030.

26. When teaching at Harvard, HA had practiced his principles, most notably by following the lead of the young German historian Rudolph Sohm. See *SKETCHES* and HA-2, all index entries under "Sohm."

27. See principal source 6 in its entirety.

28. BA wanted HA to visit Sonnenschein and lend assistance relating to the index and advertising. See letters, BA to HA, 24 Jun 1895 & 30 Jun 1895. Later HA helped as asked.

29. Kipling to HA, 30 Jun 1895. For HA and Kipling's acquaintance, see Chap. 1 and *EHA* (1907), 276, 278–79; (LoA), 1009, 1011–12.

30. BA to HA, 19 Jun 1895.

31. HA to Frewen, [14? Jul 1895], 0.1895.24. With respect to labeling themselves, HA and BA had similar but not identical tendencies. BA had recently become notorious in Boston for being an "anarchist." See BA to HA, 2 Feb 1895:—". . . people . . . look at me askance and say 'there goes an anarchist'." BA also claimed to be a "revolutionist." See BA to HA, 30 Jun 1895:—"I am a revolutionist, that is why I am treated as I am."

BA's labels for himself were humorless. Very differently, HA's labels for himself were simultaneously humorous and serious, with implied—possibly subtle—meanings. It is not a waste of effort to try to see what the meanings were.

32. In his earliest surviving letter to HA, 14 Apr 1896, young Lodge says, "You have the . . . distinction of being, except myself, the only conservative anarchist I know." He closes, "Ever yours in Conservative Anarchy."

These expressions should be compared with HA's statement in *The Education*: "Bay Lodge and Joe Stickney had given birth to the wholly new and original party of Conservative Christian Anarchists. . . ." See *EHA* (1907), 354; (LoA), 1090.

HA's attributing to Lodge and Stickney the invention of a party of Conservative Christian Anarchists is one of his innumerable self-effacing fictions. HA himself devised the form "Conservative Anarchist." When Bay Lodge first learned to use the form, HA had already shifted to "conservative and religious anarchist." It was only a short jump from the second form to the ultimate third: "Conservative Christian Anarchist." HA made the jump alone. See HA to Spring Rice, 8 Feb 1901, HA-micro 17:—"I am the original Conservative Christian Anarchist."

33. The proofs were discarded, so there is no telling what changes HA had made. One may say, however, that BA had the assistance of a highly capable editor.

34. HA to EC, 25 July [1895].

35. In HA's letters written in 1894, there are three occurrences of the word "Jew" and its variants. In 1895, there are 37; in 1896, 63. The upsurge can be seen as late and as illustrating how little willing HA was to deal with the subject till after he was heavily pressed.

His letters of 1895 and 1896 also contain seven references to Nathaniel Rothschild or Rothschilds generally and 24 to J. P. Morgan.

36. HA to EC, 3 Aug 1895.

37. BA to HA, 13 Oct 1895:—". . . that awful tragedy, which is the sum of life. The agony of consciousness."

38. HA and Schmidt had agreed that a heavy outflow of gold from the United States to England was approaching and that the "next squeeze" would occur about February 1896. Otherwise, data about what they said to each other is lacking.

39. HA to EC, 19 & 22 Aug 1895.

40. HA to EC, 29–30 Aug 1895.

41. HA to Mabel Hooper, 1 Sep 1895.

42. HA-2, 578, 871n26. The salutation appears in GCL to HA, 14 Apr 1896.

43. When he arrived at Mont Saint Michel, HA already had the idea of writing "Travels" and privately printing them. See Chap. 4. Also he had noticed an instance of an American's traveling in France and writing an instructive book. The book was *Travels through the South of France . . . in the years 1807 and 1808. . .by Lieutenant-Colonel [Ninian] Pinkney, of the North American Native Rangers*, Lond 1809. HA's copy (HAL) is inscribed: "A rare and interesting volume." and "Henry Adams./ 1893."

44. That HA differentiated education for women and education for men and that his paired books represent the differentiation he had in mind cannot be doubted. Yet nowhere in his extant writings does he provide a succinct statement as to what he believed the difference was.

45. See HA-2, 431, 463, 465, 468–72, 477–79, 484–85, 497–99, 515, 833, 835, 844.

46. HA to EC, 12 Sep 1895. There is no contradiction is saying that HA's *Mont Saint Michel and Chartres* was written for his wife and also —as the book would itself declare—that it was written for "nieces." The case involves two independent propositions: (a) HA wrote for MHA in the sense that she was the author for whom he felt himself a substitute; (b) HA wrote for "nieces" in the sense that "nieces" were the readers he thought his book might help transform.

47. The closing phrase reflects HA's feeling that Americans and Jews were currently too interested in money. The places where he most often saw money-mad Americans were New York and Paris. It could not have greatly disappointed him to think that Jews were too interested in money; but it evidently disappointed him deeply that Americans, as he saw them, were money-mad and getting more so.

48. Of the signs that HA was already writing *Mont Saint Michel and Chartres*, one was his saying in letters (as he does in this passage) that he *lived* in the Middle Ages. The statement posits a fictional ego, an "I" who has outlived many centuries and directly remembers far-gone times. The same rhetorical device appears in the completed book.

49. BA to HA, 24 Aug 1895.

50. HA to BA, 8 Sep 1895.

51. HA to EC, 18–19 Sep 1895.

52. HA to EC, 25–27 Sep 1895.

53. HA's belief in the power of British moneyed interests was strong enough to lead him to tell BA (letter of 27 Dec 1895), ". . . Wall Street *is* Rothschild."

54. HA's use of "race" and "nation" as synonyms agrees with American usage. Compare the words "a new nation" in the opening sentence of Lincoln's Gettysburg Address with the following lines spoken by Governor Hancock of Massachusetts in a story by Hawthorne—"Old Esther Dudley" (Part IV of "Legends of the Province House"): ". . . I, and these around me [Hancock's fellow revolutionaries] represent a new race of men—living no longer in the past, scarcely in the present—but projecting our lives forward into the future."

55. For a fuller outline of HA's theory of history, see Chap. 17.

56. HA to EC, 19 Aug 1895.

57. At the risk of seeming facetious when wanting to be the reverse, one can note that the Virgin appears in HA's *Mont Saint Michel and Chartres* both as a controlling person and as a means of transportation—from earth to heaven. In the latter capacity, she somewhat corresponds to the steamboat in HA's *History* and to ocean liners and automobiles in the present narrative.

58. *HUS* (Scribner), I, 176; (LoA), I, 120.

59. In his letter to Mary Curzon, 10 Oct 1895, O.1895.40, HA speaks of Hardy as "the one remaining English novelist whom I was curious to meet."

60. HA to EC, [19 Oct 1895]. HA formed a high opinion of Schmidt but a low one of other Jews he consulted in London. He said they were "beasts at Ephesus—which means the City." "They are secret and banded together; they lie; they cheat the Christians; they are gutter-Jews at that . . . and they own us all." See HA to CMG, 1 Oct 1895.

61. HA to EC, Saturday, [19 Oct 1895].

62. Three letters, King to HA, 13 Nov [1895], 21 Nov [1895], & 28 Nov [1895]; Homans, *Education by Uncles*, op. cit., 45.

63. King to HA, 28 Nov [1895].

64. O.1895.44.

65. L, IV, 346.

66. At this moment, HA may have experienced a coincidence made up of a known element and one or both of two other elements, as follows.

The known element is that HA read a Cleveland-Olney message that could appear to portend the outbreak of war between the United States and England. At the same time, possibly, he was drafting the first version of *Recognition of Cuban Independence* (principal document 7), especially the passage on pp. 20–23 that concerns the near-outbreak of war between the two countries in 1861–1862. Also at the same time, possibly, he was drafting Chap. VIII of his *Education*. This is the chapter in which "Henry Adams" learns that CFA has been appointed minister to England, is commanded by him to go to London, and is present in London during the *Trent* Affair, which strained relations between the United States and England to the near-explosion point.

If it occurred, the coincidence would help account for the passion evident throughout HA's *Recognition of Cuban Independence*. See principal source 7; also note 73, below.

The coincidence would also help account for the anti-British fervor evident in a passage in HA's letter to CFA2, 2 Feb 1896:—"The double-dyed rascality and duplicity of Lord Russell, which our father did not and could not believe, and which I only suspected, has since been proved . . . but in a worse form than I had supposed possible."

67. HA to BA, 27 Dec 1895.

68. The war-scare encouraged HA to tell Lady Curzon (letter of 30 Dec 1895) that he hoped the British navy would bombard New York. "I know no place that would be more improved by it. The chief population is Jew, and the rest is German Jew." His remark reflected his currently acute dislike of New York, his general dislike of Jews, and his special dislike of German Jews. If serious, the remark would be hideous, but it was an *irritated* remark, not a serious one.

No one need suppose that HA wanted a war with England or that he wanted New York's Jews exterminated by 13-inch shells from warships. He wanted peace.

He also wanted universal freedom from a syndicate of European and American bankers, and from the politicians who were most in league with the syndicate.

69. Levenson and his associates assert that HA in February 1896 "was giving information and advice to Gonzalo de Quesada and Horatio Rubens of the unofficial 'Cuban delegation'. . . ." See L, IV, 370n2.

The assertion appears unfounded. The available evidence does not say how many Cubans went to HA's house. It does not name those who went. It does not provide the times of their visits. It provides no clues as to who said what. It leaves open the possibility—indeed the likelihood—that HA met with some of the Cubans only to hear what they would tell him.

70. In his letter to Louisa Hooper, Saturday, 21 [Dec 1895], HA asks her to send him Vol. III of the *Transactions* of the London Missionary Society and says he already has Vols. I & II. She evidently sent the volume, for Vol. III is cited at the beginning of the chapter of the revised *Memoirs* that carries the narrative forward from its earlier stopping point. See *Memoirs of Arii Taimai*, 149.

71. HA to BA, 27 Dec 1895.

72. L, IV, 366–67.

73. HA's *Recognition of Cuban Independence* (principal source 7) is dated on p. 1:—"December 21, 1896.—Ordered to be printed." It has never been reprinted and has never been recognized for what it manifestly is: one of HA's important works.

Levenson and his associates say that the work—presumably meaning the *entire* work—was written shortly prior its being printed. See L, IV, 437n3. No evidence whatever supports their statement.

As printed, the work runs to 121 paragraphs of text in combination with 24 block quotations in small type, plus a two-part proposed joint resolution of Congress placed at the close. When studied with attention to HA's known experiences in the latter part of 1895 and all of 1896, the printed text rather obviously reveals itself to be a *second version* within which the first version survives practically intact.

In November-December 1895 and January 1896, HA had time, motive, and occasion to complete a first version and show it to certain persons. One can say he *had* to complete it. The argument is as follows.

For HA, the Cuban revolution raised afresh the issue first raised by the American Revolution: independence for the European colonies in America. (The Revolution—especially the roles played therein by John and Samuel Adams—figures vividly in HA's letter to BA, 27 Oct 1895.)

For HA, the Cuban revolution raised afresh the issue of the right of the United States to assert a strong or even deciding voice in matters relating to revolutions by colonists in the Western Hemisphere; i.e. to extend and complete the Monroe Doctrine. (That J. Q. Adams wrote the Monroe Doctrine is stated by HA in the same letter.)

For HA, the basic premise underlying the American Revolution and the Monroe Doctrine was that the revolution and the doctrine were both indispensable: neither could stand without the other; and the purpose of the two together was the creation and maintenance of an American "system" independent of Europe's imperial powers. (That American financial ineptitudes permitted European capitalists to impair and all but annihilate the independence of the American system in the period 1890–1894 is the main theme of the speeches written by HA that Cameron read to the Senate in 1893–1894 as his own. It is also the theme of HA's letters to BA from late 1893 through January 1896.)

For HA, a move by the United States assuring the independence of Cuba, the inclusion of Cuba within an American system, and the defense of Cuba against exploitation by the Europeans as a market would be a *political* counter-stroke against Europe which would help solve the problem of *financial* dominance of the United States by European capitalists. (The primacy of political action figures vividly in HA's current letters to BA and Ford.)

HA had found in Senator Cameron a dependable means of official conveyance of proposals to Congress. But in view of the gravity of the pro-Cuban resolution that he wanted Cameron to put before the Senate Foreign Relations Committee, HA could not ask the senator to introduce the resolution without first providing him written grounds for believing that the passage of the proposed measure was fully within the rights of the U. S. government, as established by American and European precedents. HA accordingly provided Cameron, in handwritten form, a full "historical summary."

The summary is easy to recognize. See paragraphs 3–112 of HA's *Recognition of Cuban Independence* as later printed, together with the text of the resolution that Cameron was to introduce.

Very persuasive and very easy to read, the summary is a bold, clear reminder to Americans concerning the value and importance of independence from Europe. Once the summary is set apart, any reader can see why Cameron felt ready to introduce the resolution and why the other members of HA's conspiracy— Mrs. Cameron and Phillips (possibly also Lee)—felt ready to follow HA's lead with respect to Cuba.

74. Principal source 7, p. 19:—"this historical summary."

75. In the summary, within the section titled "The United States and Mexico, 1861–1866," HA documents Lord John Russell's "astonishing promise of belligerence" in May 1861 to a Southern "insurrection" in the United States "before the fact of war was officially known in England to have been proclaimed by either party." HA says too that the Southern insurrection "had[,] by the latest advices of that time[,] neither a ship at sea nor an army on land."

This passage is HA's strongest charge against the British, with reference to British assistance to the rebellion that gave rise to the American Civil War.

76. One may believe that the Cubans who visited HA knew that his grandfather, Secretary of State J. Q. Adams, had developed the Monroe Doctrine for issuance by President Monroe in 1823.

One cannot believe that the Cubans asked HA to arrange what he arranged of his own accord: a move in the Senate supporting outright early Cuban independence.

77. Willy's letter is addressed to "Sweet Bandit" and signed "Bandit Bill."

6. A PHENOMENON QUITE PECULIAR

Letters by and to HA are in HA-micro 12, 13, B, or H, unless other wise indicated.

PRINCIPAL SOURCES

(1) five letters, HA to Phillips, 13 Apr–[30 Sep] 1896.
(2) eight letters, HA to Hay, 22 Apr 1896–7 Apr 1897.
(3) twenty letters, HA to Mabel Hooper, 22 Apr 1896–12 May 1897.
(4) ten letters, HA to CMG, 12 May 1896–Thursday, [22 Apr 1897].

(5) twenty-two letters and notes, EC to HA, [18 May 1896]–[7 May 1897].
(Concerning the first ones, see note 8, below.)

(6) twenty letters, HA to EC, 20 [May] 1896–28 Apr 1897.

(7) seven letters, HA to Lucy Baxter, 26 Aug 1896–10 Apr 1897, L, IV, 419–
20, 435–36, 438, 448–50, 459–61; O.1897.8–9 & 19–20.

(8) five letters, HA to Ford, 16 [Dec] 1896–10 Mar 1897, O.1896. 36–37,
O.1897.1–2, 3–6, 10–12, 13–15.

(9) [HA], *Recognition of Cuban Independence*, Senate Report No. 1160, 54th
Congress, 2d Session, ordered to be printed 21 Dec 1896. (Also see
Chap. 5, principal source 7 and note 72.)

LESSER SOURCES; CITATIONS; COMMENTS

1. One may assume that hostesses and visitors conversed in English. HA
disliked having to speak with foreigners in their own languages.

2. HA wrote more emphatically to EC, "Our Cuban friends are all right till
autumn anyway, and we will then give them a big lift." See HA to EC, 3 & 5 Jun
1896. His "then" should probably be understood to mean, not autumn, but the
coming winter, which would begin on December 22.

3. GCL to HA, 14 Apr 1896.

4. On 16 May 1896, HA wrote broadly to CFA2, "My future is to be a schoolmaster for girls, and personally conduct my scholars round the world."

5. HA can fairly be accused of distracting his surviving brothers from politics by keeping them busy as writers, CFA2 as biographer of CFA, BA as author,
reviser, even translator of *The Law of Civilization and Decay*.

6. Phillips to HA, 19 May 1896.

7. Salmon to HA, 10 Apr 1896.

8. The notes, dated only "Monday" and "Tuesday afternoon," are filmed
out of sequence in HA-micro 12 at the end of January 1896. Their dates—[18
May 1897] & [19 May 1897]—are easily established with the help of other
sources. The Knickerbocker Club entrusted the Monday note to CFA2. He sent
it to HA's former mailing address in London, the Morgan bank. There HA
chanced to find it.

9. HA to Frewen, Sunday, [14? Jul 1895].

10. To everyone's amusement, Hay at this time began to address "Uncle
Henry" in Dutch as "Oom Hendrik."

11. Someone in President Cleveland's inner circle was passing information
to Phillips. See Phillips to HA, 29 May 1896:—". . . you were right, in saying, this
Administration would not do anything [to help the Cubans] unless forced by
some great outrage on American citizens. . . . I was taken *into a corner* and told
the above, so please destroy this letter and keep [the] information to yourself."
HA did not destroy the letter but presumably kept silent.

12. Phillips was an unsparing humorist. He began his letter to HA of 19
Apr 1897, "How is your Cussedness?" The salutation in the letter of 3–4 May
1897 is "Born of Belial."

13. BA to Ford, 28 May 1896, Morgan Library, NY.

14. Beringause, 130–31, 140–43.

15. MacVeagh later remembered his and HA's interchanges in Paris as
"genuine." See MacVeagh to HA, 2 Apr 1897.

16. EC to HA, 6 Jul 1896.

17. An alternative plan for BA would make him the running mate of Senator Teller of Colorado. See Beringause, 146–47.

18. BA to HA, 12 Jul 1896.

19. HA's reaction to what he saw at churches in Ravenna, Torcello, and Murano placed him at odds not only with BA's *Law of Civilization and Decay* but also with Gibbon's *Decline and Fall of the Roman Empire*.

20. It has been very widely supposed that with respect to history HA and BA were both pessimists, HA being perhaps the more pessimistic of the two. The supposition is not supported—on the contrary is overthrown—by their surviving correspondence, read in its totality.

BA's letters to HA are the work of an outright historical pessimist. Letters by both brothers contain abundant evidence of HA's rejecting BA's pessimistic idea of history and asserting his own—which, as compared with almost any other important published idea of history, is remarkably hopeful and open-ended.

21. See the climactic paragraph beginning "Travellers in Switzerland," *HUS* (Scribner), IX, 225; (LoA), II, 1334–35.

22. Phillips to HA, 16 Jul 1896. The letter contains news about an unnamed ally of theirs in Washington. It ends, "Keep this *very dark.*"

23. HA's idea of history is an idea of the history of peoples (also termed nations or races). Civilization enters into his idea as something peoples create. A subsidiary idea is that there have been—and still are—western and eastern peoples, and that they have created divergent western and eastern civilizations.

24. HA's comments were inspired in part by recent occurrences. At a dinner the Hays attended in London, Helen Hay was assured by an English lord that Elizabeth Warder was "Miss de Rothschild." More recently, after a visit to the zoological gardens in Antwerp, Hay recorded that Elizabeth "took a hideous fancy to the pythons, and we could hardly get her away from their cage."

The episode in Antwerp was matched by another in Amsterdam. The travelers began a drive. Hay wrote: "When we came to the Zoological Gardens, Elizabeth Warder . . . said she could not live another minute without seeing one of her dear Pythons. She jumped out and Adams after her, and left Helen and me to our ride alone. We drove up and down the great canals, the magnificent wharves, the stately lines of residences, [the?] Jew quarter, and had an agreeable hour or so. We went back to find our serpent worshippers, but could not find them, and so came home." See *JHLetters*, III, 16, 21–22, 24–25.

25. HA's characterization of "the Jew" in Paris and London as an "end of civilisation" is unsimple. He evidently had in mind the bankers in London and Paris, but whether he intended "end" to mean a *result* of civilization, an *absence* of civilization, or a *failure* or *terminus* of civilization is hardly clear. What is clear is his thinking of Jews and Greeks as strong.

26. In HA's letters dating from 1896, there are 63 occurrences of "Jew" or its variants; in 1897, there are 23; and in 1898, after he began to pay close attention to the Dreyfus Affair, there are 40.

Of the 86 occurrences in 1896–1897, 70 are references to bankers, capitalists, brokers, businessmen, etc. The 70 include the reference in the passage quoted here.

It must be added that for HA the archetypal banker was Greek. See HA to EC, 13 Jul 1894, HA-micro 11:—". . . Midas, a Greek banker . . . has typified the gold-bug for three thousand years. . . ."

HA sometimes *almost* admired the world's powerful money-lords but seems never to have reached the point of actual admiration. In this connection, he and BA differed. BA had two attitudes, one hating, one admiring. He wrote that ancient Rome "was a blessed garden of paradise beside the rotten, unsexed, swindling, lying Jews, represented by P[ierpont]. Morgan and the gang who have been manipulating our country for the last four years." See BA to HA, 10 Oct 1896. Yet BA also wrote: ". . . the end of it all is that I admire my adversary. He is powerful—the only power." See BA to HA, 5 Mar 1897.

27. HA to CMG, 31 Jul 1896. HA's letters are sometimes misquoted. An instance appears at the start of Ernest Volkman's *A Legacy of Hate: Anti-Semitism in America*, NY 1982, where Volkman uses a full page at the start of Chap. 1 to juxtapose what may appear to be two legitimate quotations: "*We are in the hands of Jews who do what they please with our values.*/ Henry Adams, 1896," and "*Hitler had the best answers to everything.*/ Charles Manson, 1973."

The sentence Volkman attributes to HA is a fabrication, the raw material for which is a series of three sentences in the letter from HA to Gaskell that is here in question. In the letter, HA says: "In this situation an investment is sheer gambling. We [i.e. American and English investors] are in the hands of the Jews [i.e. American and English bankers and associated capitalists]. They can do what they please with our values [i.e. the current prices of our stocks and bonds]." By omitting the first sentence, altering the second and third, and fusing the pieces to make one sentence, Volkman makes HA seem to say something like the following: "We [i.e. the Christians] are in the hands of Jews [i.e. members of a nation, people, or race] who do what they please with our values [i.e. our Christian beliefs and moral principles]."

By adding a quotation from Charles Manson about Hitler (perhaps not fabricated), Volkman manages to treat HA and Hitler as ideological twins— either that or manages to treat HA as Hitler's teacher.

On this basis, Volkman may properly be thought an over-stepping anti-Adamsite.

28. BA to HA, 28 Oct 1896:—"McLean and Newland wanted me for vice president with Teller. Don't mention this."

29. HA to EC, 27–28 Jul 1896.

30. BA to HA, 26 Jul 1896.

31. Newspaper clipping dated 13 Aug 1896, HA-micro 13. The temperature reportedly dropped below 100° during only one day of the nine.

32. HA to Mabel Hooper, 8 Sep 1896; HA to CSR, 11 Sep 1896.

33. HA to Hay, 6 Oct 1896.

34. HA's letter is headed "Saturday." Levenson and his associates date it [30 Sep 1896], which was a Wednesday. See O.1896.31. The correct date is Saturday, [3 Oct 1896].

35. HA to Hay, 6 Oct 1896.

36. HA to EC, Friday, [9 Oct 1896].

37. Ibid.

38. Not knowing HA's newest plans, BA directed Macmillan to send copies of his book to HA in Paris and to Phillips in Washington. See BA to Macmillan Company, 11 Sep 1896, MP.

39. L, IV, 430.

40. HA to BA, [31 Jan 1896], in *Degradation*, 98–100; reprinted, L, IV, 365–66.

41. BA to HA, 21 Oct 1896.

42. Much of BA's time was being consumed in going to water cures, which seem not to have greatly helped him.

43. One may assume that HA and Ford had met and reviewed the state of the country's economy, but no record of a meeting is in evidence.

44. HA's letter illustrates a method he sometimes used when goading Hay to think or act. While professing to have no ideas, HA sketched for Hay's inspection a grim picture of a subjugated United States which at best could surrender to the Rothschilds on terms arranged through Belmont, a leading New York banker and leading Democrat.

In my view, HA did not believe the picture: he simply sketched it for effect. Its effect on Hay, even if it made him laugh, would perhaps be considerable.

45. MacVeagh to HA, 21 Oct 1896.

46. "History" is capitalized by HA both in his letter to Lucy Baxter, just quoted, and in his reply to Jameson. The capitalizations seem at least partly scornful.

47. Levenson and his associates speculate that Jameson asked HA to lecture at Brown University. See L, IV, 440n1. It can be argued in response that Jameson asked HA to write for the *American Historical Review* an article concerning the questions raised by his 1893 letter usually known as "The Tendency of History."

48. HA to CMG, 16 Nov 1896.

49. HA had written to Tati Salmon from Paris on 1 Sep 1896. The letter is missing. Its date is given in Salmon's reply, 12 Nov 1896. The reply makes clear that HA was concerned about two spears belonging to Opuhara. One spear was captured in 1815 at the time of his death in battle. The other was preserved by a chain of persons, Tahitian and European, Salmon being one, and given to the Louvre.

50. The title page bore the legends: "American Historical Society [*sic*]./ The Tendency of History./ by/ Henry Adams,/ President./ (from the Annual Report of the American Historical Association for 1894, pages 17–23.)/ Washington:/ Government Printing Office,/ 1896."

The earliest bibliography of HA's writings, as revised, contains the following statements: ". . . 'The Tendency of History' was also issued as a separate pamphlet in an edition of 50 copies which was found entire in the original package after the death of Henry Adams, he never having given away a single copy. These are now among his papers at the Massachusetts Historical Society." See JTA, *Henry Adams*, NY 1933, 224. The statements imply that, with a view to circulating his letter privately, HA arranged the printing of 50 copies in pamphlet form but reconsidered and did not distribute them.

One notices that Ford preserved a copy of the pamphlet. See FP 31. In view of his keeping a copy, one can infer that Ford—together with Jameson and possibly others—induced the Association to reprint HA's letter; that Jameson sent HA a package of 50 copies; and that HA was willing to keep them but never grew willing to distribute them.

To my mind, the guess that Ford—not HA—arranged the printing seems right. (For details about a later printing of "The Tendency of History," see Chap. 27.)

51. L, IV, 440.

52. Principal source 9.

53. Lodge's biographer describes the Cameron resolution as "a virtual declaration of war on Spain" and treats it as the work of Cameron, Lodge, and the Senate Republicans generally. See Garraty, 182.

Garraty's account is wrong on both scores. The controlling spirit behind the resolution was HA, and the resolution was not a virtual declaration of war on Spain. It was designed to precipitate either acquiescence by Spain in Cuba's independence or a declaration of war *by Spain*. HA himself placed this construction on his initiatives of 1895–1896 relating to Cuba. See Chap. 7.

54. Senator Lodge was a member of the Committee on Foreign Relations. He made a show of rebutting the criticisms voiced by outraged figures in his state. See Garraty, 182–84.

55. CFA2 to Lodge, 24 Dec 1896, quoted in L, IV, 454n5. CFA2 tells Lodge that HA's authorship lends the matter of Cameron's resolution a "humorous aspect." The elder brother's comment can be viewed as evidence of awakened envy and injured pride.

56. Garraty, 183.

57. HA's evident meaning is that he wished he were a banker. In the same ironic spirit, he had said three weeks earlier, ". . . [Bay Lodge] will, I hope, become a respectable Jew." See HA to Louisa Hooper, 12 [Dec 1896].

58. BA to HA, 8 Jan 1897.

59. CFA2 was likelier than Bigelow to talk too much and criticize HA's *Recognition of Cuban Independence*.

60. BA's letters to HA, 19 & 27 Jan 1897, make clear that BA understood his ideas about history to be ideas about "nature." He believed that "nature" creates new "types" of human beings; that each type is capable of thinking and acting only in the idiosyncratic way that is given to it when created; that the "energy" given to each type is limited; and that, in "the great war of races," each type exhausts its energies and historically dies. Thus he asserts (19 Jan 1897), ". . . now the war of races lies between Russia and India and China, and ourselves [the Americans], for Europe is exhausted. . . ."

Differently, HA believed that human beings sometimes change from one way of thinking to another, an instance being the Romans' conversion to Christianity. A word HA used for the change was "reaction." BA answered (27 Jan 1897): ". . . I'm not clear what an intellectual 'reaction' is. I dont [*sic*] know how minds can 'react.' There may be new ones [i.e. minds], but while the old ones live they always seem to me to go on in the same way."

61. Ford began his letter on January 5 and completed and mailed it on February 18. The quoted words appear in the earlier instalment.

62. Margaret Leech, *In the Days of McKinley*, NY 1959, 99–101.

63. HA to Mabel Hooper, 21 Apr 1897. The diagnosis might now be stated as myocardiomyopathy.

64. Hay to HA, 8 Apr 1897.

65. Rockhill had won Adams's admiration by making a journey to Tibet and writing an excellent account of it. See HA to Rockhill, 17 May 1895, L, IV, 282.

66. As printed by the Senate, HA's report reviews the interventions of European powers in revolutions in Greece in 1821–1827, in Belgium in 1830, in Poland in 1831, in Hungary in 1849, in the States of the Church in 1850, in the Ottoman Empire in 1878, generally in Asia, and in the Americas in 1822–1823. It reviews the interventions of England and France in the affairs of the United States and Mexico in 1861–1866. It reviews the responses of the United States to revolution in Cuba from 1869 to 1896. It differentiates European interventions from American, saying (24): "The practice of Europe in regard to intervention . . . has been almost invariably harsh and oppressive. The practice of the United States has been almost invariably mild and forebearing." It recommends intervention by the United States in Cuba in keeping with "the most moderate" of precedents (25): the one set by President Monroe in 1822. It ends by presenting a proposed joint Congressional resolution consistent with the Monroe precedent.

The report shows every evidence of being the work of a first-rate mind. It is forthright, factual, historical in method, nearly global in scope, and unrelenting in argument. Readers may find it tragically convincing about repression in Europe and Asia (Africa is overlooked) and consolingly persuasive about the progress of democracy in America.

67. For details about the breakup, see Chap. 24.

68. EC was aware of the risks. Henry Sherman, her elder brother, had died on shipboard four years earlier during a voyage to Europe.

69. Hay to Lodge, 6 May 1897, *JHLetters* (NYPL copy), III, 83–84.

70. For the Curzons' address, see Mary Curzon to HA, 2? Aug [1895].

71. HA to Mabel Hooper, 21 Apr 1897.

72. HA-micro H. Place and time of arrival appear on the message as delivered to HA.

7. MY BUSINESS IS TO LOOK AHEAD

Letters by and to HA are in HA-micro 13, 14, or H, unless otherwise indicated.

PRINCIPAL SOURCES

(1) twenty-one letters, HA to Hay, [16 May] 1897–[17?] June 1898.

(2) twelve letters, HA to BA, 17 & 18 May 1897–6 Jul 1898.

(3) sixteen letters, HA to CMG, 13 Jun 1897–26 Jun 1898.

(4) twenty-seven letters, HA to EC, [13 Jun] 1897–9 May 1898.

(5) twenty-four letters, EC to HA, [18 Nov 1897]–[8 May 1898].

LESSER SOURCES; CITATIONS; COMMENTS

1. Hay to HA, 28 May & 4 Jun 1897:—". . . you who have sat where I sit know something of my cares. . . ."

2. The U. S. government sent a commission to Europe in 1897 in hopes of making arrangements with England, France, and Germany for a conference on bimetallism. Senator Wolcott of Colorado headed the commission, which failed to achieve its object. Hay wrote to HA on 30 Oct 1897: ". . . Wolcott sails this morning with his black eye and his broken heart. I think he takes it too hard. He has put up a good fight. . . ." HA replied on 31 Oct 1897, ". . . [Wolcott] has done vast good if he has torn the mask from these Jew governments here."

How little or much HA's reply was justified may perhaps be judged most easily with the help of the account of the British response to the American commission's proposals in Youssef Cassis, *City Bankers, 1890–1914*, Camb England 1994, 291–93. Two passages are especially pertinent. "What is above all of note here is that, in a debate in which the position of the Chancellor of the Exchequer and the Treasury was firmly established from the start, the Rothschilds were nevertheless consulted and were, in fact, the only bankers to be so." ". . . the report sent by Natty Rothschild to the Chancellor of the Exchequer was not in the least ambiguous. Each [American] proposal was methodically refuted. . . ."

3. HA, memorandum written at "Brown's Hotel," [16 May 1897], O.1897. 29–30, treated by Levenson and his associates as a letter to Hay.

4. BA to HA, 10–11 May 1897.

5. Hale to HA, [June] 1897.

6. BA wrote to HA, 8 Aug 1897, that Cleveland and Olney were said to have suspected Rockhill "of sympathy with Cuba." They may also have suspected him of sympathy with HA.

7. HA to CSR, 15 Aug 1897.
8. HA to Rebecca Rae, 8 Aug 1897.
9. HA to Cunliffe, 29 Jul 1897.
10. HA to Hay, 6 Aug 1897.
11. HA's claims of needing rest were sometimes strongly worded. He wrote to CMG, 11 Aug 1897: "The years from 1890 to 1896 were trying enough to last me for life; and I want now only to get clear of all the remaining risks, and run out to sea in fair weather."
12. In his *Henry Adams on the Road to Chartres*, Camb 1971, 186–87, Robert Mane suggests how HA learned Old French. "Apart from the few pages at the end of Karl Bartsch's *Chrestomathie*, he does not seem to have had a proper syntax he could resort to. . . ."

The suggestion was written in the absence of needed evidence. HA studied Old French by obtaining a copy of *La Langue et La Littérature Françaises depuis le XIème siècle jusqu'au XIVème siècle. Textes et glossaire par Karl Bartsch précédées d'une grammaire de l'ancien français par Adolph Horning*, Paris 1887. The copy at present is in my collection. His annotations in the copy match in form those he made in his copy of the Bartsch/Horning *Chrestomathie*, 6th ed., 1895—a later publication. See notes 28–29, below.

The date when HA began to use his copy of *La Langue et La Littérature Françaises* can only be guessed.

His annotations indicate he studied four texts: "Roland," "Voyage de Charlemagne à Jérusalem et à Constantinople," "Garin de Loherain," and "Richard I [de l']Angleterre." He appears to have put the copy aside when he acquired and more heavily annotated the Bartsch/Horning *Chrestomathie*.

13. HA to Hay, 19 Oct 1897.
14. It is not suggested that HA was sole author of the plan that took him back to Egypt. It is only suggested that the Hays sought and accepted his advice and that he tailored his advice to suit their stated needs. What especially bears notice is that HA associated winter in Egypt with good health and good spirits. See HA-2, 741n47.
15. Persons wishing to trace the beginnings of the special relationship between Great Britain and the United States in the twentieth century should consider HA's provoking questions of May 1897 and CSR's extraordinary responses later in the year.
16. The analysis, HA-micro 13, was published in Gwynn, II, 235–39. There it stands in suggestive comparison with a letter that CSR wrote on 3 Nov 1897 to Theodore Roosevelt. Gwynn excises part of the letter to Roosevelt and says (II, 233n1), "What is omitted is put more fully in the next letter to Henry Adams."
17. HA began his reply to CSR, 11 Nov 1897: "Before your extremely interesting letter gets lost in my drawer under a heap of bills . . . I hasten to acknowledge and to appreciate your attention. . . ." HA's saying he might *lose* the letter perhaps served as a sufficient hint that he would do the opposite and lend it to the American authorities for reading and possible copying.

In his reply, HA also tells CSR that he needs financial data. "I can get absolutely no serious information as to the amount of credit now existing, or its equivalents in previous decades." HA's remark amounts to a request that he be treated by the British as a secret channel for continuous information-sharing.

18. In his biography of Hay, William Roscoe Thayer printed a letter from Hay to Senator Lodge, 27 Jul 1898, and while so doing suppressed a name. As printed, the relevant sentence reads: "I have been under great obligations these

last few months to X. [i.e. Spring Rice], who knows Germany as few men do, and has kept me wonderfully *au courant* of facts and opinions there." See Thayer, II, 172.

The reasons for the suppression of Spring Rice's name were many. Thayer prepared his volumes under the guidance and with the help of HA. At the time the volumes were published, World War I was in progress; the United States remained at peace; and CSR was serving as Great Britain's ambassador in Washington. If revealed, his early efforts to inform the American authorities about Germany by means of private letters to HA could be criticized as departures from ideal diplomatic practice.

In his *John Hay/ The Gentleman as Diplomat*, Ann Arbor, 1975, 126, Kenton J. Clymer retains the name when printing the sentence but gives no indication that CSR's assistance to Hay began as assistance via HA, and no indication of a departure from ideal practice.

19. EC's letter is filmed in HA-micro 13 as if written in May 1897. It is written on Brown's Hotel stationery and headed only "Thursday Eve." The suggested date, [18 Nov 1897], comports with its contents and HA's reply, [21 Nov 1897].

20. In 1857, Alice Mason had become the cousin-by-marriage of Clover Hooper. For more information concerning her importance to HA and MHA, see HA-2, index entries under "Sumner, Alice Mason."

21. HA to Mabel Hooper, 3 Dec 1897. EC learned of the meeting and told HA (letter of 13 Dec 1897) that she could imagine "nothing more incongruous" than a meeting between him and "Lady R—."

22. Ford to HA, 16 Nov 1897.

23. O.1897.57–59.

24. Ibid. Two phrases in HA's letter—"the very highest financial intelligence in Europe, Rothschilds and all" and "the best opinion of the City, from Lord Rothschild down"—need not be read as indicative of admiration. I believe they are best read as simply reflections of acknowledged status. By general consent, the Rothschilds outranked the other bankers of the world, and Nathaniel Rothschild outranked the other bankers of London.

25. HA's letters both previous and subsequent to his letter to Ford contain expressions not inimical to Jews. See for example HA to CMG, 11 Aug 1897:—". . . I can always turn Jew." Or HA to Cunliffe, 19 May 1898:—". . . the Jew is singularly impersonal . . . and can turn on himself quicker than any race I know. So I hope to cultivate the London Jew, and learn wisdom from the Synagogue."

26. HA to CMG, 28 Nov [1897].

27. Author's collection.

28. The copy is inscribed in HA's handwriting, "Henry Adams/ Paris—" That HA was reading it in December 1897 is made clear by a conjunction of evidence. He wrote to EC, 17 Dec 1897: "De ço cui calt? as my Chanson de Roland says. . . ." The version of the "Chanson de Roland" published in the copy begins with these Old French words.

29. HA's pencilings in the text and glossary indicate that he read "Vie de Saint Alexis," "Chanson de Roland," "Voyage de Charlemagne à Jérusalem et à Constantinople," "Lois de Guillaume Le Conquérant," "Traduction des Quatres Livres des Rois," "Romances," "Fragment d'un Poème Devot," "Garin de Loherain," "Amis et Amiles," "La Bataille D'Aliscans," "La Roman de Rou," "Adans de la Halle, Ou Adans Li Boçus," and "Jehan Froissart."

Before leaving for Egypt in January 1898, HA entrusted the copy to a Paris bookseller for binding in hard covers. See bill, H. Welter to Professor Adams, 14 Feb 1898, HA-micro 14. During rebinding, HA's pencilings on 631, 638, 658, 671, 707 were partly sheared off at the margins and pencilings on 589 & 622 were moved deep into the gutter. One thus may infer that HA completed his work in the copy before Welter rebound it.

30. For details given in this account, I am especially indebted to David Levering Lewis, *Prisoners of Honor/ The Dreyfus Affair*, NY 1973, 1994; Egal Feldman, *The Dreyfus Affair and the American Conscience, 1895–1906*, Detroit 1981; Jean-Denis Bredin, *The Affair/ The Case of Alfred Dreyfus*, NY 1986; and Albert S. Lindemann, *The Jew Accused/ Three Anti-Semitic Affairs (Dreyfus, Beilis, Frank) 1894–1915*, Camb England 1991.

31. In 1894, when only twenty-nine, Lazare had published a wide-ranging treatise, *L'Antisemitisme, son Histoire et ses Causes*. The book is invaluable for purposes of understanding anti-Semitism as it existed prior to the Dreyfus Affair. I have gained immeasurably from reading the English translation, *Antisemitism/ Its History and Causes*, Lincoln & Lond 1995.

32. The mention is in HA to CMG, 28 Nov [1897], in the sentence "As for me, I admire Dreifuss [*sic*]; but Sargent has just painted another Jew, Wertheimer, a worse crucifixion than history tells off [*sic*]."

The phrase "I admire Dreifuss" can be seen as equivocal, both laudatory and sarcastic. HA's linked misspellings of "Dreyfus" and "of" may be read as slurs at the expense of persons who spoke English with a German accent. Thus the sentence may seem derisory.

Read with care, HA's sentence acquires a different character. It says that an American painter, John Singer Sargent, has crucified an English Jew, Asher Wertheimer, by painting his portrait; and it implies—by juxtaposing one Jew, Wertheimer, with another, Dreyfus—that Dreyfus too has been crucified. In short, it indicates that HA in November 1897 supposed that Dreyfus was a victim of persecution and a martyr. (For details about Wertheimer, see L, IV, 497n4.)

A line in another letter by HA is apropos. See HA to Anne Fell, 18 Dec 1897:—"Paris is all Jew, yet the Jews are baited like beasts."

33. HA's impulse to take the case unseriously shows most plainly in deliberate misspellings. In his surviving letters between November 1897, when he first mentions Dreyfus, and November 1899, when he ceases to mention the case, there are 73 occurrences of "Dreyfus" and variants thereof. 71 are misspelled as "Dreifuss," "Dreifus," "Dreifussard," etc. By playing on German words, the misspellings suggest that Dreyfus is a person with three feet.

The other occurrences are misspelled "dry-fuss," obviously playing on words in English.

HA did not relent. See HA to EC, 5 Sep 1899, HA-micro 15:—"Joe Chamberlain and Dreifus convulse the world, but I still refuse to take either of them seriously."

34. HA to EC, 10 Dec 1897:—"The world, as you know, was very grateful to Captain Dreifus [*sic*] for giving it a subject of conversation for a time, but we are tired of him now, and would gladly let him out to get a new sensation." HA's "we" manifestly refers to carefree persons titillated by fashions; but if the "we" is also a reference by HA to himself, the last half of the sentence is evidence that HA could cheerfully contemplate the release of Dreyfus from Devil's Island.

35. Like the French public, HA did not know what the evidence really was until after the second court-martial of Dreyfus in 1899. While waiting to see the

evidence, he was keenly aware that at best he was weighing ill-supported rival theories. See his remarks about certain of the theories in HA to EC, 25 Sep 1899, HA-micro 15.

36. The passage appears in HA to EC, 13–14 Jan 1897. It clearly was written early on the 13th, before HA knew of the day's developments. In one respect, it may be ill-worded. The phrase "of the fact" may be supererogatory, unthinking, and/or confusing. Possibly it repeats one of Bey's locutions as remembered.

Generally speaking, the passage is clear. HA's saying he believes Bey "right" applies to Bey's assertion that there has been an enormous increase of anti-Semitism in France in consequence of French realization of a "Jew scandal," meaning use by French Jews of money and intrigue to control public opinion. HA's saying he believes Bey "right" does *not* also apply to Bey's subordinate, passing assertion about having little doubt that Dreyfus is guilty. Thus the passage does two things. It agrees with Bey that anti-Semitism has increased in France. It leaves HA's opinion about Dreyfus's guilt or innocence unstated because here irrelevant and beside the point.

In his *Henry Adams/ The Major Phase*, Cambridge 1964, 182, Ernest Samuels so quotes the passage as completely to omit Bey's reported main assertion about an increase of anti-Semitism. With the help of this omission, Samuels alleges that such doubts as HA may have had about Dreyfus's guilt or innocence "were resolved by Aristarchi Bey." ". . . Aristarchi confidently assured him that Dreyfus was guilty."

In his *Henry Adams*, Camb 1989, 320, Samuels re-draws this picture of HA's passively becoming an anti-Dreyfusite.

These depictions of HA by Samuels would be very damaging to HA if true, for if true they would make him a feckless American visitor in Paris dependent for his opinions on a helpful European diplomat. But the depictions are untrue. They mainly rest on suppression of what HA reported that Bey mostly said. They represent Bey as confident of Dreyfus's guilt, which may not be quite the same as his having "little doubt" of it. They assume that HA was predisposed to think Dreyfus guilty. (He was disposed to think the opposite. See notes 32 & 34, above.) And they state that HA, once persuaded by Bey, formed a set opinion that Dreyfus was guilty. (Within the next twenty-four hours, HA formed a more definite though still tentative opinion that Dreyfus was innocent. See especially the second instalment of HA to EC, 13–14 Jan 1898. Also see the entire body of evidence in his writings about the Dreyfus Affair.)

37. See HA to Hay, 20 Aug 1899, HA-micro 15, describing France as "our oldest ally" and describing the evident "moral collapse" of France as the "real kernel" of the Dreyfus Affair.

38. The passage appears in HA to EC, 13–14 Jan 1898, and evidently was written early on the 14th, two mornings after he talked with Bey and one morning after he read Zola's "*J'Accuse.*"

In both his accounts alleging that HA was talked into believing Dreyfus guilty (see note 36), Ernest Samuels reverses the chronology of events by recounting Zola's "sensational *J'accuse*" as occurring earlier and HA's discussion with Bey as occurring later.

Chronology is not everything in biography, but it should be correct. Samuels's erroneous chronology is the more remarkable because the evidence to which it relates is a two-part letter in which the actual chronology is given by HA with all possible plainness.

39. In his accounts of HA's opinions concerning Dreyfus (see notes 36 &

38, above), Ernest Samuels represents HA as disbelieving Zola's famous letter. We however have HA's word that he believed it. See HA to EC, 25 Sep 1899, HA-micro 15: "Hitherto I have thought that Laborie [*sic*] and Zola and Jaures were right. . . ."

Fernand Labori was the lawyer who defended Zola when he was tried for libel in February 1898. He also defended Dreyfus at his second court-martial in August–September 1899. Perhaps intentionally, HA so misspelled Labori's name as to make it seem more French.

40. The vain attempts by Ernest Samuels and other commentators to represent HA as having simple feelings about Dreyfus and the Dreyfus Affair, and especially as having a simple feeling that Dreyfus was guilty, may reflect inability to deal with HA's highly-charged complex expressions, which are concomitants of highly-charged complex ideas. HA at first tended to believe that conspirators in the French army invented a false case of treason against a French captain, a Jew. He later saw sufficient proof that the French army misread the evidence of a real case of treason, convicted the wrong officer of the crime, exonerated the actual culprit when identified, persecuted the intelligence chief who identified the culprit, and only very slowly took corrective action when forced by Zola and others to do so. In short, HA saw evidence of egregious French ineptitude. He meanwhile saw an upsurge of anti-Semitism in France such as he and others had not expected. And at every stage he saw French ineptitude in the context of an expected attempt by Germany to expand again—as in 1870—within the confines of Europe. For all these reasons, he felt that France was comparatively weak and acutely in need of support.

41. EC to HA, 31 Dec 1897. It may seem that EC meant homesick for Washington. Yet "home" was a word that EC and HA tended to use in a personal sense, as applying to places where she and he had lived in close proximity. Thus, to his ears, her "homesick" may have referred in part to their recent experiences at St. Germain, in Touraine, and in Paris.

42. EC to HA, 10 Jan 1898. Her visit to HA's house placed her in sight of her own house, diagonally across Lafayette Square. It thus was a fresh experience of what her husband had done to her.

43. EC to HA, 17–18 Jan 1898. She had not yet received HA's letter to her of 13–14 Jan 1898. Yet her reactions to the news of riots around the world and to Zola's *J'accuse* in Paris were equivalents of his and showed the compatibility of their minds.

44. The McKinley administration had taxed Hay's patience by sending special envoys to London, each of whom effectually outranked him with respect to a particular matter.

45. Finishing a letter to her on the same date, 21 Jan 1898, HA said that Rostand's work was "a fearful tour-de-force, very long, very faulty as a play, and only one rôle, which is naturally Coquelin's."

46. When recounting this moment in his *Henry Adams/ The Major Phase*, Camb 1964, 183–84, Ernest Samuels construes HA's grief (a natural emotion) as if it were a "hysterical attack" (an episode of illness). The construction is overdrawn.

Also, in matter of fact tones, Samuel speaks about the Adamses' "ill-starred wedding journey in 1872 when Marian had had a frightening nervous seizure." The alleged seizure did not occur. Samuels's unguarded passage is one of many published repetitions of a baseless fabrication. (For details about the fabrication, see HA-2, 741n47.)

In his *Henry Adams*, Camb 1989, 101, Samuels moves away from the allegation of a seizure and says instead, "... she [Marian] experienced an ominous attack of depression. ..." The 1989 allegation of an attack has no more basis in evidence than the 1964 allegation of a seizure. It too repeats the fabrication.

47. HA to EC, 11–12 Feb 1898.

48. His Egyptian paintings were presumably watercolors. They may have been few. They seem not to have survived.

49. Her letter, started on "Saturday night, 22 [Jan 1898]," is filmed out of sequence in HA-micro 14 as if dated 22 Feb 1898.

50. BA to HA, [28?] Dec 1897:—"I am to pay for all advertising. I am to pay in advance for printing, and the publisher is to take for himself half the gross proceeds." "The price of publication is cheaper than with us ... but the terms are Jewish in the extreme."

HA obviated these hardships by advancing the needed money. BA later gave him the royalties. See BA to HA, 28 Apr 1902:—"... the money is yours."

51. BA to HA, 26 Mar, 28 Dec 1898. Whether HA paid the translator's fees is unclear.

52. BA's remarks at the expense of Jews differ remarkably from HA's. BA's are offhand Yankee conversation. HA's remarks are statements by a careful thinker who chooses his words.

53. The well-publicized present-day opinion of the U. S. Navy is that the explosion was caused by a fault in the ship's design.

54. As a historian and a politician, HA thought mainly in terms of nations. He however thought also in terms of hemispheres and in terms of the Old World and the New. This outburst reflects a loss of patience with the French partly brought on by what HA was beginning to believe had been very lethal sabotage of an American battleship by the Spanish. It thus is a case of HA's thinking of two Old World nations as a bloc to which the New World stands opposed.

55. HA to EC, 30 Jan 1898. He had mentioned nevrosis—or neurosis—four years earlier. See L, IV, 172.

56. HA to EC, 26, 28 Feb 1898.

57. The only account was written later. See Hay to HA, 9 May 1898. The logic of HA's inference is not explained in Hay's letter. Hay says he at first reacted to HA's conclusion as "hard to believe" but eventually changed his mind. He says, "The case is as clear as day."

58. The Spanish envoy wrote and mailed a letter involving abusive language about McKinley. When the letter was somehow spirited to the press and published, Dupuy de Lôme quit his post. Watching what happened, Mrs. Cameron was caught between surprise and perplexity. See EC to HA, 11 Feb 1898:—"Is it not extraordinary? After these years of astuteness & caution to commit such a letter to the mails. ..."

59. HA to EC, 12–13 Mar 1898.

60. HA had wanted to see Jerusalem partly because *Mont Saint Michel and Chartres* would concern, among other persons, the enthusiasts who proposed and the warriors who waged the first crusades.

61. Hay to HA, 11 Mar 1898.

62. Letters, EC to HA, 11 Feb 1898, 24 Feb 1898, & 7 Mar 1898.

63. Letters, BA to HA, 27 Feb 1898, 11 Mar 1898, & 26 Mar 1898.

64. HA to EC, 24–28 Mar 1898:—"... tomorrow I go to Ephesus, like St[.] Paul, whose foot-steps I follow."

65. In the same letter to BA, 2 Apr 1898, HA offered his brother some

distillations of the main ideas suggested by *The Law of Civilization and Decay*. These distillations can be summarized in four words: the survival of the cheapest. An example HA gives is atheism, which, he suggests, is "still cheaper than reformed religion," and thus can be expected to supplant it. As written, these distillations can be read as if HA believed them, and there seems every possibility that BA read them in just that way.

My opinion is that HA believed none of them. Clearly he wished to tell his brother what his book appeared to say. At the same time, he wished *not* to reveal to him the historical ideas that he himself would set forth when writing *Mont Saint Michel and Chartres*.

66. *Mont Saint Michel and Chartres* (1913), 134; (LoA), 465:—"the beautiful work at Cairo."

67. See "THE STORY OF ARIITAIMAI, 1846" in *Memoirs of Arii Taimai*, 181–96.

68. HA, *Mémoires d'Arii Taimai*, Paris 1964, x.

69. For the letter's date, see Salmon to HA, 6 Jul 1898.

70. HA to EC, 10–14 Apr 1898:—"One afternoon we spent at Eleusis, really an exquisite spot." "All today we have passed in an expedition to Sunium. . . . How I wish you and Martha had been with me to see the Aegean at its best!" (Rockhill himself took part in the trip to Sunium.)

71. HA to EC, 20 Apr 1898; HA to CMG, 23 Apr 1898.

72. EC had arranged that her cousin Rosina Hoyt accompany her and Martha to Europe. The addition of the cousin did not affect HA in any significant way. On the assumption that biographies should be limited in complexity where possible, I have kept the cousin out of the narrative.

73. HA hoped also to visit Troy but learned that a visit would not be feasible during the limited time at his and Rockhill's disposal.

74. HA to EC, 13 Apr 1898. HA's plural "Reports" is confirmation that his *Recognition of Cuban Independence* was read privately in 1895 and early 1896 in a first, handwritten form and afterwards, late in 1896, was circulated, slightly revised, in a printed form.

75. The sentence in HA's letter to Hay of 5 May 1898 that begins "You have a new game to play . . ." can be read as perfectly honest; but it is followed by another sentence—"My own little game of two years ago is played out and won in far less time than I expected."—which is misleading. HA's game of 1895–1896 had not been little. It was not played out as HA intended, voluntarily by the U. S. government. It perhaps was won in less time than HA expected, but only in a way that neither he nor anyone else anticipated—a way involving an explosion.

Whether Hay would notice the dissimulations in HA's sentence may be doubted. HA so buttered the sentence that Hay might read it and not realize that any butterings were there.

76. BA to HA, 29 Apr 1898.

77. HA was also in Paris to see his dentist.

78. HA to Cunliffe, 19 May 1898.

79. In his letters written within the period embraced by this book, HA sometimes claims to have bought rare coins and antique furnishings at bargain prices and thus to have placed himself in the company of the Jews, as he imagined them. One result was his once declaring himself "the biggest Jew thief of the lot." See HA to EC, 5 Mar 1898.

8. UNDER COVER

Letters to and by HA are in HA-micro 14, 15, 16, or H, unless otherwise indicated.

PRINCIPAL SOURCES

(1) twenty-one letters, HA to BA, 19 Jul 1898–27 Dec 1899.
(2) fifty letters and a cable, HA to EC, [22 Jul 1898]–30–31 Oct 1899. (For details about a little-known letter, see note 17, below.)
(3) seven letters, HA to Rockhill, 24 Aug 1898–8 Sep 1899.
(4) seventeen letters, HA to CMG, 27 Aug 1898–31 Dec 1899.
(5) six letters, HA to Hay, 7 Sep 1898–15 Dec 1899.
(6) fifty-two letters, EC to HA, [26 Oct 1898]–1 Nov 1899. (For correct dates of eight letters, see notes 18 & 46, below.)

LESSER SOURCES; CITATIONS; COMMENTS

1. HA's letter is missing. Its gist is revealed by Rockhill's reply, 4 Aug 1898.
2. For detailed recollections of the gatherings at Surrenden Dering, see Abigail Adams Homans, *Education by Uncles*, Bost 1966, 87–96. See also HA2, Diary, 10 Sep 1898, MHS:—"The place here is enormous and the house one of those large country places that the owners cannot afford to live in." Also ibid., 11 Sep 1898:—"Mrs. Cameron is very kind to us all and entertaining."
3. HA to EC, 5–12 Nov 1891, HA-micro 9.
4. In a letter to HA, 3 Oct 1899, EC wrote about a married man and a married woman who eloped, reconsidered, and returned to their spouses. She said about them: "They both affirm that their relations have not been criminal and both beg for divorce in order that they may marry. Did you ever know such a crazy tale?"
   HA replied on 16 Oct 1899, ". . . the parties seem to have been frank enough, and foolish enough, to be ideals of virtue."
   For the parties' names, see L, V, 48n4.
5. EC had not read the letters. She however had learned to recognize the woman's handwriting on the envelopes and had discovered signs of fear in her husband's behavior. See EC to HA, 20 Aug 1899.
6. HA's account in *EHA* (1918), 318–19; (LoA), 1053–54, seems strongly worded but factually unexceptionable.
7. The phrase is drawn from HA to CMG, 4 Oct 1898. See note 9.
8. A good question is whether HA understood that he and Hay were to be equals or unequals in their new capacities. HA was sensitive to the question and answered it by invoking metaphors. He began with metaphors of extreme inferiority. He told CMG (letter of 12 Sep 1898), ". . . I am a gilded butterfly on his [Hay's] cart-wheel, or at least a house-fly on the adjoining window." He told EC (letter of 29 Nov 1898) that he was Hay's "shadow."
   Using a metaphor of extremest but ugly superiority, he told Cunliffe (letter of 19 Jan 1899): "I have grown so used to playing the spider, and squatting in silence in the middle of this Washington web . . . that I have now a little the sense of being a sort of ugly, bloated, purplish-blue and highly venomous, hairy tarantula which catches and devours Presidents, senators, diplomates [*sic*], congressmen and cabinet-officers, and knows the flavor of every generation and every country in the civilised world. Just now my poor friend John Hay is caught

in the trap, and, to my infinite regret, I have to make a meal of him as of the rest. Very glad I shall be if he escapes alive. . . ."

9. The only record of the arrangement is HA to CMG, 4 Oct 1898. The letter is carefully worded and if read casually can seem to say less, or other, than what it says. It makes four important statements: that Hay was made secretary by a "cataclysm"—the Spanish-American War; that Hay did not ask HA to become ambassador to England; that the offer of the ambassadorship was not in Hay's power to make; and that Hay asked HA to become his "associate" in the secretaryship.

That Hay and his wife agreed about the wisdom of the arrangement is clear in their later conduct and letters. That Adams adhered to the arrangement's terms is clear in his conduct and letters.

10. HA to Rockhill, 24 Aug 1898.

11. Gwynn, I, 253.

12. Thayer, II, 182; Dennett, 218–23; Clymer, 157–71.

13. See HA-2, 631–34, concerning HA's offers of proof in his *History of the United States* that the Americans were superior in intelligence.

14. BA to HA, 17 Oct 1898:—"I have today received your letter with the proof. . . . I am much pleased . . . that you are satisfied with my book in its new form. . . ."

15. L, IV, 617n1.

16. Hastily read, HA to CMG, 4 Oct 1898, may seem to indicate that Hay suggested HA as his replacement in the English mission; but careful reading supports an opposite conclusion. See note 9, above.

17. HA to EC, Wed. 11 P.M., [26 Oct 1898], filmed out of sequence in HA-micro 21 as if dated 23 Oct 1906; omitted in L & O.

18. EC's letter was written on Wednesday but she mistakenly headed it "Tuesday Evening." At a later time, EC and Ford misdated the letter and her next six letters to HA when reviewing them. The correct dates of the seven letters are: "Tuesday Evening" [actually Wednesday, 26 Oct 1898]; "Thursday Eve", [27 Oct 1898]; "Saturday night," [29 Oct 1898]; "Sunday night," [30 Oct 1898]; "Tuesday night," [1–2 Nov 1898]; "Friday," [4 Nov 1898]; and "Sunday," [7 Nov 1898].

19. HA to Rebecca Rae, 23 Aug 1898. The Spanish defenders in Cuba would not have agreed with HA that next to no one was killed.

20. HA to EC, 15 Nov 1898. The idea was groundless. In the McKinley administrations, *all* executive appointments were matters of presidential or congressional patronage.

21. HA to EC, 25–27 Dec 1898.

22. Dennett, 189:—"Hay was a day-to-day man; he was not accustomed to sit down and ponder the fundamental significance of the events which went by him. . . ."

23. HA understood that his special duty as Hay's partner was to foresee. Without telling her that he was secretly associated with Hay, he wrote to EC, 11 Dec 1898:—". . . the real job is to keep ahead of the procession. . . . I sit here, and peer into the future. . . ."

24. HA's idea of history, best consulted in his *History of the United States*, turns on the ability of humans to form "ideals," meaning chiefly visions of wanted futures. For details, see Chap. 17.

25. As printed in Paris, 1901, the words of the title appear on the title page in capital letters of five noticeably dissimilar sizes. The words in the largest type

are "Arii Taimai E." "Memoirs" is set in type almost as large. "Tauratua I Amo" is set in type large enough to be conspicuous. The lesser terms of the title—all set in smaller capitals—have meanings as follows: "Marama of Eimeo" means head chief of Moorea; "Teriirere of Tooarai" means head chief of Papara; and "Teriinui of Tahiti" means head chief of the Vaiari family.

26. A year later, on 19 Nov 1899, HA would write to Sir John Clark (L, V, 59): "It would really amuse you to visit New York now, and see what the civilisation of the future is to be. There is something magnificently energetic and big about it. The amount of energy they [the New Yorkers] control is stupendous, and dwarfs Europe."

27. For "Little Dordy," see MC to HA, Monday, [March 1899]. For the truly important meaning of "Dordy Dobbitt," see HA-2, 534–35.

28. HA to MC, 9 Dec 1898.

29. MC's relation with HA had a passionate, though innocent, aspect. In her letter to him, Monday, [March 1899], op. cit., she says nothing about Dr. Dobbitt but plainly intends to keep possession of her "Dear Little Dordy" and sends him "packs, and packs, and packs of love and kisses."

30. In his *Henry Adams*, NY & Lond 1987, 114–15, R. P. Blackmur says that there was "much gossip" and "talk" about HA's "relations with Mrs. Cameron" and that the gossip was at its "height" in "the spring and summer of 1897" (i.e. a year prior to the arrival of the Camerons and HA at Surrenden Dering). Blackmur's statement perhaps is true, but he cites no evidence. For an instance of gossip at a later time, see note 31.

31. An observer who wondered whether HA was happy with EC was Henry James. In his *Henry James/ The Treacherous Years/ 1895–1901*, Phila & NY 1959, 233–34, Leon Edel gives an impression that HJ saw HA and EC as parties to an affair. He quotes HJ as writing, evidently in 1898, that he "envied him [HA] as much as was permitted by my feeling that the affair was only what I should *once* have found maddeningly romantic." HJ's admission of envy is unfortunately so involuted that there may properly be wide disagreement about what it amounts to.

32. Three letters, Rockhill to HA, 7 Jan 1899, 25 Jan 1899, & 6 Mar 1899.

33. EC had not been told in advance where HA intended to stay. See EC to HA, Tuesday morning, [29 Mar 1899]:—"I take for granted that you are not coming here to your own appartement [*sic*], as you should, for you have not told me to notify Joseph [the man-servant]."

What arrangement they settled upon after his arrival is unclear in the evidence, which is sparse.

34. HA had already written to EC, 4 Dec 1898, "How I want a fresh baby to play Martha!"

35. Margaret Chanler, *Roman Spring/ Memoirs . . .* , Bost 1934, 294. On the same page, Mrs. Chanler recalls that HA asked Laura to call him "Deordy." One may assume that this record reflects HA's intonation when speaking the suggested name. It thus is confirmation that the name was a baby-talk form of Georgie; hence also of George.

36. HA to EC, Tuesday, [25 Apr 1899].

37. HA to EC, Saturday, [29 Apr 1899].

38. Ibid.

39. Margaret Chanler remarked that HA and the Lodges left Rome "long before you had planned to go." See her letter to HA, 23 May [1899].

40. HA to EC, Tuesday, [16 May 1899].

41. In Rome, HA had seen the ceilings that Michelangelo painted in the Sistine Chapel. In Florence, he studied sculptured figures by Michelangelo. Writing to Louisa Hooper from Florence on 20 May 1899, he said about one of the sculptor's most famous works: "Of course the Slaves are more beautiful. The struggle and the apparently happy extinction, are more to our fancy."

These lines were evidently more or less simultaneous with HA's writing a sonnet titled "The Slaves of Michelangelo." See end of HA-micro 7. The sonnet concerns the sculptor's success in representing a slave's experiencing happy extinction.

For HA, this matter of happy extinction related to questions that had been at issue for some time between him and Bigelow. The questions were: What is Nirvana? And how can one reach it?

Three months later, on 22 Aug 1899, HA would write to Louisa from Paris: ". . . Bigelow is not yet grown to real Nirwana [sic]. He still hopes to reach it by struggling. It is in vain that I point him to Michael Angelo's Slaves. I can't convince him that Nirwana is anywhere one drops; especially au cinquième Avenue du Bois."

42. During more than six weeks, from 23 May through 6 Jul 1899, HA wrote only three letters that survive. He evidently wished not to create records.

43. Margaret Chanler to HA, 23 May [1899].

44. Herbert R. Lottman, *The French Rothschilds*, NY 1995, especially 109–17.

45. Writing from Washington to Anne Fell on 24 Dec 1898, HA said he regretted not being in Paris, where people had "fits." "The fits are great fun. Some day perhaps some one will get hurt, and I never take my afternoon walk up the boulevards without looking up the Rue Laffite [sic] to see whether there is a chance to observe how a Rothschild would ornament a lamp-post." The image HA invoked is horrible but was warranted to this extent: in Paris at the time presumably were French anarchists and anti-Semites who would have liked to commit the public murder of a Rothschild.

46. See EC to HA, "Tuesday afternoon," beginning "I suppose we are half way over . . . ," filmed out of sequence in HA-micro 15 as if written in June 1899. Read together with its sequel, EC to HA, 19 Jul 1899, the letter is revealed to have been written on 10–15 Jul 1899. It makes clear that EC sailed from Cherbourg c. 8 Jul 1899.

47. EC was capable of a strong dislike of Jews. In her letter to HA, Sunday morning, [9 Jul 1899], she says, ". . . the usual percentage of israelites [sic] makes the deck nauseous."

48. HA to EC, 13 Jul 1899.

49. Four letters, HA to EC, 28 Jul 1899, 4 Aug 1899, 14 Aug 1899, & 6 & 8 Aug 1899.

50. A statement in HA's letter to EC, 14–15 Aug 1899, met the strict requirements of high comedy. ". . . just now, I replace husbands sometimes, when they want their wives looked after, provided the duties are light. . . ."

51. EC to HA, 25 Jul 1899.

52. The insanity and suicide of MHA in 1885 had been consequent to her being subjected to insupportable strains when past the age of forty-one, in a situation in Massachusetts which HA could not control. See HA-2, 487–504.

53. Hay to HA, 5 Aug 1899.

54. Possibly BA's manuscript survives in altered form as his article, "Russia's Interest in China," *Atlantic Monthly*, Sep 1900. The article was reprinted in BA, *America's Economic Supremacy*, NY 1900, 193–222.

55. Because he accepted the theory that Dreyfus was innocent, yet sympathized with the French government, army, and people, HA could count himself as pro-Dreyfus, anti-Dreyfus, both, or neither.

He appreciated the comic aspect of his position and wrote to Hay, 11 Apr 1899, "I can't find out now whether I am Dreyfussard or Anti." More negatively, he assured EC, 28 Jul 1899, that "everything said by the Dreifussards . . . as well as by the Anti-dreifussards, and other Frenchmen, if there are any," was "an obvious lie." Still more negatively, he told EC, 14 Aug 1899, that he had "not the patience to read or discuss" the Dreyfus Affair but was curious to know "the thing that comes next." What he had in mind was a very serious consideration: how the United States might fare if it could not look to France as an ally. In his words:—"Dreifuss is to be set free—that has been foreseen for a year—but what is to become of France? They can't acquit Dreifuss without condemning France. . . . That too is foreseen. . . . Then what is to become of us [the Americans]?"

56. These lines in HA to Hay, 20 Aug 1899, should be read in conjunction with HA's anonymous summary of Hay's work as secretary of state in *JHLetters*, I, xvi–xxii.

57. Feldman, *The Dreyfus Affair . . .* , op. cit, 62–64.

58. EC to HA, 19 Jul 1899:—". . . when I do go [to Washington], may I ask Maggie to put me up?" Her question needed an answer. HA's answer can be assumed but does not appear in his extant replies.

59. EC had received HA's letter of 29 Aug 1899, in which he said he had asked Misses de Wolfe and Marbury to stay with him at 50 Avenue du Bois de Boulogne, beginning about September 10. He added: "Please spread it about that I am living with actresses in your appartment [*sic*]. It will give a lurid interest to my dissolute age." As things developed, his proposed guests accepted the loan of another apartment.

60. EC added next day in the same letter, 10–11 Sep 1899: "Your house looks charming. I cannot get over my admiration of first the house and then the care these two take of it. It is wonderful."

61. Clearly the "race" HA refers to is the Americans. Their fortunes were made by Washington's army in the War of Independence and made a second time by Grant and Sherman's armies, forcing the capitulation of Confederate traitors in the Civil War. How later American armies might relate to the *French* army might seem a question, but France was the only country in Europe that had made serious pretensions to being a republic and a democracy. Thus France and the United States were historic partners. HA's reasoning is as basic as that.

62. HA to EC, 18–19 Sep 1899.

63. EC to HA, 18 Sep 1899.

64. HA to EC, 25 Sep 1898.

65. HA to EC, 25–26 Sep 1899.

66. BA to HA, 24 Sep 1899.

67. See especially BA to HA, Tuesday, [16? Oct 1899].

68. HA had recently addressed her as "the only good girl of the lot." See HA to Louisa Hooper, 22 Aug 1899.

69. HA to EC, 23 Oct 1899. Saint Gaudens seemed likely to be most remembered as the sculptor of three memorials.

The first, completed in 1891, was the memorial in Washington at HA and MHA's grave site. Designed by HA, it mainly consisted of a seated figure in bronze which to some observers was the very image of the poise of human beings when most mindful of death. HA had visited it many times.

The second, completed in 1897, was a bronze bas-relief of Colonel Robert Shaw and the black Union soldiers with whom he died. Shaw was one of MHA's cousins. HA had seen the work during a visit to Boston in March 1898. He did not express an opinion that survives.

When finished, the third would be a heroic statue of General Sherman mounted on a walking horse and preceded by an allegorical walking figure of Victory. Saint Gaudens had brought general-and-horse to Paris and caused a sensation by showing them at the Salon. Currently he was creating the Victory at a Paris studio. (The completed work was scheduled to be shown at the Paris Exposition of 1900.) HA saw the incomplete memorial at the Salon in May 1899, after returning to Paris from Rome. He did not need reminding that General Sherman was one of EC's uncles.

70. Because church spires and church windows are subjects of the first ten chapters of *Mont Saint Michel and Chartres*, one may suppose that HA had already completed first drafts of many of the ten.

71. See Chap. 4, note 5, above.

72. In HA's letters written in 1898, there are 40 occurrences of the word "Jew" and variants. In 1899, there are 55. Of the 95, 52 are references to bankers, capitalists, etc. Six are references to European socialists or communists.

73. HA's views relating to socialism are a simple matter much intertwined with the less simple matter of his views relating to capitalism and bankers, and intertwined as well with the complicated matter of his views relating to Jews.

This entire spectrum of considerations must be borne in mind when one encounters such words of HA's as the following to BA, 12 Jun 1899, "I loath the socialist . . . even more than I loath the Jew."

74. Originally Isabella Stewart, Mrs. Gardner was born in New York on 14 Apr 1840 and thus was fifty-nine and not young. She had stayed for a week with HA at 50 Avenue du Bois de Boulogne. Mrs. Cameron, in contrast, was born on 10 Nov 1857. Her age late in 1899 was forty-two—which, it happened, was the age at which Mrs. Henry Adams had died.

75. HA to CMG, 22 Nov 1899.

76. Clara Hay to HA, 10 Dec 1899.

77. The words "poisoned chalice" in HA to BA, 15 Dec 1899, are lifted from Macbeth's soliloquy beginning (1623 Folio) "If it were done, when 'tis done, then 'twer well/ It were done quickly. . . ."

78. A year earlier, HA had asked EC to understand whatever he and she were doing as it might compare with the actions set forth in one of Shakespeare's greatest plays. See HA to EC, Christmas 1898: ". . . I want you to understand better than Cleopatra did, how a world is to be well, or ill, lost."

9. Violence

Letters by and to HA are in HA-micro 16, 17, B, or H, unless otherwise indicated.

PRINCIPAL SOURCES

(1) sixty-three letters, EC to HA, 11 Jan 1900–13–15 Mar 1901. (For dates of three letters, see note 40, below.)

(2) sixty letters and notes, HA to EC, 15–17 Jan 1900–18 Mar 1901. (For details about four notes, see note 41, below.)

(3) eleven letters, HA to BA, 7 Feb 1900–7–8 Feb 1901.

(4) seven letters, HA to CMG, 1 Feb 1900–11 Jan 1901.

(5) nine letters, HA to Hay, 8 May 1900–10 Jan 1901.
(6) HA, "Prayer to The Virgin of Chartres"—incomplete; as sent to EC on 26 Feb 1901, L, V, 206–11.

LESSER SOURCES; CITATIONS; COMMENTS

1. In the same letter, 11 Jan 1900, EC tells HA, ". . . it is all wrong[,] your going away." Her protest is one of several confirmations that she was not told about the arrangement between the Hays and HA that made HA a sharer in Hay's secretaryship. See note 45, below.

2. In his second letter, HA said King was as "active as ever, if not as . . . hopeful as twenty years ago." See HA to EC, 22–23 Jan [1900].

3. HA to EC, 15–16 Jan 1900.

4. The pursuit fluttered the feelings of the Hooper nieces, who were as fond of Cousin Sturgis as they were of Uncle Henry.

5. In his biography of Hay, Dennett suggests (289) that HA had "laid the basis of Hay's Far Eastern policy" by saying in a letter to HCL, 4 Aug 1891 (HA-micro 9), that the only possible opening for expansion by the United States in the Pacific theatre would be to "Americanise Siberia." The suggestion seems overreaching. *Not* overreaching is the suggestion that Hay's resorting to informal diplomacy resulted from his difficulties with the Senate and an appeal to HA for advice. See HA to Hay, 20 Aug 1899, quoted in Chap. 8.

6. On 28 Jan 1901, HA was joined at dinner by Winty Chanler and "the Boer agent at London," then visiting in Washington. HA wrote next day to EC, "I managed to go over the whole ground with Montague White, who is intelligent, and I judge has enough Hebrew blood to be useful."

The remark is one of several instances in which HA, in the belief that a person might be all or part Jewish, supposed the person to be intelligent. For example, he spoke of "Rubens, my Cuban friend, who is I presume a Jew, and therefore has more intelligence than any fifty Americans, Spaniards, or Philippinos." See HA to EC, 12 Feb 1899, HA-micro 15.

7. Readers should take HA's talk of his and Hay's "natural pessimism" with large grains of salt. The degree to which HA was a pessimist and the degree to which he was an optimist are matters at issue in all the chapters of this biographical trilogy.

8. Cameron to HA, 29 Jan 1900.

9. HA to BA, 7 Feb 1900.

10. Salmon to HA, 10 Jan 1900.

11. Recollections by LHT, told to me several times in the 1950s and 1960s.

12. For HA's photographs of himself, Louisa Hooper, Abigail Adams, and Harriet Blaine Beale, see L, IV & V.

13. HA to Stoddard, 21 Feb 1900, HA-micro H.

14. One may speculate that Chapter VIII–XI of HA's *Education* were all drafted in the 1890s, or at least that HA knew what he would say in every one. These chapters place the crisis for his father's mission at the moment in 1863 when the British government blocked delivery of the "Laird Rams" to the Confederate navy. The crisis was identically placed by CFA2 in his biography of CFA, published in 1900. Credence in this placing was strengthened in 1918, when HA's *Education* was published. And the placing was repeated by Ephraim Douglass Adams in his *Great Britain and the American Civil War*, Lond 1925. Yet it is very evident that the crisis for the American Unionists who were in Europe at the time was the *Trent* Affair in late 1861 and early 1862.

That the crisis occurred at that early moment is one of the main suggestions advanced by the volumes of this trilogy. See HA-1, Chaps. 24–27; HA-2, Chap. 1. When the suggestion is accepted, as I expect it will be, HA's importance as a key, active figure in the American Civil War will be recognized and his many efforts to conceal and reveal his importance will be much better understood.

15. In the 1930s, when editing his *Letters of Henry Adams* (*1892–1918*) Ford deleted HA's phrase "and it makes me sick." He appears to have thought the phrase too strong for publication. See F, II, 271.

16. Her not writing a question mark after "at once" may indicate that EC felt her completed sentence as not a question but a directive.

17. Cameron to HA, 5 Apr 1900.

18. EC took advantage of being in Biarritz to visit medieval churches in the area, most notably at Lourdes, and to travel by automobile, as HA would later do.

19. In her 26 Mar 1900 letter, EC mentions being asked by a European acquaintance whether "it was true that I was divorcing Donald." (A rumor to that effect had been aired at a club in Biarritz.) She continues: "So I told him . . . there was not and never had been a question of divorce, and . . . as far as I could judge by European standards . . . I was quite respectable. Moreover that I had only left Donald in November & that I was expecting him out in May."

Her reported answer is interesting as indicating that she had come to judge her entire marital history, including her attachment to HA, by European standards concerning marital problems and their solutions, as opposed to American standards concerning the same matters.

20. BA to HA, 16 May 1900.

21. BA to HA, 22 Jun 1900; CFA2 to HA, 30 Jun 1900—misfilmed in HA-micro 16 as if dated 30 Jul 1900; BA to HA, 19 Jul 1900.

22. CFA2 to HA, 30 Jun 1900. Also see note 21, above.

23. HA to Ford, 2 May 1910, FP 13, with two of its attachments: Barron to HA, 1 May 1895, & Barron to HA, undated [1897?].

24. In his letter, HA says the researcher who helped him was "a very intelligent young fellow," which may indicate that he and Barron met. A possible date and place for a meeting is mid-July 1895 in London.

25. HA to Rockhill, 12 Jul 1900.

26. In the 1950s, LHT told me that HA was so nimble that in Paris he enjoyed outracing her down the stairs of buildings he lived in.

27. Hooper may have been ill in bed. According to HA to EC, 30–31 Jul 1900, he was suffering "one of his gastric break-downs."

28. See note 43, below.

29. Hay to HA, 22 Aug 1900.

30. HA had mentioned the idea six years earlier. See HA to EC, 10 Oct 1894, HA-micro 12: "I am rheumatic and dyspeptic, and want to be a Cardinal."

31. Donald was writing only to Martha. EC told HA, ". . . he never writes to me, but his letters to Martha are regular, and she has not now heard for a month." See EC to HA, Saturday, [15 Sep 1900], beginning "A thousand thanks. . . ."

32. Ibid.

33. For the portrait, see L, V, 151. The background possibly is evidence that EC had reoccupied 50 Avenue du Bois de Boulogne and the portrait was painted there.

34. The apartment below EC's at 50 Avenue du Bois de Boulogne was

rented by an American, Ralph Curtis. Levenson and his associates state (L, V, 151n1) that HA "rented the apartment of Mrs. Ralph Curtis' mother at 3 Rue de Traktir."

35. One is tempted to suppose that HA had wished to pay for the Zorn portrait, that EC insisted that she pay for it, and that paying Zorn put her in need of money.

36. Letters, Hay to HA, 8 Jul 1900 & 25 Sep 1900.

37. HA to EC, Monday, 29 Oct [1900].

38. The chanson appears in *MSM&CH* (1913), 227–28; (LoA), 550.

39. As a possible example of HA's writing poetry in prose, one may look at two harsh lovely sentences he had written to EC from Baalbek on 16 Mar 1898, HA-micro 14. "We had mostly come over the Lebanon by rail, in Alpine snow, and had driven five hours up a valley exactly resembling southern California or Nevada, in a freezing wind, and found ourselves at Baalbek without the means of keeping warm, and had shivered in the ruins of the Temple of the Sun for an hour or two to chill us for dinner. Baalbek is about four thousand feet above the sea; the snow is still lying in the shadows; today I amused myself by poking holes in the ice which crusted little pools of water in the temple stones; and of course there is neither a fire-place, nor wood to burn in it, in any town in Syria."

40. Her letters were headed with days but not dates. See EC to HA, Thursday, [1 Nov 1900], Saturday Eve., [3 Nov 1900], and Sunday, [4 Nov 1900].

41. Four notes written by HA on 3 Rue de Traktir stationery, one dated "Wednesday," the others undated, are filmed out of sequence in HA-micro 17, one as if written in June 1901, the other three as if written in mid-December 1901. Mostly but not entirely directed to EC, they indicate that HA sometimes gave dinner to EC or to both EC and MC at his apartment.

42. In his 5 Nov 1900 letter to Louisa Hooper, HA says of his interval at 3 Rue de Traktir, "I live up here in serene solitude with St[.] Thomas Aquinas and the Virgin of Chartres[,] who are carrying on a flirtation which at their age is hardly decorous." On this basis, HA can perhaps be accused of informing his favorite Hooper niece that a "flirtation" was in progress between himself and EC.

43. The only record of Langley's tutoring HA in Paris is a line in *The Education*: "At Langley's behest, the Exhibition dropped its superfluous rags and stripped itself to the skin, for Langley knew what to study, and why, and how. . . ." See *EHA* (1907), 331; (LoA), 1066.

44. The date of his departure is inferred from EC to HA, 22 Jan 1901.

45. When HA left, EC again protested, saying—letter of 22 Jan 1901: "Why did you go? There is absolutely no reason for it, and I do miss you so. When six o'clock comes, I am as restless as a cat." Also see note 1, above.

46. Elizabeth Lodge to HA, [26? Jan 1901], filmed in HA-micro 17 after 31 Mar 1901; GCL to HA, [25 or 26? Jan 1901], filmed in HA-micro 17 at the start of 1901. HA's yellow dragons are noted in EC to HA, Friday, [12 Oct 1900].

47. HA may have read the story. The phrase "turn of the screw" had appeared in two of his letters: HA to Ford, 19 Dec 1898, L, IV, 639; HA to EC, 29–31 Jan 1899, HA-micro 15.

48. EC to HA, Tuesday Night, [29 Jan 1901].

49. HA's arrangements at 3 Rue de Traktir were illegal. Under the laws affecting Paris apartments, Mrs. Markwald could not sublet the apartment to him, and he could not lend it to guests. But laws were one thing, practicality another. The ancient landlord would have been happy enough, as he later said, if HA had paid him a call and treated him with appropriate deference.

On Thursday, 31 Jan 1901, after much conversation, EC persuaded Joly to permit Bay and Bessy to remain but was not told by him that he already had sent them away. She then learned that they had signed a six-month lease for their Left Bank attic.

50. EC to HA, 28–29 Jan 1901.

51. Whether HA prayed to dynamos may be doubted. The story he told CSR was comic throughout.

52. Three letters, HA to EC, 5 Feb 1901, 18–19 Feb 1901, & 25–26 Feb 1901.

53. Kelly's letter is missing. For "nephew," see EC's summary letter to HA, 13–15 Mar 1901.

54. It is suggested in Chap. 3 that HA in 1893 somewhat modeled the ten stanzas after Satan's address to the sun in *Paradise Lost*, IV, 32–113. Milton reportedly wrote the address when young for an intended play and when older inserted it at a convenient place in *Paradise Lost*. Thus, if he did indeed lean on Milton in 1893, and if he inserted the stanzas of 1893 into his "Prayer to the Virgin of Chartres" in 1901, it might be said that HA took cues from Milton twice.

55. Evidence that HA had told EC he wrote *Democracy* is confined to one sentence in his letter to her of 28 Jan 1901: "I am dying to write another satire." Though slender, the evidence is sufficient.

56. Later HA said amusedly that EC fell asleep while he was reading the first chapter to her and MC. See HA to EC, 16 Apr 1901. The remark may be an instance of understatement. HA can be imagined to have given EC access to the manuscript.

57. Because Mrs. Lodge's newer travel plans tended to be precisely what HA would wish them to be, one suspects that the second trip to Italy was suggested to her by him, of course in secret.

58. When he wrote the play, Aeschylus was limited to two speaking characters in a scene. The limit may have inspired him to bring a helper onto the stage in whose nature speech is absent.

59. HA to EC, 18 Feb 1901:—". . . these French things are annoying, infuriating, and even, in the case of Bay and Bessie, may be serious; but they are superficial."

60. HA to CMG, 29 Mar [1901]:—"My apartment in Paris has got me into an exasperating situation with an 83-year old landlord, which makes me sick with white fury. . . ."

61. HA to BA, 7–8 Feb 1901.

62. Another suggestion might be that HA's violence was a delayed re-action to the jolts and disappointments imposed on him by the Dreyfus Affair. The idea tempts acceptance, but it appears that the principal cause of his violence was an inner cause, not an outer.

63. Of the lesser factors that incited HA's white wrath, one possibly was a suspicion he formed that he and EC—especially EC—had become targets of unsparing gossip. One notices that his wrath preceded by only a few days a letter in which Henry James said to a friend that EC "sucked the lifeblood of poor Henry Adams and made him more 'snappish' than nature intended." HJ continued: ". . . it's one of the longest and oddest American *liaisons* I've ever known. Women have been hanged for less—and yet men have been too, I judge, rewarded with more." See HJ to Henrietta Reubell, 27 Feb 1901, as quoted in Edel, *Henry James/ The Treacherous Years: 1895–1902*, op. cit., 234–35.

HJ's lines deserve a commentary. In the sense of first-hand observation, HJ had not known the liaison between EC and HA. During recent years, he had seen each of the parties very infrequently and can be said to have seen them together once, during a visit he made to Surrenden Dering in October 1898. See *HJLetters*, IV, 82–83.

HJ's saying that women had been hanged for less than what EC had done could be taken as an assertion of positive knowledge that she committed adultery, and his saying that men had been more rewarded than HA could be taken as an assertion of knowledge that she had not committed it enough. Yet HJ so worded his lines that they were both declarative and evasive. They could say everything or nothing. Their true importance may lie in the evidence they offer that HJ's brand of boastful gossip was highly skilled.

10. Bothered by the Slaughterhouse

Letters by and to HA are in HA-micro 17, 18, B, or H, unless other wise indicated.

PRINCIPAL SOURCES

(1) forty-one letters, EC to HA, 19–20 Mar 1901–4–5 May 1902.
(2) eighteen letters, HA to Louisa Hooper, 26 Mar 1901–28 [Apr] & 1 Jun 1902.
(3) thirteen letters, HA to CMG, 29 Mar 1901–17 Apr 1902.
(4) forty-three letters, HA to EC, 1–2 Apr 1901–27 & 29 Apr 1902. (A letter, HA to EC, c. 25–26 Mar 1901, is missing from what otherwise is an intact series.)
(5) ten letters, HA to BA, 22 Apr 1901–16 May 1902.
(6) nine letters & a cable, HA to Hay, 9 Jun 1901–28 Apr 1902.
(7) [HA], *Memoirs of Arii Taimai e/ Marama of Eimeo/ Teriirere of Tooarai/ Teriinui of Tahiti/ Tauraatua i Amo*, Paris (privately printed) 1901. (For the number of copies printed, see note 12, below.)
(8) HA, "King," in *Clarence King Memoirs*, NY & Lond 1904, 157–85.

LESSER SOURCES; CITATIONS; COMMENTS

1. HA to Anne Fell, 25 Mar 1901. He more simply told Louisa Hooper (letter of 26 Mar 1901) that "on Friday" (March 22) he "got badly shaken up" by hearing and seeing Ternina.

2. In 1955, LHT led me to the house, showed me the window from which her father threw himself, and explained that his fall was cushioned by the many lines of a rack for drying clothes.

3. The letter presumably was mailed on 26 Mar 1901. For the quoted phrase, see HA to EC, 1–2 Apr 1901.

4. Her remarks (letter to HA, 31 Mar 1901) blend offhand derogation with unqualified regard:—"He is the veriest little sheeny you ever saw in looks, but as bright as can be, & strangely enough very sympathetic and simple."

5. HA to EC, 1 Apr 1901.

6. HA unintentionally increased the likelihood of wrong impressions by asking MC in a letter sent on 9 Apr 1901, "Won't you come to Baireuth in July . . . ?"

7. Berenson changed the spelling of his first name to Bernard in 1917, when the United States entered World War I.

8. HA to Louisa Hooper, 15 Apr 1901; King to HA, Saturday, [13 Apr 1901], filmed out of sequence in HA-micro 16 at the start of 1900.

9. In a year, some of HA's relations accepted his suggestion. See BA to HA, 28 Apr 1902.

10. HA's uneasiness about the non-arrival of letters from EC coincided with an occurrence involving HA, EC, Hay, and Henry James. HA told EC (letter of 6 May 1901): "Harry James has upset me. John Hay has been greatly troubled by Harry's last volume, *The Sacred Fount.* He [Hay] cannot resist the suspicion that it is very close on extravagance [i.e. mental illness]. His alarm made me read it, and I recognised at once that Harry and I had the same disease, the obsession of the *idée fixe.*" ". . . it is insanity, and I think Harry must soon take a vacation. . . ."

HJ's novel involves continual close scrutiny of love relations between English men and women. The teller of the story is an unnamed English male narrator who has a chance to watch such men and women at a country house during a weekend. He conceives a mad theory that any love relation imparts vitality to one participant by draining vitality from the other. Hay apparently inferred that HJ could devote a novel to such a narrator's madness only if going mad himself.

The subject was one that Hay had reason to find unsettling. At an uncertain moment, apparently in 1891 when HA was not yet back from the South Seas, he became infatuated with EC. He wrote her three undated love letters beginning "Goodnight," "I have just returned," and "I had just come in"; also a sonnet, "Obedience," beginning "The lady of my love bids me not love her . . . ," of which she made a copy dated 18 Mar 1892; and two letters dated Saturday, [4 Jun 1892], and 5 Jun 1892 that may be characterized as post-love communications. See Elizabeth Cameron Papers, MHS.

The letters and sonnet were such that Hay's ardor affected EC as more verbal than real. With regard to Hay's having composed a love poem she knew Hay had addressed to Mrs. Lodge, EC wrote to HA on 19 Sep 1892, HA-micro 10: "John Hay puzzles me more and more. Do you understand him?"

That in 1901 Hay disclosed his feelings about HJ to HA was not surprising. Hay made a habit of telling HA his feelings. And there was nothing surprising in HA's reading *The Sacred Fount* and telling EC he was in agreement with Hay that HJ was bordering on insanity. When possible, HA nodded agreement with Hay's ideas as if he believed them.

Complication begins with HA's ability as a reader. Close readers of HJ's *The Sacred Fount* may realize that the narrator in the novel, his theory notwithstanding, continuously witnesses—without sensing it—an affair between an unmarried man and another man's wife (Gilbert Long and Grace Brissenden) which is uninjurious, indeed enlivening, to both participants. A possibility thus exists that Hay read the novel one way, about which he and HA could correspond, but HA read it a different and even opposite way, which he characteristically would not disclose, not even to EC.

Another complication is that HJ gossiped about HA and EC in a manner consistent with his narrator's mad theory. See Chap. 9, note 63. And such is HJ's authority that the idea of EC as a vampire imbibing HA's blood, or at least as managing him however she pleases, has been received as largely true by one of HJ's acolytes. See Edel, *Henry James/ The Treacherous Years,* op. cit., 233–35.

11. When HA sailed from New York on May 15, 1901, this letter by EC was in transit to Washington. It was forwarded to him in Europe. He may have received it in London.

12. The number of copies HA ordered is unknown. I have evidence that copies are, or were, owned or held by thirty-six agencies and persons other than myself: Massachusetts Historical Society (two copies), Adams National Historic Site (Quincy MA), Library of Congress, Bernice P. Bishop Museum (Honolulu), New York Public Library, Boston Public Library, Morgan Library (New York), British Library (London), Bibliothèque Nationale (Paris), Musée de Papeete (Tahiti), American Geographical Society, Century Association, Harvard Univ., Brown Univ., Univ. of Michigan, Univ. of Wisconsin at Milwaukee, Western Reserve Univ., Elizabeth Cameron, Margaret Chanler, Anne de Cochrain, Anne Fell, Anna Lodge, Mary Cadwalader Jones, Mabel La Farge, Princess Takau, Louisa Hooper Thoron, Brooks Adams, Alexander Agassiz, Edward T. Allen, Louis Auchincloss, Bernhard Berenson, Worthington C. Ford, Charles Milnes Gaskell, and—presumably—John La Farge. In view of the list, I hesitate to believe that HA printed more than 60 copies.

13. Persons close to Adelbert Hay were anxious to convey an impression that he died of heart failure prior to his fall. See especially Clara Hay to HA, 7 Aug 1901.

14. For details, see L, V, 260 & 260n1. Presumably HA was much disturbed by the nieces' messages. None of the messages survive.

15. HA to CMG, 2 Oct 1901.

16. This is one of the passages in his writings in which HA can appear to be seeing the Jews and the Adamses as members of two old families that stand apart from other human beings. (Another such passage is the opening paragraph of *The Education of Henry Adams*.)

The passage may elicit the question: what moved HA to write its last four words? Of the possible answers, one may be that HA—in his third life—was trying hard not to be outdated and obsolete; hence was sensitive or over-sensitive to any experiences he had that might pose for him the possibility of his falling even slightly behind.

17. Ambassador Charlemagne Tower was on leave in Switzerland.

18. HA to EC, 21–27 Aug 1901.

19. HA to EC, 1–7 Sep 1901.

20. HA to EC, Sunday, [25 Aug 1901].

21. HA attended a private school in Boston and graduated at Harvard a year ahead of Herbert's brother, Charles Sanders Peirce. It bears emphasis that, when editor of the *North American Review*, HA published a long book review by Charles Peirce which sketched the outlines of Peirce's philosophy and anticipated much of the philosophical content of HA's *Mont Saint Michel and Chartres*. See HA-2, 269.

22. HA wrote to EC, 28 Sep 1901:—"To murder him [McKinley] was a gross absurdity that makes me despair of anarchy."

Knowing that McKinley had dragged EC's Uncle John from the Senate and made him secretary of state in order to create a Senate vacancy that Mark Hanna could fill, HA added a sentence adapted to EC's feelings: "The true person to kill was Hanna,—the senator!"

23. HA to Louisa Hooper, 3 Nov 1901. The "Brice girls" were the daughters of Senator Brice, his Washington neighbor.

24. EC to HA, 7 Oct 1901.

25. Hay to HA, 13 Oct 1901. Hay says in the letter, "Destroy this indiscretion." HA disregarded the instruction.

26. HA to CMG, 2 Oct 1901:—". . . I want to make some inquiries [in London] about printing, for the printers here drive me mad."

27. HA to Hay, 2 Nov 1901:—"a tailor and a printer."

28. EC to HA, 7 Oct 1901. Before coming to England, EC again visited Washington and at HA's house saw paintings, ceramics, and other possessions of his, newly arrived from Paris. She says in her letter that they greatly improved the house.

29. Neither could a librarian to whom Taylor itemized Adams's needs. See HA to Canfield, 20 Feb 1902, O.1902.4.

30. For early support given to Kennan by HA's wife, see HA-2, 868–69.

31. In the same letter to EC, 26 Jan 1902, HA reports, "Little Quentin is very much at home in my study, and considerably older and less school-boy like than his father."

32. It may appear that HA contradicts himself, saying first that British Columbia and Manchuria are one battlefield and saying next that they are two. Apparently the two were one in that Hay and HA were considering the possibility that Americans might want to settle in two areas on opposite sides of the Pacific as a single effort of territorial expansion.

How serious HA was about such a possibility may be doubted. He wanted an American withdrawal from the Philippines and may have made much of the idea of North-Pacific expansion as a mere talking point—a delusive carrot to move the donkeys.

33. As a means of not talking, HA would sometimes monopolize a conversation. For example, HA to EC, 9 & 11 Feb 1902:—"Cabot at last came in yesterday afternoon, and I talked rapidly for an hour to prevent his saying anything. Not that I care what he says, but that I should be tempted to reply; and he who replies is lost. Perhaps a year hence it may be worth while to talk."

34. HA did not hear Hay give the eulogy, but he read it and told EC (letter of 2 & 4 Mar 1902) that it showed "my brother Brooks's influence." "It is quite in line with Brooks's paper on McKinley." Also see BA, "William McKinley: The Modern Statesman," *Boston Evening Transcript*, 21 Sep 1901, 16.

35. Apparently BA envisioned a book about the relation between the supply of precious metals and the rise and fall of empires—a relation that had been brought to his notice by HA. In this connection, see BA to HA, 18 Feb 1902:—"Rockhill told me he could find the name of the book you spoke of on Alexander's mints."

36. BA to HA, 14 Mar 1902.

37. HA to EC, 11 Feb 1902.

38. HA to EC, 23 Feb 1902.

39. HA to EC, Monday, [24 Feb 1902].

40. HA to EC, 2 & 4 Mar 1902.

41. HA to CMG, 10 Mar 1902. Gaskell would notice that HA omitted the British prime minister from his list of leaders, yet so worded the sentence as to make clear that he viewed that individual as unserious.

42. See the certificate from Western Reserve University to HA, 7 Apr 1902, acknowledging his gift of a copy. The certificate is filmed out of sequence in HA-micro 18 as if dated *1903*.

43. Steven Weissmann, a leading New York rare book dealer, advised me in 1987 that HA wrote in one of the copies, "The Library of the Century Association, with the compliments of Tati Salmon/ Papara/ Tahiti, 1902."

44. Her copies are now at Houghton Library, Harvard University. In 1956, she permitted me to photocopy the *Memoirs of Marau Taaroa*.

45. Details about this intricate situation are given in HA to EC, 16 & 19 Mar 1902.

46. HA was avoiding Lodge for two reasons especially. He believed that Lodge meant to direct the country's foreign affairs and that Lodge rivalled Roosevelt in self-servingness. With regard to the latter reason, see HA to EC, 18 Mar 1902:—"Cabot's lofty principles compel him to help no member of his family but himself."

47. BA to HA, 14 Mar 1902:—"Have you interest enough in the case to jot down your theory about the truth of negatives—as for example that parallel lines probably meet, or that force [i.e. energy?] and matter are not constant in the universe . . . [?]"

48. When replying to his brother, HA sent him a copy of a current book, John Bernard Stallo's *Concepts of Modern Science*. HA's knowing about the book was itself an instance of his meddling with science.

49. HA to EC, 23 & 25 Mar 1902.

50. HA to EC, 30 Mar 1902.

51. His closing words were an exaggeration. The Lodges had come once to dinner and were coming again that night. In each case, however, HA steered the conversation away from politics. See HA's next instalment in the same letter.

52. HA to EC, [8 Apr] 1902.

53. Before he received her letter, HA told her (letter of 13 & 15 Apr 1902) that he and she would be arriving in Paris at nearly the same time and that it would not be "worthwhile" for him to move into the apartment. What he did on his arrival is unclear, but her stated expectation that she would find him living at the apartment may have acquired a measure of persuasiveness.

54. Levenson and his associates gloss HA's phrase "a historical romance of the year 1200" by saying it "apparently refers to the *Education*." See L, V, 380n3. Their suggestion overlooks HA's "King."

55. Principal source 8. As published in 1904, HA's talk is attended by a note (159): "This paper, presented here as originally written, was intended to be read at a proposed King Memorial Meeting at the Century Club." In view of HA's tendency to do things with the utmost expedition, the suggested date of composition must be April–May 1902, prior to his leaving again for Europe.

56. Ibid., 159–61.

57. HA's "King" should not be overlooked. It was as necessary a precursor of the completed *Education* as his earlier work, "Biography of John Hay."

58. Mrs. Cameron and Martha knew. The Hays knew, for HA gave Hay an inscribed copy—now at Brown University. All or most of HA's Hooper nieces knew; presumably some La Farges knew, and perhaps Charles Warren Stoddard; but I know of no evidence that HA gave copies to CFA2 or BA or that they as yet knew anything at all about his Tahiti work.

The copy now at the Adams National Historic Site bears no inscriptions. It was taken by BA from HA's Paris library in 1912 when that library was shipped to Quincy. See Chap. 22.

59. Salmon to HA, 12 May 1904, HA-micro 19.

60. [HA], *Denkwürdigkeiten von Arii Taimai E*, translated by Paul Hambruch, Hamburg (*Mitteilungen aus dem Museum der Völkerkunde*, VIII) 1920.

61. Henry Adams, *Mémoires d'Arii Taimai*, translated by Susan & André Lebois, Paris (*Publications de la Société des Océanistes*, 12) 1964.

62. A very small facsimile edition introduced by Robert Spiller, NY 1947, is now a rare book.

11. UNDER THE SHADOW

Letters by and to HA are HA-micro 18, H, or B, unless otherwise indicated.

PRINCIPAL SOURCES

(1) sixty-five letters, EC to HA, 13 May 1902–[24 Aug] 1903. (For dating problems, see note 10, below.)

(2) eighty-seven letters, HA to EC, 16 & 22 May 1902–[24 Aug] 1903. (For dating problems, see notes 10 & 38, below.)

(3) nineteen letters, HA to Louisa Hooper, 29 May 1902–24 Aug 1903.

(4) twelve letters, HA to CMG, 11 Jun 1902–13 Aug 1903.

(5) nine letters, HA to Mabel La Farge, 17 Jun 1902–10 Jul 1903.

(6) five letters, HA to Hay, 26 Jul–6 Dec 1902.

(7) eleven letters, HA to BA, 10 Aug 1902–3 Jul 1903.

LESSER SOURCES; CITATIONS; COMMENTS

1. HA to Mabel La Farge, 17 Jun 1902.

2. HA to EC, 30 May 1902.

3. EC to HA, 2 Jul 1902.

4. Ibid.

5. HA to EC, 11 Jul 1902.

6. HA to Higginson, 2 Oct 1902.

7. HA to Hay, 26 Jul 1902; HA to CMG, 26 Jul 1902; HA to Mabel La Farge, 28 Jul 1902; HA to CMG, 6 Aug 1902.

8. EC to HA, Monday, [22 Sep 1902].

9. Later EC declared her motive. She wrote to HA from Switzerland on 25 Oct 1902, "I am coming back [to Paris] to stay with you. . . ."

10. HA's letter to EC dated only "Sunday" and beginning "Nothing to report . . ." is conjecturally dated [12 Oct 1902] in O.1902.41 but may best be dated [5 Oct 1902]. EC's letter to HA dated only "Thursday" and beginning "I wonder why . . ." is dated [16? Oct 1902] on HA-micro 18 but may best be dated [9 Oct 1902]. Her letter to him dated only "Monday" and beginning "If you leave . . ." is dated [27? Oct 1902] on HA-micro 18 but may best be dated [20 Oct 1902]. Her letter to him dated only "Saturday" and beginning "I scarcely know . . ." is dated [11? Oct 1902] on HA-micro 18 but may best be dated [25 Oct 1902].

11. BA to HA, 27 Jul 1902. One may assume that, after returning to Washington early in 1903, HA resumed his meetings with Ford; but evidence of such meetings is lacking.

12. HA to BA, 10 Aug 1902.

13. Waldo G. Leland remembered the apartment as being "on the first floor above the street" and said a "library" served as "a principal living room." See Cater, xciii. Leland's memory was partly mistaken. See HA to EC, 20 Oct 1902:—"at the top of the house."

14. Hay to HA, 19 Oct 1902.

15. HA to Hay, 26 Jul 1902. Hay could not know it, but HA's remark involved a hidden reference to the popular success of his anonymous poetical satire of 1875, *The Radical Club . . . by an Atom.*

16. Though "little," the apartment had a maid's room and a kitchen.

17. HA to CMG, 23 Oct 1902; HA to BA, 6 Dec 1902.

18. HA to Mabel La Farge, 22 Dec 1902. HA's letters about the anticipated catastrophe tended to be comically cheerful. See HA to Holt, 8 Jan 1903, Cater, 533:—"What I want is only a dynamo big enough to send us all into heaven."

19. HA to EC, 6 Jan 1903.

20. HA to EC, 11 & 13 Jan 1903.

21. Letters, EC to HA, 1 Jan 1903 & 9 Jan 1903. She later expressed astonishment. See EC to HA, 3 Feb 1903:—"Your account of your life in Washington is vertiginous. I am giddy in even listening to it. I do not see so many people in a year as you do in a day. . . ."

22. EC to HA, 13 & 19 Jan 1903.

23. HA to EC, 25 & 27 Jan 1903. To HA, HJ's writings seemed out-of-date. Sargent soon came to Washington to paint portraits of Roosevelt and Hay. He called at 1603 H Street. HA took occasion to remark, "The generation of Harry James and Sargent is already as fossil as the buffalo." See HA to EC, 1–3 Mar 1903.

24. As the months passed, HA's opinion of Roosevelt fell even lower. See HA to EC, 12 & 14 Apr 1903:—"a boarding-house bully"; and HA to EC, 19 Apr 1903:—". . . he is quite mad, and gorged with flattery."

25. HA later became convinced that the cause of Langley's depression was blackmail. See HA to EC, 12 & 14 Apr 1903.

26. HA to EC, 15 Feb 1903.

27. Ibid.

28. The portrait eventually disappeared. See L, V, 424n1.

29. With his letter to Higginson, 26 Apr 1903, HA sent "certificates of Carbon stock," asking that they be sold. Stocks did not crash in New York till July 23. He mentioned afterwards—see HA to EC, Saturday, [25 Jul 1903]—that the crash had been prophesied by Morgan. He perhaps had sold in the spring on the strength of Morgan's prophecy.

30. Letters, EC to HA, 24 Mar 1902, 27 & 29 Mar 1902.

31. The MS. moved HA to make one of his most teasing assertions. See HA to GCL, 27 Apr 1903:—"The American woman has not yet existed."

32. Evarts first appears in Chap. X, Gaskell in Chap. XIII.

33. HA had written to BA on 9 Jan 1903: "Everything behind 1900 is already bric-a-brac. In these last two months, I've read enough science to see that far, anyway."

34. EC to HA, 3 Oct [1902].

35. HA to EC, 17 Jul 1903.

36. HA to EC, Thursday, [23 Jul 1903].

37. The nearest HA came to mentioning his *Education* was his saying to BA, 2 May 1903:—"I shall put up a statue to myself as the original conservative anarchist."

In the same letter, he told BA: "The only question of serious interest to the world is the atom. What is the atom?"

38. HA's letter to EC dated only "Friday" and beginning "We had a fine day . . ." is conjecturally dated [28 Aug 1903] in O.1903.32 but may best be dated [14 Aug 1903]. His letter to her beginning "I stopped writing . . ." is dated Tuesday, 1st [Sep 1903] in O.1903.33 but involves a handwriting problem. The seeming "1st" may be "18," and the letter may best be dated [18 Aug 1903].

12. Automobiling

Letters by and to HA are in HA-micro 18, 19, or H, unless otherwise indicated.

PRINCIPAL SOURCES

(1) sixty-three letters, HA to EC, [10 Sep 1903]–[14 Oct 1904].
(2) seven letters, HA to Hay, 15 Sep 1903–8 Sep 1904; and HA to Hay, 28 Sep 1904, L, V, 612–13.
(3) sixty-two letters, EC to HA, [21 Oct 1903]–[12 Oct 1904].
(4) eleven letters, HA to CMG, 30 Oct 1903–17 [Sep 1904].
(5) letter, HA to Henry James, 18 Nov 1903.
(6) HA, "King," *Clarence King Memoirs*, NY & Lond 1904, 157–85— published by the King Memorial Committee of The Century Association.

LESSER SOURCES; CITATIONS; COMMENTS

1. HA to Louisa Hooper, 18 Dec 1903.
2. EC to HA, 25 Apr 1904:—"12,000 a year."
3. HA to EC, 2–3 Nov 1903.
4. John Morley, *The Life of William Ewart Gladstone*, Lond 1903, II, 69–86.
5. Ibid., II, 82.
6. HA disagreed with his father about Russell. CFA viewed the foreign secretary as honest.
7. HA, *Recognition of Cuban Independence*, op. cit., 4, 19–22.
8. *EHA* (1907), 139; (LoA), 867. The account in *The Education* is fictional in seeming to place HA in Washington, rather than Paris, when he first read Morley's chapter.
9. Recognition of the Confederacy by England was never workable. Prime Minister Palmerston restrained those of his colleagues who favored it. He later restrained them until joint action by several European powers also became unworkable.
10. All the questions are energetically reviewed in *EHA*, Chap. X.
11. Read carefully once, HA's letter can appear to be complimentary as well as "extremely tactful"—to use a phrase HA applies in it to HJ. Read carefully a second time, the letter can appear to be all the more uncomplimentary *because* extremely tactful.

An answer of sorts came back. See HJ to HA, 19 Nov 1903. In his letter, HJ showed awareness that HA viewed his book as insufficient. He admitted the insufficiency and blamed biography! ". . . the art of biography—devilish art!—is somehow practically *thinning*. It simplifies even while seeking to enrich. . . ."

HA later restated his opinion of HJ's book. See HA to BA, 18 Feb 1909:—"Failure matters little when it concerns only oneself. Henry James can fail as often as he likes in novels, but when he fails in biography, he leaves mighty little of William Story."

12. In its last paragraph, HA's letter contains a phrase, "The essential superficiality of Story *and all the rest* [italics added]." The phrase, in effect, restates the phrase "improvised Europeans."

Both phrases are so situated as to apply with full force to Story, to HJ, and to HA himself.

13. Hay to HA, [c. 8] Jan 1904.
14. Principal source 6.
15. Hay to HA, 2 Sep 1903.
16. Hay and HA were highly skilled in avoiding quarrels between them-selves. A remarkable instance related to Hay's purchase from HA of the land that had been the site of HA's ill-fated greenhouse. A man named Fitch disputed Hay's title to the land. There followed a comic exchange of letters between Hay and HA accusing one another of false dealings. See Hay to HA, 11 Nov 1903, enclosing Fitch to Hay, 5 Nov 1903; and HA to Hay, 22 Nov 1903. The letters parodied the dubious title obtained by the United States government to lands across the Isthmus of Panama through which the government could cut the proposed Panama Canal. By means of the parodies, Hay and HA acknowledged but by-passed the dishonesty of their country's arrangement in Panama, which was just the sort of thing about which friends might quarrel irreparably.
17. HA to EC, 8–10 Nov 1903.
18. Letters, HA to EC, 17 Jan 1904 & 24 Jan 1904.
19. HA to EC, 7–8 Feb 1904.
20. Ibid.
21. Ibid.
22. HA to EC, 14 & 16 Feb 1904.
23. HA to CMG, 14 Feb 1904.
24. HA to EC, 13–14 Mar 1904.
25. For "next of kin," see Salmon to HA, 12 May 1904. In the letter, Salmon remembers a feast held forty years earlier, when "the Tauraatua of the time (our dear old mother) was in her prime of life."
26. The second-to-last sentence of LCA's account expresses her dislike of autobiography. "I am almost ashamed of the egotism of this detailed narrative, but a traveller cannot avoid speaking in the first person while relating his own history—and this must plead my apology."
27. EC to HA, 30 May 1904. After she sent it, EC realized she had forgotten that ships of the American Line no longer stopped at Southampton and that her letter should have been addressed to Cherbourg. To counteract the lapse, she wrote and telegraphed to the latter port. See EC to HA, 3 Jun 1904.
28. HA to EC, 4 Jul [1904].
29. HA to EC, Monday, 10 A.M., [11 Jul 1904].
30. HA to MC, Sunday, 10 [Jul 1904].
31. MSM&CH (1904), 92; (1912), 93; (LoA), 436.
32. HA to CMG, 6 Aug 1904.
33. HA to CMG, 27 Aug 1904.
34. HA to EC, 26 Aug 1904.
35. EC to HA, Sat. morning, [3 Sep 1904]:—"But what a joy it is to be in Italy again. . . . Why don't you like Italy, you Yankee, and feel this with us!"
36. Salmon to HA, 13 Aug 1904.
37. Salmon to HA, 1 Apr 1904.
38. Stickney to HA, 12 Jan 1904.
39. EC to HA, 6 Jul 1904. Also see Stickney to HA, [Jul? 1904], filmed out of sequence in HA-micro 20 as if written in June 1905.
40. EC to HA, Tues., [20 Sep 1904].
41. Lucy Stickney to HA, 29 Sep 1904.

13. VEHICLES OF ANARCHISM

Letters by and to HA are in HA-micro 19, 20, H, or B, unless otherwise indicated.

PRINCIPAL SOURCES

(1) forty-three letters, EC to HA, [c. 21 Nov] 1904–[2? Nov 1905]. (For dates of problematical letters, see notes 1, 18, 73 & 76, below.)

(2) fifty-four letters, HA to EC, [c. 21 Nov] 1904–[14 Nov] 1905. (For details concerning little-known or problematical letters, see notes 71, 75, 77, 78, 84 & 85, below.)

(3) nine letters, HA to CMG, 20 Dec 1904–11 Nov 1905.

(4) four letters, HA to Hay, 3–9 May 1905.

(5) letters, HA to BA, 5 Jun, 11 Jul 1905.

(6) letter, HA to Roosevelt, 6 Nov 1905, L, V, 719–20. (HA's copy, slightly variant, is in HA-micro 20.)

(7) [HA], *Mont Saint Michel and Chartres*, Wash (privately printed) 1904.

LESSER SOURCES; CITATIONS; COMMENTS

1. EC wrote six letters to HA from the Lorraine in 1904 none of which she fully dated. They make eminent sense when dated and read in the order of composition. I believe the correct order is as follows. 1. The wholly undated letter beginning "Martha has become . . ." (conjecturally dated [Dec? 1904] as it appears in HA-micro 19) may best be dated [c. 21 Nov 1904]. 2. The letter dated only Monday and beginning "My intentions . . ." (conjecturally dated [5 Dec 1904] as it appears in HA-micro 19) may best be dated [28 Nov 1904]. 3. The letter dated only Sunday and beginning "I wandered . . ." (conjecturally dated [4 Dec 1904] as it appears in HA-micro 19), may best be dated as suggested. 4. The letter dated only Monday and beginning "I lunched . . ." (conjecturally dated [9 Jan 1905] as it appears in HA-micro 20), may best be dated [5 Dec 1904]. 5. The letter dated only Saturday and beginning "I'm going . . ." (conjecturally dated [14 Jan 1905] as it appears in HA-micro 20), may best be dated [10 Dec 1904]. 6. The letter dated only Tuesday Eve. and beginning "The train . . ." (conjecturally dated [10 Jan 1905] as it appears in HA-micro 20), may best be dated [13 Dec 1904].

2. Letters 1 & 2 as listed in note 1.

3. HA to GCL, 1 Dec 1904:—". . . it interests." HA's reaction is so terse that it may reflect anxiety to escape giving a detailed opinion. The same anxiety may be present in his writing to Charles Warren Stoddard, 20 Dec 1904:—". . . I was really interested in Bay's Cain, and thought the senator feeble as Adam and Mrs[.] Lodge *très rëussie* [i.e. triumphant] as Eve."

4. In his letter of Sunday, 4 [Dec] 1904, HA alerts EC that Mrs. Hay has begun "to take John's ailments seriously" but does not disclose that he, HA, has agreed to join in the Hays' spring vacation abroad.

5. HA later dated the Preface as written in December 1904. See *MSM&CH* (1912), v.

6. In his letter to CMG, 20 Dec 1904, HA says he has "finished printing" the book and adds that it "will run up to a pretty bulky size." The change of tenses considered, his meaning may be that the printers have finished but the binders are finishing.

7. The copies were delivered to HA on 22 Dec 1904. See Furst & Co. to

HA, 20 Jan 1911, HA-micro 25. The book was deposited for copyright on 7 Jan 1905. See Jacob Blanck, *Bibliography of American Literature*, New Haven 1955, I, 7.

8. EC's letters 2–6 as listed in note 1, above. EC planned to visit Washington on Sunday, 17 Dec 1904, and stay at a hotel, the Grafton. The same letters show that, without success, she tried to induce HA to come to New York to attend a performance of Wagner's *Parsifal*, with Augustus Saint Gaudens and Henry James as fellow guests.

9. Furst's bill (HA-micro 19) is dated 31 Dec 1904 and marked as paid 4 Jan 1905.

10. The copy HA gave to Hay is now at the John Hay Library, Brown University. It is inscribed "To John Hay from Henry Adams, Jany 1905." I assume HA gave him the copy on the 3rd. HA's letter to Anna Lodge, 3 Jan 1905, is tantalizingly worded but can be understood to say that as New Year's gifts he is giving her both a copy of *Mont Saint Michel and Chartres* and a copy of *Memoirs of Arii Taimai*.

11. Edith Roosevelt to HA, Wednesday, [4? Jan 1905], filmed in HA-micro 20 at the start of 1905.

12. The first words in the earlier book are *Travels/ Tahiti*, printed on the half-title page.

13. Writing to Louisa Hooper, 8 Jan 1905, HA said that the book as packed for mailing was "rather a terrible volume . . . because it looks pompous and puffy."

14. For a portion of her share in the effort, see EC to HA, Monday, [28 Nov] 1904 (letter 2 as listed in note 1, above):—". . .you see I do not mention you!"

15. Writing to MC, 5 Feb 1905, HA says, perhaps with a high degree of exaggeration, ". . . you know it was your book, and I read most of it to you as I wrote it."

16. In his letter to HA, 10 Mar 1905, CMG says he is waiting for the book.

17. *HJLetters*, IV, 337–39.

18. EC wrote nine letters to HA from the Lorraine in 1905. She fully dated three. Two are problematical. The letter dated only Monday Eve and beginning "Our journey . . ." (filmed out of sequence in HA-micro 20 as if dated 13 Mar 1905) may best be dated [16 Jan 1905]. The letter dated only Thursday and beginning "Mrs. Winty . . . ," conjecturally dated [12 Jan 1905] as it appears in HA-micro 20, may best be dated [23 Feb 1905]. The remaining letters are conjecturally dated in HA-micro 20, and in each case the conjectured date is evidently correct. Thus the nine are easily put in order.

19. Presumably HA gave copies to La Farge and Saint Gaudens.

20. HJ to HA, 22 Feb 1905. In the same letter, HJ characterizes HA's house as a "wonderful talk-centre." For HJ's reaction to *Mont Saint Michel and Chartres*, see Chap. 14.

21. See the first problematical letter listed in note 18, above. One may suspect that Clara Hay hinted to EC about a journey involving HA and put EC in a position to ask HA for fuller information.

22. Jusserand to HA, 12 Jan 1905.

23. Taylor to HA, 15 Jan 1905. Taylor asked HA to give a copy of *Mont Saint Michel and Chartres* to James Harvey Robinson, whom he described as "a Harvard man," a "Professor of history at Columbia," a "clever writer," and "my chief companion in the Middle Ages."

HA replied, 17 Jan 1905, by suggesting that Taylor lend his own copy to

Robinson to let him see whether he wanted one. To explain his hesitation, HA called his book a "sketch-study intended for my own and my niece's amusement" and said he wished to give it only to "personal friends."

24. The book also contains miniature biographies, notably of Saint Bernard, Abbot Suger of Saint Denis, and Eleanor of Guienne, who at different times was queen of England and queen of France.

25. *MSM&Ch* (1904), 277, 282, 333, 337; (LoA), 633, 637, 689, 693.

26. *MSM&CH* (1904), 293; (1912), 304; (LoA), 648.

27. Margaret Chanler to HA, [c. 12 Jan 1905], filmed in HA-micro 20 at the start of 1905.

28. Margaret Chanler to HA, Wednesday, [25 Jan 1905], filmed in HA-micro 20 at the start of 1905.

29. Margaret Chanler to HA, Tuesday, [7 Feb 1905], filmed in HA-micro 20 at the start of February.

30. *Constitution and List of Members of the National Institute of Arts and Letters*, HA-micro 20, filmed as if dated 15 Mar 1905.

31. Ibid. HA's inclusion presumably resulted from support by Hay, La Farge, and Saint Gaudens. I know of no evidence that HA had sought membership in the Institute—or later in the Academy.

32. Robert Underwood Johnson to HA, 25 Jan 1905; also same to HA, 15 Mar 1905. Of the first fifteen members of the Academy, five—Hay, James, La Farge, Roosevelt, and Saint Gaudens—were HA's friends, and two others—Howells and Norton—were his long-time acquaintances. The fact illustrates HA's genius for friendship.

The exclusion of women from the Institute (thus also from the Academy) riled HA sufficiently to provoke his suggesting that six "pretty actresses" be added to the Academy. See HA to Hay, 8 May 1905, listing the six. Also see a helpful comment in L, V, 657n3.

33. HA to Johnson, 27 Jan 1905.

34. Although he liked HJ and wished to extend hospitality to him, HA was not reading his novels. He apparently did not read *The Ambassadors*. On 27 Jan 1905, after learning that he and HJ had been elected to the Academy, he wrote to Margaret Chanler that he would not be reading "the Golden Fount or Mount or Count" (i.e. *The Golden Bowl*).

35. EC to HA, Tuesday Eve, [7 Feb 1905].

36. Margaret Chanler to HA, 12 Feb 1905. HA's refusal can be understood as expressive of his distrust of universities as centers of learning. He had written to CMG on 20 Dec 1904: "I am at a loss to learn what function a University now performs in the world. They are ornamental but expensive. . . ."

37. EC to HA, Thursday, [23 Feb 1905], as dated in note 18, above.

38. Butler to Margaret Chanler, 26 Feb 1905.

39. Margaret Chanler to HA, 27 Feb 1905.

40. EC to HA, 11 Feb 1905.

41. EC to HA, The Island, Monday, [13 Mar 1905]—later misdated March 14 by EC.

42. For "angina," see HA to EC, Tuesday, 14 [Mar 1905]. The note from Clara Hay to HA, dated only Monday, and filmed in HA-micro 20 as if written after c. 15 Sep 1905, may best be dated [13 March 1905]. It says the Hays cannot come to dinner because "John is feeling so seedy." It may seem a mere social note but in my view is important. HA saved it. One may assume that its arrival prompted his visiting Mrs. Hay and learning about the "angina." Possibly it marked the day when HA became entirely certain that Hay's fate was sealed.

43. Langley to HA, 9 Mar 1905; Edith Wharton to HA, n.d. (signed by her as a "niece" and dated by HA as received in April 1905); Isabella Gardner to HA, Tuesday, [14 Mar 1905], filmed out of sequence in HA-micro 20 as if written on 11 Apr 1905; HA to same, Tuesday, [14 Mar 1905]. HA may have given a copy to his niece Dorothy, which could count also as a copy for her mother, Mary Adams Quincy.

44. HA to Mary Jones, Friday, 1[7] Mar 1905.

45. HA to MC, Saturday, 18 [Mar 1905].

46. In his letter to Mary Jones, Friday, 1[7] Mar 1905, HA treats "old Sam Ward" as eligible for a copy because equivalent to Ward Thoron's youngest daughter.

47. HA to EC, Friday, 17 [Mar] 1905.

48. HA to MC, Saturday, 18 [Mar 1905].

49. HA to EC, Sunday, 9 [Apr 1905].

50. Mabel La Farge to HA, 3 Mar 1905:—"She [Sadie] wanted me to tell you [HA] if she died that you had made her last days the happiest of her life."

51. The persons who learned the secret were few. Other than Hay and his wife, HA, CMG, and EC, the most likely possibility is Rockhill.

52. HA to EC, 9 [Apr 1905]. Writing to Mabel La Farge on 23 Apr 1905, HA said, ". . . I consider my services as courier and valet at an end." The remark applies narrowly to HA's five-and-a-half week stint as the Hays' vacation companion. It leaves no doubt that, while doing what she asked, HA came to view Mrs. Hay's insistence that he travel with her and her husband as an unthinking imposition. Work in foreign affairs was one thing; servile attendance was quite another.

53. HA to EC, 23 Apr 1905.

54. Spring Rice to Hay, 26 Apr 1905, HA-micro-20. Later BA ventured a similar mistaken prophecy. See BA to HA, 2 Jul 1905:—"Russia cannot go into revolution because there is nothing to make a revolution with. If it could be revolutionized it might reorganize, but it cannot reorganize. It can, therefore, only slowly rot."

55. Hay to HA, n.d., [c. 29 Apr 1905].

56. Clara Hay to HA, Tuesday Evening, [6 Jun 1905].

57. HA to EC, 7 May 1905; EC to HA, 5 Apr 1905. What with changes of address, EC did not get his weekly letter till May 20, whereupon she wrote to say that it caused her "such a wave of homesickness that I must begin my [weekly] letter, even though the first page be stale before the last is written. O Paris! I am homesick for it. . . ."

In his letter and hers, "homesick" rather obviously has private meanings known to sender and receiver.

58. EC to HA, 1 May 1905.

59. In her previous letter to HA, 27 May 1905, EC had said: "It is a great joy to think of that apartment [50] as still mine. A wicked joy, for I ought not to have it!"

60. In her letter to HA, 24 Jul 1905, apparently in a sympathetic voice, EC excuses herself for asking him to do errands for her in Paris by saying, ". . . you have nothing else to do."

61. In a letter to HA, 14 Jul 1905, Richard Watson Gilder asked HA to write something for the *Century* about Hay. Gilder said he had in his mind an image "of you and he [Hay] walking off together." The request was malapropos. HA was reserving his ideas about Hay for use in *The Education*. Yet the image Gilder

expressed had poetic validity. When Hay died, two co-secretaries of state walked off together.

62. EC to HA, 2 July 1905.

63. Ibid.

64. HA to CMG, 28 Jun 1905; HA to EC, 2 Jul 1905; HA to Clara Hay, 4 Jul 1905.

65. HA to CMG, 28 Jun 1905.

66. When editing HA's letters for publication, Ford copied for his files HA's passage about finding Lodge repulsive. See Henry Brooks Adams file, Personal Papers (Misc.), Manuscripts & Archives Division, NYPL.

67. EC to HA, 29 & 31 Jul 1905.

68. HA told his opinion to Hay's widow. See HA to Clara Hay, 10 Aug 1905:—"Politics poisoned him. The Senate and the Diplomates [*sic*] killed him. He would have had to resign at McKinley's death if he were to save his own life."

69. EC to HA, 6 Aug 1905.

70. HA had been considering the possibility of world war for several months. See his letter to Higginson, 26 Feb 1905:—"a general war all over the world."

71. Two undated notes from HA to EC written on his Paris stationery, one beginning "I've carried Morison's address . . . ," the other "Mrs[.] Winty has sent . . . ," may belong to this interval. They are filmed in HA-micro 21 as if written in September 1906. They are omitted in both L and O.

72. I infer the probable place of the encounter from HA's stated reluctance to return to EC's apartment during the days immediately following.

73. EC to HA, n.d., [3 Nov 1905], beginning "If you. . . ." The letter is filmed out of sequence in HA-micro 20 after 11 Sep 1905 and is conjecturally dated [4? Nov 1905] in L, V, 718n1. I date it one day earlier as obviously part of a rapid exchange of notes.

74. See note 85, below.

75. HA to EC, 6:45 [P.M.], clearly written on 1 Nov 1905. Levenson and his associates suggest [2 Nov 1905]. See O.1905.42.

76. EC to HA, n.d., beginning "What is . . . ," filmed out of sequence in HA-micro 20 as if dated c. 8 Sep 1905 but evidently written late on 1 Nov 1905.

77. HA to EC, n.d., [1 Nov 1905], beginning "If it hadn't been . . . ," filmed out of sequence in HA-micro 21 at the start of September 1906; published in O.1910.47 with a mistaken date, [29? Jul 1910].

78. HA to EC, 7.30 P.M., [1 Nov 1905], beginning "I will come down . . . ," filmed out of sequence in HA-micro 21 at the start of September 1906; published in O.1910.46 with a mistaken date, [28? Jul 1910].

79. HA to EC, [2 Nov 1905]. The date suggested in O.1905.42 appears correct.

80. EC to HA, [3 Nov 1905], beginning "If you are. . . ."

81. Earlier HA had written to Hay about Hay's being the swineherd who was steering the world's pigs and hogs—the great powers. In his letter to Roosevelt, HA chooses a safer image. He pictures the president as a cowboy: "the best herder of Emperors since Napoleon." The image could seem complimentary and perhaps was so received; but, in view of Adams's dark view of Napoleon, the image involved a catch.

82. Levenson and his associates construe EC's note to HA about the Mac-Nutt intrusion as if she disagreed with HA about what to think and what to do. See L, V, 718n1. Differently, I believe there was no disagreement. By pointing to

particular aspects of the case, her note advanced a discussion between them the result of which was HA's letter to Roosevelt, written three days later. Though penned and signed by HA, the letter can properly be read, not as HA's, but as his and hers. In short, HA and EC cooperated with one another and brought their part in the affair to a shared conclusion.

83. HA to Mary Jones, 14 Nov 1905.

84. HA to EC, 4:20 P.M., [13 Nov 1905], beginning "I incline . . . ," O. 1907.42—filmed out of sequence in HA-micro 20 at the start of August 1905. Levenson and his associates date the letter [30 Sep 1907]. I believe their date is mistaken and think the date given here has a high probability of being correct.

85. After they postponed their sailing, HA chided EC:—"May I venture to suggest that this time you will say as little as possible about the steamer you are to sail in!" See HA to EC, Tuesday, [14 Nov 1905], filmed in HA-micro 20 as if dated c. 8 Sep 1905.

86. In the Editor's Preface he wrote for inclusion in the book when published, HA begins by saying that *The Education of Henry Adams* was "written in 1905." See *EHA* (1918) or any other published edition. I believe the statement is convenient and simple but untrue. One may better say that to some extent HA worked on the book during every year of his maturity, beginning in 1860.

14. EVERY OBJECT MORE THAN ATTAINED

Letters by and to HA are in HA-micro 20, 21, or H, or HA/Thoron micro, unless otherwise indicated.

PRINCIPAL SOURCES

(1) thirty-three letters, HA to EC, [4 Dec 1905]–[21 Jan 1907]. (For details about little-known and incompletely-dated letters, see notes 13, 14, 22, 29, 30, & 31, below.)

(2) thirteen letters, HA to Louisa Hooper, 4 [Dec 1905]–22 Jan 1907.

(3) twelve letters, HA to CMG, 25 Dec 1905–28 Jan 1907. (For details about a little-known letter, see note 30, below.)

(4) ten letters, HA to Isabella Gardner, 9 Feb–23 Oct 1906, L, VI, 5–6, 23, 27–28, 31; O.1906.14–16, 21–23.

(5) ten letters, EC to HA, [6 Mar]–18 [Sep] 1906. (For details about letters that are missing, little-known, or incompletely dated, see notes 15, 17, 18, & 22, below.)

(6) [HA], *The Education of Henry Adams*, Wash (privately printed) 1907.

LESSER SOURCES; CITATIONS; COMMENTS

1. HA to Mabel La Farge, 22 Feb 1906.

2. Langley to HA, 18 Dec 1905.

3. For the first instance of "hotel," see HA to Mary Jones, Thursday, [7 Dec 1905].

4. While in Boston, HA visited Fenway Court, Mrs. Gardner's private museum of the arts. He then wrote her a letter describing her as one of America's 200 creative people. She replied that his good opinion made her "eternally grateful." See HA to Isabella Gardner, 10 Feb 1906; same to HA, Monday, [19 Feb 1906].

5. Letters, HA to Mabel La Farge, 10 Dec 1905 & 22 Feb 1906.

6. Notes, Roosevelt to HA, Saturday, & Edith Roosevelt to HA, Saturday,

filmed in HA-micro 21 at the start of April 1906. HA marked the president's note "April 1906." Mrs. Roosevelt's is not logged and may be difficult to date.

7. Bancel La Farge to HA, 5 Apr 1906.

8. L, VI, 16n4, quoting an article by "R. L. S." (presumably Robert Livingston Schuyler), "From John Adams to James Monroe," NYTimes, 21 Apr 1906. The article is in part a review of a book by Edward Channing, one of HA's former students. It praises HA for having "brilliantly" made use of evidence in his *History*.

9. Letters, BA to HA, 18 Dec 1905 & 10 Apr 1906; Potter to HA, 30 Apr 1906.

10. Respectively, counting front matter, *MSM&CH* (1904) and *EHA* (1907) were 361 and 459 pages long.

11. Prior to EC's departure, HA had sent Reid a copy of *MSM&CH*. See HA to Reid, 14 May 1906; Reid to HA, 21 May 1906.

12. HA to EC, Tuesday, 12 [Jun 1906].

13. HA to EC, 3 p.m., [14 Jun 1906]. The letter is evidently the first of a pair; see also note 15. The date suggested in O.1906.15 seems correct.

14. HA to EC, n.d., [14 Jun 1906], beginning "I'm glad. . . ," filmed out of sequence in HA-micro 21 at the start of September 1906. See O.undated.9.

15. The letters between HA and EC can be viewed as sufficiently complete. Yet HA's letters to EC make clear that he received a good many letters from her that are missing. Possibly he discarded or destroyed quite a few. He usually discarded any postcards she sent him.

EC's letters to HA bear evidences in her handwriting that, when she gained access to her letters, she read them and in many instances tried to date them. It thus also seems possible that *she* culled out and destroyed some of her letters, perhaps including those she sent from London in June 1906.

16. See note 24, below.

17. Her letters of the time to HA do not say where she is; but in the letter dated 10 Aug [1906], filmed out of sequence in HA-micro 21 as if dated 10 Aug [1907], she says she is "bathing." This evidence is minimal, yet seems to place her at Bad Nauheim.

18. In a letter to HA now missing, EC evidently mentioned the unexpected death of Mary Curzon on 18 Jul 1906. In his reply, Saturday, 21 [Jul 1906], HA asked EC whether he should write a letter of condolence to Lord Curzon, or Mary's mother, or anyone. In her next missing letter, EC evidently advised HA to write to Curzon. HA did so. This four-stage development is important for showing the degree to which actions by HA or EC were sometimes actions of both.

HA did not send the letter to Curzon till 30 Jul 1906. See L, VI, 23–24. Of his many fine letters of condolence, it possibly is the best. It drew from Curzon the interesting remark, "No one but you could have written such a letter." See Curzon to HA, 6 Aug 1906. Two statements in the letter deserve review. "Some visions are too radiant for words." "I do not understand how we bear such suffering as we do when we lose them [i.e. the visions]. . . ." Though written as if meant to apply only to personal calamities such as the loss of a beloved wife, the statements can be read as also applicable to such huge calamities as the death of a great religion or a nation's losing credence in its ideals.

19. Eventually Mrs. Gardner bought the window. Without citing a basis for their statement, Levenson and his associates assert (L, VI, 31n1) that the window was "made in the early eighteenth century, and most of the pieces of glass are later replacements"—in short, that Mrs. Gardner bought a fake.

How much blame should be assigned to HA is not easily determined. When writing about the window to Mrs. Gardner, he had mixed unguarded assumptions that it was genuine, though repaired, with comic forecasts that anyone who bought it would be cheated.

20. HJ to his nephew William James, 8 Nov 1905, as reproduced in Paul C. Richards/ Autographs, Cat. 268, item 115.

It may seem odd that, in the same year in which he and HA were elected to the American Academy of Arts & Sciences, HJ described HA as having had "a disappointed and ineffectual personal career." Perhaps one should ask whether the twenty-one words in HJ's letter from "in spite of" through "career" are a case of laborious attempted humor.

21. George Monteiro's edition of *The Correspondence of Henry James and Henry Adams/ 1877–1914*, Baton Rouge & Lond 1992, prints the extant letters: six from HA to HJ; twenty-two from HJ to HA. The disproportion between six and twenty-two reflects the severity of HJ's burnings.

22. For "isolation," see EC to HA, 3 Sep 1906. HA seems not to have known how long EC would be away. His undated letter to her beginning "Are we . . . ," O.undated.8, filmed in HA-micro 21 as if dated [1 Sep 1906], may best be dated during the first six days of August 1906. It anticipates EC's return "from the south" and their having to make another Atlantic voyage.

23. The name of the hotel is given in HA to EC, 6 Aug [1906], filmed out of sequence in HA-micro 21 as if dated 6 Aug [1907].

24. It can be imagined (perhaps with some truth) that EC ceased being a tenant at 50 Avenue du Bois de Boulogne because Jews—Mr. Propper for one—had moved into the building.

25. Fragment of a letter from Louisa Hooper to one of her sisters, presumably Ellen, written prior to 20 Oct 1906. LHT recovered the fragment and in 1956 permitted me to make a copy.

26. Isabella Gardner to HA, 3 Sep 1906.

27. EC to HA, 30 Aug [1906].

28. The list of remarkable works that HA wrote but had not intended to write was interestingly long. It included his early despatches to the *New York Times*, "The Principles of Geology," "The New York Gold Conspiracy," his poem "The Radical Club," *The Life of Albert Gallatin, John Randolph, Esther,* and *"Napoléon Iᵉʳ et Saint-Domingue."*

29. Undated letter, HA to EC, [late Sep or early Oct 1906], beginning "The rent. . .," filmed in HA-micro 21 as if dated [1 Sep 1906]; omitted in both L & O.

The earliest evidence of the apartment's address is the printed letterhead at the beginning of EC to HA, 1 Nov 1908, HA-micro 22.

30. For evidence that CMG was attempting to make the visit, see the undated letter, HA to CMG, Monday, [22 Oct 1906], beginning "As the Meurice . . . ," filmed in HA-micro 21 as if written in late Sep 1907. Levenson and his associates date the letter [30 Sep 1907]. See O. 1907.42–43. I believe the date I suggest has a high probability of being correct. For confirmation that CMG and his wife came and went, see HA to CMG, 1 Nov 1906.

31. HA to EC, Monday 9 A.M. [evidently written on 7 Jan 1907 or 14 Jan 1907], beginning *"Please. . . ."* The letter is filmed in HA-micro 21 as if dated [23 Oct 1906]. It appears in O.1907.5, where it is dated [18 Mar 1907?]. That date is impossible. The letter presupposes delivery to EC in Washington. On that day, EC was in South Carolina. The earlier dates chime with what I assume was EC and MC's post-New Year's return from Coffin's Point.

32. For "Memorial," see HA to CMG, 15 Apr 1907.

33. Mrs. Hay was much better adapted to imagining what HA might do for her than imagining what she might do for him. In December 1906 and January 1907, a bibliographer, Theodore Stanton, tried to learn from Henry Holt, HA, and Clara Hay whether he might be permitted to name HA and Hay in print as the authors respectively of two anonymous novels, *Democracy* and *The Bread-Winners*. Evidently without first consulting HA, Mrs. Hay gave Stanton the desired permission in connection with *The Bread-Winners*. So doing, she went a long way to confirm that HA was the author of *Democracy*, which clearly was the reverse of what HA would have wanted her to do. See HA to Holt, 13 Dec 1906, Cater, 588; Stanton to HA, 17 Jan 1907.

34. In his letter to EC, 13 Mar 1907, HA says he was under "pressure to write a memoir of Hay." In this context, his word "memoir" could only mean a biography.

35. For "inseparable," see *EHA*, (1907), 281; (LoA), 1014.

36. The six chapters filled 82 pages. On pp. 43, 54, & 80, HA failed to correct "know" to knew, "begun" to began, and "guage" to gauge. On pp. 8, 64, & 67, he failed to correct misspellings of two names not very familiar to him: "Vassal" and "Abthorp." On p. 37, he failed to correct "Conklinian" to "Conklingian." On p. 81, he failed to correct "Provençeaux" to Provençaux. He later corrected all but the last of these errors while reading printed copies of the book, and he may have corrected the last as well while reading his Master Copy, now lost. Also he improved the chapters by making two deletions and rewording a sentence. For additional details, see Chap. 27.

37. In his letter to James Ford Rhodes, 7 Mar 1907, HA appears to recapitulate an argument he had earlier put forward when resisting Mrs. Hay's proposal that he write her deceased husband's biography. The argument also appears in HA to EC, 13 Mar 1907.

38. For "a fairly continuous autobiography," see HA to CMG, 15 Apr 1907.

39. HA was aware that speeded printing would be a breeder of errors. He apprised CFA2 (letter of 14 Jan 1907) that he might be asked to read something "in view of any errors it may contain."

40. HA's later improvement of the already-printed book is a principal subject of this narrative.

41. HA to Thwing, 26 Jan 1907, L, VI, 42.

42. Ibid.

43. Mme. Jusserand to HA, 21 Jan 1907; White House to HA, 21 Jan 1907.

44. HA to EC, Monday, [21 Jan 1907].

45. Being good-natured people, the Roosevelts and Jusserands could be counted on to treat EC well during dinner. The real question was treatment of EC by outsiders. Washington being Washington, outsiders would soon learn where the president had dined and who dined with him. The inevitable message of the occasion would be that outsiders were *not* to criticize.

46. *EHA* (1907), vi.

15. None of My Business

Letters by and to HA are in HA-micro 21, H, or B, unless otherwise indicated.

PRINCIPAL SOURCES

(1) five letters, HA to Mary Jones, 2 Feb–26 [Jul] 1907.

(2) four letters, HA to Reid, 12 Feb–1 Aug 1907, L, VI, 46–47, 77–78; O.1907.14, 28–29.

(3) letters, HA to Clara Hay, 22 Feb, 15 May 1907; also undated letter, HA to same, O.1907.5. (For the letter's date, see note 35, below.)
(4) eleven letters, HA to CMG, 4 Mar–19 Sep 1907.
(5) twenty-nine letters, HA to EC, 6 [Mar]–20 [Sep] 1907.
(6) twenty-two letters, EC to HA, 3 Jun–22 Sep 1907.
(7) [HA], *The Education of Henry Adams*, Wash (privately printed) 1907— the copy at the Massachusetts Historical Society usually known as the Thayer copy; here known also as the First Traveling Copy.

LESSER SOURCES; CITATIONS; COMMENTS

1. HJ to Clara Hay, 22 Feb 1907, in "Letters to Mrs. John Hay," Special Collections, John Hay Library, Brown University; HJ to HA, 22 Feb 1907. The first of these letters does not appear in George Monteiro, ed., *Henry James and John Hay/ The Record of a Friendship*, Providence 1965. In it, HJ told Mrs. Hay he was sending four of her husband's letters to HA, regretted finding only four, and remembered having had others. He added, "I am so very glad H. A. is doing this work."

Writing later that day, HJ told HA he was enclosing *five* letters. He added, ". . . a selection . . . of Hay's letters . . . will make the best form of commemorative record of his high wit, ability & character, & no one but you of course, should do it." Of the five letters supplied, two appear in *JHLetters*, II, 81–82; III, 266–67.

2. With regard to the diary, see note 34, below. Writing to HA, 12 Apr 1907, White says that Mrs. Hay and HA have Hay's "private letter books."

3. White to HA, 12 Apr 1907.

4. *The Letters of Mrs. Henry Adams, 1865–1883*, ed. by Ward Thoron, Bost 1936, 337.

5. For evidence and reasons supporting the assertion that HA received 100 copies of *The Education*, see Chap. 21, note 46, below.

6. HA kept Furst & Co.'s bill for printing "100 copies" of *Mont Saint Michel and Chartres* in 1904–1905 but did not keep Furst's bill for printing *The Education*.

7. HA had a precedent to follow. In the 1880s for his own use (including critical reading by relatives and friends), he had printed six copies each of portions of his *History*.

8. HA to CMG, 18 Mar 1916, HA-micro 30, recalling "the copy I . . . corrected for that purpose [i.e. publication] near ten years ago."

9. This name seems best because with time the copy acquired important features other than textual correction.

10. At a much later date, the Master Copy was lost. Its history is one of the main concerns of this narrative. While some things about the copy are established beyond a doubt by direct evidence, others must be inferred with the help of collateral evidence, and still others can only be guessed. An effort is made in the narrative to keep separate the surely known from the inferred, and both from the guessed.

11. Most of the eight copies distributed to interested persons prior to April 1907 are available. They bear no marks by HA. I accordingly think it probable that all eight were unmarked.

12. HA's letter accompanying the copy sent to Brooks and Evelyn Adams may have been addressed to both. Each is mentioned in *The Education*.

13. Mary Adams Quincy does not appear in *The Education*. Evidently HA sent his sister a copy as a courtesy, and she approved and returned it. With this

help, he was able to tell Roosevelt (letter of 11 Mar 1907) that his "family" approved the book.

14. The copy is at Houghton Library, Harvard University.

15. For the full text of CFA2's response, see L, VI, 48n1.

16. BA to HA, 24 Feb 1907.

17. CFA2 to HA, 25 Feb 1907. The elder brother's letter does not fully explain what the omitted episode was.

18. For CFA2's limited knowledge of the book, see Chapters 19 and 20. For his retaining the copy sent to him in 1907, see CFA2 to Ford, 5 Aug 1911, FP 17.

19. Cameron to HA, 10 Mar 1907.

20. EC is mentioned in *The Education* and under HA's rules was entitled to alter the book's comments about herself. She principally appears in the book as co-recipient of a sweeping compliment saying that she and Mrs. Lodge, during a "reign of sixteen years . . . led a career, without precedent and without succession, as the dispensers of sunshine over Washington." The interval meant appears to be 1881–1897. HA's words can seem to suggest that EC at the time was a tireless hostess and large-scale entertainer. I know of no evidence that she was. The actual meaning of the phrase as it relates to EC may in part have to do with the many kindnesses she paid within the circle of friends that HA, she, and others came to refer to as the "family."

21. See Chap. 19, note 55, below.

22. The copy is now owned by Catholic University of America.

23. Lodge to HA, 5 Mar 1907.

24. HA to Anna Lodge, 6 Mar 1907.

25. GCL to HA, n.d., logged by HA on its back "March 1907."

26. Sometime after she married, Louisa wrote her married name in the front of the copy and added, "Given by H. A. March 5th 1907." The copy is at the Boston Athenaeum.

27. For example, see HA to Pumpelly, 25 Mar 1907, O.1907.7, filmed out of sequence in HA-micro 21 as if dated 25 Mar 1908.

28. Eliot to HA, 8 Mar 1907. For Eliot's returning the copy, see L, VI, 719.

29. HA to Higginson, 17 Feb 1907; HA to CMG, 4 Mar 1907.

30. *EHA* (1907), vi; (LoA), 722.

31. The copy is at Beineke Library, Yale University.

32. For an expansion of the first narrative relating to assistance given to C. F. Adams by his wife, see note 44, below.

33. Mary Jones to HA, 23 Apr 1907.

34. HA's hand-copied extracts from Hay's diary are in Special Collections, John Hay Library, Brown University.

35. HA to Clara Hay, Monday, [22 Apr 1907]. The letter appears in O. 1907.5 with a suggested date, [18? March 1907]. The date is impossible. In the letter, HA says he has received approval from the president of Harvard; but Eliot had said to HA (letter of 8 Mar 1907) that he would not be able to look at *The Education* till April 15. Hence my suggested date for HA's letter. The new date comports well with Mrs. Hay's reply of 6 May 1907.

36. Eventually the copy was bought by Steven Weissman, a leading New York dealer in rare books. It changed hands and in 1990 was offered for sale by Glenn Horowitz, Bookseller, New York, for $25,000.

37. The copy is at Houghton Library, Harvard University.

38. For Trevelyan's being given a copy of *The Education*, see note 63, below.

39. For HA's linking his *Education* with St. Augustine's *Confessions* and Rousseau's *Confessions*, see Chap. 16.

40. Replying to HA on 8 Mar 1907, President Eliot echoed one of HA's expressions by saying he would be glad to look at HA's "proofs." See also HA to Higginson, 1 Apr 1907.

41. Principal source 7. Like the history of the Master Copy, the history of the First Traveling Copy is a principal concern of this narrative. From the start, the histories of the copies were intertwined but very different.

Because in time the history of the First Traveling Copy became quite complicated, I make special efforts in this and subsequent chapters to be clear and forthright about the complications.

42. Three letters, Reid to HA, 8 May, [28] May, & 28 May 1907, with a memorandum, "Suggestions of danger," and Reid's catalogue of Hay's letters.

43. Clara Hay to HA, 6 May 1907.

44. Mrs. Hay's letter may have moved HA to change his *Education* as it related to his mother. The change is a passage he inserted in his First Traveling Copy. In its entirety, it reads: "—who should have been a competent judge, since her success and popularity in England exceeded that of her husband,—" See principal source 7, p. 183; also *EHA* (LoA), 914. On the one hand, the passage weakens the image of HA's father as an unassisted hero. On the other, it gives HA's mother augmented credit of a kind she deserved.

45. In her letter to HA, 6 May 1907, Clara Hay mentions having seen Martha with Lindsay.

46. HA to CMG, 23 May 1907:—"All are noted on the margin, and will be food for printers whenever the time comes."

47. Principal source 7. This cannot be the copy HA described to CMG in 1916 as "corrected" for publication. The annotations HA made in it reveal it to be chiefly an *improvement* copy, as opposed to a *correction* copy.

48. As first printed, *The Education of Henry Adams* contained a large number of errors relating to names of persons, actual or fictional. Study of these errors as corrected in HA's First Traveling Copy yields very considerable rewards.

A glaring case of a misspelled name is the last name of William Henry Seward printed as "Seaward." It helps to notice that HA did *not* correct "Seaward" when reading the First Traveling Copy. See principal source 7, p. 112. (The misspelling was later corrected by the second annotator, but that is another story.) HA's not correcting "Seaward" appears to be a clear instance of his bypassing a misspelling because aware he had earlier corrected it in the Master Copy.

In the text and index, Charles Sumner's name appears 93 times. It is spelled correctly in 83 cases but in 10 is misspelled as "Summer." None of the Sumner misspellings appear in the first six chapters. The misspellings that appear thereafter can be read as clear indications that, beginning with Chap. VII, printing was hurried by Furst and Co. and proofreading was hurried by HA.

The first misspellings of Sumner as "Summer" are on p. 94. There are three on the page, and they are glaring. When reading the First Traveling Copy, HA let all three stand uncorrected—which is just what he would do if he remembered having corrected them in the Master Copy. (The second annotator later corrected all three.)

The fourth "Summer" is on p. 105. HA again let the error stand.

Five cases of "Summer" appear on p. 219. They are preceded on the page by two cases of Sumner spelled correctly. This is the only page on which the name is spelled both correctly and incorrectly. When he read the page, HA corrected the five misspellings as "Summer," evidently because not entirely sure whether he had corrected them in the Master Copy.

The remaining "Summer" appears alone on p. 228. HA let it stand. (The second annotator corrected it.)

In my opinion, these responses by HA to the misspelling of Seward and 10 misspellings of Sumner are decisive evidence that the annotated copy at the Massachusetts Historical Society is a traveling copy that HA read and annotated when away from his Master Copy.

49. Gaskell's "letter of correction" is missing. See note 46, above. By my count, HA made 47 corrections of simple errors (misspellings, mistaken punctuation, omitted words, etc..) in the First Traveling Copy. He nowhere indicated in the copy that a correction was suggested to him by someone else. Yet it is clear that some of the corrections were suggested by CMG. The question becomes, Which ones? Two very likely candidates are corrections relating to the date when CMG's father bought Wenlock Abbey and the date when HA first went there to visit. See principal source 7, 179.

Other candidates are misspellings of English and French names: "Newcomb" for Newcome, "Bethel" for Bethell, "Bridgenorth" for Bridgnorth, "St. James" for St. James's, "Woolsey's" for Wolsey's, and "Jaurez" for Jaurès. See principal source 7, 113, 128, 130, 152, 198, 249, 319, 371, 444.

50. Of HA's annotations in the copy, 12 are neither corrections nor improvements and may best be called references. The occasion for his writing the references is explained in Chap. 16.

51. *The Education* shows signs of having been written at the cost of sometimes extreme excitement. One consequence of excitement was expressions that HA came to dislike as overstated or too declarative. An example is two sentences he deleted. See principal source 7, 244, ink lines deleting "The problem was never solved—had no solution. Garfield and Blaine followed the failures of Grant and Sumner."

For the passage as eventually published, see *EHA* (LoA), 977, the paragraph that ends with the words "destructive political education?" Originally the paragraph ended with the two miscreant sentences.

52. For two-letter improvements, see principal source 7, 78, the annotation revising "teach" to "touch," and ibid., 397, the annotation revising "the" to "these." Made in ink, these very small changes remarkably improve the sentences in which they appear. See *EHA* (LoA), 805, sentence beginning "Yet Browning," & ibid., 1134, sentence beginning "A student of history"—the phrase "these scientific ideas."

HA's 40-word revision is made in pencil. It begins with the words "had just created a new evangel" and ends with the words "On October 13, he issued." See principal source 7, 136; *EHA* (LoA), 863.

53. Some of HA's improvements in the First Traveling Copy curb the book's slight tendency toward detraction.

54. HA to Reid, 30 May 1907.

55. Letters, EC to HA, 3 Jun 1907 & 7 Jun 1907. Martha improved enough to take a cure, whereupon EC predicted that "by autumn" she would "feel the effects of her arsenic & be much stronger." See EC to HA, Sunday, [21 Jul 1907].

56. HA's word "Democracy" in this letter is of course a reference to his novel *Democracy*.

57. Clara Hay to HA, 18 Jun 1907.
58. EC to HA, 16 Jun 1907.
59. EC to HA, 21 Jun [1907].
60. EC to HA, Saturday, 22 [Jun 1907].
61. EC to HA, 29 Jun 1907.
62. EC to HA, 17 Jul [1907]. She abbreviates cents to "cts" and draws attention to her "American parlance."
Her phrase "the human form divine" may echo the same phrase as used by Blake in his poem "The Divine Image" in *Songs of Innocence.*
63. Because Trevelyan is mentioned, though not named, in its Preface, it must be assumed that the volume sent to him was *Mont Saint Michel and Chartres.* It appears that the English historian did not hear of *The Education* till Adams paid his visit and that Adams then promised that a copy of his *Education* would be sent. A copy inscribed by HA to Trevelyan indeed was sent, via Gaskell. See HA to CMG, 16 Dec 1907, saying "the volume" is on its way. The inscribed copy was eventually listed in *American Book Prices Current,* 1974: price £550.
64. HA to EC, Friday. 5 p.m., [26 Jul 1907].
65. EC to HA, Wednesday, [14 Aug 1907].
66. CFA2 to Ford, 10 Aug 1907, FP 10; Ford to CFA2, 21 Aug 1907, FP 10.
67. Writing to Anna Lodge, 22 Aug 1907, HA says the chauffeur was "Helen Hay's." Levenson and his associates venture to correct HA. Without citing a source, they assert (L, VI, 80n2) that Josef Fritz was "chauffeur of Harry Payne Whitney (not of his sister-in-law Helen Hay Whitney)." The basis of their assertion can perhaps be assumed to be a press report. A rival source is Clara Hay's letter to HA, 27 Aug 1907. Turning to the subject of her daughter Helen and her husband, Mrs. Hay says: "I hope you saw Helen before you left Paris and of course you have heard of the deplorable accident, which cost their chauffeur his life. . . . It was reported that he was Harry's man, but that was not true." She adds: "We have not yet had a letter from Helen, only a cable to say that the chauffeur was alone in the car. I am afraid it will have upset them a good deal."

16. The Second Traveling Copy

All letters by and to HA are in HA-micro 21, 22, B, or H, or HA/Thoron-micro, unless otherwise indicated.

PRINCIPAL SOURCES

(1) twenty-eight letters, EC to HA, 22 Sep 1907–14 [Oct] 1908.
(2) four letters, HA to Reid, 27 Sep 1907–13 Sep 1908, L, VI, 86–88, 177–79.
(3) thirteen letters, HA to CMG, 28 [Sep] 1907–23 Oct 1908.
(4) eleven letters, HA to Margaret Chanler, 13 Jan–4 Sep 1908.
(5) three letters, HA to Ford, 18 Feb–10 Apr 1908; letter, HA to Ford, 10 Apr 1908, FP 10.
(6) thirty-three letters and postcards, HA to EC, 7 [Mar]–14 [Oct] 1908.
(7) three letters, HA to Wister, 20 Mar 1908, Friday, 27 [Mar] 1908, & 10 Apr 1908, L, VI, 128; O.1908.9, 11. (Concerning the second letter, see note 36, below.)
(8) [HA], *The Education of Henry Adams,* Wash (privately printed) 1907— the Thayer copy, MHS; here known also as the First Traveling Copy.
(9) [HA], biographical sketch prefacing *Letters of John Hay and Extracts*

from Diary, Wash (privately printed) 1908; reprinted in facsimile, NY 1969, I, i–xxii. (For an authoritative attestation of HA's authorship, see note 33, below.)

(10) [HA], *The Education of Henry Adams*, Wash (privately printed) 1907— the copy once known as the Athenaeum copy because on deposit at the Boston Athenaeum, now better known as the Second Traveling Copy; author's collection. (For the copy's availability to inquirers, see note 57, below).

LESSER SOURCES; CITATIONS; COMMENTS

1. Because his Master Copy is lost, there is no way of being sure whether HA had previously made the same correction in that copy. One notices, however, that he corrected the error in both his First and Second Traveling Copies. The repetition may mean he was so annoyed with himself that he wanted none of his personal copies to exhibit the "James" uncorrected. See p. 203 in principal sources 8 & 10.

2. HA's statement to Berenson that he printed one hundred copies of *The Education* is supported by other evidence. See Chap. 21, note 46, below.

3. HA to EC, 22 Sep 1908.

4. Principal 8, 329. In her *Willard Gibbs*, Garden City 1942, Muriel Rukeyser cites so many cases in which the names of Willard Gibbs and Wolcott Gibbs were confused, even by scientists, that the confusion becomes one of the main themes of her book.

5. For Gibbs's *Memoirs*, see HA-2, 338–41, 348, 648, 781, 858. For HA's adoption of a second name, see HA-2, 534–38, 856–60. For the ganoid fish and Walcott, see *EHA* (1907), 348, 453; (LoA), 1048, 1192. For HA's dealings with Walcott concerning the country's coal supply, see Chap. 11, above. Walcott succeeded Langley as head of the Smithsonian Institution.

6. HA's copy, HAL. The book's date of publication is given on the verso of the title-page. My statement that HA bought the copy while still in Paris in 1907 is a guess but I think a good one. HA scored and/or annotated 52 pages of the copy. He scored the margin next to a passage on p. 95 (the underlinings are his): ". . . d'autres Poissons, dites Ganoïds, étaient revêtus d'ecailles épaisses, ossifier, ornées d'un brillant émail, formant une enveloppe impenetrable. . . ."

7. HA's first marginal reference to Depéret appears next to his own remarkable passage, *EHA* (1907), 198; (LoA), 929:—". . . the triumph of all was to look south along the Edge to the abode of one's earliest ancestor and nearest relative, the ganoid fish, whose name according to Professor Huxley was *Pteraspis*, a cousin of the sturgeon, and whose kingdom, according to Roderick Murchison, was called Siluria."

On the same page in his First Traveling Copy (principal source 8, 198), one finds next to the same passage an additional reference: "Owens [*sic*] Palaeontology, 144." One of the books in HA's Washington library, now at MHS, is Richard Owen, *Palaeontology/ or/ A Systematic Summary of Extinct Animals. . .*, Edinburgh 1861. HA scored p. 144 next to the words: "*Genus* Pteraspis.—The buckler of Pteraspis truncatus has been found in the Silurian stratum below the Ludlow bone bed; it is *the earliest known indication of a vertebrate animal* [the underscorings of the last eight words are by HA]."

On a later page of his First Traveling Copy (principal source 8, 200), there again are references to Depéret's book and Owen's book. Still later, in the chapter "Silence," HA pencilled a very brief marginal reference (ibid., 313), "Antigone 334–375." The reference appears next to HA's comic sentence saying about silence, "Sophocles made remarks in its favor, which should have struck the Athenians as new to them. . . ." A book in HA's Washington library when he died was *Antigone* in Greek, edited on the basis of Wolff's edition by Martin L. D'Ooge, Bost 1884. In the copy, lines 334–75 are the response of the chorus to the news of Antigone's burial of her brother Polyneices—a response Walter Kaufmann translated in the 1960s as beginning, "Much is awesome, but nothing more awesome than man. . . ." See Kaufmann, *Tragedy and Philosophy*, Garden City 1968, 237.

My present opinion is that HA entered the two references to Owen and the reference to Sophocles in Washington in the winter of 1907–1908 after looking afresh at books then on his bookshelves. I suggest too that the three references point to sources HA read with interest before he wrote *The Education*. This would make them exceptions, for his references in his First and Second Traveling Copies point as a rule to works published after *The Education* was printed or works which may be regarded as new to him when the references were written.

8. See note 23, below.

9. HA to Louisa Hooper, Tuesday, 26 [Nov 1907], L, VI, 90. I assume Donald Cameron did not meet the steamer in New York.

10. Clara Hay to Houghton, Mifflin & Co., n.d., as drafted by HA, L, VI, 113. I can believe that Mrs. Hay agreed with the ideas developed in this draft. In the absence of confirmatory evidence, I shall not believe she sent any such letter to the firm.

11. HA does not tell Mrs. Jones where he encountered the formula, nor what it signifies, nor why it was so interesting to him.

12. Bancroft's copy is in Butler Library, Columbia University. It is inscribed by Bancroft on the flyleaf: "Frederic Bancroft/ From the author/ 1907."

13. HA to Burgess, 13 Jan 1908, L, VI, 103–03; Channing to HA, 21 Jan 1908; Stewart to HA, 26 Jan 1908.

14. HA to Margaret Chanler, 29 Jan 1908. For evidence that HA meant Henri—not Lucien—Poincaré, see L, VI, 110–11.

15. Margaret Chanler to HA, 29 Jan [1908].

16. EC to CMG, 14 Jan 1908, HA-micro 21.

17. HA to Rhodes, 17 Jan 1908, L, VI, 106.

18. Rhodes does not say how he learned of *The Education*. His having learned of it is evidence that word of it was circulating.

19. Rhodes to HA, 13 May 1908.

20. HA to Rhodes, 16 Mar 1908, L, VI, 125–26. The quoted sentence is HA's description of the Master Copy as annotated by mid-March 1908.

It bears emphasis that the description—"crammed with marginal notes"— does not fit any of the annotated copies of *The Education* that have so far been found but can be assumed to fit one that has not been found: the Master Copy.

21. The semi-humorous tone of his remark to Rhodes is itself evidence of HA's reluctance to refer to his personal copies, or to throw light on the methods he was using to correct and improve his book.

22. In my opinion, there are no marks in HA's First Traveling Copy of *The Education* that can be identified as inspired by Rhodes. I take this absence of evidence to be itself evidence that any changes HA made in his book in response to Rhodes's suggestions were made only in the now-lost Master Copy.

23. Four copies of *The Education* containing annotations by HA are at present available for study. None has anything glued or pasted into it by HA. A description of the contents of the lost Master Copy was given to me and my wife

orally in 1962 by Aileen Tone. She said the it was full of inserts, glued or pasted into the text where appropriate. For further details, see Chap. 27.

24. Ford to HA, 19 Feb 1908.

25. HA to Ford, 18 Feb 1908.

26. HA to Ford, 20 Feb 1908. Regrettably this important letter does not appear in the final volume of *The Letters of Henry Adams*. It was relegated to the *Supplement*.

27. Ibid. For the best version of the centipede metaphor, see HA to Rhodes, 10 Feb 1908, L, VI, 117.

28. Clara Hay to HA, 8 Mar 1908.

29. Clara Hay to HA, 9 Jul 1908.

30. Principal source 9, I, xix.

31. Principal source 9, I, xvi–xxii.

32. HA's introductory 1908 biography of Hay has been little noticed. It is very well-written. Though a mere outline, it remains far superior to other biographies of Hay with respect to authority. It tells Hay's story from within, not of course as Hay would have told it, yet with evident confidence in the truth of what it imparts.

33. In connection with the *JHLetters*, Ford later declared "The introduction is by him [HA]." See Ford to E. H. Anderson, 20 Nov 1928, inserted in Ford's annotated copy at NYPL.

34. WJ disliked an idea he found in the book. For his objection, see L, VI, 118, notes 1 & 2.

35. HA to WJ, 21 Feb 1908, L, VI, 121.

36. HA to Wister, Friday, 27 [Mar] 1908. The letter is mistakenly dated 27 Apr 1908 in O.1908.11.

37. HA had acceded to a request for a copy by Richard Olney, the former secretary of state. See HA to Olney, Thursday, 30 [Jan] 1908, L, VI, 112. Olney is mentioned in *The Education*; Laughlin is not.

38. HA to Laughlin, 6 Apr 1908, L, VI, 130–31. The copy HA sent to Laughlin is at the Houghton Library, Harvard University. One may suppose that Laughlin read it shortly after receiving it. He made many annotations. What most caught his attention was the following passage by HA: "He ["Henry Adams"] was as ignorant as a schoolboy of society. He was unfit for any career in Europe, and unfitted for any career in America, and he had natural intelligence enough to see what a mess he had thus far made of his education." See *EHA* (1907), 74; (LoA), 800.

As if he were speaking to HA, but in tones he might not have used if actually speaking to him in person, Laughlin wrote in the margin: "The real difficulty was you did not have to work for your means of subsistence and travel. As Phillips Brooks once said of a Bostonian: 'He had the disadvantage of being rich.' The sense of achievement comes most to a poor boy. . . ."

This rather strong comment by Laughlin rested on false assumptions that the Henry Adams who wrote the book and the "Henry Adams" who is its protagonist are the same and that the book is autobiographical. It rested also on ignorance of the important fact that HA *worked* from an extremely early age and by working earned his place as his parents' leading child. (For details, see Chap. 22.)

In short, Laughlin mistook a book and a man. His doing so is the more surprising because he later wrote the best description of HA ever published by anyone who knew him. See J. Laurence Laughlin, "Some Recollections of Henry Adams," *Scribner's Magazine*, May 1921, 576–85.

39. Clara Hay to HA, dated only "Wednesday," filmed in HA-micro 21 as if written in February 1908 but certainly written much later, not long before HA's departure for Europe.

40. Principal source 9, I, 1.

41. For the paragraph as printed, see any copy of *JHLetters*, I, 13. For the paragraph as written by Hay, see HA's copy, HAL, in which the names omitted in the paragraph are restored in the margin, or see the duplicate of HA's copy prepared by Ford, NYPL.

42. HA to Ford, 10 Apr 1908, FP 8. This important letter remains unpublished.

43. See note 12, above. Read with care, Bancroft's annotations in the copy can give an impression that he marked errors and possible errors only because he had a habit of correcting books when reading them. Of his 44 annotations, 27 are exclamation points, sets of brackets, and varishaped scorings indicating interest in sentences or passages; and 13 are corrections of actual or possible errors (misspellings, a case of "was was," a colloquialism, and a repeated date).

A defect of HA's book as privately printed was repetitions. In Chap. XIII, "The Perfection of Human Society," Bancroft saw HA state that in London in 1864, ". . . if any lady appeared well-dressed, she was either a foreigner or 'fast.' " Bancroft saw too that HA, forgetting what he had already written, stated five pages later, "If there was a well-dressed lady at table [in London], she was either an American or 'fast.' " Similarly in Chap. XVI, "The Press," Bancroft saw that HA likened American society in 1868 to an "earthworm" and on the next page HA likened the protagonist to an "earthworm." By writing page numbers in the margins, Bancroft noted these repetitions sufficiently to indicate that changes were needed. See his copy, 169, 174, 206, 207.

HA's available annotated copies of *The Education* do not take note of the repetitions, and the book was published in 1918 with the repetitions still in place. See *EHA* (1918), 195, 200, 237, 238; (LoA), 899, 904, 937–38. It thus might be supposed that HA never became aware of the repetitions and never modified his book to remove them.

Yet it seems more than possible that HA could read *The Education* as well as Bancroft. It thus also seems possible that HA noticed the repetitions, made appropriate changes in his Master Copy to counteract them, and later, when reading his other personal copies, by-passed them as no longer in need of work. The conclusion is that one must *guess* how completely HA corrected and improved his Master Copy. There is no alternative.

44. EC to HA, Thursday Eve, [23 Apr 1908].

45. HA to HJ, 6 May 1908.

46. Four notes, Edith Wharton to HA, [10–14 May 1908].

47. HA to EC, 24 May 1908.

48. HA to EC, 2–5 Jun 1908.

49. HA to Mabel La Farge, 4 June 1908.

50. EC to HA, 7 Jun [1908].

51. Cater, 624–25, or O.1908.22–23.

52. Isabella Gardner to HA, 20 Jun 1908.

53. HA to Isabella Gardner, 30 Jul 1908.

54. For evidence that HA had the First Traveling Copy with him in Paris in 1908 (as well as in 1907), see note 56, below.

55. Principal source 8, 346, 377, 386, 427–428.

56. HA annotated two copies of Poincaré's *La Science et l'Hypothèse*, both

published by Flammarion. Both are in HAL. Neither is dated by the publisher, but the book appeared in 1908. See printed catalogue, NYPL. The date is important. Thanks to his reference to Poincaré's book in his First Traveling Copy, one can infer that HA had the First Traveling Copy with him in Paris in 1908.

57. I bought the Second Traveling Copy from Ximenes Rare Books, New York, on 13 Jan 1987. I had it microfilmed and duplicated. A copy of the microfilm is available for study at the Massachusetts Historical Society. As a rule, I keep the book in a safe deposit box in a bank. I freely show inquirers my duplicate of the book at my home.

58. In Chap. XXIV, "Indian Summer," HA noticed a passage about "a volume by Judge Stallo, which had been treated for a dozen years by the schools, much as Wolcott Gibbs himself was treated, with a conspiracy of silence such as inevitably meets every revolutionary work that upsets the stock and machinery of instruction." In Chap. XXI, "The Grammar of Science," he also noticed a passage: ". . . for twenty years past, Stallo had been deliberately ignored, and Wolcott Gibbs himself smothered under the usual conspiracy of silence inevitable to all thought which demands new thought-machinery." The words here underscored in the two passages are words HA deleted when writing his annotations relating to "Wolcott Gibbss" in his Second Traveling Copy. The deletions are an instance of his detecting and removing an injurious repetition in his book. See principal source 10, 329, 394.

Attention should be turned as well to a wrongly repeated date, "May 22," in Chap. XXXII, "Vis Nova." HA had detected the repetition and removed it in his First Traveling Copy by changing one of the occurrences from "22" to "24." He removed it again in his Second Traveling Copy by the same means. Although admittedly small, these changes are helpful. They too show that HA was alert to the presence of hurtful repetitions in his book and was acting to remove them. See principal sources 8 & 10, 409.

It should be noted that the "May 22" repetition was discovered—apparently independently—by HA and Bancroft. See note 43, above.

In 1918, when *The Education* was readied for publication, one of its editors had possession of the First Traveling Copy. In consequence, the book was corrected with respect to "May 22" and "May 24." See *EHA* (1918), 468. Strange to say, the repetition is restored in the present standard edition. See *EHA* (LoA), 1147.

In 1918, the editors of *The Education* lacked the Second Traveling Copy. In consequence, the book as published did not reflect the deletions HA made in that copy to get rid of the "conspiracy of silence" repetition. The repetition was dealt with by other means. See *EHA* (1918), 377, 450. For further details, see Chap. 27.

59. This list is confined to those of HA's marginal references in the Second Traveling Copy that name both an author and a title.

There are also nine less-complete references in the copy. Because no work referred to by HA in the margins was published after 1908, the references can be read as evidence that he completed his work in the Second Traveling Copy in 1908 before returning to Washington.

60. HA to EC, 10–11 Aug 1908.

61. EC to HA, 18 Jul 1908.

62. HA to Margaret Chanler, 27 Aug 1908; HA to EC, 24–25 Aug 1908.

63. EC to HA, 6 Sep 1908.

64. HA to EC, 1 Sep 1908.

65. Reid to HA, 7 Sep 1908.

66. HA to Reid, 9 Sep 1908.

67. Principal source 10, 373.

68. Principal source 10, 374. In the margin, HA wrote the seven words to be inserted and also wrote below them a reminder to himself: "which Auguste Comte long afterwards enrolled in the service of his positive philosophy (Martineau. II, 152.)."

69. Principal source 10, 378.

70. The improved title for Chap. XXIX and the attendant improvements in the text of the chapter have not yet been incorporated into *The Education of Henry Adams* by editors and publishers. The same is true of other improvements HA made in his Second Traveling Copy.

The failure of HA's *Education* to appear before the public as he had wanted it to appear is the principal concern of the closing chapters of this biography.

71. HA translated extracts from Lucien Poincaré's *La Physique Modern* and Edmond Bouty's *La Verité Scientifique* relating to Gibbs. See notes attendant to the MS. of the first version of HA's "The Rule of Phase applied to History," MHS.

72. HA to Margaret Chanler, 27 Aug 1908.

73. Mrs. Keep's current address and Mrs. Cameron's former address were the same: 53 Avenue Montaigne. It thus seems possible that Mrs. Keep was living in EC's former apartment or one that EC told her about in the same building.

17. Unsatisfactory Works

Letters by and to HA are in HA-micro 22, 23, or H, unless other wise indicated.

PRINCIPAL SOURCES

(1) four letters, EC to HA, 1–2 Nov-22–23 Nov 1908.

(2) twenty-five letters, HA to EC, 3 Nov 1908–12 Dec 1908.

(3) seventeen letters, HA to Mary Jones, [4 Nov 1908]–22 Mar 1909.

(4) fourteen letters, HA to BA, 18 Nov 1908–26 Mar 1909.

(5) seven letters, HA to GCL, 2 Dec 1908–22 Apr 1909.

(6) seven letters, HA to Jameson, 14 Dec 1908–23 Mar 1909, L, VI, 197–98, 240–41; O.1908.44–45; O.1909.5, 13, 15.

(7) three letters, HA to CMG, 17 Dec 1908–2 May 1909.

(8) [HA], manuscript, "The Rule of Phase/ applied to History," dated "January 1, 1909"—the first version; filmed in sequence in HA-micro 22 (first page ends "Willard Gibbs"). (For added details, see note 19.)

(9) typed copy, "THE RULE OF PHASE/ APPLIED TO HISTORY," HAP—copied from principal source 8 (first page ends components"). (For added details, see note 21.)

(10) [HA], manuscript of a letter to "My dear Sir," dated "January 1, 1909"—filmed in sequence in HA-micro 22; published in Cater, 781–84; re-published in L, VI, 205–08. (The letter introduces principal source 8.)

(11) [HA], undated manuscript, "The Rule of Phase/ applied to History"—the second version; filmed in HA-micro Miscellaneous (first page ends "afterwards"). (For added details, see notes 29 and 44.)

LESSER SOURCES; CITATIONS; COMMENTS

1. HA to Clara Hay, 11 Nov 1908, L, VI, 190–91.

2. EC to HA, 1 Nov 1908.

3. HA to MC, 11 Nov 1908; HA to EC, 16 Nov 1908.

4. For HA, the necessity of saying such things may have begun and ended in his close friendship with Lodge's mother.

5. In 1996, I bought a copy of *Herakles* from William Reese and Co. described as follows (Cat. 153): "A very interesting association copy, with a presentation inscription on the free endsheet: 'Given by Henry Adams to Maud Howe Elliot.' The inscription is in a contemporary hand, but not Adams's. The book was published in November, and Brentano's Washington branch's small book label appears on the rear paste-down. In all likelihood, Adams's secured a number of copies of his friend's new book and directed that they be sent out. . . . It is not surprising that novelist/suffragist Maud Howe would be a recipient of such a gift from Adams."

One notices that in 1914 HA wrote to EC, "Mrs[.] Winty came last night to dinner with her odious cousin Maude Howe. I will not stand reformers. My friends may as well accept that small fact." See HA to EC, Monday, [26] Jan [1914], HA-micro 28.

6. HA to Mary Jones, 20 Dec 1908; HA to GCL, Thursday, 31 [Dec 1908]; GCL to HA, n.d. [dated Jan 1909 by HA], beginning, "I love all right-minded people . . . ," filmed in HA-micro 23 after 10 Mar 1909.

7. HA to EC, Thursday, 10 [Dec 1908]. HA later told BA (letter of 3 Feb 1909) that *Herakles* had "not had a lisp of notice although it is the most important poem since Whitman and Swinburne."

8. BA to HA, 16 Nov 1908.

9. HA to BA, 18 Nov 1908.

10. HA to Mabel La Farge, 10 Feb 1907.

11. HA to BA, 17 Feb 1909.

12. HA to EC, 10–11 Aug 1908.

13. HA to Jameson, 14 & 16 Dec 1908; also see L, VI, 198n2.

14. Note in HA's handwriting on his card, accepting an invitation to lunch with Ford on 28 Dec 1908, FP 11.

15. Clara Hay to HA, 16 Jan 1909. In her letter, Mrs. Hay verges on taking credit for HA's introductory biography as an example of her own abilities as a writer.

16. HA's set of the *Letters* is in HAL. Ford copied HA's insertions of suppressed names into another set and gave the duplicate set to the New York Public Library in 1928. My count of the names HA recovered is based on Ford's duplicate.

17. As printed, *Letters of John Hay* included 135 letters from Hay to HA, 54 to Nicolay, 48 to Reid, 33 to Clara Hay, 22 to Gilder, 19 to Howells, and smaller numbers to other recipients. HA retained the originals of the letters from Hay to himself and thus could immediately begin to write suppressed names into his set of the volumes.

The transcripts he had made for Mrs. Hay from Hay's diaries were another of HA's reliances when at work on the recovery of names. He may have retained them. If not, he was in a position to borrow them. They are now in the John Hay Library at Brown.

18. HA to BA, 3 Feb 1909.

19. Principal source 8. The paper contains upwards of thirty deletions and insertions and has more the aspect of a draft than finished work. The date HA gave his paper is a mere date of convenience. Five days before he advised BA that he was sending a "plaything," HA had said that hard work on his "dynamic theory" had confronted him with a choice between 1917 and 1922 "as the limit of our present phase of thought." See HA to BA, Friday, 29 [Jan 1909]. But no such choice appears in HA's paper as sent to BA. Instead a last phase of history is dated as beginning in 1917 and ending in 1921.

This discrepancy between HA's letter to BA and the paper seems to me good evidence that HA changed the paper in late January or early February, after writing to BA.

20. That HA's comet burned in BA's imagination should come as no surprise to readers of Chap. VI of his *Law of Civilization and Decay*, which dwells with fascinated insistence on the fate of the Templar knights, who were tortured, led to the stake, and burned alive.

21. Principal source 9. Until 1955, the Henry Adams Papers at the Massachusetts Historical Society were inaccessible to visiting researchers. In the summer of 1955, following the opening of the Adams Papers proper, I was given access to the Henry Adams Papers, 1890–1918. The papers were stored in labeled manuscript boxes. In Miscellaneous Box 2, I found a 32-page typescript titled "THE RULE OF PHASE/ APPLIED TO HISTORY." Its first page bore the words "By Henry Adams" in Ford's handwriting in the upper left-hand corner. For reasons given in Chap. 27, I believe this typescript is the one BA had made for his own use in February 1909.

22. BA especially wanted from HA any properties he had (paintings, porcelains, or whatever) that would be suitable additions to the historic Adams mansion in Quincy.

23. HA to Mary Jones, Saturday, 13 [Feb 1909].

24. Reid to HA, 5 Feb 1909.

25. Lindsay to HA, 9 Feb 1909.

26. A fragment filmed at the end of the BA-to-HA letters in HA-micro H evidently concludes BA's letter to HA, 19 Feb 1909. It ends: I sent back your manuscript yesterday after taking a copy. You've made a good job with that theory, and I have read it with a lot of pleasure. What you do with it is your affair. Evelyn sends love./ Yrs B.A."

27. HA to Rhodes, 5 Feb 1909. HA's phrase "wholly defaced by notes" cannot be a description of his First Traveling Copy, which is annotated on many pages but is by no means wholly defaced. Equally it cannot be a description of his Second Traveling Copy, which is annotated only in its later chapters. The phrase is not incompatible, however, with what I and my wife were told in 1962 about the contents of HA's Master Copy. For further information, see Chap. 27.

28. Principal source 10. The date HA affixed to the letter seems a mere date of convenience. Whether he wrote the letter before or after he wrote the first version of "The Rule of Phase applied to History" seems open to debate. My guess is after.

29. Principal source 11. In 1955, in Miscellaneous Box 2 of the Henry Adams Paper, I found in HA's handwriting a version of "The Rule of Phase applied to History" which I saw was different from the version published by BA in 1919 in *The Degradation of the Democratic Dogma*. The MS. seemed to me a very notable surprise. After studying it, I concluded that it was HA's final version and wrote a short evaluation: ". . . far more readable than the published version,

very different in content, different in what it suggests, and much more complete in the insight it affords into HA's own historical ideas."

Because I wished to write a biography of HA and had to concentrate first on his earlier writings, I was disposed not to study the MS. any longer. A second cause wholly dissuaded me from further work on it. In a sheaf of papers in the Henry Adams Library relating to "The Rule of Phase applied to History," I found evidence that Ford discovered in 1919 that there were two versions of the paper. In the papers, Ford gave it as his opinion that the version BA meant to publish was the later! I had then—and still have—a high opinion of Ford. In the absence of supporting evidence that my conclusion was right and that Ford's was wrong, I suspended my interest in the versions.

In 1996, when at last I was able to look into the problem of the versions again, evidence abounded that the conclusion Ford reached in 1919 was wrong and that the later version was indeed the unpublished one, secreted till 1955 (possibly by Ford himself) in the restricted Henry Adams Papers. For further details, see Chap. 27.

30. In the 1940s, Cater found the three-part package in George Cabot Lodge's papers. He reported that it included "several pages of the elaboration of certain ideas which were later incorporated in the body of the essay." See Cater, 781, Editor's Note.

Eventually the Lodge Papers were acquired by the Massachusetts Historical Society. In 1996, Brenda Lawson, curator of manuscripts at MHS, reviewed materials in the Society's collections relating to "The Rule of Phase applied to History." Those in the Lodge Papers included 37 pages of translations in HA's handwriting of passages about Gibbs extracted from French and German scientific writings. Clearly these 37 pages are the "several pages" that Cater had found in the 1940s.

31. GCL to HA, n.d., marked "#3 1909" and filmed out of sequence in HA-micro 23 as if written on or after 13 Mar 1909. The letter can be dated [7? Mar 1909] with the help of HA's reply, 8 Mar 1909.

32. Ibid.

33. Six letters, HA to BA, 18 Feb, 19 Feb, 23 Feb, 5 Mar, 13 Mar, 19 Mar 1909; with 82 pages of comments by HA about BA's MS., Houghton Library, Harvard. HA sent BA the comments with "a last batch of MS." See HA to BA, 5 Mar 1909.

34. HA's comments about p. 289 of BA's MS.

35. HA's comments about p. 334 of BA's MS.

36. HA's comments about p. 429 of BA's MS.

37. HA's comments about p. 495 of BA's MS.

38. Ibid.

39. HA to BA, 13 Mar 1909.

40. Ibid.

41. HA's comments about p. 202 of BA's MS.

42. BA to HA, 19 Feb 1909:—"I agree with you that biographies are best left alone, and since I have tried to write one, I see why. It is not so easy as it seems."

43. BA to Ford, 25 May 1909, FP 11:—". . . as I draw near the close of the biography, I see that I have mistaken my point of view and it must be recast." ". . . the book as it stands is not in a condition to print. Henry is right."

44. In 1955, when I came upon HA's MS. of the second version in the Henry Adams Papers, Miscellaneous Box 2, at the Massachusetts Historical Soci-

ety, xerox did not exist. I made detailed handwritten notes about the MS. My notes are silent about its having an appendix.

In 1956, I bought a Contoura—a newly developed machine for making on-the-spot copies of documents and books. Using the machine, I copied what seemed to me to be the important pages of the typed copy of the second version then kept in the Henry Adams Library, MHS. I have the copies. One page is titled "APPENDIX." It bears quotations from two authors: "Clausius" and "Whetham."

Much later, when arranging material for the *Microfilms of the Henry Adams Papers*, Stephen Riley or his aides ended the material for the reel marked "Miscellaneous" with HA's manuscript of the second version of "The Rule of Phase applied to History." See principal source 11. As filmed, HA's MS. includes *two* closing pages. The first of the two is titled "appendix" and bears the quotations from Clausius and Whetham noted above. The second of the two is headed "Electrolysis" and quotes 95 words on that subject from an unstated source.

My present impression is that the second version of HA's "The Rule of Phase applied to History" had a one-page appendix which for some reason I did not find in 1955 in Miscellaneous Box 2; that the typed copy of the second version was correct in including the one-page appendix; but that the page headed "Electrolysis" that is added to the appendix in HA-micro Miscellaneous, while pertinent to both versions of HA's essay, was never part of the appendix to the second version and instead is a mere stray note in HA's handwriting.

45. HA to Mary Jones, 22 Mar 1909.

46. HA to Reid, 1 Aug 1909:—"My copy of Hay's letters is lent to Mrs[.] Hay for her to fill in the blanks of her own copy!"

47. HA to BA, 17 Feb 1909.

48. *HUS* (Scribner), I, 174; (LoA), I, 119.

49. *HUS* (Scribner), IV, 301; (LoA), II, 1134.

50. For HA's contention that the Americans were superior to the English in intelligence, see HA-2, 633–34 & 890, notes 43–45, and the pages of the *History* cited therein.

51. *HUS* (Scribner), IX, 219; (LoA), II, 1331. HA may be imagined to have said with Charles Peirce, in Peirce's exact words, that there are "great laws of historical development . . . as practically absolute as the Second Law of Thermodynamics." See Peirce, unpublished paper, "Lecture XI. Galileo," 16, among his papers identified as 101b History of Science, Harvard University Archives. The problem for Adams, as for Peirce, was that the great laws of history were being discovered only slowly and with much difficulty.

52. *HUS* (Scribner), IX, 225; (LoA), II, 1335. To my knowledge, Chap. VI of my dissertation, *Henry Adams and History* (1954), available at University Microfilms, Ann Arbor MI, remains the only detailed review of HA's theory of history as expressed in his *History of the United States*. His is a theory of human action. In the works of historians, such theories are far from common.

53. In his presidential letter to the members of the American Historical Association, "The Tendency of History" (1893), HA did not reprove the members for their failure to notice his theory and voice opinions about it. He even came close to denying he had a theory. In a good-mannered way, he suggested that the needed theory of history was waiting in every historian's inkwell, to use a Spanish expression, and might get written at any time.

54. Edward T. Allen to HA, 18 May 1909:—"Your . . . book [on Tahiti] is of prodigious value. . . ."

55. The Teva great chief Ariifaataia, better known as Temarii, was eager to obtain gunpowder but ill-acquainted with its properties. His death in consequence of an accidental gunpowder explosion was a catastrophe for the Tevas and the Tahitians generally. See *Memoirs of Arii Taimai*, 125–29.

56. Whether or not history (or human progress) was accelerating, HA deserves credit for saying it had done so—perhaps also for being the historian who first prominently made the assertion.

57. One could endlessly question whether the pieces of his puzzle fit, do not fit, are intended to fit but do not, are intended not to fit yet possibly do, are mostly ideas he believed, are mostly ideas he disbelieved, or are not worth considering by anyone at all.

58. Attention should be drawn to passages in the first version of "The Rule of Phase applied to History" (principal source 8) that somewhat abstractly restate parts of the theory of history expressed by HA in his *History of the United States*. Three passages are the following. From paragraph 16:—". . . in history only the attractive . . . helps to construct. Only attractive forces have a positive, permanent value for the advance of society on the path it had actually pursued." From paragraph 43:—"Thought has always moved under the encumbrance of matter . . . and, unless the conditions are extremely favorable, it does not move at all . . . as in China. . . ." From paragraph 51:—". . . if man should continue to set free the infinite forces of nature, and attain the control of cosmic forces on a cosmic scale, the consequences may be as surprising as the change of water to vapor, of the worm to the butterfly, of radium to electrons."

Attention should also be drawn to a passage in the first version which sets forth an idea which some readers may feel HA could *not* have believed. From paragraph 52:—"Always and everywhere the mind creates its own universe and pursues its own phantoms; but the force behind the image is always a reality, the attractions of occult power. If values [i.e. quantifications?] can be given to these attractions, a physical theory of history is a mere matter of physical formula[s], no more complicated than the formulas of Willard Gibbs or Clerk Maxwell. . . ." The passage necessarily is part-satirical, for Gibbs's formulas are described in the second sentence of the first version as highly complicated. The passage does not reappear in the second version of HA's paper, nor does anything like it. Inquirers accordingly have two questions to consider. What did HA mean, or try to mean, when he put the passage into the first version? And why did he delete it when writing the second?

The questions are offered as samples. Questions just as difficult can be posed about many passages in the first version.

59. Close study of both versions of "The Rule of Phase applied to History" can drive a reader to the very simple conclusion that what was impressing HA most was the accelerating increase in the burning of coal to create steam. He could see the steeply rising curve of this increase. He wondered what it meant and how high it would go.

60. See note 61.

61. Different readers may react very differently to the dates that become attached to the five phases of history specified in HA's second version. Some readers may take seriously the suggestions that history can be expected to reach the beginning of its end in 1918 and reach the end itself in 1923. Other readers should be excused if they take the suggestions to be satirical or comical.

HA was not a mathematician, but he could do such things as multiply a number by itself and determine a number's square root. He had read enough science books to permit his forming an opinion about the attitudes and mental habits of scientists.

His opinion comes to the fore in paragraph 13 of the second version of "The Rule of Phase applied to History," which broaches the question of attraction and acceleration as they may enter into history. The paragraph goes on to say: "The physico-historian will certainly not trouble himself to ask whether these supposed values are real,—or in common phrase, true,—which will be to him a matter of little concern; but he will try to satisfy himself that they are convenient, especially for mathematical treatment. . . ."

The word "convenient" returns in paragraph 40. The paragraph suggests that the mind may resemble an electro-magnet. It continues, "Possibly the image may be altogether false, but its convenience may be none the less on that account, and if it be convenient, the physicist will use it."

"Convenient" makes its last appearance in paragraph 43, which says, "The most reasonable and most convenient point of departure for the new Phase [the mechanical] would . . . be the year 1600."

Yet convenience is not enough to satisfy HA when writing the second version. Using round numbers and their squares and square roots, he dances the phases of the version into chronological positions that not only suit his convenience but cater to his enjoyment. Lampooning the unseriousness of science with the abracadabra of schoolboy mathematics, he rigs the arithmetic of his paper all the way from the imminent future to the remotest past. It becomes obvious that he can end history in whatever year may most delight him.

62. Principal source 8, last paragraph.

63. A date he had newly offered was 1919 or sooner. See HA to CMG, 2 May 1909—"within ten years."

18. To Worry Historians

Letters by and to HA are in HA-micro 23, 24, or H, or HA/Thoron micro, unless otherwise indicated.

PRINCIPAL SOURCES

(1) ten letters, HA to Thoron, 15 May 1909–24 [Jan 1910].
(2) thirteen letters, HA to CMG, 6 [Jun] 1909–25 [Apr 1910].
(3) sixty-three letters, HA to EC, [16 Jun 1909]–[29 Apr 1910].
(4) four letters, HA to Elizabeth Lodge, 2 Jul 1909–14 [Jan 1910], L, VI, 267–68, 278–79, 298; O.1909.27–28.
(5) six letters, HA to Margaret Chanler, 9 Sep 1909–5 [Apr 1910]. (For details about a recovered letter, see note 37, below.)
(6) three letters, HA to Jameson, 5 Dec 1909–7 [Apr 1910], L, VI, 290–91; O.1910.2 & 21.
(7) six letters, HA to BA, 21 Dec 1909–22 Mar 1910.
(8) seventeen letters, EC to HA, [12 Jan]—[26 Mar 1910]. (For a conjecture about missing letters, see note 3, below. For a letter filmed out of sequence, see note 27, below.)
(9) letter, HA to Ford, 12 Mar 1910, L, VI, 322; & three letters, HA to Ford, 15 Mar, 22 Mar, & Friday, 25 [Mar] 1910, FP 13. (The latter three are unpublished.)
(10) typed copy, [HA], "THE RULE OF PHASE APPLIED TO HISTORY," MHS—the second version as copied for John Franklin Jameson (the

first page ends "laws of"); together with an undated, signed, 27-page criticism by Henry A. Bumstead.

(11) HA, *A Letter to American Teachers of History*, Wash (privately printed) 1910.

LESSER SOURCES; CITATIONS; COMMENTS

1. HA to Martha Lindsay, 12 Aug 1909.

2. Sent by Edith Wharton to EC, the telegram mainly repeated news cabled to John by his father. See HA to HCL, 5 Sep 1909.

3. Many letters written by EC to HA during the interval with which this chapter is concerned are missing. Perhaps HA destroyed them, once read, because replete with details concerning Martha's health. Or perhaps EC later destroyed them for the same reason.

4. HA to EC, 30 Aug 1909.

5. Clara Hay wondered whether the cause of Bay's death was "too many cigarettes." See her letter to HA, 13 Sep 1909.

6. For a very strongly stated example, see HA to CMG, 31 Aug 1909, describing Lodge as "the only poet—or person—of any genius that has come up in America for fifty years."

7. Edith Eustis to Bigelow, 27 Aug 1909, HA-micro 23.

8. HJ to HA, 31 Aug 1909.

9. Ibid.

10. Clara Hay to HA, 13 Sep 1909.

11. Berenson to HA, 17 Sep 1909, thanking HA for the "precious books" and saying about the MS., "I will fall upon it at once."

12. Cater, 650n1; Bancroft to Jameson, 24 Sep 1909, in a sheaf of MSS. relating to HA's "The Rule of Phase applied to History," MHS.

13. HA to EC, 21 Sep 1909.

14. Berenson later referred to the work HA had lent him—the second version of "The Rule of Phase applied to History"—as an "essay on humanity & the second law of thermo-dynamics." See Berenson to HA, 17 Oct 1909. The phrase may be evidence that Berenson found physics very confusing and that he had difficulty distinguishing between a paper by HA that he had read and a future book—*A Letter to American Teachers of History*—that HA had begun to describe to him.

15. Berenson to HA, Tuesday, [28 Sep 1909], filmed out of sequence in HA-micro 23 as if dated [c. 17 Sep 1909].

16. HA to Berenson, Tuesday, 28 [Sep 1909]. Professor Giacomo Luigi Ciamician of the University of Bologna is quoted in HA's *Letter*. See principal source 11, 91, 96. Also see L, VI, 282n2.

17. HA to Berenson, 6 Oct 1909.

18. Berenson to HA, 7 Oct 1909.

19. Palmer to HA, 23 Oct 1909; bill, Hugh Reese, Ltd., to Palmer, 3 Nov 1909, HA-micro 23.

20. HA to EC, Friday, 19 [Nov 1909].

21. HA to CMG, Monday, 8 [Nov 1909].

22. Ibid. See also HA to Wendell, 10 Jan 1910, L, VI, 295:—"a sort of squib, or fire-cracker."

23. HA to BA, 21 Dec 1909.

24. Clark to HA, 28 Dec 1909.

25. HA to EC, 12 Oct 1909.

26. HA to EC, 11 Jan 1910.

27. EC to HA, Wednesday, [12 Jan 1910], filmed out of sequence in HA-micro 22 as if written in November 1908.

28. Elizabeth Lodge to HA, n.d., but dated "Jan. 1910" by HA.

29. EC to HA, 16–17 Jan 1910.

30. Principal source 10.

31. In 1955, I found these documents and others in a sheaf of papers in HAL headed by a sheet bearing the words: "Typewritten manuscript of Henry Adams's 'The Rule of Phase Applied to History' with covering letters by W. C Ford, and Wilder D. Bancroft and critical comments by Henry A. Bumstead. . . ." I infer that the sheaf originally consisted only of the typescript, Bancroft's letter, and Bumstead's comments—that other materials were added later. For further details, see Chap. 27.

32. HA to Bumstead, 1 Feb 1910, L, VI, 305–06.

33. The prefatory letter is dated "16 February, 1910"—HA's seventy-second birthday.

34. HA to Frederic Bancroft, 24 Mar 1910:—". . . [I] had to make it very incomplete, especially on its sociological and socialistic side, which properly requires a volume to itself." For additional comments linking the *Letter* to socialism, see HA to Ford, 12 Mar 1910; HA to CMG, 14 Mar 1910; HA to Hadley, 15 Mar 1910; HA to Melville Bigelow, 17 Mar 1910; HA to Huntington, 24 Mar 1910; and Cater, xcv.

35. EC to HA, 1 Mar 1910.

36. Margaret Chanler to HA, 6 Mar 1910.

37. On 5 Sep 1989, James Brunner telephoned me from Geneseo, NY, offering for sale Margaret Chanler's copy of HA's *Letter* and an attendant unpublished letter by HA to her, dated 8 Mar 1910. Brunner read the letter to me, and I took detailed notes, including the full texts of what seemed to me the main sentences.

In 1999, the same materials were advertised for sale by North Star Rare Books, Great Barrington MA: price $3,700. The crucial sentence in the letter, as given in North Star's advertisement, reads, "I am the only man in America who sees the light."

38. EC to HA, 1 Mar 1910.

39. HA to Ford, 12 Mar 1910.

40. EC to HA, 17 Mar 1910.

41. EC to HA, Saturday, [19 Mar 1910].

42. EC to HA, Sunday, [20 Mar 1910]; EC to HA, Wednesday, [23 Mar 1910].

43. EC to HA, Saturday, [26 Mar 1910].

44. Lowell to HA, 11 Mar 1910; Jordan to HA, 22 Mar 1910; Dodd to HA, 14 Mar 1910; Hadley to HA, 14 Mar 1910. The fact that HA replied to Hadley (letter of 15 Mar 1910, O.1910.14) can be read as evidence that Hadley had responded to HA's book much as HA wished that readers would respond.

45. Channing to HA, 22 Mar 1910. Although they were not teachers, HA sent his *Letter* to Jameson, Ford, and Bancroft.

46. HA to Huntington, 24 Mar 1910.

47. Principal source 11, 3–4.

48. BA let no one get ahead of him in putting about the idea that HA was the discoverer of doom. He read HA's *Letter* disconsolately. See BA to HA, 1 Mar 1910:—"I have even laughed at it, though your humor is of the grimmest,—as one might laugh at one's own crucifixion."

49. BA to HA, 30 March 1910, Margaret Chanler Papers, Houghton Library, Harvard University. For other parts of the letter, see L, VI, 331n2.

BA had earlier told HA (letter of 24 Mar 1910) that the "effect" of his *Letter* was "profound" and that "the interest is beyond anything that I remember."

50. T. S. Eliot finished his senior year at Harvard in the spring and early summer of 1910. By then in Cambridge and Boston, false foundations were in place for an extraordinary dictum that Eliot would later write about HA: "Wherever this man stepped, the ground did not simply give way; it flew into particles. . . ." See "T. S. E.," "A Skeptical Patrician," *Athenaeum*, 23 May 1919, 361–62.

51. Read to HA, 20 Mar 1910.

52. HA to Ford, 22 Mar 1910.

53. Ford to HA, 24 Mar 1910.

54. HA to Ford, Friday, 25 [Mar 1910].

55. Greenslet to HA, 24 Mar 1910.

56. Baldwin to HA, 25 Mar 1910. Baldwin's employer was a magazine, *The Outlook*. In his letter, Baldwin listed HA, Roosevelt, Lodge, James B. Angell, Joseph B. Bishop, George W. Smalley, John Bassett Moore, and David Jayne Hill as persons who had been approached or recommended, in vain, as possible authors of the Hay biography.

57. HA to BA, 30 Jan 1910.

58. Elizabeth Lodge to HA, 16 Apr 1910.

19. STILL IN THE SWIM

Letters by and to HA are in HA-micro 24, 25, and H, or HA/Thoron micro, unless otherwise indicated.

PRINCIPAL SOURCES

(1) eight letters, HA to Jameson, 2 May–11 Dec 1910, L, VI, 333–34, 378–79; O.1910.31–32, 35, 56, 64–65, 75, 77.

(2) six letters, HA to Elizabeth Lodge, 3 May–24 Oct 1910.

(3) nineteen letters, HA to EC, 6 May 1910–5 Jan 1911.

(4) nine letters, HA to Anna Lodge, 17 May–25 Dec 1910.

(5) fifteen letters, HA to Louisa Hooper, [2? Jun 1910]–2 Jan 1911.

(6) eight letters, HA to Thoron, 10 Jun 1910–2 Jan 1911.

(7) five letters, HA to CMG, 2 Aug–31 Dec 1910.

(8) five letters, HA to BA, 6 Aug–24 Nov 1910.

(9) HA, *A Letter to American Teachers of History*, Wash (privately printed) 1910.

(10) HA, *The Life of George Cabot Lodge*, Bost & NY 1911.

LESSER SOURCES; CITATIONS; COMMENTS

1. HA to Ford, 22 Mar 1910, FP 13.

2. Ford to HA, 16 Apr 1910. Ford's discovery had been precipitated by an inquiry addressed to HA which HA had turned over to Ford as suited to his abilities as a researcher. See M. Alston Read to HA, 20 Mar 1910; HA to Ford, 22 Mar 1910, FP 13; Ford to HA, 24 Mar 1910; HA to Ford, 25 Mar 1910, FP 13.

3. HA to Ford, 2 May 1910, FP 13.

4. HA observed to Mabel La Farge, 6 Aug 1910, "We did not make the world, though Sturgis said we did." The remark bears on *The Life of George Cabot*

Lodge, which makes clear that, in HA's opinion, Bay Lodge shared with Bigelow—and Schopenhauer—a philosophy which held that the "Will" is "all that is"; that the Will is "knowable only as ourself"; and that "the sole tragic action of humanity is the Ego,—the Me,—always maddened by the necessity of self-sacrifice, the superhuman effort of lifting himself and the universe by sacrifice. . . ." See principal source 10, 47–48, 109–10.

5. Perhaps foreseeing that the book would be candid, HA advised Bay's mother, ". . . you may be sure that it will shock you. . . ." See HA to Anna Lodge, 21 Jun 1910.

6. HA to Elizabeth Lodge, 3 May 1910.

7. HA to Anna Lodge, 21 Jun 1910.

8. Levenson and his associates assign a mistaken date, [7? Jun 1910], to a note by HA in which he asks Bigelow for Marjorie Nott's address in "Aix," i.e. Aix-les-Bains. See O. 1910.35. A date in keeping with the available evidence is [14? Jun 1910].

9. Principal source 10, 84–85, 183–85, & 187–89. Marjorie Nott wrote six letters to HA in 1910, all from Aix-les-Bains. She dated one 26 Jun 1910. After receiving it, HA dated a second 10 Jul 1910. The two are filmed in sequence in HA-micro 24.

The other four, all undated, are filmed at the start of 1910. The one beginning "You see . . ." is best dated [c. 16 Jun 1910]; the one beginning "Yes, as my . . ." is best dated [c. 19 Jun 1910]; the one beginning "I am so . . ." is best dated [c. 22 June 1910; and the one beginning "I once read . . ." is best dated [c. Jul 1910].

Read in order, the letters are informative, as well as amusing. The letters by HA to which they reply are missing.

10. Jameson to HA, 12 May 1910.

11. For examples, see Barrett Wendell to HA, 1 May 1910; Albert Bushnell Hart to HA, 2 May 1910; Raphael Pumpelly to HA, 8 May 1910; and James Ford Rhodes to HA, 26 Sep 1910.

12. Teggart to HA, 7 Jun 1910. For an explanation of HA's dialogic method of teaching, see HA to Edward H. Davis, 3 Feb 1911:—"The mind must have a contradiction in order to act at all. My object has always been to supply the contradiction which should compel the mind to fight."

13. In 1953, I was employed by a New York bookseller specializing in books relating to economics, history, and philosophy. I bought a book from his stock: Frederick J. Teggart's *Prolegomena to History/ The Relation of History to Literature, Philosophy, and Science*, Berkeley 1916. Repeatedly during the next few months, AT told me something that required my writing a note in Teggart's book: "Aileen Tone remembered (1953–1954) that Adams told her of a historian in California who, alone, could understand him. When I suggested Teggart today, Feb. 10, 1954, she did not at all recollect the name, but said, 'I think he was an Englishman.' "

Teggart's book traverses an array of concerns that interested HA in the course of his intellectual development after 1865, including the precise matters at issue in HA's article "The Principles of Geology." The evident chief difference between HA and Teggart as thinkers about history is that HA reached very early the conclusions that Teggart did not reach till much later dates.

14. Jameson to HA, 12 & 20 May 1910; Bumstead to HA, 16 Jun 1910.

15. *Letters of William James/* edited by his son Henry James, Bost 1920, II, 344–47, includes WJ to HA, 17 Jun 1910; also WJ's postcards of 19 Jun & 26 Jun 1900 to HA and a facsimile of the latter.

When WJ visited him, HA's attention was partly fixed on a reported current condition afflicting WJ's brother Henry, which HA understood to be "melancholia." See HA to Anna Lodge, 17 May 1910.

WJ described HJ's condition as "a sort of nervous breakdown." See *Letters of William James*, II, 341.

WJ lived long enough to return to America but died on 26 Aug 1910 just after arriving at his summer home.

16. HA to CMG, 22 Sep 1910:—"Poor William James set up for our last [American] thinker, and I never could master what he thought." HA's copy of WJ's *Principles of Psychology* as reprinted, NY 1902, is in HAL. HA's markings indicate that he read the volumes carefully and doubted the clarity and/or the truth of WJ's ideas. See I, 167, 182, 220, 224, 251, 254, 256, & 271.

See especially HA's dismissing as "Twaddle" WJ's description (II, 578) of heroes who can "stand the Universe" and the brave person who "can meet it and keep up his faith in it."

17. *Letters of William James*, op. cit., II, 344, 346.

18. HA to BA, 6 Aug 1910.

19. BA to HA, 6 Mar 1909:—"Washington and he [J. Q. Adams] were the only two men who conceived America as a unity and tried practically to realize their idea. They failed and with them our civilization has failed."

20. The fullest representation of BA's new idea is "The Heritage of Henry Adams," his introduction to his ill-conceived *Degradation of the Democratic Dogma*, NY 1919, especially 103ff.

21. BA to HA, 5 Apr 1910.

22. Brett to BA, 4 May 1910, MP 49. HA was serious in addressing his books to particular audiences: his *Mont Saint Michel and Chartres* to young women, his *Education* to young men, and his *Letter to American Teachers of History* to its addressees. Neither Brett nor BA was disposed to understand, much less honor, HA's ideas in this connection.

23. BA to Brett, 7 May 1910, MP 49.

24. HA had divided his *Letter to American Teachers of History* into Chapter I, "The Problem," and Chapter II, "The Solutions." The chapter titles suggest that the book states a problem and says how it may be solved. Ironically the book does nothing of the sort. Chap. I exhibits European pessimism as revealed in the theories and writings of European scientists. Chap. II does the same!

Assuming that the book as a whole takes the problem to be European pessimism, the book has to be read as saying that no solutions are to be expected from Europe. The negative judgment is only implicit. It none the less is emphatic.

25. HA to Brett, 9 Aug 1910, O.1910.50.

26. AT told me that Ellen Warder Thoron became interested in a soldier of fortune. She did not name him. For evidence that the breakup of the marriage caused excitement, see Chap. 20.

27. In connection with this letter by HA to Thoron, Levenson and his associates state (L, VI 344n1) that MHA in 1885 left HA "for several months" to nurse her dying father in Cambridge, Massachusetts. By making this statement in the context of the breakup of the Thoron marriage, they imply that the marriage of HA and MHA also ended in a breakup. The facts are simple. HA and MHA parted in New York on 11 Mar 1885. HA returned to Washington. MHA went to Cambridge to nurse her father. HA joined her in Cambridge for four days ending on March 27 and returned to Washington. He joined her a second

time on April 4, stayed two days, and returned to Washington. Her father died on April 13. HA left for Cambridge at once, joined her, and attended the funeral. They returned to Washington together, arriving on the 19th. They had been separated for about 26 days—less than a month, During the days they were apart, they kept in touch by means of very frequent letters and telegrams. His letters survive; her letters and telegrams do not. His letters involve no indications of a tendency towards a breakup.

28. Typical statements appeared in his letter to Raphael Pumpelly, 19 May 1910 (F, II, 542):—"You want to read that drivel called my *Education.* Some men get terribly low down. Still, there are one or two ideas in that book which are fairly anarchical and sound."

29. HA to Anna Lodge, 23 Sep 1910:—". . . two Yale professors . . . profess to think well of me! What will happen to Yale!"

30. An Englishman, Arthur B. Potter, heard about *The Education* and wrote to HA from Lucerne on 20 Mar 1910, asking how he might obtain a copy. HA offered to lend him one. HA's letter is missing. On 9 May 1910, in a second letter from Lucerne, Potter thanked HA for the offer and indicated where the copy should be sent. In a third letter, sent on 7 Jun 1910 from Bristol, Potter said: ". . . I suggest that you should modify one line on page 98. You say 'that in May 1861 no one in England—literally no one—doubted that Jefferson Davis had made or would make a nation, and nearly all were glad of it.' " [The underlinings are Potter's.] Potter explained that he was born in 1852 but from an early age knew the English proponents of the Union cause in America and was positive that support for the Union existed in England at the indicated time: May 1861. HA replied. His reply is missing. In a fourth letter, sent on 17 Jun 1910 from London, Potter said he was returning the copy of *The Education* and told HA, "For all I know, you may be quite right in what you say about 1861." Yet he reported John Bright as having said in a speech in 1877 that Richard Cobden "always believed that the result of the war would be slavery abolished and the great republic still one and indivisible." HA replied. Again his reply is missing. In a postcard dated 23 Jun 1910, Potter said he had received HA's letter, "with which I agree entirely."

The importance of HA's response to Potter, to the extent that it can be adduced from the latter's communications, is that it reflects HA's resolve to make his *Education* factually accurate with respect to public events while mostly fictional with respect to himself.

The point at issue was the difference between English attitudes towards the Union in 1861 and English attitudes towards the Union in 1862. It appears that HA did not retreat from his statement on p. 98 of *The Education.* He held fast to his opinion that the most serious crises between the United States and England during the Civil War arose in 1861.

Yet it cannot be said for a fact that he kept p. 98 unchanged. His available annotated copies of *The Education* contain no modifications of p. 98, but his Master Copy remains missing. The situation underscores the seriousness of the loss of the Master Copy.

31. HA to Anna Lodge, 24 Jul 1910:—"Mrs[.] Cameron has twins to console her,—Elizabeth Hoyt and Gladys Rice,—and she was never so happy and contented . . . or so amused. . . ."

32. Ford gained access to this letter from HA to Thoron and was so struck by HA's long passage explaining how he defended himself against BA—only half of which I have quoted—that he copied it for his own use. See HA file, Misc. Personal Papers, Manuscripts & Archives Division, NYPL.

33. HCL to HA, 24 Aug 1910.

34. HA to HCL, 12 Sep 1910.

35. Koopman to HA, 16 Sep 1910.

36. CFA2 had earlier recovered it once, unexpectedly did so again, and made a record of the recoveries. ". . . when preparing the Memoir of my father published in the American Statesmen series, I came across this ante-bellum effort of my brother's, and then read it; but made no use of it. It subsequently disappeared; and, a year or so back when I again wanted it, because of a vague recollection of certain statements in it, the most careful search revealed no trace of it. I gave it up for lost; but, some ten days or two weeks ago, when looking for a cover to hold copy, I took one down, apparently empty, from a shelf, and, to my surprise, in it I found the missing manuscript. Reading it over, I was much struck both by its interest and its historical value." See MHS *Proceedings*, 43 (1909–1910), 657.

37. Ibid., 655–87. CFA2's introductory remarks include extracts, somewhat abridged, from Chap. VII of *The Education*. Also see CFA2 to HA, 28 Sep 1910.

38. HA to CFA2, 19 Sep 1910.

39. HA to CFA2, 10 Oct 1910:—"I have not read my lucubrations of half a century ago, but I have asked some other intelligent persons to read it. . . ."

40. HA to Ford, 13 Dec 1910, FP 15.

41. Evelyn Adams to HA, 3 Oct 1910.

42. Seward to Ford, 3 Jan 1911; Bigelow to Ford, 5 Jan 1911—both in FP 15.

43. HA to Thoron, 18 Sep 1910. HA studied prehistoric man in cooperation with Henri Hubert, a French palaeontologist. They apparently met through Bancel and Mabel La Farge. HA's letters to Hubert are missing. Hubert's letters to HA are in French and not very legible.

44. Mme. Whitcomb to HA, 27 Sep 1910.

45. Cater, xciii.

46. HA to Mabel La Farge, 25 Oct 1910.

47. Elizabeth Lodge to HA, 25 Oct 1910.

48. For the overall effect of *The Life of George Cabot Lodge* after undergoing last modifications in 1911, see Chap. 20.

49. BA to HA, 22 Oct 1910.

50. HA to BA, 1 Nov 1910.

51. CFA2 to HA, 28 Oct 1910. HA had written the uncompromising words: ". . . the combination of prudence with daring, patience with energy, and military skill with political foresight . . . distinguishes Washington from all other generals of whatever time or nation." See *SKETCHES*, 151.

52. HA to CFA2, 8 Nov 1910. HA presumably discovered the Pickering criticisms while assembling the materials for his compilation, *Documents Relating to New-England Federalism. 1800–1815.*, Bost 1877.

It should be noted that Pickering was one of the Adams family's enemies and that, as seen by HA, the New England Federalists ended in becoming models of political, not to mention military, incompetence.

53. CFA2 to Ford, 12 Dec 1910, FP 15; CFA2 to HA, 13 Dec 1910.

54. Cable, Mary Jones to HA, 14 Nov 1910; HA to Mabel La Farge, 19 Sep 1923; John La Farge to Miss Barnes or Miss Jones, 8 Nov [1910], HA-micro 25.

55. Without HA's knowing it, AT may have been reading a copy of *The Education* lent to her by Loulie. HA had given Loulie a copy early. Now at the Boston Athenaeum, it is signed by her and bears a note in her handwriting:

"Given by H.A. March 5th 1907." She evidently did not have it with her in Europe in the winter of 1909–1910, for she helped herself to another copy at HA's Paris apartment. Now also at the Boston Athenaeum, her second copy bears a note on the inner fly leaf in HA's handwriting: "This book was broken into, & it was carried away from Henry Adams's apartment during the great flood of January February 1910/ Paris. It is now the possession of his dear Looly." On the back of the inner fly leaf, there is also part of a note in HA's handwriting the rest of which at some point was cut off. The surviving part says "Mrs. Cam" only. One may conjecture that the copy Loulie broke into had originally been lent to Mrs. Cameron; that EC returned it to HA's Paris apartment wrapped; that Loulie tore away its wrappings and carried it off with the secret intention of lending it to her friend from New York; and that later she brought it back to HA's apartment—whereupon indulgent HA permitted her to keep it.

56. Ford to HA, 30 Nov 1910.

57. HA to Ford, 13 Dec 1910, FP 15—an unpublished letter. The occurrences of the word "Jew" and its variants in HA's letters written after 1899 is as follows: 1900—26; 1901—30; 1902—10; 1903—17; 1904—11; 1905—17; 1906—5; 1907—3; 1908—3; 1909—9; 1910—9; 1911—6; 1912—11; 1913—9; 1914—2; 1915—5; 1916—2; 1917—0; 1918—2. The frequency drops steeply with the conclusion of the Dreyfus Affair, yet the occurrences thereafter can be read as indicating that the Panic of 1893 and the Dreyfus Affair left such marks on HA that he could return to his original slight level of interest only slowly and by stages.

58. CFA2 to HA, 13 Dec 1910.

59. The address was published in an altered version. See CFA2, "The Most Critical Episode in the Civil War," *The Independent*, 5 Jan 1901, 32–37. A prefatory note says, "The following article is the substance of a paper just read before the New York Genealogical and Biographical Society. . . ." The text is followed by the words "Boston, Mass.," which may indicate that CFA2 was its abridger or editor.

60. One perhaps may assume that CFA2 sent HA his paper as published in *The Independent* or that HA otherwise acquired a copy.

If he read it, HA could quickly see that CFA2's paper (like his letter) was evidence that CFA2 had not read—or had forgotten—Chap. X of *The Education*. CFA2's paper and HA's chapter concern the same events of September–October 1862 and at points quote the same items of evidence. They are very divergent in meaning. The title of CFA2's paper, "The Most Critical Episode in the Civil War," harmonizes with a passage he twice quotes from their father's diary: "We are now passing through the very crisis of our fate." The text of the paper conveys as a certitude the idea that a particular event, the secret cancellation of a British Cabinet meeting on October 23, 1862, "proved final." "Then and there the die had unknowingly been cast."—i.e. the failure by the British to intervene in the American War at that exact moment doomed the Confederate States and assured victory for the Union.

To HA, such ideas were simply false. He knew from experience that the most critical moments for the Union occurred earlier than October 1862, and he had long since printed his opinion that each crisis had shown Palmerston to be "cautious, careful, vacillating." See *EHA* (1907), 142; (LoA), 870.

For data about an early crisis on 12 Nov 1861 (the only one that ever required a business meeting between Palmerston and CFA), see HA-2, 653n53. For

Palmerston's defeat in a secret correspondence with CFA in June 1862, see HA-2, 38–41.

61. HA to Louisa Hooper, 24 Dec 1910.

62. HA to CFA2, 18 Nov 1910; HA to Margaret Chanler, 30 Dec 1910.

63. HA to Thoron, 2 Jan 1911. HA's phrase "a few more copies" stands in contrast with a statement by Ernest Samuels that HA printed "five hundred copies" of the 1912 version of *Mont Saint Michel and Chartes* and distributed the copies "to friends and to libraries across the country." See HA, *Novels/ Mont Saint Michel/ The Education*, NY: LoA, 1983, 1218. I know of no evidence supportive of Samuels's statement.

20. "CHANSON DE GESTE"

Letters by and to HA are in HA-micro 25, 26, or H, or HA/Thoron-micro, unless otherwise indicated.

PRINCIPAL SOURCES

(1) sixteen letters, EC to HA, 6 Jan–21 Dec 1911.

(2) forty-seven letters, HA to EC, 11–12 Jan–22 Oct 1911.

(3) twenty-one letters, HA to Mary Jones, 11 Jan–8 Dec 1911.

(4) fourteen letters, HA to Thoron, 20 Jan–[3 Oct] 1911.

(5) HA, *The Life of George Cabot Lodge*, Bost & NY 1911.

(6) HA, a manuscript, "Chansons de Geste." (For details, see note 77, below.)

(7) HA, a manuscript, "Notes assembled by Henry Adams for his essay on Chansons de Geste." (For details, see note 77, below.)

LESSER SOURCES; CITATIONS; COMMENTS

1. Furst & Co. to HA, 19 & 20 Jan 1911. Changes in the book would be few. See Chap. 21. Whether HA ordered 100 copies of the new version, or less, is not known. Also see Chap. 19, note 63, above.

2. HA to EC, 17 Jan 1911. Also see Chap. 19, note 26, above.

3. HA to Thoron, 20 Jan 1911. See also HA to Jameson, 20 Feb 1911:—"My correspondents reproach me for not putting [*Mont Saint Michel and Chartres*] . . . on sale. I would rather put a few babies on sale."

4. Three letters, EC to HA, 6, 12, & 20 Jan 1911.

5. Davis to HA, 14 Jan 1911.

6. Davis to HA, 28 Jan 1911.

7. HA to Davis, 18 Jan 1911, L, VI, 403–05. Perhaps to keep his summary simple, HA did not tell Davis about Teggart's reaction.

8. Ibid.

9. Davis to HA, 28 Jan 1911.

10. Davis tried to arrange to visit HA during the Christmas holidays in 1911. HA was on the ocean, coming from Europe. Regretfully Davis wrote to HA about having missed him. HA replied. Davis was obliged to answer that he was in a "very hurried condition" and would have to resume writing "a little later." See Davis to HA, 15 Dec 1911; HA to Davis, 12 Jan 1912; Davis to HA, 21 Jan 1912.

11. CFA2 to Ford, 27 Jan 1911, FP 15.

12. Ford to CFA2, 30 Jan 1911, FP 15.

13. HA to Ford, 29 Jan 1911, FP 15.

14. Ford to HA, 9 Feb 1911.

15. HA to Ford, 11 Feb 1911, & attachments, FP 15. When HA called Mrs. Walters "the Baltimore lady," either his memory was at fault or his imagination was overactive. She lived in "West Washington," as her letter shows.

16. Edith Hoyt to HA, 9 Feb 1911.

17. EC to HA, 2 Feb 1911.

18. Edith Hoyt to HA, 9 Feb 1911.

19. HA to EC, 13–14 Feb 1911.

20. EC to HA, letter dated "15-2-11," not to be confused with her previous letter of the same day, headed "Cannes Feb. 15th 1911."

21. HA to Elizabeth Lodge, 24 Oct 1910:—"The great thing is to get it done,—that is, to get the plates ready to print. . . ."

22. HA to EC, 6–7 Feb 1911.

23. HA to EC, Sunday, 11 [Dec 1910]:—"One day the sun shone, and I couldn't find a shady corner to write in."

24. HA to Thoron, 2 Jan 1911; Thoron to HA, 5 Jan 1911 & 9 Jan 1911. In 1956, I found the two letters from Thoron in HA's copy of *Chronique de Turpin*, Paris 1835, HAL.

See also Thoron to HA, 17 Jul [1911]:—"The text of what purports to be the Pseudo Turpin exists at the Chartres Library, in a volume with three other chronicles. . . ."

25. EC to HA, 24 Feb 1911.

26. For details about the building and its accessibility, see Palmer to HA, 7 Jun 1911; Lindsay to HA, 12 Jul 1911.

27. Because scattered in his country house, the letters were difficult for Mitchell to collect.

28. Mitchell to HA, n.d., filmed in HA-micro 25 as if dated 1 Mar 1911. The things Mitchell said he most remembered about Bay were his "amazing mind, and abundant, powerful personality." He could not have known that Henry James had earlier spoken of Bay as "abundant."

29. Principal source 5, 196–201.

30. In a letter to Luquiens, 5 Mar 1911, HA wondered whether the Oxford and Cambridge scholars had been "so ignorant or indifferent for seven hundred years as not to have produced a properly edited and annotated edition of the poems of their greatest King."

Replying on 12 Mar 1911, Luquiens said he "looked everywhere" for "a critical edition of Richard's poems" but found only the prison song as published in Bartsch's *Chrestomathie*—"which you already know."

31. Letters, Luquiens to HA, 19 Mar 1911 & 22 Mar 1911:—". . . no one except yourself has ever translated [the *Chanson de Roland*] . . . successfully."

32. EC to HA, 8 Mar 1911.

33. EC to HA, 16 March 1911.

34. HA to EC, 26 & 28 Mar 1911.

35. EC to HA, 30 Mar 1911.

36. HA to Berenson, 23 Mar 1911, L, VI, 429–30.

37. HA to EC, 9 April 1911.

38. Ibid.

39. The published book is the evidence of HA's wanting his name kept off the binding. For his wanting it kept off the title page, see HA to Houghton Mifflin Co., [11? April 1911], L, VI, 438–39. When done with the *Life*, HA gave the MS. and supporting materials to Elizabeth Lodge. See his letter to her, 6.30 P.M., [15 Apr 1911]. In her reply, 19 Apr 1911, she thanks HA for writing a "magnificent book."

40. HA to EC, Sunday, [30 Apr 1911].

41. HA to EC, 6 May 1911.

42. HA to EC, 22 Jul 1911.

43. HA to Evelyn Adams, Monday, 29 [May 1911].

44. Florence Keep to HA, Friday, [9 Jun 1911], filmed out of sequence in HA-micro 26 as if written on 30 Jun 1911—an impossible date.

45. HA to Thoron, 14 Jun 1911; HA to EC, Sunday, 18 [Jun 1911].

46. HA to CMG, 16 May 1911.

47. Ibid.

48. HA to EC, Sunday, 11 [Jun 1911].

49. HA to CMG, 13 Jun 1911. The eleven presidents HA had not seen presumably were Washington, John Adams, Jefferson, Madison, Monroe, Jackson, William Harrison, Tyler, Polk, Fillmore, and Pierce.

50. HA to EC, 22 Jun 1911.

51. Ibid.

52. HA to EC, Sunday, 18 [Jun 1911]. HA later remarked to Mary Jones (letter of Sunday, 16 [Jul 1911]), that Wagner resembles Rousseau "in the avidity with which he takes his clothes off in public."

53. AT told me and my wife that in 1912, when she began to live with him, HA did not wear glasses but constantly used magnifying glasses. I infer that he began to use them in 1911 in Paris.

54. HA to CMG, 15 Jul 1911. HA's copy of Wallace's *World of Life* is missing. He presumably kept it in his Paris library.

The first London edition of Wallace's book is hard to find in the United States. The following excerpt from the third London edition, 1911, 277–78—or, alternatively, from the first New York edition, January 1911, 299–300—may be representative of the passages in the book that most attracted HA's interest.

> . . . beyond all the phenomena of nature and their immediate causes and laws there is Mind and Purpose; and . . . the ultimate purpose is (so far as we can discern) the development of mankind for an enduring spiritual existence. With this object in view it would be important to supply all possible aids that a material world can give for the training and education of man's higher intellectual, moral, and æsthetic nature. If this view is the true one, we may look upon our Universe, in all its parts and during its whole existence, as slowly but surely marching onwards to a predestined end; and this involves the further conception, that now that man *has* been developed, that he *is* in full possession of this earth, and that upon his proper use of it his adequate preparation for the future life depends, then a great responsibility is placed upon him for the way in which he deals with this his great heritage from all the ages, not only as regards himself and his fellows in the present generation, but towards the unknown multitudes of future generations that are to succeed him.

55. HA to CMG, 15 Jul 1911.

56. HA to EC, Tuesday, 18 [Jul 1911].

57. HA to Mabel La Farge, 12 August 1911.

58. HA to Thoron, 11 Jul 1911:—"I think it our duty to print the Chronicle of Turpin. . . ." Thoron carried the idea to a conclusion. In 1934, he privately printed a text of the chronicle transcribed from a MS. owned by the Vatican. See Ward Thoron, ed., *CODEX QUARTUS SANCTI JACOBI de expedimento et conversione*

yspanie et gallecie editus a beato Turpino archiepiscopo, Bost: Merrymount Press, 1934.

59. HA to CMG, 29 Jul 1911. Darwin's ideas and the extinction of vertebrates were matters HA had re-encountered in Wallace's *World of Life.*

60. See Chap. 19, note 43, above.

61. During 1911, Hubert found a small stone horse and a centipede made of reindeer bone. HA thought the finds sufficient.

62. CFA2 to Ford, 5 Aug 1911, FP 17.

63. By directing Ford to p. 411 of *Studies Military and Diplomatic* and speaking of "disclosures in Fitzmaurice," CFA2 turned Ford's attention to the ending of the essay, "Queen Victoria and the Civil War," and a footnote: "Fitzmaurice, I, 477." Together, pp. 411–13 of CFA2's essay and p. 477 of the first volume of Fitzmaurice's biography of Granville disclose that Victoria had no interest in the American Civil War but in 1864 remembered that earlier Palmerston and Russell had nearly taken "dangerous steps" and feared that her ministers might involve England in "a mad and useless combat" with Germany. Victoria offered no specifics about the steps nearly taken in the past. Presumably they too related to Germany.

By directing Ford to pages 134–53 of *The Education,* CFA2 turned his attention to parts of Chaps. X & XI that have nothing to do with Queen Victoria and nothing to do with Germany.

64. MHS *Proceedings,* 45 (1911–1912), 243–333.

65. HA to Mary Jones, 10 Aug 1911.

66. HA to EC, Tuesday, 15 [Aug 1911]. One notices that in his letter of the previous week, dated 8 Aug 1911, HA had told EC, "Ward Thoron is still working six hours a day over twelfth-century MSS. for me, in the Arsenal Library." The words "for me" may indicate that Thoron was working for HA as a paid—possibly very well paid—researcher. Thoron had independent means. Because of his marital breakup, he had left paid work in Washington and, at least to that extent, needed money. HA could easily afford to help fill the gap.

67. HA to Mary Jones, Sunday, 20 [Aug 1911].

68. For another reference to the danger that ships might collide with icebergs, see HA to BA, 22 Aug 1911.

69. MHS *Proceedings,* 45 (1911–1912), 333.

70. HA recommended publication in the *Proceedings* partly as a means of foiling the history teachers in America's universities. See HA to BA, 22 Aug 1911:—"Let us . . . keep our poor efforts out of the hands of tutors in history. They make it loathsome to their bored classes. In the Hist. Soc. Collections they can get at it if they want it, but they can't make it a text-book to learn by memory. They must use their minds on it."

71. BA to Ford, 31 Aug 1911, FP 17.

72. BA to Ford, 15 Oct 1911, FP 17:—". . . [I am] deep in Geneva[,] which I find grows on me."

73. HA to Anna Lodge, 11 Sep 1911.

74. HA to EC, Tuesday, 3 Oct [1911]:—"She gets along about as badly as most solitary widows. . . ."

75. HA to EC, 15 Oct 1911.

76. HA to Mary Jones, 27 Oct 1911. Mrs. Jones would know that the hero of the *Chanson de Roland* dies at Roncevals. She presumably would *not* know that Vivien, the hero of a comparable work, the *Chanson de Willame,* dies at Aliscans, at least in some of the story's versions.

77. In August 1955 in her Boston storeroom, LHT found a binder containing four envelopes identified in her deceased husband's handwriting. As listed by Ward Thoron, the contents of the envelopes were: "Chansons de Geste/ Unfinished Manuscript of Henry Adams"; "Notes Assembled by Henry Adams for his essay on Chansons de Geste"; "La Chanson de Willame/ Henry Adams['s] Essay at Translation"; "Chanson de Willame/ W. T.'s effort at a translation." At LHT's suggestion, I immediately copied the contents of the first three envelopes for use in writing this trilogy.

Thoron to the contrary notwithstanding, HA's "Chanson de Geste" is finished. It begins, develops, and ends, and is unfinished only in the limited sense that it contains misspellings, mistakenly repeated words, and other minor errors. When HA finished the essay is unclear. I tend to believe he drafted all of it while still in Paris in 1911 but in Washington early in 1912 modified its last pages as they bear on one of the personages in the "Chanson de Roland." See principal source 11, 163–73, and HA to Thoron, 7 Apr 1912, as it relates to Odo as the original of Tilpin.

78. HA's copy of *La Chancun de Willame*, n.p.: Chiswick Press, 1903, is in HAL. On the back flyleaf, it contains a note by Thoron and an obituary letter about Dunn clipped from the London *Times*. See also Thoron to HA, 13 Mar 1912, about the clipping.

79. The 28th page & 36th page of HA's "Chanson de Geste" indicate that he had knowledge of an Oxford MS. of the *Chanson de Roland*.

80. In HA's opinion, the authorship of the *chansons* was not susceptible of proof. He wrote—principal source 6, 150: "The best that can be done is to choose the most likely theory which will serve to reconcile the greatest number of difficulties."

On this basis, HA proposed his single-author theory. At the time he developed it, his theory was contrary to an established theory he associated with Gaston Paris: that the *chansons* originated "in popular tradition"—i.e. were developed orally by a large number of *jongleurs* in loose association. See ibid., 1.

81. Much of HA's essay is given to establishing beyond a doubt the centrality of the Abbey of Saint Denis in the work of reviving France after 950 A.D.

82. See principal source 6, last line:—"What surprises the student most [about the *Chanson de Roland*] is its violence of patriotism, and this intensity is the peculiar signature of St[.] Denis."

According to HA, the poet's shuffling of historical materials harmed Botel, the best-known count of the Spanish March and a genuine French hero, by making him lead the infidels in the second *chanson*. See ibid., 96–97, 115–18, 127–31 & 135–36.

83. HA and Thoron collected books relating to the *Chanson de Willame*. In 1956, I found in LHT's library a two-volume work: M. W. J. A. Jonckbloet, ed., *Guillaume d'Orange./ Chansons de Geste . . .* , La Haye 1854.

84. Principal source 6, 163–69.

85. Principal source 6, 49. HA took an uncensorious view of medieval forgeries. See HA to CMG, 8 Sep 1911:—". . . the Abbeys of the twelve century were the source of more literary fraud . . . than any modern syndicate of labor-unions. They were workshops of forgery. . . . Their trade in relics, their advertising, and their syndicating, were quite [as] marvelous as modern business; but they did it with wonderful art and feeling, as if they were Greeks. They harmed nobody, and amused all the world."

86. Ibid., 31.

87. CFA2 to HA, 21 Oct 1911.

88. HA to CFA2, 10 Nov 1911.

89. Ibid. HA's lines were comically at variance with the realities of his experience. The twigs to his credit included his important political actions and a long list of excellent, even superlative, writings. And he was far from being alone. Leaving men out of account, the women who in 1911 greatly valued his company included Elizabeth Cameron and Martha Lindsay, Edith and Elizabeth Hoyt, all eleven of HA's Adams and Hooper nieces, his sister Mary, his sister-in-law Evelyn Adams, Anna and Constance Lodge, Elizabeth Lodge, Clara Hay, Edith Roosevelt, Margaret White, Mary and Beatrix Jones, Edith Wharton, Margaret and Laura Chanler, Anne Fell, Rebecca Rae, Florence Keep, and Isabella Gardner, not to mention other women, such as Mrs. Henry Parkman and Charlotte Sorchan, who have gone unnamed in the body of this chapter for lack of room.

90. HA was on good terms with CFA2's daughters. They conceivably told Uncle Henry that their father had written his memoirs.

91. Mrs. Wendell Garrett, "The Published Writings of Charles Francis Adams, II (1835–1915): An Annotated Checklist," MHS *Proceedings*, 72 (1957–1960), 288, entry 438 under 1916.

92. Worthington C. Ford, "The Recall of John Quincy Adams in 1908," MHS *Proceedings*, 45 (1911–1912), 355–75. HA's compilation is cited four times in the notes.

93. CFA2 to Ford, 28 Nov 1911, FP 17.

94. Elizabeth Lodge to HA, 17 Oct 1911.

95. HA to Elizabeth Lodge, 25 Oct 1911.

96. Edith Wharton to HA, 27 Oct 1911.

97. Edith Wharton to HA, [31 Oct 1911]. Her reticence contrasts with the effusiveness of Berenson, to whom HA sent a copy of the *Life* in December. Berenson's reply could be read as flattery. See Berenson to HA, 23 Dec 1911:—"What a little masterpiece you have sent me!" "Almost it makes one long for sudden death on the chance that you would biograph one."

98. Mary Jones to HA, 8 Nov 1911.

99. HA to Mary Jones, 8 Dec 1911.

100. Ibid.

101. HA's copy of Dunn's book—*Chancun de Willame*, 1903, op. cit.—came to rest on a shelf at 1603 H Street. Hence its availability in HAL.

102. John P. Eaton & Charles A. Haas, *Titanic/ Triumph and Tragedy*, NY & Lond 1986, 92–95.

21. Room on the *Titanic*

Letters by and to HA are in HA-micro 26 or H, or HA/Thoron-micro, unless otherwise indicated. Letters, copies of letters, and cables by CFA2, Mary Quincy, and BA to EC, by HCL to Bigelow, by Bigelow to EC, by Mabel La Farge to EC, and by Clara Hay to Mary Jones were kept by EC and are in HA-micro 26.

PRINCIPAL SOURCES

(1) fifteen letters, EC to HA, 27 Dec 1911–4 Apr 1912.

(2) seventeen letters, HA to EC, 29 Dec 1911–21–22 Apr 1912.

(3) nine letters, HA to Louisa Hooper, 5 Jan–22 Apr 1912.

(4) six letters, HA to Thoron, 7 Jan–7 Apr 1912.

(5) six letters, HA to Luquiens, 25 Jan–11 Apr 1912, L, VI, 501–03, 525–26, 529–31; O.1912.14–15, 24.

(6) three letters, HA to Weeks, 3–6 Feb 1912, L, VI, 505–06, 508 11; O.1912.8–9.

(7) HA, *Mont Saint Michel and Chartres*, Wash (privately printed) 1912— second version; revised and somewhat expanded.

(8) HA, partial English translation, *La Chanson de Willame*, FTKP.

LESSER SOURCES; CITATIONS; COMMENTS

1. The note is missing. See EC to HA, 27 Dec 1911.

2. HA to EC, 29 Dec 1911.

3. From the time AT introduced me and my wife to her in 1952, LHT tended to tell us about her experience with HA on the *Olympic* on Christmas Day, 1911. The data offered here is based partly on my memories of what she then said. It rests also on some notes I took in the spring of 1955 after hearing her retell the story at her Boston apartment. But the quotations from her in this episode are all drawn from her letter to me of 17 Feb 1956, in which she put the story in writing.

4. HA to EC, 6 Jul 1909, HA-micro 23.

5. For her learning about an oriental preventive, see HA-2, 310, 765.

6. LHT to myself, 24 Feb 1966.

7. Approximately in 1934, using as sources *The Education*, the first volume of Ford's edition of HA's *Letters*, some "unpublished letters," and "family memories," LHT wrote a 29-page "Chronology/ Henry Adams." On 16 Jul 1934, she wrote for Ralph Adams Cram a 20-page biographical paper, "re Henry Adams/ Mens Sana in Corpore Sano." On 11 Aug 1967 at Cazenovia, NY, she gave me copies of both documents. Each contains information about HA that is not elsewhere available.

8. EC to HA, 11 Jan 1912.

9. HA to Jameson, 21 Jan 1912; Jameson to HA, 25 Jan 1912.

10. HA to EC, 25–26 Jan 1912.

11. Line-by-line comparison of the 1904 edition with the 1912 edition might reveal several minute corrections. E.g., a hyphen is added in the 1912 edition at the end of p. 51.

12. The unchanged or virtually unchanged chapters are I–IV, VI–VIII, and XII–XV.

13. Much of the sentence beginning "Society . . ." on p. 62 of the 1904 edition is excised on p. 62 of the 1912 edition. The paragraph beginning "The Furriers . . ." on p. 143 of the 1904 edition is prefaced with two new sentences on p. 151 of the 1912 edition. Two paragraphs beginning "That these . . ." on p. 161 of the 1904 edition are condensed into one paragraph on pp. 170–71 of the 1912 edition. The paragraph beginning "Eleanor . . ." on p. 173 of the 1904 edition is expanded and turned into two paragraphs on p. 183–84 of the 1912 edition. The paragraph beginning "Some member . . ." on p. 192 of the 1904 edition is prefaced by a new sentence on p. 203 of the 1912 edition. In the paragraph beginning "Whatever truth . . ." on p. 326 of the 1904 edition, the fifth sentence is so expanded on p. 338 of the 1912 edition that thirteen words are appended: "with which society has struggled for seven hundred years, and is still struggling." In addition, the sentence beginning "Freedom . . ." is used to start a new paragraph.

14. Compare *MSM&CH* (1904), 72–73, with *MSM&CH* (1912), 71–74. Also see *MSM&CH* (LoA), 414–17.

15. Compare *MSM&CH* (*1904*), 133–34, with *MSM&CH* (1912), 134–142. Also see *MSM&CH* (LoA), 478–86.

16. Compare *MSM&CH* (1904), 190, with *MSM&CH* (1912), 200–01. Also see *MSM&CH* (LoA), 545–46.

17. Compare *MSM&CH* (1904), 321, with *MSM&CH* (1912), 332. Also see *MSM&CH* (LoA), 676–77.

18. CFA2 to HA, 4 Jan 1912.

19. To some extent, Dana was put off by things said in CFA2's paper about his father, Richard Henry Dana, Jr., famous for having written *Two Years before the Mast*; but the principal bones of contention between Dana and CFA2 were particular events during the *Trent* Affair and their meaning.

20. HA was willing to contradict CFA2 about matters of history. In reply to CFA2's published criticisms of Washington's generalship, HA mentioned to him that Grant's capture of Richmond was "much less brilliant" than Washington's capture of Yorktown. See HA to CFA2, 19 Jan 1912.

21. For the versions of CFA2's paper, see MHS *Proceedings*, 45 (1911–1912), 35–76, and a pamphlet, CFA2, *The Trent Affair/ An Historical Retrospect*, Bost 1912. For the versions of Dana's paper, see MHS *Proceedings*, 45 (1911–1912), 508–22—with a long rejoinder by CFA2, 522–30—and a pamphlet, Richard Henry Dana, *The Trent Affair*, Bost 1912. For additional light on Dana and CFA2's different ideas and on CFA2's behind-the-scenes management of Ford as editor of the *Proceedings*, see the following documents in the CFA2 Papers, MHS, and FP 18 & 61: CFA2 to Ford, 13 Mar 1912; CFA2 to Dana, 14 Mar 1912; Ford to CFA2, 16 Mar 1912; CFA2 to Ford, 18 Mar 1912; Ford to CFA2, 18 Mar 1912; Ford to Julius H. Tuttle, 18 Mar 1912; CFA2 to Ford, 1 Apr 1912; Ford to CFA2, 1 Apr 1912; CFA2 to Ford, 1 Apr 1912; CFA2 to Ford, 4 Apr 1912; Dana to Ford, 4 Apr 1912; Dana to CFA2, 8 Apr 1912; CFA2 to Dana, 10 Apr 1912; Ford to CFA2, 10 Apr 1912; Dana to CFA2, 12 Apr 1912; CFA2 to Ford, 12 Apr 1912; CFA2 to Dana, 16 Apr 1912; Dana to CFA2, 22 Apr 1912; Dana to CFA2, 1 May 1912; CFA2 to Dana, 3 May 1912; Dana to CFA2, 22 May 1912.

22. The great point of CFA2's essay was that the leaders of the Union in 1861 could have gained great credit for themselves and the country if they had anticipated and conformed to the advice he was able to give fifty years later about the Union's best response to the demands of the British government.

The great point of Dana's essay was that England "was threatening war" with the United States and "making preparations for it" from the moment news arrived in England that a boarding party from a Union warship had removed Confederate envoys from a British mail ship. This was a point that CFA2's essay had failed to make. It was also a point with which HA had agreed from the time the *Trent* Affair began.

The great point of HA's last and best analyses of England's conduct in 1861 was that Lord John Russell, England's foreign minister, sought ways of extending recognition to the Confederacy even before news arrived in England that armed rebellion had started in the United States, and continued to seek such ways, while always pretending to do otherwise. See HA, *Recognition of Cuban Independence*, op. cit., 19–22, and *EHA* (1907), 128–43; (LoA), 855–72; in combination with HA to BA, 23 Aug 1911:—". . . I dealt with Earl Russell,—very gently, for a damneder scoundrel for a diplomate [*sic*] I do not know."

23. Serious considerations stood in the way of HA's criticizing or replying

to CFA2's paper "The Trent Affair." Dana became involved, and friction between Dana and CFA2 did not subside until late May 1912. By then, HA was in no condition to enter into quarrels.

24. On 1 Feb 1912, HA mentioned in a letter to EC that Mrs. Jones, Mrs. Lodge, Mrs. Rae, Charles's daughter Elsie, and the Whites had joined him for breakfast and his table "was once again fairly full." HA went on to say, "It has not the spring that you gave it, when Nanny Lodge was twenty years younger, but it is amusing on account of the political muddle[,] which grows funnier every day."

His remark should serve as a corrective to misunderstandings of the passage in *The Education* in which HA speaks of "a reign of sixteen years, during which Mrs. Cameron and Mrs. Lodge led a career, without precedent and without succession, as the dispensers of sunshine over Washington." See *EHA* (1907), 290; (LoA), 1024. The passage has often been read to say that Mrs. Cameron conducted a salon and Mrs. Lodge perpetually entertained. In my opinion, the passage mainly reflects two facts: that, after the death of his wife, HA when in Washington was a perpetual offerer of informal midday meals; and that Mrs. Cameron and Mrs. Lodge proved enlivening participants in many of these occasions.

25. Luquiens to HA, 28 Jan 1912.

26. Taylor to HA, 2 Feb 1912.

27. Weeks to HA, 6 Feb 1912.

28. HA to EC, 11–12 Jan 1912.

29. EC to HA, 23 Jan 1912.

30. EC to HA, 31 Jan–1 Feb 1912.

31. EC to HA, 7 Feb 1912.

32. Weeks to HA 14 Feb 1912.

33. HA to EC, 18 Feb 1912.

34. Thoron hesitated to accept the assignment. See Thoron to HA, 23 Mar 1912:—"How much use I can make of a visit to Barcelona without you to inspire me . . . troubles me. . . . Why don't you come down there too?"

35. Luquiens to HA, 20 March 1912.

36. Principal source 8. HA translated verses 557–743, 935–1135 (some verses omitted), 1178–1398, 1432–1567, & 1614–1673 as presented in his copy of *La Chancun de Willame*, n.p.: Chiswick Press, 1903, HAL.

37. Principal source 8.

38. Luquiens to HA, 6 Apr 1912, enclosed in the envelope containing principal source 8.

39. Weeks to HA, 14 Mar 1912.

40. George R. Agassiz to HA, 14 Jan 1912.

41. See note 46, below.

42. CMG to HA, 2 Apr 1912:—". . . if you liked [I] could present one in your name[,] for which they would be very grateful."

43. EC to HA, 20 Mar 1912.

44. For HA's characterizations of Roosevelt as a would-be American Napoleon, see two letters, HA to EC 24 & 26 Mar 1912 and 31 Mar–1 Apr 1912; also HA to BA, 10 Apr 1912.

45. EC to HA, 4 Apr 1912.

46. The statement that HA burned copies of his *Education* is new. It is an inference made possible by a protracted inquiry the results of which are presented here in minimum, yet sufficient, detail.

In 1907, HA did not preserve his bill from the printer saying how many privately printed copies of *The Education* he ordered and/or how many were delivered. When he felt he had to tell people about the number of copies he obtained, he said "a few" or used words to the same effect. He strengthened the impression that there were few by telling many persons that copies he had lent them must be returned. When he gave people copies outright, he did so quietly or secretly.

An exception to this pattern of behavior was a letter HA wrote to Berenson on 26 Sep 1907—noticed in Chap. 16—in which he seemed to say he had obtained "a hundred copies" of his *Education*. This number might seem at odds with his phrase "a few."

In February 1916, HA wrote an "Editor's Preface" for *The Education* signed "H. C. L."—the initials of Henry Cabot Lodge. He felt obliged to say how many copies were printed. His opening sentence says the book had been printed "to the number of one hundred copies."

The Education was published in 1918 a half-year after HA's death. For fifteen years thereafter, the public had no reason to doubt how many copies of the book were privately printed. All published copies of the book began with the "Editor's Preface." All said the author had privately printed "one hundred copies."

In 1933, the following entry appeared in a bibliography of HA's writings published at the back of the first biography written about him: *Henry Adams*, by James Truslow Adams (no relation):

> *The Education of Henry Adams*, privately printed
> (40 copies only), Washington, 1907, vi, 453pp.

James Truslow Adams had first published the bibliography in 1930 as a pamphlet. The pamphlet's title page bore the words "Compiled by James Truslow Adams." In both its forms, the bibliography supplied few details. In the 1930 version, the entry relating to *The Education* was silent about the number of copies privately printed. The entry in the 1933 version offered definite information— "40 copies only"—but did not disclose the source of the information.

The difference between "one hundred" and "40 copies only" drew the notice of Harold Dean Cater. He reacted as if both numbers had to be true and as if a theory was needed to explain how both could be so. He invented such a theory and in 1947 stated it on p. 591 of his book, *Henry Adams and His Friends, A Compilation of His Unpublished Letters*. He said, "At first he [HA] had only forty copies printed, but the demand for it became so great that he had to have more copies of it made later." He did not explicitly say that sixty more copies were printed. Neither did he repeat the familiar words "one hundred." But he said enough to float a myth that HA first ordered forty copies of *The Education* and later ordered sixty, which, although printed later, were dated 1907 and were not distinguishable from the original forty.

That Cater's myth about two printings of *The Education* rested on no better evidence than two published expressions—"one hundred" and "40 copies only"—was not apparent to Cater's readers and not apparent even to Cater, who evidently was so charmed by the elegant simplicity of his theory that he worded it as an indubitable fact: ". . . [HA] had to have more copies made. . . ."

Cater's myth became received opinion. Jacob Blanck quoted it in his authoritative *Bibliography of American Literature*. See *BAL* 32. Ernest Samuels repeated it in an attempted definitive edition of *The Education* published by Houghton Mifflin Company in 1974. See p. 539. Book dealers garnished the myth with details. See William Reese Co., Cat. 119, item 5:—"A strong case has been made that Adams initially had forty copies printed for distribution within a small circle of interested readers whose opinions and suggestions for revisions he solicited, and then had an additional printing of sixty copies made at a later date, possibly as late as 1913 or 1914. . . ."

A most assiduous searcher for information about HA was his niece-by-marriage Louisa Hooper Thoron. On May 31, 1953, she advised me by letter: ". . . I'm looking at the Bibliography, p. 225, of Truslow Adams' *Henry Adams*. Mᵣ William Jackson told me he prepared it."

Jackson was the person in charge at Harvard University's Houghton Library. I soon had a chance to meet him in his office. He told me what he had told LHT: that *he* compiled the bibliography published in 1930 as "Compiled by James Truslow Adams" and reissued, revised, in 1933 in the latter's *Henry Adams*.

Listening to Jackson did not make me feel any certainty about the authorship of the bibliography, but it all but convinced me that HA's words "one hundred" in the "Editor's Preface" were misleading, and it led me to assume that the phrase "40 copies only" was inserted in 1933 on the basis of information obtained from HA's printer.

In subsequent years, while looking into other matters relating to HA, I accumulated evidence about particular privately printed copies of *The Education*. As evidence piled up in my files, a new idea came to the fore. Why not track as many copies as possible, if only to see what their histories might indicate?

In January 1987, I unexpectedly became the owner of HA's Second Traveling Copy. Beginning at once, I tried to learn everything there was to learn about the other copies HA had annotated. I continued to gather information about still other copies.

In July 1987, I sought access to the newly-opened Worthington C. Ford Papers at the New York Public Library. Among other things, I found evidence about the compilation of James Truslow Adams's bibliography of HA's writings. The evidence made clear that Jackson's boast to LHT and me that he had written it was empty. Yet I clung to the idea that HA might have printed "40 copies only."

At last, in the spring of 1998, the number of copies I had traced passed the 40 mark. HA's own number—100—was perforce revived, and a new question came to mind. What could an inquirer learn by closely analyzing the evidence about particular copies?

The following is a summary of the evidence so far amassed about particular copies. The summary leads to a series of conclusions.

We need a list of the copies concerning which there is good data. We start with the copies HA treated as his own. He is presumed to have annotated No. 5 very completely. He annotated the others in varied amounts, except No. 6, which is wholly unmarked.

1.	First Traveling Copy	Lent to W. R. Thayer, 1914. Given by him to MHS, 1918, in exchange for No. 3.
2.	Second Traveling Copy	Part of HA's Paris library, shipped to BA in 1912. Present owner: Edward Chalfant.
3.	Substitute Copy	Given to MHS, 1916. Exchanged by MHS, 1918, for No. 1. Present owner: Abernethy Library, Middlebury College.

4.	Signed Copy	Given to William Wilmer, 1916. Present owner: Eden R. Martin.
5.	Master Copy	Given to AT, 1917. Entrusted by her to Egisto Fabbri, 1927. Irretrievably lost.
6.	Attendant Clean Copy	Given to AT, 1917. Given by her, 1969, to the present owner: Louis Auchincloss.

We add copies HA gave to libraries.

7.	Mass. Hist. Society	Gift arranged, 27 Jan 1911. Copy was used as publisher's copy, 1918, then destroyed.
8.	Library of Congress	Gift accepted, 27 Nov 1915.
9.	New York Public Library	Sent to intermediary Rives, 25 Mar 1916.

We add copies variously obtained by Adams & Hooper relatives.

10.	Louisa Hooper	Given to her by HA, 1907. Lent by her to the Harvard College Library, 9 May 1910; later recovered by her. Present owner: Boston Athenaeum.
11.	Evelyn Adams	Lent by HA to BA & EA, 1907; kept by EA; later sold. Present owner: Harvard.
12.	Mabel Hooper La Farge	Given a copy taken by her sister Louisa from HA's stock. Present owner: Mary La Farge.
13.	Louisa Hooper	Her second copy; taken by her from HA's Paris apartment, 1910. It evidently had been lent by HA to Elizabeth Cameron & returned. Present owner: Boston Athenaeum.

We add inscribed copies given by HA to friends.

14.	Anna Lodge	Given, 1907, for "Sister Anne." Present owner: Catholic University of America.
15.	Mary Jones	Given, 1907, for "Mrs. Mary Cadwalader Jones." Present owner: Yale University.
16.	O. W. Holmes, Jr.	Given, 1907, for "Oliver Wendell Holmes." Present owner: Harvard University.
17.	Henry Cabot Lodge	Given, 1907, for "H. Cabot Lodge." Sold at a late date; offered in 1990 by Glenn Horowitz Books, NY. Price: $25,000.
18.	Lucy Frelinghuysen	Given, 1911, for "Lucy Frelinghuysen." Present owner: Lehigh University.
19.	Carolyn D. Phillips	Given, 1914; later sold. In stock at Wm Reese Co., New Haven, 26 Mar 1998.
20.	Rebecca Dodge Rae	Undated gift, for "Rebecca Rae." Present owner: Northwestern University.

We add unmarked copies lent or given by HA to friends.

21.	Frederic Bancroft	Given, 1907. Annotated by Bancroft. Present owner: Columbia University.
22.	Ward Thoron	Given c. winter of 1907–1908. Present owner: Boston Athenaeum.

23.	J. Laurence Laughlin	Lent, 1908; not returned. Annotated by Laughlin. Present owner: Harvard.
24.	Beatrix Jones via Mary Cadwalader Jones	A second copy evidently lent or given to Mary Cadwalader Jones, 1908; lent or given by her to her daughter; eventually given by Beatrix to the present owner: University of Pennsylvania.
25.	Henry Osborn Taylor	Lent, 1909; not returned. Present owner: Harvard.
26.	Isabella Gardner	Inscribed by Mrs. Gardner: ". . . from Henry Adams, January 1910." Presently at Fenway Court, Boston.
27.	Bernhard Berenson	Given, 1910. Presently at I Tatti near Florence (subdivision of Harvard).
28.	Worthington C. Ford	Given, 1910. Annotated by Ford, 1918. Present owner: Harvard.
29.	Florence Keep	Signed on flyleaf, "Florence S. Keep." Present owner: Morgan Library, NY.

We add other copies held by libraries.

30.	John Hay Library, Brown University	Copy given by a collector, who bought it from Goodspeed, Bost.
31.	New York Pub. Library	Second copy; given by a collector, Joseph Halle Schaffner. (See No. 9, above.)
32.	Dartmouth College	Copy acquired [1957?] from Harvard College Library. Bears label, ". . . from Prof. A. C. Coolidge"; stamp, back of t.p.," Harvard College/Jun 2 1918/Library."
33.	Univ. of Illinois	Copy bought from Seven Gables, 1960.
34.	Univ. of Virginia	Given by a collector, C. Waller Barrett.
35.	Univ. of Virginia	second copy; provenance not obtained.
36.	Newberry Library	unmarked copy; provenance not obtained.
37.	Newberry Library	second copy; provenance not obtained.

We exclude from our list a copy that did not belong to HA.

	—Johns Hopkins Univ.	Printer's copy, given to the university by J. H. Furst, Co., Baltimore.

We add additional copies presently held by dealers.

38.	Wm. Reese Co., New Haven	Copy listed in Cat. 119 Literature, with letter, HA to "My Dear Sir [possibly Rev. George William Douglas, formerly rector, St. John's Church, Wash]," 14 Apr 1908. [*Not* the letter to "My dear Sir, 17 Apr 1908, O.1908.9–10]. Price: $9,500.
39.	19th Century Bookshop	Cat. 20, p. 3. Excellent condition; evidently unmarked. The copy was bought for a client by the shop at the Doheny sale & was later turned back by the client for sale by the shop. Price: $10,000.
40.	David O'Neal, Boston	Copy in stock.
41.	" " "	" " "
42.	" " "	" " "

Of the 42 copies so far traced, the ones numbered 30–37 do not—for me—have complete provenances at present. These eight and the copies numbered 38–42 may have been lent or given to persons whose names appear in the lists of persons that follow.

As requested, ten persons returned copies lent to them by HA. (Copies so returned could be lent or given to other persons.)

a.	James Donald Cameron	Lent & returned, 1907.
b.	Elizabeth Cameron	See copy no. 13, above.
c.	Charles W. Eliot	Lent & returned, 1907.
d.	Clara Hay	Lent & returned, 1907.
e.	James Ford Rhodes	Lent & returned, 1907. (Another request by Rhodes is listed below.)
f.	Edith Morton Eustis	Lent & returned, 1908.
g.	Fred & Blanche Tams	Lent & returned, 1908.
h.	John L. Stewart	Lent, 1908; evidently returned, 1909.
i.	T. Jefferson Coolidge	Lent & returned, 1909.
j.	Arthur B. Potter	Lent & returned, 1910.

Copies lent or given by HA to the following 28 persons have—for me—incomplete histories. I am yet to learn the copies' whereabouts. An unknown number of these persons returned the copies to HA, who then could lend or give the copies to other persons.

a.	C. F. Adams, Jr.	Lent, 1907.
b.	Theodore & Edith Roosevelt	Lent or given, 1907.
c.	Henry Lee Higginson	Lent, 1907.
e.	Baron Hermann Speck von Sternburg	Shown or lent a copy, 1907.
d.	Chas. Milnes Gaskell	Given, 1907. Possibly lost after CMG's death, when Thornes House burned.
e.	Chas. Milnes Gaskell	Second copy held by CMG, 1912. Possibly lost in the same fire.
f.	Sir George Trevelyan	Given; inscribed by HA. Listed, *American Book Prices Current*, 1974. Price: £550.
g.	George Cabot Lodge & Elizabeth Lodge	Lent or given, 1907.
h.	Augustus Saint Gaudens	Copy sent, 1907.
i.	Elisabeth Marbury	Copy lent or given, 1907. Possibly meant also for Elsie de Wolfe & Anne Morgan.
j.	William James	Copy lent, 1907.
k.	John W. Burgess	Copy lent or given, 1908.
l.	Edward Channing	Copy lent or given, 1908.
m.	Richard Olney	Copy lent, 1908.
n.	Owen Wister	Copy lent, 1908.
o.	Henry James	Copy lent, 1908.
p.	Calvin S. Brice	Copy lent or given, 1908.
q.	Whitelaw Reid	Copy sent, 1908.
r.	Anne Palmer Fell	Copy evidently lent, 1908.
s.	Barrett Wendell	Copy lent for an indefinite term, 1909.
t.	John Franklin Jameson	Copy evidently given, 1909.
u.	Raphael Pumpelly	At HA's direction, Jameson sent Pumpelly a copy, 1910.

v.	James Ford Rhodes	Promised a copy by HA, 1910, to be sent by Jameson.
w.	George R. Agassiz	Copy given, 1912.
x.	James B. Angell	Evidently received copy, 1913.
y.	Albert H. Washburn	Copy sent, 1914.
z.	Edward Sanford Martin	Copy sent, 1914.
aa.	James Byrne	Copy sent, 1914.
aa.	John La Farge & Florence La Farge	Given to John La Farge; redirected by HA in 1915 (after John La Farge's death) to Florence La Farge.

HA refused to lend or give copies to the following persons.

a.	Constance Lodge	Copy refused, 1907.
b.	Lindsay Swift as representative of Boston Public Library, appealing to HA via CFA2	Copy refused, 1915.
c.	Prof. Stephens, Hist. Dept., U. of California, appealing to HA via James Ford Rhodes	Copy refused, 1916.

With unknown results, HA received requests from the following persons.

a.	Henry J. Gensler	Copy requested, 1907.
b.	Josephine Lazarus	Copy sought via Margaret Chanler, 1908.
c.	Charlotte H. Sorchan	Copy requested, 1909.
d.	Charles T. Thwing	Copy requested, 1910.
e.	Samuel Swett Green	Copy requested, 1910.
f.	Albert Bushnell Hart	Copy requested, 1910.
g.	[Illegible] W. Pennypacker as representative of Hist. Soc. of Pennsylvania	Copy requested, 1911.
h.	E. Marion Bryce [Mrs. James Bryce]	Copy requested, 1912.
i.	E. E. King as representative of Bryn Mawr College	Copy requested, 1914.
j.	Henry Osborn Taylor as representative of the Century Association.	Copy requested, 1916.
k.	John Thomas Lee	Copy requested, 1916.
l.	[Illegible] Wellman, Springfield, MA	Loan requested for personal use, 1916.
m.	Charles L. Pierson.	Data re availability requested, 1916.

CONCLUSIONS

—HA was right in saying that 100 copies were printed in 1907.

—The 1933 report that there were "40 copies only" was false.

—Cater's 1947 claim that HA began by printing 40 and printing more later was false.

—HA kept to a minimum the number of copies given outright.

—He preferred to lend copies—return requested.

—He recovered many lent copies, which he again could lend.

—By this means, he kept a surplus on hand at 1603 H Street.

—The destruction of many copies (perhaps as many as 35, or even more) could seem to him appropriate or needful.

—Assuming that he destroyed the surplus copies in early April 1912, he could do so with the hope of continuing to recover copies he had lent.

—In view of the presently available evidence, the copies sent to Angell, Washburn, Martin, and Byrne in 1913–1914 can be assumed to have been lent before April 1912 and to have been tardily returned.

47. See the last lines of note 46, above.

48. Histories of the copies are given in this narrative. Each copy is given a name or other clear identification. They appear as the Attendant Clean Copy, the copy given to the Library of Congress, the Substitute Copy, the Signed Copy, and the copy given to the New York Public Library.

49. In 1956, while we were looking together at a photocopy of H. H. Richardson's plan for the top floor of 1603 H Street, AT told me that the cedar closet in the hall was used only for storing trunks. She said that one of the trunks contained things that had belonged to MHA, and she mentioned what some of them were.

At Cazenovia, New York, Faith Thoron Knapp later showed me items that had been stored in the trunk, notably MHA's green Worth dress. For added details relating to the trunk, see Chaps. 26 & 27.

50. HA had long since had the idea of putting a book in a closet. He had remarked to BA about the latter's *La Lois de Civilisation et de la Decadence*, "Probably you will get tired of the toy, and put it in a dark closet at last. . . ." See HA to BA, 6 Apr 1899, HA-micro H.

51. My statement that HA hid his Master Copy and the Attendant Clean Copy in the trunk is a well-informed inference which I arrived at only after many years of reflection. See Chap. 27, note 113.

After drawing the inference, I began to find supporting evidence above and beyond the evidence by which I had been guided. I am now entirely sure that the inference is correct.

There is of course the question of the date of HA's action. The evidence that HA hid the copies in the trunk very shortly before the time he expected to go New York and board the *Titanic* is in my opinion compelling. The evidence is mental: HA's loss of memories. For details about which he lost and why he lost them, see Chap. 25.

52. It goes without saying that no one other than HA would be likely to open the trunk while HA was alive; and further that, if copies of his *Education* were discovered in the trunk after he died, the discoverers would be forced to infer that the copies had been valued highly by HA and for that reason were to be valued highly by other persons.

53. CFA2 to Ford, 1 Apr 1912, FP 61.

54. HA to EC, 16 Apr 1912.

55. Ibid. The image of a "shoreless ocean" had earlier appeared at an important place in HA's writings, the opening paragraph of Chap. VIII of *Democracy*.

56. HA to EC, 21 Apr 1912.

57. HA to Mary Jones, 20 Apr 1912; *EHA* (1907), 432; (LoA), 1172.

58. HA to EC, 22–23 Apr 1901, HA-micro 17.

59. It bears repeating that HA had anticipated the destruction of passenger ships by collisions with icebergs. See Chap. 20.

It should be noticed too that EC, writing to HA on 23 Jan 1912, mentioned that the *Adriatic* had carried J. P. Morgan and other Wall Street financial magnates to Europe in a body. She went on to say, "What a shock Wall St. would have if that ship went down."

60. This account of HA's illness is based mostly but not entirely on the many papers concerning the illness that EC preserved. A particular detail in the account may be drawn from any of these papers; but always, when words are quoted, the source is given.

61. Unsigned typed copy, HCL to Bigelow, 25 Apr 1912.

62. Ibid.

63. CFA2 to EC, 29 Apr 1912; unsigned typed copy, HCL to Bigelow, 3 May 1912.

64. Unsigned typed copy, HCL to Bigelow, 12 May 1912.

65. Mabel La Farge to EC, 21 May 1912.

66. Bigelow wrote letters of his own to Mrs. Cameron. For reasons best known to him and her, he addressed her only as "Dear Hostess." See letters, Bigelow to EC, 26 Apr 1912 & 19 May 1912.

67. CFA2 to EC, 29 Apr 1912. In 1956, AT told me that the telephone was located where it could be used by William Gray. She could not remember whether it was on the ground floor in the kitchen or on the main floor in the pantry.

68. On 4 Jun 1966, LHT informed me by phone that she had recovered a letter of hers to her sister Mabel, written in 1912, affirming that she arrived in Washington "a week" after HA fell ill.

69. Unsigned typed copy, HCL to Bigelow, 4 May 1912.

70. HA to EC, 25–26 Jan 1912,

71. HA to EC, 31 Mar–1 Apr 1912.

72. Unsigned typed copy, HCL to Bigelow, 9 May 1912.

73. Ibid.

74. Ibid.

75. Ibid.

76. HA to Anne Fell, Thursday, 18 [Apr 1912].

77. CFA2 to Ford, 18 Mar, 1 Apr 1912. CFA2's disparagement of Dana as small was simultaneous with HA's concerning himself about a fictional character who was small. HA translated verses of the *Chanson de Willame* that involve the fatal peril of Willame's son Vivien, verses that concern Willame himself and his wife Guiborc, and also verses that concern their other son, Guy, an untried fifteen-year-old. In the last verses HA translated, Guy is judged to be too small in body to be a warrior, yet insists on becoming a warrior, and is accepted as an adequate, even superior, replacement for lost heroic Vivien. These verses are HA's only extended statement on the subject of human physical smallness.

78. BA's effort to "make over the Old House into a museum" is a subject in itself. For a brief summary, see Beringause, 303–04.

79. BA to Ford, 11 May 1912, FP 19.

80. Clara Hay to Mary Jones, 12 May 1912. Clearly Mrs. Hay was speaking of a second visit by CFA2 to HA. HCL dates this visit as having occurred on May 2. See HCL to Bigelow, 3 May 1912, unsigned typed copy:—"Charles saw Henry yesterday. . . ." CFA2 advised EC (letter of 8 May 1912) that he recently had visited HA "for a few minutes only, and I do not think it did him any good."

81. Unsigned typed copy, HCL to Bigelow, 13 May 1912.
82. CFA2 to EC, 21 May 1912.
83. The message of Bigelow's cable of May 17 is repeated in his letter to EC, 19 May 1912. In the same letter, Bigelow tells EC that HA is having "attacks of violent delirium . . . but not, as I understand it, more than once in any one day." He says that the attacks "are in a way the most hopeful thing in sight, as it is possible that the struggle and muscular effort might break another blood vessel and end it." Bigelow says too that HA is "now beyond reach, and getting farther and farther away."
84. Undated cable, Mary A. Quincy to EC, filmed in HA-micro 26 after 29 May 1912.
85. CFA2 to EC, 24 May 1912.
86. CFA2 to EC, 25 May 1912.
87. BA to EC, 26 May 1912.

22. Recoveries

Letters by and to HA are in HA-micro 26, 27, or H, or HA/Thoron micro, unless otherwise indicated. Letters and cables by CFA, BA, Bigelow, Clara Hay, and Mabel La Farge to EC are in HA-micro 26 & 27.

PRINCIPAL SOURCES

(1) twenty-five letters, HA to EC, 24 Jun 1912–28 Jan 1913.
(2) forty letters, EC to HA, 18 Jun 1912–1 Feb 1913.
(3) eight letters, HA to Thoron, 27 Jul 1912–29 Jan 1913.
(4) three letters, HA to CSR, 27 Jul 1912–4 Mar 1913, L, VI, 546–48, 560–61, 582–83.
(5) three letters, HA to AT, 29 Jul–8 Sep 1912.
(6) five letters, HA to Berenson, 1 Aug 1912–28 Jan 1913, O.1912. 36–37; L, VI, 556–58, 565–66, 572–73, 586–87.

LESSER SOURCES; CITATIONS; COMMENTS

1. Jameson to Ford, 28 May 1912, FP 19.
2. CFA2 to EC, 21 Jun 1912.
3. Speaking for herself and Martha, EC said in her letter to HA, 18 Jun 1912, "We both wanted to write but they wouldn't let us."
4. EC to HA, 18 Jun 1912.
5. EC's copy of EC to "Mr. Adams" [CFA2], 3 Jun 1912, HA-micro 26; EC to HA, 27 Jun 1912.
6. EC to HA, 18 Jun 1912.
7. All the letters HA dictated to Miss Horne were so worded as to raise no eyebrows if read by CFA2 or others, conceivably in the form of carbon copies.
8. Mabel La Farge to EC, 21 May 1912:—". . . his mind wanders much to the South Seas & Japan & Mr La Farge. . . ."
9. EC to HA, 27 Jun 1912. EC's words "Mine is yours" may need a second look. They may partly mean that her apartment is his, as perhaps it was, in the sense of his having paid the rent until she could sublet it at high rates for short intervals to Americans even richer.
The words may also state a rule applicable in all situations. In that event, if applied to plans, the words can mean that, once known, a plan of his is also by willing adoption a plan of hers.

10. Letters, EC to HA, 5 Jul 1912 & 8 Jul 1912. The return cable considered, responsibility for the shipment of HA's possessions rested, not with EC, but with CFA3 and any other persons whose advice he may have sought. For lack of evidence, it is impossible to say whether there were other persons and, if so, who they were.

11. BA to HA, 28 Jul 1912.

12. Evelyn Adams to HA, 13 Jul 1912:—"Mrs. Cameron was here [in London] on the day before she was to sail on the 'Adriatic,' in accordance with Mr. Cameron's commands."

13. HA to Anna Lodge, 27 Jul 1912:—"Mrs. Cameron was summoned over suddenly by the unexpected announcements of Colgate Hoyt's marriage, and she got here just in time to attend it."

14. HA to Berenson, 1 Aug 1912:—"I have Mrs. Cameron here . . . and my niece, Miss Hooper, both of them really Parisian, and I am afraid they are staying here chiefly on my account. . . ."

15. Weeks to HA, 9 Jun 1912.

16. Thoron was contemplating a trip to Barcelona in the fall but remained anxious that HA go with him. See letters, Thoron to HA, 21 July 1912 & 11 Aug 1912.

17. HA to EC, 15 Aug 1912.

18. HA to Anna Lodge, Saturday, [17 Aug 1912], misdated by HA "Saturday, 18," and filmed out of sequence in HA-micro 27 as if written on 18 Sep 1912.

19. EC to HA, 17 Aug 1912.

20. HA's letter to BA is missing. For the quoted words, see BA to Ford, 18 Aug 1912, FP 19.

21. HA to Storey, 1 Sep 1912.

22. HA to Thoron, 6 Sep 1912.

23. Letters, EC to HA, 16 Oct 1912 & 25 Oct 1912.

24. EC to HA, 29 Aug 1912:—"No word from the man who owns me."

25. HA to CMG, 30 Aug 1912:—"I can't read newspapers or magazines owing to the type."

26. Ford had urged the selection of Thayer for the position on the basis of the biography of Cavour. See Ford to A. B. Hart, 8 Mar 1912, FP 61.

27. BA to HA, 25 Sep 1912.

28. BA to HA, 15 Nov 1912. Levenson and his associates state as a matter of undoubted fact that HA's disorder was a "cerebral thrombosis." See L, VI, 540n1. But the alleged fact was never more than an initial medical assumption impossible to verify with then-existing pre-mortem tests. If BA and CFA2 can be believed, the assumption came to be wholly discounted by the consulted physicians.

29. EC to HA, 5 Oct 1912.

30. Robert Bliss was currently first secretary at the U. S. embassy in Paris. HA knew him and his wife Mildred well enough to have given them a copy of the 1904 edition of *Mont Saint Michel and Chartres*. The copy is presently in my collection. It bears the bookplates of husband and wife inside the front cover.

31. HA to Lindsay, 28 Sep 1912.

32. HA to Mary Jones, 5 Oct 1912.

33. EC to HA, 25 July 1912.

34. HA to EC, 13 Sep 1912.

35. EC to HA, 5 Jul 1912.

36. HA to CSR, 20 Sep 1912.

37. HA to Jameson, 27 Sep 1912.

38. Louisa Hooper was one of the club's founding members.

39. Talking with me and my wife, AT several times remembered the purple velvet.

40. HA to Berenson, 13 Nov 1912.

41. HA to CFA2, 7 Nov 1912.

42. CFA2 to HA, 8 Nov 1912.

43. Ibid.

44. CFA2 to Ford, 17 Jul 1912, FP 60.

45. MHS *Proceedings*, 46 (1912–1913), 24; HA, *Historical Essays*, NY 1891, 237–78.

46. MHS *Proceedings*, 46 (1912–1913), 23–81, especially 24–25, 64–66, 68–70 & 72.

47. Read in the order of their composition, HA's principal writings about the British government's dealings with the United States in 1861 reveal that he arrived by stages at a well-based conviction that a policy of concealed hostility to the Union and support for the Confederacy was pressed by Gladstone, attemptedly executed by Russell under cover of a feigned neutrality, and decisively opposed at critical moments by Palmerston, if only to temporize.

In contrast, CFA2's new paper attempted a defense of the British government's dealings with the United States in 1861 by omitting both Gladstone and Palmerston and by taking Russell's professed neutrality at face value—a procedure not merely self-defeatingly selective but also willfully superficial.

48. See note 50, below.

49. HA to Louisa Hooper, 8 Dec 1901:—"As twelfth-century music[,] I should hardly call it artistically correct. . . ."

50. The only contemporary account of AT's arrival is HA's letter to Thoron, 13 Dec 1912. HA says, "She brought music, and especially a publication by J. B. Wekerlin, 'Echos du Temps Passé,' Vol. I, quite lately published. . . ."

HA's misspelling of Weckerlin's name conforms to a misspelling of the name by the publisher on the volume's title page. AT's copy of the volume is missing, but the Music Division of the New York Public Library owns a reprint of *Échos du Temps Passé/ Volume I/ Recueil de chansons, noëls, madrigaux . . . du XIIme au XVIIIme siècles/ Transcrits avec accompagnement de piano par J. B. Wekerlin* [i.e. Jean-Baptiste-Théodore Weckerlin], Paris; Durand & Cie, n.d. The reprint says on its cover that it was readied in Paris for distributors in London and Philadelphia. Everything about it supports belief that copies of the reprint were available for sale in New York in 1912 and were—in HA's phrase—"quite lately published."

In his account to Thoron, HA continues by describing contents of the volume. What he lists matches what appears on pp. 4–10 of the Weckerlin volume preserved in New York at Lincoln Center.

Beginning in 1952, AT several times told me and my wife things she could remember about her going to Washington to stay a month with HA. Invariably she said that she took with her a music book she bought at the last chance at Schirmer's store. She said it proved to be HA's introduction to the music of medieval songs. But she did not mention Weckerlin. She said nothing about other music books and nothing about Kurt Schindler.

In the 1940s when compiling his *Henry Adams and His Friends*, Cater interviewed AT and understood her to say she took to Washington in 1912 *one* book of music; that it had been given to her by Kurt Schindler; and that it included songs by the Chatelain de Coucy and Thibaud of Champagne. In his Biographical Introduction, xcvii–xcviii, Cater offered these particulars and added, "Footnotes at the bottom of the pages gave the catalogue numbers of the original manuscripts in the Bibliothèque Nationale and the Arsenal Library in Paris." But Cater did not name the book's author and did not provide its title.

No footnotes appear in the Weckerlin volume.

Study of Cater's account can encourage the conclusion that AT told him more things than he could keep straight, that statements about two books became confused in his mind and turned into assertions about one book, and that he further confused matters by making guesses. Yet his account has value. It establishes the point that Schindler had a role in the story. It suggests that Schindler gave AT a book (other than Weckerlin's first volume) and that she took the book to HA's house. And it creates a mystery:—What was the second book?

I am indebted to Siegmund Levarie for the suggestion that the book was Schindler's *6 Old French Christmas Carols* and for the general comment that Schindler's publications, though useful, were transitory and commercial. No copy of *6 Old French Christmas Carols* appears to survive in libraries I can reach. I thus cannot report whether the book had footnotes or whether it was based in any measure on Weckerlin's first volume, as seems probable.

51. BA to HA, 22 Oct 1912.

52. BA to HA, 5 Nov 1912. BA also says in his letter that he found three unbound copies of HA's *Tahiti* and would be sending them—with some of HA's other books—to Paris for binding. He says too that all the books were currently stacked on the floor of the Stone Library, pending the building of a bookcase in which to shelve them.

In 1956, while seaching at Quincy for materials relating to HA, I found the three unbound copies of the *Tahiti* in a trunk in an upstairs room in the Old House. I found no trace of a separate bookcase made to shelve the books that belonged to HA's Paris library. I infer that BA's intended efforts to have the copies bound and to take proper care of the library were somehow impeded or simply dropped.

53. Letters, BA to HA, 8 Dec 1912 & 18 Dec 1912.

54. *MSM&CH*, all editions, second-to-last paragraph of Chap. XI.

55. HA to Ford, 23 Nov 1912, FP 19.

56. Jameson to HA, 8 Oct 1912.

57. For HA's reactions and for "*Moorish*," see HA to Anna Lodge, 26 Jun 1910; also HA to Thoron, 3 Jul 1911.

58. HA to Cook, 19 Jul 1910, O.1910.43.

59. HA to Elizabeth Lodge, 3 Aug 1912.

60. Cram to HA, 29 Nov 1912. In the same letter, Cram told HA that he had spoken to two leading English architects and told them that HA's *Mont Saint Michel and Chartres* was "a perfect and unique revelation of the essential elements in Mediaevalism."

61. Cram to HA, 4 Dec 1912.

62. Cram to HA, 27 Jan 1913.

63. AT's accounts to me and my wife of the scolding she got from HA were among the vividest of the recollections we heard her voice. She made it clear that his disapproval could be frightening.

64. After a talk with AT on 29 Feb 1952, I wrote the following note: "He [HA] forbade her to read his books while she lived in his house. There would be time when he was dead. MSM&Ch was the exception."

65. During conversations with me and my wife, AT remembered HA's ordering the new piano but did not give a date. She was specific about the date of his making her an actual niece, saying that he did so when she had stayed a month and promised to stay indefinitely.

66. HA seems to have sent EC his translation of the first stanza. See the loose folded sheets headed *Merci clamant"* (the original) and "Merci clamant" (the translation) in HA-micro 27, filmed after EC to HA, 6–7 Jan 1913. His translation begins, "Beseeching mercy for my mad excesses. . . ."

67. HA to Luquiens, 10 Dec 1912, L, VI, 570.

68. AT mentioned several times to me and my wife that the comings and goings of the Library of Congress wagon struck her as exceptional. The library seemed to treat HA as a privileged official.

69. Putnam to HA, 14 Dec 1912.

70. Luquiens to HA, 22 Dec 1912.

71. Ibid.

72. Luquiens to HA, 1 Jan 1913.

73. HA to Berenson, 28 Jan 1913; HA to EC, 7 Jan 1913.

74. Picard supplied the *Bibliographie*. See HA to Thoron, 29 Jan 1913. The copy is presently in my collection. For information about HA's annotations in the copy, see Chap. 23.

75. Raynaud, *Bibliographie*, II, 201, within entry 1891.

76. Thoron to HA, 19 Jan 1913; HA to Thoron, 29 Jan 1913.

77. CFA2 to HA, 20 Dec 1912.

78. HA to CFA2, 21 Dec 1912.

79. Carbon copy of CFA2 to Ford, 31 Dec 1912, CFA2P.

80. HA to EC, 14 Jan 1913.

81. CFA2 to HA, 7 Feb 1913.

82. HA to CFA2, 7 Feb 1913, F, II, 609.

83. Letters, EC to HA, 4 Nov 1912 & 27 Nov 1912.

84. EC to HA, 22 Dec 1912.

85. For "somnolent," see EC to HA, 19 Dec 1912.

86. EC to HA, 31 Dec 1912–1 Jan 1913.

23. OUR PARIS

Letters by and to HA are in HA-micro 27, 28, & H, or HA/Thoron-micro, unless otherwise indicated.

PRINCIPAL SOURCES

(1) forty-two letters and a note, HA to EC, 5 Feb–22 Dec 1913.

(2) forty-five letters and a postcard, EC to HA, 5 Feb–18 Dec 1913.

(3) fourteen letters and two cables, HA to Thoron, [5 Feb]–17 Dec 1913.

(4) nine letters, HA to Mary Jones, 16 Feb–21 Dec 1913.

(5) four letters, HA to AT, [14 Mar]–10 [Dec] 1913. (HA's letter to AT dated "Friday, 12" and beginning "Your account . . ." is mistakenly published in O.1913.16 as if written in 1913. The correct date is Friday, 12 [Feb 1915].)

(6) five letters, HA to CMG, 5 Mar–1 Nov 1913.

(7) HA, *Mont-Saint-Michel and Chartres*, Bost 1913—HA's annotated copy of the first published edition, MHS.

LESSER SOURCES; CITATIONS; COMMENTS

1. Thoron to HA, 24 Jan 1913.
2. HA to Thoron, 7 [Feb 1913].
3. HA to Thoron, [5 Feb 1913].
4. HA to Cram, 21 Feb 1913. Also see Siegmund Levarie, "Henry Adams, Avant-gardist in Early Music," *American Music*, v. 16., no. 4 (Winter 1997), especially 440–42.
5. HA to Mabel La Farge, 24 Jan 1913.
6. The edition later became the property of LHT. She gave it in the late 1950s to Bruce Brooks Pfeiffer, presently Director of the Frank Lloyd Wright Archives, for use at Taliesen West in Arizona.
7. Recollections of AT, 29 Feb 1952.
8. The parts included transcriptions by Aubry of some of the songs. HA's copy of a lesser work, Pierre Aubry, *Trouvères et Troubadours, deuxième édition, revue et corrigée*, Paris 1910, is presently in my collection. It contains no annotations.
9. In August 1969, LHT asked me in a letter, "Did you know that there was a famous duel over the songs[?]" Her question was occasioned by excitement and surprise. A musicologist had just told her a little about the intended duel, and she was not sure what happened, nor aware that Beck was one of the principals. Her letter continues: "Aubry[,] who got out the Chansonier [*sic*] de l'Arsenal[,] was challenged by someone who disagreed with him about some theory. . . . Aubry . . . felt that he had to fight and then either got killed or killed himself in the shuffle."
10. HA to Cram, 21 Feb 1913, O.1913.12:—". . . there is no one in France to rival him. He can hardly have come away to better himself at Champagne, Ill."
11. Recollections of AT, 29 Feb 1952. The phrase "a sense of the North" is AT's. She said that HA was "uncanny" in his knowledge of Rock Creek Park; also in his knowledge of French forests.
12. HA to EC, 30 Jan 1911. Ruth Draper later became an overnight guest. See HA to EC, 14 Jan 1913:—"I have had Ruth Draper for a night."
13. HA to EC, 25 Feb 1913.
14. CFA2 to HA, 1 Mar 1913.
15. A copy of a letter to Prof. J. H. Latan, of Johns Hopkins University, evidently written by CFA2's secretary, 15 Jan 1914, CFA2P, provides the title of the lecture-series—*1643–1865: A Nationality: Its Inception; Its Development; Its Birth*—and the title of each lecture. With the help of this outline, one can see that CFA2's conception of the achievement of American nationality was wholly at variance with HA's, set forth in his *History of the United States*.
16. The copy is in my collection. The inscription reads "For/ niece Aileen/ from/ uncle Henry/ March 25. 1913."
17. The evidence is clear that HA arranged the creation of the trust fund with CFA3 in March 1913 but did not tell AT about the arrangement till November and then gave AT a wrong impression that the arrangement had just been made.

HA's letter of instruction to CFA3 is not in evidence, but CFA3 wrote two replies to HA, dated 25 Mar and 3 Apr 1913. CFA3 does not say in the replies that the desired arrangement relates to AT, but he takes HA's instructions very seriously, says a codicil need not be added to HA's will, and says, ". . . your letter will produce the result which you want with the least fuss."

I can document the incompleteness of AT's knowledge. On 28 Apr 1957, I had a conversation with her that resulted in my writing two notes. "After she had been a year with him [i.e. in November 1913], Adams gave A. T. . . . a trust fund—not in the will—which has since supported her." "The stocks A. T. got were U. S. Steel, A.T. and T. and Calumet Copper."

In other conversations with me and my wife, AT said HA told her that his object was to make her an actual niece, and that when given to her the stocks were worth $25,000. She said too that CFA3 managed during many years to send her wondrously large amounts but that the trustee who replaced him when he died did not work similar wonders.

AT was never poor. My wife and I remained in close touch with her till her death on 13 July 1969 in her 91st year. She maintained her accustomed standard of living to the end.

18. To my mind, there is something not fully clear about the relation that HA and AT formed with one another. In January 1914, HA permitted John Briggs Potter—husband of HA's niece-by-marriage Ellen Hooper Potter—to make matching drawings of himself and AT. In the 1950s and till a late date in the 1960s, when she gave it to the Massachusetts Historical Society, visitors to AT's apartment, 10H, at 151 East 83 Street, New York, saw above her living room fireplace the drawing of HA. (The drawing of AT was placed near the end of the opposite wall.) To that extent, HA was ever-present to AT.

This simple fact may dispose inquirers to ask whether AT was HA's informally adoptive niece or his adoptive-daughter in the guise of an adoptive-niece. HA was capable of such a deception. So, perhaps, was AT. But the question seems difficult. Adoptive niece or daughter? I feel quite unsure.

My uncertainty is increased by a postscript added to a letter from Thoron to HA dated only Friday and beginning "This perfectly . . ."—filmed in HA/Thoron-micro as written in 1915. The writer of the postscript was Niece Loulie—newly Thoron's wife. It ends with the words "Most lovingly your daughter."

19. Recollection of AT, 29 Feb 1952. AT said that HA spent hours at a time in Picard's Paris bookshop in 1913 and 1914. To her, the shop seemed cold, and HA seemed always to ask for books that were long out-of-print or hopelessly rare. A man named Rattier poked around the shop for him.

20. EC to HA, 20 Mar 1913.

21. EC to HA, 30 Mar 1913.

22. Thoron had photographs made of many of the songs but by no means all. On this point, see HA to Thoron, 22 Jan 1914.

If one may judge from HA's annotations in his copy of Raynaud's *Bibliographie des Chansonniers Française,* op. cit., three collections of songs Thoron arranged to have photographed were: Oxford, Bodleian Library, Douce 308, and Paris, Bibliothèque Nationale, Pb[5] and Pb[12]. Each collection was large.

23. HA to EC, 18 May 1913.

24. HA to EC, 2 May [1913]; HA to Anna Lodge, 15 May 1913. In a subsequent letter to Mrs. Lodge, 2 Jul 1913, HA said, "I am trembling as usual for fear of war."

25. EC to HA, 25 May 1913. Soon after I first met her, AT told me she had photographs taken by HA in Egypt. She showed them to me and my wife. Mounted on sheets of stiff gray cardboard, they evidently were good extra prints that HA had wanted to preserve.

In 1965, AT gave me the entire series. They did not include his photograph of Abu Simbel seen from the side but included a photograph of the temple's figures seen face to face. I am inclined to believe that the photographs HA sent to EC at Stepleton were drawn from this series, that EC returned the photographs to HA, and that he took them back to Washington.

In 1982, to expedite the completion of the second volume of this trilogy by obtaining an IBM word-processing system (then an expensive acquisition), I sold the series to a dealer, with the exception of a duplicate. I do not know the present whereabouts of the series.

26. EC to HA, 11 Jun 1913.

27. EC to HA, 3 Jul 1913.

28. HA to Anna Lodge, 2 Jul 1913; HA to EC, 6 Jul 1913.

29. HA to EC, 27 [Jul 1913].

30. HA to CMG, 7 Aug 1913.

31. During conversations with me and my wife, AT recollected that, to his and her satisfaction, HA made efforts to identify conjecturally the composers of unattributed songs.

Some penciled notes support her assertion and appear to date one such effort as having occurred in August 1913. On the back of the second page of a letter from CFA2 dated 5 Aug 1913 and received at the Château de Marivault c. 12 Aug 1913, HA wrote in pencil in two columns and in reverse order a series of numbers from 168 to 135. Next to each number, he wrote the name of a composer, the word "anon.," or a straight line.

These annotations correspond to, but do not always match, annotations HA made on pp. 181–83 of his copy of Raynaud's *Bibliographie des Chansonniers Français*, op. cit., presently in my collection. On these pages, Raynaud concludes a list of songs—all anonymous—in a MS. in the Bibliothèque Nationale identified as Pb[12].

Full analysis of this evidence would best be attempted by a music specialist. Here it may be noted that both on the back of the page of the letter and on page 181 of the *Bibliographie*, HA attributes one of the songs to "Richart"; i.e. Richard Coeur de Lion.

32. HA to Thoron, 27 Aug [1913].

33. EC to HA, 13 Aug 1913.

34. The dinner on 2 Sep 1913 at 6 Square du Bois de Boulogne brings to mind HA's statement in his letter to HJ, 29 May 1913: "Only women are worth cultivating. . . ."

35. BA was trustful of Ford. He wrote Ford a letter, 23 Dec 1913, FP 22, about the ability of the English to "reduce the destruction of compromising documents to a system" and to do the same with "private letters." He goes on to say, "The English are a wonderful people for whitewashing." He names two Americans—CFA2 and Hay—who, in his opinion, accepted England's whitewashed history as real. He declares: "The Russell family is . . . making gigantic efforts . . . to get Lord John canonized by my brother Charles. They [the English] are a great people; by all odds sharper in this world's wisdom than we. And how they have got their story told for them by judicious suppression on the one hand and bribery and flattery on the other! Even in politics—just think of the pocketing of John Hay!"

36. E.g., many letters in the Ford Papers, NYPL, testify to the energy of CFA2 and Ford in attempting to get access to the journal of Benjamin Moran—a constant witness of HA during much of that period.

37. Thayer to Ford, 8 Aug 1913, FP 21.

38. How Ford had arrived at this very important judgment is unknown and might be very hard to guess with even a modicum of correctness.

39. Thayer to Ford, 2 Sep 1913, FP 21.

40. One has to imagine that gossip about Hay and Anna Lodge and gossip about Hay and Elizabeth Cameron had reached Boston-Cambridge. Gossip was in order. Hay had gone through the motions—at least the *literary* motions—of being in love with both women.

41. Thayer to Ford, 2 Sep 1913, FP 21. Thayer's tendency to make negative judgments was evident in the letter. He lamented what he took to be James Huneker's unwarranted interest in composers' sexual vices; and he said about HJ's *A Small Boy and Others*: ". . . it's the most wilfully affected of Jamesian productions, & shows a deterioration of mental power. I call it an *auto*-description of a remarkable case of elephantiasis of the Ego."

42. Thayer to Ford, 9 Oct 1913, FP 21.

43. HA to EC, 5 [Oct 1913].

44. EC to HA, 26 Oct 1913.

45. HA to CMG, 1 Nov 1913.

46. HA to EC, 4 Nov [1913].

47. For "Woodruff," see HA to Anna Lodge, 15 May 1913; HA to Margaret Chanler, 3 Aug 1913. In conversations with me and my wife, AT liked to imitate HA's gruff voice when using the mistaken name.

48. HA to EC, 24 Nov 1913. Perhaps in attempted agreement with HA, Levenson and his associates describe Cram's Note as "fulsome." See L, VI, 623n1.

49. HA, *MSM&CH* (1913), vi–vii.

50. Principal source 7. HA's copy is the authoritative text of the book, superseding all others. The improvement stands first, on p. 72, line 9. Corrections follow on 72, 76, 90, 91, 96, 97, 101, 103, 135, 166, 189, 202, 206, 222, 229 (2), 231, 235, 251, 252, 268, 291, 299, 302, 306, 307, 327, 328 (2), 330, 335, 357. The improvement deserves notice. In a sentence about the west portal at Chartres cathedral, HA inserts 'human' before 'misery,' with the following result: ". . . everything is there except human misery." The improvement does not appear in the present standard edition: *MSM&CH* (LoA), 407, line 18.

51. Letters, EC to HA, 8 Nov 1913, 16 Nov 1913, & 26 Nov 1913.

52. EC to HA, 4 Dec 1913.

53. HA to Morison, 28 Nov 1913, L, VI, 624.

54. HA to Ford, 29 Nov 1913, FP 22.

55. HA's comic morning greetings were one of AT's favorite recollections of him. She imitated his inflection.

56. HA to Cross, 16 Dec 1913, L, VI, 627; HA to Berenson, 10 Dec 1913, O.1913.54. Berenson had the marvelous grace to reply (letter of 23 Dec 1913): "Noël, noël, noël. I wish I were with you, to have Miss Tone sing us a Noël from the days when people believed the whole blessed fairy tale."

57. Thayer to HA, 23 Dec 1913.

58. Ibid. Thayer's letter is valuable evidence that HA was not long in Washington before he was chafing to be back in Paris.

59. Ibid. One of the effects of HA's privately printing his books was to induce in other persons strong, even inordinate, desires to collect them.

60. CFA2 to HA, 24 Dec 1913. One may assume that the letter was taken directly from 1701 Massachusetts Avenue to 1603 H Street on the day it was written.

61. HA to Thayer, 26 Dec 1913.

24. WAR

Letters by and to HA are in HA-micro 28, 29, or H, or HA/Thoron-micro, unless otherwise indicated.

PRINCIPAL SOURCES

(1) twenty-nine letters and a telegram, HA to EC, Tuesday, 16 [Dec 1913]–26–30 Nov 1914. (See note 2, below, concerning the first letter in the series.)
(2) thirty-eight letters and a postcard, EC to HA, 26 Dec 1913–22 Nov 1914.
(3) four letters and a cable, HA to Thoron, [22 Jan]–28 [Jul] 1914.
(4) nine letters, HA to CMG, 19 Feb–18 [Oct] 1914.

LESSER SOURCES; CITATIONS; COMMENTS

1. Letters, HA to EC, 18–19 [Feb 1913] & 18 Mar 1913, HA-micro 27.
2. HA's note to EC is written on his Washington stationery, dated only "Tuesday, 16," and begins "A line to say. . . ." It advises EC that Rachel has "taken legal steps to obtain a separation." It is filmed out of sequence in HA-micro 24 as if written after 14 Jan 1910. Its correct date is Tuesday, 16 [Dec 1913]. It is omitted from L & O.
3. EC to HA, 26 Dec 1913.
4. Letters, EC to HA, 8 Jan 1914 & 15 Jan 1914.
5. EC to HA, 23 Jan 1914.
6. Thayer later recorded that they met in "January 1914" but did not specify a day or days. See his inscription on the flyleaf of the "Thayer copy" of The Education, MHS. Also see note 7.
7. Hazen, 242, quoting a letter from Thayer to his wife, 19 Jan 1915:—". . . I called on Mr. Charles Adams, who took me down to lunch with his brother Henry. That arch-egoist was interesting, and very expansive, compared with last year. . . ."
8. HA to Louise Boit, 15 Mar 1913, O.1913.16.
9. Ford's copy of the *JHLetters*, with enclosure, Rare Books Division, NYPL.
10. For evidence supporting this account and for further details, see Chap. 27.
11. BA to HA, 7 Jan 1914. BA said of the furniture, "I doubt that anything so good exists in New York"; also that some of the pieces were "better than anything I have seen in the Louvre."
12. Potter's drawing became AT's property after HA's death. On 29 Feb 1952, I recorded points she made that day in conversation. She said that HA "might have commissioned a portrait [by a recognized artist], had it not been that with one exception there was no painter whose work he liked. He did like Zorn." It was implicit in what AT said that Potter's drawing was not HA's idea. She remembered that the drawing was done "while he was cross." "He told Potter it was now or never, and to pay no attention to his grousiness." She added that John Singer Sargent saw Potter's portrait of HA and said it was "all out of drawing." She went on to say: "Well, Sargent's things are all out of drawing too." She stressed that HA would "never let Sargent near him"—i.e. paint his portrait—because Sargent arbitrarily "chose things to emphasize."

For other details about Potter's drawing of HA and a companion drawing of AT, see Chap. 23, note 18, above.
13. HA to EC, 9 Feb 1914.

14. EC to HA, 12–13 Feb 1914.

15. The entry is quoted in HA-1, 1.

16. For HA's inheriting the coins from CFA, see CFA2 to Tuttle, 22 Feb 1914, FP 62.

17. HA to EC, 5–6 Apr 1914:—"The world . . . [is] bothered to know what her duties are as private secretary. She explains as well as she can, that she sings."

18. HA to EC, Monday, [26] January [1914].

19. EC to HA, 19 Feb 1914.

20. EC to HA, 6 Mar 1914.

21. BA to Ford, 16 Jan 1914, FP 22.

22. Elizabeth Hoyt to EC, 18 Apr 1918, HA-micro 31:—"There is a pretty complete history of our times in those drawers of Dordy's downstairs—letters from every part of the world & from every sort of person."

23. HA to EC, 22 Mar 1914. This is the second instance of HA's preparing to return EC's letters.

24. HA to EC, 1–2 Mar 1914.

25. BA to Ford, 21 Jan 1914, FP 22. If made, HA's remark could have been meant by him to apply in part to a *future* work, Thayer's life of Hay.

26. HJ to HA, 21 Mar 1914.

27. The fallout of HJ's act can be seen in such statements as one by Leon Edel about a character in HJ's *The Ambassadors*: "Waymarsh seems to possess the gloom of Henry Adams. . . ." See Edel, *Henry James/ The Master: 1901–1916*, Phila & NY 1972, 72.

28. Berenson's visit occurred soon after HA wrote to CMG, 19 Feb 1914: "The atmosphere [in America] really has become a Jew atmosphere. It is curious and evidently good for some people, but it isolates me. I do not know the language, and my friends are as ignorant as I. We are still in power, after a fashion. . . . We keep Jews far away, and the anti-Jew feeling is quite rabid. We are anti-everything and we are wild uplifters, yet we somehow seem to be more Jewish every day."

HA's remarks were noticeably detached. He added two sentences that much increased the detachedness. "This is not my own diagnosis. I make none." The sentences can be taken literally. HA stayed home and talked with people who visited him. They told him a great deal about the Jews and "anti-Jew feeling" in America. He felt disposed to accept what he was told.

29. HA to EC, 5–6 Apr 1914; HA to EC, 12–13 Apr 1914.

30. HA to Anna Lodge, 13 May 1914.

31. Flexner to HA, 24 Apr 1914.

32. HA to EC, Monday, 25 [May 1914].

33. EC to HA, 27 May 1914.

34. HA to EC, Sunday, 31 [May 1914].

35. HA to CMG, 1 Jun 1914.

36. Ibid.

37. Recollection by AT, 24 Jan 1967.

38. EC to HA, 12 Jul 1914.

39. HA to Thoron, Tuesday, 28 [Jul 1914].

40. CMG to HA, 3 Aug 1914; Elizabeth Lodge to HA, 3 Aug 1914.

41. Recollection by AT, 17 Sep 1966.

42. Ibid. Also see Cater, c.

43. Cater, c.

44. HA to Curtis, 10 Aug 1914, Dartmouth College Library; EC to HA, 12 Aug 1914.

45. BA to HA, 7 Aug 1914.

46. HA to Curtis, op. cit.

47. HA to CMG, 13 Aug 1914.

48. Louisa Hooper to "Dear Roger," 15 Aug 1914. LHT found the letter in May 1958 and sent it to me to copy and use in this narrative.

49. EC to HA, 21 Aug 1914.

50. EC to HA, 27 Aug 1914.

51. HA to CMG, Friday, [28 Aug 1914].

52. HA to EC, 5 Sep 1914.

53. HA to Martha Lindsay, 18 Sep 1914.

54. EC called the dog "Swartz." See EC to HA, 13–14 Sep 1914. HA wrote of him as "Swarz." See HA to Lindsay, 23 Sep 1914. But Martha changed his name to "Smuts." See EC to HA, 24 Sep 1914.

55. Recollection by AT, often repeated by her in connection with a snapshot she owned of HA, herself, and the dog at Stepleton. In the snapshot, HA is looking at his watch.

56. EC to HA, 16 Oct 1914.

57. *HJLetters*, IV, 722.

58. EC to HA, 28 Oct 1914.

59. Davis to HA, 7 Nov 1914.

60. HA's memory erred, substituting c for b. He clearly meant the MS. at the Bibliothèque Nationale listed in Raynaud's *Bibliographie des Chansonniers Français*, op. cit., I, 110–22, as Pb⁵. It contains 141 songs. In his copy of Raynaud's book (presently in my collection), HA heavily annotated the relevant pages.

25. LOSSES MISAPPREHENDED

Letters by and to HA are in HA-micro 29, 30, or H, or in HA/Thoron-micro, unless otherwise indicated.

PRINCIPAL SOURCES

(1) fifty-nine letters, EC to HA, 29 Nov 1914–9 Feb 1916.

(2) thirty-four letters, HA to EC, 7–8 Dec 1914–6 Feb 1916.

(3) four letters, HA to CMG, 26 Dec 1914–18 Mar 1916.

(4) four letters, HA to Thayer, 6 Jul 1915–6 Feb 1916.

LESSER SOURCES; CITATIONS; COMMENTS

1. Letters, EC to HA, 31 Dec 1914 & 8 Jan 1915; HA to EC, 13 & 15 Dec 1914.

2. Letters, EC to HA, 29 Nov 1914 & 3 Dec 1914.

3. HA to EC, 7 Dec 1914.

4. HA to EC, 13 Dec 1914.

5. Fay to HA, 14 Dec 1914.

6. HA to EC, 20 Dec 1914.

7. HA to CMG, 26 Dec 1914. HA appreciated his advantages. He said in the same letter, "I am better off than anyone else I know, of my age, which is epitaph enough."

8. HA to Thoron, 21 Dec 1914.

9. HA to Taylor, 15 Feb 1915. Possibly the stoic philosopher whom HA had most in mind was Marcus Aurelius.

10. Ibid.

11. HA to EC, 25 & 29 Dec 1914.

12. Clipping of a newspaper story headed "MRS ROOSEVELT RECALLS HENRY ADAMS' REMARK." LHT gave me the clipping on 5 Apr 1963 and told me she had clipped it from a Boston paper without recording the name of the paper or the date of the issue. Datelined "WASHINGTON, June 2 (A. P.)," the story says Mrs. Roosevelt recalled HA's reply on June 3 while addressing a graduating class.

13. HA to EC, 25 & 29 Dec 1914; HA to Berenson, 11 Jan 1915, O.1915.1.

14. Florence La Farge to HA, [15 Jan 1915]; HA to Mary Jones, Wed., [19 Jan 1915]; Florence La Farge to HA, Tuesday, [26 Jan 1915].

15. Thayer to HA, 24 Jan 1915:—"I leave herewith the bundle of Hay's letters which you kindly lent to me."

16. HA to EC, 22 Jan 1915:—"The dormouse sleeps sounder than ever, but he dreams of unpleasant things. . . ."

17. EC to HA, 5 Feb 1915.

18. HA to EC, 16 Feb 1915.

19. HA to AT, Sat., [20 Feb 1915]; HA to EC, 25 Feb 1915.

20. HA to EC, 26 Mar 1915.

21. On 28 Apr 1957, after listening to comments by AT about CFA2 and his last illness and death, I made the following notes: "Died after riding three days w. pneumonia, and a fever. Could not dismount. Said he would die in the saddle." In addition, I recorded a general comment: "Miss T. does not remember Charles [ever] smiling."

See also Edward Chase Kirkland, *Charles Francis Adams, Jr./ 1835–1915/ The Patrician at Bay*, Camb 1965, 221:—"Pneumonia set in."

22. HA to Higginson, Sunday, 21 [Mar 1915]:—"It was I who expected the summons. . . ."

23. Recollections of AT, 20 Jun 1963. AT also said there was a song which she sang exclusively for HA and which he said "*was* him." She remembered it as saying that the singer had been blind, deaf, dumb, and frivolous all through life but at last was cured; that "light was breaking through."

24. HA to Luquiens, 29 Dec 1914, L, VI, 677; HA to EC, 9 Apr 1915.

25. HA to EC, 9 Apr 1915. AT preserved the programs in the form of six-song lists, each on a page. Late in life, she gave the lists to Bruce Brooks Pfeiffer for use at Taliesen West by Frank Lloyd Wright's assistants and students. Pfeiffer eventually gave photocopies of the lists to Siegmund Levarie, author of "Henry Adams, Avant-gardist in Early Music," the pioneer article on HA as the musical forerunner who brought secular medieval music to the United States. See *American Music*, v. 25, no. 2 (Winter 1997), 429–45.

When finished with the photocopies, Levarie gave them to me. The first page is dated 8 Mar–10 Apr 1915.

In my opinion, HA and AT should be credited equally as co-authors of the programs.

26. EC to HA, 7 Mar 1915.

27. Louise Amory to HA, 14 Mar 1915.

28. EC to HA, 25 Apr 1915.

29. For the quoted phrase, see EC to HA, 21 Apr 1915.

30. HA to EC, 5–6 Feb 1915.

31. HA to EC, 15–16 Apr 1915.

32. HA to EC, 26 May 1915.

33. EC to HA, 22 May 1915.

34. The act had an important smaller meaning. It permitted HJ to live more comfortably under very strict British wartime regulations.

35. AT several times told me and my wife the story of HA's reaction and each time remembered HA's using the words here quoted.

36. Typed passage headed "Quotation from letter of Mrs. Winthrop Chanler to her daughter Laura, September 7, 1915," sent to me in March 1971 by Louis Auchincloss with the following advice:—"Mrs. C. was always inclined to pounce on the least evidence in HA of religiosity—so take it *cum grano salis*." (The word beginning "alon" is typed as if Mrs. Chanler wrote "along." I think it likely she wrote "alone.")

37. HCL to Ford, 6 Jul 1915, FP 66. The phrase "Autobiographical Memoir" is Lodge's.

38. CFA2 appears to have been the originator of the mistaken idea that the Adamses, the Hays, and King joined together as the Five of Hearts while they were living in Washington. The available evidence leaves no doubt that they formed the association *after* King and the Hays left the capital and that they did so with a view to keeping closely tied to each other when no longer neighbors. For details, see HA-2, pages indexed under "Five of Hearts."

In his biography, Thayer later published the following lines about *Democracy*: "Clarence King is still commonly regarded as its author; and there are many supporters of Hay; but I believe that only Mr. [Henry] Adams possessed the substance, and style, and the gift of Voltairean railery which distinguish it." See Thayer, II, 59.

39. Greenslet eventually published an autobiography. The book can suggest that HA's supposed autobiography became a near-obsession for him.

40. An admission should be made to persons who persist in imagining that HA's *Education* is an autobiography. The book is autobiographical in that it provides at a few junctures information about the actual Henry Adams that HA could expect might be difficult or impossible for his biographers to get. An outstanding example is a sentence in Chap. VIII: "He had written pretty frequently to Henry J. Raymond, and Raymond had used his letters in the *New York Times*." See *EHA* (1907), 103; (LoA), 829.

Ironically the sentence also illustrates the degree to which *The Education* is not autobiographical. Reading the sentence, one might get the impression that HA was not a paid contributor to the *New York Times*; that he occasionally wrote letters to Raymond as an unpaid volunteer. His actual status was very different. The news despatches he wrote were paid, systematic, and numerous. Those that ended the series were exceedingly important. For details, see HA-1.

41. Not long after he printed his *Education*, HA began to serve as the target of ill-informed jokes asserting that he was the man who wrote his autobiography and forgot to include his marriage. Really the joke was on the jokers; for HA was the man who wrote and printed a book which—while telling a story about an essentially fictional "Henry Adams"—leaves out or radically minimizes *all* the noteworthy achievements of the actual Henry Adams. The omitted achievements included a happy marriage, which, even when tragically ending, remained a signal success with respect to HA's conduct, as his wife's last known words make very clear. See HA-2, 503.

42. HCL to Ford, 1 Sep 1915, FP 66. The word "Autobiography" is Lodge's.

43. Ibid.
44. HCL to Ford, 18 Sep 1915, FP 66.
45. HCL to Ford, 21 Sep 1915, FP 66.
46. HA to CMG, 15 Aug 1915.
47. Two of EC's letters were evidently lost on ships sunk by submarines.
48. Anna Lodge to AT, 25 Sep 1915, HA-micro 29.
49. HA to HCL, 28 Sep 1915.
50. HA to HCL, 5 Oct 1915.
51. EC's memory somewhat erred. The first version of HA's paper refers explicitly to "1917" but sets "1921" as its main terminal date.
52. EC's easy grasp of HA's "The Rule of Phase applied to History" bears comparison with Abraham Flexner's easy grasp of HA's *Letter to American Teachers of History*, noted in Chap. 24.
53. HA to Ford, 11 Nov 1915, FP 26:—"I warmly hope that Thayer's Hay will be a success. I have not yet read it, but so much of our status in Paradise depends on it, that I wait anxiously for judgment."
54. She employed the stenographer for purposes other than writing to HA. See EC to HA, 18 Jan 1916.
55. The address can prove different from what a reader expects. On 11 Nov 1963, LHT informed me: "I have just been reading . . . 16 pages of the Memorial Address given by Henry Cabot Lodge. . . . I'd never read it before, & I'm astounded at the number of pages it takes before it comes to grips with . . . the subject. . . . It has nothing but evasion and uncomplimentary things to say [about CFA2] until the account gets him to Harvard when the young man begins to feel that he found congenial contemporaries & a life he didn't have to find fault with!!"
56. *Autobiography*, lv.
57. For details relating to MHA, see HA-2, 362–63, 375–76.
58. *Autobiography*, lvi.
59. HCL to Ford, 26 Nov 1915, FP 66:—"Ever since my college days[,] he has been one of my dearest and most intimate friends—no one more so—and there is no one whose criticism and somewhat rare approval I have so much valued throughout my life."
60. Putnam to HA, Saturday morning, [27 Nov 1915].
61. Ibid.
62. HA to Thayer, 17 Dec 1915. One searches the biography in vain for a passage of the sort that HA praised Thayer for writing. Instead one finds a passage (Thayer, II, 53–63) that credits HA with an important innovation. The passage includes the following lines (62): "The group which gathered round Mr. Adams has had no counterpart on this side of the Atlantic. It was free alike from the academic flavor which prevailed in Boston and Cambridge, and from the Bohemianism which New Yorkers seemed to affect. Its leading members had the Renaissance stamp of versatility."
63. Greenslet to HA, 22 Dec 1915. The word "autobiographic" is Greenslet's.
64. HA to Thayer, 29 Dec 1915.
65. Undated draft of a letter, HA to Dear Sir, replying to "your letter of the 22d," filmed in HA-micro 30 as if written on 18 Feb 1916.
   The first page of the document bears a query—"Feb 18?"—in Ford's handwriting. With no better grounding in evidence than Ford's query, which they pass over in silence, Levenson and his associates date the document "[Early February 1916]." See L, VI, 719.

A date consistent with the evident date of Greenslet's letter and HA's usual promptness in replying is late December 1915.

Levenson and his associates say (720n1) the document "may be a draft." Their remark makes room for an implication that the document *may be a letter HA mailed.* Yet everything about the document shows it to be a mere draft. Appropriately, it was found in HA's papers.

66. HA appears later to have used his draft of the never-sent letter to Greenslet as a starting point when writing the "Editor's Preface" for *The Education.* For the contents of the latter, see Chap. 26.

67. Thayer to HA, 4 Feb 1916.

68. Ibid. On 5 Feb 1916, Thayer wrote a letter to EC saying (Hazen, 272–73): ". . . many persons told me . . . that Mr. Adams really guided Hay's policy as Secretary of State. There is nothing to indicate this in the record. The great pilot after 1901 was Roosevelt, who put through several of the chief measures which were commonly attributed to Hay. The policy of the Open Door, and the preservation of China, were Hay's diplomatic triumphs."

The true question, in my view, was never whether Hay was subjected to HA's control. It was whether Hay asked HA to share his office and work with him. This was something that Hay and HA could do without leaving a record that Thayer would be able to see. It also was something they could do while holding very different views about which policies might be best. But Thayer and his purported informants seem not to have weighed the possibility of such secrecy, in combination with such intelligent and considerate sharing. They seem to have known Hay only dimly and HA not at all.

69. EC to HA, 23 Feb 1916:—". . . [Jack Carter] wants some one to write a volume on Henry Adams & his Friends. . . . With you as the central figure, and with Mr. Hay, Clarence King, Theodore, Spring-Rice, your brothers & many others spinning like fretful midges around you, some thing [*sic*] pretty could be done. Only . . . *you* ought to be the one to do it."

70. HA to Thayer, 6 Feb 1916.

71. Much later, Greenslet claimed to have been shown a copy of *The Education* in 1907 by Richard Watson Gilder and to have "read it nearly all night." See his *Under the Bridge/ An Autobiography,* Bost 1943, 144–45. For remarks about the credibility of other claims by Greenslet, see note 77, below.

72. Copy of letter, Greenslet to Thayer, 29 Feb 1916, CaterP. Part of the letter is worded somewhat as a parody of a formal receipt, affirming that Greenslet has the copy of *The Education* in his possession, is responsible for it, and will hold it "until further notice."

The wording of this part of the letter can be read as evidence that Thayer let Greenslet retain the copy only after the latter had been trusted with it temporarily, had read it, had visited HA, and had written to HA asking final approval of the plan-of-publication they agreed upon at 1603 H Street.

73. The "Thayer Copy" of *The Education,* op. cit., MHS, also known here as the First Traveling Copy, contains annotations in the text in HA's handwriting and in another handwriting. I attribute 178 of the annotations to HA, 21 to the other writer. For additional details, see Chap. 27.

74. Copy of letter, Greenslet to Thayer, 7 Feb 1916, CaterP.

75. Hazen, 242.

76. Greenslet to Thayer, 7 Feb 1916, op. cit. Greenslet's phrase "the role of inspirer of statesmen" can seem gratuitous, as if devised by someone who knew almost nothing about HA and felt free to have any idea about him that

came to mind. Equally it can seem an unthinking or perverse misreading of the statement in *The Education* that can seem to clamor most for notice. In Chap. XXI, "Twenty Years After," one finds the statement: ". . . as far as he [Adams] had a function in life, it was as stable-companion to statesmen, whether they liked it or not." (Nearby sentences involve the words "horse," "stable," and "John Hay.") See *EHA* (1907), 277; (LoA), 1010.

The emotional coloring of the statement is partly determined by the phrase "whether they liked it or not." The phrase is certainly amused, confident, assertive, even aggressive.

The meaning of the statement is determining most by the stable-companion metaphor and by two plurals, "statesmen" and "they." It may be helpful to consider what the meaning of the metaphor really is.

Stable-companions necessarily are horses.

Those in the metaphor are evidently carriage horses, used for moving human beings in quantity, as opposed to riding horses, at the service of single riders, or farm horses, used for such things as plowing.

All carriage horses have some or all of the attributes and the abilities expected of carriage horses.

In turn, their attributes and abilities fit them to be companions.

Stables are of different sizes. A large stable may house many carriage horses. A small one might house two horses who are teamed.

At first sight, the metaphor can be wonderfully misleading. It can seem to suggest that HA was confined to the role of *mere* companion of statesmen and hence was *never* a statesman. But sooner or later the metaphor reveals an inescapable but opposite meaning.

In the metaphor, all the stable inhabitants are carriage horses: i.e. all are statesmen. In the metaphor, HA always inhabits stables. Therefore HA is always a statesman.

The conclusion can be factually supported as follows.

Successive stables that HA inhabited were JQA's library at Quincy in the 1840s; CFA's work-spaces in Boston, Washington, and London from the late 1840s to 1868; and the Hay-Adams houses in Washington from 1898 to 1905, when Hay died. In each of the instances, HA was teamed with another horse.

Eleven horses with whom HA was teamed only transiently were Henry J. Raymond (in 1861–1862), Thurlow Weed (in 1861–1862), Richard Cobden (in 1863), William Evarts (on and off in 1863–1870), Salmon P. Chase (in 1869–1870), John Bright (in 1869–1870), Henry Cabot Lodge (from 1873 to 1876), Carl Schurz (incompatibly in 1876), Wayne MacVeagh (in 1881), James Donald Cameron (1892–1894), and William Phillips (1895–1896). With the possible exceptions of his teamings with Weed and Cobden, HA figured in each of the teams as the abler horse.

Very large stables HA shared with other statesmen, whether they liked it or not, were Washington in the winter of 1860–1861; London in the period 1861–1868; Washington in combination with London from 1868 to 1870; and Washington—often in combination with U. S. legations and embassies abroad—from 1877 until he died in 1918.

A stable HA shared with successive presidents of the United States from 1877 to 1918 was Lafayette Square, each of the presidents being stalled transiently on the south side in the publicly-provided White House, HA being stalled perennially on the north side, first in a rented private house, then in a private house he built and owned.

That HA could be a statesman and find it open to himself to be also other things—a great traveler, a great writer, an educator of future Americans, etc.—is left open by the metaphor, which suggests that one must start somewhere and that HA made his start by becoming, and by never ceasing to be, what he first had to be: one of America's politicians—or, in politer language, a statesman.

77. Greenslet later tried to create an impression that *The Education* was published by Houghton Mifflin Company as a result of his having repeatedly visited the author. In his *Under the Bridge*, op. cit., 145–46, he says he paid HA a surprise visit in 1907; that later he was invited to come to 1603 H Street for noon meals "when possible"; and that he appeared there "once or twice a year." As if to substantiate his claim, he remarks that the furniture in HA's house was not large enough to afford comfortable seating for male guests.

I doubt his claim to have visited HA at times other than 11 Feb 1916. The claim has no support in any evidence I know of, apart from the claim itself. I notice too that his allegation that HA's chairs were not large enough for men repeats an allegation made not long after HA's death in an anonymous article, "At Mr. Adams's," published in the *New Republic* on 25 May 1918.

According to Ford (letter to Lodge, 21 Jun 1918, LP 104), the article was written by Philip Littell with the help of Mrs. Victor Sordeau and Mrs. Ralph Ellis. Evidence that Littell or Mrs. Sordeau ever entered HA's house is lacking. Elizabeth Warder Ellis knew HA well enough to visit him, but her relations with him were apparently not of a sort that leaned towards factualness. See L, IV, 664.

78. Greenslet to HA, 15 Feb 1916.

79. Greenslet to Ford, 15 Feb 1916, with envelope, FP 26.

80. AT remembered the desk in HA's main-floor study as having double banks of drawers to the right and left at both front and back, making as many as thirty-two drawers. Some presumably could be locked.

81. My inference that HA believed that the First and Second Traveling Copies were in his house in February 1916—that is, until he found them to be "missing"—is based on three considerations: (a) his later saying "books" were "missing out of sets"; (b) the arithmetical fact that the imagined retention of the traveling copies would make possible imagined sets large enough to be thought of as sets; and (b) the absence of evidence that HA ever sought to recover the First Traveling Copy from Thayer or the Second Traveling Copy from BA.

82. HA to CMG, 18 Mar 1916.

83. Ibid. HA told CMG the story of his shock a month after the shock occurred and after he had completed the important actions he thought his situation required of him. Hence his being able to write a partly humorous account.

26. COPIES GIVEN, COPIES FOUND

Letters by and to HA are in HA-micro 30, 31 & H, unless otherwise indicated.

PRINCIPAL SOURCES

(1) 101 letters, EC to HA, 17 Feb 1916–27 Mar 1918.

(2) twenty-four letters, HA to EC, 1 Mar 1916–1 Mar 1918.

(3) five letters, HA to CMG, 18 Mar 1916–19 Feb 1918.

(4) letter, HA to HCL, 1 Mar 1916.

(5) photocopies of all pages bearing HA's handwriting in [HA], *The Education of Henry Adams*, Wash (privately printed) 1907—the Abernethy

Copy, known here also as the Substitute Copy. (Courtesy of the Abernethy Library, Middlebury College)

(6) photocopies of the half title page and all other pages bearing HA's handwriting in [HA], *The Education of Henry Adams,* Wash (privately printed) 1907—the copy known here as the Signed Copy. (Courtesy of R. Eden Martin)

(7) [HA], separately preserved 15-page MS. in two parts: "Editor's Preface." [i–ix] & "Contents." [x–xv], MHS.

LESSER SOURCES; CITATIONS; COMMENTS

1. On 29 Feb 1952 after a talk with AT, I wrote the following summary of things she said: "Adams was partly blind. He went to the great oculists . . . and had glasses made but would not wear them, because oculists made poor glasses. Instead, he had a great variety of magnifying glasses, thick, thin, large, small, and pocket ones, which he would whip out on occasion."

2. With respect to where he started work, see note 8, below. With respect to the secrecy of his action, see note 34, below.

3. He had corrected the misspelling in the First Traveling Copy and presumably also in the Master Copy.

4. Vassall was the last name of the person who built the Old House, the clapboard mansion in Massachusetts eventually bought by JA as his residence. Conceivably HA's error had been pointed out to him by BA and/or CFA2.

5. The words deleted were "came afterwards to him and." HA may have deleted them in the now-lost Master Copy. He had not deleted them in the First Traveling Copy. He had been the grandchild most desirous of fixing attention on his father's mother. He went to great lengths both to reveal and to conceal his relation with her, which as felt by him was tantamount to their sharing a single identity. The evident purpose of his deletion is to make their combinedness less obtrusive.

6. HA had not deleted the sentence in the First Traveling Copy. I think it inconceivable that he deleted it in the Master Copy. The point of the passage in which the sentence appears is that few healthy amusements were available to men and boys in Massachusetts in the 1840s. The deletion of the sentence does not lessen the passage's effectiveness.

7. *Autobiography,* xix.

8. Principal sources 5 & 6. An account of the emergence of principal source 6 is in order.

In early April 1998, after first drafting this chapter, I resumed my efforts to trace privately printed copies of *The Education.* I phoned The 19th Century Shop in Baltimore to ask what happened to an excellent unmarked copy the Shop had listed in 1991 in Catalogue 20: price $10,000. The Shop advised me that it was sold to a collector whose name could be disclosed only with the collector's permission.

On April 10, I received a call from R. Eden Martin of Glencoe, Illinois. He told me the Shop had given him my phone number. He said that in 1991 he bought from the Shop, not the advertised copy, but a copy signed by HA and containing annotations by him of the sort made by authors preparing works for publication.

This news came as a great surprise. By phone, Mr. Martin shortly gave me details about the annotations. Also he mailed me a page of data furnished by the Shop, including a detailed provenance. The provenance is mainly interesting for saying that HA lent the copy to Dr. William Wilmer "in 1907"; that the loan was shortly turned into a gift; that Wilmer kept the copy; that it passed to a grandson; and that its first buyer was The 19th Century Shop. In view of the words "in 1907," Mr. Martin and I at first assumed that HA's annotations were written in 1907.

On April 24, I received from Mr. Martin complete photocopies of the pages in his copy bearing marks by HA. The marks—most notably HA's signature— were matches of examples of HA's handwriting in the shaken form it acquired in 1916. This was a second surprise. A quick check revealed the telling fact that the 10 corrections and one improvement in Mr. Martin's copy reappear in HA's Substitute Copy, the one he sent to Lodge on 1 Mar 1916.

While guessing mistakenly that Mr. Martin's copy was annotated in 1907, I had guessed that the copy was an *assistant* copy. Everything I have since learned about it confirms me in thinking this idea correct.

I also guessed from the start that HA pressed an assistant copy into service to permit his reading the book in both his studies without seeming to read it in either, which meant without carrying a copy between them. I believe this idea too is correct.

I assume that Mr. Martin's copy was the downstairs copy. I may be wrong. HA may have read Mr. Martin's copy upstairs. But the distribution makes little difference. What matters is that HA did something he had done before. He read and annotated *The Education* in separate places in linked copies.

9. The evidence that HA read the copies in the way suggested here is the presence or absence in Mr. Martin's copy of annotations relating to particular chapters. Admittedly the evidence is minimal.

10. Evidently while reading the assistant copy (principal source 6), HA saw that the first entry in the Index, "Abthorp," was a misspelling of "Apthorp." He corrected the error in that copy. Later in the main copy (principal source 5) with the help of the page numbers already printed in the entry, he corrected seven misspellings of "Apthorp" in the text.

This is a simple example of a correction-and-improvement procedure HA knew how to use. The procedure was to annotate sufficiently in an assistant copy and later annotate more fully or better in a main copy. His use of the procedure in 1916 matters greatly. It indicates that his lost Master Copy was more completely corrected and more artfully improved than his First and Second Traveling Copies.

11. My suggestion that HA had a servant convey the copy is a guess consistent with HA's evident desire to keep his reading secret.

12. Writing his name and address in books he owned was far from usual with HA. This instance is an exception.

13. Principal source 5—the Substitute Copy—contains 37 annotations. All 37 have been ascribed to HA, but three are in a handwriting not his. The three were written by Ford. For details, see Chap. 27.

The 34 annotations in HA's handwriting appear in twenty chapters and relevant index entries. That HA made no marks in the other fifteen chapters may be confirmative of rapid reading.

14. Howard M. Munford was the first person to study the annotations in principal source 5—known here as the Substitute Copy. He studied them by themselves and as compared with those in the First Traveling Copy. He worked under handicaps, some self-imposed. He assumed that the First Traveling Copy was HA's "original corrected copy" and failed to consider that it might be some-

thing less, a sort of assistant copy. He did not know of the existence of the Second Traveling Copy. For these and other reasons, he could not fully understand the annotations in the First Traveling Copy, and he ended by dismissimg the annotations in the Substitute Copy as no better than "perfunctory." See his "Thayer, Ford, Goodspeed's, and Middlebury: A Missing Copy of *THE EDUCATION OF HENRY ADAMS* Found," MHS *Proceedings*, 83–84 (1971), 148–53, especially 149.

15. HA made non-correction a guiding rule. He ignored errors in the text that cried for correction, including misspellings of Sumner as "Summer." He let "James McKinley" stand uncorrected. Examples can be multiplied.

16. See page 256 in each of the three copies.

17. Principal source 5, 329 & 394.

18. This judgment is based on principal source 5, 329 & 393–94, but not on the uncorrected index entry for "Gibbs, Wolcott."

In each of the available annotated copies of *The Education*, HA let the mistaken "Gibbs, Wolcott" index entry stand uncorrected.

In my view, the uncorrected index entries are added evidence that HA cut corners when working in the First and Second Traveling Copies, thereby saving time and energy he would need when trying to correct his book completely and improve it perfectly in his Master Copy.

19. Because the Master Copy is lost, how many of its corrections and improvements HA could not remember in 1916 cannot be known. The best one can do is compare his annotations in principal sources 5 & 6 with those he made in his First and Second Traveling Copies. The results of the comparison are very stark. In 1916, he could remember some corrections that appear in the First Traveling Copy but really none of the improvements. He could remember virtually none of the corrections that appear in the Second Traveling Copy and none of the improvements, not even the changed chapter title.

The corrections and improvements he made in the First Traveling Copy deserve a second look. By and large, the corrections appear in ink. Most are simple. By and large, the improvements appear in pencil. All are important. Many are subtle. It can be strongly argued that, generally speaking, HA made the ink corrections earlier, the pencil improvements later. If so, in 1916—as shown by his annotations in the Substitute Copy (principal source 5)—HA could remember some of his simple early work as corrector-and-improver but lost all memory of his important, often subtle, later work.

In my opinion, this pattern is too manifest and too dismayingly disastrous not to have revealed itself to HA in 1916 as he was reading the Substitute Copy and the Signed Copy (principal sources 5 & 6).

20. Principal source 7.

21. Ibid.

22. HA wished the seals to be respected. See his letter to Rhodes, [24?] May 1916:—". . . I have left with Cabot Lodge a corrected copy for the Hist. Soc., sealed, to protect it in case of trespass."

23. Principal source 4. The letter was first published in 1947. See Cater, 769–70. In his text (769) and in his "Biographical Introduction" (xc), Cater misdated the letter "March 1, 1915." Other writers accepted the mistaken date and repeated it. Examples are Samuels in his *Henry Adams: The Major Phase*, Camb 1964, 560ff, and Munford in the article (1971) cited in note 14, above.

In 1973, Samuels attributed the erroneous date to bad penmanship on HA's part. He told Munford he learned the correct date only after scrutinizing "with a magnifying glass repeatedly" the last digit in HA's "1916." See Howard M. Munford, "A Third Annotated Copy of *THE EDUCATION OF HENRY ADAMS*," MHS *Proceedings*, 85 (1973), 107n2.

The excuse Samuels offered was a poor one. The last digit in HA's "1916" is not hard to read. See the MS. in HA-micro 30. Moreover, an account by Greenslet in his *Under the Bridge/ An Autobiography*, NY & Bost 1943, 144–52, had long since pointed towards 1916 as the correct year; and Cater had cited the account. See his cxvii, note 190. Thus the fault was Cater's (also Samuels's), and not HA's.

24. In the 1950s and 1960s, AT several times told me and my wife about the delivery. Always she said *she* made the delivery to Lodge's house. The point needs notice, for in 1947 Cater had published a different account of what happened. See Cater, xc & cxvii, note 190.

The different account was obtained at two removes. Cater got it from Elsie—Elizabeth Ogden Adams, youngest daughter of CFA2—who, he said, got it from Senator Lodge. (Lodge died on 9 Nov 1924.)

According to the account, HA made the delivery, found Lodge at home, and told him what the packet had in it. The account is very detailed. A speech of HA's to Lodge and a reply of Lodge's to HA are quoted by Cater as if Lodge remembered them word-for-word and could repeat them to Elsie; also as if Elsie two decades later could repeat them word-for-word to Cater for him to take down. That the account is fiction seems not occur to Cater. He passes it off as fact.

His presentation is complicated by his knowledge of a letter from HA to HCL which he says "documents" what Elsie told him she got from Lodge. See Cater, xc. The letter is principal source 4, which Cater misdated "March 15, 1915." See note 23, above.

Cater had found the letter with its envelope and thought the condition of the envelope needed explanation. He offered a theory:—"The letter was found in the Lodge papers, and since the envelope containing it shows no sign of having been mailed, it evidently was placed by Adams in the sealed package. . . ." See Cater, xc–xci.

If he had asked himself about the credibility of the word-for-word speeches he claimed Elsie told him she got from Lodge, and if he had recognized that HA's letter to Lodge was what it says it is, a *covering* letter mainly stating what is in a sealed packet, Cater might have realized that the envelope showed no sign of having been mailed because it and the letter it contained were kept *outside* the packet, to be hand-delivered by someone other than HA.

Clearly the condition of the envelope as reported by Cater in 1947 is supportive of AT's assertions in the 1950s and 1960s that *she* made the delivery. Just as clearly, Cater's theory about the placement of the envelope-and-letter can be set aside as valueless.

25. See note 8, above.

26. I am indebted to the Rare Books Division of the New York Public Library for information about Rives and the conditions imposed by HA. The copy bears no marks by HA.

I infer that HA thought the copy the last in his house from the absence of evidence that he ever again distributed a copy.

Here I do not count the copies later recovered and gave to AT.

27. Principal source 4. The letter has aspects of lesser moment. See L, VI, 725.

28. The argument that HA did not let Lodge see the "Editor's Preface" before sealing it in the packet rests securely on two telling facts.

When he saw it in 1918, the message of the added preface came to Ford as a complete surprise. See Chap. 27.

The covering letter HA sent *outside* the packet (principal source 4) and the "Editor's Preface" HA sent *inside* the packet (principal source 7) flatly contradict each other.

HA wanted Lodge to be deceived while he, HA, continued to live but wanted the world to learn the truth after he was dead. The covering letter was meant for immediate reading by Lodge. It deceived. It said the copy of *The Education* inside the packet was "corrected and prepared for publication." Urgently HA wished Lodge to receive the letter, read it, and believe its misleading message.

The "Editor's Preface" was meant for eventual reading. It told the truth. It said that HA was obliged to permit the publication of his book despite its being "unprepared and unfinished"—"declaredly incomplete"—in short, that the copy in the sealed packet was *not* prepared for publication. So HA made very sure to put the "Editor's Preface" *inside* the packet, preparatory to sealing the packet and sending packet-and-letter to Lodge's house.

29. On the verso of its title-page, the third edition of CFA2's *Autobiography* bears the words "Published March 1916" and the further words "Second Impression, March, 1916/ Third Impression, May, 1916."

30. Principal source 7.

31. The means HA used in the "Editor's Preface" to bring forward the terms "unity" and "multiplicity" was to disguise himself as Lodge and quote from his own book—from Chap. XXIX of *The Education*. Some readers may find this procedure humorous.

32. Principal source 7.

33. That HA in 1916 wrote contradictory documents—principal sources 4 & 7—which said he prepared his *Education* for publication and said he left it unprepared is in my view good evidence that he had strongly wished to create a Publisher's Copy, made one in 1907, turned it into a Master Copy, and failed to make a new Publisher's Copy late in 1912 or thereafter mainly because much affected—and perhaps discouraged—by the loss of the *Titanic* and his month-long collapse.

I believe this evidence underpins my otherwise minimally supported assertion that HA in 1912 hid both his Master Copy and an Attendant Clean Copy that he hoped he might turn into a Publisher's Copy.

34. In my estimation, whatever HA would not reveal to EC he would be even surer not to reveal to AT.

Hindsight confirms me in this judgment. When I consider all that AT ever told me she knew about the privately-printed copies of *The Education*, I am most impressed by how little she knew, how little her curiosity was roused, and how little she must have been told.

35. Villard to Ford, 6 Mar 1916, FP 27.

36. Ford to Villard, 8 Mar 1916, FP 27.

37. EC to HA, 12 Jun 1916.

38. HA to EC, 28 Mar 1916.

39. HA to EC, 28 Mar 1916; HA to EC, 23 & 25 Apr 1916.

40. HA to EC, 1 Jun 1916.

41. EC to HA, 23–24 May 1916.

42. AT several times told me that HA made the prophecy but did not recall whether he made it immediately after the outbreak of war or somewhat later.

43. HA to Gaskell, 18 Mar 1916. Also see HA to EC, 1 Jul 1916:—"I sit dumb and green with fear."

44. HA to Ford, 12 Aug 1916, FP 27. With the permission of the Manuscripts & Archives Division, New York Public Library, the letter is published here for the first time,

45. HA to CMG, 3 Oct 1916; HA to EC, 2 Nov 1916.

46. HA to EC, 3 Jan 1917. Drives were a necessity, not a pleasure. On 29 Feb 1952 after a talk with AT, I wrote a note:—"Adams especially hated the idea of being read to, and taking carriage drives, and had to submit to both." During later talks, AT said that the worst aspect of the drives, when long continued, was lack of new places to go.

47. HA to EC, 3 Jan 1917. Evidence that HA attached great importance to his friendship with the envoy leads me to assume that the lunches were restricted to the persons named and that Elsie did not appear.

48. When telling me and my wife about this success, AT did not date it. She only said she made her effort during a drive and after keeping silent for a very long time.

When describing HA's loquacity about his wife, AT imitated his voice and invented remarks of the sort she said he made. Each remark contained the words "your Aunt Clover."

49. HA to EC per AT, 1 Feb 1917.

50. HA to EC per AT, 1 Mar 1917.

51. Ibid.

52. AT to LHT, 5 Mar 1917. The letter is one of a series from AT to LHT which LHT in the 1960s gave me permission to copy and which both AT and LHT gave me permission to quote.

53. After a talk with AT on 29 Feb 1952, I wrote a summary of things she had said:—"Adams was especially standoffish with intellectually pretentious people. . . . When French doctors came to meals, he would speak English, and force them to speak bad English in return, though his French was excellent. He would not place himself in a disadvantageous position."

54. I am not suggesting that HA gives a true account of their efforts in *The Education*. I only suggest that he knew the truth; that no one else did, Hay being gone; and that his knowledge must have helped him decide how much to say and not say in his book about a subject he knew was fraught with problems. Also see note 61, below.

55. HA to EC per AT, 7 May 1917.

56. HA to EC per AT, 2 Jun 1917.

57. HA to CMG per AT, 8 Jun 1917. HA apparently viewed the building of the Community of Atlantic Powers as partly a result of strenuous exertions by American and British leaders. In the same letter, he said, ". . . we have established one great idea even though we have pulled all the stars out of their courses in order to do it."

58. HA to Henry Watkins Anderson, 17 Jul 1916, L, VI, 735.

59. EC to HA, 16 Mar 1916.

60. HA-1, 364.

61. I have limited to one sentence this statement of the object HA set himself when working with Hay because I think the subject so complex that I should try to deal with it only in broadest outline.

62. I believe the best evidence of HA's outlook is the last phrase in the last sentence of his last letter to CMG, sent 19 Feb 1918. The phrase also appears as the title of this narrative.

63. HA to EC per AT, 5 Sep [1917].

64. Ibid.

65. MHA's fineries later became the property of Louisa Hooper Thoron. She left them to her daughter, Faith Thoron Knapp. At her home in Cazenovia, NY, Mrs. Knapp showed me many of them, notably the dress, which is valuable in part for indicating MHA's measurements.

66. For grounds underlying this inferential account of the recovery of the Master Copy and Attendant Clean Copy, see Chap. 27, note 113.

67. AT told Cater about the moment in the 1940s. She repeatedly told me and my wife about it in the 1950s and 1960s. In this paragraph with one exception, I rely upon the story as presented in Cater, cv–cvi, which comports exactly with what AT told me and my wife. The exception concerns Cater's date. He says the dinner took place "just after the United States entered the war"; i.e. in April 1917.

I am sure his date is mistaken. To me it seems a guess that Cater impulsively set down and was not circumspect enough to erase. It is rendered implausible by the standard work on Lodge, which says the senator was supportive of President Wilson for an interval after the declaration of war. See Garraty, 336.

When telling me and my wife about the moment, AT did not supply a date and only indicated that the moment occurred while the United States was a participant in the war. The approximate November date suggested here is supported by *dated* evidence supplied by HA about a November dinner at which Lodge was present. For additional dated evidence, see note 69, below.

68. *HUS* (Scribner), VIII, 308; (LoA), II, 1122. The visitor was George Ticknor.

69. An echo of the moment seems to be audible in HA's letter to Mabel La Farge per AT, 14 Dec [1917], L, VI, 774–75. In the letter, HA says he is "buffeted from morning till night by no thought except war or the quarrels and suspicions and *treasons* which are supposed to be the result of our corrupt nature [italics added]."

70. Loring to HA, [c. 12 Dec 1917], filmed in HA-micro 31 at the start of December.

71. For details concerning AT's disclosures to other persons about her owning the copies, see Chap. 27.

72. For further details about the Master Copy as remembered by AT, see Chap. 27.

73. HA to EC per AT, 2 Nov 1917.

74. EC to HA, 16 Nov 1917, 20 Dec 1917.

75. In the 1950s and 1960s, when telling me and my wife about the occasion, AT emphasized that HA answered the bell.

76. HA to EC per AT, 1 Feb 1918.

77. AT to LHT, 26 Jan 1918. See note 52, above.

78. HA to CMG per AT, 19 Feb 1918.

79. AT to LHT, 20 Feb [1918]. See note 52, above.

80. Ibid.

81. Ibid.

82. Ibid.

83. HA's remark about Mabel's respect for the conversation can seem to

imply that others at the table—he himself, AT, and perhaps Elizabeth Hoyt—felt little or no respect for the parts of the conversation that Lodge contributed.

84. HA to Thayer per AT, 21 Feb [1918].

85. The copy evidently remained under Greenslet's guardianship at the Houghton Mifflin office.

86. HA to Jameson, 2 May 1910.

87. HA to Thayer per AT, 15 Mar [1918]—the last known letter by HA. It is partly valuable for his saying that, by writing and distributing his *Letter to American Teachers of History*, he hoped to initiate "some sort of open alliance or still opener antagonism" between America's historians and "the biologists of the Jacques Loeb type."

88. Ibid.

89. When preparing to write the "Biographical Introduction" to his *Henry Adams and His Friends* (1947), Harold Dean Cater noticed that there was a lack of evidence concerning the last weeks of HA's life. By means of interviews, he tried to develop an account of the last weeks and especially of the day and evening before HA's death. The result was a paragraph beginning, "On the twenty-first of March, 1918. . . ." See Cater, cvi. While some of the less important assertions in the paragraph may be credible, or not obviously incredible, statements appear in it that would be very important if true but in my view are surely false.

The paragraph is supported—attemptedly—by a note (cxviii, note 206): "Unless otherwise indicated, the material in the remainder of this essay was furnished by Miss Tone."

One notices the following passage: "On the afternoon of Wednesday, March 26, Spring-Rice and some other friends dropped in and they had a long talk about the war. . . ."

On 26 Mar 1918, Spring Rice had been dead for six weeks. Since his death was forcibly impressed on AT at the time it occurred and during a funeral service in Washington, I disbelieve Cater's claim that AT was his source for the passage.

One especially notices the following sentences:—"The battle of the Marne depressed everyone, but Adams seemed to suffer from it more than any of his friends. He was convinced that the Germans would defeat the allies and his worst fears—the débâcle itself—the final chaos he found in his studies, but had refused to believe—would all be realized."

Since HA's letters provide powerful evidence that he anticipated Germany's *defeat*, I disbelieve Cater's claim to the contrary. I also disbelieve the depiction of HA as "convinced that . . . his worst fears —the débâcle itself—the final chaos . . . would all be realized."

The picture presented is one of a Henry Adams who did not exist in 1918, yet in the 1940s could seem to have then existed, but only in the mind of a researcher impressed by misleading publications for which Brooks Adams was responsible and sufficiently rattled by fears of Nazi victory in World War II to impose his fears on the victim he had chosen as his biographical subject. The inventor of the false statements in Cater's account very obviously was Cater, yielding to imagination and willingness to say things he did not know.

27. SINS OF THE HEIRS

PRINCIPAL SOURCES

(1) originals & carbons of eighty-two selected letters & two telegrams, HCL to Ford, 27 Mar 1918–10 Oct 1924, LP 104 & FP 67.

(2) originals & carbons of thirty-nine selected letters, Ford to HCL, 28 Mar 1918–26 Sep 1924, FP 67 & LP 104.

(3) [HA], "Editor's Preface"—copy typed by Ford, revised by Ford & HCL, separately filed, MHS.

(4) photocopies of all annotated pages of *The Education of Henry Adams*, Wash (privately printed) 1907—the Abernethy copy, known here also as HA's Substitute Copy, (Courtesy of Abernethy Library, Middlebury College)

(5) [HA], *The Education of Henry Adams*, Wash (privately printed) 1907— the Thayer copy, MHS; known here also as HA's First Traveling Copy.

(6) [HA], "THE RULE OF PHASE/ APPLIED TO HISTORY"—BA's 32-page typed copy; originally stored in HAP, Misc. Box 2; not filmed in HA-micro Misc.; separately filed, MHS.

(7) HA, *A Letter to American Teachers of History*, Wash (privately printed) 1910—HA's copy, MHS, with insertions by him on pp. 12, 84, 106, 132, 172, 194 & 201.

(8) [HA], *The Education of Henry Adams/ An Autobiography*, Bost & NY 1918—the first published edition.

(9) *The Degradation of the Democratic Dogma/ by Henry Adams/ with an introduction by/ Brooks Adams*, NY 1919.

(10) HA, *The Tendency of History*, NY: Macmillan, 1928; also NY: Book League of America, 1929.

LESSER SOURCES; CITATIONS; COMMENTS

1. *Egisto Fabbri/ 1866–1933, with a memoir by Mabel La Farge*, New Haven (privately printed} 1937, 43–44—hereafter cited as *Fabbri*.

In 1952, soon after I and my wife met AT, I became aware that a book bound in blue and titled *Egisto Fabbri* in gold was on a top shelf in her living room. AT never mentioned the book to us, but she told us she had taken books from HA's library after his death, and she showed us those that most interested her. In 1969, after her death, I secured permission from her executor to take away the fifteen books that had belonged to HA. For reasons given in this chapter, I shrank from asking for the book titled *Egisto Fabbri*.

In 1987, I bought a copy from a dealer. I have since realized that the book is more relevant to AT than it may seem. E.g. the book documents Fabbri's support of the effort made by an American, Justine Ward, to teach European children to sing medieval music. AT too was supportive of Ms. Ward's effort. During her last years, she played for me and my wife a recording of music sung at Mont Saint Michel in 1966 by 3,800 *"écolliers-ward"* at the *"Premiere Manifestation du Millenaire en l'Eglise Abbatiale."* In 1969, her executor let me have the recording, in addition to the fifteen books.

2. AT never said to me and my wife that she sang at a Fabbri benefit, but when we first knew her she mentioned that while HA was alive she once sang medieval songs at a place in America other than his house.

With heavy emphasis, she went on to say that HA urged her *never* to commercialize their work as recoverers of medieval music—*never* to make it pay. I assume that HA expressed this idea to her just before she left for New York or just after her return, and I believe that singing at the benefit came near enough to money-earning to make her take his stricture everlastingly to heart.

For an example of her supporting a non-commercial enterprise late in life, see Chap. 25, note 25, above.

3. The nieces who discovered that HA had died wrote accounts of his death in four letters still extant: AT to Mabel La Farge, Good Friday [29 Mar 1918], Cater, 778–79; Elizabeth Hoyt to "Dilly" [i.e. EC], 1 Apr 1918, HA-micro 31; typed copy of AT to Thwing, n.d. (1? Apr 1918), FP 29; Elizabeth Adams to CMG, 6 Apr 1918, HA-micro 31 & Ford, II, 650–51. A fifth account, evidently based on information provided by AT and Elizabeth Hoyt, appears in Mary Jones's letter to EC, 19 Apr 1918, HA-micro 31.

My account of HA's death, begun in Chap. 26 and completed here, is based on their five accounts and treats them as collectively true.

Their accounts agree in many respects, differ in others. Mrs. Jones's account alone states time of death: ". . . the doctor seemed to think he died in his sleep about seven. . . ." AT's account to Thwing divulges something the others suppress: the stain on HA's head and face. Elizabeth Hoyt's account debates the question of a noise. "Aileen thinks she heard Dordy moving about his room earlier in the morning, and thought he may have gotten up & feeling badly had gone back to bed. Personally I am inclined to think that it was something else she heard. I don't believe he got up at all or felt any sensations of illness."

4. This was one of the first recollections AT imparted to me and wife when accepting us as friends in 1951–1952. Her imparting it made us feel she had unexpected secrets to tell. She later told us other secrets, but an extremely long time passed before I began to realize that the disclosures she evidently most cared about were parts of a unified story.

5. Cater, civ.

6. *Family Vista/ the memoirs of Margaret Chanler Aldrich*, New York 1958, 194–95. Mrs. Aldrich attended the funeral. She says in her account that she later asked Dr. Smith why he read the psalms in a Puritan version and learned from him that he chose the version himself when readying the service for CFA2; also that Elsie had told him that, after the service for CFA2, when walking back to 1603 H Street, she was told by HA that he wanted the same service for himself.

I disbelieve this account as it relates to a request by HA. The account conflicts with AT's saying that HA did not attend CFA2's funeral. See Chap. 25.

I believe Elsie needed a justification for arranging a service for HA and also needed a means of linking HA satisfyingly to her father. I infer that she met both her needs by inventing a story about HA and telling it to Dr. Smith.

7. Elizabeth Hoyt to EC, 1 Apr 1918, HA-micro 31.

8. Elsie may have phoned.

9. In my opinion, Lodge's writings subsequent to November 1917 are untrustworthy at points as they relate to HA and AT. I especially disbelieve his account of the discovery of HA's death.

Lodge says the maid heard HA "get up and go into his bath room to take his bath." But did *anyone* hear HA go to his bathroom?

The nieces evidently slept one floor below HA in the best bedrooms in the house. AT slept in the room originally intended for HA, to the east on the front. I believe one cannot assume that Mary Baily, the maid, was in a better position than AT to hear HA get up, if he did get up; and what AT reportedly thought she heard was only HA's "moving about his room"—i.e. *within* his room. See note 3, above.

A speculative explanation of Lodge's account can be offered, as follows. Elsie told Lodge that AT believed she heard HA move about his room. One of the unfortunate effects of the terrible moment at HA's dinner table in November 1917 was that Lodge wished no longer to acknowledge AT as a reality in

HA's life. Accordingly when writing to Ford, he transformed AT to "the maid." After making one change, Lodge made more. He had HA go to the bathroom to take his bath. Elaborations were needed. Spinners of fictions hope that fiction will seem less like fiction if swelled with "facts."

A more overt instance of Lodge's erasing AT appears in the body of this chapter.

10. In response to this passage, Ford asked Lodge to write a statement about his friendship with HA, to be read on Lodge's behalf at the next meeting of the Society. Lodge sent one. See HCL to Ford, 4 Apr 1918, FP 67, beginning, "I cannot be present. . . ." While admirable for much that it says about HA, Lodge's statement can be faulted for seeming to imply that HA never ceased to value Lodge as a friend. The truth was otherwise. The senator may not have known it or wished he did not know it, but HA wholly lost his early good opinion of Lodge.

11. This important passage states Lodge's belief that, by means of a letter to him dated 1 Mar 1916, HA had given ownership of *The Education* and *Mont Saint Michel and Chartres* to the Massachusetts Historical Society and had given him, Lodge, exclusive control of the former book's publication. For Lodge's later assertion of ownership of *The Education* solely by himself, see carbon of HCL to Ford, 26 Apr 1918, LP 104.

12. Ford to HCL, 28 Mar 1918, LP 104. Lodge did not return the letter. When Cater learned of it in the mid-1940s, the letter, with envelope, was in the Lodge Papers. See Cater, xci, misdating the letter 1 Mar 1915. At a later time by an unknown process, the letter drifted to the Henry Adams Papers. See HA-micro 30.

13. Ford to HCL, 28 Mar 1918, LP 104:—"Friend he was; for he came of his own accord . . . when I was in the Treasury Department, and when I needed some friendly recognition and encouragement. . . . There was no one in Washington like him. . . ."

14. Ford to HCL, 1 Apr 1918, LP 104.

15. Greenslet to Ford, 1 Apr 1918, FP 67.

16. Principal source 3.

17. Ford to HCL, 1 Apr 1918, LP 104.

18. Ibid. In the right margin of p. 67 in the sealed copy (principal source 4), Ford had written question marks opposite "Sinfony" and "*Haus-fraus.*"

19. The evidence that the copy was destroyed is its disappearance from the Society's shelves and records.

20. Principal source 4, 446.

21. As this chapter shows, Ford later wrote to Thayer as if he shared Thayer's opinion. Also see Greenslet to Ford, 17 Jul 1918, FP 30:— ". . . Thayer turned his copy over to you to print from. . . ."

22. Principal source 5. I believe that Ford quickly noticed the second hand-writing because in a parallel situation I did so myself. Out of respect for the copy's importance, I avoided asking the Massachusetts Historical Society to permit me to see the "Thayer copy"—HA's First Traveling Copy—until August 1987. By then I had become the owner of HA's Second Traveling Copy and was accustomed to studying marks made by HA when correcting and improving his *Education.*

Very soon after opening the First Traveling Copy, I realized that its text was marked in two handwritings: a form of HA's (sometimes in ink, sometimes in pencil) and a different handwriting (always in ink). The presence of a second handwriting surprised me, for in his attemptedly definitive edition of *The Education*, Bost 1974, Ernest Samuels had listed all the annotations in the text of the Thayer copy as "revisions and corrections made by Henry Adams." See 519, opening words of Appendix B.

That Samuel failed in this respect can seem unaccountable. The handwritings in the Thayer copy are glaringly different. Samuels similarly failed to notice that three annotations in principal source 4—HA's Substitute Copy—are in a second handwriting, Ford's.

23. Three and a half months later, Greenslet informed Ford that Jameson had visited the Houghton Mifflin office and asked "whether we were using in the printing of 'The Education of Henry James [*sic*]' the corrigenda covering certain mis-prints which he discovered and sent us about two years ago." Greenslet added, "Our memory is that we entered them in pencil in Mr. Thayer's copy of 'The Edu[c]ation. . . .'" See Greenslet to Ford, 17 Jul 1918, FP 30.

Greenslet's words "in pencil" are erroneous. The corrections were made in ink.

Greenslet's words "we entered them" are ambiguous. They may mean either that the corrections were entered by Thayer or that they were entered by a Houghton Mifflin employee.

The information that it was Jameson who discovered the necessity of the intruded corrections brings an interesting fact into play. In 1918 in one way or another, the following persons were related to *The Education of Henry Adams*: HA, CFA2, Jameson, Ford, and Thayer. The first three had been presidents of the American Historical Association in 1893–1894, 1901, and 1907. Ford had been president for 1917. The incumbent president was Thayer.

24. Principal source 5. By my count, there are 199 annotations in the text of the copy brought to Ford by Thayer—the First Traveling Copy. 178 are in HA's handwriting. Of these, 166 correct or improve the text. 12 are references in the margins to works by other writers. By my count, there are 21 annotations *not* in HA's handwriting. Of these, 20 correct misspellings. One corrects mistaken punctuation.

25. On page 430 of principal source 5—the First Traveling Copy—HA indicates in the margin that a phrase, "perhaps no more than," should be inserted in the text but fails to indicate where the phrase is to go. This is one of many instances of his cutting corners when making improvements in his First and Second Traveling Copies.

In my view, his cutting corners in the copies is good evidence that he considered an improvement made only after he had entered it in final form in his Master Copy.

26. In their letters, Thayer, Greenslet, and Ford never explicitly mention the references in the margins of the First Traveling Copy. The three men seem not to have wanted to learn why HA wrote them.

27. Charles Sumner's surname appears 87 times in *The Education*. In the text as privately printed, the name was spelled correctly 77 times and misspelled 10 times as "Summer." In Thayer's copy, by my count, HA had corrected five of the misspellings on page 219 and let the others stand uncorrected on pages 94, 105, and 228. As Ford could see, the five misspellings HA failed to correct were corrected in the second handwriting by someone else. Ford could see as well that many other misspellings ("Appenines," "Cherburg," "La Marck," and "Nietshe" are examples) were corrected in the second handwriting. He could not infer from this evidence that HA had been incapable of correcting the mis-

spellings. He knew that HA, both before his illness and for a considerable time thereafter, was as capable a corrector of texts as anyone who could be found. E.g. see HA's corrections in his copy of *Mont-Saint-Michel and Chartres*, Bost & NY 1913, MHS.

Given time to think, Ford might perhaps have inferred that HA in places left words misspelled in Thayer's copy because he had already corrected them in another copy—i.e. an actual master copy.

The essential point is that Lodge, Ford, Thayer, and Greenslet knew nothing about the method HA devised for himself when correcting and improving his *Education* and were in too much haste to try to learn what the method must have been.

28. Thayer to Ford, 3 Apr 1918, FP 30.

29. HCL to Ford, 4 Apr 1918, FP 67.

30. Four letters, HCL to Ford, 30 Mar, 4 Apr, 5 Apr & 6 Apr 1918, FP 67; & carbon copy, HCL to Ford, 8 Apr 1918, LP 104.

31. Carbon copy, Ford to Lodge, 8 Apr 1918, FP 67.

32. In his own copy, now at Harvard, Ford duplicated marks he found in Thayer's copy and marks that appear in Bancroft's copy, now at Columbia. The errors Bancroft detected were few. Rather than send Ford his copy, he may have sent a list.

33. Ford to HCL, 29 Apr 1918, LP 104.

34. As published, the book bore the legend "An Autobiography" where it would be most visible: on the title page and on the backstrip. The legend was omitted on the front cover and on the half title page.

35. BA to Ford, 19 Apr 1918, FP 30.

36. HCL to Ford, 26 Apr 1918, FP 67.

37. HCL to Ford, 27 Apr 1918, FP 67. Lodge seems to have obtained the exact advice he wanted.

38. AT may already have left Washington. If not, she left very soon.

39. Greenslet to Ford, 30 Apr 1918, FP 30.

40. HCL to Ford, 1 May 1918, FP 67.

41. The list is filed at MHS with Ford's typed copy of HA's "Editor's Preface" (principal source 3). According to my identifications of the handwritings in the Thayer copy at MHS (principal source 5), 15 of the 28 entries on Ford's list reflect misspellings Jameson had noticed and asked Houghton Mifflin Company to correct. See note 23, above.

42. Carbon copy, Ford to Thayer, 3 May 1918, FP 30.

43. Principal source 5, inscription on its flyleaf dated 5 May 1918, written & signed by Thayer:—". . . from/ Henry Adams/ Washington/ January 1914./ Given by me to the Massachusetts Historical Society, in exchange for another copy."

44. Lodge corrected an error concerning the place where a codfish was displayed in the Massachusetts legislature and an error concerning the place where he himself was married. See *EHA* (1907), 37 & 309; *EHA* (1918), 46 & 353. Also see HCL to Ford, 15 Jun 1918, FP 67.

45. Letters, HCL to Ford, 18 Jul 1918 & 1 Aug 1918, FP 67.

46. BA to Ford, 20 Jun 1918, FP 30. It did not trouble BA that HA in his late books had presented no hard-and-fast theory about history or anything else and instead brought forward a wide range of theories, some devised by himself, most by other writers.

47. BA to Ford, 27 Aug 1918, FP 30.

48. Warren to Ford, 18 Oct 1918, FP 29; Ford to HCL, 29 Jun 1918, LP 104.

49. *The Piper*, issue subtitled *Contents October, 1918*, FP 29. The announcement continues by saying that HA's book might just as well be fiction. "He [HA] tells the whole story in the third person, as if Henry Adams were not himself, but a hero of fiction. . . . He tells it, however, with a vividness and freshness of detail which makes the book as fascinating to read as any novel."

50. The figures given are based on my own reading of the Thayer copy and are tentative only as they relate to the few instances in which the handwritings are hard to distinguish.

51. With the help of Samuels's attemptedly definitive edition (Tables 3 & 4 where accurate), contemporary letters between Lodge and Ford, the annotations in Ford's copy of *The Education* at Harvard, those in Bancroft's copy at Columbia, and my own findings here and there in Houghton Mifflin's 1918 edition, I have listed 113 such changes. My guess is that a word-by-word comparison of the 1907 printing and the 1918 edition would reveal other changes worth knowing about, but I think my present list is long enough to represent fairly well what was good and what bad about Ford's work.

52. By my count, 34 of the 39 changes correct indubitable errors of wording, spelling, punctuation, or fact. The other five are parts of a reversal by Ford of HA's misidentification of Willard Gibbs as Wolcott Gibbs. This reversal is similar to the one HA achieved in his Second Traveling Copy, to which Ford did not have access.

53. Ford's corrections of HA's spellings are offset by a gratuitous injury. He changed HA's correct "oneself" to an incorrect "one's self." See *EHA* (1907), 116, line 29; (1918), 135.

54. An especially wrong-headed and high-handed change made by Ford was his substitution of "Socrates" for "Sophocles" in a passage about "the merits of silence" in Chap. XXIII. See *EHA* (1907), 313; (1918), 358.

One of the few merits of Samuels's attemptedly definitive edition, op. cit., is its restoration of readings that Ford had rejected.

55. The comment is quoted in a Houghton Mifflin advertisement of the book that Ford clipped from a newspaper (not identified). See FP 29.

56. BA to Brett, 24 Dec 1919, MP 49.

57. Principal source 6.

58. Carbon copy, Ford to HCL, 21 Nov 1918, FP 67.

59. HCL to Ford, 23 Nov 1918, FP 67. In the letter, Lodge mentions that he has "never seen" HA's reported "essay on 'Phase in History.'"

I find it very hard to imagine that Richards would have offered the opinion Lodge reports him to have offered if four conditions were different: if HA were alive, if HA and Richards were face to face, if Richards read the books about thermodynamics that HA is known to have assembled, and if Richards read carefully the direct quotation from Lord Kelvin that appears in HA's *Letter*, 3–4.

As for the opinion Lodge reports Thayer to have offered, perhaps the less said the better.

60. Greenslet to Ford, 22 Nov 1919, FP 30:—". . . [I] wanted to publish the Letter to Teachers and had considered Senator Lodge's objection . . . ill-founded. I gather that you . . . agreed with me. . . ." Also see letters BA to Ford, 14 Apr 1920 & 20 Apr 1920, FP 31.

61. Carbon copy, Ford to HCL, 21 Nov 1918, FP 67.

62. HCL to Ford, 10 Jan 1920, FP 67. Levenson and his associates published 83 letters from HA to Lodge in L, I–VI and none in the *Supplement*. They pub-

lished 29 letters to Mrs. Lodge in L, I–VI and 27 in the *Supplement*, for a total of 56. Thus, if Lodge was more or less right in saying that the letters to his wife were "equal in number" to those to himself, roughly 27 letters from HA to Mrs. Lodge appear to have been destroyed.

63. Brett had agreed to publish HA's *Letter* on condition that the book be given a title that would "more sufficiently indicate its contents." See carbon copy, Brett to HA, 4 Apr 1910, MP 49.

64. BA to Brett, 10 Dec 1918, MP 49.

65. BA to Brett, 14 Dec 1918, MP 49.

66. Principal source 6, 32.

67. Mabel La Farge to Ford, 11 Dec 1918, FP 31.

68. In a letter, 10 Mar 1920, Misc. Personal Papers, Manuscripts & Archives Division, NYPL, Mabel asks Ford, ". . . will you kindly correct it [i.e. the "Prayer" in printed proof] from the manuscript?"

69. *Fabbri*, 49.

70. Ibid., 52.

71. Carbon copy, Ford to HCL, 13 Jan 1920, FP 67.

72. Mabel La Farge to Ford, 25 Mar 1920, Misc. Personal Papers, Manuscripts & Archives Division, NYPL.

73. See the sequence of contents in *Letters to a Niece and Prayer to the Virgin of Chartres/ by Henry Adams/ with a Niece's Memories by Mabel La Farge*, Bost & NY 1920.

74. Ford to HCL, 11 Jun 1920, LP 104.

75. Ibid. For authoritative information about the murder of Paul and Malcolm's suicide, see L. H. Butterfield, "Worthington Chauncey Ford, Editor," MHS *Proceedings*, 83–84 (1971), 57.

76. Brett to BA, 20 Dec 1918, CFA2P 34.

77. Principal source 7. HA's changes in the *Letter* more completely illustrate some points in the argument but do not change it.

78. BA to Brett, 20 Dec 1918, MP 49.

79. James Donald Cameron died on 30 Aug 1918, aged eighty-five.

80. Recollections of Henry S. Sherman, August 1956.

81. Draft, Ford to EC, 10 Feb [19]19, FP 31.

82. In her reply to Ford, 2 Mar 1919, FP 31, EC offered a comment:—". . . this is the moment when public interest is awakened to the fact that a great man lived close by, unrecognized and almost unknown."

83. On the back of EC's letter giving her collection to the Society, Ford wrote a note: "The mss. were given to the Adams Collection, not the Mass. Hist. Socy." See EC to Ford, 15 Mar 1920, FP 58.

84. Copy of letter, EC to Huntington Cairns, 9 Jan 1930, FP 55.

85. Frederic Bancroft sketched the problem. See Bancroft to Ford, 10 May 1920, FP 36:—"What his [HA's] best fame needs is a thorough study of the man *and his whole work* by someone with both admiration and a critical faculty [italics added]."

86. BA to Brett, 10 Dec 1918, MP 49.

87. *Degradation*, 1.

88. Ford to BA, 21 Apr 1919, filed with principal source 6, MHS.

89. The typed version Ford supplied to Macmillan was evidently used in printing and then destroyed.

90. Bumstead to Ford, 3 May 1919, HAL; Ford to BA, 5 May 1919, HAL; BA to Bumstead, 8 May 1919, CaterP.

The decision to correct HA's supposed "error" rested on a false assumption that his paper was uncomical and mathematically solemn. A far truer assumption would have taken the paper to be farcical and all the better for waving a mis-chosen formula before the reader's eyes.

To see BA's doctoring, compare all that follows "simple formula" and ends with "square of the time" in principal source 6, page 24, lines 23–24, with all that follows "simple formula" and ends with "centre of the sun" in *Degradation*, page 30l, lines 19–22.

91. BA to Brett, 12 Dec 1918; Brett to BA, 13 Dec 1918; BA to Brett, 20 Dec 1918—all in MP 49.

92. Three letters, BA to Brett, 17 Apr, 29 Jul, & 31 Jul 1919, MP 49.

93. [CFA, CFA2 & HA], *A Cycle/ of Adams Letters/ 1861–1865*, Bost & NY 1920.

94. For a contemporary reaction, see Frederic Bancroft to Ford, 7 Jan 1921, FP 37: "The volumes are indeed a very important demonstration of our friend's [CFA2's] rugged and manly character." Bancroft says too that the volumes reveal an "unfortunate early weakness" in HA that "became more and more a ruling passion." The "weakness" he had in mind perhaps was HA's resorting, when possible, to anonymity.

95. *Fabbri*, 60–61. Fabbri had shown an aptitude for understanding the problems that *The Education* puts before a reader. He had asked Mabel (ibid., 52) whether the "Dynamic Theory of History" outlined near the end of the book was intended by HA to be taken as only "suggestive," rather than as straightforwardly declarative.

96. *Fabbri*, 80.

97. Ibid., 81.

98. Ibid., 91.

99. Sales were sufficient to require a second printing.

100. Anonymous review, NYTimes, 20 Jun 1920, preserved by Ford, FP 41.

101. The first two chapters bore the titles HA had given the two chapters of his book, *A Letter to American Teachers of History*. Macmillan's editors retained the chapters with their titles but deleted the title and date of the book, thus concealing the *book's* existence! Moreover, by dating their concocted *three*-chapter work as finished on 1 Jan 1909, they falsified the date of its Chaps. I and II, which were first printed in 1910.

102. A rough Shakespearean equivalent would be a single work made up of the folio text of *King Lear* (without its title) and the first quarto of *Hamlet* (complete) under an easy-to-read title, *The Tragedy of Romeo and Juliet*.

103. HA2 to Ford, 12 Nov 1929, FP 55.

104. Carbon copy, Ford to HA2, 5 Dec 1929, FP 55.

105. HA2 to Ford, 14 May 1937, FP 59.

106. When studying evidence relating to HA during the summer of 1955 at the Massachusetts Historical Society, I arranged to submit questions that would be put to HA's aged nephew Henry while I listened to his answers. My first question concerned the whereabouts of HA's Paris library, which seemed to have disappeared. I heard HA2 say in answer that, as a means of preventing the complete dispersal of the library among members of the Adams family, he arranged to have the remaining books put up for auction so that he could anonymously buy them all. He seemed to indicate that he remained their owner when he spoke.

At the time, I did not have knowledge enough to ask a follow-up question:

whether the books he bought included an annotated copy of his uncle's *Education*. Such a question might have opened a way to the Society's effecting an early recovery of HA's Second Traveling Copy.

107. The secret of the engagement was so deep that Mabel La Farge never learned it. Source: information from her daughter-in-law, Mrs. Henry Adams La Farge, May 1998.

108. *Fabbri*, 96.

109. Ibid., 101, 103.

110. AT told Louis Auchincloss the story of her broken engagement in a way that included the details given here about her being on a train scheduled to proceed to Rome, her being intercepted by one of Egisto's sisters when the train reached Florence, the place of the talk with the sister, and Aileen's staying on the train. Auchincloss kindly confirmed these details to me by telephone on 28 Jan 1998.

In 1952–1953, AT had told me and my wife the story in very general terms. (She included the detail about the French word "*dot*.")

In 1962, AT had told me and wife the story again, this time in much greater detail, yet still in a way that left much out.

Until Auchincloss told me the story as AT more fully told it to him, I had no idea where the engagement was broken or what AT did after the break occurred. I consider these additions important.

111. En route to Maine, AT wrote a letter to me, Sunday, [June 1962], beginning: "Just a word—to tell you that my letter to the Principessa Caffarelli is on its way to Rome— But [—] as I wrote—my mind was counting the stretch of years since my last visit to that lovely Baggazzano [*sic*]—and the book was left there in 1927!! Is there any chance of its survival? Let us hope! [—] books *do* survive!"

112. Tecla [Caffarelli] to AT, 16 Aug [1962], in my collection. The letters begins: "You can't imagine how pleased I was to hear from you after all these years. I will certainly look for the book . . . at Bagazzano when I go there in the autumn. The library there has become very large. . . ."

113. I should explain that my principal interest is in great stories. I have studied HA and written about him because I believe he enacted one of America's greatest stories by managing to initiate and complete three great lives in one long lifetime.

I want to mention also that my work was helped in its early stage by a succession of personal favors so advantageous to me that I have never ceased being amazed by their occurrence.

In 1945 at the Twentieth Air Force Headquarters on Guam, I became friendly with a fellow sergeant, William Goldsmith. He learned that, when I was not at work as an Air Force historian, I was studying HA materials I had brought with me to the western Pacific. He told me that, at the first chance after the war, he would introduce me to a direct descendant of CFA2.

In December 1945, Goldsmith invited me to meet him and Mrs. Lewis Teague, originally Mary Abbott, in New York at P. J. Clarke's Bar on Third Avenue at 55 Street. Mary had been told about my interest in her great-great-uncle. While we leaned over a checked tablecloth and drank beer, Mary told me I had to marry a friend of hers, a fellow artist who was collecting and reading HA books, Eleni Petrou.

Soon Mary and her husband invited me to dinner at their apartment on Spring Street. The other guest was Eleni Petrou. Later that night she and I walked to her apartment house on Commerce Street. She asked me to come upstairs. When I saw her HA books, shelved just inside the door of her apartment, I noticed that in some cases her copies were better than those I had been able to obtain. I remarked, "We'll have to get married."

We did, and later Eleni introduced me to a Russian friend of hers, Svetlana Alexieff, who in Paris had married an American our age, Paul Rockwell. It eventually developed that Paul had a friend, Benjamin Tone, who was Aileen Tone's great nephew. Paul introduced us to Ben, and Ben firmly instructed me to telephone his great-aunt with his backing and ask her to let me and Eleni visit her at her apartment. I did as directed. A maid answered, Miss Tone came to the phone, heard what I had to say about Ben, and said she no longer gave interviews. When I promised that I would not ask questions, she somewhat relented. When I asked whether my wife could come, she gave way entirely and named a time. I believe Ben's support made the needed difference.

When we paid our visit, AT and Eleni became intimates at once. I kept my promise and did not ask questions.

Very soon Eleni and I got a call from Mary's aunt, Mrs. George Grinnell, arranging for us to take an apartment at 140 East 83 Street. Our new home looked across the street to AT's windows.

During our innumerable later meetings with AT, I continued not to ask questions about HA. The result was a phenomenon which I have come fully to appreciate only after long experience of its effects.

The phenomenon was very simple. AT talked to Eleni and me about HA only when she wished to do so and practically always about matters relating to HA that interested her very strongly.

The things she told us were in one way troublesome. They seemed miscellaneous. They did not appear to connect with one another.

After her death, I very gradually began to sense that the things she told us were parts of a disassembled story.

At last I began to assemble it. It grew evident that one part, perhaps the central part, was missing—was left untold. Finally I realized that the part she never told could be inferred from the many that she did tell.

The never-told part was her and HA's recovery of his Master Copy of *The Education* and the Attendant Clean Copy late in 1917, followed by HA's giving her both copies with a request that she take them to New York and not read either copy till after he was dead.

The main things that permitted my making this complex inference are the following.

—AT told us that, when she began to live with him, HA required that she not have, read, or talk about his books while she continued to be with him. He made one exception: his *Mont Saint Michel and Chartres*. He especially prohibited her having his *Education*. She made the point so firmly that I assumed she did not have a copy of *The Education* as printed in 1907.

—AT told us that, when she had been with him for a year, HA gave her an inscribed copy of *Mont Saint Michel and Chartres* as reprinted in 1912. She made it clear that she greatly valued the copy, but she did not show it to us.

—AT gradually let us know that, after all, she had a copy of *The Education* as privately printed in 1907—not inscribed. She made it clear that she greatly valued this volume also.

—Her disclosure that she had copies of both *Mont Saint Michel and Chartres* and *The Education* led me to expect that she would show them to us. During the eighteen years of our friendship, she never did; and, in keeping with my policy of not asking questions, I never asked to see them. Instead I silently wondered where she kept them. I could see that they were not in her living room bookcase. I assumed she was keeping them in her bedroom closet.

—AT repeatedly told us that in 1916, when the time came for him to give his *Education* to the Massachusetts History Society, HA had instructed her to carry the packet to Senator Lodge's house, and she had done so. She never quite dropped the subject. I came to think it was strangely vivid in her mind that HA had asked her to carry a copy of *The Education* away from his house.

—AT told us that, late in the years she spent with him, she one day induced HA to talk to her about his wife, from which time he did so very freely.

—AT told us that, when HA died, she asked the right to clothe his body and went to a top-floor closet used as a trunk room, opened the trunk containing MHA's clothes, accessories, etc., and took from it a long, fine-woven white shawl from India. It was clear that she had earlier become very familiar with the contents of the trunk.

—When I obtained photocopies of surviving architectural plans of HA's house, AT welcomed the chance to examine the plans in my company and offer comments. She was most interested in telling me details about the top floor, including details about the cedar closet off the hall, used as the storage room for trunks. She said again that there was a trunk filled with Aunt Clover's things.

—AT repeatedly told us that there was a terrible moment at HA's dinner table when HA told Lodge he had to stop talking treason.

—Early in our friendship, AT had told us in sketchy terms that sometime after HA's death she became engaged to a man who belonged to a European family and that a family representative put an end to the engagement by telling her in her fiancé's absence that she lacked the necessary "*dot.*" As she told it, the story of the engagement did not involve a copy of *The Education*. I at first inferred from what she said that her fiancé's family was French.

—In June 1962, AT told us to our amazement that she had owned a second copy of *The Education*, in fact a most extraordinary copy; that she became engaged to an Italian-American, Egisto Fabbri; that she and Egisto agreed to own the copy together; that she last saw the copy in his library at his and his family's villa near Florence; and that the copy was fascinating to both of them. I got an initial wrong impression that she suffered two broken engagements!

—When I came to my senses, I realized that she had told the story of one failed romance but had told it disjointedly, one part when she first knew us, the other much later. When told the first time, the story involved something she was informed she lacked: a sufficient "*dot.*" When told the second time, the story involved something she had come to own: a fascinating copy of *The Education*. Reconsidered, the second telling acquired a still more striking feature. It became a loud reminder that AT had not disclosed how, when, and why she got either or both of her copies of *The Education*. This seemed to be one thing she simply could not disclose.

—Shortly before her death in 1969, aged ninety-one, AT told us that she intended to leave her remaining copy of *The Education* to her friend Louis Auchincloss and her inscribed copy of *Mont Saint Michel and Chartres* to me.

—At the last moment, AT restated her wishes to her close friend Frederika Landon. Mrs. Landon gave the copies to Auchincloss and me. I think it significant that AT kept the copies as long as possible, that she treated them as a pair, and that one copy of the pair was unmarked and the other copy bore words in HA's handwriting.

INDEX

Adams, Abigail (niece of HA; daughter of JQA2; later Mrs. Robert Homans), 87, 142, 261, 446, 558, 560, 598
Adams, Abigail Brooks (mother of HA), 10, 301, 385, 442, 472, 506, 622
Adams, Abigail Smith (great-grandmother of HA; wife of JA), 15, 367, 373
Adams, Arthur G. (nephew of HA; son of JQA2), 190
Adams, Brooks (younger brother of HA), 17, 39–42, 47, 61, 68–69, 72–73, 76, 84–85, 87, 91–92, 94–99, 101, 103, 107–08, 111, 113–14, 116–17, 119–22, 124–25, 130, 133–36, 138, 140, 142, 146–47, 150–51, 156–57, 161, 171, 173–74, 178, 180–81, 185, 189–90, 200, 219–21, 223–24, 226–27, 234–36, 238, 250–51, 253–54, 260–61, 263, 269, 271–73, 283, 289, 293, 332–41, 351–52, 357–58, 363, 367–68, 377–78, 380, 383–84, 394, 398–401, 404, 421–30, 432–34, 438, 440–41, 464–65, 467, 471–74 , 496, 505–07, 511, 529–39, 541–42, 557–60, 562–63, 569, 573–74, 577–81, 583, 590–91, 593, 605–06, 608, 614, 620, 632–33, 638, 641, 643, 648, 652–53, 660–61, 663, 665, 669, 671, 677, 679–80, 692, 695
Adams, Charles Francis (father of HA), 15, 21, 32, 39, 72, 87–88, 116, 134, 164, 185, 187, 297–98, 301, 332, 368, 398–400, 404, 441–42, 451, 466, 506, 513, 539–40, 572, 576, 598, 609, 622, 643–45, 678
Adams, Charles Francis, Jr. (older brother of HA), 17–18, 21, 25, 39–40, 47, 72, 85, 87–88, 116, 121–22, 124, 140, 161, 171, 178, 180–81, 185, 187, 190–91, 204, 253–54, 263, 266, 293, 306, 313, 315, 320, 332, 337, 381–84, 386, 390, 398–400, 404, 410, 412, 419, 421–22, 424–29, 432, 434, 437–38, 441, 445–46, 451, 457, 462, 466, 474, 480–82, 484–86, 489–90, 492, 494, 498, 502, 505, 510, 513, 523–24, 531, 539–40, 551, 557, 559, 572, 579, 583, 598, 606, 619, 643–45, 648, 650, 652–53, 661, 663–64, 667, 669, 671, 674–77, 680, 689, 691, 695
Adams, Charles Francis, III (nephew of HA, son of JQA2), 190, 211, 429, 452, 512, 523, 529–31. 536, 540, 663, 667–68
Adams, Elizabeth (niece of HA; youngest daughter of CFA2), 47, 87, 282, 421, 434–35, 437–38, 444, 452–53, 456, 460, 466, 468–75, 477,

495, 498, 505, 507, 511–13, 519, 522–23, 529, 539–40, 542, 683, 685, 689
Adams, Evelyn (wife of BA), 40, 42, 61, 68, 76, 84, 87, 89, 98, 101, 111, 120, 124, 130–31, 133, 135–36, 142, 146, 150, 156, 171, 173–74, 185, 189, 219–21, 227, 238, 250–51, 260, 263, 283, 289, 293, 332–33, 351–52, 358, 382, 396, 398, 400, 421, 429–30, 471–74, 573, 620, 663
Adams, George Caspar (nephew of HA; son of JQA2), 190
Adams, George Washington (uncle of HA), 15, 190, 310–11, 424, 445–46

Adams, Henry
As writer, 288, 322. Also *see* WRITINGS, below
As partner with Elizabeth Sherman Cameron, 5–6, 8–9,18–19, 159–60, 167–68, 181–82, 222, 277–78, 342, 351, 387, 447–48, 459–60, 516–17, 520–21, 599–600, 615–17. Also *see* Cameron, Elizabeth Sherman (all entries)
As politician, 7, 16, 18–19, 33, 40–46, 50–54, 57, 64–69, 72–73, 90–91, 96, 102, 105–10. 113, 116–18, 120, 123–25, 129–30, 132, 134–36, 138–39, 142, 147–49, 154–56, 160, 163–65, 167–68, 173–75, 184–86, 188, 190, 195–96, 200, 211–12, 215, 220–22, 225, 227, 236, 238, 240, 250–52, 255, 257, 270–75, 277, 288–90, 396, 419, 513–14, 573, 576–78, 582–83, 585–86, 590–93, 598–99, 613–15
As economist, 24–25, 33–34, 41–46, 64–67, 69, 87, 90, 100, 102, 107, 118, 126–27, 134–36, 140–42, 151, 166, 180, 210, 560, 568, 573, 576–78
As traveler, 287. Also *see* planned travels, 9; travels in Egypt & the Middle East, 38, 146–52, 590–91, 668–69; in Japan, 4–5, 38, 662; in South Seas, 4–6, 9, 662; in British Isles, 3–6, 22–24, 89, 93, 117, 119, 162, 232–33; in Caribbean & Mexico, 28, 62–63, 76–78, 80–85, 104, 109–10; in Switzerland, 31, 38–39, 235; to India (never made), 49–50, 54; to Yellowstone & Grand Tetons, 64, 68–73; to Pacific Northwest, 71–73; in France, 89–90, 95–99, 113, 117, 137, 218–19, 256–58, 322–23; in Holland, 112–13; in Italy & Sicily, 113–15, 126, 131, 169–70, 258, 594; in Germany, 117–18, 214; in Greece & Turkey, 142, 150–54, 216, 591; in the Balkans, 142, 150–51, 153–54, 156, in Hungary & Austria, 155–56, 214–15, in Russia, 142, 150, 174, 210, 214–17; in

Poland, 214; in Sweden, Norway & Denmark, 215–18; to Africa and Central Asia (imagined; never made), 427, 429
As hospitable Washingtonian, 5, 13, 18–20, 27–28, 40, 51–53, 60–61, 68–69, 75, 85, 87–89, 103, 111, 121, 124–26, 128–33, 145–46, 151, 163, 167–68, 170, 175–76, 185–87, 189, 211–12, 219–21, 223, 226–27, 238–39, 250–52, 258, 260–64, 267–68, 281–82, 287, 289, 291, 313, 320–21, 331–33, 354, 356, 358–60, 391, 394–95, 410, 412, 414, 422, 436–37, 439–40, 442–443, 449–52, 462, 464–65, 468, 475–76, 478–81, 507–09, 512–15, 517–19, 551, 605, 608, 612, 616, 619, 653, 670, 672, 674, 679, 685–87
As visitor & resident in Paris & its environs, winter of 1891–92, 4, 6, 9–10, 14–17; summer of 1895, 97, 99–100; summer of 1896, 112–13, 115–17, 119; summer of 1897 through late January 1898—Pavillon d'Angoulême, 134–37, 16 Rue Christophe Colomb, 137–42; 146; summer of 1898, 153–54, 156–57; summer of 1899 through 6 Jan 1900—50 Ave. du Bois de Boulogne, 166, 168, 171–72, 174–82; summer of 1900—20 Rue de Longchamps, 183–84, 189–90, 50 Ave. du Bois de Boulogne, 192–94; autumn of 1900—3 Rue de Traktir, 194–98, 201–02, 204–06, 600–01; summer & autumn of 1901—50 Ave. du Bois de Boulogne, 211–13, 218–20; summer & autumn of 1902—50 Ave. du Bois de Boulogne, 227, 232–34, 23 Ave. du Bois de Boulogne, 235, 237; nine successive summers & autumns —23 Ave. du Bois de Boulogne: 1903, 242–44, 246, 249; 1904, 254–59; 1905, 270–80; 1906, 284–88; *1907*, 300, 303, 305–06, 309–12; 1908 till October 28, 320–27; 1909, 341–42, 348–57; summer of 1910 through 5 Jan 1911—23 Ave. du Bois de Boulogne, 362–64, 369, 373–74, 382–83, 88 Ave. du Bois de Boulogne, 383–87; summer and autumn of 1911—88 Ave. du Bois de Boulogne, 393, 395–402, 406–08; summer and autumn of 1913, 449, 53 Ave. Montaigne, 452, 6 Square du Bois de Boulogne, 452, 461, 669, Château de Marivault, 455–56, 669; summer of 1914—40 Ave. de Trocadero, 469–73, Château de Coubertin, 470–72
As fearer and hater of egoism, 11–12, 90, 301–02, 550–51
As practical optimist, 348–49, 362–63, 388–90, 510, 638, 685
As president and former president of the American Historical Association, 54,73–74, 76–80, 91–92, 122–23, 314–15, 325, 333–39, 341–49, 571; his theory of history, 343–45, 571, 580, 583, 590, 593, 634–35
As conservative Christian anarchist, 60–61, 93, 112, 127, 145, 175–76, 217, 222, 225, 265, 278, 281, 291, 357, 567, 574, 604, 608
As opponent of socialism, 329, 362, 379, 389, 483, 597, 638
As fugitive from Boston, 84, 282, 446
Relations with closest American friends. *See* entries for John Hay, Clarence King, William Phillips, Anna Cabot Lodge, George Cabot Lodge
Relations with closest British friends. *See* entries for Charles Milnes Gaskell, Sir John & Lady Clark, Sir Robert Cunliffe, Sir Arthur Cecil Spring Rice
Relations with Adams relatives, 24, 28. Also *see* all entries under Adams except those for Herbert Baxter Adams and James Truslow Adams
Relations with Hooper relatives. *See* all entries under Hooper and those for Ellen Hooper Gurney, Louisa Hooper Thoron, and Mabel Hooper La Farge

Adams, Henry
WRITINGS
Aaron Burr, 339
"Biographical Sketch [of John Hay]" (prefaced to *Letters of John Hay*—see below), 317–18, 331, 627
"Biography of John Hay," 31–32, 555–56, 606
"Buddha and Brahma," 535–36
Cameron speeches. *See* Speeches, below
Chanson de Willame (translations from), 407, 412–13, 415–16, 653, 661
"Chanson of Thibaud," 196–97
"Chansons de Geste," 392, 394, 399, 401–04, 411–16, 431, 646, 647–50
"Count Edward de Crillon," 69, 91–92
Cycle of Adams Letters, A (posthumous; includes letters by HA), 539–40
"Declaration of Paris. 1861, The," 438
Degradation of the Democratic Dogma, The (posthumous; assembled & titled by BA), 534–39, 541–42
Democracy, 12–13, 203, 288, 303, 409, 485–86, 511, 555, 601, 619, 623, 660
Documents Relating to New-England Federalism. 1800–1815, 405, 643, 650
"Editor's Preface" & "Contents" (for *The Education of Henry Adams*), 501–03, 524–25, 527, 529, 616, 677, 684
Education of Henry Adams, The (1907 version), 7, 12–14, 16, 20, 25–28, 32, 47–48, 52–53, 75, 88, 96, 102, 138, 152, 179, 228, 231–32, 241–42, 244, 247–48, 250–51, 254–56, 265, 267, 270, 272–73, 280, 283–84, 288–303, 309–10, 312–28, 330, 333, 345, 354, 362–63, 367–69, 375, 379, 386, 390, 399–400, 409, 416–19, 443, 460, 462, 464, 469, 478, 480, 485–86, 490–93, 495, 498, 501–03, 509, 515–16, 519, 524, 529, 550–51, 554–55, 559, 570, 576, 601, 604, 608, 616, 619–20, 625, 628, 641–42, 643–44, 652–53, 675, 684–85, 690–92, 695
Master Copy, 293, 300, 311–12, 315–16, 324–25, 330, 334, 337–38, 416–19, 460, 464, 492, 495–96, 499, 503, 511, 512, 515–16, 522, 530, 542–44, 614, 617, 620, 622–23, 625–28, 632, 642, 656, 660, 680–82, 684, 691–92, 697–98
Attendant Clean Copy, 419, 496, 503, 512, 515–16, 656, 660, 684, 697–98
First Traveling Copy, 299–300, 302–303, 308–313, 315, 323–25, 330, 416, 418, 460, 464–65, 492–97, 499, 526–28, 530–32, 622–23, 625–26, 629, 632, 677, 679–82, 690–93
Second Traveling Copy, 324–25, 327–28, 330, 341–42, 401, 416, 418, 464, 492, 495–

97, 499, 530, 625–26, 629–30, 632, 679, 681–82, 690–91, 693, 696
Copies HA destroyed, 418, 481, 516, 653–60
Substitute Copy, 498–504, 524–32, 681–82, 691
Signed Copy, 499–501, 503–04, 680–82
Education of Henry Adams, The (1918 version), 524–32, 535–37, 598, 616, 628–29, 692–93
Esther, 96, 409–10, 618
"Great Secession Winter of 1860–61, The," 381–82, 643
History of the United States of America, 7–8, 10, 12–13, 20–22, 53–54, 61–62, 69, 78, 80, 92, 95, 101–02, 114, 123, 129, 283, 288, 309, 339, 343–44, 361–62, 375, 475, 478–79, 511, 514, 552–54, 576, 593, 617, 620, 634–35, 667
John Randolph, 339, 445, 618
"King," 228, 249, 289, 606
Letter to American Teachers of History, 342, 348–52, 354–69, 375–79, 381, 383–84, 388–90, 397, 469, 490–91, 515, 519–20, 531–34, 541, 637–39, 641, 676, 687, 694–95; HA's annotated copy, 536–37, 694
Letter to Langley re molecules, 34–37
Letters & other literary remains, HA's, collected by Ford, 530–31, 533–38, 540
Letters of John Hay, 289–93, 298, 300–01, 303–06, 312, 317–20, 326, 331, 334, 336, 342, 354, 381, 383, 392, 445, 457, 461, 464, 480, 619–20, 631, 634
Letters to a Niece . . . (contains letters & a poem by HA; collected by Mabel La Farge), 535–36
Life of Albert Gallatin, The & *The Writings of*, 33, 333, 339, 554, 618
Life of George Cabot Lodge, The, 354, 358–59, 368–69, 373–75, 380–83, 392–93, 395, 406, 409, 445, 639–40, 646
Memoirs of Arii Taimai (1901) together with *Memoirs of Marau Taaroa, Last Queen of Tahiti* (the preliminary version—1893), 7, 10–11, 20, 27–31, 37, 55–64, 75, 111, 122–23,164, 186, 189–90, 192, 201, 213, 219, 226, 228–30, 253, 262, 265, 288, 292, 344–45, 354, 367–68, 409, 441, 511, 554–55, 566–67, 570, 577, 591, 593–94, 604–06, 612, 634, 665
Memorandum [for the Treasury Dept.?] beginning "The instructions . . . ," 33–34, 556
Mont Saint Michel and Chartres (1904 version), 96–98, 102, 136–38, 141–42, 151–53, 165, 172, 175, 178–80, 190, 193, 196, 203, 211, 213, 219, 221, 228, 231, 233, 236, 238–39, 250–53, 255, 261–67, 269, 271–73, 276, 281, 283–84, 288–89, 292, 295–96, 298–99, 301, 305, 308–09, 313, 315–18, 327, 342, 345, 354, 362, 367, 379, 388, 402, 409, 411, 417–18, 441–42, 502–03, 511, 519, 570, 575, 576, 590, 597, 604, 611–13, 617, 620, 641, 645, 651–52, 690
Mont Saint Michel and Chartres (1912 version), 379, 382–83, 385–86, 388, 392–93, 395, 397, 402, 407, 410–11, 414–18, 441–43, 452, 478, 502–03, 511, 519, 570, 576, 611, 645, 651–52, 690
Mont Saint Michel and Chartres (1913 version), 442, 445, 460, 462, 469, 490–92, 502–03, 511, 519, 531, 576, 670, 692
"Napoleon I$^{\text{er.}}$ et Saint-Domingue," 618

"New York Gold Conspiracy, The," 618
New York Times, The, HA's despatches to, 555, 618, 675
Poetry in prose, HA's, 218, 600
"Prayer to the Dynamo," 48–49, 203, 557, 564–66, 601
"Prayer to the Virgin of Chartres," 187, 201–03, 206, 531, 535–36
"Principles of Geology, The," 618
Radical Ciub, A Poem . . . , *The*, 48, 556, 564–65, 607, 618
Recognition of Cuban Independence, 108, 113, 123–25, 129–130, 154, 156, 562, 576–78, 583–84, 591, 652–53
"Rule of Phase applied to History, The" (first version), 334–39, 345, 347–48, 368–69, 378, 393, 488, 532, 632–33, 635, 676
"Rule of Phase applied to History, The" (BA's typed copy of first version), 336–37, 369, 378, 532–36, 538, 632, 693; as retyped & doctored by BA, 538
"Rule of Phase applied to History, The" (second version; also copy typed for Jameson), 338, 341–42, 345–48, 354–55, 359–60, 369, 376, 538, 632–37
Speeches to U. S. Senate: (No. 1) "Remonetization of Silver" [given 25 Sep 1893], 44–46, 50, 56; (No. 2) [given 30 Oct 1893], 50–54; (No. 3) [given 18 Apr 1894], 54, 65, 70, 72, 562–63, 566, 568
Tahiti. See *Memoirs of Arii Taimai*
"Tendency of History, The," 78–80, 91, 123, 537, 541, 571, 634; *1896* offprint, 582
Tendency of History, The (a fabricated book, published 1928), 541–42, 695

Adams, Henry, II (nephew of HA; son of CFA2), 161, 190, 542, 592, 695–96
Adams, Herbert Baxter, 54, 74, 78, 570
Adams, James Truslow, 582, 654–55
Adams, John (great-grandfather of HA), 14–15, 72, 129, 311, 373, 384, 441, 513–14, 578, 680
Adams, John, II (uncle of HA), 15
Adams, John (nephew of HA, son of CFA2), 161, 190
Adams, John Quincy (grandfather of HA), 14–16, 72, 85, 129, 164, 215, 254, 318, 332, 334, 337, 339–40, 368–69, 373, 378, 405, 441, 446, 451, 466, 506, 513, 538, 551, 555, 578–79, 641, 678
Adams, John Quincy, II (oldest brother of HA), 17, 21, 39–42, 64, 70–72, 75, 87, 116, 140, 274, 570
Adams, Louisa Catherine, II (older sister of HA; later Mrs. Charles Kuhn), 245, 476
Adams, Louisa Catherine Johnson (grandmother & most-loved blood relation of HA; wife of JQA), 15, 85–86, 191–92, 206, 215, 253, 373, 390, 423–24, 498, 610, 680
Adams, Marian (Clover) Hooper (wife of HA), 3–5, 19, 21, 54, 95–96, 111, 119–20, 146, 164, 186, 209, 293, 352, 447, 454, 476, 485, 489, 491, 500, 504, 507, 510, 512, 523, 575, 586, 589–90, 595, 597, 641–42, 660, 675, 685–86
Adams, Mary (younger sister of HA). *See* Quincy, Mary Adams
Adams, Mary Ogden (wife of CFA2), 47, 421, 425, 427, 430, 437, 453

Adams, Mary (niece of HA; middle daughter of CFA2), 87
Adams Memorial (or Monument), 5–6, 20–21, 111, 119, 186, 200, 248, 362, 489, 491, 523, 596
Adams Real Estate Trust, 28, 39–40, 64
Aeschylus, 204
Agassiz, Alexander, 211, 416, 557
Agassiz, George, 416, 557
Agassiz, Louis, 29
Alger, Russell A., 167
American Academy of Arts & Sciences, 266–67, 480, 613, 618
American Historical Association, 54, 73–74, 76–77, 91, 123, 333, 537, 541, 570, 582, 634, 691
Ames, Frederick, 41
Anarchists, 60, 171, 173–76, 217, 561, 595
Anderson, Henry Watkins, 510, 685
Anderson, Larz, 8–9, 17
Anderson, Nicholas, 8, 26
Anti-Semites, (French) 144, 171, 173, 175, 561; 587–88, 595; (American) 672
Arii Taimai, 11, 27, 30, 56–57, 60, 106, 111, 152, 229–30, 253, 258, 550, 610
Arthur, Chester A., 72, 303
Arthur, Frank, 470
Asquith. Herbert, 93
Atwater, Dorence, 192
Aubry, Pierre, 444, 450, 667
Augustine, Saint, 318, 320, 477, 479

Balfour, Arthur, 161, 509
Ball, Sir Robert, 22
Bancroft, Frederic, 313, 320–21, 438, 528, 626, 628–29, 638, 692, 694, 695
Bancroft, George, 340
Bank of England, 24
Baring, Thomas, 25
Baring Brothers, 25, 43, 129, 133
Barron, Oswald, 85–86, 191, 390–91, 599
Barrymore, Ethel, 231
Baxter, Lucy, 10, 17, 47, 60, 69, 118, 121–22, 125, 127, 129–30
Bayard, Thomas, 38–39, 75, 93, 105
Beale, Harriet Blaine (Mrs. Truxton Beale), 19, 105, 107–08, 598
Beck, Jean-Baptiste, 444, 450–51, 667
Belmont, August, 121, 582
Belmont, Perry, 407, 436
Berenson, Bernhard, 211–12, 251, 255–56, 309–10, 317, 329, 350–51, 354–56, 394, 430–31, 437, 447, 453, 455, 461, 468, 480, 625, 637, 650, 663, 670, 672; spelling of first name, 602
Beretania, 75
Bergson, Henri, 508
Bernstein, Eduard, 180–181
Berry, Walter, 397, 471
Bey, Aristarchi, 143–44, 588
Bigelow, John, 382, 386, 595, 598
Bigelow, William Sturgis, 19–20, 22, 42, 125, 130–31, 133–34, 184, 197, 199, 246, 351–54, 367, 381, 421–23, 425, 427–28, 430, 583, 640, 661–62
Blaine, Harriet. See Beale, Harriet Blaine
Blaine, James G., 19, 67, 293, 552, 623
Bliss, Mildred, 452, 505, 663
Bliss, Robert, 452, 663
Boit, Louise, 464

Boston Athenaeum, 283
Boston Public Library, 283, 480–81
Bougainville, Louis, 65
Brett, George, 378–79, 534–39, 694
Brice, Calvin, 51, 321–22
Brice girls (Helen & Palmyre), 218–19, 326, 604
Bright, John, 88, 412, 642, 678
Bryan, William Jennings, 114, 116, 121, 323, 329, 380, 436, 460–61, 475
Bryce, James, 439
Buchanan, James, 308–09
Bumstead, Henry A., 359–60, 376, 538, 638
Burgess, John W., 263, 268, 313
Burr, Aaron, 461
Butler, Nicholas Murray, 267–68

Cabot, George, 514
Cameron, Elizabeth Sherman (partner of HA during his final life; wife of James Donald Cameron), 4–8, 13–14, 16–19; 28, 31, 38–40, 42–44, 47, 50, 52, 61, 63, 69–75, 77, 80, 82–85, 89–90, 92–97, 99, 101–04, 108–22, 126, 128, 130, 142–54, 156–73, 175–90, 192–206, 209–28, 231–47, 249–52, 254–56, 258–64, 267–70, 272–84, 286–89, 291, 295, 297, 302–07, 311, 313, 315, 317, 321–23, 325–33, 341–42, 348, 350–54, 356–64, 369, 374, 379–80, 383, 385–88, 391–402, 406–11, 414–15, 417, 420–22, 425–36, 438–39, 446–61, 463–83, 487–89, 491–93, 504–13, 516–17, 519–21, 523, 537, 542, 552, 568, 578, 584, 589–93, 597–98, 602–05, 607, 610, 612, 614–17, 621, 623–24, 630, 637, 642, 644, 653, 661–63, 670–71, 676–77, 684, 694
Cameron, James Donald, 4, 6, 18–19, 28, 31, 38–41, 44–45, 50–53, 60, 65–68, 70–71, 73–75, 83, 92–94, 99, 103–04, 108–10, 115, 117, 119–20, 123–24, 130–32, 137, 146, 150, 157–59, 161–62, 164, 172, 175–76, 183, 185, 188–89, 194–95, 202. 205, 212–13, 217 , 220–21, 224, 232–33, 243–46, 257, 260–61, 272, 277, 279, 282, 295, 311, 317, 321, 329, 341, 356–61, 363–64, 392, 430, 432–33, 435, 463, 467–68, 471, 520, 562–63, 568, 578, 582, 592, 599, 663, 678, 694
Cameron, Martha (only child of James Donald Cameron and Elizabeth Cameron; later Mrs. Ronald Lindsay), 6, 18, 31, 40, 61, 75, 84, 92, 96–97, 99, 103, 110, 115, 117, 119, 130–32, 137, 140, 148, 150, 159, 164, 167–72, 175–76, 181, 183, 185, 188–90, 192–93, 195–97, 202–04, 210, 217, 219, 232–36, 242–46, 249, 254, 257–64, 267–69, 272, 278–82, 284, 286–89, 295, 297, 302–07, 311, 313, 317, 321–22, 326, 329–33, 336, 341–42, 348, 350–52, 356–57, 360, 364, 369, 374, 380, 383, 385–88, 391–95, 401, 406–07, 417, 432, 439, 447, 449, 452–57, 460, 468, 471, 473–74, 477, 481, 483–84, 488, 516, 519–21, 537, 591, 593, 599, 602, 612, 623, 637, 662
Cameron, Rachel (daughter of James Donald Cameron by a previous marriage; later Mrs. Chandler Hale), 117, 130–31, 463, 671
Capet, Hugh, 402–03, 413–14
Carlisle, John G., 33–34
Carnegie, Andrew, 71
Carroll, Lewis (Alice's Adventures in Wonderland), 481, 674

Chamberlain, Joseph, 13, 161, 222, 236, 551, 587
Chanler, Laura, 169, 171, 263–68, 278, 300, 321–22, 456–57, 484, 594
Chanler, Margaret, 169, 171, 177, 238, 261, 263, 265–68, 277–78, 289, 313–14, 321–22, 329, 342, 354, 362, 451, 483–86, 508, 511, 594, 613, 631, 638, 675
Chanler, Winthrop, 169, 238, 322, 598
Channing, Edward, 313, 364, 378, 617
Chanson de Roland, 379, 402–04, 413–16, 431, 585–86, 646, 648–49
Chanson de Willame, 402–04, 407, 412–16, 430–31, 648–50
Chase, Salmon P., 678
Choate, Joseph, 188
Churchill, Jennie Jerome, Lady Randolph, 140, 466, 586
Clark, Lady Charlotte Coltman, 3–4, 6, 22, 39, 85, 93, 119, 138
Clark, Sir John, 3–4, 6, 20, 22, 25, 39, 85, 93, 119, 138–39, 162, 181, 233, 306, 357, 369, 594
Clemenceau, Georges, 144, 357
Clemens, Samuel Langhorne, 266, 284, 532
Cleveland, Grover, 27, 33, 38–39, 42–44, 50, 53, 60, 62, 67, 71–72, 97, 105–09, 117, 123–24, 148, 154, 224, 303, 358, 567, 576, 579, 584
Cobden, Richard, 88, 642, 678
Congress, U. S., 44, 50–51, 53, 55, 62, 64, 67, 87, 103, 105, 107–10, 117, 121–23, 154, 157
Constitution, U. S., 25
Cook, Albert S., 379, 383
Cook, Captain James, 58–59
Copley, Mrs. John Singleton, 14–15,
Cram, Ralph Adams, 442, 460, 665, 670
Crillon, Count Édward de (pseudonym), 69, 92
Croly, Herbert, 445, 457
Cross, Wilbur, 461
Crowninshield, Benjamin, 7, 26
Cuban delegates, Gomez, Maceo & Campos, 104, 106–08; Gonzalo de Quesada, 120, 127, 167, 221; Horatio Rubens, 131, 167, 598; delegates generally, 577–79
Cunliffe, Sir Robert, 6, 22, 39, 69, 81, 93, 104, 109, 136, 138, 156, 195, 255, 274, 551, 592
Curtis, Lisa, 447, 465–66, 469, 471
Curtis, Ralph, 447, 465–66, 468–69, 472, 600
Curzon, Lady Mary Leiter, 88, 102, 131, 181, 576, 617
Curzon, Lord George, 88–89, 93, 131, 573, 617
Czolgosz, Leon (alias Fred Niemand), 217

Dana, Richard Henry, III, 412, 424, 652–53, 661
Darwin, Charles, 22, 242, 378, 648; Darwinism, 320
Davis, Edward H., 388–89, 476, 640, 645
Day, William, 145, 156, 158
Debs, Eugene, 71, 75
Descartes, René, 242, 328
de Wolfe, Elsie, 172, 231, 238, 255, 257, 281–82, 300, 306–07, 309, 320, 331, 596
Disraeli, Benjamin, 88
Draper, Ruth, 451, 667
Dreyfus, Alfred; also the Dreyfus Affair, 142–48, 171, 173–78, 580, 587–89, 596, 601, 644
Dupuy de Lôme, Enrique, 103, 106, 109, 147–49, 590
Dwight, Theodore Frelinghuysen, 5, 9, 17–18

Eddy, Spencer, 146, 163, 171
Edward VII, King, 284, 350, 374
Eliot, Charles W., 21–22, 296, 298, 534, 552, 621–22
Eliot, T. S., 639
Emerton, Ephraim, 79
Emmons, Samuel Franklin, 210, 220, 226, 394
Endicott, Mary (Mrs. Joseph Chamberlain), 88, 551
Engels, Friedrich, 181
Eustis, Edith, 323, 353–54, 410
Evarts, William Maxwell, 242, 293, 608, 678
Everett, Sydney, 74
Everett, William, 224
Expositions: Chicago—1892, 31, 38, 42, 47–48, 190, 193, 555, 564; Paris—1900, 189–90, 193, 197–98, 200; St. Louis—1904, 252, 254

Fabbri, Egisto, 522, 535, 540–44, 688, 695–96
Faraday, Michael, 29, 35, 265, 314, 327, 555
Fay, Sigourney W., 478–79
Fell, Anne Palmer, 5–6, 17, 30, 75, 127, 209, 236, 254, 284, 423, 595, 602
Fish, Hamilton, 500
Fitch, John, 343
Five of Hearts, the, 485, 675
Flexner, Abraham, 469, 676
Ford, Paul Leicester, 10, 78, 556; murder of, 536, 694
Ford, Worthington Chauncey, 10, 78, 91, 104, 113, 123–24, 126–29, 138, 140, 166, 234, 306, 316, 320, 333, 363, 367, 373, 382, 384–85, 390–91, 399–401, 404–05, 419, 424–25, 432, 434, 438, 441, 446, 451–52, 457–58, 461–62, 464, 467, 486–87, 491, 504, 506, 524–38, 540, 542, 556, 578, 580, 582, 599, 607, 615, 631, 638–39, 642, 648, 650, 663, 669, 676, 678, 684, 690–95
Foster, Dewitt C., 80–81
Franklin, Benjamin, 314, 318–19, 513; *Memoirs*, 26, 299, 319, 554
Frelinghuysen, Lucy, 238
Frewen, Moreton, 51
Froude, James Anthony, 83
Fulton, Robert, 343

Gallatin, Albert, 33, 37
Gardner, Isabella Stewart, 181, 269, 285–87, 325, 597, 616–18
Garfield, James A., 72, 216, 308, 623
Gaskell, Charles Milnes, 3–7, 18, 22, 24, 39, 41, 61, 72, 75, 83, 87, 93, 103, 106–07, 109, 116, 119–20, 124, 128, 138–40, 151–53, 159, 162, 168, 175, 181, 194–95, 209–10, 233, 242, 244, 251, 255, 257, 263–64, 275, 281, 283–85, 288, 292, 296, 301–02, 305–06, 315, 322, 329–30, 349–50, 357, 360–61, 396–98, 401, 416–17, 459, 470–71, 473–74, 479, 487, 495–97, 506–07, 510, 513, 518–19, 549–51, 592–93, 605, 608, 613, 623–24, 637, 653, 672, 679, 686
Gaskell, Lady Catherine Milnes, 305
Gibbon, Edward, 318; *Decline & Fall*, 203, 580
Gibbs, Willard, 310–14, 324, 329–30, 346, 349, 355, 359, 500, 625, 633, 635, 693
Gilder, Richard Watson, 119–20, 269, 303, 614–15, 631, 677
Gladstone, William, 88, 246–47, 399, 664

Gold, flows of, 28, 31, 33–34, 39, 41, 91, 100, 103–104, 124, 127–28, 140
Gould, Jay, 25, 37, 309
Goya, 189
Grant, Julia, 37
Grant, Ulysses S., 72, 320, 500, 623, 652
Gray, William, 18, 22, 146, 151, 176, 354, 356, 375, 418, 420–21, 428, 432, 476, 596, 661
Greenslet, Ferris, 368, 445, 485, 491–95, 498–99, 525–29, 533, 675–79, 683, 687, 690–93
Gresham, Walter, 38, 42, 75, 105
Grétry, André, 16
Gurney, Ellen Hooper (sister of HA's wife; Mrs. E. W. Gurney), 3–4, 19, 209
Gurney, Ephraim Whitman, 21, 274

Hale, Chandler, 76, 80–83, 85, 130–31, 134, 570
Hanna, Mark, 224, 227, 604
Hankey, Thomson, 25
Harcourt, Sir William, 43, 93, 141
Hardin, B. Lauriston, 421–22, 523, 689
Hardy, Thomas, 102, 576
Harrison, Benjamin, 19, 27, 33, 303
Harvard College/University, 21–22, 40, 78, 283, 534–35, 552, 558
Hawthorne, Nathaniel, 575
Hay, Adelbert, 70–71, 115, 213, 220, 604
Hay, Alice (later Mrs. James W. Wadsworth), 70, 146, 469
Hay, Clara Stone (Mrs. John Hay), 13, 32, 70, 137–39, 146, 158–59, 168, 181, 183, 188, 193, 200, 220, 223, 226, 235, 238, 240, 261, 264, 268–71, 273, 275, 289–90, 293, 298–304, 306, 313, 317–20, 331, 334, 336–37, 342, 381, 383, 410, 420, 425, 427, 445, 447, 461–62, 468, 485, 585, 593, 604, 611–13, 615, 619–20, 624, 626, 631, 637, 661, 675
Hay, Clarence, 469
Hay, Helen. See Whitney, Helen Hay
Hay, John, 5, 13–14, 17–18, 21, 31–32, 41, 44, 47, 50, 55, 61, 64, 68–71, 74–75, 84, 100, 104, 106, 108–16, 119–22, 124–31, 133–35, 137–39, 146–52, 154–61, 163–68, 170–71, 181, 183–86, 188–89, 193, 195–98, 200, 204–05, 213, 215–16, 219–223, 225–27, 234–36, 238, 240, 249–52, 257–58, 261, 264, 266–71, 273–74, 276–77, 289–93, 297–98, 300–01, 303–04, 306, 317–20, 331, 334, 336, 349, 368, 381, 447, 457–58, 461–62, 464, 485, 489–90, 492–93, 504, 509, 510–11, 513–14, 519, 529, 533, 554–55, 573, 579–80, 582, 584–86, 589–93, 596, 598, 603–06, 610–16, 619, 627, 669–70, 672, 674–78, 685
Hayes, Rutherford B., 72
Hearn, Lafcadio, 84
Herlem, Marie, 270, 283–84, 386–87
Hewitt, Lucy, 243, 255, 439, 447
Hewitt, Peter Cooper, 447
Hickox, Annie, 388, 466
Higginson, Henry, 296, 615
Hitt, Reynolds, 115, 121, 234–35, 239
Holmes, Oliver Wendell, Jr., 238, 299, 446
Holt, Henry, 619
Homans, Abigail Adams. See Adams, Abigail
Hooper, Edward (brother of HA's wife), 4, 17, 19–21, 27–28, 30, 39–40, 42, 71, 87, 103, 122, 137, 151, 192–93, 204, 209, 212–13, 424, 570, 599, 602

Hooper, Ellen (niece of HA's wife; later Mrs. John Briggs Potter), 4, 22, 26, 30–31, 68, 187, 323, 465, 668
Hooper, Fanny (Mrs. Edward Hooper), 4
Hooper, Fanny (niece of HA's wife), 4, 26–27, 121–22
Hooper, Louisa. See Thoron, Louisa Hooper
Hooper, Mabel. See La Farge, Mabel Hooper
Hooper, Marian (Clover). See Adams, Marian (Clover) Hooper
Hooper, Mary (niece of HA's wife), 4, 26–27
Hooper, Robert William (HA's father-in-law), 209
Houghton Mifflin Company, 87, 89, 178, 334, 368, 395, 406, 442, 445, 457–58, 485–86, 492–93, 498–99, 524–26, 528–29, 531–32, 535–36, 540, 646, 679, 687, 691–93; The Piper, 531–32, 693
Howard, George, 200
Howe, Maude, 631
Howells, William Dean, 266, 321, 613, 631
Hoyt, Annie (niece of Mrs. Cameron), 364, 430
Hoyt, Colgate, 395, 430, 663
Hoyt, Edith (cousin of Mrs. Cameron), 231, 391–92, 394, 414, 437, 450, 460
Hoyt, Elizabeth (niece of Mrs. Cameron) 231, 238, 364, 380, 383, 391–92, 394–95, 401, 406–08, 414–15, 430, 432, 451, 456, 482–83, 516, 523, 537, 642, 672, 687, 689
Hoyt, Lida Sherman (sister of Mrs. Cameron; Mrs. Colgate Hoyt), 89, 188–90, 194, 202, 212–13, 231, 236, 238, 321, 325–26, 328, 430
Hubert, Henri, 398, 643, 648
Huntington, Ellsworth, 365–66

Ibsen, Henrik, 17
Iddings, Joseph, 70–71

Jackson, Andrew, 15, 461
James, Alice, 17
James, Henry, Sr., 467
James, Henry, Jr., 8–9, 12, 17, 39, 131, 138–39, 260, 263, 267, 293, 300, 309, 321, 323, 353, 467–68, 475, 484, 500, 603, 608, 612–13, 620, 641, 646, 675; Daisy Miller, 235; Portrait of a Lady, 303; Turn of the Screw, 199, 600; Wings of the Dove, 234–35, 237–38; Ambassadors, 247, 613, 672; Wm. Wetmore Story, 247–49, 609; Golden Bowl, 267, 613; Small Boy & Others, 452, 455, 670; Notes of a Son & Brother, 467; Sacred Fount, 603; on HA, 285–86, 612, 618; on his Mont Saint Michel & Chartres, 285–86; on his Education, 353; on his relation with EC, 594, 601–02
James, William, 39, 309, 318–19, 328, 374, 377, 640–41
Jameson, John Franklin, 91–92, 122–23, 333, 341, 355, 357, 359–60, 375–76, 411, 436, 441, 582, 638, 691–92
Jay, Augustus, 7
Jefferson, Thomas, 7, 15, 37, 318, 339–40
Jesus Christ, 479
Jews, 43, 83, 92–93, 97, 100, 107, 115–16, 124–25, 139, 141, 143–45, 147, 157, 210–11, 214, 273, 286, 396, 468, 560–63, 567, 571, 574–76, 580–81, 583, 586–87, 590–91, 595, 597–98, 604, 618, 644, 672
Johnsons (forebears of Louisa Catherine Adams), 385, 390

Johnson, Catherine Nuth (mother of LCA), 85–86, 191, 373, 385, 390
Johnson, Joshua (father of LCA), 85–86, 191, 390
Johnson, Samuel, 200
Johnson, Underwood, 480
Jones, Beatrix, 263, 267–68, 278, 282, 321
Jones, John Percival, 51
Jones, Mary Cadwalader, 260, 263, 267–69, 276, 278, 282, 297–98, 312, 321, 332, 334, 336, 341, 384, 388, 391, 399–400, 402, 406–07, 417, 425, 435, 450–52, 472, 647, 649, 689
Jusserand, Elise R., 291, 619
Jusserand, Jean-Jules, 263–64, 291, 619

Keep, Florence Boardman, 304, 329, 331, 362, 368, 393, 395–96, 402, 410, 431–34, 444, 449–54, 465, 468, 483, 648
Keep, Frederic, 304, 329, 331, 362, 368, 393–96, 433
Kelly, Edmond, 183, 188, 201, 204, 210–11, 213, 219, 235
Kelvin, William Thomson, Lord, 29, 35, 227, 242, 326, 349, 350, 355–56, 365–66, 377–78, 556, 693
Kennan, George, 221
Kidd, Benjamin, 77
King, Clarence, 5, 13, 20, 22, 27, 29, 31–32, 42, 55, 61–65, 68–70, 73–74, 76, 100, 103. 106, 147, 183, 199, 204–05, 209–210, 215, 220, 226, 228, 236, 240, 249, 267, 289, 394, 485, 490, 529. 554, 557, 598, 675, 677
Kipling, Rudyard, 17, 92
Knox, Philander, 336. 356, 436
Kuhn, Louisa Adams. See Adams, Louisa Catherine, II

La Farge, Bancel, 68, 155, 282–83, 351, 472, 643
La Farge, Florence, 480
La Farge, Grant, 442
La Farge, John, 5, 17, 27, 68, 103, 155, 181, 211, 238, 251, 260, 263, 266–67, 269, 286, 298, 351, 369, 384, 429, 442, 480, 606, 612–13, 662
La Farge, Mabel Hooper (niece of HA's wife), 4, 17, 19, 26–27, 30–31, 38–39, 68–69, 73–74, 115, 119, 121–22, 124, 126, 127–28, 131, 133–35, 137, 139–40, 155, 158, 170, 198, 231, 238, 245, 263, 270, 280, 282–83, 322–23, 351–52, 391, 398, 421, 432, 470, 472, 519, 522, 535–36, 540–41, 643, 662, 686, 688, 694–96
Langley, Samuel F., 34–37, 193, 198, 220, 233, 238, 269, 281–82, 519, 556, 600, 608, 625
Laughlin, J. Laurence, 319, 627
Lee, Thomas, 108–10, 578
Leiter, Mary Victoria. See Curzon, Lady Mary Leiter
Library of Congress, 166–67, 234, 316, 333, 443–45, 449, 491, 495, 660, 666
Lincoln, Abraham, 5, 21, 293, 319–20, 481, 507, 510, 575
Lincoln, Robert, 7, 17, 26, 100, 308
Lindsay, Ronald, 282, 287, 289, 302, 304–05, 307, 321–22, 326, 330–33, 336, 341–42. 348, 350–51, 356–57, 369, 385–86, 392, 394, 397, 401, 435, 439, 446, 452, 460, 468, 474–75, 481, 488, 520
Lodge, Anna Cabot Mills (Mrs. Henry Cabot Lodge), 12, 17, 40, 42, 89–90, 92–93, 95, 99, 110, 120, 124, 128, 130–31, 133, 135, 165, 168, 170–71, 173, 177, 186, 189, 204, 209–10, 213–16, 220, 223, 226, 238–40, 245, 251, 260–61, 263, 276, 295–96, 313, 332, 350, 352, 354, 375, 379–81, 383, 393, 397, 401, 410, 420–21, 425, 432, 454, 458, 472, 482, 487–89, 491, 533–34, 601–603, 611–12, 621, 624, 631, 640, 653, 668, 670, 693–94
Lodge, Constance, 96, 295, 488, 512, 515
Lodge, Elizabeth Davis (Mrs. George Cabot Lodge), 193–94, 197–201, 204, 206, 211, 213–14, 238, 260, 295, 332, 352–54, 358–59, 369, 374, 379–80, 383, 392–93, 406, 410, 420, 453, 471–72, 511, 519, 601
Lodge, George Cabot, 93, 96, 110, 112, 125.131, 142, 180, 186, 193–94, 197–98, 200–02, 204, 206, 212–14, 238, 240–41, 259, 295–97, 332, 338–39, 341–42, 351–54, 356, 358, 368–69, 373–75, 380–83, 392–93, 406–07, 574, 583, 601, 608, 611, 631, 633, 637, 640, 646
Lodge, Henry Cabot, 5, 12, 42, 51, 67, 75, 93, 104, 107–08, 120, 124–25, 164–71, 177, 186, 189, 201, 204–05, 209–10, 213–15, 219–22, 225–27, 238–39, 252, 260, 275–76, 281, 295, 297, 299, 334, 358, 380–81, 392–93, 410, 420–25, 427, 432, 446, 481–82, 484, 486–92, 498–99, 501–05, 507, 511–15, 519, 524–36, 569, 582–83, 585, 605–06, 611, 615, 637, 675–76, 678, 682–84, 686, 689–90, 692–94
Lodge, John, 96, 260, 295, 351–52, 472, 637, 661
Loring, Harriet, 125
Loring, William L., 515–16
Lowell, James Russell, 39, 248
Luquiens, Frederick B., 379, 383, 393, 413, 415–16, 443, 444–45, 450, 646
Lyall, Sir Alfred, 24–25, 93
Lyell, Sir Charles, 242, 357

Mach, Ernst, 313
MacNutt, Francis, 278–80, 615–16
Macmillan & Company, 98, 107, 113, 119, 246, 378, 391, 404, 534, 536, 539, 541–42, 694–95
MacVeagh, Franklin, 38, 359
MacVeagh, Virginia Cameron (Mrs. Wayne MacVeagh; sister of James Donald Cameron), 27, 52, 113, 115, 117–18, 359, 361, 468
MacVeagh, Wayne, 27, 38, 41–44, 50, 52, 75, 113, 115, 117–18, 121, 300, 359, 361–62, 468, 678
Madison, James, 37, 90, 309
Marau Taaroa, Queen, 10–11, 20, 27–30, 55–56, 61, 63–64, 75, 111, 152, 186, 550, 554–55, 568
Marbury, Elisabeth, 172, 238, 255, 257, 260, 272–73, 275–76, 281–82, 300, 306–07, 309, 320–21, 596
Marie Antoinette, Queen, 63
Marshall, John, 32, 467
Marx, Karl, 77, 181, 361, 570–71
Mason, Alice, 140, 586
Massachusetts Historical Society, 211, 306, 315–16, 333, 367, 373, 382, 384, 390, 400–01, 405, 412, 424, 434, 446, 451, 462, 464, 481, 484, 486, 494, 501–03, 515, 524–26, 528–34, 536–538, 542, 563, 582, 623, 629, 648, 682, 690, 692, 694–96
Maupassant, Guy de, 17
Maxwell, James Clerk, 29–30, 34–37, 265, 348–49, 555–57, 635

McHenry, James, 309
McKinley, William, 104, 112–13, 120–21, 125,
   127–28, 136, 147–48, 153–55, 157–59, 163–
   64, 166, 190, 204, 216–19, 223, 273, 276, 303,
   308, 589–90, 593, 604–05, 615
Michelangelo, 74, 215, 595
Milton, John, 48
Mitchell, Langdon, 375, 420, 646
Moetia, 192, 194
Monroe Doctrine, 105, 108, 129, 577–78
Moran, Benjamin, 669
Morgan, Anne, 272, 275–76, 300, 306–07
Morgan, J. P., 66, 87, 106, 211, 224, 227, 272, 321,
   374, 398, 452, 574, 581, 608, 661
Morison, Samuel Eliot, 461

Napoleon I, 344, 436, 615, 653
New York Public Library, 501, 556, 631, 660, 683
New York Stock Exchange, 34, 39, 74, 106, 236,
   239–40, 243, 392, 394, 398, 401, 608. Also see
   Panics
Newspapers: Aurore, 144; Boston Transcript, 382;
   Herald (Paris), 161, 245; New York Herald, 44,
   52, 65, 562, 568; New York Evening Post, 532;
   New York Sun, 44, 51–52, 65, 67, 562; New York
   Times, 44, 66, 283, 510, 541, 555, 562, 675;
   New York Tribune, 31; The Times (London),
   161, 274; Washington Evening Star, 108; Wash-
   ington Post, 70
Newton, Isaac, 33, 242, 328,
Nicolay, John, 5, 21, 31–32, 631
Nobody, Fred. See Czolgosz, Leon
Norton, Charles Eliot, 467, 613
Nott, Marjorie, 375, 383, 640
Nuth (untraced grandfather of LCA; possible em-
   igrant from Germany), 385, 390–91

Oberea. See Purea
Olney, Richard, 105–07, 123–25, 127, 148, 154,
   156, 576, 584, 627
Opuhara, 60, 106, 111, 123, 582

Palgrave, Francis Turner, 138
Palmer, Ralph, 160, 165, 168, 193–94, 356
Palmerston, Viscount, 88, 246–47, 386, 399, 609,
   644–45, 648, 664
Panics: 1893, 42–43, 50, 100, 104, 140, 644; 1903,
   243–44; 1907, 306–07, 312
Parkman, Francis, 54
Pascal, Blaise, 327–28
Paul, Saint, 590
Pearson, Charles Henry, 77, 570–71
Peirce, Charles, 237, 604, 634
Peirce, Herbert, 215–16
Periodicals: American Historical Review, 91–92, 122,
   333, 341, 582; American Journal of Science, 29;
   Atlantic Monthly, 529; Century, 119–20, 269,
   614–15; Forum, 100, 174; Nation, 29; North
   American Review, 11, 29, 604; Scribner's, 255,
   358; Yale Review, 461, 535
Phillips, William Hallett, 17, 21, 28, 30, 43, 47,
   70–71, 73, 106, 108–13, 115, 119, 127–29,
   131–35, 162, 166, 423–24, 567, 578–80, 678
Pickering. Timothy, 384, 643
Poincaré, Henri, 313, 624–25
Polk, James K., 340
Potter, Arthur B., 642
Potter, John Briggs, 283, 323, 465, 668, 671
Prescott, William, 57

Presidential elections: 1788, 14; 1792, 14; 1792,
   14; 1800, 15; 1824, 15; 1828, 15–16; 1860,
   125; 1876, 19; 1880,19; 1884,19, 67; 1892, 27;
   1896, 104, 112–14, 116, 120–22, 151; 1900,
   189, 261; 1908, 329, 331; 1912, 395, 402,
   419–20, 428, 436
Pullman, George M., 71
Pumpelly, Raphael, 429, 557, 642
Pupin, Michael, 313–14
Purea, 57–58, 65–66, 152, 228, 562, 568
Putman, Herbert, 491

Quincy, Dorothy (niece of HA), 245–46, 252,
   268, 282
Quincy, Elinor (niece of HA), 286, 397
Quincy, Josiah, 42
Quincy, Mary Adams (younger sister of HA),
   245–46, 252–53, 286, 293, 385, 397, 421,
   425, 506, 620–21

Rae, Rebecca Dodge, 5–6, 17, 118, 136, 163, 238
Ramsden, Frederick, 62, 74
Randolph, John, 340
Raphael, Henry, 92–93
Raymond, Henry Jarvis, 675, 678
Reid, Whitelaw, 7, 284, 293, 300, 303–06, 326–27,
   327–28, 336–37, 452, 631; Mrs. Reid, 464
Rhodes, James Ford, 315, 619, 626–27, 682
Richard Coeur de Lion, 16, 393, 440, 443–45,
   449, 451, 455, 646, 669
Richards, Theodore, 533–34, 693
Richardson, H. H., 13, 96, 177, 331, 551, 661
Rockhill, Caroline A., 136, 152, 158
Rockhill, William W., 105, 126, 129, 132–33, 135–
   36, 142, 149–53, 158–59, 162, 164, 166–68,
   170, 181, 183–84, 189–90, 192, 222, 224,
   583–84, 591, 605
Rodin, Auguste, 99, 198
Roosevelt, Alice, 223, 282, 517
Roosevelt, Edith Kermit, 219–23, 238–39, 260–
   61, 282, 291, 295, 323, 352, 517, 619
Roosevelt, Eleanor, 479, 507, 517, 674
Roosevelt, Franklin D., 479–80
Roosevelt, Quentin, 220, 223, 605
Roosevelt, Theodore, 5, 13, 27, 70, 75, 132–33,
   156, 158, 163, 173, 189, 204, 216–25, 235–36,
   238–39, 250, 252, 261, 263, 267, 273–74,
   280–82, 284, 291, 295–98, 308, 323, 329–30,
   334, 340, 374. 380, 398, 402, 405, 417, 420,
   428, 436, 476, 479, 510–11, 517, 585, 606,
   608, 613, 615–16, 619, 621, 653, 677
Root, Clara F. W., 225
Root, Elihu, 224–25, 227, 250–51, 306, 462, 464
Rostand, Edmond, Cyrano de Bergerac, 146, 149,
   589
Rothschilds in general, 24, 92, 121, 148, 243,
   574–75, 582, 595
Rothschild, Mayer Alphonse de, Baron, 121, 144–
   45, 171,
Rothschild, Lionel de, 210, 252, 602
Rothschild, Nathaniel Meyer de, Baron, 43, 141,
   574, 584, 586
Rousseau, Jean Jacques, 26, 63, 299, 318, 320, 554,
   647
Russell, Lord John, 88, 246, 386, 399, 576, 578,
   609, 648, 652, 664, 669

Sadie (HA's servant), 241, 243, 268, 270, 614
Saint Gaudens, Augustus, 5, 179, 248, 258, 263, 266–67, 269, 306, 489, 491, 596–97, 612–13
Sala, Count Maurice, 82
Salisbury, Lord, 93, 105
Salmon, Tati, 11, 20, 27–28, 30, 60, 63–64, 75, 106, 111, 152, 186, 192, 226, 228, 253, 258, 268–69, 550, 568, 582, 610
Sargent, John Singer, 318, 587, 608, 671
Schmidt, Hermann, 92, 94–95, 102–03, 575–76
Schopenhauer, Rudolf, 101, 361, 640
Schurz, Carl, 321, 678
Scott, Sir Walter, 455
Sedgwick, Ellery, 529
Sévigné, Mme. de, 103
Seward, Frederick W., 382
Seward, William Henry, 88, 222, 319–20, 382
Shakespeare, William, *Antony & Cleopatra*, 597; *Hamlet*, 32, 48, 340; *Julius Caesar*, 61, 567; *Macbeth*, 24, 181–82, 340, 597; *Merchant of Venice*, 562; *Othello*, 181, 340
Shaw, Robert, memorial to, 597
Sherman, Charles (nephew of Mrs. Cameron), 246
Sherman, Henry (nephew of Mrs. Cameron), 516, 537
Sherman, John (uncle of Mrs. Cameron), 8, 104–05, 125, 127–29, 145, 148, 156, 196, 217, 604
Sherman, William Tecumseh (uncle of Mrs. Cameron), 8, 281, 597
Ships, trans-Atlantic: *Adriatic*, 329, 341–42, 348, 357, 385–87, 429–30, 433–35, 447, 661, 663; *Amerika*, 278; *Baltic*, 271, 362–63, 368–69; *Cedric*, 475–76; *Cretic*, 268–70; *Gallia*, 18; *George Washington*, 463; *Kaiser Wilhelm II*, 329–31; *La France*, 449, 452; *Lapland*, 393, 395; *Lucania*, 39; *Majestic*, 27; *New York*, 92, 278, 288; *Oceanic*, 364; *Olympic*, 402, 407–08, 415, 420, 429, 455, 459, 466, 468, 475, 651; *Paris*, 38, 119; *Philadelphia*, 231, 298–300, 332; *St. Louis*, 117, 163, 213, 249, 254, 278, 280, 307, 311, 320, 329; *St. Paul*, 117–18, 128, 130–33, 140, 150, 188–89, 237; *Teutonic*, 8, 18, 20, 22, 26–27, 110–12, 159, 267, 551, 553, 561; *Titanic*, 415, 417, 419–20, 422–24, 428, 496, 660; *Umbria*, 40
Ships, other: *Benjamin Franklin*, 424; *Dolphin*, 57; *Endeavor*, 58; *Maine*, 147–50, 154, 590–91; *Mediana*, 74, 76
Slidell, John, 21
Smith, Cotton, 523, 689
Smithsonian Institution, 34, 76, 556, 625
Soubiran. *See* Crillon, Count Édward de
Speck von Sternburg, Baron Hermann, 252
Spring Rice, Sir Cecil Arthur, 70, 93, 119, 136, 138, 159–60, 200, 267, 271, 431, 436, 439, 478, 507, 509, 512, 514, 517–19, 585–86, 677, 687
State Department, 19, 134–35, 139, 145, 157, 163, 166, 173, 336
Stevenson, Robert Louis, 187, 534
Stickney, Joseph Trumbull, 142, 171, 197, 199, 234, 243–44, 259–60, 375, 574
Stickney, Lucy, 259–61
Stoddard, Charles Warren, 187, 606, 611
Storey, Moorfield, 433
Story, William Wetmore, 247–49, 609
Sumner, Charles, 248, 315, 412, 623

Swan Sonnenschein & Company, 87, 89, 92–94, 98, 101, 103
Swift, Lindsay, 480

Taft, William Howard, 329, 331–32, 336, 356–59, 374, 380, 395, 398, 402, 410, 417, 419–20, 428, 436
Tams, J. Frederic, 220
Tams, Blanche Cruger, 220, 269, 313
Tams, Violet, 269
Taura-atua i Amo. *See* Arii Taimai
Taura-atua i Amo (HA's Tahitian name & title), 11, 56–57, 60
Taura-atua i Patea (grandfather of Arii Taimai), 11, 59–60, 106, 111, 123
Taylor, Henry Osborn, 221, 263–65, 413, 479, 612–13
Teggart, Frederick J., 376, 389, 640, 645
Ternina, Milka, 184, 187–88, 197, 199, 209–10, 213, 602
Thayer, William Roscoe, 434, 457–58, 461–62, 464–65, 469, 480, 484–86, 488, 491–92, 498–99, 504, 519–20, 526–28, 533, 585–86, 663, 670–72, 674–77, 679, 687, 690–93
Thibaut, Count, 440–41, 449, 455–56, 459
Thomson, William. *See* Kelvin, Lord
Thoron, Ellen Warder (first wife of Ward Thoron), 304, 306, 379, 388, 395, 463, 641–42
Thoron, Louisa Hooper (niece of HA's wife; second wife of Ward Thoron), 4, 22–23, 26–27, 31, 38, 47, 68–69, 81, 106, 124, 126, 135, 137, 139–40, 152–53, 155, 165, 179, 186–87, 194, 197–98, 200, 209, 211, 213, 219, 226, 233, 237, 242–43, 254, 263, 283, 287, 296, 313, 317, 322–23, 351–52, 384–85, 391, 395, 398, 400, 402, 407–10, 415, 420–22, 425, 428, 430, 434–39, 442, 444, 446, 452–53, 456, 470, 472–73, 483–84, 511, 517–18, 577, 595–96, 598–600, 602, 606, 643–44, 649, 651, 655, 661, 663–64, 667–68, 674, 676, 685–86
Thoron, Ward, 304, 315, 317, 322–23, 350–52, 356, 379, 380, 383–85, 388, 394–96, 398, 400–01, 404, 415, 433–34, 440, 442, 444–45, 449–51, 453–56, 463, 465, 470–71, 479, 483, 511, 641–42, 647–49, 653, 663, 664, 668
Thwing, Charles F., 31, 290–91, 689
Tone, Aileen, 351, 384–85, 395, 400, 439–40, 442–46, 449–53, 455–56, 459–61, 465, 468–77, 481–82, 484, 487, 495, 498, 505–09, 511–513, 515–20, 522–23, 529–31, 535, 540–44, 627, 641, 643–44, 647, 660–61, 664–75, 678, 680, 683–90, 696–98
Tower, Charlemagne, 155–56, 604
Treasury Department, 33, 39, 45, 91, 100, 121, 140, 690
Trevelyan, Sir George Otto, 299, 305–06, 326, 624
Tutaha, or Tu (or Pomare), 58–59
Twain, Mark. See Clemens, Samuel Langhorne

Vanderbilt, William, 168
Velasquez, 200
Victoria, Queen, 99–100, 199, 399, 510, 648
Vignaud, Henry, 7

Wade, Maggie, 18, 47, 146, 151, 176, 289, 342, 354, 596
Wadsworth, James W., 476
Wagner, Richard, *Götterdämmerung*, 209–10, 213;

Parsifal, 612; *Ring,* 210, 213–14; *Tristan &*
   Isolde, 184, 187–88; autobiography, 397, 647
Walcott, Charles D., 241, 311, 534, 625
Wallace, Alfred Russel, 397, 647–48
Wallis, Samuel, 57–58, 63
Walpole, Horace, 300
Ward, Mary, 4
Warder, Elizabeth, 109–116, 580
Warner, Roger S., 473
Warren, Winslow, 531
Washington, George, 14–16, 32, 310–11, 318–19,
   378, 384, 405, 481, 513, 538, 641, 643, 652
Washington Monument, 323
Waters, Chester, 85
Weed, Thurlow, 678
Weaver, James B., 43
Weeks, Raymond, 413–16, 430–31
Western Reserve University, 31, 69, 164, 552–53
Wharton, Edith, 14, 146, 260, 267–69, 300, 321,
   350, 352, 356, 358, 379, 406–07, 461, 471,
   637, 650
White, Henry, 7, 26, 128, 130–31, 293, 300, 304,

   321, 331–32, 352, 357, 374, 387, 397, 410,
   464, 483, 620
White, Montague, 221, 598
White, Stanford, 5
White House, 5, 15, 167, 329, 344, 410, 480
Whitney, Helen Hay, 70, 109–14, 133, 139, 146,
   200, 205, 222, 231, 238, 306–07, 533, 580,
   621
Whitney, Payne, 222, 231
Wilhelm II, Kaiser, 142, 210, 225, 236, 252, 271,
   273, 476
Wilmer, William, 395, 412, 499, 501, 504, 681
Wilson, Woodrow, 380, 436, 460, 480–81, 509,
   511–12, 514, 518, 670, 686
Winsor, Justin, 79
Wister, Owen, 238, 318–20
Wood, Leonard, 238

Yarrow, Harry C., 421–23, 425–26

Zola, Emile, 144–48, 150, 588–89
Zorn, Anders, 194, 600, 671